Volume 1

The Story of
AMERICA

Beginnings to 1877

GEOGRAPHY CONSULTANT

Phillip Bacon
Professor Emeritus of Geography and Anthropology
University of Houston

ACADEMIC REVIEWERS

Willard Bill
University of Washington

Ray A. Billington
Late of the Huntington Library

John Morton Blum
Yale University

Robert Farrell
Indiana University

Eric Foner
Columbia University

William H. Harbaugh
University of Virginia

Michael Holt
University of Virginia

Ari Hoogenboom
Brooklyn College, CUNY

Arthur S. Link
Princeton University

Robert Middlekauff
University of California, Berkeley

Edmund Morgan
Yale University

Robert V. Remini
University of Illinois, Chicago

Richard White
University of Washington

AFRICAN AMERICAN HISTORY

John H. Bracey, Jr.
University of Massachusetts,
  Amherst

Thomas R. Frazier
Baruch College
City University of New York

Asa G. Hilliard, III
Georgia State University

Norman McRae
Former Director of Fine Arts
  and Social Studies
Detroit Public Schools
Detroit, Michigan

William J. Marks, Sr. Ed. D.
Consultant, Social Studies Education/
  Curriculum
Dallas, Texas

George C. Wright
University of Texas

HISPANIC STUDIES

Frank De Varona
Associate Superintendent
Dade County Public Schools
Miami, Florida

HISPANIC AND WOMEN'S STUDIES

Gloria Contreras
University of North Texas

HISTORY OF RELIGION

Timothy L. Smith
Johns Hopkins University

MEXICAN AMERICAN HISTORY

Alan Knight
University of Texas

Linda K. Salvucci
Trinity University

Volume 1
The Story of AMERICA
Beginnings to 1877

JOHN A. GARRATY
Gouverneur Morris Professor of History
Columbia University

HOLT, RINEHART AND WINSTON, INC.
HARCOURT BRACE JOVANOVICH, INC.
Austin • Orlando • San Diego • Chicago • Dallas • Toronto

JOHN A. GARRATY is a distinguished historian and writer and the Gouverneur Morris Professor of History at Columbia University. His books include the widely adopted college textbook *The American Nation*, biographies of Henry Cabot Lodge and Woodrow Wilson, *The Great Depression*, and the popular *1,001 Things Everyone Should Know About American History*. He has held Guggenheim, Ford, and Social Science Research Council Fellowships. Professor Garraty is a former president of the Society of American Historians, editor of the *Dictionary of American Biography,* and coeditor of the *Encyclopedia of American Biography.*

PHILLIP BACON is Professor Emeritus of Geography and Anthropology at the University of Houston. He served on the faculties of Columbia University and the University of Washington and is former Dean of the Graduate School of Peabody College for Teachers at Vanderbilt University.

INSTRUCTIONAL REVIEWERS

Tim Beatty
History Teacher
Roehm Middle School
Berea, Ohio

Wayne Beddow
Social Studies Teacher
Hellgate High School
Missoula, Montana

Gloria Foster
History Teacher
Upland High School
Upland, California

Michael Gallagher
Social Studies Teacher
Mead Junior High School
Glenview, Illinois

David Vigilante
History Teacher
Gompers Secondary School
San Diego, California

Karen Tindel Wiggins
Director of Social Studies
Richardson Independent
  School District
Richardson, Texas

ADVISORY COMMITTEES

Jack Bovee
Social Studies Coordinator
Lee County Schools
Fort Myers, Florida

Arthur Cheatham
History Teacher
Roosevelt Middle School
Decatur, Illinois

Luis Cuevas
Adjunct Professor of History
Santa Fe Community College
Gainesville, Florida

William Curnow
History Teacher
Nolan Middle School
Detroit, Michigan

Dr. W. G. Freeman, Jr.
History Teacher
Montera Junior High School
Oakland, California

Kathleen Johnson
History Teacher
Area E Magnet School
Detroit, Michigan

Nelda Krohn
History Teacher
Oak Grove Middle School
Concord, California

Malcolm W. Moore, Jr.
Social Studies Teacher
Thomas Jefferson Middle School
Decatur, Illinois

Evelyn Nash
Social Studies Supervisor
Detroit Public Schools
Detroit, Michigan

Frank Taylor
Social Studies Supervisor
Fairfax County Schools
Annandale, Virginia

Mark Zink
Social Studies Teacher
Hampton Middle School
Detroit, Michigan

Cover: © B. Gelberg, 1989 Sharpshooters

Maps: R.R. Donnelley Company Cartographic Services

Copyright © 1992 by Holt, Rinehart and Winston, Inc.

Printed in the United States of America

ISBN: 0-03-072896-7

23456   041   9876543

Contents

Unit One
THE AMERICAN COLONIES
Beginnings to 1770

Unit Two
THE AMERICAN NATION
1770-1798

Unit Three
A GROWING AMERICA
1790-1840

Contents   **vii**

Unit Four
A WESTERING AMERICA
1816-1860

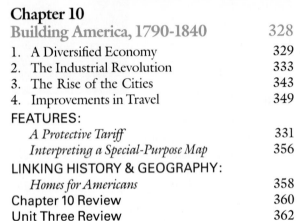

Unit Five
A DIVIDED AMERICA
1850-1877

Epilogue
THE DEVELOPMENT OF MODERN AMERICA
1877 to the Present

REFERENCE SECTION

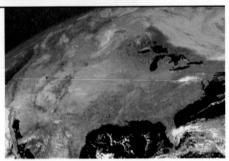

STRATEGIES FOR SUCCESS

FEATURES

CHARTS, GRAPHS, TABLES, & DIAGRAMS

To the Student

The Story of America tells our story because it is important in itself. It is a great epic and the unique tale of how hundreds of millions of people took possession of a vast continent, often at the expense of the original inhabitants. There are other reasons for telling our story. It may be read as a grand lesson that permits us to understand how past affects present. Our story is composed of many pasts that allow us to explain how our present experiment in democracy has gone on for more than 200 years. Thus we read history knowing full well that those who study the past can come to understand who we are and how far we've come and are sometimes able to caution us about our present course toward the future. But we also realize that historians have never been any better at telling the future than politicians, economists, or fortune tellers.

The Story of America was written especially for you, young Americans born in the last half of the 20th century. It provides the background to help you know about the people and values that make America great. It also presents the many controversies and challenges that have faced Americans from time to time throughout history. You can learn from their successes—and failures.

The author of *The Story of America* is ever mindful that chronology is the spine of history. Events are presented in the order in which they occurred. Time lines at the end of each chapter help you see and remember the chronology of important events.

The Story of America contains many original documents and lengthy excerpts from primary and secondary sources. These include eyewitness accounts, poems, song lyrics, diary entries, and excerpts from a variety of other sources. These materials can give you special insight into the thinking and attitudes of Americans. *The Story of America* also is filled with striking and memorable illustrations. These paintings, photographs, and other illustrations may indeed be worth a thousand words. Each captures a bit of the history of its time. The illustrations in *The Story of America* also show changing aspects of American life such as dress, art, and architecture.

An integral part of the story of America is the relation of people to the landscape. The beautifully detailed maps and special geography features in *The Story of America* illustrate this relationship and show its importance in the unfolding of our nation's story. The textbook also introduces you to the five themes of geography: location, place, relationships within places, movement, and regions. Charts, graphs, tables, and diagrams highlight the economic and sociological trends. Together, they portray a nation that has grown dramatically from such small beginnings.

When you have finished *The Story of America* you should understand the democratic values and ethical ideas that guide the American people and appreciate the civic responsibilities of all Americans to participate in American democracy. *The Story of America* will help you recognize the multicultural character of the American society and have empathy for the struggles of people to secure a place in society. With this information you will be able to take your place in society as an informed voter, more appreciative of the legacy that is the story of America.

HOW TO USE *The Story of America*

The Story of America contains a vast amount of information. It has many useful features to help you understand and use this information. Some features help you preview what you are about to read. Others help you read for that information or find additional information. Still other features help you review what you have read. Using the features of *The Story of America* wisely will help you become a better student of history.

Using the Textbook's Features

To get the most from *The Story of America,* here are some guidelines.

1. **Use the Table of Contents.** Make yourself familiar with the **Table of Contents** (pages v-xii). A quick skimming shows you how the book is organized and helps you anticipate what you will be reading. It shows that *The Story of America* is organized into five units, **A** and the units are further divided into 17 chapters and an Epilogue. As its name implies, the Table of Contents shows the content of each chapter, the special features the textbook contains, and the page on which each unit, chapter, and feature can be found. To the right is a sample.

2. **Study the unit opening pages.** Each unit gives a preview of its content with a unit title, an illustration, an introduction, and a list of chapters that are included. Take time to study the **B** unit opening page. It contains clues to what you are about to read. For example, after studying the opening page of Unit One on page 1, what can you tell about the people and times covered in this unit?

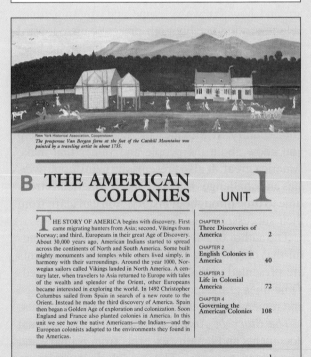

New York Historical Association, Cooperstown
The prosperous Van Bergen farm at the foot of the Catskill Mountains was painted by a traveling artist in about 1735.

B **THE AMERICAN COLONIES** UNIT 1

THE STORY OF AMERICA begins with discovery. First came migrating hunters from Asia; second, Vikings from Norway; and third, Europeans in their great Age of Discovery. About 30,000 years ago, American Indians started to spread across the continents of North and South America. Some built mighty monuments and temples while others lived simply, in harmony with their surroundings. Around the year 1000, Norwegian sailors called Vikings landed in North America. A century later, when travelers to Asia returned to Europe with tales of the wealth and splendor of the Orient, other Europeans became interested in exploring the world. In 1492 Christopher Columbus sailed from Spain in search of a new route to the Orient. Instead he made the third discovery of America. Spain then began a Golden Age of exploration and colonization. Soon England and France also planted colonies in America. In this unit we see how the native Americans—the Indians—and the European colonists adapted to the environments they found in the Americas.

CHAPTER 1
Three Discoveries of America 2

CHAPTER 2
English Colonies in America 40

CHAPTER 3
Life in Colonial America 72

CHAPTER 4
Governing the American Colonies 108

1

CHAPTER 2

English Colonies in America

C

The wealth and splendor of Spain's American empire attracted other Europeans the way flowers in springtime attract honeybees. The English in particular were envious of Spain. They longed to build an empire in the Americas. They hoped for a share of the gold and silver that almost everyone believed was so plentiful in the new land, and they wanted American products such as sugar and rice, which could not be grown in their cold climate. The English colonists came to America to trade and sell, to practice their religions, and to find work. Would they find a better life in a New World?

Preview & Review

Use these questions to guide your reading. Answer the questions after completing Section 1.
Understanding Issues, Events, & Ideas. Explain the English rise to power and its first journeys to America, using the following words: sea dog, Spanish Armada, charter, Roanoke, enclosure movement, northwest passage, joint-stock company.

D

1. How did Queen Elizabeth try to weaken Spain?
2. Why did the first settlers on Roanoke Island want to return to England?
3. Why were each of the following interested in colonizing America: the queen? landowners? merchants? explorers?

Thinking Critically. Imagine that you find a lost diary explaining what happened to the colonists of Roanoke Island. What does it say?

At right is Nicholas Hilliard's 1572 miniature portrait of Elizabeth I.

1. WHY COLONISTS CAME TO AMERICA

England Challenges Spain

In 1497, not very long after the news of Columbus' discovery reached England, its king, Henry VII, sent John Cabot on a voyage of exploration. Cabot sailed along the coast of Newfoundland, giving England a claim to the northern regions of America. At that time Spain seemed too powerful to challenge. But in the 1550s, after Elizabeth I inherited the throne, the English became seriously interested in America.

Elizabeth, ruling England alone in a world dominated by men, was a person of the strongest will and ambition. She was a shrewd ruler and a clever diplomat who paid little attention to right and wrong. Elizabeth never married, perhaps because no man could be her equal. She had a temper to match her fiery red hair and a tongue to match her sharp features. She was well aware of England's limited strength compared to Spain's. She proceeded with caution.

National Portrait Gallery, London

40 ENGLISH COLONIES IN AMERICA

3. **Read the chapter introduction.** Every chapter of *The Story of America* begins with an introduction that provides an overview and states the main ideas of the chapter. When you read the introduction, begin forming questions you may have about the chapter's content.

C

4. **Use the section Preview & Review to guide your reading.** Every section of *The Story of American* begins with a **Preview & Review.** These contain key words and questions that can help guide your reading of the section. The questions are *the same ones* you use to review your mastery of the information in the section. The symbol shows you when you have reached the end of the section. A note in the margin tells you to return to the Preview & Review to begin your review of the section. By carefully reading the Preview & Review *before* beginning the section, you can identify important words or terms and major questions or ideas discussed in the section.

D

E

4. "A CITY UPON A HILL"

The Puritans

While the London Company was making plans to settle Virginia, another joint-stock company, the Virginia Company of Plymouth, or the Plymouth Company, tried to establish a settlement far to the north near the mouth of the Kennebec River in what is now Maine. The settlers arrived in 1607 but remained only one winter. However, fishermen and traders continued to set up temporary camps in the area. In 1614 the Plymouth Company sent John Smith to explore the region further. It was Smith who first called the area **New England.**

F

In the early 1620s the Plymouth Company, now called the Council of New England, gave away several tracts of land in the northern regions, including much of what are now Maine and New Hampshire.

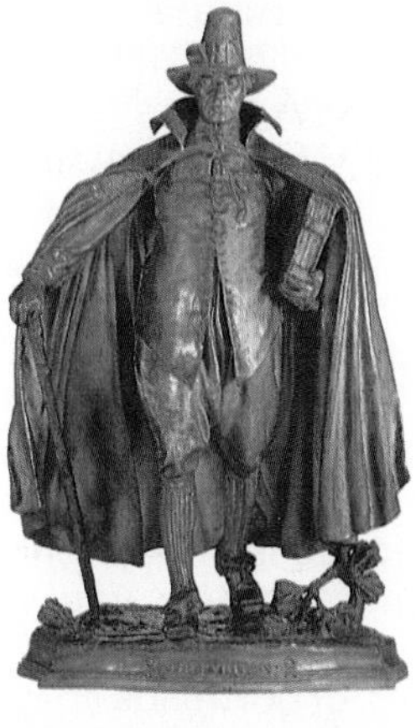

Preview & Review

Use these questions to guide your reading. Answer the questions after completing Section 4.
Understanding Issues, Events, & Ideas. Use the following words to compare Puritan settlements with Jamestown: New England, Puritans, Massachusetts Bay Company, freemen, commonwealth, Fundamental Orders, proprietary colony, Toleration Act.

1. Who were the Puritans? How did the Puritans differ from the Pilgrims? Why did they leave England?
2. Why did Puritan leaders expel Roger Williams? Anne Hutchinson?
3. What kind of powers did the king's grant give Lord Baltimore? Why were these powers never used?

Thinking Critically. You are a Puritan living in Massachusetts in 1634. Write a letter to your cousins in England, convincing them to come to America.

Metropolitan Museum of Art

The great 19th-century American sculptor, Augustus Saint-Gaudens, made this bronze, "The Puritan." What does this sculpture show you about Puritan life?

"A City upon a Hill" 57

5. **Read the chapters and sections.** *The Story of America* has many features that make reading it easier. First, the headings and subheadings provide a kind of outline of the main ideas and important details.

E

Second, pay special attention to words printed in bold black type. These **boldfaced terms** call your attention to important history words. A definition follows most, right in that sentence or the next. You can also check a word's meaning in the glossary.

F

Third, study the illustrations and read the captions. Relate what you see to what you read. All of the pictures are chosen carefully to help you better understand what you are reading. One picture can be worth a thousand words.

A STRATEGIES FOR SUCCESS

READING GRAPHS

The successful student is able to gather information from a variety of sources, including graphs. *The Story of America* contains many graphs. Graphs present information visually. There are several types of graphs, each used to present a certain type of data. A *pie*, or *circle*, graph is used to show proportions. A *line* graph shows changes in two factors. It most often shows changes over time. A *bar* graph shows comparisons, making highs and lows stand out. A *picture graph*, or *pictograph*, uses pictures to illustrate amounts.

Because graphs can contain so much information and are so common in histories, it is important to know how to read them.

How to Read a Graph
Follow these steps to read a graph.
1. **Read the title.** The title will tell you the subject and purpose of the graph. It may also contain other information, such as dates.
2. **Study the labels.** Line and bar graphs show two sets of data, one set displayed on the horizontal axis and the other on the vertical axis. The *horizontal* axis is the line at the bottom of the graph that runs across the page. The *vertical* axis is at the left side of the graph and runs up and down. Labels on these axes identify the type of data and the unit of measurement, when appropriate.

3. **Analyze the data.** Note all trends, relationships, and changes among the data. Note increases and decreases in quantities.
4. **Put the data to use.** Use the information to form generalizations and hypotheses and to draw conclusions.

Applying the Strategy
You may have heard the expression, "A picture is worth a thousand words." The picture graph may also be worth a thousand words. Study the picture graph below. Note that small figures are used to make a simple comparison of the population of the American colonies in 1730. Each symbol stands for 10,000 persons. A partial figure represents a fraction of 10,000. For example, the population of Delaware in 1730 was 9,170 persons, so it is represented by part of a figure. What is the population of Virginia? New York? If you said 1,014,000 for Virginia and 48,000 for New York, you have read the graph correctly!

There also are examples of other types of graphs in this unit. The pie graph on page 89 shows the ethnic makeup of the colonial population. (For an example of a bar graph, turn to page 139 in the next chapter.)

For independent practice, see Practicing the Strategy on page 107.

COLONIAL POPULATIONS, 1730ᵃ

New Hampshire		Maryland	
Massachusetts		Virginia	
Connecticut		North Carolina	
Rhode Island		South Carolina	
New York			
New Jersey		= 10,000 persons	
Pennsylvania		= 8,000 persons	
Delaware		= 6,000 persons	
		= 4,000 persons	
		= 2,000 persons	

ᵃGeorgia not yet founded

Source: *Historical Statistics of the United States*

78   LIFE IN COLONIAL AMERICA

B HEROES OF THE REVOLUTION

In the flush of victory Americans celebrated their first national heroes. Benjamin Franklin had been widely known for his experiments with electricity and for *Poor Richard's Almanack.* Now he was admired everywhere for his staunch support of the Revolution.

Thomas Jefferson had also become a national hero by the 1780s. American pride in the Declaration of Independence swelled when the Revolution succeeded and the courage of the document's signers could be fully appreciated.

The greatest hero of all was Washington. "The Father of His Country" was, by all accounts, a stern man who stood alone and said little. Yet all Americans admired his personal sacrifice and his careful use of power. One admirer called him "no harum

"John Paul Jones" by Charles Willson Peale.

Starum ranting Swearing fellow but Sober, steady, and calm."

A Scot, John Paul Jones, was revered as the founder of the strong United States naval tradition. In his little ship *Bon*

Homme Richard ("Poor Richard," named in admiration of Franklin), Jones came upon a British convoy led by the powerful *Serapis.* He lashed his ship to the *Serapis* and fought from sunset into moonlight until both ships were seriously damaged. Still Jones refused to surrender. "I have not yet begun to fight," he proclaimed. Finally the British vessel surrendered and was boarded by Jones as the *Bon Homme Richard* sank in a storm of fire.

All men and women who had been brave enough to take up arms against the British were now heroes. One, Andrew Jackson, was only a boy of nine when war broke out. For refusing to black the boots of a British officer, he was struck sharply in the face with the flat of a sword. He carried the scar to his grave.

...hode... ...pro-duced, because, as a result of, the source of, For independent, on page 134. ...cing the Skill

INTERPRETING HISTORY: The American Revolution

Historians study the past much like detectives solve crimes. Like a detective, an historian gathers evidence, such as letters, diaries, newspaper articles, and eyewitness accounts, interprets it, and reaches a conclusion. But different historians may interpret that evidence differently.

For example, historians have debated for nearly 200 years the reasons behind the American Revolution. Many historians, such as James Franklin Jameson, support the theory that the Revolution was an economic and social struggle. In his book *The American Revolution Considered as a Social Movement* he stresses that democratic ideals were growing among the colonists and the Revolution brought about significant economic and social changes. Historian Mary Beth Norton agrees in her

book *Liberty's Daughters: The Revolutionary Experience of American Women 1750–1800.* She points out that even the status of women in America improved after the Revolution.

Historian Gordon Wood in *The Creation of the American Republic 1776–1787* takes a contrasting view. He maintains that the colonists were motivated by patriotism. Historian Edmund S. Morgan supports this, arguing that the colonists were united by the principles expressed by Patrick Henry's "Give me liberty or give me death!"

Whether the Revolution was prompted by economic reasons or patriotic ones will always remain open to debate. Historians will continue to pursue the answers. This detective work makes history exciting.

132   GOVERNING THE AMERICAN COLONIES

6. Study the special features. *The Story of America* has many features that enrich history and help you develop the tools of the historian. These features appear on tinted backgrounds.

A On blue pages are **Strategies for Success.** These features appear in each chapter. They present additional information related to the specific chapter content and provide an opportunity for you to develop or sharpen your study skills.

B Most chapters also contain one or more brief features that highlight an important person, event, or idea. These features are easily identified by their three-column format and special heading. They are meant to give the reader a chance to pause and to consider their significance in our history.

C A third feature, **Interpreting History,** teaches the historian's craft by discussing interpretations of events or ideas that have created historical controversy. Examples include the causes of the American Revolution, the motives of the writers of the Constitution, and the political intrigue behind the Monroe Doctrine.

Every chapter of *The Story of America* uses the words of historical figures whenever possible. Besides lengthy primary source quotations, marked with large red quotation marks, you will often find a **Point of View** in the margin. **D** This feature presents a brief statement about a key event, person, or situation. Sometimes opposing opinions are presented as **Points of View.**

Another key feature is the map program. The maps illustrate physical, cultural, and historical information clearly and accurately. Almost every map contains relief shading showing major physical features, so you are constantly aware **E** of the interplay of history and geography. Several Strategies for Success will help you hone your map-reading skills. In addition, a special section titled **Maps: Portraying the Land** in the Reference Section provides a variety of information about maps and mapmaking.

The Story of America highlights the ethnic and cultural contributions of different groups **F** to American culture. To help you visualize some of the many contributions, you will find four pictorial essays, or portfolios, that contain the art and artifacts of some of the groups that

Page sample D (left top)

seen far more of the world than any of the other settlers. He had fought in a number of wars in eastern Europe against the Turks. In one war he was captured, taken to Constantinople, and sold into slavery. However, he managed to kill his master and escape. After many other remarkable adventures Smith found himself in the colony of Virginia.

In 1608 Smith was elected president of the Virginia council. Once in charge, he bargained with the Indians for food. He stopped the foolish searching for gold. Instead he put people to work building shelters and planting food crops. Hard work and strict discipline became the order of the day.

Reforms for Virginia

Virginia's difficulties finally convinced the merchant adventurers in England that the London Company needed to be reorganized. In 1609 Sir Edmund Sandys, a councilor who was also a member of Parliament, England's legislative body, obtained a new charter from King James. This charter called for the appointment of a governor who would rule the colony in Jamestown rather than from London.

The London Company then raised a good deal more money and outfitted a fleet of nine ships to carry about 600 new settlers across the Atlantic. Those who paid their own fare received one share of stock in the company. Those who could not pay agreed to work as servants of the company for seven years in return for their passage. Until 1616 everything the colonists produced was to be put into a common storehouse or fund. On that date the servants would have worked off their debt to the company. Then the profits of the enterprise were to be divided among the shareholders—both the investors back in England and the settlers. Every shareholder would also receive a grant of Virginia land.

These were fine plans but hard to put into effect. Conditions in Virginia got worse and worse. The first governor, Lord De La Warr, put off coming to Jamestown. Smith returned to England for supplies and colonists, and to convince company managers to invest more money in the colony. Without his firm hand, the organization and rules he had begun quickly fell apart. The years from 1609 to 1611 were a **starving time.** As Smith described it:

John Smith was 27 years old when he took command of the Jamestown settlement. This engraving portrays him at the age of 33. Does time seem to have taken an early toll for this bold adventurer?

Point of View

An Algonquin leader asked John Smith why the colonists used force with the Indians.

❝Why will you take by force what you may have quietly by love? Why will you destroy us who supply you with food? What can you get by war? We can hide our provisions and run into the woods; then you will starve for wronging your friends. Why are you jealous of us? We are unarmed, and willing to give you what you ask, if you come in a friendly manner.❞

Powhatan, 1607

❝By their [the Indians'] cruelty, our Governours indiscretion [poor judgment] and loss of our ships, of five hundred [colonists] within six months after Captaine Smith's departure, there remained not past sixtie men, women and children, most miserable and poore creatures; and those were preserved for the most part, by roots, herbes, acornes, walnuts, berries, now and then a little fish . . . yea, even the very skinnes of our horses. . . . This was that time,

D

48   ENGLISH COLONIES IN AMERICA

Page sample E (right top)

And how was the new, larger empire in America to be governed? The old system of 13 separate colonies, each controlled from London, worked well enough when the colonies were separated from one another by thick forests. Now the wilderness was shrinking. Four colonies—Virginia, Pennsylvania, Connecticut, and Massachusetts—each claimed parts of the Ohio Valley just won from France. Each based its case on a royal charter drafted before anyone knew much about American geography. Who would untangle these conflicting claims?

There were also the Indians in the Ohio Valley. Everyone expected them to stop fighting when the French surrendered. Instead they organized behind Pontiac, a chief of the Ottawa, and tried to drive the settlers back across the Appalachians. How could an area claimed by so many different colonies be defended? Who would pay the cost of British troops were used?

These last questions were the most pressing ones. The answers were that the British put down **Pontiac's Rebellion** and paid the cost of doing so. To keep the peace the British stationed 6,000 soldiers in the land won from the French and closed the entire region beyond the Appalachian Mountains to settlers. This decision was announced in the **Proclamation of 1763.** Only licensed fur traders might enter the Ohio region. No one could purchase Indian lands.

Most American colonists did not like the Proclamation of 1763. It seemed to put the great West as far out of reach as it had been when the forts built by Governor Duquesne had first barred the way ten years earlier. 🔲

LEARNING FROM MAPS. *The French and Indian War significantly changed the face of North America. Study these maps. What changes can you discover?*

Return to the Preview & Review on page 116.

NORTH AMERICA IN 1754

British · French · Spanish · Russian · Unexplored

Azimuthal Equal-Area Projection

NORTH AMERICA IN 1763

British · French · Spanish · Russian · Unexplored · Proclamation Line of 1763

Azimuthal Equal-Area Projection

E

Page sample F (left bottom)

America's Indian Heritage

MAJOR CULTURAL REGIONS AND INDIAN TRIBES OF NORTH AMERICA, c. 1500

Albers Equal-Area Projection

This map shows the geographic location of the major cultural groups into which American Indian tribes have been divided. It also shows some of the hundreds of tribes in each group. Of course many tribes moved about a great deal, so the locations shown are approximate.

This stone pipe found in Oklahoma shows a man playing chunkey, a game popular everywhere in the region of the Mound Builders. Games lasted all day. Chunkey was a bit like bowling, a bit like the javelin toss.

St. Louis Science Center

Peabody Museum of Archaeology and Ethnology, Harvard University

The Hopewell mounds yielded this mica serpent. Mica is a mineral silvery in color and so fine it is translucent—diffused light passes through.

F

10   THREE DISCOVERIES OF AMERICA

Page sample F (right bottom)

America's Pacific Heritage

Since ships first sailed or land caravans carried off its treasure, westerners have been fascinated by the East. Marco Polo was bedazzled even though he came from Venice, a western jewel. The art of the Orient is the oldest in the world, but it was hidden behind the walls of Forbidden Cities. Emigrants from Asia were too poor to own eastern treasures such as we see on these pages, but traders like John Ellerton Lodge filled the holds of the *Kremlin* and *Magnet* with china, silk, ivory, even fireworks that bloomed like chrysanthemums to bring Pacific culture to America.

This dragon comes from a Chinese embroidered chair of the 18th century. Eastern dragons seldom breathed fire and were seen as protectors.

St. Louis Art Museum

Chinese porcelain has long been prized. The export ware below is an Orange platter in the "Fitzhugh" pattern.

Four little lads in holiday dress were photographed on the teeming streets of San Francisco's Chinatown before the earthquake of 1906.

F

America's Pacific Heritage   757

A

LINKING HISTORY & GEOGRAPHY

CROSSING THE ATLANTIC

By the 15th century Europe had two groups of sea powers. One, the Italian city states, located on the relatively calm and sheltered waters of the Mediterranean Sea, traded with China, the Indies, and India. The second group, the Hanse Towns, which later became the Hanseatic League, sailed the North and Baltic seas, carrying goods from Russia and Siberia to the towns of northern Europe. Both groups developed from unique geographic environments—the linking of great overland trade routes from the east with the indented coastlines of tideless seas. Captains and crews sailed in comparative security, knowing land lay not too far away.

Looking to the Atlantic

1. Why did the other nations of Europe begin to look for their own trade routes?

The merchants in Italy and the Hanse Towns charged other Europeans very high prices for the goods they traded. Because these merchants held monopolies, other nations had difficulty establishing their own trade routes. Slowly the leaders of the other European nations began to realize that their only realistic alternative was to look westward—to the Atlantic Ocean. But that meant facing a landless horizon and the vastness of an uncharted watery wilderness.

It is interesting to note that only those nations that actually faced the Atlantic—Spain, Portugal, England, France, and the Netherlands—actually met the challenge of the Atlantic (as Norway had centuries earlier). They, and they alone, took the knowledge of navigation, map making, and shipbuilding and applied it to a much sterner test of seamanship in the open Atlantic Ocean.

Geography of the Ocean Frontier

2. What manner of watery frontier did these early sailors find as they ventured westward?

We can get some sense of what lay ahead by looking at a map or globe. As you can see, the Atlantic covers one fifth of the earth's surface. And you can see it occupies a unique space on Planet Earth, separating Europe and Africa from the Americas and creating a barrier—or, for some, a highway—between those continents.

A map or globe shows you, too, that the Atlantic is a long body of water that resembles an hourglass. The widest part of the ocean, spanning some 4,150 miles (6,640 kilometers), stretches between Spain and Florida. It was precisely this expanse crossed by Columbus in 1492! The narrowest part lies between Norway and Greenland in the north. Here the distance is a mere 930 miles. Across this narrowest section, with islands scattered like stepping stones, the Vikings sailed around the year 1000.

Mixing the Waters of the Atlantic

3. How else is the Atlantic's geography unique?

Perhaps the most amazing aspect of the Atlantic's geography is its huge *drainage basin,* the area of land whose rivers flow into an ocean. Most of the world's great rivers empty their waters into the Atlantic.

In North American the Atlantic basin stretches all the way to the Rocky Mountains. There, in western North America, the many tributaries of the mighty Mississippi begin. At mid-continent they join to form the river that drains two thirds of the continent toward the Gulf of Mexico, an arm of the Atlantic.

In South America the Atlantic's drainage area extends across the continent to the soaring Andes Mountains. Among those towering peaks the world's greatest flow of water begins its journey to the Atlantic. So great is this rush of water—carried by the Amazon River—that the volume of water is greater than that of the Mississippi, Nile, and Yangzte rivers *combined.*

The Atlantic also gathers much of the water from Africa. Waters of the Nile, Congo, and Niger rivers eventually reach the Atlantic. The Atlantic also claims the Rhine and the other great rivers of Western Europe as well as many of those of Eastern Europe and central Russia.

The immense size of the drainage basin opened the way to yet-to-be-explored lands. In North America, the Gulf of St. Lawrence, Hudson Bay, and Gulf of Mexico carried sailing vessels from Europe to the continent's edge. Rivers carried explorers to its very heart.

Sailing West

4. What propelled the early sailing ships from Europe to the Americas?

One other aspect of the Atlantic's geography

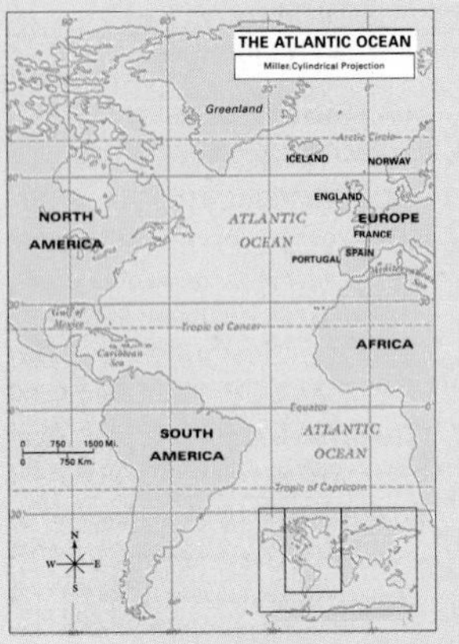
THE ATLANTIC OCEAN
Miller Cylindrical Projection
Greenland
Arctic Circle
ICELAND
NORWAY
ENGLAND
EUROPE
FRANCE
SPAIN
PORTUGAL
NORTH AMERICA
ATLANTIC OCEAN
Tropic of Cancer
AFRICA
Equator
SOUTH AMERICA
ATLANTIC OCEAN
Tropic of Capricorn
0 750 1500 Mi.
750 Km.
N
W
E
S

played a vital role in the discovery and exploration of the New World. Winds and ocean currents helped transport people and cargoes from Europe to the Americas and back.

As you can see from the map on page 24, Columbus first headed south to the Canary Islands before turning westward. This was no accident. Early explorers voyaging southward along Africa's west coast found strong and steady winds from the northeast between 30° and 5° north of the equator. These winds carried the sleek sailing ships ever westward.

What causes these winds? Air always flows from centers of high atmospheric pressure to areas of lower pressure. The winds along the African coast result from air flowing from zones of high pressure near 30°N to a low-pressure zone always found near the equator.

Of course, if the world did not turn on its axis, the air would simply flow from north to south in the Northern Hemisphere and south to north in the Southern Hemisphere. The earth's rotation causes the winds to deflect, or bend.

These wonderful winds, among the steadiest and most reliable on earth, soon became invaluable for ships sailing westward. Within a remarkably short period of time they were known to sailors everywhere as the *trade winds.*

The Return Trip

5. Once in the Americas, how did people return to Europe?

Just as the trade winds carried ships westward, the Gulf Stream helped propel them back to Europe. The Gulf Stream begins in the eastern portions of the Gulf of Mexico. It flows northward along the eastern seaboard of the United States. At about 40°N the current swings eastward across the Atlantic toward the British Isles. It is one of the strongest and most consistent ocean currents. Coupled with the northeast trade winds, it provided knowledgeable navigators with the means to complete roundtrip voyages between Europe and the New World.

The geography of the Atlantic made it ideal as a pathway of discovery. Winds and currents moved the sailing ships on just the right paths. Plentiful bays and gulfs, fed by huge rivers, provided entrances into continents. Soon the forbiddingly vast waters of the Atlantic became one of the most heavily traveled routes in the world.

APPLYING YOUR KNOWLEDGE

Your class will work in three groups to create a profile map of the Atlantic Ocean. One group should map the major ocean currents. Another should identify and label on a map the major rivers eventually draining into the Atlantic. The third group should measure distances across the ocean from various spots (such as Virginia) in North America to Norway, Spain, and England. You will then combine the groups' findings to create your profile map of the Atlantic.

176 THE REVOLUTIONARY WAR

Linking History & Geography 177

B

CHAPTER 3 REVIEW

Enlightenment

Triangular Trade

1600 COLONIAL AMERICA 1650 1700 1750

1619 First Africans brought to America

1676 Bacon's Rebellion erupts

1706 Benjamin Franklin is born

1740 The Great Awakening

1750 Enlightenment in America

★ Settlement reaches the Appalachians

1754 Franklin's Albany Plan of Union

Chapter Summary

Read the statements below. Choose one, and write a paragraph explaining its importance.

1. The American land held many blessings for the first settlers.
2. Early colonists relied on rivers as transportation routes, and early cities grew on river banks.
3. Although colonial women could not vote and worked very hard, American life offered more opportunities than it did in Europe.
4. Most early settlers obtained land and worked hard to improve it, qualifying them to vote.
5. Africans were first brought to America to work as slaves.
6. Slavery was inhuman; educated slaves were more likely to run away or revolt.
7. Cash crops such as tobacco were the major southern products and required much labor.
8. Triangular trade became very profitable.
9. Intellectual movements such as the Great Awakening and the Enlightenment involved Benjamin Franklin and many Americans.
10. As settlers moved west, many controversies arose.

Reviewing Chronological Order

Number your paper 1-5. Then study the time line above and place the following events in the order in which they happened by writing the first next to 1, the second next to 2, and so on.

1. The Great Awakening
2. Bacon's Rebellion
3. Albany Plan of Union
4. First Africans brought to America
5. The Enlightment in America

Understanding Main Ideas

1. Why did the colonists have to be self-reliant? Give at least two examples of ways the colonists were self-reliant.
2. What hardships did women in colonial America face?
3. What geographical feature did all the large towns have in common?
4. Why did working people in the colonies earn more and get better treatment than workers in England? Why did indentured servants agree to come to America to work? How were African slaves usually treated by their owners in the American colonies?
5. How was American slavery different from slavery elsewhere?
6. Why was the Enlightenment welcomed in America?

Thinking Critically

1. **Synthesizing.** Imagine that you are the 26-year-old widow Martha Dandridge Custis. What advantages might you have over a European woman of your time? What major advantages does a twentieth-century American woman have over a colonial woman?
2. **Drawing Conclusions.** How did the availability of land and the scarcity of labor help make life in colonial America more democratic than it was in England?
3. **Evaluating.** Do you think "Yankee ingenuity" was a positive or a negative quality? Why? How did northern colonists use it to find a means of paying for the European goods they wanted? Do you think Americans still have "Yankee ingenuity"? Explain your answer.

Writing About History

An important point in this chapter is that the great amount of land in America affected the lives of the colonists. Suppose you are an American colonist. Write a letter to a friend in Europe explaining how the abundance of land affected one of the following: women, indentured servants, slaves, American Indians.

Practicing the Strategy

Review the strategies on pages 78 and 103.

Reading Graphs. Study the pie graph on page 89 and answer these questions.

1. What percentage of the colonial population was African? Where does that percentage rank?
2. The English, Scotch-Irish, and Scottish were all British. What percentage of the total population did the British make up?
3. What three groups represent the smallest percentages of the colonial population?

Creating a Graphic Representation. Reread the information on the Great Awakening on pages 95 to 98. Then create a word web of at least five terms centered on The Great Awakening.

Using Primary Sources

Being a freed slave in the South often meant being on your guard. Southerners began to fear the large number of freed slaves living in their midst. North Carolina and other states passed laws providing a reward for the capture and resale of "illegally" freed slaves. In 1797 Thomas Pritchet and three other freed slaves petitioned the House of Representatives for federal protection. After some debate the House voted to not accept the petition, leaving the fate of freed slaves to the individual states. Read the excerpt from the *Annals of the Congress of the United States,* 4th Cong., 2nd Sess. (1796–97) to get a sense of the struggle slaves faced. Then answer the questions.

> *I, Thomas Pritchet, was set free by my master Thomas Pritchet, who furnished me with land . . . where I built myself a house, cleared a sufficient spot of woodland to produce ten bushels of corn; . . . this I was obliged to leave . . . being threatened by Holland Lockwood, who married my said master's widow, that if I would not come and serve him, he would apprehend me, and send me to the West Indies; Enoch Ralph also threatening to send me to jail, and to sell me. . . . Being thus in jeopardy, I . . . escaped by night into Virginia. . . . where shipping myself to Boston, I was landed in New York, where I served as a waiter for seventeen months; but my mind being distressed on account of the situation of my wife and children, I returned to Norfolk in Virginia, with the hope of seeing them; but finding I was advertised in the newspaper, twenty dollars the reward for apprehending me, my dangerous situation obliged me to leave Virginia.*

1. Give two examples from the excerpt to show that Pritchet's freedom was often threatened.
2. How might you defend Pritchet's argument that he was a free person? How might you defend Holland Lockwood's belief that Pritchet was not a free person?
3. Why did Pritchet return to Virginia? Why did he leave again?

Linking History & Geography

Almost all of the early cities in America developed on a body of water. Research the location of the first colonial cities and draw a map showing their locations. Then in a brief essay explain why the first cities developed on bodies of water, using one city as a specific example.

Enriching Your Study of History

1. **Individual Project.** Some colonial business leaders advertised in England to persuade more European settlers to come to America. Draw an eye-catching poster with an attention-getting slogan for a group of these business leaders.
2. **Cooperative Project.** On page 99 there are examples of slogans or wise sayings from *Poor Richard's Almanack.* With your classmates write three of your own slogans. Consider such subjects as good health, friendship, and good study habits. Put your slogans on a poster and compare them with those of the rest of the class. What do you conclude makes a good slogan? Try to reach a class consensus in your discussion.

106 LIFE IN COLONIAL AMERICA

Chapter 3 Review 107

have come to America. These four portfolios are titled: America's Indian Heritage, America's West African Heritage, America's Hispanic Heritage, and America's Pacific Heritage. The first contains unique works by American Indian artisans. The last three present beautiful and representative works of art from the native lands of their group's members.

A   **Linking History & Geography** features appear on beige pages. A six-page section before Unit One describes key elements of American geography, defines the five basic themes of geography with examples from American history, and discusses the development of the United States and important geographic concepts. In addition, two-page features that are part of the narrative appear in each unit. They highlight the importance of geography in the unfolding of America's history. Most contain beautifully detailed maps.

7. **Study the Epilogue.** The **Epilogue** briefly continues America's story to the present. It provides a brief description of the major events of United States history from 1877 to the present and gives you a quick glimpse at what you will study in your next American history course.

8. **Reviewing your study.** To check your understanding and to help you remember what you have learned, always take time to review. **B** When you finish a section, return to the Preview & Review and answer the questions. Complete the **Chapter Review** when you finish your study of the chapter. Do the same for the **Unit Review.**

9. **Use the Reference Section.** *The Story of America* provides a **Reference Section.** When you want to know the meaning of a boldfaced term, turn to the **Glossary,** which begins on page 718. Entries are listed alphabetically, with page references for pages in the text where the word appears in boldface type. When you need to know on which page something is mentioned, turn to the **Index,** which begins on page 736. Index entries are always in alphabetical order. Become familiar with the rest of the Reference Section, which contains an atlas and charts and graphs full of data about the story of America.

Studying Primary Sources

There are many sources of historical information. They include diaries, journals, and letters; memoirs and autobiographies; paintings and photographs; editorials and editorial cartoons. All of these are *primary sources.* They give firsthand eyewitness accounts of history.

Primary sources appear frequently in *The Story of America,* for they are the historian's most important tool. You should use primary sources, usually bracketed by large quotation marks, to gain an understanding of events only eyewitness accounts can provide.

How to Study Primary Sources

To study primary sources, follow these guidelines.

1. **Read the material carefully.** Look for main ideas and supporting details. Note what the writer or speaker has to say about the atmosphere or the mood of the people.

2. **Ask yourself questions.** Ask *who* or *what* is described. If sources conflict, and they often might, *who* is speaking and *what special insights do they have?* You may also want to ask *why* an action took place.

3. **Check for bias.** Be alert for words, phrases, or information that present a one-sided view of a person or situation when it seems evident that more than one point of view is possible.

4. **When possible, compare sources.** Study more than one primary source on a topic if available. By comparing what they have to say, you can get a much more complete picture than by using only one source.

Also, remember that historians use *secondary sources* as well as primary sources. These are descriptions or interpretations of events written after the events have occurred. History books such as *The Story of America,* biographies, encyclopedias, and other reference works are examples of secondary sources.

Developing Historical Imagination

When we read history, we tend to form opinions about events in the past. Sometimes these opinions can keep us from fully understanding history. To judge people and events of the past using today's standards can lead to a false picture of history. We need instead to develop our historical imagination.

To develop historical imagination, we need to put ourselves in the place of those who lived in the past. In that way we can better see why they thought and acted as they did. Remember that science, education, and all other fields of endeavor have advanced greatly in a relatively short time. So it is important to keep in mind what people in the past knew and *what they did not know.* Throughout *The Story of America* you will have the opportunity to use your historical imagination, to take yourself back to another time.

Writing About History

Writing is an important intellectual process. It helps us clarify our thoughts, learn information, and discover new ideas. *The Story of America* contains numerous writing opportunities. Although you may not always have time to use them all, the guidelines that follow can help you improve your writing. This is especially true of longer writing assignments.

How to Write More Effectively

To write more effectively, follow these guidelines.

1. **Prewrite.** Prewriting includes all the thinking and planning that you do before you write. Before you write, ask yourself these questions: Why am I writing? Who will read my writing? What will I write about? What will I say about the topic? How will I organize my ideas?
2. **Collect information.** Do research if necessary. You can write more effectively if you have many details to choose from.
3. **Write a first draft and evaluate it.** In your first draft, remember to use your prewriting plan as a guide. Write freely, but consider your purpose and audience.

   As you review and evaluate your first draft, note places where you need to add or clarify. It may help to read your draft aloud or to exchange it with a partner.
4. **Revise and proofread your draft.** Add, cut, replace, and reorganize your draft as needed to say what you want to say. Then check for proper spelling, punctuation, and grammar.
5. **Write your final version.** Prepare a neat and clean final version. Remember that appearance is important. Although it does not affect the quality of your writing itself, it can affect the way your writing is perceived and understood.

Many writing opportunities in *The Story of America* ask you to create a specific type of writing —a diary entry, a letter, an advertisement, a poem, or a newspaper editorial. Most of these opportunities ask you to use your historical imagination—to write from the point of view of a person living then rather than now.

A diary is a personal log of your experiences. Each entry is dated and is a brief statement of what has happened and your reactions. Your diary entries should be the personal recollections of a person *at a particular time in history.*

You are probably familiar with writing letters. When you write a letter, be sure to indicate to whom you are writing and include in your letter the specific details called for in the assignment.

You also are probably familiar with advertisements. An effective advertisement captures the attention and highlights an important feature of the "product." When you develop an advertisement, make it memorable and to the point.

Writing a poem often can seem difficult. Remember, however, that poems do not have to rhyme. An example of such free verse is Whitman's "Leaves of Grass" on pages 496-97. Notice that although the lines do not rhyme, they are organized in a specific way. That is what makes it poetry. When you write a poem, let the words flow but keep them focused.

A newspaper editorial is a statement of opinion or point of view. It states a stand about an issue and provides the reasons for that stand. You might wish to read the eidtorial page of your local paper to see how the editorials are written there.

Using the guidlines listed in this section together with those developed in the Strategies for Success should help you write with confidence as you study *The Story of America.* Remember to have a plan and to use historical imagination when it is called for. Now, enjoy *The Story of America.*

LINKING HISTORY & GEOGRAPHY

An important part of America's story is the land. We live in one of the most magnificent nations on earth. Over the years this vast and varied nation has offered its treasures to generations of Americans. Its physical features have influenced the nation's history. As you read, keep the following questions in mind:

1. Why do historians note the geography of places where historical events occur?
2. What are the major physical features of the United States?
3. How did these features influence settlement patterns and land use?
4. What are the five themes of geography?

THE HISTORY-GEOGRAPHY CONNECTION

History is played out in specific times and places. What those places are like can influence historical events. In planning battlefield strategy generals must take the lay of the land into account. Settlers usually consider the availability of water and other resources when they locate their new homes. The process works the other way too: people can leave their mark on a place. Just as the physical landscape influences decisions made by settlers, settlers also shape the land. They cut forests down for lumber and clear land to plant crops. They dig wells and carve mines out of mountainsides.

And historical events can actually shape geography. Development of the steel plow made farming the tough sod of the Great Plains profitable. Soon thousands of farmers rushed onto this "last frontier," pushing aside the Indians.

So to understand history, it is important to understand the **geography** of the places where historical events occurred. Geography is more than a description of the earth's physical features. It is the study of both the physical setting and cultural setting. The physical setting includes landforms and waterways, weather and climate, and wildlife and natural vegetation. The cultural setting includes human activities and their impact on the **environment**—the natural surroundings.

THE AMERICAN LAND

Where is America? You can look on a map and find it. But early explorers had little accurate information to go on. In fact, Columbus and others had no way of knowing that two large bodies of land lay between Europe and Asia.

These explorers also had no idea that North America and South America are large landmasses called **continents**. Geographers divide the earth's

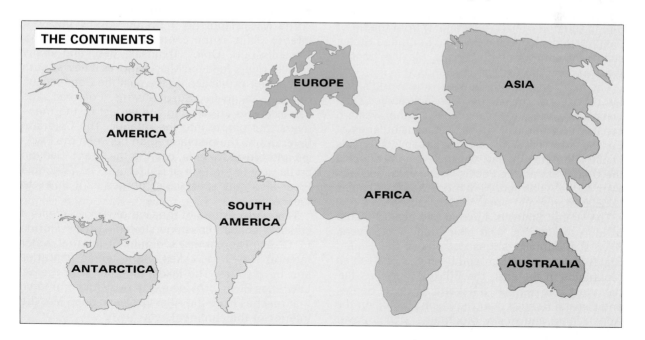

THE CONTINENTS

NORTH AMERICA

EUROPE

ASIA

SOUTH AMERICA

AFRICA

ANTARCTICA

AUSTRALIA

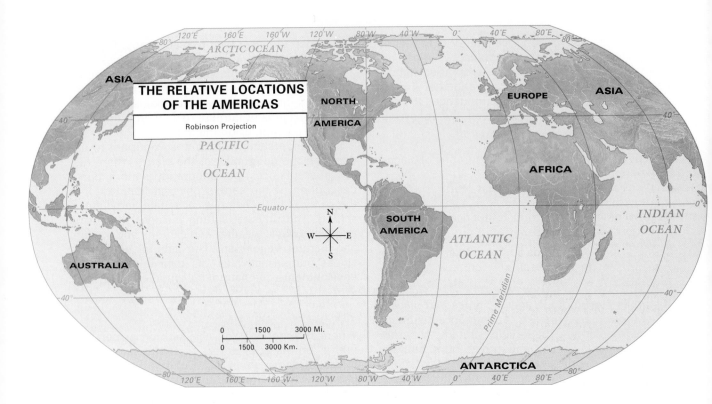

THE RELATIVE LOCATIONS
OF THE AMERICAS

Robinson Projection

land areas into seven continents—North America, South America, Europe, Africa, Asia, Australia, and Antarctica. North America stretches more than 4,500 miles (7,200 kilometers) from the tip of Panama to the icy Arctic Ocean. The United States shares the continent with Canada, Mexico, Central America, and the Caribbean islands.

The two Americas lie between the world's two largest oceans. The Atlantic Ocean stretches eastward from the American coast to the western coasts of Europe and Africa. The coastal lands of Europe and West Africa are more than 3,000 miles (4,600 kilometers) away. On the western edge of the United States, the Pacific Ocean extends westward to the Asian continent more than 8,000 miles (12,800 kilometers) away.

The United States is a varied and beautiful land of high mountains, vast plains, and long rivers. Several mountain ranges cut across the United States from north to south—the Appalachian Mountains in the east, the Rocky Mountains farther west, and the Sierra Nevada, Cascade Range, and Coastal Ranges near the Pacific. Between the Appalachian and Rocky mountains, plains cover much of the interior part of the United States. They stretch more than 1,000 miles east to west and more than 1,200 miles north to south.

The Mississippi River system drains this vast interior plain at the center of the United States. The Missouri, Ohio, Arkansas, Red, and many smaller rivers feed the Mississippi as it flows south to the Gulf of Mexico. In the east the Connecticut, Hudson, Delaware, Susquehanna, Potomac, and James rivers are among the largest of the many rivers that empty into the Atlantic. The Colorado River drains the plateau region between the Rockies and Sierra Nevada, carving the Grand Canyon on its way to the Gulf of California. The Columbia River also cuts spectacular gorges as it flows to the Pacific.

The warm waters of the Gulf of Mexico create a crescent-shaped coastline stretching from Florida to Texas. The country's dominant internal water feature, the Great Lakes, were carved centuries ago by glaciers. The lakes, together with the St. Lawrence River, provide a waterway for commerce that reaches from the Atlantic Ocean deep into the interior of the continent.

SETTLING AMERICA

People from every continent but Antarctica have come to live in North and South America. The first Americans came from Asia to Alaska across a land bridge that once linked the continents. Thousands of years later Europeans and Africans crossed the Atlantic Ocean and Asians crossed the Pacific to America. They brought with them ideas and customs that give American society its special multicultural flavor.

Just as immigrants came to the United States from every part of the inhabited world, so settlers moved about within the country. European pioneers established villages along the East Coast, then moved across the Appalachians into America's heartland. Spaniards and later Mexicans came from the south and west. Africans came as explorers, then as slaves, and still later as immigrants to all parts of the country. Settlers from Canada moved south to settle around the Great Lakes and the northern plains. Russian trappers and traders followed the Pacific coast southward. Hundreds of thousands—perhaps millions—of native Americans were displaced by the movement of these settlers.

POPULATION PATTERNS

The American population is different from that of most nations. Americans represent many groups with different backgrounds and customs. Except for the Indians, all are immigrants or descendants of people who came to America after 1500.

For much of its history the American population grew rapidly. The colonial population almost doubled every 20 years, increasing from less than 100,000 in 1650 to nearly 3,000,000 in 1776. It grew even more rapidly between 1820 and 1910 as large numbers of immigrants entered the country. Today declining birth rates and limited immigration have resulted in slower population growth.

Until recently the majority of Americans lived in **rural** areas—on farms and in small villages. The first census in 1790 showed that 94 percent of all Americans lived in rural areas. But people moved continuously and in large numbers from rural to **urban** areas—cities and towns. According to the 1920 census, for the first time in our history more Americans lived in urban than rural areas. And the 1990 census showed that urban areas accounted for more than 76 percent of the population.

LAND USE

Since the earliest times people coming to America found a richness in nature unsurpassed by any place on earth—vegetation, wildlife, water, minerals, and even the soil itself. We call these riches **natural resources.** In various combinations these resources help provide what humans need to survive and prosper.

The first American Indians used only crude tools of stone and bone to hunt, till the soil, and clear the land. Since then, Americans have developed an amazing array of technological advances to harvest and use the nation's many resources.

Americans used the fertile soil, fresh water, valuable mineral deposits, forests, and other resources to build the nation's strong economy. In so doing they have changed the nature of America's landscape—cutting the forests, redirecting rivers, carving mines out of hillsides, and paving thousands of acres of land.

At first Americans transformed the landscape with little concern for the future. But about 1900 they became sensitive to the effects of what they were doing to the environment. Conservationists, such as John Muir and Theodore Roosevelt, alerted the public to the dangers facing the country's natural beauty and resources. Scientists began studying **ecology**—the interrelationships of organisms and their environments. They began to warn people to develop sensitive areas cautiously. The government established national parks and **conservation** efforts—planned management of resources to prevent their depletion—to protect the nation's natural gifts.

THE FIVE THEMES OF GEOGRAPHY

The topics you have just read about represent only a small part of the information geographers collect. They organize this information according to five themes: location, place, relationships within places, movement, and region. Categorizing the information in this way helps us to analyze facts and to see the relationships among them.

Absolute and Relative Location

Geographers describe location in two ways. The first is **absolute location**—exactly where on earth a place is. The second is **relative location**—where a place is in relation to other places.

Geographers have marked maps and globes

with a grid of imaginary horizontal and vertical lines. These are the lines of latitude and longitude. To describe the absolute location of a place, geographers state its latitude first, then its longitude. For example, San Antonio is located at 29°25′30″N, 98°29′8″W. We read this as "twenty-nine degrees twenty-five minutes thirty seconds north, ninety-eight degrees twenty-nine minutes eight seconds west." You will learn more about latitude and longitude and the grid they form in the Strategy for Success on page 46.

Geographers usually describe relative location in terms of distance and direction from a given point of reference. For example, you may live 3 miles west of your school. Or, Houston is 245 miles southeast of Dallas. You can generally determine the relative location of a place by studying a map of the region that includes that place.

The shifting location of the American West provides another example of relative location. Americans have usually applied the term "The West" to the frontier—the edge of settlement. To the first colonists along the Atlantic coast, the west was just a few miles inland. A century later it was the Ohio Valley on the other side of the Appalachians. From there the term applied to areas progressively farther west. The relative location of "the West" changed as the frontier moved with the American pioneers and settlers.

Place

Every location on earth is unique. The features that make it unique are called **place** characteristics. Some of these are physical characteristics—landforms, climate, and vegetation. Others are cultural characteristics—the roads, farms, and buildings created by humans.

Early settlement patterns in America demonstrate the importance of place. Pioneers looked for just the right site for their settlement, one with the physical characteristics they were looking for. For pioneers, important site features included level land to build on, enough space to expand, and the availability of water. As elsewhere, American settlements developed along rivers, lakes, and bays, which provided the earliest transportation routes as well as a protective barrier in case of attack. For example, Fort Pitt grew into the city of Pittsburgh largely because it was located where the Allegheny and Monongahela rivers join to form the Ohio River.

Relationships Within Places

People adapt the environment to their needs. Early Americans cleared sites for settlement, hunted wildlife, and tilled the soil. The first settlers in Plymouth soon found their new environment was quite different from that of their British homeland. Summers were hotter, and winters were far more severe. The crops with which they were most familiar grew poorly. They were forced to plant different crops, build new types of homes, and make other adjustments to their new environment. We continue to interact with our environment today. The theme of **relationships within places** studies such human-environment interactions.

Movement

As people and goods continually move across the earth, ideas and information travel with them. The geographic theme of **movement** describes such activities. Because the United States is a nation of immigrants, movement has been a key to the American experience.

Technology has had a great influence on movement. The printing press and new designs in sailing ships quickened the flow of people, goods, and ideas. Road improvements and the railroad, and then automobiles, airplanes, television, and computers sped their movements even further.

Regions

Broad areas of the earth often contain one or more common characteristic features. Geographers call these areas **regions**. They use cultural features such as language or architecture to define cultural regions and physical features such as landforms and climate to define physical regions.

People have been powerfully influenced by their ideas about regions. In the early 1800s most white southerners—those who owned no slaves as well as those who did—felt that "cotton was king" and that slavery was necessary to the southern way of life. Recognizing such regional thinking will help you interpret people's actions and decisions.

Geographers often identify—and historians constantly refer to—seven major physical regions of the United States: Coastal Plains, Appalachian Highlands, Canadian Shield, Interior Plains, Rocky Mountains, Intermountain Region, Pacific Coast, and the Hawaiian Islands. The physical features of each of these regions have dominated their development.

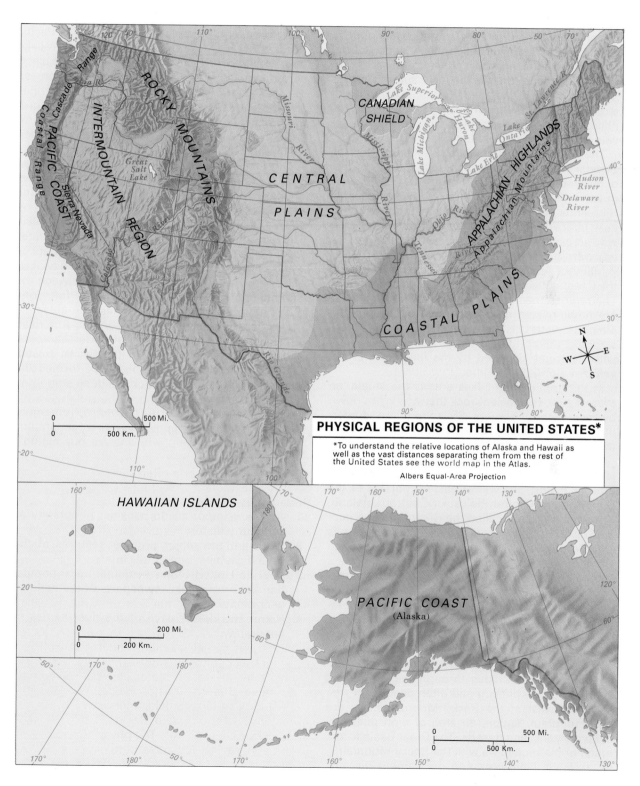

PHYSICAL REGIONS OF THE UNITED STATES*

*To understand the relative locations of Alaska and Hawaii as well as the vast distances separating them from the rest of the United States see the world map in the Atlas.

Albers Equal-Area Projection

HAWAIIAN ISLANDS

PACIFIC COAST
(Alaska)

The **Coastal Plains** are a continuous lowland. To the north this region is called the Atlantic Coastal Plain. It is quite narrow and interrupted by numerous bays. Southward the plain spreads across much of Georgia and all of Florida. Southwestern stretches of the region are called the Gulf Coastal Plain. Most of the first European settlements developed on the Coastal Plains.

The **Appalachian Highlands** rise just beyond the Coastal Plains. The highlands consist of eroded, or worn-down, mountains of an older and once much higher mountain chain. The Appalachian Highlands posed a difficult challenge to early settlers interested in moving west. They found their way across the highlands through gaps carved by eastward-flowing rivers.

Many of America's first large cities grew where the Coastal Plains join the Appalachian Highlands. The regions meet at the **fall line,** along which rivers flowing east drop from the foothills to the plains in waterfalls and rapids. These cities were shipping points for farmers and planters inland. Later factories powered by the falling water developed along the fall line.

In the upper Great Lakes area is the **shield,** an area of exposed ancient rock that was worn down by the weight of glaciers. Soils are thin and infertile, but the exposed rock is rich in minerals. It is the oldest part of the North American land.

Pioneers who crossed the Appalachian Highlands entered the lowland area that forms the **Interior Plains**. The wetter eastern portion of the region is the Central Plains, or Central Lowland. The western part is called the Great Plains. A general dividing line between these two sections is 100° W longitude. The first Europeans viewed the Great Plains as a virtual desert, but later farmers turned the region into America's "breadbasket."

Towering over the western edges of the Great Plains are the **Rocky Mountains**. The Rocky Mountains stretch from Texas and New Mexico all the way to Alaska. Magnificent peaks and deep, narrow valleys dominate the landscape. These dramatic landforms formed a barrier to pioneers heading west. Journeys through the mountains were extremely difficult and often deadly.

To the west of the Rocky Mountains lies the **Intermountain Region,** an area of high plateaus, deep canyons, and deserts. The Great Basin forms much of the region. As with the Rocky Mountains, its dramatic landforms and dry climate discouraged pioneers; most pushed on to the Pacific Coast. Only a few settlements, such as Salt Lake City, thrived before technology made it possible to dam rivers and pump water to fields and homes.

Two high and roughly parallel mountain ranges and the plateaus and valleys between them form the **Pacific Coast** region. To the east the Sierra Nevada and Cascade Ranges are part of a steep mountain chain that extends north into Canada. Along the Pacific Ocean rise the Coastal Ranges. These mountains are still forming and are frequently subject to earthquakes such as the one that struck Oakland, California, in 1989, and to volcanic eruptions such as Mount St. Helens in 1980. The San Andreas Fault—where two tectonic plates meet—cuts across the mountains from east of Los Angeles to San Francisco. The plates grind against each other, resulting in earthquakes. Between the mountain chains lie fertile valleys that form one of the nation's most productive farming areas.

The **Hawaiian Islands** form a unique American landscape. They are the tops of undersea volcanoes rising from the floor of the Pacific Ocean. Centuries of volcanic eruptions have formed the islands, and the volcanic rock has been smoothed by erosion and weathering.

As you read *The Story of America*, remember the themes of geography and other geographic factors. They will help you analyze our nation's development.

Geography Review

1. Why is it important to consider geography as you study history?
2. What are the major physical features of the United States?
3. How do United States settlement and population patterns reflect key aspects of the nation's geography?
4. Name and define each of the five themes of geography.

New York Historical Association, Cooperstown

The prosperous Van Bergen farm at the foot of the Catskill Mountains was painted by a traveling artist in about 1735.

THE AMERICAN COLONIES

UNIT 1

T HE STORY OF AMERICA begins with discovery. First came migrating hunters from Asia; second, Vikings from Norway; and third, Europeans in their great Age of Discovery. About 30,000 years ago, American Indians started to spread across the continents of North and South America. Some built mighty monuments and temples while others lived simply, in harmony with their surroundings. Around the year 1000, Norwegian sailors called Vikings landed in North America. A century later, when travelers to Asia returned to Europe with tales of the wealth and splendor of the Orient, other Europeans became interested in exploring the world. In 1492 Christopher Columbus sailed from Spain in search of a new route to the Orient. Instead he made the third discovery of America. Spain then began a Golden Age of exploration and colonization. Soon England and France also planted colonies in America. In this unit we see how the native Americans—the Indians—and the European colonists adapted to the environments they found in the Americas.

Three Discoveries of America

America was discovered three times, each time by accident. The first time was about 30,000 years ago, when people from northern Asia touched foot on American soil in what is now Alaska. The second discovery of America occurred about the year 1000, but we know little about the Viking sailors who reached Newfoundland. The third discovery, 500 years ago, was made by a persistent Italian who sailed under the colors of Spain and claimed what he believed to be the Indies for King Ferdinand and Queen Isabella. Thus began a Golden Age of discovery and conquest of the Americas by Spain. Would Spain come to dominate the New World?

1. THE FIRST AMERICANS

The Ice Age

Preview & Review

Use these questions to guide your reading. Answer the questions after completing Section 1.
Understanding Issues, Events, & Ideas. Use the following words to compare early American Indians: Ice Age, historical imagination, society, culture, Stone Age, clan, adobe, pueblo, Mound Builders, Five Nations, confederation, artifact, archaeologist, carbon-14 dating, anthropologist, folk tale.
1. How did the Ice Age lead Asian people to the first discovery of America?
2. Why did the first immigrants to America come in waves?
3. Give three examples of how environment influenced the customs of early American Indian societies.
Thinking Critically. 1. Compare the way of life of farmers with that of hunters and wanderers. **2.** You know that the peoples of North and South America spoke many different languages. Other than speaking, how could people from two different tribes communicate?

Today Asia is separated from America by the Bering Strait, a body of water between Alaska and Siberia more than 50 miles (80 kilometers) wide. When early people first came to America from Asia, the strait was dry land. The earth was then passing through a great **Ice Age,** a period when the weather was much colder than at present. What in warmer times would have fallen as rain and drained back into the oceans fell as snow instead. Gradually, enormous amounts of this snow piled up in the northern and southern regions of the earth, far more than could melt during the short summers. Vast ice fields called glaciers formed. So much water was trapped in these thick glaciers that the water level of the oceans dropped sharply, exposing a land bridge between Asia and North America.

Plants froze, but their seeds and spores lay dormant until warmer weather came. With each period of warmth the plants that grew from the seeds and spores spread to new areas. Eventually they spread across the land bridge into North America. The animals that fed on them followed. The bones of ancient Asian elephants, called mammoths, and of saber-toothed tigers have been found in dozens of places in the United States. Following the animals came people, the first Americans.

The exact year, decade, or century when the first Americans arrived will never be known, for no historian recorded the adventures of these pioneers. Their graves are unmarked. The ashes of their campfires have been scattered by the winds of the ages. These were accidental discoverers, hunters following wild game or herders driving their flocks over the next hill to find greener pastures.

The first American immigrants came in waves, for there were warmer periods when some of the ice melted and the water level rose. The last crossed about 10,000 years ago. At about that time the great glaciers began to melt, and the Bering land bridge was flooded over by the rising ocean.

The Great Migration

What did it feel like to be among the first people to reach this great, empty land? We know what the first astronauts experienced when they set foot on the moon. They were aware that they were doing something no one had ever done before. We do not know exactly what the first Americans experienced. They did not know that they were exploring a new continent. Understanding the difference calls for an act of **historical imagination.** Having a good historical imagination means being able to look at past events, keeping in mind what

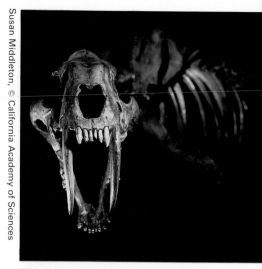

This jaw of a saber-toothed cat was found in the La Brea Tar Pits in Los Angeles. This and other fossils from the Pleistoscene era may be viewed today at the museum on Wilshire Boulevard. How do fossils help us understand the past?

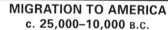
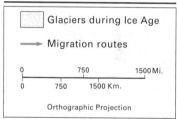

MIGRATION TO AMERICA
c. 25,000–10,000 B.C.

☐	Glaciers during Ice Age
→	Migration routes

0 _____ 750 _____ 1500 Mi.
0 _____ 750 _____ 1500 Km.

Orthographic Projection

LEARNING FROM MAPS. *The Asiatic wanderers who came to the Americas spread slowly across the lands. What physical barriers hindered their spread to the east and west in North America?*

The First Americans 3

the people of the day knew, but at the same time remembering what they did not know.

Once in North America, the wanderers moved slowly southward and to the east, following the life-giving game. The distances they covered were enormous. It is 15,000 miles (24,000 kilometers) from their homeland in Asia to the southern tip of South America and 6,000 miles (9,600 kilometers) to what is now New England. Many thousand years passed before they had spread over all this land.

As they advanced and multiplied, the first Americans gradually changed their ways of life. Some made their homes in fertile valleys, others in tropical jungles. Some settled in mountainous regions or in deserts. Each group had different problems, and each learned to see the world in different ways. As a result each society created its own culture. A **society** is a group of people who live in a specific geographic area and who have a common culture. The **culture** of a society consists of those values and behavior patterns held in common: language, government, family relationships, how they make a living, how they educate their children, and the objects they create.

Some sense of how many different cultures developed comes from the fact that the peoples of North and South America spoke between 1,000 and 2,000 languages.

A few researchers think that people from other continents may have arrived in the Americas many hundreds of years ago. They point out that the Chinese and Polynesians were excellent sailors and had boats capable of making the voyage. And pottery found in Ecuador is quite similar to that being made in Japan during the same period. Others claim that free Africans came to America long before the first black slaves were brought. They find evidence in the Negroid features of ancient statues found in Mexico. Still others say Roman coins found in Venezuela suggest that Europeans reached the New World even before the Vikings.

Early American Cultures

By the 1400s there were perhaps 50 million people living in North and South America. Only about 1 or 2 million of these inhabited what is now the United States and Canada. Partly because they were so few in number and spread over such a huge area, these people had developed a number of distinct cultures.

Many cultural differences stemmed from the ways groups dealt with the basic problem of scarcity. Like all societies these groups had to make choices about how best to use their limited resources to meet basic needs. Some hunted and gathered wild plants. Others turned to farming. Those who planted seeds and cultivated the land were able to develop a more secure and comfortable life than those who relied on hunting and gathering. People who had mastered farming, or agriculture, could settle in one place instead of roaming in

This agate point was made into a weapon sharp enough to kill mammoths and bison. When the point was attached to a spear, and the spear was flung by an atlatl—a device for holding and throwing—it changed the way people hunted. Use your historical imagination to describe two hunts: one before these weapons existed and one after.

Lee Boltin, © American Museum of Natural History

This water jar was one of the pieces of clay pottery made by the Zuñi who lived in the desert of the Southwest. After reading page 6 about the Zuñi environment, why do you think it was important that jars were watertight?

constant search of food. They built permanent houses. Their societies grew to include more members.

None of the groups made much progress in developing simple machines or substituting mechanical or even animal power for their own muscle power. They had no wagons or other vehicles with wheels and no horses or oxen to help plow the land. Their tools and weapons were made of wood or stone or bone. Aside from a few copper objects and some gold and silver jewelry, they had no metals. Anthropologists call this stage of development the **Stone Age.** It ended with the arrival of Europeans and their technology.

Most leaders, or chiefs, were chosen in a fairly democratic manner. That is, most chiefs ruled with the consent of their societies, not by force or written law. Life was mostly governed by tradition and custom. People tended to work in groups rather than alone. Usually they did not own their land as individuals. Their "hunting ground" or homeland was the general region in which the group lived. It was not an area with specific boundaries. This was true even of the farmers, who could not go far from the crops they tended.

These agricultural people were mostly peaceful, though they could fight fiercely to protect their fields. The hunters and gatherers, on the other hand, were quite warlike because their need to move about brought them frequently into conflict with other groups.

Some early American cultures were matrilineal, which means that kinship was traced through the female side. When a man and woman married in such a society, the man became a member of his wife's social group, or **clan.** A typical household might consist of an older woman, her daughters, and her granddaughters. Of course, the woman's husband, her sons-in-law, and her grandsons would also

What is this animal with horns? Nobody today seems to know. It was carved around the first century by the early residents of the Hopewell site in Ohio. The tail has a rattle, the head is horned, and little feet are pressed to the body. How do you suppose the early Americans used this carving?

The First Americans   **5**

© John Running

Pueblo Bonito was the greatest Anasazi village in Chaco Canyon, New Mexico. At least 1,200 people lived there once. Drought ended most great pueblos in the last years of the 13th century. How might modern environmental studies have helped save Pueblo Bonito?

live in the household group. But only the female members were truly permanent members of the clan.

All of these statements are **generalizations,** broad statements that link loosely associated facts. They are true of most of the groups we are discussing. Yet every one of these communities was somewhat different from all the others. No generalization about them can be completely accurate. History is full of such "mostly but not entirely true" statements. This is unfortunate, but we must learn to live with this weakness. Remember, as you read, to add words like "usually" or "nearly always" when you spot a generalization.

Early American Societies

Land and climate strongly influenced the way the first Americans lived. They adjusted to nature—their **environment**—far more than they tried to change it. A brief look at some of the early American societies gives us an idea of the variety of American Indian cultures that evolved over hundreds of years.

The Southwest. As much as 1,000 years ago in the Southwest, the Hopi and Zuñi were building with **adobe**—sun-baked brick plastered with mud. Their homes looked remarkably like modern apartment houses. Some were four stories high and contained quarters for perhaps a thousand people, along with storerooms for grain and other goods. These buildings were usually put up against cliffs, both to make construction easier and for defense against enemies. They were really villages in themselves, as later Spanish explorers must have realized since they called them **pueblos.** *Pueblo* is Spanish for town.

The people of the pueblos were peaceful and gentle. They raised what they called the three sisters—corn, beans, and squash. They made excellent pottery and wove marvelous baskets, some so fine that they could hold water. The Southwest has always been a dry country, with water scarce. The Hopi and Zuñi brought water from streams to their fields and gardens through irrigation ditches. Water was so important that it played a major role in their religion. They developed elaborate ceremonies and religious rituals to try to bring rain.

The Great Basin. The way of life of less settled groups was simpler and more strongly influenced by nature. Small tribes such as the Shoshone and Ute wandered the dry and mountainous lands between the Rocky Mountains and the Pacific Ocean. They gathered seeds and hunted small animals such as rabbits and snakes.

The Far North. In Alaska and northern Canada the ancestors of today's Eskimos hunted seals, walruses, and the great whales. They lived in igloos built of blocks of packed snow. When summer came, they fished for salmon and hunted the lordly caribou.

Field Museum of Natural History

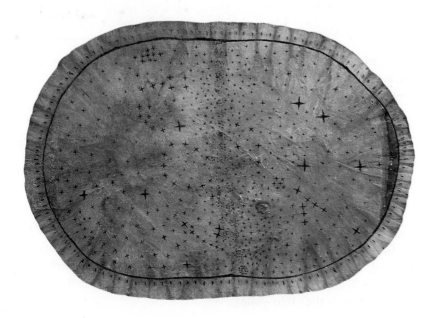

An early Pawnee astronomer painted this star chart on buckskin to show the stars and planets of the night sky. A reverence for the heavens was a part of the Pawnee tradition. How might the star chart have been used?

This Kwakiutl ceremonial mask was carved from wood and painted. One head contains another. When opened, its heads look in three directions—perhaps to past, present, and future. Early Americans of the Northwest carved masks and totem poles to represent their ancestors. How many different works of art in this chapter would you classify as religious? How many are made for everyday use? Can you make a generalization about the kinds of artifacts that are usually preserved?

The Northwest. Fishing was the mainstay of the Kwakiutl, Nootka, and Tlingit tribes. These people lived mostly on salmon and other fish caught in northwestern coastal waters. The magnificent forests of redwood, pine, and cedar that grew right down to the ocean supplied them with lumber to build their homes and canoes and to carve their ancestral totem poles.

The Great Plains. The Cheyenne, Pawnee, and Sioux tribes, known as the Plains Indians, lived on the grasslands between the Rocky Mountains and the Mississippi River. They hunted bison, commonly called buffalo. Its meat was the chief food of these tribes, and its hide was used to make their clothing and the covering of their tents and teepees. Every part of the animal was used, even its waste, which when dried served as fuel for cook fires in that treeless region. Little wonder that the buffalo was an important symbol in the religious life of the Plains Indians!

The Southeast. The Ohio Valley was once the home of the ancestors of such important tribes as the Choctaw and the Creek. They were called the **Mound Builders** because they buried their dead in elaborate earthen mounds built in the shape of birds or snakes, or in human form. These were very large, as high as an eight-story building, and one has been found that covers an area as large as 50 modern city blocks. We know that the people of the mounds traded with tribes as far away as the Rocky Mountains and the Gulf of Mexico because objects made of stone and ornaments made of the teeth of sharks and alligators have been found in their settlements. Tribes such as the Cherokee, Natchez, and Choctaw gradually moved southeast from the Ohio Valley.

The Eastern Woodlands. The Mohawk, Oneida, Onondaga, Cayuga, and Seneca made up a group of tribes that was later called the **Five Nations** or League of the Iroquois. They lived in the densely wooded central region of what is now New York State. The Iroquois **confederation,** a loose association of tribes, was very powerful because it could assemble many warriors. The Iroquois men were hunters, the women farmers. The Iroquois women also participated in tribal decision making, choosing new chiefs, for example.

For thousands of years these tribal societies knew nothing of the rest of the world. They were as isolated from their original homeland in Asia and from Europe and Africa as if they were on the moon.

Uncovering the Past

Since the first Americans did not record their history in books, we must reconstruct it from those objects they created that have survived the centuries. These include campsites and buildings, engraved stones, clay pots, tools and weapons, jewelry—what are known as **artifacts.** Putting together these fragments is like solving an enormous jigsaw puzzle with many missing pieces. It is a difficult but fascinating task.

Scientists called **archaeologists** search for and study artifacts. In America archaeologists have located and carefully dug up ancient camps, burial grounds, and entire cities. They have found hundreds of thousands of artifacts from arrowheads to huge stone statues.

We can estimate the age of these artifacts by using the technique called **carbon-14 dating.** Carbon is present in all living things, and some of this carbon takes a form called carbon-14. When a living thing dies, its carbon begins to break down at a very slow but steady rate. Thus, by measuring what remains of the carbon-14 in, say, a human bone or even a piece of charcoal from a campfire, an expert can tell about how long ago the person was alive or the fire put out. Carbon-14 dates are accurate only to within a few hundred years. They are not much use for studying recent events. But for learning the history of the peoples who first settled America, the method is most useful.

In addition to what archaeologists can tell us about the first Americans, we can also learn by studying their living descendants. The scientists who do this research are called **anthropologists.** Some anthropologists live with and observe the descendants of the first Americans. They ask how these people explain their relation to one another. What are their religious ideas and other values? Do they tell stories called **folk tales** that have been handed down from generation to generation? What are their habits and traditions? The answers to these questions throw light on how early Americans lived and thought. In such ways historians have been able to learn a great deal about these first settlers of America.

© John Running

The Anasazi of the Pueblo period around 1100 made this classic pottery in black on white. The vessels were painted with a dye.

Return to the Preview & Review on page 2.

America's Indian Heritage

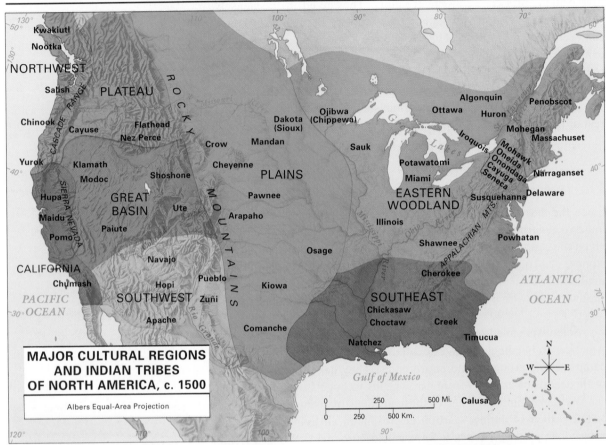

Kwakiutl
Nootka
NORTHWEST
Salish   PLATEAU
Chinook   Cayuse   Flathead
          Nez Perce
Yurok   Klamath
         Modoc   Shoshone
Hupa
Maidu   GREAT
              BASIN   Ute
Pomo   Paiute
CALIFORNIA   Navajo
Chumash   Hopi   Pueblo
PACIFIC   SOUTHWEST Zuñi
OCEAN
           Apache

ROCKY

CASCADE RANGE
SIERRA NEVADA

MOUNTAINS

Crow
Cheyenne
PLAINS
Pawnee
Arapaho

Osage

Kiowa

Comanche

Dakota (Sioux)
Mandan

Ojibwa (Chippewa)
Sauk

Potawatomi
Miami

Illinois

EASTERN
WOODLAND

Shawnee

Algonquin
Ottawa   Huron   Penobscot
Iroquois   Mohegan   Massachuset
          Mohawk
          Oneida
          Onondaga   Narraganset
          Cayuga
          Seneca
Susquehanna   Delaware

APPALACHIAN MTS.

Powhatan

Cherokee

SOUTHEAST
Chickasaw
Choctaw   Creek
Natchez
Timucua

Calusa

ATLANTIC
OCEAN

Gulf of Mexico

Rio Grande

Mississippi River
Ohio River

MAJOR CULTURAL REGIONS AND INDIAN TRIBES OF NORTH AMERICA, c. 1500

Albers Equal-Area Projection

0   250   500 Mi.
0   250   500 Km.

N
W   E
S

This map shows the geographic location of the major cultural groups into which American Indian tribes have been divided. It also shows some of the hundreds of tribes in each group. Of course many tribes moved about a great deal, so the locations shown are approximate.

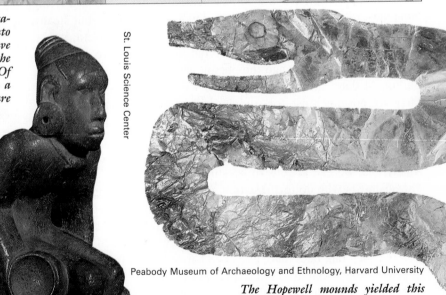

This stone pipe found in Oklahoma shows a man playing chunkey, a game popular everywhere in the region of the Mound Builders. Games lasted all day. Chunkey was a bit like bowling, a bit like the javelin toss.

The Hopewell mounds yielded this mica serpent. Mica is a mineral silvery in color and so fine it is translucent—diffused light passes through.

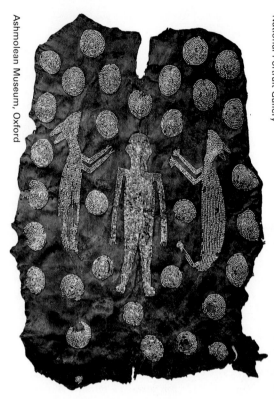

Maloaks als Rebecka daughter to the mighty Prince
Powhatan Emperour of Attanoughkomouck als Virginia
converted and baptized in the Christian faith, and
Wife to the wor.ll Mr Tho: Rolff.

Ætatis suæ 21. Aº. 1616.

Powhatan's Mantle was worn by the
great leader of the Algonquins, who
lived on the Virginia tidewater—
lands just inland from the ocean. It
is the oldest historical example of
American Indian art. The cloak is
made of tanned buckskin and decorated with shells.

Pocahontas, daughter of the great
Powhatan, is seen here in a 1616
painting. She married John Rolfe of
Jamestown and was taken to England. In 1617 she died of smallpox.

This painted fish bowl was made by
the Mimbres, a Mogollon people of
southern New Mexico. The Mogollon
were among the first people of the
Southwest to make pottery. They are
best remembered for their black-on-
white ware.

A fragment of a woven basket was
found at Hogup Cave near the Great
Salt Lake in Utah. The baskets were
so tightly woven that they could hold
water into which hot stones were lowered to boil stews.

America's Indian Heritage   **11**

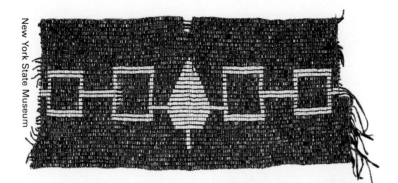

The Hiawatha Belt shows the unity of the five Iroquois tribes. The squares are connected to a central tree, or heart. The beads from which the belt is fashioned were probably brought to America by Europeans.

The mask of painted wood below depicts the moon. It was carved by the Haida, a people of the Queen Charlotte Islands, which are west of British Columbia.

The men of the Hopi spun cotton yarn on a spindle. Weaving was also primarily man's work.

The wooden deer mask was made by inhabitants of Key Marco, off Florida's swampy coast.

A thunderbird—the mythical creator of the storms that rolled over the Great Plains—swoops out of the sky, hurling lightning flashes on this Pawnee ceremonial drum.

Those who knew the old ways wove this Navajo blanket.

The great photographer of the American West was Edward Sheriff Curtis. He took "A Piegan Dandy" showing traditional Indian dress and hairstyle. More recently Norman New Rider, a Pawnee Indian, was expelled from school for refusing to cut his braided hair. The Court held that his hair style had no direct link to long-standing tradition or religious identity.

George Catlin was one of America's greatest painters of western Indian life. His 1832 portrait of Black Rock shows Catlin's attention to detail. The chief of the Two Kettle tribe of the Blackfoot Nation wears a split-horn ermine cap with a trail of eagle feathers, the mark of the bravest of leaders.

America's Indian Heritage 13

Preview & Review

Use these questions to guide your reading. Answer the questions after completing Section 2.

Understanding Issues, Events, & Ideas. Use the following words to describe the first European ventures outside Europe: Viking, saga, Vinland, manor, serf, feudal system, Crusades, Holy Land, Islam, Moslems, Indies, Commercial Revolution, compass, astrolabe.

1. What problems are there with using the Viking Sagas as a historical source?
2. Explain the relationship between serfs and lords.
3. How did Europe change during the Commercial Revolution?
4. What inventions made longer sea voyages possible? How?

Thinking Critically. 1. Imagine you are a member of Leif Ericson's crew. Describe what you see when you set foot on Vinland for the first time. **2.** Do you think the Crusades were successful? Why or why not?

National Archives of Norway, Oslo

A Norse ship such as the Vikings might have sailed to America is shown on the seal of the city of Bergen, Norway. It was carved in about 1300. Why do you think the Vikings crossed the ocean?

2. EUROPE AWAKENS

The Viking Sagas

The second discovery of America was much less important than the first. It occurred about the year 1000, less than a thousand years ago, but we know little for certain about the event or the European people who took part in it. The discoverers were Norwegian sailors who were called **Vikings.**

In 982 a redheaded Viking named Eric the Red sailed from Iceland and in 986 founded a settlement near the southern tip of the island of Greenland in the North Atlantic. The story of Eric and his family and their adventures was passed down from generation to generation in **sagas,** a traditional Scandinavian story form. These sagas were told and retold. They were not written down until 200 years after the events they describe.

The two major sagas about their adventures, *Eric the Red's Saga* and the *Greenlanders' Saga,* contradict each other at many points. They are obviously a mixture of fact and fancy. Nevertheless, there is little doubt that either Leif Ericson, Eric's son, or another Viking sailor was the first European to set foot on the North American continent.

Archaeologists have discovered the remains of only one Viking camp in North America. It is at a place called L'Anse aux Meadows (the Creek of the Meadows) in Newfoundland. But the sagas speak of a land called **Vinland** (Wine Land) which must have been farther south since grapes do not grow as far north as Newfoundland. According to the *Greenlanders' Saga,* Leif sailed to Helluland (Baffin Island today) and Markland (Labrador). He then passed around a large island (Newfoundland) and reached a country "so choice, it seemed to them that none of the cattle would require fodder for the winter." There he found the grapevines. Leif and his crew loaded their boat with grapes and vines and timber before they sailed back to Greenland.

Next, the saga tells us, Leif Ericson's brother Thorvald sailed to Vinland. While exploring, he and his party encountered nine men in kayaks. A kayak is a kind of canoe. They killed eight of the men but the ninth escaped, soon to return with a larger force. Although the Vikings drove them off, Thorvald was killed in the battle.

According to the sagas, other expeditions followed, one led by Eric's daughter Freydis. The Vikings gathered grapes, traded for furs with the natives, whom they called *Skraelings,* and fought with them repeatedly. Sometime around the year 1010 the Vikings stopped visiting Vinland, perhaps because of these troubles with the Skraelings. Outside Norway and Iceland no one knew of their adventures. Nearly five hundred more years passed before the original Americans were again disturbed by outsiders.

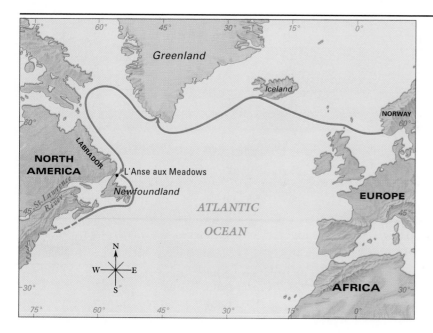

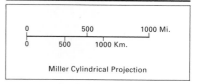

0   500   1000 Mi.

0   500   1000 Km.

Miller Cylindrical Projection

LEARNING FROM MAPS. *The Vikings crossed the Atlantic at one of its narrowest points. In what direction did they sail to reach Vinland?*

Europe in the Year 1000

If the Vikings could make their way to North America, why did no other Europeans attempt to explore the western seas for such a long time? There were several reasons for the delay. Life in Europe was slow paced. Little changed from one year to the next. The people were mostly poor and uneducated. Curiosity about the rest of the world was at a low point. Each village, or **manor,** was a tiny world in itself, ruled by a lord. The lord's fields were cultivated by peasants called **serfs.** Serfdom was a condition halfway between freedom and slavery. Serfs could not leave their village. They were said to be bound to the soil. They labored to feed themselves and their families, but a large part of what they produced went to the lord of the manor. In exchange the lord protected his serfs against enemies and acted as lawgiver and judge for the community.

Nations as we know them did not yet exist. True, there were kings of places called England and France, but these rulers had relatively little power. The lesser nobles, the lords of the manor, owed their power to a great duke or count, he in turn to a king. Under what was called the **feudal system** each lord owed certain payments or services to a higher authority. In return for these "feudal dues" the higher noble protected him. But the lords of the manors controlled the land and the people, which meant that more often than not they were practically independent.

There was little trade between one manor and the next. Nearly everything that was eaten, worn, or used was made right in the community. Such a life had advantages. Everyone knew what to expect of everyone else. Misunderstandings were rare. But it was a

This mural was painted on a castle wall in Trent, Italy. It is titled, "The Month of August." The 15th-century artist represented the feudal system with some ladies of the manor in the foreground, poor villagers going to market in the middle ground, and serfs harvesting grain in the background. Give a brief description of each of these three classes in the feudal system.

narrow existence in a small world. People lacked not only the wealth and free time to explore but even the urge to do so.

The Crusades

Outside pressures eventually ended Europe's slumber. One was a series of religious wars, the **Crusades,** organized by the Roman Catholic popes in order to get control of the city of Jerusalem and the rest of the **Holy Land** of Palestine. This region had been overrun by the followers of the Arab prophet Mohammed, founder of **Islam,** a new religion. *Islam* means "submission to God." Believers in Islam are called **Moslems.** The Moslems created a huge empire extending from India in the East through the Holy Land and across North Africa to the Atlantic Ocean. They also conquered most of Spain.

About the time that the Vikings were exploring the lands west of Greenland, the Moslem ruler of Palestine, the Caliph Hakam, began to persecute Christians in his domain. It became impossible for Europeans to visit the Holy Land.

Therefore, in 1095 Pope Urban II summoned Catholics to take up the cross (*crusade* means "marked with a cross") and drive the Moslems out of Palestine. All over Europe lords and serfs responded. Thousands sewed crosses to their garments and marched off, first to Constantinople, which is today the city of Istanbul in northwestern Turkey, and then on to Palestine. In 1099 the crusaders captured Jerusalem and founded the Christian Kingdom of Jerusalem. Crusaders sought not only a visit to the Holy Land but also the relics of the life and death of Christ—the Holy Grail used at the Last Supper, the Crown of Thorns, and the cross on which Christ was crucified.

The Moslems did not meekly submit to Christian control of a region that was equally holy to their faith. For the next 200 years war raged almost continuously. The sultan Saladin recaptured Jerusalem in 1187. Gradually the Moslems pushed the Christians back. Crusade after Crusade was organized in Europe to help the Christian Kingdom and regain the lost territory. Finally, in 1291, the last Christian stronghold, the city of Acre, was forced to surrender.

The Commercial Revolution

The Crusades caused great changes in the ways that Europeans thought and acted. The tens of thousands who traveled by land and sea to the Holy Land saw another world and heard new ideas. In the markets they tasted new foods such as dates and rice and oranges. They discovered pepper and cinnamon, ginger, nutmeg, cloves, and other spices to flavor and preserve foods. They bought garments made of silk and cotton, finer and more comfortable than the wool they wore. Jewels, rugs, and countless other beautiful objects excited them. Almost all of these treasures of the Orient came to the Holy

From a French manuscript hand colored in 1584 comes the "Capture of Alexandria." The crusaders in their armor are about to enter the ancient city in Egypt that once housed the world's greatest library. How does the artist show that this was a voyage on sea as well as on land?

In *A Distant Mirror* an historian studied the 14th century. She gave this neat summary.

> **"Stimulated by commerce, a surge took place in art, technology, building, learning, explorations by land and sea, universities, cities, banking and credit, and every sphere that enriched life and widened horizons. . . ."**
>
> Barbara Tuchman

Art Resource

Marco Polo, shown here in traditional Tartar dress, learned much about the Orient in his 17 years there. For much of the time, he served as an ambassador for Kublai Khan. Why might this be an excellent way to learn about a foreign country?

Land by old trade routes from India, China, and the islands off the east coast of Asia, the **Indies.**

When the crusaders returned to their homelands, they brought goods from Asia for others to see. Amidst this excitement, travelers from Venice—Marco Polo, his father, and uncle—set out for China in 1271. They returned 25 years later with riches and amazing stories. The desire for more Asian goods quickly spread. European society began to pass through what we call the **Commercial Revolution.** Imagine the excitement people felt when they read Marco Polo's descriptions of mysterious new Asian lands:

> **"** After going thirty miles in a westerly direction, through a country filled with fine buildings, among vineyards and many cultivated and fertile fields, we arrived at a handsome and considerable city, named Gouza. The townspeople lived by commerce and manual arts. They manufactured the finest kind of cloth.
>
> From the city of Gouza we journeyed ten days through Cathay [China]. . . . We saw many vineyards and much cultivated land. From here grapes were carried to Cathay, where the vine does not grow. Here we found an abundance of mulberry trees, the leaves of which allow the inhabitants [worms] to produce large quantities of silk. We noticed a degree of civilization which existed among all the people of this country, because of their frequent contacts with the towns, which are not far from each other. To these towns the merchants continually traveled carrying their goods from one city to another.
>
> At the end of ten days journey from the city of Gouza we arrived at the kingdom of Ta-in-fu, whose chief city, the capital of the province, bears the same name. Ta-in-fu is very large and beautiful. A great deal of trade is carried on in this city. A variety of articles are manufactured, including weapons which are used by the grand Khan's armies. There are many vineyards from which large quantities of grapes were gathered. Although this is the only district within the borders of Ta-in-fu that has vineyards, there is still enough supply for the entire province. Other fruits also grow here in plenty, as does the mulberry tree, together with the worms that yield the silk.
>
> Upon leaving Ta-in-fu, we traveled several days through a fine country in which there were many cities, where commerce and manufacturing prevailed. We reached a large city named Pi-an-fu, which is very famous. Like Ta-in-fu, this city contains numerous merchants and artisans. Silk is produced here also in great quantity.[1] **"**

[1]From *The Travels of Marco Polo: The Venetian*, edited by William Marsden

To pay for Asian goods, Europeans had to produce more goods of their own. They manufactured more woolen cloth, trapped more fur-bearing animals, cut more lumber. The isolated life of the self-sufficient manor ended. People left the manors. Towns grew into cities. Since townspeople produce no food, the remaining farmers increased their production to feed them. Lords of the manor cleared more land. To get their serfs to do more work, the lords had to grant them more privileges. In addition there were artisans of every sort to be housed and fed while they erected Europe's soaring cathedrals. By custom no serfs or slave laborers were used to build these mighty structures.

Life became more exciting—and more uncertain and dangerous, too. Trade between East and West made merchants and bankers more important. They needed strong rulers who would build roads, protect trade routes against robbers, and keep the peace. They willingly lent money to these rulers. The rulers used the loans to raise armies to protect their lands against foreign enemies and also against robbers who preyed on traveling merchants. Thus, merchants and kings helped one another. The kings became more powerful, the merchants richer. The European economy expanded.

This is how books were printed in the late 16th century. Typesetters pick movable type from trays called fonts on the left. The press is on the right. Explain how printing broke down barriers between ordinary people and the rich.

Europe Stirs to New Ideas

The religious ideals that inspired the Crusades were not forgotten. But some Europeans became more concerned about their own world, less about the hereafter. More people were buying and selling, enjoying luxuries, appreciating art, gaining scientific knowledge. Advances in printing made by Johannes Gutenberg of Germany in the 1450s did still more to break down barriers. With Gutenberg's press, used first to print a Bible, a printer could make any number of copies of a book simply by setting the type once. It was no longer necessary to copy manuscripts by hand. Books became much cheaper. As a result ordinary people as well as rich learned to read. They improved their minds with the powerful new knowledge found in books.

Great improvements were soon made in designing and sailing ships. The Vikings had crossed the Atlantic without navigation instruments. They steered by watching the stars and the sun, hoping for the best. By about 1100 the **compass** had been invented. Its magnetized needle always pointed north, which enabled sailors to know their direction even when sun and stars were hidden by clouds. By the 1400s sailors were also using the **astrolabe,** an instrument that measured a ship's latitude—that is, its distance north or south of the equator. These instruments made navigation more accurate.

Soon larger ships were designed and built. The stage was set for the third and final discovery of America and for the exploration and invasion of many other parts of the world by Europeans.

National Maritime Museum, Greenwich

This beautiful astrolabe with case from the 16th century no doubt made many a sea voyage. It was used to reckon a ship's latitude. What other important navigational instrument had been invented about 1100?

Return to the Preview & Review on page 14.

Portuguese carracks combined European square foresails with aftermasts adapted from the Arabs.

Preview & Review

Use these questions to guide your reading. Answer the questions after completing Section 3.
Understanding Issues, Events, & Ideas. Contrast the search for eastern routes with the Viking voyages, using the following words: middlemen, geography, navigation, San Salvador, Hispaniola, Line of Demarcation.
1. What made Europeans search for a new route to the Indies?
2. What contributions did Henry the Navigator make to the Age of Discovery?
3. What was Columbus' goal? In what way was he well qualified for his undertaking?
Thinking Critically. 1. Use your historical imagination to describe the arrival of Columbus and his crew as it appeared to the "Indians" living on San Salvador. **2.** Compare Columbus' reception when he first returned to Spain with the treatment he received in the last years of his life.

3. THE AGE OF DISCOVERY

The Search for Eastern Routes

As we said at the beginning, all of the discoveries of America were made by accident. The third one was made by explorers who were looking for a better way to get to China.

Trade between Europe and the East was dominated by Italian merchants whose ships sailed from Venice, Naples, and other ports. Their ships carried cloth, furs, metals, and other European products to Constantinople and brought back the silks, spices, jewels, and other Oriental goods that Europeans craved. These goods were very costly.

The merchants of Constantinople justified their high prices by pointing out how dangerous and expensive it was to bring goods to Constantinople from places half the world away. Their caravans had to crawl through high mountain passes infested with bandits and cross burning deserts where bands of roving thieves might strike at any time. Goods passed through many **middlemen.** Each of these earned a profit, adding to the final cost. Local lords taxed the travelers and their goods. There were tolls to be paid at bridges and ferries. Little wonder that the people of western Europe were eager to find easier and less expensive routes to the East.

The obvious path east was by no means the shortest. It was the all-sea route around Africa to India, the Indies, and China. This longer route had many advantages. Ships sail day and night, while

STRATEGIES FOR SUCCESS

READING A TIME LINE

Historians say that "the skeleton of history is chronology." The dictionary defines *chronology* as "the science that deals with measuring time by regular divisions and that assigns to events their proper dates." In other words, historians arrange events in *chronological order,* or the order in which they happened.

One of the best ways to show chronological order is by a *time line.* Time lines appear at the end of each chapter of *The Story of America.* These time lines show the order in which the events mentioned in each chapter happened and complement the written summary.

How to Read a Time Line

In reading a time line, follow these steps.

1. **Determine its framework.** Note the years covered and the intervals of time into which the time line is divided. The time lines in *The Story of America* are divided into years, except those in this first unit, which are divided by 100-year periods (centuries) because they cover such broad spans of time. Colored bars show long-term events.
2. **Study the sequence carefully.** A time line is proportional. The space between each date—the *interval*—is always the same. In this way you can visually see the span of time between events. Remember that sometimes the length of time between events is an important historical fact. (Also note that each year is marked on the time line, even when no event is listed.)
3. **Fill in the blanks.** Time lines usually list only key events. Study those listed. Think about the events and the people, places, and other events associated with them. In this way, you can "flesh out" the framework provided by the time line.
4. **Note relationships.** Ask yourself how each event relates to the other events. This will help you recognize cause-effect relationships.
5. **Use the time line as a summary.** Use the listed events to weave a summary of the time period.

Applying the Strategy

Study the time line below. Note that the years covered are 900 to 1500. The time line has intervals of 100 years. The time line lists events related to the Age of Discovery. As you know from your reading, each journey was built on the experiences of previous journeys. Eventually this spirit of exploration led to the discovery of a "New World." What other relationships among the events can you discover? Remember to "fill in" important events not listed on the time line.

For independent practice, see Reviewing Chronological Order on each Chapter Review page.

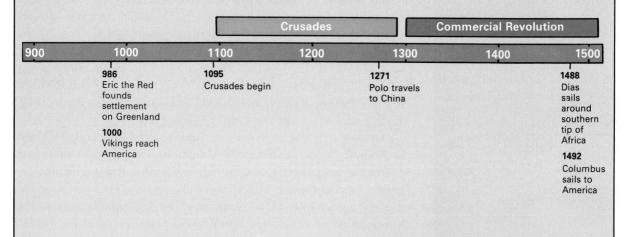

THE AGE OF DISCOVERY

Crusades	Commercial Revolution

| 900 | 1000 | 1100 | 1200 | 1300 | 1400 | 1500 |

986
Eric the Red founds settlement on Greenland

1000
Vikings reach America

1095
Crusades begin

1271
Polo travels to China

1488
Dias sails around southern tip of Africa

1492
Columbus sails to America

Prince Henry of Portugal led scholars in studying geography and navigation. He became known as Henry the Navigator. This miniature was painted in the middle 15th century. Why did Henry establish his school?

This oil portrait is believed to be an accurate likeness of Christopher Columbus, although none was painted during his lifetime. His face seems proud and strong willed. Why was Columbus more apt than most sailors to find a new route to the Far East?

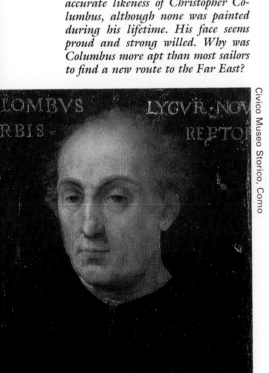

Civico Museo Storico, Como

land travelers and the horses, donkeys, and camels that haul their belongings must stop each night to rest. The sea route would save time and labor. Once packed in a vessel's hold, goods would not have to be unloaded and reloaded until a port was reached. Still more important, only one shipper would profit from the sea voyage, and no tolls or taxes need be paid along the way.

No one had ever sailed from Europe all the way to the Orient. There were no maps or charts, little knowledge of winds and currents. Indeed, no European had even seen the west coast of Africa below the Sahara. Prince Henry of Portugal, who became known as Henry the Navigator, took the lead in finding a route around the continent of Africa.

Henry created a kind of research center for scholars to share their knowledge of **geography,** the study of the earth and its surface features, and **navigation,** the science of sailing ships. Experts came from many lands. Their information about tides and the position of the stars in different regions was of great value to Henry's captains. Armed with this information and financed by Henry, brave sailors gradually explored the African coast. In 1445 one of Henry's ships reached the site of present-day Dakar, in Senegal, where the great western bulge of Africa turns to the south and east.

By the 1470s, after Henry's death, Portuguese ships had reached the equator. In 1488 Bartolomeu Dias managed to sail around the southern tip of the continent, only to turn back when the crew panicked, afraid to venture into the unknown seas ahead. Finally, in 1498, Vasco da Gama sailed around Africa and on to India.

Christopher Columbus

Meanwhile, another explorer traveled in a different direction. His name was Christopher Columbus. Instead of sailing far to the south around Africa, he headed for Asia by sailing directly west. This possibility had attracted little attention. Educated people no longer believed that the world was flat. They did not think a ship sailing too far to the west would reach the edge and "fall off." But they believed that there was no land on the "other side" of the globe. Since it was at least 10,000 miles (16,000 kilometers) from western Europe to Asia, no ship could carry enough food and water to make the journey. The trip was out of the question.

Or was it? Columbus did not think so, and few captains knew the Atlantic Ocean as well as he. Columbus was a sturdily built man of above-average height, red-haired, and with a ruddy complexion. He was born in Genoa, in northern Italy, in 1451. He went to sea at an early age. While still a young man, he had sailed south to the Guinea coast of Africa and north to the waters around the British Isles. He may even have visited Iceland.

In 1476 Columbus was shipwrecked off Portugal. He settled in Lisbon and along with his brother Bartholomeo became a chart maker. Columbus studied every map and book of geography he could get his hands on. A doctor who knew him wrote that Columbus had a "noble and grand desire to go to the places where the spices grow." He was particularly fascinated by the famous tales of Marco Polo. If Columbus could get to China and the Indies by sailing west, fame and fortune would be his.

There were islands in the Atlantic—the Madeiras 350 miles (560 kilometers) from southern Portugal, the Azores 600 miles (960 kilometers) farther west. Columbus heard stories about an island called Antila, only 1,000 miles (1,600 kilometers) from Japan. He persuaded himself, moreover, that China was only 4,500 miles (7,200 kilometers) west of Spain and Portugal, Japan nearer still.

When he decided to sail westward, Columbus first sought the backing of the king of Portugal, John II. John believed, quite correctly, that Columbus was greatly underestimating the distance to be covered. He refused to invest in such a foolhardy expedition. Columbus, he said, was a "big talker and boastful . . . and full of fancy and imagination." The Columbus brothers then attempted to interest Henry VII of England, Charles VIII of France, and the Spanish monarchs, Ferdinand and Isabella. All rejected their proposals.

But Columbus persisted. Finally, early in 1492, Queen Isabella agreed to outfit three tiny ships. The *Santa María,* which Columbus personally commanded, was about 85 feet (about 26 meters) long and had a crew of 39. The *Pinta* and the *Niña* were somewhat smaller than the *Santa María.* The entire expedition consisted of 87 men.

On Friday, August 3, 1492, the little fleet set sail from Palos, Spain. After a stopover in the Canary Islands off northwestern Africa, the ships headed into the unknown. For over a month they sailed westward, always toward the setting sun, always alone, never another sail in sight. Columbus was a magnificent sailor. The *Santa María*'s compass guided him, but to judge his position he had only a sandglass that had to be turned each half hour to measure time and only his years of experience at sea to estimate his speed. Yet he reckoned the distance traveled each day with amazing accuracy.

As day followed day into mid-October, Columbus' men grew tense. They had sailed far beyond where land was supposed to be, and before them lay only the endless ocean. They demanded that Columbus turn back. He would not. Be of good hope, he urged them. Finally he promised to abandon the search if they failed to sight land by October 12.

The breeze freshened and the three ships picked up speed. Now broken branches, land birds, and other hopeful signs began to appear. At last, by moonlight at two o'clock in the morning of October 12, the lookout Rodrigo de Triana spotted the foam of waves breaking on a distant shore. "*Tierra! Tierra!*" he shouted. Land! Land!

Photo MAS

Why do you think Isabella, shown here, outfitted Columbus' tiny fleet when so many others had refused him?

Columbus in America

When day broke, Columbus approached the land, which was a small island. He was absolutely certain that he had reached the Indies. Now he had earned the title given him by Ferdinand and Isabella— Admiral of the Ocean Sea. He named the island **San Salvador,** or Holy Savior, out of gratitude for having reached it safely. He found no spices there, no silks or rugs. Except for tiny bits that some of the inhabitants wore in their noses, he found no gold.

The natives of the island of Guanahaní, for that was its name in their language, were astonished and awed by the Europeans. Columbus, certain in his belief that he was in the Indies, called them Indians. All native Americans would thereafter be thus mistakenly described. They came forth shyly, bearing gifts. "They invite you to share everything they possess," Columbus recorded. He in turn gave them small presents—beads, bits of cloth, and tiny brass bells that particularly delighted them. When Luis de Torres, a member of the crew who knew Arabic, tried to speak to these "Indians," not a one understood him. This seemed odd, for Arabic was a common language in the Indies.

By signs the Indians told Columbus that many other islands lay to the west and south. So he pushed on, taking a few Indians along

LEARNING FROM MAPS. *During his four voyages Columbus became quite familiar with the lands bordering the Caribbean Sea. Name the Caribbean lands he visited.*

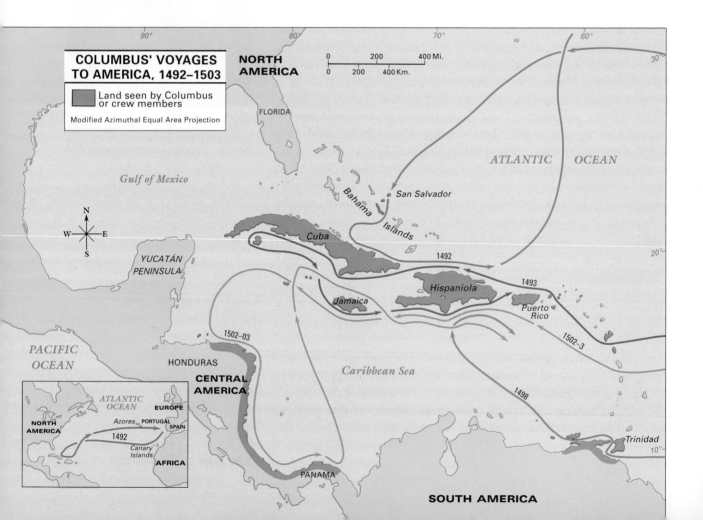

COLUMBUS' VOYAGES TO AMERICA, 1492–1503

Land seen by Columbus or crew members

Modified Azimuthal Equal Area Projection

as interpreters. Everywhere he found the same charming, generous people. But he found no spices and very little gold.

Soon the explorers reached Cuba. Perhaps this was China! At every harbor along this large landmass, Columbus expected to find a fleet of Chinese junks. Some of the local people told him that gold could be found at *Cubanacan,* by which they meant "in the middle of Cuba." Columbus thought they were saying *El Gran Can*—in Spanish, "the Great Khan"—and sent a delegation headed by de Torres to present his respects to the Emperor of China! Of course, the delegation found only tropical jungle.

Finally, in December 1492, Columbus reached an island which he named **Hispaniola,** the Spanish Isle. It is presently occupied by Haiti and the Dominican Republic. There the inhabitants had substantial amounts of gold; one chief gave him a belt with a solid gold buckle. The Spaniards could not find the source of the gold, but there was enough of it to convince them that there must be mines nearby. When the *Santa María* ran aground and had to be abandoned, Columbus left some of his crew on the island and ordered them to build a fort with the remains of the ship and to look for the gold. He then sailed home in the *Niña,* still certain that he would find gold but not certain he had reached the Far East.

Columbus Returns to Spain

Columbus landed a hero at Palos, Spain, on March 15, 1493. Everywhere crowds lined his route, gazing in wonder at the Indians he was bringing to show the king and queen. When he reached Barcelona, Ferdinand and Isabella showered honors upon him. They made him their personal representative, or viceroy, in the Indies.

No one yet had a very clear picture of where these new territories were. Columbus had made the Spanish claim, but Portugal, which already owned the Azores, claimed rights to lands farther into the Atlantic. The two Catholic countries turned to Pope Alexander VI to decide the issue. In May 1493 the Pope divided the ocean about 300 miles (480 kilometers) beyond the Azores. The dividing line was called the **Line of Demarcation.** New lands to the west of the line were to belong to Spain, those to the east to Portugal. In 1494 Spain and Portugal signed a treaty that moved the line farther west.

When Brazil, which extends well east of the Line of Demarcation, was discovered in 1500, it became Portuguese. This explains why today Brazilians speak Portuguese while most other South Americans speak Spanish.

Meanwhile, in September 1493 Columbus again sailed westward, this time with a fleet of 17 ships and 2,000 colonists. When he reached Hispaniola, he discovered that the crew members he had left there had been killed by the Indians. Columbus built a new settlement, named Isabella, then sailed off on a further futile search for China.

A sorrowful Isabella and a sober court is the subject of "Columbus before the Queen." Emanuel Leutze did this oil painting in 1843. Columbus wrote of his experience in chains: "I am here and in such a state that even persons of the lowliest condition must despise me. Surely someone in the world will not allow this to be. If I had taken over the Indies and given them to the Moors, I should meet no greater hostility." What proved to be Columbus' fatal flaw?

Return to the Preview & Review on page 20.

When he returned to Isabella, he found the town in very bad condition. Many colonists were sick, others were squabbling with one another. More fighting had broken out with the Indians. Little gold had been collected. Much discouraged, Columbus sailed back to Spain.

Columbus was a great sailor and a brave and determined man. But he was not good at politics or business. He made two more trips across the Atlantic. On one he discovered the island of Trinidad off the north coast of South America. On the other he explored the coast of Central America from Honduras to Panama and spent more than a year on the island of Jamaica. He never obtained the wealth he had hoped for. The king took away most of his power. The great discoverer even spent a short time in jail. He died, almost forgotten, in 1506. He never accepted the fact that he had not reached the Indies. 📧

4. SPAIN'S GOLDEN AGE

Preview & Review

America: A New World

News of Columbus' voyage and the wonderful things he had brought back with him spread rapidly through Europe. Gradually more new lands were discovered as explorers ventured across the Atlantic. On one of these voyages an Italian named Amerigo Vespucci visited the northern coast of South America. Later he traveled along the coast of Brazil. The voyages were not in themselves path breaking, and Vespucci was more a tourist than an explorer. But he wrote a description of his adventures that attracted much attention. Europeans were beginning to realize that an entire new continent existed out there in the Atlantic Ocean. Amerigo Vespucci did not mention "the Indies." He wrote about a **New World.**

In 1507 a German geographer who had read Amerigo's account suggested that the New World should be called America in his honor. The idea caught on, and by the 1530s people in every European country except Portugal and Spain were calling the new regions America. But 500 years after Columbus, we still call the islands discovered by Columbus the West Indies.

Balboa and Magellan

Vespucci showed that America was very large. Two Spanish explorers soon proved that it was nowhere near Asia.

The first was Vasco Núñez de Balboa. Balboa was the governor of a Spanish settlement in what is now the Republic of Panama, in Central America. In 1513 he set out with about 200 Spanish soldiers and several hundred Indians to explore the area. The party made its way through a thick jungle that was infested with insects and poisonous snakes. They crossed tangled swamps and climbed up rugged mountains. In three weeks they covered only about 60 miles (96 kilometers). Finally, when they neared the top of the mountains, Balboa ordered his men to stop. He climbed to the summit alone. There before him, glittering in the sun as far as the eye could see, stretched what seemed to be an endless ocean.

After giving thanks to God, Balboa and his men pushed onward until they reached the shore. Where breakers came roaring in over the sand flats, he waded in, sword in hand, and took possession of the new ocean for Spain.

Balboa had crossed the Isthmus of Panama, where the Panama Canal would be dug 400 years later. His discovery that another great body of water lay beyond America proved that it was a long way to the Indies. To get there by sailing west, one would have to find a passage through or around the land barrier.

Use these questions to guide your reading. Answer the questions after completing Section 4.
Understanding Issues, Events, & Ideas. Use the following words to discuss Spanish adventures in America: New World, America, isthmus, strait, Pacific Ocean, circumnavigate, Aztecs, conquistadors, mission, Incas, immunity, economy.
1. What was the significance of Vespucci's voyages to the "New World"?
2. What did the voyage of Magellan and El Cano prove?
3. How did disease help the Europeans "conquer" the native Americans?
4. What made Spain's empire so rich? What drained away its riches? What brought Spain's Golden Age to an end?
Thinking Critically. 1. Predict what might have happened to Aztec culture and civilization if the Aztecs had not been conquered by the Spaniards. **2.** If you were a member of the party of any Spanish conquistador, which one would you choose to follow? Why?

The Granger Collection

The inscription circling this 17th-century engraving reads: "This is Vasco Núñez Zerez de Balboa who discovered the Sea of the South." What did Balboa's discovery tell the world?

Spain's Golden Age   27

Ferdinand Magellan's portrait was probably made in the 16th century. Who was his partner in his round-the-world voyage?

Juan Sebastian El Cano was able to complete Magellan's voyage around the world. Do you think this portrait shows the will power it must have taken to head home with the 17 survivors on the ship Victoria?

Since Balboa had shown that only a narrow neck of land, or **isthmus,** separated the oceans at Panama, surely somewhere there must be a narrow water passage, or **strait,** connecting the Atlantic to Balboa's ocean. In 1518 a Portuguese captain named Ferdinand Magellan presented Emperor Charles V of Spain with a plan to find such a route. Magellan was a short, stocky man, dark, bearded, and very, very tough. He was a veteran of several wars in the East and knew the area well. He approached Charles after his own king, Manuel I of Portugal, had refused to back his expedition.

Charles V agreed to finance Magellan's voyage. On September 20, 1519, the explorer set sail from Sanlúcar de Barrameda, Spain, with five ships and 237 men. Their first stop was in the Canary Islands. From there they sailed to Brazil, then southward along the coast of South America, searching always for a water passage to the west.

Off what is now Argentina Magellan's fleet ran into a terrible storm. One of the ships sank. This disaster so frightened the sailors that they urged Magellan to turn back. When he refused, some mutinied. Magellan crushed this rebellion before it could spread, and he put the leaders to death. Then he sailed on.

Finally the voyagers reached the southern tip of South America. As the fleet entered the narrow passage between the land and the island of Tierra del Fuego (Land of Fire), fierce storms and huge waves tossed the ships about wildly. The sailors on one ship, shaken and discouraged, turned tail before the tempest and fled homeward. Sadly, this vessel contained a large part of the expedition's supplies.

The three remaining ships battled head winds and powerful currents in the strait for 38 days. At last they made their way through the passage, which we now call the Strait of Magellan, into a broad and tranquil sea. Because it seemed so calm and safe after the long struggle with the turbulent strait, Magellan named it the **Pacific Ocean.** (*Pacific* means "peaceful.")

Magellan now happily pointed his fleet toward the west. But the greatest ordeal lay ahead. For 98 days the three ships sailed onward. They sighted only two uninhabited islands. When their food ran out, the hungry sailors ate the rats in the ships' holds, then leather from the rigging, then sawdust. Many died. Those who remained grew steadily weaker and weaker.

Finally, early in 1521, the fleet reached the island we call Guam. Magellan was now directly south of Japan. After seizing food and water from the peaceful inhabitants, he pushed on to the Philippine Islands. There, in a battle against local warriors, Magellan was killed. Following Magellan's death, Juan El Cano assumed command.

The fleet wandered about the Indies for many months. Two more ships were lost. Only the *Victoria* remained to sail across the Indian Ocean, around the tip of Africa, and home to Sanlúcar, Spain. On September 6, 1522, almost three years after they had set out, El Cano and the other 17 who were still alive set foot again on Spanish soil.

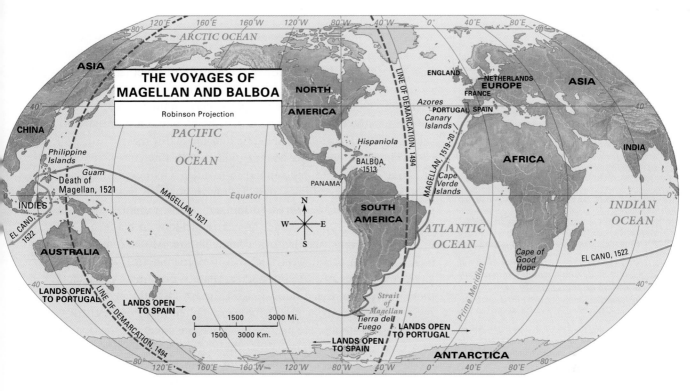

THE VOYAGES OF
MAGELLAN AND BALBOA

Robinson Projection

They were the first to **circumnavigate,** or sail around, the entire earth.

This was one of the greatest sea voyages of all time, which is reason enough for remembering it. But it brought few benefits to Spain. By proving that Asia was so far west of Europe, the expedition demonstrated that sailing there in that direction was much more dangerous and expensive than anyone had imagined. So ended Columbus' dream of capturing the rich trade of Asia by sailing west.

LEARNING FROM MAPS. *The circumnavigation of the earth by Magellan, El Cano, and their crew was an amazing feat. Why was the voyage across the Pacific Ocean the most trying part of the journey?*

Cortés and Montezuma

While Magellan and El Cano were making their great voyage, the Spaniards were extending their control in America. Colonies were founded on all the larger islands of the Caribbean Sea. By 1519 most of the coastline around the Caribbean had been explored, and some knowledge of the peoples of the Americas had been gathered.

The most powerful state was the Aztec empire of central Mexico. In 1519 Hernán Cortés and about 450 soldiers set sail from the Spanish colony of Cuba to make contact with the Aztecs. The Aztec society and culture was mighty and wealthy. They had built great stone temples and had mastered mathematics and astronomy. Their capital city, Tenochtitlán, located on an artificial island, housed 200,000 people.

The Aztecs were also warlike. They had conquered most of the other people of Mexico. Only a few groups, such as the Tarascan, had successfully resisted them. According to their religion, human sacrifices had to be offered to the god of war to keep the sun moving

This drawing from an early Aztec manuscript shows the meeting of Cortés and Montezuma. Montezuma is seated at the left with members of his court, Cortés at the right with his interpreter Doña Marina, whom the Aztecs called Malinche. In contrast to this peaceful greeting, what was the outcome of the conquistadors' discovery of the Aztecs?

in the sky. Each year thousands were slaughtered for this purpose. The victims were chosen from among the captives taken in wars. The Aztecs forced those they had conquered to pay heavy taxes.

As Cortés and his handful of Spanish soldiers marched inland from the coast, many local people eagerly joined forces with him. By the time he reached Tenochtitlán, he had an army of many thousands. With this army Cortés defeated the Aztecs.

The Aztec emperor, Montezuma, was a thin, fair-skinned man of about 40, delicate and refined in manner. His people treated him as a kind of god. Nobles had to bow low three times before approaching him. They addressed him as "Lord, my lord, great lord" and spoke with eyes lowered, not daring to look at his face.

Here we must use historical imagination. Montezuma probably believed that Cortés, with his steel armor, powerful weapons, and large war horses, was also a god. Perhaps Cortés was Quetzalcoatl, the chief rival of the Aztec war god. In any case the Aztecs did not resist the Spaniards at first. Montezuma gave them rich gifts of gold and precious stones. He became a virtual prisoner, and the Spaniards took control of his empire. Why did he do this? In this excerpt from his letter to Emperor Charles V of Spain, Cortés claimed among other things that the Aztecs willingly gave their treasure away:

❝I spoke to Montezuma one day, and told him that Your Highness [Charles V] was in need of gold, . . . and I besought him to send some of his people . . . to . . . those lords who had there submitted themselves to your Highness to pray them to assist Your Majesty with some part of what they had. Besides Your Highness's need, this would testify that they began to render service, and Your Highness would the more esteem their good will; and I told Montezuma that he also should give me from his treasures, as I wished to send them to Your Majesty. He asked me afterwards to choose the Spaniards whom I wished to send, and two by two, and five by five, he distributed them through many provinces and cities. He sent some of his people with them, ordering them to go to the lords of those provinces and cities and tell them that I had commanded each one of them to contribute a certain measure of gold. Thus it was done, and all those lords to whom he sent gave very compliantly, as had been asked, not only in valuables, but also in bars and sheets of gold, besides all the jewels of gold, and silver, and the feather work, and the stones, and the many other things . . . so marvelous that, because of their novelty and strangeness, they have no price, nor is it probable that all the princes ever heard of in the world possess such treasures.[1]❞

[1]From *Fernando Cortes, his five letters of relation to the Emperor Charles V*, Vol. 1

Compare Cortés' claim with this view, taken from a written Aztec history of the conquest.

    ❝ Then Montezuma dispatched various chiefs to meet the Spaniards. They gave the 'gods' emblems of gold and feathers, and golden necklaces. And when they were given these presents, the Spaniards burst into smiles; their eyes shone with pleasure; they were delighted by them. They picked up the gold and fingered it like monkeys; they seemed to be transported by joy, as if their hearts were illumined and made new.

    The truth is that they longed and lusted for gold. Their bodies swelled with greed, and their hunger was ravenous; they hungered like pigs for that gold. They snatched at the golden emblems, waved them from side to side and examined every inch of them.

    They went to Montezuma's storehouse, where his personal treasures were kept. The Spaniards grinned like little beasts and patted each other with delight.

    When they entered the hall of treasures, it was as if they had arrived in Paradise. They searched everywhere and covered everything; they were slaves to their own greed. All of Montezuma's possessions were brought out: fine bracelets, necklaces with large stones, ankle rings with gold bells, the royal crowns and all the royal finery—everything that belonged to the king and was reserved to him only. They seized these treasures as if they were their own, as if this plunder were merely a stroke of good luck. And when they had taken all the gold, they heaped up everything else in the middle of the patio.[1] ❞

For a time Cortés permitted Montezuma to remain as emperor while the Spaniards looted the Aztec treasure. But in 1520 the Aztecs suddenly revolted. They drove the Spaniards out of the city. Montezuma apparently was killed in the fight. The Spaniards quickly regrouped and, aided by their native allies, surrounded Tenochtitlán. In August 1521 they recaptured it. By 1540, when he returned to Spain, Cortés controlled much of modern Mexico, and Spanish soldiers continued to conquer more of the region.

The Conquistadors

Cortés was one of the important Spanish **conquistadors,** or conquerors. There was no excuse for his invasion of Montezuma's empire. The conquistadors were greedy and ruthless. Yet the terrible reputation of the conquistador is overstated. The Spaniards were no more

---

[1]From *The Broken Spears, The Aztec Account of the Conquest of Mexico*, edited by Miguel Leon-Portilla

❝I had [the Aztec] idols taken from their places and thrown down the steps. . . . I had images of Our Lady and of other saints put there, which caused [Montezuma] and the other natives some sorrow. . . . They believed that those idols gave them all their worldly goods.❞
Hernan Cortés, c. 1520

Points of View

❝Ixtlilxochitl [an Aztec ally] went to his mother . . . to bring her out to be baptized. She replied that he must have lost his mind to let himself be won over so easily by that handful of barbarians, the conquistadors. . . . He told her that she would receive the sacrament, even against her will.❞
An Aztec account, c. 1519

STRATEGIES FOR SUCCESS

READING MAPS

Your study of history is greatly enriched by geography. To fully understand geographic information, you must be able to read a map. All of the maps in *The Story of America* have four parts: a *title;* a *key,* or *legend;* a *scale;* and a global *grid.* If you understand the information provided by these four parts, you will be able to read a map with confidence.

How to Read a Map

To gather information from a map, follow these guidelines.

1. **Read the title.** The title of a map tells the subject of the map and what parts of the earth are shown. Some map titles include a date.
2. **Study the key, or legend.** The legend explains what the colors and special symbols on the map mean.
3. **Note the distance scale.** The map scale is used to measure distances. Maps in *The Story of America* have a bar scale. The length of the line on the scale represents that number of miles and kilometers on the earth's surface.
4. **Use the grid.** The grid of latitude and longitude helps you locate places on the earth through a special numbering system based on a unit of measure called a degree. Most of the maps in this textbook have grid "tics" around the map's border to indicate the presence of the complete grid.
5. **Note other map features.** Most maps show other information in special ways as well. The maps in *The Story of America* use a compass rose to indicate direction. *Italic* type marks physical features while regular type labels political features. Be sure to look for all the features of each map.

Applying the Strategy

Study the map below. The title, "Spanish Explorations and Conquests," tells you that the map illustrates the routes of Spanish explorers and areas of conquest in America. Although no special symbols are used on the map, colors mark the locations of the Aztec and Inca empires. You can use the compass rose to determine the directions the explorers moved. For example, De Vaca and Esteban traveled first generally west, then south. You can use the scale to measure the distance the explorers traveled.

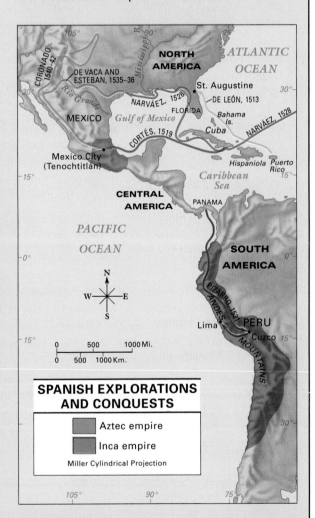

For independent practice, see *Practicing the Strategy* on pages 38–39.

greedy and ruthless than the British, French, or Dutch, or for that matter, the Aztecs. Indeed, in their attempt to bring Christianity to America, the Spanish taught many Indians to read and write and introduced useful products of many kinds.

Cortés and his men had mixed motives. Adventure for its own sake was one of these, and who can blame them? Uncovering the secrets of two vast, unknown continents was the greatest adventure in human history. Especially after gold and the other rich resources of America were discovered, most Spaniards believed that America was a paradise, a kind of Garden of Eden where they could live splendidly while also doing good. They developed a sense of special purpose, or **mission**—a belief that God had appointed them to do His work in this entirely new world. Here were people to be converted to Christianity, even if the task was a bloody one.

One of Cortés' soldiers summed up the motives of the conquistadors in a sentence: "We came here to serve God and the King, and also to get rich." The conquistadors were not only brave and ambitious but absolutely sure they were right. This gave them the energy to accomplish great deeds—and also to do great harm. By the 1530s they had gained a foothold that grew into an empire.

Already, in 1513, Juan Ponce de León had made the first Spanish landing on the mainland of North America. De León was searching for the Fountain of Youth, a magical spring that was said to prevent anyone who bathed in it from growing old. Of course, he did not find such a magic fountain, but he did claim Florida for Spain.

And in the same year that Cortés landed in Mexico, Alonzo Alvarez de Piñeda explored the coasts of Florida and Texas. Piñeda's reports led Pánfilo de Narváez to mount another expedition. In 1528 Narváez sailed from Florida in search of treasure. He died, and his men became hopelessly lost in the wilderness. Only 15 survived, among them Cabeza de Vaca and an African named Estaban. De Vaca's *La Relacion* (1542), the first book about lands that would become part of the United States, and Estaban's expedition into the American Southwest led to further explorations. In 1540 Francisco Vásquez de Coronado and a large army sought gold in what would become Arizona, New Mexico, Texas, Oklahoma, and Kansas. Meanwhile, Hernando de Soto and an even larger army explored much of what became the southern United States, also looking for gold.

In South America in 1531 Francisco Pizarro marched into the snow-capped Andes Mountains. There he found the **Incas,** a people with a culture as rich and complex as the Aztecs. Pizarro and his men defeated the Incas, seized a huge treasure of silver, and forced the Incas to work their mines for Spain's benefit.

The European Invasion

When Columbus stepped ashore on Guanahaní Island in October

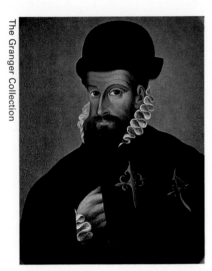

The artist of the handsome portrait of Francisco Pizarro is unknown. It was probably painted in the 16th century.

1492, he planted the Spanish flag in the sand and claimed the land as a possession of Ferdinand and Isabella. He did so despite the obvious fact that the island already belonged to someone else—the "Indians" who gathered on the beach to gaze with wonder at the strangers who had arrived in three great, white-winged canoes. He gave no thought to the rights of the local inhabitants. Nearly every later explorer—French, English, Dutch, as well as the Spanish—thoughtlessly dismissed the people they encountered. What we think of as the discovery of America was actually the invasion and conquest of America.

In these new lands Europeans felt ten feet tall. Here were discoveries to be made, fame and fortune to be won. They were sure that the native people would offer little or no resistance. Of what use were spears and arrows against men clad in steel astride horses and armed with guns and cannon? How could "savages" who worshipped many different gods, even animals, resist good Christians.

Perhaps some natives at first thought the Europeans were superior. With historical imagination it is not hard to see the Spanish conquerors as some Indians must have seen them. Here were gods come from heaven to rule them. In the hands of these gods, flaming, roaring "firesticks" could strike down an animal or human, invisibly, across great distances. These gods looked down at frail canoes from enormous floating fortresses.

In reality the Europeans were not so mighty, the Indians not so ignorant and powerless. The Europeans learned much from the native people—how to live, travel, hunt, and fight in a different environment, what to plant and how to grow it. Of the dozens of products never before seen by Europeans, corn was by far the most important.

Of course the Indians also learned from the Europeans. Textiles, and metal tools of every sort from fish hooks to shovels, knives, guns, and steel traps were highly prized. But the Indians also learned that the visiting "gods" were all too human. When the Europeans tried to conquer and enslave them, they resisted bitterly. In the end they were defeated. But the main reason was not European firepower but disease. When Cortés invaded the land of the Aztecs in 1519, there were perhaps as many as 25 million people in Mexico. A hundred years later, there were barely 1 million! Smallpox, measles, and typhoid fever—not Spanish guns—accounted for so many deaths.

The germs that caused these diseases were brought to America from Europe, where people had suffered from them for countless generations. But while many Europeans died each year from diseases like smallpox, most people had developed considerable resistance, called **immunity.** The inhabitants of America lacked immunity. Measles was a "childhood disease" in Europe. Adults seldom caught it. But it struck down Americans by the thousands. No one can blame the Europeans for this terrible destruction. Indeed, the causes of the plagues were not then known. Nevertheless, this terrible loss of life was another tragic result of the third discovery of America.

The End of Spain's Golden Age

By 1536, when Pedro de Mendoza founded the city of Buenos Aires in Argentina, Spain had control of the mightiest empire in the world. The inhabitants of lands 20 times the size of Spain recognized the Spanish king as overlord. The red and gold Spanish flag flew on staffs all over the Caribbean islands and from Buenos Aires to the land of the Zūni. This empire made Spain enormously rich. Gold and silver poured into the royal treasury. With this wealth and the weapons it could buy, Spain seemed all powerful.

But there were cracks in the Spanish armor. Spain's own ability to produce goods—its **economy**—was weak and inefficient. In the 1500s about 95 percent of the Spanish people were peasant farmers. Even so, because of poor soil and bad farming methods, they could not raise enough food to support the rest of the population. Spain had to import wheat from other parts of Europe. Manufactured articles had to be imported too, because Spain had almost no industry. Instead of using the gold and silver of America to improve farmland and finance manufacturing, the Spanish government bought what it needed abroad, paying for its imports with the treasure of America. While the flow continued, all was well. When the flow slowed to a trickle in the early 1600s, the Golden Age ended.

Meanwhile, however, aspects of Spanish culture had been permanently planted in what has ever since been called the "Latin" lands of South and Central America. Chief among these cultural traditions was the Roman Catholic Church. For more than 200 years Catholic missionaries worked to convert the Indians to the Christian faith. Although at first the missionaries had little success in winning over the Indian tribes who lived in mountainous areas—particularly the Maya and the Inca—many Indian families converted to Catholicism. Most remained loyal to it in one way or another until the end of the 19th century. Missionaries established large churches in the cities that emerged in Latin America as well as in smaller towns and villages. Missionary priests spent much of their time educating the converts and training new missionaries from the native and Spanish and Portuguese populations.

As the frontier of Spanish control and settlement expanded northward from Mexico into California and New Mexico, the conquistadores relied heavily on the missions established by the Catholic priests. Mission life brought the Indians under Spanish political rule and created farms and ranches that raised food for the settlements. These settlements included soldiers stationed in nearby forts, called *presidios*. Slowly a Latin American civilization emerged. It was made up of a combination of Catholic ritual, Indian agriculture, and Spanish political and military organization.

Aztec metalworkers crafted beautiful works, such as this gold figure of the god of Regeneration. Their Spanish conquerors melted down many such pieces and used the precious metals in their own works.

This 16th century Spanish bowl was shaped from captured Aztec silver. How did reusing these precious metals steal from our knowledge of the Aztec culture?

Return to the Preview & Review on page 27.

LINKING HISTORY & GEOGRAPHY

THE COLUMBIAN EXCHANGE

Imagine the excitement when Europeans first met American Indians. Curiosity seized both sides. Almost immediately a great exchange of material items and ideas, which we call the Columbian Exchange in honor of Christopher Columbus, began to take place.

Europeans dominated the exchange in many ways. Their plants and animals, styles, methods, and beliefs were brought to the New World by conquerers and colonists alike. Of course, plants and animals native to the Americas, such as tobacco and turkeys, new ideas, and even native people crossed the Atlantic to become established in Europe. But the greatest impact of the exchange was felt in the New World.

A Truly New World

1. How did the environment of the New World begin to change?

Not only people crossed the Atlantic Ocean to take up residence in the New World. A key aspect of the Columbian Exchange was a biological transfer. An entire collection of lifeforms was transported, both intentionally and unintentionally, by explorers, colonists, indentured servants, and slaves. What finally resulted from the mixing of these lifeforms created a unique environment in the Americas.

When Europeans first set foot on the western shores of the Atlantic, they found a biological world that was considerably different from the ones in their homelands. There were none of the Old World crops, such as wheat and peas, grasses, or even weeds that the Europeans recognized. They were unfamiliar with many of the trees, and there were absolutely no domesticated horses, sheep, goats, cattle, or even cats. Even such common creatures as rats, mice, sparrows, starlings, and honey bees were missing in the New World.

Europeans also brought with them germs that were totally new to America. Certainly the American Indians did not live in a germ-free paradise, but they had never known smallpox, measles, chickenpox, influenza, malaria, yellow fever, diptheria, whooping cough, scarlet fever, and a number of other diseases that plagued the inhabitants of the Old World. Accordingly, they had developed no immunities. European diseases soon ravaged the American Indians.

Impact on the New World

2. What was the impact of the new environment on the American Indians?

The Europeans brought many things to the New World that they hoped would help them— seeds of crops to provide food, horses for muscle and transportation. But did the native people benefit from what the Europeans brought?

There is no doubt that the American Indians did profit from European crops and livestock, especially the horse. Many tribes grew more food than they had ever known. But the toll exacted on the Indians in sickness and death from the new diseases, along with the destruction of their hunting grounds, farmland, and wild game far outweighed any of the benefits.

New Plants Take Root

3. Where and how were the first European plants introduced in the Americas?

It seems likely that the first Old World plants to spread to the New World found their first home in Newfoundland. It was here that European fishers put ashore to dry the cod and other fish taken from the waters of the Grand Banks. Before loading the dried and salted fish aboard their ships, sailors would clean out the holds of their vessels. Among the sweepings were the seeds of many European grasses, plants, and weeds that soon flourished in the new land.

Fishing vessels were putting into harbors along Newfoundland's coast nearly a century before the Jamestown and Plymouth colonies were established. In fact, in 1534, when Cartier "discovered" the St. Lawrence River, he found European fishing vessels already there! So Europe's plants began to spread on the new continent even before its people did.

A New Ecology Emerges

4. How rapidly and how far did new plants spread?

The European plants that spread most quickly over the widest area were white clover and what we call Kentucky blue grass. Mixed together they were known by the colonists as "English grass." They spread from Nova Scotia to the Carolinas and by the 1760s had crossed the Appalachians into Kentucky and Tennessee. Wherever white clover and blue grass encountered

White clover, left, blue grass, right

native American grasses, they overpowered them. They grew westward to the 100th meridian, where lack of rainfall created an environment in which they could not survive.

So dramatic was the spread of white clover and blue grass that when the famous English naturalist Charles Darwin met Mr. Asa Gray, an American botanist, he teased Gray about the ability of European grasses and weeds to overtake the American landscape. Mr. Gray answered that American grasses and weeds were "modest, woodland, retiring things; and no match for the intrusive, pretentious, self-asserting foreigners." (Later historians would note that his comments also described the interactions of Europeans and American Indians!)

A Zoological Revolution

5. How did European animals cause a zoological revolution in the New World?

Mr. Gray's comments were true of animals as well. Regardless of their purpose—meat, milk, leather, power, or speed—European domesticated animals were quickly established in America. The only truly domestic animals raised by American Indians were the dog and turkey. As a result, a vast array of European livestock,

many of which were simply turned loose to fend for themselves, created a zoological revolution in America.

Swine, cattle, and horses, released or escaped from European masters, soon roamed the New World. Swine, brought from Cuba by de Soto in the 1540s, evolved into long-legged, sharp-snouted, vicious-tusked, "razorbacks."

Within a century they ranged from semitropical Florida to the cool French colonies in Canada. Within 30 years of the founding of Maryland, settlers there also were complaining about herds of wild cattle. In Virginia young men hunted wild cattle just as they hunted deer.

In Europe horses were expensive and worth taking care of. In America they were comparatively less expensive and wandered free. Wild horses were considered a nuisance in many of the colonies. The majority were unmarked and could legally be claimed by anyone who could catch them. Most, however, were so shy and swift that catching them was difficult.

Oddly, as with plants, only a few creatures native to America have ever been established in the wild in Europe. The list is confined to the grey squirrel, the muskrat, and a few insects like the Colorado potato beetle.

A New Environment

6. How was the environment in colonial America a new one?

Environments are always evolving. Within 100 years of the arrival of the first Europeans, a new environment had developed in the Americas. European plants and animals had spread, replacing or mixing with many native species. The children of colonists, indentured servants, and slaves—and of American Indians—grew up in a truly new world of plants and animals.

Applying Your Knowledge

Your class will create an encyclopedia of the flora and fauna of your local area. As a class, develop a list of the plants and animals living in your area. You will select or be assigned an item from the list to research. Write a brief insert for the class encyclopedia explaining where your item originated. You may wish to add a sketch to your article. Donate the encyclopedia to your school or community library.

CHAPTER 1 REVIEW

Crusades

25,000 B.C.   1000   1100   THE AGE OF DISCOVERY   1200

25,000 B.C.
Great
Migration
begins

1000
Vikings sail
to America

1095
Crusades begin

1100
Compass invented

Chapter Summary
Read the statements below. Choose one, and write a paragraph explaining its importance.
1. The first Americans arrived in waves from Asia beginning 30,000 years ago.
2. Environment strongly influenced the American Indian cultures.
3. In about the year 1000 the Vikings made the second discovery of America.
4. The Crusades led to the Commercial Revolution, which caused Europeans to venture into the world outside of Europe.
5. Explorers looking for a better trade route to China made the third discovery of America.
6. The years between 1450 and the early 1600s became known as the Age of Discovery.
7. The Portuguese and Spanish were the first world explorers.
8. The Spanish led the early exploration of America, claiming vast areas and conquering the Indians.

Reviewing Chronological Order
Number your paper 1-5. Then study the time line above and place the following events in the order in which they happened by writing the first next to 1, the second next to 2, and so on.
1. The Crusades
2. Columbus discovers America
3. The Great Migration
4. Cortés conquers the Aztecs
5. Vikings sail to America

Understanding Main Ideas
1. Why did the first Americans develop so many cultures? Give three examples to support your answer.
2. What is a generalization? What words should the reader of history add?
3. What is our source of information about the Vikings?
4. How did Gutenberg's printing press help Europeans discover new ideas?

5. How did the native Americans view the Europeans when they first met them? How did their view change?
6. How did the conquistadors treat the American Indians? How did their "sense of mission" seem to excuse the conquistadors' behavior?

Thinking Critically
1. **Selecting Alternatives.** If you could have been one of the first Americans, would you rather have been one of the Indians of the Southwest, the Northwest, or the Great Plains? Why? (To support your reasoning, cite information you have learned about the effect of environment on these cultures.)
2. **Analyzing.** Why do you think it is important to use historical imagination when studying the past?
3. **Drawing Conclusions.** Which of the three discoveries of America do you think was the least important? Why?
4. **Evaluating.** Do you agree with the author's view that the discovery of America by Europeans was "actually the invasion and conquest of America"? Why or why not?

Writing About History: Expressive
Imagine you are one of the following: one of the first Asians to arrive in America, a Viking explorer, a member of Columbus' crew, or an Indian witnessing Columbus' arrival in America. Write a letter to a friend describing what you see and your thoughts and feelings. Use the information in Chapter 1 to help you develop your letter.

Practicing the Strategy
Review the strategies on pages 21 and 32.
Reading a Time Line. Study the time line on page 21, then answer the following questions.
1. What are the intervals of time that divide this time line?
2. Name the first and last events on this time line and give their dates.

Commercial Revolution

1300	1400	1500	1600

1271 Polo travels to China

1291 Crusades end

1420 Henry establishes navigation school

1450 Gutenberg improves printing press

1492 Columbus discovers America

1513 Balboa sights Pacific Ocean

★ De León explores Florida

1519 Magellan's voyage begins

★ Hernán Cortés conquers the Aztecs

1522 El Cano completes circumnavigation

1528 De Vaca, Esteban explore Texas

1531 Pizarro conquers the Incas

Reading Maps. Study the map on page 3. Then answer the following questions.

1. In what general direction did the first Americans crossing the Bering Strait travel?
2. In miles and kilometers, what is the distance from the coast of Asia to the coast of South America?

Using Primary Sources

On his first voyage, in 1492, Columbus kept a journal, which is now lost. Luckily a Spanish priest copied parts of it before it disappeared. As you read the following excerpt from *The Journal of Christopher Columbus (During His First Voyage, 1492–1493)* by Clements R. Markham, note Columbus' attitude toward the Indians. Then answer the questions to the right.

> Friday, October 12 *At two hours after midnight the land was sighted. The vessels stayed in place, waiting for daylight. On Friday they arrived at a small island of the Lucayos Indians, called Guanahaní in the Indians' language. . . .*
>
> *The island was rather large and very flat with bright green trees, much water, a very large lake in the center, and without any mountains. The whole land was so green that it is a pleasure to look on it. The people are very friendly. They long to possess our things, but having nothing to give in return they take what they can get, and presently swim away.*
>
> *Still they give away all they have in return for whatever may be given to them, even broken bits of crockery and glass. I saw one of them trade 16 skeins of cotton for three small Portuguese coins, the skeins weighing as much as 25 pounds of cotton thread. . . . I think it is grown on this island, though my short stay did not allow me to find out for sure. Here also is found the gold that the people wear fastened in their noses. But in order not to lose time, I intend to depart from here and see if I can discover the island of Cipango*.*

*Present-day Japan

1. What evidence in this excerpt suggests that the Indians were unfamiliar with people from cultures and regions different from their own?
2. From Columbus' description of the geographic features of the island, what kind of foods do you think the Indians lived on?
3. What evidence indicates that Columbus did not realize he had discovered a land previously unknown to most Europeans?

Linking History & Geography

Many of the earliest explorers in the New World came from Spain, Portugal, England, France, and the Netherlands. Study the map on page 177 and note the location of each of these countries. Then in a brief paragraph explain how the geographic location of these countries helped them to lead the Age of Discovery and to be among the first to send sailors across the Atlantic to the Americas.

Enriching Your Study of History

1. **Individual Project.** Using the maps in this chapter as a guide, trace on an outline map of the world the explorations of Leif Ericson, Columbus, Balboa, Magellan and El Cano, Narváez and Esteban, Coronado, and de León.
2. **Cooperative Project.** With three of your classmates, choose one of the American Indian groups mentioned in this chapter, and research its way of life. Your group might prepare a booklet about them including drawings and stories, or build a model of a typical village. If the group originally lived nearby, arrange a visit to a local museum.

Chapter 1 Review 39

English Colonies in America

The wealth and splendor of Spain's American empire attracted other Europeans the way flowers in springtime attract honeybees. The English in particular longed to build an empire in the Americas. They hoped for a share of the gold and silver that almost everyone believed was so plentiful in the new land, and they wanted American products such as sugar and rice, which could not be grown in their cold climate. The English colonists came to America to trade and sell, to practice their religions, to convert the Indians, and to find work. Would they find a better life in a New World?

Preview & Review

Use these questions to guide your reading. Answer the questions after completing Section 1.
Understanding Issues, Events, & Ideas. Explain the English rise to power and its first journeys to America, using the following words: sea dog, Spanish Armada, charter, Roanoke, enclosure movement, northwest passage, joint-stock company.
1. How did Queen Elizabeth try to weaken Spain?
2. Why did the first settlers on Roanoke Island want to return to England?
3. Why were each of the following interested in colonizing America: the queen? landowners? merchants? explorers?
Thinking Critically. Imagine that you find a lost diary explaining what happened to the colonists of Roanoke Island. What does it say?

At right is Nicholas Hilliard's 1572 miniature portrait of Elizabeth I.

1. WHY COLONISTS CAME TO AMERICA

England Challenges Spain

In 1497, not very long after the news of Columbus' discovery reached England, its king, Henry VII, sent John Cabot on a voyage of exploration. Cabot sailed along the coast of Newfoundland, giving England a claim to the northern regions of America. At that time Spain seemed too powerful to challenge. But in the 1550s, after Elizabeth I inherited the throne, the English became seriously interested in America.

Elizabeth, ruling England alone in a world dominated by men, was a person of the strongest will and ambition. She was a shrewd ruler and a clever diplomat who paid little attention to right and wrong. Elizabeth never married, perhaps because no man could be her equal. She had a temper to match her fiery red hair and a tongue to match her sharp features. She was well aware of England's limited strength compared to Spain's. She proceeded with caution.

National Portrait Gallery, London

One way to weaken Spain without openly going to war was to attack Spanish merchant ships on the high seas. In those days a ship out of sight of land was at the mercy of any more powerful vessel. There was no way to call for help or even to send an alert. A fast, powerfully armed ship could overtake a clumsy Spanish galleon loaded with treasure. The crew would be easily overcome, the cargo taken off, and the ship sent to the bottom. No one could prove that the ship had not run on a rocky reef in a fog and been dashed to pieces, or gone down in a storm, as in fact frequently happened.

The Spanish considered such attackers pirates, and rightly so. Nevertheless, Elizabeth encouraged English captains to roam the trade routes between Spain and its colonies in America in search of such prey.

The most famous of what the English affectionately called their **sea dogs** was Francis Drake. In 1577 Drake began the most famous of his many escapades. From England he sailed his ship, the *Golden Hind,* across the Atlantic and through the Strait of Magellan. In the Pacific he captured the *Cacafuego,* a Spanish galleon carrying a fortune in silver from Peru. Then he sailed north to California, which he claimed for England.

Also by Nicholas Hilliard is this 1581 miniature of Sir Francis Drake. What might be some reasons for the popularity of such miniatures?

"Cabot Leaving the Port of Bristol" was painted in 1906 by Ernest Board. How many figures from religious life can you identify in this blessing of Cabot's ship?

From California Drake crossed the Pacific and Indian Oceans, rounded Africa, and returned home. When he reached England in 1580, Drake presented Queen Elizabeth with a treasure worth twice her annual income. Little wonder that Elizabeth made him a knight of the kingdom right on the deck of the *Golden Hind*.

Drake sailed again into Spanish waters in 1585. This time he terrorized Spanish towns in the Caribbean islands. "Drake the Dragon," the Spanish called him. Philip II, the king of Spain, was furious. He collected the largest fleet the world had ever seen—130 ships carrying 30,000 men and armed with 2,400 cannon. In 1588 this mighty **Spanish Armada** sailed from Spain to invade England.

While Elizabeth and her troops awaited the Armada, she urged her men to fight for the glory of England:

> " I know I have but the body of a weak and feeble woman; but I have the heart of a king, and of a king of England, too; and think foul scorn that Perma [the Spanish military leader] of Spain, or any prince of Europe, should dare invade the borders of my realms: to which, rather than any dishonor should grow by me, I myself will take up arms; . . . and by your valor in the field, we shall shortly have a famous victory over the enemies of my God, of my kingdom, and of my people.[1] "

Elizabeth's ships were fewer and smaller, but easier to maneuver and more powerful. They sank many of the attackers. Storms finished off still more. Not one Spanish sailor or soldier set foot on English soil, except as a captive. Only about half the Armada limped back to Spanish ports. With Spain's navy shattered, the stage was set for England to carve a place for itself in America.

False Starts in America

Even before the defeat of the Spanish Armada, English sailors were visiting North American waters in increasing numbers. By the 1570s about 50 vessels were catching fish on the Grand Banks off the coast of Newfoundland. Some of the fishermen established temporary camps ashore. In 1578 Queen Elizabeth issued a document called a **charter** to Sir Humphrey Gilbert. This charter gave Gilbert the right to establish and control a colony in America. Operating under the charter, Gilbert landed on Newfoundland with a party of 200. He officially claimed the island for England. This group did not stay, and Gilbert was drowned when his ship went down in a storm.

When Humphrey Gilbert was eight, his father had died. Later his mother married a man named Raleigh. They had a son, Walter, Humphrey's half-brother. He grew up to be the handsome and charm-

Another miniature by Nicholas Hilliard, this one is of Sir Walter Raleigh around 1585. He was a particular favorite of Elizabeth's at this time. Based on the three miniatures, what generalization can you make about clothing in Elizabeth's court?

[1]From *A Treasury of the World's Great Speeches,* selected and edited by Houston Peterson

ing Sir Walter Raleigh, a close adviser of Queen Elizabeth. Two years after Humphrey Gilbert's death, Raleigh sent seven ships carrying over a hundred men to America. Under Gilbert's charter they were to establish a colony and look for gold.

Raleigh did not accompany the group. Some said Queen Elizabeth was in love with him at this time and would not let him leave her court. His colonists passed the winter on an island called **Roanoke** off the coast of what is now North Carolina. One of them, an artist and mapmaker named John White, painted many watercolors of the Indians of the region and of the plants and animals there.

No gold was found at Roanoke. The colonists fought with the local Indians. Life was hard. When Sir Francis Drake arrived at Roanoke in June 1586 on his way back from his raid in the Caribbean, the colonists eagerly accepted his offer of passage back to England.

Ever hopeful, in 1587 Raleigh dispatched another hundred-odd colonists to Carolina, headed by John White. For the first time women were sent out, among them White's married daughter, Ellinor Dare. These colonists landed at Roanoke in July, and on August 18 Ellinor Dare gave birth to a daughter, Virginia, the first English child born in America.

A few days later John White sailed back to England for more supplies. He intended to return promptly, but he could not because of the national crisis caused by the attack of the Spanish Armada. Other delays followed and White did not get back to Roanoke until 1590. The island was deserted. No one has ever discovered what happened to the inhabitants of this "Lost Colony" of Roanoke.

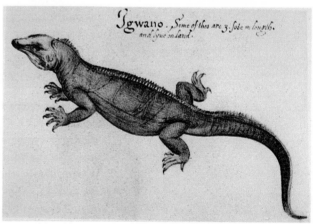

New Hopes in America

Despite the setbacks, many important people in England remained very interested in America. For the queen and other political leaders, a major attraction was the hope of finding gold and silver to increase England's wealth and power. Another was to reduce the power of Spain, which already controlled so much of the Americas. For upper-

Three of John White's watercolors made around 1585 are shown here. These may have been the first views the English had of the Atlantic loggerhead turtle, the iguana, and the pineapple. How do the watercolors show that White was a careful observer of nature?

Why Colonists Came to America   43

class gentlemen like Raleigh and Gilbert, the chief goals were adventure, honor, fame, and riches—especially gold.

There were practical, down-to-earth reasons for more ordinary English people to colonize America. Many people were out of work in England. Because of a rising demand for woolen cloth, many landowners had stopped farming and begun raising sheep. They fenced in, or enclosed, their fields and planted them in grass for the sheep. This was known as the **enclosure movement.** Raising sheep took much less labor than growing grain, so many serfs and tenants had to look for work elsewhere. Some found jobs in the towns. Others wandered about the countryside, often disturbing the peace.

A nursery rhyme that appeared at about this time warned that homeless people, put out of work and home by the enclosure movement, were draining the strength of England:

> “ Hark, hark, the dogs do bark;
> The beggars are coming to town,
> Some in rags and some in tags
> And some in velvet gowns. ”

Perhaps they could be resettled and made useful workers again in America. People who thought this way saw America as a safety valve for troublemakers and to keep English jails from overflowing.

In addition, the expanding cloth industry in England gave a boost to foreign trade and made many merchants rich. These merchants were eager to invest their profits in colonial ventures. For them America was a new business opportunity. Finally, there was still the hope for a practical westward route to the Indies. Although the trip around South America was too long to be profitable, maybe sailors would discover a **northwest passage** through North America.

Merchant Adventurers

The experiences of men like Gilbert and Raleigh proved that founding a colony was expensive and risky. Most English merchants and manufacturers were shrewd and cautious in business, not daring adventurers or high-born court favorites. Instead of outfitting expeditions as individuals, they organized what they called **joint-stock companies.** These companies were the ancestors of our corporations. They were owned by many stockholders who shared in the profits and losses.

The London merchant Sir Thomas Smythe was typical of these merchant adventurers. Smythe backed the first English attempt to sail around Africa. In 1600 he helped found the British East India Company, which received exclusive rights from the English government to trade with the Indies. He also invested money in a number of expeditions into Arctic waters in search of the northwest passage. Smythe became the treasurer and guiding spirit of the Virginia Company of London, often called the London Company.

The true focus of this country scene is the fence. It separates the wheat field from the sheep who are yielding up their wool to the shearers. When the enclosure movement made work scarce, some Englishmen looked to America. What caused the landowners to enclose their fields and graze sheep?

The joint-stock Virginia Company was given charters by James I, who became king of England after his cousin Queen Elizabeth died in 1603. In l606 James gave the London Company the right to develop a huge area of North America. The region was named Virginia in honor of Queen Elizabeth, who because she never married was known as the Virgin Queen.

Virginia extended along the Atlantic Coast from about the latitude of New York City to what is now South Carolina, and west "from sea to sea"—that is, all the way to the Pacific Ocean! Obviously neither King James nor anyone else in England had the slightest idea of how enormous this grant was. The country had never been explored. The charter shows what big ideas the colonizers had, as well as their disregard for the rights of the native Americans. Because a few of his explorers had nosed their way along the Atlantic beaches, King James claimed the right to the whole continent. 🔳

Return to the Preview & Review on page 40.

STRATEGIES FOR SUCCESS

USING LATITUDE AND LONGITUDE

One of the basic tasks in both history and geography is to locate exactly what is where on the earth. To do this, you must identify the *absolute location* of each place, or its precise spot on the earth. Cartographers, or map makers, have created a grid system of imaginary lines to make this task easier.

Most maps are drawn with the North Pole at the top and the South Pole at the bottom. The *equator* is the line halfway between the North and South poles. Several shorter imaginary lines circle the earth parallel to the equator and on both sides of it. They are called *parallels,* or *lines of latitude.* Parallels are used to locate places north and south of the equator. They are numbered from zero degrees (0°) at the equator to 90 degrees (90°) north (N) at the North Pole and 90° south (S) at the South Pole.

A second set of imaginary lines called *meridians,* or *lines of longitude,* crisscrosses the parallels. In 1884, an international agreement set the meridian passing through the Royal Observatory in Greenwich, England, near London, as 0° longitude, or the *prime meridian.* The meridian directly opposite the prime meridian, on the other side of the globe, is the 180° meridian. Meridians are used to locate places east and west of the prime meridian. Meridians east of the prime meridian are numbered from 0°E at the prime meridian to 180°E and those to the west are numbered from 0°W to 180°W. By noting latitude and longitude, you can quickly find exact locations on earth.

How to Find Exact Location

To use latitude and longitude to find the exact location of a place, follow these guidelines.
1. **Use the global grid.** The grid provides lines of latitude and longitude marked with corresponding degrees.
2. **Find the equator.** Check the lines of latitude, those running from east to west, until you find 0°. This marks the equator.
3. **Locate the correct parallel.** Continue to check the lines of latitude until you find the one you are looking for. Remember that northern latitudes are above the equator and southern latitudes are below it.
4. **Find the prime meridian.** Check the lines of longitude by reading along the top or bottom of the map. The prime meridian is marked 0°.
5. **Locate the correct meridian.** Continue to read along the grid until you find the meridian you are looking for. Remember that west is to the left of the prime meridian and east is to the right.

Applying the Strategy

Study the map below. It shows the voyages of Cabot and Raleigh and the locations of the first colonies. You can note that Jamestown is located at about 37°N, 77°W while Plymouth is at about 42°N, 70°W. See if you can find the exact locations of other colonies as well.

For independent practice, see Practicing the Strategy on pages 70–71.

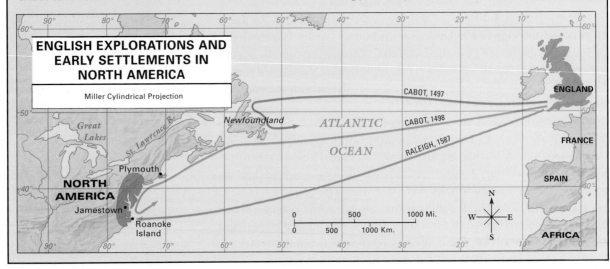

ENGLISH EXPLORATIONS AND EARLY SETTLEMENTS IN NORTH AMERICA

Miller Cylindrical Projection

2. THE SETTLEMENT OF VIRGINIA

Jamestown: The First Colony

A few days before Christmas 1606, the London Company sent off three ships, the *Discovery*, the *Susan Constant*, and the *Godspeed*, bearing 104 settlers. Their destination was Virginia, their purpose to build a town and search for gold, silver, and copper.

The three little ships reached Virginia on April 26, 1607. They sailed up a river, which they named after King James. A few days later they chose a place to build a fort on a peninsula jutting out into the river. They called this settlement **Jamestown.**

From the start life in Jamestown was an endless series of troubles. The site was easy to defend but swampy and infested with fever-bearing mosquitoes. By the end of summer half the colonists had died, and many of those who remained were sick with malaria. Because the planting season had ended before the colonists had finished building houses and walling the town, they were unable to plant a crop. Soon they were desperately short of food. When the first ship from England arrived the next spring, only 38 colonists were alive to greet it.

The colony also suffered from poor leadership. King James named a council to rule it. He appointed mostly stockholders in the London Company. They did not go to Jamestown and knew almost nothing about the difficulties the settlers faced. For example, there was no sign of gold in the area around Jamestown. Yet the London authorities insisted that the colonists spend much of their energy searching for the precious metal. The Londoners did create a local council in Virginia, supposedly to handle day-to-day problems, but they gave the councilors no real authority.

Still worse, the Virginia councilors quarreled among themselves and allowed the colonists to neglect the basic tasks of planting crops and making the settlement safe.

The Jamestown settlers were poorly prepared for the great challenge of living in the new country. The 36 so-called gentlemen among them had none of the skills needed by pioneers, such as carpentry and farming. They were unaccustomed to hard labor of any kind. As for the others, there were goldsmiths, perfumers, and jewelers, who were certainly skilled—but in the wrong trades. Not one of them had ever been a real farmer. Too many settlers apparently believed that in America wealth grew on trees. They did not realize that it was necessary to work hard if they wished to stay alive.

Fortunately, one man among these colonists had the courage to take command. He was John Smith. Smith was a swashbuckler, a **soldier of fortune,** who was ready to fight for whoever would pay him. He was a short, bearded fellow of 27, a man of action. He had

Use these questions to guide your reading. Answer the questions after completing Section 2.
Understanding Issues, Events, & Ideas. Use the following words to to describe events in Jamestown: Jamestown, soldier of fortune, starving time, headright, House of Burgesses, indentured servant.
1. Why did so many of the first settlers in Jamestown die?
2. What helped conditions in Jamestown begin to improve? What changes did John Smith make when he became president of the Virginia council?
3. How did wealthy settlers profit from the headright system?
4. How did the Indians help the Jamestown colonists? Why did they attack the colonists?
Thinking Critically. 1. You are an indentured servant in Virginia. Write a letter to a relative in England, telling about your life. **2.** You are a Virginia colonist in 1618. What crop would you plant in order to assure your success as a farmer? Why would you choose this crop?

The Settlement of Virginia   47

John Smith was 27 years old when he took command of the Jamestown settlement. This engraving portrays him at the age of 33. Does time seem to have taken an early toll for this bold adventurer?

Point of View

An Algonquin leader asked John Smith why the colonists used force with the Indians.

66Why will you take by force what you may have quietly by love? Why will you destroy us who supply you with food? What can you get by war? We can hide our provisions and run into the woods; then you will starve for wronging your friends. Why are you jealous of us? We are unarmed, and willing to give you what you ask, if you come in a friendly manner.99

Powhatan, 1607

seen far more of the world than any of the other settlers. He had fought in a number of wars in eastern Europe against the Turks. In one war he was captured, taken to Constantinople, and sold into slavery. However, he managed to kill his master and escape. After many other remarkable adventures Smith found himself in the colony of Virginia.

In 1608 Smith was elected president of the Virginia council. Once in charge, he bargained with the Indians for food. He stopped the foolish searching for gold. Instead he put people to work building shelters and planting food crops. Hard work and strict discipline became the order of the day.

Reforms for Virginia

Virginia's difficulties finally convinced the merchant adventurers in England that the London Company needed to be reorganized. In 1609 Sir Edwin Sandys, a councilor who was also a member of Parliament, England's legislative body, obtained a new charter from King James. This charter called for the appointment of a governor who would rule the colony in Jamestown rather than from London.

The London Company then raised a good deal more money and outfitted a fleet of nine ships to carry about 600 new settlers across the Atlantic. Those who paid their own fare received one share of stock in the company. Those who could not pay agreed to work as servants of the company for seven years in return for their passage. Until 1616 everything the colonists produced was to be put into a common storehouse or fund. On that date the servants would have worked off their debt to the company. Then the profits of the enterprise were to be divided among the shareholders—both the investors back in England and the settlers. Every shareholder would also receive a grant of Virginia land.

These were fine plans but hard to put into effect. Conditions in Virginia got worse and worse. The first governor, Lord De La Warr, put off coming to Jamestown. Smith returned to England for supplies and colonists, and to convince company managers to invest more money in the colony. Without his firm hand, the organization and rules he had begun quickly fell apart. The years from 1609 to 1610 were a **starving time.** As Smith described it:

66 By their [the Indians'] cruelty, our Governours indiscretion [poor judgment] and losse of our ships, of five hundred [colonists] within six months after Captaine Smith's departure, there remained not past sixtie men, women and children, most miserable and poore creatures; and those were preserved for the most part, by roots, herbes, acornes, walnuts, berries, now and then a little fish . . . yea, even the very skinnes of our horses. . . . This was that time, which still to this day (1624) we call the starving time; it

Virginia Museum of Fine Arts

were too vile to say, and scarce to be believed, what we endured. . . .[1] **"**

At one point the colonists almost decided to abandon the settlement and return to England.

Things began to improve in 1611 when the council appointed Thomas Dale, a solider with a reputation for sternness, as governor. Dale arrived with fresh supplies and a new group of settlers in March. He promptly resumed the tough course set by John Smith. He also established laws requiring church attendance and regulating moral behavior. Dale soon became very unpopular because of his harsh rule. A man convicted of stealing some oatmeal was chained to a tree and allowed to starve to death. The colonists charged that Dale was a tyrant. Nevertheless, they began to plant corn, repair the fort, and work to make sure that the colony would survive.

Headrights and Indentures

In 1618 the London Company launched a campaign to attract more investors and settlers to Virginia. Colonists who paid their own way

"Landing at Jamestown" was painted by John Gadsby Chapman in 1841. It depicts the arrival of the second group of Jamestown settlers.

[1]From *The General Historie of Virginia* by Captain John Smith

or that of others would receive 50 acres (20 hectares) of land for each "head" transported. This was called a **headright.** The company relaxed the rigorous discipline that Thomas Dale had imposed as governor of the colony. It guaranteed all settlers the same legal rights that English subjects had at home. It also gave settlers a voice in the local government of the colony. They would be allowed to elect representatives to an assembly known as the **House of Burgesses.** This was the first elected government body in America. Along with the governor's council, the House was given the power to make laws for the colony. It first met at Jamestown in 1619.

The London Company made an all-out effort to develop many kinds of products in the colony. But tobacco remained Virginia's most important commodity by far. As the price of tobacco rose, everyone rushed to plant more of it. The broad, green leaves of tobacco plants could be seen growing in the streets of Jamestown.

Growing tobacco required a great deal of labor. In Jamestown laborers to work the land were in short supply. Those settlers who had money had a tremendous advantage in obtaining workers because of the headright system. Poor people who wanted to come to Virginia signed contracts called indentures. They agreed to work for seven years to pay off the cost of getting to America. These contracts of indenture could be bought and sold. The newcomer, who was called an **indentured servant,** had to work without wages for the person who owned the indenture. The owner also received the headright issued by the colonial government for bringing the newcomer to Virginia. He could therefore claim 50 acres (20 hectares) of land. In other words, the person who paid the passage of the immigrant received for one price both land and the labor needed to farm it.

Treatment of indentured servants varied, as these letters written to parents back in England show[1]:

To Mr. John Sprigs White Smith in White Cross Street near Cripple Gate London

Maryland Sept'r 22d 1756

Honred Father

O Dear Father, believe what I am going to relate the words of truth and sincerity, and Ballance my former bad Conduct [to] my sufferings here, and then I am sure you'll pity your Distress[ed] Daughter. What we unfortunate English People suffer here is beyond the probibility of you in England to Conceive. Let it suffice that I, one of the unhappy Number, am toiling almost Day and Night, and very often in the Horses druggery . . . and then tied up and whipp'd to that Degree that you'd not serve an Animal.

---

[1]From Public Record Office, London, High Court of Admiralty, 30:258, no. 106, and 30: 258, no. 90

[There is] scarce any thing but Indian Corn and Salt to eat and that even begrudged. Nay, many Neagoes are better used. [I have] no shoes nor stockings to wear. . . . What rest we can get is to rap ourselves up in a Blanket and ly upon the Ground. This is the deplorable Condition your poor Betty endures. And now I beg, if you have any Bowels of Compassion left, show it by sending me some Relief. Clothing is the principal thing wanting, which if you should condiscend to, may easely send them to me by any of the ships bound to Baltimore Town, Patapsco River, Maryland. And give me leave to conclude in Duty to you and Uncles and Aunts, and Respect to all Friends,

Honred Father,

Your dutifull and Disobedient Child,

Elizabeth Sprigs

To Mr. Tuggey at Low Tewting in Surrey

Anoplis November 2, 1756

Honred Father and mother

I take this opertinewtey of riting to you to Lett you know that i am in Maryland and a footman to the Honrable Colnall Taskur and i am in a Good Place. . . . I live as well as aney one Can. But to be so Long fron hering or seeing from you, i think you are Ded. I shall be Glad to heer from you, but as i have sent 2 Letters to you and never Receved an Answer i Expect you are Ded.

I live [as] well as aney one Can in the world. I am marrad since i Come heer, and I hope to be in England in a bout 12 mounths and shall bring my wife with me. And Pray send to me som knives som buckls and Butins and Aney thing you think Proper for i Can make Good money heer. . . .

Pray send me a Letter by the first ship Com'g to maryland and Drict it to mr Toeggett att the Honrable Collnl. Taskers in Anoplis i Maryland

PS: I have marrad as sweat a gall [as] Ever was Born. Shee Is as trew to me as the verelle Sun an i [shall] bring hur to England will me plees God i Live. . . . Pray excuse the bad riting to you for you know i am a bad [scholar].

Your Dewtful Sun,

Richard Tuggeyy

The great tobacco boom did the London Company little good. By the time the boom began, the original colonists had already served their seven years and were no longer working for the company.

A COLONY BUILT UPON SMOKE

In the long run what made Virginia prosper was tobacco. When the colonists realized that there was no gold nor silver to be found, they looked for other sources of wealth. They tried to raise silkworms, to make glass, to grow wine grapes—all without success. Tobacco was a different story. Here was a plant native to America. The Indians prized it highly, using it for personal enjoyment and in their ceremonies. Sir Francis Drake brought tobacco to England from the West Indies after his raid, and Sir Walter Raleigh made smoking fashionable in high society. The habit spread quickly in England.

It is interesting that from the very start many people argued that smoking was unhealthy. King James himself opposed the use of tobacco. Although he

considered it beneath his dignity to engage in public debate, he published anonymously an essay on the subject. This "Counterblast to Tobacco" described smoking as a "vile and stinking" habit that would injure the lungs and the brain. Thousands of King James' subjects ignored his warning. Demand for tobacco soared in England.

The Indians of Virginia grew and smoked tobacco, but this local plant had a harsh and bitter taste. A colonist named John Rolfe, who came to Jamestown about 1610, solved the problem by bringing in tobacco seeds from the Spanish colonies. This variety of tobacco flourished in Virginia and produced a much milder smoke. In 1616 Virginia farmers exported about 2,200 pounds (1,000 kilograms) of tobacco to England. Two years later they exported more than 20 times that amount.

The Virginians now had a cash crop they could sell in England. They were able to purchase the manufactured items they could not yet produce themselves: cloth, tools, furniture, guns. Little wonder that King Charles I, who succeeded James I in 1625, joked that Virginia was "built upon smoke."

Bloodshed in Jamestown

The colonists treated their Indian neighbors far worse than they treated their indentured servants. In the early days Jamestown could not have survived without the Indians. They gave the starving colonists food. They taught them how to live in the wilderness. The land around Jamestown was a dense forest. Corn, a native American plant grown by the Indians, would not grow for the colonists in forest shade. It would take years to cut down the huge trees and root out their stumps. The Indians showed the colonists how to kill the trees by cutting a ring around the trunks. Sunlight could then shine through the dead and leafless branches, and corn planted by the colonists sprouted between the trunks.

The colonists accepted the Indians' help and advice and then tried to take control of their homelands! The Indians resisted. In a sudden attack in 1622 they killed about 350 colonists, almost one third of Virginia's European population. The bloodshed convinced King James that the colony, which was already being mismanaged, should be taken away from the London Company. In 1624 he canceled the charter and put Virginia under direct royal control. The Company was bankrupt, the stockholders' investment lost.

Return to the Preview & Review on page 47.

3. THE SETTLEMENT OF MASSACHUSETTS

The Pilgrims

In 1617 Sir Edwin Sandys was trying to put Virginia's affairs in order. A community of people who were living in Holland asked him for permission to settle in America somewhere within the London Company's grant. These **Pilgrims,** as we now call them, had left England in 1608 to escape religious persecution. Pilgrims were **Separatists,** people who had ''separated'' themselves from the Anglican Church, the Church of England. The Anglican Church had been established when Henry VIII broke from the Pope in Rome and the Roman Catholic Church. Separatists opposed the Anglican Church because it was sponsored by the state. It also seemed to them dominated by what had been Catholic rituals and not to be accomplishing the true goals of the **Protestant Reformation** that had taken place in Europe.

In Holland the Dutch had not interfered with the Pilgrims' religious practice, but still the Pilgrims were not happy in their new home. They could not get good jobs. Their children were beginning to speak Dutch instead of English.

Sandys admired the Pilgrims, but other company officials considered them dangerous **radicals.** (Radicals are people who favor sudden and widespread changes.) There were long delays, but finally in 1619 the London Company and the king granted the Pilgrims permission to migrate. Because the Pilgrims were poor people without money to pay for their voyage, they accepted a proposal by a group of English merchant adventurers. The merchants would put up the money to found a new settlement. The Pilgrims would do the work. In September 1620 a party of 35 Pilgrims and 66 other colonists sailed from Plymouth, England, on the *Mayflower* bound for Virginia.

Plymouth Plantation

The little party on the *Mayflower* never reached Virginia. On November 9 they sighted land on Cape Cod Bay, north of the London Company's territory. With winter so near, they decided not to test their ship any longer in the stormy waters of the Atlantic and to settle where they were.

Because Cape Cod was outside the region controlled by the London Company, there was no existing government. Therefore, the Pilgrims decided to draw up a document which would provide a legal basis for governing the area and themselves. This document is called the **Mayflower Compact.** Its signers first acknowledged the authority of King James. They were not seeking to create a new nation. They

Preview & Review

Use these questions to guide your reading. Answer the questions after completing Section 3.
Understanding Issues, Events, & Ideas. Describe the Pilgrim arrival in America, using the following words: Pilgrims, Separatists, Protestant Reformation, radical, Mayflower Compact, Plymouth, Thanksgiving Day.
1. Why were the Pilgrims called Separatists? Why did the Pilgrims leave Holland?
2. How were the experiences of the Pilgrims similar to those of the first Jamestown settlers?
3. How did the Pilgrims differ from the Jamestown settlers?
Thinking Critically. You are one of the Pilgrims who came to Plymouth on the Mayflower, and you are helping to write laws for your colony. Write the law you think is the most important. Explain why your law is the most necessary. Suggest some possible consequences for the colony if your law is not included.

The Granger Collection

This colored engraving of the May-flower at full sail was probably made in the 19th century. What do you suppose life was like for the more than 100 people aboard?

then pledged "submission and obedience" to the officers they would themselves elect and to the laws they might pass. They wrote:

66 In the name of God, Amen. We whose names are under-written, the loyal subjects of our dread sovereign Lord King *James,* by the grace of God, of Great Britain, France, and Ireland, King, Defender of the Faith, etc., having under-taken, for the glory of God, and advancement of the Chris-tian faith, and honor of our king and country, a voyage to plant the first colony in the northern parts of Virginia, do by these Presents solemnly and mutually promise in the presence of God, and one of another, covenant and combine ourselves into a civil Body Politik for our better ordering and preservation and furtherance of the ends aforesaid; and by Virtue hereof, to enact, constitute, and frame such just and equal Laws, ordinances, acts, constitutions, and offices from time to time, as shall be thought most meet and con-venient for the Good of the Colony unto which we promise all due submission and obedience. 99

The Mayflower Compact is a short and simple document. To us it might seem a rather obvious and unnecessary statement, made by decent and honest people about to settle in a new land. Yet the Compact tells us a great deal about life in America, then and later.

So far as any record shows, this was the first time in history that a group of people consciously created a government where none had existed before.

The Pilgrims decided to settle at a place they called **Plymouth.** The rock on which they are thought to have landed is now a national monument. They came ashore with almost nothing, no "butter or oil, not a sole to mend a shoe." They were true pilgrims, these wanderers, uncertain of what lay over the next hill.

In some respects the Pilgrims were like the first immigrants from Asia, people who owned little more than what they had on their backs, isolated in an unknown land. The Pilgrims were totally dependent on one another, but this was their strength. They recognized their common purpose and the need for unity. Above all they trusted in "the good providence of God." They were ready to give up the familiar world for the uncertain wilderness. One of the Pilgrims, William Bradford, described their lot:

❝ Being thus arrived in a good harbor, and brought safe to land, they fell upon their knees and blessed the God of Heaven who had brought them over the vast and furious ocean, and delivered them from all perils and miseries thereof, again to set their feet on the firm and stable earth, their proper element. . . .

But here I cannot but stay and make a pause, and stand half amazed at this poor people's present condition; and so I think will the reader, too, when he well considers the same. Being thus passed the vast ocean, and a sea of troubles before in their preparation (as may be remembered by that which went before), they had now no friends to welcome them nor inns to entertain or refresh their weather-beaten bodies; no houses or much less towns to repair to, to seek for succor [relief]. It is recorded in Scripture as a mercy to the Apostle and his shipwrecked company [Acts: 28], that the barbarians showed them no small kindness in refreshing them, but these savage barbarians when they met with them (as after will appear), were readier to fill their sides full of arrows than otherwise. And for the season it was winter, and they that know the winters of that country know them to be sharp and violent, and subject to cruel and fierce storms, dangerous to travel to known places, much more to search an unknown coast. Besides, what could they see but a hideous and desolate wilderness, full of wild beasts and wild men—and what multitudes there might be of them they knew not. . . . Which way soever they turned their eyes (save upward to the heavens) they could have little solace or content in respect of any outward objects. For summer being done, all things stand upon them

"Signing the Compact" was painted by Percy Moran. What does this picture say about the roles of men and women in the Pilgrim society?

with a weather-beaten face, and the whole country, full of woods and thickets, represented a wild and savage hue. If they looked behind them, there was the mighty ocean they had passed and was now as a main bar and gulf to separate them from all the civil parts of the world.

What could sustain them now but the Spirit of God and His Grace? May not and ought not the children of these fathers rightly say: 'Our fathers were Englishmen which came over this great ocean, and were ready to perish in this wilderness; but they cried unto the Lord, and He heard their voice and looked upon their adversity.'[1] 🙶

[1]From *History of Plimoth Plantation, 1620–1647* by William Bradford

Their early experiences were similar to those of the Jamestown settlers. Disease swept through the exhausted party. The survivors might well have starved to death if an Indian named Squanto had not befriended them. Squanto taught the Pilgrims how to grow corn. He showed them the best streams for fishing.

Things changed for the better in the spring. Unlike the first Virginians, the Pilgrims worked hard, planted their crops, and in the autumn gathered in a bountiful harvest. For this, in November 1621, the settlers came together to give thanks to God. Thus was established the American tradition of **Thanksgiving Day.**

However, Plymouth remained a very small colony. Life there was hard. The courage, determination, dignity, and piety of the Pilgrims—not wealth or power—has assured them a permanent place in our nation's history.

The Pilgrims came to America for very different reasons than the settlers of Virginia. Even at this early date it was clear that America attracted ordinary people. For nearly all, there was hope of finding a better life in the land of opportunity. 🖳

Return to the Preview & Review on page 53.

4. "A CITY UPON A HILL"

The Puritans

While the London Company was making plans to settle Virginia, another joint-stock company, the Virginia Company of Plymouth, or the Plymouth Company, tried to establish a settlement far to the north near the mouth of the Kennebec River in what is now Maine. The settlers arrived in 1607 but remained only one winter. However, fishermen and traders continued to set up temporary camps in the area. In 1614 the Plymouth Company sent John Smith to explore the region further. It was Smith who first called the area **New England.**

In the early 1620s the Plymouth Company, now called the Council of New England, gave away several tracts of land in the northern regions, including much of what are now Maine and New Hampshire.

The great 19th-century American sculptor, Augustus Saint-Gaudens, made this bronze, "The Puritan." What does this sculpture show you about Puritan life?

Use these questions to guide your reading. Answer the questions after completing Section 4.
Understanding Issues, Events, & Ideas. Use the following words to compare Puritan settlements with Jamestown: New England, Puritans, Massachusetts Bay Company, freemen, commonwealth, Fundamental Orders, proprietary colony, Toleration Act.

1. Who were the Puritans? How did the Puritans differ from the Pilgrims? Why did they leave England?
2. Why did Puritan leaders expel Roger Williams? Anne Hutchinson?
3. What kind of powers did the king's grant give Lord Baltimore? Why were these powers never used?

Thinking Critically. You are a Puritan living in Massachusetts in 1634. Write a letter to your cousins in England, convincing them to come to America.

"A City upon a Hill"   57

Maine remained a part of Massachusetts until 1820, but in 1679 New Hampshire was proclaimed a separate royal colony. The most significant grant made by the Council of New England was to a group of religious reformers. Like the Pilgrims, these people were critical of the Church of England. But they were not Separatists. They had not given up hope of reforming the Church from within. They sought to purify it. Hence they were known as **Puritans.**

The efforts of the Puritans to reform the Church of England met strong resistance. Puritan ministers were even denied the right to preach. When they were persecuted, many Puritans began to think of moving to America. Perhaps there they could create a perfect church and community. As one of their leaders explained, they sought to build "a city upon a hill," a community other people could look up to and admire and eventually copy.

Before taking advantage of the council's grant, the Puritans obtained a new charter from the king and organized the **Massachusetts Bay Company.** Under the charter their colony was to be practically self-governing. They planned their venture carefully. Their first group was large—about a thousand people—and adequately supplied. In 1630 their 11-ship convoy reached Massachusetts.

The governor of Massachusetts Bay, John Winthrop, was well aware of the difficulties involved in founding a settlement in a wilderness. He was a practical person who preferred compromise and persuasion to force. The charter put all political power in the hands of the stockholders. But Winthrop feared that unless ordinary colonists had some share in governing the settlement, there would be trouble. Therefore he and the other stockholders decided to make about a hundred additional settlers **freemen**, which meant that they could vote for the governor of the colony and for members of its legislature, which was called the General Court. The new freemen were church members, which violated the charter. Freemen were required to be church members until this regulation was changed in 1664.

The Puritans were not democratic in the modern sense of the term. They did, however, try earnestly to create a **commonwealth,** a society devoted to the common welfare of all.

Within a year of their arrival the Puritans had "planted," as they called it, several communities centered around their chief town, Boston. During the next ten years, about 15 or 20 thousand people came, far more than to any earlier colony. Soon some groups, or congregations, were pushing out on their own. In 1635 the Reverend Thomas Hooker led his congregation from Massachusetts to the fertile valley of the Connecticut River. There in Connecticut they established the town of Hartford. Other "river towns" sprang up in the valley. These towns formed a common government and drafted a written constitution, the **Fundamental Orders.** The system outlined in the Fundamental Orders was not especially different from the government of

John Winthrop, the first governor of Massachusetts Bay, sat for this portrait in the 17th century. Compare this portrait with the miniatures of Sir Francis Drake and Sir Walter Raleigh at the beginning of the chapter. In what ways does Winthrop resemble an Englishman of Queen Elizabeth's court? How does he differ?

Massachusetts Bay. Its main distinction was that it allowed male residents who were not church members to become freemen. The document is very important historically because it was the first written frame of government in America, a kind of ancestor of all the state constitutions and of the Constitution of the United States.

Religious Conflicts

Because religion was so important to the Puritans, they would not tolerate anyone whose religious beliefs differed from their own. They believed theirs was the true faith and thought all others must be the work of the devil. Our concept of freedom of religion would have made little sense to them at all. Thomas Hooker left Massachusetts because of religious disagreements that now seem quite trivial. These differences were certainly unimportant compared with those of another minister, Roger Williams.

Williams was charming. But he was impulsive and easily excited. He was very stubborn about anything he considered a matter of principle, and he was a man of many principles. He was out of place in Massachusetts because he questioned many Puritan beliefs. He did not believe the government should have any power over religious questions, whereas the Puritans thought it should enforce all the provisions of their strict faith as well as the Ten Commandments and civil law. He even insisted that, despite their charter, the colonists had no right to the land of Massachusetts until either they or the king purchased it from the Indians who lived there.

The oil painting above shows the journey of Thomas Hooker and company from Plymouth to Hartford in 1636.

Banished from Massachusetts, Roger Williams casts a determined look backward as he sets out to found Rhode Island. How is his appearance like that of "The Puritan" on page 57?

Anne Hutchinson is shown on trial in this 19th-century engraving. What impression does she seem to make on her all-male jury?

By 1635 the members of the General Court had heard enough of Williams' criticisms. They ordered him to leave the Commonwealth. He went off with a few followers and the next year founded the town of Providence, on Narragansett Bay. There he put his theories about religious freedom and fair treatment of the Indians into practice. In 1644 he obtained a charter for the colony to be known as Rhode Island and Providence Plantations.

No sooner were the Puritans rid of Williams than they had to face another attack on their religious beliefs. This one came from Anne Hutchinson. Mrs. Hutchinson was one of the most remarkable of all the early colonists. She was both learned and deeply emotional. She and her husband William arrived in 1634, and soon she became known for her many acts of kindness and for her thorough knowledge of the Bible. She was very strong willed and, if possible, even more strict about matters of principle than Roger Williams. When she disagreed with some of the sermons delivered by her minister, she said so openly. She also began to hold meetings in her home to discuss religious questions. She told the people who attended these meetings that formal religion, church attendance, and prayer were less important than leading a holy life. One could go to Heaven without them.

These ideas horrified the Puritans. In 1637 Anne Hutchinson was brought to trial. Although she was able to defend her ideas brilliantly, she was found by the court to be "a woman not fit for our society." She too was banished, or expelled, from Massachusetts. Later, she and other exiles bought an island from the Narragansett Indians and founded Portsmouth, Rhode Island.

Maryland

By this time another English colony had been founded in the region immediately to the north of Virginia. It had a different origin than any of the others, being essentially the property of a single person. The English rulers claimed America as their private possession to do with as they wished. For this reason few people objected when Charles I gave 10 million acres (4 million hectares) of land around Chesapeake Bay to an important English nobleman, George Calvert, Lord Baltimore. The grant gave Calvert enormous power. He could found manors such as had existed in feudal times and hold the residents as serfs. He could act as the prosecutor and judge of anyone accused of breaking the law. He was known as the proprietor, or owner, of the area, and his colony was thus a **proprietary colony.**

Calvert died before the king's seal was attached to the charter making the grant. His son Cecilius Calvert became the first proprietor of the colony, which was called Maryland in honor of Queen Henrietta Maria, the wife of Charles I. The Calverts were Catholics and hoped to make Maryland a Catholic colony.

The first settlers landed in 1634 and founded the town of St.

Maryland Historical Society

Mary's. Life was relatively easy for them because Virginia, now prosperous, was nearby. They could get food and other supplies without waiting for ships from distant England. They scarcely searched for gold. Instead they turned promptly to growing tobacco.

Despite the charter Cecilius Calvert soon realized that he could not rule Maryland like a feudal lord. In order to attract settlers, he had to allow people to own land and to have some say in the government. Although he encouraged Catholics to settle in Maryland, a majority of the people who came there were Protestants. The Catholics received large land grants and held most of the important positions in the colony. The Protestants resented this favoritism. To have made the Catholic Church the official church of Maryland might have caused a revolution.

Calvert dealt with this problem shrewdly. He encouraged the local legislature to pass the **Toleration Act** of 1649, which guaranteed freedom of religion to all Christians. On the surface the Catholics were "tolerating" the Protestants. In fact, the Catholic minority was protecting itself. 🔁

"The Settlement of Maryland" was painted by Emanuel Leutze. What does this scene say about religious life in Maryland? What does it say about relations between the colonists and the local Indians?

Return to the Preview & Review on page 57.

"A City upon a Hill" 61

George Catlin was one of the greatest painters of the American West. In 1847 he painted the chief of the Taensa Indians receiving Robert La Salle in 1682. What ceremonial trappings of power do the Indians display?

Preview & Review

Use these questions to guide your reading. Answer the questions after completing Section 5.

Understanding Issues, Events, & Ideas. Compare the activities of European colonizers in America other than England, using these words: Quebec, New Netherland, patroon, New Sweden, Viceroy, New Spain.

1. What French claims were made in America at the time of the English claims?
2. What was the success of the early Dutch and Swedish settlements in America?
3. What were the geographic boundaries, east and west, of the Spanish colonies in the New World?

Thinking Critically. Did Peter Minuit pay a fair price to the Indians for Manhattan Island? Support your answer with sound reasoning.

5. OTHER EUROPEAN COLONIES IN NORTH AMERICA

The French in America

In 1524, not long after John Cabot's voyage in the service of Henry VII of England, the French king, François I, sent an Italian explorer, Giovanni da Verrazano, along the Atlantic Coast from North Carolina to Nova Scotia in search of a northwest passage. Eleven years later Jacques Cartier sailed up the St. Lawrence River as far inland as the present site of Montreal. In 1608, while the English settlers were struggling at Jamestown, Samuel de Champlain founded the first permanent French settlement in America at **Quebec.**

In 1673 Father Jacques Marquette and Louis Joliet explored the upper Mississippi River. Soon after, in 1679, Robert La Salle set sail aboard the first vessel on the Great Lakes. By 1700 French explorers had sailed through the Great Lakes, down the Mississippi River to the Gulf of Mexico, and up the Missouri River to the Rocky Mountains. In addition to what is now Canada, France claimed the entire Mississippi valley, lands also covered by grants of the English king to Virginia. Many wars would be fought for control of these overlapping territories.

National Gallery of Art, Paul Mellon Collection

From the beginning Jesuit missionaries made great efforts to bring Catholic culture to the Indians of Canada's St. Lawrence River valley. They established a farming colony near Quebec city and spent a great deal of time and energy Christianizing the Indians and teaching them how to farm and to settle down and live in villages. The friendship that developed between the French and the Indians helped the French to hold on to their North American territories. They depended heavily on their Indian allies in their wars with England over control of North America.

Dutch and Swedish Colonies

By 1620 the English had founded only two tiny settlements in America—Jamestown and Plymouth. Nevertheless, they claimed all the territory from Newfoundland to Florida, which of course had already been claimed by Spain. The English claim, however, was impossible to enforce. The first to challenge it were the Dutch people from Holland, also called The Netherlands. The Dutch were excellent sailors and master shipbuilders. Like the English they were dependent for their prosperity on foreign trade. The English rightly considered them their greatest rival on the high seas.

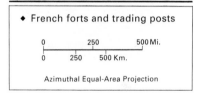

FRENCH EXPLORATIONS AND NON-ENGLISH SETTLEMENTS IN NORTH AMERICA

◆ French forts and trading posts

Azimuthal Equal-Area Projection

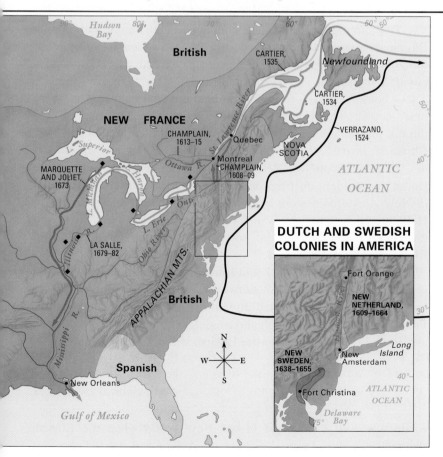

LEARNING FROM MAPS. *French explorers traveled farther inland than explorers from other nations. What route did they follow? Why did this make it easier for them to explore inland areas?*

The Dutch claimed the region drained by the Hudson River. They based their right to it on Henry Hudson's 1609 explorations of the river, which had been discovered by Portugal's Estaban Gómez in the 1520s. They called it **New Netherland.** In 1624 Dutch fur traders opened a post at Fort Orange, the site of present-day Albany. Two years later they founded New Amsterdam, on Manhattan Island at the mouth of the Hudson. Peter Minuit, the governor of the colony, bought Manhattan from its Indian inhabitants for some knives, beads, and trinkets. Eventually the island became the center of what is New York City, one of the most valuable pieces of property in the world. It has become fashionable to call Minuit's purchase the greatest real estate bargain of all time.

In 1629 Kiliaen Van Rensselaer, a jeweler from Amsterdam who owned stock in the Dutch West India Company, persuaded the company to issue a "Charter of Freedom and Exemptions" to encourage American settlement. A **patroon** was a landholder with powers like those of a feudal lord of the manor. Anyone who brought 50 new settlers to New Netherland was to receive a great estate in the Hudson River Valley and the powers to rule it. Rensselaer's patroonship, Rensselaerswyck, was the most successful one under the charter. Because the Dutch West India Company ruled the colony with an iron hand, not many people came to New Netherland.

Two directors of the Dutch company, Peter Minuit and Samuel Blommaert, were also involved in a New Sweden Company that founded **New Sweden** on the Delaware River near what is now the city of Wilmington. The Swedes built the first log cabins in America. These homes, so easy to build in a land covered with forests, were much copied. The Swedes traded for furs with the Indians, but they did not prosper. When a Dutch force captured their settlement, Fort Christina, in 1655, the region became a part of New Netherland.

The history of New Netherland was brief. The English saw the Dutch as intruders on English soil. Worse, Dutch merchants based in New Amsterdam were buying Virginia tobacco and selling it in Holland, much to the annoyance of English tobacco merchants. And the Dutch colony's excellent harbor at the mouth of the Hudson River was a tempting target.

In 1664 King Charles II sent four English warships carrying 400 soldiers to capture New Amsterdam. The town had only 1,500 inhabitants, and the people had no will to fight. When their governor, Peter Stuyvesant, tried to organize a defense, they pushed him aside and turned the town over to the English without firing a shot.

Spanish Settlements

Spain was well established in the New World when the English colonists arrived. Lucas Vásquez de Ayllón had started the first

Peter Stuyvesant appears a confident leader in this 19th-century engraving. However, his heavy-handed rule may have contributed to the loss of New Amsterdam to the English. Geographically, why was it difficult for the Dutch to hold New Amsterdam?

Daughters of the Republic of Texas Library

European settlement in America, San Miguel de Gualdape, on the coast of Georgia. That settlement did not survive. But in 1565 Pedro Menéndez de Avilés founded St. Augustine, Florida, a fort that became the first *permanent* European settlement in America. There the Spanish built the first schools and homes. The first European baby to be born in America, Martin Arguelles, was born in St. Augustine. Over the years Spain built more missions and forts as far up the Atlantic Coast as Virginia.

Spanish influence also spread into the northern part of what was then Mexico. In 1598 Don Juan de Oñate, son of a wealthy mine owner in Mexico, set out to settle the area known as New Mexico. He took with him many soldiers and Catholic missionaries. After conquering the Indians who lived in the Acoma pueblo, Oñate claimed New Mexico for Spain. In 1609 Santa Fe became the permanent capital of the area.

The Spanish influence spread slowly westward. In 1602 Sebastián Viscaíno explored the California coast. By 1700 many Spanish ranchers were living in southern California. In 1769 Gaspar de Portolá and Father Junípero Serra built a chain of missions and presidios up the Pacific Coast as far north as San Francisco.

Many Spanish colonists claimed large grants of land called *encomiendas*. To work the land, Spanish landowners claimed those Indians who lived on it. At best these Indians received meager wages. At worst they became almost like slaves. Roman Catholic priests and missionaries, most notably Friar Bartolomé de Las Casas, fought for freedom and justice for the Indians.

As with most English colonies, power to govern the Spanish colonies was centered on the king. His representatives, or **viceroys,** ruled in his name. The viceroy for **New Spain**—Central America, the Caribbean, and Spanish North America—lived in Mexico City. The viceroy in Lima, Peru, ruled the colonies in South America. Lesser officials enforced the laws. Spanish influence in the United States lasts in the names of many cities and in Spanish, the second most commonly spoken language. 🖫

Theodore Gentilz painted these Mexican couples dancing the fandango. The men hold candles aloft in their right hands. One enthusiast is firing his pistol into the ceiling.

The Granger Collection

Bartolomé de Las Casas arrived in America in 1502. He became the first Catholic priest ordained in America. He fought enslavement of the Indians and worked to help them.

Return to the Preview & Review on page 62.

European Challenges to England   65

Use these questions to guide your reading. Answer the questions after completing Section 6.
Understanding Issues, Events, & Ideas. Use the following words in a description of the other colonies: Quakers, trustee.
1. Where did the proprietors of Carolina hope to find settlers?
2. How did the proprietors intend to run Carolina? Why did their plan fail?
3. Why did William Penn found a colony in America? Why was it unusual for someone like Penn to be granted a charter?
4. Why did many Europeans come to Pennsylvania?
5. Why was Georgia founded?
Thinking Critically. 1. Of the colonies described in this section, which would you have most liked to live in? Why? Which would you have least liked to live in? **2.** You know that New York was named for the Duke of York and Jamestown for King James I. If you could name a colony in honor of someone, who would it be and why? What name would you give the colony?

6. LATER COLONIAL SETTLEMENTS

The Carolinas

In 1663 Charles II gave the land between Virginia and Spanish Florida to eight noblemen, among them Sir George Carteret, who was probably the richest person in England, and Sir Anthony Ashley Cooper. The grateful proprietors named the region Carolina in honor of Charles I, whose name in Latin was *Carolus*. In order to avoid the expense of financing expeditions from England, the Carolina proprietors hoped to attract settlers from the older colonies, especially from Virginia and Maryland.

A number of Virginians did drift into the northernmost part of the grant, but settlement there was scattered and isolated. There were few roads and practically no villages, churches, or schools. Most of the colonizers became small farmers who grew food crops and a little tobacco.

When it became clear that settlers from the older colonies were not moving to the Carolinas in any number, Sir Anthony Ashley Cooper brought in people from the island of Barbados in the West Indies. In 1670 Charleston (originally Charles Town) was founded. Charleston soon became a busy trading center, as well as the social and political center of Carolina.

The proprietors of Carolina had broad political authority—on paper. They dreamed of creating a land of great estates where lords with feudal titles reigned over lowly tenants. Two fifths of the land was to be owned by the noble class.

The system was "almost unbelievably ill-suited to the American scene," as a modern historian has written. Most of the intended tenants quickly obtained land of their own. In 1719 the settlers rebelled against the proprietary government and asked the king to take over the colony. Ten years later the area was separated into North Carolina and South Carolina, each under the authority of a royal governor.

Immigrants from Europe came mostly through Charleston. They and people drifting down from Virginia's Shenandoah Valley settled the Piedmont back country of both colonies. They carved out farms for themselves in this remote region. They were people of many faiths—Anglicans, Baptists, Scotch-Irish Presbyterians, Lutherans, and Moravians. At first, the most important was the Anglican Church of England, which was the established (tax-supported) religion in many of the colonies. But by the end of the colonial period, Methodist circuit riders—preachers who traveled from town to town—had converted large numbers of Anglicans and a considerable number of the African slaves in the region.

New York and New Jersey

When New Netherland was taken over by the English in 1664, the name of the colony was changed to New York in honor of the Duke of York, its new proprietor. The duke had control of the entire region between Connecticut and Delaware. He immediately began to hand out generous chunks of it to his friends. The largest prize was New Jersey, which included everything between the Hudson and Delaware rivers. He gave this region to Sir George Carteret and another of the Carolina proprietors, John, Lord Berkeley.

To attract colonists, Carteret and Berkeley offered land on easy terms. They also promised settlers religious freedom and the right to elect a legislature. In 1674 Berkeley sold his half interest to two Quakers. **Quakers** were one of the Separatist groups. They were religious enthusiasts. They believed that everyone could communicate directly with God. For this reason they did not depend upon ministers or church services. They relied on direct communication with the Holy Spirit as much as on the Bible. They stressed religious tolerance, kindness among Christians, and simplicity. They were opposed to warfare and any use of force.

Another group of Quakers bought the rest of New Jersey in 1681 from the heirs of George Carteret. In 1702 the two sections were reunited as one colony.

Pennsylvania and Delaware

Another large colonial grant was awarded to a very unlikely candidate, William Penn. Penn was a person of great wealth and high social status, the son of a much-decorated English admiral. While at Oxford University, he became a Quaker.

Because of their peaceable and anti-establishment beliefs, Quakers, both at home and in America, were often imprisoned, tortured, or even hanged. Penn himself spent some time in jail. To protect other Quakers from such persecution, Penn hoped to create a refuge in America. Charles II was agreeable. He owed a large sum of money to Penn's father, who had died in 1670. To cancel this debt, in 1681 he gave William the region between New York and Maryland, suggesting that it be called Pennsylvania in honor of Penn's father.

William Penn was strongly religious and held to high ideals. He also had a solid understanding of the value of money and how to make it. Pennsylvania was to be ''a holy experiment'' in Christian living and self-government. Penn personally came to Pennsylvania to oversee the laying-out of Philadelphia, his city of ''brotherly love.'' Like Roger Williams, he insisted that the Delaware Indians be paid for their land and treated fairly by the settlers.

Penn was shrewd in business. To attract settlers he wrote glowing accounts of Pennsylvania's soil and climate and circulated them

Point of View

William Penn's biographer tells of Penn's respect for American Indians.

> **''From what Penn had read or heard or seen of Indians, he had formed a highly favorable opinion of them. They were quiet folk, much like typical Quakers, serious, reserved, and taciturn, qualities Penn admired. . . .''**
> Harry Emerson Wildes

throughout Europe. These, along with his promises of a voice in the government and religious liberty, lured settlers from many lands. Among these were large numbers of Germans, who were popularly known as the Pennsylvania Dutch. "Dutch" was the way English settlers pronounced the word *Deutsch*, which means German.

Pennsylvania prospered from the start. Farmers produced large crops of wheat and other foodstuffs. They exported their surplus through Philadelphia. Penn in 1682 obtained a grant of land on Delaware Bay. This region was called the Three Lower Counties because it was farther down the Delaware River. As you have read, the British had obtained it along with the rest of New Netherland in 1664 (see the map, page 63). The Three Lower Counties were represented in the Pennsylvania legislature. But as Pennsylvania continued to expand westward, delegates from the Three Lower Counties asked Penn for permission to form a government of their own. Penn consented and in 1704 the Three Lower Counties became Delaware.

Georgia

The last of the English colonies in America, Georgia, was not settled

Benjamin West, the most highly regarded artist of his day, went to Europe on the eve of the Revolution and never returned to America. He painted "Penn's Treaty with the Indians" around 1770. Do you think this painting gives an accurate picture of the meeting between Penn and the Indians? Explain.

FOUNDING OF THE THIRTEEN COLONIES		
Colony	Founded	Reason for Founding
New England Colonies		
Massachusetts	1620	Religious freedom
New Hampshire	1622	Profit from trade and fishing; religious freedom
Connecticut	1635	Religious and political freedom; expand trade
Rhode Island	1636	Religious freedom
Middle Colonies		
New York (New Netherland)	1624	Expand trade (Dutch)
Delaware (New Sweden)	1638	Expand trade (Swedish)
New Jersey	1664	Investment by founders; religious and political freedom
Pennsylvania	1682	Investment by founders; religious and political freedom
Southern Colonies		
Virginia	1607	Expand trade and agriculture
Maryland	1632	Investment by founders; religious and political freedom
North Carolina	1663	Profit from trade and agriculture
South Carolina	1663	Profit from trade and agriculture
Georgia	1732	Investment; haven for debtors; buffer against Spanish

until 1733. It was founded by a group of well-to-do, charitable Englishmen who hoped to provide a new start for English people who had been imprisoned for debt. Their leader was James Oglethorpe, a man deeply committed to helping victims of political, economic, and religious oppression.

Armed with a charter granting him and his associates the authority to manage Georgia as **trustees** for 21 years, Oglethorpe came to America in 1733 with about a hundred settlers. They founded the town of Savannah. Each settler was given 50 acres (20 hectares) of land, tools to work it with, and enough supplies for the first year. Oglethorpe was stubborn and very straitlaced. He tried to make the settlers grow things like olive trees and silkworms that would not flourish in Georgia. He demanded that no lawyers be allowed in the colony, insisting that all lawyers were born troublemakers. He attempted to ban liquor.

Georgia was an out-of-the-way colony. A hostile Spanish settlement in Florida on its southern border kept it from growing very fast. Few people lived there. The people who did come to Georgia resented the strict rules. They made it impossible to keep out liquor, or even lawyers. In 1752, a year before their charter was due to run out, the discouraged trustees turned the colony over to the king.

LEARNING FROM TABLES. *This table shows how the colonies are often grouped. Although there were no formal ties between the colonies in each group, geographical and cultural factors drew them together. What were the two most common reasons for founding colonies?*

Return to the Preview & Review on page 66.

CHAPTER 2 REVIEW

Spain's Golden Age			
1500	**1550**	**1600**	

1497 Cabot explores America

1513 Ponce de León explores Florida

1540 Coronado expedition begins

1565 Menéndez founds St. Augustine

1585 Roanoke founded

1588 Spanish Armada defeated

1607 Jamestown founded

1608 Quebec settled by French

Chapter Summary
Read the statements below. Choose one, and write a paragraph explaining its importance.
1. Defeat of the Spanish Armada by the English led to Spain's decline and England's rise.
2. The first English settlements in America suffered severe setbacks.
3. People came to America to trade and sell, to practice their religion, and to find work.
4. Joint-stock companies invested in colonies such as Virginia.
5. John Smith's leadership and the popularity of tobacco saved Virginia.
6. The Pilgrims who settled Massachusetts came to America to escape religious persecution.
7. The Mayflower Compact represents the first attempt to create a government where none existed before.
8. The Puritans settled New England, where several religious conflicts eventually arose.
9. The French, Dutch, Swedes, and Spanish also established colonies in America.
10. The Middle Colonies and Georgia were established under royal grants and charters.

Reviewing Chronological Order
Number your paper 1-5. Then study the time line above and place the following events in the order in which they happened by writing the first next to 1, the second next to 2, and so on.
1. Jamestown founded
2. First Thanksgiving
3. Cabot explores America
4. Spanish Armada defeated
5. Penn granted Pennsylvania

Understanding Main Ideas
1. For what various reasons did the English want to establish colonies in America?
2. How did forming joint-stock companies help the English explore and colonize America?
3. Why are the Mayflower Compact and the Fundamental Orders important documents in American history?
4. By 1700, what French claims had been made in America? What Dutch claims? What Swedish claims? What was the extent of Spanish settlement in America?
5. How were colonists attracted to New Jersey? To Pennsylvania? To Georgia?

Thinking Critically
1. **Interpreting.** The English saw Sir Francis Drake as a hero; the Spanish saw him as a villain. In your opinion, which view was more accurate? Cite facts to support your point of view.
2. **Synthesizing.** Imagine that you are one of the colonists of Jamestown, Virginia—either a jeweler or an indentured servant. What is your attitude toward Captain John Smith as leader of your colony? Use information from this book, combined with historical imagination, to support your view of Smith.
3. **Evaluating.** How did Roger Williams, Anne Hutchinson, and William Penn differ from other colonists in their dealings with American Indians? Do you think their methods were more ethical or less ethical than those of the Jamestown colonists? Why?

Writing About History: Expressive
Read about the Lost Colony of Roanoke in an encyclopedia or reference book. Then use your historical imagination to create a diary with at least ten entries that one of the settlers might have kept hidden in a tree.

Practicing the Strategy
Review the strategy on page 46.
Using Latitude and Longitude. Look at the map on page 29 and answer the following questions.
1. How many degrees are there between the parallels of latitude? Between meridians?
2. Which continent lies between approximately 40W° and 80W°?

1620
Mayflower
Compact

1621
First Thanksgiving

1629
Massachusetts
Bay founded

1634
Maryland settled

1635
Connecticut settled

1636
Rhode Island
settled

1663
The Carolinas
established

1664
England takes over
New Netherland

1681
Penn granted
Pennsylvania

1704
Delaware
becomes
a separate
colony

1732
Georgia
established

3. What are the approximate coordinates of Plymouth? of Jamestown?
4. Approximately what is the latitude and longitude of present-day Florida?

Using Primary Sources

In 1621 Edward Winslow, one of the Pilgrim settlers in Plymouth, wrote the first account of the settlement's beginnings, including this of the first Thanksgiving. Note that rather than blood-thirsty savages, Winslow describes a peaceful civilized people. To better understand life in these early colonies, read the excerpt from Winslow's *Relation or Journall, etc.* in Alexander Young's *Chronicles of the Pilgrim Fathers* and answer the questions that follow it.

> *Many of the Indians came to visit us, including their greatest king, Massasoit, who brought about 90 of his followers. We entertained and feasted them for three days. The Indians went out and killed five deer, which they presented to our governor. Although food is not always this plentiful, yet by the goodness of God we are so far from want that we often wish you were here to share our plenty.*
>
> *We have found the Indians very faithful in their pact of peace with us, very kind, and ready to please us. We often go to them, and they come to visit us. Some of us have traveled 50 miles inland with them. We walk as peaceably and safely in the woods as on the roads of England. We entertain the Indians in our homes, and they give their deer meat to us.*

1. Why do you think the Indian king presented the deer to the colonial governor?
2. How did the Indians demonstrate their commitment to peace with the colonists?
3. How do you think Winslow's account of colonial life may have influenced people in England? Support your answer with two specific examples from the excerpt.

Linking History & Geography

In the first two chapters you have read about trade routes and routes of exploration. Routes are paths by which people, goods, and culture travel from place to place. Routes usually develop where people can travel easiest and least expensively. Use the map of French Explorers in America on page 63 to answer the following questions.

1. By what route did the French explorers travel from Quebec to New Orleans?
2. European settlers often found natural waterways made the best routes. Why would lakes, rivers, and streams provide good routes?
3. What do you notice about the geographic location of all the French settlements, forts, and trading posts?

Enriching Your Study of History

1. **Individual Project.** The first Jamestown settlers had the wrong trades and skills needed for survival. Some were goldsmiths and jewelers. Use historical imagination to make a list of five occupations that would have made Jamestown stronger. Explain the reasons for each choice. Make a similar list for a group today going to an unexplored area. Are your lists similar? Why or why not?
2. **Cooperative Project.** In small groups, gather information on all the colonies and settlements in America described in Chapters 1 and 2. List the name of the colony, its date of founding, and other important information. Then pool your information with that of the other groups to create a large chart of all the colonies and settlements. Then work together to make a large map of North America that shows the Spanish, English, Dutch, and Swedish colonies, and the French settlements.

Chapter 2 Review 71

Life in Colonial America

T he English colonies in North America were separate communities scattered along the Atlantic Coast from New England to Georgia. Few people in the Carolinas ever saw or spoke with a person from Massachusetts or New York or Pennsylvania. People did not often use the word "American" to describe themselves or their country. Most thought of themselves as English or Dutch or French— whatever their homeland was. Yet they and their children soon became more American than European, for they were changed by the land. Alas for others, the Africans first brought to America in 1619, there was slavery. What hope had the African American children born thereafter?

Preview & Review

Use these questions to guide your reading. Answer the questions after completing Section 1.
Understanding Issues, Events, & Ideas. Explain the influences of land and rivers on American settlers, using the following words: town common, public school, southern hospitality, frontier, squatter, democracy, political equality, seaport.
1. How did the great amount of land in America influence the size of the family?
2. How did rivers shape life in the South? Why were seaports essential in the North?
3. What was the attitude toward women in colonial America?
4. In what ways were rural people self-sufficient?
Thinking Critically. 1. Why did most colonists believe that people who owned a country should have a say in running it? **2.** Suppose that you are a colonial person who does not own property. Make an argument for your right to vote.

1. AN AMERICAN CIVILIZATION

Land and People

In the beginning America was a very large country with a very small population. There was much work to be done and few people to do it. This situation had enormous effects on the colonists. For one thing it tended to make them more flexible. To succeed, one needed to be

New York State Historical Assn., Cooperstown

open-minded. Historical imagination can help us to see why this attitude was important. Everything was so different in America. Those who were willing to experiment, to try new ways of doing things, usually did better than those who insisted on following traditional paths. For the same reason, Americans had to be jacks-of-all-trades. Farming in the wilderness meant being one's own carpenter, tailor, butcher, even one's own doctor.

With so much land to farm and with the woods and streams full of game and fish, there was always plenty to eat. Children grew big and strong. Sons and daughters were usually taller than their parents. The grandchildren grew taller still. Because there was so much work to be done, another child was an asset, not merely another mouth to feed. A six-year-old could tend the chickens, a ten-year-old weed vegetables or milk cows. Large families were the rule. There was plenty of land. When they were grown, the children could have farms of their own.

Children were well treated and given much love by most American parents. Europeans claimed that American children were spoiled. Compared to how children were treated in Europe, this may have been so, but by modern standards it was far from true. American youngsters worked hard, and family discipline was quite strict.

Point of View

Young Martha Dandridge of Virginia became a skillful rider. She once rode her horse Fatima up the stairs at her Uncle William's house. Her father called her by a pet name when he defended her.

"Let Patsy alone! She's not harmed William's staircase. And, by heavens, how she can ride."
John Dandridge, c. 1745

Rivers Shape Life

In a country without roads the first colonists relied on rivers to get themselves and their goods from place to place. In Virginia, rivers like the James and the Potomac were broad, deep, and slow moving. Oceangoing vessels could sail up them for many miles. The ships brought the products of Europe to inland tobacco farmers and took away barrels of cured tobacco for sale in England. For this reason the population of Virginia was scattered thinly over the land. Farms

For many years this painting of the Van Bergen farm in the Hudson Valley around 1735 hung over the fireplace mantle, so proud were those who lived on the prosperous farm. Where in the painting can you find the owner and his family?

"The Plantation" was painted in about 1825. It reminds us of another great Virginia plantation, Mount Vernon. All roads run to the river's edge for easy shipping. How is this both a picture and a kind of map?

spread along the riverbanks. Land between the rivers lay untouched for many years. There were few towns because buying and selling could take place at each farmer's riverside dock.

In New England the rivers were shallow and full of rapids. Ships could not sail up them. Seaports were essential from the beginning. Boston, New Haven, Newport, and other coastal towns became quite large early in their histories. Inland transportation had to be by road.

Building roads was an expensive business. Settlers remained close together so that few had to be built. The New England village made its appearance. Around a small, parklike town square—the **town common**—the villagers built their church, meeting house, and school. Each family received a small plot of land for a house and a garden around this town common. Outside the village lay the fields where crops were grown. Workers went out each morning, tilled their strips of land, and returned at day's end to their snug homes.

Thus, people in New England were community minded. In Virginia and other southern colonies people were more family centered. There were more schools in New England, not only because Puritans believed that education was very important, but also because enough families lived within walking distance of the schools to support them. In 1647 Massachusetts began the first organized educational system in the colonies, requiring all towns with 100 families to set up the first **public schools.**

Colonists in the Middle and Southern Colonies also saw the value of an education. In the Middle Colonies churches and families started private schools. These schools charged fees so only children of wealthy colonists could attend. Wealthy southerners were more apt to educate their children at home with tutors, or private teachers. These children received an excellent education, but most other southern children received almost none. Southern education soon lagged far behind that of other sections, a condition that continued until after the Civil War. Also, perhaps because their lives were more isolated, southerners tended to welcome strangers with a special warmth. This was one origin of **southern hospitality.**

Women in Colonial America

Most of the first settlers were young men. Once a colony was established, however, it was important to these men and to the merchant adventurers or colonial proprietors that more women be recruited. The London Company shipped whole boatloads of unmarried women to Virginia. When the women married, their husbands would pay the cost of their passage. Women often came to America as indentured servants and frequently ended up marrying their masters. Colonists tended to take a practical rather than a romantic view of marriage.

Yet people familiar with European attitudes almost always noticed that American men were more respectful of women and more considerate of their wives than European men were. In America women were needed as workers and mothers—and companions too.

This oil painting shows "Abigail Gerrish and Her Grandmother" in about 1750. It was painted by John Greenwood, who with a handful of other New England painters broke with English traditions to create art that was truly American. Like Abigail, when colonial children were dressed up they appeared as miniature adults. How were most colonial children treated?

Keturah Rawlins of Boston made this needlepoint around 1749. What are some other crafts made by colonial Americans?

Compared to their status today, women had few rights in colonial times. They were kept by law and custom under the thumb of men. Married women could not own property. If they earned any money, it belonged legally to their husbands. Almost none had the right to vote. Divorce was next to impossible. Needless to say, wives also worked very hard. In addition to keeping house, rearing children, and performing hundreds of farm chores, the typical colonial woman had to devote much time to teaching her children, to making clothing for the whole family, and to caring for anyone who was sick. If men were jacks-of-all-trades, women were surely jills-of-all-trades. The advantages of having many children in America were not weighed against the health of the mothers of these children. Constant child-bearing caused many women to die at an early age.

Yet, when all these things have been said, it remains true that America offered women more opportunities than was common in Europe. Women learned to handle guns and to defend themselves against attack. Some women ran large farms and plantations because "the man of the house" was away or had died. Martha Dandridge Custis, still in her twenties when her husband died, became one of the wealthiest women in America. Women in America ran newspapers, served as lawyers in colonial courts, and did other things that would have been almost impossible for women in Europe.

In the churches, which were often the social as well as religious centers of the colonies, women often outnumbered men. They also equalled men in their power to affect religious practices. Quakers, of course, carefully preserved the right of women to preach and to carry on especially assigned missionary work. Still, few women became ministers. Yet women directed most religious aspects of family life, and they influenced the moral standards of the community. This gave them a much higher place in American congregations than women enjoyed in Europe.

Land and Labor

In Europe landowners were the kingpins of society. Membership in the nobility meant control of large territories and the people who lived in them. For lesser people, owning land brought prestige as well as whatever profit could be made from it. Except for highly skilled artisans, laborers in Europe tended to be poor.

In America there was so much unused land that without labor land was worth almost nothing. With labor it could be used productively. This meant that working people earned more than European workers and were better treated by their employers. In 1698 Gabriel Thomas, an English visitor, wrote of the value of labor and the abundance he saw in America:

66 What . . . serves Man for Drink, Food and Rayment [clothes], is cheaper here than in *England*, or elsewhere;

Martha Dandridge Custis was one of the richest women in America. This detail is from an oil portrait painted by John Wollaston. In 1757 Mrs. Custis' husband died and she became the owner of the Custis lands in Virginia. She is the same "Patsy" Dandridge who rode her horse up her uncle's staircase. When she next appears in our story, she will be married to the commander in chief of the American army in the Revolutionary War.

but the chief reason why Wages of Servants of all sorts are higher here than there, arises from the great Fertility and Produce of the Place; besides, if these large Stipends [payments] were refused them, they would quickly set up for themselves, for they can have Provision very cheap, and Land for a very small matter, or next to nothing in comparison of the Purchase of Lands in *England;* and the farmers there can better afford to give that great Wages than the farmers in England can, for several reasons very obvious.

At First, their Land costs them (as I said but just now) little or nothing in comparison, of which the Farmers commonly will get twice the encrease of [as much] Corn for every Bushel they sow, that the Farmers in *England* can from the richest Land they have.

In the Second place, they have constantly good price for their Corn, by reason of the great and quick vent [market] into the *Barbados* and other Islands; through which means Silver is become more plentiful there than here in *England,* considering the Number of People, and that causes a quick Trade for both Corn and Cattle; . . .

Thirdly, They pay no *Tithes,* and their Taxes are inconsiderable; the Place is free for all Persuasions [religions], in a Sober and Civil way, for the Church of *England* and the *Quakers* bear equal Share in the Government. They live Friendly and Well together; there is no Persecution for Religion, nor ever like to be; 'tis this that knocks all Commerce on the Head [in England], together with the high Imposts [duties], strict Laws, and cramping Orders. Before I end this paragraph, I shall add another Reason why Womens Wages are so exorbitant; they [women] are not yet very numerous, which makes them stand upon high terms for their several services, in *Sempstering* [seamstressing], *Washing, Spinning, Knitting, Sewing,* and in all other parts of their Imployments. . . .

Reader, what I have written, is not *Fiction, Flam, Whim,* or any sinister *Design,* either to impose upon the Ignorant, or Credulous [those tending to believe too easily], or to curry favour with the Rich and Mighty, but in meer pity and pure Compassion to the Numbers of Poor Labouring Men, Women, and Children in *England,* half starv'd, visible in their meagre looks, that are continually wandering up and down looking for Employment without Encouragement or reward for their Work. . . . Here there are no Beggars to be seen (it is a Shame and Disgrace to the state that there are so many in *England*) nor indeed have any here the least Occasion or Temptation to take up that Scandalous Lazy Life. . . .

STRATEGIES FOR SUCCESS

READING GRAPHS

The successful student is able to gather information from a variety of sources, including graphs. *The Story of America* contains many graphs. Graphs present information visually. There are several types of graphs, each used to present a certain type of data. A *pie,* or *circle,* graph is used to show proportions. A *line* graph shows changes in two factors. It most often shows changes over time. A *bar* graph shows comparisons, making highs and lows stand out. A *picture* graph, or *pictograph,* uses pictures to illustrate amounts.

Because graphs can contain so much information and are so common in histories, it is important to know how to read them.

How to Read a Graph
Follow these steps to read a graph.
1. **Read the title.** The title will tell you the subject and purpose of the graph. It may also contain other information, such as dates.
2. **Study the labels.** Line and bar graphs show two sets of data, one set displayed on the horizontal axis and the other on the vertical axis. The *horizontal* axis is the line at the bottom of the graph that runs across the page. The *vertical* axis is at the left side of the graph and runs up and down. Labels on these axes identify the type of data and the unit of measurement, when appropriate.

3. **Analyze the data.** Note all trends, relationships, and changes among the data. Note increases and decreases in quantities.
4. **Put the data to use.** Use the information to form generalizations and hypotheses and to draw conclusions.

Applying the Strategy
You may have heard the expression, "A picture is worth a thousand words." The picture graph may also be worth a thousand words. Study the picture graph below. Note that small figures 🛇 are used to make a simple comparison of the population of the American colonies in 1730. Each symbol stands for 10,000 persons. A partial 🛇 figure represents a fraction of 10,000. For example, the population of Delaware in 1730 was 9,170 persons, so it is represented by part of a figure. What is the population of Virginia? New York? If you said 114,000 for Virginia and 48,000 for New York, you have read the graph correctly!

There also are examples of other types of graphs in this unit. The pie graph on page 89 shows the ethnic makeup of the colonial population. (For an example of a line graph, turn to page 139 in the next chapter.)

For independent practice, see Practicing the Strategy on page 107.

COLONIAL POPULATIONS, 1730*		
New Hampshire	Maryland	
Massachusetts	Virginia	
Connecticut	North Carolina	
Rhode Island	South Carolina	
New York	🛇 = 10,000 persons	
New Jersey	🛇 = 8,000 persons	
Pennsylvania	🛇 = 6,000 persons	
Delaware	🛇 = 4,000 persons	
	🛇 = 2,000 persons	*Georgia not yet founded

Source: *Historical Statistics of the United States*

What I have deliver'd about this *Province*, is indisputably true, . . . in the Year 1681.[1] **"**

High wages and cheap land meant that most Americans owned land. In Massachusetts and the other New England colonies the legislatures gave large tracts of land to groups of settlers who wanted to found new towns. The people then cleared as much of this land as they could farm and divided it up among the families. The rest, the commons, remained town property. As the town grew, newcomers were given some of the common land so that they could have farms.

In other colonies people got land in many ways. Those with headrights received it for nothing. Others bought land or got large grants from the king or from colonial authorities. Indentured servants could get money to buy land by working for wages after their terms of service were completed. Those who were impatient and willing to live under crude and dangerous conditions moved west to the edge of the settled area. This region, vaguely defined and shifting always westward, was called the **frontier.** On the frontier a settler could clear a tract of wild land, build a cabin, and plant a crop. Such people were called **squatters.** By the time settlement had expanded to their region, most squatters had made enough money to buy their property. If not, they usually sold their "improvements" to a newcomer and moved farther west to repeat the process.

Land and the Right to Vote

The fact that most Americans owned land affected in unexpected ways how the colonies were governed. Today we believe that all adult citizens should have the right to vote. One does not have to be rich or own property to participate in elections. This principle is known as **political equality,** a basic element of what we call **democracy.**

During the colonial era people did not believe in democracy as we now know it. For example, women were usually not allowed to vote. Nor could slaves or Indians. Only men who owned a certain amount of land or had other substantial wealth qualified to vote.

There was almost no difference between the attitudes of the English and the Americans on this point. Most colonists believed that the people who *owned* a country should have a say in running it, not those who merely *lived* in a country. Yet, since a majority of the colonists owned land, having to meet a "property qualification" to vote did not disqualify many.

Thus, while the colonists did not believe in the idea of democracy, in practice their governments were quite democratic. In most of the colonies about as large a percentage of the adult men voted in elections as does today. With time, people became accustomed to voting. Since the property requirement had so little practical effect,

[1]From *An Historical and Geographical Account of the Province and Country of Pennsylvania* by Gabriel Thomas

"Burning Fallen Trees in a Girdled Clearing, Western Scene" is the title of this fine engraving by W. J. Bennett. The girdle is the band cut in the tree in the foreground. It was a way of killing trees learned from the Indians by the first settlers of Jamestown. What name was given settlers who cleared wild land and planted crops on it?

An American Civilization   79

it ceased to seem important. Gradually, the *idea* of democracy began to catch up with what was actually happening.

In the early days settlers could remember England, where a handful of great landowners completely dominated elections. These settlers considered voting a privilege that they had gained by coming to America. Their grandsons, who grew up in a society where nearly every man voted, began to see voting as a natural right, not a privilege. This was one of the most important results of the ease of obtaining land in America.

Rural and Town Life in America

Both the northern colonies and the southern were mostly rural. In 1690 Boston was the largest town in North America, but it had a population of only about 7,000. Most colonists were farmers.

Despite the importance of trade and the foreign manufactured goods that trade made available, most farm families made many of the things they needed right in their own homes. They spun wool sheared from their sheep into thread. They wove the thread into cloth from which they made their coats and dresses and shirts and trousers. They used the skins of deer for "buckskin" leggins and moccasins. They carved buttons out of bone and made plates and spoons of wood. They built most of their own furniture, oftentimes using homemade tools. All this was especially true of families on the frontier and those living in districts far removed from rivers and roads. These people had to be almost entirely self-sufficient.

The towns were centers of activity, really the hearts and minds of the colonies. In even the smallest villages there were religious congregations and group activities like discussion clubs and sewing circles that people enjoyed.

The largest towns, in addition to Boston, were New York, Philadelphia, Charleston, and Newport. All were **seaports,** their economy based upon sea trade and shipbuilding. Though small by modern standards, all were bustling, vital communities. Their harbors were forests of ships' masts and spars. Their docks were piled high with barrels, boxes, crates, chests, and bales of every sort. In New York and Philadelphia one could hear many languages spoken. "We are a people thrown together from various quarters of the world," one proud citizen of Philadelphia explained.

In the shops and warehouses of the towns could be found fine English cloth and chinaware, tea from India, wine from Portugal and the Madeira islands, molasses from the sugar islands, as well as products from all the mainland colonies. Their taverns were crowded with sailors and dockworkers and artisans of all sorts. Every colonial town of any size had a weekly newspaper. Some had theaters too. The wealthy merchants built fine houses in the towns and filled them with good furnishings, some made by colonial artisans. 🔲

Mrs. Samuel Chandler, shown in an oil painted by Winthrop Chandler around 1780, was married to a merchant wealthy enough to supply her fine clothes from abroad. How does this painting show that Mrs. Chandler was wealthy?

Return to the Preview & Review on page 72.

America's West African Heritage

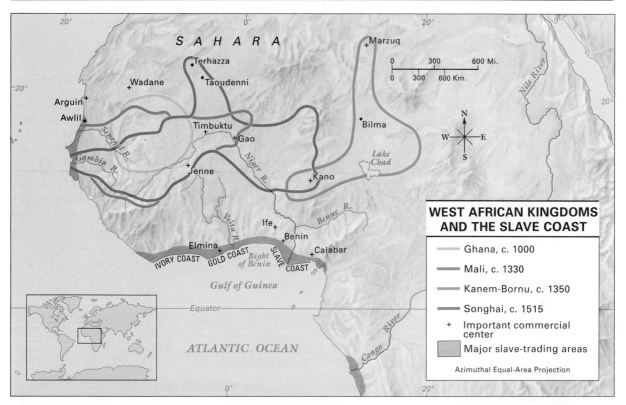

West Africa was the site of several great trading kingdoms. For centuries they traded mostly with Arab merchants who traveled in camel caravans. When Europeans began to explore the coast in the early 1500s, many turned to coastal trade. They soon discovered that captured Africans, sold as slaves, were a valuable commodity.

WEST AFRICAN KINGDOMS AND THE SLAVE COAST

⎯⎯	Ghana, c. 1000
⎯⎯	Mali, c. 1330
⎯⎯	Kanem-Bornu, c. 1350
⎯⎯	Songhai, c. 1515
+	Important commercial center
▨	Major slave-trading areas

Azimuthal Equal-Area Projection

For more than a thousand years great civilizations rose and fell in West Africa south of the Sahara. Why these kingdoms came to be—the will of a powerful ruler, a favorable place to trade—and why so little of their grand architecture remains—is as much a mystery to us as why Egypt and Rome declined and fell, or, closer to home, what fate befell the Mayan civilization.

Our African heritage is not that of a "dark continent" but rather that of the place where civilizations developed and culture advanced. Consider Egypt, one of the world's greatest civilizations. Consider Ghana, Mali, and Songhai, in the Western Sudan. Each of these kingdoms had an elaborate court life with artisans organized into guilds before Europe's Renaissance.

Other West African kingdoms—Asante, Dahomey, the Yoruba, and Benin—flourished in the forest lands farther south toward the West African Coast. Trade was important to their economies, and travelers to Africa wrote descriptions of the regal courts, especially in Benin, where magnificent bronzes were cast. Only with the permission of the king could artisans cast brass.

In eastern Africa later kingdoms—Zimbabwe and Mwanamutapa—grew powerful. Recent research shows that slaves preserved many aspects of their culture. However, because slaves were forbidden to speak their own tongues and produce their own art, much of our African heritage was lost. But their voices still speak to us of Africa's past in the art we look at here.

The Brooklyn Museum

A hornblower from Benin summons us to our study of Western African culture. This figure was cast in brass in the 17th century.

81

Below is the figure of a king of the Asante culture in Ghana. He was carved from wood in the 19th century and wields the symbol of his authority.

Royalty's pride is evident in this dark bronze altarpiece displayed in Benin City in Nigeria. To this day the Nigerian king wears a cap and choker similar to that in this 16th-century work.

Again from the 19th century, this beaded stool, surely fit for a ruler, comes from the Cameroons. It may have been fashioned by workers from Benin or Yoruba.

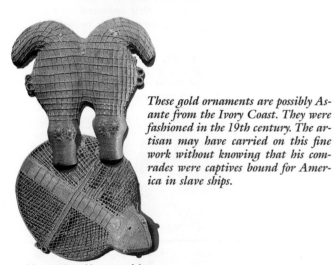

These gold ornaments are possibly Asante from the Ivory Coast. They were fashioned in the 19th century. The artisan may have carried on this fine work without knowing that his comrades were captives bound for America in slave ships.

Asante kings drank their palm wine from this 19th-century calabash vessel decorated with gold.

© Lee Boltin

Earlier than its sister civilizations, Egypt produced this 12th-dynasty head of a sphinx made of polished stone in about 1900 B.C.

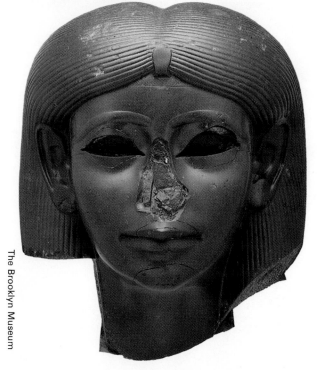

Metropolitan Museum of Art

What grace there is in this wooden antelope head! It would have been attached to a cap made of basketry for ceremonies commemorating tyi wara, *who taught humans the secret of agriculture. The head comes from the Bambara culture of Mali.*

Metropolitan Museum of Art

An ivory spoon in the figure of a man was made in Sierra Leone (in the style of Portuguese explorers) in the 16th century.

America's West African Heritage   **83**

This woman's wrapper woven from costly threads was made by the Asante people of Ghana in the early part of this century.

These dolls, probably made between 1880–1900, consist of fabric, leather, ceramics, and metal. They may recall earlier dolls held secretly in slumber by slave children.

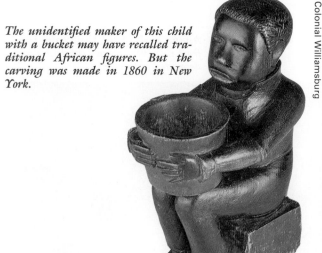

The unidentified maker of this child with a bucket may have recalled traditional African figures. But the carving was made in 1860 in New York.

Romare Bearden used his African American heritage for inspiration to make this 1970 collage, SHE-BA. The artist has clothed the woman in a contemporary fashion but he also recalls the famous Queen of Sheba.

84   LIFE IN COLONIAL AMERICA

2. SLAVERY AND THE ECONOMY

The Origins of Slavery

Indentured servants got land and eventually political power in America. Other laborers in America were cruelly used. These were the slaves brought from Africa. It takes a strong historical imagination to think as the European colonizers did about slavery. Most had certain deep-seated prejudices about people and their rights. Most believed that some people were better than others, that the values and customs of their society were better than any others. Being Christians, they felt certain that Christianity was the only true religion. Non-Christians were ''heathens,'' sinful and evil by nature.

We have seen how this point of view affected the way other Europeans dealt with the Indians. In the English colonies, however, the newcomers were not often able to make the Indians work for them. The land was large, the Indian population small. In most cases the Indians—those who were not wiped out by warfare or disease—eventually gave up their lands and moved west. A few Indians were enslaved. A few took on European ways. Most simply melted into the forest rather than submit to white control. There was nothing the colonists could do to stop them from leaving.

Another source of labor then became available—that of African

Use these questions to guide your reading. Answer the questions after completing Section 2.
Understanding Issues, Events, & Ideas. Explain why American slavery was a southern institution, using the following words: slave, British, peculiar institution, cash crops, tidewater, naval stores, fur trade, Yankee ingenuity, free enterprise, triangular trade.

1. Why did the colonists originally prefer indentured servants to African slaves? What caused a change in attitude?
2. What made growing cash crops profitable for the South?
3. Why did African slaves become the chief labor source in raising southern cash crops?
4. How was the triangular trade conducted? What were some variations of the triangular trade?

Thinking Critically. 1. Why do you think Africans brought to America as slaves were less likely to revolt than those born in America? **2.** Suppose that you are a Virginia tobacco planter. What similarities do you share with a South Carolina rice grower or a Pennsylvania wheat farmer?

The slave cabins of Mulberry Plantation stand in orderly rows behind the main house in this oil painting on paper by Thomas Coram. Do you think most slave cabins looked like the ones in this painting?

Gibbes Museum of Art

slaves. The story of how these innocent people were brought to America and compelled to work as slaves is the most tragic and shameful chapter in our history. It is even more shameful than the ill use of the Indians, who at least had the means of fighting back.

The Spaniards brought slaves from Africa to their American colonies before the founding of Jamestown. It may be that the English colonists got the idea of enslaving Africans from the Spanish example. In any case the first Africans were brought to the English colonies by Dutch traders, who sold them to the Jamestown colonists in 1619. Records are few, but these twenty Africans may have been treated as indentured servants rather than slaves because slavery was not legal according to English laws of the times.

At first few slaves were imported. Tobacco farmers and others in need of laborers much preferred indentured servants to Africans. Most indentured servants were **British**—from England, Scotland, Wales, or Ireland—and were familiar with the English language and life style. The Africans could not speak English. Many lacked the skills needed by farmers. And it cost much more to buy a slave than to purchase the labor of a servant for a limited period of time.

For a long time there were plenty of indentured servants. When they completed their service, most of them became independent farmers. They then competed with their former masters. The more servants a tobacco planter hired, the more small farmers would be planting tobacco for themselves seven years later. The price of tobacco and other crops tended to fall as production increased. Under slavery this kind of competition did not occur.

Slave Life

By 1690 there were slaves in all the English colonies. The **peculiar institution,** as some slaveholders called it, was firmly fixed in American society. It was to last for another 175 years.

Slavery was not unique to America. Many societies—the Greeks, Romans, Arabs, some African tribes—enslaved prisoners of war. Many came to look on their slaves as members of the household. But American slavery was different. It was based on race. Americans considered Africans inferior, and slaves as property rather than human beings.

It is hard for persons in a free society to conceive of what it was like to be a slave. We must use historical imagination carefully. The idea that slaves were constantly beaten or worked to death like prisoners in a concentration camp is incorrect. Slaves were too valuable to be treated like that—unless they refused to work or rose up against their owners. They were usually given adequate food, clothing, and shelter, again because they were expensive property. But slaves had absolutely *no rights*. Not only could they not vote or own property, their owners had complete control over their lives. An owner could separate a husband and wife, or sell a child and keep the child's parents. Slaves worked for the exclusive benefit of their owners. Slavery was inhuman, but those who were enslaved were human beings.

Most who became slaves were prisoners taken in wars in Africa or unsuspecting villagers captured by African slave hunters. These people marched their captives in chains to prison pens on the coast, then sold them to slave traders. Venture Smith described his experiences when as a six-year-old boy he and his family were captured by slave hunters from a neighboring African tribe:

66 They then came after us in the reeds, and the very first salute I had from them was a violent blow on the back of the head with the fore part of a gun, and at the same time a grasp around the neck. I then had a rope put about my neck, as had all the women in the thicket with me, and was immediately led to my father, who was likewise pinioned [held down] and haltered for leading. In this condition we were all led to the camp. The women and myself being pretty submissive, had tolerable treatment from the enemy, while my father . . . was cut and pounded on his body with great inhumanity. . . . I thus saw him tortured to death. The shocking scene to this day fresh in my mind, and I have often been overcome thinking of it. . . .

The enemy army was large, I should suppose consisting of about six thousand men. . . . The enemy had remarkable success in destroying the country wherever they went. For as far as they had penetrated, they had laid the habitations [villages] waste and captured the people. . . . They pinioned the prisoners of all ages and sexes indiscriminately, took their flocks and all their effects, and moved on their way towards the sea. On the march the prisoners were treated with clemency [mercy], on account of their being submissive and humble. Having come to the next tribe, the enemy laid siege and immediately took men, women, children, flocks, and all their valuable effects. They then went on to the next district which was contiguous [next] to the sea, called in Africa, Anamaboo. . . . The enemies' provisions were then almost spent, as well as their strength. The inhabitants knowing what conduct they had pursued, and what were their present intentions, improved the favorable opportunity, attacked them, and took enemy, prisoners, flocks and all their effects. I was taken for a second time [by Africans]. All of us were put in a castle, and kept for market. On a certain time I and other prisoners were put on board a canoe, under our master, and rowed away to a

A British warship captured a Spanish slaveship on its way to the West Indies in the 18th century. A young English naval officer, Lt. Francis Meynell, went below and made this watercolor sketch on the spot. In what ways do these prisoners appear more comfortable than other Africans who sailed the Middle Passage?

vessel belonging to Rhode Island, commanded by Captain Collingwood, and the mate Thomas Mumford. While we were going to the vessel, our master told us to appear to the best possible advantage for sale. I was bought on board by one Robertson Mumford, steward of said vessel, for four gallons of rum, and a piece of calico, and called VENTURE, on account of his having purchased me with his own private venture. Thus I came by my name. All the slaves that were bought for that vessel's cargo, were two hundred and sixty.[1] **99**

Next came the dreadful **Middle Passage,** the voyage across the Atlantic. The Africans were crowded below deck as closely as the captain thought possible without causing all to smother. How many died on the crossing was usually a matter of luck. If the winds were strong and favorable, the trip would be reasonably short. Most would survive. If the ship was delayed by bad weather, or if smallpox or some other contagious disease broke out, the death toll would be

[1]From *A Narrative of the Life and Adventures of Venture, A Native of Africa but Resident about Sixty Years in the United States of America* by Venture Smith

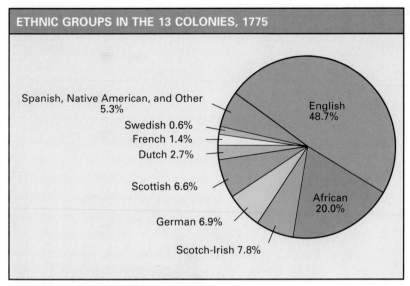

ETHNIC GROUPS IN THE 13 COLONIES, 1775

Spanish, Native American, and Other 5.3%
Swedish 0.6%
French 1.4%
Dutch 2.7%
Scottish 6.6%
German 6.9%
Scotch-Irish 7.8%
English 48.7%
African 20.0%

Source: *Historical Statistics of the United States*

LEARNING FROM GRAPHS. *Only nine ethnic groups had a sizeable number of people in the British colonies. What percentage of the total population did the British—English, Scotch-Irish, and Scottish—and their African slaves make up? What two other groups had the largest numbers?*

enormous. Olaudah Equiano, a slave who later bought his freedom, described the Middle Passage thus:

66 When the ship had loaded all its cargo, we were all put below deck. The number of people was so great that each person barely had room to move. The stale air and the heat almost choked us. Everyone was dripping sweat, so that the air became unfit to breathe, from a variety of foul smells. These conditions caused sickness among the slaves, and many died—in this way becoming victims to the short-sighted greed of their purchasers.

This wretched situation was made even worse by the rubbing of the chains against the slaves' skin, which became unbearable, and by the filth of the tubs, into which the children often fell and were almost drowned. The screams of the women, and the moans of the dying, made this a scene of horror almost beyond belief.[1] 99

Once in America, the slaves were put on public display and sold to the highest bidder. They were prodded and poked at by prospective buyers the way traders examine an old horse.

One can imagine how confused and depressed most new slaves were after these experiences. Separated from home and family, unable to communicate, drained of strength and hope, there was little likelihood that they would try to resist or run away. Where could they run to? You might think children born into slavery probably bore its weight with less pain, having never known freedom.

Not so. It is one of the many strange aspects of slavery that

[1]From *The Interesting Narrative of the Life of Olaudah Equiano, or Gustavus Vassa, The African*, vol. 1, by Olaudah Equiano

Slavery and the Economy   89

In the West Indies slaves refine sugar by boiling cane under the watchful eyes of the overseers who inspect the sugar drying in bins. An English artist made this colored lithograph in the 19th century. With your classmates, describe what you imagine these working conditions to be.

those who were born into slavery and particularly those who had the highest places in the system, such as those skilled at crafts like carpenters, were the ones who most frequently ran away or tried to organize slave revolts. Another puzzle is that by teaching slaves specific skills, their owners increased their usefulness but made them less willing to accept being slaves. Slaves who could read and write and practice a trade were far less willing to accept their condition than illiterate "field hands."

Southern Agriculture

What the colonists needed most were European manufactured goods. The money to buy these goods could be earned if the colonists raised crops that Europeans wanted but could not grow themselves. These were called **cash crops** because they brought the growers money to buy farm tools, furniture, clothing, guns and ammunition, pots and pans, books, glassware. The southern colonists had an advantage in the search for cash crops because of their warm climate. The island settlements in the West Indies, for example, raised sugarcane, a tropical plant that Europeans wanted badly but could not grow. By selling sugar refined from the sugarcane to their home countries, Spanish, English, French, and Dutch colonists in the West Indies could get money to buy European manufactured goods.

Tobacco provided a cash crop for the colonists of Maryland, Virginia, and the Carolinas. The seeds of tobacco are so small that a tablespoon will hold about 30,000 of them. The colonists planted these tiny seeds in beds of finely powdered soil. When the seeds sprouted, the little plants were moved to the fields. The best tobacco was made from the largest leaves. As the plants matured, the side shoots of each plant were cut off. At a certain point the top bud was clipped to stop growth. This pruning concentrated the plant's energies in the big leaves. In the fall these leaves were removed and carefully cured, or dried, in airy sheds. Then the tobacco was packed in barrels for shipping.

When tobacco first became popular in England, the price of American tobacco was very high. Anyone with even a small plot of land could make a good living growing it. More and more tobacco was planted as the tobacco colonies expanded. Gradually the price fell. The large planters could still live well enough earning a small profit on each barrel of tobacco. But many small farmers were forced to sell out and move west. When the news of this change reached Europe, poor people were less eager to come to America as indentured servants. With fewer Europeans coming to the tobacco colonies, African slaves became the chief source of labor on the tobacco plantations.

In parts of South Carolina and later in Georgia too, rice became the chief cash crop. Rice needs a warm climate and much water. It grew well in swamps and low-lying lands along the Atlantic Coast. The fields were flooded by building dikes and canals and trapping river water that was backed up by the incoming ocean tides. Coastal areas of the South were called the **tidewater** because their rivers were affected in this way by the ocean tides.

Malaria and other tropical fevers struck down many of the people who had to work in the rice fields. For this reason slave labor was used almost exclusively. Owners claimed that slaves were immune to these diseases because of their African origin. It may have been that they suffered less because of natural immunity, but large numbers of Africans caught malaria and many died. Working knee-deep in mud with the temperature in the nineties and humidity high, the air swarming with mosquitoes, was not good for anyone.

South Carolina farmers also grew indigo, a plant that produced a blue dye used by the English cloth manufacturers. Indigo was first grown in the English colonies by Eliza Lucas, who while still in her teens was running three large South Carolina plantations owned by her father, a colonial official in the British West Indies. An inventive person, Lucas also produced silk and experimented with other products, although without much success.

The great pine forests of the South yielded tall, straight logs that became the masts of ships in the Royal Navy. The sap, or resin, of pine trees was made into tar and pitch that were used to preserve rope and make the hulls of ships watertight. These products were called **naval stores.**

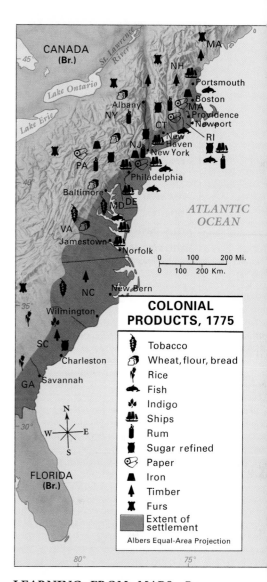

LEARNING FROM MAPS. *By 1775 the colonies produced an amazing number and variety of goods. What area was the manufacturing center? Why do you think manufacturing developed there?*

You read on page 91 of young Eliza Lucas' attempt to cultivate indigo. An historian took this view.

"Indigo proved more really beneficial to Carolina than the mines of Mexico or Peru were to Spain. . . . The source of this vast wealth . . . was the result of an experiment by a mere girl. . . ."
Edward McCrady

Northern Products

The northern colonies also produced naval stores, but the climate from Pennsylvania to Massachusetts Bay and New Hampshire was too cold to grow most of the southern cash crops. Put differently, the climate in these colonies was similar to the climate in England. And England already produced all it needed of the crops that grew best in the North—wheat, barley, and oats.

One American product, more northern than southern, highly valued in Europe was fur. Fur-bearing animals were scarce in Europe but abundant in the forest wildernesses of America. Americans hunted and trapped beaver, deer, and other animals and sent the skins to Europe, where they were made into coats and wraps or converted into felt for hats. The colonists also traded for furs with the Indians. The **fur trade** was essentially a frontier activity. As the colonies grew larger, fur traders and hunters had to go farther and farther west. And there the English often encountered angry French and unfriendly Indians, who claimed those lands and especially the fur trade for themselves.

Northerners did a great deal of fishing, especially in the waters off Newfoundland. The English worked that area too, so there was no market in England for the American catch. The Americans instead exported large quantities of dried and salted fish to southern Europe. But only a few northerners trapped fur-bearing animals or fished. Most had to find other means of paying for the European manufactured goods they craved. The problem turned out to be a great advantage, for it encouraged northerners to try different things. It stimulated their imagination, or what has come to be called **Yankee ingenuity**—a knack for solving problems in clever and creative ways. This is a quality highly valued in the American **free enterprise** economic system, which encourages people to develop and market their ideas for profit with little government.

Since most people were farmers, the northern colonists produced much more food than they could eat. Where could they sell this surplus? The answer they came up with was the sugar-producing islands of the West Indies. These islands were all small. Every acre of fertile soil was devoted to raising sugarcane. Moreover, producing sugar requires a great deal of labor. The islands were densely populated, mostly by African slaves. The sugar planters worked their slaves very hard. They realized that the slaves had to have plenty to eat if they were to work well.

American merchants and sailors soon discovered that they could make excellent profits shipping grain and fish to the sugar islands, and also horses for plowing and hauling and barrels to pack sugar in. They could invest the profits of this trade in sugar and carry the sugar to England. When the sugar was sold, they could buy English manufactured goods and sell these at another fat profit at home.

The Triangular Trade

The trade between the northern colonies, the sugar islands, and England was called the **triangular trade** because three separate voyages were involved. The trade did not operate as neatly as its name suggests. There were many variations, some quite complex. American merchants frequently bought molasses in the sugar islands instead of sugar. Molasses is what is left over after the crystallized sugar has been boiled out of the sugarcane. It was almost a waste product in the islands, and very cheap. The Americans took it back to the mainland, most frequently to Rhode Island, where it was distilled into rum, a powerful alcoholic drink. The rum was then shipped to West Africa, where it was traded for slaves. The slaves, in turn, were taken to the West Indies, or perhaps to the colonies in America. Then the cycle might be repeated: slaves for molasses, molasses into rum, rum for slaves. If the African slaves were sold in Virginia, the captain of the vessel might buy tobacco and take that to England. He might then purchase manufactured goods for sale back home.

The triangular trade was extremely profitable. The Americans bought things where they were plentiful and cheap and sold them where they were in great demand. Each leg of the voyage added to the gain. The more complicated the route, the more money that could

Sea captains relax in port on a leg of their triangular trade. This oil painting on bed ticking was done by John Greenwood in the late 18th century. Called "Sea Captains Carousing in Surinam," its title shows that the artist disapproved of such behavior. Why do you think the artist painted a scene that doesn't meet with his approval?

The St. Louis Art Museum

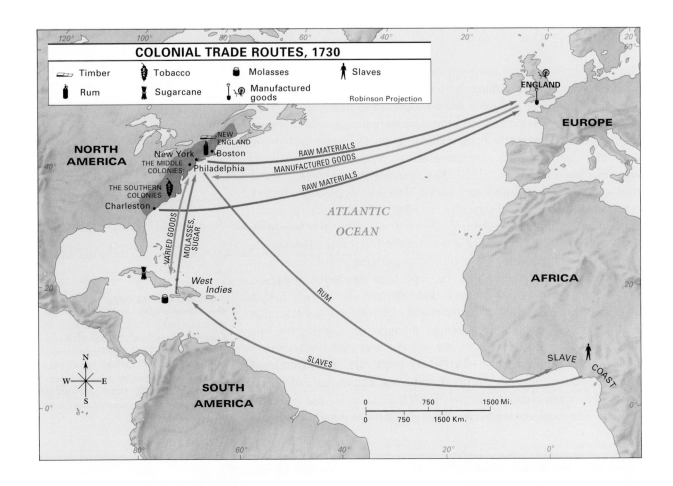

COLONIAL TRADE ROUTES, 1730

Timber Tobacco Molasses Slaves
Rum Sugarcane Manufactured goods

Robinson Projection

ENGLAND

EUROPE

NORTH AMERICA

NEW ENGLAND
New York Boston
THE MIDDLE COLONIES
Philadelphia

THE SOUTHERN COLONIES
Charleston

RAW MATERIALS
MANUFACTURED GOODS
RAW MATERIALS

ATLANTIC OCEAN

AFRICA

VARIED GOODS
MOLASSES, SUGAR

West Indies

RUM

SLAVE COAST

SLAVES

N
W E
S

SOUTH AMERICA

0   750   1500 Mi.
0   750   1500 Km.

LEARNING FROM MAPS. *This map of colonial trade routes helps us see how logical British economic policies were. Raw materials were sent to England to be transformed into finished products. Manufactured goods were sent to the colonies. Why did England discourage the growth of colonial industries?*

Return to the Preview & Review on page 85.

be made. Sometimes a ship was away from its home port for years. When it finally returned, the owners were rich indeed.

Thus what looked like a disadvantage—the fact that England did not need what northern colonists could produce—became an advantage, especially for the merchants and shipowners. A typical example was Thomas Amory, Irish born, who settled in Boston in 1720. Amory's ships traded with the West Indies, the Azores, England, and several European nations. He manufactured rum and naval stores and also built ships. He was so wealthy that when he married the daughter of a Boston tavern keeper, he could speak of his wife's fortune as *only* £1,500, although that was quite a large sum at the time. (£ is the symbol for the British monetary unit "pound.") Another Boston merchant, James Bowdoin, son of a French Protestant who came to America to escape religious persecution, acquired a fortune of over £182,000.

Trade was the key to prosperity in the northern colonies, just as cash crops were the key to prosperity farther south. For this reason merchants were the most admired people in the North, the leaders of society, and often the political leaders too. In the South the planter, owner of a large estate and many slaves, played a similar role.

3. AMERICANS SHARE NEW IDEAS

The Great Awakening

Most colonists were deeply religious and made great efforts to maintain their congregations. This was true even on the frontier, where the people were spread thinly over wide areas. In seasons of revival people traveled for miles to attend religious services. In Virginia and the Carolinas, and later in western Pennsylvania and New York, frontier Presbyterian and Baptist ministers—the Methodists had not arrived yet—sometimes rode from place to place on horseback, preaching and holding meetings wherever a group could be brought together. In this way the religious life of the scattered people was maintained.

Just how deeply many colonists felt about religion was revealed in a long series of events often called the **Great Awakening.** These events began among Dutch settlers around New Brunswick, in northern New Jersey, in the 1720s. The movement spread in the late 1730s to the Congregationalists under Jonathan Edwards in the Connecticut valley, and to Presbyterian revivalists, many of whom had come directly from northern Ireland to eastern Pennsylvania and southern New York. These Scotch-Irish, as they were called, carried the movement with them wherever they settled, mostly along the frontier from Maine to Georgia.

Then in 1739 a young English preacher named George Whitefield arrived in Philadelphia. He was on his way to Savannah, Georgia,

Preview & Review

Use these questions to guide your reading. Answer the questions after completing Section 3.
Understanding Issues, Events, & Ideas. Explain the significance of the following words: Great Awakening, Enlightenment, Albany Plan of Union, orrery.

1. What was the Great Awakening? In what way was the Great Awakening a force for religious toleration?
2. What was the Enlightenment? Why was its spirit welcome in the colonies?
3. For what reasons was Benjamin Franklin the greatest American of the Enlightenment?
4. How did self-taught Americans add to the spirit of the Enlightenment in the colonies?

Thinking Critically. Imagine that you are attending a town meeting in North Carolina. One of the topics discussed is Benjamin Franklin's Albany Plan. Would you be for or against uniting the colonies? Why?

National Portrait Gallery, London

Salvation is in the hands of George Whitefield in this early painting done at the time of the Great Awakening. Read the description of Reverend Whitefield on the next page to see how well the oil painting matches the historical account.

where the colony's English trustees had appointed him minister. He had intended to found an orphanage there. Instead he spent almost 30 years preaching throughout the colonies. He died in Massachusetts in 1770.

Whitefield was a small, fair-skinned man with deep-blue eyes. While preaching, he radiated energy and enthusiasm, bounding about and waving his arms to emphasize his points. His sermons urged "sinners" to have faith in the Lord and repent their sins. Sometimes he held services outdoors, but most of the time he was invited to preach in larger churches, especially in Boston, New York, Philadelphia, and Charleston. Everywhere he went, he stirred intense religious emotion in his listeners. During his meetings, thousands of colonists confessed their sins and resolved to lead blameless lives.

Next to Whitefield, the best-known preacher of the Awakening was Edwards. On July 8, 1741, he delivered his most memorable sermon, "Sinners in the Hands of an Angry God." Imagine how his listeners trembled as he said:

Jonathan Edwards, Whitefield's disciple, has a surprisingly gentle appearance for the prophet of an "Angry God."

❝ [T]here is nothing between you and Hell but the air; it is the only power of and mere pleasure of God that holds you up. . . .

Your wickedness makes you as it were heavy as lead, and to tend downwards with great weight and pressure towards Hell; and if God should let you go, you would sink immediately and swiftly descend and plunge into the bottomless gulf, and your healthy constitution [body], and your own care and prudence [sensibility], and best contrivance [plans], and all your righteousness [good behavior], would have no more influence to uphold you and keep you out of Hell than a spider's web would stop a falling rock. . . . There are the black clouds of God's wrath now hanging directly over your heads, full of the dreadful storm, and big with thunder; and were it not for the restraining hand of God it would immediately burst forth upon you. The sovereign [supreme] pleasure of God for the present stays [holds back] his rough wind; otherwise it would come with fury, and your destruction would come like a whirlwind, and you would be like the chaff [seed coverings] on the summer threshing [process used to separate the grain from the useless pieces collected at harvest] floor.

The wrath [anger] of God is like great waters that are dammed for the present; they increase more and more, and rise higher and higher, till an outlet is given; and the longer the stream is stopped, the more rapid and mighty is its course when once it is let loose. 'Tis true that judgment against your evil works has not been executed hitherto [recently]; the floods of God's vengeance have been withheld; but your guilt in the meantime is constantly increasing; and you are every day treasuring up more wrath; the waters are continually rising and waxing [growing] more and more mighty; and there is nothing but the mere pleasure of God that holds the waters back that are unwilling to be stopped, and hard press to go forward; if God should only withdraw his hand from the floodgate, it would immediately fly open, and the fiery floods of the fierceness and wrath of God would rush forth with inconceivable [unimaginable] fury, and would come upon you with omnipotent [unlimited] power; . . .

The bow of God's wrath is bent, and the arrow made ready on the string, and justice bends the arrow at your heart, and strains the bow, and it is nothing but the mere pleasure of God, and that of an angry God, without any promise or obligation at all, that keeps the arrow one moment from being drunk with your blood. . . .

The God that holds you over the pit of Hell, much as one holds a spider, or some loathsome insect, over a fire, abhors [rejects] you, and is dreadfully provoked [angered]; his wrath towards you burns like fire; he looks upon you as worthy of nothing else but to be cast into the fire; . . .

Therefore let everyone that is out of Christ now awake and fly from the wrath to come! . . .[1]”

Dozens of ministers followed in the steps of Whitefield, Edwards, and Gilbert Tennent, a Presbyterian preacher in the Middle Colonies. Waves of religious enthusiasm swept towns from Georgia to New Hampshire. Most of these preachers downplayed the differences that separated the various Protestant sects. All that mattered, they promised, was sincere repentance and reliance on God's grace for forgiveness.

The religious excitement aroused by the Great Awakening continued up to the eve of the American Revolution. The Baptists, who had come to North Carolina and Virginia in large numbers, organized revivals wherever they went. Methodist preachers newly arrived from England spread the Awakening to the frontier. Because Methodists at that time urged freedom for the slaves, they gained many black converts. In fact, revivals in the Carolinas and Virginia shaped popular religion among African Americans and whites profoundly, spreading to Kentucky, Ohio, and later to the deep South.

The Great Awakening was one of the first truly national events in colonial history. It was a force for religious toleration because of its come-one-come-all spirit. Many people were carried away by the excitement in the crowd when they heard a dynamic speaker like

[1]From *Jonathan Edwards: Representative Selections, with Introduction, Bibliography and Notes,* edited by Clarence Faust and Thomas H. Johnson

Whitefield preach. They announced that they were converted. They swore to lead saintly lives in the future. In rural areas some of the people who gathered to listen were attracted more by the festival atmosphere that surrounded the meetings than by the desire to save their souls. Although the Awakening slowly faded after 1750, it had permanently changed American religious attitudes.

The Great Awakening also had important political consequences. The Christian and Jewish traditions of most Americans had always encouraged democracy. Religious teachings stressed that people were created equal in the eyes of God. The power of the state was not absolute because Jews and Christians believed they owed an important part of their allegiance to the "kingdom of God." The Protestant Reformation had emphasized the importance of individual conscience. Some congregational Protestant denominations were even set up according to democratic models of government. Now, the Great Awakening encouraged these democratic ideals. People experienced freedom of choice in their religious lives. Soon they sought the same in their political lives.

The Search for Knowledge

By the 1750s many people in the colonies were caught up by the spirit of what is known as the **Enlightenment.** The name describes a belief that in an orderly universe human reason will prevail. This time is sometimes called the Age of Reason because "enlightened" people believed that they could improve themselves and the world around them by careful study and hard thought.

Two great scientific advances set the stage for the Enlightenment. One was the invention of the telescope by the Italian scientist Galileo in 1609. Using his telescope, Galileo was able to arrive at a much better understanding of the size of the universe and makeup of our own solar system than was earlier possible. The other advance was Sir Isaac Newton's discovery of the laws of gravity, which explained why the stars and planets behaved as they did.

The work of Galileo and Newton and other scientists changed the way educated people thought and the value they gave to thinking. The orderliness of the movements of the planets seemed to suggest that the universe was like a gigantic watch, complicated but operating according to fixed laws. If laws or rules governed the universe, surely no mystery of nature was beyond human solution. Surely humans, once they had solved the mysteries of nature, were destined to march steadily forward to greater and greater achievements.

These ideas found a welcome home in the colonies. It was easy to believe in progress in America because the colonies were so obviously making progress. The dense forest was being pushed back. The people were growing richer and more numerous. It was easier still to believe that thought and study would push forward the frontiers of knowledge. Explorers and scientists were constantly finding new rivers and mountains, new plants and animals. Americans produced clever new ideas and ingenious ways of doing things.

Benjamin Franklin

The greatest American of the Enlightenment was Benjamin Franklin. The story of his life begins in Boston, where he was born in 1706. His father was a soap and candle maker. Benjamin was the fifteenth of 17 children. He had only two years of schooling. At ten he became an apprentice in his father's shop, but after two years he shifted to the printer's trade, working for one of his nine older brothers.

When he was 17, Benjamin left Boston to seek his fortune in Philadelphia. Soon he owned his own printing shop, then also a newspaper, the *Pennsylvania Gazette*. He published books and wrote

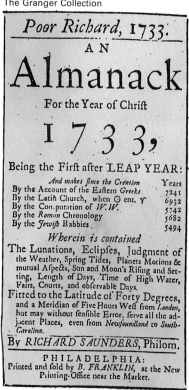

the annual *Poor Richard's Almanack,* each volume full of practical advice, weather predictions, odd bits of information, and what he called "scraps from the table of wisdom." One of the best-known examples of these "scraps" was the slogan "Early to bed, and early to rise, makes a man healthy, wealthy, and wise." Other typical examples are "God helps them that help themselves," "One today is worth two tomorrows," and "When the well is dry, they know the worth of water." He was so successful that by the time he was 42 he had enough money to live comfortably for the rest of his life.

Fogg Art Museum, Harvard University Portrait Collection

This is the earliest known portrait of Benjamin Franklin, painted around 1746 by Robert Feke. Based on this painting, would you say Franklin is a successful man? Why?

At this point Franklin retired from the printing business so that he could pursue his other interests. These were almost endless. He invented a cast-iron fireplace (the Franklin stove) which radiated most of its heat into the room instead of allowing it to escape up the chimney. He invented bifocal eyeglasses so that people who were both nearsighted and farsighted need have only one pair. His famous experiment with a kite in a thunderstorm proved his theory that lightning was a form of electricity. This alone made his reputation among the leading European scientists of the time.

In addition to his scientific discoveries, Franklin was an outstanding citizen and public servant. He helped found the first library in Philadelphia, and the first fire department, and the first hospital, and a school—the Academy for the Education of Youth, which became the University of Pennsylvania. He was the town postmaster and later, by appointment of the king, postmaster for all the colonies.

In 1754 Franklin drafted a scheme for uniting the colonies—the **Albany Plan of Union.** At this time he had no idea that the colonies might break away from England. Under his proposal England would still have had the final say about American affairs. But long before most other colonists understood the need, Franklin realized that the common interests of the different colonies were making it necessary for them to have some sort of common government. To make the point he drew a sketch of a snake divided into many pieces representing the different colonies. He attached to this drawing the title *Join, or Die*.

In 1754 Franklin was already world famous. But, as we shall later see, the most important and exciting part of his life still lay ahead of him.

Self-Taught Americans

Colonial America had only a few colleges, such as Harvard in Massachusetts, William and Mary in Virginia, Yale in Connecticut, and the College of New Jersey, now called Princeton. But many colonists, caught up by the spirit of the Enlightenment, taught themselves.

David Rittenhouse was a clockmaker who made valuable contributions to the construction of telescopes and other instruments. He also built an **orrery,** a mechanical model of the sun and planets which copied their movements exactly.

John Bartram was a farm boy who had little formal education but a passionate interest in all growing things. He traveled far and wide in America, collecting strange plants for his garden outside Philadelphia. He sent carefully packed samples of his discoveries to the leading European naturalists and received from them their own unusual finds. Distinguished visitors from Europe made detours to see his collection, and prominent Americans like George Washington and Benjamin Franklin came frequently to his garden.

Princeton University Observatory

David Rittenhouse, a clockmaker, made this beautiful orrery which copied the movements of the sun and planets exactly. Why would a clockmaker have been particularly comfortable with the European ideas of the Enlightenment?

Return to the Preview & Review on page 95.

4. EAST-WEST DISPUTES

Conflicts over Land and Government

America was indeed a land of opportunity. In England the cities and highways were crowded with ragged beggars and tramps. Few free people in America were that poor and hopeless. Some colonists were rich by any standard, but none was nearly as rich as the great English noble families or the merchant princes of London. Most Americans had what was called "middling" wealth. They lived comfortably, not lavishly. And they worked hard. Even the rich were rarely idle rich.

Yet colonial society was not really the "peaceable kingdom" that the Quaker artist Edward Hicks liked to portray. Sharp conflicts frequently occurred. Some even led to bloodshed.

By about 1750 settlement in most colonies had reached the eastern slopes and valleys of the Appalachian Mountains—that long range that runs from Georgia to New York and New England. In those days this was "the West" to the English colonists. It was only 100 miles (160 kilometers) or so from the seacoast where settlement had begun. But travel was slow and difficult. Most people rarely saw anyone from outside their own communities.

Most colonists did not like Franklin's Albany Plan of Union. They were afraid of losing some of their independence to what seemed to them a "foreign" institution. The average person was loyal to only one colony and to only one village or county in particular. If the colonists had any common loyalty beyond that, it was to England or to the British Empire of which they were a part.

Colonial governments sometimes engaged in bitter disputes with each other over territory. Boundaries were vague, mostly because the original land grants were made before the territories involved had been explored. The boundary between Maryland and Pennsylvania caused endless disputes and court battles. The dispute was finally settled in the 1760s when surveyors Charles Mason and Jeremiah Dixon set the boundary at a line that came to be called the **Mason-Dixon line.** David Rittenhouse designed some of the instruments used by Mason and Dixon to survey this boundary. Disagreements of this type occurred so frequently that during his career Rittenhouse served on boundary commissions for more than half the English colonies.

Different interest groups in a single colony often came into conflict with one another. In areas already settled people tended to think that defense against attack was a local matter. They argued that frontier settlers were responsible for their own troubles and should have to face the consequences without outside help.

The Quakers of Philadelphia, who opposed war as a matter of principle, often blamed the "hotheaded" Scotch-Irish settlers in the frontier sections of Pennsylvania for conflicts with the local Indians.

Preview & Review

Use these questions to guide your reading. Answer the questions after completing Section 4.
Understanding Issues, Events, & Ideas. Use the following words to discuss colonial east-west disputes: Mason-Dixon Line; one person, one vote; Bacon's Rebellion.
1. Why did colonial governments have so many disputes among themselves over territory?
2. Why did people in the frontier sections of most colonies resent the eastern sections?
3. What was the cause of Bacon's Rebellion?
4. Why did many Virginians consider Bacon a hero?
Thinking Critically. 1. Do you think our electoral system today is similar to that of our colonial past? Explain the similarities or differences and the reasons for them. **2.** Use your historical imagination to describe what nonviolent methods Nathaniel Bacon might have used to protest the Indians' attacks.

American Philosophical Society

David Rittenhouse designed many tools for surveyors. Why were his services so often in demand in the English colonies?

Edward Hicks painted "The Peaceable Kingdom" in the early 19th-century. He was a preacher and a painter who made over 100 views of wide-eyed animals living in harmony with settlers of America. William Penn's meeting with the Delaware Indians can be seen in the background. How did colonial society differ from the world that Hicks portrayed?

Whether the Quakers were correct or not, pioneers whose fields were burned or neighbors slain in surprise attacks were furious at the attitudes of these easterners, who were safe from such attacks.

People in the frontier sections favored policies that made it easy for them to get land cheaply. Eastern landowners usually objected to such policies. If land was cheap in the West, the value of their own property would go down. A seaport merchant in the fur trade might sell guns to the Indians because guns made them better hunters. Westerners opposed such sales because they were afraid the Indians might use the guns to shoot settlers rather than deer or bear.

There were many such honest differences between the West and the East. The problem was that easterners made the policies because they controlled the colonial governments. The Quakers were secure because they had a large majority in the Pennsylvania colonial legislature. They and similar groups in most colonies had more representatives than their numbers should have entitled them to.

STRATEGIES FOR SUCCESS

CREATING A GRAPHIC REPRESENTATION

Students are required to read and remember a great deal of information. One of the best ways to help you remember all you read is to develop a graphic representation. A graphic representation is a kind of diagram that links related words, terms, or concepts together, a visual illustration of a verbal statement.

There are many types of graphic representations. You are familiar with several: flow charts, pie charts, and even family trees. Other types include spider maps, continuum scales, and compare/contrast matrices. One of the most useful in American history is a word web.

How to Develop a Word Web

To develop a word web, follow these steps.
1. **Identify the main ideas.** Read the information and list the heading or title of each major idea or topic. If no heading or title is given, create your own.
2. **Note supporting details.** Review the material to identify details that support each main idea.
3. **Structure the headings.** Form a word web by placing each main idea in a circle. Then place supporting details or related ideas in separate circles and connect them to the main idea. Continue to connect ideas and details to complete a web similar to the one below.
4. **Use the information.** Note the relationships among the data. Draw conclusions, make inferences, and form hypotheses.

Applying the Skill

Review Section 2 of this chapter on the origins of American slavery. Note that the section covers five main ideas: the origins of slavery, slave life, southern agriculture, northern products, and triangular trade. To make a word web, place those five ideas in circles.

What are the subtopics? Reread the section.

Note that under the origins of slavery, three topics are discussed: European prejudices, slaves as an improved labor source, and the arrival of the first slaves in 1619. Choose a term to indicate each of these topics, such as "prejudices," "labor source," and "first slaves." Place these terms in circles and connect them to your central term: origins of slavery. A word web for the first subsection would resemble the one below. You may wish to expand your web by finding additional terms to include on your web. (For example, "heathens" has been linked to prejudices in the web below.) Review the rest of Section 2 and create word webs for the other topics.

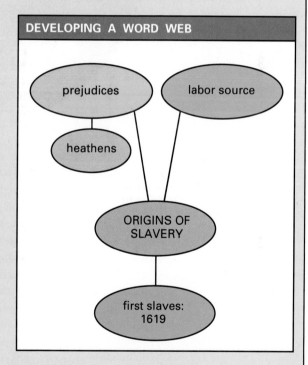

DEVELOPING A WORD WEB

For independent practice, see Practicing the Strategy on page 107.

Museum of Fine Arts, Boston

Look carefully at this "Quaker Meeting," which took place in London. How does it differ from the religious paintings you saw in Chapter 2?

The American system was and still is to elect legislators by geographical districts. Today, under the principle **one person, one vote,** all election districts must have approximately the same number of residents. A city district may be very small in area, one in farm country quite large. But their populations must be about equal.

When the first assemblies were formed in any colony, the election districts were fairly even in population. As the colony grew, people moved westward beyond the boundaries of the original districts. Soon these western settlers were demanding the right to elect representatives. They asked the assemblies to create new election districts.

Because of the East-West disagreements, colonial assemblies were often reluctant to create new election districts, except in New England, where all the townships were the same size. Therefore, a western legislator would have to represent several times as many voters as an eastern legislator did. In this way the East continued to control the colonial government long after the western population greatly exceeded the eastern.

Because they were under-represented, westerners deeply resented laws regulating land, road construction, and other matters that conflicted with their interests. Sometimes they even resorted to force to correct the injustice.

104   LIFE IN COLONIAL AMERICA

Bacon's Rebellion

A good example of an East-West conflict occurred in Virginia in May of 1676. The trouble began along the Maryland-Virginia border when Indians killed a shepherd. Settlers responded by killing 24 Indians, including several of the Susquehanna tribe. Since the Susquehannas had not been involved in the murder, they were furious. Sweeping south out of Maryland, they killed at least 36 frontier settlers.

One of the men killed in this raid worked for a tobacco planter named Nathaniel Bacon. Not much is known about Bacon except that he was a thin, dark, rather sad-faced man who had come to Virginia from England only two years earlier. He had considerable money and was related to the wife of the governor of Virginia, Sir William Berkeley. Bacon promptly took charge of a large force of volunteers and marched them off to punish the Indians.

Governor Berkeley tried to stop the violence. When Bacon refused to heed his order to lay down his weapons, the governor proclaimed him a rebel. Bacon's force, in the meantime, had wiped out the Occaneechi, an Indian community that had nothing to do with the troubles. Indians, Bacon insisted, were "all alike." Then Bacon turned on the government. He drove the governor out of Jamestown and burned the town. He resumed his assaults on the Indians. In October 1676 Bacon died. The rebellion collapsed.

Nathaniel Bacon was not a pure villain, despite his slaughter of innocent people and his refusal to obey the governor's orders. Most of the western planters considered him a hero. Many people felt that the legislature—the House of Burgesses—was not responsive to their needs. There had not been an election in Virginia in 15 years.

Governor Berkeley had a long and distinguished career, but he had grown bad tempered in his old age. His wish to protect the Indians may not have been based entirely on his sense of justice. He seems to have had a considerable investment in the fur trade. If so, this would help explain why he did not want to see the Indians, on whom this profitable trade depended, killed or driven off.

After **Bacon's Rebellion** there were new elections in Virginia. The local Indians, most of whom had abandoned their lands when faced by Bacon's bloodthirsty army, were allowed to return after they agreed that they held the land under the authority of "the Great King of England." Some of their descendants still live on these lands. The conflict might have been avoided and many lives saved if the House of Burgesses had represented the interests of all the people.

Fortunately, incidents like Bacon's Rebellion were rare in the colonial period. Displacing the Indians, slavery, unfair representation, and other sources of conflict seemed to be balanced by the opportunities that a new country made possible. America was not paradise. Life was hard and often dangerous. Yet the future seemed promising. 🖎

Return to the Preview & Review on page 101.

CHAPTER 3 REVIEW

1619
First Africans
brought to America

1676
Bacon's
Rebellion
erupts

Chapter Summary
Read the statements below. Choose one, and write a paragraph explaining its importance.
1. The American land held many blessings for the first settlers.
2. Early colonists relied on rivers as transportation routes, and early cities grew on river banks.
3. Although colonial women could not vote and worked very hard, American life offered more opportunities than it did in Europe.
4. Most early settlers obtained land and worked hard to improve it, qualifying them to vote.
5. Africans were first brought to America to work as slaves.
6. Slavery was inhuman; educated slaves were more likely to run away or revolt.
7. Cash crops such as tobacco were the major southern products and required much labor.
8. Triangular trade became very profitable.
9. Intellectual movements such as the Great Awakening and the Enlightenment involved Benjamin Franklin and many Americans.
10. As settlers moved west, many controversies arose.

Reviewing Chronological Order
Number your paper 1-5. Then study the time line above and place the following events in the order in which they happened by writing the first next to 1, the second next to 2, and so on.
1. The Great Awakening
2. Bacon's Rebellion
3. Albany Plan of Union
4. First Africans brought to America
5. The Enlightment in America

Understanding Main Ideas
1. Why did the colonists have to be self-reliant? Give at least two examples of ways the colonists were self-reliant.
2. What hardships did women in colonial America face?
3. What geographical feature did all the large towns have in common?
4. Why did working people in the colonies earn more and get better treatment than workers in England? Why did indentured servants agree to come to America to work? How were African slaves usually treated by their owners in the American colonies?
5. How was American slavery different from slavery elsewhere?
6. Why was the Enlightenment welcomed in America?

Thinking Critically
1. **Synthesizing.** Imagine that you are the 26-year-old widow Martha Dandridge Custis. What advantages might you have over a European woman of your time? What major advantages does a twentieth-century American woman have over a colonial woman?
2. **Drawing Conclusions.** How did the availability of land and the scarcity of labor help make life in colonial America more democratic than it was in England?
3. **Evaluating.** Do you think "Yankee ingenuity" was a positive or a negative quality? Why? How did northern colonists use it to find a means of paying for the European goods they wanted? Do you think Americans still have "Yankee ingenuity"? Explain your answer.

Writing About History: Informative
An important point in this chapter is that the great amount of land in America affected the lives of the colonists. Suppose you are an American colonist. Write a letter to a friend in Europe explaining how the abundance of land affected one of the following: women, indentured servants, slaves, American Indians.

	Enlightenment

Triangular Trade

1700	1750

1706
Benjamin Franklin
is born

1740
The Great
Awakening

1750
Enlightenment in America

★
Settlement reaches the Appalachians

1754
Franklin's Albany Plan of Union

Practicing the Strategy

Review the strategies on pages 78 and 103.
Reading Graphs. Study the pie graph on page 89 and answer these questions.

1. What percentage of the colonial population was African? Where does that percentage rank?
2. The English, Scotch-Irish, and Scottish were all British. What percentage of the total population did the British make up?
3. What three groups represent the smallest percentages of the colonial population?

Creating a Graphic Representation. Reread the information on the Great Awakening on pages 95 to 98. Then create a word web of at least five terms centered on The Great Awakening.

Using Primary Sources

Being a freed slave in the South often meant being on your guard. Southerners began to fear the large number of freed slaves living in their midst. North Carolina and other states passed laws providing a reward for the capture and resale of "illegally" freed slaves. In 1797 Thomas Pritchet and three other freed slaves petitioned the House of Representatives for federal protection. After some debate the House voted to not accept the petition, leaving the fate of freed slaves to the individual states. Read the excerpt from the *Annals of the Congress of the United States,* 4th Cong., 2nd Sess. (1796–97) to get a sense of the struggle slaves faced. Then answer the questions.

I, Thomas Pritchet, was set free by my master Thomas Pritchet, who furnished me with land . . . where I built myself a house, cleared a sufficient spot of woodland to produce ten bushels of corn; . . . this I was obliged to leave . . . being threatened by Holland Lockwood, who married my said master's widow, that if I would not come and serve him, he would apprehend me, and send me to the West Indies; Enoch Ralph also threatening to send me to jail, and to sell me. . . . Being thus in jeopardy, I . . . escaped by night into Virginia. . . .

where shipping myself to Boston, I was landed in New York, where I served as a waiter for seventeen months; but my mind being distressed on account of the situation of my wife and children, I returned to Norfolk in Virginia, with the hope of seeing them; but finding I was advertised in the newspaper, twenty dollars the reward for apprehending me, my dangerous situation obliged me to leave Virginia.

1. Give two examples from the excerpt to show that Pritchet's freedom was often threatened.
2. How might you defend Pritchet's argument that he was a free person? How might you defend Holland Lockwood's belief that Pritchet was not a free person?
3. Why did Pritchet return to Virginia? Why did he leave again?

Linking History & Geography

Almost all of the early cities in America developed on a body of water. Research the location of the first colonial cities and draw a map showing their locations. Then in a brief essay explain why the first cities developed on bodies of water, using one city as a specific example.

Enriching Your Study of History

1. **Individual Project.** Some colonial business leaders advertised in England to persuade more European settlers to come to America. Draw an eye-catching poster with an attention-getting slogan for a group of these business leaders.
2. **Cooperative Project.** On page 99 there are examples of slogans or wise sayings from *Poor Richard's Almanack.* With your classmates write three of your own slogans. Consider such subjects as good health, friendship, and good study habits. Put your slogans on a poster and compare them with those of the rest of the class. What do you conclude makes a good slogan? Try to reach a class consensus in your discussion.

Chapter 3 Review 107

Governing the American Colonies

As their colonies in America developed, the English worked out a system to govern and control them. The system applied to all the English colonies, not just those that eventually became the United States. Jamaica and Barbados in the West Indies, Bermuda, English possessions everywhere in the world, including its colonies in North America—all were part of one whole, the British Empire. The people of Massachusetts Bay may have felt a little closer to the people of Virginia than to the sugar planters of Jamaica, but the difference must have been small. All were British, and all were colonists. All recognized the same king, all flew the same flag. But how long could the English hold their far-flung colonies?

1. THE ENGLISH COLONIAL SYSTEM

Royal Grants and Charters

In theory the colonies belonged to the king himself, not to the English government. At one time the king owned all the land. He could dispose of it in whatever way he wished. Over the years, as we have seen, the kings established colonies in America in various ways. James I granted Virginia to the London Company in a kind of business deal. James gave the company the right to look for gold and silver, and in return the company was supposed to pay James one fifth of the gold and silver it found.

Charles II gave captured New Netherland to his brother, the Duke of York, as a present. He used Pennsylvania to pay off his debt to William Penn's father.

Each royal grant or charter was different from the others. But in every case the king remained the ruler, and his government supervised colonial affairs. The colonies remained English. They were not independent nations. England was an ocean away, but decisions made by the king and British lawmakers affected every colonist in one way or another.

Preview & Review

Use these questions to guide your reading. Answer the questions after completing Section 1.
Understanding Issues, Events, & Ideas. Describe the English colonial system, using the following words: Privy Council, Parliament, governor, assembly, legislature, town meeting, county court, justice of the peace.
1. Why could the king dispose of the American colonies as he wished?
2. Which groups made policies and passed laws that governed England's colonies in America?
3. Which groups assisted the governors of the English colonies?
4. Who handled local government in New England? Who handled local government in the southern colonies?
Thinking Critically. In your opinion, which benefitted more from the colonial system, the colonies or Britain? Explain your reasoning.

Franklin Institute, Boston (Photo: Gabor Demjen)

Of course, the kings did not personally manage the everyday affairs of the colonies. Ever since King John signed the Magna Carta, or Great Charter, in 1215 at Runnymede, the English rulers had shared power with lawmaking bodies. And it is important to keep in mind that colonial concerns were much less important to the kings and to the English government than dozens of local matters. Colonial policy was set by the king's principal advisers, who made up what was called the **Privy Council.** *Privy* originally meant "private." A subcommittee of the council, the Lords of Trade, made the major decisions and handled particular colonial problems as they arose. All were subject to the lawmaking body of England, **Parliament.** Parliament consisted of the king or queen, the House of Lords, and the House of Commons, which controlled government finances. Parliament passed the laws that applied specifically to the colonies.

Benjamin Franklin stands at the bar of the English House of Commons in 1766. Members of Parliament have assembled for Franklin's report from the American colonies. His red-robed questioner is Prime Minister George Grenville. The members of Parliament include William Pitt and Edmund Burke, who both spoke for better treatment of the colonies. Compare this picture with those you can find of the present-day House of Commons in session.

Government in the English Colonies

There were also governments in each English colony. These carried out the policies and enforced the laws of England and attended to all sorts of local matters that were of no direct concern to England. The colonial governments were modeled after the government of England. At the head of each colony was a **governor.** The governor was the chief executive. He represented the king. He was supposed to oversee the colonial government and make sure that the laws were executed, or enforced. Some governors were American born but most were English. Governors received orders and policies from London and put them into effect. When local problems arose, they decided what was to be done. For example, when Nathaniel Bacon raised a force to attack the Indians in Virginia, Governor Berkeley, on his own authority, ordered Bacon to put down his arms.

Point of View

Free men in America were encouraged to carry arms. The governor of Virginia complained bitterly.

> **How miserable that man is that Governes a People wher six parts of seaven at least are Poore Endebted Discontented and Armed.**
> Sir William Berkeley, c. 1676

Governors were assisted by councils, which had roughly the same powers and duties that the king's Privy Council had in England. In most of the colonies members of the council were appointed, not elected by the voters. Councilors tended to be picked from among the wealthiest and most socially prominent people in each colony. This was true also of colonial judges.

Local laws were made by elected bodies. These **assemblies,** or **legislatures,** were modeled on the House of Commons in England. On paper their powers were strictly limited. Both the colonial governor and the government in England could disallow, or cancel, any law passed by an assembly. In practice the assemblies, like the House of Commons, had a great deal of power because they controlled the raising of money by taxes and the spending of that money too. Governors could call the assemblies into session and dismiss them at their pleasure. They could order new elections, thus ending the terms of the legislators. A governor could not, however, make the legislators pass any law the legislature did not want to pass.

Because the assemblies had control over money, they could control the governor. They would refuse to spend money on projects the governor wanted unless he agreed to approve laws they wanted to enact. In extreme cases they could attach a sentence providing money for the governor's salary to a bill he had threatened to disallow. Then, if the governor disallowed the law, he got no pay!

Local Government

Each town or community also had a government of its own. In New England townships the inhabitants ran their affairs through what were called **town meetings.** Almost all citizens were entitled to take part in these gatherings. At the meetings they set the rate of town taxes, approved applications of new settlers, set aside land for the newcomers, hired teachers and ministers, and settled local issues.

In the Southern Colonies local government was in the hands of **county courts.** These courts decided when and where to build roads, license taverns, raise taxes, try criminals, and settle lawsuits. In general they oversaw all local matters. The chief officials of the county courts were **justices of the peace.** They were appointed by the governor.

The colonial system of government was quite well suited to the needs and wishes of all involved. The king and his advisers in London made the major decisions and appointed the people who put these decisions into effect. The colonists, however, were able to influence the decision makers in many ways. Purely local questions were left in the hands of the community. It was a complicated system, and often those who ran it were not efficient. But for about 150 years it worked reasonably well. The raw materials of America flowed to England in exchange for manufactured goods. The colonies grew and prospered.

Return to the Preview & Review on page 108.

2. ENGLISH COLONIAL POLICIES

The Dominion of New England

Most colonists liked the fact that the British Empire was divided into so many separate parts. It allowed each colony a great deal of control over its own affairs. British leaders felt differently. If they could combine the colonies into a few regional groups, it would be easier to manage them.

The most serious attempt to unify a group of colonies occurred after the death of Charles II in 1685. Since Charles had no children, his brother James, the Duke of York, became king. James was already proprietor of the colony of New York. In 1686 he created the **Dominion of New England.** When organized, the Dominion included New York, New Jersey, Connecticut, Rhode Island, Massachusetts, and New Hampshire. Sir Edmund Andros, a soldier who had formerly been governor of New York, was appointed governor of the Dominion.

Each of the colonies in the Dominion resented the loss of its independence. Moreover, the new governor was given enormous power. He could make laws on his own, including tax laws. Indeed, he ruled like a dictator, deciding by himself all questions of importance. The colonial assemblies ceased to meet.

Fortunately for the citizens of the Dominion, Andros' rule did not last very long. James II proved to be extremely unpopular in England. He ignored laws that Parliament had passed and adopted a strongly pro-Catholic policy that alarmed the many powerful Protestant groups in the nation. When his second wife, Queen Mary of Modena, gave birth to a son who would be raised a Catholic, the leaders of Parliament staged what was soon known as the **Glorious Revolution.** They invited James' daughter Mary, who was a Protestant, and her Dutch husband, William of Orange, to become joint

Use these questions to guide your reading. Answer the questions after completing Section 2.
Understanding Issues, Events, & Ideas. Use the following words to explain the economic benefits to Britain of the colonies: Dominion of New England, Glorious Revolution, mercantilism, favorable balance of trade, Navigation Acts, enumerated articles.
1. Why did the English government want to combine the colonies into a few regional groups? How did the colonists react?
2. What effect did the Glorious Revolution have on the Dominion of New England?
3. What was the overall purpose of the Navigation Acts?
Thinking Critically. How would our economy be different today if the British still controlled the American colonies?

When the news came to America that William and Mary were England's monarchs, the Glorious Revolution that brought them to power was already several months old. These portraits of William and Mary were painted in the late 17th century. What was the religious question that brought William and Mary to the throne?

GROWTH OF COLONIAL TRADE WITH ENGLAND

Value (in pounds sterling)

☐ Exports
◼ Imports

	1700	1763
Exports	395,000	345,000
Imports	1,100,000	1,630,000

LEARNING FROM GRAPHS. *Many British laws had a major effect on the colonial economy. How does the chart illustrate the growth of a favorable balance of trade for Britain and an unfavorable one for the colonies?*

rulers of England. James was so unpopular that he could not raise an army to put down the revolution. It was won without a shot being fired. William and Mary crossed the English Channel from the Netherlands in November 1688 to take the throne.

When news of the Glorious Revolution reached Boston the next April—the delay provides a good example of the slowness of communication between England and America—an angry crowd gathered. Andros and other Dominion officials were arrested. A council of leading citizens took over the government. The other colonies in the Dominion also revolted. The Dominion quickly fell apart.

Thereafter the English authorities gave up trying to unify the colonies. The new king, William III, had little interest in America. He relied on the Lords of Trade to manage the colonies, but that committee was made up of weak and inefficient men. Local self-government once again flourished in America.

Mercantilism

The English did not give up the idea of regulating their American colonies. Colonies were supposed to be profitable. The English expected to add to their national wealth by developing and using American raw materials. They passed laws designed to control what the colonists produced and where they sold it. The object was to have the colonists concentrate on goods that England needed and to make sure that these goods were sold in England rather than in another country. This economic program is called **mercantilism.**

Another way of explaining English policy is to point out that all the European nations were trying to obtain as much gold and silver as possible. Gold and silver seemed at the time to be the true source of national power and wealth. Since neither England nor its colonies had gold or silver mines, England had to trade for these metals. Foreigners would pay gold and silver for English and colonial goods. The more the colonies could produce, the more there was to sell. Moreover, it was important to have what is called a **favorable balance of trade.** That is, England must sell more than it bought. A favorable balance was important because every English purchase of foreign goods reduced the amount of gold and silver that could be held in the country. Trading goods for gold and silver was the key to prosperity. Trade, said Daniel Defoe, the author of *Robinson Crusoe*, was "the Wealth of the World." Colonies were helpful in making trade grow. That is why the Lords of Trade had been put in charge of them.

The Navigation Acts

To make sure that the colonies raised the right products and sold them in the right places, Parliament passed many laws regulating

colonial commerce, or the buying and selling of goods. These laws—
the Acts of Trade and Navigation—were known as **Navigation Acts.**
The first Navigation Act was passed in 1651. The last important one
was enacted in 1733. We need not consider each law separately
because they were all part of one system, known as the Old Colonial
System.

The Navigation Acts provided that all goods passing between
England and the colonies must be carried in ships that had been built
either in Britain or in the colonies. The owners of these vessels must
be British or American. The captain and most of the crew must be
British or American too. For example, a Boston merchant could own
a ship made in London or Philadelphia and carry goods from Virginia
to New York or to any port in Britain. But the merchant could not
use a French-made ship for these voyages or hire a Dutch or Portuguese captain.

*Many British ships sailed from Bris-
tol, shown in this painting, on their
voyages to explore and colonize America. At this broad quay ships took on
provisions or unloaded cargo from the
colonies. After reading page 114, list
some of the enumerated articles these
ships might have brought from American colonies.*

English Colonial Policies 113

European goods could be brought into the American colonies *only* after being taken to England. American colonists could import French wine, for instance, but only after it had been brought to England. Once in England, of course, the wine could only be carried to the colonies in a British or colonial ship because of the first rule.

Colonial producers could sell certain products only within the British Empire. The names of these products were listed, or enumerated, in various ways. These items were known as **enumerated articles.** Only goods that England needed but could not produce at home were enumerated. Sugar, tobacco, furs, naval stores, cotton, and the dye indigo were the most important enumerated articles. Many very important colonial products, such as fish and wheat, were not enumerated because England already had adequate supplies. Colonists could sell these products anywhere they could find a buyer.

In addition, the British could buy enumerated products only from their own colonies. British sugar planters in the West Indies and tobacco planters in Virginia and Maryland could not sell their crops in France or Spain or Holland. In return British consumers could not buy sugar or tobacco raised in colonies controlled by the French, Spanish, or Dutch.

Parliament put restrictions on a few colonial manufactured products that competed with British goods. Although the manufacture of woolen cloth and fur hats for local sale was legal, their exportation was prohibited. Late in the colonial period the construction of any new forges, or shops to make iron products, was outlawed. The British believed that these laws were perfectly fair to the colonists. They were trying to make their empire self-sufficient. If the colonies concentrated on producing raw materials that England needed, and if England concentrated on manufacturing, each would benefit. No precious gold or silver would have to be spent for foreign goods. The favorable balance of trade could be maintained.

LEARNING FROM GRAPHS. *Compare the chart of the destinations of colonial exports with the map of colonial trade routes on page 94. What exports did the colonists send to the West Indies? What did they send to Great Britain and Ireland?*

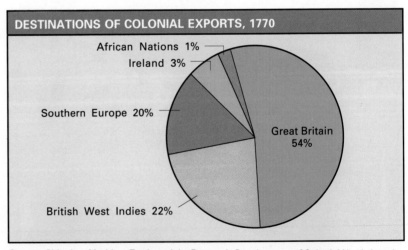

DESTINATIONS OF COLONIAL EXPORTS, 1770

African Nations 1%
Ireland 3%
Southern Europe 20%
Great Britain 54%
British West Indies 22%

Source: *Shipping, Maritime Trade and the Economic Development of Colonial North America*

The need to channel the flow of colonial raw materials into England—and to keep foreign goods and vessels out of colonial ports—became obvious in the 1650s when the Dutch built a magnificent merchant fleet of 10,000 ships. They dominated trade wherever they sailed: coastal France, the North Atlantic, South America, India, and the East and West Indies.

The Navigation Act system worked quite well for more than a hundred years. The complicated triangular trade described in Chapter 3 did not conflict with it. The laws followed the natural trends of trade. The colonies were not well enough developed at this time to produce large amounts of manufactured goods. England, on the other hand, was by far the most efficient producer of manufactured goods in the world.

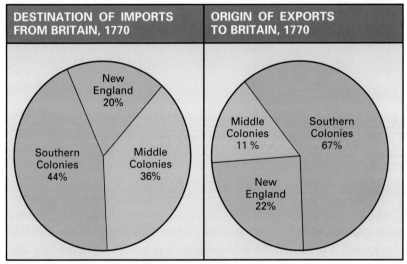

DESTINATION OF IMPORTS FROM BRITAIN, 1770	ORIGIN OF EXPORTS TO BRITAIN, 1770

New England 20%
Southern Colonies 44%
Middle Colonies 36%

Middle Colonies 11%
Southern Colonies 67%
New England 22%

Source: *Shipping, Maritime Trade and the Economic Development of Colonial North America*

LEARNING FROM GRAPHS. *By comparing the two graphs at the left you can draw conclusions about the economies of the three colonial regions. Which region was the most self sufficient? Why did the Middle Colonies account for such a small proportion of the exports to Britain?*

Moreover, the Navigation Acts were not enforced very strictly. Smuggling was common. America was far from England. It had a long coastline with many isolated harbors and tiny coves where small ships could slip in under cover of night and easily unload their cargoes of contraband goods.

For many years the English government did not try very hard to prevent smuggling. Most Americans obeyed the laws. England was getting all the colonial products it needed. It hardly seemed worth the effort and expense to stop shippers who tried to sneak past the British navy with a cargo of tobacco bound for Amsterdam, or with French wine or silk that had not been taken first to England.

Although American smugglers considered the Royal Navy their natural enemy, most colonists believed that the British army and navy were vital to their safety and well-being. Like children, the colonists were under the control of a mother country, and they needed its protection. 🖳

Return to the Preview & Review on page 111.

Photo: Dan McCoy/Rainbow

In this watercolor France's Indian allies are shown attacking Deerfield, Massachusetts. Already much of the town is in flames in this scene. What do you suppose was the function of the red building in the center of town?

Preview & Review

Use these questions to guide your reading. Answer the questions after completing Section 3.

Understanding Issues, Events, & Ideas. Use the following words to cite the significance of French challenges to England in America: King William's War, Schenectady, Queen Anne's War, Deerfield, King George's War, French and Indian War, Fort Pitt, Seven Years' War, Pontiac's Rebellion, Proclamation Line of 1763.

1. How were French colonies different from English colonies?
2. Why did France win most of the early battles in America?
3. What were the results of the French and Indian War?
4. What was the purpose of the Proclamation of 1763? How did most colonists react to it?

Thinking Critically. 1. Why did the building of forts by the French obstruct westward expansion of the British colonial frontier? **2.** Using your historical imagination, write Robert Dinwiddie's message, to Marquis Duquesne. Explain Dinwiddie's objection to building forts west of Virginia.

3. FRANCE CHALLENGES ENGLAND

The French and English Wars

From the time of the Glorious Revolution until the 1760s, England was almost constantly at war in Europe, always against France. Americans were involved in these wars because the French had also become a colonial power in North America.

The French, who had begun their explorations of America in 1524, did not build many permanent settlements in America. While the English were clearing land and planting crops along the Atlantic Coast, the French were ranging deep into the continent, hunting, trapping, and setting up trading posts where they bought furs from the American Indians.

Whenever war broke out in Europe between England and France, French and English colonists fought in America. It was difficult for them to get at each other because their posts and settlements in America lay far apart in the wilderness. Most of the battles consisted of sneak attacks and raids on frontier outposts. Relatively few colonists actually took up arms. Much of the fighting was done by Indians allied with one side or the other.

The first colonial conflict was known as **King William's War.** It went on with interruptions from 1689 to 1697. The French, with Indian support, attacked **Schenectady** in New York and a few villages in New England. American colonists responded by marching against

Port Royal in Nova Scotia, which they captured and then lost. An attempted invasion of Canada failed miserably. When the war ended, the treaty of peace returned all captured territories to their colonial owners.

Both sides followed a similar strategy in **Queen Anne's War,** which began in 1702 and ended in 1713. France's Indian allies attacked several New England settlements and destroyed **Deerfield,** Massachusetts. The English colonists responded by making raids on Nova Scotian villages. Once again they captured Port Royal. Far to the south a force of Carolinians struck a blow at France's ally, Spain, by burning St. Augustine, Florida. The outcome of this war was decided in Europe, where England won a series of decisive victories. The Treaty of Utrecht in 1713 gave England control of Nova Scotia, Newfoundland, and Hudson Bay.

The third English-French clash in America, **King George's War,** lasted from 1744 to 1748. Once again Indians friendly to France crossed the St. Lawrence and attacked settlements in New England. New Englanders sailed north and captured Louisbourg, a fort on Cape Breton Island that guarded the mouth of the St. Lawrence River. England fared badly in the European phases of this war. To the New Englanders' disgust Fort Louisbourg was given back to France at the peace conference ending the war.

The French and English wars involved few of the colonists. Still, they increased tensions between settlers from both nations, who blamed each other for their troubles on the frontier. We can easily see the attitudes of both sides from the following excerpts. The first is from a letter written in 1718 by Alexander Spotswood, deputy governor of Virginia to the British Board of Trade.

     " The French have built so many forts that the British settlements almost seem surrounded by French trade with the numerous Indian tribes on both sides of the lakes. The French may, in time, take over the whole fur trade. But even if they do not they can, whenever they please, send bands of Indians to the outskirts of our settlements and greatly threaten His Majesty's subjects there. If the French should increase their settlements along these lakes, in order to join their lands in Canada to their new colony in Louisiana, they might take over any English settlements they please.

     Nature, it is true, has formed a defense for us with that long chain of mountains which runs from the west of South Carolina as far north as New York and which is passable only in a few places. But even this natural defense may become a danger to us, if we do not take over before the French do. Now, while both nations are at peace, is the time to prevent all such dangers caused by the growing power of the French which threaten His Majesty's holdings. While the French are still unable to seize all that vast area west of our lands, we should attempt to make some settlements along the Great Lakes. At the same time we should also take over the passes of the mountains in order to safeguard communications with such settlements. . . . We could also cut off or disturb the communication between Canada and Louisiana if a war should break out. Once such a settlement was made, I can't see how the French could dispute our right of possession. The law of nations recognizes the right of the first nation that settles an area. And if the French should try to make us leave the area by force, we are closer to our settlements and aid than they are to theirs.[1] "

The English acted on Spotswood's advice, building forts along the Great Lakes. But the French reacted strongly as we see in this excerpt from a letter written in 1750 by a French settler in Canada.

" The St. Lawrence River and the lakes which supply the waters of that great river stretch across the interior of Canada. Its navigation and trade can be halted more easily than people may think. One of the best ways to avoid this misfortune is further to strengthen not only Quebec and Montreal, but also Fort Frederic. It is essential to establish at that fort a large, well-fortified French village in time of peace and to attract an Indian village in time of war. This effort will cost little if we settle some farmers on Lake Champlain at the same time and form some villages there.

Fort Frontenac is at the outlet of Lake Ontario, on which the English have established a post or fort called Oswego. This is clearly illegal, and is a serious threat to Canada. This Oswego post is located on a lake that has long been claimed by France. And it has been built by the English during a period of peace. The Governor of Canada has protested but taken no further action. Although it ought to have been pulled down in the beginning by using force, the post is still there.

This post, which has been regarded as of little importance, can, in fact, destroy Canada, and it already caused the greatest harm. . . . It is there that the English hand out rum to the Indians, even though the King of France has forbidden this trade. It is there that the English try to win over all Indian nations. They not only try to corrupt them with gifts but also urge them to kill the French traders throughout the vast forests of New France.

[1]From *The Official Letters of Alexander Spotswood*, edited by R.A. Brock

As long as the English occupy Fort Oswego, we must distrust even those Indians who are most loyal to the French. . . . Shipping on the lakes will always be exposed to danger. Agriculture will make very slow progress, and will be limited to the heart of the colony. In short, we will face all the difficulties of war and none of its advantages. Everything possible, then, must be done to destroy this dangerous post.

We must also have free and dependable communication from Canada to the Mississippi. This chain, once broken, would leave an opening where the British would doubtless move in. . . .[1]"

The French Menace

Though considerable blood had been spilled between 1689 and 1748, neither England nor France had gained much from the other in America. In 1752 the French governor of Canada, the Marquis Duquesne de Menneville, ordered the construction of a new chain of forts running from Lake Erie south to the Ohio River, in what is now western Pennsylvania. These forts, Duquesne believed, would keep English fur traders and settlers from crossing the Appalachian Mountains into territory claimed by France.

Duquesne's action alarmed many people in the English colonies, none more so than Lieutenant Governor Robert Dinwiddie of Virginia. Dinwiddie was very interested in buying land beyond the frontier, which could later be sold to settlers at a big profit.

When Dinwiddie learned what the French were doing, he sent a young planter and land surveyor named George Washington to warn them that they were trespassing on Virginia property. Washington was only 21 years old, but as a surveyor he knew the western land well. In November 1753 he set out with a party of six to find the French commander. After weeks of tramping through the icy western forests, Washington delivered Dinwiddie's message. But Duquesne rejected it with contempt.

In the spring of 1754, Dinwiddie sent another group of Virginians to build a fort where the Monongahela and Allegheny join to form the Ohio River. He also appointed Washington as lieutenant colonel of the Virginia militia and ordered him to lead a force of 150 soldiers to protect the new post against a possible French attack.

Before Washington could reach the Ohio, the French drove off the construction party and completed the post on their own, naming it Fort Duquesne. They occupied it with a force of about 600 men.

Washington should have turned back at this point or at least called for reinforcements. But he was young, ambitious, and head-

[1]From *Documents Relative to the Colonial History of the State of New York,* Vol. X, edited by E.B. O'Callaghan

The war that started to shape North America began with a headstrong young colonel named George Washington holed up in a place called Fort Necessity.

Early in 1755 Major General Edward Braddock arrived in Virginia with two regiments of red-coated British soldiers. He was under orders to drive the French out of Fort Duquesne. Braddock was a veteran with over 40 years in the British army. But his long military experience proved a disadvantage in America. Instead of moving swiftly along forest trails, guided by Indian scouts, he carved a road through the wilderness so that he could haul heavy cannon for the attack on the French.

Under such conditions surprise was impossible. As the

Washington/Custis/Lee Collection,
Washington and Lee University

troops approached Fort Duquesne, the French were ready for them. When Braddock's force of 1,400 men was passing through a narrow gulch about 8 miles (13 kilometers) from the fort, the woods suddenly exploded with gunfire. Redcoats fell by the hundreds. Panic spread among the survivors. Braddock fought bravely but finally was shot in the lungs.

Colonel Washington, who was serving under Braddock, miraculously escaped injury. A big man, well over six feet, he must have presented a tempting target as he tried to rally and organize the British soldiers. Two horses were shot out from under him. After he had finally led the 500 survivors back to safety, he discovered four bullet holes in his coat.

strong. He marched straight toward Fort Duquesne. On the way he surprised a small French scouting party, killing their leader. The main French force then advanced against him. He set up a defensive post, Fort Necessity, but the French easily surrounded it. After an all-day attack Washington had to surrender. The French commander then allowed him and his men to go free. They returned to Virginia, leaving the disputed territory to the French.

The French and Indian War

With Washington's retreat the war began in earnest. In all North America there were no more than 90,000 French settlers. The population of the English colonies was about 1.5 million. Thousands of British soldiers took part in the struggle. Yet for about two years the outnumbered French won most of the battles. They were experts at forest warfare. Most of the Indians sided with them, for unlike the English the French colonists were mostly interested in the fur trade. They did not try to force the Indians to give up their lands or abandon their ways of life.

The British were not easily discouraged. The tide began to turn after a brilliant English politician, William Pitt, took over management of the war effort. In 1758 English troops finally captured Fort

Duquesne. They changed its name to **Fort Pitt,** which is why the modern city on the site is named Pittsburgh.

Gradually other key French posts were taken. The most decisive battle occurred at the city of Quebec in 1759. Quebec is located on a cliff overlooking the St. Lawrence River. The British attack force, led by General James Wolfe, could not at first find a way to get up the cliff without being exposed to murderous fire.

Then one day Wolfe noticed some women washing clothes on the bank of the St. Lawrence. The next day he saw the same clothes hung out to dry on the cliff above. There must be a hidden path up the cliff! Wolfe investigated, found the path, and in the dead of night moved his army up to the city. There on a field outside the city called the Plains of Abraham the battle took place. Both Wolfe and the French commander, General Louis Joseph de Montcalm, were killed in the fight, which ended with the surrender of the city to the English.

By this time the conflict had spread throughout the world, including Europe, where it has been called the **Seven Years' War.** Everywhere the British were victorious. French outposts in Asia and Africa were captured. Spain entered the conflict on the side of France in 1761, only to see its colonies in Cuba and the Philippine Islands overwhelmed by the British.

When the war ended in 1763, the British were able to redraw the map of the world. Outside North America they were remarkably generous. They returned most of the lands they had conquered.

LEARNING FROM MAPS. *Note that most of French lands were north and west of the British colonies. Despite this, a strong rivalry existed. Why were the British concerned with French control of this area?*

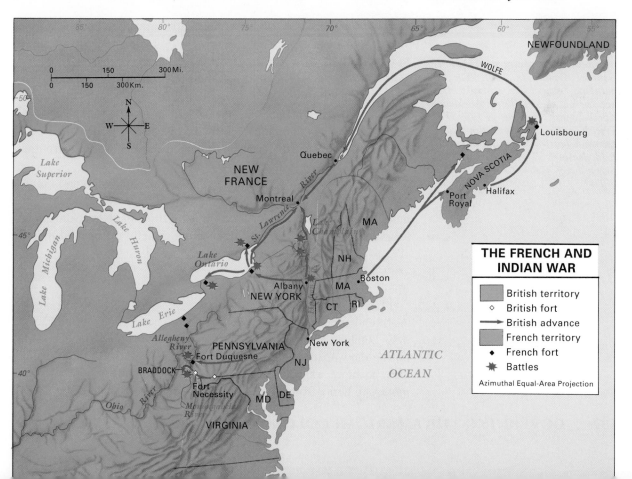

THE FRENCH AND
INDIAN WAR

British territory
◇ British fort
→ British advance
French territory
◆ French fort
✳ Battles

Azimuthal Equal-Area Projection

Benjamin West painted "Death of General Wolfe" in 1771. The oil painting shows the general's last breaths on the Plains of Abraham, where he was the victor in 1759. The French commander Montcalm died in the same battle. Do you think battlefield deaths were really like the one shown here? How did they probably differ?

France had to surrender Canada and all claims to the Ohio and Mississippi Valleys. Spain turned over to the British Florida and the Gulf Coast as far west as the Mississippi River.

Nearly everyone in the English colonies in America was delighted with the outcome of the war. The French threat had been removed. Spain had been pushed back from the southern frontier. The way to the West lay open.

Although some of the colonies had contributed men and money to the conflict, British soldiers and sailors had done most of the fighting. The Royal Treasury paid most of the bills. Never did Americans feel more loyal to the king or more grateful to England than in 1763.

Postwar Problems

As often happens after wars, peace brought new problems and caused new conflicts. The British government had borrowed huge sums during the war to pay its heavy costs. The new, larger empire would also be more expensive to maintain and defend. Where was the money to come from?

And how was the new, larger empire in America to be governed? The old system of 13 separate colonies, each controlled from London, worked well enough when the colonies were separated from one another by thick forests. Now the wilderness was shrinking. Four colonies—Virginia, Pennsylvania, Connecticut, and Massachusetts—each claimed parts of the Ohio Valley just won from France. Each based its case on a royal charter drafted before anyone knew much about American geography. Who would untangle these conflicting claims?

There were also the Indians in the Ohio Valley. Everyone expected them to stop fighting when the French surrendered. Instead they organized behind Pontiac, a chief of the Ottawa, and tried to drive the settlers back across the Appalachians. How could an area claimed by so many different colonies be defended? Who would pay the cost if British troops were used?

These last questions were the most pressing in 1763. The answers were that the British put down **Pontiac's Rebellion** and paid the cost of doing so. To keep the peace the British stationed 6,000 soldiers in the land won from the French and closed the entire region beyond the Appalachian Mountains to settlers. This decision was announced in the **Proclamation of 1763.** Only licensed fur traders might enter the Ohio region. No one could purchase Indian lands.

Most American colonists did not like the Proclamation of 1763. It seemed to put the great West as far out of reach as it had been when the forts built by Governor Duquesne had first barred the way ten years earlier. 🖐

LEARNING FROM MAPS. *The French and Indian War significantly changed the face of North America. Study these maps. What changes can you discover?*

Return to the Preview & Review on page 116.

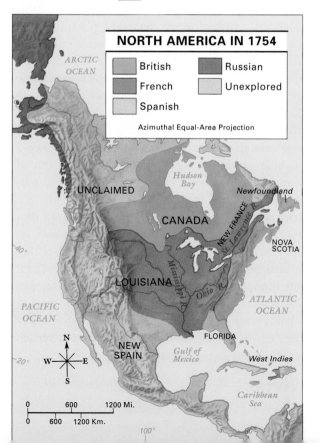

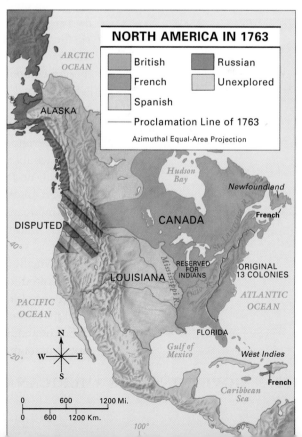

Use these questions to guide your
reading. Answer the questions
after completing Section 4.
**Understanding Issues, Events, &
Ideas.** Use the following words to
describe colonial protests to British
tax policies: Sugar Act, duty,
taxation without representation,
Stamp Act, Sons of Liberty,
boycott, Declaratory Act, indirect
tax, tariff, Townshend Acts,
Circular Letter, Boston Massacre.
1. For what two reasons did colonists dislike the Sugar Act?
2. What caused the Stamp Act to
   be repealed?
3. What did Parliament say about
   taxation without representation?
4. How did the conflicts draw colonists together?
Thinking Critically. 1. Could conflicts between the British and the
colonists before 1772 have been
resolved peacefully? Explain your
reasoning. **2.** You are a reporter
who witnessed the Boston Massacre. Write an article and headline
on it.

4. TAXATION WITHOUT REPRESENTATION

The Sugar Act

The Proclamation of 1763 made sense as a temporary policy designed to make peace with the Indians and to buy time to untangle complicated colonial claims in the Ohio Valley. The problem of governing the empire as a whole and paying the costs involved proved much more difficult to manage.

In 1763 the British prime minister was George Grenville. Grenville had the mind of a bookkeeper: he saw the colonies in terms of money taken in, money spent. Running the colonies was expensive. Most of the tax money collected in the colonies was also spent in the colonies. They were no longer so profitable for the mother country. In England taxes were high. In America taxes were low. To Grenville the conclusion was obvious: Parliament should raise the money to run the colonies by taxing the colonists.

The first of Grenville's tax measures was the **Sugar Act** of 1764. Under this law sugar, coffee, and a number of other products the colonists imported were to be taxed upon entry into any colonial port. These import taxes, called **duties,** were not high. One of the most controversial, the duty on foreign molasses, actually reduced the existing molasses tax from sixpence a gallon to threepence.

Although the Sugar Act resembled many of the earlier laws regulating colonial trade, it actually marked a drastic change in British policy. The old sixpenny tax on foreign molasses, put into effect by the Molasses Act of 1733, was not designed to raise money. It was passed to protect planters in the British sugar islands from foreign competition by making foreign molasses so expensive that no American would buy it. In other words, the tax was not supposed to be collected. The Molasses Act of 1733 was one of the Navigation Acts, part of the effort to make the Empire self-sufficient and hold down the importing of foreign products. A tax of only threepence a gallon would not be high enough to keep French molasses out of America, and England would receive duties from *all* imported molasses, regardless of where it came from.

Americans did not want to pay any new taxes. They were particularly alarmed by Grenville's determination to crack down on smugglers so that the new taxes could be collected. Remember that the Navigation Acts had never been strictly enforced. A merchant who wanted to import French molasses could slip into a remote cove at night and bring his kegs ashore. If caught and brought to trial, a local jury would probably set him free. Or, more likely, he could pay bribes of about a penny a gallon to the customs officials and in perfect safety unload at his own wharf in broad daylight.

STRATEGIES FOR SUCCESS

RECOGNIZING CAUSE AND EFFECT

Determining cause-and-effect relationships is crucial for the reader of history. A cause is a condition, person, or event that makes something happen. An effect is the outcome of a cause. A cause may have many effects. An effect may itself be the cause of other effects. For example, because of high costs of the French and Indian War, Britain levied taxes on the colonies. The costs were a cause and the taxes were the effect. But the taxes resulted in colonial unrest, becoming a cause of the Revolution. Visually, the relationship would look like this:

CAUSE		EFFECT/CAUSE		EFFECT
Cost of French and Indian War	→	New taxes levied	→	Colonial protests

To fully understand the reasons for an event, you must be able to recognize the cause-effect relationships.

How to Recognize Cause-Effect Relationships

Follow these steps to recognize cause-effect relationships.

1. **Look for cause-effect clues.** Certain words are immediate clues to cause and effect. Cause clues include *led to, brought about, produced, because, as a result of, the source of,* and *the reason why*. Some effect clues are the *outcome of, as a consequence, resulting in, gave rise to,* and *depended on*.

   Remember, however, that writers do not always state the link between cause and effect. Sometimes you must read closely to see the relationship between the events.

2. **Check for complex connections.** Note that many cause-effect relationships have complex connections. A single cause may have many effects. Likewise, a single effect may have root in many causes. And remember that an effect may itself be a cause.

Applying the Strategy

Read pages 130–133 and identify at least one cause-effect relationship. Then draw a cause-effect diagram similar to the one in the first column.

There are numerous cause-and-effect relationships presented in the material. For example, the stationing of troops in Boston caused tensions to mount. The situation flared into the Boston Massacre. Can you find other relationships, both stated and unstated, in the excerpt?

For independent practice, see Practicing the Skill on page 134.

The Sugar Act contained regulations requiring shippers to file papers describing their cargoes in detail. Persons accused of smuggling could be tried in admiralty courts, which had jurisdiction over all affairs of the sea. In British admiralty courts there were no juries and the judges were stern. If convicted, offenders lost both the cargo involved and the ship that carried it.

Americans disliked the Sugar Act, both for selfish reasons and because an important principle was involved. That they did not want to pay new taxes was understandable but hard to justify. The money raised was to be spent in the colonies and for the defense and development of the colonies. That the colonists should bear part of the expense was certainly a reasonable thing for the English to ask, particularly since it was for the protection of the colonies.

The moral principle behind their objection, however, was very important. Did Parliament have the right to tax people who had no say in the election of its members? *No*, most Americans answered. It was **taxation without representation.** People should be taxed only by legislative bodies that they had themselves elected. The Sugar

Act violated the laws of God and nature. Taxing people without their consent was little different from outright robbery. A Boston lawyer named James Otis put the issue clearly in his essay *The Rights of the British Colonies Asserted and Proved.*

James Otis

❝ I have waited for years to hear some friend of the colonies pleading in public for them [in England]. I have waited in vain. One privilege after another is taken away. Where we shall end up only God knows. I trust He will protect and provide for us, even if we are driven and persecuted—as many of our ancestors were driven to these once inhospitable shores of America. . . .

It is unjust that a heavy burden should be laid on the trade of the colonies to maintain an army of soldiers, customhouse officers, and fleets of guardships. All the wealth both from trade and the colonies themselves was not enough to support these groups last war. How can anyone suppose that all of a sudden the trade of the colonies alone can bear such a heavy burden? . . .

To say that the Parliament has absolute and arbitrary power does not make sense. Parliament cannot make two and two equal five. Parliament can declare that something is being done for the good of the whole, but this declaration by Parliament does not make it true. There must be a higher power—that is, God. Should any act of Parliament be against any of His natural laws, which are eternally true, such an act would be contrary to eternal truth and justice. Therefore, it would be void. . . .

We regard ourselves as happy under Great Britain's rule. We love, esteem, and revere our mother country, and honor our king. If the colonies were offered a choice between independence and subjection to Great Britain upon any terms other than absolute slavery, I am convinced they would accept subjection. The British government in all future generations may be sure that the American colonies will never try to leave Britain's rule unless driven to it as the last desperate action against oppression. It will be an oppression that will make the wisest person mad and the weakest strong. . . .

I hope these hints . . . will not be misunderstood. They are delivered in pure affection to my king and country, and are not a reflection on any individual. The best army and the best people may be led into temptation. All I know is that it is easier to prevent evil than to escape it once it is here.[1] ❞

[1]From "The Rights of the British Colonies Asserted and Proved," by James Otis

Not all colonists agreed with Otis' ideas. Martin Howard, a Rhode Island lawyer, spoke for those still loyal to Britain.

> " Our personal rights of life, liberty, and property are guaranteed to us by the law of England. These form the birthright of every citizen, whether born in Great Britain, on the ocean, or in the colonies. The political rights of the colonies are more limited. The nature, quality, and scope of these political rights depend completely upon the charters which first established them.
>
> I am aware that this reasoning will be argued against by quoting the saying "No English subject can be taxed without his consent, or the consent of his representatives."
>
> It is the opinion of the members of the House of Commons that they are the representatives of all British subjects, wherever they may live. From their point of view, the saying about taxation is fully respected, and its benefit applies to the colonies. And indeed, the saying must be viewed in this way, for in a strict sense taxation with consent always was and always will be impractical. . . .
>
> Believe me, my friend, it causes me great pain to see that the colonies are so ungrateful to the mother country, whose army and money have just rescued them from being ruled by a French government. I have been told that some colonists have gone so far as to say that, the way things are, they would even prefer a French government to an English one. Heaven knows I have little ill will for anyone. Yet for a moment I wish that those unworthy subjects of Britain could feel the iron rod of a Spanish inquisitor or a French tax agent. This would indeed be a punishment suited to their ungrateful feelings.[1] "

The Stamp Act

Most colonists did no more than complain about the Sugar Act. So Prime Minister Grenville moved ahead with his plans to raise money in America. In March 1765 Parliament passed another tax measure, the **Stamp Act.** This law taxed the use of all sorts of printed matter—deeds to land, marriage licenses, advertisements, newspapers, diplomas, customs documents, even packets of playing cards. Actual stamps or special stamped paper had to be purchased and attached before any of these items could be sold.

Seldom has a political leader been so wrong about what the public would accept. When the terms of the law became known in America, nearly all the colonists spoke out in opposition. The colo-

The Granger Collection

This is one of the hated stamps used to tax all kinds of goods in the American colonies. What items were taxed under the Stamp Act?

[1]From *A Letter from a Gentleman at Halifax, . . . The Rights of Colonies Examined,* by Martin Howard

Points of View

nial assemblies wrote petitions urging that the law be done away with. They drafted stern resolutions denying Parliament's power to tax the colonies. A Stamp Act Congress attended by representatives of nine colonies met in New York and passed 14 polite but firm resolutions. Laws such as the Stamp Act, one resolution stated, "subvert the rights and liberties of the colonists."

The first open resistance to British authority now occurred. Groups calling themselves **Sons of Liberty** began to organize. These "Liberty Boys" believed in action rather than talk. Grenville had appointed a stamp master who was to receive the stamps and sell them to the public. In Boston the Liberty Boys stormed the house of stamp master Andrew Oliver even before he had received any stamps to sell. They broke his windows and made off with many of his valuables. Similar Stamp Act Riots erupted in other colonies. Many of the stamp masters found their very lives in danger. No one could safely distribute the hated stamps.

Colonists also began to refuse to buy anything English until the law was repealed. A thousand merchants agreed to **boycott,** or not import, British goods. This boycott was effective because it hurt the business of exporters in England. These exporters were soon urging Parliament to back down. Finally, since the law was not bringing a single penny into the treasury, Parliament repealed it.

The Declaratory Act

The issue was far from settled. The British were puzzled by the colonial argument against taxation without representation. Many older laws of Parliament applying to the colonies, such as the Molasses Act of 1733, had been tax laws. If representation was so important, what was the difference between the Stamp Act and any of the English laws that colonists had been obeying without argument for the past 150 years?

Furthermore, English leaders claimed, Parliament *did* represent the colonies. Every member of Parliament was said to represent every person in the Empire. The fact that no colonist sat in Parliament or voted for members seemed unimportant. Many thousands of people living in England could not vote for members of Parliament. Many parts of England, including some entire cities, were not represented in Parliament.

The members of Parliament did not think the colonists' objections were sincere. Nor did they want the repeal of the Stamp Act to seem like a surrender. They therefore passed the **Declaratory Act** at the same time that they repealed the Stamp Act. The act was only a statement of power, not an exercise of power. It had no specific effects. The colonies, it said, were "subordinate"—that is, under the control of Parliament. Parliament could pass *any* law regarding the colonies that it desired.

The colonists were so happy to learn that the Stamp Act had been repealed that they ignored the threat contained in the Declaratory Act. Still, they did not accept the principle that Parliament was supreme. When the colonies were tiny and isolated settlements struggling to survive, they had submitted to Parliament in return for aid and protection. By the 1760s the colonies were strong and solidly established. Like children, they were now growing up. The mother country no longer commanded their unquestioning obedience. If trouble was to be avoided, England would have to recognize that time had changed its relationship with its American offspring.

The Declaratory Act was not merely ill-advised. It was both untrue and unwise—untrue because the colonies were in fact no longer completely "subordinate" and unwise because by claiming that the colonies were subordinate, it was sure to encourage them to prove that they were not.

The Townshend Acts

The Declaratory Act did nothing about Great Britain's need for money. In 1767 Charles Townshend, the chancellor of the exchequer, or finance minister, made yet another attempt to tax the colonists.

Paul Revere's engraving of Boston in 1768 shows British troopships landing the Redcoats. To Bostonians unaccustomed to the presence of British soldiers, this seemed like an invasion.

Henry Francis du Pont Winterthur Museum

Fiery radical Sam Adams is the subject of this 1771 oil by the great John Singleton Copley, who also painted Paul Revere below.

Silversmith, engraver, firebrand, later hero of the Midnight Ride, Paul Revere sat for this Copley portrait around 1770. He is musing over a piece of his handsome silver. This is one of the first portraits to celebrate the work of a tradesman rather than an aristocrat. Why is Revere a good subject for this new kind of portrait?

Townshend was an attractive, witty person, the kind of man often described as clever. But he was short of common sense. Like many upper-class English of that time, he had a low opinion of colonists, whom he thought crude and rather dull.

If the colonists considered direct taxes like the stamp duties beyond Parliament's authority, Townshend reasoned, then let them pay **indirect taxes.** Taxes on imports collected from shippers and paid by consumers in the form of higher prices were indirect taxes. The Sugar Act taxes were an example. The colonists had not liked that law, but they had not done much about it but grumble.

Townshend therefore proposed a number of additional **tariffs,** or taxes, on colonial imports. The **Townshend Acts** of 1767 taxed glass, lead, paper, paint, and tea—all things in everyday use that were not produced by Americans. Like Grenville before him, Townshend also tried hard to collect the taxes. He appointed a Board of Customs Commissioners with headquarters in Boston to enforce the law. The commissioners turned out to be greedy racketeers.

Under the law the customs officials received a third of the value of all ships and cargoes seized for violations. But these commissioners were not satisfied with what they could collect by enforcing the regulations strictly. They trapped merchants by allowing minor technical violations to go unpunished for a time and then cracking down when the merchants had grown used to doing business this way. They brought false charges of smuggling against shippers and paid witnesses to testify falsely to obtain convictions. When their thievery caused local citizens to riot against them, they demanded that the British government send troops to Boston to protect them.

The colonists responded to the Townshend Acts and the greed of the customs commissioners by organizing another boycott. After all, no one could collect the taxes if no tea or glass or paint was imported. The Massachusetts legislature also sent a **Circular Letter** to the other colonial assemblies. No more taxation without representation, it said. Let us take action together.

The British minister in charge of colonial affairs, Lord Hillsborough, ordered Massachusetts to rescind, or cancel, the Circular Letter. When the legislature refused, he ordered the assembly dissolved by the governor. He also moved two regiments of British soldiers from the frontier to Boston.

The Boston Massacre

Before the French and Indian War, British troops had never been stationed in the colonies. Now, during peacetime, several thousand ''Redcoats,'' so called because of their red uniforms, were suddenly quartered in Boston. Tensions mounted. Most people in Boston did not hesitate to show their dislike for the soldiers, but they avoided violence. On March 5, 1770, serious trouble erupted. A squad of

soldiers guarding the hated customs house was being taunted by a crowd of sailors, loafers, and small boys. The crowd threw snowballs and rocks, and some attacked the British soldiers. The Redcoats began to fire into the crowd. When order was restored, three Americans lay dead on the ground. Two others died later of their wounds. One of the first patriots to die in the cause of American independence was Crispus Attucks, a black man.

The captain of the guards, Thomas Preston, and eight of his men were arrested and accused of murder. A few Boston radicals, led by Sam Adams, now began to hint that the colonies should declare their independence. Adams was a founder of the local Sons of Liberty and one of the authors of the Massachusetts Circular Letter. Another radical, the silversmith Paul Revere, made and distributed an en-

Paul Revere quickly published "The Boston Massacre" after the Redcoats fired in March 1770. From your reading what are some ways in which this engraving may be considered to give only one point of view? What is art or printed matter of this type generally called?

Taxation Without Representation   **131**

INTERPRETING HISTORY: The American Revolution

Historians study the past much like detectives solve crimes. Like a detective, an historian gathers evidence, such as letters, diaries, newspaper articles, and eyewitness accounts, interprets it, and reaches a conclusion. But different historians may interpret that evidence differently.

For example, historians have debated for nearly 200 years the reasons behind the American Revolution. Many historians, such as James Franklin Jameson, support the theory that the Revolution was an economic and social struggle. In his book *The American Revolution Considered as a Social Movement* he stresses that democratic ideals were growing among the colonists and the Revolution brought about significant economic and social changes. Historian Mary Beth Norton agrees in her

book *Liberty's Daughters: The Revolutionary Experience of American Women 1750–1800.* She points out that even the status of women in America improved after the Revolution.

Historian Gordon Wood in *The Creation of the American Republic 1776–1787* takes a contrasting view. He maintains that the colonists were motivated by patriotism. Historian Edmund S. Morgan supports this, arguing that the colonists were united by the principles expressed by Patrick Henry's "Give me liberty or give me death!"

Whether the Revolution was prompted by economic reasons or patriotic ones will always remain open to debate. Historians will continue to pursue the answers. This detective work makes history exciting.

graving of this **Boston Massacre** that portrayed Captain Preston commanding his sneering soldiers to fire at unarmed American civilians.

The Calm Before the Storm

Cooler heads took control. Sam Adams' cousin John Adams, a respectable lawyer, was a prominent Boston critic of British policy. Nevertheless, he came forward to defend the accused soldiers to make sure they had a fair trial. He was successful and eventually obtained their freedom.

Frustrated once again in its effort to raise money in America, Parliament repealed all the Townshend duties except the tax on tea. That tax was kept, not for the money it might bring, but to demonstrate to colonial leaders and all English subjects that Parliament still claimed the right to tax the colonies.

The crisis seemed to have ended. Lord Hillsborough announced that the government would not try to raise any more money in the American colonies. Normal trade relations between the colonies and England resumed. Business was good. Colonial merchants even imported a good deal of tea, in most cases quietly paying the threepenny duty.

This period of calm hid a basic change in attitude in both Great Britain and in the colonies. Until the late 1760s few colonists had considered England unfair to them. Most were proud to be known as English. They might complain about this or that action of the government in London, but only in the way that citizens today may complain about their political leaders in Washington. Hardly anyone had thoughts of breaking away from England.

The conflicts resulting from the Sugar, Stamp, and Townshend Acts drew colonists together. Many began to fear that the English might try to take away their rights or destroy their liberty. This fear led them to cooperate more with people in other colonies. They recognized that they had common interests. During the calm following the repeal of the Townshend duties, the colonists were less fearful. Yet they remembered the heavy hand of the British. When new threats appeared, the colonists would readily join together to protect themselves.

The English leaders had failed to make Americans pay reasonable taxes for their own defense and administration. This struck a terrible blow to English pride. They could do nothing about it at the moment. Their frustration made them boil inside. They too would react differently—and forcefully—when a new crisis developed.

Religious Controversy with England

Events slowly pushed many American pastors to the side of independence. Many wrote pamphlets criticizing Parliament and the king. They wrote on subjects that ranged from taxation without representation to the right of people to select their own ministers without guidance from church or political officials. Americans, they wrote, feared that bishops and pastors appointed by the British would have strictly English points of view. More and more congregations—even Anglicans and Quakers, who supported the English side in most controversies—felt increasingly alienated from England.

Another reason why the Americans were moving steadily toward a break with Great Britain was the Great Awakening. The Awakening instilled in people a greater sense of personal dignity and their duty to be responsible for their own salvation. This had led them to want to establish their own congregations and appoint their own ministers—without interference from England. Of course, most English church leaders disagreed. So ministers and laypeople alike began to add religious oppression to their grievances against England.

In the early 1770s most people who had lived through the turmoil of the previous ten years thought that the threat to the peace and stability of the British Empire had ended. Nearly all were genuinely relieved. Nearly all were convinced that no serious trouble would ever again disturb this happy state of affairs. Of course they were wrong. On both sides of the Atlantic people were ready in their minds for separation, whether they knew it or not. More and more they were thinking of those on the other side of the ocean as "them" rather than "us." John Adams had this idea in mind when he wrote, "The revolution was complete in the minds of the people, and the Union of the colonies, before the war commenced." ▣

Return to the Preview & Review on page 124.

CHAPTER 4 REVIEW

1651
First Navigation Act passed

1686
Dominion of New England created

1688
Glorious Revolution

1689
English-French conflict in colonies begins

Chapter Summary

Read the statements below. Choose one, and write a paragraph explaining its importance.

1. English monarchs and their advisers felt they had complete control of the colonies.
2. Each colony was led by a governor, who represented the king or queen and who was assisted by a council and an assembly.
3. Town meetings in New England handled local matters while in the Southern Colonies county courts headed by justices of the peace were the local government.
4. The colonies were a key part of England's trade and economy.
5. Parliament passed many laws regulating colonial commerce.
6. European wars between France and England often spilled over into the colonies.
7. England's victory over France in the French and Indian War drove France from North America.
8. Postwar problems such as large debts and conflicting western claims created problems for England.
9. Taxation without representation led to serious conflicts between the colonists and the English government.
10. The first warning of upcoming violence erupted in the Boston Massacre.

Reviewing Chronological Order

Number your paper 1-5. Then study the time line above and place the following events in the order in which they happened by writing the first next to 1, the second next to 2, and so on.
1. The Boston Massacre
2. The first Navigation Act is passed
3. Parliament passes the Stamp Act
4. The French and Indian War ends
5. Dominion of New England created

Understanding Main Ideas

1. Explain how the colonies were governed from England.
2. What was the purpose of the Navigation Acts?
3. Why did most Indian tribes side with the French rather than the English?
4. What was the Declaratory Act? Why did Parliament pass this law?
5. How did the colonists respond to the Townshend Acts of 1767?

Thinking Critically

1. **Synthesizing.** Imagine that you are an American Indian at the time of the French and Indian War. Would you prefer to fight on the side of the French or the British? Support your choice with sound reasoning based on fact.
2. **Solving Problems.** If you were an American colonist in 1764, you probably would be opposed to the Sugar Act and similar new British tax laws. In your opinion, what could the British have done to appease the colonists and to avoid provoking their discontent?
3. **Evaluating.** In your own words, explain what John Adams meant when he wrote, "The revolution was complete in the minds of the people . . . before the war commenced."

Writing About History: Persuasive

Use your historical imagination to put yourself in the boots of one of the British soldiers accused of the Boston Massacre. Write a letter to your family in England to present your side of the story.

Practicing the Strategy

Review the strategy on page 125.
Recognizing Cause and Effect. Review "France Challenges England" on page 116–23 and answer these questions.
1. What caused the English and French colonists in America to start fighting.
2. What was the effect of Queen Anne's War on the French and English colonies?
3. What effects did Duquesne's decision to build forts have? What was the final outcome?

1752
French fortify
Ohio Valley

1754
French and Indian
War starts

1759
Quebec falls to
British troops

1763
French and Indian
War ends

★
Proclamation of 1763

★
Britain acquires East
and West Florida

1764
Sugar Act passed

1765
Stamp Act enacted

★
Sons of Liberty formed

1767
Townshend Acts

1768
Circular Letter sent

1770
Boston Massacre

Using Primary Sources

Mercy Otis Warren's play *The Adulateur* was written to protest the Boston Massacre and other British acts. It was first printed in *The Massachusetts Spy* in 1773. Its heroes, Brutus and Cassius, were patriots opposed to a greedy ruler. Brutus has often been identified as Warren's brother, James Otis, and Cassius as Samuel Adams. Brutus and Cassius also were the Roman senators who assassinated Julius Caesar in hopes of preserving the Roman republic. As you read the excerpt, compare the sentiments of the characters to those of the Patriots. Then answer the questions.

Brutus: *I sprang from men who fought, who bled for*
       freedom:

    From men who in the conflict laugh'd at danger:
    Struggl'd like patriots, and through seas of blood
    Waded to conquest—I'll not disgrace them.
    I'll show a spirit worthy of my sire.
    Tho' malice dart her stings—tho' poverty
    Stares full upon me;—tho' power with all her thunder
    Rolls o'er my head,—thy cause my bleeding country
    I'll never leave—I'll struggle hard for thee,
    And if I perish, perish like a freeman.
Cassius: *You're not alone—there are, I know, ten*
       thousand,
    Ne'er bow'd the knee to idol power—Repeated insults
    Have rous'd the most lethargic [lazy].

1. Compare the speech of Brutus with Otis' essay on page 126.
2. Why might a play be an excellent form of propaganda for the Patriots' cause?

Linking History & Geography

In today's world of instant communications and supersonic flight, it takes historical imagination to understand what it was like when ships powered only by wind and ocean currents were the one way to travel between America and Europe. Then the geographic location of America meant that time and distance had a major effect on life. To understand how geographic location affected the colonists, complete the following activities.

1. Research how long it took to sail from England to America in 1750.
2. Then in a paragraph discuss some of the problems this travel time caused both rulers and colonists.
3. In a second paragraph, explain why time and distance helped foster a sense of independence in the colonies.

Enriching Your Study of History

1. **Individual Project.** Prepare a chart with a column headed *Cause* and a column headed *Effect* to show the consequences of British actions from the Proclamation of 1763 to the Boston Massacre of 1770. Include the following example in your chart:

Cause		*Effect*
Townshend Acts	→	Colonists organize a boycott

2. **Cooperative Project.** With four other classmates, write and perform a skit in which you attend a meeting of the Sons of Liberty. What actions of the British upset you? What actions might you take? Have at least one member argue for proceeding with caution.

Chapter 4 Review   **135**

UNIT ONE REVIEW

Summing Up and Predicting
Read the summary of the main ideas in Unit One below. Choose one statement, then write a paragraph predicting its outcome or future effects.
1. America was discovered at least three times— by Asian wanderers, by the Vikings, and by Columbus.
2. Early American Indian cultures were strongly influenced by the environment and developed many unique life styles.
3. Europeans came to America for many reasons—economic opportunity, religious freedom, and adventure among them.
4. Most Africans were brought to America as slaves.
5. At first life in the colonies was hard, but it improved as the colonies grew.
6. Grants and charters permitted colonial settlement, but the kings themselves had complete authority over the colonies.
7. The British defeated other European colonial threats in America, but postwar problems caused conflicts with the colonies.

Connecting Ideas
1. Contrast ways in which native Americans affected the environment with ways in which European colonists affected it.
2. Compare reasons that people first came to North America with reasons that people immigrate to the United States today.
3. If you could colonize another planet, name three things you would do to avoid mistakes made by the early colonists of America.

Practicing Critical Thinking
1. **Analyzing.** Explain how the Commercial Revolution in Europe after the Crusades led to Columbus' voyage to the New World.
2. **Synthesizing.** The year is 1606. You are in charge of leading a group of English people to America to start a colony. Name three types of skilled workers you would take with you, and three objects that you would pack, all to help assure your colony's survival. Explain your reason for each choice.
3. **Drawing Conclusions.** Benjamin Franklin was one of the greatest Americans of the Enlightenment, or Age of Reason, a time of belief in human progress. Which achievement in Franklin's life do you think is the best example of the Enlightenment's spirit of progress? Why?

4. **Evaluating.** You know that many of the tax laws that outraged colonists were made by Britain's prime minister, George Grenville, and the finance minister, Charles Townshend. If you could advise these men to change their attitudes in order to avoid conflict with the colonies, how would you recommend they behave?

Exploring History Together
1. Study the time lines at the end of each of the chapters in Unit One. Then your group will create its own time line of the most important events in the unit. Members of your group may wish to illustrate the time line.
2. Your group will prepare a debate on taxation in the colonies. One side will explain the British reasons for taxing the colonists. The other side will give the American argument against taxation by Britain. After the debate, your class will vote on which side presents the best argument.
3. Your class will prepare a panel discussion to present to the class. Various members will portray John Smith, Anne Hutchinson, William Penn, and Pontiac. The topic of the discussion: "Life in the Colonies." Actors should conduct research to gain knowledge about their characters' lives and points of view.

Reading in Depth
Alderman, Clifford L. *Colonists for Sale: The Story of Indentured Servants in America.* New York: Macmillan. Provides a close-up view of indenture and the people who became indentured servants.

Curtin, Philip D., ed. *Africa Remembered: Narratives by West Africans from the Era of the Slave Trade.* Madison: University of Wisconsin Press. Presents personal accounts of Africans who were sold as slaves.

Hampden, John, ed. *New Worlds Ahead: First Hand Accounts of English Voyages.* New York: Farrar, Straus, & Giroux. Tells the story of the early voyages to America in the words of the people who made them.

Hooks, William H. *The Legend of White Doe.* New York: Macmillian. Tells a fictional tale about the fate of Virginia Dare and the small band of settlers with her.

Syme, Ronald. *La Salle of Mississippi; Champlain of the St. Lawrence.* New York: Morrow. Provides accounts of the journeys of these two great French explorers.

"Raising the Liberty Pole" shows how excited the American colonists had become at the prospect of freedom.

THE AMERICAN NATION

UNIT 2

Revolution and the creation of the United States of America is the subject of this unit. The Revolution began even before the American colonists first took up arms against their British rulers. The war was only part of the Revolution and it was not complete until the United States government was established under the Constitution. This unit tells how the Declaration of Independence explained America's revolt to the rest of the world. It describes the fight for freedom and the struggle of the nation to govern itself under the weak Articles of Confederation. And it describes the writing and acceptance of the Constitution. It answers important questions raised by the Revolution, among them: How should the United States be governed? What roles would men and women, free and slave, play in a society that proclaimed "all men are created equal"?

The Revolutionary War

Ordinary people rarely protest when the cost of living goes down. Yet such was the American character that its revolt from Britain began when the price of tea was lowered. For at the same time a British company was given nearly total control of the tea market. What did this mean for the future of American self-government? This chapter explains how the struggle for the colonists' rights as Englishmen became the American Revolution. The Declaration of Independence was published to explain to the world the complaints the colonists had with the British government and why they wanted to create a government of their own. Major persons and events of the Revolutionary War as well as the impact of war on everyday life are described here. Battles fought in the Northeast, South, and West gradually brought America its freedom. But what was the price of victory for the Americans who won this freedom in 1781?

Preview & Review

Use these questions to guide your reading. Answer the questions after completing Section 1.
Understanding Issues, Events, & Ideas. Use the following words to explain the beginning of the Revolution: Tea Act, East India Company, monopoly, Boston Tea Party, Coercive Acts, Intolerable Acts.
1. What was the purpose of the Tea Act?
2. Why did the British think the colonists would be pleased with the Tea Act? Why did the colonists resent it?
3. How did Great Britain react to the Boston Tea Party?
Thinking Critically. You wish to protest the Tea Act, but you disapprove of the method used by those involved in the Boston Tea Party. What would you do instead?

1. THE REVOLUTION BEGINS

The Tea Act

The calm before the storm of the revolution ended in 1773. In May of that year Parliament passed a law known as the **Tea Act.** This law was designed to help the British East India Company, which was in very bad shape. After its founding in 1600, the **East India Company** had prospered, bringing riches to its stockholders and employees by its trade with India. But by 1773 the company had fallen upon hard times. King George III and Parliament felt that something must be done to revive the company's fortunes.

One of the chief products of the East India Company was tea. In 1773 it had about 17 million pounds (7.65 million kilograms) of unsold tea stored in English warehouses. Normally the company sold its tea at auction in London to wholesale merchants. The merchants then sold the tea to English storekeepers or to American wholesalers, who in turn sold it to retail merchants in the colonies. These merchants sold the tea to the colonists. The tea was taxed first in England and then again—the threepenny Townshend duty—in the colonies.

The Tea Act authorized the East India Company to sell tea directly to American retailers. This would eliminate the handling charges and profits of both British and American wholesalers. In addition, the act repealed the English tax on tea so that only the Townshend tax remained.

Frederick, Lord North, who had become prime minister of England in 1770, assumed that the colonists would not object to the Tea Act. The cost of tea would be greatly reduced for Americans, and opposition to paying the Townshend duty had been gradually dying out. Now, with the price much lower because of the elimination of the middlemen's profits and the English tax, surely the colonists would not mind paying the threepenny charge. East India tea, even with the tax, would be as cheap as tea from the Dutch East Indies, which smugglers were selling in America. Many people thought the prime minister's reasoning made sense.

The East India Company promptly shipped 1,700 chests containing about 500,000 pounds (225,000 kilograms) of tea to its agents in Boston, New York, Philadelphia, and Charleston.

Contrary to Lord North's hopes, news of the Tea Act caused great resentment in the colonies. What bothered most people was not only the tea tax but the fact that Parliament had given an English company what amounted to a **monopoly** of the tea trade in America. A monopoly is the exclusive control of a product or service in a given market. American importers of English tea would be cut out of the business. Even smugglers of foreign tea could not beat the company's price. Both groups were furious.

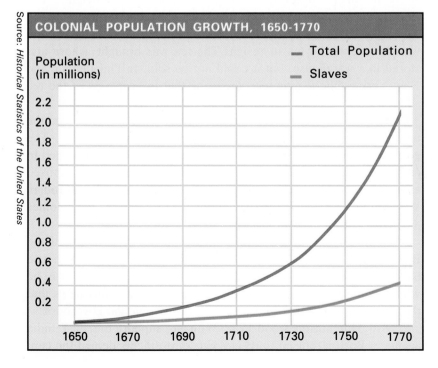

COLONIAL POPULATION GROWTH, 1650-1770

Population (in millions)

— Total Population
— Slaves

2.2
2.0
1.8
1.6
1.4
1.2
1.0
0.8
0.6
0.4
0.2

1650   1670   1690   1710   1730   1750   1770

LEARNING FROM GRAPHS. *The colonial population grew very rapidly, almost doubling every 20 years! Artisans and craftsmen of every type came to America. By 1770 the colonies were no longer a wilderness and could produce the food and most of the goods they needed. How did this affect the move toward independence?*

Other merchants were angry too. If Parliament could give the East India Company a monopoly of the tea business, could it not give other monopolies to the company or to any favored group? "Every Tradesman will groan under dire Oppression," warned one excited Philadelphian.

The American merchants were very influential people. No doubt their dislike of the Tea Act affected how other citizens responded to it. As we said earlier, ordinary people rarely protest when the cost of living goes down. Yet in this case they did. The strength of the public reaction showed how mistrustful the Americans were of the British by 1773.

The Tea Act seemed part of a devilish plot to make the colonies totally subordinate to England. Had not Parliament itself revealed that intention in the Declaratory Act back in 1766? Only recently, in 1772, the British government had begun to pay the salaries of colonial governors. Now the governors were no longer dependent upon the colonial assemblies, which had been able to threaten not to pay governors who disregarded colonial opinion. For years English leaders had been complaining about the high cost of governing the colonies. Why were they now taking on an additional expense? Many Americans believed that Lord North and his associates intended to crush local self-government in America.

The Boston Tea Party

When the ships carrying the East India Company's tea began to arrive in American ports, public protest rose to new heights. The ship *London* arrived in Charleston, South Carolina, on December 2. An angry crowd gathered and persuaded the company agent who was to receive the tea to resign. The tea was brought ashore and stored in a warehouse, but it could not be sold. In Philadelphia and New York public feeling was so strong that the captains of the tea ships did not dare unload. Instead they sailed back to England.

In Boston, however, an explosive situation developed when the tea ship *Dartmouth* tied up in the harbor on November 27. The governor of Massachusetts, Thomas Hutchinson, was determined to enforce the law. Hutchinson was American born. He had opposed all the British efforts to tax the colonies after the French and Indian War. But he believed that Parliament had the *right* to tax the colonies and to pass laws like the Tea Act.

Over the years Hutchinson had become the chief target of the Boston Sons of Liberty and of Sam Adams in particular. His house had been looted by rioters during the Stamp Act crisis. It was he who had announced, with obvious pleasure, the alarming news that the English had decided to pay the salaries of colonial governors.

Now Hutchinson stood firm. With his support the East India agents in Boston refused to resign. Customs officers denied the cap-

The Granger Collection

tains of tea ships permission to leave the port. For more than two weeks tension mounted in the town. Crowds milled in the streets. Sam Adams and other radicals stirred public feeling at mass meetings.

Finally, on the night of December 16, Adams gave the signal to a group of townspeople disguised as Mohawk Indians. They boarded three tea ships and dumped the tea chests into the harbor. Tea worth about £15,000, a considerable fortune, was destroyed while a huge crowd watched silently from the shore.

Overboard go the chests of East Indies tea while Boston citizens watch from the harbor. Many probably recognized the thinly disguised "Mohawks." The artist has made an attempt to set the scene at night with lights in the windows. Look closely at the crowds on the piers. How did the Boston Tea Party bring people from different levels of society together?

The Coercive Acts

The **Boston Tea Party** was, as the name suggests, a kind of celebration in the eyes of those who participated in it. In British eyes (and, it must be admitted, to any neutral observer) it was a serious crime. Obviously it had been carefully planned. The "Mohawks" had gathered at the home of Benjamin Edes, editor of the Boston *Gazette,* to put on their costumes and await Sam Adams' signal.

When the news reached England, government leaders were furious. Parliament promptly passed a series of laws to force Massachusetts to pay for the tea.

The Revolution Begins   141

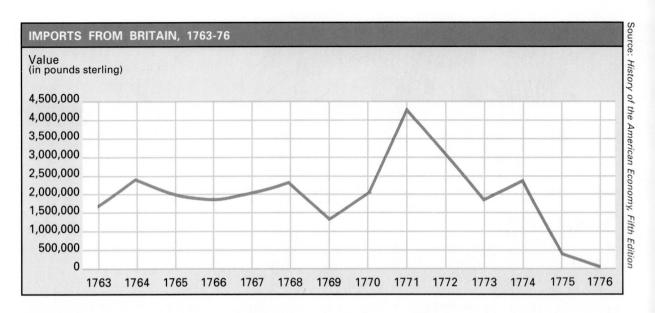

IMPORTS FROM BRITAIN, 1763-76

Value
(in pounds sterling)

Source: *History of the American Economy, Fifth Edition*

LEARNING FROM GRAPHS. *Much of the conflict between England and the colonies grew out of economic policies. What was the general trend of imports from England before 1771? What was the trend after 1771? What caused the change?*

The first of these laws, known collectively as the **Coercive Acts,** was the Boston Port Act. It provided that no ship could enter or leave Boston harbor until the town had paid for the tea. The second, the Administration of Justice Act, gave the governor power to transfer the trials of soldiers and royal officials accused of serious crimes to courts outside of Massachusetts. This would be done when the governor felt that a fair trial could not be had in the colony.

The third law, the Massachusetts Government Act, further increased the governor's power by giving him control over town meetings, and it replaced the elected colonial council with a council appointed by the king. Another law, not directly related to the Tea Party but equally disliked by the colonists, ordered citizens to house British soldiers in their homes. A general, Thomas Gage, commander of British troops in America, replaced Thomas Hutchinson as governor of Massachusetts. Hutchinson promptly set sail for England to report to the king. He never returned to America.

Many Americans who had been critical of British policies spoke out against the Tea Party as an unnecessary act of violence. But the Coercive Acts angered and frightened everyone. To punish the entire community because some tea had been destroyed by extremists was the act of tyrants. Benjamin Franklin wrote that if the English government wanted to make up for the East India Company's loss, it ought to pay the money itself. It could subtract the sum from the far larger amount it had "extorted" from the colonies by its many illegal policies.

The Americans called the Coercive Acts the **Intolerable Acts.** The two names reflect the two views of the crisis. To the British the time had come to *coerce,* or force, the colonists into obedience. To the colonists the use of such force was *intolerable*—more than they could be expected to put up with. 🖘

Return to the Preview & Review on page 138.

2. SHOTS HEARD ROUND THE WORLD

Preview & Review

Use these questions to guide your reading. Answer the questions after completing Section 2.

Understanding Issues, Events, & Ideas. Use the following words to describe the outbreak of the Revolutionary War: Committee of Correspondence, First Continental Congress, Patriot, Minute Man, Concord, Lexington, Revolutionary War, Battle of Bunker Hill.

1. What did Lord North hope to accomplish by punishing Massachusetts so severely?
2. What actions did the First Continental Congress take?
3. When and why did Parliament declare Massachusetts to be in a state of rebellion?
4. Why were British troops sent to Concord?
5. Why did the Americans occupy Bunker Hill and Breed's Hill?

Thinking Critically. 1. After Lexington and Concord, could a peaceful solution to the problems between the colonists and the British government still have been found? Why or why not? 2. Imagine that you are a resident of Boston. From your roof you are watching the Battle of Breed's Hill. In your diary, describe what you see and your reaction.

The First Continental Congress

Lord North hoped to accomplish two things by punishing Massachusetts so severely. One was to frighten the other colonies into accepting more British control over their affairs. The second was to tempt the other colonists to take advantage of Massachusetts' suffering. Ships that could not unload at Boston could unload at New York or Philadelphia or Baltimore to the benefit of those towns.

Lord North was assuming that the colonies were still separate societies. He was quite mistaken. Even before the Tea Act, radicals in Boston had formed a **Committee of Correspondence** to keep in touch with radicals elsewhere in Massachusetts and in the other colonies. A network of such committees existed by the time news of the Coercive Acts reached America. Almost without intending to, these committees were becoming an informal central government, a kind of United States waiting to be born.

The leaders of the other colonies did not even consider taking advantage of Massachusetts' misfortune. When the Massachusetts committee sent out a message in June 1774 calling for a meeting of colonial leaders, all but Georgia sent delegates. In September these delegates gathered in Philadelphia for what we now call the **First Continental Congress.**

The Congress took a firm but moderate position. It condemned the Intolerable Acts, and it urged full support for the citizens of Boston. It passed resolutions demanding the repeal of all the British laws aimed at raising money in the colonies. Only the colonial assemblies, it declared, had the right to tax Americans. The delegates denounced the British practice of maintaining an army in the colonies in peacetime. The Congress also set up a Continental Association to enforce a ban on importing British products of all kinds.

No one spoke openly about independence. Indeed, the delegates sent off a "loyal address" to George III, asking him politely to help them in their struggle for the rights of English subjects. Yet the Congress concluded its session in October with this stern warning: "We have *for the present* only resolved to pursue . . . peaceable measures." Then they adjourned, agreeing to meet again the following May if their demands had not been met.

Lexington and Concord

Meanwhile, in Massachusetts hatred of the Intolerable Acts had turned the colony into an armed camp. General Gage ruled in Boston, supported by his regiments of British Redcoats. Outside the city no

British law could be enforced. With the colonial legislature no longer functioning, local groups calling themselves **Patriots** took over. In the towns and villages citizens began to form militia companies. These civilian-soldiers could soon be seen drilling on town commons all over the colony. They were called **Minute Men** because they were supposed to be ready for action on a moment's notice.

Parliament now declared Massachusetts to be in a state of rebellion. The government decided to send more Redcoats to General Gage in Boston and ordered him to "arrest and imprison" the radical leaders. On the night of April 18, 1775, Gage sent a force of 700 men commanded by Lieutenant Colonel Francis Smith to seize a supply of weapons that the Patriots had gathered at **Concord,** a town about 15 miles (24 kilometers) west of Boston. On the way the troops could also arrest Sam Adams and the merchant John Hancock, another Patriot leader, who were at **Lexington.**

When the British troops set out, Paul Revere, who had made the engraving of the Boston Massacre, and another Patriot, William Dawes, rode ahead to rouse the countryside. Revere reached Lexington at midnight and warned Adams and Hancock to flee. Dawes reached the town about half an hour later. They then rode on toward Concord, accompanied by Dr. Samuel Prescott, a young man from Concord who had been visiting a lady in Lexington. Revere and Dawes were captured by a British patrol. Prescott escaped by jump-

This scene of the "Occupation of Concord" is taken from a larger engraving by Ralph Earl. Row upon row of Redcoats march past the Concord cemetery. How did this orderly march collapse when the Minute Men assembled?

ing his horse over a stone wall, and he got to Concord in time to warn the people of the coming attack.

The British advance guard under Major John Pitcairn reached Lexington at dawn. Before them, lined up on the common, were some 70 Minute Men. The group included a number of men in their sixties as well as youngsters in their teens. Such a tiny force could not hope to stop the Redcoats.

Major Pitcairn rode forward and with a sneer ordered the Minute Men to move off. They were about to do so when someone fired a shot. British accounts say it was an American, American accounts blame a British soldier. More shots followed, and suddenly the Redcoats, "so wild," as one witness put it, "they could hear no orders," fired a volley directly into the American line.

When the smoke cleared, eight Minute Men lay dead. Ten other Americans and one Redcoat were wounded. The Britishers then marched on to Concord. They managed to occupy the town and destroyed whatever supplies the Americans had not carried off or hidden after the warning that the Redcoats were coming.

It was now mid-morning. The Redcoats had been on the march since midnight. Outside Concord, Minute Men from every nearby town were rapidly gathering. One group drove back three British infantry companies guarding Concord's North Bridge. Two more Americans were killed in this skirmish, but three Redcoats also fell. Colonel Smith decided to head back to Boston.

The march back was like a trip through the corridors of Hell. The Americans used their knowledge of the natural landscape to great advantage. All along the route they hid behind trees, along river banks, and in hollows. Snipers peppered the weary Redcoats with

The Minute Men at Lexington fall before the Redcoats led by Major John Pitcairn on April 19, 1775. This is the first of a series of hand-colored engravings made by Amos Doolittle. What is the response of the Minute Men here? How did it quickly change?

Shots Heard Round the World   145

STRATEGIES FOR SUCCESS

TRACING MOVEMENTS ON A MAP

Oftentimes a map shows routes of movement. Maps in Chapter 1, for example, show the migration of the first Americans (page 3) and the voyages of discovery of Columbus (page 24) and of Magellan and El Cano (page 29). Other maps in this book show the movement of troops in wartime. Studying routes on a map will give you a great deal of information about the course of events and will help you understand how the story unfolded.

How to Trace Movements on a Map

To trace movements on a map, follow these guidelines.
1. **Read the map's title.** The title will tell you what general information is shown on the map.
2. **Study the legend.** Lines indicate routes. Arrows indicate the directions of movement. In the case of troop movements, the routes and arrows may be colored differently to represent each army. Battle sites will be shown and will often indicate by color which army was victorious.

3. **Note the routes and related events carefully.** The routes tell you a great deal about the geography of an area as well as the overall picture of the historical event. For example, by studying troop movements closely you gain a sense of the sweep of an army from battle to battle—the victors in pursuit, the defeated in retreat. You can see where armies gathered strength and where desperate fighters played out their final hours.

Applying the Strategy

Like all good maps, the one on this page tells a story. But the story may be fully appreciated only by carefully reading the descriptions in your book on pages 143–47. Then turn to the map to see Revere, Dawes, and Prescott riding across Massachusetts ahead of the advancing British army. Note the site of the American victory at North Bridge near Concord and the retreat of the British troops to Boston.

For independent practice, see Practicing the Strategy on pages 178–79.

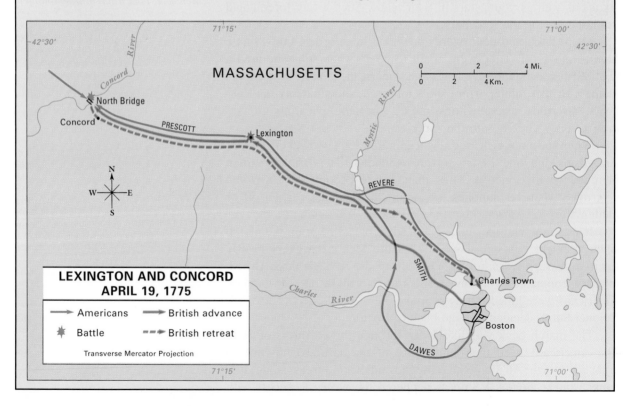

MASSACHUSETTS

**LEXINGTON AND CONCORD
APRIL 19, 1775**

→ Americans   → British advance
★ Battle   --→ British retreat

Transverse Mercator Projection

bullets. Hundreds and hundreds of local citizens picked up their muskets and followed the sound of gunfire to join in the fight. By the time the British were safely back in Boston, they had suffered 273 casualties. American losses came to just under 100.

Breed's Hill

The **Revolutionary War** had begun. Within 48 hours nearly 20,000 angry American militiamen had gathered in and around Cambridge, across the Charles River from Boston. The new Massachusetts Provincial Assembly appointed Artemas Ward, a veteran of the French and Indian War, to command this large force. Ward, however, was not a good organizer. Militiamen from other New England colonies had their own commanders. Everywhere there was confusion.

Fortunately for the Americans the one important British force in America was penned up in Boston. In May Ethan Allen and the "Green Mountain Boys," militiamen from Vermont, took Fort Ticonderoga on Lake Champlain, capturing some valuable heavy cannon. Then, on June 16, the Americans occupied Bunker Hill and Breed's Hill, two high points near Charles Town, on the peninsula across the harbor from Boston. Working all night, they built an earthen *redoubt*, or fort, on Breed's Hill.

From this strong point cannon would be able to pound Boston and the British warships in the harbor. The British realized at once that they must clear the Americans from this position or abandon the city.

Three weeks earlier, three leading English generals had arrived in Boston to advise Gage. One of them, Major General William Howe, a veteran of King George's War and the French and Indian War, was assigned the task of driving the Americans back. Howe was a brave man and a skillful soldier. It was he who had led General Wolfe's advance guard during the surprise attack on the French at Quebec in 1759.

On the morning of June 17, Howe ferried 1,500 Redcoats across the bay on barges. He himself led one force around the base of Breed's Hill, hoping to cut off the Americans' retreat and attack their position from the rear. The rest of the Redcoats, commanded by Brigadier General Robert Pigot, marched straight up Breed's Hill. They advanced in three broad lines, pushing through tall grass and climbing over fences as they went.

It was a dramatic sight. Across the bay hundreds of Bostonians watched the brewing battle from their windows and rooftops. The Americans on Breed's Hill were tired and hungry after their night's labor with spades and shovels. Fresh troops were supposed to relieve them, but none arrived. The inexperienced civilian soldiers now faced hardened professional troops—skilled British bayonet fighters eager to avenge the bloody retreat from Concord.

The Americans knew how to shoot, and their commander, Colonel William Prescott, knew how to maintain discipline. Legend has it that the men were told not to fire until they could see the whites of the enemy's eyes. The British came on, firing with no effect against the earthen wall of the redoubt. They were prepared to take losses until they could scale the wall and end the battle with their bayonets. When the British were almost to the wall, Prescott gave the signal. A wall of flames erupted as the Americans fired. The heavy musket balls tore through the British lines. A second volley sent the Redcoats back down the hill in confusion. The field before the redoubt was littered with dead and dying men.

Meanwhile, General Howe's force had met a similar fate in front of an American defense line along the shore. Both British generals then regrouped and sent their brave soldiers forward once more against the American defenses. Once more they were thrown back.

Instead of landing behind the two hills as he could easily have done, Howe had probably attacked the Americans directly to shock them. He thought the untrained colonials would turn and run when faced by his disciplined veterans. Once the Redcoats had taken the

"Attack on Bunker Hill with the Burning of Charles Town" is the title of this oil painting. However, the real battle is being fought on Breed's Hill, to the right, which the orderly rows of Redcoats are attempting to scale. Can you spot the flaming shells being launched from Boston?

National Gallery of Art

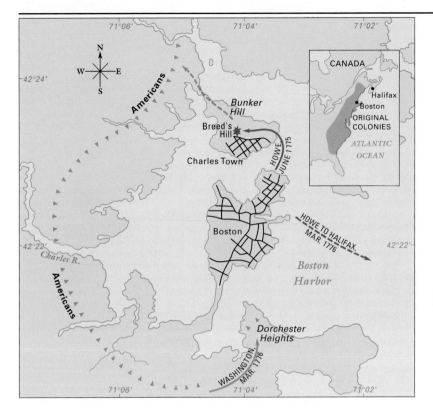

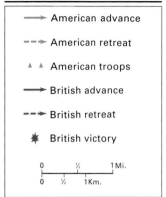

→	American advance
- - →	American retreat
▲ ▲	American troops
→	British advance
- - →	British retreat
✸	British victory

0   ½   1 Mi.

0   ½   1 Km.

LEARNING FROM MAPS. *The Americans held a very strong position around Boston, forcing Howe to retreat to Halifax, Nova Scotia. What made the American position so strong? If Washington had been able to capture Howe and his retreating Redcoats, the war may have ended quickly. How did the British escape?*

hill by direct assault, the weakness and cowardice of the defenders would be exposed. The rest of the rebel army would melt away and the war would be over. After all, American militiamen had proved very poor soldiers in earlier wars. Howe's former commander, General Wolfe, had described the American soldiers attached to his command during the French and Indian War as "the dirtiest, most contemptible cowardly dogs you can conceive."

After two charges Howe knew that he had made a terrible mistake. Now he *had* to take the hill or face a defeat that would shatter morale. Reinforced by fresh troops, the Redcoats advanced up the hill for the third time. Inside the redoubt the Americans were almost out of ammunition. Those who had no more bullets loaded their muskets with nails and pieces of glass. Their last volley tore fresh holes in the British line. Then the Redcoats were over the wall.

Now American blood flowed freely as the veteran Redcoats proved their skill in hand-to-hand fighting. Among those killed was Dr. Joseph Warren, leader of the Massachusetts Patriot government.

The battle ended with the British in control of the vital high ground. For some reason it has been remembered as the **Battle of Bunker Hill** rather than Breed's Hill. Over a thousand English soldiers were dead or wounded, more than four out of every ten in the battle. About a hundred Americans were killed. Three hundred more were wounded or taken prisoner. Most of the American casualties came after the men had used up their ammunition. 🖰

Return to the Preview & Review on page 143.

Shots Heard Round the World   **149**

The delegates attending the Second Continental Congress in 1776 were painted by Robert Pine and Edward Savage. A weary Benjamin Franklin is in the center.

Historical Society of Pennsylvania

Use these questions to guide your reading. Answer the questions after completing Section 3.
Understanding Issues, Events, & Ideas. Contrast the divided sentiments of the Tories and the Whigs, using the following words: Second Continental Congress, Olive Branch Petition, Dorchester Heights, Loyalist, Tory, Whig.
1. What was the mood of the Second Continental Congress? Why?
2. What were Washington's major assets as a general?
3. What was the condition of the American army when Washington took command? What changes did he make?
4. Why was discipline of ordinary British soldiers so harsh?
5. Why did Washington allow Howe to leave Boston?
Thinking Critically. Compare the British and American soldiers during the Revolutionary War. From your comparison, predict who might be the winner.

3. "LIBERTY OR DEATH"

The Second Continental Congress

Lexington, Concord, and Bunker Hill had been fought by Massachusetts with some help from neighboring New England colonies. The rest of the colonies were now to enter the conflict. In May the **Second Continental Congress** met in Philadelphia. Some of the most important men in America had been elected delegates. Others not yet well known would soon become important. The Massachusetts radicals Sam Adams, John Adams, and John Hancock were there. So was Benjamin Franklin of Pennsylvania. Virginia sent its fiery orator Patrick Henry, who had just urged the arming of the Virginia militia in a speech ending:

❝ We are not weak if we make proper use of the means which the God of nature has granted us. Three million people, armed in the holy cause of liberty, and in such a country as ours, cannot be conquered by any force which our enemy can send against us. Besides, we shall not fight our battles alone. There is a just God who rules the fates of nations. He will raise friends to fight our battles for us.

 The battle is not won by the strong alone. It is won by the alert, the active, the brave. Besides, we have no choice. Even if we were cowardly enough to desire it, it is now too late to back down from the conflict. There is no retreat but in submission and slavery! Our chains are forged! Their clanking may be heard on the plains of Boston! The war is inevitable—and let it come! I repeat, let it come!

It is in vain to drag the matter out. Gentlemen may cry peace, peace. But there is no peace. The war is actually begun! The next gale that sweeps from the north will bring to our ears the resounding clash of arms! Our brethren are already in the [battle]field! Why stand we here idle? What is it that gentlemen wish? What would they have? Is life so dear, or peace so sweet, as to be purchased at the price of chains and slavery? Forbid it, Almighty God! I know not what course others may take; but as for me, give me liberty or give me death![1] 99

Virginia was also represented by George Washington, well known for his role in the French and Indian War, and by a young lawyer named Thomas Jefferson. Jefferson had recently attracted attention by writing a pamphlet, *A Summary View of the Rights of British America,* in which he argued that kings should be "the servants of the people," not their masters.

Not all the delegates took such extreme positions. The Congress proceeded cautiously. It sent an **Olive Branch Petition** asking the king to protect them against Parliament. (An olive branch is a symbol of peaceful intentions.) It issued a "Declaration of the Causes and Necessity of Taking Up Arms." Earlier, on June 15, two days before the Battle of Bunker Hill, Congress had created an official American army and appointed George Washington as its commander in chief.

Washington looked like a general. He was over six feet tall, strong, a fine athlete, yet dignified and reserved. His bravery had been demonstrated in the western wilderness on the day the French ambushed General Braddock. Yet Washington was also known for his sound judgment and his sense of responsibility. He was the kind of person people trusted and respected from the first meeting.

Actually, Washington had much to learn about warfare and running an army. The other possible commanders, however, knew still less. The fact that Washington was from Virginia, the most powerful of the southern colonies, was another reason why he was chosen. The appointment symbolized the union of the colonies that was rapidly taking place.

Washington accepted the assignment eagerly and, in fact, so expected it that he had arrived in his uniform. He set out at once for Massachusetts. It was typical of the man that he refused to take a salary. His conviction that a commander in chief should not profit from the war was so strong that he stood fast on the issue.

[1]From *Sketches of the Life and Character of Patrick Henry,* 3d ed., edited by William Wirt

Washington carried this miniature of his "dear Patsy" throughout the Revolutionary War. It was painted by Charles Willson Peale in about 1776. Below, Washington stands in 1782 with his horse Nelson. John Trumbull painted this picture in 1790.

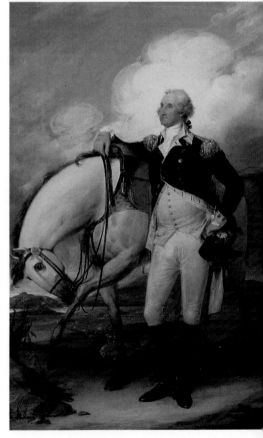

Henry Francis du Pont Winterthur Museum

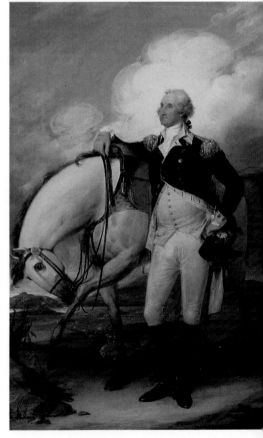

The American Army

When Washington arrived outside Boston on July 3, 1775, he found himself in charge of an army of about 14,000 men. Some were living in dormitories on the campus of Harvard College. Others were in private homes. A few units had set up tents. Nearly all the men wore their ordinary outdoor clothing. There were no American uniforms. The soldiers even had to supply their own guns. Most of them were armed with muskets, a weapon that fired a round bullet with murderous effect at close range. Beyond 50 yards (about 46 meters) it was wildly inaccurate. Some soldiers had only spears or axes. Gunpowder and cannon were scarce.

There was very little discipline. Men commanded by leaders like Colonel Prescott, the hero of Breed's Hill, made good soldiers. Those with lazy or cowardly officers seldom performed well. Most units had elected their own officers and treated them as equals rather than as their superiors. This was not a force for military efficiency.

Washington was very unhappy with the army he found. As a southern planter and slave owner he was accustomed to ordering men about and being obeyed. He set out at once to turn what he called "this mixed multitude" into his own idea of an army. He made the men build barracks and taught them to march in step. He weeded out officers who could not maintain discipline. Any soldier found drunk was given a good whipping.

Then Washington sought to persuade the men to sign up for a year's service in the new Continental Army. Only about 10,000 did so. Many had families to support at home. Moreover, Washington's stern discipline was not popular with many units. Officers in this army were appointed, not elected. Washington chose mostly men like himself from the upper classes of society. He believed that ordinary soldiers would obey their "betters" more readily than people of their own level. There were 28 regiments, each with 8 companies of about 90 men. Units from the more distant colonies arrived, and gradually a national army emerged.

Rifle companies from the Southern Colonies were particularly impressive in Washington's army. Their guns, called "Pennsylvania rifles," had grooved barrels which set a bullet spinning when fired. In the hands of sharpshooters, these rifles were accurate at 150 yards (135 meters) or more. They were greatly feared by the British, especially when snipers began to pick off sentries at what seemed to be incredible distances. The British sent one captured rifleman back to England to demonstrate his weapon. His aim proved so deadly that the exhibition was said to have discouraged many English civilians from enlisting.

Pennsylvania rifles still had to be loaded and fired in the same slow and cumbersome way that muskets were. Gunpowder was poured down the barrel. Then the bullet and some kind of wadding

Anne S.K. Brown Military Collection, Brown University

The American "sharpshooter" on the left and Pennsylvania regular infantryman on the right were drawn in 1784. Although officers are pictured in gray and tan, the Continental Army was actually encouraged to wear brown. Why would this have been a good color for soldiers fighting in America?

were packed in with a ramrod. Next a small amount of powder was sprinkled on the firing pan. When the marksman pulled the trigger, a sparking arrangement similar to that of a cigarette lighter ignited the powder in the pan. That flame entered a small hole in the barrel and exploded the main charge, firing the bullet. Occasionally the powder in the pan "flashed" without causing the gun to fire. This is the origin of the expression "a flash in the pan."

Obviously it was difficult and dangerous for a soldier to reload either a rifle or a musket while moving and under fire.

The British Army

In July 1775 the British had fewer than 4,000 soldiers in Boston. It was a force much different from the army Washington commanded. The generals were members of the aristocracy. Often they were prominent in politics too. William Howe and two other generals then in Boston—John Burgoyne and George Clinton—were members of Parliament. Such men paid little heed to instructions from London that did not please them.

Officers of lower rank normally obtained their commissions by buying them. Prices were high. A colonel's post might go for £5,000, a substantial fortune in the 1700s. This meant that only wealthy men

Howard Pyle illustrated the Battle of Bunker Hill with such attention to detail that we have a good idea of British fighting techniques. How is this picture a kind of closeup of the painting on page 148? Which do you find more helpful in picturing the battle in your mind?

PRAISE TO WASHINGTON

In October 1775 George Washington received a remarkable poem that was written by Phillis Wheatley, a young slave who was brought to Boston from Africa when she was about seven. The Wheatleys, who gave her their name, taught her to read and write. Soon she began to write what became the first widely applauded American poems. Here are some lines from "To His Excellency George Washington," a poem written in the classical manner:

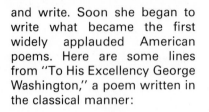

In bright array they seek the work of war,
Where high unfurl'd the ensign waves in air.
Shall I to Washington their praise recite?
Enough thou know'st them in the fields of fight.
Thee, first in peace and honours,—we demand
The grace and glory of thy martial band. . . .
Proceed, great chief, with virtue on thy side,
Thy ev'ry action let the goddess guide.
A crown, a mansion, and a throne that shine,
With gold unfading, WASHINGTON! be thine.[1]

Independence National Historical Park Collection

Washington was greatly impressed. He wanted to publish the poem himself, but he was too modest to do so. Instead he wrote to Phillis to say he would "be happy to see a person so favored by the Muses" and invited her to visit him at the Continental Army camp. We know she made the visit, but we do not know what was said between the Father of the Country and the first African American poet.

New York Public Library Picture Collection

could hope to be officers. The gap between officer and enlisted man could not be bridged.

Ordinary soldiers were mostly drawn from the very bottom of society. Criminals were often allowed to enlist to avoid jail or execution. Vagrants and idle persons of all sorts were frequently "pressed" into service. Discipline was brutal, in part because it seemed the only way to control such types. A marine in the Boston garrison who was convicted of punching an infantry officer was sentenced to receive 800 lashes with a cat-o'-nine-tails. Nearly 1,000 slaves fought with the British for a promise of freedom.

The principal weapon of the British infantry was a musket similar to that used by colonial troops but heavier and equipped with a bayonet. Soldiers "leveled" their muskets before firing, but they did not really try to aim. The guns did not even have rear sights. If a whole line fired at once in the general direction of the enemy, some damage would be done. The smoke alone caused by the exploding gunpowder could screen the soldiers as they plodded methodically ahead. The object was to get close enough to the foe to go for him with cold steel. Their bright red uniforms made British soldiers easy

[1]From "To His Excellency George Washington" by Phillis Wheatley

targets for marksmen, but against the inaccurate muskets of the day what the men wore made little difference. The attack on Breed's Hill is an excellent example of the strengths and weaknesses of British tactics.

Despite the harsh treatment of enlisted men, the British army was an excellent fighting machine. Both officers and men were brave, enduring, effective. The system reflected English society just as the American system reflected American society. Conditions that today might seem cruel and mindless were accepted as normal and necessary by most of those on the bottom as well as by their leaders. Perhaps the typical soldier took a kind of pride in his ability to stand up to the punishing life he had to lead. All ranks could take pride in being English, members of the most powerful nation in the world.

Washington's First Victory

For long months after the Battle of Bunker Hill, the British army sat pinned down in Boston. The American forces ringing the city greatly outnumbered them. Washington was eager to attack, but he was persuaded not to assault the city directly. In January 1776 Colonel Henry Knox, a very stout but energetic and talented young artillery officer, reached camp with the heavy brass and iron cannon that had been captured at Fort Ticonderoga. Using sleds and teams of oxen, Knox and his men had dragged the cannon nearly 300 miles (480 kilometers), a tremendous achievement. In March Washington had these guns pulled up **Dorchester Heights,** south of Boston. He built strong defenses to protect them. From this position the cannon could have blown the British positions in the city below to bits.

General Howe realized at once that he must either capture Dorchester Heights, a task far more difficult than the capture of Breed's Hill, or abandon Boston. He had neither the men nor the desire to attack. He let the Americans know that if they did not allow him to leave peacefully, he would destroy the city. Washington wisely agreed to let Howe move his troops. On March 17, 1776, the British departed for their naval base at Halifax, Nova Scotia, there to await reinforcements and supplies from home. With the fleet went more than 1,500 Americans. These people preferred exile to rebellion against a king and country they considered their own. They and others like them, perhaps a fifth of the American population, were called **Loyalists,** or **Tories.** Americans who believed in the patriotic resistance to King George were called **Whigs.**

For the moment the thirteen colonies were entirely clear of British troops. But the struggle was just beginning. By July 1776 General Howe was back on American soil with a powerful army. By then the colonies had given up trying to persuade England to treat them more fairly. Instead they had declared their independence and become the **United States of America.** 🖎

Return to the Preview & Review on page 150.

4. INDEPENDENCE IS DECLARED

Use these questions to guide your reading. Answer the questions after completing Section 4.
Understanding Issues, Events, & Ideas. Use the following words to describe the sentiments of the colonists: tyranny, Declaration of Independence, Fourth of July, democracy.
1. What was the significance of Thomas Paine's *Common Sense?*
2. Why did Congress appoint a committee to prepare the Declaration of Independence?
3. What did the Declaration of Independence tell the world?
4. Why must we use historical imagination to understand the first "self-evident" truth of the Declaration?
Thinking Critically. 1. What do you consider to be the two most important ideas of the Declaration of Independence? Why? **2.** If you had been one of the framers of the Declaration of Independence, name one other "unalienable right" that you would have included. Explain your choice.

The Movement for Independence

Once large numbers of Americans had been killed by British soldiers, the conflict was bound to turn into a war for independence. Bayonets had been used on the brave defenders of Breed's Hill after their ammunition had run out. Any peaceful solution seemed unlikely.

For many months the colonists had tried to believe that King George was their friend. He was being misled by evil advisers, the argument ran. Of course, this was not true, and eventually the colonists realized that it was not.

The person most responsible for opening the colonists' eyes was an Englishman who had just recently immigrated to America. His name was Thomas Paine. In January 1776 Paine published a pamphlet, *Common Sense.* In it he attacked not only George III, whom he called a "Royal Brute," but the whole *idea* of monarchy. *Any* king was a bad thing, Paine insisted. People have "a natural right" to rule themselves. Therefore, the colonies should throw off all connection with Great Britain and create a republic of their own.

National Portrait Gallery

Paine opposed **tyranny,** which is the cruel and unjust use of power. He wrote:

> Alas! We have been long led away by ancient prejudices and [have] made large sacrifices to superstition. We have boasted the protection of Great Britain, without considering that her motive was *interest* not *attachment* and that she did not protect us from *our enemies* on *our account,* but from *her enemies* on *her own account.* . . .
>
> But Britain is the parent country say some. Then the more shame upon her conduct. Even brutes do not devour their young, nor savages make war upon their families. . . . This New World has been the asylum [a place of security] for the persecuted lovers of civil and religious liberty from *every part* of Europe. Hither have they fled, not from the tender embraces of the mother, but from the cruelty of the monster; and it is so far true of England that the same tyranny which drove the first emigrants from home pursues their descendants still. . . .

A brooding Thomas Paine is shown in the portrait above by John Wesley Jarvis.

A government of our own is our natural right; and when a man seriously reflects on the precariousness [uncertainty] of human affairs, he will become convinced that it is infinitely wiser and safer to form a constitution of our own, in a cool, deliberate manner, while we have it in our power, than to trust such an interesting event to time and chance. . . .

O ye that love mankind! Ye that dare oppose not only the tyranny but the tyrant, stand forth! Every spot of the old world is overrun with oppression. Freedom has been hunted round the globe. Asia and Africa have long expelled her. Europe regards her like a stranger, and England has given her warning to depart. . . .

Wherefore, instead of gazing at each other with suspicious or doubtful curiosity, let each of us hold out to his neighbor the hearty hand of friendship, and unite in drawing a line, which like an act of oblivion [pardon], shall bury in forgetfulness every former dissension. Let the names of Whig and Tory be extinct; and let none other be heard among us, than those of a good citizen, and open and resolute friend, and a virtuous supporter of the RIGHTS OF MANKIND, and of the FREE AND INDEPENDENT STATES OF AMERICA.[1]**

Common Sense was an immediate best seller. Nearly everyone in the colonies read it or heard it discussed. Once the idea of independence was freely talked about, more people accepted it.

By June 1776 nearly all the members of the Second Continental Congress were ready to act. Richard Henry Lee of Virginia introduced a resolution for independence on June 7:

" RESOLVED: That these United Colonies are, and of right ought to be, free and independent States, that they are absolved from all allegiance to the British Crown, and all political connection between them and the State of Great Britain is, and ought to be, totally dissolved.**"**

Before passing this resolution, Congress appointed a committee to prepare a statement explaining why independence was necessary. The members of this committee were Benjamin Franklin of Pennsylvania, John Adams of Massachusetts, Roger Sherman of Connecticut, Robert Livingston of New York, and the youngest delegate, 33-year-old Thomas Jefferson of Virginia. The document they drafted, the **Declaration of Independence,** was written mainly by Jefferson. On July 2, voting by states, the delegates resolved to declare their independence. Then, on the **Fourth of July,** they officially approved the Declaration.

[1]From *Common Sense* by Thomas Paine

The Granger Collection

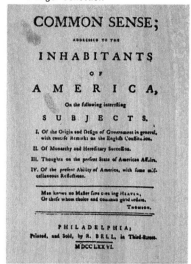

COMMON SENSE;

ADDRESSED TO THE

INHABITANTS

OF

AMERICA,

On the following interesting

SUBJECTS.

I. Of the Origin and Design of Government in general, with concise Remarks on the English Constitution.

II. Of Monarchy and Hereditary Succession.

III. Thoughts on the present State of American Affairs.

IV. Of the present Ability of America, with some miscellaneous Reflections.

Man knows no Master save creating Heaven,
Or those whom choice and common good ordain.
Thomson.

PHILADELPHIA;
Printed, and Sold, by R. BELL, in Third-Street.
MDCCLXXVI.

This is the title page of Paine's widely read Common Sense. *What was the main idea of Paine's essay?*

"The Declaration of Independence" was painted by John Trumbull in 1786. Thomas Jefferson and Benjamin Franklin may be found near the center of the painting.

THE DECLARATION OF INDEPENDENCE
In Congress, July 4, 1776
The unanimous Declaration of the thirteen united States of America,

Thomas Jefferson wrote the first draft of the Declaration in a little more than two weeks. He was 33 years old.

In the first paragraph, the signers state that the colonists must break their political ties with Britain. They feel that it is important to justify why they are making the separation.

impel: force

endowed: provided

"Laws of Nature" and "Nature's God" refer to Isaac Newton's belief that certain patterns are invariable and predictable. Natural or "unalienable" rights (the rights to life, liberty, and the pursuit of happiness) cannot be taken away. This protection, reasoned the English philosopher John Locke, is called natural law. People created governments to protect their natural rights. A government, therefore, must have the consent of the governed. If a government abuses its powers, it is the right as well as the duty of the people to do away with that government.

When in the Course of human events, it becomes necessary for one people to dissolve the political bands which have connected them with another, and to assume among the powers of the earth, the separate and equal station to which the Laws of Nature and of Nature's God entitle them, a decent respect to the opinions of mankind requires that they should declare the causes which impel them to the separation.—

We hold these truths to be self-evident, that all men are created equal, that they are endowed by their Creator with certain unalienable Rights, that among these are Life, Liberty, and the pursuit of Happiness.—

That to secure these rights, Governments are instituted among Men, deriving their just powers from the consent of the governed,—

That whenever any Form of Government becomes destructive of these ends, it is the Right of the People to alter or to abolish it, and to institute new Government, laying its foundation on such principles and organizing its powers in such form, as to them shall seem most likely to effect their Safety and Happiness. Prudence, indeed, will dictate that Governments long established should not be changed for light and transient causes; and accordingly all experience hath shown, that mankind are more disposed to suffer, while evils are sufferable, than to right themselves by abolishing the forms to which they are accustomed. But when a long train of abuses and usurpations, pursuing invariably the same Object evinces a design to reduce them under absolute

Despotism, it is their right, it is their duty, to throw off such Government, and to provide new Guards for their future security.—

Such has been the patient sufferance of these Colonies; and such is now the necessity which constrains them to alter their former Systems of Government. The history of the present King of Great Britain is a history of repeated injuries and usurpations, all having in direct object the establishment of an absolute Tyranny over these States. To prove this, let Facts be submitted to a candid world.—

He has refused his Assent to Laws, the most wholesome and necessary for the public good.—

He has forbidden his Governors to pass Laws of immediate and pressing importance, unless suspended in their operation till his Assent should be obtained; and when so suspended, he has utterly neglected to attend to them.—

He has refused to pass other Laws for the accommodation of large districts of people, unless those people would relinquish the right of Representation in the Legislature, a right inestimable to them and formidable to tyrants only.—

He has called together legislative bodies at places unusual, uncomfortable, and distant from the depository of their public Records, for the sole purpose of fatiguing them into compliance with his measures.—

He has dissolved Representative Houses repeatedly, for opposing with manly firmness his invasions on the rights of the people.—

He has refused for a long time, after such dissolutions, to cause others to be elected; whereby the Legislative powers, incapable of Annihilation, have returned to the People at large for their exercise; the State remaining in the meantime exposed to all the dangers of invasion from without, and convulsions within.—

He has endeavored to prevent the population of these States; for that purpose obstructing the Laws for Naturalization of Foreigners; refusing to pass others to encourage their migrations hither, and raising the conditions of new Appropriations of Lands.—

He has obstructed the Administration of Justice, by refusing his Assent to Laws for establishing Judiciary powers.—

He has made Judges dependent on his Will alone, for the tenure of their offices, and the amount and payment of their salaries.—

He has erected a multitude of New Offices, and sent hither swarms of Officers to harass our people, and eat out their substance.—

He has kept among us, in times of peace, Standing Armies without the Consent of our legislatures.—

He has affected to render the Military independent of and superior to the Civil power.—

He has combined with others to subject us to a jurisdiction foreign to our constitution, and unacknowledged by our laws; giving his Assent to their Acts of pretended Legislation:—

For quartering large bodies of armed troops among us:—

---

despotism: unlimited power

usurpations: wrongful seizures of power

tyranny: oppressive power exerted by a government

candid: fair

Here the Declaration lists the charges that the colonists had against King George III. How does the language in the list of grievances in the Declaration appeal to people's emotions?

relinquish: release, yield

inestimable: priceless

formidable: causing dread

Why do you think the king had his legislatures in the colonies meet in places that were hard to reach?

annihilation: destruction

convulsions: violent disturbances

naturalization of foreigners: the process by which foreign-born people become citizens

appropriations of land: setting aside land for settlement

tenure: term

a multitude of: many

What wrongful acts does the Declaration state have been committed by the king working with the British Parliament?

quartering: lodging, housing

For protecting them, by a mock Trial, from punishment for any Murders which they should commit on the Inhabitants of these States:—

For cutting off our Trade with all parts of the world:—

For imposing Taxes on us without our Consent:—

For depriving us in many cases, of the benefits of Trial by Jury:—

For transporting us beyond Seas to be tried for pretended offences:—

For abolishing the free System of English Laws in a neighboring Province, establishing therein an Arbitrary government, and enlarging its Boundaries so as to render it at once an example and fit instrument for introducing the same absolute rule into these Colonies:—

For taking away our Charters, abolishing our most valuable Laws, and altering fundamentally the Forms of our Governments:—

For suspending our own Legislatures, and declaring themselves invested with power to legislate for us in all cases whatsoever.—

He has abdicated Government here, by declaring us out of his Protection and waging War against us.—

He has plundered our seas, ravaged our Coasts, burnt our towns, and destroyed the Lives of our people.—

He is at this time transporting large Armies of foreign Mercenaries to complete the works of death, desolation and tyranny, already begun with circumstances of Cruelty & perfidy scarcely paralleled in the most barbarous ages, and totally unworthy the Head of a civilized nation.—

He has constrained our fellow Citizens taken Captive on the high Seas to bear Arms against their Country, to become the executioners of their friends and Brethren, or to fall themselves by their Hands.—

He has excited domestic insurrections amongst us, and has endeavored to bring on the inhabitants of our frontiers, the merciless Indian Savages, whose known rule of warfare, is an undistinguished destruction of all ages, sexes and conditions.

In every stage of these Oppressions We have Petitioned for Redress in the most humble terms: Our repeated Petitions have been answered only by repeated injury. A Prince, whose character is thus marked by every act which may define a Tyrant, is unfit to be the ruler of a free people.

Nor have We been wanting in attentions to our British brethren. We have warned them from time to time of attempts by their legislature to extend an unwarrantable jurisdiction over us. We have reminded them of the circumstances of our emigration and settlement here. We have appealed to their native justice and magnanimity, and we have conjured them by the ties of our common kindred to disavow these usurpations, which would inevitably interrupt our connections and correspondence. They too have been deaf to the voice of justice and of consanguinity. We must, therefore, acquiesce in the necessity, which denounces our Separation, and hold them, as we hold the rest of mankind, Enemies in War, in Peace Friends.—

We, therefore, the Representatives of the united States of America, in General Congress, Assembled, appealing to the Supreme Judge of the

What was the rallying cry of the colonists to protest the king's tax policies?

The "neighboring Province" that is referred to here is Quebec.

arbitrary: not based on law

render: make

abdicated: given up

foreign mercenaries: soldiers hired to fight for a country not their own

perfidy: violation of trust

insurrections: rebellions

petitioned for redress: asked formally for a correction of wrongs

Notice that the Declaration has 18 paragraphs beginning with "He has" or "He is." What is the effect of this repetition?

unwarrantable jurisdiction: unjustified authority

magnanimity: generous spirit

conjured: called upon

consanguinity: common ancestors

acquiesce in: consent to

Most American people thought that completely breaking ties with Great Britain should be a last resort. Why do you think they felt that way?

world for the rectitude of our intentions, do, in the Name, and by Authority of the good People of these Colonies, solemnly publish and declare, That these United Colonies are, and of Right ought to be Free and Independent States; that they are Absolved from all Allegiance to the British Crown, and that all political connection between them and the State of Great Britain, is and ought to be totally dissolved; and that as Free and Independent States, they have full Power to levy War, conclude Peace, contract Alliances, establish Commerce, and to do all other Acts and Things which Independent States may of right do.—

And for the support of this Declaration, with a firm reliance on the protection of divine Providence, we mutually pledge to each other our Lives, our Fortunes and our sacred Honor.

John Hancock	*Benjamin Harrison*	*Lewis Morris*
Button Gwinnett	*Thomas Nelson, Jr.*	*Richard Stockton*
Lyman Hall	*Francis Lightfoot Lee*	*John Witherspoon*
George Walton	*Carter Braxton*	*Francis Hopkinson*
William Hooper	*Robert Morris*	*John Hart*
Joseph Hewes	*Benjamin Rush*	*Abraham Clark*
John Penn	*Benjamin Franklin*	*Josiah Bartlett*
Edward Rutledge	*John Morton*	*William Whipple*
Thomas Heyward, Jr.	*George Clymer*	*Samuel Adams*
Thomas Lynch, Jr.	*James Smith*	*John Adams*
Arthur Middleton	*George Taylor*	*Robert Treat Paine*
Samuel Chase	*James Wilson*	*Elbridge Gerry*
William Paca	*George Ross*	*Stephen Hopkins*
Thomas Stone	*Caesar Rodney*	*William Ellery*
Charles Carroll	*George Read*	*Roger Sherman*
of Carrollton	*Thomas McKean*	*Samuel Huntington*
George Wythe	*William Floyd*	*William Williams*
Richard Henry Lee	*Philip Livingston*	*Oliver Wolcott*
Thomas Jefferson	*Francis Lewis*	*Matthew Thornton*

rectitude: rightness

In this paragraph, the signers stated their actual declaration of independence. What rights would the new United States of America now have as an independent nation?

Congress adopted the final draft of the Declaration of Independence on July 4, 1776. A formal copy, written on parchment paper, was signed on August 2, 1776.

The following is part of a passage that was taken out of Jefferson's original draft by the Congress: "He has waged cruel war against human nature itself, violating its most sacred rights to life and liberty in the persons of a distant people who never offended him, captivating and carrying them into slavery in another hemisphere, or to incur miserable death in their transportation thither." Why do you think the Congress wanted to delete this passage?

While on the committee to prepare the Declaration, John Adams received a letter from his wife, Abigail Adams. The last sentence said, "If particular care and attention is not paid to the ladies, we are determined to foment a Rebellion, and will not hold ourselves bound by any laws in which we have no voice, or Representation." Did the writers of the Declaration heed her advice?

The Declaration of Independence

Jefferson's Declaration of Independence is one of the best-known and most influential political documents ever written. No one has expressed so well the right of a people to overthrow a government they do not like and make a new one they do like. This idea comes from the thinkers of the Enlightenment. So does the phrase "Laws of Nature and of Nature's God," which refers to the belief that certain patterns follow natural law and do not change. Jefferson based this idea on the works of Isaac Newton and Francis Bacon, who hoped to develop a science of human and political behavior.

Jefferson originally wrote that the truths set forth in the Declaration were "sacred and undeniable." In polishing the Declaration, Franklin changed the phrase to read "self-evident"—that is, obvious. The truths make up only a small part of the document. Nevertheless, they are the part that makes the Declaration so important. For the first time in history, a group of revolutionaries were carefully explaining why they had the right to use force to change their government.

The Declaration of Independence is a superb statement of the principles on which democratic government is based. (Political power in a **democracy** comes from the people and is for the benefit of all.) Using historical imagination reminds us that the Declaration was also wartime propaganda. As a description of the causes of the Revolution, the Declaration is one-sided. Many of the charges made against George III were strongly exaggerated. Some were untrue. The king had many faults. But he was not a tyrant.

Those who put their names on the Declaration of Independence were burning bridges behind them. In English eyes they were now traitors. If they lost the war, they could expect the treatment commonly given traitors—death.

Self-Evident Truths

Over the years people have argued heatedly about what Jefferson meant by the first of his self-evident truths in the Declaration of Independence—"that all men are created equal." Historical imagination can help us understand. First of all, Jefferson surely meant by *men* "people," just as when he spoke of "the opinions of mankind," he meant the opinions of all people, women and men alike.

This is not to suggest that Jefferson or any other signer of the Declaration believed in equal rights for women as the term is used today. The delegates who signed the Declaration believed that women were entitled to life, liberty, and the pursuit of happiness so long as they behaved as men thought they should behave.

During the Revolution women held many jobs usually performed by men in peacetime. Many ran farms and shops while their husbands, fathers, and brothers were at war. Abigail Adams called herself a "farmeress" and really did manage the Adams farm. Some women served as nurses in the army. A few actually fired guns in defense of liberty. Martha Washington joined her husband in winter camp and encouraged other women to do war work. "Whilst our husbands and brothers are examples of patriotism," she wrote, "we must be patterns of industry." Women were not the legal equals of men, and no movement to improve the position of women grew out of the Revolution.

On the other hand, Jefferson certainly meant that only free men were created equal. Jefferson believed that for free men there were certain *unalienable* rights, God-given rights that no just government could take away for *any* reason. How could he, a slaveholder, claim that liberty was a God-given right of "all men"?

During the Revolutionary War about 5,000 Africans served in the American army and navy. Crispus Attucks fell in the Boston Massacre. Peter Salem, Caesar Ferrett, Samuel Craft, and Prince Estabrook were among the militiamen on the Lexington common when the first shots were fired. Salem Poor, Cato Howe, and Cesar Jabor were among the defenders of Breed's Hill. Indeed, Africans, slave and free, fought in every major battle. Still, most Americans tolerated slavery.

Nearly every European person in America of the 1770s was in some ways prejudiced against Africans by today's standards. Further, most men of all origins were "male chauvinists" by today's standards. We must use our historical imagination if we want to understand these men and their times. To condemn George Washington for owning slaves and taking control of his rich wife's property would only show that we did not understand Washington and the Revolution. We would be equally wrong if we took the Declaration so literally as to believe that the signers were perfect democrats.

Reaction to the Declaration

Many Americans, particularly the Patriots (also known as Whigs), rejoiced at the news that independence had been declared. Throughout the colonies Whigs celebrated, holding festive banquets and demonstrations to show their support of the Declaration. Some Americans greeted the news with indifference. These people did not care one way or another. The Loyalists (or Tories), strongly opposed the sentiments expressed in the Declaration and regarded the Whigs as traitors.

Despite Paine's plea to "let the names of Whig and Tory be extinct," arguments between the Whigs and the Tories continued throughout the Revolutionary War. In many cases, the Tories openly welcomed the British troops and did all they could to hurt the Patriots' cause. In other cases they fled to Canada or returned to England as the revolution and the war spread.

"I desire you would Remember the Ladies, and be more generous and favourable to them than your ancestors. Do not put such unlimited power into the hands of the Husbands. Remember all Men would be tyrants if they could. . . ."
Abigail Adams, 1776

Points of View

"Depend upon it, We know better than to repeal our Masculine systems. Altho they are in full Force, you know they are little more than Theory. . . . We have only the Name of Masters, and rather than give up this, which would compleatly subject Us to the Despotism of the Peticoat, I hope General Washington, and all our brave Heroes would fight."
John Adams, 1776

Return to the Preview & Review on page 156.

Independence Is Declared   **163**

Preview & Review

Use these questions to guide your reading. Answer the questions after completing Section 5.
Understanding Issues, Events, & Ideas. Use the following words to describe the progress of the war: Battle of Long Island, sunshine patriot, mercenary, battles of Trenton and Princeton, Battle of Saratoga, treaty of alliance.
1. Why did the British want to capture New York?
2. What was the British strategy for 1777?
3. In what way was General Washington a victor in 1777?
4. What was the most important result of the Battle of Saratoga?
5. What did the French promise in the 1778 treaty of alliance?
Thinking Critically. 1. Why do you think the author refers to 1776–77 as "America's dark hour"? 2. Suppose you are a German mercenary serving under General Burgoyne at Saratoga. Write a letter to a friend describing this leader and telling what you think of him.

America's Dark Hour

The British were now determined to crush the American rebellion. General Howe had left Boston in March 1776 with 4,000 soldiers. He returned to New York City in July 1776 with 32,000. This army was supported by a huge fleet of over 400 warships and transports under the command of General Howe's brother, Richard, Lord Howe.

By capturing New York and patrolling the Hudson River with their warships, the British could split New England from the rest of what they still called "the colonies." General Howe first established a base on Staten Island. Then, late in August, he landed 20,000 soldiers on Long Island. Instead of attacking directly, he brilliantly outmaneuvered Washington's army. Then he struck from two directions. The **Battle of Long Island** revealed that Washington was inexperienced at managing a complicated operation. He barely managed to withdraw his battered troops across the East River to New York City.

The victory greatly heartened the British. Howe became a national hero. King George knighted him. Sir William, as he was thereafter called, again proceeded slowly and carefully. Apparently the losses he had suffered in the Battle of Bunker Hill had made him overly cautious.

After delaying several weeks, Howe finally moved his army across the East River. Once more the British troops routed Washington's force. The Americans fled to the northern end of Manhattan Island, leaving Howe in control of New York City. New York was not like Boston. A large proportion of the citizens were Loyalists. They welcomed the British with open arms.

This was one of the low points of the war for the Americans. If Howe had been more aggressive, he could probably have destroyed Washington's army completely.

Yet, after more fighting, Washington crossed the Hudson to New Jersey, where Howe could not use the British fleet to maneuver around him. Half of Washington's army had been captured by now, nearly 3,000 at Fort Washington at the northern end of Manhattan Island. Washington had left this garrison behind when he moved his main force to New Jersey. Through late November and into December, the disheartened army retreated in the direction of Philadelphia, followed by Howe. The Continental Congress, thoroughly alarmed, shifted its sessions from Philadelphia to Baltimore. In mid-December the exhausted American army retreated across the Delaware River into Pennsylvania.

In this dark hour Washington devised a daring and brilliant plan. Winter was closing in. The enlistments of most of his men were about to expire. Something had to be done to revive their spirits and raise

the hopes of the people. As Thomas Paine wrote in another of his powerful pamphlets, too many Americans were **sunshine patriots,** enthusiastic for independence when things were going well, cowards and shirkers when the future looked grim.

Across the Delaware River in Trenton, New Jersey, 1,400 of General Howe's soldiers were encamped. These men were not English but Hessians—German troops from the principality of Hesse-Cassel. Americans hated and feared the Hessians, partly because they were tough soldiers known to be fond of looting and mistreating civilians, partly because they were **mercenaries,** hired soldiers, killing for money. Actually, the Hessians were not really mercenaries. The real mercenary was their ruler, Prince Frederick II of Hesse-Cassel. It was the prince who had ordered his soldiers to America, and it was he who pocketed the money paid by the British.

Washington decided to attack the Hessian camp. On Christmas night, amidst a snowstorm, he led his men back across the Delaware River, 9 miles (about 15 kilometers) above Trenton. The soldiers marched swiftly on the town. At dawn they overwhelmed their astonished foe. More than 900 Hessians were taken prisoner. So complete was the surprise that only 30 Hessians were killed before the brief **Battle of Trenton** was over. Not a single American was killed.

Washington quickly struck the British again, this time in the **Battle of Princeton,** where he drove two British regiments from the town, with heavy losses. Then he made camp for the winter at Morristown, New Jersey, only about 30 miles (48 kilometers) west of New York.

"The Death of General Mercer at the Battle of Princeton" was painted by John Trumbull in 1789. How did Washington spark his army with the battles of Trenton and Princeton?

Americans Hold Together 165

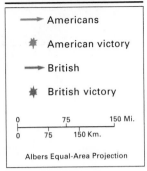

TURNING POINT OF THE WAR, 1776–77

→ Americans

✳ American victory

→ British

✳ British victory

0   75   150 Mi.

0   75   150 Km.

Albers Equal-Area Projection

CANADA

Quebec

Montreal

Fort St. John

MAINE (Part of MA)

Lake Champlain

BURGOYNE

GREEN MTS.

Connecticut R.

St. Lawrence R.

Lake Ontario

NEW YORK

Fort Ticonderoga

Saratoga

ARNOLD

NH

Oriskany

GATES

Albany

MA

Boston

CT

RI

West Point

Hudson R.

PENNSYLVANIA

White Plains

BRITISH FLEET FROM HALIFAX

WASHINGTON

Morristown

Princeton

Trenton

Germantown

New York

Monmouth Court House

Valley Forge

Brandywine

CLINTON

Philadelphia

MD

NJ

DE

HOWE

VIRGINIA

Chesapeake Bay

Susquehanna R.

Delaware R.

CANADA

St. Lawrence R.

Halifax

ORIGINAL COLONIES

ATLANTIC OCEAN

LEARNING FROM MAPS. *The American army spent most of 1776 and 1777 retreating from the British. They won several key victories, however. What American victories are shown on this map? Burgoyne's troops were captured by the victorious Americans at Saratoga. Why was this a geographically important victory for the Americans?*

1777: The Year of Decision

When the snows melted, the war resumed. The British developed a complicated strategy for 1777. General George Clinton would hold New York with a small force while General Howe took the bulk of his troops by sea to Chesapeake Bay in order to attack Philadelphia from the south. At the same time another British army led by General John "Gentleman Johnny" Burgoyne would march down from Canada toward New York.

Howe carried out his part of the plan. He moved slowly, as usual, but effectively. He landed his men in Maryland on the Chesapeake in August. Washington hurried southward as soon as he learned where Howe was. The two armies clashed at Brandywine Creek, southwest of Philadelphia, on September 11.

The Battle of Brandywine near Philadelphia resembled the Battle of Long Island both in the tactics used and the result. Howe cleverly outmaneuvered Washington. He sent part of his force around the American right side and then struck from two directions. The Americans were badly defeated. On September 26 Howe marched into Philadelphia.

In October Washington staged a surprise counterattack. At the Battle of Germantown north of Philadelphia he gave a better account of himself than at Brandywine, but his battle plan was too complicated. A heavy fog led to much confusion. Once more the British held the field when the shooting stopped.

These losses were very discouraging. Nevertheless, at year's end Washington still held his army together. Its will to fight had not been broken. Howe won the battles, but he failed to smash the American army. With the approach of winter, Washington and his men retreated into camp at Valley Forge, northwest of Philadelphia.

The Battle of Saratoga

The British were able to occupy and hold seaport towns and the surrounding countryside because of their powerful navy. However, it was gradually becoming clear that fighting in the interior was much more difficult for them. The fate of General Burgoyne illustrates this point effectively.

Burgoyne was a typical upper-class Englishman of his day—rich, pleasure loving, accustomed to having his own way. He was, however, more talented than most. He wrote a number of plays that were good enough to be performed in London. He had fought with distinction in Europe during the Seven Years' War. Ordinary soldiers loved him because he treated them as human beings, not as the scum of the earth.

Yet like General Braddock in the 1750s, Burgoyne did not adapt well to American conditions. He set out from Montreal in June 1777 with 6,000 regulars (half of them German mercenaries), a small force of Loyalists, and about 500 Indians. He also brought with him 138 pieces of artillery and an enormous amount of baggage of every sort. Burgoyne's personal baggage alone filled 30 carts.

A large crowd of peddlers and other civilians tagged along behind the army. Some of the officers brought their wives. Baron von Riedesel, commander of the German troops, and Frederika von Riedesel even brought their three small children, the youngest only a year old.

This cumbersome army sailed smoothly enough down Lake Champlain and recaptured Fort Ticonderoga on July 5. But thereafter, moving overland, the advance slowed to a crawl. The retreating Americans chopped down huge trees to block the forest paths. It took the army 24 days to reach Fort Edward, 23 miles (about 37 kilometers) south of Ticonderoga.

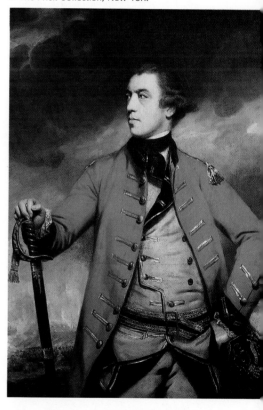

The English general John Burgoyne is the subject of this splendid oil portrait by Sir Joshua Reynolds. What five words would you choose to describe General Burgoyne after studying this painting?

This bronze medal was ordered struck by Congress to commemorate the surrender of the British at Saratoga. General Burgoyne is handing his sword to General Horatio Gates.

With every passing day more and more American militia gathered. Like the Minute Men at Concord, these were local farmers who picked up their rifles or muskets and gathered to defend their own districts. Burgoyne noted with dismay: "Wherever the King's forces point, three or four thousand [militiamen] assemble in twenty-four hours."

The commander of the regular troops facing Burgoyne was General Horatio Gates. Gates was very cautious. He avoided a major battle as long as possible. On September 19 the two armies finally clashed in the **Battle of Saratoga,** or Freeman's Farm. American units led by Colonel Daniel Morgan and Major General Benedict Arnold, dealt Burgoyne's army a smashing blow. The British advance was stopped. On October 7 Burgoyne was defeated again.

By this time Burgoyne's army was surrounded. Supplies were running low. On October 17 he surrendered at Saratoga. The Americans took 5,700 prisoners. British losses were heavy.

The Alliance with France

The Battle of Saratoga was probably the great victory that won the United States independence. It greatly increased the Americans' confidence.

But the most important result of the Battle of Saratoga occurred in France. When the news of the victory reached Paris, the French officially recognized the government of the United States. By March Benjamin Franklin and two other American diplomats had negotiated a **treaty of alliance.** The proposed alliance discouraged the British so much that they offered to never again try to tax the colonists if they would lay down their arms. This offer was refused. In the treaty France promised to fight to protect the United States. So France declared war on Great Britain.

The French were eager to see the Americans win their independence because that would weaken their enemy, Great Britain. They had been helping the Americans with loans and war supplies from the start of the revolution. Many French officers had already come to America to fight. The best-known of these was the youthful Marquis de Lafayette, who was only 19 when he joined the American army. Now the French army and navy joined in the conflict directly. By the summer of 1778, a French fleet was operating in American waters. In 1780 an army of 5,000 men under Count Rochambeau landed in Rhode Island.

Spain entered the war against England in 1779. Bernardo de Gálvez, governor of Louisiana, sent gunpowder, guns, food, medicine, and money to the rebelling colonies. Later he captured the British fort at Pensacola. Spanish-born Jorge Farragut fought in both the Continental navy and army. Two Polish officers—Casimir Pulaski and Thaddeus Kosciusko—also served with great distinction.

Return to the Preview & Review on page 164.

The Valley Forge Historical Society

6. THE WAR IS WON

Winter at Valley Forge

We can see now that the American victory was almost certain after the Battle of Saratoga. This happy future was much less clear to Washington and the weary soldiers wintering at **Valley Forge.** Supplies of food and especially of clothing were scarce. According to Washington himself, 2,898 of his men were barefoot in December 1777. Many were ill.

The problem was bad organization and not enough horses and wagons to bring supplies to Valley Forge. Nearby, civilians had plenty to eat and adequate clothing. Knowing this made Washington boil with rage and discouraged his men. Thousands deserted.

The soldiers who did not leave were strengthened by their suffering. They also benefited from the training they got from a German volunteer, General Friedrich von Steuben. Von Steuben was something of a faker. He claimed to be a baron and a former lieutenant general in the army of King Frederick of Prussia. Actually, he had no noble title, and he had been only a captain in the Prussian army. He was perfectly sincere, however, in his wish to help the American cause. And he was an excellent soldier.

Von Steuben taught Washington's veterans how to maneuver in the field and how to use bayonets properly. He was a stern taskmaster who made the soldiers drill for hours. He lost his temper frequently, and since he knew very little English, he tended to shout at the Americans in a mixture of German and French, substituting curses for clear instructions. Nevertheless, the Americans came to love him. He worked himself as hard as the men he was drilling. His devotion

Preview & Review

Use these questions to guide your reading. Answer the questions after completing Section 6.
Understanding Issues, Events, & Ideas. Use the following words to report on the American victory in the Revolutionary War: Valley Forge; Battle of Monmouth Court House; King's Mountain; Battles of Cowpens and Guilford Court House; Vincennes; Yorktown.
1. Why were the conditions at Valley Forge so bad?
2. What were the American tactics in the war in the South?
3. In what area did George Rogers Clark fight the British?
4. Why was Washington able to defeat the British at Yorktown?
Thinking Critically. 1. In your opinion, what were the three most important reasons for the Americans' victory in the Revolutionary War? Explain. 2. Who do you think is the most important American hero of the Revolutionary period? Why?

"The March to Valley Forge, December 16th," above, was painted by William B. Trego. Imagine that you are riding next to General Washington on his white horse. What are your impressions of the troops who pass before you?

This fine engraving shows Francis Marion, the "Swamp Fox," crossing the Pee Dee River in South Carolina. How can you tell that his soldiers are "irregulars"?

to them was obvious. Despite his foreign background, he knew how to manage the Americans. And he understood something of American democracy. He said:

> In Prussia, when an officer says, 'Do this,' the soldiers do it without argument. In America, I am obliged to say, 'This is the reason why you ought to do that.'

The War in the South and West

In May 1778 General Howe resigned his command. General Henry Clinton replaced him. Clinton marched the British army in Philadelphia back to New York. The Americans then put General Benedict Arnold, one of the heroes of the Battle of Saratoga, in charge of the American troops in reoccupied Philadelphia. While Clinton's troops were marching across New Jersey, Washington attacked. His victory at the **Battle of Monmouth Court House** was a small one, but it gave a valuable boost to American morale.

Thereafter the British concentrated their efforts in the South, where they hoped to find many Loyalists. Using the navy effectively, the British captured Savannah, Georgia, in 1778. In 1780 another naval expedition led by Clinton captured Charleston, South Carolina. Clinton took as many Americans prisoner in Charleston as the British had lost at Saratoga. He then returned to his base at New York, leaving General Charles Cornwallis in charge of the southern campaign. Later in 1780 Cornwallis routed an American army under the command of General Horatio Gates at Camden, South Carolina.

The British in the South counted on local support, but they soon found guerrilla bands picking away at them. These irregular soldiers, led by men like Francis Marion, the "Swamp Fox," and Thomas Sumter, continued to resist the Redcoats. Soon Cornwallis was in serious trouble in the South.

After Gates' defeat at Camden, Nathanael Greene was put in charge of the American forces in the South. General Greene used hit-and-run tactics against Cornwallis with brilliant results. A band of militiamen had already destroyed a Tory force at **King's Mountain** in South Carolina. Now Greene divided his forces and staged a series of scattered raids. At the **Battle of Cowpens** in South Carolina one flank soundly defeated the British. They then rejoined Greene and attacked Cornwallis' army at **Guilford Court House,** forcing the British to retreat to the coast. There Cornwallis would be supported and

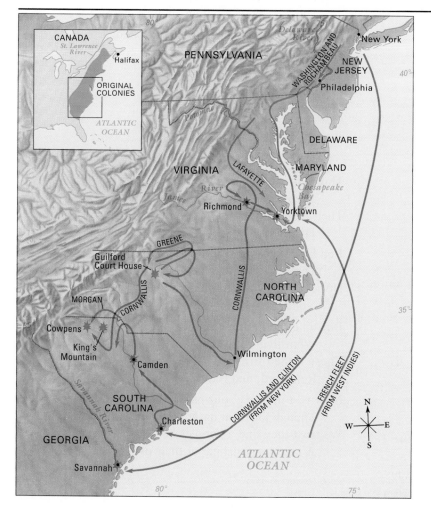

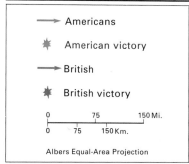

THE WAR IN THE SOUTH, 1778–81

→ Americans

✴ American victory

→ British

✴ British victory

0   75   150 Mi.
0   75   150 Km.

Albers Equal-Area Projection

LEARNING FROM MAPS. *The British relied on the navy to move the army into strategic position. How is this illustrated on the map? Note the locations of the British and American victories. Do you think the American army intentionally avoided major confrontations along the coast? Why?*

The War Is Won   171

Philip Freneau served as a soldier in the American Revolution. He was one of the first professional American journalists, and a great supporter of the Revolution and of the Jeffersonian democracy.

supplied by the Royal Navy. But soon most of Georgia and the Carolinas were back in American hands.

The Patriots won control of the interior of South Carolina with the Battle of Eutaw Springs. In this battle, which was the last major encounter in South Carolina, the colonists attacked the British, who fell back to Charleston. The American poet Philip Freneau memorialized the sacrifices of the Americans who fought the battle in his poem, ''To the Memory of the Brave Americans.'' Freneau wrote:

Under General Greene, in South Carolina, who Fell in the Action of September 8, 1781.

> At Eutaw Springs the valiant died;
>   Their limbs with dust are covered o'er—
> Weep on, ye springs, your tearful tide;
>   How many heroes are no more!
>
> If in this wreck of ruin, they
>   Can yet be thought to claim a tear,
> O smite your gentle breast, and say
>   The friends of freedom slumber here!
>
> Thou, who shalt trace this bloody plain,
>   If goodness rules thy generous breast,
> Sigh for the wasted rural reign;
>   Sigh for the shepherds, sunk to rest!
>
> Stranger, their humble graves adorn;
>   You too may fall, and ask a tear;
> 'Tis not the beauty of the morn
>   That proves the evening shall be clear.—
>
> They saw their injured country's woe;
>   The flaming town, the wasted field;
> Then rushed to meet the insulting foe;
>   They took the spear—but left the shield.
>
> Led by thy conquering genius, Greene,
>   The Britons they compelled to fly;
> None distant viewed the fatal plain,
>   None grieved, in such a cause to die—
>
> But, like the Parthian, famed of old,
>   Who, flying still their arrows threw,
> These routed Britons, full as bold,
>   Retreated, and retreating slew.
>
> Now rest in peace, our patriot band;
>   Though far from nature's limits thrown,
> We trust they find a happier land,
>   A brighter sunshine of their own.[1]

[1]From *American Literature Survey: Colonial and Federal to 1800,* edited by Milton Stern and Seymour Gross

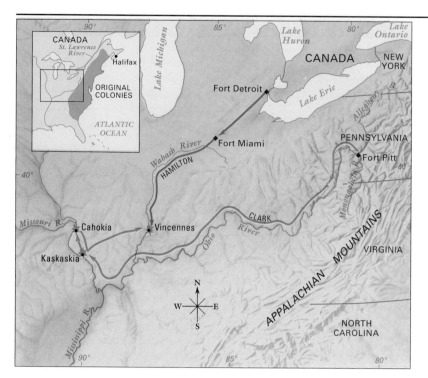

Americans

American victory

British

0   100   200 Mi.

0   100   200 Km.

Albers Equal-Area Projection

LEARNING FROM MAPS. *As the map shows, few battles of the Revolutionary War were fought west of the Appalachian Mountains. Why? Most of Clark's military expenses were financed by the state of Virginia. Why do you think Virginia was interested in insuring American control of the Ohio Valley?*

The Americans' fortunes also improved in the West, while fighting in the North was at a standstill. George Rogers Clark, financed by Virginia's governor, Patrick Henry, swept into Illinois country. There he won several battles against the British and their Indian allies. He took **Vincennes,** on the Wabash River, in 1778 and recaptured it in February 1779. Clark built Fort Nelson, now Louisville, Kentucky, and planned a campaign to march upon Fort Detroit. But he was unable to proceed when adequate supplies did not arrive from Virginia.

In the North there was treason. Benedict Arnold had persuaded Washington to make him commander of the key American fort at West Point, on the Hudson River north of New York City. He had secretly agreed to turn over the fort to the British for a large sum of money and a commission in their army.

Fortunately for the United States, a British officer, Major John André, was captured while returning from West Point with papers confirming Arnold's treachery. André was hanged as a spy, but Arnold escaped to New York and later became a British general.

In May 1781 Cornwallis marched north into Virginia, hoping for a decisive victory. Again local militiamen and regular army units began to pick away at his army. Again he retreated to the sea. This time he fortified himself at **Yorktown,** a small tobacco port located where the York River flows into Chesapeake Bay. An American force under General Lafayette took up positions outside the town to keep the British under observation.

George Rogers Clark, the conqueror of the Northwest, was painted by James Barton Longacre.

The War Is Won   173

In the flush of victory Americans celebrated their first national heroes. Benjamin Franklin had been widely known for his experiments with electricity and for *Poor Richard's Almanack.* Now he was admired everywhere for his staunch support of the Revolution.

Thomas Jefferson had also become a national hero by the 1780s. American pride in the Declaration of Independence swelled when the Revolution succeeded and the courage of the document's signers could be fully appreciated.

The greatest hero of all was Washington. "The Father of His Country" was, by all accounts, a stern man who stood alone and said little. Yet all Americans admired his personal sacrifice and his careful use of power. One admirer called him "no harum

"John Paul Jones" by Charles Willson Peale.

Starum ranting Swearing fellow but Sober, steady, and calm."

A Scot, John Paul Jones, was revered as the founder of the strong United States naval tra-

dition. In his little ship *Bonhomme Richard* ("Poor Richard," named in admiration of Franklin), Jones came upon a British convoy led by the powerful *Serapis.* He lashed his ship to the *Serapis* and fought from sunset into moonlight until both ships were seriously damaged. Still Jones refused to surrender. "I have not yet begun to fight," he proclaimed. Finally the British vessel surrendered and was boarded by Jones and his crew.

All men and women who had been brave enough to take up arms against the British were now heroes. One, Andrew Jackson, was only a boy of nine when war broke out. For refusing to black the boots of a British officer, he was struck sharply in the face with the flat of a sword. He carried the scar to his grave.

Surrender at Yorktown

Now came the final act of the long struggle. Washington had originally intended to assault New York City with the support of the French army that Count Rochambeau had brought to Rhode Island. Rochambeau urged a joint attack on Yorktown instead. Washington finally agreed. Leaving a small force to trick General Clinton into thinking the Americans intended to attack New York, the combined American and French armies marched swiftly south.

At the same time two French fleets, one from the West Indies, the other from Newport, Rhode Island, came together off Yorktown. The squadron from the West Indies landed 3,300 more French soldiers outside the Yorktown defenses. After Washington and Rochambeau arrived in early September 1781, there were 16,000 allied soldiers and 36 warships in position. Cornwallis had only 8,000 men, and many of them were ill. When a British fleet sought to relieve him, it was driven off by the French. Cornwallis' army was doomed.

Washington's grasp of the lay of the land at Yorktown was excellent. The Americans had pinned the British on a swampy peninsula with their backs to the Chesapeake Bay. On October 9 Washington began to batter Cornwallis' fortifications with heavy artillery.

The assault was under the able direction of French gunners and of the same Henry Knox, now a general, who had brought the guns of Fort Ticonderoga to Boston to make possible Washington's first victory back in 1776. Cornwallis sent off a last message to General Clinton: "If you cannot relieve me very soon, you must be prepared to hear the Worst." No relief arrived.

Cornwallis had to surrender on October 19. His men marched out, their flags furled, while the band played "The World Turned Upside Down." The French troops, in beautiful white uniforms, were lined up on the right. On the left were the Americans. Only the front ranks wore the buff and blue uniform of the Continental Army. The rest were, in the words of General von Steuben, "a ragged set of fellows." As the British soldiers threw down their arms angrily in formal surrender, Lafayette told the band to strike up "Yankee Doodle." This dramatic scene took place on a field no more than 10 miles (16 kilometers) from Jamestown, where the first English settlers had landed 174 years before.

The last battle was over. The British still had control of New York City, Charleston, Savannah, and some frontier posts, but they no longer had the will to fight. Public opposition in England to the war was growing, and British Whigs were gaining strength against the Tories and the King. In March Parliament voted to give up "further prosecution of offensive war on the Continent of North America." A few days later Lord North resigned as prime minister. Although a peace treaty was still to be signed, the Revolutionary War had been won. 🖹

For Cornwallis' British troops this is "The World Turned Upside Down" as they surrender to the Americans at Yorktown in October 1781. At the center is General Benjamin Lincoln leading the Redcoats past the Americans, in buff and blue, on the right. General Washington is in front of the flag. On the left are French allies, in buff, with Polish and Prussian fighters behind. John Trumbull painted this oil. How do you suppose regular American soldiers looked at the time of the surrender?

Return to the Preview & Review on page 169.

The War Is Won   175

LINKING HISTORY & GEOGRAPHY

CROSSING THE ATLANTIC

By the 15th century Europe had two groups of sea powers. One, the Italian city states, located on the relatively calm and sheltered waters of the Mediterranean Sea, traded with China, the Indies, and India. The second group, the Hanse Towns, which later became the Hanseatic League, sailed the North and Baltic seas, carrying goods from Russia and Siberia to the towns of northern Europe. Both groups developed from unique geographic environments—the linking of great overland trade routes from the east with the indented coastlines of tideless seas. Captains and crews sailed in comparative security, knowing land lay not too far away.

Looking to the Atlantic

1. Why did the other nations of Europe begin to look for their own trade routes?

The merchants in Italy and the Hanse Towns charged other Europeans very high prices for the goods they traded. Because these merchants held monopolies, other nations had difficulty establishing their own trade routes. Slowly the leaders of the other European nations began to realize that their only realistic alternative was to look westward—to the Atlantic Ocean. But that meant facing a landless horizon and the vastness of an uncharted watery wilderness.

It is interesting to note that only those nations that actually faced the Atlantic—Spain, Portugal, England, France, and the Netherlands—actually met the challenge of the Atlantic (as Norway had centuries earlier). They, and they alone, took the knowledge of navigation, mapmaking, and shipbuilding and applied it to a much sterner test of seamanship in the open Atlantic Ocean.

Geography of the Ocean Frontier

2. What manner of watery frontier did these early sailors find as they ventured westward?

We can get some sense of what lay ahead by looking at a map or globe. As you can see, the Atlantic covers one fifth of the earth's surface. And you can see it occupies a unique space on Planet Earth, separating Europe and Africa from the Americas and creating a barrier—or, for some, a highway—between those continents.

A map or globe shows you, too, that the Atlantic is a long body of water that resembles an hourglass. The widest part of the ocean, spanning some 4,150 miles (6,640 kilometers), stretches between Spain and Florida. It was precisely this expanse crossed by Columbus in 1492! The narrowest part lies between Norway and Greenland in the north. Here the distance is a mere 930 miles. Across this narrowest section, with islands scattered like stepping stones, the Vikings sailed around the year 1000.

Mixing the Waters of the Atlantic

3. How else is the Atlantic's geography unique?

Perhaps the most amazing aspect of the Atlantic's geography is its huge *drainage basin,* the area of land whose rivers flow into an ocean. Most of the world's great rivers empty their waters into the Atlantic.

In North America the Atlantic basin stretches all the way to the Rocky Mountains. There, in western North America, the many tributaries of the mighty Mississippi begin. At mid-continent they join to form the river that drains two thirds of the continent toward the Gulf of Mexico, an arm of the Atlantic.

In South America the Atlantic's drainage area extends across the continent to the soaring Andes Mountains. Among those towering peaks the world's greatest flow of water begins its journey to the Atlantic. So great is this rush of water—carried by the Amazon River—that the volume of water is greater than that of the Mississippi, Nile, and Yangzte rivers *combined.*

The Atlantic also gathers much of the water from Africa. Waters of the Nile, Congo, and Niger rivers eventually reach the Atlantic. The Atlantic also claims the Rhine and the other great rivers of Western Europe as well as many of those of Eastern Europe and central Russia.

The immense size of the drainage basin opened the way to yet-to-be-explored lands. In North America, the Gulf of St. Lawrence, Hudson Bay, and Gulf of Mexico carried sailing vessels from Europe to the continent's edge. Rivers carried explorers to its very heart.

Sailing West

4. What propelled the early sailing ships from Europe to the Americas?

One other aspect of the Atlantic's geography

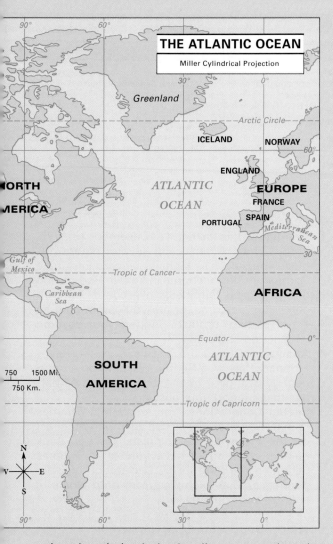

THE ATLANTIC OCEAN
Miller Cylindrical Projection

Greenland

Arctic Circle

ICELAND   NORWAY

ENGLAND

NORTH
AMERICA

ATLANTIC
OCEAN

EUROPE
FRANCE
SPAIN
PORTUGAL
Mediterranean
Sea

Gulf of
Mexico

Tropic of Cancer

Caribbean
Sea

AFRICA

Equator

SOUTH
AMERICA

ATLANTIC
OCEAN

750   1500 Mi.
750 Km.

Tropic of Capricorn

N
W—E
S

areas of lower pressure. The winds along the African coast result from air flowing from zones of high pressure near 30°N to a low-pressure zone always found near the equator.

Of course, if the world did not turn on its axis, the air would simply flow from north to south in the Northern Hemisphere and south to north in the Southern Hemisphere. The earth's rotation causes the winds to deflect, or bend.

These wonderful winds, among the steadiest and most reliable on earth, soon became invaluable for ships sailing westward. Within a remarkably short period of time they were known to sailors everywhere as the *trade winds.*

The Return Trip

5. Once in the Americas, how did people return to Europe?

Just as the trade winds carried ships westward, the Gulf Stream helped propel them back to Europe. The Gulf Stream begins in the eastern portions of the Gulf of Mexico. It flows northward along the eastern seaboard of the United States. At about 40°N the current swings eastward across the Atlantic toward the British Isles. It is one of the strongest and most consistent ocean currents. Coupled with the northeast trade winds, it provided knowledgeable navigators with the means to complete roundtrip voyages between Europe and the New World.

The geography of the Atlantic made it ideal as a pathway of discovery. Winds and currents moved the sailing ships on just the right paths. Plentiful bays and gulfs, fed by huge rivers, provided entrances into continents. Soon the forbiddingly vast waters of the Atlantic became one of the most heavily traveled routes in the world.

APPLYING YOUR KNOWLEDGE

Your class will work in three groups to create a profile map of the Atlantic Ocean. One group should map the major ocean currents. Another should identify and label on a map the major rivers eventually draining into the Atlantic. The third group should measure distances across the ocean from various spots (such as Virginia) in North America to Norway, Spain, and England. You will then combine the groups' findings to create your profile map of the Atlantic.

played a vital role in the discovery and exploration of the New World. Winds and ocean currents helped transport people and cargoes from Europe to the Americas and back.

As you can see from the map on page 24, Columbus first headed south to the Canary Islands before turning westward. This was no accident. Early explorers voyaging southward along Africa's west coast found strong and steady winds from the northeast between 30° and 5° north of the equator. These winds carried the sleek sailing ships ever westward.

What causes these winds? Air always flows from centers of high atmospheric pressure to

CHAPTER 5 REVIEW

1773	1775	1777

1773
Parliament passes Tea Act
★
Boston Tea Party

1774
Intolerable Acts
★
First Continental Congress

1775
Battles of Lexington and Concord
★
Battle of Bunker Hill
★
Second Continental Congress
★
Washington appointed commander of Continental Army

1776
Common Sense published
★
Declaration of Independence
★
American victory at Trenton

1777
American victory at Princeton
★
Battle of Saratoga
★
Winter at Valley Forge

Chapter Summary

Read the statements below. Choose one and write a paragraph explaining its importance.
1. British economic policies and other attempts to control colonial life angered the colonists.
2. Lexington and Concord were the first battles of the Revolutionary War and ended chances for peaceful settlement.
3. The American Army was small, inexperienced, and ill-equipped to fight the British.
4. Washington's leadership and the cause of freedom helped Americans endure dark days.
5. The Declaration of Independence told the world of America's grievances.
6. Successes at Saratoga and elsewhere in 1777 turned the tide of war in America's favor.
7. Help from France and other Europeans bolstered the colonists.
8. The American victory at Yorktown convinced England to end the war.

Reviewing Chronological Order

Number your paper 1-5. Then study the time line above and place the following events in the order in which they happened by writing the first next to 1, the second next to 2, and so on.
1. The Battle of Saratoga
2. The British surrender at Yorktown
3. The Boston Tea Party
4. Lexington and Concord
5. The Declaration of Independence

Understanding Main Ideas

1. Why were the Committees of Correspondence important?
2. How did Lord North misjudge the other colonies when he punished Massachusetts?
3. Why was the Battle of Saratoga so critical to the American cause.
4. What was the last major battle of the war? Explain the role of the French in this battle.
5. Use your historical imagination to explain what "all men are created equal" meant to the leaders of the American Revolution.

Thinking Critically

1. **Evaluating.** It is the night of December 16, 1773. You, Samuel Adams, and several others disguise yourselves as Mohawks, board East India Company ships anchored in Boston Harbor, and dump English tea chests overboard. Are you committing a crime, or are you committing an act of political protest? Support your position with sound reasoning.
2. **Analyzing.** During the first years of the Revolutionary War, was George Washington a good general or a poor one? Why? Name three battles that support your answer.
3. **Seeing Connections.** You know that Thomas Paine's *Common Sense* had an important effect on the views of the colonists. Do you think Paine's ideas could have influenced Thomas Jefferson's writing in the Declaration of Independence? Cite examples from both works to support your opinion.

Writing About History: Informative

Write your own eyewitness account of the Boston Tea Party, either as a member of the Sons of Liberty or as a captain of one of the tea ships. Use the information in Chapter 5 to help you develop your account. Begin with a draft copy. Write freely. Then be sure to evaluate the content, organization, and style of your draft, taking care to check spelling and punctuation. After making any changes you feel necessary, write out your final copy.

Practicing the Strategy

Review the strategy on page 146.
Tracing Routes on a Map. Study the map on page 166 and answer the following questions.
1. From what city did Washington leave? What two battles did he win?

1778
Treaty with France signed

★
American victories in South and West

1781
British surrender at Yorktown

2. Along what route did British troops travel to reach Saratoga? How can you tell the Americans won?

3. In what general direction did Gates lead his troops from Albany to Saratoga?

4. What aspects of Howe's route are different from those of the other commanders shown on the map?

Using Primary Sources

It remains a mystery who fired the first shots of the revolution at Lexington. Even eyewitness accounts, such as those of militiaman Ebenezer Munroe of Lexington and British commander Colonel Francis Smith, contradict each other. To see how their accounts differ, read the following excerpts. Then answer the questions below.

About seventy of our company had assembled when the British troops appeared. Some of our men went into the meeting house where the town's powder was kept. . . . When the regulars had arrived within eighty or one hundred rods (438 to 547 yards), they . . . halted, charged their guns, and doubled their ranks, and marched up at quick step. Captain Parker ordered his men to stand their ground, and not molest the regulars unless they meddled with us. The British troops came directly in our front. The commanding officer advanced within a few rods of us and exclaimed, "Disperse, you . . . rebels! You dogs, run!—Rush on my boys!" and fired his pistol.

Corporal Ebenezer Munroe, Lexington militia

Our troops advanced toward them, without any intention of injuring them, further than to inquire the reason of their being thus assembled, and if not satisfactory, to have secured their arms; but they in confusion went off, principally to the left—only one of them fired before he went off, and three or four more jumped over a wall and fired from behind it among the soldiers; on which the troops returned it.

Colonel Francis Smith, British Tenth Infantry

1. What evidence in Munroe's account leads you to believe that the British approached the Lexington militia aggressively?

2. According to Colonel Smith's account why did the British troops approach the colonists?

3. Note the contradiction between the two accounts. Which version do you think is closer to the truth? Why do you think so?

Linking History & Geography

In every war geography plays a key role. It helps shape where battles are fought and often influences their outcomes. The Americans' familiarity with their native land was a major factor in their success against the British. Review the map on page 149 and read General Burgoyne's description of the Boston landscape. Then explain how geography helped and hindered each side in the fighting to control Boston.

Boston is a penninsula, joined to the main land only by a narrow neck. . . . Arms of the sea and the harbor surround the rest. . . . On one of these arms, to the north is Charlestown and over it is a large hill (Breed's Hill). . . . To the south is an even larger scope of land, containing three hils, joining also to the main by a tongue of land and called Dorchester Neck. The heights . . . north and south . . . command the town.

Enriching Your Study of History

1. **Individual Project.** Make a recruiting poster for Washington's army. Make up a slogan for your poster. (A slogan is a short phrase that catches people's attention and advertises a group's purpose.) Display your poster.

2. **Cooperative Project.** Prepare with your classmates a map of the major battles of the Revolutionary War. Make your map large enough to display in the classroom. Decide whether or not you will show troop movements and how you will distinguish on your map between American forces and British forces.

Chapter 5 Review 179

Creating the United States

Yorktown was the last battle of the Revolutionary War. Great Britain gave up its thirteen American colonies, and the fighting ended. But the Battle of Yorktown did not end the American Revolution that had begun in the early 1770s. Ending the Revolution was something only the Americans could do. The British had tried to stop the Revolution by force. When they failed, the Revolution went forward. In other words, there was more to the Revolution than the war. Breaking free from British control did not answer this question: What kind of government shall America have instead? Nor did it answer these questions: What kind of society should the people of America create? What kind of economic system?

1. SELF-GOVERNMENT

A Central Government

The most obvious task facing Americans after the war was creating a new system of government. This task had two parts. One was to change the governments of the individual colonies into governments that were independent of England. The other was to find a substitute for the British colonial system—that is, to establish a new central government that could deal with common problems and advance the common interests of the new independent governments. Several political and intellectual traditions helped shape these governments. Some of these traditions were anchored in English history. In 1215, for example, English nobles had forced King John to sign the Magna Carta, which limited the power of the king and protected the liberties of the nobles. The document also dealt with the rights of the ordinary people. It established the principle that the king could not levy taxes without the consent of the Great Council, a body of nobles and church leaders who advised the king. It guaranteed an accused person a trial by a jury of peers, or equals. The Magna Carta provided the basis for establishing parliamentary democracy in England and later in the United States. American leaders also looked to the traditions of parliamentary government in England and to the English Bill of

Preview & Review

Use these questions to guide your reading. Answer the questions after completing Section 1.
Understanding Issues, Events, & Ideas. Use the following words in discussing plans to govern the new nation: constitution, legislature, executive, court, Bill of Rights, conservative, public servant.
1. What two tasks lay before the Americans who were creating a new system of government?
2. Why did the state constitutions give legislatures power?
3. Why was the creation of the state constitutions the most significant event of the Revolution?
4. In what ways was the Second Continental Congress the first central government of the United States?
Thinking Critically. Imagine that you are a state governor at the time a new state constitution has been written. What powers do you wish to be granted?

Rights of 1689, which declared that the monarch could not proclaim or suspend any law, impose any tax, or maintain an army in peacetime without Parliament's consent.

The Enlightenment (see page 98), with its emphasis on reason and the rule of law, also influenced American leaders. Many Americans believed, as Bacon, Newton, and other political philosophers had, in an orderly government based on the consent of the governed.

Other traditions rested on colonial practices. The Mayflower Compact (see page 54), for example, had established the people, not the government, as the ultimate source of authority. And the tradition that the people should play a major role in making and agreeing to laws had long been practiced in New England town meetings and the Virginia House of Burgesses.

Many Americans looked back even further to the democratic ideals of Greek and Roman governments and to the moral responsibilities taught by the early Jewish and Christian writers of the Bible.

All of these traditions, then, influenced Americans as they took the first steps toward forming lasting governments for the young nation. The first step was to create the states. The second was to create the United States. The first step was more important in those days because the state governments affected the lives of the people much more than the central government. The second step was more difficult because it meant deciding what power the United States should have over the separate states that made it up.

Americans enjoyed the engravings of William and Thomas Birch, particularly those of Philadelphia, where revolutionary ideas for self government were put forth. This view is of the Arch Street Ferry.

Self-Government 181

State Governments

Changing a colony into a state meant getting rid of all British controls on local government and then deciding what, if any, new controls should be substituted. The original colonial charters had been grants of power by the king. In place of these royal charters, the people of the states substituted **constitutions.** These constitutions were written descriptions of the system of government the people wanted and of the powers that each part of the government was to have.

The constitutions were all more or less alike, although each state made its own. They divided government into three parts: an elected **legislature,** where proposed laws were to be debated and either passed or rejected; an **executive,** who was to carry out the laws and manage the day-to-day operations of the government; and a system of **courts,** where the laws could be enforced.

The state legislatures replaced the colonial assemblies. The assemblies had always been the part of the colonial governments most influenced by public opinion. They had become centers of popular opposition to British control. Naturally the new constitutions gave the legislatures a great deal of power.

On the other hand, state governors were given very little power by the constitutions. They lost the right to dismiss the legislatures and the power to keep a particular legislature in office for years without its members having to stand for reelection. The powers to declare war, to conduct foreign relations, and to appoint government officials were generally assigned to the legislatures, not to the governors. Governors, in other words, were intended to be mere administrators, not rulers or even policy makers. This change was a natural result of the widespread resentment of the way colonial governors had tried to dominate the assemblies.

One state, Pennsylvania, decided not to have a governor at all. The work usually done by a governor was to be done by a supreme executive council of 12 persons elected by the people. Another state, Virginia, dealt with the problem of controlling the governor by having the legislature elect him. Even with this control the Virginia constitution went on to order that the governor's salary be "adequate *but moderate.*"

The powers of state judges were also limited by the constitutions. Even the legislatures were subject to strict checks. They were increased in size so that individual representatives would have less power. Terms of office were usually only one year, kept short so that voters could quickly get rid of representatives whose actions they disapproved of. Most of the constitutions also contained **Bills of Rights,** lists of what the state governments could *not* do and liberties that the people could not be deprived of. The troubles that led to the Revolution had made Americans suspicious of *all* government.

Some of the constitutions were more **conservative,** or less likely to encourage change. Some made greater changes in the colonial patterns. Qualifications for voting varied. The Pennsylvania constitution gave the right to vote to all adult free men who paid taxes. In South Carolina property qualifications for voting were kept high, and a person running for office needed a considerable fortune.

What was common to all constitutions and what made them all fundamentally democratic was that the people were establishing the rules by which political life was to be organized and run. The constitutions were contracts, written legal agreements. They demonstrated that governments existed to do what the people wanted them to do, but no more. They made government officials **public servants,** not the public's masters. It was a "government of law, not men."

The creation of these constitutions also proved that people could change their government peacefully. The American states were created in an orderly, legal manner. Making constitutions caused hot debates and sharp arguments, but there was no rioting and bloodshed, no use of any kind of force. It was particularly remarkable that governments could be changed in this peaceful and orderly way even while the people were fighting a war for survival. The creation of the state constitutions was the most significant event of the Revolution.

Representing the People

The new governments did not try to make radical changes. Many people worried about the government being controlled by a few "aristocrats." By aristocrats they meant the rich and socially prominent people of their communities. Other groups feared control by "the mob," meaning the artisans and manual laborers of the towns and other relatively poor people who owned little or no property. Since the great majority of the people were neither "aristocrats" nor members of "the mob," most of the constitutions tried to protect the owners of property and at the same time to prevent these well-to-do citizens from using their wealth and influence to take advantage of the poor. The result was usually to keep things more or less as they had been in colonial times.

In some cases the constitutions were written by special assemblies called conventions elected by the voters specifically for that purpose. This method made sure that the ideas and intentions of those who prepared the constitutions were known and approved of in advance. The convention system was one of the most original political ideas to come out of the Revolution.

Most of the new governments finally gave their western districts fairer representation in the state legislatures. Many did away with state support for one particular region. The constitutions did not attempt, however, to do away with slavery.

The high ideals of the times had led many owners to free their slaves, but they did so as individuals, not in response to state law.

Point of View

An English writer whose books take us backward *and* forward in time made this observation about the American Revolution.

"From the point of view of human history, the way in which the Thirteen States became independent is of far less importance than the fact that they did become independent. And with the establishment of their independence came a new sort of community into the world. It was like something coming out of an egg. . . . It had no dukes, princes, counts, nor any sort of title-bearers claiming to ascendancy or respect as a right. Even its unity was as yet a mere unity for defence and freedom. It was in these respects such a clean start in political organization as the world had not seen before. . . ."

From *The Outline of History,* H. G. Wells, 1920

However, in the northern states the legislatures gradually passed laws to free the children of slaves born after a certain date. These laws did not deprive owners of any existing human property. No such laws were passed in the South, where nine of every ten slaves were held. Indeed the Revolution had transformed slavery from a national to a sectional institution. The movement to free slaves was probably caused more by the high cost of maintaining slavery than by a belief in freedom for all inspired by the Declaration of Independence. Even in Virginia, for example, the price of tobacco was very low in the 1770s and 1780s, so owning slaves was not very profitable. When conditions changed, the attitudes of southern slave owners changed also, as we shall see later.

Forming a Central Government

Forming a central government for all the states was much more complicated. In a sense it began with the Plan of Union drafted by Benjamin Franklin at the Albany Congress in 1754. The Stamp Act Congress was another step. So were the colonial committees of correspondence and the informal organizations designed to enforce bans on importing British goods. The First Continental Congress followed. All these attempts at union were responses to the same pressures that led Benjamin Franklin to say, ''we must indeed all hang together, or, most assuredly we shall all hang separately.''

The Second Continental Congress was the first central government, the first true United States. It had a continuing existence, and it ran the country on a day-to-day basis. In the beginning this government had no constitution or specific duties. Then the new state constitutions provided for the regular election of representatives to the Congress, and it was firmly and legally established.

From the start the Congress assumed a great deal of power. It appointed Washington commander in chief of the army and selected other generals. It drafted the Declaration of Independence. It operated a postal service. It sent representatives to foreign countries to obtain support. The diplomats who negotiated the crucial treaty with France after the Battle of Saratoga were assigned by the Continental Congress. The Congress also figured out how much money would be needed each year to carry on the war and perform other government functions. It decided how much each state should contribute to this total. It then sent bills for these amounts, called requisitions, to the states. These were often ignored by the states and rarely paid in full. Congress had to borrow large sums of money to make up the difference. It even printed paper money.

The Congress was a kind of American parliament. But there was no American equivalent to the English king or the prime minister. Instead committees of Congress carried out the functions of the head of state and executive leader of the country.

Return to the Preview & Review on page 180.

2. SETTING NEW BOUNDARIES

The Articles of Confederation

By November 1777 a committee of Congress had drafted a written constitution, the **Articles of Confederation.** This charter made no important change in the way what it called "The United States of America" was already operating. It put in writing the powers that the Continental Congress was already exercising. It stressed the independence of the separate states. The United States was to be only a "league of friendship"—that is, a kind of alliance. The Articles of Confederation provided that each state should have but one vote in Congress. All laws passed by Congress had to be approved by 9 of the 13 states. The Articles themselves could not be amended unless all the states agreed.

Limits were set on the power of the United States, even while the nation was fighting a war for its very survival. This reveals how suspicious people were of a central government. In particular they feared being taxed by the central government. This was obviously a result of their resentment of the Stamp Act and the other taxes that Parliament had tried to make them pay. Thus Section 8 of the Articles of Confederation said Congress should decide how much money had to be raised, but actual tax laws would have to be passed by the state legislatures.

Many states were reluctant to give Congress the authority that the Articles proposed, even though it was severely limited. However,

Preview & Review

Use these questions to guide your reading. Answer the questions after completing Section 2.
Understanding Issues, Events, & Ideas. Use the following terms to describe America's first government: Articles of Confederation, ratify, Peace of Paris, Land Ordinance of 1785, township, Land Ordinance of 1787 or Northwest Ordinance, territory, republican.
1. How did the Articles of Confederation stress the independence of the states?
2. How would new states come into being under the Land Ordinance system?
3. What two limitations did Congress place on states that were formed from territories?
Thinking Critically. You are John Jay negotiating the Treaty of Paris. Before your meeting with Richard Oswald of Britain, decide what you want to achieve for the United States. Then write a list of the points you will try to make.

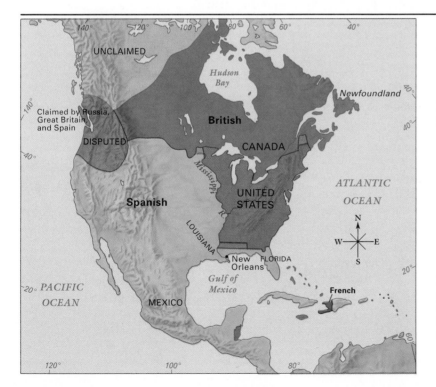

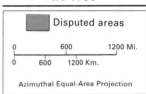

NORTH AMERICA IN 1783

Disputed areas

| 0 | 600 | 1200 Mi. |

| 0 | 600 | 1200 Km. |

Azimuthal Equal-Area Projection

LEARNING FROM MAPS. *The end of the war added a large area to United States control. What problems might this large area cause for the new nation?*

185

after a little more than a year had passed, all the states except Maryland had **ratified** the document. To ratify means to approve. Maryland's objections had nothing to do with the fear of a central government. In fact, it was demanding an increase in the power of Congress.

At issue was the old question of who should control the western lands. Maryland's colonial charter did not include a "sea-to-sea" land grant such as that of Virginia, Massachusetts, and other colonies. Maryland insisted, therefore, that all state claims to lands beyond the Appalachian Mountains be turned over to the United States. Some of the states agreed, but Virginia, which had enormous western claims, refused to do so. Maryland was equally stubborn. Therefore the Articles of Confederation could not go into effect. Finally, in January 1781, Virginia gave up its western claims, and Maryland ratified the Articles.

No one could have known this at the time, but the decision to put all western lands under the control of the central government was one of the most important in the entire history of the United States. The incident is an example of how the give-and-take of political compromise in a democratic system can have unintended results. In this case the results were all good.

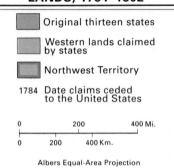

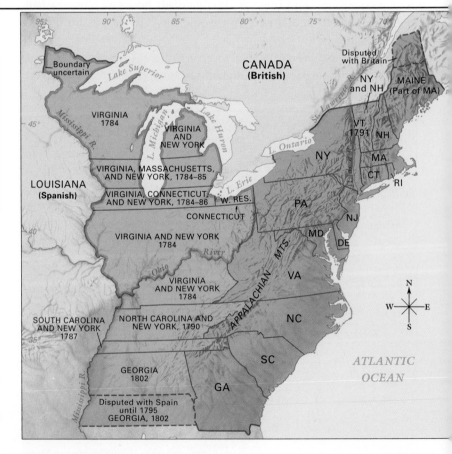

LEARNING FROM MAPS. *As the map shows, many of the original colonies claimed western lands. On what were these claims based? Why was it geographically and politically important for the new nation to settle these western claims immediately?*

Maryland had held out for national control of the western lands for selfish reasons. People in the state seeking to make a fast profit buying and selling land, including the governor himself, hoped to get huge tracts of Indian land in the Ohio Valley. Virginia gave up its claims for equally selfish reasons. Benedict Arnold's raiders had invaded the state in December 1780. Cornwallis was preparing to march his powerful army north from the Carolinas. Virginia was obviously going to need the help of the other states. Giving up its western claims was a kind of goodwill gesture.

The Treaty of Paris

The importance of settling the western claims became fully clear only after a peace treaty was signed with Great Britain officially ending the Revolutionary War. Negotiating the treaty was complicated because the struggle had become another world war. Spain and France were deeply involved, and their interests were not always the same as America's. Spain, for example, wanted to extend its control in America into what are now Mississippi and Alabama. France was not eager to see the United States become too large and powerful either. Both these nations wished to settle many issues with the British. In the complicated negotiations they might sacrifice American goals to advance their own.

Another problem was that the British leaders resented having lost a war to colonists. Their pride was hurt. To have to negotiate with "rebels" was a bitter pill for them to swallow. They might prefer to give more to the French and Spanish to avoid giving in to the Americans.

The peace negotiations took place in Paris in 1782 and 1783. Congress appointed an extremely distinguished delegation consisting of Benjamin Franklin, Thomas Jefferson, John Adams, Henry Laurens, and John Jay. Franklin, Jefferson, and Adams were probably the best-known and most respected Americans of their generation. Henry Laurens had made a fortune as a merchant and planter in South Carolina. He had served as president of the Continental Congress. During the war he had been captured by the British while sailing to Holland on a diplomatic assignment. He had spent more than a year locked up in the Tower of London. Finally he was released in exchange for General Cornwallis, who had surrendered after the Battle of Yorktown.

John Jay, a New York lawyer and drafter of the first New York state constitution, had also been a president of the Continental Congress. Jay came to Paris directly from service as United States minister to Spain. He was a humorless person but extremely intelligent and a shrewd diplomat. Franklin tended to accept the suggestions of the French foreign minister, Count Vergennes. Jay did not trust Vergennes, and he was right not to.

Point of View

The king of England made his separate peace with John Adams after the Revolutionary War with these words.

"I wish you, Sir, to believe, that it may be understood in America, that I have done nothing in the late contest but what I thought myself indispensably bound to do by the duty which I owed my people. I will be very frank with you. I was the last to consent to the separation; but the separation having been made, and having become inevitable, I have always said, as I say now, that I would be the first to meet the friendship of the United States as an independent power."

George III

Fortunately for the United States, Jay did the most important negotiating with the chief British delegate, Richard Oswald. He persuaded Oswald that a strong United States in North America would be less of a threat to England than a strong France or Spain.

In the end Oswald accepted Jay's argument. In November 1782 he signed an agreement that gave the United States nearly everything it hoped for. Besides official recognition of the United States, the British accepted the Great Lakes as the northern boundary of the new nation and the Mississippi River as the western boundary. The southern boundary was set at 31 north latitude. Louisiana remained under Spanish control while the British returned control of Florida and the southern parts of present-day Alabama and Mississippi to Spain.

The British also agreed to remove their armies from American soil "with all convenient speed." In return the Americans promised not to seize any more property from American Loyalists. They would urge the state governments to give back property that had already been taken. Finally, they agreed not to try to prevent British subjects from recovering debts owed them from before the Revolution by Americans. This agreement, the **Peace of Paris,** was officially accepted by both sides in September 1783.

Benjamin West had to leave unfinished his portrait of the delegates to the Paris Peace Convention. The British delegates refused to pose. The Americans, from left, are John Jay, John Adams, Benjamin Franklin, Henry Laurens, and Franklin's grandson, who was secretary to the delegation. As you read this book, think how this picture symbolizes that the quarrel between the United States and Britain was also unfinished.

Courtesy, Cincinnati Historical Society

CINCINNATI-1800.

The Land Ordinances

With peace and with the United States recognized as a member of the family of nations, Congress turned to other problems. One of the most important was the organization of the territory beyond the Appalachian Mountains. As early as 1780 Congress had decided that western territories under its control should be "formed into distinct republican States which shall become members of the Federal Union." After the war was won, Congress put the policy into effect by passing two laws called Land Ordinances.

The first, the **Land Ordinance of 1785**, established a method of selling the land. This method combined the New England idea of carving up the wilderness into large townships and the southern practice of giving land in smaller units to individuals. Unsettled regions were to be surveyed into squares 6 miles (about 10 kilometers) on a side. Half of these **townships** would then be subdivided into 36 sections, each 1 square mile (640 acres, or 256 hectares) in area. The townships and sections were to be sold at public auction. The money would go into the treasury of the United States, but the money from the sale of one section in each township would be given to the local community for the support of its schools. Thus America committed itself early to an educated population as the foundation of a democratic society. In the words of Thomas Jefferson:

“ If a nation expects to be ignorant and free, in a state of civilization, it expects what never was and never will be. ”

The **Land Ordinance of 1787**, better known as the **Northwest Ordinance,** was a plan to govern the lands bounded by the Ohio and Mississippi Rivers and the Great Lakes while they were growing from territory to statehood. The new regions could have been carved up into colonies the way the English had done with their American possessions. But the American people had just fought a war to get

Cincinnati, on the Ohio River, lay in the new Northwest Territory. A. J. Swing painted this view in 1800. Fort Washington is in the background. If you can, compare this early view with a contemporary picture of Cincinnati. Another group might find out the origins of the name Cincinnati and try to decide why it was chosen for this frontier settlement.

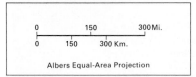

```
0        150        300 Mi.
0    150   300 Km.
```

Albers Equal-Area Projection

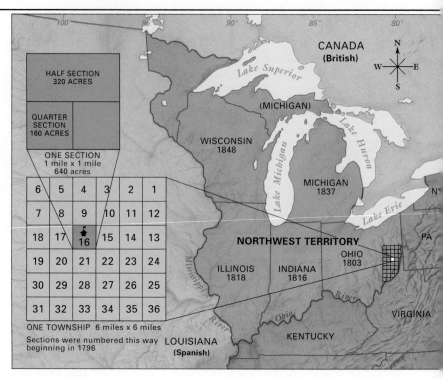

HALF SECTION
320 ACRES

QUARTER
SECTION
160 ACRES

ONE SECTION
1 mile x 1 mile
640 acres

6	5	4	3	2	1
7	8	9	10	11	12
18	17	16	15	14	13
19	20	21	22	23	24
30	29	28	27	26	25
31	32	33	34	35	36

ONE TOWNSHIP 6 miles x 6 miles
Sections were numbered this way
beginning in 1796

CANADA
(British)

Lake Superior

(MICHIGAN)

Lake Huron

WISCONSIN
1848

Lake Michigan

MICHIGAN
1837

Lake Erie

NORTHWEST TERRITORY

PA

OHIO
1803

ILLINOIS
1818

INDIANA
1816

Mississippi River

Ohio River

LOUISIANA
(Spanish)

KENTUCKY

VIRGINIA

LEARNING FROM MAPS. *Compare this map to the one on 186. Note that the ordinance settled claims to lands in the Northwest Territory. What states had claimed lands there? Why were the lands divided into townships and sections?*

rid of colonialism. The Ordinance provided that the Northwest be divided into units called **territories.** Each territory was to be ruled by a governor, a secretary, and three judges appointed by Congress. When 5,000 men of voting age had settled a territory, they could elect a local legislature to deal with their own affairs and a nonvoting delegate to represent their interests in Congress.

When the population of the territory reached 60,000, the voters were to draft a state constitution. After Congress approved this document, the territory would become a state, equal to all the other states. The only limitations placed by Congress were that the state government must be **republican**—that is, its power must lie in representatives elected by the people—and that slavery must be prohibited in all land north of the Ohio River.

Under the Northwest Ordinance, the states of Ohio, Indiana, Illinois, Michigan, and Wisconsin were eventually formed. As the nation expanded westward, the same method was used again and again. Thus the original 13 states became the present 50. This development was not always smooth. Many controversies marked the history of westward expansion. Slavery, for example, was not ruled out in all new territories. Bitter conflicts erupted over this issue, as we shall see.

Without the Land Ordinance system there would surely have been far more bitter conflicts. If Congress had tried to give the West less power than the original states, the United States would almost certainly have become a number of separate nations.

3. PEACETIME TROUBLES

Hard Times

The end of the Revolutionary War was a great blessing. The bloodshed stopped. Normal life could resume. American ships could sail the seas without fear of attack. Merchants could buy and sell in markets such as China that formerly had been closed to them.

However, peace brought out the weaknesses of a government that was only a "league of friendship." When the need to "hang together" to save their necks ended, the states tended to go off in different directions. The great Land Ordinances could never have been passed if Virginia had not given up its western claims. And the Virginians would never have given them up if they had not felt threatened by the coastal invasions of General Cornwallis.

Once the war was over, rivalries between the various states became more troublesome. As every American sports fan knows, members of leagues, however friendly, can compete with one another fiercely! There was a brief economic downturn, or **depression.** War had disrupted both farming and trade. Farmers and merchants experienced hard times. This depression lasted from 1784 to 1786. During the hard times the states were stingier than ever about supplying the money that the United States needed to run its affairs. Each state would pay only for direct benefits and ignore national needs. States like North Carolina and Georgia had frontier districts where there could be fighting with the Indians or possible invasion by Spanish forces. These states were willing to contribute to national defense. South Carolina, geographically protected from danger by its neighbors Georgia and North Carolina, was unwilling to pay its share of national defense.

The Trade Problem

Many Americans were hurt by British regulations of trade with the United States after the war. To the British the United States had become a foreign country. They therefore applied the Navigation Acts to American commerce. They barred American dried and salted fish from the sugar islands in the British West Indies. This hurt New England fishermen. The British required that other American products be carried to the West Indies in British ships. This hurt American merchants and shipbuilders.

British manufacturers had not been able to sell their products in America during the war. Local manufacturing had begun to spring up to supply the needs of the people. With peace restored, the British began to sell goods in America at extremely low prices in order to win back the customers they had lost.

Preview & Review

Use these questions to guide your reading. Answer the questions after completing Section 3.
Understanding Issues, Events, & Ideas. Use the following words to explain the nation's problems under the Articles of Confederation: depression, tariff, Continental dollar, hard money, inflation, unconstitutional, Shays' Rebellion.
1. What were some of the peacetime troubles for the "league of friendship"?
2. How did British restrictions on trade hurt Americans after the war had ended?
3. Why did Congress begin to print paper money? Why did Americans prefer "hard" money to paper money? What was the fate of paper money in Rhode Island?
4. Why did the farmers in western Massachusetts rise up against their government?
Thinking Critically. 1. If you were a storekeeper at the end of the Revolutionary War, would you accept Continental dollars? Why or why not? 2. Of the problems discussed in this section, which do you think was the most difficult? Why?

This practice, called dumping, could have been checked by taxing British imports. High **tariffs,** or taxes on imports, might also have persuaded the British to remove the restrictions on American trade with the West Indies. But the United States government did not have the power under the Articles of Confederation to put tariffs on foreign goods.

One need only recall how Americans felt about the Townshend duty on tea to understand why the states had been unwilling to allow the central government to tax imports. And if one or another individual state taxed British goods, British merchants would simply ship their products to a port in a state that had not passed tariff laws.

Soon many Americans began to suggest that Congress be given the power to tax foreign goods. This could be done only if all the states agreed to change the Articles of Confederation. Despite many attempts this unanimous consent could not be obtained.

The Money Problem

Another power denied the United States under the Articles of Confederation was the power to tax. The system of asking the states for money never worked well, even during the war. To pay its bills Congress printed more and more paper money, called **Continental dollars.** This money fell in value because people had no confidence

In another Philadelphia scene by William and Thomas Birch, we see shipbuilders busily at work on the frigate Philadelphia. *You will read about this famous ship in the war with Tripoli on page 275 of Chapter 8. "Preparation for WAR to defend Commerce," was the engravers' title. What do you think the title means?*

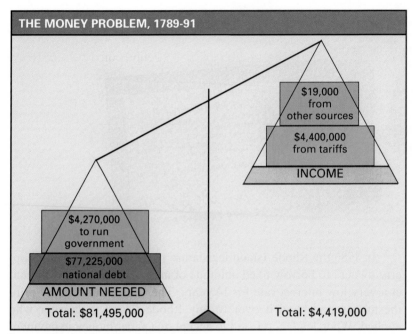

THE MONEY PROBLEM, 1789-91

$19,000 from other sources

$4,400,000 from tariffs

INCOME

$4,270,000 to run government

$77,225,000 national debt

AMOUNT NEEDED

Total: $81,495,000

Total: $4,419,000

Source: *Historical Statistics of the United States*

LEARNING FROM DIAGRAMS. *Part of the money problem for the young nation was the money borrowed during the Revolutionary War. According to the diagram, what was the national debt? In what ways could the United States bring the scales into balance?*

in it. They preferred **hard money**—gold and silver coins that simply as metal were worth the value stamped on them. The lower the real value of the Continental dollar, the more dollars the government had to print. A vicious cycle developed. Soon people were using the expression "not worth a Continental" to mean "worthless."

The state governments did have the power to tax their citizens. They could issue paper money too, and all did so. This increase in the amount of paper money caused **inflation.** Inflation happens when prices rise because the amount of dollars in people's pockets is increased without an increase in the amount of goods available for sale. People lost confidence in state money for the same reason that they distrusted Continentals.

Some states therefore cut down on their paper money issues. To pay their expenses, they increased taxes. Money paid in taxes was money that otherwise might have been spent on goods, so the demand for goods declined. Sellers then had to lower their prices.

Not everyone benefited from lower prices, not even all the people who could buy things more cheaply. People who had borrowed money in the past preferred inflation, which made it easier for them to pay their debts. A farmer who borrowed $10 when wheat was selling for 25 cents a bushel would have to grow 40 bushels to pay his debt. If the price of wheat went up to 50 cents a bushel, he would only have to produce 20 bushels to pay it.

Popular pressure for "cheap" paper money was particularly strong in Rhode Island. That state had been hard hit by the postwar depression. Taxes were a heavy burden on the farm population.

All the states issued paper money. We see that there once was a three dollar bill in Rhode Island and that "to counterfeit is Death" in New Jersey. Study the other bills carefully for their different messages.

In 1786 the Rhode Island legislature passed a bill allowing property owners to borrow fixed amounts of money from the government at a very low interest rate for 14 years. The state would simply print the money and hand it over to any Rhode Island landowner who applied. When lenders refused to accept this paper money in payment of debts, the legislature passed a law allowing the debtors to deposit the money with local judges, who would declare the loan repaid. When storekeepers refused to accept the paper at face value, the legislature passed a law to heavily fine them.

These laws caused business in Rhode Island to come to a standstill. Storekeepers closed their shops rather than sell goods for money they believed worthless. People who were owed money went into hiding. Some fled the state. One jokester suggested that instead of paper the state issue money made of rope. Then people who refused to accept it could be whipped with the rope, and if they continued to refuse, hanged with it.

One tough-minded butcher, John Weeden of Newport, Rhode Island, refused to accept paper money from a customer, John Trevett. When he was fined for refusing, Weeden went to court. In the case of *Trevett v. Weeden,* the Rhode Island Supreme Court refused to make Weeden pay the fine on the grounds, never before used by an American court, that the law was **unconstitutional.** It violated the state constitution. The constitution had not given the legislature the power to pass the law. After the court's decision people refused to accept Rhode Island paper money. It fell rapidly in value.

Shays' Rebellion

Cautious people in all the states had been greatly concerned by the actions of the Rhode Island legislature. Events in Massachusetts soon brought more cause for alarm. There the reverse of the Rhode Island situation existed. The Massachusetts legislators were determined to pay off the large state debt by raising taxes.

The Granger Collection

Daniel Shays brought his protest against taxes to the steps of the state supreme court in Springfield, Massachusetts in 1786. Howard Pyle recreated the drama 100 years later. Study the engraving carefully. What differences do you see between Shays (at the center, top right) and his opponents?

These taxes hit people in the western part of the state very hard. Poor farmers who did not have the money to pay them had their farms seized and sold. Resentment mounted. Crowds gathered to prevent local courts from meeting to condemn the property of debtors so that it could be sold to pay the taxes. In September 1786 a mob marched on Springfield, Massachusetts, to prevent the state supreme court from meeting.

The leader of the protesters was Daniel Shays, a veteran of the Revolutionary War. Shays had fought at Lexington, Bunker Hill, and Saratoga. Although he was uneducated, he had risen to the rank of captain. He was a poor man, much troubled by the determination of the state to prevent inflation and pay off the debt.

After breaking up the meeting of the supreme court, Shays tried to attack the Springfield arsenal in order to get more weapons. However, his force of 1,200 men was routed by militia units. A second battle with the militia in January 1787 had the same result. **Shays' Rebellion** collapsed and Shays fled to Vermont. 🖾

Return to the Preview & Review on page 191.

Use these questions to guide your reading. Answer the questions after completing Section 4.

Understanding Issues, Events, & Ideas. Use the following words to report on the Constitutional Convention: Constitutional Convention, national government, Preamble, nationalism, federalism.

1. What surprising result came from the meeting to revise the Articles of Confederation?
2. Why did the delegates agree so quickly to a new Constitution?
3. What are some of the powers the Constitution gave to the United States government?

Thinking Critically. You are a supporter of having a strong central government. What arguments would you use to sway others to your side?

As a historical record of the signing of the Constitution, this painting is not a very good one. Even the tapestry of the sunburst that hangs behind Washington is fanciful. The actual sunburst was painted on the president's chair. Why do you suppose artists "touch up" history in this way?

4. "WE, THE PEOPLE"

The Constitutional Convention

The financial disturbances in Rhode Island and Massachusetts raised questions in the minds of many conservatives about the future of republican government. Was this what happened when the people were allowed to govern themselves? Would debtors always use their votes to cheat the rich when they had the votes to do it, as in Rhode Island, or resort to force when they did not, as in Massachusetts?

One result of such questions was to make people want to increase the power of the United States government at the expense of the states. Then it would be more difficult for a minority to frighten the majority or for one group to get control of the government.

A stronger central government could maintain order better. It could develop a unified policy for the whole country. Those who favored giving the national government control over foreign trade expected prosperity to result. These objectives—unity, order, and prosperity—made a powerful combination. The time had come to revise the Articles of Confederation.

In September 1786 delegates from five states met at Annapolis, Maryland, to discuss the foreign trade problem. They could do nothing about it unless all the states participated. One of the men present was Alexander Hamilton of New York, a young lawyer who had served on General Washington's staff during the war. He suggested that the group call another meeting. Delegates to this meeting should consider a plan for revising the entire Articles of Confederation.

Congress voted to recommend this proposal to the states. All the legislatures except Rhode Island's sent delegates to the meeting. The sessions began at the Pennsylvania State House in Philadelphia on May 25, 1787.

Independence National Historical Park

The delegates' first decision was to elect George Washington president, or chairman, of the conference. The presence of Washington, who was 55, and of Benjamin Franklin, who was over 80, added prestige to the group. But most of the work was done by much younger people like James Madison of Virginia, who was 36.

The next major step was the decision to try to draft a new constitution. The delegates had been authorized by the state legislatures only to try to patch up the Articles of Confederation. Instead they decided to wipe the slate clean. The meeting then became the **Constitutional Convention.** This was technically illegal. The delegates justified their action by pointing out that they were only recommending changes. The states could always reject their proposals.

The Supreme Law of the Land

On May 30, only five days after beginning their first discussion, the delegates agreed in principle to the most fundamental change. The Articles of Confederation had created a "league of friendship." A league is a kind of treaty signed by basically independent nations. The delegates at Philadelphia proposed a **national government** instead. Gouverneur Morris of Pennsylvania, one of the best speakers at the convention, explained the difference between the two. The "league of friendship" was "a mere compact resting on the good faith of the parties." A national government was "a complete and compulsive" authority, able to enforce its laws directly on the people.

This principle was spelled out in the famous first sentence of the Constitution, the **Preamble.** It reads: "We the *People* of the United States . . . do ordain and establish this Constitution," not "We the states . . ." In Article VI the Constitution further states that it is to be "the supreme Law of the Land." Judges in the states are to be bound by it without regard for anything in the state constitutions. Even the members of the state legislatures were to be required to take an oath to support the United States Constitution.

Such a drastic change was agreed upon so quickly because the delegates were determined to create a more effective central government. Of course, some Americans disapproved of the change. When Sam Adams, who was not a delegate, saw that the Preamble to the Constitution began "We the People" rather than "We the states," he remarked, "As I enter the Building I stumble at the Threshold." Nevertheless, the Philadelphia delegates had been appointed by *state* legislatures. The legislatures would not have selected them if they were not prepared to see the United States made stronger.

Historical imagination helps us to understand another reason why people were ready for a more powerful government. The Revolutionary War had stirred **nationalism,** a feeling of national pride. It had given people their first heroes and their first flags. Thousands of soldiers had traveled far from home and seen other parts of the country. They had fought alongside soldiers from other states. Their horizons had been broadened. Afterwards, they were less likely to think of themselves as Virginians or Pennsylvanians or New Yorkers. They had become first of all Americans.

No one wanted the central government to swallow up the states. The state governments should remain strong and active and independent. However, to the powers already possessed by the United States, the delegates now added several. The most important were the power to tax and the power to regulate trade between the states and between all the states and foreign countries. The Constitution also took away from the separate states the right to coin money and print paper money and the right to tax imports and exports. Such a system of shared powers is known as **federalism.**

Now the United States could raise money to pay its expenses without depending on the state legislatures. Therefore it could avoid printing too much money. The dollar would be worth a dollar, whether in silver or gold coins or in the form of a dollar bill.

Now the United States could place tariffs on imported goods, either to raise money or to regulate foreign trade. These were powers Parliament had tried to exercise before the Revolution. Now Congress was to exercise them.

Moreover, reducing the power of the states to "make" money meant that incidents like Rhode Island's paper money problems could no longer occur. Any future Daniel Shays could be checked by the power of the whole nation if necessary.

The states, however, would still have enough power to manage their local affairs. They could not print money, but they could obtain money by taxing their citizens. The states and the local communities within them could continue to have their own police, and state governors could call up militia units in emergencies.

LEARNING FROM CHARTS. *Federalism is the term used for the sharing of power by the national and state governments. "Delegated powers" are given to the national government. "Reserved powers" are held by the states. Why are delegated powers best held by the national government? Why are reserved powers best held by the states?*

FEDERALISM

Powers Delegated to National Government	Powers shared by National and State Governments	Powers Reserved to States
Declare war		Establish and maintain schools
Maintain armed forces		Establish local goverments
Regulate interstate and foreign trade	Maintain law and order	Conduct elections
Admit new states	Levy taxes	Create corporation laws
Establish post offices	Borrow money	Regulate business within the state
Set standard weights and measures	Charter banks	Make marriage laws
Coin money	Establish courts	Provide for public safety
Establish foreign policy	Provide for public welfare	Assume other powers not delegated to the national government or prohibited to the states
Make all laws necessary and proper for carrying out delegated powers		

THE ARTICLES OF CONFEDERATION AND THE CONSTITUTION	
The Articles	**The Constitution**
THE EXECUTIVE BRANCH	

No executive to administer and enforce legislation
Executive committee to oversee government
  when Congress out of session
Congress with sole authority to govern
	President chosen by electors, who in turn are
	  chosen by the states
	Administers and enforces federal laws

THE LEGISLATIVE BRANCH	
A unicameral legislature (one house) Each state with one vote, regardless of population Nine votes (of original 13) to enact legislation	A bicameral legislature (two houses) Each state having equal representation in the Senate Each state represented according to population in the House of Representatives Simple majority to enact legislation
THE JUDICIAL BRANCH	

No national court system
Congress to establish temporary courts to hear
  cases of piracy
	National court system, headed by the Supreme Court
	Courts to hear cases involving national laws,
	  treaties, the Constitution; cases between states,
	  between citizens of different states, or between
	  a state and citizens of another state

OTHER MATTERS	

Admission to the Confederation by nine votes (of 13)
Amendment of Articles must be unanimous
	Congress to admit new states
	All states must have a republican form
	  of government
	Amendment of the Constitution by two-thirds vote
	  of both houses of Congress or by a national con-
	  vention and ratified by three-fourths of the states

The Preamble of the Constitution neatly summarizes what these changes were meant to accomplish. "We the People" were creating "a more perfect Union" where "Justice" would be assured and order maintained (the founders used the term "domestic Tranquility"). The new system would "provide for the common defense" against foreign enemies too. It would "promote the general Welfare" and secure for Americans and their descendants "the Blessings of Liberty." In other words, the Constitution would supply the nation with the *unity, order,* and *prosperity* lacking under the Articles of Confederation.

The Constitution embodied the ideas and ideals of the European Enlightenment. That governments must be created by and subject to the will of the people was basic to the political philosophies of John Locke and Jean-Jacques Rousseau. Baron de Montesquieu proposed a government of three branches with the powers divided among them. Voltaire contributed the ideals of personal liberties and "unalienable rights" guaranteed by the government. The complete text of the Constitution, with commentary, follows on pages 201–18. 🖅

LEARNING FROM CHARTS.
This chart illustrates the weaknesses of the Articles of Confederation and the parts of the Constitution aimed at avoiding those weaknesses. Which of the weaknesses of the Articles do you think was the most serious? Why?

Return to the Preview & Review on page 196.

THE CONSTITUTION

"Although it had flaws and is still not perfect, our Constitution has allowed a system of government to flourish with freedom and opportunity unequaled anywhere in the world before or since. The United States has no need for walls or laws to keep people from moving elsewhere; and for over 200 years countless millions of people have come here from all parts of the globe, creating a society of pluralism and diversity resting on liberty.

For being an American and enjoying the fruits of our Constitution—the liberty and opportunity that our system of self-government makes possible—is a lifelong adventure. It is a privilege to be an American, and a privilege that carries responsibilities we must all fulfill.[1]"

Warren E. Burger

When the delegates arrived at the Constitutional Convention in Philadelphia, their instructions were to revise the Articles of Confederation. Instead they wrote a brilliant new document that has come to embody the true meaning of democracy. Even more astonishingly, what the framers wrote more than 200 hundred years ago still applies today. The United States is the only country in the world that has been governed under the same basic law for so long. The flexibility of the Constitution has allowed the United States to function smoothly through the past two centuries of tremendous change and growth while it developed into a great world power.

Most of the debates at the convention were about protecting the rights of the states from the powers of the federal government, the small states from large states, the powers of Congress from a strong president, and the rights of minorities from the will of the majority. Even though the Articles of Confederation gave the federal government no real power, the delegates still feared a central government that could become *too* powerful.

To restrict power, the men who wrote the Constitution devised ways to balance each branch of government against the others. They believed that if each branch of government could check, or put limits on, the other branches, then the central government would be efficient without taking away the liberties of the people. The writers also had foresight to provide a means of amending, or changing the Constitution. They made the amendment process part of the Constitution. It was important that the amendment process not be made too easy. If it were, the Constitution would not be a basic law at all. So the amendment process was made diffi-

[1] From *The Constitution: Foundation of Our Freedom* by Warren E. Burger

cult but not impossible. As a result, the Constitution as originally written has been amended only 26 times in 200 years. The parts of the Constitution that are no longer in effect are marked in blue. Some of these have become inactive due to the passage of time. Others have been removed by amendments. As you read these changes, consider why they happened.

The first part of the Constitution consists of seven Articles. The Articles describe the three branches of government, discuss states' rights, and explain the amendment procedure, the concept of "national supremacy," and the ratification process. The second part of the Constitution consists of the 26 amendments.

CONTENTS

THE CONSTITUTION OF THE UNITED STATES OF AMERICA

Preamble

We the People of the United States, in Order to form a more perfect Union, establish Justice, insure domestic Tranquility, provide for the common defense, promote the general Welfare, and secure the Blessings of Liberty to ourselves and our Posterity, do ordain and establish this Constitution for the United States of America.

Preamble
The short and dignified Preamble explains the goals of the new government under the Constitution.

Article I

Section 1. All legislative Powers herein granted shall be vested in a Congress of the United States, which shall consist of a Senate and House of Representatives.

Section 2. The House of Representatives shall be composed of Members chosen every second Year by the People of the several States, and the Electors in each State shall have the Qualifications requisite for Electors of the most numerous Branch of the State Legislature.

No Person shall be a Representative who shall not have attained to the Age of twenty-five Years, and been seven Years a Citizen of the United States, and who shall not, when elected, be an inhabitant of that State in which he shall be chosen.

Representatives and direct Taxes shall be apportioned among the several States which may be included within this Union, according to their respective Numbers, ~~which shall be determined by adding to the whole Number of free Persons, including those bound to Service for a Term of Years, and excluding Indians not taxed, three fifths of all other Persons.~~ The actual Enumeration shall be made within three Years after the first Meeting of the Congress of the United States, and within every subsequent Term of ten Years, in such Manner as they shall by Law direct. The Number of Representatives shall not exceed one for every thirty Thousand, but each State shall have at Least one Representative; ~~and until such enumeration shall be made, the State of New Hampshire shall be entitled to choose three; Massachusetts eight; Rhode Island and Providence Plantations one; Connecticut five; New York six; New Jersey four; Pennsylvania eight; Delaware one; Maryland six; Virginia ten; North Carolina five; South Carolina five; and Georgia three.~~

When vacancies happen in the Representation from any State, the Executive Authority thereof shall issue Writs of Election to fill such Vacancies.

Legislative Branch
Article I explains how the legislative branch, called Congress, is organized. The chief purpose of the legislative branch is to make the laws. Congress is made up of the Senate and the House of Representatives. The decision to have two bodies of government solved a difficult problem during the Constitutional Convention. The large states wanted the membership of Congress to be based entirely on population. The small states wanted every state to have an equal vote. The solution to the problem of how the states were to be represented in Congress was known as the Great Compromise.

The number of members of the House is based on the population of the individual states. Each state has at least one representative. The current size of the House is 435 members, set by Congress in 1929. If each member of the House represented only 30,000 American people, as the Constitution states, the House would have more than 6,000 members.

The House of Representatives shall choose their Speaker and other Officers; and shall have the sole Power of Impeachment.

Section 3. The Senate of the United States shall be composed of two Senators from each State, ~~chosen by the Legislature thereof,~~ for six Years; and each Senator shall have one Vote.

Immediately after they shall be assembled in Consequence of the first Election, they shall be divided as equally as may be into three Classes. The Seats of the Senators of the first Class shall be vacated at the Expiration of the second Year, of the second Class at the Expiration of the fourth Year, and of the third Class at the Expiration of the sixth Year, so that one third may be chosen every second Year; ~~and if Vacancies happen by Resignation, or otherwise, during the Recess of the Legislature of any State, the Executive thereof may make temporary Appointments until the next Meeting of the Legislature, which shall then fill such Vacancies.~~

No Person shall be a Senator who shall not have attained to the Age of thirty Years, and been nine Years a Citizen of the United States, and who shall not, when elected, be an Inhabitant of that State for which he shall be chosen.

The Vice President of the United States shall be President of the Senate, but shall have no Vote, unless they be equally divided.

The Senate shall choose their other Officers, and also a President pro tempore, in the Absence of the Vice President, or when he shall exercise the Office of President of the United States.

The Senate shall have the sole Power to try all Impeachments. When sitting for that Purpose, they shall be on Oath or Affirmation. When the President of the United States is tried, the Chief Justice shall preside: And no Person shall be convicted without the Concurrence of two thirds of the Members present.

Judgment in Cases of Impeachment shall not extend further than to removal from Office, and disqualification to hold and enjoy any Office of honor, Trust or Profit under the United States: but the Party convicted shall nevertheless be liable and subject to Indictment, Trial, Judgment and Punishment, according to Law.

Section 4. The Times, Places and Manner of holding Elections for Senators and Representatives, shall be prescribed in each State by the Legislature thereof; but the Congress may at any time by Law make or alter such Regulations, except as to the Places of choosing Senators.

The Congress shall assemble at least once in every Year, and such Meeting shall be on the first Monday in December, unless they shall by Law appoint a different Day.

Section 5. Each House shall be the Judge of the Elections, Returns and Qualifications of its own Members, and a Majority of each shall constitute a Quorum to do Business; but a smaller Number may adjourn from day to day, and may be authorized to compel the Attendance of absent Members, in such Manner, and under such Penalties as each House may provide.

Every state has two senators. Senators serve a six-year term, but only one third of the senators reach the end of their terms every two years. In any election, at least two thirds of the senators stay in office. This system ensures that there are experienced senators in office at all times. The framers wanted to make sure that changes in our government would only be made after careful study.

The only duty that the Constitution assigns to the vice president is to preside over meetings of the Senate. Modern presidents have given their vice presidents more and varied responsiblity.

The House charges a government official of wrongdoing, and the Senate acts as a court to decide if the official is guilty.

Congress has decided that elections will be held on the Tuesday following the first Monday in November of even-numbered years. The Twentieth Amendment states that Congress shall meet in regular session on January 3 of each year. The president may call a special session of Congress whenever it is necessary.

Each House may determine the Rules of its Proceedings, punish its Members for disorderly Behavior, and, with the Concurrence of two thirds, expel a Member.

Each House shall keep a Journal of its Proceedings, and from time to time publish the same, excepting such Parts as may in their Judgment require Secrecy; and the Yeas and Nays of the Members of either House on any question shall, at the Desire of one fifth of those Present, be entered on the Journal.

Neither House, during the Session of Congress, shall, without the Consent of the other, adjourn for more than three days, nor to any other Place than that in which the two Houses shall be sitting.

Section 6. The Senators and Representatives shall receive a Compensation for their Services, to be ascertained by Law, and paid out of the Treasury of the United States. They shall in all Cases, except Treason, Felony and Breach of the Peace, be privileged from Arrest during their Attendance at the Session of their respective Houses, and in going to and returning from the same; and for any Speech or Debate in either House, they shall not be questioned in any other Place.

No Senator or Representative shall, during the Time for which he was elected, be appointed to any civil Office under the Authority of the United States, which shall have been created, or the Emoluments whereof shall have been increased during such time; and no Person holding any Office under the United States, shall be a Member of either House during his Continuance in Office.

Section 7. All Bills for raising Revenue shall originate in the House of Representatives; but the Senate may propose or concur with Amendments as on other Bills.

Every Bill which shall have passed the House of Representatives and the Senate, shall, before it become a Law, be presented to the President of the United States; If he approve he shall sign it, but if not he shall return it, with his Objections to that House in which it shall have originated, who shall enter the Objections at large on their Journal, and proceed to reconsider it. If after such Reconsideration two thirds of that House shall agree to pass the Bill, it shall be sent, together with the Objections, to the other House, by which it shall likewise be reconsidered, and if approved by two thirds of that House, it shall become a Law. But in all such Cases the Votes of both Houses shall be determined by Yeas and Nays, and the Names of the Persons voting for and against the Bill shall be entered on the Journal of each House respectively. If any Bill shall not be returned by the President within ten Days (Sundays excepted) after it shall have been presented to him, the Same shall be a Law, in like Manner as if he had signed it, unless the Congress by their Adjournment prevent its Return, in which Case it shall not be a Law.

Every Order, Resolution, or Vote to which the Concurrence of the Senate and House of Representatives may be necessary (except on a question of Adjournment) shall be presented to the President of the United States; and before the Same shall take Effect, shall be approved

Congress makes most of its own rules of conduct. The Senate and the House each have a code of ethics that members must follow. It is the task of each house of Congress to discipline its own members. Each house keeps a journal, and a publication called the *Congressional Quarterly* records what happens in congressional sessions. The general public can learn how their representatives voted on bills.

The framers of the Constitution wanted to protect members of Congress from being arrested on false charges by political enemies who did not want them to attend important meetings. Neither did the framers want members of Congress to be taken to court for something they said in a speech or in a debate.

The power of taxing is the responsibility of the House of Representatives. Because members of the house are elected every two years, the framers felt that representatives would listen to the public and seek its approval.

The veto power of the president and the ability of Congress to override a presidential veto are two of the important checks and balances in the Constitution.

by him, or being disapproved by him, shall be repassed by two thirds of the Senate and House of Representatives, according to the Rules and Limitations prescribed in the Case of a Bill.

Section 8. The Congress shall have Power To lay and collect Taxes, Duties, Imposts and Excises, to pay the Debts and provide for the common Defense and general Welfare of the United States; but all Duties, Imposts and Excises shall be uniform throughout the United States;

To borrow Money on the credit of the United States;

To regulate Commerce with foreign Nations, and among the several States, and with the Indian Tribes;

To establish an uniform Rule of Naturalization, and uniform Laws on the subject of Bankruptcies throughout the United States;

To coin Money, regulate the Value thereof, and of foreign Coin, and fix the Standard of Weights and Measures;

To provide for the Punishment of counterfeiting the Securities and current Coin of the United States;

To establish Post Offices and post Roads;

To promote the Progress of Science and useful Arts, by securing for limited Times to Authors and Inventors the exclusive Right to their respective Writings and Discoveries;

To constitute Tribunals inferior to the supreme Court;

To define and punish Piracies and Felonies committed on the high Seas, and Offences against the Law of Nations;

To declare War, grant Letters of Marque and Reprisal, and make Rules concerning Captures on Land and Water;

To raise and support Armies, but no Appropriation of Money to that Use shall be for a longer Term than two Years;

To provide and maintain a Navy;

To make Rules for the Government and Regulation of the land and naval Forces;

To provide for calling forth the Militia to execute the Laws of the Union, suppress Insurrections and repel Invasions;

To provide for organizing, arming, and disciplining, the Militia, and for governing such Part of them as may be employed in the Service of the United States, reserving to the States respectively, the Appointment of the Officers, and the Authority of training the Militia according to the discipline prescribed by Congress.

To exercise exclusive Legislation in all Cases whatsoever, over such District (not exceeding ten Miles square) as may, by Cession of particular States, and the Acceptance of Congress, become the Seat of the Government of the United States, and to exercise like Authority over all Places purchased by the Consent of the Legislature of the State in which the Same shall be, for the Erection of Forts, Magazines, Arsenals, dock-Yards, and other needful Buildings;—And

To make all Laws which shall be necessary and proper for carrying into Execution the foregoing Powers, and all other Powers vested by this Constitution in the Government of the United States, or in any Department or Officer thereof.

Section 9. ~~The Migration or Importation of such Persons as any of the States now existing shall think proper to admit, shall not be prohibited by the Congress prior to the Year one thousand eight hundred and eight, but a Tax or duty may be imposed on such Importation, not exceeding ten dollars for each Person.~~

The Privilege of the Writ of Habeas Corpus shall not be suspended, unless when in Cases of Rebellion or Invasion the public Safety may require it.

No Bill of Attainder or ex post facto Law shall be passed.

No Capitation, or other direct, Tax shall be laid, unless in Proportion to the Census or Enumeration herein before directed to be taken.

No Tax or Duty shall be laid on Articles exported from any State.

No Preference shall be given by any Regulation of Commerce or Revenue to the Ports of one State over those of another: nor shall Vessels bound to, or from, one State, be obliged to enter, clear, or pay Duties in another.

No Money shall be drawn from the Treasury, but in Consequence of Appropriations made by Law; and a regular Statement and Account of the Receipts and Expenditures of all public Money shall be published from time to time.

No Title of Nobility shall be granted by the United States: And no Person holding any Office of Profit or Trust under them, shall, without the Consent of the Congress, accept of any present, Emolument, Office, or Title, of any kind whatever, from any King, Prince, or foreign State.

Section 10. No State shall enter into any Treaty, Alliance, or Confederation; grant Letters of Marque and Reprisal; coin Money; emit Bills of Credit; make any Thing but gold and silver Coin a Tender in Payment of Debts; pass any Bill of Attainder, ex post facto Law, or law impairing the Obligation of Contracts, or grant any Title of Nobility.

No State shall, without the Consent of the Congress, lay any Imposts or Duties on Imports or Exports, except what may be absolutely necessary for executing its inspection Laws: and the net Produce of all Duties and Imposts, laid by any State on Imports or Exports, shall be for the Use of the Treasury of the United States; and all such Laws shall be subject to the Revision and Control of the Congress.

No State shall, without the Consent of Congress, lay any Duty of Tonnage, keep Troops, or Ships of War in time of Peace, enter into any Agreement or Compact with another State, or with a foreign Power, or engage in War, unless actually invaded, or in such imminent Danger as will not admit of delay.

Article II

Section 1. The executive Power shall be vested in a President of the United States of America. He shall hold his Office during the Term of

If Congress has implied powers, then there also must be limits to its powers. This section lists powers that are denied to the federal government. Several of the clauses protect the people of the United States from unjust treatment. The *Writ of Habeas Corpus* means that people have the right to appear before a judge to determine if they are being held legally. This section prohibits a *bill of attainder*, a legislative act by which a person is declared guilty and punished before a trial has been held. Also prohibited is an *ex post facto law*, which is a law that punishes a person for doing something that was legal before the law was passed.

Section 10 lists the powers that are denied to the states. In our system of federalism, the state and federal governments have separate powers, share some powers, and are denied other powers. The states may not exercise any of powers that belong to Congress.

Executive Branch

The president is the chief of the executive branch. It is the job of the president to enforce the laws. The framers wanted the president and vice president's term of office and manner of selection to be different from those of members of Congress. They decided on four-year terms, but they had a difficult time agreeing on how to select the president and vice president. The framers finally set up an electoral system, which varies greatly from our electoral process today. The Twelfth Amendment changed the process by requiring that separate ballots be cast for president and vice president. The rise of political parties has since changed the process even more.

In 1845 Congress set the first Tuesday after the first Monday in November of every fourth year as the general election date for selecting presidential electors.

The youngest elected president was John F. Kennedy; he was 43 years old when he was inaugurated. (Theodore Roosevelt was 42 when he assumed office after the assassination of McKinley.) The oldest elected president was Ronald Reagan; he was 69 years old when he was inaugurated.

four Years, and, together with the Vice President, chosen for the same Term, be elected, as follows.

Each State shall appoint, in such Manner as the Legislature thereof may direct, a Number of Electors, equal to the whole Number of Senators and Representatives to which the State may be entitled in the Congress: but no Senator or Representative, or Person holding an Office of Trust or Profit under the United States, shall be appointed an Elector.

The Electors shall meet in their respective States, and vote by Ballot for two Persons, of whom one at least shall not be an Inhabitant of the same State with themselves. And they shall make a List of all the Persons voted for, and of the Number of Votes for each; which List they shall sign and certify, and transmit sealed to the Seat of the Government of the United States, directed to the President of the Senate. The President of the Senate shall, in the Presence of the Senate and House of Representatives, open all the Certificates, and the Votes shall then be counted. The Person having the greatest Number of Votes shall be the President, if such Number be a Majority of the whole Number of Electors appointed; and if there be more than one who have such majority, and have an equal Number of Votes, then the House of Representatives shall immediately choose by Ballot one of them for President; and if no Person have a Majority, then from the five highest on the List the said House shall in like Manner choose the President. But in choosing the President, the Votes shall be taken by States, the Representation from each State having one Vote; A quorum for this Purpose shall consist of a Member or Members from two thirds of the States, and a Majority of all the States shall be necessary to a Choice. In every Case, after the Choice of the President, the Person having the greatest Number of Votes of the Electors shall be the Vice President. But if there should remain two or more who have equal Votes, the Senate shall choose from them by Ballot the Vice President.

The Congress may determine the Time of choosing the Electors, and the Day on which they shall give their Votes; which Day shall be the same throughout the United States.

No Person except a natural born Citizen, or a Citizen of the United States, at the time of the Adoption of this Constitution, shall be eligible to the Office of President; neither shall any Person be eligible to that Office who shall not have attained to the Age of thirty-five Years, and been fourteen Years a Resident within the United States.

In Case of the Removal of the President from Office, or of his Death, Resignation, or Inability to discharge the Powers and Duties of the said Office, the Same shall devolve on the Vice President, and the Congress may by Law provide for the Case of Removal, Death, Resignation or Inability, both of the President and Vice President, declaring what Officer shall then act as President, and such Officer shall act accordingly, until the Disability be removed, or a President shall be elected.

The President shall, at stated Times, receive for his Services, a Compensation, which shall neither be increased nor diminished during the

Period for which he shall have been elected, and he shall not receive within that Period any other Emolument from the United States, or any of them.

Before he enter on the Execution of his Office, he shall take the following Oath or Affirmation:—"I do solemnly swear (or affirm) that I will faithfully execute the Office of President of the United States, and will to the best of my Ability, preserve, protect and defend the Constitution of the United States."

Section 2. The President shall be Commander in Chief of the Army and Navy of the United States, and of the Militia of the several States, when called into the actual Service of the United States; he may require the Opinion, in writing, of the principal Officer in each of the executive Departments, upon any Subject relating to the Duties of their respective Offices, and he shall have Power to grant Reprieves and Pardons for Offenses against the United States, except in Cases of Impeachment.

He shall have Power, by and with the Advice and Consent of the Senate, to make Treaties, provided two thirds of the Senators present concur; and he shall nominate, and by and with the Advice and Consent of the Senate, shall appoint Ambassadors, other public Ministers and Consuls, Judges of the supreme Court, and all other Officers of the United States, whose Appointments are not herein otherwise provided for, and which shall be established by Law: but the Congress may by Law vest the Appointment of such inferior Officers, as they think proper, in the President alone, in the Courts of Law, or in the Heads of Departments.

The President shall have Power to fill up all Vacancies that may happen during the Recess of the Senate, by granting Commissions which shall expire at the End of their next Session.

Section 3. He shall from time to time give to the Congress Information of the State of the Union, and recommend to their Consideration such Measures as he shall judge necessary and expedient; he may, on extraordinary Occasions, convene both Houses, or either of them, and in Case of Disagreement between them, with Respect to the Time of Adjournment, he may adjourn them to such Time as he shall think proper; he shall receive Ambassadors and other public Ministers; he shall take Care that the Laws be faithfully executed, and shall Commission all the Officers of the United States.

Section 4. The President, Vice President and all civil Officers of the United States, shall be removed from Office on Impeachment for, and Conviction of, Treason, Bribery, or other high Crimes and Misdemeanors.

Article III

Section 1. The judicial Power of the United States, shall be vested in one supreme Court, and in such inferior Courts as the Congress may from time to time ordain and establish. The Judges, both of the supreme and inferior Courts, shall hold their Offices during good Behavior, and

Emolument means "salary, or payment." In 1969 Congress set the president's salary at $200,000 per year. The president also receives an expense account of $50,000 per year. The president must pay taxes on both.

The oath of office is administered to the president by the chief justice of the United States. Washington added "So help me, God." All succeeding presidents have followed this practice.

The framers wanted to make sure that an elected representative of the people controlled the nation's military. Today, the president is in charge of the army, navy, air force, marines, and coast guard. Only Congress can decide, however, if the United States will declare war. This clause also contains the basis for the formation of the president's cabinet. Every president, starting with George Washington, has appointed a cabinet.

Most of the president's appointments to office must be approved by the Senate.

Every year the president presents to Congress a State of the Union message. In this message, the president explains the legislative plans for the coming year. This clause states that one of the president's duties is to enforce the laws.

Judicial Branch
The Articles of Confederation did not make any provisions for a federal court system. One of the first things that the framers of the Constitution agreed upon was to set up

a national judiciary. With all the laws that Congress would be enacting, there would be a great need for a branch of government to interpret the laws. In the Judiciary Act of 1789, Congress provided for the establishment of lower courts, such as district courts, circuit courts of appeals, and various other federal courts. The judicial system provides a check on the legislative branch; it can declare a law unconstitutional.

Congress has the power to decide the punishment for treason, but it can punish only the guilty person. *Corruption of blood* means punishing the family of a person who has committed treason, and is expressly forbidden.

The States
States must honor the laws, records, and court decisions of other states. A person cannot escape a legal obligation by moving from one state to another.

shall, at stated Times, receive for their Services, a Compensation, which shall not be diminished during their Continuance in Office.

Section 2. The judicial Power shall extend to all Cases, in Law and Equity, arising under this Constitution, the Laws of the United States, and Treaties made, or which shall be made, under their Authority;—to all Cases affecting Ambassadors, other public Ministers and Consuls;—to all Cases of admiralty and maritime Jurisdiction;—to Controversies to which the United States shall be a Party;—to Controversies between two or more States;—between a State and Citizens of another state;—between Citizens of different States;—between Citizens of the same State claiming Lands under Grants of different States, and between a State, or the Citizens thereof, and foreign States, Citizens or Subjects.

In all Cases affecting Ambassadors, other public Ministers and Consuls, and those in which a State shall be Party, the supreme Court shall have original Jurisdiction. In all the other Cases before mentioned, the supreme Court shall have appellate Jurisdiction, both as to Law and fact, with such Exceptions, and under such Regulations as the Congress shall make.

The Trial of all Crimes, except in Cases of Impeachment, shall be by Jury; and such Trial shall be held in the State where the said Crimes shall have been committed; but when not committed within any State, the Trial shall be at such Place or Places as the Congress may by Law have directed.

Section 3. Treason against the United States, shall consist only in levying War against them, or in adhering to their Enemies, giving them Aid and Comfort. No Person shall be convicted of Treason unless on the Testimony of two Witnesses to the same overt Act, or on Confession in open Court.

The Congress shall have Power to declare the Punishment of Treason, but no Attainder of Treason shall work Corruption of Blood, or Forfeiture except during the Life of the Person attainted.

Article IV

Section 1. Full Faith and Credit shall be given in each State to the public Acts, Records, and judicial Proceedings of every other State. And the Congress may by general Laws prescribe the Manner in which such Acts, Records and Proceedings shall be proved, and the Effect thereof.

Section 2. The Citizens of each State shall be entitled to all Privileges and Immunities of Citizens in the several States.

A Person charged in any State with Treason, Felony, or other Crime, who shall flee from Justice, and be found in another State, shall on Demand of the executive Authority of the State from which he fled, be delivered up, to be removed to the State having Jurisdiction of the Crime.

No Person held to Service of Labor in one State, under the Laws thereof, escaping into another, shall, in Consequence of any Law or Regulation therein, be discharged from such Service or Labor, but shall

~~be delivered up on Claim of the Party to whom such Service or Labor may be due.~~

Section 3. New States may be admitted by the Congress into this Union; but no new State shall be formed or erected within the Jurisdiction of any other State; nor any State be formed by the Junction of two or more States, or Parts of States, without the Consent of the Legislatures of the States concerned as well as of the Congress.

The Congress shall have Power to dispose of and make all needful Rules and Regulations respecting the Territory or other Property belonging to the United States; and nothing in this Constitution shall be so construed as to Prejudice any Claims of the United States, or of any particular State.

Section 4. The United States shall guarantee to every State in this Union a Republican Form of Government, and shall protect each of them against Invasion; and on Application of the Legislature, or of the Executive (when the Legislature cannot be convened) against domestic Violence.

This section permits Congress to admit new states to the Union. When a group of people living in an area that is not part of an existing state wishes to form a new state, it asks Congress for permission to do so. The people then write a state constitution and offer it to Congress for approval. The state constitution must set up a representative form of government and must not in any way contradict the federal Constitution. If a majority of Congress approves of the state constitution, the state is admitted as a member of the United States of America.

Article V

The Congress, whenever two thirds of both Houses shall deem it necessary, shall propose Amendments to this Constitution, or, on the Application of the Legislatures of two thirds of the several States, shall call a Convention for proposing Amendments, which, in either Case, shall be valid to all Intents and Purposes, as Part of this Constitution, when ratified by the Legislatures of three fourths of the several States, or by Conventions in three fourths thereof, as the one or the other Mode of Ratification may be proposed by the Congress; Provided that ~~no Amendment which may be made prior to the Year One thousand eight hundred and eight shall in any Manner affect the first and fourth Clauses in the Ninth Section of the first Article; and that~~ no State, without its Consent, shall be deprived of its equal Suffrage in the Senate.

Amendments
America's founders may not have realized just how enduring the Constitution would be, but they did make provisions for changing or adding to the Constitution. They did not want to make it easy to change the Constitution. There are two different ways in which changes can be proposed to the states and two different ways in which states can approve the changes and make them part of the Constitution.

Article VI

All Debts contracted and Engagements entered into, before the Adoption of this Constitution, shall be as valid against the United States under this Constitution, as under the Confederation.

This Constitution, and the Laws of the United States which shall be made in Pursuance thereof; and all Treaties made, or which shall be made, under the Authority of the United States, shall be the supreme Law of the Land; and the Judges in every State shall be bound thereby, any Thing in the Constitution or Laws of any State to the Contrary notwithstanding.

The Senators and Representatives before mentioned, and the Members of the several State Legislatures, and all executive and judicial Officers, both of the United States and of the several States, shall be bound by Oath or Affirmation, to support this Constitution; but no

National Supremacy
One of the biggest problems facing the delegates to the Constitutional Convention was the question of what would happen if a state law and a national law conflicted. Which law would be followed? Who decided? The second clause of Article VI answers those questions. When a national and state law disagree, the national law overrides the state law. The Constitution is the supreme law of the land. This clause is often called the "supremacy clause."

religious Test shall ever be required as a Qualification to any Office or public Trust under the United States.

Article VII

The Ratification of the Conventions of nine States, shall be sufficient for the Establishment of this Constitution between the States so ratifying the Same.

DONE in Convention by the Unanimous Consent of the States present the Seventeenth Day of September in the Year of our Lord one thousand seven hundred and Eighty seven and of the Independence of the United States of America the Twelfth. IN WITNESS whereof We have hereunto subscribed our Names.

George Washington—
President and deputy from Virginia

Ratification
The Articles of Confederation called for all 13 states to approve any revision to the Articles. The Constitution required that the vote of nine out of the 13 states would be needed to ratify the Constitution. The first state to ratify was Delaware, on December 7, 1787. The last state to ratify the Constitution was Rhode Island, which finally did so on May 29, 1790, almost two and a half years later.

New Hampshire
John Langdon
Nicholas Gilman

Massachusetts
Nathaniel Gorham
Rufus King

Connecticut
William Samuel Johnson
Roger Sherman

New York
Alexander Hamilton

New Jersey
William Livingston
David Brearley
William Paterson
Jonathan Dayton

Pennsylvania
Benjamin Franklin
Thomas Mifflin
Robert Morris
George Clymer
Thomas FitzSimons
Jared Ingersoll
James Wilson
Gouverneur Morris

Delaware
George Read
Gunning Bedford, Jr.
John Dickinson
Richard Bassett
Jacob Broom

Maryland
James McHenry
Daniel of St. Thomas Jenifer
Daniel Carroll

Virginia
John Blair
James Madison, Jr.

North Carolina
William Blount
Richard Dobbs Spaight
Hugh Williamson

South Carolina
John Rutledge
Charles Cotesworth Pinckney
Charles Pinckney
Pierce Buttler

Georgia
William Few
Abraham Baldwin

Attest: *William Jackson*, Secretary

THE AMENDMENTS

ARTICLES in addition to, and Amendment of the Constitution of the United States of America, proposed by Congress, and ratified by the Legislatures of the several States, pursuant to the fifth Article of the original Constitution.

First Amendment

[The First through Tenth Amendments, now known as the Bill of Rights, were proposed on September 25, 1789, and declared in force on December 15, 1791.]

Congress shall make no law respecting an establishment of religion, or prohibiting the free exercise thereof; or abridging the freedom of speech, or of the press; or the right of the people peaceably to assemble, and to petition the Government for a redress of grievances.

Second Amendment

A well regulated Militia, being necessary to the security of a free State, the right of the people to keep and bear Arms, shall not be infringed.

Third Amendment

No Soldier shall, in time of peace, be quartered in any house, without the consent of the Owner, nor in time of war, but in a manner to be prescribed by law.

Fourth Amendment

The right of the people to be secure in their persons, houses, papers, and effects, against unreasonable searches and seizures, shall not be violated, and no Warrants shall issue, but upon probable cause, supported by Oath or affirmation, and particularly describing the place to be searched, and the persons or things to be seized.

Fifth Amendment

No person shall be held to answer for a capital, or otherwise infamous crime, unless on a presentment or indictment of a Grand Jury, except in cases arising in the land or naval forces, or in the Militia, when in actual service in time of War or public danger; nor shall any person be subject for the same offence to be twice put in jeopardy of life or limb; nor shall be compelled in any criminal case to be a witness against himself, nor be deprived of life, liberty, or property, without due process of law; nor shall private property be taken for public use, without just compensation.

Bill of Rights

One of the conditions set by several states for ratifying the Constitution was the inclusion of a Bill of Rights. Many people feared that a stronger central government might take away basic rights of the people that had been guaranteed in state constitutions. If the three words that begin the preamble—*We the people*—were truly meant, then the rights of the people needed to be protected.

The first ten amendments to the Constitution are called the Bill of Rights.

The First Amendment protects freedom of speech and thought, and forbids Congress to make any law "respecting an establishment of religion" or restraining the freedom to practice religion as one chooses.

A police officer or sheriff may enter a person's home with a search warrant, which allows the law officer to look for evidence that could convict someone of committing a crime.

The Fifth, Sixth, and Seventh Amendments describe the procedures that courts must follow when trying people accused of crimes.

The Fifth Amendment guarantees that no one can be put on trial for a serious crime unless a grand jury agrees that the evidence justifies doing so. It also says that a person cannot be tried twice for the same crime.

Sixth Amendment

The Sixth Amendment makes several promises, which include a prompt trial and a trial by a jury chosen from the state and district in which the crime was committed. The Sixth Amendment also states that an accused person must be told why he or she is being tried and promises that an accused person has the right to be defended by a lawyer.

In all criminal prosecutions, the accused shall enjoy the right to a speedy and public trial, by an impartial jury of the State and district wherein the crime shall have been committed, which district shall have been previously ascertained by law, and to be informed of the nature and cause of the accusation; to be confronted with the witnesses against him; to have compulsory process for obtaining witnesses in his favor, and to have the Assistance of Counsel for his defense.

Seventh Amendment

The Seventh Amendment guarantees a trial by jury in cases that involve more than $20, but in modern times, usually much more money is at stake before a case is heard in federal court.

In Suits at common law, where the value in controversy shall exceed twenty dollars, the right of trial by jury shall be preserved, and no fact tried by a jury shall be otherwise reexamined in any Court of the United States, than according to the rules of the common law.

Eighth Amendment

Excessive bail shall not be required, nor excessive fines imposed, nor cruel and unusual punishments inflicted.

Ninth Amendment

The Ninth and Tenth Amendments were added because not every right of the people or of the states could be listed in the Constitution.

The enumeration in the Constitution, of certain rights, shall not be construed to deny or disparage others retained by the people.

Tenth Amendment

The powers not delegated to the United States by the Constitution, nor prohibited by it to the States, are reserved to the States respectively, or to the people.

Eleventh Amendment

[Proposed March 4, 1794; declared ratified January 8, 1798]

The Judicial power of the United States shall not be construed to extend to any suit in law or equity, commenced or prosecuted against one of the United States by Citizens of another State, or by Citizens or Subjects of any Foreign State.

Twelfth Amendment

[Proposed December 9, 1803; declared ratified September 25, 1804]

The Electors shall meet in their respective states and vote by ballot for President and Vice President, one of whom, at least, shall not be an inhabitant of the same state with themselves; they shall name in their ballots the person voted for as President, and in distinct ballots the person voted for as Vice President, and they shall make distinct lists of all persons voted for as President, and of all persons voted for as Vice President, and of the number of votes for each, which lists they shall sign and certify, and transmit sealed to the seat of the government of the United States, directed to the President of the Senate;—The President of the Senate shall, in the presence of the Senate and House of Representatives, open all the certificates and the votes shall then be counted;—The person having the greatest number of votes for President, shall be the President, if such number be a majority of the whole number of Electors appointed; and if no person have such majority, then from the persons having the highest numbers not exceeding three on the list of those voted for as President, the House of Representatives shall choose immediately, by ballot, the President. But in choosing the President, the votes shall be taken by states, the representation from each state having one vote; a quorum for this purpose shall consist of a member or members from two thirds of the states, and a majority of all the states shall be necessary to a choice. And if the House of Representatives shall not choose a President whenever the right of choice shall devolve upon them, before the fourth day of March next following, then the Vice President shall act as President, as in the case of the death or other constitutional disability of the President;—The person having the greatest number of votes as Vice President, shall be the Vice President, if such number be a majority of the whole number of Electors appointed, and if no person have a majority, then from the two highest numbers on the list, the Senate shall choose the Vice President; a quorum for the purpose shall consist of two thirds of the whole number of Senators, and a majority of the whole number shall be necessary to a choice. But no person constitutionally ineligible to the office of President shall be eligible to that of Vice President of the United States.

The Twelfth Amendment changed the election procedure for president and vice president. This amendment became necessary because of the growth of political parties. Before this amendment, electors voted without distinguishing between president and vice president. Whoever received the most votes became president, and whoever received the next highest number of votes became vice president. A confusing election in 1800, which resulted in Thomas Jefferson's becoming president, caused this amendment to be proposed.

Thirteenth Amendment
[Proposed January 31, 1865; declared ratified December 18, 1865]

Section 1. Neither slavery nor involuntary servitude, except as a punishment for crime whereof the party shall have been duly convicted, shall exist within the United States, or any place subject to their jurisdiction.

Section 2. Congress shall have power to enforce this article by appropriate legislation.

Although some slaves had been freed during the Civil War, slavery was not abolished until the Thirteenth Amendment took effect.

In 1833 Chief Justice John Marshall ruled that the Bill of Rights limited the national goverment but not the state governments. This ruling meant that states were able to keep blacks from becoming state citizens. If blacks were not citizens, they were not protected by the Bill of Rights. The Fourteenth Amendment defines citizenship and prevents states from interfering in the rights of citizens of the United States.

Fourteenth Amendment
[Proposed June 13, 1866; declared ratified July 28, 1868]

Section 1. All persons born or naturalized in the United States, and subject to the jurisdiction thereof, are citizens of the United States and of the State wherein they reside. No State shall make or enforce any law which shall abridge the privileges or immunities of citizens of the United

States; nor shall any State deprive any person of life, liberty, or property, without due process of law; nor deny to any person within its jurisdiction the equal protection of the laws.

Section 2. Representatives shall be apportioned among the several States according to their respective numbers, counting the whole number of persons in each State, ~~excluding Indians not taxed.~~ But when the right to vote at any election for the choice of electors for President and Vice President of the United States, Representatives in Congress, the Executive and Judicial officers of a State, or the members of the Legislature thereof, is denied to any of the ~~male~~ inhabitants of such State, being ~~twenty-one years of age, and~~ citizens of the United States, or in any way abridged, except for participation in rebellion, or other crime, the basis of representation therein shall be reduced in the proportion which the number of such ~~male~~ citizens shall bear to the whole number of ~~male~~ citizens ~~twenty-one years of age~~ in such State.

Section 3. No person shall be a Senator or Representative in Congress, or elector of President and Vice President, or hold any office, civil or military, under the United States, or under any State, who, having previously taken an oath, as a member of Congress, or as an officer of the United States, or as a member of any State legislature, or as an executive or judicial officer of any State, to support the Constitution of the United States, shall have engaged in insurrection or rebellion against the same, or given aid or comfort to the enemies thereof. But Congress may by a vote of two thirds of each House, remove such disability.

Section 4. The validity of the public debt of the United States, authorized by law, including debts incurred for payment of pensions and bounties for services in suppressing insurrection or rebellion, shall not be questioned. But neither the United States nor any State shall assume or pay any debt or obligation incurred in aid of insurrection or rebellion against the United States, ~~or any claim for the loss of emancipation of any slave;~~ but all such debts, obligations and claims shall be held illegal and void.

Section 5. The Congress shall have power to enforce, by appropriate legislation, the provisions of this article.

Fifteenth Amendment
[Proposed February 26, 1869; declared ratified March 30, 1870]

The Fifteenth Amendment extended the right to vote to black males.

Section 1. The right of citizens of the United States to vote shall not be denied or abridged by the United States or by any State on account of race, color, or previous condition of servitude.

Section 2. The Congress shall have power to enforce this article by appropriate legislation.

Sixteenth Amendment
[Proposed July 12, 1909; declared ratified February 25, 1913]

The Sixteenth Amendment made legal the income tax described in Article I.

The Congress shall have power to lay and collect taxes on incomes, from whatever source derived, without apportionment among the several States, and without regard to any census or apportionment among the several States, and without regard to any census or enumeration.

Seventeenth Amendment
[Proposed May 13, 1912; declared ratified May 31, 1913]

The Senate of the United States shall be composed of two Senators from each State, elected by the people thereof, for six years; and each Senator shall have one vote. The electors in each State shall have the qualifications requisite for electors of the most numerous branch of the State legislatures.

When vacancies happen in the representation of any State in the Senate, the executive authority of such State shall issue writs of election to fill such vacancies: *Provided*, That the legislature of any State may empower the executive thereof to make temporary appointments until the people fill the vacancies by election as the legislature may direct.

This amendment shall not be so construed as to affect the election or term of any Senator chosen before it becomes valid as part of the Constitution.

The Seventeenth Amendment required that senators be elected directly by the people instead of by the state legislature.

Eighteenth Amendment
[Proposed December 18, 1917; declared ratified January 29, 1919; repealed by the Twenty-first Amendment December 5, 1933]

Section 1. After one year from the ratification of this article the manufacture, sale, or transportation of intoxicating liquors within, the importation thereof into, or the exportation thereof from the United States and all territory subject to the jurisdiction thereof for beverage purposes is hereby prohibited.

Section 2. The Congress and the several States shall have concurrent power to enforce this article by appropriate legislation.

Section 3. This article shall be inoperative unless it shall have been ratified as an amendment to the Constitution by the legislatures of the several States, as provided in the Constitution, within seven years from the date of the submission hereof to the States by the Congress.

Although many people felt that Prohibition was good for the health and welfare of the American people, the amendment was repealed 14 years later.

Nineteenth Amendment
[Proposed June 4, 1919; declared ratified August 26, 1920]

The right of citizens of the United States to vote shall not be denied or abridged by the United States or by any State on account of sex.

Congress shall have power to enforce this article by appropriate legislation.

As you have read, Abigail Adams was disappointed that the Declaration of Independence and the Constitution did not specifically include women. It took almost 150 years and much campaigning by women's suffrage groups for women to finally achieve voting privleges.

Twentieth Amendment
[Proposed March 2, 1932; declared ratified February 6, 1933]

Section 1. The terms of the President and Vice President shall end at

In the original Constitution, a newly elected president and Congress did not take office until March 4, which was four months after the November election. The officials who were leaving office were called "lame ducks" because they had little influence during those four months. The Twentieth Amendment changed the date that the new president and Congress take office. Members of Congress now take office on January 3, and the president takes office on January 20.

noon on the 20th day of January, and the terms of Senators and Representatives at noon on the 3rd day of January, of the years in which such terms would have ended if this article had not been ratified; and the terms of their successors shall then begin.

Section 2. The Congress shall assemble at least once in every year, and such meeting shall begin at noon on the 3rd day of January, unless they shall by law appoint a different day.

Section 3. If, at the time fixed for the beginning of the term of the President, the President elect shall have died, the Vice President elect shall become President. If a President shall not have been chosen before the time fixed for beginning of his term, or if the President elect shall have failed to qualify, then the Vice President elect shall act as President until a President shall have qualified; and the Congress may by law provide for the case wherein neither a President elect nor a Vice President elect shall have qualified, declaring who shall then act as President, or the manner in which one who is to act shall be selected, and such persons shall act accordingly until a President or Vice President shall have qualified.

Section 4. The Congress may by law provide for the case of the death of any of the persons from whom the House of Representatives may choose a President whenever the right of choice shall have devolved upon them, and for the case of the death of any of the persons from whom the Senate may choose a Vice President whenever the right of choice shall have devolved upon them.

~~*Section 5.* Sections 1 and 2 shall take effect on the 15th day of October following the ratification of this article.~~

~~*Section 6.* This article shall be inoperative unless it shall have been ratified as an amendment to the Constitution by the legislatures of three-fourths of the several States within seven years from the date of its submission.~~

Twenty-first Amendment
[Proposed February 20, 1933; declared ratified December 5, 1933]

The Twenty-first Amendment is the only amendment that has been ratified by state conventions rather than by state legislatures.

Section 1. The eighteenth article of amendment to the Constitution of the United States is hereby repealed.

Section 2. The transportation or importation into any State, Territory, or possession of the United States for delivery or use therein of intoxicating liquors, in violation of the laws thereof, is hereby prohibited.

~~*Section 3.* This article shall be inoperative unless it shall have been ratified as an amendment to the Constitution by conventions in the several States, as provided in the Constitution, within seven years from the date of the submission hereof to the States by the Congress.~~

Twenty-second Amendment
[Proposed March 24, 1947; declared ratified March 1, 1951]
Section 1. No person shall be elected to the office of the President

more than twice, and no person who has held the office of President, or acted as President, for more than two years of a term to which some other person was elected President shall be elected to the office of the President more than once. ~~But this Article shall not apply to any person holding the office of President when this Article was proposed by the Congress, and shall not prevent any person who may be holding the office of President, or acting as President, during the term within which this Article becomes operative from holding the office of President or acting as President during the remainder of such term.~~

~~*Section 2.* This article shall be inoperative unless it shall have been ratified as an amendment to the Constitution by the legislatures of three fourths of the several States within seven years from the date of its submission to the States by the Congress.~~

From the time of President Washington's administration, it was a custom for presidents to serve no more than two terms of office. Franklin D. Roosevelt, however, was elected to four terms. The Twenty-second Amendment made into law the old custom of a two-term limit for each president, if reelected.

Twenty-third Amendment
[Proposed June 16, 1960; declared ratified April 3, 1961]

Section 1. The District constituting the seat of Government of the United States shall appoint in such manner as the Congress may direct:

A number of electors of President and Vice President equal to the whole number of Senators and Representatives in Congress to which the District would be entitled if it were a State, but in no event more than the least populous state; they shall be in addition to those appointed by the States, but they shall be considered, for the purposes of the election of President and Vice President, to be electors appointed by a State; and they shall meet in the District and perform such duties as provided by the twelfth article of amendment.

Section 2. The Congress shall have power to enforce this article by appropriate legislation.

Until the Twenty-third Amendment, the people of Washington, D.C., could not vote in presidential elections.

Twenty-fourth Amendment
[Proposed August 27, 1962; declared ratified February 4, 1964]

Section 1. The right of citizens of the United States to vote in any primary or other election for President or Vice President, for electors for President or Vice President, or for Senator or Representative in Congress, shall not be denied or abridged by the United States or any State by reason of failure to pay any poll tax or other tax.

Section 2. The Congress shall have power to enforce this article by appropriate legislation.

Twenty-fifth Amendment
[Proposed July 6, 1965; declared ratified February 23, 1967]

Section 1. In case of removal of the President from office or of his death or resignation, the Vice President shall become President.

Section 2. Whenever there is a vacancy in the office of the Vice Pres-

The illness of President Eisenhower in the 1950s and the assassination of President Kennedy in 1963 were the events behind the Twenty-fifth Amendment. The Constitution did not provide a clear-cut method for

ident, the President shall nominate a Vice President who shall take office upon confirmation by a majority vote of both Houses of Congress.

Section 3. Whenever the President transmits to the President pro tempore of the Senate and the Speaker of the House of Representatives his written declaration that he is unable to discharge the powers and duties of his office, and until he transmits to them a written declaration to the contrary, such powers and duties shall be discharged by the Vice President as Acting President.

Section 4. Whenever the Vice President and a majority of either the principal officers of the executive departments or of such other body as Congress may by law provide, transmit to the President pro tempore of the Senate and the Speaker of the House of Representatives their written declaration that the President is unable to discharge the powers and duties of his office, the Vice President shall immediately assume the powers and duties of the office as Acting President.

Thereafter, when the President transmits to the President pro tempore of the Senate and the Speaker of the House of Representatives his written declaration that no inability exists, he shall resume the powers and duties of his office unless the Vice President and a majority of either the principal officers of the executive department or of such other body as Congress may by law provide, transmit within four days to the President pro tempore of the Senate and the Speaker of the House of Representatives their written declaration that the President is unable to discharge the powers and duties of his office. Thereupon Congress shall decide the issue, assembling within forty-eight hours for that purpose if not in session. If the Congress, within twenty-one days after receipt of the latter written declaration, or, if Congress is not in session, within twenty-one days after Congress is required to assemble, determines by two-thirds vote of both Houses that the President is unable to discharge the powers and duties of his office, the Vice President shall continue to discharge the same as Acting President; otherwise, the President shall resume the powers and duties of his office.

Twenty-sixth Amendment
[Proposed March 23, 1971; declared ratified July 5, 1971]

Section 1. The right of citizens of the United States, who are eighteen years of age or older, to vote shall not be denied or abridged by the United States or by any State on account of age.

Section 2. The Congress shall have power to enforce this article by appropriate legislation.

INTERPRETING THE CONSTITUTION

You Be the Judge

Listed below are 6 fictional situations. Decide if each situation is allowed by the Constitution. Then, on a separate piece of paper, tell if each situation is allowed or not allowed and write the part of the Constitution that supports your decision.

1. You are a 33-year-old lawyer running for a seat in the House of Representatives. You immigrated to the United States 15 years ago and became a United States citizen five years later.

2. Because the state of New York has more people than Alabama, Congress has decided to tax the people of New York at a higher rate than the people of Alabama.

3. Congress has passed a law making it illegal to purchase or smoke cigarettes. In addition, the law states that anyone who smoked cigarettes before the law was passed will be sentenced in court to pay a $500 fine.

4. You were born in the United States and have lived here all your life. Now, at age 40, you decide to run for president of the United States.

5. You are a Supreme Court justice. A senator who disliked your ruling on a case is writing a bill to cut the salaries of the Supreme Court justices in half.

6. The states of Oregon and Washington declare that they are now one state named Orewash. The legislatures of both states agreed to the formation of the new state, as did Congress.

Classifying Amendments

Carefully read the 26 amendments. Then, classify the amendments according to the headings in the chart below.

Protect Rights   Extend Rights   Solve a Problem

Thinking Critically

Ratification of the Constitution was a long fight for public opinion. Much of the battle took place in newspapers. About 70 newspapers were for the new Constitution and about 12 newspapers were against it. Imagine that you are a newspaper editor in 1787. What would you say to your readers? Write a short editorial expressing your opinion—either for or against the Constitution.

INTERPRETING HISTORY: The Constitution

Did you know that the Constitution has been a source of continuing controversy among historians? Few people do. The debate centers on the reasons the United States Constitution was written as it was.

Times in America were perilous in the years from 1781 to 1787. Economic problems and interstate squabbles threatened the future of the weak new nation. But the Articles of Confederation established no central governing authority. Political power was divided equally among the states. Such a system had great difficulty dealing with these problems. So why from this setting did the Constitution emerge?

Historians disagree about the answer. The major theories focus on the same two motives—economics and patriotism—that historians debate in their study of the American Revolution. The traditional view holds that the Constitution was written by patriots who wanted nothing more than to help the struggling nation survive. These patriots recognized the weaknesses of the Articles of Confederation and felt if they were not revised the security of the nation—if not the nation itself—was at stake. They met to revise the Articles. But noting its basic weakness, they wrote a new document—the Constitution—creating a stronger central government. Historian John Fiske, who wrote *The Critical Period in American History,* insisted that the nation would not have survived under the Articles of Confederation.

Noted historian Charles A. Beard disagreed with Fiske. In his *An Economic Interpretation of the Constitution of the United States* Beard claimed that the writers of the Constitution were wealthy men who had loaned the government large sums of money. If the government failed, they would lose their investment. In writing the Constitution, with its stronger central government, Beard said they were protecting their economic interests. He called the Constitution "an economic document drawn with superb skill by men whose property interests were at stake."

In more recent years other historians with other interpretations have tried to solve the mystery. But the controversy continues. As historians quickly learn, people's motives are difficult to gauge accurately and are often open to interpretation.

5. "A MORE PERFECT UNION"

Use these questions to guide your reading. Answer the questions after completing Section 5.
Understanding Issues, Events, & Ideas. **a.** Create a word web around the word *Constitution* using the following words: Virginia Plan, New Jersey Plan, president, Congress, Senate, House of Representatives, judiciary, Supreme Court, Great Compromise. **b.** Write a brief analysis of the Constitution using the following words: Three-Fifths Compromise, elector, advice and consent, district court, appellate court, checks and balances, veto, override, impeachment, ratifying, convention, Federalist, Antifederalist, Federalist Papers.
1. Why did the delegates give so much power to the president?
2. What was the reasoning behind the electoral system?
3. How does the Constitution guard against misuse of power?
Thinking Critically. If you were Alexander Hamilton, how would you persuade Samuel Adams and John Hancock to ratify the Constitution?

The Great Compromise

Giving new power to the United States was relatively simple. Deciding who should control and use the power was more difficult. The problem was complicated. Should the authority of the United States government remain concentrated in Congress? Or should it be separated into executive, legislative, and judicial branches as in most state constitutions? Further, should each state have an equal weight in electing representatives to the United States as was true under the Articles of Confederation? Or should representation depend upon population? That would give the larger states more representatives and thus more influence than the smaller ones.

Early during the Convention, Governor Edmund Randolph of Virginia, a member of that state's delegation, presented the **Virginia Plan.** It provided for a government with three separate branches and for representation by population. William Paterson then offered the **New Jersey Plan,** which would have left all power in Congress and continued the one-state, one-vote system.

The delegates adopted the basics of the Virginia Plan with little debate. There was to be an executive branch headed by a **president** of the United States; a legislative branch, the **Congress,** with two chambers, a **Senate** and a **House of Representatives;** and a system of courts, the **national judiciary,** including the **Supreme Court.**

The delegates from the smaller states, however, dug in their heels on the question of representation by population. The debate went on for weeks. Both camps realized they must find some way to agree or the entire Constitution would be defeated. Finally they worked out the so-called **Great Compromise.** Members of the House of Representatives would be elected on the basis of population. (In the first House, Virginia, the largest state, elected 11 representatives, New Hampshire chose 3, Pennsylvania 8, and so on.) But each state was to have two seats in the Senate. Further, to protect the influence of the state governments, the Constitution provided that senators were to be elected by the state legislatures, not by the people.

Slavery in the Constitution

When the delegates spoke of "the People," they were not talking about slaves. The delegates decided to allow each state to determine who could vote and who could not. The only limit they imposed was a clause saying that the same rules must apply to the elections to Congress as to the "most numerous" branch of the state's own legislature. Because they did not qualify to vote in Congressional elections, almost no Africans in America could vote, not even those who were free.

Mrs. B. S. Church painted this fine oil portrait of William Paterson.

The delegates to the Convention completed the Constitution on September 15, 1787. On September 17 they held their final meeting to sign the document. They were painfully aware that it was not perfect. Benjamin Franklin expressed the general attitude when he said, "There are several parts of this Constitution which I do not at present approve, but I am not sure that I shall never approve them."

Franklin urged doubters to accept the view of the majority. They should not, he said, be like the French woman who, during an argument with her sister,

Bradley Smith/Laurie Platt Winfrey

Benjamin Franklin by Duplessis

said, "I don't know how it happens, Sister, but I meet with nobody but myself that's always in the right." Nearly all of the delegates took Franklin's advice.

As the last of the delegates were adding their signatures, Franklin looked up at the now-empty president's chair, where George Washington had sat throughout the sessions. On its back was painted a rising sun. Turning to some of the others, Franklin said, "I have often looked at that without being able to tell whether it was rising or setting. But now I know that it is a rising and not a setting sun."

Northern and southern delegates did clash over whether slaves should be counted in determining the number of representatives a state should have in Congress. The issue was decided by what is called the **Three-Fifths Compromise**—three fifths of the slaves were counted in the population of a state. Actually, the delegates were very squeamish about slavery. They did not even mention the word in the final document. The Three-Fifths Compromise provided for counting "the whole Number of free Persons" and "three fifths of all other Persons." In another so-called compromise Congress was denied the power to outlaw bringing slaves from abroad until 1808. Still another clause required the free states to return any person "held to Service or Labor" who managed to escape into a free state.

The ban on importing slaves did not effectively end slavery. Why did the delegates avoid deciding the fate of the peculiar institution? Historical imagination helps us here. Some of the delegates surely had guilty consciences about allowing slavery to exist in a nation where "all men" were supposed to be equal and where the government was committed to providing "the people" with "Blessings of Liberty." But their feelings of guilt did not prevent them from protecting the interests of slave owners in the ways just mentioned. Political considerations also influenced them. They believed that if slaves were banned, the southern colonies would not stay in the Union. Probably more important, nearly all of them believed that blacks were fundamentally inferior to whites. They might deserve to be free, but they did not merit being treated as equals. In short, the Founding Fathers could not escape the prejudices of their times.

Other delegates in 1787 thought that slavery was a dying institution in North America. They agreed to the compromises because they felt slavery would not be a problem by 1808. But the framers of the Constitution were profoundly mistaken! Preserved by the constitutional compromises, slavery expanded and became more important to the South, and affected the lives of hundreds of thousands of African Americans. For more than seventy years the nation struggled with the moral and legal issues of slavery. Not until a bloody civil war erupted was slavery finally brought to an end.

Women and the Constitution

Just as the framers of the Constitution allowed slavery to exist in a nation where "all men were created equal," they provided no further guarantees for women. The enlightened political views expressed in the Declaration of Independence and Constitution did give women in America hope for future changes. But the Constitutional guarantees were not specific. Women were not specifically given the right to vote, or to hold office, or other rights seemingly reserved for men. As with slavery, this situation would create problems for America as the nation matured.

The Presidency

The most drastic change put into effect by the Constitutional Convention was the creation of a powerful presidency. As we have seen, under the Articles of Confederation there was no chief executive. In discussing the new office, the delegates were torn in two directions. They wanted a national leader. But they did not want to make the chief executive too powerful. Neither did they want a figurehead.

Some delegates wanted to give the executive power to a group. Others preferred a president sharing authority with an elected council. Some suggested that the state legislatures choose the president.

The delegates settled for one president—and a president with a great deal of power. Besides being responsible for administering the laws passed by Congress, the president was to be commander in chief of the army and navy. He alone was in charge of foreign relations. He was to appoint judges and other important government officials. And the president was also given the power to veto laws passed by Congress.

Everyone assumed that the first president would be George Washington. This was one reason why the office was given so much power. Washington was so admired and trusted that the delegates made the presidency worthy of his talents. For example, who but Washington could serve as commander in chief of the army?

Of course, Washington would not be president forever. Looking

In the heart of Wall Street stands this statue in bronze of Geroge Washington by J. Q. A. Ward. It marks the site where the first president took the oath of office.

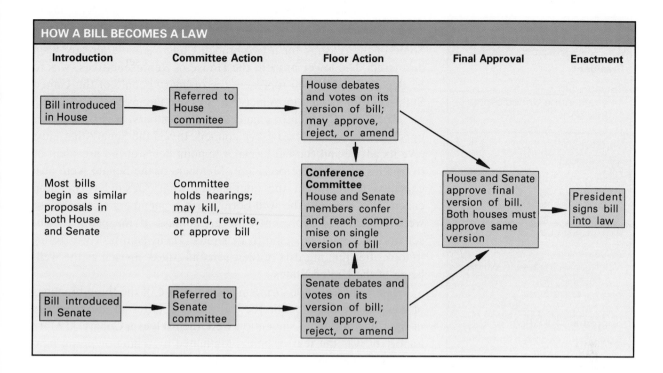

HOW A BILL BECOMES A LAW

Introduction	Committee Action	Floor Action	Final Approval	Enactment

Bill introduced in House → Referred to House commitee → House debates and votes on its version of bill; may approve, reject, or amend

Most bills begin as similar proposals in both House and Senate

Committee holds hearings; may kill, amend, rewrite, or approve bill

Conference Committee House and Senate members confer and reach compromise on single version of bill

House and Senate approve final version of bill. Both houses must approve same version → President signs bill into law

Bill introduced in Senate → Referred to Senate committee → Senate debates and votes on its version of bill; may approve, reject, or amend

ahead, the delegates worked out a complicated system for choosing his successors. Each state was to select in whatever manner its legislature wished as many **electors** as it had senators and representatives in Congress. The electors in each state would then meet to vote for president. Each elector would vote for two people, only one of whom could be a resident of that state. The votes would then be counted and the results forwarded under seal to the national capital. On an appointed day the ballots from the different states would be opened and counted in the presence of the Senate and the House of Representatives. The person with the largest number of votes would become president, the second largest, vice president. However, if the leading candidate did not receive a majority, the House of Representatives would choose a president from among the five persons with the largest number of votes. In this voting each state delegation in the House would have only one vote.

There were good reasons why the delegates created such a complicated system of election. The country was large. Communication was slow and limited. It seemed unlikely that any person less famous than a Washington could be well-known all over the country. Yet it was important that the president be a person of outstanding character as well as ability. If candidates were selected in each region by persons who knew them well, the high standard needed could probably be met. Then the people's representatives in Congress could discuss the merits of the best of these and make a final selection. The rule that the House of Representatives vote by states was another concession to the smaller states.

LEARNING FROM CHARTS. *A bill is sent to the president for approval or veto only after it passes both houses. Why must both houses approve the same version of a bill?*

"A More Perfect Union" 223

LEARNING FROM CHARTS.
The requirements to hold public office in the federal government vary depending on the office. Which office has the strictest requirements? Why might this be?

The Congress

Some of the reasons for a two-branch Congress have already been discussed. The lower branch, the House of Representatives, was to be popularly elected to represent the ordinary people of the United States. It alone could introduce bills to raise money.

The Senate, which originally had 26 members, was seen as the upper house, a kind of advisory council. It was the Senate that must give its **advice and consent** to major appointments of the president or to treaties made by the president. Members of the Senate were also expected to represent the interests of what Alexander Hamilton called "the rich and the well-born," just as members of the House were expected to represent "the great mass of the people." But senators were not expected to be snobs. Their main task was to try to look after the interests of their separate states as well as the well-being of the United States.

The Congress, not surprisingly, is the first of the three branches of government described in the Constitution. After all, the members of the Constitutional Convention were themselves a Congress. More important was the fear of being dominated by a king or prime minister. The Americans who drew up the Constitution remembered vividly what had happened to the colonies under English rule.

The Judiciary

The Constitution also provided for a system of United States courts, separate from the courts of the individual states. It only mentioned specifically a **Supreme Court.** It left it to Congress to decide how many judges to have on the Supreme Court and how many lower courts to set up under the Supreme Court. (There are now nine Supreme Court Justices and two kinds of lower federal courts—the **district courts** and the **appellate courts,** or appeals courts.)

Under the Constitution all United States judges serve "during good Behavior." This means that they cannot be removed once appointed unless they commit a crime or are unable to perform their duties for some reason, such as insanity. The Constitution gives the federal courts the responsibility of hearing all cases involving the laws and treaties of the United States and also cases involving foreigners, two or more states, and the citizens of different states.

Checks and Balances

Although they were creating a more powerful government, the delegates at Philadelphia were very concerned about the possible misuse of power. They tried to prevent misuse by dividing power among many people and institutions and by a clever system of **checks and balances.** Here are a few examples of how the president's powers are checked. The other branches are subject to similar restraints.

The president can **veto,** or reject, bills passed by Congress. This is a check on the power of Congress, but Congress can **override** a veto. If both houses pass the bill again by two-thirds majorities, it becomes law.

The president is commander in chief of the army and navy. But Congress controls the raising of money to maintain the armed forces, and Congress alone has the power to declare war.

The president or representatives of the president can negotiate treaties with foreign countries. But such treaties become law only when approved by two thirds of the Senate.

The president has the power to appoint judges, ambassadors, and other important officials. But the Senate can vote to reject any of these appointments.

Finally, if the president commits a serious crime, he can be brought to trial by a process called **impeachment.** In such cases the House of Representatives brings the charges against the president, and the Senate acts as judge and jury. A two-thirds vote is necessary for conviction and removal from office.

LEARNING FROM CHARTS. *Two of the key aspects of the Constitution are its separation of powers and its checks and balances. Make a list of the checks each branch has on the others. Which check is the most powerful? Why?*

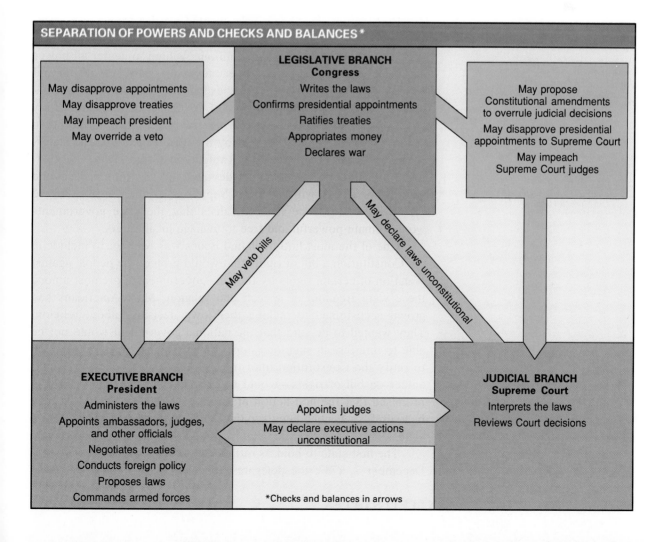

SEPARATION OF POWERS AND CHECKS AND BALANCES *

LEGISLATIVE BRANCH
Congress
Writes the laws
Confirms presidential appointments
Ratifies treaties
Appropriates money
Declares war

May disapprove appointments
May disapprove treaties
May impeach president
May override a veto

May propose Constitutional amendments to overrule judicial decisions
May disapprove presidential appointments to Supreme Court
May impeach Supreme Court judges

May veto bills

May declare laws unconstitutional

EXECUTIVE BRANCH
President
Administers the laws
Appoints ambassadors, judges, and other officials
Negotiates treaties
Conducts foreign policy
Proposes laws
Commands armed forces

Appoints judges
May declare executive actions unconstitutional

JUDICIAL BRANCH
Supreme Court
Interprets the laws
Reviews Court decisions

*Checks and balances in arrows

Ratifying the Constitution

The Constitution was to go into effect when nine states (two thirds) had approved it. Interest in the document was high. Everywhere citizens read and discussed the new form of government. They elected representatives to state **ratifying conventions** where the decision to approve or disapprove was to be made. Since it was complicated and involved many important changes, the Constitution did not win everyone's approval. Opinions were sharply divided. Yet since there was no nationwide vote on the Constitution nor public opinion polls to sample popular attitudes, it is impossible to know whether or not a majority of the people favored the new system. In some states there was little organized opposition. In others opponents were quite vocal.

Supporters of the Constitution called themselves **Federalists.** Those who opposed it are known as **Antifederalists.** The second name is confusing because a *federal* form of government is one that involves a combination of independent states. We speak of the United States today as the federal government. The so-called Antifederalists actually were federalists in this sense.

Both groups, in other words, wanted a federal form of government. They differed about how strong the federation known as the United States should be. Almost no one wanted to center all power in the federal government, and very few were satisfied with the old "league of friendship" of the Articles that the Constitution proposed to replace. Those who disapproved of the Constitution did so mostly because they were afraid the new central government would be so powerful that it would soon destroy the independence of the states. The Constitution, one excited Antifederalist said, was "a beast, dreadful and terrible," which "devours, breaks into pieces, and stamps [the states] with his feet." Supporters of the Constitution did their best to persuade Antifederalists that the state governments would remain powerful and free to manage local affairs.

One of the most hotly debated issues was whether to include in the Constitution a bill of rights that would protect the people against violation of certain rights by the new government. Foremost among these were freedom of speech and religion. Most Americans had grown accustomed to making their own decisions about religion. They wanted to be sure that the national government would not be able to interfere in such decisions. Several states, in fact, hesitated to ratify the Constitution until they were promised that such guarantees—a bill of rights—would be included. When James Madison promised that the first action of the newly elected Congress would be to draft such amendments to the Constitution, votes for ratification squeaked by in several key states.

The first state to hold its ratifying convention was Delaware. On December 7, 1787, the delegates voted unanimously to accept the

Constitution. By February, four more states had ratified by large margins—Pennsylvania, New Jersey, Georgia, and Connecticut.

Sentiment in a number of other states was also running strong for ratification. Nine states would be enough to put the Constitution into effect, but how effective could the government of the United States be if Massachusetts, New York, and Virginia refused to join the Union? The Antifederalists in these important states were numerous and well organized.

The Massachusetts convention met in early January 1788 and debated the question for nearly a month. At first the Antifederalists seemed to have a majority. The memory of Shays' Rebellion was on everyone's mind. Representatives from the troubled districts were strongly against ratification. The men Paul Revere had gone to Lexington to warn in April 1775, Sam Adams and John Hancock, were delegates. They were believed to oppose the Constitution.

The Federalists, however, proved to be shrewd politicians. They organized a mass meeting in Boston in favor of ratification. This show of support in his home district persuaded Sam Adams to vote for the Constitution in spite of his doubts. The Federalist leaders promised Hancock, who was very ambitious, that they would not oppose him for governor in the next election if he would vote for the Constitution. They even hinted that he might be a good candidate for vice president if the new government was accepted.

Hancock then came out for the Constitution. He also made an important practical suggestion that helped persuade others in Massachusetts and other states to go along: once the Constitution was accepted, amendments should be submitted dealing with objections to it. The convention then voted 187 to 168 to ratify.

The contest was also close in Virginia, but again the Federalists won out. By the end of June ten states had ratified. Only Rhode Island, North Carolina, and New York had yet to act.

New York was crucial. Because of its geographical location the nation would be split almost in two if New York did not join. And 46 of the 65 delegates at the New York convention were Antifederalists. These Antifederalists had numerous supporters who wrote lively articles for New York newspapers. One such writer submitted his articles under the pen name "Brutus." Although historians are uncertain of Brutus' real identity, many people think that he was Robert Yates, a New York judge. In one typical Antifederalist essay Brutus wrote:

    66 Let us now proceed to enquire, as I at first proposed, whether it be best the thirteen United States should be reduced to one great republic, or not? It is here taken for granted that all agree in this, that whatever government we adopt, it ought to be a free one; that it should be so framed as to secure the liberty of the citizens of America, and such

RATIFICATION OF THE CONSTITUTION	
State	Date
Delaware	1787
Pennsylvania	1787
New Jersey	1787
Georgia	1788
Connecticut	1788
Massachusetts	1788
Maryland	1788
South Carolina	1788
New Hampshire*	1788
Virginia	1788
New York	1788
North Carolina	1789
Rhode Island	1790

*Ninth state, guarantees ratification

LEARNING FROM TABLES. *Delaware became the first state, ratifying the Constitution in December of 1787. Within the next year several other states joined Delaware. Why was New Hampshire's ratification especially important?*

an one as to admit of a full, fair, and equal representation of the people. The question then will be, whether a government thus constituted, and founded on such principles, is practicable, and can be exercised over the whole United States, reduced into one state? . . .

History furnishes no example of a free republic, any thing like the extent of the United States. The Grecian republics were of small extent; so also was that of the Romans. Both of these, it is true, in process of time, extended their conquests over large territories of country; and the consequence was, that their governments were changed from that of free governments to those of the most tyrannical that ever existed in the world.

Not only the opinion of the greatest men, and the experience of mankind, are against the idea of an extensive republic, but a variety of reasons may be drawn from the reason and nature of things, against it. In every government, the will of the sovereign [supreme authority] is the law. In despotic governments, the supreme authority being lodged in one, his will is law, and can be as easily expressed to a large extensive territory as to a small one. In a pure democracy the people are the sovereign, and their will is declared by themselves; for this purpose they must all come together to deliberate, and decide. This kind of government cannot be exercised, therefore, over a country of any considerable extent; it must be confined to a single city, or at least limited to such bounds as that the people can conveniently assemble, be able to debate, understand the subject submitted to them, and declare their opinion concerning it. . . .

The territory of the United States is of vast extent; it now contains near three millions of souls, and is capable of containing much more than ten times that number. Is it practicable for a country, so large and so numerous as they will soon become, to elect a representation, that will speak their sentiments, without their becoming so numerous as to be incapable of transacting public business? It certainly is not.[1] 🙶

Defeat seemed certain.

The leader of the Federalists at the convention was young Alexander Hamilton. Although he did not have a very high opinion of the Constitution—he thought it too weak rather than too strong—he was determined to see it ratified. He, John Jay, and James Madison had already written a series of newspaper articles explaining and

[1]From *The Anti-Federalist Papers and the Constitutional Convention Debates,* edited by Ralph Ketcham

defending the Constitution, the now-famous **Federalist Papers.** In Federalist Paper 9, for example, Hamilton wrote:

❝ A Firm Union will be of the utmost moment to the peace and liberty of the States as a barrier against domestic faction and insurrection. It is impossible to read the history of the petty Republics of Greece and Italy, without feeling sensations of horror and disgust at the distractions with which they were continually agitated, and at the rapid succession of the revolutions, by which they were kept in a state of perpetual vibration, between the extremes of tyranny and anarchy. If they exhibit occasional calms, these only serve as short-lived contrasts to the furious storms that are to succeed. . . .

A distinction, more subtle than accurate has been raised between a *confederacy* and a *consolidation* of the States. The essential characteristic of the first is said to be, the restriction of its authority to the members in their collective capacities, without reaching to the individuals of whom they are composed. It is contended that the national council ought to have no concern with any object of internal administration. An exact equality of suffrage between the members has also been insisted upon as a leading feature of a Confederate Government. These positions are in the main arbitrary; they are supported neither by principle nor precedent. It has indeed happened that governments of this kind have generally operated in the manner, which the distinction, taken notice of, supposes to be inherent in their nature—but there have been in most of them extensive exceptions to the practice, which serve to prove as far as example will go, that there is no absolute rule on the subject. And it will be clearly shewn, in the course of this investigation, that as far as the principle contended for has prevailed, it has been the cause of incurable disorder and imbecility [stupidity] in the government.

The definition of a *Confederate Republic* seems simply to be, an "assemblage of societies" or an association of two or more States into one State. The extent, modifications and objects of the Federal authority are mere matters of discretion. So long as the separate organization of the members be not abolished, so long as it exists by a constitutional necessity for local purposes, though it should be in perfect subordination to the general authority of the Union, it would still be, in fact and in theory, an association of States, or a confederacy. The proposed Constitution, so far from implying an abolition of the State Governments, makes them constituent parts of the national sovereignty by allowing

STRATEGIES FOR SUCCESS

SQ3R—A HELPFUL STUDY PLAN

One of your most important tasks is to remember what you learn. SQ3R is a strategy that makes that task simpler. SQ3R stands for *Survey, Question, Read, Recite,* and *Review.* It is a study plan that can make you a more efficient reader. With practice it will save you time and help you remember important information.

How to Use SQ3R

To use the SQ3R method to study, follow these steps.

1. **Survey the sections.** When you begin a reading assignment in *The Story of America,* skim over the section titles, Preview & Review, boldface words, and illustrations and their captions. Surveying helps you prepare to read the assignment.

2. **Question what lies ahead.** Use the information from your survey to question what lies ahead. Turn section heads into questions. Ask who? what? when? where? why? and how? Write down your questions as a study guide for yourself.

3. **Read to answer the questions.** You needn't try to remember everything you read. Usually the answers to the questions you have formed will give you the main ideas and the most important details.

4. **Recite what you find.** Write down answers to your questions in your own words. This gives you an immediate check on your understanding and helps you not to forget what you read. Using your own words makes you think carefully about the material.

5. **Review your work.** There are two times for useful review—immediately and later. When you finish writing down answers to all your questions, *immediately* answer the questions a second time without looking at your written answers. Reread any parts of the chapter that give rise to questions you still find difficult to answer.

    A few days later, perhaps while preparing for a test, review again by answering your set of questions without looking back to your written answers. Again reread if necessary.

SQ3R GUIDELINES	
STEP	WHAT TO DO
Survey	Read the Preview & Review. Read the headings. Scan for specific details. Skim for unfamiliar words. Look at illustrations and their captions.
Question	Make up a set of questions from your survey. Turn titles into questions. Ask who? what? when? where? why? how?
Read	Read to find answers to your questions.
Recite	Write the answers to your questions in your own words.
Review	Immediately answer your questions without looking at your earlier answers. Reread if necessary. Later answer your questions again. Reread if necessary.

SQ3R may seem to take a great amount of time and effort. But as you learn to use it, you will see that it actually saves both reading and study time. Use the chart on this page to help you organize your use of SQ3R.

Applying the Strategy

Use SQ3R to help you study "A More Perfect Union" on pages 220–31. The Preview & Review on page 220 introduces new words about the Constitution. The Preview & Review questions indicate the section focuses on the writing of the Constitution and its ratification. The section headings, such as "The Great Compromise," "Slavery in the Constitution," and others can be turned into questions such as "What was the Great Compromise?", "What did the Constitution say about slavery?", and other questions to help you understand the Constitution. Reviewing your answers to these questions and those in the Preview & Review will help you study the section.

For independent practice, see Practicing the Strategy on page 232.

them a direct representation in the Senate, and leaves in their possession certain exclusive and very important portions of sovereign power. This fully corresponds, in every rational import of the terms, with the idea of a Federal Government.[1] **99**

At the ratifying convention Hamilton advanced all the arguments developed in the Federalist essays and invented some new ones on the spot.

Although Hamilton probably did not change many minds, the Antifederalists were in a difficult position. If the United States needed New York, so did New York need the United States. Moreover, opinion in New York City was strong for the Constitution. Hamilton and other city leaders threatened to break away from the state and join the Union on their own if the Constitution was rejected. For practical reasons rather than because their minds had been changed, enough Antifederalists voted on July 26, 1788, to ratify the Constitution, 30 to 27.

[1]From *The Federalist Papers* by Alexander Hamilton, James Madison, and John Jay

The United States of America

Now the new system would have its chance. The first Congress was elected early in 1789. The state legislatures chose their presidential electors. On April 6, on order of the last Continental Congress, the new Congress gathered for the formal counting of the electoral votes in New York City, the temporary national capital. No one was surprised that George Washington was the unanimous choice of the 69 electors. John Adams, who received 34 votes, was declared vice president.

On April 30 Washington stood on the balcony of Federal Hall, at the corner of Broad and Wall Streets in New York City, and took the oath of office as president. A fine statue of Washington marks the site today. The oath he recited has been repeated by every president, for it is part of the Constitution:

66 I do solemnly swear that I will faithfully execute the Office of president of the United States, and will, to the best of my ability, preserve, protect, and defend the Constitution of the United States. **99**

Thus ended the Revolution. Thirteen English colonies in America had become one independent nation. That new nation was to be guided by a rare and special type of government—one based on consent of the governed. What would the Americans make of their independence and their new union? 🔲

Return to the Preview & Review on page 220.

CHAPTER 6 REVIEW

1775   FOUNDING THE UNITED STATES   1780

1777
Articles of
Confederation
drafted

1781
British
surrender
at Yorktown

Chapter Summary
Read the statements below. Choose one, and write a paragraph explaining its importance.
1. The first task Americans faced after the war was creating a new system of government. The system included both a central and state governments to represent the people.
2. At first the states formed a "league of friendship" under the Articles of Confederation.
3. The Treaty of Paris in 1783 gave lands in the Ohio Valley to the colonies, who settled troublesome colonial claims to the lands through land ordinances.
4. Hard times hit Americans after the war, making them realize they needed a stronger bond than the Articles of Confederation.
5. The Constitution of the United States is the supreme law of the nation.
6. The Constitution is in large part a document of compromises.
7. Debates between Federalists favoring the Constitution and Antifederalists opposing it took place throughout the country before the states voted on ratification.
8. The United States of America was created when New Hampshire became the ninth state to ratify the Constitution.

Reviewing Chronological Order
Number your paper 1-5. Then study the time line above and place the following events in the order in which they happened by writing the first next to 1, the second next to 2, and so on.
1. Washington elected first president
2. Northwest Ordinance
3. Articles of Confederation drafted
4. United States of America established
5. Treaty of Paris

Understanding Main Ideas
1. Why did the new state constitutions give more power to the legislatures than to governors?
2. How might a tariff on British goods have helped Americans immediately after the war?
3. What are some of the major duties of each of the three branches of the federal government under the Constitution?
4. Explain the difference between the American Revolution and the Revolutionary War.

Thinking Critically
1. **Analyzing.** Explain in your own words what Benjamin Franklin meant when he said, "We must all hang together, or we shall surely all hang separately."
2. **Synthesizing.** Imagine that you are a poor Massachusetts farmer in 1786. Would you be likely to follow Daniel Shays to prevent the state supreme court from meeting? If so, why? If not, why not?
3. **Evaluating.** On the question of ratification of the Constitution, how would you vote if you were a ship's captain from Boston? A bank clerk from New York City? A plantation owner from Georgia? In each case, explain why you would vote for or against ratification.

Writing About History: Classificatory
You are a delegate to the Constitutional Convention. Write a letter to the people of your state outlining the differences between the Constitution and the Articles. Explain why you feel the Constitution is an improvement. Use the information in Chapter 6 to help you write your letter.

Practicing the Strategy
Review the strategy on page 230.
SQ3R—A Helpful Study Plan. SQ3R can be helpful in studying important documents. This is certainly true of the United States Constitution. Apply the strategy to the Constitution on pages 201–18. Then answer the following questions.
1. Into what major sections is the United States Constitution divided?
2. What questions would you use to review each of the sections of the Constitution?
3. How would you answer each of your questions?
4. How would this process help you study the Constitution?

| 1785 | 1790 |

83
eaty
Paris
ned

1784
Economic
depression
hits America

1785
Land
Ordinance
of 1785

1786
Shays'
Rebellion in
Massachusetts

1787
Northwest
Ordinance

★
Constitutional
Convention
meets

1788
New Hampshire
ratifies
Constitution

★
United States of America
established

★
New York ratifies the Constitution

1789
Washington elected first president

Using Primary Sources

Review the following excerpts from the United States Constitution to understand the workings of the document. Then complete the activities below each.

> ARTICLE I, Section 8. *The Congress shall have the Power . . . To make all Laws which shall be necessary and proper for carrying into Execution the foregoing Powers, and all other Powers vested by this Constitution in the Government of the United States, or in any Department or Officer thereof.*

1. *Article I, Section 8* lists all the many powers assigned to Congress. The last entry on the list is called the "necessary and proper clause." Its intent and scope have been the subject of heated debate throughout the nation's history. What do you think the framers of the Constitution had in mind when they included this clause among the powers of Congress?
2. Give an example of a situation in which Congress might use the necessary and proper clause. (You may wish to review the other powers listed in *Section 8* on pages 204–05.)

> ARTICLE V. *The Congress, whenever two thirds of both Houses shall deem it necessary, shall propose Amendments to this Constitution, or, on the Application of the Legislatures of two thirds of the several states, shall call a Convention for proposing Amendments, which, in either Case, shall be valid to all Intents and Purposes, as Part of this Constitution, when ratified by the Legislatures of three fourths of the several States, or by Conventions in three fourths thereof, as the one or the other Mode of Ratification may be proposed by the Congress; Provided that no Amendment which may be made prior to the Year One thousand eight hundred and eight shall in any Manner affect the first and fourth Clauses in the Ninth Section of the first Article; and that no State, without its Consent, shall be deprived of its equal Suffrage in the Senate.*

1. *Article V* describes two methods for amending the Constitution. What are the basic steps in amending the Constitution?
2. Create a chart illustrating the steps in the two ways to amend the Constitution. What is the difference in the two methods?
3. Which method of amending the Constitution do you think is most often used? Why?

Linking History & Geography

The new United States of America faced a serious geographic problem at the end of the Revolutionary War. The country had new territory west of the Appalachian Mountains to govern. The new government faced conflicting colonial claims to these lands and decisions about their settlement. Study the map on page 186 and review the information about the land ordinances. Then in a brief paragraph, explain how the nation's leaders dealt with the serious geographic problem of settling the new territory.

Enriching Your Study of History

1. **Individual Project.** Clip articles from current newspapers and magazines that deal with activities of the three branches of the federal government. Group the articles that deal with each branch and add them to bulletin board charts. See how many different kinds of activities you can find for each branch of the government.
2. **Cooperative Project.** In your group, choose one branch of the federal government—legislative, executive, or judicial—and make a chart illustrating the duties of that branch. Combine your chart with charts from groups choosing the other branches to illustrate the system of checks and balances.

Chapter 6 Review   233

Governing the United States

Under the Constitution a federal government began to develop. As the first president, George Washington made decisions that to this day shape the highest office in the land. He set up a cabinet of advisers. His secretary of the treasury attempted to pay off the national debt and restore the credit of the United States. He avoided foreign wars and put down a small rebellion. When he left office, he delivered a famous Farewell Address urging national unity and neutrality. Would those who came after him be able to follow this advice?

Preview & Review

Use these questions to guide your reading. Answer the questions after completing Section 1.
Understanding Issues, Events, & Ideas. Use the following words to describe Washington's presidency: precedent, department of state, department of the treasury, department of war, attorney general, cabinet, amendment, Bill of Rights, natural rights, legal rights, human rights.
1. Why was Washington especially careful about the precedents he established?
2. What was Washington's view on the use of presidential power?
3. What is the purpose of the Bill of Rights?
Thinking Critically. 1. Imagine that you live during the administration of George Washington. Which of his qualities as president do you admire most? Why? **2.** The United States government has been called "a government of law, not men." How does this affect you as an American citizen?

1. A GOVERNMENT IS FORMED

Establishing Precedents

Like all later presidents, Washington's first task was to appoint officials to run the government departments. He also had to decide what jobs needed to be done and how the work should be organized and supervised. The task was complicated by the need to cooperate with the Congress. Of course, the Senate had to approve the major appointments. In addition, laws had to be passed to create the positions and provide money to pay salaries. Washington's government seems simple when compared to the enormous federal government of today. It was not so simple to design and staff it back in 1789.

Washington was extremely conscientious. He knew that as the first president he was establishing a **precedent,** a guide for later action, every time he made a decision. The Constitution had given him a great deal of power. He was a strong and determined person. He wanted to use his power to the full. Yet he wanted to assure citizens who were worried about the misuse of presidential power.

Washington sincerely believed in the separation of powers. In particular he was careful not to tread on the toes of Congress. It was the job of Congress to make the laws. His job was to execute, or carry out, the laws.

Congress created three main departments: the **department of state,** the **treasury,** and a **war department.** Each of these was headed by a secretary appointed by the president. Today the secretary of

The Granger Collection

DEVELOPMENT OF THE CABINET	
Office	Date Established
State	1789
Treasury	1789
War[1]	1789
Attorney General[2]	1789
Navy[3]	1798
Postmaster General[4]	1829
Interior	1849
Agriculture	1889
Commerce and Labor[5]	1903
Commerce	1913
Labor	1913
Defense	1947
Health, Education, and Welfare[6]	1953
Housing and Urban Development	1965
Transportation	1966
Energy	1977
Health and Human Services	1979
Education	1979
Veterans Affairs	1989

▢ Original Members
[1]Lost cabinet status, 1947
[2]Not head of Justice Dept. until 1870
[3]Lost cabinet status, 1947
[4]Lost cabinet status, 1970
[5]Divided, 1913
[6]Divided, 1979

state has charge of the relations of the government with foreign countries. In 1789 the secretary also had to manage all domestic affairs except those handled by the war and treasury heads. Yet Jefferson, the first secretary of state, had a staff of only five persons.

The war department headed by General Henry Knox maintained a small army and navy, but in peacetime five people could carry out its functions. Only the treasury department, under Alexander Hamilton, had a fairly large staff. It collected taxes and tariffs and attempted to make a farsighted economic plan for the United States. By 1790 the treasury department had 70 persons. Washington made Edmund Randolph, presenter of the Virginia Plan at the Constitutional Convention, **attorney general.** Randolph, a part-time employee, was a legal adviser to the president.

Washington called upon the secretaries for advice, but he did not meet with them as a group. What we call the **cabinet,** a group of department heads meeting regularly with the president to discuss current issues, did not exist in Washington's day.

General Knox, who worshiped Washington, his former commander, ran the war department efficiently. He was mostly a follower who merely agreed with whatever decision Washington made. Jefferson was just the opposite. He disliked routine office details and sometimes neglected his duties as head of the state department. He

LEARNING FROM CHARTS.
This chart illustrates the steady growth in the size of the cabinet. Why do you think the president today has more advisers than the first presidents did?

often disagreed with Washington about important matters. Hamilton was a bundle of energy and wide ranging in his interests. He was eager to increase his own power. Gradually he became Washington's most influential adviser.

Washington as President

Washington would have preferred to serve without salary, as he had during the Revolutionary War, but Congress voted him a salary of $25,000. That was a very large sum for the time. Congress did not give him an expense account, however, so the salary was not as generous as it seemed. Washington actually spent about $5,000 a year of his own money on official business.

Congress did rent a fine three-story mansion near the federal building for the president. The house was, according to the first lady, Martha Custis Washington, "handsomely furnished, all new." Washington supplied his own servants. He brought seven of his slaves up from Mount Vernon, his Virginia plantation. He hired another 14 servants locally. He served the best food and wines at official dinners. He drove about in a fine carriage drawn by six horses. At receptions he appeared in rich formal clothes and wore his dress sword.

On the other hand, the small size of the government made for simplicity. New York City, the nation's capital, was still a small town of about 30,000 people in 1789. On Tuesday afternoons from three to five o'clock, President Washington received guests. Every Friday evening Martha Washington gave a tea party. No invitations were necessary for these affairs. Anyone who was properly dressed could

Martha Washington received guests at tea parties on Friday evenings in the presidential mansion in New York City. This oil painted by Daniel Huntington turns the tea party into "The Republican Court." All eyes are on the first lady at left center. President Washington is near the center. Does this picture suggest that America had found its own style or does the gathering look more European?

The Brooklyn Museum

simply walk in. Washington particularly hated the afternoon affairs, which were for men only. The visitors tended to stand and stare in awe at the Great Man, or else they ignored him and spent their time gobbling up the refreshments.

The tea parties were different. Washington enjoyed chatting with the women at these affairs very much. The president was a tall, powerfully built man. Women often found him charming. According to Abigail Adams, the wife of the vice president, Washington was much more dignified and well mannered than King George III of England. Of course, Abigail Adams was an ardent patriot. She may have been prejudiced!

To many people of the time Washington seemed more like a statue on a pedestal than a human being. That is still the case. He seemed almost too formal and dignified to be a real person. This was because he was so aware of his responsibilities. He could hardly ever relax. Americans considered him the greatest hero of their Revolution. He felt that he had to live up to the almost godlike image the people had made of him.

This must have made life difficult for Washington at times. He frequently complained of the burdens of his office. He looked forward to the day when he could retire to his plantation at Mount Vernon. Yet he never neglected his duties. Although he only looked like a perfect man, he was as close to a perfect first president as the young nation could have hoped for.

Abigail Smith Adams is shown as a young woman in this watercolor. She wrote wise and warm letters to her husband John during the Continental Congress.

The Bill of Rights

One of the first tasks Congress took up was preparing the **amendments** to the Constitution that the Federalists had promised the Antifederalists. The purpose was to reassure people who were afraid that the new government had too much power. About 80 proposed amendments had been suggested by one or another state. After debating through the summer of 1789, the Congress passed 12. Ten of these were ratified by the states.

These first ten amendments are known as the **Bill of Rights.** They did not give rights to the people or to the states. The rights already existed. The amendments stated simply and clearly that the government had no authority to take them away. The First Amendment begins, ''Congress shall make no law . . .'' That was the basic principle.

The First Amendment protects the freedoms of religion, speech, and the press, and the right of people to gather together in groups peacefully—that is, the right to assembly. The Second Amendment guarantees the rights of American citizens to own firearms. It prevents the government from absolutely prohibiting such ownership. It also protects the right and duty to serve in the armed forces. The Third Amendment provides that in peacetime no soldiers can be lodged in private homes without the consent of the owners. In wartime soldiers can be quartered in private homes only according to specific laws passed by Congress at the time. The Fourth Amendment protects the right to privacy—no ''unreasonable searches and seizures'' are permitted.

Several amendments deal with the rights of people accused of committing crimes. The Fifth Amendment prohibits forcing people to testify against themselves and bans ''double jeopardy''—prosecuting again a person acquitted of a crime for the same crime, and guarantees ''due process''—standard procedures applied in all cases to all accused persons. The Six, Seventh, and Eighth Amendments guarantee speedy trial, trial by jury, and protection from excessive bail and from torture. All accused persons are entitled to be told in advance what crime they are accused of. All have the right to be helped by a lawyer.

The Ninth Amendment says that the rights mentioned in the Constitution and the first eight amendments are not the only rights of the people. Civil liberties are not taken away from the people simply because they are not mentioned. The Tenth Amendment states that all powers not given to the United States government by the Constitution or denied by the Constitution to the States are ''reserved'' to the states or to the people as individuals.

Two points about the Bill of Rights are particularly important. One is that most of the amendments did not protect people's rights against violation by the state governments. The First Amendment says that *Congress* may not interfere with freedom of religion, speech, or the press. It did not prevent Massachusetts or South Carolina or any other state from doing so. Some states permitted and protected slavery, the most complete denial of human rights one can imagine.

The second point is that the rights protected were what the people of that day called **natural rights.** People also have **legal rights,** those given them by laws. For example, our present old-age pension law gives persons over a particular age fixed amounts of money each month. The people have a right to these payments. But the law can be and many times has been changed by Congress. If for some reason Congress voted to repeal the old-age pension law, that right would disappear. The right of free speech, however, is one of our natural rights, or **human rights.** Under the Constitution the government cannot take that right away.

The insistence of many Americans on the addition of the Bill of Rights illustrates how concerned Americans were with human rights and ethical behavior of government. Stating these ideals in the Constitution focused attention on principles which were becoming worldwide concerns. It also alerted all Americans to their civic responsiblities. If the nation were to remain free and democratic, each citizen would have to participate.

THE BILL OF RIGHTS

AMENDMENT 1	Guarantees freedom of speech, religion, and the press, and the right to assemble peacefully, and to petition the government.
AMENDMENT 2	Guarantees the right to bear arms and to organize state militia.
AMENDMENT 3	Prohibits quartering of troops.
AMENDMENT 4	Prohibits unreasonable searches and seizures of property.
AMENDMENT 5	Guarantees that no one may be deprived of life, liberty, or property without due process of law; prohibits forcing accused persons to testify against themselves; requires a grand jury for serious criminal charges; prohibits military trial for civilians.
AMENDMENT 6	Guarantees the right to a speedy trial in criminal cases, the right to know all charges, the right to obtain and question witnesses, and the right to have counsel.
AMENDMENT 7	Guarantees a trial in most civil cases.
AMENDMENT 8	Prohibits excessive fines and bail, and cruel and unusual punishment.
AMENDMENT 9	Gives rights not specifically mentioned in the Constitution to the people.
AMENDMENT 10	Reserves the powers not delegated to the national government for the states.

LEARNING FROM CHARTS. *The Bill of Rights grew out of the ratification debate. Its intent was to guarantee individual rights. Study the chart and refer to the amendments on pages 211–12. Then restate in your own words what is guaranteed by each of the first ten amendments.*

But how would Americans know what their responsibilities were? How could they be relied on to make intelligent and ethical decisions? That was the role of education. Educated voters were the key to preserving a democratic society. From the beginning leaders linked education to America's social and civic values—freedom, justice, self-reliance, and prosperity. Informed Americans could better solve economic and political problems and advance technologically. At the time, of course, formal education was still mostly limited to boys and young men. Girls and young women would struggle for more than 50 years to gain access to the educational system.

The Living Constitution

The writers of the Constitution had hoped to create a government that would guide the nation forever. But they were mindful that as America grew the needs of society might change. They believed that later generations of Americans should be able to change, or amend, the Constitution if they needed to. Therefore, they included the amendment process as part of the Constitution itself. It is this process that makes the Constitution flexible, allowing it to adapt to the tremendous changes in America over 200 years.

Return to the Preview & Review on page 234.

A Government Is Formed 239

Historical Society of Pennsylvania
(photo: Bradley Smith/Laurie Platt Winfrey)

Alexander Hamilton, the genius of finance who put the United States on a firm financial foundation, was painted by John Trumbull. With other class members, prepare a series of reports on how the United States is financed today. Then contrast today's financial arrangements with Hamilton's plan.

Use these questions to guide your reading. Answer the questions after completing Section 2.
Understanding Issues, Events, & Ideas. Use the following words to explain the nation's early financial system: government bond, speculator, Bank of the United States, security, bank note, necessary and proper clause, elastic clause.
1. How did Hamilton propose to pay off the national debt?
2. How did speculators profit when the government paid its debts?
3. Why did Hamilton want a Bank of the United States?
4. Why did Jefferson oppose the bank bill?
Thinking Critically. 1. Which term, *necessary* or *proper,* would you emphasize to interpret the elastic clause? Why? **2.** During Alexander Hamilton's term as secretary of the treasury, would you rather be a speculator or a war veteran? Why?

2. FINANCING THE NATION

Hamilton and the National Debt

One of the main reasons for strengthening the national government was the poor condition of the finances of the United States. Congress therefore acted quickly to use its new power to tax. In 1789 it placed a tariff, or tax, of 5 percent on all foreign goods entering the country. This law was quite similar to the measures Parliament had employed in the 1760s to raise money in America. Those laws had caused a revolution. The Tariff Act of 1789 was accepted by everyone. The vital difference was that the new taxes were agreed to by the people's own representatives. These taxes were not imposed by an outside power.

These taxes raised enough money to meet the day-to-day expenses of the government. They did not deal with the problem of paying off the large debts that the government had accumulated during and after the Revolutionary War. This debt included money lent by foreign governments and bonds sold to private citizens by the government to raise money during the Revolution. It included bonuses and other payments promised to soldiers. The government also owed money to merchants and manufacturers who had supplied it with various goods.

Because of the large national debt, investors were unwilling to lend the government more money. They considered the United States

240   GOVERNING THE UNITED STATES

a poor credit risk. The **government bonds,** certificates representing the money the national government had borrowed, had fallen far below their face value. A person who owned a $1,000 bond might not be able to sell it for even $500.

It was the responsibility of the secretary of the treasury, Alexander Hamilton, to find a way to pay off the debt and restore the credit of the government. Many people admired Hamilton extravagantly during his lifetime. Others considered him a villain. This division of opinion remains today.

Everyone recognizes that Hamilton was a genius of finance. But his ideas about government and about human nature remain controversial. Hamilton had a low opinion of the average person's honesty and judgment. He believed that most people were selfish and easily led astray by crafty, power-hungry leaders.

Hamilton did not trust the rich any more than he did what he called "the great mass of the people." If "aristocrats" had power, they would oppress the rest of society. If the poor controlled the government, they would use their power to seize the property of the rich. A good government, he thought, was one that balanced rival interests. This attitude was not unusual, as we have seen. However, Hamilton went beyond most political thinkers of his day. He thought that the selfish desires of the rich could be used to strengthen the government and thus the whole nation.

Many of the people who had bought government bonds had sold them at a loss. Others had been forced to accept the government's promises to repay them when the money owed them became available. They had sold these paper promises to investors for less than their face value. These investors were what we call **speculators.** They were gambling that some day the government would be able to pay off its bonds and other debts at full value. Speculators were wealthy or well-to-do people who had spare cash.

Hamilton proposed gradually raising enough money by taxes to pay off all the national government's debts. He also wanted the United States to assume, or take over, the debts of the states. He wanted to pay all at their face value. A speculator who had bought a $1,000 bond for $500 would receive $1,000. Hamilton reasoned that by doing this he would make the wealthy bond owners enthusiastic supporters of the national government. With such powerful people behind it, the government would be strong.

Some Americans felt that this policy was unfair to the former soldiers and other owners of bonds or government promises who had sold them cheaply. They wanted the original owners of these securities to receive at least some of their increased value. Hamilton refused. The speculators had paid what the bonds were worth at the time they bought them, he pointed out. They had taken the risks. Now they were entitled to the profits. After some hesitation Congress passed the necessary laws.

The Roots of Capitalism

Hamilton's view that the risk-takers deserved the rewards and that the desire of rich people to get richer would strengthen the country echoed the ideas of the Scottish philosopher Adam Smith. Smith was the first modern economist. In his book *An Inquiry into the Nature and Causes of the Wealth of Nations*, published in 1776, Smith argued that self-interest was the force that could bring about a free, orderly, and progressive society. If left free of government regulations, producers who wanted to make money would have to compete with one another. This competition would result in the highest quality goods and services at the best price for the consumer.

This economic philosophy later came to be called **capitalism,** the system that is the core of the American economy. Under capitalism, most businesses are privately owned and the owners are motivated by a desire for **profit,** the gain resulting from sales of goods or services. Rival businesses compete for customers and profits in the **market.** The business that provides the highest quality product to consumers at the best price makes the largest profit. The least efficient fail. Smith warned against government intervention and control. Free competition should determine the "wealth of nations." Hamilton, on the other hand, believed that government and business could work together for the benefit of both. Hamilton's handling of the government bond issue as well as the rest of his economic plan demonstrated this belief. However, like Smith he believed that government involvement in the economy should be limited—the basis of the free enterprise system in the United States today.

The Bank of the United States

The next step in Hamilton's plan was the establishment of a **Bank of the United States.** In 1790 there were almost no banks of any kind in the country. Hamilton argued that the government could use the bank to deposit the money it received from taxes. The bank would also be able to print new paper money, called **bank notes,** to represent the money it had on deposit. It could lend them to merchants and manufacturers, thus speeding the growth of business. For example, a manufacturer of shoes might ask the bank for a loan to buy leather. The leather and the shoes made from it would be **security** for the loan. If the shoemaker did not repay the loan, the bank would seize the goods. Thus the manufacturer would be able to produce more shoes, earn more money, and repay the loan. Without such a bank the shoe manufacturer and all sorts of other people in business would have to operate on a much smaller scale. Once again Hamilton's scheme would greatly benefit the nation, especially the rich.

In 1791 Congress passed a bank bill. But President Washington did not sign it immediately. He hesitated because he could find noth-

The First Bank of the United States issued this $10 bank note in 1796. The X-marks probably show that it was redeemed, or turned in to the Bank for gold or silver. Notice that at the bottom of the note the name of the holder and the date were written in by hand. Which branch of the government has the power to coin money and issue bank notes?

ing in the Constitution authorizing Congress to create a bank. So he asked Hamilton and Secretary of State Jefferson if they thought the bill was constitutional.

Hamilton, naturally enough, said the bill was constitutional. Jefferson, however, insisted that it was not. What is most interesting about their arguments is that they relied on the *same* clause in the Constitution—**the necessary and proper clause.** Yet they reached opposite conclusions.

Besides spelling out the powers of Congress, such as the power to tax and the power to borrow money, the Constitution says that Congress can "make all laws which shall be necessary and proper" to put its powers into effect. This clause means, for instance, that since Congress has the power to coin money, it may also build and operate a mint. But the necessary and proper clause is vague. Hamilton concluded that the bank had "a natural relation" to the power to collect taxes and regulate trade. A bank was a *proper* way to make use of that power.

On the other hand, Jefferson claimed that Congress could only pass laws that were *necessary,* "not those which are merely '*convenient.*'" Since the government could function without a bank, a bank was "not *necessary* and consequently not authorized," Jefferson said.

Washington accepted Hamilton's argument. He signed the bank bill. In most cases since, government leaders have done the same. The necessary and proper clause is often called the **elastic clause** because it has been used so often to stretch the powers of Congress. Yet the clause can be read two ways. If only the Constitution had said "necessary *or* proper," many later arguments would have been avoided.

Critics of Hamilton's financial policies objected more to his desires to help already powerful interests than to the policies themselves. The policies were so effective that almost everyone approved of them. The credit of the United States was soon as good as that of any nation in the world. The Bank proved a most valuable institution, both to the government and to business. 🖮

Return to the Preview & Review on page 240.

Financing the Nation   243

Use these questions to guide your reading. Answer the questions after completing Section 3.

Understanding Issues, Events, & Ideas. Use the following words to explain America's dilemma in staying neutral: French Revolution, privateer, Battle of Fallen Timbers, Jay's Treaty, Treaty of Greenville, right of deposit, Pinckney's Treaty, special interest group.

1. How did Americans greet news of the French Revolution in 1789?
2. What reasons were there for America to side with France in the war?
3. What actions of "Citizen" Genet made Washington's neutrality policy harder to maintain?
4. What did the country gain from Jay's Treaty? Pinckney's Treaty?
5. What arguments did Washington make for unity in his Farewell Address? For neutrality?

Thinking Critically. **1.** Predict the effect on future relations between Indians and settlers caused by the fate of the Indian Confederacy. Support your prediction with facts from the textbook. **2.** In your opinion, what was Washington's greatest achievement?

3. THE NATION IS TESTED

The French Revolution

The first serious political conflicts in the United States were not caused by Hamilton's schemes but by events that occurred on the other side of the Atlantic Ocean. The American Revolution had been very popular in France. Of course, it had weakened France's chief European rival, Great Britain. But the Revolution also seemed a great step forward to the liberal-minded French people. Washington and Jefferson were almost national heroes to them.

Thus the American Revolution was one of the causes of the **French Revolution,** which began in 1789. That revolution, in turn,

was greeted with enormous enthusiasm in America. Did it not prove that America's republican ideas were spreading?

This enthusiasm slackened, however, when the French Revolution took a more radical turn. By 1793 extremists were in control of France. They executed King Louis XVI and many members of the nobility. They began to put radical social changes into effect. Then, in 1793, war broke out between France and Great Britain.

The United States had signed a treaty of alliance with France in 1778. French help had made it possible for America to win its independence. The treaty was still in effect. Furthermore, the United States had not yet managed to get the British to live up to all the terms of the treaty that had ended the Revolutionary War. Was the United States duty bound to side with France?

Musée de Versailles

Point of View

The opening lines of *A Tale of Two Cities* capture the mood in France on the eve of its great revolution.

> "It was the best of times, it was the worst of times, it was the age of wisdom, it was the age of foolishness, it was the epoch of belief, it was the epoch of incredulity, it was the season of Light, it was the season of Darkness, it was the spring of hope, it was the winter of despair, we had everything before us, we had nothing before us, we were all going direct to Heaven, we were all going direct the other way—. . ."
>
> Charles Dickens, 1859

The French Revolution erupted in 1789. Here we see the revolutionaries storming the Bastille, where political prisoners were held. Hubert Robert painted the large oil from which this scene is taken. Why did Americans support the citizens of France in their uprising?

The Neutrality Proclamation

Edmond Genet preferred to call himself simply "Citizen" Genet. This oil portrait by Ezra Amos, a traveling painter, shows an older, less meddlesome Genet. Compare this portrait with the description of Genet at age 30 on this page.

Albany Institute of History and Art

Should the United States come to the aid of France by declaring war on Great Britain? Many Americans thought that was the honorable course the country should follow. But Washington felt otherwise. He issued a neutrality proclamation warning American citizens not to aid either side. The government would try to be "friendly and impartial" to both.

The revolutionary government in France paid little attention to this proclamation. It sent a special diplomatic representative, Edmond Charles Genet, to rouse support for France in the United States.

Genet was a charming, red-haired man of 30, an enthusiastic supporter of his country's cause. He spoke English fluently. Although the son of an important French diplomat, he called himself simply "Citizen" Genet. He arrived at Charleston, South Carolina, in April 1793. While making his way northward to present himself to President Washington, he persuaded a number of Americans who owned merchant ships to mount guns on their vessels and sail off to attack unarmed British ships on the high seas. These ships and the men who sailed them were called **privateers.** They flew the French flag and carried papers issued by the French government making them part of the French navy.

Privateering was a common practice at the time. Americans had often engaged in it under the British flag in earlier wars. Privateering was possible during the days of wooden sailing ships because the differences between a warship and a merchant vessel were slight. A small privateer was designed for speed and easy maneuvering. Armed with a few cannon, it could capture or destroy an unarmed cargo vessel. It could also escape large pursuing warships. Since Genet's privateers were entitled to keep two thirds of the value of the cargo and ships they captured, the business could be very profitable.

A privateer was certainly not acting in a neutral manner. When Washington learned what Genet was up to, he was furious. When Genet reached the capital, which had been moved to Philadelphia, Washington ordered him to stop these activities at once. Genet ignored the orders. Privately he called Washington *le vieillard,* which is French for "the old man." He continued to recruit and arm privateers. He tried to persuade several Americans to organize private armies to attack Spanish Florida and Louisiana, since Spain was also at war with France at this time. He even tried to raise an army to invade Canada. Washington finally demanded that the French replace him.

The removal of Genet did not stop the efforts being made to involve the United States in this latest European war. Washington and his advisers believed that neutrality was the proper policy for America. Maintaining neutrality was not easy. Both France and Great

Britain wanted to trade with the United States. Since they were at war with each other, each also wanted to prevent the other from getting American products. The navies of both began to seize unarmed American merchant ships on the Atlantic. In a single year several hundred American vessels loaded with valuable goods were captured. The British attacks were much more damaging than the French because Great Britain had a much larger navy than France.

The Indian Confederacy

Americans were also troubled by the refusal of the British to remove their troops from forts on American soil in the Great Lakes area. These outposts were not important in themselves, but American frontier settlers claimed that the British were supplying the Indians of the area with guns to use against them.

The Revolutionary War had not won the Indians of the country their independence. During the conflict Indians fought on each side. When the war ended, the British coldly betrayed those Indians who had helped them. They did so by signing the peace treaty granting all the land between the Appalachian Mountains and the Mississippi River to the United States. The Indians properly claimed that they, not the British, owned this land.

The tribes of the region north of the Ohio River resisted the invasion of American settlers who pressed into the area after 1783. They joined together in a confederacy and pledged not to sell any territory to the settlers. Unlike the tribes who lived by hunting, many of these Indians had taken up farming. For them, moving would mean more than having to find another hunting ground.

By the late 1780s 10,000 settlers were pouring into the Ohio Valley each year. They disregarded the fact that the land had always been owned by the Indians. These settlers demanded that the government protect them. Finally in 1790 an army of 1,400 led by General Josiah Harmar advanced against the Indian confederacy.

The artist who drew Little Turtle is unknown but the likeness is thought to be accurate. His adversary Arthur St. Clair was painted by Charles Willson Peale. Little Turtle appears peaceful in this portrait. How do we know the truth to be different?

The leader of the Indian confederacy was Michikinikua, or Little Turtle, chief of the Miamis. Despite his mild name, Little Turtle was a brave and skillful fighter. He defeated Harmar's force badly. The next year Little Turtle and his warriors defeated an even larger army commanded by Major General Arthur St. Clair. They killed over 600 of St. Clair's 2,000 men and wounded 250 others. These battles were among the fiercest

Smithsonian Institution

Independence National Historical Park

General Anthony Wayne orders a charge at the Battle of Fallen Timbers where he routed Little Turtle.

and bloodiest in the entire history of warfare between settlers and Indians.

In 1792 Washington placed General "Mad Anthony" Wayne in command of the army. Wayne was "mad" only in the sense that he was a tough professional soldier. He loved a good fight, but he was certainly not crazy.

Wayne had more than 3,600 soldiers under his command. He spent months training and drilling them. In October 1793 he headed north from a base on the Ohio River near Fort Washington (present-day Cincinnati). As he advanced, he built a series of forts to protect his rear guard. Scouts ranged ahead and on each side to protect the army against surprise. The army passed the winter at Fort Greenville, about halfway between Fort Washington and Lake Erie.

Observing Wayne's careful preparations, Little Turtle decided that it would be hopeless to resist. "The Americans are now led by a chief who never sleeps," he warned his fellows. But hotter heads prevailed. Led now by Blue Jacket, a chief of the Shawnees, in June 1794 the Indians attacked part of Wayne's force near the place where St. Clair had been routed. They won a minor victory. Still, Wayne continued his slow, steady advance. The showdown battle occurred in August near Fort Miami, one of the British posts a few miles southwest of Lake Erie.

This **Battle of Fallen Timbers** was a great victory for Wayne. He had more men and he "outgeneraled" Blue Jacket. The Indians fled in disorder. When they sought safety in Fort Miami, the British commander refused to let them in. Wayne then set fire to the Indians' cornfields and homes. Their defeat was total, their spirits broken. Soon their ancestral lands were settled by whites.

The distrust between Indians and whites continued, and in many cases increased. Some people used the situation for profit. Swindlers became rich cheating government Indian agents. One ingenious method was to "create" an "Indian chief" to receive government goods and money.

> You have heard of the Indian nations to the westward, that occasionally make war upon the frontier settlements? It has been the policy of government, to treat [sign treaties] with these, and distribute goods. Commissioners are appointed for that purpose. Now you are not to suppose that it is an easy matter to catch a real chief, and bring him from the woods; or if at some expense one was brought, the goods would go to his use; whereas it is much more profitable to hire substitutes and make chiefs of our own; and as some unknown gibberish [nonsense language] is necessary, to pass for Indian language, we generally make use of Welsh, or Low Dutch, or Irish [languages]; or pick up an ingenious fellow here and there, who can imitate a language by sounds of his own. . . . If your man is tractable [easily taught], I can make him a Kickapoo [Indian] in about nine days. . . . He must have a part of his head shaved, and painted, with feathers on his crown; but the paint will rub off, and the hair grow in a short time, so he can go about with you again.[1]

Is it any wonder the great chief Tecumseh came to think most white men were evil? He said:

> I admit that there are good white men, but they bear no proportion to the bad; the bad must be the strongest, for they rule. They do what they please. They enslave those who are not of their color, although created by the same Great Spirit who created them. They would make slaves of us if they could; but as they cannot do it, they kill us. There is no faith to be placed in their words. They are not like the Indians, who are only enemies [of each other] while at war, and are friends in peace. They [whites] will say to an Indian, "My friend; my brother!" They will take him by the hand, and, at the same moment, destroy him. . . . Remember that this day I have warned you to beware of such friends as these. I know the Long-Knives. They are not to be trusted.[2]

[1] From *Modern Chivalry* by Hugh Henry Brackenridge
[2] From *A Century of Dishonor* by Helen Hunt Jackson

Jay's Treaty

Earlier in 1794 Washington had sent John Jay, chief justice of the United States, to England to try to work out a solution to all the conflicts that had developed between the two nations. Jay had done well in the negotiations leading to the treaty of 1783 ending the Revolutionary War. This time he was far less successful.

Jay got the British to agree to withdraw their troops from the western forts. They also agreed to let American ships trade with British colonies in Asia. And they promised to pay damages to the shipowners whose vessels they had illegally seized in the West Indies. But that was all.

The British refused to stop attacking American merchant ships elsewhere in the world. They would not allow American ships to trade with the British sugar islands in the West Indies. They rejected the American view of the trading rights of neutral nations during wartime. They would not pay for the slaves who had fled to their lines during the Revolutionary War.

Most Americans disliked **Jay's Treaty.** Many leading politicians urged Washington to reject it. Washington, however, decided to accept it, and he managed to persuade the Senate to ratify it. He considered it unfair and in some respects insulting. Americans had proper claims that the British had flatly refused to recognize. Nevertheless, he realized that the United States had some gains from the treaty. More important, the treaty made it possible to avoid going to war again. Washington knew that time was on the nation's side. Each year the United States was becoming larger, richer, and stronger. A war with Great Britain, or any other European nation, would cost much and could gain little.

The removal of the British troops and the defeat of the Indians at the Battle of Fallen Timbers opened the northwest to peaceful settlement. In August 1795 General Wayne and 92 leading chiefs signed the **Treaty of Greenville.** The Indians agreed to turn over the entire southern half of what is now Ohio to the American settlers.

America obtained an additional and unexpected benefit from Jay's Treaty. Relations between the United States and Spain were not good. The Spanish government had refused to recognize the boundary between Florida and the southern United States that had been fixed by the peace treaty ending the Revolutionary War. The Spanish also controlled the west bank of the Mississippi River and both sides of the mouth of the river, including the city of New Orleans.

The Spanish refused to allow Americans to load and unload cargo freely at New Orleans. This especially hurt the western farmers. They needed what they called the **right of deposit** at New Orleans in order to transfer their farm products from river craft to ocean-going ships.

When the Spanish read Jay's Treaty, they were greatly alarmed. They suspected that the published version was incomplete. Perhaps there was a secret clause outlining a joint British-American attack on Spain's possessions in North America. They decided to try to make friends with the United States. In 1795 they signed a treaty accepting the American version of the Florida boundary line and granting Americans the right to ship goods freely down the Mississippi. This agreement is known as **Pinckney's Treaty** because it was negotiated for the United States by Thomas Pinckney, a son of Eliza Lucas Pinckney, who first cultivated indigo in America.

Washington's Farewell Address

By 1796 Washington could justly feel that he had set the United States well on its way as an independent nation. The Jay and Pinckney Treaties had assured the United States the boundaries first laid out in the treaty of 1783. The bloody fighting between settlers and Indians had been ended, at least for the moment. Settlers were pushing west across the Appalachian Mountains. Kentucky had enough people to become a state by 1792. Tennessee entered the Union in 1796. Ohio would soon follow.

Besides his sense of having completed his main tasks, Washington was tired after serving two terms as president. Political bickering was beginning to affect his reputation as a national hero. Although he could surely have been elected to a third term had he wished one, Washington decided to retire.

His Farewell Address of September 1796 announced his decision. It also contained his final advice to the American people. That advice can be boiled down to two ideas—unity at home, neutrality abroad. Washington said:

> The name of American, which belongs to you in your national capacity, must always exalt the just pride of patriotism more than any appellation [name] derived from local discriminations. With slight shades of difference, you have the same religion, manners, habits, and political principles. You have in a common cause fought and triumphed together. . . .
>
> In contemplating the causes which may disturb our union, it occurs as matter of serious concern that any ground should have been furnished for characterizing parties by *geographical* discriminations—*Northern* and *Southern*, *Atlantic* and *Western*—whence designing men may endeavor to excite a belief that there is a real difference of local interests and views. . . . You cannot shield yourselves too much against the jealousies and heartburnings which spring from these misrepresentations; they tend to render alien [unfriendly] to each other those who ought to be bound together by fraternal affection. . . .

Imagine the president of the United States, on horseback, leading an army westward across the United States, with the secretary of the treasury as second in command. In 1794 this surprising turn of events came about when western farmers rioted to protest a tax placed on the manufacture of whiskey. This was the so-called Whiskey Rebellion.

Congress had placed a tax of about 25 percent on the value of any whiskey distilled, or manufactured, in the United States. The tax was one of the measures designed by Hamilton to pay off the debts of the United States and the states. This very heavy tax angered frontier farm-

ers, who usually distilled a large part of their corn and other grain into whiskey. They did so because land transportation was so difficult and expensive. There were few roads and they were rough and impassable in bad weather. It was much cheaper to ship whiskey than bulky farm products the long distances to market over these bad roads.

In 1794 farmers in western Pennsylvania rioted to protest the tax. They bullied tax collectors, prevented courts from meeting, and threatened to march on Pittsburgh. Washington promptly called up 12,900 militiamen to duty and marched westward. Alexander Hamilton was his second in command.

When the soldiers reached the troubled area, not a single "rebel" could be found. No one dared to stand up before this huge force, which was actually larger than any army Washington had commanded during the war! The "rebellion" ended, or perhaps it would be more accurate to say it disappeared.

Some historians feel that Washington overreacted to the Whiskey Rebellion. Perhaps he did. Still, the contrast was sharp between his swift and painless enforcement of the law and the bloodshed of Daniel Shays' rebellion only eight years earlier. This time there was a strong central government backed by the new Constitution.

Observe good faith and justice toward all nations. Cultivate peace and harmony with all. . . .

Against the insidious wiles [sly tricks] of foreign influence (I conjure [beg] you to believe me, fellow citizens) the jealousy [suspicion] of a free people ought to be constantly awake, since history and experience prove that foreign influence is one of the most baneful foes of republican government. But that jealousy, to be useful, must be impartial, else it becomes the instrument of the very influence to be avoided, instead of a defense against it. . . .

The great rule of conduct for us, in regard to foreign Nations, is in extending our commercial relations, to have with them as little Political connection as possible. So far as we have already formed engagements let them be fulfilled with perfect good faith. Here let us stop. . . .**

Washington's advice was far-sighted. His main points bear repeating. First, *unity.* Washington disliked political squabbling, but his argument mostly concerned conflicts between **special interest groups** in different sections of the country. Too often northerners, southerners, and westerners thought only of what was best for their own region and tried to gain their objectives no matter what the effect on other sections. Washington called these rivalries "the jealousies and heartburnings" of "geographical discriminations." Such attitudes were shortsighted. Northern manufacturers needed southern raw

The Metropolitan Museum of Art

materials. Southern farmers sold their crops in northern markets. East and West had common interests. All sections of the country profited from the increase in trade that resulted. To understand why Washington put so much emphasis on so obvious a point, one must remember how new the United States was. Local pride remained strong. Washington stressed the argument that national unity was "a main pillar . . . of real independence."

As for *neutrality,* Washington urged a policy of avoiding "passionate attachments" to any foreign country. The United States was fortunate. Its "detached and distant" location meant that it did not have to become involved in European conflicts. To do so would be very costly. The "great rule of conduct" for America ought to be to encourage trade with the rest of the world but to "steer clear of permanent alliances."

Washington did not mean by this last statement that the United States should isolate itself from the rest of the world, as the Jay and Pinckney Treaties provided. He was against *permanent* ties with any particular nation but the president did not oppose evenhanded dealings with all foreign countries.

President Washington, on his white horse, rode to put down the Whiskey Rebellion in 1794. This oil painting is probably by F. Kemmelmeyer. How was the central government threatened by this rebellion?

Return to the Preview & Review on page 244.

The Nation Is Tested   253

Preview & Review

Use these questions to guide your reading. Answer the questions after completing Section 4.
Understanding Issues, Events, & Ideas. Use the following terms to explain the development of political parties: two-party system, Federalist, Democratic-Republican, reactionary, District of Columbia, XYZ Affair, Alien and Sedition Acts.
1. Why did Jefferson distrust Hamilton? Why did Jefferson distrust all government?
2. Explain the events of the election of 1796 to illustrate how the growth of political parties ruined the election process set up in the Constitution.
3. Why did President Adams send commissioners to France?
4. How was the Sedition Act motivated by politics?
Thinking Critically. You are a newspaper editor. Write an editorial expressing your opinion about French actions in the XYZ Affair.

4. THE TWO-PARTY SYSTEM

The First Political Parties

The election of a president to succeed Washington was the first in which political parties played a role. Today we think of political parties as the machinery by which office seekers work out programs and present issues to the voters. The **two-party system**—today the Democratic and Republican parties—makes it possible for this large country to have an effective national government. If every candidate or local group set up a different organization, no one would ever have a majority. No satisfactory decisions could be made.

The framers of the Constitution, however, disliked and distrusted political parties. They made no provision for them. They called parties *factions.* The word suggests fringe groups conspiring to dominate the rest of society. The framers believed that individuals representing small districts could arrive at agreements based on the national interest. In their eyes political parties meant corruption. Leaders, they thought, should take personal responsibility for their decisions.

Yet very soon after the Constitution was ratified, political parties began to form. They did so because the Constitution created a strong

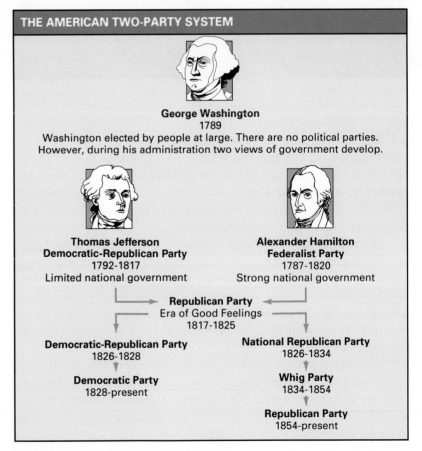

THE AMERICAN TWO-PARTY SYSTEM

George Washington
1789
Washington elected by people at large. There are no political parties. However, during his administration two views of government develop.

Thomas Jefferson
Democratic-Republican Party
1792-1817
Limited national government

Alexander Hamilton
Federalist Party
1787-1820
Strong national government

Republican Party
Era of Good Feelings
1817-1825

Democratic-Republican Party
1826-1828

National Republican Party
1826-1834

Democratic Party
1828-present

Whig Party
1834-1854

Republican Party
1854-present

LEARNING FROM DIAGRAMS. *This chart illustrates the development of the two-party system in America. Why did different political parties develop? How does a two-party system help preserve democracy?*

national government. Because it was powerful, the government made important decisions. National politics therefore *mattered*. People joined together in parties to attempt to control the decisions of the government.

The first parties were influenced more by personalities than by issues. The principal figures were Secretary of the Treasury Hamilton and Secretary of State Jefferson. Members of Congress who favored Hamilton's financial policies took the name **Federalists.** They began to vote as a group on most issues, even those not related to Hamilton's programs.

Those who opposed Hamilton and his ideas began to call themselves **Democratic-Republicans.** James Madison, at the time a congressman from Virginia, was the chief organizer and manager of the Democratic-Republican party. Jefferson was its best-known leader. He was the person most responsible for the ideas it stood for.

Jefferson and Hamilton

Thomas Jefferson considered Alexander Hamilton to be a dangerous **reactionary.** A reactionary is one opposed to political or social change. Jefferson thought that Hamilton wished to undo the gains of the Revolution and go back to a less democratic form of government. He even thought that Hamilton wanted to make the United States into a monarchy, perhaps with George Washington as king.

Yet Jefferson himself was not a democrat in the modern sense. He distrusted human nature almost as much as Hamilton did. Because governments consisted of people, Jefferson distrusted *all* government. He wanted to keep the government as small as possible. Hamilton, on the other hand, wanted to use the government to control the weak and selfish elements in human nature.

In Jefferson's opinion the best way to keep government small was to keep society simple. The United States was a free country, he believed, because it was a nation of farmers. The population was spread out. Most families owned their own land. They managed their own affairs. Countries with crowded seaports and industrial towns needed more government controls to preserve order. City workers seldom owned land. They had less interest in protecting property and in having orderly government. "When we get piled upon one another in large cities," Jefferson said, "we shall become corrupt." Hamilton disagreed with all these ideas. He wanted the United States to have a strong and varied economy. He urged the government to do everything it could to encourage the growth of industry.

When Hamilton proposed paying off the national debt, Jefferson did not oppose him. Jefferson also went along with the plan to take over the state debts. In exchange Hamilton agreed that the permanent capital of the United States—the **District of Columbia**—should be located in the South, on land donated by Maryland and Virginia.

Thomas Jefferson wanted to keep government as small as possible. This fine miniature portrait is by John Trumbull. Later Jefferson stopped wearing powdered wigs.

Jefferson *did* object to Hamilton's Bank of the United States and to the Whiskey Tax. Those measures favored eastern merchants and other city interests. Southern and western farmers had little to gain from a national bank, and they were the ones who had to pay the Whiskey Tax.

The Election of 1796

The growth of political parties ruined the complicated system for choosing the president established by the Constitution. Instead of voting for local electors whose judgment they trusted, voters in 1796 were presented with lists of names. The party leaders drew up these lists. They picked persons who had promised to vote for the party's choice for president. Ballots containing the names of the party's electors were sometimes printed and handed out to voters in advance.

John Adams, who had been Washington's vice president, was the logical choice of the Federalists for president. Jefferson was the Democratic-Republican favorite. For vice president the Federalist party leaders decided to run Thomas Pinckney of South Carolina, who had negotiated the popular treaty with Spain. The Democratic-Republican candidate for vice president was Senator Aaron Burr of New York.

The campaign to succeed Washington was a bitter one. The election became a struggle for national power between the Federalists and the Democratic-Republicans. The following political broadside—a large sheet of paper printed on one side—urged Democratic-Republicans in Pennsylvania to vote for Jefferson and the other Democratic-Republicans. Such attacks on Adams and the Federalists would soon lead to the first challenge of the freedoms guaranteed by the first Amendment.

❝ FELLOW CITIZENS!
The first concern of freemen, calls you forth into action.— Pennsylvania was never yet found wanting when Liberty was at stake; she cannot then be indifferent when the question is, *Who shall be President of the United States?* The citizen who now holds the office of President [Washington], has publicly made known to his fellow citizens that he declines to serve in it again. Two candidates are offered for your choice, as his successor; THOMAS JEFFERSON of Virginia, and JOHN ADAMS of New England.—No other candidate is proposed, you cannot therefore mistake between them. THOMAS JEFFERSON is the man who was your late Secretary of State, and Minister of the United States to the French nation; JOHN ADAMS is the man who is now Vice President of the United States, and was the late Minister to the king of Great Britain.—THOMAS

John Adams, elected president in 1796, was painted by John Singleton Copley. In contrast to Washington, Adams was short and stocky.

JEFFERSON is a firm REPUBLICAN,—JOHN ADAMS is an avowed MONARCHIST. . . .

Thomas Jefferson first drew the declaration of American independence;—he first framed the sacred political sentence that all men are *born* equal. *John Adams* says this is all a farce and a falsehood; that some men should be Kings, and some should be born Nobles. Which of these, freemen of Pennsylvania, will you have for your President? Will you, by your votes, contribute to make the avowed friend of monarchy, President? or will you, by neglectfully staying at home, permit others to saddle you with Political Slavery? . . . *Adams* is a fond admirer of the British Constitution, and says it is the first wonder of the world. *Jefferson* likes better our Federal Constitution, and thinks the British full of deformity, corruption, and wickedness. Once more, fellow citizens! Choose ye between these two, which you will have for your President, *Jefferson* or *Adams*. . . . Put in your tickets for fifteen good REPUBLICANS, and let the watch word be LIBERTY and INDEPENDENCE![1] **""**

Elbridge Gerry was one of the three American commissioners who negotiated with the French in the XYZ Affair.

Hamilton, who was very influential in the Federalist party, disliked Adams. However, he dared not openly oppose him for president. Instead he worked out a clever, but very shady, scheme. The Federalists seemed likely to win a majority of the electors. If all these electors voted for Adams and Pinckney, both would have the same number of electoral votes. Since Adams was known to be the presidential candidate, he would be chosen president and Pinckney vice president. To prevent this from happening, Hamilton persuaded a few Federalist electors in South Carolina not to vote for Adams. If Pinckney got even one more vote than Adams, according to the rules he would be president and Adams vice president.

Unfortunately for Hamilton, news of his plan leaked out. A large number of Federalist electors who were friendly to Adams reacted by not voting for Pinckney. When the electoral votes were counted in the Senate, Adams had 71, Pinckney only 59. Jefferson, who had the united support of the Democratic-Republican electors, received 68 votes. He, not Pinckney, now became the new vice president!

The XYZ Affair

From the beginning of his presidency, John Adams had to deal with a serious problem with the French. France was still at war with Great Britain. French leaders were angry at the United States for agreeing to the Jay Treaty. French warships and numerous French privateers called picaroons were stopping American merchant ships on the high seas and seizing their cargoes. In 1795 alone they captured 316

[1]From *The People Make a Nation* by Sandler, et al.

STRATEGIES FOR SUCCESS

SEPARATING FACT FROM OPINION

Being able to distinguish fact from opinion is a key strategy for the successful student. Reading history presents us with many facts. A *fact* is something known to be true. For example, you read on page 235: "By 1790 the treasury department had 70 persons." This is a statement of fact. It can be proven from records that exist. Also a fact is the statement on page 236: "Washington would have preferred to serve without salary, as he had during the Revolutionary War, but Congress voted him a salary of $25,000." Again, records verify this information.

But history also presents us with opinions. An *opinion* is a personal belief. When the facts are sorted through, it remains for the historian to offer an opinion about larger events. For example, in describing Washington's approach to his responsibilities as president, the author states: "Washington was extremely conscientious." This statement is the historian's opinion that Washington was very conscientious about his duties. People at the time and other historians might disagree with this assessment. It is important to know when the ideas you are reading are facts and when they are opinions.

How to Separate Fact from Opinion

To separate facts from opinions, follow these guidelines.

1. **Ask "can it be proven?"** Determine whether the idea can be checked for accuracy in other sources. If so, it is probably factual. If not, it probably contains an opinion.
2. **Look for context clues.** Opinions are sometimes signaled in writing by words like *believe* or *think.* Other clues that signal opinions include **loaded words** intended to stir your emotions, such as *extremely, ridiculous,* or *most important.*

Applying the Strategy

Read the following excerpt from *The Story of America.* List the sentences that contain the opinions of the historian who wrote the excerpt.

The election of a president to succeed Washington was the first in which political parties played a role. Today we think of political parties as the machinery by which office seekers work out programs and present issues to the voters. The two-party system—today the Demo-cratic and Republican parties—makes it possible for this large country to have an effective national government. If every candidate or local group set up a different organization, no one would ever have a majority. No satisfactory decisions could be made.

The framers of the Constitution, however, disliked and distrusted political parties. They made no provision for them. They called parties factions. The word suggests fringe groups conspiring to dominate the rest of society. The framers believed that individuals representing small districts could arrive at agreements based on the national interest. In their eyes political parties meant corruption. Leaders, they thought, should take personal responsibility for their decisions.

Yet very soon after the Constitution was ratified, political parties began to form. They did so because the Constitution created a strong national government. Because it was powerful, the government made important decisions. National politics therefore mattered. People joined together in parties to attempt to control the decisions of the government.

The first parties were influenced more by personalities than by issues. The principal figures were Secretary of the Treasury Hamilton and Secretary of State Jefferson. Members of Congress who favored Hamilton's financial policies took the name Federalists. They began to vote as a group on most issues, even those not related to Hamilton's program.

Those who opposed Hamilton and his ideas began calling themselves Democratic-Republicans.

You should note that the historian claims that the framers of the Constitution "disliked" and "distrusted" political parties. The author is basing his statements on a consensus of the sources he has studied. It is a valid interpretation of the situation, but it is an opinion because it cannot be proven with absolute certainty.

Continue to reread the discussion of the first American political parties. Note that the historian claims these early parties were more influenced by personalities such as Hamilton and Jefferson than by issues. Is this an example of an opinion? Why or why not? What other examples of opinions can you find in the section?

For independent practice, see Practicing the Strategy on page 263.

The Granger Collection

vessels. When President Washington sent Charles Pinckney, Thomas Pinckney's brother, to France to try to settle these problems, the government refused to receive him. The French even ordered him out of the country.

When he became president, Adams decided to make another effort to reach an understanding with France. He sent three special commissioners to France: Charles Pinckney, the former ambassador; John Marshall, a Federalist from Virginia; and Elbridge Gerry of Massachusetts, a personal friend of his who happened to belong to the Democratic-Republican party.

In those days diplomats had much greater responsibilities than they do today. It took Marshall almost seven weeks to get from Philadelphia to Paris. Without radios or telegraphs diplomats could not send back home for new instructions. They had to make many important decisions on their own. This explains why the negotiations between the French and the three American commissioners developed as they did.

The French foreign minister, Talleyrand, was brilliant, but he could not be trusted. He was of noble birth and had been a bishop of the Catholic church before the French Revolution. During the revolution he became a leading diplomat of the new republican

The XYZ Affair is the subject of this American political cartoon of 1798. It is titled "Cinque-Têtes, or the Paris Monster." The five-headed monster stands for the Directory, the French government. The three American commissioners, Pinckney, Marshall, and Gerry, are on the left. A symbolic monster sits top right in front of a guillotined citizen. The interesting "Civic Feast" on the right seems to consist of live frogs. Why does the five-headed monster say, "Money, money, money"?

government. When the revolution became more radical, however, Talleyrand had to flee the country to save his life. He spent nearly two years in the United States. In 1796 he returned to France after a more conservative government, known as the Directory, took office. Soon thereafter he was named foreign minister.

The three Americans expected Talleyrand to be friendly because the United States had given him refuge. They were completely wrong. He had disliked America. "If I have to stay here another year," he had written to a French friend, "I shall die." Moreover, Talleyrand loved money. He would not discuss the issues unless he received a large bribe.

The Americans did not know what to do. For weeks they had a series of meetings and exchanged letters with three secret agents of Talleyrand—one a Swiss banker, another a German merchant, the third a French diplomat. Besides the outright bribe, Talleyrand expected the United States to make a large loan to France that would be practically a gift. The United States must also apologize to France for certain harsh remarks about the French nation that President Adams had made in a speech to Congress.

Bribing officials was not as frowned upon then as it later became. Yet Talleyrand wanted $250,000, a huge sum. (At today's prices it would have amounted to several million dollars.) He would not stop the attacks on American ships or even begin to negotiate until the money was promised. "It is money," the Swiss banker reminded the Americans. "It is expected that you will offer money." Pinckney, the only American commissioner who could speak French properly, burst out angrily, "No, no. Not a sixpence!" Finally the commissioners gave up. Pinckney and Marshall returned home very much discouraged by Talleyrand's greed.

Gerry remained in Paris because he feared that France would declare war on the United States if the negotiations were broken off. President Adams was very upset by the request for a bribe. He ordered Gerry to return to America. He published the letters of the commissioners, substituting the letters X, Y, and Z for the names of Talleyrand's secret agents.

The publication of the XYZ correspondence created a sensation. Congress ordered 10,000 additional copies distributed free in rural areas where there were few newspapers. When John Marshall reached Philadelphia, Federalist members of Congress gave a huge banquet in his honor. "Millions for defense, but not one cent for tribute"—that is, for bribes—became a Federalist slogan. Congress created a department of the navy and appropriated money for 40 new warships. It increased the size of the tiny United States army from 3,500 to about 10,000 men. It officially suspended the treaty of alliance with France.

War seemed unavoidable. Public feeling against France was bitter. Children in the streets played games of French against Americans. Washington came out of retirement to command the army. Suddenly Adams, who had been elected president by such a narrow margin, became a national hero.

The Alien and Sedition Acts

War with France would certainly have been popular in 1798. President Adams, however, wished to avoid it. He was right to do so. France had the most powerful army in the world. Its commander, Napoleon Bonaparte, was a military genius. The French navy completely outclassed the American navy. Although three powerful new warships called frigates were being built, the largest American warships ready for action were tiny coast guard patrol boats with crews of only six men. French privateers waited outside American harbors and picked off merchant ships almost at will.

Nevertheless, many Federalist leaders, including Hamilton, hoped for war. War would give them an excuse to destroy what they called their "internal enemies." Jefferson's Democratic-Republicans had long been supporters of France and some of the radical ideas of the French Revolution. Would they not side with France if war broke out? It was time to crack down on "Demo*crats* and 'all other kinds of rats,' " these Federalists claimed.

Taking advantage of the war scare and the public anger over the XYZ Affair, the Federalists pushed several laws through Congress in the summer of 1798. These laws are known as the **Alien and Sedition Acts** because they were aimed at foreigners in the United States and at people who were supposedly trying to undermine the government in order to help France.

One of these laws increased from 5 to 14 years the length of time foreigners had to live in the United States before they could become citizens. Another gave the president the power to jail or order out of the country foreigners who he thought were "dangerous to the peace and safety of the United States."

Still more severe was the Sedition Act, which outlawed conspiracies against the government and attempts to start riots or uprisings. The act made it a crime for anyone to "write, print, utter, or publish" even merely "scandalous" statements critical of the government, of either house of Congress, or of the president. So much for the First Amendment!

The Sedition Act was an attempt to frighten the Democratic-Republicans into silence. In practice it made criticism of the Federalists a crime but not criticism of the Democratic-Republicans. It was against the law to "defame" the president but not the vice president.

Such an attack on freedom of speech and of the press was a threat to everything the American Revolution had sought to protect. In 1798 the American experiment in republican government was little more than 20 years old. Was it about to end in a new tyranny? 🗐

Return to the Preview & Review on page 254.

CHAPTER 7 REVIEW

		Washington's Presidency
1785	ESTABLISHING AMERICAN PRECEDENTS 1790	

1789
Washington inaugurated
as president

★
French Revolution begins

★
Tariff Act of 1789

1791
Bill of Rights
adopted

★
Bank of U.S.
is chartered

1792
Kent
beco
a sta

Chapter Summary

Read the statements below. Choose one, and write a paragraph explaining its importance.

1. Washington took great care in each decision because he realized that as the first president he was setting precedents.
2. The Bill of Rights, the first ten amendments to the Constitution, protect natural rights.
3. Hamilton and Jefferson disagreed over the interpretation of the "necessary and proper clause" of the Constitution.
4. Americans at first cheered the French Revolution but remained uninvolved as it took a radical turn.
5. Settlers crossing the Appalachians into the Ohio Valley faced conflicts with the Indians until General Wayne's victory at Fallen Timbers.
6. The Jay and Pinckney Treaties were beneficial to the young nation because they kept it out of war.
7. In his farewell address, Washington stressed unity and neutrality.
8. The country developed a political system with two opposing parties, leading to the unusual results of the 1796 election.
9. The XYZ Affair created a sensation and led to the Alien and Sedition Acts.

Reviewing Chronological Order

Number your paper 1-5. Then study the time line above and place the following events in the order in which they happened by writing the first next to 1, the second next to 2, and so on.
1. Bill of Rights adopted
2. Genet comes to the United States
3. The XYZ Affair
4. Washington becomes the first president
5. The Battle of Fallen Timbers

Understanding Main Ideas

1. Why were Washington and other Americans concerned about the precedents the first president established?
2. Why did Hamilton want the national government to assume state debts and pay state and national debts at face value?
3. Why did Washington want to avoid going to war against Great Britain or aiding the French?
4. What were Washington's accomplishments as president?
5. How did the views of Jefferson and Hamilton contrast on the uses of government?
6. What actions did Congress take after the XYZ correspondence was published? How did ordinary Americans respond?

Thinking Critically

1. **Interpreting.** Explain the difference between natural rights and legal rights. Which of these are protected by the Bill of Rights?
2. **Contrasting.** Contrast the views of Hamilton and Jefferson as they applied the "necessary and proper clause" to the bank bill.
3. **Analyzing.** Explain the two main ideas expressed in Washington's Farewell Address.
4. **Determining Cause and Effect.** Why did political parties begin to form so soon after the Constitution was ratified?
5. **Evaluating.** According to the treaty of alliance with France, the United States was to join France in the war against Britain. Washington, however, urged neutrality and the country refused to join France. Was that the proper action? Explain your answer.

Writing About History: Expressive

Imagine you are an eyewitness to one of the following: a tea party with President Washington, Washington's meeting with Citizen Genet, the Battle of Fallen Timbers, or the negotiation between American diplomats and secret agents X, Y, and Z. In a brief essay describe what you see and your thoughts and feelings. Use the information in Chapter 7 to help you develop your essay.

	1795				1800

93	1794	1795	1796	1797	1798
net comes the ted States	Battle of Fallen Timbers	Treaty of Greenville	Two-party system develops	XYZ Affair	Alien and Sedition Acts passed
	★	★	★		
utrality clamation ssued	Jay's Treaty	Pinckney's Treaty	Adams elected president		
	★		★		
	Whiskey Rebellion		Tennessee enters the Union		

Practicing the Strategy

Review the strategy on page 258.

Separating Fact From Opinion. Number your paper 1–5. Then read the following list of statements. If you think the statement is a fact, write an *F* next to the number. If you think it is an opinion, write an *O*.

1. Washington was America's greatest president.
2. By the late 1780s 10,000 settlers were pouring into the Ohio Valley each year.
3. Most Americans disliked Jay's Treaty.
4. Genet was a charming, young gentleman.
5. By 1796 Washington could justly feel that he had set the United States well on its way.

Using Primary Sources

Washington presented his farewell address on September 17, 1796. In it he stated his recommendations for the nation's future course. Read the following excerpt from Washington's Farewell Address and answer the questions in the next column.

The great rule of conduct for us, in regard to foreign Nations, is, in extending our commercial relations, to have with them as little Political connection as possible. So far as we have already formed engagements, let them be fulfilled with perfect good faith. Here let us stop.

Europe has a set of primary interests, which to us have none, or a very remote relation. Hence she must be engaged in frequent controversies, the causes of which are essentially foreign to our concerns.

Our detached and distant situation invites and enables us to pursue a different course. . . . 'T is our true policy to steer clear of permanent alliances, with any portion of the foreign world.

1. Why did Washington recommend America avoid foreign alliances?
2. What advantages might "detached and distant" political relations provide to the United States? What disadvantages might have resulted from the situation?
3. Do you think Washington's views on trade with foreign nations would be acceptable policy for the United States government to follow today? Why or why not? Support your opinion with at least two reasons.

Linking History & Geography

Geography, as you have learned, influences people's actions. For example, it helps determine how they make their living and how they get their goods to market. Review the information about the Whiskey Rebellion on page 252 and study the map on 186. Then explain how geographic factors contributed to the Whiskey Rebellion.

Enriching Your Study of History

1. **Individual Project.** Do research in your library to prepare a short report on the life of one of the following persons: Thomas Jefferson, James Madison, Alexander Hamilton, Aaron Burr, Anthony Wayne, John Adams, John Jay, Thomas Pinckney.
2. **Cooperative Project.** Research with your classmates the Battle of Fallen Timbers. Then use your historical imagination to prepare interviews with members of both armies—the Indian confederacy and the United States. Questions and answers should explain why each side fought, describe the battle itself, and explain the results and consequences of the battle. Your group should present its interviews to the class as television interviews.

Chapter 7 Review   263

UNIT TWO REVIEW

Summing Up and Predicting

Read the summary of the main ideas in Unit Two. Choose one statement, then write a paragraph predicting its outcome or effect in the future.

1. Vast distance and the need for self-sufficiency separated the colonists from Britain.
2. Objections to British policies led to the independence movement.
3. Shots fired at Lexington and Concord started the Revolutionary War.
4. The Declaration of Independence stated American principles of democratic government and listed colonial grievances against Britain.
5. American forces suffered early setbacks but eventually defeated the British.
6. The major task after the war was establishing government—state and national. The Articles of Confederation failed to deal with serious problems, prompting development of the United States Constitution.
7. As the first president, Washington established many precedents.
8. Americans cheered the spirit of the French Revolution, but it caused them problems.

Connecting Ideas

1. You know that Thomas Jefferson did not mention women in the Declaration of Independence. In what ways have women's rights been expanded today?
2. James Madison said, "In framing a system which we wish to last for ages, we should not lose sight of the changes which ages will produce." In your opinion, why has the Constitution lasted for more than 200 years? How does the Constitution provide for changes?
3. If you could repeal an amendment to the Constitution, which one would it be? Why? If you could add an amendment to the Constitution, what would it be?

Practicing Critical Thinking

1. **Drawing Conclusions.** As you know, the American Revolution helped inspire the French people to revolt. From what you have learned, how was the French Revolution different from the American Revolution?
2. **Synthesizing.** You are a delegate to the Constitutional Convention in 1787. What do you think is the most serious flaw in the Articles of Confederation? How is it being corrected by the new Constitution? Cite the article and section of the Constitution that will correct this flaw.
3. **Evaluating.** You are a member of the ratifying convention for Rhode Island, the only state that has not yet ratified the Constitution. Write the speech that you would deliver to persuade your fellow members to ratify.

Exploring History Together

1. Prepare a notebook or bulletin board display on the United States government today. Members of your group should collect newspaper and magazine clippings dealing with the activities of each branch of government.
2. Together with nine classmates, analyze the Bill of Rights. Have each member of your group study one amendment. Prepare a report, skit, or other presentation that explains the protections provided by that amendment. Use current examples whenever possible.
3. With several classmates, prepare and present a skit illustrating a key scene from the Revolutionary War, Constitutional Convention, or XYZ Affair. Review Unit Two to be sure you present accurate points of view.

Reading in Depth

Borden, Morton. *George Washington.* Englewood Cliffs, NJ: Prentice-Hall. Traces Washington's life as general and president.

Bowen, Catherine Drinker. *Miracle at Philadelphia.* Boston: Atlantic Monthly Press. Presents a dramatic account of the debates, quarrels, and compromises that resulted in the United States Constitution.

Chidsey, Donald Barr. *Valley Forge.* New York: Crown. Tells the gripping story of the Continental army at Valley Forge in the winter of 1777.

Davis, Burke. *Black Heroes of the American Revolution.* San Diego: Harcourt Brace Jovanovich. Recounts the many contributions of African Americans to the independence movement.

———. *Three for the Revolution.* San Diego: Harcourt Brace Jovanovich. Contains information about Patrick Henry, George Washington, and Thomas Jefferson.

Williams, Selma R. *Demeter's Daughter: The Women Who Founded America, 1587–1787.* New York: Antheneum. Describes the exploits of both famous and everyday women in the founding of America.

The Thomas Gilcrease Institute, Tulsa
"Indian Village" by Jules Tavernier

A GROWING AMERICA

UNIT 3

Thomas Jefferson is the central figure of this unit. Like George Washington, the Hero of the Revolution, and Andrew Jackson, who became the hero of the common man, Jefferson used the presidency to protect the interests of people with differing points of view. When he became president, political power shifted from the Federalists to the Democratic-Republicans. The United States more than doubled in size with the Louisiana Purchase, the annexation of Florida, and the establishment of new boundaries with Spain to the south and west and Britain to the north. This expansion had enormous social, political, and economic consequences. The War of 1812 gave Europe notice that the United States was well established. Meanwhile the Industrial Revolution led to the rise of cities and the creation of a more complex economy based on both agriculture and industry.

265

The Age of Jefferson

I n his inaugural address in 1801, Thomas Jefferson called the United States "the world's best hope." Since the people *were* the government, they were eager to protect and defend it. America's leaders realized this was a rare, indeed unique, form of government. Jefferson's greatest accomplishment was the purchase from France of the Louisiana Territory for $15 million. This chapter describes the expedition of Lewis and Clark to explore the Louisiana Purchase and concludes with troubles on the high seas with Britain. Would the young nation find itself at war again?

1. THE FALL OF THE FEDERALISTS

Attacks on the Sedition Act

In 1798 the Federalists pushed the Sedition Act through Congress. Although the law was passed because of the war scare abroad with France, its real motives had to do with politics at home. The Sedition Act made it a crime to criticize the president, who was a Federalist, but not a crime to criticize the vice president, who was a Democratic-Republican. In that sense the act was purely political.

Only about ten people were convicted of violating the Sedition Act. Not one of these was accused of plotting against the government. All the convictions were for *criticizing* the government or some important Federalist leader. Charles Holt, a newspaper editor, published an article calling the United States army "a band of disorganized . . . ruffians, a burden, a pest, and a terror to the citizens." For this and similar statements he was sentenced to six months in jail and fined $200. James Callender, another editor, claimed that President Adams was "repulsive," a "fool," and "the blasted tyrant of America." His punishment was nine months in jail and a $200 fine.

Such statements were untrue and in very bad taste. Still, the right to make them was protected by the **First Amendment** of the Constitution, which guarantees freedom of speech and of the press. Moreover, equally unfair criticisms of Jeffersonian leaders were made by Federalist editors. These were ignored by the government.

Preview & Review

Use these questions to guide your reading. Answer the questions after completing Section 1.
Understanding Issues, Events, & Ideas. Discuss reasons for the attacks on the Sedition Act, using the following words: First Amendment, unconstitutional, Kentucky and Virginia Resolutions, nullify, doctrine of nullification, repeal, states' rights, Convention of 1800, dictator, Twelfth Amendment.
1. What was the political purpose of the Sedition Act?
2. What was the historical importance of the Kentucky and Virginia Resolutions?
3. Why did the election of 1800 and the growth of political parties lead to the Twelfth Amendment to the Constitution?

Thinking Critically. 1. You are to fill in for Charles Holt while he is in jail for sedition. Write an editorial defending Holt, using the First Amendment to support your view. 2. Do you agree that Adams was heroic in reestablishing negotiations with the French? Why or why not?

A Federalist editor strikes phrases from America's great documents in this 1799 political cartoon. 'Peter Porcupine' says, "I hate this country and will sew this seeds of discord in it." Liberty weeps at the tomb of Benjamin Franklin. At right the devil himself whispers, "Let us destroy this idol liberty," while the British lion purrs, "Go on, dear Peter, my friend, and I will reward you." How do you think those who favored the Sedition Act felt about this cartoon?

Vice President Jefferson reacted swiftly to the obvious political bias of the Sedition Act against his party. Above all, he believed that Congress did not have the power under the Constitution to pass any of the Alien and Sedition Acts. They were **unconstitutional,** in his opinion. That is, they violated the intent of the framers of the Constitution. He wrote out a series of statements called *resolutions* which explained his reasoning. A friend of his introduced these resolutions at a session of the legislature of the new state of Kentucky, where the Jeffersonians had a large majority. The legislature voted to approve them in November 1798.

At the time the public did not know that Jefferson had written the resolutions. They were called the *Kentucky Resolutions.* About a month later a similar set of resolutions was passed by the Virginia legislature. These were written by James Madison.

The **Kentucky and Virginia Resolutions** did not claim that the rights of free speech and free press had no limits. The issue was whether the federal government had the power to limit them. Jefferson and Madison argued that because of the First Amendment, it could not. Only the state legislatures could restrict these rights.

When Congress goes beyond its legal powers, what can be done? Jefferson had a simple answer. The Constitution, he wrote, was a contract. It was an agreement made by separate states. It gave certain powers to the federal government created by the states. What if Congress broke the contract by passing a law that the Constitution did not give it the power to pass? Jefferson argued that any state could **nullify,** or cancel, the law. The law would no longer exist within that state. Each state, said Jefferson, "had an equal right to judge for itself" whether or not a law of Congress was constitutional.

James Madison was author of the Virginia Resolutions. Gilbert Stuart painted Madison in the early 1800s.

The Fall of the Federalists   267

If put into practice, this **doctrine of nullification** would have meant the end of the United States as one nation. If any state could refuse to obey a law of Congress, the national government would soon collapse. Even the friendly Kentucky legislature found the idea of nullification too radical. It changed that resolution. Instead it urged Congress to **repeal,** or revoke, the unconstitutional law. The Virginia Resolutions took the same position.

The Kentucky and Virginia Resolutions had no practical effects. The other states did not respond favorably to them. Congress did not repeal the Alien and Sedition Acts. The resolutions are important, however, because they put forth an argument about **states' rights** that reappears many times in the story of America, most notably over the issue of slavery.

The Heroism of John Adams

The Federalists, of course, did not think that the Alien and Sedition Acts were unconstitutional. President John Adams had special reason for believing them both legal and desirable. The coarse personal attacks of Democratic-Republican editors like James Callender made him very angry. He was understandably delighted to see such people punished.

Adams also wanted to be reelected president in 1800. He knew that his strong stand against France at the time of the XYZ Affair had made him very popular. The people saw him as the defender of the nation's honor and security during a national crisis. The danger of war with France was a political advantage for him. If war actually broke out, he would almost certainly be reelected.

John Adams, however, was too honest and too patriotic to put personal gain ahead of duty. He learned that the French foreign minister, Talleyrand, was eager to repair the damage caused by the XYZ Affair. Adams decided to try again to solve the nation's difficulties with France by negotiation. Late in 1799 he sent three new commissioners to Paris.

This made Hamilton and his Federalist supporters furious. They wanted the conflict between America and France to continue. But they could not prevent Adams from acting.

The American commissioners were greeted "with a friendly dignity." After months of discussion the diplomats signed a treaty known as the **Convention of 1800.** Peace was restored between the two nations. France agreed to release the United States from its obligations under the treaty of alliance of 1778. Little else was gained, for the French would not agree to pay for the damages their warships and privateers had done to American vessels and their cargoes.

On October 4, 1800, Napoleon Bonaparte, who was now **dictator,** or absolute ruler, of France, gave an enormous party for the American commissioners. It took place at his brother's estate outside

Paris. There were 180 guests, including all the high officials of the French government. A magnificent meal was eaten. Champagne toasts were drunk to "perpetual peace," to "freedom of the seas," and to President John Adams. Later there were fireworks and a concert.

The Election of 1800

President Adams had stopped the threat of war with France. He was quite rightly proud of what he had done. Many years later he said that the treaty was his greatest achievement—"the most splendid diamond in my crown" was the way he put it. Peace ended the crisis that had led to passage of the Alien and Sedition Acts. Equally important, it ended the threat to democracy these laws posed. It also lessened the fear of many Americans that the Jeffersonians preferred France to their own country. This helped Jefferson in his campaign for the presidency in 1800.

The political divisions evident in the election also reflected sharp religious divisions. Because of his well-known belief in freedom of thought and his opposition to government support of religion, many conservatives were afraid that Jefferson would oppose any form of religion and would suppress churches wherever he could. This was especially true in New England, stronghold of the Federalists. On the other hand, large numbers of deeply religious Methodists and Baptists as well as many Presbyterians voted for Jefferson.

The Democratic-Republican party again nominated Jefferson for president and Aaron Burr for vice president. The Federalists ran Adams for president and Charles C. Pinckney of XYZ fame for vice president. In the campaign the Jeffersonians were united, the Federalists badly divided. Hamilton disliked Adams so much that he

Thomas Jefferson, left, and Aaron Burr, right, were the Democratic–Republican candidates for president and vice president in 1800. Jefferson was painted by Rembrandt Peale about the year of the election and Burr was painted by John Vanderlyn in 1809. Who were their Federalist opponents?

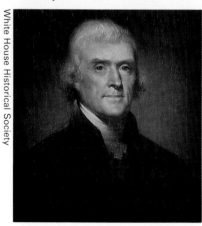
White House Historical Society

New-York Historical Society

Jefferson was the first president to be inaugurated in the new capital city, which was named after George Washington, who had died in 1799. The land on which Washington was built, which is called the District of Columbia, had been chosen by President Washington himself. He selected a site a few miles up the Potomac River from his plantation, Mount Vernon. The land was surveyed by two former clockmakers, Andrew Ellicott and Benjamin Banneker, who was probably the first black civil servant employed by the federal government.

Washington also selected the designer of the capital, Pierre Charles L'Enfant, a French-born engineer who had come to America to serve in the Revolutionary Army. L'Enfant had remodeled Federal Hall, the first home of Congress, in New York City. Washington liked his work and asked him to design the permanent capital. It was a remarkable opportunity, and L'Enfant did a brilliant job.

L'Enfant's plan provided for broad avenues reaching out like spokes in a wheel from two main centers where the president and Congress would be located. The plan left generous room for parks as well. It has been widely regarded as one of the finest examples of city planning in the world.

In 1801, however, Washington was a tiny village. Only one wing of the Capitol building had

The New York Public Library

Benjamin Banneker, a clockmaker and scientist, and Andrew Ellicott surveyed the District of Columbia.

been erected. The Treasury Department building and the still-unfinished president's mansion

published a pamphlet on "The Public Conduct and Character of John Adams," in which he described Adams as jealous, vain, and stubborn. According to Hamilton, John Adams was totally unfit to be president.

Once again Hamilton tried to manage the votes of the Federalist electors in order to make the Federalist candidate for vice president get more votes than Adams. Again this trick failed. The Democratic-

LEARNING FROM GRAPHS.
These charts show the electoral vote in the 1800 and 1804 presidential elections. According to the graphs, how had the balance of political power shifted by 1804?

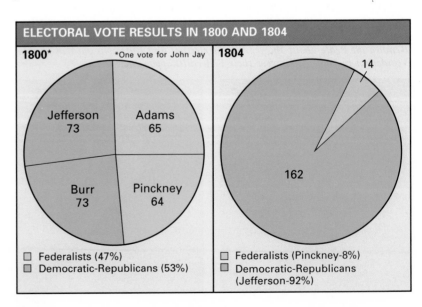

ELECTORAL VOTE RESULTS IN 1800 AND 1804

1800*   *One vote for John Jay

- Jefferson 73
- Adams 65
- Burr 73
- Pinckney 64

☐ Federalists (47%)
☐ Democratic-Republicans (53%)

1804

- 14
- 162

☐ Federalists (Pinckney-8%)
☐ Democratic-Republicans (Jefferson-92%)

were the only other solidly constructed buildings. There were a few clusters of houses and shops. The streets were unpaved, dusty in dry weather, ankle-deep in mud after every rain. Living was uncomfortable. Members of Congress slept and ate in rough hotels called boarding houses. A room and three meals a day in one of these places cost about $15 a week. There was little to do after sessions of Congress. Most senators and representatives hurried back to their home districts as soon as Congress adjourned. In summer the village was almost deserted. President Jefferson flatly refused to stay there in July and August because of the heat and humidity.

Republican party won the election. Jefferson received 73 electoral votes, Adams only 65.

Because the Democratic-Republicans were well organized, all their electors had voted for Burr as well as Jefferson. He, too, had 73 electoral votes! The electors intended, of course, that Burr be vice president. Nevertheless, the tie meant that the House of Representatives would have to choose between them. Under the Constitution each state, no matter how many representatives it had, would have one vote. Since there were 16 states, 9 were needed for a majority. The Democratic-Republicans controlled 8 states. The Federalists had 6, and 2 were divided evenly. The Federalists voted for Burr, partly to make trouble for the opposition, partly because they thought Burr less radical than Jefferson. Thus, on the first ballot Jefferson got 8 votes and Burr 6. The votes of the equally divided states cancelled each other. For an entire week all the delegates held firm. They voted 35 times without anyone changing his vote. Finally, Federalist James A. Bayard of Delaware, that small state's only representative, changed to Jefferson. That gave Jefferson the presidency, 9 states to 6. Burr became vice president.

Everyone now realized that the development of well-organized political parties meant tie votes between members of the same party would become common. The **Twelfth Amendment** was added to the Constitution. Thereafter the electors voted separately for president and vice president. 🖳

Return to the Preview & Review on page 266.

The Fall of the Federalists   271

Use these questions to guide your reading. Answer the questions after completing Section 2.
Understanding Issues, Events, & Ideas. Use the following words to discuss Jefferson's presidency: *Marbury v. Madison,* Barbary pirate, right of deposit, Louisiana Purchase, secession.
1. What did Jefferson mean by "We are all Republicans—we are all Federalists"?
2. What was established by John Marshall's ruling in *Marbury v. Madison?*
3. Why was the United States at war with the Barbary States?
4. Why were New England Federalists upset over the Louisiana Purchase? What was their plan? How was Vice President Burr involved?

Thinking Critically. 1. You are a farmer in the Ohio River valley in 1802. Write a letter to President Jefferson that explains how the loss of the right of deposit has affected you and your fellow farmers. 2. In your opinion, did Jefferson take his presidential powers too far? Explain your answer.

2. JEFFERSON AS PRESIDENT

Jefferson's Inaugural Address

Jefferson's inaugural address, delivered in the Senate chamber of the Capitol on March 4, 1801, was a fitting beginning for the new city and his administration. Jefferson believed that his election was a kind of second American Revolution that had checked the Federalists' attempt to make the United States into a monarchy. The speech, however, showed that he intended to make few changes. The tone was similar to that of Washington's Farewell Address. Like that speech, its main themes were unity at home and neutrality abroad.

Majority rule was the first principle of democracy, Jefferson reminded his audience. But minorities also have rights and "to violate [them] would be oppression." His main point was that political differences could be smoothed over by discussion and compromise. He said:

    “ Every difference of opinion is not a difference of principle. We have called by different names brethren of the same principle. We are all Republicans—we are all Federalists.**”**

With this clever reference to the political parties, he was reminding people that everyone wanted America to be a *republic* rather than a monarchy, and also that everyone believed in a *federal* system, with power divided between the central government and the states.

As for the rest of the world, Jefferson tried to show that he did not intend to make the United States dependent on France, as the Federalists had claimed during the campaign. His policy would be "honest friendship for all nations, entangling alliances with none."

The United States Capitol with its handsome proportions was designed by a Quaker architect and doctor, William Thorton. He presented this drawing to President Washington in 1793. The building features a copper dome. Jefferson said that it "captivated the eyes and judgment of all."

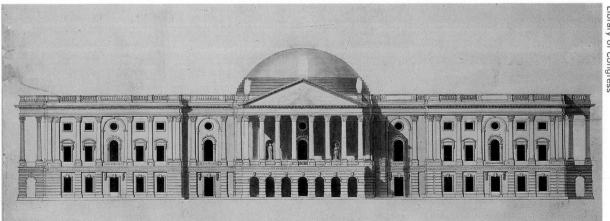

Library of Congress

He also spoke with deep feeling about American democratic ideals. The United States, he said, was "the world's best hope." It had "the strongest government on earth" because the people felt that they were part of the government. They were therefore eager to protect and defend it.

Jefferson's speech promised a moderate and reasonable program. The Alien and Sedition Acts were either repealed or allowed to expire. By 1802 all were gone. Jefferson got Congress to repeal the Whiskey Tax too. And he canceled the Federalists' program for expanding the army and navy. On the other hand, he continued Hamilton's policy of paying off the national debt and made no effort to do away with the Bank of the United States.

The author of the Declaration of Independence had no taste for pomp and ceremony in the White House. He sometimes wore a frayed coat and carpet slippers to greet the representatives of foreign nations who presented themselves in powdered wigs, bemedaled coats, and silver-buckled shoes. Plain citizens and foreign diplomats were each seen in their turn, for Jefferson told them all, "Nobody shall be above you, nor you above anybody."

Jefferson and the Judiciary

The only serious trouble Jefferson encountered in his first term involved the courts. He believed that judges must be independent. But he feared what he called their "habit of going out of the question before them, to throw an anchor ahead, and grapple further hold for future advances of power."

Jefferson, like many presidents, had to contend with a Supreme Court whose members had been appointed by his political opponents. The chief justice, John Marshall, whom Jefferson particularly disliked, was appointed by John Adams. Adams also appointed numerous other judges unfriendly to the Jeffersonians. Several of these appointees were known as "midnight justices" because Adams had signed the commissions appointing them during the final hours of his presidency.

In the confusion of Adams' last hours the commissions of a number of justices of the peace for the new District of Columbia were not distributed. When Jefferson found them, he refused to let them be released to the appointees. This led William Marbury, one of Adams' appointees, to ask the Supreme Court to order the secretary of state, James Madison, to issue the commissions. The case of **Marbury v. Madison** (1803) provided a great test for the court and Chief Justice Marshall. Marshall ruled against Marbury. The law allowing Marbury to sue, he announced, was not authorized by the Constitution. Thus, Jefferson had his way. But this case established the power of the Supreme Court to declare an act of Congress unconstitutional, which was much more important.

National Portrait Gallery

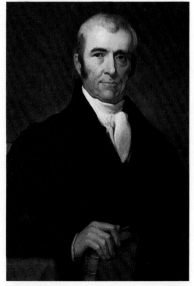

John Marshall was painted by Henry Inman in 1781. Why is Marshall's name so often linked to Constitutional law?

STRATEGIES FOR SUCCESS

INTERPRETING A PHYSICAL MAP

A *physical map* is a special-purpose map that shows the natural landscape, or *topography,* of an area. It shows the location and extent of physical features such as rivers and mountain chains. It also illustrates the relative locations of various features. Because elevation, access to water, and the "the lay of the land" often influence human activities, a physical map can help you better understand how the history of an area unfolded.

How to Understand a Physical Map

To understand a physical map, follow these guidelines.

1 **Use basic map reading skills.** Review the strategy on page 32. Study the title, key, scale, and grid for important information.
2. **Note the colors used to show elevation.** The distance above or below sea level is *elevation.* Look at the colors on the map to get a "feel" for the landscape. Check the elevation key to associate colors to elevations. Note also that special shading called "cartographic art" highlights mountain and valley areas.
3. **Study shapes.** Look closely at the shapes of the features shown on the map—how steep a mountain range is and how far it stretches, how wide and long a river is.
4. **Read the labels.** Learn the names of the key features.
5. **Note relative locations.** *Relative location* is the position of a feature in relation to other features. Note where each major feature appears in relation to other major features. Use this information to draw conclusions about the effect of the topography on movement, settlement patterns, and economic activity.

Applying the Strategy

Study the physical map to the right. It shows the topography of the lands of the eastern seaboard of the United States. Note that the Appalachian Mountains form a wall to the west of the region. What effect did they have on settlement? Note also that the area is drained by several rivers. What are the major ones? How did they affect settlement? Along which did important cities begin to grow? How did rivers affect farming and transportation for the early settlers? Note the physical features shown on the map of the Louisiana Purchase on page 285.

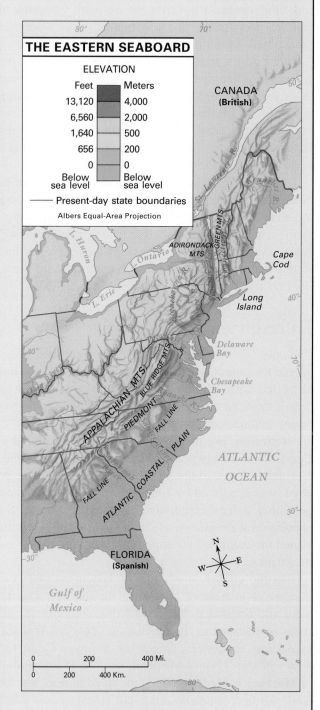

THE EASTERN SEABOARD

ELEVATION

Feet		Meters
13,120		4,000
6,560		2,000
1,640		500
656		200
0		0
Below sea level		Below sea level

—— Present-day state boundaries

Albers Equal-Area Projection

For independent practice, see Practicing the Strategy on pages 292–93.

The Barbary Pirates

Aside from his problems with the courts, Jefferson's first term was a parade of triumphs. Despite cutbacks he had made in the navy in order to save money, he managed to fight a small war with the **Barbary pirates.**

For decades the North African Arab states of Morocco, Algiers, Tunis, and Tripoli had made a business of piracy. They seized ships, crews, and passengers all over the Mediterranean Sea and held them for ransom. European countries found it simpler and cheaper to pay annual protection money called tribute than to crush the pirates. Under Washington and Adams, the United States had paid this tribute as well. However, the practice went against Jefferson's grain. "When this idea comes across my mind," he said, "my faculties are absolutely suspended between indignation and impatience." So when the pasha of Tripoli tried to increase the tribute, Jefferson refused to pay. Tripoli then declared war in May 1801, and Jefferson sent a naval squadron to the Mediterranean.

In the words of one historian, the action was "halfhearted and ill-starred." The pirates were not overwhelmed. The war dragged on for several years. In 1804 Lieutenant Stephen Decatur, who had captured two pirate ships, performed one of the boldest acts of the war. He and ten sailors secretly slipped into Tripoli harbor and set fire to the *Philadelphia,* an American warship that had been captured by the pirates. Their bravery is remembered in the famous phrase of the *Marine's Hymn:* "To the shores of Tripoli."

The navy then blockaded Tripoli harbor and forced the pasha to

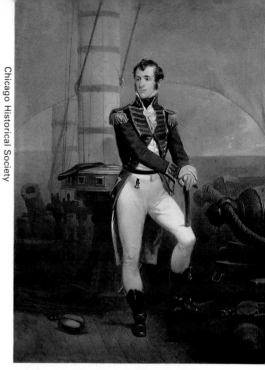

Stephen Decatur, after forcing Algiers to sign a peace treaty, stands on the deck of his man-of-war. Alonzo Chappel painted this portrait. Lord Nelson, England's greatest naval hero, called Decatur's secret burning of the Philadelphia *"the most bold and daring act of the age." Decatur was killed in a duel in 1820.*

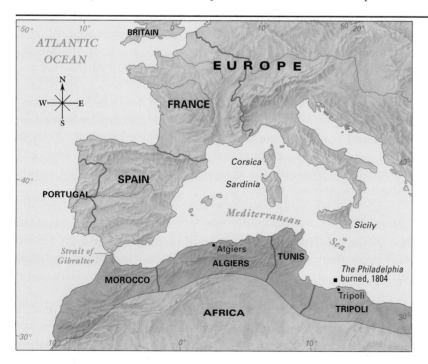

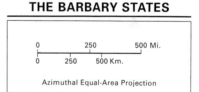

THE BARBARY STATES

0	250	500 Mi.
0	250	500 Km.

Azimuthal Equal-Area Projection

LEARNING FROM MAPS. *Although the Barbary states were tiny and far from the United States, they caused problems. How did their location make it possible for them to harm United States trade?*

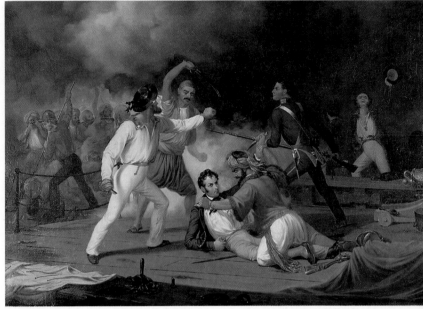

"Decatur at Tripoli," by W. A. Martin, also celebrates the triumph of the American hero. Finally through Decatur's efforts the pasha of Tripoli and the rulers of Algeria and Tunisia left American vessels unharmed. Can you think of a modern example of the United States being treated as the pasha treated the young nation?

stop attacking American ships. The United States continued to pay tribute until 1815, but the firm action of the American government strengthened its reputation.

The Louisiana Purchase

Jefferson's most important accomplishment was adding a huge new western region to the nation. This came about in a most unexpected manner. The settlers who crossed over the mountains into Kentucky, Tennessee, and the lands north of the Ohio River cleared the land and planted crops. As the country developed, traffic on the Mississippi River increased rapidly. Frontier farmers floated their wheat, lumber, tobacco, and other produce down the river on log rafts. These goods had to be stored in warehouses and on docks in New Orleans while waiting to be reshipped to East Coast ports or to Europe on oceangoing vessels. As we have seen, Pinckney's Treaty of 1795 with Spain guaranteed Americans what was called the **right of deposit** at New Orleans. Without the right of deposit, western settlers could not get their produce to market.

All went well until 1800, when Spain, under pressure from the powerful Napoleon Bonaparte, agreed to give New Orleans and the rest of the land called Louisiana back to France. For more than a year Spain continued to govern New Orleans. But France was obviously preparing to take over the city as part of a general expansion of its overseas empire. Napoleon planned to use Louisiana as a breadbasket to feed the French West Indian sugar islands. France's most important island colony, Santo Domingo, had broken away during the French Revolution. Slaves led by Toussaint L'Ouverture

Toussaint L'Ouverture astride his horse led so strong an uprising in Santo Domingo that it took 20,000 of Napoleon's French soldiers to quiet the rebellion. The French later seized him and he died a year later. Why was Napoleon determined to crush L'Ouverture's rebellion?

took control of the island. In l80l Napoleon had sent 20,000 soldiers to put down the rebellion.

Jefferson had long been an admirer of France and of French civilization. He disliked the English. Yet the mere thought of France controlling New Orleans made him willing to consider an alliance with Great Britain against France. If France canceled the right of deposit, he wrote to his diplomatic representative in Paris, Robert R. Livingston, we must "marry ourselves to the British fleet."

Spain was a weak nation. It could not seriously threaten American interests. If Spain closed New Orleans to Americans, the city could probably be captured by a force of arms. With a great military power such as France in control, the result might be very different. To solve the problem, Jefferson instructed Livingston to offer to buy the city of New Orleans from France.

Livingston spent the greater part of 1802 trying to arrange a deal. Talleyrand, who was still in charge of French foreign relations, looked down his nose at him. He would not even tell Livingston whether or not Spain had also given Florida to France. Napoleon seemed to be the only person able to make decisions, and he was hard to reach. "He seldom asks advice," Livingston complained in a letter to James Madison, the secretary of state. "His ministers are mere clerks."

"Raising the Flag at New Orleans" shows the Stars and Stripes replacing the French tricolor after the Louisiana Purchase. The scene is the Vieux Carre (old square), now Jackson Square. In the background are the landmark St. Louis Cathedral, built in 1795, and the Cabildo, the government headquarters built in 1794. Fire recently ravaged the third floor of the Cabildo but its contents were saved and it will soon open again to the public. Why was New Orleans so important to the United States?

In October 1802 Spain canceled the American right of deposit at New Orleans. The situation was at once critical. Much alarmed, Jefferson sent a trusted adviser, James Monroe, to join Livingston in France. He authorized Monroe to offer Napoleon $10 million for New Orleans. Meanwhile, the French expedition to Santo Domingo had been wasted by yellow fever and jungle warfare.

Now Napoleon needed money. Soon he planned to resume his long war with England. The French possessions in America would then be easy targets for Britain's powerful navy. Early in 1803 he ordered Talleyrand to offer to sell New Orleans and all the rest of Louisiana to the United States. The Americans quickly took the offer.

When Napoleon offered to sell Louisiana, he did not simply mean what is now the state of Louisiana. Rather he meant all the land between the Mississippi River and the Rocky Mountains! When Talleyrand, the French foreign minister, passed this news on to Robert Livingston, the American negotiator was dumbfounded. But he recovered swiftly. He offered $5 million for the territory. Not enough, said Talleyrand. He urged Livingston to think the matter over.

The very next day James Monroe arrived in Paris to represent President Jefferson. After considerable discussion he and Livingston decided to offer $15 million. If Jefferson thought $10 million a fair price for New Orleans, surely $15 million was not too much to pay for that city and the entire western half of the Mississippi Valley. Talleyrand accepted the offer.

This **Louisiana Purchase** was one of the greatest real estate bargains in history. When the Americans asked Talleyrand about the exact boundaries of Louisiana, he could not tell them. No one knew. "You have made a noble bargain for yourselves," Talleyrand said. "I suppose you will make the most of it."

Hamilton and Burr

Adding all this new territory to the United States alarmed many of the leaders of the Federalist party. Jefferson was popular with farmers and with western settlers in general. Federalist strength was greatest in New England and among merchants and other city residents. When people began to settle Louisiana, and new states were formed beyond the Mississippi, the power and influence of the Federalists in Congress seemed sure to decline.

A group of angry Federalists in the New England states, led by Timothy Pickering, a former secretary of state, began to scheme to withdraw their states from the Union. Such a withdrawal, the technical name for which is **secession,** would be more likely to succeed if New York joined the movement. Then a strong northeastern confederacy could be formed. Pickering and his friends therefore tried to persuade Vice President Aaron Burr of New York to join them.

Burr did not enjoy being vice president. He had decided to seek

The Granger Collection

With steady aim Aaron Burr has just fired the fatal shot in his duel with Alexander Hamilton, who had fired his pistol into the air. What events led to this duel?

election as governor of New York. When he was approached by the Federalists, he did not agree to join the plot, but he did not reject the idea either. However, he was defeated in the New York election, which took place in April 1804. Without the support of New York, the secession scheme had to be abandoned.

During his campaign for governor, Burr had become very angry with Alexander Hamilton, who had criticized him in a most insulting manner. Hamilton had strongly opposed the idea of secession. He disliked Burr even more than he disliked Jefferson. After Burr had lost the election, Hamilton continued to make insulting remarks about him. Finally Burr challenged Hamilton to a duel.

Dueling was against the law in New York and in many other states. Hamilton had performed bravely during the Revolutionary War. Therefore no one could accuse him of cowardice. Like many Americans of his day, Hamilton believed that a challenge to duel could not honorably be refused. He accepted. On July 11, 1804, the two men met secretly in New Jersey, across the Hudson River from New York City. At the signal to fire, Hamilton discharged his pistol into the air. Burr aimed his gun carefully. Hamilton fell. The bullet had passed through his liver and come to rest against his backbone. Nothing could be done. The next morning, he died.

In a way, this senseless tragedy marked the decline of the Federalist party that Hamilton had created. The Louisiana Purchase was popular nearly everywhere. Jefferson was easily reelected president in 1804. Four years later his friend and adviser, James Madison, became president. Madison served two terms, and then another of Jefferson's friends, James Monroe, was president for eight more years. 🖅

Return to the Preview & Review on page 272.

Jefferson as President 279

Use these questions to guide your reading. Answer the questions after completing Section 3.
Understanding Issues, Events, & Ideas. Describe the Lewis and Clark expedition, using the following words: Corps of Discovery, continental divide.
1. What kinds of instructions were Lewis and Clark given for their expedition?
2. What was Sacagawea's surprise discovery when the Lewis and Clark Expedition met the Shoshone Indians?
3. How did Captain Lewis maintain harmony? Why was such harmony unusual?
4. What were some achievements of Lewis and Clark?
5. On what explorations did Pike travel?
Thinking Critically. 1. You are a soldier on the Lewis and Clark Expedition. Write a diary entry describing your visit to the Shoshone camp. **2.** What is a modern voyage of discovery that you would consider to be as great as that of Lewis and Clark? Why?

3. THE LOUISIANA TERRITORY

The Lewis and Clark Expedition

President Jefferson began promptly to plan for the development of the Louisiana Territory. In fact, he first asked Congress for money to explore the region even before Spain had returned it to France. Congress supplied him with $2,500. He then appointed his private secretary, a young ex-soldier named Meriwether Lewis, to head the expedition. According to Jefferson, Lewis was brave, careful, and "habituated to the woods."

Lewis persuaded another soldier, William Clark, to become co-leader of the expedition. The two had met while both were fighting under General Anthony Wayne against the Indian confederacy in the Ohio Valley. These two experienced outdoorsmen made an excellent team.

Jefferson gave the explorers very detailed instructions. These instructions reflected his own interests, which were as varied as Benjamin Franklin's. Besides describing and mapping the country, Lewis and Clark were to keep careful records of its climate—the temperature, the number of rainy days, wind directions, and so on. They were to locate and map the course of all rivers in order to find "the most direct . . . water connection across this continent." In addition, Jefferson ordered them to take note of soil conditions and to look for traces of valuable minerals. They were to collect plant and animal specimens and even to bring back the bones of any "rare or extinct" animals they could find.

Jefferson was particularly interested in the many American Indian cultures. As a young man he had been one of the first people to find and excavate a settlement of the ancient civilization of the Mound Builders. He instructed Lewis and Clark to gather all sorts of information about the western Indians. He wanted to know about their languages, their clothing, what they ate, how they lived, their diseases. He gave Lewis and Clark a list of basic English words and told them to take note of the corresponding words in the languages of the Indians they met.

Lewis and Clark prepared for their journey carefully. They consulted with leading scientists. They gathered the necessary equipment, such as guns, warm clothing, gifts for Indians, and medicines. They even secured navigational instruments so that they could map the country accurately.

They chose with equal care the members of what they called their **Corps of Discovery.** They employed a half-French, half-Indian interpreter who was skilled in the sign language used by Indians of different tribes to communicate with one another. One member was an expert at repairing guns, another a carpenter. Twenty-one members of the Corps were army men. The secretary of war had authorized Lewis to "detach" from their military duties any volunteers he wanted. Only strong men used to living in the woods were chosen, for as Lewis said, hard work was "a very essential part of the services required of the party." The group finally chosen consisted of 45 people. One of these, an enormously strong man named York, became the first person of African descent to cross the continent. He was a slave owned by William Clark.

Westward to the Pacific

On May 14, 1804, the explorers set out from their base at the junction of the Mississippi and Missouri Rivers. Up the Missouri they went. They traveled in three boats, the largest a 55-foot (about 17-meter) keelboat manned by 22 oarsmen. Their first objective was the "mountains of rock that rise up in the West."

By August they had reached what is now Council Bluffs, Iowa. There they had their first meeting with Indians belonging to the tribes of the Great Plains. Lewis and Clark put up the United States flag, which at the time had 17 stars. Through an interpreter Lewis told the Plains Indians that "the great Chief of the seventeen nations of America" wanted to live in peace and was eager to trade with them for their furs. He then gave out gifts and left them an American flag, but Jefferson's hopes for peace were doomed to disappointment.

By October the explorers were deep in the northern plains. Cold weather was fast approaching. They built Fort Mandan, and in this snug, easily defended post they passed a long, bitterly cold winter.

When spring came, Lewis and Clark shipped the many boxes of plants, Indian craft objects, and animal bones and skins that they had collected back to St. Louis in the keelboat. Everything was carefully labeled. Then they pushed on. A Canadian, Toussaint Charbonneau, accompanied them as an interpreter, as did Sacagawea (Bird Woman), a Shoshone Indian married to Charbonneau.

Sacagawea became a very important member of the party. High in the Rockies, near the present-day border of Montana and Idaho, the expedition met up with the Shoshone. Lewis had pushed ahead with Charbonneau and the guide who knew Indian sign language. Most Indians of the region were very wary and difficult to find, but the explorers came upon three Shoshone women. After giving them gifts, they persuaded these Shoshone to lead them to their camp. There they found 60 warriors on horseback. The Shoshone people greeted the explorers in friendly fashion, giving them food and smoking a ceremonial pipe of peace. When Sacagawea and the rest of the party reached the Shoshone camp, she discovered to everyone's delight that the chief was her brother!

The Shoshone sold Lewis and Clark 29 horses for the trip across North America's **continental divide,** the ridge of the Rocky Mountains that separates the streams that flow east into the Mississippi Valley

Some names in history—Lewis and Clark among them—seem forever paired. James Meriwether Lewis is at the top, William Clark is below. Both were painted by Charles Willson Peale. Lewis was Jefferson's secretary, an ex-soldier. Clark was also a soldier. As you read on, decide whether this team was well chosen.

from those that flow west to the Pacific Ocean. Equally important, one of the warriors, whom the explorers called Toby, guided them through the Bitterroot Mountains. Without Toby's help they might have become hopelessly lost in the rugged High Plateau country.

Lewis and Clark were the first outsiders to describe the Shoshone people and many of the other Indians of the mountain area. They obtained more horses from a tribe called the Flatheads. Eventually they reached the great Columbia River. In November 1805, having floated down the Columbia in dugout canoes carved from the trunks of great ponderosa pine trees, they reached the Pacific.

They settled for the winter near the mouth of the Columbia River. There they built Fort Clatsop, named after the local Indians. The fort was 50 feet (15 meters) square. It consisted of two rows of huts made of pine logs facing each other across a courtyard. During the rainy winter months when food was scarce, the men ate a good deal of dog meat and whale fat, called blubber. According to Captain Lewis, the men became "extremely fond" of dog meat. "For my own part," Lewis added, "I think it is an agreeable food and would prefer it vastly to lean venison or elk."

After a long, rainy winter the explorers began the trip back. They had been gone nearly two years. Most people, even President Jefferson, had lost hope of their return. The group reached St. Louis late in September 1806. Crowds lined the river to greet them. Their exciting but difficult adventure had been remarkable for its harmony. There had been no serious clashes with the many Indians they met along the way. The explorers had managed to get along with one another too, even when cooped up far from home with little to do during two winters.

Charles Marion Russell was a famous painter of the American West. Once a trapper and cowboy, Russell lived for a time with the same people visited by Lewis and Clark. In this Russell painting Sacagawea, who became a new mother on the journey, greets her Shoshone relatives. The 1805 scene is set near the present-day border of Idaho and Montana. Although this is a reunion, what signs of tension can you find in the painting?

Amon Carter Museum

In this Charles Russell painting leaders of the Corps of Discovery encounter Indians—perhaps Clatsops—in the lower Columbia River in 1805. Sacagawea signs their greetings. Why do you think it was important that the corps members included an Indian interpreter?

Captain Lewis deserves much of the credit for this harmony. He was a firm but considerate leader. He treated all members of the party fairly. He was careful not to exclude the slave York or Sacagawea, as when he called for a vote on where to build Fort Clatsop.

Lewis and Clark's Achievement

Besides giving the United States a claim to territory in the Northwest, this remarkable expedition produced an amazing amount of new information about the Great West. Lewis and Clark discovered the true course of the Missouri River. They proved that the continent was much wider than most people had thought. They found and mapped a number of passes through the Rockies. In later years their maps would help settlers make their way through the mountains and on to the Pacific. Hundreds of hunters, trappers, scientists, and ordinary settlers profited from Lewis and Clark's maps and reports.

Lewis and Clark also discovered and brought back many new plants. They saw animals in their natural habitats. They sent back large numbers of skins of animals as well as many live animals of the region for scientific study. The journals and diaries of the journey contained many fantastic stories and adventures. Lewis recounted a day that included a hair-raising encounter with a bear and the near-loss of the expedition's supplies:

    ❝ In an instant this monster ran at them with open mouth. The two who had reserved their fires discharged their pieces [guns] at him as he came towards them. Both of them struck him, one only slightly and the other fortunately broke his shoulder. This however only retarded [slowed] the bear's motion for a moment.

    The men unable to reload their guns took to flight, the

Missouri Historical Society
President Jefferson specifically asked for information on new flora (plants) and fauna (animals). One of William Clark's sketches is shown below.

The Louisiana Territory   **283**

bear pursued and had very nearly overtaken them before they reached the river. Two of the party betook themselves to a canoe, and the others separated and concealed themselves among the willows. Reloading their pieces, each discharged his piece at him as they had the opportunity. They struck him several times again but the guns served only to direct the bear to them.

In this manner he pursued two of them separately so close that they were obliged to throw themselves into the river altho' the bank was nearly twenty feet perpendicular [high]. So enraged was this animal that he plunged into the river only a few feet behind the second man he had forced to take refuge in the water. Finally one of those who still remained on shore shot him through the head and killed him. They then took him to shore and butchered him. They found that eight balls [bullets] had passed through him in different directions. The bear being old, the flesh [meat] was indifferent not tasty. They therefore only took the skin and fleece, [the fat] of the latter made us several gallons of oil.

It was after the sun had set before these [men] came up with us, where we had halted by an occurrence, which I have now to describe. Altho' the occurrence happily passed without ruinous injury, I cannot recollect it but with the utmost fear and horror. This is the upsetting and narrow escape of the white perogue [canoe].

It happened unfortunately for us this evening that Charbono was at the helm of this perogue, . . . Charbono cannot swim and is perhaps the most timid waterman in the world. Perhaps it was equally unluckey that Capt. C [Clark], and myself were both on shore at that moment. . . . In this perogue were embarked our papers, instruments, books, medicine, and great part of our merchandize and in short almost every article indespensibly necessary . . . to ensure the success of the enterprise in which we were now launched to the distance of 2200 miles [3520 kilometers]. . . . A sudon squal [sudden gust] of wind struck her obiquely [at an angle], and turned her considerably.

The steersman alarmed, instead of puting her before the wind, lufted her up into it. The wind was so violent that it drew the brace of the squarsail out of the hand of the man attending it, and . . . would have turned her completely topsaturva [upside down], had it not been for the resistence made by the oarning [sail] against the water.[1] ""

[1]From *Original Journals of the Lewis and Clark Expedition,* edited by Ruben Gold Thwaites

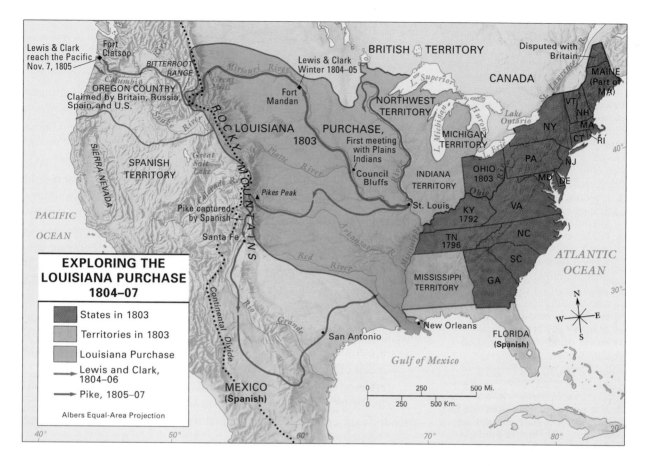

EXPLORING THE
LOUISIANA PURCHASE
1804-07

States in 1803
Territories in 1803
Louisiana Purchase
Lewis and Clark, 1804–06
Pike, 1805–07

Albers Equal-Area Projection

Lewis and Clark's accounts of the Indian tribes they met, such as the one on page 293, provided much fresh information. In some cases the very existence of large tribes was unknown until the reports of Lewis and Clark were published. All in all, their expedition was one of the great voyages of discovery of modern times.

Pike's Adventures

The success of Lewis and Clark did not open wide the gates of Louisiana. But their discoveries spurred other explorations. In 1805, a year before the return of Lewis and Clark, Zebulon Pike led an expedition north from St. Louis. He traveled up the Mississippi, searching for the river's source. Although Pike was not successful, he learned much about the upper Mississippi region.

In 1806 Pike explored the southern part of the Louisiana Purchase. His party traveled up the Arkansas River, and in November Pike sighted the mountain in Colorado that was later named Pikes Peak. Pike then went on to Santa Fe and across the Rio Grande. He returned to Louisiana through Texas. Although Pike's notes added to the information being collected about the American West, he was not nearly so careful an observer as Lewis and Clark.

Return to the Preview & Review on page 280.

LEARNING FROM MAPS. *The Louisiana Purchase almost doubled the size of the United States. Trace the route Lewis and Clark took. What were the major obstacles they encountered? Do the same for Pike's journey.*

Zebulon Pike is the subject of this Charles Willson Peale portrait.

Independence National Historical Park

The Louisiana Territory   285

Preview & Review

Use these questions to guide your reading. Answer the questions after completing Section 4.

Understanding Issues, Events, & Ideas. Create a chronological outline of President Jefferson's foreign policy, using the following words: impressment, Embargo Act, Non-Intercourse Act, Macon's Bill Number Two.

1. How did the war between France and England affect the United States on the high seas?
2. For what purpose was impressment originally intended? Why were Americans sometimes victims of impressment?
3. Why did America still have troubles on the high seas even after the Non-Intercourse Act and Macon's Bill Number Two?

Thinking Critically. 1. What do you think President Jefferson should have done differently to make his foreign policy more successful? Explain your answer.
2. The year is 1807. Before the Embargo Act, you were a manufacturer who sold cloth to England. Now you are unemployed. Are you sympathetic toward a ship captain arrested for smuggling sugar? Why or why not?

Jefferson and the Navy

Only a few weeks after selling Louisiana to the United States, France was again at war with England. Once again the struggle between these two European nations had powerful effects upon the United States.

America's prosperity depended to a large extent on foreign trade. Americans still needed foreign manufactured goods, and farmers sold a great deal of their produce abroad. French and British warships and privateers hurt this trade by capturing American merchant ships bound for each other's ports.

During 1806 the British seized 120 American ships carrying cargoes to and from the French West Indies. The British also claimed the right to seize American ships headed for European countries that Napoleon had conquered, such as Holland and Belgium. Napoleon, in turn, issued orders to his captains to capture any neutral vessel that had allowed itself to be inspected on the high seas by a British warship. Such vessels "have become English property," Napoleon announced in his Milan Decree of 1807.

Jefferson had said in his inaugural address that he favored "honest friendship" with all nations. How could the United States be friendly with countries that attacked its ships in this manner? What could be done to prevent these attacks?

One obvious way to protect American shipping would be to build a navy powerful enough to escort convoys of merchant ships and drive off or sink privateers. When John Adams was president, a naval building program had been undertaken. The frigates *Constitution, Constellation,* and *United States* had performed well against French armed vessels in the late 1790s. They were without doubt the most powerful warships of that type afloat at the time. But frigates cost several hundred thousand dollars each and were expensive to maintain. Once peace with France had been reached, Jefferson saw no need to expand the navy further. He preferred to rely on small gunboats, which cost only about $10,000 apiece to build. These tiny gunboats were useless on the high seas or in combat with a large warship. This is one reason the war with the Barbary pirates had dragged on so long.

Jefferson's trouble was that although he was very upset when foreign powers threatened the rights of American citizens, he was unwilling to spend large sums of public money to defend those rights. In a way, the whole country suffered from the same confusion. War in Europe caused attacks on American ships. These attacks were a blow to American pride. Yet the war greatly increased the demand for American goods in Europe. Sales doubled between 1803 and 1805. The foreign war was making America prosperous.

The Granger Collection

Trouble on the High Seas

Merchants could protect themselves against the loss of ships and their cargoes by insuring them. Insurance rates were high in wartime, but the prices merchants could get for their goods were high too. More alarming was the loss of men.

For hundreds of years the Royal Navy had claimed the right to *impress* any British civilian into the navy in a national emergency. **Impressment** was a hit-or-miss way of drafting men for military service. As the system developed in the 1700s, a ship's captain in need of sailors would send what he called a *press gang* ashore. Perhaps some of his crew had been killed in a battle at sea. More likely, some may have deserted when the vessel reached port.

The press gang, composed of members of the warship's crew, would go ashore armed. They would roam the waterfront area searching for men who looked as though they were experienced sailors. The press gang seized anyone they wanted and carried the men away to their ship. Sometimes they found it easiest just to drag off drunks from shoreside bars. The unfortunate men who were impressed received one shilling, called press money, to "compensate" them for having been forced to serve in His Majesty's navy.

Press gangs were not supposed to take anyone who was not a British subject. But sometimes they made mistakes. Particularly in British ports in the West Indies, American sailors on shore leave were often taken. These men naturally protested loudly that they were Americans. But Englishmen who wanted to avoid being impressed frequently claimed that *they* were Americans. Because they spoke the same language, it was not always easy to tell the difference.

The captain of H.M.S. Leopard *is impressing four angry American seamen after capturing the U.S.S.* Chesapeake *in 1807. Howard Pyle made this illustration. Use historical imagination to think what it might have been like to be impressed—a long voyage ahead—in the navy of another country.*

English sailors sometimes even carried false papers, pretending that they were Americans. Real Americans often did not have any way of proving they were citizens when grabbed by a press gang. The gangs seldom troubled to check carefully in any case. They took any man they wanted. When the captains of British warships sent press gangs ashore, they were not accustomed to having them come back empty-handed. By the time an American was reported missing, he would be far at sea, beyond reach of rescuers.

The United States government did not deny the right of the British to impress British sailors from American merchant ships. But most Americans considered the practice shameful, even if no sailors were taken. British naval officers were often arrogant and domineering. Sometimes they treated the Americans rudely and with contempt. "On board our good old ship *Leander*," one British officer later admitted, "we had not enough consideration for the feelings of the people we were dealing with."

The Embargo Act

In December 1807 Congress passed the **Embargo Act.** This law prohibited all exports from the United States. Jefferson reasoned that if

"You shall be king hereafter," says the emperor Napoleon, standing just behind President Jefferson. This English political cartoon is a satire on the Embargo Act and its effects on American merchants. The profits go to the French. Look closely. "My warehouses are full," says one man. Says another, "My family is starving." Yet Jefferson tells his audience: "This is a Grand Philosophical Idea. If we continue this Experiment for about fifteen or twenty years, we may begin to feel the good effects." This is all too much for one man, who remembers 'Great Washington.' Even the little dog is angry. What complaint do the merchants have?

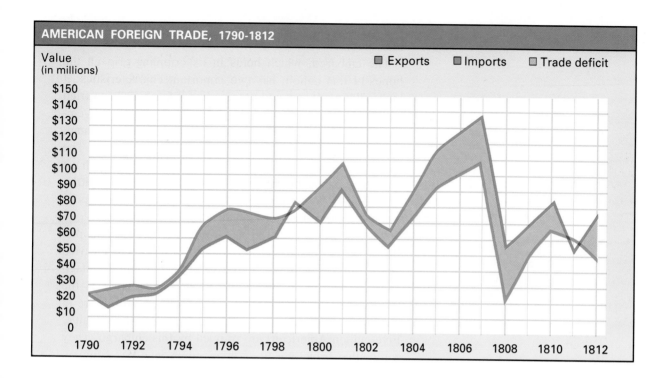

AMERICAN FOREIGN TRADE, 1790-1812

Value (in millions)

☐ Exports ☐ Imports ☐ Trade deficit

merchant ships could not carry goods abroad, no American sailor could be forced into a foreign navy. This was, of course, a drastic way of dealing with the problem, like trying to kill a fly on a window by throwing a brick at it.

Stopping exports caused unemployment among sailors and among workers who had been making goods that were usually exported. The busy shipbuilding industry nearly came to a standstill. More workers were unemployed. Even more serious, foreign shipowners would not carry goods to America if they had to return to their home ports empty. The value of all the goods imported in 1808 was less than half that of 1807. The embargo policy was an economic disaster.

People in the New England states and in other areas where foreign trade was important deeply resented the Embargo Act. Josiah Quincy, a Massachusetts Federalist in Congress during the embargo crisis, was a vocal opponent of the embargo. Quincy and other opponents of the embargo felt it was doing great economic damage to the United States as a whole, and especially to trading interests in New England. In a speech before Congress Quincy explained his concerns:

66 The entire nation is suffering under a most serious oppression, the embargo. All the business of the nation is in disorder. All the hopes of the people are frustrated. All the nation's industry is at a standstill. Its many products hastening to market are stopped in their course. With every

LEARNING FROM GRAPHS.
This line graph illustrates trends in American foreign trade. As you can see, Americans imported more than they exported even in the early 1800s. What general trend do you note for American trade between 1790 and 1807? Then what happens? Why?

passing hour the desire of the citizens to resist the embargo increases.

The embargo, which holds in its crippling grip all the hopes of this nation, has two important characteristics: it hurts all Americans, and nothing like it has ever been tried before. Every interest in the nation is affected by the embargo. The merchant, the farmer, the planter, the craftsman, the laboring poor—all are sinking under its weight. The embargo especially hurts the poor. From those who have much, it takes something. But from those who have little, it takes all. What hope is left to the hard-working poor when they lose their jobs because of the embargo?

The embargo affects the hopes and interests of all people. But it is also remarkable because it has never been tried before. In fact it never before entered into human imagination! There is nothing like it in all of history or in the tales of fiction. All the habits of our mighty nation are at once frustrated. All property of our people sinks in value. Five million Americans are trapped by this embargo. They can neither travel nor trade outside our once free country.

I ask whether the embargo, which affects so many Americans and which is so new, and which interferes with the desires and interests of the whole nation, ought to be left in effect. Who can predict when the British and French will honor American trading rights and bring an end to the embargo? And who can guarantee that the patience of the citizens will not soon give out and lead them to resist the embargo?[1]"

Many people broke this law because they considered it unwise and unfair. There were many ways of doing so. Trade by sea between one American port and another was allowed. A captain could sail from Boston to New York or from Philadelphia to Charleston or to any other American port. Many announced that they were sailing on such a voyage and went instead to Europe or the West Indies. If caught, they claimed that a storm had driven them off course.

The captain of the merchant ship *Commerce,* supposedly headed for New Orleans, sailed to Havana, Cuba. The excuse he gave was that he had run out of water for his crew. At the same time that he filled his water barrels, he sold his cargo and bought sugar.

Besides tricks such as these, many Americans resorted to direct smuggling in order to sell their goods abroad. Large amounts of American products were carried illegally from the northern states to Canada. That long and still almost unsettled border was very difficult to patrol. When smugglers were caught and brought to trial, juries

[1]From "How Jefferson's Embargo Paralyzed Trade" by Josiah Quincy in *America: Great Crises in Our History Told by Its Makers*, Vol. V

made up of their fellow citizens usually found them not guilty. It was as hard to convict a merchant charged with violating the Embargo Act as it had been in the 1770s to convict someone of violating the Townshend Act by importing Dutch tea to avoid the tea tax.

America on the Eve of War

In the fall of 1808, James Madison, Jefferson's longtime friend, was elected to succeed him as president. After the election Jefferson gave up the struggle to enforce the Embargo Act. Early in 1809 Congress repealed it. Congress then passed a law to permit reopening trade with all foreign countries except France and Britain. Under this **Non-Intercourse Act** no English or French ship could enter an American harbor nor could Americans sell goods to those countries. The law also gave the president the power to end the boycott against either nation whenever it "shall cease to violate the neutral commerce of the United States."

The Non-Intercourse Act was even harder to enforce than the Embargo Act. A ship's captain could set out officially for Spain or Holland or any other nation and then land his cargo in whatever country he liked—including Britain or France. English and French attacks on American ships continued.

In desperation a congressman from North Carolina, Nathaniel Macon, proposed a bill allowing American ships to trade with England and France but prohibiting English and French ships from trading with the United States. How this would reduce attacks on American ships and sailors was hard to see. Congress did not pass Macon's bill. But in 1810 it did pass **Macon's Bill Number Two.**

This law removed all restrictions on trade with England and France. It also provided that if either nation stopped attacking American merchant ships, the president could cut off all trade with its rival nation unless it also stopped its attacks. For example, if the English would leave American ships alone, the Americans would boycott England's rival—France.

Macon's Bill Number Two seemed to treat England and France in exactly the same way. In fact, trade with England quickly became as great as it had been before the Embargo Act. But there was little trade with France because by 1810 the British navy dominated the Atlantic Ocean. Few neutral merchant ships dared try to get to French-controlled ports. And the British practice of impressing American sailors continued. The policies of Jefferson and Madison had failed. To more and more people it seemed that the only way to protect the right to trade freely was to go to war. 🖅

Return to the Preview & Review on page 286.

CHAPTER 8 REVIEW

Federalist Era	Adams Presidency	
1795		**1800** THE AGE OF JEFFERSON

1798
Kentucky
and Virginia
Resolutions

1800
Convention
of 1800

★
Jefferson elected president

1801
Tripoli declares
war on U.S.

Chapter Summary
Read the statements below. Choose one, and write a paragraph explaining its importance.
1. Federalist attempts to continue to control the government failed.
2. The Kentucky and Virginia Resolutions emphasized the idea of nullification and states' rights.
3. The first Democratic-Republican president, Thomas Jefferson, was elected in 1800.
4. Federalist attempts to control electors led to passage of the Twelfth Amendment, which provided for electors to vote separately for president and vice president.
5. *Marbury v. Madison* set a precedent for declaring an act of Congress unconstitutional.
6. The United States purchased the Louisiana Territory from France in 1803, doubling the nation's size.
7. New England Federalists were alarmed that the Louisiana Purchase would lessen the influence of their section.
8. Lewis and Clark explored the northern region of the new territory while Pike explored the southern reaches.
9. War between Britain and France caused serious problems for Americans.
10. The Embargo Act, Non-Intercourse Act, and Macon's Bill Number Two failed to protect American shipping and sailors.

Reviewing Chronological Order
Number your paper 1–5. Then study the time line above and place the following events in the order in which they happened by writing the first next to 1, the second next to 2, and so on.
1. Embargo Act passed
2. Jefferson elected president
3. *Marbury v. Madison*
4. Kentucky and Virginia Resolutions
5. Lewis and Clark expedition begins

Understanding Main Ideas
1. Why was the Twelfth Amendment needed? How did it improve national elections?
2. What was Jefferson's doctrine of nullification?
3. Why did Jefferson want to buy Louisiana? Why did Napoleon want to sell it?
4. Why was Sacagawea important to the success of the Lewis and Clark Expedition?
5. What was impressment? Why did it anger many Americans?
6. Why did many Americans break the Embargo Act of 1807?

Thinking Critically
1. **Seeing Relationships.** Write a note to Thomas Jefferson, explaining why you think his doctrine of nullification is dangerous to the Union. Explain your view of states' rights.
2. **Evaluating.** You know that Aaron Burr killed Alexander Hamilton in a duel. If dueling were still practiced today, would you be for or against legalizing it? Why?
3. **Synthesizing.** Imagine that you are either York, the slave of William Clark, or Sacagawea. From your point of view, what was the most important achievement of Lewis and Clark's famous expedititon?

Writing About History: Persuasive
Suppose you are one of the following: A Federalist supporting the Sedition Act or a Democratic-Republican supporting the Kentucky and Virginia Resolutions. Write a letter to a newspaper stating your views. Use the information in Chapter 8 to help you develop your letter.

Practicing the Strategy
Review the strategy on page 274.
Interpreting a Physical Map. Study the map on page 285 and answer the following questions.
1. Why were rivers so important to Lewis and Clark's expedition?

	Jefferson Presidency					
	1805				1810	

803
Marbury v.
Madison

★
U.S. purchases
Louisiana

★
France and Britain go to war

1804
Lewis and Clark begin expedition

★
Burr shoots Hamilton in duel

1806
Pike explores
southwestern
territory

1807
Embargo Act

1809
Non-Intercourse
Act

1810
Macon's Bill
Number Two

2. Using your historical imagination and the map, describe the landscape Lewis and Clark encountered on the second half of their journey. How does the map show this?

Using Primary Sources

In the following entry from the *Original Journals of the Lewis and Clark Expedition,* Clark describes trading with a group of Indians. He compares these people to the other Indians he had described earlier in his journal. (Clark's original spelling and punctuation have been retained.) As you read the excerpt, think how you would interpret Clark's descriptions.

November 7th Thursday 1805

A cloudy foggey morning Some rain. we Set out early proceeded . . . under a high rugid hills with Steep assent the Shore boalt and rockey, the fog so thick we could not see across the river, two cano[e]s of Indians met and returned with us to their village, they gave us to eate Some fish, and Sold us, fish, Wap pa to *roots three dogs and 2 otter skins for which we gave fish hooks principally of which they were verry fond.*

Those people call themselves War-ci-â-cun *and Speake a language different from the nativs above with whome they trade the* Wapato *roots of which they make great use as food. their houses differently built, raised entirely above ground eaves about 5 feet from the ground Supported and covered in the same way of those above, dores about the Same size but in the Side of the house in one corner, one fire place and that near the opposit end, around which they have their beads [beds] raised about 4 feet from the flore which is of earth, under their beads they Store away Baskets of dried fish Berries & Wappato. . . . Their Canoes are of the Same form as those above.*

1. What evidence in this excerpt from Clark's journal indicates that the Indians he met were peaceful?

2. In what ways did the Indians Clark met differ from the other natives he described?

3. In what ways do you think the geographic features of the area that Clark refers to limited the diet of the Indians?

Linking History & Geography

Lewis and Clark encountered many geographical obstacles in their quest to reach the Pacific. Using the information in this chapter and on the map on page 285, answer the following questions:

1. How long did it take Lewis and Clark to reach the Pacific Ocean? About how great a distance had they traveled?

2. What major physical obstacles made their trip difficult?

3. How did climate affect the expedition? Why?

Enriching Your Study of History

1. **Individual Project.** Read further about the Lewis and Clark expedition in an encyclopedia or other reference book. Then use historical imagination to prepare diary entries that you might have written as a member of the expedition. Try to describe one ordinary day and one very exciting day.

2. **Cooperative Project.** Using historical imagination and problem-solving skills, have your group prepare and present a skit for the class. The scene is a public meeting in an American port city. It is 1807. The British have seized 120 American ships. Now the French will capture any American ship that allows itself to be searched on the high seas by the British. Members of your group should explain why American ships must sail the Atlantic and offer several points of view about ways to protect America's shipping. Then your classmates will vote on which course of action is best.

Chapter 8 Review   293

War and Peace, 1812-1823

This Shoshone encampment at Trapper's Rendevouz of Green River fades into the horizon it is so vast. Alfred Jacob Miller painted the scene in 1837. The Shoshone ranged as far as the Rocky Mountains, where their meeting with the Lewis and Clark expedition occurred. How does this peaceful scene betray no hint of what lies ahead for Indians and settlers?

When America declared war on Great Britain in 1812, the people of the Northeast were bitterly opposed. Strangely enough, they were also the people most injured by British attacks on American ships and their crews. Those who favored the war were westerners and southerners, called War Hawks, many of whom had never even seen the Atlantic Ocean. If war broke out, these "hawks" hoped to gobble up British-owned Canada. They also expected to take Florida from Spain, because Spain had now taken the side of England in the long war the British were fighting against Napoleon. Trouble began on the frontier with fighting between settlers and American Indians. Then, when the War of 1812 broke out, Britain and America battled inconclusively at sea and on land. When peace was made in 1815, the Stars and Stripes still flew over the land. But how would the world react when put on notice that the United States now intended to police the whole Western Hemisphere?

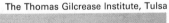

The Thomas Gilcrease Institute, Tulsa

1. WAR IN THE NORTHWEST

War Hawks on the Frontier

The **War Hawks** and other frontier settlers blamed England for the troubles between Indians and settlers in the Northwest Territory. They felt that the British in Canada kept the Indians riled up to make trouble. They correctly believed that if war broke out, the Indians in the Great Lakes region would side with the British. Henry Clay, a young senator from Kentucky was a leading War Hawk. The following is an excerpt from the speech Clay delivered in the Senate on February 22, 1810, expressing the attitude of the War Hawks:

66 No man in the nation wants peace more than I. But I prefer the troubled ocean of war, with all its disasters and desolation, to the calm decaying pool of dishonorable peace. If we can settle our differences with one of our enemies— Britain or France—I should prefer it be Britain. But if with neither, and we are forced into a selection of our enemy, then I choose war with Britain. I believe her first in aggression and her injuries and insults to us are extremely cruel in character.

Britain stands out in her outrage on us, by her violation of the sacred personal rights of American freemen, in the arbitrary and lawless imprisonment of our seamen.

But we [Congress] are asked for the means of supporting the war, and those who oppose it triumphantly appeal to the empty vaults of the Treasury. We have, I am credibly informed, in the city and vicinity of New Orleans alone, public property sufficient to pay off the debt noted in the Treasury report. And are we to regard as nothing the patriotic offers so often made by the States, to spend their last cent, and risk their last drop of blood, in the preservation of our neutral privileges?

It is said, however, that it is hopeless to go to war with Great Britain. If we go to war, we are to estimate not only the benefit gained for ourselves, but the injury to be done the enemy. The conquest of Canada is in your power. I trust that I shall not be thought to be bold when I state that I truly believe that the militia of Kentucky are alone competent to place Montreal and Upper Canada at your feet. Is it nothing to the pride of the King, to have the last of the immense North American possessions held by him in the beginning of his reign taken from him? Is it nothing to us to put out the torch of Indian warfare? Is it nothing to gain the entire fur trade connected with Canada? . . .

Preview & Review

Use these questions to guide your reading. Answer the questions after completing Section 1.
Understanding Issues, Events, & Ideas. Use the following words to describe troubles on the frontier from the Indian point of view: War Hawk, Red Stick Confederacy, Battle of Tippecanoe.
1. Why was Tecumseh so opposed to the Indian land sale in 1809? What else did he oppose?
2. What did Tecumseh do to organize the tribes east of the Mississippi River?
3. Why was sentiment for declaring war on England stronger on the frontier than elsewhere in the country by 1812?
Thinking Critically. Imagine that you are a member of a hunting tribe in the early 1800s. Do you agree with Jefferson's theory that your standard of living will improve if you become a farmer? How will your way of life change?

STRATEGIES FOR SUCCESS

SYNTHESIZING INFORMATION

To synthesize information you must combine ideas from several sources. *The Story of America* is a synthesis. The author studied many historical sources and used that information to create this textbook. You, too, are asked to synthesize information in this and other courses. Each time you are directed to read information *and* study a map to gain a new understanding, you are synthesizing information.

How to Synthesize Information

To effectively synthesize information, follow these guidelines.

1. **Select sources carefully.** Make sure that the sources you are studying cover the same information and complement, or add to, each other.
2. **Read for understanding.** Identify main ideas and important supporting evidence in each source.
3. **Compare and contrast.** Note where sources agree or build on each other. More importantly, note where they differ.
4. **Interpret all the information.** Use what you have found to interpret the information. This is the key step in synthesizing.

Applying the Strategy

You know that after the end of the Revolutionary War, settlers moved into the lands beyond the Appalachian Mountains. Here troubles erupted. Study the map on this page and then reread "War in the Northwest" on pages 295–99.

By studying these two sources, you should be able to answer some key questions about these events. Why were so many settlers attracted to these lands? What would most of the settlers do with the land? The map shows the area beyond the Appalachians as gently rolling, with abundant streams and rivers. Could this be what many of the settlers were looking for? As you know, many of these pioneers were farmers. They were looking for fertile soil on which to start farms. Do you think they found what they were searching for?

This surge of land-hungry settlers across the mountains caused trouble with the Indians already there. Why? Synthesize the information by using your prior knowledge about how the Indians and settlers differed on their view of land

ownership and the information from your reading and the map to answer this question.

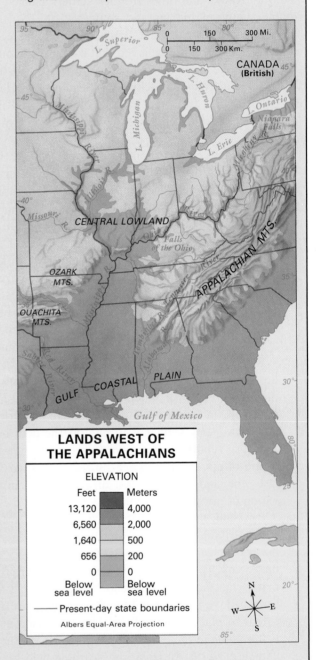

LANDS WEST OF THE APPALACHIANS

ELEVATION

Feet		Meters
13,120		4,000
6,560		2,000
1,640		500
656		200
0		0
Below sea level		Below sea level

—— Present-day state boundaries

Albers Equal-Area Projection

For independent practice, see Practicing the Strategy on page 326.

If we surrender without a struggle to maintain our rights, we forfeit the respect of the world and (what is worse) of ourselves.[1] **"**

The huge area of land in southern Ohio that was turned over to the settlers by the Indians in the Treaty of Greenville in 1795 was not enough to satisfy the land-hungry pioneers for long. Their most cold-blooded leader was General William Henry Harrison. Harrison was governor of the Indiana Territory, the region directly west of the new state of Ohio. He considered the Indians "wretched savages" blocking the forward march of what he called "civilization." By "civilization" Harrison meant his own way of life.

Harrison used trickery, bribery, and military force to push Indians off more and more land. Other government leaders who seemed milder and more tolerant than Harrison did the Indians almost as much harm. They tried to get Indians to settle on farms and become "good Americans." They wanted Indians to give up their customs and religions and copy the largely European culture of the newly arriving settlers. They claimed that the change would be the best thing that could happen both to the Indians and to their new neighbors on the frontier. They did not care that this would destroy the Indians as a distinct group of people.

As President Jefferson put it, if the Indians farmed the land and gave up hunting, more land would be available for the new settlers. By becoming farmers, the Indians would increase what Jefferson called their "domestic comforts"—that is, their standard of living.

Many Indians found some parts of the European way of life attractive. Guns, for example, made them more efficient hunters and warriors. Knives and metal tools, bright-colored cloth, whiskey, cheap jewelry, and other trinkets appealed to them powerfully. Sharp-eyed traders took great advantage of the Indians' desire for these things, swapping nearly worthless goods or whiskey for their valuable furs.

Tecumseh and the Prophet

By about 1809 a brilliant leader was rising among the Indians of the Ohio Valley. He was Tecumseh, a Shawnee chief. Tecumseh is Shawnee for Panther Lying in Wait. He had fought under Chief Little Turtle against United States troops in the 1790s. He took part in the Battle of Fallen Timbers, where one of his brothers was killed.

Tecumseh was against all grants or sales of land to settlers. He believed that God, "the Great Spirit," had created the land for all Indians to *use,* not to own. He claimed Indians had no right to sell the land, even to one another. He asked:

Field Museum

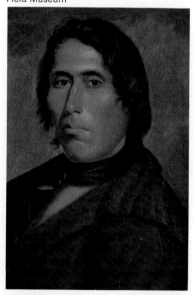

We believe this to be a portrait of Tecumseh, the great leader of the Red Stick Confederacy. What view did Tecumseh take on land ownership? Who did he believe "owned" the land?

[1]From *Annals of Congress*, 11th Congress, 1st Session (1809–10)

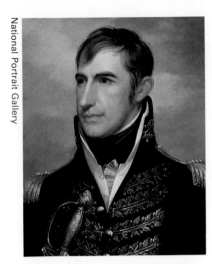

William Henry Harrison here is painted as a young soldier by Rembrandt Peale. In your opinion, which more describes Harrison—diplomat or warrior?

The portrait in oil of Tenskwatawa, known as the Prophet, is by George Catlin. It was painted in the 1830s by the great 19th century painter of American Indians.

“ Why not sell the air, the clouds, and the great sea? . . . White people are never satisfied. . . . They have driven us from the great salt water, forced us over the mountains. . . . We are determined to go no farther. ”

Tecumseh was also against torture and other forms of cruelty in warfare.

In September 1809 General Harrison signed a treaty with the chiefs of a number of tribes. The Indians gave up 3 million acres (1.2 million hectares) in return for about $10,000. That was not even half a cent an acre. The United States government was selling similar land for $2 an acre. Clearly, the Indians were being cheated.

Tecumseh was furious. No Shawnees signed the treaty. He went to see General Harrison. He warned the general not to try to take over the lands just purchased. The local "village chiefs" who had signed the treaty had no right to do so. "We are prepared to punish those chiefs who . . . sell their land," Tecumseh said. And he added sternly, "If you continue to purchase . . . it will produce war."

Tecumseh realized that war was likely to break out between the United States and Great Britain. He intended to organize the many Indian tribes south of the Great Lakes. Then he would threaten to side with the British forces in Canada. Perhaps that would persuade the Big Knives, as he called the soldiers because of their swords and bayonets, to allow the Indians to hold their land in peace.

Tecumseh made this promise to Harrison: If the United States would give up its claims to the Indian lands purchased by the 1809 treaty, the Indians would become loyal allies and help the United States in any war against the British in Canada.

Harrison told Tecumseh frankly that the president would never agree to this. Tecumseh then said that he hoped the Great Spirit would put some sense in the president's head. Otherwise, "he may sit still in his town and drink his wine," but "you and I will have to fight it out."

Tecumseh then set out to organize all the Indian tribes east of the Mississippi to resist expansion onto their land. The alliance he formed was called the **Red Stick Confederacy,** possibly after the Creeks, also known as Red Sticks, who joined the Confederacy.

Tecumseh was an inspiring leader. He was a tall, handsome man with a long, thin face. He wore simple deerskin clothing with few decorations. Usually he had a single eagle's feather in his hair. He was a marvelous speaker and very intelligent. Even General Harrison admitted that Tecumseh was "one of those . . . geniuses which spring up occasionally to produce revolutions."

All along the southern and western frontiers Tecumseh preached Indian unity and resistance to expansion onto Indian land. Resistance meant more than fighting with gun and tomahawk. Indians, he said, must cast off every sign of other cultures. Tecumseh was aided in

The Granger Collection

his crusade by his brother Tenskwatawa, known as the Prophet. Tenskwatawa had been a heavy drinker and troublesome as a young man. He was sometimes called Laulewasikaw, which in Shawnee means Loud Mouth. In 1805 he experienced a religious vision. He dropped all his bad habits and began to preach against drinking and against copying other cultures. He claimed to have magical powers and to be able to see the future.

The Prophet attracted many Indians to the Red Sticks, but he was a poor leader. General Harrison marched against his headquarters at the village called Prophetstown in the fall of 1811. The Prophet ordered a night attack. The battle took place in Indiana, near where Tippecanoe Creek joins the Wabash River. On November 7 the battle raged among the tall oaks and thickets along the rivers. The fighting was fierce and extremely bloody. Harrison squeezed the Indians back against the streams until they fled. Harrison then destroyed their town, but almost a fifth of his own force of about a thousand men were killed or wounded.

The chief result of this **Battle of Tippecanoe** was to make Harrison a popular hero. Tecumseh had been away from Prophetstown recruiting more men for the Red Stick Confederacy. He was annoyed with his brother, who should not have started the fighting. But he did not think that the battle was very important. He referred to it as a "scuffle with the Big Knives."

No one could doubt, however, that the Red Sticks were preparing to fight the Big Knives. The British in Canada would probably help the Indians in such a contest. Because western settlers blamed the British for the Indians' warlike behavior, sentiment for declaring war on England was strong on the frontier by 1812.

The fierce fighting, much of it at close quarters in the Indiana woods, can be seen in this lithograph by Kurz and Allen. General Harrison, at far left, urges his men on in the bloody battle. According to the lithograph, why would it seem the soldiers had the advantage at Tippecanoe?

Return to the Preview & Review on page 295.

2. THE WAR AT SEA

Use these questions to guide your reading. Answer the questions after completing Section 2.
Understanding Issues, Events, & Ideas. Using the following words, describe the early United States navy: War of 1812, frigate, ship of the line, Old Ironsides.
1. Why did northeastern members of Congress vote against war with Britain?
2. In what European conflict was Britain involved in 1812?
3. Why were so many battles at sea won by the United States?
Thinking Critically. Imagine that you are a young American sailor aboard the *Constitution*. Write a letter to a relative in Great Britain, explaining how you and your crew defeated the *Guerrière*.

The War of 1812 Begins

In June 1812 Congress declared war on Great Britain. The vote was fairly close in both the Senate and the House of Representatives. Nearly all the members of Congress who voted against the war came from the northeastern states, where shipping and foreign trade were important. Although these people were angered by the impressment of sailors and by British attacks on American ships, they realized that war with England would seriously injure their trade. They would rather suffer the insults and losses and wait for the war in Europe to come to an end.

The War Hawks continued to defend the war, even after the fighting had begun. Henry Clay stated in Congress in 1813:

&6 What cause, Mr. Chairman, which existed for declaring the war has been removed? . . . Indian hostilities, which were before secretly instigated [caused] now openly encouraged; and the practice of impressment unceasingly . . . insisted upon. . . . An honorable peace is attainable only by an efficient war. My plan would be to call out the ample resources of the country, give them a judicious [sensible] direction, prosecute [fight] the war with the utmost vigor, strike wherever we can reach the enemy, at sea or on land, and negotiate the terms of a peace. . . .[1]99

Still opposition to the war grew. Newspaper editorials such as the following one appeared all over the Northeast. Compare the sentiments expressed in it to those in Clay's speeches urging war.

&6 The feeling is growing by the hour that we are in a condition no better in relation to the South than that of a conquered people. We have been forced, without the least necessity, to give up our habits, occupations, means of happiness, and means of support. We are plunged into a war without feeling that there has been sufficient cause for it. We are obliged to fight the battles of a conspiracy which, while pretending to defend republican equality, aims at trampling into the dust the weight, influence, and power of trade.

We, whose ships were the training ground of sailors, are insulted with the pretense of a devotion to sailors' rights by those whose region knows nothing of navigation beyond the size of a ferryboat or an Indian canoe. We have no interest in fighting this sort of war, at this time and under these circumstances, under the command of Virginia.

[1]From *Annals of Congress*, 12th Congress, 2nd Session (1811–13)

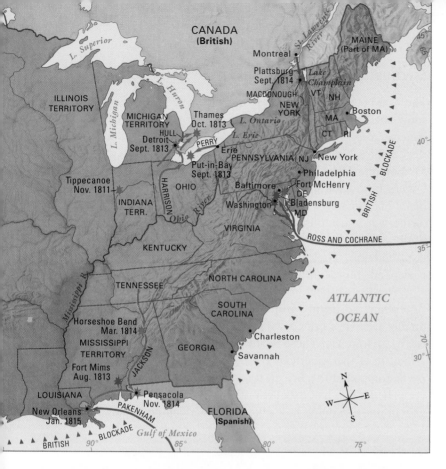

THE WAR OF 1812

→ Americans

✳ American victory

→ British

✳ British victory

0	200	400 Mi.
0	200	400 Km.

Albers Equal-Area Projection

LEARNING FROM MAPS. *This map well illustrates the British strategy in the War of 1812. At what three points did they attempt to attack the United States? Why did they choose these points?*

The consequences must be either that the southern states must drag the northern states farther into the war or we must drag them out of it, or the union of our nation will break apart. We must no longer listen to those foolish outcries against a separation of the states. It is an event we do not desire. But the states are separated in fact when one section continues in actions fatal to the interests and opposed to the opinions of another section because of a geographical majority.[1] 99

Probably those opposing the war were correct in thinking that this **War of 1812** was a mistake. The British were engaged in a life-and-death struggle with Napoleon, now emperor of France. Napoleon was seeking to conquer and control all Europe. French attacks on American commerce were fewer in number than British attacks only because France had a much smaller navy.

The British had no real quarrel with the United States. Nor could the United States gain anything by fighting Britain that it would not get anyway once the war between Great Britain and France was over. By forcing Britain to fight in America, the United States was obviously making it more difficult for the British to bring the war in Europe to an end.

[1]From *Columbian Sentinel* (Boston), Jan. 13, 1813

The War at Sea 301

Victories at Sea

The first battles of the War of 1812 occurred at sea. They resulted in some spectacular American victories. The most powerful ships in the American navy were its seven **frigates.** These three-masted, square-rigged ships varied in length from about 140 to 175 feet (about 42 to 53 meters). The *Chesapeake* was one of the vessels in this class. Others bore such names as *Constitution, United States,* and *President.* The frigates were all quite new. They had been built as a result of the war scare following the XYZ Affair of 1797. They were beautifully designed—fast, easy to maneuver, and armed with 40 to 50 or more cannon. Their officers were young but highly skilled and experienced. Morale in the navy was very high.

The British fleet in the Atlantic was many times larger than the American. To begin with, there were seven **ships of the line.** Ships of the line were armed with 60 to 70 or more cannon. Then there were 34 frigates. These were somewhat smaller and less heavily armed than the American type. Dozens of smaller ships and transports completed the British force.

The British had excellent officers and sailors. Their one mistake was in not reckoning how able the American navy had become.

The Constitution, *America's prized frigate, commenced firing on the British* Guerrière *on August 12, 1812. Under the deadly blaze of its cannon the* Guerrière *was smashed. Thomas Birch is thought to have painted this scene. Can you explain in your own words the maneuver known as "crossing the T" that helped Americans in the battle?*

U.S. Naval Academy

In August 1812 the *Constitution* met with the British frigate *Guerrière* off the coast of Maine. The *Guerrière,* a French-built ship, had been captured by the British in 1806. Captain Isaac Hull of the *Constitution* held his fire until the two ships were side by side. Then he said to his gun crews, "Now, boys, pour it into them."

The *Constitution*'s first volley broke the *Guerrière*'s mizzenmast. With sails and rigging trailing over its stern, the *Guerrière* could not be managed. Captain Hull then crossed in front of the crippled ship. This maneuver, called crossing the T, enabled him to fire broadsides while the British ship's guns could not be aimed at the *Constitution*. The Americans' cannon fired again and again, splintering the Britishers' hull and smashing down masts, sails, and rigging. From above, perched high in the *Constitution*'s rigging, American riflemen picked off sailors on the *Guerrière*'s deck. After half an hour the British captain surrendered. His ship was a total wreck. Of its crew of over 270, 79 were killed or wounded. Only 14 Americans died.

The *Constitution* later defeated the frigate *Java* in another famous battle. **Old Ironsides,** as it is now called, is the most famous ship ever to have flown the American flag. It has been preserved as a museum and monument at the Boston Navy Yard.

In October 1812 the American frigate *United States* sighted H.M.S. *Macedonian* near the Azores. Captain Stephen Decatur of the *United States* was already famous for his exploits while fighting North African pirates when Jefferson was president. Now he outmaneuvered the captain of the *Macedonian* brilliantly. Taking advantage of the fact that he had more powerful, long-range guns, he pounded the *Macedonian* from a distance. When the *Macedonian* finally surrendered, 100 cannon holes were counted in her hull. Decatur put an American crew aboard the captured ship and sailed it to New York. There the vessel was sold for $200,000, the money going, according to the custom of the time, to the crew of the *United States.*

These and other victories at sea were won because the American frigates were better fighting machines than the British ships. The American sailors proved to be superior fighters too. The fire of their guns was extremely accurate, and the tactics of the American captains were often brilliant.

After early losses the British high command ordered captains to avoid single-ship battles with American frigates. Instead the huge British navy was used to bottle up most American warships in their home ports. By early 1813 the British fleet in American waters had been increased to 17 ships of the line, 27 frigates, and about 50 other warships.

The frigates *Essex* and *President* both got to sea, the latter to be defeated by a squadron of four British ships.

Dozens of American privateers roamed the oceans during the

Point of View

The opening and closing stanzas of a 21-year-old scholar's first poem show how he fought to save the *Constitution* in 1830.

Old Ironsides

Ay, tear her tattered
    ensign down!
    Long has it waved on
    high,
And many an eye has
    danced to see
    That banner in the sky;
Beneath it rung the
    battle shout,
    And burst the cannon's
    roar—
The meteor of the ocean
    air
    Shall sweep the clouds
    no more.
. . . .
    Oh, better that her
    shattered hulk
    Should sink beneath
    the wave;
Her thunders shook the
    mighty deep,
    And there should be
    her grave;
Nail to the mast her
    holy flag,
    Set every threadbare
    sail,
And give her to the god
    of storms,
    The lightning and the
    gale!
           Oliver Wendell
           Holmes, 1830

A WOLF AGAINST SHEEP

The Essex

Captain David Porter was one of the American naval captains whose tactics were particularly brilliant. One time, while captain of the frigate *Essex,* Porter saw a British ship approaching. He turned the *Essex* away and set more sails to make the enemy captain think he was trying to escape. At the same time he ordered weights dragged from the stern so that in fact the ship was moving more slowly.

The commander of the British ship, the 22-gun *Alert,* fell for this trick and sped after the *Essex.* Then, when the *Alert* was in range, Porter turned and let loose with his 46 cannon. Within eight minutes the battle was over, the *Alert* a wreck. In two months on the high seas, Captain Porter captured seven British ships.

The *Essex* later managed to slip past the British in the Atlantic and sail around South America into the Pacific Ocean. There it destroyed or captured many English ships that were hunting whales. The *Essex,* one historian writes, "was like a wolf in a pasture of unguarded sheep." Eventually, British "guardians" arrived. Then the *Essex* was trapped off the coast of Chile by three British warships and forced to surrender.

war. These privateers were fast, light, and beautifully designed. They could easily outsail the best frigates of the Royal Navy. One privateer, the *True-Blooded Yankee,* captured 27 British merchant ships off the coast of Ireland and Scotland in a little more than one month. By the war's end privateers were capturing an average of nearly two ships a day. All told, they took about 1,300 vessels during the war. 🖹

Return to the Preview & Review on page 300.

3. THE WAR ON LAND

The Fight for Canada

The fighting on land during the War of 1812 was a seesaw struggle. It seemed at the start that Canada would be an easy target. The population was small, and many Canadians sympathized with the United States. Yet when a force commanded by General William Hull, an uncle of Captain Isaac Hull of the *Constitution*, crossed the border from Detroit, it quickly ran into trouble. Indians under Tecumseh ambushed one militia unit. Confused, Hull retreated to Detroit without making a real fight. Far worse, he surrendered the fort to a small Canadian force commanded by General Isaac Brock. Brock then announced that Michigan had been annexed to the British Empire! And for the moment it had. Indeed, by the end of 1812, most of what are now Indiana and Illinois was also controlled by Canadian troops.

In 1813 the Indian-hater William Henry Harrison, who was a competent general, was put in charge of the war on the border. Before he could invade Canada, however, a British naval squadron had to be cleared from Lake Erie. The officer who accomplished this task was Oliver Hazard Perry.

Perry came from a navy family. His father, his four brothers, and two of his brothers-in-law were naval officers. To win control of Lake Erie, he built a fleet, including two 20-gun ships, right on the scene. Finally, in September 1813, in the bloody **Battle of Put-in-Bay,** he defeated the British squadron. "We have met the enemy, and they are ours," he informed General Harrison. About a quarter of Perry's

Use these questions to guide your reading. Answer the questions after completing Section 3.
Understanding Issues, Events, & Ideas. Explain the significance of the following words: Battle of Put-in-Bay, Battle of the Thames, Plattsburg, Creek War, Battle of Horseshoe Bend, Bladensburg, Fort McHenry, Battle of New Orleans.
1. Why were the British able to burn Washington in 1814?
2. Why was the defense of Fort McHenry so important?
3. Why were the British defeated at the Battle of New Orleans?
Thinking Critically. 1. You are a member of Jackson's frontier militia. Write a letter to a friend, describing your opinion of Jackson. 2. You are a reporter on the night of August 24, 1814, in Washington, D.C. From a safe hiding place you observe the events. Write your observations in a newspaper article.

Oliver Hazard Perry, 28 years old, is shown transferring the United States colors from his sinking ship, the Lawrence, *to the* Niagara. *William Powell painted this view of the "Battle of Lake Erie."*

U.S. Capitol Historical Society

brave men were African Americans, which led him to comment that "the color of a man's skin" was no more an indication of his worth than "the cut and trimmings" of his coat.

Harrison was then able to capture Detroit and advance into Canada. At the Thames River, which flows through southern Canada to Lake Erie, he defeated Canadian troops and their Indian allies in the **Battle of the Thames.** The victory won back the Great Lakes region for the United States. But the most significant result of the battle was the death of Tecumseh. Without the great chief it was easier for the United States to gain full control of the northwestern region.

American forces also turned back a combined land and naval attack from Canada. The Americans, anticipating an invasion from Montreal, built a fleet of ships on Lake Champlain. British troops swept into New York and reached **Plattsburg.** There they fought American forces while awaiting naval support that never came. In a hard-fought battle on Lake Champlain the Americans under Commodore Thomas Macdonough defeated the British. The invading British army then scurried back to Canada.

The Creek War

The southern Indians were also soon crushed. Tecumseh, it will be remembered, had traveled extensively in the South persuading the Indian tribes there to join his Red Stick Confederacy. He had won many supporters among the younger Creek warriors in Alabama and Georgia.

These Indians, with some support from both British and Spanish agents, began to attack southern frontier outposts. The most serious of their assaults during this **Creek War** occurred in August 1813 when Red Eagle, leader of the warring Creeks, surprised and overwhelmed the defenders of Fort Mims in western Alabama. Red Eagle's warriors killed between 400 and 500 persons, many of them women and children.

General Andrew Jackson, commanding a force of Tennessee militiamen, then marched into Creek country. Jackson had fought in the Revolutionary War while still a boy. After the Revolution he had moved to Tennessee, where he prospered as a lawyer and plantation owner. He served for a time in both houses of Congress, and he was a judge of the Tennessee Supreme Court.

Jackson was at heart a fighting man, a natural leader of soldiers. Most frontier militia units were hard to discipline. Being used to living on their own, frontiersmen disliked taking orders and being controlled in any way. Jackson's soldiers, however, accepted his orders without question. This was because they both feared and respected him. He had a reputation for being very tough. The men called him "Old Hickory" because the wood of the hickory tree is

The Granger Collection

extremely hard. But he was also known for his loyalty to his men and for his concern for their welfare.

In a series of battles Jackson's army smashed the Creek forces. The climax came in March 1814 at the **Battle of Horseshoe Bend,** on the Tallapoosa River in Alabama. There 1,200 of Red Eagle's Red Sticks had dug in, protected, they thought, by the curve of the river and a wall of earth. Jackson's soldiers swept over the wall and killed 700 of the Indians, losing only 26 of their own men. Jackson forced the Creeks to surrender 20 million acres (8 million hectares) of their land. The Indians in the South could resist no longer.

Creek chief Red Eagle, also known as William Weatherford, surrenders to Andrew Jackson after the Battle of Horseshoe Bend. Red Eagle had escaped but surrendered when he realized that the Indian situation was hopeless. The Creeks agreed to leave southern and western Alabama. Why do you think they were asked to leave?

The Burning of Washington

The British had thus far depended mostly upon Canadian militia units and Indian allies to fight the United States. But by the spring of 1814 Napoleon had been defeated in Europe. The British then sent 14,000 soldiers to fight in America.

The British set out to destroy Washington. The capital city was supposed to be protected by a fleet of 26 gunboats on Chesapeake Bay. When a British squadron led by a 74-gun ship of the line entered the bay, the gunboats' commander hastily pulled his tiny ships back

The British burned most federal buildings in Washington. They spared the Patent Office because the superintendent, Dr. William Thorton, in the second-story window, threatened to charge them with vandalism. The president's house nearby went up in flames. Dolley Madison, below, saved the Stuart portrait of Washington from the burning White House, but little else.

into a shallow stream. There they were out of range of the British cannon but useless for the defense of Washington.

In August an army of 4,500 Redcoats came ashore south of Washington. It was commanded by General Robert Ross, who had fought against Napoleon under the great British general the Duke of Wellington. At the village of **Bladensburg,** Ross's troops attacked a large but poorly organized force of American militiamen. The Americans fled in panic. On the night of August 24 the British marched straight into Washington and set fire to all the public buildings. Even the president's mansion, the White House, was set afire. A British officer, George R. Glieg, wrote of the city's conquest:

❝ While the two brigades which had been engaged [at Bladensburg], remained upon the field to recover their order, the third, which had formed the reserve, and was consequently unbroken, took the lead, and pushed forward at a rapid rate towards Washington.

As it was not the intention of the British government to attempt permanent conquests in this part of America; and as the General [Ross] was well aware that, with a handful of men, he could not pretend to establish himself for any length of time, in an enemy's capital, he determined to lay it under contribution [destroy it], and return quietly to the shipping [British troop ships]. . . .

Such being the intention of General Ross, he did not march the troops immediately into the city, but halted them upon a plain in its immediate vicinity, whilst a flag of truce was sent in with terms. But whatever his proposal might have been, it was not so much as heard; for scarcely had the party bearing the flag entered the street, than they were fired upon from the windows of one of the houses, and the horse of the General himself, who accompanied them, killed. . . . All thoughts of accomodation [mercy for Washingtonians] were instantly laid aside; the troops advanced forthwith [immediately] into the town, and having first put to the sword [executed] all who were found in the house from which the shots were fired, and reduced it to ashes, they proceeded, without a moment's delay, to burn and destroy every thing in the most distant degree connected with government. In this general devastation were included the Senate-house, the President's palace, an extensive dock-yard and arsenal, barracks for two or three thousand men, several large store-houses filled with naval and military stores, some hundreds of cannon of different descriptions, and nearly twenty thousand stand of small arms. . . . The powder magazines were of course set on fire, and exploded with a tremendous crash, . . . whilst quantities of shot, shell, and hand-grenades, which could not otherwise be rendered useless, were thrown into the [Potomac] river. . . .

Had the arm of vengeance been extended no further, there would not have been room given for so much as a whisper of disapprobation [disapproval]. But, unfortunately, it did not stop there; a noble library, several printing offices, and all the national archives were likewise committed to flames, which, though no doubt the property of the government, might better have been spared.[1] 99

President James Madison had been at the battlefield at Bladensburg. He escaped by fleeing up the Potomac River into Virginia. Dolley Madison, the first lady, protected by a slave named Jennings, got away from the White House only minutes before the British entered. All she could save was some silverware and an oil painting of George Washington.

The Defense of Baltimore

The British had no intention of remaining in Washington. Their next objective was Baltimore, Maryland, at the head of Chesapeake Bay.

[1]From *The Campaigns of the British Army at Washington and New Orleans* by George Robert Glieg

Maryland Historical Society

Typical of the battles of the War of 1812, bombs really did burst in air. Flags told of victory and loss. This is the bombardment of Fort McHenry, which Francis Scott Key made so memorable.

Transport ships of their fleet put General Ross' army ashore on September 12 about 14 miles (about 23 kilometers) south of the city. Then the ships advanced toward **Fort McHenry,** which guarded the entrance to Baltimore Harbor.

Unlike the assault on Washington, the attack on Baltimore was a failure. Ross' troops ran into stiff resistance about 7 miles (about 11 kilometers) from the city. When the general himself rode forward to investigate, he was killed by a sharpshooter. The Americans retreated a few miles, but their line held.

Meanwhile, the fleet could not get within cannon range of Fort McHenry. The water was too shallow for most of the warships. Five special ships armed with rockets and bombs did get to within 3 miles (about 5 kilometers) of the fort. At dawn on September 13 Admiral Sir Alexander Cochrane ordered these vessels to open fire.

After a day and night of firing on Fort McHenry, the British fleet withdrew. Baltimore was safe. Now the tide of the war was turning. The shame of having the nation's capital destroyed roused people to fight harder. The defense of Baltimore showed their new determination. Thousands of young men came forward to enlist in the army.

The Battle of New Orleans

Now the British were planning a still greater attack. This one came in the South, near the city of New Orleans. During the fall of 1814 they gathered an army of 11,000 veterans of the war against Napoleon

THE STAR-SPANGLED BANNER

The bombardment of Fort McHenry, which began at dawn, went on all that day and the following night. It had little effect. The distance was too great for accurate fire. Many of the bombs burst harmlessly in the air. Only four soldiers in the fort were killed. Its walls remained unbroken.

Francis Scott Key

While the firing was in progress, Francis Scott Key, a Washington lawyer, was aboard one of the larger British vessels. He had been sent to try to obtain the release of an American doctor who had been arrested by the British after the Battle of Bladensburg. Admiral Cochrane had agreed to let the doctor go free, but he would not allow the Americans to go ashore until the battle was over.

Key watched the attack on Fort McHenry. Until darkness fell, he could see the fort's flag, an enormous banner 36 feet long and 29 feet wide (about 11 meters by 8 meters). During the night the continuing glare of the British rockets and the bursting bombs gave proof that the Americans were holding out. Then, when dawn came, Key could again see the flag, waving proudly over Fort McHenry. He was so inspired by the sight that he wrote "The Star-Spangled Banner." This poem, when set to

National Museum of American History
The flag that flew over Fort McHenry is now shown in a patriotic flourish at selected times of the day.

the music of an English song, became our national anthem (see page 327). The great flag, the original "star-spangled banner," hangs in the Smithsonian Institution in Washington.

at a base on the island of Jamaica in the Caribbean Sea. A fleet of 60 ships carried this force to the Louisiana coast.

The Redcoats landed east of the mouth of the Mississippi River and marched through the swampy country without being discovered. They were only 7 miles (about 11 kilometers) from New Orleans when muddied messengers with the news burst in upon the American general who was in charge of defending the city. The date was December 23, 1814.

The American general was Andrew Jackson, who had been put in command of southern defenses after his victories over the Creeks. He had marched south, captured Pensacola in Spanish Florida so the British could not use it as a base, and then prepared to defend New Orleans. Although surprised by the British advance, Jackson reacted at once. "Gentlemen," he announced, "the British are below. We must fight them tonight." Quickly he ordered every available unit forward. A force of cavalry advanced on the left. Down the Mississippi went a warship to bombard the enemy from the right. In the center went Jackson's regular troops along with hastily organized

Andrew Jackson on the eve of his great national popularity is shown here in a portrait by Ralph Earl.

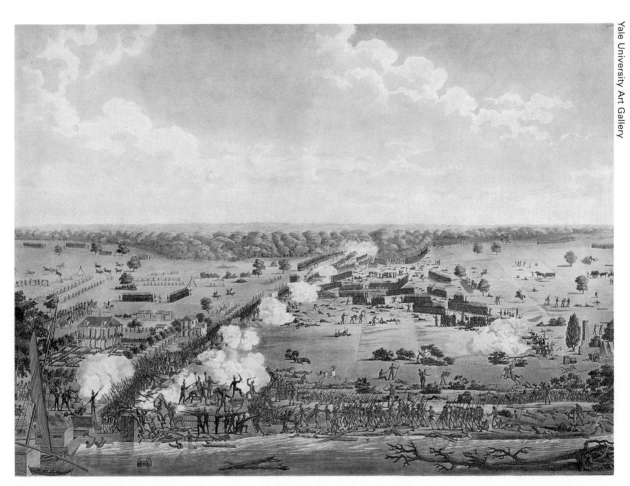

Hyacinthe Laclotte went into the thick of the fighting to make this drawing of the Battle of New Orleans. Later it was colored. The British and Americans can be seen fighting hand-to-hand with sabers. Use your historical imagination to describe the sights and sounds of this battlefield.

militia units. Among the militiamen was a company of free African American citizens of New Orleans. A group of pirates came forward "patriotically" to defend the city in exchange for Jackson's promise not to arrest them.

The battle began at 7:30 that very evening. It lasted for two hours and ended in a draw. Jackson then retreated and began to build an earth-wall defense line behind a canal only 5 miles (8 kilometers) from New Orleans.

The sudden American attack made the British delay their advance. They should have abandoned it altogether. Jackson had brought up many cannon and had his men properly positioned to defend the wall. When the British commander, General Sir Edward Pakenham, finally attacked on January 8, 1815, his men were mowed down by a hail of iron and lead. They suffered over 2,000 casualties in about an hour. General Pakenham and both his second and third in command were killed. When the smoke cleared, even the toughest American veterans were stunned by the sight of the battlefield. "You could have walked a quarter of a mile . . . on the bodies," one of them reported. Only 71 Americans were killed, wounded, or missing in action in this **Battle of New Orleans.**

Return to the Preview & Review on page 305.

4. PEACE AND NEW BOUNDARIES

Preview & Review

Use these questions to guide your reading. Answer the questions after completing Section 4.
Understanding Issues, Events, & Ideas. Explain the importance of each of the following words: Peace of Ghent, Hartford Convention, Rush-Bagot Agreement, Negro Fort, Transcontinental Treaty.
1. What were the terms of the Peace of Ghent?
2. What did the Rush-Bagot Agreement provide?
3. Why did General Jackson march into Florida?
4. Why did Luis de Onis agree to negotiate the Florida question with John Quincy Adams?
5. What were the terms of the Transcontinental Treaty? What claims did the United States make for the territory west of the Louisiana Purchase?
Thinking Critically. 1. Why do you think the Federalist Party lost popularity after the War of 1812? **2.** Imagine that you are Luis de Onís in 1818. Write a journal entry that describes your negotiations with John Quincy Adams.

The Peace of Ghent

The loss of life at New Orleans was particularly tragic because the battle should never have been fought. Although the soldiers did not know it, the war was officially over!

Since August 1814 five American commissioners had been trying to negotiate a peace treaty with British diplomats at the city of Ghent in Belgium. The British demanded that the United States return most of the Northwest Territory to the Indians. The Americans wanted the British to give up the right to impress sailors from American ships. Neither side would compromise.

The discussions dragged on for months. Finally everyone realized that the reasons for fighting had simply disappeared. With Napoleon defeated, the British did not need to stop American ships from carrying goods to Europe. There was no longer any need to impress sailors into the Royal Navy.

On December 24, 1814, the day after Jackson had rushed his men out from New Orleans to stop the British advance but two weeks before the final battle, the delegates signed the **Peace of Ghent.** The terms of this treaty were simple. Peace was restored. No territory changed hands. No promises were made. The United States did not get what it had set out for in 1812. As one witty historian has said, "It surrendered nothing except the right to shoot Englishmen." That was a right no one any longer wished to exercise.

Nowadays, of course, the whole world would have known about the treaty within hours after the signing. But in 1814 it took weeks for the news to reach Washington and more weeks for word to be sent to the troops around New Orleans. Thus, the brave men who fell before Jackson's defense wall died needlessly.

The Battle of New Orleans did serve some purpose. It restored American military morale, which had been badly damaged by the ill-organized battles along the Canadian border and by the burning of Washington. It also made a popular hero of Andrew Jackson.

The peace treaty itself was equally popular. In New England, where most people had been opposed to fighting Great Britain, some Federalist leaders had revived talk of seceding from the Union. Late in 1814 they held a meeting, the **Hartford Convention,** to consider this step. Fortunately, moderates at the convention managed to prevent such an extreme act. When the war ended without serious loss to the United States, the Federalist party suddenly seemed out of date and almost unpatriotic. Trade with Europe also picked up rapidly after the war. In the 1816 presidential election, Rufus King, the Federalist candidate, got only 34 votes in the electoral college to James Monroe's 183.

Solving Problems with England

Still another result of the War of 1812 was that it convinced Europe that the United States was here to stay. The British no longer dreamed of regaining their former colonies. This did not mean that England and the United States suddenly became allies or even particularly friendly. The new attitude was one of respect rather than friendship.

Many sore spots remained between the United States and Great Britain. After 1815, however, these conflicts were solved by diplomats, not by soldiers and sailors.

The first step was to negotiate a treaty in 1815 removing many restrictions on trade between the two nations. Then, in 1817 they signed the **Rush-Bagot Agreement,** which provided that neither would maintain a fleet of warships on the Great Lakes. Each was to have four small vessels on the lakes to act as a kind of police force, but the border between the United States and Canada—one of the longest in the world—was to remain forever unfortified.

A difficult problem was deciding on the exact boundary between Canada and the United States. American and British experts worked on this. In 1818 one of these commissions fixed the northern boundary of the Louisiana Purchase at 49° north latitude. At this time the two nations also agreed to joint control of the area west of the Louisiana territory, known as the Oregon Country.

Jackson's Invasion of Florida

Many westerners had hoped that the War of 1812 would pry Florida from Spanish control. They were disappointed. But soon after the war the United States got possession of both Florida and a huge chunk of Spanish territory west of Louisiana.

Settlers who lived along the southern frontier of the United States complained of raids by Seminoles from Florida, reinforced by many Creek warriors who had gone there after their terrible defeat by Andrew Jackson at the Battle of Horseshoe Bend.

The settlers also complained that many of their slaves were escaping into Florida. About 250 of these runaways, often called Maroons, controlled what was known as the **Negro Fort** on the Apalachicola River, about 60 miles (96 kilometers) south of the American border. Knowing there was a fort controlled by runaways encouraged other slaves to try to escape. In 1816 an American force marched into Florida—Spanish territory—and blew up the fort, killing most of its occupants.

Early in 1818 Jackson was sent to crush the Seminoles and their Maroon allies. Again ignoring the boundary line, he boldly pursued them into Florida at the head of an army of 3,000 soldiers and 2,000 Indian allies. The Seminoles and Maroons fell back, avoiding a battle.

Jackson was furious. When two Indian chiefs were captured by trickery, he had them hanged. At the town of St. Marks on the Gulf of Mexico he seized Alexander Arbuthnot, a harmless, 70-year-old British trader. Arbuthnot's crime had been to warn the Seminoles that the army was coming. Shortly thereafter Jackson captured another British civilian, Robert Ambrister, a former British marine who was indeed working with the Seminoles.

Jackson believed that all the conflicts with the Indians were caused by foreign agents. He decided to put Arbuthnot and Ambrister on trial. It was obviously illegal to try English civilians before an American military court on territory belonging to Spain. Jackson nevertheless did just that. The two men were found guilty and sentenced to death. Arbuthnot was hanged. Because he had been a soldier, Ambrister was executed by a firing squad.

Since he was unable to find any Indians or Maroons to attack, Jackson next marched into West Florida and captured the capital, Pensacola, which had been returned to the Spanish by the Treaty of Ghent. He dashed off a letter to President Monroe explaining what he had done. Then he went home to Tennessee.

The Transcontinental Treaty

Jackson's invasion proved that Spain could no longer control Florida. In Washington the Spanish minister to the United States, Luis de Onís, bitterly protested the seizure of Pensacola. It was "an outrage," he said. Jackson must be punished.

President Monroe was embarrassed. He did not want to approve of what Jackson had done. But he did not want to give up the territory Jackson had taken. He dared not criticize the popular general publicly. So he told Onís that he agreed that Jackson had gone beyond his orders, but had done so because of military necessity.

Onís knew then that the United States was not going to give back West Florida. The rest of Florida was surely lost as well.

Onís was already negotiating with John Quincy Adams, the secretary of state, about the boundary between the Louisiana Purchase and Spanish Mexico. Perhaps he could get better terms in this discussion by agreeing to give up Florida.

John Quincy Adams, the son of ex-president John Adams, had been in public service since he was a teenager. Like his father he was very intelligent, hard-working, stubborn, and as shrewd as a Yankee trader. He suggested to Onís that Spain should give up Florida. The United States would then be willing to postpone settling the Louisiana boundary. As Adams well knew, this was exactly the opposite of what Onís wanted.

Onís was afraid that a delay would only increase American demands in the West. Already Adams was claiming that the Mexican

The young John Quincy Adams sat for this oil portrait by John Singleton Copley a few years after the Revolutionary War. Copley's paintings were said to mirror his subjects with great accuracy. What negotiation did Adams successfully complete?

province of Texas was part of the Louisiana Purchase. So Onís insisted that a "safe and permanent" line be agreed to quickly.

Adams pressed Onís to accept the Rio Grande as the line. Since this would have given Texas to the United States, Onís practically spat out his refusal. After further dickering Adams suggested a compromise. A western boundary would be drawn that left Texas in Spanish hands. But he added the idea that from a point north of Texas the boundary line should extend west *"straight to the Pacific Ocean."*

This would give the United States a boundary all the way across North America. Onís tried to get Adams to give up this claim. He failed. Finally he wrote his superiors in Spain: "If His Majesty . . . hasn't sufficient forces to make war on this country, then I think it would be best not to delay making the best settlement possible."

In October 1818 the Spanish government gave in. It agreed in principle to Adams' demand. In a few months the details were ironed out by Adams and Onís. Spain ceded Florida to the United States. In return the United States canceled $5 million in claims against the Spanish in Florida. The line between Mexico and the United States followed roughly the present eastern and northern boundaries of Texas, then went north to 42° north latitude, then west to the Pacific Ocean.

Adams drove such a hard bargain that he forced Onís to agree that where the boundary followed rivers, it would run along the Spanish side of the river, not the middle of the stream as most such boundaries do.

The **Transcontinental Treaty** was a great triumph for Adams and for the United States. Great Britain's Proclamation of 1763 had set the western boundaries of the American colonies at the Appalachian Mountains. In 1783 the peace treaty ending the Revolutionary War extended that boundary to the Mississippi River. The Louisiana Purchase of 1803 extended the boundary to the Rocky Mountains. Now this treaty with Spain pushed the line on to the Pacific Ocean. In little more than 50 years the nation had grown from a string of settlements along the Atlantic Coast to a powerful country a continent wide. John Quincy Adams was not exaggerating when he said that the day he and Onís signed the treaty was "the most important day of my life."

The Whole Continent One Nation

When Adams first suggested extending the boundary line between Mexico and the United States west to the Pacific, Onis argued that there was no need for such a boundary. He insisted that the entire Pacific Coast belonged to Spain. He denied that the United States had a right to any territory west of the Louisiana Purchase.

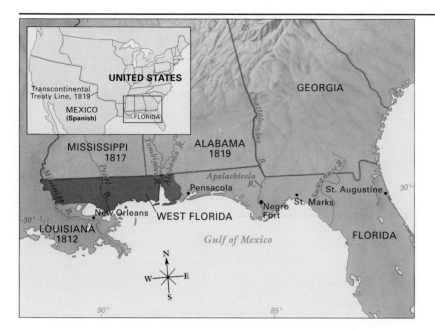

Occupied by U.S., 1810

Ceded to U.S. by Spain, 1819

| 0 | 100 | 200 Mi. |
| 0 | 100 | 200 Km. |

Albers Equal-Area Projection

LEARNING FROM MAPS. *Florida, which was a British colony at the time of the Revolutionary War, had again become a Spanish possession. Why was it important for American defenses that Florida become part of the United States? Did the United States gain or lose land by signing the Transcontinental Treaty in 1819?*

Adams declared that Onís' argument was "nonsense." He reminded the Spaniard that Great Britain claimed the Oregon Country and was willing to share control of it with the United States. Russia also had a number of trading posts along the northern Pacific Coast.

Adams, of course, won the argument. But his success was more a sign of Spain's weakness than of the correctness of his argument. Aside from the explorations of Lewis and Clark, the United States had little on which to base its claims in the region beyond the Rocky Mountains. Jefferson had *purchased* Louisiana from France. Was this not proof that the nation had not owned that land before 1803? How could it claim a right to land still farther west?

The answer to this question was very simple. The people were pushing steadily westward. They assumed that the land beyond the mountains was eventually to be a part of the United States. John Quincy Adams, for example, was convinced that God intended the United States to control all of North America. He wrote in 1811:

❝ The whole continent appears to be destined . . . to be peopled by one nation. . . . The acquisition of a definite line of boundary to the [Pacific] forms a great epoch in our history. ❞

No European country was strong enough or determined enough to resist United States claims very vigorously. Of course, the native Americans of the Northwest were another matter. They fought hard to protect their own claims. But that came much later. When Adams and Onís divided the land by drawing a line on a map, the actual invasion of the region by white settlers lay far in the future.

Return to the Preview & Review on page 313.

America's Hispanic Heritage

"Princess Margarita after Veláz-quez" was painted by Fernando Bot-ero of Colombia in 1978. His figures with large heads satirize the Spanish nobility and their displays of wealth.

The "Maids of Honor" shows Princess Margarita surrounded by her friends and dwarf. Velázquez himself stands to the left, holding a brush. The mirror at the back reflects the smiling king and queen.

More than 300 years pass before our eyes when we see these two paintings of the same little Spanish princess. The first is by Diego Rodriquez de Silva y Velázquez. In 1656 he painted *Las Meñinas* ("Maids of Honor") in the court of Philip IV of Spain. The second portrait of Princess Margarita was painted in our time by Fernando Botero of Colombia. His painting, like the others on these pages, shows our Hispanic heritage. Botero is modern and at the same time pays homage to the American Indians whose art and architecture flourished long before the painted sails of Columbus' ships hove into view.

From Colombia comes this Quimbáya gilded pendant fashioned in 500–1000 A.D. The medallions cover the likeness of a woman whose face we see but whose torso is demurely covered.

The Brooklyn Museum

sala miel Paxdei

New Orleans—a Spanish frontier city—seems an appropriate home for "Archangel with a Gun," painted on cotton in the 17th century by a Peruvian disciple in the circle of an artist known as the Master of Calamarcha. The artist contrasts finery typical of Europe with an essential tool of the frontier–the rifle.

America's Hispanic Heritage   319

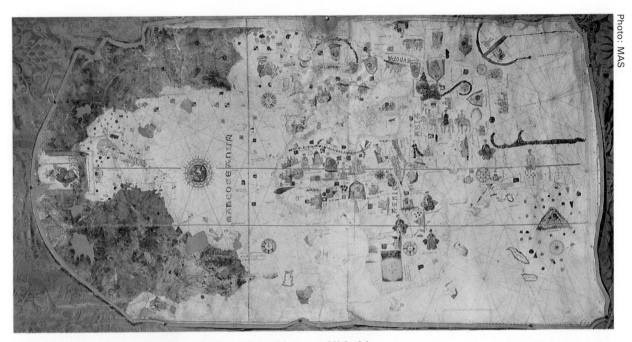

From Juan de la Cosa, a Spaniard, we have this world map published in 1500. It shows for the first time the islands and coasts of the Americas.

A Spanish-trained Indian artist made this Peruvian miniature of "Atahualpa, Last King of the Incas."

The first great native-born Puerto Rican painter was José Campeche. His "Dama a Caballo" ("Lady on Horseback") shows how strong the Spanish influence was in 1785.

Amelia Pelaez del Casal is a Cuban painter who studied for a time in Europe. There she was influenced by the Cubist style of Pablo Picasso of Spain and Georges Braque of France. To these influences she brought the vivid colors of her Caribbean homeland, as seen in "Fishes," on the right, painted in 1943.

One of Mexico's greatest artists was Diego Rivera, best known for his murals. "Women Washing Clothes in a River among Zopilotes" was painted in 1928.

Miguel Martinez, a contemporary Hispanic American who lives in Taos, New Mexico, is the artist of this contemporary painting entitled "Taos Mesa."

5. A LATIN AMERICA POLICY

Preview & Review

Use these questions to guide your reading. Answer the questions after completing Section 5.

Understanding Issues, Events, & Ideas. Compare Monroe's foreign policy with Washington's, using the following words: Latin America, Monroe Doctrine, historical significance.

1. Why did the revolutions in Latin America delight most people in the United States?
2. What joint statement did Great Britain want to issue with the United States? Why did the United States refuse?
3. What were the major principles of the Monroe Doctrine?

Thinking Critically. Why might nations of Latin America have supported the Monroe Doctrine? Why might they have opposed it?

Revolution in Latin America

Spain ceded Florida to the United States and signed the Transcontinental Treaty because it was no longer strong enough to protect its vast holdings in the Americas. The great Spanish empire was falling apart. Revolutionary leaders like Simón Bolívar and Francisco de Miranda in Venezuela, José de San Martín in Argentina, Bernardo O'Higgins in Chile, and Miguel Hidalgo y Costilla in Mexico inspired the people to break from their colonial masters. By 1822 most of Spain's colonies in the Americas as well as Portuguese Brazil, often called **Latin America,** had revolted and declared their independence.

Just as the American Revolution had stirred revolutionary feelings in France, it had a profound effect on Latin America. More and more people were demanding the "natural rights" described in the Declaration of Independence and the Constitution. One by one the Spanish colonies in South and Central America threw off their colonial bonds and established governments based on these values.

These Latin American revolutions delighted most people in the United States. The new nations seemed to be copying the example of their North American neighbor. As free countries they would be open to ships and goods from the United States. This had not been so under Spanish rule. President Monroe promptly established diplomatic relations with the new republics.

Great Britain also profited from Spain's declining influence. But it did not intend to recognize the new republics officially, as the United States had done. The British found themselves in a difficult position. On the one hand, they did not want to encourage revolutions or the formations of republics anywhere. British leaders feared that revolutionary ideas might spread and "infect" their own colonies. On the other hand, they did not want to see the South American republics destroyed. They were worried about other European powers that did not trade heavily with South America. Might they not help Spain regain control of its former colonies? Already there was talk of a large French army being sent to South America.

In 1823 George Canning, the British foreign minister, proposed that the United States and Great Britain issue a joint statement warning other nations not to try to restore Spanish control in America. The two countries themselves should promise not to try to take over these former colonies, Canning added.

This was most flattering for the United States—this opportunity to issue with Great Britain a joint statement of international policy. But this particular statement was not really one that the United States wished to make. Secretary of State Adams had two reasons for rejecting Canning's suggestion. The island of Cuba was still a Spanish

Simón Bolívar is the great revolutionary hero of South America. He is often called The Liberator. With his comrades he drove the Europeans out of Latin America.

colony. Someday, Adams hoped, the United States might be able to take it over. Canning's plan would rule out this possibility. And why should the United States help the British increase trade with the new republics?

Why trail along like a rowboat in the wake of a warship? It would be better, Adams advised President Monroe, for the United States to issue a statement of its own. The statement, he added, should deal with the whole question of relations between the United States, the other countries of the Western Hemisphere, and the nations of Europe. After much discussion the president agreed.

On December 2, 1823, the members of Congress gathered to hear the president's annual State of the Union message. The message, like most such speeches, dealt with many subjects. What Monroe said about foreign relations made up a relatively small part of it. He did not stress the subject in any special way.

The Monroe Doctrine

What the president said in his State of the Union message came to be known as the **Monroe Doctrine.** It consisted of the following principles:

The United States would not interfere with any existing European colony in North or South America. In other words, the United States had no intention of trying to force Great Britain to give up Canada, or Spain to give up Cuba.

The colonial period of North and South American history was now over. No more colonies could be founded in the Americas.

The United States would consider any attempt to create a new colony "dangerous to [its] peace and safety." In other words, the United States might go to war to prevent such an attempt.

The United States and Europe had different political systems that should not be mixed. Therefore, the United States would not become involved in purely European affairs.

In 1823 no one realized how important this statement of principles was. It was many years before anyone referred to it as the Monroe Doctrine. Even the person most responsible for the statement, John Quincy Adams, thought it a small matter compared to the Transcontinental Treaty and many of the lesser diplomatic affairs he handled as secretary of state. In 1824, when Adams was running for president, he did not even list the Monroe Doctrine among his achievements.

European leaders were more amused than annoyed by Monroe's speech. If the United States could not even protect its capital city from a raiding party, how could it police the whole Western Hemi-

INTERPRETING HISTORY: The Monroe Doctrine

Why do people act as they do? This is one of the most difficult of all questions to answer, especially for historians who can rarely interview the participants. What may appear to be a dull proclamation written long ago may conceal an interesting "behind-the-scenes" political story. Such was the case of the Monroe Doctrine. Did President James Monroe issue his statement because he feared European involvement in the Western Hemisphere? Or were there other reasons behind it?

In *The Making of the Monroe Doctrine* (1975) Ernest May investigated Monroe's motivations and those of his secretary of state, John Quincy Adams. May claims that no real European threat existed. Monroe's statement offered moral support to the newly independent American republics and boosted United States prestige as a world power without risking war. But May also offers another side of the story. He claims that Adams had his sights set on the upcoming presidential election of 1824 when he urged Monroe to issue his famous statement. May says Adams was keenly aware that as secretary of state he would be held responsible for the administration's foreign policy. If Monroe's policy was successful, it would be a feather in Adams' cap.

But why did Monroe reject Britain's offer of a joint statement? According to May, Adams thought that an alliance with England was unnec-essary and might prove unpopular. Many people in the United States were anti-British. Memories of the American Revolution and the War of 1812 remained strong. May points out that Adams was worried about the public's mistaken opinion that he was pro-British. He feared that they would re-call that he had once been a member of the Federalists, a party that had favored strong ties with England.

May points out that the situation was complicated by the fact that two of Adams' rivals for the presidency—John C. Calhoun and William Crawford—were also members of Monroe's cabinet. Both were aware of Adams' image problem and used it to their own political advantage when they met with Monroe to discuss the British proposal. May claims that both men hoped Monroe would accept the British offer, as did former president Thomas Jefferson, who was supporting Crawford for the presidency. They all knew that if Adams' image was hurt, it would improve Crawford's chances. May insists, however, that none of the policymakers tried to help themselves at the expense of what they believed was right for the country.

Ernest May offers one interpretation of the events that led to the Monroe Doctrine. Other historians might provide different interpretations as they explore the motivations behind the doctrine.

Thomas Jefferson said, "Monroe was so honest that if you turned his soul inside out there would not be a spot on it." To the Monroes fell the sad task of refurnishing the rebuilt White House, and when we visit the president's home today we see much of their taste reflected. Monroe was painted by John Vanderlyn. Elizabeth Monroe was painted by Benjamin West.

National Portrait Gallery

White House Historical Society

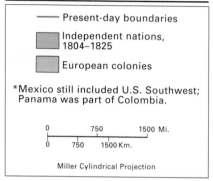

Present-day boundaries

Independent nations,
1804–1825

European colonies

*Mexico still included U.S. Southwest;
Panama was part of Colombia.

0   750   1500 Mi.

0   750   1500 Km.

Miller Cylindrical Projection

LEARNING FROM MAPS. *By the mid-1820s revolutions in Latin America modeled on the American Revolution produced many new countries. According to the map, what countries remained in the possession of Europeans?*

sphere? The new Latin American republics felt the same way. They approved of the ideas in President Monroe's statement. They hoped he was sincere. But could the United States really protect them in time of crisis?

Yet the Monroe Doctrine was one of the most important statements of American foreign policy ever issued. It provides a good example of how people closest to an event sometimes cannot appreciate its significance. The **historical significance** of events is seldom entirely clear when the events occur. This is because the significance usually depends upon the results of the event. These results occur over time and seldom can be predicted. The Declaration of Independence of July 4, 1776, for example, was a fine statement of principles. But its historical significance was clear only when the new nation fought and won the Revolutionary War.

Similarly, only after the United States had grown powerful enough to back its words with actions did it become clear that President Monroe had issued a kind of second Declaration of Independence. This one said to the nations of Europe: "Hands off the Western Hemisphere."

Return to the Preview & Review on page 322.

CHAPTER 9 REVIEW

1795	1800	1805

1795
Treaty of Greenville

Chapter Summary
Read the statement below. Choose one, and write a paragraph explaining its importance.
1. The War Hawks and frontier settlers blamed England for continuing troubles with the Indians in the Northwest Territory.
2. Tecumseh, the great Indian leader, organized many of the Indians in the Ohio Valley.
3. General William Henry Harrison defeated the Indians at Tippecanoe.
4. Many Americans, especially northeastern merchants, opposed the War of 1812.
5. The United States navy was very successful, and despite the burning of Washington, D.C., American land forces finally won the war.
6. American pride was heightened by the defense of Fort McHenry and Andrew Jackson's heroic leadership at the Battle of New Orleans.
7. Negotiations after the war solved problems with England and added Florida and other territory to the United States.
8. Between 1804 and 1825 many nations in Latin America became independent. In the Monroe Doctrine the United States insisted that Europe no longer involve itself in the affairs of the Western Hemisphere.

Reviewing Chronological Order
Number your paper 1–5. Then study the time line above and place the following events in the order in which they happened by writing the first next to 1, the second next to 2, and so on.
1. British troops burn Washington
2. The Monroe Doctrine
3. The Transcontinental Treaty
4. Tecumseh organizes the Indians
5. War of 1812 begins

Understanding Main Ideas
1. In which region of the country was the War of 1812 bitterly opposed? Why was this opposition surprising?
2. What were the causes of conflicts between settlers and Indians on the frontier?
3. How did General Harrison try to gain land from the Indians? What method did other government leaders propose?
4. What were the major provisions of the Peace of Ghent? What were some outcomes of the war that were not part of the treaty?
5. Why had so many Latin American nations broken from Spanish rule by 1822?
6. What did the Monroe Doctrine state?

Thinking Critically
1. **Synthesizing.** Imagine that you are an African Amerian sailor serving under Oliver Hazard Perry. In your diary, write a personal account of the Battle of Put-in-Bay, including your appraisal of Perry and his treatment of you.
2. **Evaluating.** You know that when Dolley Madison fled the burning White House moments before the British arrived, she saved some silverware and a portrait of George Washington. If you were in the first lady's situation today and could save only two objects, which would you choose? Why?
3. **Analyzing.** If the telegraph had existed on December 24, 1814, how might the Battle of New Orleans have been different? Why?

Writing About History: Expressive
You are one of the following: Dolley Madison escaping from the White House, Francis Scott Key watching the bombardment of Fort McHenry, an American soldier fighting at New Orleans. Write a diary entry describing what you see and your thoughts and feelings. Use the information in Chapter 9 to help you write your entry.

Practicing the Strategy
Review the strategy on page 296.
Synthesizing Information. Reread "Peace and New Boundaries" and study the maps closely. Then write a paragraph describing how and why the boundaries of the United States changed, using information from those two sources.

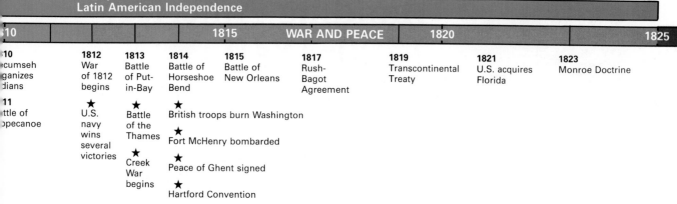

	1812	1813	1814	1815		1817		1819	1821	1823

War of 1812

Latin American Independence

$10				**1815**	**WAR AND PEACE**		**1820**			**1825**

$10	1812	1813	1814	1815	1817	1819	1821	1823
cumseh ganizes dians	War of 1812 begins	Battle of Put-in-Bay	Battle of Horseshoe Bend	Battle of New Orleans	Rush-Bagot Agreement	Transcontinental Treaty	U.S. acquires Florida	Monroe Doctrine
11 ttle of opecanoe	★ U.S. navy wins several victories	★ Battle of the Thames ★ Creek War begins	★ British troops burn Washington ★ Fort McHenry bombarded ★ Peace of Ghent signed ★ Hartford Convention					

Using Primary Sources

On the night of September 13, 1814, Francis Scott Key watched the shelling of Fort McHenry. Deeply moved, Key composed a poem describing the events he had witnessed. The poem was later set to music and entitled "The Star-Spangled Banner." Ferdinand Durang first sang the tune in public in 1815. It was officially adopted as the national anthem by an act of Congress on March 3, 1931. As you read Key's words, note how they keep alive the image of the American flag. Then answer the questions.

> *"Oh, say can you see by the dawn's early light*
> *What so proudly we hail'd at the twilight's last gleaming*
> *Whose broad stripes and bright stars through the perilous fight*
> *O'er the ramparts we watched were so gallantly streaming?*
> *And the rockets' red glare, the bombs bursting in air*
> *Gave proof through the night that our flag was still there*
> *Oh, say does that star-spangled banner yet wave*
> *O'er the land of the free and the home of the brave?"*

1. Although Key watched the battle at night, he still could see the flag flying over Fort McHenry. What enabled him to see it? What does the flag symbolize?
2. What do the words "broad stripes and bright stars . . . were so gallantly streaming" suggest about Key's attitude toward his country?
3. Which line describes the United States and the American people?

Linking History & Geography

Relative location is a geographic term that refers to the positions of places in relation to other places on earth. The most common way to express relative location is in terms of distance and direction. For example, San Francisco is about 340 miles (544 kilometers) northwest of Los Angeles. The principles behind the Monroe Doctrine are based in part on relative location. Review the Monroe Doctrine on page 324 and study the map on page 325. Then in a brief paragraph, explain the geographic reason why the United States felt closely linked to the countries of Latin America.

Enriching the Study of History

1. **Individual Project.** Build a model or make a sketch of the U.S.S. *Constitution* ("Old Ironsides"). Use your model or sketch to illustrate a short oral report on this famous ship.
2. **Cooperative Project.** Create and present a half-hour biographical play about Tecumseh. Have six groups prepare and present five-minute scenes, with different classmates in the role of Tecumseh. Show Tecumseh (a) meeting with General Harrison after Harrison has made a treaty with other Indian tribes, (b) with the Prophet, planning the Red Stick Confederacy, (c) recruiting for the Redsticks on the frontier, (d) recruiting in the South, (e) meeting with the Prophet sometime after the Battle of Tippecanoe, and (f) with some of his warriors just after the Battle of the Thames.

CHAPTER 10

Building America, 1790-1840

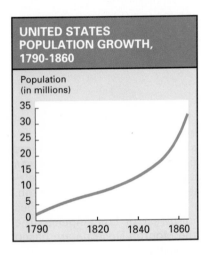

UNITED STATES POPULATION GROWTH, 1790-1860

Population (in millions)

Americans who lived between 1790 and 1840 must have been amazed by the changes that had taken place before their eyes. The population of the nation had grown from 4 million to 17 million. In 1790 the country was already larger in area than England, France, Spain, and several other European countries *combined*. By 1840 it had doubled its size. In 1840 America was still a rural society, a nation of farmers. But the picture was beginning to change. In 1790 nine out of ten people depended on the soil for their livelihood. Only about 5 percent lived in urban centers—that is, in places with a population of at least 2,500. By 1840 the percentage of Americans engaged in farming had dropped. Only about six out of ten made their living from the soil. The number of people living in towns and cities had risen to almost 11 percent. Nearly 10 percent of the labor force was working in factories in 1840. In 1790 the first factories were just being built. Clearly the nation was changing in significant ways. How would these changes come about and how would they affect American society?

Clayville, Rhode Island, as it appeared in 1850.

Rhode Island Historical Society

After grazing in greener pastures the cows come home for the night. Asher Durand painted this picture about 1845.

Metropolitan Museum of Art

1. A DIVERSIFIED ECONOMY

Nature's Nation

What strikes us most today about the economic development of the United States is the speed with which the country changed from a land of farmers into a nation of factory workers and city dwellers. The change came about so swiftly that it seems there could have been no stopping it. But was it in fact unstoppable? If so, how can we explain the fact that most Americans of that time *opposed* the development of manufacturing and the growth of cities?

Ever since the first settlements were established in the 1600s, land had been the chief source of wealth in America. It was still so in the early 1800s. Most people wanted to own land, even if only a small plot. To own land was a sign that a person was free and independent and held a stable place in society.

Thomas Jefferson and countless other writers and speakers of the period sang the praises of the American farmer. "Those who labor in the earth," Jefferson wrote in 1785, "are the chosen people of God, if ever He had a chosen people. . . . " Little wonder that

Preview & Review

Use these questions to guide your reading. Answer the questions after completing Section 1.
Understanding Issues, Events, & Ideas. Describe changes in the American economy in the early 1800s, using the following words: diversified economy, protective tariff, duty.
1. Why did most people in America want to own land?
2. Why did some Americans want a diversified economy?
3. Why did American manufacturers want the government to place protective tariffs on imported goods?
Thinking Critically. Imagine that you are a British manufacturer in 1816. Write a letter to your cousin in America, explaining how the Tariff of 1816 has affected your business.

Until they became extinct, passenger pigeons blackened the sky in flight. In the spring of 1794, in central New York, the fictional Leatherstocking—six feet tall, gray-eyed, sandy-haired, with but a single tooth left in his enormous mouth—foresees the birds' fate.

"This comes of settling a country!" he said—"here have I known the pigeons to fly for forty long years, and, till you made your clearings, there was nobody to scare or hunt them. I loved to see them come into the woods, for they were company for a body; hurting nobody; being, as it was, as harmless as a garter snake. But now it gives me sore thoughts when I hear the frighty things whizzing through the air, for I know it's only a motion to bring out all the brats in the village at them. Well! the Lord won't see the waste of his creatures for nothing, and right will be done to the pigeons, as well as others, by-and-by."

From *The Pioneers*,
James Fenimore Cooper,
1823

America was referred to as "Nature's nation." Agriculture was the foundation on which the nation was built. Most people believed that manufacturing and big cities would simply destroy the peaceful farming society that was the American ideal. Americans had only to follow the "laws of nature" heralded by the Enlightenment to be successful.

The Turn Toward Manufacturing

A small but determined group of Americans did see the need to develop manufacturing. Alexander Hamilton was the first to speak for them. They favored a **diversified economy,** one in which manufacturing existed side by side with agriculture. They argued that manufacturing would make America independent of European suppliers. Not surprisingly, the supporters of manufacturing first gained a wide audience during the crisis that led to the American Revolution.

Political freedom would mean little without economic independence. This was the warning of Dr. Benjamin Rush, who was the president of the United Company of Philadelphia for Promoting American Manufactures. Many people agreed when Rush said:

The Granger Collection

Benjamin Rush

" A people who are *entirely* dependent upon foreigners for food and clothes must always be subject to them."

After the first battles of Lexington and Concord there was no argument against American manufacturing. It was now a necessity. The Continental Congress was especially anxious to encourage the production of weapons. But guns and ammunition remained scarce, as the soldiers at the Battle of Bunker Hill and in other early campaigns sadly learned. The Continental Army had to depend upon foreign supplies. The Americans could not have won the war without this assistance.

The American Revolution brought the nation political independence. But did it have economic independence? No sooner had the war ended than the British began selling cloth, chinaware, and every sort of manufactured product at bargain prices in order to win back American customers. Consumers purchased these goods eagerly. American producers lost business as a result. They wanted the government to place high taxes, called **protective tariffs,** on imported goods. Then those goods could not be sold so cheaply. As we have seen, the wish to have only one set of laws to regulate all trade and

A PROTECTIVE TARIFF

A protective tariff works this way: Suppose a hat manufacturer in Danbury, Connecticut, could make a hat for $3. After adding a profit the hat might be sold for $4. But an English hat manufacturer, having lower labor costs, might be able to make a similar hat for $2.50. Even after adding a dollar for profit, the English manufacturer could undersell the American. As a result the American manufacturer would be driven out of business.

The Tariff of 1816, therefore, put a tax of 30 percent on imported hats. Because 30 percent

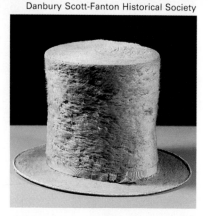

Danbury Scott-Fanton Historical Society

of $3.50 is $1.05, the English hat would now cost $4.55. The American manufacturer's business would be safe. Even if the

English hatmaker sold hats at cost, the duty—30 percent of $2.50—would raise the price to $3.25, still leaving the American with a small advantage.

Of course, American consumers had to pay higher prices because of the new tariff. But the theory was that the whole country would benefit. Business activity would increase because of the protection given to manufacturers. More people, for example, would be employed in making hats. And these hatmakers would spend their earnings, thus helping other businesses grow.

---

commerce was one of the most important reasons for revising the Articles of Confederation.

Americans continued to depend on foreign-made goods until Jefferson's Embargo Act of 1807 and the War of 1812 made importing them almost impossible. With European goods unavailable, quick

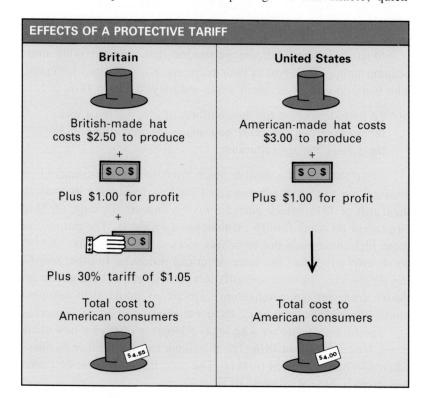

EFFECTS OF A PROTECTIVE TARIFF

Britain

British-made hat costs $2.50 to produce
+
$ ○ $
Plus $1.00 for profit
+
≡ ○ $
Plus 30% tariff of $1.05
Total cost to American consumers
$4.55

United States

American-made hat costs $3.00 to produce
+
$ ○ $
Plus $1.00 for profit

Total cost to American consumers
$4.00

LEARNING FROM PICTO-GRAPHS. *What does the pictograph to the left illustrate? Why is the measure called a protective tariff?*

Collection IBM Corporation, Armonk, N.Y.

The Yankee peddler was a welcome visitor in New England homes. His horse-drawn wagon carried an enormous variety of the goods essential for everyday life. What might each of the two women be thinking as they look at his wares?

profits could be made by anyone who could produce articles that were usually imported. People put money into manufacturing. Before 1808 there were only 15 cotton mills in the nation. In 1809 alone, 87 mills were built.

Most Americans became persuaded that manufacturing must become an important part of their economy. Even Thomas Jefferson, who had opposed government aid to industry, wrote in 1816:

66 To be independent for the comforts of life, we must make them ourselves. We must now place the manufacturer by the side of the agriculturalist. 99

After the war the British again tried to dump manufactured products on the American market. Congress responded by passing the Tariff of 1816, which placed a tax on imports, or **duty,** of 20 to 30 percent on many foreign manufactured products. The purpose of these high duties was not to collect money. It was to make foreign goods cost more than the same American products. In other words, the duties were protective tariffs intended to protect American industry from foreign competition. Americans could then compete among themselves to produce the goods demanded by consumers.

To aid manufacturers with loans, Congress created a new Bank of the United States in 1816. The first Bank had gone out of business when its charter expired in 1811. The new Bank, like the first one, was given a 20-year charter.

Return to the Preview & Review on page 329.

2. THE INDUSTRIAL REVOLUTION

Mass Production

American manufacturers had a treasure store of natural resources to draw on. Abundant forests provided lumber for buildings and machines and also logs for fuel. There was iron for making tools and nails. Swift-running streams supplied waterpower to run machinery.

Still, American manufacturers had to overcome many obstacles. It was difficult to turn out goods in large quantities. The shoemakers of Lynn, Massachusetts, made boots one pair at a time for particular customers. The clockmakers of Philadelphia made timepieces only after individuals placed their orders. Americans did not yet have the manufacturing know-how to **mass produce,** or make large numbers of articles. Their **industrial technology**—that is, the tools, machines, and other things used to produce goods—was very inefficient.

One of the first Americans to improve the nation's industrial technology was Eli Whitney. When war threatened between the United States and France in the 1790s, Congress decided to purchase 7,000 muskets. Muskets were still in short supply in America. The new government arsenal at Springfield, Massachusetts, had turned out only about 1,000 muskets in three years.

Here in Whitneyville, Connecticut, Eli Whitney built his gun factory to make muskets with interchangeable parts.

Yale University Art Gallery

Preview & Review

Use these questions to guide your reading. Answer the questions after completing Section 2.

Understanding Issues, Events, & Ideas. Describe early factory production in the United States, using the following words: mass produce, industrial technology, interchangeable parts, Industrial Revolution, spinning jenny, water-frame, putting-out system, Rhode Island system, Lowell system.

1. What assets did American manufacturers have? What obstacles did they have to overcome?
2. How did Eli Whitney set out to improve the nation's industrial technology?
3. What ws the benefit of the spinning jenny?
4. How did the British government try to protect the secrets of its Industrial Revolution?
5. Why did Lowell not want to copy British labor methods?

Thinking Critically.   **1.** If you were a worker in the early 1800s, would you have preferred to work under the putting-out system, the Rhode Island system, or the Lowell system? Explain your answer.   **2.** You are a young mother who has taken a job in a factory. How does your standard of living change?

Muskets were made by hand. A gunsmith shaped each barrel and fitted it with its own trigger and other parts. If a part broke, a new one had to be made and fitted to that particular gun. The barrel or trigger of one musket could not be substituted for another. It would not fit.

Whitney decided that he could manufacture muskets by the thousands if he could make them from **interchangeable parts.** If all triggers and barrels for a certain model of gun were exactly the same, the parts from any musket could be used with those of any other.

In 1798 Whitney wrote to Oliver Wolcott, the secretary of the treasury. He offered to turn out 10,000 muskets. His offer must have astonished Wolcott, but the government needed the guns badly. Whitney got the contract and an advance payment of $5,000 to get his business started.

It took Whitney two years to produce the grinders and borers and lathes that would enable him to produce identical parts. By September 1801 his shop in New Haven, Connecticut, had produced 500 muskets. He took ten of these to Washington. There he appeared before an amazed but delighted group of officials, which included President John Adams and Vice President Thomas Jefferson. Whitney took the muskets apart. He mixed the parts so that it was no longer possible to know which trigger went with which barrel, and so on. Then, choosing pieces at random, he reassembled the parts into ten muskets. Whitney's demonstration led to a revised contract. The new contract gave him an advance of $30,000.

James Hargreave's spinning jenny was first built in 1765. The one pictured is an improved model. At it a spinner could operate all the spindles at once by cranking the wheel. When the cotton fibers were stretched, fine thread was made. What were some advantages of the spinning jenny?

Machines Replace Hand Tools

While Whitney was developing his method of producing interchangeable parts, English manufacturers were shifting their work from hand tools to power-driven machinery. This was the **Industrial Revolution.**

The process began in the 1700s. In those days almost every home had a spinning wheel for making thread and a loom for weaving cloth. Families made a good deal of their own clothing, working in their spare time. But it took about six times as long to make thread as it took to weave the same thread into cloth. This meant that one weaver used all the thread that six spinners could produce.

In 1765 an English weaver and carpenter named James Hargreaves built a machine called the **spinning jenny.** (Some say the machine was named after his wife. Others say the name came from "gin," a short form of the word "engine.") The spinning jenny was a mechanical spinning wheel. It was small, cheap, and easy to build. It could be operated by hand. Soon Hargreaves's invention found its way into thousands of English homes.

The spinning jenny increased output, but it did not reduce the price of cotton cloth very much. Because cotton fibers are not very strong, cotton could only be used for the short threads running across the cloth. Linen had to be used for the thousands of threads running lengthwise. And linen, which was made from the flax plant, was much more expensive than cotton.

In 1768 Richard Arkwright, a barber, solved this problem. He invented a spinning machine that produced much stronger cotton thread. Now cloth could be made entirely of cotton. The price fell.

Arkwright's machine was much bigger and heavier than Hargreaves's jenny. It could not be kept in a home or operated by hand. It required a mechanical force, such as waterpower, to run it. Thus it was called the **water-frame.** In 1771 Arkwright formed a partnership and constructed what the English called a "mill." Americans sometimes called mills factories.

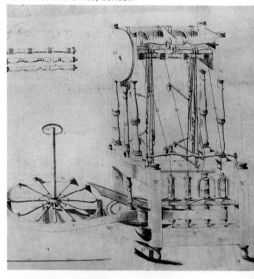

Here is the 1769 patent drawing for the spinning machine invented by Richard Arkwright. Cotton fibers were twisted between its rollers to produce strong thread. Why was Arkwright's spinning machine a product of the Industrial Revolution, but not Hargreave's spinning jenny?

The Factory Comes to America

Arkwright's water-frames proved so successful that by the late 1780s over 100 cotton mills in England were using them. Cotton cloth production increased greatly. Soon English cloth was being exported to every part of the world.

The British government had no intention of sharing the secrets of its Industrial Revolution with other countries. It would not allow the export of textile-making machinery. Nor would it allow workers who were familiar with the machines to leave the country. But a number of these skilled workers, called mechanics, still made their way to America. The most important was Samuel Slater, who at one time had worked for Arkwright. When Slater decided to go to Amer-

Samuel Slater came to America in 1789 after memorizing plans for cotton-spinning machinery. Today he would be considered an industrial spy. Do you think it was right for him to memorize his employer's designs to take to another country?

The Industrial Revolution   335

Moses Brown is one of America's early benefactors of education. He built the factory to house Samuel Slater's spinning machines. Brown prospered and later gave large sums of money to the Quakers and to Brown University, which is named for his brother. You might inquire in your own state to see how much financial support must come from private sources for colleges and universities, large and small.

ica, he memorized the designs for the new cotton-spinning machinery.

Slater landed in New York in 1789, the year the new Constitution went into effect. He soon met up with Moses Brown of Providence, Rhode Island. Brown was a member of a family that had been engaged in commerce and small-scale manufacturing in Rhode Island for generations. Slater agreed to build cotton-spinning machines for Brown in Pawtucket, Rhode Island, on the Blackstone River. By 1791 the work was done. Slater's machines spun cotton thread, using waterwheels turned by the current of the Blackstone for power. This thread was both better and cheaper than homespun cotton. The day of the factory had arrived in America.

Slater's machines made only thread. Brown sold some of this thread in his Providence store. The rest he supplied to workers who wove it into cloth on looms in their own homes. This was known as *putting out* the thread. The weavers returned the cloth to Brown, who paid them so much a yard for their work. He then sold the cloth in his store.

The **putting-out system**—families producing finished items at home—was widely used in America. It persisted long after factories became common. Hats, shoes, stockings—many products as well as cloth—were made in this manner. The system made one workshop out of many homes. Brown's weavers worked for wages, but they did so at home. They were less dependent upon Brown than the workers in Slater's factory were on Slater. They owned their own tools and had control over when and how hard they worked.

The Changing Role of Women

The beginnings of industrialization had both positive and negative effects on women. Women had long been respected and even idolized for their role in the family. Women in the colonies had worked at jobs ranging from shopkeepers and journalists to "doctoresses" and midwives. But by the late 1700s their status and even their opportunities had begun to slip. Some of the professions began requiring college training and licensing. Because women weren't permitted in college, they could not get licenses. So they could no longer practice, no matter how much practical training they had.

Generally speaking, American women accepted their lot in life. Most were content to marry, have children, and keep house. They realized the hard work and lack of status that being a housewife meant.

Industrialization meant many changes for women. The shift from homemade goods to factory-made goods changed women's economic role. In colonial America women on farms had worked side by side with their husbands as partners. Nineteenth-century farm women continued to do so, but as factories sprang up, more and more families left the farm. The men entered the business world and their wives became dependent on their husband's earnings to buy factory-made goods and food. But with husbands away at work six days a week, wives asserted more control over the day-to-day activities of their families.

As the American economy moved steadily from an agricultural base to manufacturing, family life changed. How a city woman lived was determined by her husband's wealth and by the type of job he held. Even prosperous farm women did much the same things that poorer farm women did. Raising and educating their children, tending chickens and a garden, sewing, cooking, and other household chores occupied the time of nearly all. But the wives of the well-to-do city husbands had a great deal of leisure time compared to farm women because they could employ servants and buy more things in stores. These women eventually became the leaders of the women's rights movement.

Beginning in the late 1700s there was also a growing interest in education for women. Several "Ladies Academies" were founded. Young girls who had brothers in school were allowed to study along side them and receive the same training. In 1787 Dr. Benjamin Rush, a professor at the University of Pennsylvania, spoke out on the need for education for women. Among the subjects he suggested they study were the English language and writing, geography, history, biography, travel, vocal music, dancing, and religious instruction. Then in the 1820s the city of Boston opened an "experimental" high school for girls that taught the same subjects as were taught in the boys schools.

Recruiting a Labor Force

Who wanted to work in factories? In England most factory jobs were filled by former tenant farmers who had been thrown out of work when owners fenced the land and planted grass in order to raise sheep. But there had been no enclosure movement in the United States. Most American farmers worked their own land for themselves. They were self-employed. So were most artisans, such as carpenters and shoemakers. Few people in America worked for wages. Still fewer were willing to work in factories.

American manufacturers tried to solve this problem in two ways. The **Rhode Island system** made much use of children. Slater's first spinning machines were operated by seven boys and two girls ranging in age from 7 to 12. Slater could use these young children because his machinery was relatively easy to operate. He could pay them much less than adults. Children in the Slater mills received between 33 and 67 cents a week, while adult workers in Rhode Island were earning between $2 and $3 a week. As late as 1820 more than half of the workers in the Rhode Island mills were children.

This gentle watercolor cannot reproduce the noisy waterfall from the Blackstone River which turned Samuel Slater's spinning machines at Pawtucket Falls, Rhode Island. By today's standards how is this an ecologically sound operation?

FAMILY WANTED,
To work in a Thread-Mill:

THE Mill is four miles and a half from Providence, on the Turnpike road leading from Providence to Chepachet, und que fourth of a mile from Messrs. Richard Anthony & Son's Cotton-Mill. For particulars, enquire of ASA SAYLES, on the premises. A. SAYLES & Co.
North-Providence, March 7 . 18W.

Child labor seemed perfectly reasonable to most people. Farm children had always worked. In those days children were not required by law to go to school. Poor families were delighted to have any money their children could earn. Often entire families, parents and children together, worked in the early factories, answering advertisements like the one on the left from a Providence newspaper.

The second method of getting workers for the factories was invented by Francis Cabot Lowell, a prominent Boston merchant. In 1810 Lowell visited spinning and weaving mills in England. He was deeply impressed by their efficiency. Like Slater, he carefully memorized the layout of the mills. He hoped to be able to reproduce them in New England.

Lowell's opportunity to test his memory came sooner than he had expected. When he returned to America, the War of 1812 was under way. Foreign trade had come to a standstill. No English goods were available. Lowell therefore organized a group of investors called the Boston Associates and hired a brilliant young engineer named Paul Moody.

Lowell and Moody spent a year constructing power looms copied from English designs. Meanwhile, the Associates built a factory at Waltham, Massachusetts, where they could use the waterpower of the Charles River. By the end of 1813 the factory and machinery were ready to operate. This plant both spun cotton into thread *and* wove it into cloth by machine.

Lowell did not copy British labor practices. He and other manufacturers were disturbed by the poverty of English workers during the Industrial Revolution in England. Lowell was as much concerned with the well-being of his workers as with his own profits. He was determined not to use children and poor families, as was being done in England and Rhode Island.

Instead, the **Lowell system** employed young unmarried girls from neighboring farms. Many of these young women were willing to work for wages before settling down. Many found they were far better off than if they had stayed at home. Eben Jennison wrote to his daughter Elizabeth in Lowell:

> 66 The season with us has been very Dry and the Drough[t] verry severe. The crops are very light indeed and business verry Dull [slow]. If you should be blessed with your health and are contented I think you will do better where you are than you could do here.[1] 99

Many were able to save part of the wages, and some even sent money home. In a later letter Jennison thanked his daughters (Amelia had joined her sister in Lowell) for sending $5, and promised to repay them with interest "some day or other." He also instructed Elizabeth to "look out for" another younger sister, Emily, who was coming to Lowell:

> 66 A few words in relation to Emily. She had got about ready to come to Lowel. . . . I should not consent to hir coming at any rate if you was not there. She is young [16] and needs a mothers care and a mothers advise. You must se to hir and give hir such council as you thinks she needs. She may be homesick for a spell but if you comfort hir up she will soon get the better of it.[2] 99

And the young girls who had left their families and friends did get homesick! Sarah Hodgdon wrote to her mother Mary:

> 66 Give my love to farther. Tell him not to forget me and to my dear sister and to my brothers and to my grandmother. Tell her I do not forget her. And to my Aunts and to all my enquiring friends.
>
> > I want to se you more I think
> > Than I can write with pen and ink.
> > But when I shall I cannot tell
> > But from my heart I wish you well.
> > I wish you well from all my heart

[1]From *The Underside of American History*, edited by Thomas R. Frazier
[2]*Ibid.*

Although we are so far apart.
If you die there and I die here,
Before one God we shall appear.[1] ”

But homesick or not, the idea of life in the factory community seemed interesting and even exciting to most of the young girls. In addition, religious leaders started churches and Sunday schools and organized local social activities, giving milltowns such as Lowell a reputation for being stiffly formal and proper communities. This reputation for respectability attracted additional farm girls to the factory towns. Most found, however, that life was hard.

Occasional revivals helped the rapidly expanding congregations to establish what many thought was a Christian culture in these towns. It surrounded the young women from the farms with the symbols of their religion. But the effects were not merely spiritual. Women employed in the mills became active in workers' associations of various sorts in Lowell. Slowly they developed feelings of independence. Soon many were resisting their employers' insistence that owners must control the lives of their workers.

Families sometimes moved to mill towns too. Making a living at farming was increasingly hard, especially in New England. Factories offered new hopes—and new frustrations.

Conditions varied from mill to mill. Some were far more pleasant than others. The English novelist Charles Dickens described several Lowell factories in his *American Notes for General Circulation*, written in 1842. In general, he felt conditions in these factories were much better than those in English factories, with which his readers were all too familiar. Dickens wrote:

“ The girls were returning to their work; . . . They were all well dressed, but not to my thinking above their condition. . . . The rooms in which they worked, were as well ordered as themselves. In the windows of some, there were green plants, which were trained to shade the glass; in all, there was as much fresh air, cleanliness, and comfort, as the nature of the occupation would possibly admit of. Out of so large a number of females, many of whom were only then just verging on womanhood, it may be reasonably supposed that some were delicate and fragile in appearance; no doubt there were. But I solemnly declare, that from all the crowd I saw in the different factories that day, I cannot recall or separate one young face that gave me a painful impression, not one young girl whom, assuming it to be a matter of necessity that she gain the daily bread by the

[1]From *The Underside of American History*, edited by Thomas R. Frazier

labour of her hands, I would have removed from those works if I had had the power. . . .

In this brief account of Lowell . . . I have carefully abstained from drawing a comparison between these factories and those of our land [England]. . . . The contrast would be a strong one, for it would be between the Good and Evil, the living light and the deepest shadow. . . . But I only more earnestly adjure [urge] all those whose eyes may rest on these pages, to pause and reflect upon the difference between this town [Lowell] and those great haunts of desperate misery [in England].[1] "

Not all the "Lowell girls" would agree with Dickens. Not all thought their situation was "Good" or "the living light." The following lines are from a letter written in 1845 by a Lowell girl known simply as Julianna. In it she expresses the despair often felt by some of the factory workers. Compare her feelings with those expressed in Dickens' observations:

" THE EVILS OF FACTORY LIFE. NUMBER ONE
. . . All is hurry, bustle and confusion in the street, in the mill and in the overflowing boarding house. If there chance to be an intelligent mind in that crowd which is striving to lay up [learn] treasures of knowledge, how unfavorably it is situated! Crowded into a small room, which contains three bed and six females, all possessing the "without end" tongue of woman, what chance is there for *studying?* and much less so for thinking and reflecting? . . .

Incarcerated [imprisoned] within the walls of a factory, while as yet mere children—drilled there from five [A.M.] until seven o'clock [P.M.], year after year—thrown into company with all sorts and descriptions of minds, dispositions and intellects, without counsellor or friends to advise—far away from a watchful mother's tender care or father's kind instruction . . . what *must*, what will be the natural, rational result? What but ignorance, misery, and *premature decay* of both *body* and *intellect?* Our country will be but one great hospital filled with worn out operatives [Lowell girls] and colored slaves. . . . What we would ask, . . . will be the mental and intellectual character of the future generations of New England? What but a race weak, sickly, imbecile, both mental and physical? A race fit only for corporation tools and time-serving slaves. . . . "
                                                        JULIANNA
Lowell, October, 1845[2]

[1]From *American Notes for General Circulation* by Charles Dickens
[2]From *America's Working Women: A Documentary History 1600 to the Present,* compiled and edited by Rosalyn Bauxhall, Linda Gordon, Susan Reverby

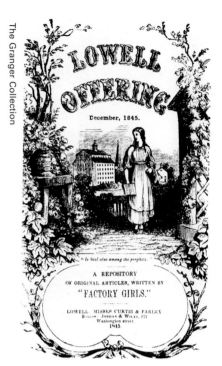

Contributors to the Lowell Offering *were the young women who worked in the Lowell factories.*

The first mill operations spun wool and cotton into thread, but soon weaving was also done by machines. Do you think the child working under the spindles at left had a safe job?

Growth of the Factory System

Much of America's early industry developed in New England. The successes of Slater and Brown meant other Americans soon wanted to build factories. The locations of these factories, and later of the cities that would grow up around them, was influenced partly by America's unique geography and partly by history. The machinery in the first American factories was driven by water. These factories sprang up at waterpower sites in New England and the Middle Atlantic states. Especially ideal were sites on the fall line. Along this line rivers drop from the Appalachian foothills to the Atlantic Coastal Plain in small waterfalls. Water rushing over these falls provided the power to run the factory machinery. All along the eastern seaboard owners built factories to take advantage of this power source.

By 1812, however, steam-powered machines were replacing water-driven ones in America. Location directly on lakes, rivers, and streams remained important, however. Such waterways provided another advantage—cheaper water transportation. Bulky materials moved more easily on water in barges and ships than in wagons over land. Mills that used bulky raw materials such as iron, timber, or coal or that produced bulky products such as steel continued to open along the shores and banks of navigable waterways. Cities such as Pittsburgh, Buffalo, and Richmond soon spread from clusters of factories. 🖙

Return to the Preview & Review on page 333.

3. THE RISE OF THE CITIES

Preview & Review

Use these questions to guide your reading. Answer the questions after completing Section 3.
Understanding Issues, Events, & Ideas. Describe the growth of American cities, using the following words: immigrant, nativist, urban frontier, urban center, tenement.
1. Where did most immigrants come from between 1820 and 1840?
2. Why did nativists fear too much immigration?
3. In what sense were western cities an urban frontier?
4. What caused slums to develop in cities?
Thinking Critically. **1.** Imagine that you are an immigrant in Boston in 1830. Use your historical imagination to describe the kind of job you would look for and the skills that would be necessary for that job. Then list the steps you would take to find the job. **2.** The year is 1835. You have decided you want to move to the urban frontier. What service would you most like to provide farmers? Why? How would you set up your service to make it profitable?

Immigration from Europe

Many women walked out of factories to protest wage reductions in 1834 and 1836. They were replaced by men and women recently come from Europe. These **immigrants** were very poor and willing to take any jobs they could find. The number of people coming to America was increasing yearly. Only about 250,000 immigrants had entered the United States between the end of the Revolutionary War and 1820. During the next 20 years more than 700,000 crossed the Atlantic.

The majority of these immigrants came from England, Ireland, and Germany. Most came as families. Nearly all came to the United States because they were poor and hoped to earn a better living in what Europeans considered "the land of opportunity." Both the Roman Catholics and Protestants among them contributed much to the growth of American religion during the 1820s and 1830s.

The Roman Catholics, especially, became an important element in cities like Boston, Philadelphia, and New York. Considerable friction between German and Irish Roman Catholics emerged. Soon the Irish gained dominance over the Germans, a fact easily seen in the growth in the number and power of Irish bishops in America.

Religious activity offered a relief from the pressures of factory labor and city life. The churches provided opportunities for newcomers to make friends, most often among people like themselves in religion and ethnic background.

No one rolled out the red carpet for these newcomers. Some Americans opposed unlimited immigration. These **nativists** believed that too much immigration would destroy American institutions. They wanted to keep the country for "native Americans." They conveniently forgot that the only real native Americans were the Indians!

The nativists were members of various Protestant churches. They were particularly hostile to Irish Catholics, who were entering the country in large numbers. Disease had destroyed most of the potato crop in Ireland, and thousands of Irish, facing starvation, turned to America. In 1834 a nativist mob burned a Catholic convent near Boston. Similar shameful incidents occurred in other parts of the country. Andrew M. Greeley, a contemporary writer, discusses the typical nativist view of the Irish Catholics who came to America:

" It is no secret that the Irish were not especially welcomed when they entered the United States. One can understand this reaction. Most earlier immigrants were, if not wealthy, at least reasonably skilled workers or artisans. They were the most ambitious and vigorous of the Europeans seeking

Blood flows in the streets of the City of Brotherly Love in this 1844 engraving of an anti-Catholic riot in Philadelphia. Why was the mob so threatened by new arrivals to America?

to make new lives for themselves in a richer country. But the famine Irish [people who left Ireland because disease destroyed the potato crop] were poor, uneducated, and confused. They fled not to a better life but from almost certain death. They were dirty, undernourished, disease-ridden, and incapable of anything but the most unskilled labor. That they arrived in great numbers and filled up whole sections of cities almost overnight did not go unnoticed by native Americans [Those already living there]. . . .

If the Irish were to be accepted into American society they must be sober, industrious, and ambitious, like the Protestant immigrants who had come before them. There, of course, was the heart of the problem. Not only were they poor, sick, dirty, and uneducated. They were also Catholic.

The Irish Catholics, with their unmarried clergy, had an equally strange tendency not to send their children to public schools, where every effort would be made to turn them into good Americans—this meant, of course, good Protestant Americans. From the nativist point of view, it was no wonder that churches were burned and that Catholics were occasionally murdered in riots.[1]

[1]From *That Most Distressful Nation: The Taming of the American Irish* by Andrew M. Greeley

Meanwhile people continued to leave their homes in Ireland, miserable and downtrodden. Many sang this farewell to their homeland:

> " Farewell to thee, Erin mavoureen [Ireland dear],
> Thy valleys I'll tread never more;
> This heart that now bleeds for thy sorrows
> Will waste on a far distant shore.
> Thy green sods lie cold on parents,
> A cross marks the place of their rest,
> The wind that moans softly above them
> Will waft [blow] their poor child to the West.[1] "

[1]From *The Irish in America* by James E. Johnson

City Life in America

Most of the immigrants who came to America between 1820 and 1840 settled in the cities of the Northeast. These were still communities where a person could easily walk from one end to the other in half an hour—places where church steeples stood out on the skyline and the masts and spars of ships at the wharves towered over the roofs of the houses, shops, and warehouses. There were no skyscrapers

LEARNING FROM GRAPHS. *These charts show the total number of immigrants coming to the United States between 1820 and 1860 and their places of origin. What are some trends in immigration during those years illustrated by the charts?*

Source: *Historical Statistics of the United States*

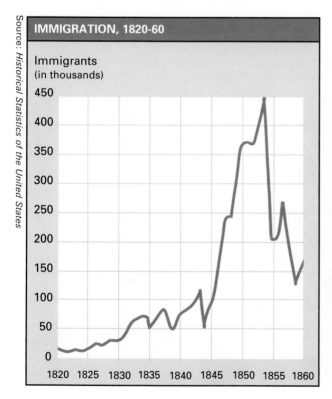

IMMIGRATION, 1820-60

Immigrants (in thousands)

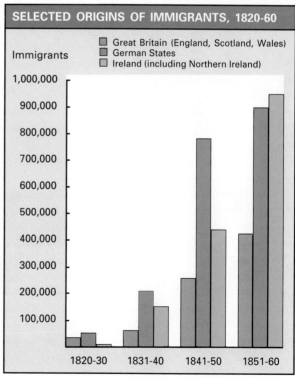

SELECTED ORIGINS OF IMMIGRANTS, 1820-60

Immigrants

- Great Britain (England, Scotland, Wales)
- German States
- Ireland (including Northern Ireland)

or great factories. The largest manufacturer in New York City in the 1830s employed only about 200 people.

These eastern cities were mainly shipping centers. Manufacturing was not very important. Most industries which did exist, such as shipbuilding and barrel making, were linked to trade and commerce.

The cities to the west were also mainly commercial centers. We think of cities as developing in already settled areas, but these western cities developed on the edge of settlement. They made up what may be called an **urban frontier.** They were founded even before most of the surrounding forests were cleared by farmers. Indeed, they acted as outposts and depots from which settlers spread out. Many people went west not to farm but to live in these communities and supply the needs of farmers.

All American cities underwent similar growing pains in this period. Since few city streets were paved, there was always mud in rainy weather. This gave rise to a famous joke about the poor condition of city streets: A passing citizen offers help to a man who has sunk up to his neck in a huge mud puddle. "No need to worry," replies the man. "I have a horse under me."

Many a stockbroker may have lifted a cup to his lips at the Tontine Coffee House, right, since it also served as the Stock Exchange. Meanwhile, the life of New York City, as it always has, goes on in all its variety. Down Water Street is a forest of masts and spars from the wharves of the East River. Describe some of the problems of city life illustrated by this picture.

New–York Historical Society

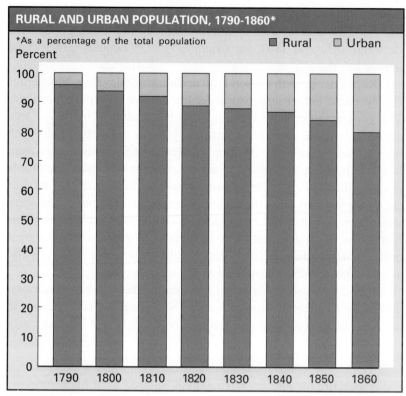

RURAL AND URBAN POPULATION, 1790-1860*

*As a percentage of the total population ■ Rural □ Urban

Percent

Source: *Historical Statistics of the United States*

LEARNING FROM GRAPHS.
Originally the United States was a nation of farmers. But almost immediately that began to change. Why were people attracted to cities?

Garbage littered city streets. In all parts of the country, goats and hogs were allowed to roam about rooting through the waste. Charleston, South Carolina, passed a law against shooting turkey buzzards because these scavengers ate the dead cats and dogs and rotting food left lying about the town.

Polluted water and the lack of sanitation often led to epidemics of contagious diseases. The most dreaded was cholera. This terrible disease is caused by bacteria and is spread in polluted water, but no one knew this at the time. During cholera epidemics people living in dirty, crowded slums died by the hundreds. Many people, therefore, thought the disease was a punishment for poverty.

Many American cities had neither police nor fire departments. Even the largest cities had no more than a dozen police officers, and these were only part-time employees. They refused to wear uniforms, arguing that uniforms were for servants.

Fires were put out by volunteer fire companies. There was often much competition between these associations. When fires broke out, fire companies sometimes fought each other rather than the blaze. More than glory was at stake. Cash prizes were frequently awarded to the companies that responded most quickly to alarms.

In 1790 there were only 24 **urban centers** in the United States with a population of 2,500 or more. By 1840 there were 131. Many

The Rise of Cities 347

people moved into the cities, but many left them too. There was, in other words, a great deal of turnover among the urban population. Between 1830 and 1840, for example, 35,775 families either came into or left the city of Boston.

Rapid city growth caused crowded slums to develop. Most cities simply could not absorb people as fast as the newcomers arrived. The poor crowded into the attics and basements of houses. Large apartments were broken up into many small ones. Buildings with many families crowded together were called **tenements.** Rents were low. But because there were so many apartments in each, the profits made by owners of tenements could be very large. Little, if any, of the profit went to keep the tenement buildings in repair. They were unsanitary and unsafe. An American reformer declared in 1840: "One half of the world does not know *how the other half lives*." The great crusader for housing reform, Jacob Riis, made the phrase popular some 50 years later, as we shall see.

Education also was a major concern in cities. Urban educators, especially those in Boston and other New England cities, came to see their schools as a "community in miniature." One historian says of these schools:

“ There, the child could mature in an environment created especially for him, in surroundings tailored to fit his needs as separate from those of the adult community. There, . . . the schoolmaster could impart the moral instruction that had once come from the pulpit. . . . The public school was to be a classroom, a family room, a church house—all things to all children. The school was to nurture the child to adulthood, equip him with necessary skills of a livelihood, and familiarize him with the rigors and dangers of life in the city. In short, the school was to be the social incubator [a device providing a safe and controlled environment] of responsible citizens.[1] ”

[1] From *The Culture Factory: Boston Public Schools* by Stanley K. Schultz

By the late-1820s many cities had year-round primary schools. Nearly 45 percent of Boston's school-age population was in school. Boston provided a Latin high school for boys, an English high school for boys and a similar experimental school for girls (schools with less emphasis on the classics than the Latin schools), and two separate schools for African Americans. Other large cities soon followed Boston's lead.

Despite all of these problems, the cities remained the cultural centers of American life. Cities, with their theaters, cafes, taverns, and libraries, attracted people in large numbers—artists, writers, ordinary people searching for excitement and adventure. 🖻

Return to the Preview & Review on page 343.

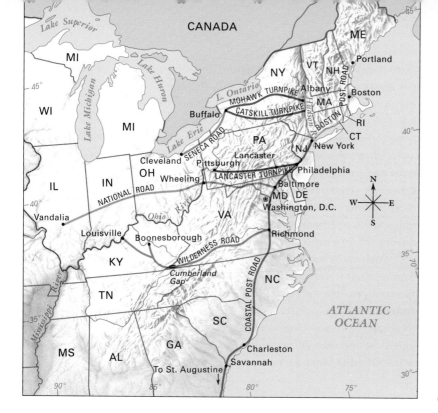

MAIN ROADS, 1840

0   150   300 Mi.

0   150   300 Km.

Albers Equal-Area Projection

LEARNING FROM MAPS. *Note the pattern of America's earliest roads. Why do most of the roads run from east to west?*

4. IMPROVEMENTS IN TRAVEL

New Roads and Turnpikes

As the cities expanded, it was no longer easy to walk from one end to the other. A new means of transportation was necessary. In 1827 Abraham Brower began running a stagecoach up and down Broadway in New York City. By 1833 there were about 80 stagecoaches in New York. The coaches were drawn by two horses and seated 12 passengers. In the winter some drivers replaced their wheels with runners, turning them into sleighs. Stagecoaches could soon be found in every city, and service between many cities was also available.

Travel overland could be efficient only if there were good roads. America's roads were poor indeed. Most were unpaved. They turned into seas of mud after every heavy rain. In dry weather they were bumpy and rutted, and every passing wagon sent up clouds of dust. An inexpensive way to build weatherproof roads had not yet been found. Most roads were built by private companies that hoped to earn profits. The roads these companies built marched straight up and down hill and dale rather than around them in a more level but longer and more expensive way.

Builders collected tolls from people who traveled over their roads. The tollgate was usually a pole, or pike, blocking the road. When the traveler paid the toll, the pike was raised or turned aside to let the traveler pass. Hence these toll roads were called **turnpikes.**

Travel overland was both expensive and time-consuming. In the

Preview & Review

Use these questions to guide your reading. Answer the questions after completing Section 4.
Understanding Issues, Events, & Ideas. Use the following words to discuss travel in the 1800s: turnpike, Cumberland Road or National Road, canal, Erie Canal, *Fulton's Folly, Tom Thumb,* Transportation Revolution.
1. In what ways were America's early roads poor? Why was the National Road built?
2. What problem was there in traveling inland?
3. What were some early uses of steam power?
4. What were some advantages of railroads? How did railroads boost the economy?

Thinking Critically.   1. You are a merchant in New York after the building of the Erie Canal. Write a letter to your brother in Georgia, explaining how the canal has improved your business.   **2.** Briefly explain how the railroad would affect you if you were: a farmer; a mine owner; a land owner in a remote area.

early 1800s it cost more to haul a ton of goods only 9 miles inland (about 14 kilometers) than to bring the same ton all the way across the Atlantic Ocean. Little wonder that in the 1790s the rebellious farmers of Pennsylvania had turned their corn into whiskey! In bulk form corn was far too expensive to ship to eastern markets.

During the War of 1812 a wagon drawn by four horses took 75 days to go from Worcester, Massachusetts, to Charleston, South Carolina. It would have been quicker to sail to Europe, stay a week or two, and return to America—and cheaper too. Any profits that might have been earned would have been eaten up by the four horses during the 75-day trip.

The roads of this period did not unite the country. In 1806 Thomas Jefferson took the first steps to link the eastern regions with the western. He authorized the building of the **Cumberland Road,** or **National Road.** Construction began in 1811 at Cumberland, Maryland. The route crossed over the mountains in southern Pennsylvania and ended at the site of present-day Wheeling, West Virginia. Later it was extended west to Vandalia, Illinois.

With the crack of a whip the driver of this stagecoach urges his horses westward. The wheels of the stagecoach sink into the muddy road, which is marked by the stumps of the trees probably felled to build the bridge at right. Whenever the horses galloped around a curve such as this, there was always the chance the overland travelers would "be stumped"—or stopped by stumps that broke the coach's wheels. How were America's first roads a good example of private enterprise in action?

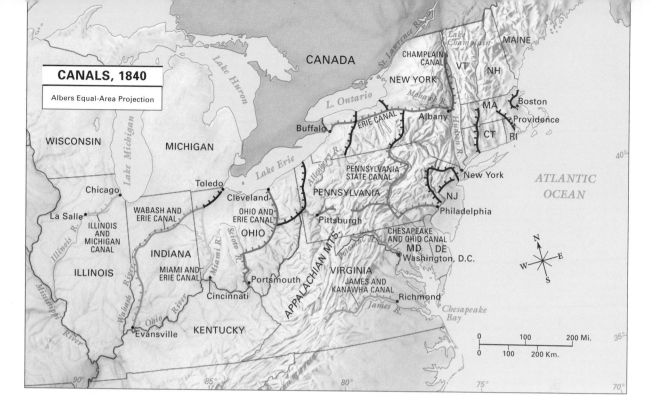

CANALS, 1840

Albers Equal-Area Projection

The National Road was a remarkable engineering achievement. It was built on a solid stone foundation with a gravel topping. Over it rolled an almost endless caravan of coaches, carts, and wagons. Its sturdy stone bridges still carry traffic today.

Canals

The easiest means of moving goods and people was by water. But like its roads, America's rivers and lakes were not connected. Fortunately many of them could be joined by digging **canals.**

Goods were carried through canals on barges towed by horses or mules. The animals plodded patiently along what were called towpaths on the bank of the canal. A mule could pull a load 50 times or more heavier on water than it could over any road. Thus, canal transportation was much cheaper than transportation by road.

Canals were very expensive to build. They could not be dug without government support. In 1816 De Witt Clinton, the canal commissioner of New York, persuaded the state legislature to build a canal running from the Hudson River across the state all the way to Lake Erie. This route offered the most attractive passage from the Atlantic Coast to the Great Lakes. It passed through the Mohawk Valley, a gap in the Appalachian Mountains. There the land was relatively level. The water did not have to be raised and lowered very much by canal locks. In 1817 work on Clinton's "Big Ditch" began. Much of the digging was done by European immigrants.

The first section was opened to traffic in 1819, and in 1825 the **Erie Canal** was completed. It was an engineering wonder: 363 miles

LEARNING FROM MAPS. *Canals helped form a transportation network that included the early roads. Why were canals particularly important to farmers and merchants?*

This plate celebrates the building of the Erie Canal with its view of the entrance of the canal at the Hudson River.

Improvements in Travel 351

long, 40 feet wide, and 4 feet deep (about 580 kilometers long, 12 meters wide, and 1 meter deep). It cost the state $7 million, an enormous sum for those days, but it attracted so much traffic that the tolls collected soon paid its cost. Because of this high volume, the rates charged for using the canal were very low. The cost of shipping a ton of goods fell from 19 cents a mile before the canal was built to 1 cent. The canal became the busiest route for goods and people moving between the Atlantic Coast and western cities and farms.

When other states saw how profitable the Erie Canal was, they hastened to build canals of their own. Soon a wave of canal building was under way. In 1816 there were only about 100 miles (160 kilometers) of canals in the entire nation. By 1840 there were more than 3,300 miles (5,280 kilometers). This meant that the combined length of the canals of the United States was greater than the distance across North America between the Atlantic and Pacific Oceans.

The canals created a network that united the different sections of the country and stimulated their economies. Bulky farm products could now be shipped cheaply to distant markets. Eastern manufactured products no longer had to be lugged over the Appalachians.

In 1849 when this scene was captured by its artist, Pittsburgh was often called the "Gateway to the West." From its crowded docks steamboats set out to carry settlers on the Ohio River as they began their journeys westward. In the years after Fulton sailed his Clermont, steamboats became huge floating palaces, gliding from city to city, practically cities in themselves. Read descriptions of steamboat travel. In what ways is travel today superior and in what ways is it not?

Steamboats

Travel by canal was slow. It still depended on animal power. Mules would only walk about 3 miles an hour (about 5 kilometers) pulling a barge. Keelboats, pushed along by poles or by the wind in a small sail, were not much faster. What was needed was a new source of power. Once again, British technology supplied the answer. In the 1760s a Scot named James Watt had invented a practical steam engine. Watt's invention used the energy of burning wood and coal to replace the energy of beasts and human beings. When the steam engine was used to run machines in factories, it replaced waterpower. This meant that factories did not have to be located near dams or swiftly moving rivers. They could be built anywhere.

If steam can move machines, can it not be used to move boats? One of the first Americans to ask this question was John Fitch, a silversmith and clockmaker. In 1787 Fitch launched a steamboat propelled by 12 paddles on the Delaware River. Among the many spectators who witnessed the launching of Fitch's smoke-belching monster were several of the delegates from the Constitutional Convention in nearby Philadelphia. Shortly afterwards, Fitch built a

AVERAGE FREIGHT RATES* BETWEEN LOUISVILLE AND NEW ORLEANS, 1810-59		
*per 100 pounds	**Upstream**	**Downstream**
1810-1819	$5.00	$1.00
1820-1829	$1.00	$0.62
1830-1839	$0.50	$0.50
1840-1849	$0.30	$0.25
1850-1859	$0.25	$0.25

Source: *History of the American Economy*

New York State Historical Association, Cooperstown

Robert Fulton's portrait is by Benjamin West. Fulton had himself been a Philadelphia portrait painter before he turned his mechanical aptitude to canal engineering and steamboats. What did Fulton's steamboat prove?

second boat which carried passengers between Philadelphia and Burlington, New Jersey. But this enterprise was a commercial failure.

For another 20 years steamboats were neither efficient nor reliable. Then, in 1807, Robert Fulton, an artist turned inventor, began building a steamboat on the East River in New York City. Fulton called it the *Clermont*, but those who had watched it being built called it **Fulton's Folly.** In August the boat made its first voyage up the Hudson River from New York City to Albany. The 300-mile trip (480 kilometers) took 62 hours, but the *Clermont* soon proved that a steam vessel could earn a profit.

In 1811 Nicholas Roosevelt, an associate of Fulton and a distant relative of two future presidents, built the *New Orleans* at Pittsburgh. In the winter of 1811–12 this boat made the 1,950-mile trip (3,120 kilometers) from Pittsburgh to New Orleans in only 14 days. Previously the journey had taken four to six weeks.

An even more dramatic breakthrough occurred in 1815 when the *Enterprise* was piloted up the Mississippi from New Orleans to Pittsburgh against the current. Before that time a trip upstream by sail or keelboat from New Orleans to Pittsburgh took more than four months. Soon dozens of steamboats were sailing up and down the western rivers. In 1817 there were only 17. By 1840 there were 536.

New forms of transportation such as the steamboat had a certain glamour about them. People, especially young boys, were fascinated by them. Here is how Mark Twain described his fascination:

❝ When I was a boy, there was but one permanent ambition among my comrades in our village on the west bank of the Mississippi. That was to be a steamboatman.

After all these years, I can picture that old time myself now, just as it was then: the white town drowsing in the sunshine of a summer's morning; the streets empty, or pretty near so; . . . the great Mississippi, the majestic, magnificent Mississippi, rolling its mile-wide tide along, shining in the sun; the dense forest away on the other side; the 'point' [of land] above the town and the 'point' below. Presently a film of dark smoke appears above one of those remote 'points'; instantly a Negro drayman [wagon driver], famous for his quick eye and prodigious [mighty] voice, lifts up the cry, 'S-t-e-a-m-boat acomin'!' and the scene changes! . . . All in a twinkling, the dead town is alive and moving. Drays, carts, men, boys, all go hurrying from many quarters to a common center, the wharf. Assembled there, the people fasten their eyes upon the coming boat as upon a wonder they are seeing for the first time.

And the boat is rather a handsome sight, too. She is long and sharp and trim and pretty. She has two fancy-topped chimneys, with a gilded device of some kind swung between them, and a fanciful pilothouse, all glass and ''gingerbread'' [fancy wood designs] perched on the top of the ''texas'' deck [the deck with the largest cabins; steamboat decks were named after states, according to size]. The paddle boxes are gorgeous with a picture or with gilded rays above the boat's name; the boiler-deck, the hurricane-deck, and the texas deck are fenced and ornamented with clean white railings. There is a flag gallantly flying from the jack-staff; the furnace doors are open and the fires glaring bravely. The upper decks are black with passengers. The captain stands by the big bell, calm, imposing, the envy of all. Great volumes of the blackest smoke are rolling and tumbling out of the chimneys; . . . the pent steam is screaming through the gauge cocks [devices for measuring the steam pressure]. The captain lifts his hand, a bell rings, the wheels stop; then they turn back, churning the water to foam, and the steamer is at rest. . . .

Ten minutes later the steamer is under way again, with no flag on the jack-staff, and no black smoke issuing from the chimneys. After ten more minutes the town is dead again, . . .[1]''

Alexis de Tocqueville of France visited America in 1831. His observations about the young nation became the classic *Democracy in America*.

"The roads, the canals, and the mails play a prodigious [mighty] part in the prosperity of the Union. . . . In the Michigan forests there is not a cabin so isolated, not a valley so wild, that it does not receive letters and newspapers at least once a week. . . . Of all the countries of the world, America is the one where the movement of thought and human industry is the most continuous and the most swift."

Alexis de Tocqueville, 1831

Railroads

Soon after the canals and steamboats, there came a still more significant technological advance—the railroad. The first steam-driven locomotive, the *Tom Thumb*, was built by Peter Cooper for the Baltimore & Ohio Railroad in 1830. The track on which the *Tom Thumb* made its first run had been used by horse-drawn coaches. To demonstrate the engine, Cooper raced *Tom Thumb* against a horse-drawn coach. The locomotive swept ahead from the start. But it broke down before the finish line. The horse won the race.

[1]From *Life on the Mississippi* by Mark Twain

STRATEGIES FOR SUCCESS

INTERPRETING A SPECIAL-PURPOSE MAP

Special-purpose maps, as their name tells you, contain specific information. The map on page 351 is a special-purpose map that illustrates the growth of the canal system in America. Interpreting the information contained on a special-purpose map will help you to understand that aspect of history or geography.

How to Interpret a Special-Purpose Map

To interpret a special-purpose map, follow these guidelines.

1. **Use map basics.** Read the title, check the legend, and scale. These map parts will tell you the subject of the map and its extent.
2. **Note special symbols.** Special-purpose maps often use symbols to illustrate information.

Study the key to make sure you understand what the symbols on the map represent.

3. **Read the labels.** Identify each feature portrayed on the map.
4. **Study the map as a whole.** Note the overall pattern of the information. Is it concentrated in one area? Does it seem to be influenced by geographic factors?

Applying the Strategy

Study the map below. Note that it illustrates the railroad network in the United States in 1860. The paths of railroads are marked by ——and the main ones are labeled. What area of the country had the most railroad mileage? Why?

For independent practice, see Practicing the Strategy on page 360.

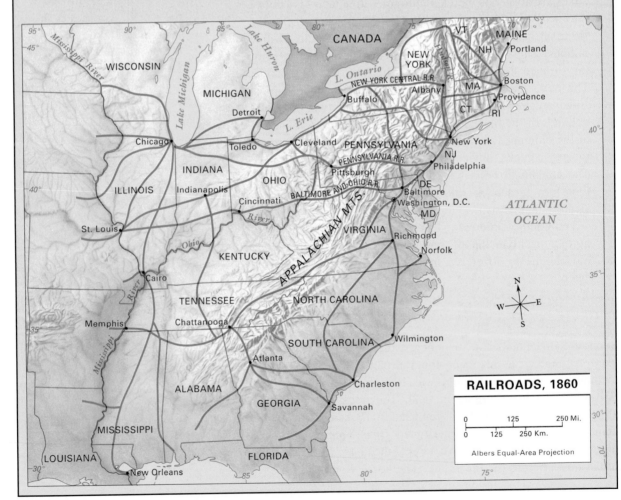

RAILROADS, 1860

The Chessie System, B & O Railroad Museum Archives

"The Race of the Tom Thumb" was painted as part of a series for the Fair of the Iron Horse held in celebration of 100 years of operation by the Baltimore & Ohio Railroad. The horse won this race. What does this tell us about making generalizations from too few instances?

Trains had many advantages over canals and steamboats. They could go practically anywhere. They were much faster. They could pull greater loads. And they could operate all year round in the northern states, where the canals and many rivers were frozen solid in the winter months.

In the beginning many Americans considered trains dangerous. The sparks from their engines set fields afire and frightened farm animals. The engines often jumped their tracks. But the advantages of railroads could not be resisted. In 1830 the Baltimore & Ohio, the nation's only railroad, had 13 miles (about 21 kilometers) of track. By 1840 there were dozens of lines operating more than 3,300 miles (5,280 kilometers) of track, most of it in the Northeast.

Railroads gave the economy a great boost. Besides reducing travel time and cost, they caused many other businesses to expand. The demand for iron for engines and rails greatly increased the mining and smelting of iron. Remote areas boomed once the railroads reached them. Farmers expanded output. Land prices rose.

The railroads completed the web of transportation which began with turnpikes. This **Transportation Revolution** brought about dramatic changes. It tied westerners to easterners. It made it easier for people in one region to know and do business with people in other regions. It made nearly everyone more prosperous. In a way, the Transportation Revolution had almost as much to do with creating the *United* States as the American Revolution itself.

Return to the Preview & Review on page 349.

Improvements in Travel 357

HOMES FOR AMERICANS

It is easy to overlook the importance of houses in the study of history. They are so common, fulfilling a basic need—shelter. In today's cities and suburbs they seem to stretch for miles in no particular pattern, holding no historical clues. But to those who study such houses, they tell a great deal about us.

Houses and the Cultural Landscape

1. What is the cultural landscape? Why is housing of special interest to those studying the cultural landscape?

Every inhabited part of the earth has both a physical and a cultural landscape. Physical features such as the mountains, deserts, plants, and animals make up the *physical landscape.* The imprint or effect a group of people leaves on its *human habitat*—the place where it lives—creates the *cultural landscape.*

Housing interests geographers and other scientists because the design and construction of a house often shows how people adapt to their physical setting. The ancestors of the Hopi built pueblos, ancient apartment houses, in the cliffs. The Arapaho stretched buffalo hide on poles to make teepees to provide shelter on the treeless plains. Later settlers on the Plains cut chunks of sod to build their houses.

Housing also often reflects the cultural heritage of its builders. The Hopi were farmers and built permanent structures. The Arapaho were hunters. Their teepees could be quickly taken down as they pursued buffalo herds. Size and style made a statement about the owner's place in society. No one who saw a plantation mansion could mistake the wealth of a southern planter!

Housing and the Environment

2. How do houses reflect the environment?

Environment influenced European settlers as it had the Hopi and Arapaho. Builders developed many styles to deal with particular conditions. In places with heavy snowfall, settlers often sharply pitched the roof to cause the snow to slide off easily. In areas with long rainy seasons, such as the Pacific Northwest, Indians and later settlers frequently built roofs with a broad overhang or a porch to provide a dry walkway beside the house. Where there was little rainfall, as in the Southwest, rooflines were flat. There overhangs provided shade from the relentless sun and large windows caught every breeze.

The Log Cabin

3. Why was the log cabin the typical pioneer home east of the Mississippi?

Perhaps the best example of a house reflecting the American environment is the log cabin. When we think of houses on the early frontier, log cabins instantly come to mind. It was the most common housing for pioneers until the frontier reached the Great Plains, an area too dry to support the trees needed to build log cabins.

In many ways the log cabin was nearly perfect housing for the frontier environment. With its notched logs, joined at the corners, it was easy to construct. And the building material—trees—surrounded the pioneers. Often a family, using little more than an axe as a tool, could put together a simple log cabin in a few days.

Building a Log Cabin

4. How did settlers adapt log cabins to their needs?

Nature influenced the style and construction of log cabins. Pioneer families could handle only logs of a limited size. They could not lift or move the largest into place. The natural taper of the logs also created a built-in limit to the size of the cabin for a builder using only an axe.

The simplest cabins consisted of one room with a chimney at the end. To add space the family might put planks over part of the rafters to create a loft. Such lofts, reached by ladder from the main floor, often became the bedroom for the children. An ambitious family might also build a second log room attached to the first.

American Housing and European Culture

5. How does culture and tradition influence housing design?

Some architectural designs reflect cultural traditions rather than environmental concerns. As you might expect, European—especially British—influences dominated housing styles in the colonies in the 1700s and 1800s. The frame construction common to New England reflected European traditions. First, a heavy frame of vertical, horizontal, and diagonal timbers was

raised. The open spaces of this skeleton were filled with materials such as mud and stone.

It did not take long before New England builders found that, unlike in their homelands, timber was abundant. Soon the framework was covered with horizontal sidings called clapboard. The New England frame house was born.

The plantation home characteristic of the South in the late 1700s evolved from the English cottage. American builders quickly adapted their cottages. It became common to add a front porch and rear shed with its own chimney as the kitchen. Later, as the wealth of the planters increased, porches surrounding the entire building were added along with balconies, a great number of rooms, and massive columns reaching upward to the overhanging roofline.

The "Shotgun House"

6. Why is the shotgun house unique?

One of the most unique designs in American homes is the long, narrow house found in many southern cities. It is called a "shotgun house." It is unique because it is of African origin and was brought to the United States from Haiti. It is a distinctive and significant African contribution to the American cultural landscape.

The shotgun house is a narrow, one-story house, one room in width, and three or four rooms deep. It has a narrow, frontward-facing gable. The term *shotgun* refers to the interior arrangement of the house. Each room is directly behind the room in front. The doorways are in a straight line so, as the story goes, "a shotgun can be fired in the front door and the bullet will travel out the back without hitting anything."

The first shotgun homes were probably built in New Orleans. Haitians began pouring into the city in the early 1800s. Many were the descendants of African slaves from the Yoruba area of West Africa, in modern-day Nigeria. The characteristic Yoruba house consists of two or three rooms, one directly behind the other. The Haitian descendants of the Yoruba brought the style to New Orleans.

By 1810 there were almost twice as many African Americans as Europeans in New Orleans, and most were free. Many were skilled craftsman, especially carpenters and stone masons. Slowly, New Orleans took on a distinctive flavor strongly influenced by African American styles. By the 1830s independent African American contractors were busily constructing shotgun houses throughout the city.

American Houses

7. Why did the American environment create unique houses?

As with most things brought from Europe, settlers found that their traditional housing styles did not quite fit the new environment. Trial and error helped them invent styles that were better for America. Soon new styles of houses, each reflecting both environmental and cultural aspects of their builders, dotted the American cultural landscape.

Applying Your Knowledge

Your class will create a display of traditional American houses. Each group will research a different housing style: New England, plantation, log cabin, shotgun, sod, and others. Reports should explain cultural links to housing style and descriptions of typical building materials. Groups should prepare a model or detailed drawing of the styles they research.

Linking History & Geography 359

CHAPTER 10 REVIEW

1765
Spinning jenny invented

1768
Water-frame developed

1787
Fitch's
steam-
boat

1789
Samuel Slater
comes to U.S.

1791
Slater and
Brown's mi
opens

Chapter Summary

Read the statements below. Choose one, and write a paragraph explaining its importance.

1. Americans recognized the need for a diversified economy during the wars with England.
2. In the early 1800s the government began to help American businesses with protective tariffs and the Bank of the United States.
3. In the early 1800s Americans imported and invented the technology to mass produce goods.
4. Finding industrial workers was often a problem until waves of immigrants began to arrive in the United States in the 1820s.
5. Despite nativist opposition, immigrants poured into growing American urban areas.
6. During the 1800s the United States gradually changed from a rural to an urban nation.
7. Rapid city growth caused slums to develop.
8. Building new roads, canals, and railroads led to a Transportation Revolution.

Reviewing Chronological Order

Number your paper 1–5. Then study the time line above and place the following events in the order in which they happened by writing the first next to 1, the second next to 2, and so on.

1. Whitney demonstrates interchangeable parts
2. Lowell develops Lowell system
3. Erie Canal completed
4. Samuel Slater comes to U.S.
5. National Road begun

Understanding Main Ideas

1. How does a protective tariff work? Use an example to illustrate your answer.
2. What were some of the major changes that occurred during the Industrial Revolution?
3. Why did some Americans fear the large number of immigrants that began to arrive in the United States in the 1820s?
4. Why was immigration important to both the Industrial and Transportation revolutions?

Thinking Critically

1. **Judging.** When Samuel Slater memorized designs for English cotton-spinning machinery and moved to America, was he committing a crime, or was he ignoring unjust laws? Explain your answer.
2. **Synthesizing.** The year is 1840. You have immigrated to New York, where you live in a tenement with your parents and four brothers. Compose a letter to your grandmother back in Ireland, describing your new home.
3. **Inventing.** You are one of the workers who helped build Clinton's "Big Ditch." Write a song or poem praising the wonders of the Erie Canal.

Writing About History: Informative

You are a newspaper reporter in 1801. Use your historical imagination to join the onlookers as Whitney takes apart and reassembles the ten muskets. Write a report of the event and the reactions of the audience. Use the information in Chapter 10 to help you develop your report.

Practicing the Strategy

Review the strategy on page 356.

Reviewing Special-Purpose Maps. Study the map on page 351, then answer the following questions.

1. This special-purpose map illustrates which specific mode of transportation? What time frame is indicated?
2. How would a shipment of coal be transported from Pittsburgh, Pennsylvania, to Chicago, Illinois? Name each part of the water route that would be used for the journey.
3. Which river is connected to the Great Lakes by five of these canals?

Using Primary Sources

One sign of America's economic growth was the development of improved methods of transpor-

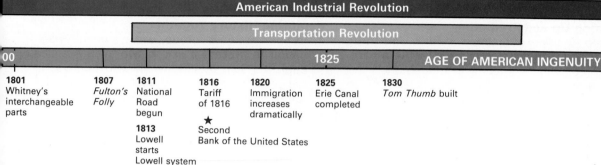

American Industrial Revolution

Transportation Revolution

00   1825   AGE OF AMERICAN INGENUITY   1850

1801
Whitney's
interchangeable
parts

1807
Fulton's
Folly

1811
National
Road
begun

1813
Lowell
starts
Lowell system

1816
Tariff
of 1816

★
Second
Bank of the United States

1820
Immigration
increases
dramatically

1825
Erie Canal
completed

1830
Tom Thumb built

tation. During the early 1800s water transportation was especially important. Timothy Flint, a missionary and writer, described a journey he took on a keelboat in his book *Recollections of the Last Ten Years*.

> *Our keelboat was between 80 and 90 feet [24 and 27 meters] in length, had a small but comfortable cabin, and carried 17 tons. It was an extremely hot afternoon when we left. The river was almost to the top of its banks, and the current was very rapid. We looked out over a deep, green forest with a richness of plants and trees and a grandeur of size and height, that characterizes the forest in this part of Ohio.*
>
> *We started this trip under favorable signs. We experienced in a couple of hours what has so often been said of all earthly enjoyments—how near to each other are the limits of happiness and trouble. Banks of thunderclouds were on the horizon when we left Cincinnati. They gathered over us, and a violent thunderstorm followed. We had no time to reach the shore before it burst upon us, accompanied by strong gusts of wind. The gale [wind] was too violent for us to think of landing on a rugged, rockbound shore. We protected the open part of the boat as well as we could, and began scooping out the water the boat took in from the waves. We had women passengers on board, whose screams added to the uproar outside. . . . The patron [skipper], who had done this work for many years and who had been, as he said, "boatwrecked" half a dozen times, kept perfectly cool! . . .*

1. From Flint's description of the keelboat, how do you think this craft helped in the settlement and trade of the West?
2. Why would a thunderstorm such as the one described be especially dangerous to a keelboat?
3. Use Flint's description to sketch what you think a keelboat looked like.

Linking History & Geography

As the nation developed, geography had less and less influence on transportation. To understand how the Transportation Revolution helped change even the direction goods were carried in the United States, answer the following questions.

1. Study the map on page 296. Into what major river do most of the rivers in the Ohio Valley flow? In what direction does that river flow?
2. Look at the map on page 351. Why had farmers in central Ohio begun to send their produce down the Ohio and Mississippi rivers? What general direction would their route follow?
3. Use the map on page 356. What two railroads might you use to move goods from central Ohio to New York City? In what general direction would your goods travel?
4. How did the development of canals and railroads change the *direction* of transportation in the eastern United States?

Enriching Your Study of History

1. **Individual Project.** Young women in the factories of Lowell worked 12 hours a day, six days a week. Each shared a bedroom with six other women. Although wages in Lowell were higher than women could earn in any other occupation, factories were hot, damp, and stuffy, and the work was usually boring. Use historical imagination to write a letter home to your family on the farm describing what you like and dislike about Lowell.
2. **Cooperative Project.** As a class project, prepare a bulletin board or multimedia display to show the scope of the Transportation Revolution in the United States. Each group will be responsible for one form of transportation. When completed, the display should show major rivers, canals, roads, and railroads that made up the American network by 1840.

UNIT THREE REVIEW

Summing Up and Predicting

Read the summary of the main ideas in Unit Three below. Choose one statement, then write a paragraph predicting its outcome or future effect.

1. The *Kentucky and Virginia Resolutions*, in response to the Sedition Act, put forth the doctrine of nullification and states' rights.
2. The Louisiana Purchase in 1803 and the Transcontinental Treaty in 1819 more than doubled the area of the United States.
3. Troubles continued with England, pushing the countries to the brink of another war.
4. The Indians in the Ohio Valley attempted to resist the onslaught of settlers from the east but were eventually defeated.
5. Despite opposition to the War of 1812 by many Americans, a war was declared in which the United States defeated Britain.
6. Revolutions throughout Latin America produced many independent countries and prompted the Monroe Doctrine.
7. The Industrial Revolution, European immigration, and the Transportation Revolution began to rapidly change American society in the early 1800s.

Connecting Ideas

1. John Adams called his part in the Convention of 1800 "the most splendid diamond in my crown." Would this statement have alarmed a Democratic-Republican? Why or why not?
2. How did the Louisiana Purchase, the death of Alexander Hamilton, and the American victory in the War of 1812 weaken the Federalist Party?
3. Which idea expressed in the Monroe Doctrine do you think is the most important to the United States today? Why?

Practicing Critical Thinking

1. **Drawing Conclusions.** Soon after the Revolutionary War, the young United States had trouble with England and France. Which of these two countries do you think was the greater threat? Cite specific examples to support your answer.
2. **Evaluating.** In your opinion, which battle in the War of 1812 was the most important to the Americans? Why?
3. **Synthesizing.** Write a conversation between two twelve-year-olds: Jane, a thread mill worker, and John, a farm boy. Have Jane describe her job; have John describe his chores.

Exploring History Together

1. In your assigned group, use historical imagination to present a skit in two acts. Act One depicts a visit by city dwellers to relatives in the country in the early 1800s. Act Two is a return visit by the country relatives to the city. Your skit should show the merits of city life and of country life.
2. You and members of your group will conduct research to create a display comparing problems faced by cities today with those in the years 1790–1840. Some students will find newspaper and magazine articles to show problems that have continued to the present. Others will report on solutions to city problems of the past and of today.
3. Have some members of your group research and prepare a bulletin board showing some of the problems faced by cities in 1790–1840. Add newspaper and magazine articles to illustrate problems which continue to this day. Other members may report on the solutions found to some city problems of 1790–1840 and of today.

Reading in Depth

Adams, Samuel H. *Chingo Smith of the Erie Canal.* New York: Random House. Relates the experiences of a homeless boy in the early days of the canal.

Blos, Joan W. *A Gathering of Days: A New England Girl's Journal, 1830–1832.* New York: Scribner's. Portrays the life of a young factory worker.

Chidsey, Donald Barr. *Lewis and Clark: The Great Adventure.* New York: G. P. Putnam's Sons. Contains a detailed description of the journey with many interesting sidelights.

Cooney, Barabara. *Island Boy.* New York: Viking. Traces New England's history, culture, and social changes through four generations of a local family.

Cooke, David C. *Tecumseh: Destiny's Warrior.* New York: Messner. Presents an account of the great Indian leader's life.

Leckie, Robert. *The War Nobody Won: 1812.* New York: Putnam. Describes events surrounding the war, including American opposition to it.

Tallant, Robert. *Louisiana Purchase.* New York: Random House. Investigates the politics of the purchase and the American reaction to the "Great Bargain."

Butler Institute of American Art
"The Oregon Trail" by Albert Bierstadt is an oil painting done in 1869. Its golden sunset captures the romance of a westering America.

A WESTERING AMERICA

UNIT 4

Unit Four describes America's growth and sectional conflicts in the years 1820–1850. Andrew Jackson's presidency marked the increased influence of the "common man" and of the West. Westward expansion and the removal of southern Indians from their homelands begun under Jackson culminated in the period of manifest destiny, when the nation overspread the continent. The addition of new western territories aggravated the slavery question and led again to attempts to solve it, this time by the Compromise of 1850. The abolitionist movement was one of the many reform movements in the 1830s–1850s, which was known as the Age of Reform.

The Age of Jackson

James Monroe's presidency came to be known as the Era of Good Feelings. The Republicans had little political opposition; the nation was prosperous, at peace, and growing rapidly. The era ended when regional differences between the Northeast, the South, and the West caused sectional conflicts. These conflicts set the stage for Andrew Jackson's rise to power. This chapter compares and contrasts the democratic ideals of Thomas Jefferson and Andrew Jackson. It describes the three main concerns of Jackson's presidency—the preservation of the Union, his battle against the Bank of the United States, and Indian removal. Finally the chapter raises questions about the new style of political campaigning started by Jackson's supporters and made traditional by the Whigs in the Log Cabin Campaign of 1840. Would such changes in politics be for the better?

Preview & Review

Use these questions to guide your reading. Answer the questions after completing Section 1.
Understanding Issues, Events, & Ideas. How did the writings of Irving and Cooper reflect the American character and experience?
1. What was the Era of Good Feelings?
2. How did advances in technology improve Americans' lives?
3. What were advantages of regional specialization?
Thinking Critically. What characters in modern stories or movies does Deerslayer remind you of?

1. THE ERA OF GOOD FEELINGS

Monroe's Presidency

President James Monroe was one of the luckiest persons ever to hold high office in the United States. He got on easily with most people, but he was really quite an ordinary fellow. He was little brighter than the next person. He seldom had an original idea. Nevertheless, in his long and happy life he advanced from one success to another. He achieved nearly every goal he set out after. Because the Federalists were so unpopular after the War of 1812, Monroe was elected president in 1816 without serious opposition.

In 1817 he made a goodwill tour of New England. That part of the country had been a Federalist stronghold. Yet everywhere the president went, enthusiastic crowds gathered. Local officials—Federalists and Republicans alike—greeted him warmly. As one Boston newspaper wrote, ''an **Era of Good Feelings**'' had begun. When Monroe ran for reelection in 1820, no one ran against him. Only one presidential elector refused to vote for him.

The country was at peace with all nations. It was prosperous and growing rapidly. There were 15 stars in the flag that Francis Scott Key saw waving over Fort McHenry in 1814 when he wrote ''The

Pennsylvania Academy of Fine Arts

Star-Spangled Banner." By 1821 the flag that flew over the fort had 22 stars. Ohio and Louisiana had become states before the war, but their stars had yet to be added to the flag. Indiana, Illinois, Alabama, Mississippi, and Maine had been admitted to the Union as states in the seven years since the British had fired on Fort McHenry.

American Literature

During the Era of Good Feelings Americans became more aware of the unique qualities of their own culture. At this time the first works of truly American literature were written. There had long been American writers and many books had been published in America. But they were more European in style and content. Now authors wrote about the unique American past, with an emphasis on nature, that was part of the American spirit.

The first American writer to receive worldwide literary acclaim

This Fourth of July celebration in Philadelphia's Centre Square around 1815 is certainly more formal than one imagines the frontier salutes to freedom that must have taken place the same day. Farmers would have come in from the fields and merchants closed up their shops to picnic and watch fireworks. During the Era of Good Feelings, there was probably little of the political speechmaking that later came to be a large part of Fourth of July celebrations.

The Era of Good Feelings   365

was Washington Irving. Irving wrote books on a variety of American subjects: histories of the fur trade, a record of his personal tour of the West, and a four-volume biography of George Washington. Although Irving is often considered one of the early writers of the Romantic Age, he did not believe that a creative artist must be "original." In fact, he is most renowned for two stories from his

Washington Irving

The Sketch Book of Geoffrey Crayon, Gent., published in 1819. Both "Rip Van Winkle" and "The Legend of Sleepy Hollow" draw on old German folktales. But their setting is all American: the Hudson River and Catskill Mountains of Irving's New York home.

Irving's writings are noted for their wit, their portrayal of the American spirit, and their wonderful descriptions of the American landscape. Notice the detailed geographic description in this excerpt from "The Devil and Tom Walker" from *Tales of a Traveler* (1824):

❝ One day that Tom Walker had been to a distant part of the neighborhood, he took what he considered a shortcut homeward, through the swamp. Like most shortcuts, it was an ill-chosen route. The swamp was thickly grown with great gloomy pines and hemlocks, some of them ninety feet high, which made it dark at noonday, and a retreat for the owls in the neighborhood. It was full of pits and quagmires, partly covered with weeds and mosses, where the green surface often betrayed the traveler into a gulf of black, smothering mud; there were also dark and stagnant pools, the abodes [homes] of the tadpole, the bullfrog, and the water snake; where the trunks of pines and hemlocks lay half drowned, half rotting, looking like alligators sleeping in the mire.

Tom had long been picking his way cautiously through this treacherous [dangerous] forest; stepping from tuft to tuft of rushes and roots, which afforded precarious footholds among the deep sloughs [a muddy, swampy area]; or pacing carefully, like a cat, along the prostrate [fallen] trunks of trees; startled now and then by the sudden screaming of the bittern [a bird], or the quacking of a wild duck rising on the wing from some solitary pool. At length he arrived at a firm piece of ground, which ran out like a peninsula into the deep bosom of the swamp. It had been one of the strongholds of the Indians during their wars with the first colonists. Here they had thrown up some kind of

The Granger Collection

fort, . . . used as a place of refuge for their squaws and children. Nothing remained of the old fort but a few embankments, gradually sinking to the level of the surrounding earth, and already overgrown in part by oaks and other forest trees, the foliage [leaves] of which formed a contrast to the dark pines and hemlocks of the swamp. . . .[1]"

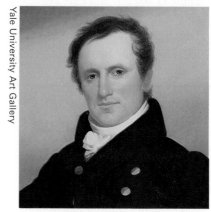

James Fenimore Cooper

Tales of a Traveler celebrated a truly American experience. So did the writings of another notable author of this period, James Fenimore Cooper. Cooper's best-known work, the Leatherstocking tales, is five related novels written about the American frontier. The series includes *The Pioneers, The Last of the Mohicans, The Prairie, The Pathfinder*, and *The Deerslayer*. They portray the life of Natty Bumpo as he journeys westward with the frontier.

Cooper's views of the first Americans is not realistic. Historians have criticized his distortion of historical fact about the Indians. They are either too good or too vicious to be believable. His portraits of conditions on the frontier are more accurate. They represent the first descriptions of the frontier read by a large segment of the American public. His novels also present a range of social conflicts faced by Americans—conflicts between the individual and society, between civilization and the wilderness, and between two different societies (settlers and Indians).

In *The Deerslayer* (1841), the last of the Leatherstocking tales, Bumpo, who was raised by the Delaware Indians, is passing from adolescence to manhood. In this excerpt he has been captured by the Huron Indians and charged with killing one of their warriors. He suddenly makes a daring escape and is chased by the Hurons. Note that although much of the story has the unrealistic quality of a folk tale, the descriptions seem real enough:

" Deerslayer had thrown a bit of dead branch in the canoe, and this was within reach of his arm. Removing the cap he wore, he put it on the end of this stick, and just let it appear over the edge of the canoe, as far as possible from his own person. This ruse [trick] was scarcely adopted before the young man had a proof how much he had underrated the intelligence of his enemies. In contempt of an artifice [trick] so shallow and commonplace, a bullet was fired directly

[1]From *Tales of the Traveler* by Washington Irving

through another part of the canoe, which raised [caused a welt on] his skin. He dropped the cap, and instantly raised it immediately over his head, as a safeguard. It would seem that this second artifice was unseen, or what was more probable, the Hurons, feeling certain of recovering their captive, wished to take him alive.

Deerslayer lay passive a few minutes longer, his eye at the bullethole, however, and much did he rejoice at seeing that he was drifting further and further from the shore. When he looked upward, the treetops had disappeared, but he soon found that the canoe was slowly turning, so as to prevent his getting a view of anything at his peephole but the two extremities of the lake. He now bethought him of the stick, which was crooked, and offered some facilities for rowing, without the necessity of rising. The experiment succeeded on trial, better even than he had hoped, though his great embarrassment [test] was to keep the canoe straight. That this present maneuver was seen soon became apparent by the clamor [loud noise] on the shore, and a bullet entering the stern of the canoe, traversed [traveled] its length, whistling between the arms of our hero, and passed out at the head [of the canoe]. This satisfied the fugitive that he was getting away with tolerable speed and induced [caused] him to increase his efforts. . . . As the sound of voices seemed to grow more distant, however, Deerslayer determined to leave all to drift, until he believed himself beyond the reach of bullets. This was nervous work, but it was the wisest of all the expedients [ways] offered; and the young man was encouraged to persevere [continue] in it by the circumstance that he felt his face fanned by the air, a proof that there was a little more wind.[1] 〟

Technology and Progress

American creativity and ingenuity in technology also soared. Many of America's first technological advances had been borrowed from Great Britain. But soon Americans were innovating on their own. Eli Whitney's revolutionary new method of making muskets with interchangeable parts was used to produce watches, clocks, sewing machines, farm machinery, and even the famed Colt revolver.

Technological breakthroughs seemed to advance every possible activity but none more than farming and manufacturing. Plows made from the new alloys (a mixture of metals) and shaped for differing soil conditions helped farmers cultivate more land. New and better crop varieties and breeds of livestock, the use of crop rotation, and the

[1]From *The Deerslayer* by James Fenimore Cooper

development of fertilizers—such as the marl and guano used by southern tobacco growers—allowed farmers to grow crops on worn out land or in areas that were marginally fertile. Contour plowing and improved drainage techniques protected the topsoil in many areas. These and other advances contributed to the farming boom in America before the Civil War.

American industry enjoyed similar successes. Oliver Evans built a high-pressure steam engine that could be adapted for many purposes. Within a few years it was being used not only in steamboats but to run sawmills and printing presses. Evans also used his engine to power an amazingly modern flour mill he designed. Charles Goodyear discovered vulcanization, a process that toughened rubber. Jacob Perkins developed a nail-making machine. Furnaces and rolling mills replaced local forges in Pennsylvania's iron industry, and the shoe industry was mechanized. Of this burst of American creative genius an English visitor said:

66 We find Americans producing a machine even to peel apples; another to beat eggs; a third to clean knives; a fourth to wring clothes; in fact there is scarcely a purpose to which human hands have been ordinarily employed for which some ingenious attempt is not made to find a substitute in a cheap and efficient labor-saving machine.[1] 99

[1]From *A History of the American People* by Stephan Thernstrom

He did not exaggerate! Only 41 patents were granted to American inventors in 1800; in 1860, 4,357—more than 100 times as many—were issued.

As mechanical devices and innovation played increasingly important roles in the lives of Americans, the study of applied science became part of American education. Beginning in Boston in 1795 a network of mechanics' institutes spread through American cities to train men to build and repair machines. President Madison urged the creation of a national university as a "temple of science." At Harvard and Yale lectures on the exciting frontier of technology became increasingly popular with students. And in 1824 Rensselaer Polytechnic Institute opened "for the purpose of instructing persons who may choose to apply themselves in the application of science to the common purpose of life."

As the United States grew larger and richer, people noticed more differences between one region and another. These differences were in many ways for the good. People in one section produced one thing, those in another section something else. A large percentage of the nation's shoes were made in or near Lynn, Massachusetts. Fairfield County, Connecticut, especially the town of Danbury, was a center of hat manufacturing. Such **specialization** meant that there was a great deal of trading, not only of goods but also of ideas.

Point of View

An English poet viewed America's vigor and self sufficiency with some sorrow.

In the States
With half a heart I
  wander here
    As from an age gone
    by,
A brother—yet though
  young in years,
    An elder brother, I.
You speak another tongue
  than mine,
    Though both were
    English-born.
I toward the night of
  time decline;
    You mount into the
    morn.
Youth shall grow great
  and strong and free,
    But age must still
    decay;
Tomorrow for the
  States—for me,
    England and
    Yesterday.
Robert Louis Stevenson,
1887

Return to the Preview & Review on page 364.

Preview & Review

Use these questions to guide your reading. Answer the questions after completing Section 2.

Understanding Issues, Events, & Ideas. Explain the issues of the election of 1824, using the following words: sectional conflicts, overseer, Conestoga wagon, American system, internal improvements.

1. What caused sectional conflicts? Into which sections did the nation seem divided?
2. Describe differences among the regions.
3. How was the outcome of the election of 1824 determined?
4. What kind of government did the second President Adams believe in?

Thinking Critically. 1. Of the four candidates for president presented in the section, for whom would you have voted? Why? 2. You are heading westward in a Conestoga wagon in 1817. Describe the benefits and drawbacks of this method of travel.

Regional Differences

The Industrial Revolution helped strengthen and diversify the nation's economy and the Transportation Revolution tied its far-flung parts together. Americans were developing a sense of their national identity. Yet regional differences persisted. As American author Thomas Kettell explained in 1860:

❝ The Northern or New England States are endowed [given] by nature with a mountainous and barren soil, which poorly rewards the labor of the farmer. However, its wooded slopes, and tumbling streams, which fall into spacious harbors, showed the first settlers the direction in which their industry [hard work] was to be employed. Shipbuilding and navigation at once became the leading industry, bringing with it wealth.

The harsh rule of the mother country forbade a manufacturing development, and that branch of industry never got a footing in the colonies. Independence from Britain opened up manufacturing, and also provided a large market for the sale of manufactures to the agricultural laborers of the more fertile fields of the Middle and Southern States.

The genius of Northern industry was quick in applying profits earned in commerce to the development of manufacturing. With every increase in population, and every extension of national territory, the New England States gained a larger market for their wares, while the foreign competing supply has been restricted by high duties on imports.

The mountain rivers of New England have become motors, by which annually improving machinery has been driven. These machines require only the attendance of females, but a few years since a non-producing class, to turn out immense quantities of textile fabrics. In the hands of the male population, other branches of industry have multiplied, in a manner which shows the stimulant of an ever-increasing demand.

At about the time that New England became free to manufacture, . . . Charleston, S.C., was no longer regarded as the nearest port to Europe, and New York assumed its proper position, as the leading seaport. The commerce of the Middle States rapidly increased, and with that increase a larger demand for the manufactures of New England was created.

When population spread west of the Allegheny Mountains, and the annexation of Louisiana opened up the Mississippi River to a market for western produce, a new demand for New England manufactures was felt. This was further enhanced by the opening of the Erie Canal. In later years, the vast foreign immigration, pouring over new lands opened up by railroads, has given a further stimulus to the demand for New England manufactures.[1]

These regional differences came to cause conflicts and arguments over government policies. New leaders emerged who tended to represent their own sections of the country rather than the country as a whole. The Era of Good Feelings ended, to be replaced by an era of **sectional conflicts.** The nation seemed divided into three geographic regions: the Northeast, the South, and the West.

The Northeast

The northeastern section, consisting of the New England states, New York, New Jersey, and Pennsylvania, became the major manufacturing area of the United States. Most of the important seaports were also located in this section.

These seaports and other towns were growing rapidly. New York City had 200,000 people by 1830. Europeans began coming to the United States in increasing numbers about 1830, and many settled in New York City and other eastern cities. The hustle and bustle of city life was exciting. Theaters and concert halls were built, book and magazine publishing flourished. But overcrowding turned older neighborhoods into slums. The rich seemed to get richer while the poor grew poorer.

But this was not really the case. Although the rich seized a larger share of the pie than before, the pie itself was larger. The poor were actually getting richer too, in terms of their purchasing power. Wages rose for most people, even laborers and servants. There was a greater variety of consumer goods than ever before.

So the industrial changes in the Northeast brought dramatic improvements in the standard of living of the average family. By 1840 the industrial surge had lifted income per person in the region 35 percent above the national average and almost double the southern average.

These gains made life for people in the Northeast more comfortable and satisfying in many ways. People had a far more varied diet: less bread and more meat, fruit and vegetables most of the year, and more milk for growing children. Homes were larger, warmer, and better lighted. Machine-made clothing fit better and was easier to launder than homespun garments. More low-cost books, magazines, and newspapers were available.

[1]From *Southern Wealth and Northern Profits* by Thomas P. Kettell

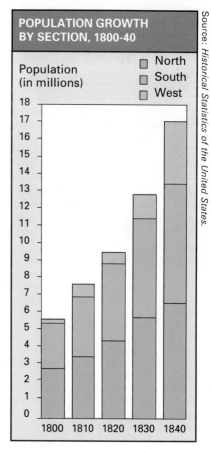

POPULATION GROWTH BY SECTION, 1800-40

Source: *Historical Statistics of the United States.*

LEARNING FROM GRAPHS. *The American population grew rapidly in the 19th century. This graph reflects how much of that growth happened in the nation's three major sections. How does the graph illustrate the increasing attraction of the West?*

Sectional Conflicts   371

But who was the average resident of the Northeast—a Boston merchant who collected fat dividends on textile stocks, a young woman who toiled 72 hours a week in a mill in Lowell, the owner of a large tenement in New York or Philadelphia, or an immigrant laborer living in the slum? In this region there really was no typical, average resident. And because city life had such variety, it is not possible to describe a typical city resident, particularly the poor. Far more is known about a well-to-do family like that of John Ellerton Lodge and Anna Cabot Lodge of Boston.

The Lodges of Boston. The Lodges lived in a big, square stone house in a quiet residential neighborhood. Their home was surrounded by a beautiful garden. There were stables where the Lodge horses and carriage were kept. The house was full of fine English and early American furniture. John Lodge was a merchant whose ships were mostly engaged in trading with China. His business was located on Commercial Wharf. From his office overlooking the harbor, he could see the masts and spars of his many ships. These vessels brought in varied Chinese goods—tea, silk, chinaware, ginger and other spices, even fireworks, which Lodge sold in America.

John Ellerton Lodge was an extremely hard worker who was also active in charitable affairs. Private charity was especially important in those days, for there were few government welfare programs. Lodge was interested in the cultural life of Boston too. He was president of the board of directors of the local opera house.

Despite the growth of cities in the Northeast, agriculture remained the occupation of a large majority of the people. Farmers grew wheat, corn, and other grains and raised cattle, sheep, and hogs. Farms tended to be small, run by a single family with perhaps one or two "hired hands." Since most people had large families, many sons and daughters of farmers moved to the towns and cities when they grew up. Others headed west to seek their fortunes.

John Ellerton Lodge and his wife Anna Cabot Lodge are among those remembered in the popular Boston ditty: "Cabots speak only to Lowells and Lowells speak only to God." But the Lodges, founders of a political dynasty, were great supporters of Boston's cultural life.

The South

The aristocratic traditions and plantation economy of the South made life there dramatically different from life in the Northeast or West. By the South we mean the states south of Pennsylvania and east of the Mississippi River. These were the states where slavery was still legal. As in colonial times, tobacco was the most important cash crop in Maryland, Virginia, and North Carolina. By 1815 and after, cotton replaced rice as the main crop of South Carolina, Georgia, and, as the country grew, of Alabama, Tennessee, and Mississippi too. Southern farmers also grew grain and other food crops and raised hogs and cattle.

Tobacco and cotton were especially important to the South. There was a great demand for these crops in Europe and in the northern states. Southerners did not develop much manufacturing.

The Abbey Aldrich Rockefeller Folk Art Center, Colonial Williamsburg

They could buy the clothing, tools, and other manufactured goods they needed with the money earned by exporting cotton and tobacco.

Cotton was grown on small family farms of a few dozen acres and on large plantations worked by a hundred or more slaves. There were far more small farms than plantations, but the great cotton plantation was the ideal of southern society. The planters were the most influential leaders of the region.

These planters were rich and influential indeed. They had big houses, dozens of slaves, and thousands of acres of prime land. In 1860 only 22 percent of the white population lived in the South, yet two thirds of all the men with estates valued at $100,000 were southerners. Three quarters of the white families had no slaves. Most did own their own small farms. But the most fertile lands with access to transportation were controlled by the planters. Slaveless white families scratched out a living on the less-desirable lands. The richest 10 percent of the farmers in the South owned almost 65 percent of the farm wealth. In addition, the average slaveholder was five times as wealthy as the average northerner and more than ten times richer than the average slaveless southern farmer. Slave labor was the basis of almost every southern fortune.

Planters liked to think of themselves as aristocrats. They proved to be as dominant politically as they were economically. They held more political offices than the slaveless majority. The more powerful the office, the more likely it was held by a planter. Generally non-slaveholders supported the planters politically. As you have read, there were few southern schools and not everyone could attend. The children of wealthy families usually attended college. Few others had a good chance to go to school. Only about 15 percent of school age whites attended school, averaging a mere 11 days of school each year! Half of the white people of Southern Carolina could not read or write in 1850. No wonder the planters controlled politics as well as economics.

Greenville, South Carolina, in 1825 already shows the prosperity of the plantation economy as three-story buildings rise amidst its fields. Notice how these early southern buildings were dramatically different from those in the rest of the country. What were some practical reasons for the South to adopt a different architecture than the Northeast or the West?

John C. and Floride Calhoun managed a 550-acre plantation called Fort Hill; the mansion is now part of the Clemson College campus. Since Calhoun was usually in Washington, it fell to Floride Calhoun to attend to the daily life at Fort Hill. Describe what you imagine a typical day in her life was like.

But the planter was not the typical southerner. Only 16,000 families—one percent of the southern population—had plantations with 40 or more slaves. As in the North, life styles varied so from group to group that no typical southerner emerged. Still, the South was identified with its planters.

The Calhouns of South Carolina. A good example of an important planter was John C. Calhoun, master of Fort Hill plantation in South Carolina. Fort Hill is in the northern part of the state, in hilly country within sight of the Blue Ridge Mountains. John and Floride Calhoun built their place in 1825, after he had been elected vice president of the United States.

Despite their wealth, their many slaves, and his importance as vice president, the Calhouns' life was not that of the idle rich. Floride was responsible for managing the entire household. Besides raising her nine children, she had to make sure that any slave who was ill or injured was properly cared for. She made some of the clothing worn by women slaves. She rarely had a free moment.

When not in Washington, the vice president worked at dozens of farm chores. He was up at dawn and in the fields by 7:30. He checked with his plantation manager, the **overseer.** He experimented with new varieties of crops. He had to keep his eye on every detail of a very large operation.

The West

The West had an amazingly important influence on America's politics, economy, and culture. The flow of people west changed the nation's perspective.

In the early 1800s so many families were moving west that an Englishman on the way to Ohio in 1817 wrote:

> Old America seems to be breaking up and moving westward. We are seldom out of sight as we travel . . . of family groups, behind and before us.

People of every sort were on the move. In the South well-to-do planter families accompanied by a dozen or more slaves shared the roads with poverty-stricken farmers who had nothing more than the clothes on their backs and a few tools. Along the National Road, which crossed the mountains, individuals on horseback passed weary couples pulling handcarts. Many discontented or poor people actually walked all the way from the eastern states to Ohio and Indiana.

Sometimes several families banded together for the trip. One traveler described a group that included 42 children crowded into three wagons. The **Conestoga wagon** was developed to handle the heavy loads of the pioneers. It was built with strong, wide wheels to withstand the ruts and mud and bumps of unpaved roads. A canvas cover protected the travelers from rain and snow and sheltered them

at night. The wagons were not known for speed or comfort. But they were tough, roomy, and not very expensive. A good one cost less than the horse that pulled it.

Of course, after the opening of the Erie Canal across New York in 1825, traveling west became far less difficult. But the trip was never easy. Soon wagons and canals had carried enough people west to populate vast new markets for eastern merchants.

What attracted the hundreds of thousands of settlers—most of them farmers, and some artisans—away from the cleared fields and established towns and cities of the East? The chief answer is: the seemingly unlimited land and opportunity offered by the West.

Throughout the West nearly everyone began as a farmer. For the settlers of Indiana or Alabama the work of clearing land and building a house was little different from what it had been 200 years earlier. Huge trees had to be chopped down, or at least killed by stripping their bark, so that sunlight could shine on the pioneers' first crops. Their first houses were usually made of logs. No one could spare the time or energy to saw logs into boards. The kitchen was often an open shed or lean-to on the side of the cabin. The rugged self-reliance of these frontier settlers has become part of America's self-image.

Historians have long noted the importance of the West on the American character. Westerners seemed the model of self-sufficiency, a trait most Americans considered part of the national identity. There was also a community spirit—everyone pitched in to help out. This made economic, social, and political arrangements more democratic. One settler boasted that "a pleasing feature of western life is the perfect social equality."

Weary travelers were glad to stop their Conestoga wagons at the Fairview Inn on Old Frederick Road. There they could swap stories and get supplies before beginning again on their long journey west. Surely an overnight stay was a luxury. How much do you think a Conestoga wagon or a span of horses cost? Where would you find the answer?

The Fine Arts Museums of San Francisco, M. H. DeYoung Memorial Museum

Mission San Gabriel Arcangel was founded in 1771.

By 1820 there were almost as many people west of the Appalachian Mountains as there had been in the original 13 states at the time of the American Revolution. Settlers thought of this area between the Appalachians and the Mississippi River as the West. It was indeed the western frontier of the United States. By 1850 the land called the Northwest Territory lay in the eastern half of the Middle West. Its location, like other areas of the growing nation, was redefined by the rush west. In this way the meaning of the term "the West" kept changing as the United States grew westward.

The first Americans had lived in western America for perhaps 30,000 years or more. By the 1770s there were many Spanish and Russian settlements, mostly trading posts and missions, in the Far West along the Pacific coastline. These western peoples either had separate societies or were colonists of Spain, Russia, or Great Britain. Some would later come to refer to themselves as Americans. But they did so only after the United States had grown to include them at the western edge of the continent. Then the West came to mean the land between the Rockies and the Pacific Ocean.

Even the present-day use of the terms "West" or "Far West" is not particularly accurate when talking about the nation. What of those most western of all the states—Alaska and Hawaii?

Most western residents owned and operated their own family farms. And although wealth was not evenly distributed, it was not as unequal as in many more-settled areas. Because the price of land was cheaper in the West, it was easier to work one's way up from hired hand to farm owner. In the West it seemed a person, through hard work and ingenuity, could succeed faster than in other sections of the country.

The typical American frontiersman was a rugged individualist, venturing into the unknown wilderness. He moved often, clearing new land and building new shelters. His mobility and self-sufficiency preserved his freedom and independence. Of course westerners wanted to produce and sell surpluses to trade for manufactured goods. Few were any more self-sufficient than city people. But the "typical frontiersman" was a reminder to all Americans of the strength and determination required to open new lands for settlement.

Natty Bumpo, the hero of James Fenimore Cooper's immensely popular Leatherstocking tales, and Daniel Boone are perfect examples of the westerner. Their amazing mobility was a unique characteristic of the American West. Restless movement from place to place was common. Most people moved to find more fertile land or to take advantage of rising land values. But almost always they moved to "get ahead."

Such mobility often affected western community life. Wrote one pioneer:

> 66 Everything shifts under your eye. The present occupants sell, pack up, and depart. Strangers replace them. Before they have gained the confidence of their neighbors, they hear of a better place, pack up, and follow their neighbors.[1] 99

And though the environment was new and unique, the earliest settlers built institutions they had been familiar with. Small western towns often resembled much larger eastern cities in this respect. When 23-year-old Abraham Lincoln arrived in New Salem, Illinois, in 1831, the town had fewer than 150 residents but already supported a school, a Sunday school, even a debating society.

Western life held some advantages for women. They had no more political and legal rights than their eastern sisters. In general they still had few opportunities to engage in work commonly reserved for men. Why was this so? Frontier life was a physical challenge, and more so for women. Aside from helping in the field, women did all the cooking, making and repairing of clothing, and laundering. They cut firewood, carried water, tended the garden and chickens, and made cheese, butter, soap, and candles. And they had children, whom they looked after. An 1862 report by the commissioner of agriculture stated that "on three out of four farms, it is safe to say, the wife works harder, endures more, than any other on the place; more than the husband, more than the farm hand, more than the hired help of the kitchen." But on the frontier there was usually a shortage of labor. It was therefore more common for women to manage large farms, run general stores, and undertake other activities defined as men's work in other parts of the country.

The Lincolns of Indiana. A famous example of the hardships faced by these pioneers is the story of Thomas and Nancy Lincoln, who settled with their two children in Indiana in the winter of 1816. The land was covered with dense forest. Thomas Lincoln, a carpenter as well as a farmer, began by building a "half-faced camp." This was a crude, three-sided shelter of logs and branches, entirely open on the south. It was December when Thomas Lincoln built his camp.

[1]From *A History of the American People* by Stephan Thernstrom

"Settler's Cabin in Indiana" is the work of Karl Bodmer, a Swiss artist, who left his sketch unfinished. But we clearly see the rustic cabin, a spring house for storing provisions in the cool earth, and split rail fences. As this family prospered, how might they improve their cabin and farm?

The family survived only by keeping a roaring fire going day and night in front of the camp. Thomas hastened to build a more permanent log cabin, complete with a stone fireplace and chimney.

That winter the family lived on deer, turkey, and other forest animals shot by Thomas Lincoln. The Lincolns' young son Abraham, who was only seven when they arrived, had to fetch their water from a spring some distance from the cabin. Once the cabin was finished, Abraham helped his father clear land for their first crop. He soon became expert with an axe. (Later, when Abraham Lincoln became a politician, he was known as "the Rail-Splitter" because of his skill at splitting long logs into fence rails.)

The Lincolns suffered many hardships of the frontier. Nancy Lincoln died of a mysterious disease called "the milk sickness." Abraham had almost no formal schooling. He loved to read, but there were few books to be bought or borrowed. After ten years of back-breaking labor, Thomas sold the farm for only $125.

Abraham Lincoln was an exceptional person who would surely have made his mark in any situation. He rose easily in the rough-and-tumble frontier world. He was able to become a lawyer and make an excellent living, despite his humble origins and lack of education. Westerners respected ability and paid little mind to a person's origins.

Corn was usually the first crop planted in the West. It was easy to grow and could feed both the pioneers and their farm animals. After the work of clearing and fencing the land was finished, wheat, tobacco, and cotton would be grown in one place or another. And although the West remained mostly agricultural, small-scale manufacturing of all kinds soon sprang up everywhere. Transportation was so expensive at first that westerners made all kinds of goods for themselves. Everything from nails and pots and stoves to paper and barrels and clocks was made in shops and small plants in dozens of western communities.

The Election of 1824

By 1824 the three sections of the United States had produced strong leaders, each of whom was favored by a particular section. No one had opposed Monroe for president in 1820. Four candidates, each strong in his section of the country, competed for the office when Monroe retired four years later.

One candidate was John Quincy Adams. He seemed the logical choice in 1824 because he was Monroe's secretary of state. Monroe had been Madison's secretary of state before becoming president, and Madison had been Jefferson's. Adams had also been very successful as secretary. The Adams name and his long career of public service were other advantages. But he had few supporters outside New England and the other northeastern states.

The favorite in the southern states was William H. Crawford of Georgia. Crawford was Monroe's secretary of the treasury. Like Adams he had been a diplomat. He had served in the Georgia legislature and in the United States Senate.

Crawford was a tall, attractive man who got on easily with all sorts of people. He was a politician's politician, a master of all the ins and outs of that craft. Although his support was mainly southern, some important northern leaders backed him for president. He seemed likely to be elected, until he suffered a stroke that left him partly paralyzed.

The other two candidates were westerners. One was General Andrew Jackson. He was one of the few nationally popular persons of the time. He was not much of a politician, and he had relatively little interest in sectional issues like roads and tariffs. The second western candidate was Henry Clay of Kentucky. Like Crawford, Clay was handsome and charming. He loved the give-and-take of political debate and the behind-the-scenes negotiations that were necessary to get important bills through Congress.

Clay had been a prominent War Hawk in 1812, but he was best known for his superb ability to solve sectional conflicts by working out clever compromises. Clay was the father of a plan for sectional cooperation that he called the **American System.** Easterners wanted the government to place high tariffs on foreign manufactured goods that competed with their own

Chicago Historical Society

Three times Henry Clay saved the Union when sectional conflict led to crisis. For his efforts he was known as the Great Compromiser. Why is it sometimes hard for people to reach a compromise?

products. Westerners wanted the government to help pay for what were called **internal improvements**—the roads and canals needed to get western goods to market cheaply.

Clay proposed that western members of Congress vote for high tariffs in exchange for eastern votes for internal improvements. By helping each other, he explained, both sections would profit. In 1824 Clay was well known throughout the country because he was speaker, or presiding officer, of the House of Representatives. But his support in the election was only in the West.

When the electoral votes were counted, Jackson had 99, Adams 84, Crawford 41, and Clay 37. Since no one had a majority, under the Constitution the House of Representatives had to choose the president from among the three candidates with the most votes. This meant that Henry Clay was eliminated. But although he could not hold the office himself, Clay decided who would be president. He urged his supporters to vote for Adams, who was then elected.

The Second President Adams

John Quincy Adams, like his father, President John Adams, was intelligent, strong willed, energetic, and totally dedicated to serving his country. Naturally he had been brought up a Federalist. But in the early 1800s he realized that Federalist ideas were out of date. He switched to the Jeffersonian Republican party.

Adams believed firmly, like Alexander Hamilton, that the federal government should encourage the development of manufacturing and stimulate all kinds of economic activity. He considered Clay's American System an excellent idea. He also hoped to establish a national university in Washington, and he urged Congress to spend large sums on scientific research and exploration.

Like his presidential father, John Quincy Adams put service to country ahead of personal gain. He lacked the common touch, and critics found him hard and stern. You might be interested in researching Adam's political career and contributions after he left the presidency.

National Portrait Gallery

Adams favored a government that would look after national interests, but the country was still sharply divided. People were mostly caught up in their own sectional interests. Even as brilliant a politician as Clay or Crawford would have found it difficult to bring the people together. And Adams was a very poor politician. His administration was a disaster.

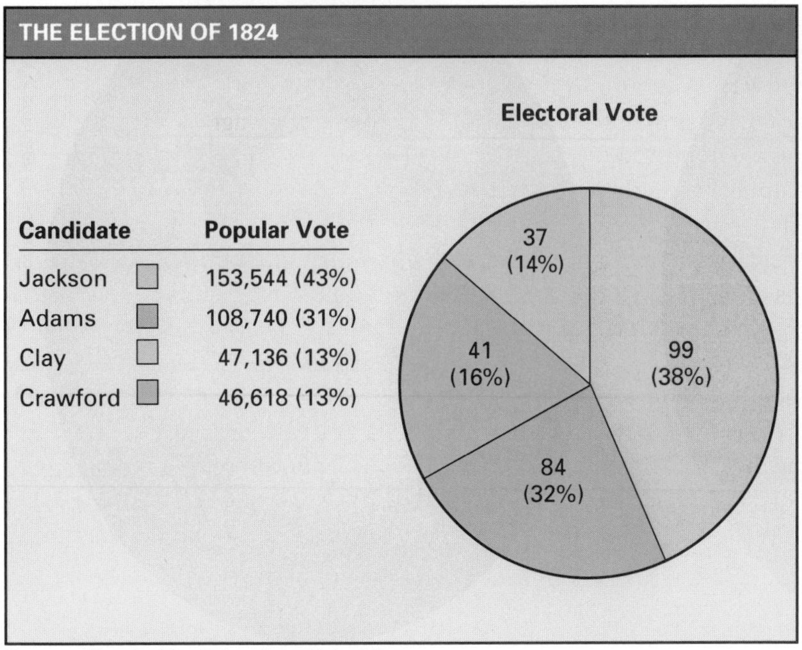
THE ELECTION OF 1824
Electoral Vote
Candidate
Popular Vote
Jackson 153,544 (43%)
Adams 108,740 (31%)
Clay 47,136 (13%)
Crawford 46,618 (13%)
37 (14%)
41 (16%)
99 (38%)
84 (32%)
Source: *Historical Statistics of the United States*

LEARNING FROM GRAPHS. *The figures from the 1824 presidential election show that none of the candidates gained a majority of either the electoral or popular votes, although clearly Jackson received the most of each. Why did Adams become president? How do you think most Americans felt about that outcome?*

Adams was extremely hardworking. Every morning he got up at five o'clock. In the dead of winter he would throw open his window and take a sponge bath with ice-cold water to prepare for his day's work. He assumed that everyone in government was as devoted to duty and as energetic as he was. When his associates did not live up to his expectations, he managed, without intending to, to make them feel guilty.

An example of Adams' clumsiness as a politician was his appointment of Henry Clay as secretary of state. Clay was certainly able, and he had some diplomatic experience. But naming him looked like a political payoff. It had been Clay's friends in the House of Representatives who had cast the votes that made Adams president. Furthermore, the last four secretaries of state had moved up from that office to the presidency. The supporters of Andrew Jackson were outraged. They charged Adams with making a "corrupt bargain" with Clay by promising to try to make Clay his successor in return for votes in the election.

Once in office, Adams quickly showed that he did not know how to use the power of the presidency to get his program adopted. He would not replace government officials who resisted his policies with people who supported them. When he was sure he was right, he was rigid and stubborn. And he was nearly always sure that he was right.

His plan for a national university had no chance of being accepted by Congress. "Let us not recommend anything so unpopular," the practical-minded Henry Clay suggested. But Adams made the recommendation anyway. "I feel it is my indispensable duty," he explained to Clay.

Return to the Preview & Review on page 370.

Andrew Jackson and his wife, Rachel, who died shortly before his inauguration.

Preview & Review

Use these questions to guide your reading. Answer the questions after completing Section 3.
Understanding Issues, Events, & Ideas. Describe Jacksonian democracy, using the following words: Democrats, common man, popular vote, nominating convention, spoils of office, spoils system, rotation in office.

Write a newspaper editorial explaining the conflict over protective tariffs, using some of the following terms: tariff question, Tariff of Abominations, ordinance, ordinance of nullification, ticket, Nullification Crisis.

1. Why did Jackson win in 1828?
2. Why did some people argue that protective tariffs were unconstitutional?
3. Why did Jackson oppose the South Carolina Ordinance of Nullification?

Thinking Critically. Would you have been a supporter of Jeffersonian democracy or Jacksonian democracy? Give reasons for your answer.

3. JACKSON AS PRESIDENT

The Election of Andrew Jackson

By 1828 Adams was discouraged and depressed. None of his policies had succeeded, but he was determined to seek reelection. This time he faced only one opponent, Andrew Jackson. The Jacksonians were now calling themselves simply **Democrats** instead of Democratic-Republicans. This was the formal beginning of the Democratic party.

In those days candidates for president did not themselves campaign. To do so was considered undignified. Their supporters were not so restrained. The campaign of 1828 was bitterly fought and mean spirited.

The Jacksonians said little about issues like the tariff and internal improvements. They again accused Adams of having made a "corrupt bargain" in 1824. When they discovered that he had bought a chess set and a billiard table for the White House, they charged him with wasting public money on gambling devices. One Democratic newspaper claimed that Adams was so pro-British that he intended to move to England and buy a noble title when he retired.

The president's supporters replied with lies of their own. Jackson was a gambler and a murderer, they said. They told shady stories about his mother and his wife, Rachel. Understandably, by the end of the campaign Jackson and Adams were furious with each other.

These lies and wild charges probably had little effect on the election, nor did any of the real issues. Jackson won the election chiefly because he was so popular, while Adams was so ramrod straight and remote from ordinary voters.

Jacksonian Democracy

Jackson's victory marked a turning point in American history. Although he was neither poor nor ordinary in any sense, he presented himself as being in tune with the **common man.** (Women were not counted in politics at that time because they could not vote.) Jackson's position was shrewd politically, and there was some truth to it. He was not an ignorant man, but he was poorly educated. He wrote with a terrible scrawl. His spelling was even worse. He had the manners of a gentleman, but he was capable of behaving like a rowdy. He was in these respects unlike any earlier president.

Jackson was also the first ''westerner'' to occupy the White House. His election signified the beginning of a shift of political power to the West.

After Jackson delivered his inaugural address on March 4, 1829, he held an open house at the White House. Anyone could come. The mansion became so crowded that Jackson was almost crushed to death. Furniture was broken, mud tracked over expensive carpets.

In the Era of the Common Man the White House was open to all. Robert Cruikshank made this clever caricature titled "The President's Levee, or all Creation going to the White House." How did Jackson finally escape his well wishers on inauguration day? Do you think such events should be open to everyone?

Library of Congress

INTERPRETING HISTORY: Jacksonian Democracy

Historians sometimes disagree about the causes of events and the motives of participants. They also sometimes present widely different opinions of historically important people. Andrew Jackson is an example. Historians have portrayed Jackson as an ignorant bully; a military hero; a cruel and ruthless Indian fighter; a champion of "the common man;" and a wise statesman who preserved the Union by resisting nullification. But which of these images is closest to the true man?

No historian would deny that Jackson was a key figure in American history and that he at least reflected the growing spirit of democracy. But the conflicting images of Jackson reflect the fact that he was an extremely complicated man and often an inconsistent one.

To Frederick Jackson Turner, Old Hickory was a frontier hero and a champion of the common citizen. Turner emphasized the role the frontier played in molding Jackson's character and democratic beliefs. Arthur M. Schlesinger's *The Age of Jackson* (1945) and Robert Remini's three-volume biography of Jackson added to Turner's image of Jackson as the great man of the people. Both Schlesinger and Remini credited Jackson with challenging the power of the privileged class and bringing the common citizen into government as never before.

In his famous *Life of Andrew Jackson* (1860), James Parton claimed that while Jackson did much good, he was personally headstrong and "not capable of being convinced" by argument. Jackson's spoils system resulted in widespread governmental corruption, Parton insisted. It discouraged educated people who were qualified for public service from seeking office. Thomas P. Abernethy's *From Frontier to Plantation in Tennessee* (1932) agreed with this unsavory image of Jackson. Abernethy described Jackson as a shrewd politician, an opportunist who preached democracy only to win votes. He was a self-made aristocrat, who opposed the democratic movement in his home state of Tennessee.

Many historical figures like Andrew Jackson present complex and at times contradictory personal and public images. Historians investigate actions and motives in an attempt to provide as accurate a picture of them as possible.

Huge amounts of food and drink were consumed. Jackson finally had to escape out a side door of the White House and spend the night in a nearby hotel.

This was a new kind of democracy, quite different from that of Thomas Jefferson. Jefferson had tried to teach people that public officials were their servants. No person had *rights* superior to those of anyone else. The Jeffersonians believed that the people should have the right to choose their leaders. Yet they assumed that the people would choose exceptional persons to lead them.

The Jacksonians claimed that any ordinary person could be a leader. The common sense of the common man was all that was required to handle public office or a government job.

This faith in ordinary people had already led to important reforms. State property qualifications for voting and holding office were dropped, allowing more people—almost exclusively white males—than ever to vote. More and more, presidential electors were chosen by **popular vote,** or by the people, not by the state legislatures.

Soon national meetings of party leaders began to be held. These **nominating conventions** were attended by delegates from all over the nation. The delegates chose the party's presidential and vice presidential candidates. Then, at the presidential election, voters cast ballots for the electors in their states who were pledged to vote for the candidates selected at the party conventions. Both the Democrats and their opponents adopted this method of choosing candidates.

Not all results of this new faith in the good sense of the common man were for the good. Politicians soon learned to attract voters by slogans and flattery rather than by discussing the issues. Probably this was bound to come with the spread of democratic ideas and the pressures of closely fought elections.

In Jackson's case there was no way to avoid making personality more important than issues. No party had been led by as popular and colorful a figure as "Old Hickory" Jackson, ex-Indian fighter and Hero of New Orleans. Since then, "personality"—and sometimes the lack of it—has decided many an election.

Election campaigns were becoming a spectator sport with voters watching from the sidelines while office seekers competed for what became known as the **spoils of office.** The Jacksonian Democrats went further. They made politics a team sport which a great many ordinary citizens could play. When they won an election, elected officers appointed as many supporters as possible to government jobs. This became known as the **spoils system.**

The Jacksonians then added the idea known as **rotation in office.** After a certain length of time, usually four years, most jobholders were replaced by other members of the team. The purpose was to get as many people as possible involved in party politics by holding out to all loyal party workers the possibility of a government job.

Southerners did not share as fully as those from other sections in the egalitarian urge of Jacksonian democracy and later political reforms. Aristocratic traditions held that only the planter class was qualified to hold office. Few, if any, outside their ranks were ever elected or appointed.

The Idea of Nullification

Jackson was popular in all parts of the country, but sectional disagreements did not end when he was elected president. The **tariff question** was particularly troublesome. Many members of Congress represented districts whose products had to compete with foreign-made goods, such as cotton and woolen cloth. These districts, mostly in the northeastern states, favored high protective tariffs. The southern states produced few such products. They opposed tariffs that would raise the prices of goods they had to buy.

A few months before the presidential election, Congress had passed a tariff law with very high duties. People who opposed it called it the **Tariff of Abominations.** They considered it abominable, or disgusting. Most southerners were among this group.

What made the tariff argument so serious was the belief of some experts that protective tariffs were unconstitutional. They argued

Point of View

A lifetime studying Andrew Jackson led one modern historian to this view.

"At one time in the history of the United States, General Andrew Jackson of Tennessee was honored above all living men. And most dead ones, too. The American people reserved to him their total love and devotion. . . . Nothing within their sovereign power did they deny him. Nothing satisfied the need to acknowledge his greatness or the enormous debt they owed him. As a mark of their devotion and confidence—if not the mark of madness—some men continued to vote for him for President of the United States nearly fifteen years after his death. As the nation stumbled toward the crisis of the Civil War these voters desperately sought to summon him from his tomb to rescue once again his beloved country.[1]"

Robert Remini, 1976

[1]*Andrew Jackson and the Course of the American Empire,* Copyright © 1977 by Robert V. Remini. Harper & Row.

that the Constitution gave Congress the power to tax imports only in order to raise money. To tax imports to keep foreign goods out of the country was an abuse of power and therefore illegal, they said.

One person who considered the Tariff of Abominations unconstitutional was Vice President John C. Calhoun, whose South Carolina cotton plantation we have described. In 1828 Calhoun wrote an essay insisting that a state had the right to prevent an unconstitutional law from being enforced within its territory.

Jefferson and Madison had made a similar argument in the Kentucky and Virginia Resolutions in 1798. But Calhoun went further. He described an orderly way for a state to be free of a law it found unconstitutional. When a state legislature considered a law of Congress unconstitutional, he wrote, it could order a special election to choose delegates to decide the question. If the delegates agreed, they

"Sun of intellectual light & liberty, stand ye still, in masterly inactivity, that the Nation of Carolina may continue to hold Negroes & plant Cotton till the day of Judgment!"

This caricature of John C. Calhoun shows him as the Biblical Joshua commanding the sun to stand still. He wants to hold back time so that "The nation of Carolina may continue to hold Negroes and plant cotton till the day of Judgement." What position of Calhoun's was the cartoonist attacking? What clause in the Constitution would have contributed to Calhoun's distress?

could pass an act, or **ordinance,** called an **ordinance of nullification.** The law would then be *nullified*—that is, cease to exist—in the state.

Neither South Carolina nor any other state tried to nullify the Tariff of Abominations. Calhoun believed that Jackson agreed with him about tariffs. He supported Jackson for president in 1828 and was himself elected to a second term as vice president, running this time with Jackson on the Democratic **ticket,** as the list of candidates was called. He assumed that after the election Congress would pass a new law lowering the tariff.

But the influence of manufacturers in Congress was growing steadily. When a new tariff was finally passed in 1832, it lowered the duties only slightly. Southerners were disappointed and angry.

The Nullification Crisis

The South Carolina legislature decided to put Calhoun's theory of nullification into practice. It ordered a special election. The delegates chosen by the voters met in November 1832 and passed an ordinance nullifying the tariff laws. After February 1, 1833, the collection of tariffs would be prohibited in South Carolina. (The delay was decided upon in hopes that Congress would avoid a showdown by lowering the tariff before the deadline.) When the ordinance was passed, Calhoun resigned as vice president and returned to South Carolina. The legislature then elected him a United States senator.

President Jackson was not particularly interested in tariffs. Unlike Calhoun, he was not brilliant at political theory. But he knew the United States would fall apart if a state could refuse to obey any federal law it did not like. As president he had sworn to protect and defend the Constitution. He therefore acted as decisively as he had acted in 1815 when he learned that General Pakenham's Redcoats were approaching New Orleans.

First Jackson issued a *Proclamation to the People of South Carolina.* This warned them that he would use the army if necessary to enforce tariff laws if nullification was actually tried. Then he announced that he would march personally into South Carolina at the head of his troops and hang the leading nullifiers. "Union men, fear not," he said. *"The Union will be preserved."*

If other southern states had supported South Carolina by nullifying the tariff, civil war would probably have resulted. But most southerners were not ready to break up the Union over tariffs. Northerners were also eager to avoid a fight. In Congress, Calhoun and Henry Clay worked out a compromise tariff bill with a gradual lowering of duties. When it passed and was signed by Jackson, the South Carolina legislature repealed the Ordinance of Nullification.

The **Nullification Crisis** was over. But the question remained unanswered. Did a state have the right to refuse to obey a federal law that it considered unconstitutional? 🖅

Return to the Preview & Review on page 382.

Preview & Review

Use these questions to guide your reading. Answer the questions after completing Section 4.

Understanding Issues, Events, & Ideas. Explain the significance of the following words: Second Bank of the United States, bank note, hard money, bankrupt, "pet bank," inflationary spiral, boom, Panic of 1837, depression.

1. Why did state-chartered banks dislike the Bank of the United States? Why did Jackson dislike it?
2. Why was Jackson's bank veto so popular?
3. How did Jackson try to close the Bank of the United States?
4. What was the result of reckless lending and putting more bank notes into circulation?

Thinking Critically. **1.** You are a student of economics in 1830. Do you agree with Jackson's "hard money" theory? Why or why not? **2.** Imagine that you are Nicholas Biddle. Write a letter to the president of a state bank, explaining the dangers of his issuing too many bank notes. Warn him of what you will do if he persists.

Nicholas Biddle is shown in a fine miniature painted by Henry Inman, c. 1831.

The Bank of the United States

The Nullification Crisis showed Andrew Jackson at his best. He was determined, coolheaded, and confident. He stood firm for the great principle of saving the Union. Yet he was willing to compromise on the particular issue of the tariff. The same cannot be said for his handling of another controversy of his presidency. This was the question of whether or not to renew the charter of the **Second Bank of the United States.**

After the Second Bank of the United States was founded in 1816, many state-chartered banks lost business to it. Several states therefore passed laws placing heavy taxes on branches of the Bank within their borders. The Bank refused to pay these taxes. In the case of *McCulloch v. Maryland* (1819), the Supreme Court declared that the Bank was constitutional and therefore that no state could tax it. That appeared to answer the constitutional question first raised by George Washington when Alexander Hamilton proposed the first Bank of the United States in 1790. After 1819 the new Bank prospered.

Courtesy Nicholas Biddle, Jr.

The president of the Bank, Nicholas Biddle, was an excellent financier. He used the resources of the powerful Bank to stimulate the nation's economy by lending money to businesses to expand their operations. At the same time he tried to prevent state banks from lending money too recklessly.

Banks made loans by issuing paper money to borrowers who put up some sort of security, such as a deed to land, to guarantee that the loan would be repaid. Each bank created its own paper money, with its name printed on the bills. This paper money, called **bank notes,** was supposed to represent gold or silver coins in the bank's safe. These bank notes passed from hand to hand, as money does today. Anyone who received any bank's note had the right to go to that bank and exchange the note for coins, called **hard money.**

So long as people were sure a bank would exchange hard money for bank notes, few would trouble to make the exchange. For this reason banks issued far more notes than they had gold and silver in their vaults. Up to a point this was reasonable and safe.

But some banks were tempted to issue very large amounts of

notes. The more notes issued, the more loans there were earning interest for the bank. This was dangerous, for if people suddenly began turning in these notes, the bank would not have enough gold and silver. It would then be **bankrupt,** and people who owned its paper money or who had deposited their savings in it would be hurt.

However, Nicholas Biddle had a way to force state banks to be conservative about making loans. He could threaten to turn in all of the state bank notes that the Bank of the United States received in the course of its far-flung activities and demand payment in gold or silver in return.

Many state bankers objected to Biddle's policies. They wanted the government to let the Bank go out of business when its 20-year charter ran out in 1836. Then they would be able to make loans more freely and thus earn larger profits.

Andrew Jackson also wanted to do away with the Bank of the United States. His reasoning, however, was far different from that of the state bankers. Jackson was what was called a hard-money man. His reasoning went this way: Bank notes were supposed to represent gold and silver coins. A bank that issued more notes than it had gold and silver in its vaults was committing a fraud. Since *all* banks did so, including the Bank of the United States, Jackson considered them all dangerous. "I do not dislike your Bank any more than all banks," the president told Biddle. And he added that he was "afraid of banks." For this tough old frontier fighter to admit that he was afraid of anything was most unusual. The Bank of the United States was in deep trouble.

Jackson also had more logical reasons for disliking the Bank. He believed that its conservative policies had caused a depression in 1819. And he was convinced that a private corporation ought not to have so much power over the nation's economy. The fact that Biddle had used the Bank to influence political events angered him further. Biddle had employed Senator Daniel Webster and other opponents of Jackson, and he made loans to newspaper editors who supported anti-Jackson candidates.

The Bank Veto

Biddle and supporters of the Bank in Congress knew that Jackson hoped to destroy it. They decided to introduce a bill in Congress to recharter the Bank in 1832, four years before its charter would expire. This would extend the charter before campaigning began for the presidential election of 1832.

Jackson could sign the bill if he believed the Bank was popular, or he could veto it. If he signed it, the Bank would be safe. If he vetoed it, his decision could be used against him in the election. Perhaps he would be defeated. Then Congress could pass another recharter bill which the new president would sign.

New York Historical Society

President Jackson in a cloak attacks the many-headed Bank of the United States. Nicholas Biddle in his top hat is at the center. The heads of the 24 bank directors spring up from the "nasty varmit." Jackson defends himself with his "veto stick," aided by Vice President Van Buren, who is choking Massachusetts and Delaware. Research the story of the Hydra, the many-headed monster of mythology, to see how it was the inspiration for the monster in this cartoon.

Source: *Historical Statistics of the United States*

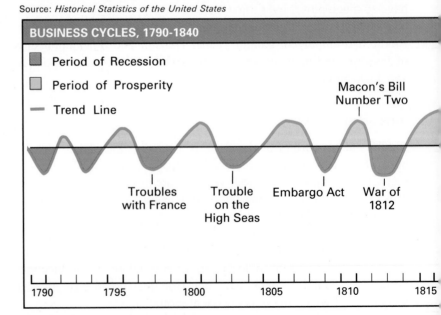

BUSINESS CYCLES, 1790-1840

Period of Recession
Period of Prosperity
Trend Line

Troubles with France

Trouble on the High Seas

Embargo Act

War of 1812

Macon's Bill Number Two

1790   1795   1800   1805   1810   1815

390   THE AGE OF JACKSON

Jackson vetoed the bill. He gave reasons: The Bank was unconstitutional. It was a dangerous financial monopoly. The arguments defied the Supreme Court's ruling in *McCulloch v. Maryland*. This was one of several confrontations between Jackson and the Court.

He also claimed the Bank had allowed a few wealthy investors to make profits from ''the earnings of the American people.'' Many of its stockholders were foreigners.

Some of these arguments made little sense. But most ordinary people were impressed by Jackson's attack on monopoly and uncontrolled wealth. The veto was very popular. The Bank was still in business, but its charter was running out. In the election Jackson defeated his opponent, Henry Clay, by 219 electoral votes to 49.

Boom and Bust

Jackson then set out to close down the Bank of the United States. He began to withdraw the government money that was already in the Bank to pay bills. At the same time he stopped depositing government money in the Bank. Instead he ordered that the income from taxes and land sales be deposited in various state banks. Jackson's opponents charged that the government was showing favoritism in this matter. They called banks that received these deposits ''Jackson's pets'' or **''pet banks.''** This was somewhat unfair because the money was soon spread out among nearly 100 different state banks.

Biddle tried to fight back by forcing state banks to convert their paper money to gold. This was done to limit the number of business loans they could make. His policies only turned more people against the Bank. Many of the banks began to lend money recklessly. More and more bank notes were put into circulation.

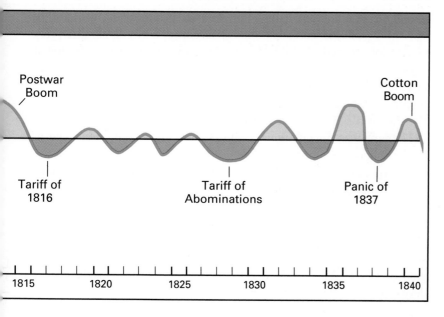

Postwar Boom

Cotton Boom

Tariff of 1816

Tariff of Abominations

Panic of 1837

1815   1820   1825   1830   1835   1840

LEARNING FROM GRAPHS. *American business continually goes through a series of ups and downs known as the business cycle. This graphic shows the cycles between 1790 and 1840. How many recessions did the nation experience in those years? What is one generalization you can make about periods of prosperity?*

The Panic of 1837 has brought hard times to this family with its hungry mother and starving children.

Return to the Preview & Review on page 388.

With so much paper money available, prices began to rise rapidly. Many people borrowed money in order to buy land. The price of city lots soared. As the price of land rose, more people hastened to buy land. The federal government sold undeveloped western lands in enormous amounts. In 1832 government land sales came to $2.6 million. Four years later the total was nearly $25 million.

Jackson's battle with the Bank outlasted his time in office. In 1837 there was an **inflationary spiral**—that is, a continuous rise in prices when the higher cost of one product or service causes the prices of other goods and services to go up too. This inflationary spiral, called a **boom,** ended as most booms do in a sudden collapse of prices and business activity. This collapse, the **Panic of 1837,** was followed by a period when economic activity generally slowed down. This is called a **depression.** Worried depositors all over the country suddenly began rushing to the banks to change their bank notes into gold or silver. Banks swiftly ran out of coin and had to close their doors.

5. JACKSON'S INDIAN POLICY

The Southern Indians

The third great issue of Jackson's presidency was the removal of the southern Indians to undeveloped territory west of the Mississippi River. In 1830 about 120,000 Indians still occupied parts of Florida, Georgia, Alabama, and Mississippi.

Few Americans at the time knew much about these or any Indians beyond what they read in novels such as the Leatherstocking tales and stories they heard. These often portrayed Indians as savages on the warpath. Most people had little or no idea about what the Indians valued. The Cherokee stressed honor, dedication, and bravery. The Shawnee lived by two basic rules: "Do not injure or kill your neighbor, for it is not him or her you injure but yourself," and "Do not wrong or hate your neighbor, for Moneto, the Grandmother, the Supreme Being, loves him or her also as she loves you." To the Shawnee, absolute honesty was the basis for all character. Dishonesty was a crime, the greatest dishonor. These same values were shared by many Indian societies. Surely many Americans would have been surprised at how similar those rules are to the Ten Commandments honored by Christians and Jews.

Ordinary people knew little about Indian religions. Most Indian societies were guided by shamans, or religious leaders. Cherokee shamans conducted religious ceremonies and ministered to the special needs of families. They also reminded the people of Cherokee traditions and the examples set by their ancestors. Shamans continually told Indian parents to teach their children the importance of tribal ideals such as honesty, the rights of others, and bravery. Miami Indian shamans took the boys of the village on vision quests. During these four-day fasts the young braves waited for visions of their personal guardian spirits. The values of their personal guardians were to guide them through life. Girls also had visions of spirits.

Few people realized how the Indians lived. Some Indians east of the Mississippi continued to hunt regularly after settlers began crossing the Appalachians in the 1790s. But most were farmers, tending tribal lands. The Cherokee lived in houses grouped in small settlements or towns. They farmed fields owned by the community. Families were assigned specific farm plots in the field. The entire Cherokee family worked at farming. Even the children had certain tasks, such as cleaning harvested crops or helping to carry tools or produce. Indian societies that wanted to retain a culture based on hunting and gathering asked the United States government to be permitted to move west. By 1807 the Shawnee, Wyandot, Delaware, and Miami had made such requests. The Miami adapted to their new home in an interesting way. Each summer they would leave their forest villages and go west to the prairies to hunt buffalo.

Use these questions to guide your reading. Answer the questions after completing Section 5.
Understanding Issues, Events, & Ideas. Describe Jackson's policy to remove the southern Indians, using the following words: Cherokee Nation, Removal Act, Treaty of Dancing Rabbit Creek.

Write a political analysis of the election of 1840, using the following terms: Whig, Independent Treasury System, Log Cabin Campaign.

1. In what sense did the southern Indians have governments within governments?
2. What did Jackson offer in an attempt to persuade the southern Indians to move west?
3. What was the outcome of the Treaty of Dancing Rabbit Creek?
4. What tactic did the Whigs use to win the election of 1840?

Thinking Critically. 1. You are a Choctaw Indian making the trip west from Mississippi during the winter of 1831–32. Tell about your experiences. 2. In your opinion, did the Log Cabin Campaign of 1840 present General Harrison as a man qualified to be president? Give reasons for your answer.

THE TRAIL OF TEARS

Travelers on the Trail of Tears surely hadn't such warm blankets and sturdy ponies. Yet this is how a later artist came to romanticize the relocation of the Cherokees. Read the excerpt on page 403 for an eyewitness account.

The most tragic story of Indian removal was that of the Cherokees of Georgia. Of all the American Indians, the Cherokees made the greatest effort to accept new customs. They developed a written language and published their own newspaper. They drafted a written constitution for the Cherokee Nation. Many took up farming. Some built houses in the style of southern plantation owners. They even copied their southern neighbors by buying a considerable number of slaves!

The Cherokees would not surrender their independence. They fought against removal in the federal courts. When the Supreme Court upheld their claims, President Jackson ignored the court's decision. In 1835 a small group of Cherokees agreed to go west, but the vast majority still refused.

In 1838 Martin Van Buren, Jackson's successor as president, sent General Winfield Scott to Georgia with orders to round up the Cherokees and force them to leave the area. Seven thousand soldiers swiftly herded together 15,000 Cherokees and marched them off. They were forced to leave nearly all their possessions behind. About 4,000 of them died on the long Trail of Tears to Oklahoma. It was, one white soldier later recorded, "the cruelest work I ever knew."

The southern Indian tribes would not agree to blend into the United States. They insisted on keeping their tribal governments, so there were what amounted to governments within governments in these states. The Indians' attitude was understandable. The southern states treated Indians almost as harshly as they did slaves. They did not allow Indians to vote or testify in court. Yet they wished to tax them and make them serve in the state militia. They refused to recognize the existence of tribal governments.

Jackson backed up the states in these matters. In the opinion of Chief Justice John Marshall in the case of *Worcester v. Georgia* (1832), Georgia law did not extend to the **Cherokee Nation,** which was located entirely within that state. Jackson considered Marshall's decision wrong. Although he had been a fierce Indian fighter, Jackson did not hate Indians. He respected their courage and fighting ability. But since they were unwilling to give up their tribal governments and become merely Georgians, he believed they should move to open territory west of the Mississippi River. The fact that their right to their lands was guaranteed by treaty, Jackson ignored.

This seemed a reasonable proposal to the president. After all, he explained, every year thousands of Americans left family and friends "to seek new homes in distant regions."

But since it would be unfair and maybe dangerous to try to force the Indians to move, Jackson set out to persuade them to go. He offered to pay for their present lands, to transport them west at government expense, and to give them new land beyond the frontier. The place chosen was west of Arkansas in what is now Oklahoma.

Not all Americans favored Jackson's removal policy. State laws passed by Georgia, Alabama, and Mississippi shattered the terms and spirit of treaties between the Indians and the United States. Many Americans felt it was unfair and unjust to break the treaties that granted these Indians the right to live on their lands *forever.* These people blamed Jackson for not protecting the rights of Indians guaranteed by the treaties. Edward Everett, a Massachusetts congressman, was a strong defender of Indians' rights. In a speech to Congress in 1831 Everett expressed the feelings of many of those who opposed removing the Cherokee and other Indian tribes from lands granted to them by treaty. Everett said:

> 66 I cannot disguise my impression that it [the cancellation of the previous Indian treaties] is the greatest question which ever came before Congress, short of the question of peace and war. It concerns not an individual, but entire communities of men, whose fate is wholly in our hands, . . . As I regard it, it is a question of inflicting the pains of banishment [exile] from their native land on seventy or eighty thousand human beings, the greatest part of whom are fixed and attached to their homes in the same way that we are. . . .
>
> The Indians, as was natural, looked to the Government of the United States for protection. It was the quarter [place] whence they had a right to expect it—where, as I think, they ought to have found it. They asked to be

protected in the rights and possessions guaranteed to them by numerous treaties, and demanded the execution [making], in their favor, of laws of the United States governing the intercourse [interactions] of our citizens with the Indian tribes. They came first to the President, deeming [claiming], and rightly, that it was his duty to afford them this protection. They knew . . . he had but one constitutional duty to perform toward the treaties and laws—the duty of executing [enforcing] them. The President refused to afford the protection demanded. . . .

The President acquiesces [accepts passively] in this course, on the part of the States, although it is his sole duty, in reference to this matter, to enforce the law, of which these treaties are a part. Congress last winter made express provision against their violation. They are violated. Let us either make provision to execute [the treaties], or let us abrogate [abolish] them.[1] 99

Of course, many Indians also spoke out against the policy. Speckled Snake, a Creek more than 100 years old, responded in 1829 to Jackson's announcement:

66 Brothers! I have listened to many talks from our great father [American leaders]. When he first came over the wide waters, he was but a little man . . . very little. His legs were cramped by sitting long in his big boat, and he begged for a little land to light his fire on. . . . But when the white man had warmed himself before the Indians fire and had filled himself with their hominy, he became very large. With a step he bestrode the mountains, and his feet covered the plains and the valleys. His hand grasped the eastern and western sea, and his head rested on the moon. Then he became our Great Father. He loved his red children, and he said, 'Get a little further, lest I tread [step] on thee. . . .'

Brothers I have listened to a great many talks from our great father. But they all begin and ended in this: 'Get a little further; you are too near me.'[2] 99

Indian Removal

In 1830 Congress passed a **Removal Act** providing money to carry out Jackson's policy of Indian removal. The first Indians approached were the Choctaws, who lived in central Mississippi. In September 1830 government agents organized a great conference at Dancing Rabbit Creek in Mississippi. Between 5,000 and 6,000 Choctaws

[1]From *Congressional Debates*, 21st Congress, 2nd Session
[2]From *Red Men Calling on the Great White Father* by Katherine C. Turner

attended. The agents supplied food for this huge gathering. They distributed cloth, soap, razors, and other gifts. They promised the Choctaws land in the West, free transportation, expense money for a year while they were settling in their new home, and annual grants to support the tribal government. Any Choctaw who wished to remain in Mississippi as an individual farmer would be given a plot of land. Failure to move, agents warned, could mean destruction of their society. The federal government could offer them no protection.

In the **Treaty of Dancing Rabbit Creek** the Choctaws accepted these terms. The Indians gave up a battle they could not win. Most were filled with a sadness we cannot feel. George M. Harkins, a district chief of the Choctaw Nation, expressed the sadness of his people and the hope that this would be the last injustice toward his tribe:

Under a tin roof are gathered America's last outdoor dwellers of the South. Here council members from 17 tribes have been assembled in 1843 at Tahlequah, the new Cherokee capital in Oklahoma. Some 10,000 delegates attended this meeting. Cherokee chief John Ross called upon his people to promote friendship between the southern exiles and the Plains Indians, their new neighbors.

National Museum of American Art

❝ TO THE AMERICAN PEOPLE:
I ask you in the name of justice for repose [rest], for myself and my injured people. Let us alone—we will not harm you, we want rest. We hope, in the name of justice that another outrage may never be committed against us. . . .

Friends, my attachment to my native land is strong—that cord is now broken; and we must go as wanderers in a strange land! I must go—let me entreat [beg] you to regard us with feelings of kindness, and when the hand of oppression is stretched against us, let me hope that every part of the United States, filling the mountains and valleys, will echo and say stop. . . .[1] ❞

[1]From *Touch the Earth: A Self-Portrait of Indian Existence* by T.C. McLuhan

Colonel Cobb, another Choctaw chief, expressed similar feelings. His was one of the last groups to head westward. Here he addresses a government agent who has come to prepare the tribe for removal:

" Brother! We have listened to your talk, coming from our father, the Great White Chief, at Washington, and my people have called upon me to reply to you. . . .

Brother! we have, as your friends, fought by your side, and have poured out our blood in your defense, but our arms are now broken. You have grown large. My people have become small, and there are none who take pity on them.

Brother! my voice is become weak—you can scarcely hear me. It is not the shout of a warrior, but the wail of an infant. I have lost it in mourning over the desolation and injuries of my people. These are their graves which you see scattered around us, and in the winds which pass through these aged pines we hear the moanings of their departed Ghosts. Their ashes lie here, and we have been left to protect them. Our warriors are nearly all gone to the West, but here are our dead. Will you compel us to go too, and give their bones to the wolves?

Brother! . . . you speak the words of a mighty nation. I am a shadow, and scarcely reach to your knee. My people are scattered and gone; when I shout, I hear my voice in the depths of the forest, but no answering voice comes back to me—all is silent around me! My words therefore must be few. I can now say no more.[1] "

Not many Americans heard or read these sad speeches, or knew to what they referred. Indians as Americans' allies? Few realized that the Oneida and Tuscarora had fed Washington's starving men at Valley Forge when white settlers refused supplies because the army had no money. Few knew Washington had once said: "If these Indians had been our enemies instead of our friends, the war would not have ended in American independence."

So removal proceeded. Jackson was eager to carry out the removal smoothly. As one government agent put it, if the removal could be handled well, it would "break the ice and pave the way for future removals." A full year was devoted to preparations. Still, the move was badly managed.

The first group of Indians set out during the winter of 1831–32. That winter turned out to be bitterly cold, even in Mississippi and Arkansas. Many died of exposure and starvation. Later groups in 1832 and 1833 fared better. All in all, about 15,000 Choctaws settled

[1]From "A Chieftain's 'Farewell Letter' to the American People" in *The American Indian*, vol. 1, no. 3

STRATEGIES FOR SUCCESS

USING PHOTOGRAPHS AS PRIMARY SOURCES

Photographs are important primary sources. Studying them for details can tell you much about a person, event, or time.

On this page are the photographs of the first three presidents of the United States to sit before the camera: John Quincy Adams, *upper right,* Andrew Jackson, *below,* and Martin Van Buren, *lower right.* It is hard today to believe that the camera lets us see so far into the past. In fact, we are able to view the actual images of all but 5 of the 41 presidents.

How to Use Photographs as Primary Sources

Follow these steps to use photographs as primary sources.

1. **Study the subject.** Identify the person, event or location in the photograph.
2. **Check for details.** Note the expression, action, or setting. Look closely at the style of dress and other details.
3. **Don't be misled.** Remember that many scenes are posed and exclude more than is included. Remember also that early photography took such a long time for the exposure that subjects appear unnaturally stiff.

Applying the Strategy

Study the photographs on this page. What do they tell you about these former presidents? About the early to mid-1800s?

For independent practice, see Practicing the Strategy on pages 402–03.

Metropolitan Museum of Art

National Portrait Gallery

George Eastman House

beyond the Mississippi. The federal government had cut costs of the relocation wherever possible. Sometimes the Indians were supplied with spoiled meat and other bad food. Even so, the move still cost much more than had been expected. Nevertheless, Jackson went ahead with the Indian removal policy. More than 45,000 southern Indians were resettled.

The Seminoles refused to sign a treaty of removal. Led by their great chiefs Phillip and Osceola, the Seminoles fought. Joseph Hernández, Florida's first congressional delegate and the first Hispanic in Congress, raised an army of volunteers. Within a few short months, Hernández had captured all the Seminole leaders. By 1842 the Second Seminole War was over.

By the 1840s scarcely an Indian remained in the southern states. The tribes that were removed had suffered heavy losses. For the moment the survivors were free to go their own way, but not for long.

The Log Cabin Campaign of 1840

Martin Van Buren had been secretary of state during Jackson's first term and vice president during his second. Van Buren came from New York. He was a small, red-haired man, one of the shrewdest politicians of his day. He was so clever at political dealing that he was frequently called "the Little Magician" or "the Red Fox."

In 1836, with Jackson's approval, the new Democratic party nominated Van Buren for president. When the opposition, now calling itself the **Whig** party, put up three different presidential candidates, Van Buren won the election easily. He got 170 electoral votes, while his closest opponent, General William Henry Harrison, received only 73.

As president, Van Buren was hurt by the economic depression that followed the Panic of 1837. Many state banks closed. Others had shaky finances. The federal government had no safe place to store tax payments and other income. At Van Buren's urging, Congress established an **Independent Treasury System.** Thereafter, all money due the government was to be paid in gold or silver. This money was simply stored in government vaults until needed.

In 1840 Van Buren sought reelection. This time the Whigs united behind General Harrison. They correctly guessed that this old Indian fighter would have an appeal to voters similar to that of Andrew Jackson. Their strategy was the **Log Cabin Campaign.**

In 1828 the Democrats had ignored most issues and concentrated on describing the virtues of that friend of the common man and savior of his country, Andrew Jackson. Now the Whigs sang the praises of "Old Tippecanoe," the conqueror of Tecumseh. Harrison was a simple man of the people, the Whigs claimed. He lived in a log cabin and always had a warm welcome for strangers. He drank that won-

Part of the hoopla of the 1840 presidential campaign is this sheet music, "General Harrison's Log Cabin March and Quick Step." If you're musical you might try to play this song to hear how a tune sung at a political rally might have sounded over 100 years ago.

derful beverage of the people, homemade hard cider, right out of the jug. On the other hand, the Whigs insisted, Van Buren was an aristocrat who dined off gold plates in the White House and misused the people's money on expensive French wines. When Van Buren tried to discuss issues such as the tariff and banking policy, they shouted, "Van, Van, is a used-up man." Then they launched into speeches describing the Battle of Tippecanoe. At every Whig gathering cider flowed freely.

These tactics worked perfectly. The campaign was mindless but very exciting. Voters by the thousands were fascinated. In the election of 1836, 1.5 million citizens had gone to the polls. In 1840 the total soared to 2.4 million. Harrison won by a big margin, 234 electoral votes to 60. The ideas set in motion by the Jacksonians in 1828 had proved unbeatable. American politics would never be the same.

Return to the Preview & Review on page 393.

CHAPTER 11 REVIEW

Era of Good Feelings

1815					1825

1816
Era of
Good Feelings

★
American
System
adopted

1817
First Seminole
War begins

1818
Jackson
enters
Florida

1824
John Quincy Adams elected

Chapter Summary

Read the statements below. Choose one, and write a paragraph explaining its importance.

1. The Era of Good Feelings after the War of 1812 was brought to an end by sectional quarrels.
2. The nation became divided into the Northeast, South, and West by regional interests.
3. President John Quincy Adams was not very successful at ending sectional conflicts.
4. The election of Andrew Jackson, champion of the common man, in 1828 was a turning point in American history.
5. After 1828 elections and government in general were more democratic, involving more people than ever before.
6. The Tariff of Abominations led to the Nullification Crisis, which Jackson forcefully ended.
7. Jackson's opposition to the Bank of the United States and his banking policies led to a depression called the Panic of 1837.
8. Jackson hoped to move the southern Indians to open western lands, but removal attempts were disasters.
9. The Log Cabin Campaign of 1840 changed election campaigning.

Reviewing Chronological Order

Number your paper 1–5. Then study the time line above and place the following events in the order in which they happened by writing the first next to 1, the second next to 2, and so on.

1. Tariff of Abominations
2. Jackson elected president
3. Trail of Tears
4. Log Cabin Campaign
5. Ordinance of Nullification

Understanding Main Ideas

1. Why were the years after 1817 known as the Era of Good Feelings? Why did it end?
2. How was Henry Clay's American System intended to help both westerners and easterners?
3. Describe the major economic differences among the Northeast, the South, and the West.
4. How did the Tariff of Abominations lead to the Nullification Crisis?
5. Why did Jackson veto the rechartering of the Second Bank of the United States?
6. Describe Jackson's removal of the southern Indians to western lands.
7. Who was "Old Tippecanoe"? Describe his campaign in the election of 1840.

Thinking Critically

1. **Synthesizing.** Imagine that you are Abraham Lincoln at age 18. Write the brief part of your autobiography beginning with the winter of 1816 and ending with the sale of the farm.
2. **Defending a Point of View.** Do you agree or disagree with the Jacksonians' claim that the "common sense of the common man" was the only requirement necessary for working in government? Why?
3. **Solving Problems.** If you had been Van Buren's campaign manager before the election of 1840, how would you attempt to win? Cite specific examples of tactics you would use.

Writing About History: Informative

A Cherokee named Sequoyah invented what is called a syllabary—a system that permitted writing the sounds of spoken Cherokee with 85 different characters. By 1828 a weekly newspaper was published in the Cherokee language. Use your historical imagination and the information in Chapter 11 to write reports for the Cherokee newspaper about events leading to Indian removal.

Practicing the Strategy

Review the strategy on page 399.
Reviewing Photographs as Primary Sources. Study the photographs on page 399, then answer the following questions.

| 8 ff of minations drew Jackson cted president | 1830 Congress passes Removal Act | 1831 First group of Choctaws removed | 1832 Jackson vetoes Bank charter ★ Ordinance of Nullification | 1833 Compromise tariff passed | 1835 Second Seminole War begins | 1836 Martin Van Buren elected | 1837 Financial Panic sweeps country | 1838 Trail of Tears | 1840 Log Cabin Campaign ★ Harrison elected president |

1. How do years of military service and battle show on Andrew Jackson's face?
2. What do John Quincy Adams' posture, clothing, and furnishings tell you about his status and way of life? About the time in which he lived?
3. How would you have felt in the presence of Martin Van Buren if you had been granted an interview with him in 1836?

Using Primary Sources

Many Americans were upset by the removal of the Indians. Among the most outspoken were missionaries who had lived and worked among these Indians. As you read the following excerpt—written by Mr. Jones, a Baptist missionary—think about why the route was called the Trail of Tears. Then answer the questions.

Camp Hetzel, near Cleveland (Miss.), June 16 [1838]. *The Cherokees are nearly all prisoners. They have been dragged from their houses, and encamped at forts and military posts, all over the nation. In Georgia, especially, multitudes were allowed no time to take anything with them, except the clothes they had on. Well-furnished houses were left a prey to plunderers, who like hungry wolves, follow in the train of the captors. These wretches rifle the houses, and strip the helpless, unoffending owners of all they have on earth. Females, who have been habituated to comforts and comparative affluence are driven on foot before the bayonets of brutal men. . . . It is a painful sight. The poor captive . . . his weeping wife almost frantic with terror, surrounded by a group of crying, terrified children . . . is in most cases stripped of the whole [of his property], in one blow.*

1. According to Mr. Jones, what way of life did the Cherokee Indians have before they were taken captive?

2. If you had been a soldier assigned to help capture the Cherokees, why might you not allow the captives to take their belongings with them?
3. Do you think Mr. Jones viewed the American soldiers any differently than he viewed the plunderers? Support your opinion with two examples from the excerpt.

Linking History & Geography

Completion of the National Road gave the economy of the West a boost. By 1853 the road had almost reached the Mississippi River. In order to understand the importance of the National Road, complete the following activities.

1. Draw a map showing the route of the National Road and the cities through which it passed.
2. Write a brief statement relating each of the following to the National Road: carrying freight became cheaper and easier, more people moved to the west, cities in the Ohio Valley grew larger, and land values west of the Appalachians rose.

Enriching Your Study of History

1. **Individual Project.** Prepare a brief campaign speech to endorse John Quincy Adams, William H. Crawford, Andrew Jackson, or Henry Clay for the presidency in 1824. Present your speech to the class, which will hold a mock election after all the speeches have been given.
2. **Cooperative Project.** Work as a team to prepare multimedia presentations. Each team will cover one region—Northeast, South, or West—in the early 1830s. Give an accurate picture of work and home, reporting on as many details as you can find through research.

Chapter 11 Review   403

CHAPTER 12

Manifest Destiny

This chapter describes the popular attitude of the 1840s that the United States was destined to dominate the entire continent, all the way west to the Pacific. First, Texas joined the Union. After war with Mexico, California and the territories of the Southwest became part of the United States. Oregon was settled and the boundary dispute with the British was resolved by compromise in 1846. Early settlers in the West included Spanish missionaries and the *rancheros* in California, the people who followed the Oregon Trail in caravans of covered wagons, the Mormons of Utah, and the Forty-Niners who flocked to California during the Gold Rush of 1849. As new territories came into the Union, the old question of slavery again arose: Which lands should be free, which slave?

1. THE TEXAS QUESTION

A Troubled President Eyes Texas

William Henry Harrison took the oath of office as president on March 4, 1841. He was 68 years old, then the oldest man elected president. Exactly one month later, on April 4, he died of pneumonia. His successor, Vice President John Tyler of Virginia, was 51, the youngest president up to that time.

John Tyler was the first vice president to become president because of the death of his running mate. He was not a success as president. The Whig party had nominated him only because he was a former Democrat who had opposed the policies of Andrew Jackson. They had not studied his position on important issues. One of these was adding Texas to the Union, which Tyler favored but most Whigs opposed.

National Portrait Gallery

John Tyler

Preview & Review

Use these questions to guide your reading. Answer the questions after completing Section 1.
Understanding Issues, Events, & Ideas. Briefly describe Texas history from 1820 to 1844, using the following words: dark horse, annexation, *ranchero, rancho, presidio, empresario,* Alamo, Goliad, Republic of Texas, San Jacinto.
1. How was life in New Spain somewhat different than life elsewhere in the United States?
2. How did the issue of annexing Texas affect the presidential election of 1844?
3. Why did immigrants to Texas from the United States feel little loyalty to Mexico?
4. Why did President Jackson oppose statehood for Texas?
Thinking Critically. Imagine that you are Stephen F. Austin in 1834. You are in Mexico City to explain the feelings of the Texans about Texan–Mexican conflicts. What would you say to the Mexican leaders.

Tyler's troubles first began when Henry Clay and other Whigs in Congress attempted to push through a bill creating a new Bank of the United States. The Whigs discovered that Tyler considered a federal bank unconstitutional. He vetoed the bill.

The Whig politicians were furious. They referred to Tyler as "His Accidency" instead of "His Excellency." Unfortunately, neither they nor later political leaders learned from this experience. Even today much less attention is paid to the qualifications of vice presidential candidates than presidential ones. Yet eight vice presidents have become president after the death or resignation of their running mates.

Should Texas Join the Union?

Since they disliked him so much, the Whigs did not nominate Tyler for a second term in 1844. Instead they chose Henry Clay, even though he had been defeated for that office twice before, in 1824 and 1832. The Democrats were expected to nominate former president Van Buren.

But a new issue had developed by 1844 that caught even experienced politicians like Clay and Van Buren by surprise. This issue caused Van Buren to lose the Democratic nomination to James K. Polk, a former governor of Tennessee. Polk was what is called a **dark horse** candidate. A dark horse is one who seems to have no chance at the start of a convention but wins the nomination when the favored candidate or candidates cannot obtain the required majority of the delegates.

The new issue was **annexation.** Should the Republic of Texas be annexed, or added to the Union as a state? As we have seen, Texas lay on the Spanish side of the boundary negotiated in the Transcontinental Treaty of 1819. Two years later, Texas became part of independent Mexico when that nation revolted against Spain.

At that time hardly any United States citizens lived in Texas, but pioneers were beginning to trickle in. Their arrival set off a chain of events that eventually led the United States to acquire the vast area of the American Southwest.

This daguerreotype of James K. Polk and his wife, Sarah, is the first taken of a president and first lady. Sarah Polk often advised the president on speeches and correspondence.

Texas' Roots in New Spain

The northern lands of Mexico were mostly inhabited by Indian tribes and by Spanish missionaries and *rancheros*—wealthy ranchers who worked the large *ranchos* (ranches) awarded them by the Mexican government. These were the lands that we know today as the states of Texas, New Mexico, Arizona, California, Nevada, Utah, and part of Colorado and Wyoming. Indians, of course, still controlled much of the region.

Interestingly, the people from the United States were called

Americans, but their neighbors in Mexico were not. This made about as much sense as Columbus calling the first Americans Indians.

The Spaniards based their claim to northern Mexico on the explorations of Coronado and other early travelers. This meant little to the Indians, who tended to send the Spanish on wild goose chases for the Seven Cities of Cibola and other lands of dubious wealth. The Spanish controlled the area only by making alliances with some Indians. This area was part of the Viceroyalty of New Spain, which also included Mexico and all of Central America except Panama. Its capital was Mexico City.

Mexico City lay so far from the new Spanish territory that a nothern capital was created in Santa Fe. The Spanish also began the complicated task of connecting the towns and missions of New Spain by building *El Camino Real* (the King's Road), which joined Mexico City with Veracruz, Santa Fe, and many of the missions in California. Travelers today still follow *El Camino Real*.

The labors and movements of the Spanish did not go unnoticed by the French, Russians, and British in the area. For protection the Spanish began an ambitious program of building forts called presidios, missions, and settlements of various sizes.

The center of life in what is now California lay in the missions and the ranchos. Franciscan priests of the Catholic Church hoped to bring the message of Christianity to the local Indians. To attract followers, they built their missions as cities unto themselves, the church at the center. The influence of this architecture of adobe and tile is much with us today. Covered walkways connected the various buildings. They led to the priests' simple living quarters and to workshops where the Indians were taught to weave, blacksmith, and farm. In the fields outside the mission walls the Indians grew grain and grapes and tended sheep and cattle. Trusted Indians had their own farms nearby.

For the Franciscan priests the one true religion was Catholicism. Missionaries taught the Indians to read and write in their own language as well as in Spanish, explained the mysteries of the church, and taught them to remember the feast days which commemorated the saints. Surely all at Mission San Juan Capistrano could recall that the swallows returned every year on the Feast of St. Joseph. But for some Indians mission life was forced labor. They fled to return to the old ways.

The ranchos placed as deep an imprint on the Spanish communities as the missions. These isolated communities developed far from Mexico City. These were powerful estates with thousands of cattle and sheep to tend. On the ranchos the young men learned to ride and developed nearly all the tools of the American cowhands who came later to the Great Plains.

Spanish traditions and Catholic teachings were strong among the settlers of New Spain. Yet, like the English colonists along the Atlantic Coast, the Spaniards found themselves a far distance from their capital and rulers. They began to think that the lands they worked belonged to them, not to the wealthy governors who mounted horses on saddles trimmed in silver and whose wives wore jeweled combs in their hair. They also began trading with the United States which attracted American families to the area.

Spanish Americans had a strict racial system which they wished to keep intact. Highest were Spaniards born in Spain. Next came Creoles, descendents of the Spanish born in America. These groups held all the power of New Spain. Mestizos, people of Spanish and Indian ancestry came next, then mulattos (people of white and black ancestry), then African Americans. The Indians came last. They were treated as children by the missionaries and abused by the foremen of mines and ranches where they worked.

Revolution in New Spain

Like the American colonists, the settlers of New Spain came to deeply resent the heavy hand of the government in Mexico City. When revolutions began to topple governments in Europe late in the 1700s and early in the 1800s, the Spanish and Portuguese colonies in America also revolted. In 1821 New Spain successfully won its independence and became the independent Republic of Mexico. But sadly in the flush of these victories, Mexicans found that the original purpose of the revolution—to free those who were oppressed by the racial power structure—was hard to put into practice.

Most Spaniards returned to Spain, leaving the leadership of the Republic to Creoles. The struggle to organize the government took three years. Finally Mexico's republic was organized and a constitution proclaimed in 1824. It strictly outlawed slavery, a change that would come to have important consequences when American settlers began to stream into northern Mexico.

Life in Northern Mexico

By 1830 perhaps as many as 50,000 Mexicans, mostly mestizos, lived in the northern part of the territory. Already living on these lands were more than 250,000 Indians. Some, such as the Hopi and Zuñi, married newcomers, became Mexican citizens, and merged their ways of life. Others, the Navajo, Ute, and Apache especially, moved or did battle for their ancestral territories with the new arrivals.

Life in northern Mexico was not much different than life elsewhere in Mexico. Rich landowners still controlled vast *ranchos* and large herds of sheep or cattle, as well as silver or copper mines. Most people worked for the landowners. The missions also owned huge tracts of land and large herds. Here, Indians did most of the work.

There were not many large towns in northern Mexico. Ranches

were far apart and most settlements had only a few buildings. People counted on each other. Men headed the households. They handled the trading and worked outside the home. Upper-class women did not usually go out in public except to go to market or to church. But inside the home the mother made most of the day-to-day decisions, and her children helped and obeyed her. A Mexican boy or girl was expected to be *respetuoso* and *bien educado*—to be respectful of others and to do well the work others depended on.

Before he was very old, a boy joined his father in the fields or rode beside him as he gave orders to his workers. A girl helped her mother go to market, bake, weave, and take care of the younger children. Of course, if the family was wealthy, servants might do many of these jobs. Quite often many members of the same family—grandparents, aunts and uncles—lived close together. A large family meant more hands to help do the work. People learned to work with others and to do what was best for the family. They also learned that when one member of the family did something wrong, all members were disgraced.

Americans in Texas

Into this setting came settlers from America. Moses Austin of Missouri, after losing his money overnight in a financial panic, struck out for Texas. He respected and admired the Mexicans and felt his future lay with them. He was granted a colony in 1821 in what is now Texas, but he died of pneumonia the year following. On his deathbed Moses Austin asked his son Stephen to carry out his dream of colonizing Texas.

As some Americans in the United States did, some Mexicans opposed immigration. Others thought settlers should be attracted to Texas, where they could eventually become citizens. Trade would increase, particularly over what came to be known as the Santa Fe Trail. The second group won the argument and Stephen F. Austin was given a renewal of his father's grant. He thus became an *empresario*—the Mexican term used to describe people who made a business of bringing in settlers. Each empresario received 23,000 acres (9,315 hectares) of land for every 300 families brought into Texas. Austin and his group, the "Old Three Hundred," joined about 6,000 Tejanos—Texans of Mexican descent—living near San Antonio and other small Texas towns. Despite their different backgrounds, Austin and Juan Seguín, a Tejano leader, became friends.

The families who followed Austin each received a grant of land. Most grew cotton on it. They prospered. By 1830 about 20,000 Americans had come to Texas, bringing 2,000 slaves with them.

Stephen F. Austin became a citizen of Mexico and urged that Catholicism be the religion of the colony. Austin was a powerful empresario in Texas, then part of the Mexican state of Coahuila. But

Texans see this painting of Stephen F. Austin at their capitol in Austin. He is shown in his cabin in 1824. Why is Austin considered a hero in Texas? What makes a person a hero?

Austin had difficulty inspiring loyalty to Mexico among the settlers from America. The friendship with the Tejanos aside, most Americans came to feel that Texas was *their* country and that they were the real Texans. Few troubled to learn Spanish. When the Mexican government abolished slavery and sought to end immigration from the United States, the Texans found ways to evade these laws.

The trickle of colonists from the United States and the third-generation Tejanos in Texas gave people a feeling of independence and nationalism. Why should they report to a foreign capital as far away as Mexico City? Hadn't they earned the land by farming and ranching as others had in the westward-moving United States?

Texas Wins Its Independence

Government leaders in Mexico City naturally disliked the Texans' attitude. They tried to stop further immigration to Texas. When Austin came to Mexico City to explain the feelings of the Texans, he was thrown in jail and held for a year without trial. Finally, in 1835, the Texans revolted.

This painting by Theodore Gentilz is thought to be the most accurate view of the final Mexican assault on the Alamo. The original 1885 oil painting is lost. Can you locate the Mexican soldiers and the Texas defenders of the Alamo?

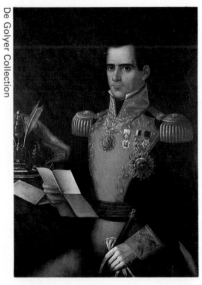

De Golyer Collection

Antonio López de Santa Anna was the general who called himself the Napoleon of the West. In 1836 he led the Mexican army's siege of the Alamo. Why did Santa Anna feel he was right in leading the Mexican army into Texas? Do you think he was right?

To the Mexican government this was a civil war. The president of Mexico, Antonio López de Santa Anna, marched northward at the head of his army to put down the rebellion. In February 1836 he captured San Antonio. But 155 people from the town retreated into the Alamo, the stronghold built by Spanish missionaries. They refused to surrender. Others joined them, including Seguin and nine other Mexicans who were eager to see Texas independent.

Santa Anna's army attacked the Alamo repeatedly. Meanwhile, Seguin and others left the fort to request reinforcements. After ten days of siege, Santa Anna's army broke into the Alamo. Every one of the defenders, who the Mexicans considered traitors, was killed on the spot. Among the dead were Davy Crockett, a colorful frontier character who had represented Tennessee in Congress, and James Bowie, who designed the Bowie knife. A similar blood bath occurred at **Goliad** when some 350 Texans were shot by firing squads.

On March 2, Texans had declared themselves an independent country—the **Republic of Texas.** They set up a temporary government with David G. Burnet as president and Lorenzo de Zavala, a Tejano, as vice president. They then appointed Sam Houston commander of the Texas army. For a time Houston retreated eastward. Then, at **San Jacinto,** he turned and attacked the Mexicans. It was a small battle. Houston had only 783 soldiers, Santa Anna about 1,300. Yet this battle determined who would win the war. On the afternoon of April 21, 1836, Houston surprised the Mexican soldiers. The Texans broke through Santa Anna's defenses. "Forward!" Houston shouted. "Charge! Remember the Alamo! Remember Goliad!"

The Texans rushed into the Mexican camp, this slogan on their lips. The Mexicans fought bravely but were soon defeated. Many died. The others fell back in disorder, calling out fearfully "*Me no*

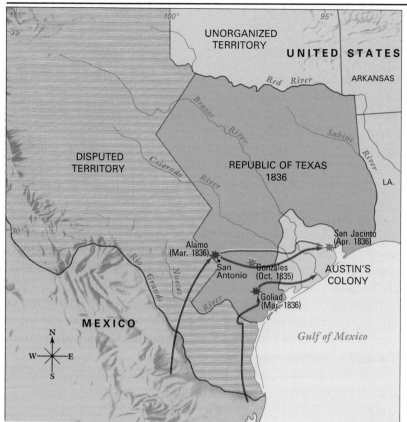

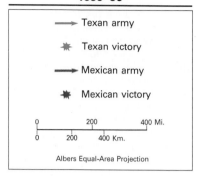

TEXAS WAR
FOR INDEPENDENCE,
1835–36

→ Texan army

✳ Texan victory

➤ Mexican army

✳ Mexican victory

| 0 | 200 | 400 Mi. |
| 0 | 200 | 400 Km. |

Albers Equal-Area Projection

LEARNING FROM MAPS. *Although Texas was still part of Mexico, many Texans viewed Santa Anna's campaign as an invasion. Where did the Texans win battles?*

San Jacinto Museum Association

Sam Houston commanded the Texas army. He sits astride his horse in this oil painting by Steven Seymour Thomas. Why did Houston grant Santa Anna his freedom in 1836?

Alamo," although in fact many of these men were the very ones who had killed the defenders of the mission.

The victory was total. "The fierce vengeance of the Texans could not be resisted," Houston explained. Over 600 Mexicans were killed, and Santa Anna was captured. Houston wisely gave him his freedom in exchange for his promise to take his army out of Texas. The Republic of Texas then elected Houston its first president.

The people of the republic, however, were eager to see Texas become one of the United States. Andrew Jackson, who was still president at the time, was unwilling to accept Texas. He was worried about the political problem that might result if another slave state were admitted to the Union. The next president, Van Buren, took the same position. That is why the Democrats rejected Van Buren as their 1844 presidential candidate.

President Tyler, being a southerner, favored admitting Texas. He had his secretary of state negotiate a treaty of annexation in 1844. The Senate refused to ratify this agreement. In 1844 the Democrats nominated Polk, who favored both slavery and the annexation of Texas. To balance this pro-southern policy, Polk proposed ending the agreement with Great Britain for joint control of the Oregon country. The United States would take over all that area, which extended far beyond the present northern boundary of the nation. 📧

Return to the Preview & Review on page 404.

The Texas Question 411

2. WESTWARD MOVEMENT

Preview & Review

Use these questions to guide your reading. Answer the questions after completing Section 2.
Understanding Issues, Events, & Ideas. Use the following words to describe the westward movement: manifest destiny, Willamette Valley, Sutter's Fort, Oregon Trail.
1. What obstacles faced westward travelers seized with the spirit of manifest destiny?
2. How was the Willamette Valley region in Oregon settled? Why did Sutter's Fort in California attract settlers?
3. How were the wagons moving westward on the Oregon Trail a "community on wheels"?
4. How did Texas and the Oregon Territory enter the Union?
Thinking Critically. 1. You know that many easterners had "Oregon fever" in the 1830s. What do you think attracted pioneers to the Willamette Valley in Oregon? **2.** How does the verse from the song on page 414 express the settlers' view of manifest destiny?

Manifest Destiny

In the 1840s westward expansion became a hot political issue. For 200 years moving west had seemed like climbing up a steep incline—slow and difficult work. It was as though North America were an enormous plank balanced just west of the Mississippi River like a seesaw. Once the midpoint was passed, the balance tilted. The road ahead now seemed downhill, therefore easy.

People rushed westward eagerly. Suddenly it appeared possible that the entire continent might be theirs! This new attitude was given a name by a writer named John L. O'Sullivan. It was, O'Sullivan announced, **manifest destiny**—that is, the obvious future role of the people of the United States—"to overspread the continent." To many Americans this also meant it was God's will that they conquer the Indians, a convenient religious and political idea.

The way west only seemed easy. Wild animals and mighty forests lay in the path of eastern travelers. John Adams had written of "conquering" the West "from the trees and rocks and wild beasts." The pioneers of the 1840s had to cross rugged and dangerous country to reach the Pacific Coast. But neither the Rocky Mountains nor the great western desert could stop them. One enthusiastic speaker referred to the Rockies as "mere molehills."

Beyond the Rocky Mountains lay an enormous land of towering mountains, magnificent forests, and fertile valleys drained by rivers teeming with fish. This area is now called the Pacific Northwest. In the 1800s it was known as the Oregon Country or simply as Oregon. Oregon stretched northward from 42°N—the northern border of California—to 54°40′N—the southern boundary of Alaska.

Until the early 1820s Oregon had been claimed by four countries—Spain, Russia, Britain, and the United States. Spain gave up its claim in 1819 in the Transcontinental Treaty. Russia, which had built several forts to protect its fur trappers, withdrew in 1825. The United States and Great Britain agreed to joint occupation.

Sailors and fur traders were the first Americans interested in Oregon. Soon after the Lewis and Clark expedition the Rocky Mountain Fur Company started business. It hired rugged "mountain men" who roamed the West collecting animal skins, or pelts. These mountain men followed Indian trails or cut new ones through the mountains, establishing paths that were later used by settlers moving west. Another successful venture was the American Fur Company, started by John Jacob Astor a German immigrant. By the 1820s it controlled most of the western fur trade.

The movement west began in the 1830s when a few Christian missionaries settled in the **Willamette Valley** in Oregon. Among the first to make the six-month journey was Jason Lee, a Methodist sent

William Henry Jackson, who painted this view of Sutter's Fort in 1941, was a photographer who 'painted in' the historical additions of mules and mounted horsemen. What are some reasons pioneers might have been attracted to Sutter's Fort?

to preach to the Indians. Samuel Parker, a Presbyterian minister, followed a year later. Then in 1836 four Presbyterian missionaries—Marcus Whitman, Narcissa Prentice Whitman, Henry Spalding, and Elizabeth Spalding—made the long, hard trip across the mountains to minister to the Flathead and Nez Perce Indians. In 1840 Father Pierre de Smet, a Jesuit priest, arrived in the Oregon country.

The missionaries had little success in persuading the local Indians to become Christians. But their descriptions of the country began to attract more easterners. They described a fertile valley, where water was plentiful. Abundant rain fell on the western slopes of the Cascade Range, feeding numerous streams and the Willamette River. By 1840 about 120 families were living there. As you will read, such availability of water was crucial to western settlement.

Others were making their way to the Mexican province of California. John A. Sutter was one of the first from the United States to do so. Sutter had immigrated to America from Switzerland in 1834. From New York he had made his way to Oregon. Then he sailed to the Hawaiian Islands. In Hawaii he purchased a ship and transported a cargo of local produce to San Francisco.

Somehow Sutter persuaded the Mexican governor of California to grant him a large tract of land in the Sacramento River valley. He settled on the American River, a branch of the Sacramento, in 1839. Gradually he built a fortified town, which he called **Sutter's Fort.** The entire place was surrounded by a thick wall 18 feet high (about 6 meters) topped with cannon for protection against unfriendly Indians. Sutter's Fort attracted weary, westward-moving pioneers the way a magnet attracts iron.

The Oregon Trail

From small beginnings there came a mass movement westward by 1843. All over the northern states people, many ruined by the Panic of 1837, caught what they called "Oregon fever" and prepared to move west. They gathered in groups in western Missouri to make the 2,000-mile voyage (3,200-kilometer) over the **Oregon Trail.** This trail followed the Platte River to Fort Laramie in Wyoming and then crossed the Rockies by way of South Pass before descending to Oregon along the Snake and Columbia rivers.

One such group set out on May 21, 1843. One of its guides was Marcus Whitman, the early missionary settler in Oregon who had returned east on church business. Almost a thousand people were involved. They rode in 120 canvas-covered wagons pulled by oxen. About 5,000 cattle and a small army of dogs accompanied them.

Such a large group was really a community on wheels. Because much of the trail crossed Indian territory, the caravan had to be ruled like an army. An elected council of ten settled disputes. A guide or pilot planned the route and decided where and when to stop for food and rest. Each wagon had its special place in the caravan. A bugler summoned everyone to rise at dawn and signaled the time to settle down for the night. Each night the wagons were formed in a great circle as protection against possible Indian attack.

The group traveled 15 or 20 miles (24 to 32 kilometers) on an average day. Getting the entire company across a river could take as long as five days, for there were no ferries or bridges along the way. Nevertheless, progress was steady. On October 27, 1843, the caravan reached the Willamette Valley safely.

The next year five groups made the trip overland to Oregon and California. Although California belonged to Mexico and control of Oregon was in dispute with the British, these pioneers gave no thought to the fact that they were going to foreign countries. In this respect they were like the people who were settling Texas. On the Oregon Trail people sang:

❝ The hip-hurrah for the prairie life!
Hip-hurrah for the mountain strife!
And if rifles must crack, if swords we must draw,
Our country forever, hurrah, hurrah! ❞

Still, leaving home was a bittersweet experience for many of the pioneers. Elizabeth Goltra wrote in her diary as she was leaving Kansas for Oregon in 1853:

❝ Today we started across the dreary plains. Sad are the thoughts that steal over the reflecting mind. I am leaving my home, my early friends and associates never to see them again, exchanging the disinterested solicitude [attention] of fond friends for the cold and unsympathetic friendship of strangers. . . . Hard indeed that heart that does not drop a tear as these thoughts roll across the mind.[1] ❞

[1]From "Diaries and Reminiscences of Women on the Oregon Trail: A Study in Consciousness," an unpublished essay by Amy Kesselman

STRATEGIES FOR SUCCESS

LEARNING FROM ART

Many books you study, as *The Story of America* does, contain reproductions of famous paintings and other artwork. Gathering information from these sources is a key strategy to understanding history. An engraving such as Currier & Ives' "Westward the Course of Empire Takes Its Way," shown below, can provide a great deal of historical information. This engraving, made by Fanny Palmer and James M. Ives in 1868, gives the artists' view of manifest destiny. More importantly, such a work of art can help shape the ideas of a nation. This Currier & Ives print has appeared in more history books than any other and greatly influenced the way Americans in the 1870s and 1880s viewed westward expansion.

How to Gather Information from Art

To effectively gather information from art, follow these steps.

1. **Determine the subject of the work.** Check its title or caption. Study the people, objects, and actions it depicts.
2. **Examine the details.** If it is a painting or drawing, study the background. Remember that *all* the visual evidence is important to understanding the historical event or period.

3. **Note the artist's point of view.** If possible, determine whether the events are portrayed favorably or unfavorably. Ask what impact the work might have on other viewers.
4. **Use the information carefully.** Remember that a work of art may be an artist's *interpretation* of an event. Try to determine how accurately it depicts the event before deciding how to use the information.

Applying the Strategy

James M. Ives and Nathaniel Currier were America's most popular makers of hand-colored prints (pictures from engravings). Carefully study their print below. The main title is "Across the Continent." Close study discloses a picture full of clues to the artists' optimistic view of the westward movement. Note the locomotive puffing on its endless tracks, hardworking men and women building their community, covered wagons heading for further frontiers, and the vast open spaces of yet-to-be-settled America. See if you can spot other historical details.

For independent practice, see Practicing the Strategy on page 446.

Museum of the City of New York

People were leaving their families, their friends behind. Most had a great sense of loss. Imagine what Mary Stewart felt when she began the following poem as her first diary entry:

To Martha

    " Oh friend, I am gone forever, I cannot see you now
        The damp comes to my brow. . . .
        Ah, then I think how different our fates in life were cast,
        I think how oft we sat and played
        Upon some mossy stone,
        How we would act and do when we were big girls grown
        And would always live so near
        That I could always come to you,
        And you would come to me, and this we would always do
        When sickness came in fevered brow and burning through each
          vein . . .[1] "

The trip was long, tiring, and hazardous. Men drove the wagons, herded the cattle, scouted the trail for Indians, and made the decisions on where to camp. Women did the cooking and washing and much more. Martha Ann Morrison, a girl of 13, remembered:

    " The women helped pitch the tents, helped unload, and
        helped yoking up the cattle. Some of the women did nearly
        all the yoking; many times the men were off [away from
        camp, usually scouting for Indians]. One time my father

Benjamin Franklin Reinhart painted "The Emigrant Train Bedding Down for the Night" in 1867. Pioneers did not use cumbersome Conestoga wagons to cross the country nor find water this easily. What does the painting suggest about the roles of women and children in wagon trains?

[1]From ''Diaries and Reminiscences of Women on the Oregon Trail: A Study in Consciousness,'' an unpublished essay by Amy Kesselman

The Corcoran Gallery of Art

was away hunting cattle driven off by the Indians, and that left Mother and the children to attend to everything. . . .[1]"

Children were also called upon to do their share of heavy jobs. Most, when they stayed healthy, saw the trip as a great adventure. But along the way thousands of people died, many of them children. Lodisa Frizzel, headed to California in 1852, remarked:

"That this journey is tiresome no one will doubt, that it is perilous, the deaths of many will testify, and the heart has a thousand misgivings, and the mind is tortured with anxiety, and often as I passed the freshly made graves, I have glanced at the side boards of the wagon, not knowing how soon it might serve as the coffin for some one of us. . . .[2]"

[1]From *Women's Diaries of the Westward Journey* by William Schlissel
[2]From "Diaries and Reminiscences of Women on the Oregon Trail: A Study in Consciousness," an unpublished essay by Amy Kesselman

Taking Texas and Oregon

Manifest destiny was a national mood, but people in different sections wanted different parts of the West. Southerners had little interest in Oregon. They wanted Texas and some even hoped to annex Cuba and parts of Central America. More important, many northerners were strongly opposed to adding Texas to the Union because that would mean opening more territory to slavery. In short, manifest destiny could be both a divisive and a unifying force.

This was the situation when the presidential election of 1844 was held. James K. Polk emerged the winner. Polk had promised to bring both Texas and Oregon into the Union. He was soon able to do so.

Congress voted to annex Texas by treaty a few months after the election. In December 1845 Texas became a state. At the same time Polk began diplomatic negotiations with the British about Oregon. He made it clear that if England did not agree to a satisfactory settlement, he was ready to take the territory by force. The British had no stomach for a fight over Oregon. But they were unwilling to surrender all of the area. In 1846, after considerable discussion, the negotiators reached a compromise. The territory was divided by extending the already existing boundary between the United States and Canada to the West Coast.

Polk also had hoped to take New Mexico and California. Unfortunately, he could not claim, as he had with Texas and Oregon, that the lands were already peopled by Americans. There were almost none in New Mexico and less than 700 in California, compared with 11,000 Mexicans. General Santa Anna, back in power in Mexico City, refused to discuss the sale of the two provinces. To gain those territories would take a little longer. 🖅

Texas State Library and Archives

The Lone Star flag was adopted as the national banner of Texas in 1839. It is today the state flag. By what process did Texas become a state in 1845?

Return to the Preview & Review on page 412.

3. WAR WITH MEXICO

Use these questions to guide your reading. Answer the questions after completing Section 3.
Understanding Issues, Events, & Ideas. Describe the war with Mexico, using the following words: Rio Grande, Nueces River, Battle of Buena Vista, Santa Fe, Bear Flag Revolt, Republic of California, Veracruz, Cerro Gordo, Puebla, Mexico City, Treaty of Guadalupe Hidalgo.
1. Why did the United States go to war with Mexico?
2. How did California respond to the Mexican War?
3. Why did Polk put General Scott in command of the army sent to capture Mexico City?
Thinking Critically. **1.** You are Nicholas P. Trist in the midst of negotiating a treaty with Mexico when you receive Polk's message to break off discussions. Why do you ignore Polk's message? **2.** You are an American rancher in Texas. Write a letter to your family in Boston describing the differences between your former way of life in New England and your new life influenced by your Mexican neighbors' culture. Also list aspects of your culture that your neighbors have adopted.

At right is Taylor's 1847 portrait by William Garl Brown, Jr.

Message to Congress: "War Exists"

Annexing Texas led to war. Although Mexico had not been able to prevent Texas from becoming independent, the Mexicans did not accept the Texans' claim that the new republic extended all the way to the **Rio Grande,** the "Great River." They insisted that the **Nueces River,** a river farther to the north and east, was the boundary between Mexico and Texas.

After Texas was annexed, President Polk sent troops commanded by General Zachary Taylor across the Nueces River. Then he sent a diplomatic representative, John Slidell, to Mexico City. The Mexican leaders were unwilling even to discuss the boundary question. National pride was involved. The Mexicans again stated their claim for all of Texas. Polk then ordered General Taylor to march straight to the Rio Grande. When he did so, a Mexican force crossed the river and attacked one of his patrols. When word of this skirmish reached Washington, Polk informed Congress: "War exists." Congress promptly declared war on Mexico on May 13, 1846.

Chicago Historical Society

Despite the Texas and Oregon gains, war with Mexico was instantly unpopular with easterners who opposed slavery. Polk had deliberately provoked the war, critics argued—and many historians today agree. They thought the true cause of the war was Polk's determination to have New Mexico and California for the United States. Abraham Lincoln, a young Illinois lawyer serving his only term in Congress, introduced his Spot Resolutions. In them he questioned whether the "spot" on the north bank of the Rio Grande where American blood had been shed was actually United States soil. If we were going to declare war, he said, we'd better be sure.

Not even everyone in the army agreed with the war. Years later, in his autobiography, then Captain Ulysses S. Grant remembered, "I was bitterly opposed to the measure [war], and to this day regard the war . . . as one of the most unjust ever waged by a stronger against a weaker nation."

The Early Fighting

United States forces fought the Mexican War on land and sea. They had the easiest time in California and New Mexico, which included present-day Arizona. For one thing, the Mexicans had not kept strong forces at their presidios in this region. Equally important, many wealthy Mexican families had political, economic, even ties by marriage with American settlers. Many did not resist the invaders.

In the summer of 1846 troops led by General Stephen Kearny marched southwestward from Fort Leavenworth on the Missouri River. They took Santa Fe, winning control of New Mexico. Kearny then pushed on to sourthern California. There Mexican resistance was stiff, but Kearny managed to get the upper hand. From San Diego he advanced his army up the coast to Los Angeles and Santa Barbara.

In California John C. Frémont joined the U.S. naval squadron and a militia force raised by residents of the area around Sutter's

"The Battle of Buena Vista," painted in 1847 by Carl Nebel, shows General Zachary Taylor astride 'Old Whitey' at the center.

Fort to defeat the local Mexican forces. For this **Bear Flag Revolt,** they designed a simple flag, a grizzly bear on a plain background and proclaimed themselves the **Republic of California.** By February 1847 the important towns of San Francisco, Los Angeles, and San Diego had been won from Mexico.

CALIFORNIA REPUBLIC

California Printing Office

The war did not go quite as smoothly in Mexico. Mexico was a large country far from the supply depots of the United States. The fighting was often fierce, especially in the region just south of the Rio Grande. Yet the U.S. forces quickly defeated the Mexicans. General Taylor was not a brilliant commmander, but his well-trained troops were devoted to him. By autumn of 1846 they had won three major battles. In February 1847, in the **Battle of Buena Vista,** they routed the last important force in northern Mexico.

The Capture of Mexico City

These early victories posed a political problem for President Polk. General Taylor had become a national hero. He was a plain, unassuming soldier made in the mold of William Henry Harrison and Andrew Jackson. His troops affectionately called him ''Old Rough and Ready.'' Taylor belonged to the Whig party. Polk was afraid that Taylor might decide to run for president in 1848. The president had no intention of seeking a second term himself, but as a loyal Democrat he did not want Taylor to be too successful on the battlefield. He therefore put a different general, Winfield Scott, in command of the army which had the task of capturing Mexico City.

General Scott, a powerful man nearly six feet, six inches tall, was also a Whig. He lacked Taylor's easy-going style. He was stuffy and rather vain. Behind his back his troops called him ''Old Fuss and Feathers.'' Scott therefore seemed less of a threat to the Democrats than Taylor. Fortunately for the nation, Scott was an excellent general, actually far more competent than Taylor.

Scott approached Mexico City from the sea. In March 1847 his fleet of 200 ships put 10,000 men ashore near the city of **Veracruz** on Mexico's east coast. The United States army captured Veracruz easily and then marched inland, following the route of Cortés. They won an important battle at **Cerro Gordo** and another at **Puebla.** By September they were at the outskirts of **Mexico City.**

There the showdown clash occurred. It was hard fought with 1,000 United States soldiers and 4,000 Mexican soldiers killed or wounded. But again Scott's troops were victorious. The capital city was occupied, the Mexicans forced to surrender.

The Treaty of Guadalupe Hidalgo

Polk had attached a state department official, Nicholas P. Trist, to Scott's army. Trist's task was to negotiate a peace treaty once the Mexicans had been defeated. In addition to insisting on the Rio Grande boundary of Texas, he was told by Polk to offer as much as $30 million if Mexico would sell California and the rest of the Southwest to the United States.

Trist proved to be an excellent negotiator. He persuaded the defeated Mexicans to turn over all that territory for a little more than $18 million. The negotiations took a great deal of time, however, because there was great confusion in Mexico City. The government had almost collapsed.

The Stars and Stripes flies over the shore near Veracruz as an artist of the day depicts the landing of some of the 200 ships and 10,000 men who came ashore in eastern Mexico. Explain how this painting might be considered patriotic.

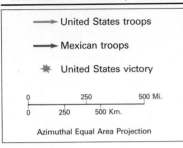

THE MEXICAN WAR, 1846–47

→ United States troops

→ Mexican troops

✳ United States victory

```
0        250        500 Mi.
0     250    500 Km.
```

Azimuthal Equal Area Projection

LEARNING FROM MAPS. *Notice the disputed area between the Nueces River and the Rio Grande. Judging from the map, how did the United States navy contribute to the victory?*

President Polk became impatient and also somewhat greedy. Mexico had been so thoroughly beaten that he began to think of demanding even more territory. He sent Trist a message ordering him to break off the discussions and return to Washington. Trist ignored the order. He completed the negotiations with the Mexican government and sent the resulting **Treaty of Guadalupe Hidalgo** back to the United States.

President Polk was furious. Out of pure spite he had Trist fired from his state department job. He would not even pay Trist his salary for the time he had spent in Mexico.

Nevertheless, Polk found that he had to agree to the Treaty of Guadalupe Hidalgo. The terms, after all, were better than he had hoped for. And the war had become extremely unpopular in some parts of the country. Particularly in the North, many people felt that there had been no reason for seizing so much of Mexico over what was really a minor boundary dispute. In Congress Senator Thomas Corwin expressed their feelings:

❝ Mr. President, . . . I voted for a bill somewhat like the present at the last session—our army was then in the neighborhood of our line [border]. I then hoped that the President did sincerely desire peace. Our army had not then penetrated far into Mexico, and I did hope, that with the two millions [dollars] then proposed, we might get peace, and avoid the slaughter, the shame, the crime, of an aggressive, unprovoked war. But now you have overrun half of Mexico—you have exasperated and irritated her people— . . . and boldly ask her to give up New Mexico and California; and as a bribe to her patriotism, seizing on her property, you offer three million [dollars] to pay the soldiers she has called out to repel your invasion, on condition she will give up to you at least one-third of her whole territory. . . .

What is the territory, Mr. President, which you propose to wrest from Mexico? It is consecrated to the heart of the Mexican by many a well-fought battle with his old Castilian master [against the Spanish in the Mexican Revolution]. His Bunker Hills, and Saratogas, and Yorktowns, are there! The Mexican can say, "There I bled for liberty! and shall I surrender that consecrated home of my affections to the Anglo-Saxon [descendants of the English] invaders? What do they want with it? They have Texas already. They have possessed themselves of the territory between the Nueces and the Rio Grande. What else do they want? . . .

What would be the response? . . . The Senator from Michigan says he must have this. Why, my worthy Christian brother, on what principle of justice? "I want room!"

Sir, look at this pretense [unsupported claim] of want of room. With twenty millions of people, you have about one thousand millions of acres of land, inviting settlement by every conceivable argument, bringing them down to a quarter of a dollar an acre, and allowing every man to squat where he pleases. But the Senator from Michigan says we will be two hundred millions in a few years, and we want room. If I were a Mexican I would tell you, "Have you not room in your own country to bury your dead men? If you come into mine, we will greet you with bloody hands, and welcome you to hospitable graves. . . ."[1]

Adding more territory where slavery might be established was another concern in the North. Polk therefore swallowed his anger and submitted the treaty to the Senate, which ratified it after heated debate.

A Blending of Cultures

After the treaty had been signed, more and more Americans moved into the Southwest. They brought their own language, laws, and ways

[1]From *Appendix to the Congressional Globe,* 29 Congress, 2nd Session

of behaving. Differences in the cultures of the Americans and the Mexicans—75,000 or more in the new U.S. lands—created problems at first.

For families with ties to Americans, adjusting was usually fairly easy. Other Mexicans did not do as well. Many lost their property. To get the prime land held by Mexicans, Americans challenged land titles that had been granted by Spanish or Mexican authorities and held for years. This started long and costly court battles. Whatever the decision, hard feelings resulted.

Under the treaty Mexicans were granted all the rights of American citizenship. Yet their culture, which blended Spanish, Mexican, and Indian ways of life, often was viewed as inferior. Traditions of family loyalty, personal honor, and devout Catholicism were not respected by the newcomers. Poor Mexican Americans suffered most. Many of these newcomers were forced to take low-paying jobs on American ranches, railroads, or in American mines. Mexican American bandits, many of them trying to recover their stolen property or livestock, raided American settlements.

In time, though, the two groups helped change each other's way of life. They borrowed ideas from each other. The Americans learned from the Mexicans how to mine the rich hills of the Southwest. Because they had no mining laws of their own, Americans also used Mexican laws to form their own. They also learned sheep ranching. The tough *churros* of the Mexicans were well-adapted to thrive in dry lands of the Southwest. These sheep had already changed the lives of some of the Indian tribes in the area. Navajo women learned to weave their wool into beautiful, warm blankets colored with Navajo dyes and woven into traditional patterns. Seeing that they could trade their blankets for horses and other things they needed, the Navajo decided to settle down and raise sheep. Now the Americans began to raise sheep too. As you will read later, American cowhands also learned their craft from Mexican *vaqueros*.

The Americans brought tools, seeds, and livestock with them. They had the latest inventions and business techniques. Mexicans adopted the best of these and many other things despite the fact that Americans often treated them like second-class citizens. A new way of life was formed in the Southwest, a system of values and behavior shared by most of the people there. You can see this special way of life today throughout the Southwest. You see it in the music of people like Santiago and Flaco Jiménez and Laura Canales, in the art of Amado Peña and Joan Miró, in the clothes the people wear, in their laws, in their architecture, and in the words they use. It is a way of life with deep roots in three cultures—Indian, Mexican, and American.

Return to the Preview & Review on page 418.

Thomas Gilcrease Institute, Tulsa

The pride of the Spanish rancheros is evident in this color lithograph titled "Hacendado y Su Mayordomo," "The Landowner and His Foreman." The Mexican artist is Julio Michaud. Judging from these riders, were most rancheros wealthy people? How can you tell?

4. THE GOLDEN WEST

California and the Rancheros

The great prize that the United States won in the Mexican War was the province of California. In the 1840s most of the region beyond the Rocky Mountains was untouched by any other than its native Indians. But, as we have seen, the Spanish had been living in California and New Mexico since the late 1700s. By the 1830s there were 21 mission settlements in a kind of broken string from San Diego to Sonoma, north of San Francisco. The landholdings of the missions were enormous.

Around the missions founded by the Spanish were clustered large Indian villages, for Father Junípero Serra and other priests had converted thousands of Indians to Christianity. Life for these Indians was very regimented. They did all the work that supported the missions. They tended large herds of cattle and grew corn, grapes, and other crops. They also made cloth, leather goods, wine, soap, and many other manufactured products.

The missions were so prosperous that other Mexicans demanded that the government open the rich mission lands to settlers. In the early 1830s it did so. Thereafter many Mexican citizens with cattle obtained *ranchos* free. These landholders were called *rancheros*. Within a few years 700 *ranchos* were established in California, most of them

Preview & Review

Use these questions to guide your reading. Answer the questions after completing Section 4.
Understanding Issues, Events, & Ideas. Contrast the settlement of Utah with that of California, using the following words: Mormons, Nauvoo, Salt Lake City, Mormon Trail, Law of Riparian Rights, Law of Prior Appropriation, prospector, Gold Rush, Forty-Niner, clipper ship, stake a claim, mining camp, Negro Hill, ghost towns.
1. Compare life in a California mission with life on a *rancho*.
2. How were Mormons able to move so many people westward?
3. Define two laws of water rights.
4. What were some of the means of travel used by the Forty-Niners?
Thinking Critically. You are a prospector who has struck gold in California. Write a letter persuading a relative to join you.

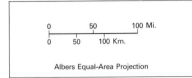

SPANISH MISSIONS IN CALIFORNIA, 1830

```
0        50        100 Mi.
0     50    100 Km.
```

Albers Equal-Area Projection

San Francisco Solano
(Sonoma) 1823
San Rafael 1817
San Francisco
(Mission Dolores) 1776
Santa Clara 1777
San José de Guadalupe 1797
Santa Cruz 1791
San Juan Bautista 1797
San Carlos 1770
La Soledad 1791
CALIFORNIA
San Antonio de Padua 1771
San Miguel 1797
PACIFIC OCEAN
San Luis Obispo 1772
Santa Inés 1804
La Purísima Concepción 1787
San Fernando 1797
Santa Bárbara 1786
San Buena Ventura 1782
San Gabriel Arcángel 1771
San Juan Capistrano 1776
San Luis Rey 1798
San Diego 1769

NEVADA
CALIFORNIA
PACIFIC OCEAN
MEXICO

N
W — E
S

LEARNING FROM MAPS. *The missions were located no more than one day's travel apart. Why are most near the coast?*

about 50,000 acres (20,000 hectares) in area. Each *ranchero* had an enormous amount of land.

Life on one of these great ranches was rich but simple. People ate enormous quantities of meat at every meal. Horses were so plentiful that travelers merely lassoed a new one when their own mounts became tired. Most of the hard work of caring for the herds and raising crops was still done by the Indians, who were even worse off than when they had lived outside the missions.

Yet in spite of their wealth, the ranchers had few comforts and conveniences. Their homes were unheated and poorly furnished. Window glass was scarce. Most homes had dirt floors. People lived so far apart that they had few visitors. There were no newspapers. The days stretched out one after another.

The Mormons of Utah

The signing of the Treaty of Guadalupe Hidalgo increased interest in westward expansion. During the Mexican War one of the most remarkable migrations of American history had taken place into what is now Utah. This was the settlement that spread out next to the

Great Salt Lake. It consisted of members of a uniquely American religious sect, the **Mormons.**

The Mormon religion was begun in the 1820s by Joseph Smith, a young farmer in western New York. According to Smith, an angel named Moroni gave him golden tablets on which was written the *Book of Mormon.* Smith's English version of the book was published in 1830. It became the basis of the Mormon Church.

Smith attracted many followers, and in 1831 he founded a new community in Ohio. In 1837 the Mormons moved to Missouri. In 1839 they moved again to a town they called **Nauvoo,** in Illinois. The close-knit, cooperative society that the hard-working Mormons developed enabled them to prosper. Nauvoo grew rapidly. By 1844 it was the largest city in Illinois, with a population of 15,000.

The Mormons adopted religious practices that tended to set them apart. One was polygamy, which permitted a man more than one wife at the same time. Smith also became quite domineering as the church grew. He organized a private army, the Nauvoo Legion. He refused to allow critics of his group to publish a newspaper in Nauvoo. By 1844 opposition to the Mormons in Illinois led to Smith's arrest. Then a mob formed. Smith was dragged from jail and lynched.

"Handcart Pioneers" was painted on linen about 1870 by C.C.A. Christensen, who himself pulled his belongings westward. He later traveled with his paintings to portray the Mormon Exodus. What is an exodus?

The Church of Jesus Christ of Latter-Day Saints Museum

A DESERT IN BLOOM

"View of Great Salt Lake City" is an 1867 toned lithograph by Christian Inger.

The valley near the Great Salt Lake was almost a desert. It was here upon the salt flats under the strong sun that the Mormons made their home. The streams running down from the nearby mountains were ordered dammed by Brigham Young. Irrigation ditches were dug so that fields could be watered and crops planted.

As more groups of Mormons arrived, the place became a beehive of activity. Indeed, a beehive is one of the symbols of the Mormon religion. Everything was organized to serve the common good.

Salt Lake City was a planned community. By 1849 it had broad streets lined with neat houses that were set off by well-tended gardens. The surrounding fields were rich with wheat, corn, and potatoes. There were large herds of cattle, horses, and sheep.

Passing travelers marveled at the Mormons' prosperity and at the speed with which they made the desert bloom and caused their mighty temple and tabernacle to rise.

After the murder of Smith the Mormons decided that to practice their religion they would have to find a place far removed from other people. Brigham Young became their new leader. Young was devoutly religious, handsome, and tremendously strong. He was also an excellent organizer. He realized that moving 15,000 people across the country would require very careful planning.

First he divided the Mormons into small groups. He himself led the first group west in 1846. The party proceeded slowly across Iowa, stopping to build camps and to plant crops at several points so that those who followed would have food and shelter. In western Iowa they built a large camp on the Missouri River. It contained nearly a thousand cabins.

Then, in April 1847, Young led a small advance party west. Now they moved swiftly. In July they reached a dry, sun-baked valley near Great Salt Lake. There they established **Salt Lake City,** their permanent home. Their route, followed by many later pioneers, came to be known as the **Mormon Trail.** The ruts worn by their wagons may still be seen today.

The Mormons' success was possible because Brigham Young had almost total control over the community. He headed both the church and the government. Most Mormons believed that Young was inspired by God. They considered him all-wise and devoted to their happiness. They accepted his leadership without questions.

Regulating Water Rights

Even today we wonder why the Mormons chose to build Salt Lake City in a desert where the available water conditions could best be described as *semiarid*—that is, very dry. We know, after the lynching of Joseph Smith in Nauvoo, that the Mormons wanted to go as far away from "civilization" as possible. And we know that the Mormons were not simply led to their destination by seagulls: too much careful planning had been ordered by Brigham Young to leave such matters to chance. No, there were two reasons for the Mormon's success: their industry and the regulation of water rights.

Water is essential to life. Without it, no crops can be grown, no cattle and sheep grazed, no shade trees planted. Most of the earlier settlers of the West put down roots beside river banks or mountain streams. Hardly anyone ventured out of the river valleys.

Settlers of the eastern United States had developed a law that governed the use of water. There rainfall and rivers were abundant, yet the easterners wanted to be sure water ran freely. They applied what is known as the **Law of Riparian Rights.** The term *ripa* comes from the Latin for "riverbank." Basically the law says that property owners whose land borders a stream or river have the right to a steady flow of water in the stream and may use its water reasonably. But the landholders may not decrease or increase the flow of water by changing its direction, nor may they alter its quality. Imagine the consequences of doing so for those living downstream! In the East, the principle applied to manufacturing more than farming. A water-wheel could turn the lathes and looms of factories, but the water must pass freely to the next location.

The Granger Collection

For the Mormon settlers in Utah here was a terrible dilemma. To survive they had to dam streams, flood land, and create a system of canals and irrigation ditches. In doing so, they violated the Law of Riparian Rights. Yet this was the only way to make their desert blossom and attract passersby to an oasis where fresh fruits and vegetables could be bought for the hungry children of the wagon caravans.

Since water resources were so different in the West, the Mormons began to develop a new law to govern the use of water. Brigham Young insisted that land set aside for farming adjoin an irrigation ditch connected to a stream from a nearby mountain. Church councils

Brigham Young sat for this daguerreotype in his later years. How would you describe his appearance?

The Golden West   429

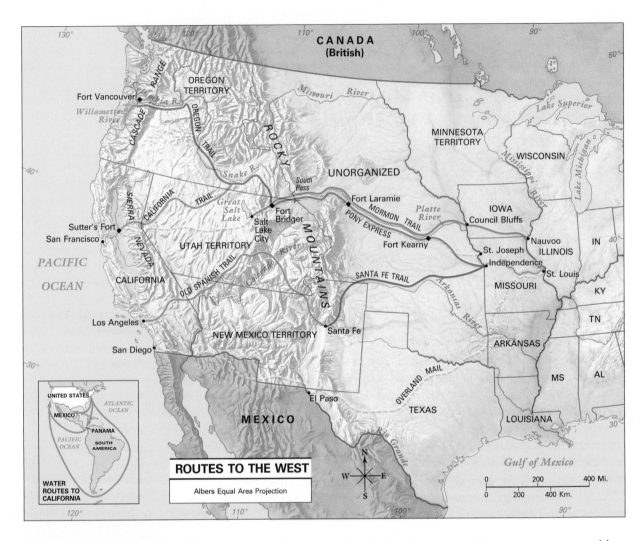

ROUTES TO THE WEST

Albers Equal Area Projection

LEARNING FROM MAPS. *Note from the inset map that there were three water routes to the west. Why did most people travel one of the land routes?*

supervised the ditches. Within two years the system was working smoothly and there seemed to be water for all.

The Law of Prior Appropriation

Brigham Young understood that he was violating the law by irrigating. He set about developing a new legal concept that would meet the realities of the West. This he called the **Law of Prior Appropriation.** The law says that rights to water use belong to the person who first uses the water, as long as it is for beneficial purposes such as farming, mining, manufacturing. It also says that the community good outweighs the good of individuals. A limited resource such as water must be divided among as many people as have need of it. It is the basic water law in all western states.

Water laws are as important to California fruit growers as range watering holes are to ranchers. Today even easterners must rethink their water laws, but in their case it is because so much free-running water has been polluted.

Gold in California

By 1848 the Oregon travelers, the Mormons, and other westward-moving pioneers had made crossing the continent a fairly common experience. The trip was still long and tiring. Sometimes it could be dangerous. But the routes were well marked, and there were a number of forts and settlements along the way where travelers could rest and obtain fresh supplies.

After the Mexican War California attracted more easterners. Many of them settled in and around John A. Sutter's well-known fort on the American River. As the area developed, Sutter, with an eye to new business, expanded his activities. To supply lumber for new settlers, he decided to build a sawmill about 40 miles (64 kilometers) up the river from Sutter's Fort.

First the river bed next to the mill had to be dug out so that a large water wheel could be installed to produce power to run the saws. James W. Marshall was in charge of building the mill. During the digging he noticed bits of shiny yellow metal shimmering in the water. He collected some of them and had them tested. They were pure gold.

How did the discovery of gold nuggets like this one set the nation abuzz in 1848?

The golden hills of California rise above Sutter's Mill in this colored drawing. The site may be visited today. What was the result of the surprise discovery made here?

This discovery took place in January 1848. Soon other people began to prospect, or search for, gold. When they found gold, they told friends about their good luck. More people became **prospectors.** By May the town of San Francisco was buzzing with the news. "Gold! Gold! *Gold* from the American River!"

By the end of the year the whole country had the news. Then, in December 1848, President Polk himself announced that the gold was "more extensive and valuable" than had been thought.

The Forty-Niners

After the President's announcement the **Gold Rush** was on. In 1849 at least 80,000 people came to California to look for gold. The historian Samuel Eliot Morison described "the gold-fever of '49" this way:

66 Farmers mortgaged their farms, workmen downed their tools, clerks left counting-rooms, and even ministers abandoned their pulpits. 99

Most of these **Forty-Niners** followed the overland trails across the Rocky Mountains. Some, however, took longer but more comfortable water routes. Some sailed from the East to Panama, crossed the isthmus on foot, and then sailed north to San Francisco. Others took the all-water route around South America.

Sometimes it took half a year to make the long ocean voyage. But for those who could afford the fare (about $1,000), **clipper ships** made the trip around in much less time. The sleek, three-masted clippers were incredibly fast. Several are known to have sailed over

What name is given people such as the miner panning for gold?

Thomas Gilcrease Institute, Tulsa

The Marine Arts Collection, Seamen's Bank for Savings

The fleet clipper ship "Flying Cloud" was painted by Frank Vining Smith. What advantages did these ships offer western travelers?

Charles Christian Nahl and August Wenderoth painted "Miners in the Sierras"
in 1851. What does this view tell you about the physical features of California's
gold-mining areas?

400 miles (640 kilometers) in 24 hours. The best modern racing yachts
have rarely approached their records.

The clipper ships were 200 to 300 feet (60–90 meters) or more in
length. Their towering masts supported clouds of sails. Their sharp,
graceful bows knifed through the seas smoothly. The most famous
clipper ship was *Flying Cloud* designed by Donald McKay. In 1851
Flying Cloud sailed from Boston to San Francisco in 89 days, less
than three months. Remember that it had taken Magellan 38 days
just to sail through the Straits of Magellan!

Mining Camps

Gold was worth $16 an ounce in 1849. About 10 million ounces (28
million grams) were mined in California that year. Production increased in 1850 and 1851. By 1852 100,000 prospectors were mining

in California. They found 81 million ounces (2.3 billion grams) during that one year. Some miners became millionaires. Others made smaller fortunes. But most made very little.

When a miner found gold, he would **stake a claim** by driving wooden stakes in the ground to mark the spot. Then no one else could legally work that place. Soon dozens of other prospectors would flock to the surrounding area to stake out claims. Disputes about boundaries and other rights frequently broke out.

Villages called **mining camps** sprang up wherever gold was found. These camps were given colorful names such as Whiskey Flat, Hangtown, Roaring Camp, and Volcano. Life in the camps was uncomfortable, expensive, and sometimes very dangerous. A person could be flat broke one day and worth thousands of dollars the next. Such an up-and-down life, combined with the hardships the miners faced, encouraged a devil-may-care attitude. Many miners were heavy drinkers and reckless gamblers. This situation attracted all sorts of thieves and tricksters, as well as shrewd business dealers, saloon-

Charles Christian Nahl of Rough and Ready painted "Sunday Morning in the Mines" in 1872. This is an allegorical painting. It shows evil on the left and good on the right. The bad miners break the Sabbath by rough riding to the gambling tent. But the good miners hear the Bible read and wash clothes. Do you suppose mining camp life was more like that on the left side of the picture or the right?

Sutter's Fort State Historical Monument

At the head of the Auburn Ravine in 1852, American and Chinese miners posed for this rare picture. How might the sluice that divides the miners be a symbol of a deeper division?

keepers, and merchants who sold the miners everything from pick-axes, blue jeans, and tents to liquor, fancy clothes, and fine horses at extremely high prices. These types made far more money than the miners. Fighting in the mining camps—with fists, knives, and guns—was common.

People from all over the United States, from Mexico and South America, from Europe, and from as far away as China and Australia flocked to the gold regions. With so many people crowding into the camps, disputes of all kinds occurred. Mexican Californians were badly treated and often prevented from prospecting. The Chinese and free African Americans were also mistreated, although none of the gold seekers were more hard working. The local Indians were driven off by brute force, although as always they were the original settlers of the land.

Nevertheless, some from these various groups found gold, and a few became rich. Two African American miners, digging in a most unpromising spot, hit a deposit so rich that the site was named **Negro Hill.** These two men found gold worth $80,000 in four months. By 1852 there were 2,000 African Americans in California, half of them working in the mining area.

Despite the problems of camp life the majority of the prospectors and storekeepers in the mining country were not villains. The difficulty was that most of the camps sprang up too quickly to establish orderly governments. Most early miners did not intend to put down roots. They left the camps when the gold ran out and rushed off to other strikes in other regions. The old camps became **ghost towns,** inhabited only by a stray cat or two or a few hermits or vagabonds.

Perhaps 1,000 of the prospectors in California were African Americans. How were they treated by the majority of the miners?

Return to the Preview & Review on page 425.

The Golden West 435

Use these questions to guide your reading. Answer the questions after completing Section 5.
Understanding Issues, Events, & Ideas. Explain the issue of the spread of slavery, using the following words: free state, slave state, Missouri Compromise, popular sovereignty, Free-Soil, Wilmot Proviso, secede, Compromise of 1850.
1. What had the Missouri Compromise decided about free and slave states? What problems would arise if California were added to the Union?
2. Why did northern Democrats form the Free-Soil party?
3. Why did southerners oppose the Wilmot Proviso?
4. What did the Compromise of 1850 seem to accomplish?
Thinking Critically. You are a reporter witnessing the debates between Clay, Calhoun, and Webster. In a newspaper article, describe the arguments of each man, the attitude of the audience, and the atmosphere in the room.

5. FREE AND SLAVE TERRITORIES

Slavery in the Southwest

Adding California to the Union caused new problems. In the past the movement of white settlers into new lands had forced most of the native Indian population to retreat westward. But the California Indians had their backs to the ocean. As a result those who had not been forced to labor on the great Califonia ranches were almost wiped out by the invading white settlers.

In earlier times most new territories had been added to the United States before many settlers had entered them. But California already had a well-established Spanish population. Then the Gold Rush, as we have just seen, greatly increased the state's population. Everyone realized that California did not need to go through the territorial stage of development. Like Texas, it would enter the Union directly as a state. But should California be a **free state** prohibiting slavery or a **slave state** allowing it?

Always in the past, northern territory had become free, southern slave. The Northwest Ordinance of 1787 had declared that the land north of the Ohio River and east of the Mississippi should be free. Kentucky and the territory south of the Ohio became slave states.

"Slaves Escaping Through the Swamp" was painted in 1863 by Thomas Moran.

Philbrook Art Center

In 1820 a sharp conflict had developed over the admission of Missouri as a state. Missouri, which was part of the Louisiana Purchase, extended far north of any slave state. But most of its citizens wanted slavery. The **Missouri Compromise** of 1820 allowed Missouri to become a slave state. Congress balanced this decision by creating a free state, **Maine,** which had been part of Massachusetts.

The Missouri Compromise also divided the rest of the Louisiana Purchase into free and slave territory. The land south of Missouri's southern border—latitude 36° 30′—was opened to slavery. The land west and north of Missouri was to be free.

After the Treaty of Guadalupe Hidalgo some people favored extending this line dividing free territory from slave all the way to the Pacific. That would have split California in two. Californians did not want any of it to become a slave state. In fact, many people hoped to keep blacks out of the region altogether. The Spanish in California had never been slaveholders. The gold miners were opposed because they were afraid that big mining companies would bring in large numbers of slaves to compete.

If California became a free state, what would the eastern slave states expect in return? And what about slavery in the rest of the territory obtained from Mexico? These questions led to a great debate in Congress and throughout the country.

The Election of 1848

The debate over free and slave territories began even before the discovery of gold. It played an important part in the presidential election of 1848. Since President Polk did not seek a second term, the Democrats nominated Senator Lewis Cass of Michigan. Cass had been secretary of war in Andrew Jackson's cabinet. He favored a system known as **popular sovereignty.** This system would let settlers in new territories make their own decision about slavery.

Many northern Democrats were unhappy about the nomination of Cass. They considered popular sovereignty a victory for slavery because it would allow southerners to bring their slaves into new land. These Democrats founded a new organization, the **Free-Soil** party. Their candidate was former president Martin Van Buren.

The Whig party chose General Zachary Taylor as its candidate. President Polk's worst fears had come true. "Old Rough and Ready" had no political experience, but he was very popular. He refused to express an opinion on any of the controversial issues of the day. During the campaign the Whigs stressed his victories in the war, his courage, and his personal honesty. As had been the case with General Harrison in 1840, this tactic worked perfectly. In the election Taylor got 163 electoral votes to Cass's 127. Van Buren received about 10 percent of the popular vote but no electoral votes because he did not get a majority in any state.

National Portrait Gallery

Zachary Taylor, twelfth president, was the popular 'Rough and Ready' of the Mexican War. This lithograph is by Francis D'Avignon, made while Taylor was president. What qualities did the Whigs stress when Taylor campaigned? Are these the same qualities you would look for in a president? Explain your reasoning.

Free and Slave Territories   437

The Compromise of 1850

After the election the debate continued. Besides the future of California and the other new territory, every aspect of the slavery issue was discussed. There were lengthy arguments on the question of the slave trade in Washington, D.C., and on the question of how to force northern officials to return slaves who had escaped into their states.

On each issue there was a northern and a southern position. Many northerners hoped to keep slavery out of all the new territory. In August 1846, long before the end of the Mexican War, Congressman David Wilmot of Pennsylvania introduced the **Wilmot Proviso** in the House of Representatives. The proviso called for prohibiting slavery "in any territory [taken] from the Republic of Mexico." The object was to make all the land available to northern settlers.

Southerners, or course, wanted to be able to take their slaves into all such territory. They controlled enough votes in Congress to defeat the Wilmot Proviso.

As we shall see in the next chapter, many northern people believed strongly that it was sinful for one person to own another. Few of these northerners believed that it was legally possible to abolish slavery in states where it already existed. But large numbers were determined that it should not spread into new lands. Since Congress had always had the power to decide whether or not to allow slavery in new territories, people who felt this way were urging their representatives and senators to support measures like the Wilmot Proviso that would ban slavery in the entire Southwest.

Congress also controlled the city of Washington because the District of Columbia was not part of any state. Those who disliked slavery urged Congress to abolish the institution there. At the very least they wanted Congress to prohibit the buying and selling of slaves in the capital.

The more extreme southerners wanted a law guaranteeing the right of owners to bring their slaves into all the new territories. Even moderate southerners would not agree to the abolition of slavery in Washington. Some were not opposed to a law which would prohibit buying and selling of slaves there. In return they demanded that Congress pass a stricter fugitive slave law. They argued, with considerable truth, that many northern police officials and northern judges were refusing to help in the capture and return of slaves who had escaped into the free states.

All the important members of Congress took part in the debate over these issues. Old Henry Clay, three times an unsuccessful candidate for president and now senator from Kentucky, worked out the compromise that was eventually accepted.

Congress should admit California as a free state, Clay urged. The rest of the land obtained from Mexico should be organized as New Mexico Territory. Slavery should neither be prohibited nor

specifically authorized there. In other words, Clay supported Lewis Cass's popular sovereignty plan for this territory.

To please antislavery northerners, Clay suggested that the buying and selling of slaves in the District of Columbia be prohibited. To please southerners, he proposed a very harsh fugitive slave bill. Another of Clay's bills provided that some lands claimed by Texas were to be transferred to New Mexico Territory. In exchange the debts that Texas had built up while it was an independent republic were to be paid by the United States.

Clay's proposals caused one of the most famous debates in American history. The bitterest attack came from John C. Calhoun, the father of nullification. Calhoun, old and ill, his once-powerfull voice broken by the throat cancer that would soon kill him, sat grim and silent as another senator read his words:

> ❝ How can the Union be saved? There is but one way by which it can with any certainty; and that is, by a full and final settlement, on the principle of justice, of all the ques-

Henry Clay, 72 years old and ailing, pleads with the Senate to reach the Compromise of 1850. Seated at left, his ear cupped, is Daniel Webster, who supported Clay. His attackers are John C. Calhoun, standing third from right, and William Seward, seated in the left front. Vice President Fillmore presides. What was debated?

Free and Slave Territories   439

Points of View

tions at issue between the two sections [North and South]. The South asks for justice, simple justice, and less she ought not to take. She has no compromise to offer but the Constitution; and no concession or surrender to make. She has already surrendered so much she has little left to surrender. Such a settlement would go to the root of the evil, and remove all cause of discontent, by satisfying the South she could remain honorably and safely in the Union, and thereby restore the harmony and fraternal feelings between the sections which existed anterior to [before] the Missouri agitation [compromise in 1820]. Nothing else can, with any certainty, finally and forever settle the question, terminate the agitation, and save the Union.

But can this be done? Yes, easily; not by the weaker party [the South], for it can of itself do nothing—not even protect itself—but by the stronger. The North has only to will it to accomplish it—to do justice by conceding to the South an equal right in the acquired territory, and to do her duty by causing stipulations [rules] relative to fugitive slaves to be faithfully fulfilled [followed]—to cease the agitation of the slave question, and to provide for the insertion of a provision in the Constitution, by an amendment, which will restore the South in substance [reality] the power she possessed of protecting herself, before the equilibrium [balance] between the sections was destroyed by the action of this Government. There will be no difficulty in devising [creating] such a provision—one that will protect the South and which at the same time will improve and strengthen the Government, instead of weakening and impairing it.

But will the North agree to this? It is for her to answer the question. But, I say she cannot refuse, if she has half the love of the Union which she professes [claims] to have, . . . At all events, the responsibility for saving the Union rests on the North, and not on the South. The South cannot save it through any act of hers, and the North may save it without any sacrifice whatever, unless to do justice and to perform her duties under the Constitution should be regarded by her as sacrifice. . . .[1]**"**

Calhoun claimed the North now controlled the government, which was making laws that took away the rights of southerners. All citizens had the right to take their property into all the territories of the United States. Unless Congress allowed owners to bring their slaves into the territories, the southern states would **secede,** or leave the Union. There was nothing evil or immoral about slavery, Calhoun argued. Northerners must accept the fact that it exists. If they want

[1]From the *Congressional Globe,* 31st Congress, 1st Session

to live at peace with the South, they must stop criticizing slavery. The South would compromise no more. Calhoun would die on March 30, croaking sadly, "The South, the poor South!"

Also attacking the compromise was Senator William Seward of New York. He spoke against making any concessions to the slave interests. Clay's fugitive slave bill must not pass, said Seward. Although the Constitution of the United States required the return of fugitives, a "higher law," the law of God, would keep decent people from helping to capture an escaped slave.

Daniel Webster of Massachusetts sat for this oil painting done in 1846 by G.P.A. Healy. How did Webster support Clay's Compromise of 1850?

Then, on March 7, three days after Calhoun's speech, Daniel Webster, the important and famous senator from Massachusetts, rose to answer Calhoun's remarks. He delivered a powerful speech in support of Clay's compromise proposals. In part he said:

    " Mr. President, I wish to speak to-day, not as a Massachusetts man, nor as a northern man, but as an American, and as a member of the Senate of the United States. . . . It is not to be denied that we live in the midst of strong agitations, and are surrounded by very considerable dangers to our institutions of government. The imprisoned winds are let loose. The East, the West, the North, and the stormy South, all combine to throw the whole ocean into commotion [noisy confusion], to toss its billows to the skies, and to disclose its profoundest depths. I do not affect [pretend] to regard myself, Mr. President, as holding, or as fit to hold, the helm [a steering device for a ship] in this combat of political elements; but I have a duty to perform, and I mean to perform it with fidelity [faithfulness]. . . . I speak to-day for the preservation of the Union. "Hear me for my cause" I speak to-day out of a solicitous [concerned] and anxious heart, for the restoration to the country of that quiet and that harmony which makes the blessings of this Union so rich and so dear to us all. . . .

    There has been found in the North, among individuals and among legislators, a disinclination [unwillingness] to perform fully their constitutional duties in regard to the return of persons bound to service [fugitive slaves] who have escaped into the free States. In that respect, the South, in my judgment, is right, and the North is wrong. . . .

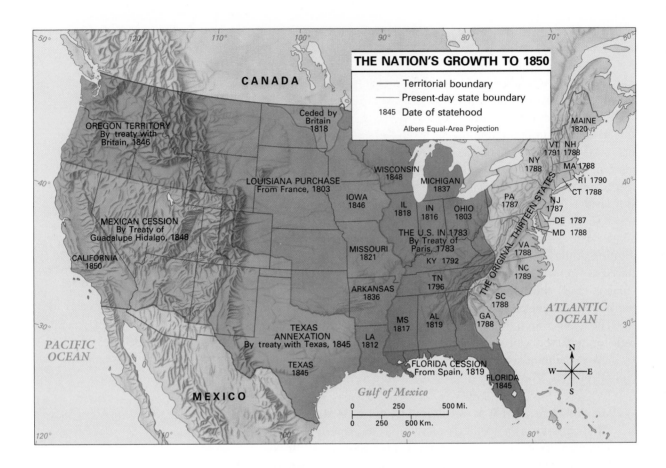

THE NATION'S GROWTH TO 1850

——— Territorial boundary
——— Present-day state boundary
1845 Date of statehood
Albers Equal-Area Projection

CANADA

OREGON TERRITORY
By treaty with
Britain, 1846

Ceded by
Britain
1818

MAINE
1820

LOUISIANA PURCHASE
From France, 1803

WISCONSIN
1848

MICHIGAN
1837

VT NH
1791 1788

NY
1788

MA 1788

RI 1790

CT 1788

MEXICAN CESSION
By Treaty of
Guadalupe Hidalgo, 1848

IOWA
1846

IL
1818

IN
1816

OHIO
1803

PA
1787

NJ
1787

DE 1787

MD 1788

CALIFORNIA
1850

MISSOURI
1821

THE U.S. IN 1783
By Treaty of
Paris, 1783

KY 1792

VA
1788

NC
1789

THE ORIGINAL THIRTEEN STATES

ARKANSAS
1836

TN
1796

SC
1788

ATLANTIC
OCEAN

PACIFIC
OCEAN

TEXAS
ANNEXATION
By treaty with Texas, 1845

MS
1817

AL
1819

LA
1812

GA
1788

N
W   E
S

TEXAS
1845

FLORIDA CESSION
From Spain, 1819

FLORIDA
1845

MEXICO

Gulf of Mexico

0   250   500 Mi.

0   250   500 Km.

LEARNING FROM MAPS. *By
1853 the continental United States
was complete. How was the land in
your state acquired?*

Now, as to California and New Mexico, I hold slavery
to be excluded from these territories by a law even
superior to that which admits and sanctions Texas—I mean
natural law—of physical geography—the law of the formation of the earth. That law settles forever, with a strength
beyond all terms of human enactment, that slavery cannot
exist in California or New Mexico. . . . I look upon it,
therefore, as a fixed fact, to use an expression current at
this day, that both California and New Mexico are destined
to be free, so far as they are settled at all, which I believe,
especially in regard to New Mexico, will be of very little
for a great length of time—free by the arrangements of
things by the Power Above us [God]. . . . I will say further,
that if a resolution, or a law, were now before us, to provide
a territorial government for New Mexico, I would not vote
to put any prohibition [of slavery] into it whatever. . . . I
would not take the pains to reenact the will of God. . . . I
would put into it no evidence of the votes of superior power
[the North], . . . to wound the pride of the gentlemen who
belong to the Southern states. I have no such object—no
such purpose. They would think it a taunt [insult]—an in-

dignity. They would think it to be an act of taking away from them what they regard as a proper equality of privilege; and whether they expect to realize any benefit from it or not, they would think a theoretic wrong—that something more or less derogatory [insulting] to their character and their rights had taken place. I propose to inflict no such wound on any body, unless something essentially important to the country, and efficient to the preservation of liberty and freedom, is to be effected. . . .

And now, Mr. President, instead of speaking of the possibility or utility [usefulness] of secession, instead of dwelling in these caverns of darkness, instead of groping with those ideas so full of all that is horrid and horrible, let us come out into the light of day; let us enjoy the fresh air of liberty and union; let us cherish those hopes which belong to us; let us devote ourselves to those great objects that are fit for our consideration and our action; let us raise our conceptions [thoughts] to the magnitude [high level] and importance of the duties that devolve upon [pass to] us; let our comprehension be as broad as the country for which we act, our aspirations [goals] as high as its certain destiny; let us not be pigmies in a case that calls for men. Never did there devolve, on any generation of men, higher trusts than now devolve upon us for the preservation of this Constitution, and the harmony and peace of all who are destined to live under it.[1] **"**

[1]From the *Congressional Globe,* 31st Congress, 1st Session

In the midst of the debate on Clay's bills, President Taylor fell ill and died. Vice President Millard Fillmore of New York succeeded him. Fillmore favored Clay's compromise. Nevertheless, the arguments dragged on into the summer months.

Finally the various proposals came to a vote. California was admitted to the Union as a free state. The rest of the former Mexican lands were organized into two large territories, Utah and New Mexico, where slavery was not restricted. Texas was given $10 million to pay its debts. The slave trade in the District of Columbia was abolished. A new Fugitive Slave Act was passed.

Few Americans, North or South, approved of all these laws. But nearly all who followed the debate were pleased with the result as a whole. The **Compromise of 1850** appeared to finally put an end to the conflict between the free and slave states. All the territory owned by the United States had now been organized. Never again would Congress have to decide the future of slavery on American soil. As Senator Stephen A. Douglas of Illinois put it, a "final settlement" had been reached. At least that was how it seemed in 1850.

Millard Fillmore completed Zachary Taylor's term as president. This daguerreotype was taken about 1850. What stand did Fillmore take on the Compromise of 1850?

Return to the Preview & Review on page 436.

Free and Slave Territories 443

LINKING HISTORY & GEOGRAPHY

THE NATION MOVES WEST

During the mid-1800s hardy pioneers, looking ever westward, ventured beyond the Mississippi into an entirely new frontier. The West was an enormous land of many physical regions— grass-covered but treeless plains, parched deserts, and towering snowcapped mountains.

Each region was different in landforms, climate, soil, and vegetation from anything the pioneers had seen east of the Mississippi. These were lands whose mysteries had to be probed and tested before permanent settlements could be fully undertaken.

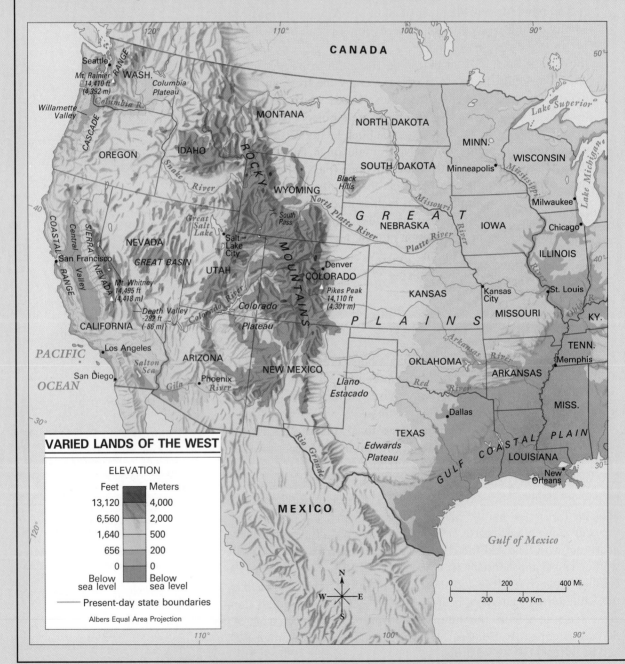

VARIED LANDS OF THE WEST

ELEVATION

Feet	Meters
13,120	4,000
6,560	2,000
1,640	500
656	200
0	0
Below sea level	Below sea level

— Present-day state boundaries

Albers Equal Area Projection

The Great Plains

1. How did the pioneers view the Plains? Why?

The first geographic region the pioneers encountered was a grassy region that became known as the Great Plains. The Plains feature level to rolling land with few trees. The dry region receives too little rain to support forests, but enough for a carpet of low-growing grasses to flourish.

Travelers who crossed the Great Plains reacted in many different ways to the vast empty space. Pioneers raised in the eastern United States were struck by the lack of trees and apparent worthlessness of its dry landscape. Familiar with abundant rainfall and thick forests, they agreed with Major Stephen H. Long, who labeled the region the Great American Desert. Days and weeks of dry weather greeted travelers. Because many sought farmland, few stayed to farm the seemingly too-dry plains. In fact, the Great Plains would be the last area of the United States to be fully settled—awaiting farming advances such as the steel plow and the windmill that would help make the dry land of the plains productive.

A Geographic Explanation

2. What natural forces created the Plains?

The geographic explanation for this broad, dry grassland lies in the nature of the western landscape. In the United States the prevailing wind blows from west to east. This wind crosses the Pacific Ocean, picking up moisture. As the rain-bearing air blows onto North America, it runs headlong into the towering Cascade and Sierra Nevada mountain ranges. The mountains force the air to rise and cool. Because cool air cannot hold as much moisture as warm air, the now-cool air drops its moisture as rain or snow. Thus, rain or snow falls frequently on the western slopes of the Cascades and Sierra Nevadas.

The drier and lighter air crosses the peaks and slides down the eastern slopes. With its downward rush, the air warms, snatching whatever moisture it can from the land between the Pacific Ranges and the Rocky Mountains. The warming air thus dries the landscape as far as the western slopes of the Rockies. Then the air is once again forced to rise, cool, and lose its moisture. The air slides down the eastern slopes of the Rockies, becoming the warm dry winds that cross the western Great Plains.

The Rocky Mountains

3. Why did the trails west follow irregular routes rather than straight lines?

Looming in the path of the pioneers who crossed the plains rose the great masses of the Rocky Mountains. This mountain range extends from Alaska into Texas and southward. Rain and snow, available from the air that was forced to rise over the mountain peaks, support the dense forests of pine, fir, and spruce covering the mountainsides. Most of the precipitation, however, occurs as snow during the late winter and early spring. Depths of 25 feet (7.6 meters) or more are common. Pioneers trapped in such snows faced death from cold and starvation, so journeys were planned to cross the Rockies before winter. To the early pioneers, the Rocky Mountains seemed more suited to trappers and miners than farmers, so they pushed on.

The Intermountain Region

4. Why did most of the pioneers find the Intermountain landscape forbidding?

Travelers now crossed the vast desert area that fills the entire country between the Rockies and the Pacific ranges. Jagged rocks and dry sands characterize this Intermountain Region. It is hardly a landscape that the early pioneers found attractive, especially the farmers used to the lush green of the lands east of the Mississippi. Hardy prospectors, however, soon uncovered the region's valuable treasury of minerals.

The Pacific Coast

5. What attracted settlers to the Pacific Coast?

Near the western edge of the continent the pioneers discovered many fertile valleys. In the northwest, sheltered by the Cascades from winter blasts, lie valleys watered by broad rivers and streams. To the south in California, between the Sierra Nevada and the Coastal Ranges, stretch great valleys of rich soil and water for irrigation. The pioneers, their descendants, and other newcomers turned this westernmost edge of the United States into a land of great abundance.

Applying Your Knowledge

You will work in groups to plan a trip by wagon train across the West. Your group should prepare a list of items you will need on the journey. Create a class list by combining the items on individual group lists.

CHAPTER 12 REVIEW

1820		MANIFEST DESTINY		1830	

1820	**1821**	**1824**	**1828**	**1834**
Congress ratifies Missouri Compromise	Austin leads settlers into Texas	Adams elected president	Jackson elected president	Settlement of Oregon begins

Chapter Summary

Read the statements below. Choose one, and write a paragraph explaining its importance.

1. Texas independence focused the nation's attention on expansion and the West.
2. Manifest destiny encouraged eager pioneers to head west.
3. Victory in the Mexican War gave the United States a huge new territory that included most of present-day California, Arizona, Nevada, Utah, and New Mexico.
4. The Mormons and other pioneers followed established trails to western destinations.
5. The discovery of gold in California caused a rush of people to the West.
6. The acquisition of new territory raised questions about the spread of slavery.
7. First the Missouri Compromise, then the Compromise of 1850, attempted to solve the problems surrounding slavery's spread.

Reviewing Chronological Order

Number your paper 1-5. Then study the time line above and place the following events in the order in which they happened by writing the first next to 1, the second next to 2, and so on.

1. California Gold Rush begins
2. Mormons found Salt Lake City
3. Compromise of 1850
4. Republic of Texas proclaimed
5. Missouri Compromise

Understanding Main Ideas

1. Describe the events that led Texans to declare their independence from Mexico.
2. In your own words, explain what manifest destiny meant to Americans in the mid-1800s.
3. What was the chief cause of the war with Mexico? What were the major outcomes?
4. What events led the Mormons to move from western New York to Utah?

5. How did the Gold Rush add to the push of Americans westward?
6. How did the Compromise of 1850 differ from the Missouri Compromise?

Thinking Critically

1. **Drawing Conclusions.** When Travis and the other defenders of the Alamo refused to surrender to Santa Anna, were they brave or foolish? Why do you think so?
2. **Synthesizing.** You and your family are part of a wagon train headed for Oregon in 1843. What is your greatest fear as you journey from your Missouri home? What tasks will you take on in order to help your family arrive safely in the Willamette Valley?
3. **Evaluating.** Several presidents—Jackson, Harrison, and Taylor, for example—were elected because of their popularity as military leaders. In your opinion, does war experience qualify a person for the presidency? Why or why not?

Writing About History: Classificatory

Imagine you are a newspaper reporter. Prepare a news article that explains point by point the provisions of the Compromise of 1850. Finish your article with a paragraph that tells why most people felt this was the final settlement of the slavery question. Review the information on the compromise on pages 438–43.

Practicing the Strategy

Review the strategy on page 415.
Learning from Art. Study the painting on page 425 and answer the following questions.

1. What is the subject of the painting?
2. What, in your opinion, is the artist's point of view about the subject of the painting?
3. Do you feel that this painting is a fairly accurate representation? Explain your answer.

1836
Mexican army
defeats Texans
at the Alamo
★
Republic
of Texas
proclaimed

1840
Harrison
elected
president

1841
Tyler
succeeds
Harrison
as president

1844
Polk
elected
president

1845
Texas
enters
the
Union

1846
Oregon
boundary
dispute
settled

1847
Mormons
found
Salt Lake
City
★
Republic
of
California
declared

1848
Treaty of
Guadalupe
Hidalgo
★
Free-Soil party
runs presidential
candidate
★
Taylor elected
president

1850
Fillmore
succeeds
Taylor
★
Compromise
of 1850
★
California
enters the
Union

Using Primary Sources

On February 23, 1836, a large Mexican army sur-rounded the Alamo. Inside was a force of fewer than 200 Americans, mostly Texans, under the command of William Barret Travis. A messenger carrying a letter from Travis slipped through Mex-ican lines in the darkness of the night after the siege began. As you read Travis' message, think how historians might judge his words and actions. Then answer the questions that follow it.

Lt. Col. Travis

P.S. The Lord is on our side. When the enemy appeared in sight, we had not three bushels of corn. We have since found in deserted houses 80 or 90 bushels, and got into the walls 20 or 30 head of beeves.

T.

COMMANDANCY OF THE ALAMO
*BEJAR, Feb. 24, 1836

To the people of Texas & all Americans in the world
Fellow Citizens & Compatriots:

I am besieged, by a thousand or more of the Mexicans under Santa Anna. I have sustained a continual bom-bardment & cannonade for 24 hours & have not lost a man. The enemy has demanded a surrender at discre-tion, otherwise the garrison is to be put to the sword, if the fort is taken. I have answered the summons with a cannon-shot and our flag still waves proudly from the walls. I shall never surrender or retreat. Then I call on you, in the name of Liberty, of Patriotism, & of every thing dear to the American character, to come to our aid with all dispatch. The enemy is receiving reinforce-ments daily & will no doubt increase to three or four thousand in four or five days. Though this call may be neglected, I am determined to sustain myself as long as possible, and die like a soldier, who never forgets what is due to his honor & that of his country.

VICTORY OR DEATH

William Barret Travis

Lieutenant Colonel, Commanding

* The Mexican name for the area surrounding present-day San Antonio.

1. Why do you think Travis addressed his letter not only to the people of Texas but to all Amer-icans in the world?
2. What do you think Travis meant by his refer-ence to the "American character"?
3. What evidence in Travis' letter suggests that he was willing to make every sacrifice for the lib-erty of Texas?

Linking History & Geography

On an outline map of the United States, label with their names and dates of admission to the Union the states carved out of the lands won from Mex-ico, and trace the major trails to the West.

Enriching the Study of History

Individual Project. Prepare a report on the Alamo, telling its history from the time of its founding to 1836. You might include brief biographies of Davy Crockett, James Bowie, Antonio López de Santa Anna, or one of the Tejano fighters at the Alamo. You might also make a sketch or model of the Alamo to illustrate your report.

Cooperative Project. Your class will hold a Mexican American festival highlighting Mexican contribu-tions to American culture. The festival should in-clude Mexican foods, games, stories, art, music, and other contributions. Each group will research a different category for the festival.

Chapter 12 Review   **447**

CHAPTER 13

Slavery and Abolition

While slaves wait on benches, the white men make their bids to the auctioneer, with his arm outstretched. Yet surely this 1852 oil painting by Eyre Crowe is "prettified"—the freshly starched aprons, the smiling mother, the boy in his Sunday best. Who knows if these children will still sit in Mother's lap when the auctioneer raps down his gavel?

After the American Revolution slavery seemed to be dying out. The northern states passed laws gradually doing away with it. Many individual southerners gave up slavery voluntarily. Methodists north and south were expected to free their slaves. In 1808 Congress prohibited bringing any more slaves into the country. Yet slavery persisted. Southerners argued that slavery was essential for their economy based largely on growing cotton. When cotton production increased after the invention of the cotton gin, the demand for slaves and land grew. Was this a time when southerners would listen to arguments for the abolition of slavery?

Bradley Smith/Laurie Platt Winfrey

1. COTTON AND SLAVERY

200 Years of Slavery

Since no African slaves could be brought into the United States after 1808, by 1850 most of the slaves in America were native born. Nevertheless these slaves struggled to preserve their African heritage.

Some people who thought that slavery was bad for the country proposed freeing the slaves and sending them back to Africa. In 1817 they founded the **American Colonization Society.** They purchased land in Africa for former slaves to settle on. Most free African Americans were not interested in living in Africa. However, the American Colonization Society did persuade several thousand to make the move to what became the nation of **Liberia,** on the west coast of Africa.

Few of the sponsors of colonization genuinely wanted to help freed slaves. The colonization movement was mostly aimed at getting rid of the former slaves. Nevertheless, the movement was another sign that many people in the South, as well as the North, were unhappy with slavery.

Free African Americans

Most of the free African Americans lived in the North. There they found opportunities in almost every field of endeavor. Many joined the armed forces. Almost half the seamen aboard U.S. ships in 1850 were African Americans. Others blazed trails west. James Beckwourth, Pierre Bonza and his son George, and two African American missionaries—John Marrant and John Stewart—helped lead the westward movement.

Several became notable inventors and writers. Benjamin Banneker, an expert surveyor and mathematician, contributed to science, medicine, and politics. He also wrote a popular almanac that included antislavery essays as well as information about the tides, the moon, crops, and the weather. Lewis Temple invented a harpoon that was hailed as the most important invention in the history of whaling. James Forten, a veteran of the U.S. navy and of the Revolutionary War, invented a device for controlling sails. Thomas Jennings developed a process for cleaning clothes and became wealthy. William Wells Brown became the first African American novelist and playwright. He also wrote three travel books and several short histories of the African American people.

But most free African Americans in the North faced prejudice and discrimination. Northern laws kept them from voting and serving on juries and from becoming judges and law officers. In Ohio they could not even testify in court. Laws also barred them from schools in many states and from being buried in most "whites-only" cemeteries.

Preview & Review

Use these questions to guide your reading. Answer the questions after completing Section 1.
Understanding Issues, Events, & Ideas. Tell what a slave and a slaveowner might have said about the following words: American Colonization Society, Liberia, cotton boll, Sea Island cotton, upland cotton, cotton gin.
1. What was the purpose of the American Colonization Society?
2. Why did the demand for cotton suddenly increase in the 1790s?
3. How did the cotton gin make it profitable to grow cotton?
4. Why did cotton increase the demand for slave labor but not the supply of slaves?
Thinking Critically. 1. As a free African American in 1817, you have the choice of moving to Liberia or staying in America. What do you decide? Why? 2. Imagine that you are Eli Whitney's father. Write a letter to your son agreeing or disagreeing with Eli's claim that the cotton gin would be a "great thing" for the country.

They were forced to ride in separate railway cars and sit in separate parts of the theaters, usually at the back of the balcony. Finding work was even more discouraging. In 1819 one teenager asked classmates in his graduating class:

> **"** What are my prospects? To what shall I turn my hand? Shall I be a mechanic? No one will employ me; white boys won't work with me. Shall I be a merchant? No one will have me in his office. Can you be surprised at my discouragement?[1] **"**

He and other African Americans struggled in the decades before the Civil War for opportunities and rights available to other Americans.

And what of the more than 100,000 free African Americans in the South? A few rose to fame and importance. Norbert Rillieux helped revolutionize sugar refining. Henry Blair patented a seedplanter for corn. Daniel A. Payne established a school for free African Americans with a curriculum that included arithmetic, literature, science, chemistry, zoology, astronomy, and geography as well as reading and writing.

Many southern whites saw free African Americans as a threat. They watched them carefully and blocked many of their attempts to achieve. Like their brothers in the North, southern free African Americans could not vote or participate in the legal system. They could not own businesses in many places or secure loans or otherwise use banks. Despite these frustrations most southern free African Americans chose to stay in the South to help others—free and slave.

The Importance of Cotton

Southern attitudes about slavery changed after the discovery of a new crop that greatly increased the need for slave labor. This crop was cotton. In the 1790s cotton was in great demand in many parts of the world because of the new spinning machinery that had been invented in England. It was just at this time that Samuel Slater was building the first spinning machines in America. These machines could produce thread so rapidly that they were soon using up cotton faster than the world was producing it.

Most cotton came from Egypt. Egyptian cotton was of very high quality. It had long, soft fibers that grew around and protected the seeds of the plant. When the plant ripened, the **cotton boll** burst open. Then the fluffy white fibers could easily be separated from the shiny black seeds.

A little of this cotton was grown in America on the Sea Islands along the coast of Georgia and South Carolina. The winters there were very mild. But **Sea Island cotton** would not grow on the mainland. The plants were so tender that they were killed by the slightest spring frost.

New York Public Library Picture Collection

In a single engraving we see the blossom of a cotton plant and the boll ripe for picking.

[1]From *Eyewitness: The Negro in American History* by William Katz

Another variety of cotton, called **upland cotton,** could withstand colder temperatures. It was hardy enough to be grown almost anywhere in the southern states. Unfortunately, the fibers of this plant were short and tightly woven about the seeds. It took a whole day for a skilled person to remove the seeds by hand from a single pound of this cotton.

If only someone would invent a machine for removing the seeds from upland cotton! Many farmers in South Carolina and Georgia were expressing this hope in one way or another in the 1790s. Rice cultivation could not be increased much in those states. Rice needed a great deal of water. It could only be grown where the fields could be flooded. Indigo, the plant introduced in the 1740s by Eliza Lucas, was not worth growing after the Revolution because the British government no longer paid a bounty for producing it.

Eli Whitney and the Cotton Gin

In 1793 Eli Whitney was visiting a friend on a plantation near Savannah, Georgia. Whitney had just graduated from Yale College. He had learned about metalworking from his father, a nail maker. He had not yet turned his inventive mind to thinking about making guns from interchangeable parts.

During his visit he talked with a number of Georgia farmers. They mentioned their interest in growing cotton and showed him how difficult it was to remove the seeds from upland cotton bolls. Young Whitney had never seen a cotton plant before. Perhaps that was an advantage. He studied the plant carefully. He wrote to his father in Connecticut:

> 66 If a machine could be invented that would clean the Cotton, it would be a great thing both to the Country and to the inventor. 99

After a few days of thinking, Whitney designed a machine that he called a **cotton gin.** It consisted of a box that opened at the top and had rows of narrow slits down one side. The box was stuffed with cotton, seeds and all. Against the side of the box Whitney set a roller or cylinder. The cylinder had rows of wire teeth around it. These rows of teeth were arranged so that when someone turned the cylinder, the teeth passed into the box through the slits. The cotton in the box caught on the teeth as they turned. As the teeth came out of the box, they pulled the cotton fibers with them.

But the seeds, which were wider than the slits in the box, could not pass through with the fibers. The fibers therefore pulled free of the seeds. A second cylinder, turning in the other direction, brushed the fibers from the teeth. As the first cylinder continued to turn, the teeth reentered the box to catch up more of the cotton.

One person turning the handle of a cotton gin could remove the

Eli Whitney had just graduated from Yale when he designed and tested the cotton gin. How do you think he would have reacted if he had known the cotton gin would increase the demand for cotton and make slavery more economically necessary for the South?

Cotton and Slavery   451

This sketch of Eli Whitney's 1793 cotton gin shows how easily one slave could operate the rollers while others emptied baskets of newly picked cotton. What do the drawings in the border show you about cotton and slavery?

seeds of not one pound of cotton in a day but of fifty! A gin was easy to make and cheap. Even a small farmer could afford one. The owners of large plantations soon were building large gins powered by horses or mules. Quickly it became profitable to grow cotton.

Effects of the Cotton Gin

All over the South farmers began to plant cotton. In 1793 they grew about 10,000 bales, each containing 500 pounds (225 kilograms) of cotton. In 1801 American production reached 100,000 bales. By 1835 it had passed a million bales. Cotton was worth about 25 cents a pound in the 1790s. The price remained in the 15- to 20-cent range even after supply of cotton had increased enormously. Cotton planters prospered.

Most of the people who flocked westward into Alabama, Mississippi, Arkansas, Louisiana, and on into Texas became cotton planters. Of course they also raised large quantities of corn, wheat, cattle, and other food products. But cotton was their most important crop. Indeed, it became the key to prosperity for the South and almost as important for the rest of the country.

Cotton cultivation made possible the rapid growth of the northern cotton cloth industry. Citizens everywhere benefited from cheap cotton clothing, which was cool in summer and much easier to keep clean than woolen garments. Exports of cotton to England and other countries paid for badly needed foreign imports of all kinds.

The great cotton boom increased the need for workers to culti-vate the fields and to pick and gin the fluffy white fibers when the crop was ripe. Cotton growing seemed especially well suited for the institution of slavery because it kept the slaves busy the year round. (Slaveowners always feared that if their workers had too little to do, they would get into trouble!)

The year began with spring planting, whether on a small farm worked by a single family and one or two slaves or on a large plantation with a hundred slaves. First, corn and other food crops were planted in March. When these were in the ground, the cotton seeds were sown. Once sprouted, the corn needed little care, but the small, tender cotton plants required much labor. The young shoots had to be thinned out. As the plants grew, the soil had to be hoed and cultivated frequently to keep down weeds. Insect pests had to be killed before they could do serious damage to the crop. This work kept all hands busy during the long southern summers.

By September it was time to harvest the corn. The cornstalks were gathered and stored away to make winter food for cows and pigs. Picking the cotton took up the rest of the fall because the cotton bolls did not all ripen at the same time. Unless the white fluff was gathered as soon as the bolls burst open, rain and dust would dirty it and thus reduce its value. The slaves had to go through the fields almost daily.

Picking took skill and patience but not a great deal of strength. Women and children worked the fields side by side with the men. A skilled worker could gather 200 pounds (90 kilograms) in a day. Solomon Northrup, a free African American kidnapped and sold into slavery, describes cotton picking on a Louisiana plantation in late August:

> When a new hand, one unaccustomed to the business [of picking cotton], is sent for the first time into the field, he is whipped up smartly and made for the day to pick as fast as he possibly can. At night it is weighed so that his capability in cotton picking is known. He must bring in the same weight each night following. If it falls short, it is considered evidence that he has been laggard [lazy], and a greater or less number of lashes [with the whip] is the penalty.
>
> An ordinary day's work is two hundred pounds. A slave who is accustomed to picking, is punished, if he or she brings in a less quantity than that. . . . The hands are required to be in the cotton field as soon as it is light in the morning, and, with the exception of ten or fifteen minutes, which are given them at noon to swallow their allowance of cold bacon, they are not permitted to be a moment idle until it is too dark to see, and when the moon is full, they often times labor till the middle of the night. They do not

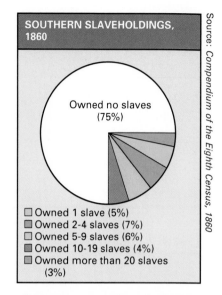

SOUTHERN SLAVEHOLDINGS, 1860

Owned no slaves (75%)

☐ Owned 1 slave (5%)
☐ Owned 2-4 slaves (7%)
☐ Owned 5-9 slaves (6%)
☐ Owned 10-19 slaves (4%)
☐ Owned more than 20 slaves (3%)

Source: *Compendium of the Eighth Census, 1860*

LEARNING FROM GRAPHS. *We often think that all southerners owned slaves. How does this graph change that notion?*

Cotton and Slavery   453

dare to stop even at dinner time, nor return to the quarters, however late it be, until the order to halt is given by the driver [overseer].

The day's work over in the fields, the baskets are 'toted,' or in other words carried to the gin-house, where the cotton is weighed. . . . This done, the labor of the day is not yet ended, by any means. Each one must then attend to his respective chores. One feeds the mules, another the swine—another cuts wood, and so forth, beside, the packing [of the cotton] is all done by candlelight. Finally, at a late hour, they reach the quarters, sleepy and overcome with the long day's toil. Then a fire must be kindled in the cabin, the corn ground in the small hand-mill, and supper, and dinner for the next day in the field, prepared. All that is allowed them is corn and bacon, which is given out at the corncrib and the smoke-house every Sunday morning. Each one receives, as his weekly allowance, three and a half pounds of bacon, and corn enough to make a peck [8 quarts; 8.9 liters] of meal. That is all—no tea, coffee, sugar, and, with the exception of a scanty sprinkling now and then, no salt. . . .[1] **99**

"Cotton Plantation on the Mississippi" shows slaves picking cotton while their overseer watches from his mule. It is typical of Currier & Ives that this scene shows no more passion than a Sunday outing. Yet what does historical imagination suggest was truly the case?

[1]From *Twelve Years a Slave* by Solomon Northrup

The Granger Collection

After picking, the cotton had to be put through the gin to remove the seeds. Then it was packed in bales. This was done in a cotton press, a box-like affair with a heavy screw-down top. The bales were bound in burlap and tied with wire or twine.

Harvesting was usually over by Christmas time. Then, for about a week, all work stopped. During this brief period the harsh and cruel side of slavery was put aside, if not forgotten. There were feasts, singing and dancing, a Christmas tree bright with candles. One South Carolina slave described a tree he remembered as "a picture of beautifulness." There were also small presents for everyone. Some masters even dressed up as Santa Claus and distributed gifts to the slave children.

After this brief holiday it was time to clear new land. Fences had to be repaired, tools sharpened. Thus the winter passed. Soon it was time for the next spring planting.

Although cotton increased the demand for slave labor, there could be no sudden increase in the supply of slaves. Congress had forbidden bringing any more slaves into the country. Farmers therefore competed with one another for American-born slaves. The natural increase of the population could not satisfy the demand. The price of slaves rose rapidly. By 1850 slaves were selling for three or four times as much as they had cost before the invention of the cotton gin. 🖻

Cotton is packed into bales under pressure from the screw-down top of this cotton press. A mule can turn the heavy screw by patiently plodding its circular path. Where would the baled cotton most likely be sent?

Return to the Preview & Review on page 449.

Use these questions to guide your reading. Answer the questions after completing Section 2. **Understanding, Issues, Events, & Ideas**. Use the following words to describe a visit to a southern plantation: ''Cotton is King,'' Fourth of July.

1. How did the cotton gin make life more difficult for slaves?
2. How did some southerners justify slavery?
3. What did southerners mean by boasting that ''Cotton is King''?
4. Why did southerners believe that criticism of slavery was unpatriotic and dangerous?

Thinking Critically. **1.** Plan a film that shows life for a slave on a cotton plantation. What props and details will you include on your ''set''? **2.** You are a northern newspaper reporter at a Fourth of July celebration in the South in 1830. Write an interview with a slave who saw the celebration.

2. "COTTON IS KING"

How Cotton Affected Slaves

In some respects the fact that slaves were becoming more valuable meant that their owners treated them better. Prosperous owners could afford to feed, clothe, and house slaves adequately. Probably most did so, if only because it made sense to take good care of such useful property.

The slaves ate simple food. It consisted mainly of corn, pork fat, and molasses. This did not make a balanced diet, for no one at that time understood the importance of vitamins and minerals for good health. Fortunately, most slaves were allowed to have small vegetable gardens of their own. They could fish in the streams and hunt and trap small forest animals, such as opossums and raccoons. They got enough to eat, even if their food was plain and simple.

The slaves wore clothing that was also simple but sufficient—overalls, cotton and woolen shirts, a pair of heavy work shoes, a hat for protection against rain and summer heat.

Slave cabins were small and poorly furnished. Most families lived in a single room. The cabins had fireplaces for cooking and to provide heat in winter. Some had board floors, but many were built directly on the earth. Windows rarely had panes of glass. These

Hampton University Archives

This photograph of the remains of a slave cabin in Georgia reveals little of the life—and death—that would have taken place inside. Imagine the voices once heard here—and perhaps the whispered longings for freedom.

STRATEGIES FOR SUCCESS

COMPARING STATISTICS

Statistics are numerical facts. They are often organized into tables, charts, or graphs so they are easier to analyze. Comparing statistics from two or more sources will help you understand relationships among the statistics.

How to Compare Statistics

To effectively compare statistics, follow these guidelines.

1. **Identify the types of data being compared.** Read the titles, headings, labels, and footnotes of each source (chart, graph, or table.)
2. **Examine the data.** Note the specific statistics for each heading.
3. **Be sure you know what is being compared.** Check quantities and values. They may vary from column to column or source to source and may be misread if not noted carefully.
4. **Notice both similarities and differences.** Observe how the numbers are alike or how they differ.
5. **Look for relationships.** Note *trends*—if quantities seem to increase or decrease at the same time or rate. Make inferences and draw conclusions. Form hypotheses to explain the trends you discover. Consider cause and effect relationships.

Applying the Strategy

Study the bar graphs below. The bottom graph shows cotton production and the top graph measures the size of the slave population of the United States. Both contain statistics for the years 1820 to 1860. How do the statistics compare? Note that both graphs show a steady increase during the years they cover. How might the statistics for cotton production and the size of the slave population be related? Would increasing cotton production require more slaves? Would more slaves increase production? Are both possible?

The map below shows the major cotton-producing areas in 1839 and in 1859. Note that this area has increased. How is the information on this map related to the statistics on the graphs? What are some conclusions you can draw from the information shown on the map and charts on this page?

For independent practice, see Practicing the Strategy on page 474.

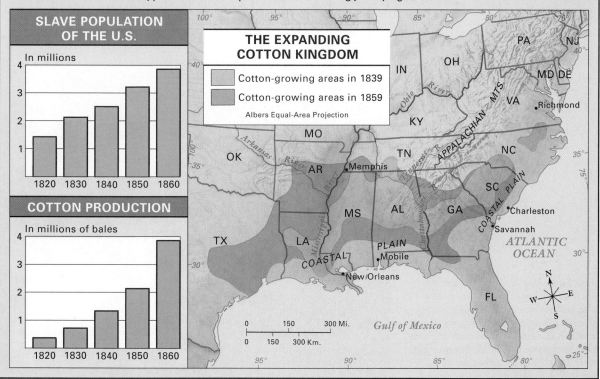

SLAVE POPULATION OF THE U.S. (In millions): 1820, 1830, 1840, 1850, 1860

COTTON PRODUCTION (In millions of bales): 1820, 1830, 1840, 1850, 1860

THE EXPANDING COTTON KINGDOM
- Cotton-growing areas in 1839
- Cotton-growing areas in 1859
Albers Equal-Area Projection

living conditions were primitive by modern standards. They were not, however, unhealthy. They tended to improve as time passed. Poor farm people, in the North as well as in the South, were not much better off in these respects.

However, the cotton gin also made life much more difficult for most slaves. When slaves were worth more, owners changed their attitude toward slavery. The number of slaves who were freed by their owners declined after 1800. Most southern state governments even passed laws making it difficult for owners who wanted to release their slaves to do so. Owners also tended to try to make their slaves work harder. The high price of cotton encouraged them to increase production by any possible means.

The westward expansion of cotton cultivation was extremely hard on thousands of slaves. Owners and slaves moved west together from Virginia and the Carolinas to Alabama, Mississippi, and Texas. But they made the move under very different circumstances.

American pioneers endured the dangers and hardships of the frontier willingly. They hoped to obtain a better way of life. They were prepared to take risks and suffer inconveniences to do so. The slaves whom they brought with them faced the same dangers and hardships. But they had no hope of benefiting as a result.

At a Slave Auction

No aspect of slavery brought home the inhumanity of it more than the slave auction. Slaves waited as buyers looked them over, deciding their fate and often that of their families. Josiah Henson recalled:

This is one half of a stereopticon slide, once very popular, that would show a three-dimensional image of these slaves picking cotton. Imagine viewing the slide in the comfort of your northern home in 1850. How might your future life be different from the lives of these children held as slaves?

458

"The crowd collected round the stand [auctioneer's platform], the huddling group of Negroes, the examination of muscle, teeth, the exhibition of agility, the look of the auctioneer, the agony of my mother—I can shut my eyes and see them all.

My brothers and sisters were bid off first, and one by one, while my mother, paralyzed by grief, held me by the hand. Her turn came, and she was bought by Isaac Riley of Montgomery County. Then I was offered to the assembled purchasers. My mother, half distracted with the thought of parting forever from all her children pushed through the crowd, while the bidding for me was going on, to the spot where Riley was standing. She fell at his feet, and clung to his knees, entreating [begging] him in tones that a mother could only command, to buy her baby as well as herself, and to spare to her one, at least, of her little ones. Will it, can it be believed that this man, thus appealed to, was capable not merely of turning a deaf ear to her supplication [request], but of disengaging himself from her with such violent blows and kicks, as to reduce her to the necessity of creeping out of his reach, and mingling the groan of bodily suffering with the sob of a breaking heart? As she crawled away from the brutal man I heard her sob out, "Oh, Lord Jesus, how long, how long shall I suffer this way!" I must have been then between five and six years old.[1]"

New Orleans claimed one of the largest slave markets in the South. Solomon Northrup recounted what he called a typical scene at an auction:

"David and Caroline were both bought by a Natchez planter. They left us, grinning broadly. They were happy because they had not been separated. Lethe was sold to a planter of Baton Rouge, her eyes flashing with anger as she was led away. The same man also purchased Randall. The little fellow was made to jump and run across the floor, and to perform many other acts to show his activity and condition. All the time the trade was going on his mother Eliza was crying aloud and wringing her hands. She begged the man not to buy him unless he also bought her and her daughter. . . . The man answered he could not afford it, and then Eliza burst into sobs. Freeman [the auctioneer] turned around to her savagely, with his whip in his uplifted hand, ordering her to stop her noise or he would whip her. Unless

The master of Tombee, a cotton plantation of St. Helena Island, South Carolina, made this entry in his diary.

"I will be compelled to send about ten prime Negroes to town next Monday, to be sold. . . . I never thought I would be driven to this very unpleasant extremity. Nothing can be more mortifying and grieving to a man than to select out some of his Negroes to be sold. You know not to whom, or how they will be treated by their new owners. And Negroes that you find no fault with—to separate families, mothers & daughters, brothers & sisters—all to pay for your own extravagances. People will laugh at your distress, and say it serves you right, you lived beyond your means. . . ."

Thomas B. Chapin,
May 3, 1845

SOLD DOWN THE RIVER

Kennedy Galleries

"Slave Auction at Richmond," above, is also by Eyre Crowe. With the rap of the autioneer's hammer the young woman on the platform will become the property of the highest bidder in this close, narrow hall.

Pioneers often left loved ones behind. Young men and women setting out for the West had to bid farewell to parents and friends knowing they would probably never see them again. It was very sad. For slaves these separations were cruel rather than sad. They had no choice in the matter. Since few could read or write, they did not even have the possibility of writing letters to those left behind.

It was bad enough for slaves whose owners took their human property west along with the farm tools, furniture, and other goods. Much worse was the fate of those who were sold to professional slave traders. These traders made a business of buying slaves wherever they could find them. They herded the poor captives together, chained them, and carted them off to regions where their labor was in

great demand. Busy markets developed in cities like New Orleans, where slaves from the Upper South were collected.

At these markets the slaves were sold at auction, one by one, to the highest bidder. Mothers were often separated from their children, wives from their husbands—all by the fall of the auctioneer's gavel. To be sold down the river in this way was a terrible fate.

she stopped that minute, he would not have such whining, he said. He would take her out into the yard and give her a hundred lashes. Yes, he would take the nonsense out of her pretty quick.

Eliza cringed and tried to wipe away her tears, but it was all in vain. She wanted to be with her children, . . .[1]"

Slaves never stopped trying to locate and rejoin their families. Many slaves ran away in an effort to join loved ones sold away. Reward notices printed in many southern newspapers described these

[1]From *Twelve Years a Slave* by Solomon Northrup

460   SLAVERY AND ABOLITION

attempts. Theodore Dwight Weld, a leading abolitionist, collected hundreds of such notices in his book *American Slavery As It Is. Testimony of A Thousand Witnesses*. Weld used the book to counter southern claims that slaves were basically happy. Many notices such as these appeared:

" *Macon (Ga.) Messenger,* November 23, 1837. $25 Reward—Ran away, a Negro man, named Cain. He was brought from Florida, and has a wife near Mariana, and probably will attempt to make his way there.

Richmond (Va.) Compiler, September 8, 1837. Ran away from the subscriber, Ben. He ran off without any known cause, and I suppose he is aiming to go to his wife, who was carried [moved] from the neighborhood last winter.

Richmond (Va.) Enquirer, February 20, 1838. Stop the Runaway!!!—$25 Reward. Ran away from the Eagle Tavern, a Negro fellow named Nat. He is no doubt attempting to follow his wife, who was lately [recently] sold to a speculator named Redmond. The above reward will be paid by Mrs. Lucy M. Downman, of Sussex County, Va.

Lexington (Ky.) Observer and Reporter, September 28, 1838. $50 Reward.—Ran away from the subscriber, a Negro girl, named Maria. She is of copper color, between 13 and 14 years of age—bare headed and bare footed. She is small of her age—very sprightly and very likey. She stated she was going to see her mother at Maysville.[1] "

The Peculiar Institution

By the 1830s most southerners were convinced that slavery—"the peculiar institution"—was absolutely necessary to their well being. They thought their whole way of life depended upon their ownership of slaves. They even persuaded themselves that slavery was good for the slaves as well as for the owners. They wrongly argued that their slaves were childlike by nature and of lower intelligence. They reasoned that under slavery they could protect and guide these "inferior" people. Compare the life of the slave with that of the northern free worker, they urged. Did slaves ever have to worry about where their next meal was coming from? Did anyone ever see a slave begging in the South? Sick slaves were cared for by their masters. Old slaves were certain of support as long as they lived and a decent burial when death finally came.

Southerners especially liked to compare the living conditions of plantation workers with those of poor immigrants and low-paid factory workers in northern cities. They insisted that the workers who

[1]From *American Slavery As It Is. Testimony of a Thousand Witnesses* by Theodore Dwight Weld

While growing up in Hannibal, Missouri, Sam Clemens, the future Mark Twain, once saw an angry overseer strike a clumsy slave.

66He was dead in an hour. Nobody in the village approved of murder, but of course no one said much about it. . . . Considerable sympathy was felt for the slave's owner, who had been bereft of valuable property by a worthless person who was not able to pay for it.99

Mark Twain

planted and picked cotton were better fed, better housed, and better clothed than the workers in the northern textile factories who spun the cotton into thread and wove it into cloth.

Yet even in the South people were still debating the evils and merits of slavery. In 1831 and 1832 delegates to the Virginia legislature held a year-long debate. Those who supported slavery used many arguments—economic, social, even religious. One of the most unusual was this one entered in the record of the debate:

66 We have no hesitation in affirming [claiming to be true], that throughout the whole slaveholding country, the slaves of a good master are his warmest, most constant, and most devoted friends; they have been accustomed to look up to him as their supporter, director and defender. Every one acquainted with southern slaves, knows that the slave rejoices in the elevation and prosperity of his master. . . . Have no doubt that they form the happiest portion of our society. A merrier being does not exists on the face of the globe, than the negro slave of the United States. . . .¹99

Of course, every debate has two sides, as this one did. Those opposed to slavery pointed to its many ''evils.'' Speaking during the Virginia debates, one delegate focused on the economic and social problems slavery caused for the South.

66 Slavery is ruinous to whites—retards improvement—roots out industrious population, banishes [throws out] the yeomanry [farmers] of the country—deprives the spinner, the weaver, the [black]smith, the shoemaker, the carpenter of employment and support. The evil admits no remedy—it is increasing, and will continue to increase, until the whole countryside will be inundated with one black wave, covering the whole extent, with a few white faces here and there floating on the surface. The master has no capital to invest but what is invested in human flesh—the father instead of being richer for his sons, is at a loss how to provide for them; there is no diversity of occupations, no incentive to enterprise. Labor of every species is disreputable because performed mostly by slaves . . . and the general aspect [look] of the countryside marks the curse of a wasteful, idle, reckless population who have no interest in the soil, . . .²99

Few southerners, however, spoke of the negative effects of slavery on the slaves. Their cause would be championed by northerners—white and black.

¹From *Review of the Debate on the Abolition of Slavery in the Virginia Legislature of 1831 and 1832* by Thomas R. Dew
²From *Niles' Weekly Register*, vol. 43, Sept. 8, 1832

AFRICAN AMERICANS IN THE U.S. POPULATION, 1790-1860				
Year	African Americans in the U.S. Population	Percentage of Total U.S. Population	Free African Americans	Percentage of Total African Americans
1790	757,208	19.3	59,527	7.9
1800	1,002,037	18.9	108,435	10.8
1810	1,377,808	17.9	186,446	13.5
1820	1,771,656	17.8	233,634	13.2
1830	2,328,642	17.6	319,599	13.7
1840	2,873,648	16.9	386,293	13.4
1850	3,638,808	15.6	434,495	11.9
1860	4,441,830	14.0	488,070	11.0

Source: *Historical Statistics of the United States*

LEARNING FROM TABLES. *This chart contains data about African Americans—both free and slave—in the U.S. population. What surprising trend can you note in the percentage of the total population made up of slaves from 1790 to 1860? What do you think might have caused this?*

Pride and Prejudice

Slaveholders also took pride in the importance of American cotton to the whole world. **"Cotton Is King"** was a southern slogan. Southerners meant by this slogan that their cotton was essential to the prosperity of the United States and to most of Europe as well. Since cotton depended on slavery, criticism of slavery seemed to them unpatriotic and downright dangerous.

Of course, cotton was *not* king in the sense that southerners imagined. It was the nation's most valuable export, but the national economy would not have collapsed if no cotton were grown. Still, southerners were hardly alone in boasting about the importance of their system. Like Americans in all sections, they were proud of their country and their way of life.

That pride was understandable. The United States was a rich and growing country. The American experiment in republican government was proving a success. Most ordinary people in other nations greatly admired America. European reformers studied the Declaration of Independence and the Constitution. They looked forward to a time when they might create similar governments in their own lands. Each year more and more foreigners were crossing the Atlantic Ocean hoping to find wealth and happiness in the United States.

Noticing these things, Americans tended to sing the praises of their country and of themselves. Frontier settlers in particular liked to brag about their own abilities. One western character explained:

> 66 I am a real ring-tailed roarer . . . from the thunder and lightning country. I make my breakfast on stewed Yankee and pork steak and rinse them down with spike nails. I can lick my weight in wildcats or raccoons. . . . I can out-eat, out-drink, out-work, out-grin, out-snort, out-run, out-lift, out-sneeze, out-lie anything in the shape of man or beast from Maine to Louisiana. 99

The sketch shows a ring-tailed roarer on his diet of spike nails, an image that comes from the bragging voices of the American frontier.

"Stump Speaking" shows a politician campaigning in rural Missouri. His speech may have lasted hours and genuinely interested his attentive listeners. George Caleb Bingham, who painted this picture in 1854, was a politician himself as well as a fine American painter.

It was this kind of thinking that explains the foolish confidence of the western War Hawks who had expected to conquer Canada so easily when war broke out with Great Britain in 1812.

Most easterners and southerners were more restrained than western types like the War Hawks and the "ring-tailed roarer." But Americans in every section felt deep national pride. Each **Fourth of July** people gathered in towns and villages to celebrate the anniversary of the signing of the Declaration of Independence. There were fireworks, parades, brass bands, and many stirring speeches by politicians, ministers, and war veterans. The words of the Declaration were sometimes read aloud, reminding listeners that "all men are created equal." On the outskirts of plantation lawns and city parks slaves heard these words as they tended the horses and waited for their owners. How did they feel? As Frederick Douglass, a former slave, said:

❝ What to the American slave is your Fourth of July? I answer, a day that reveals to him, more than all the other days of the year, the injustice and cruelty of which he is the constant victim. . . .[1]❞

[1]From *The Life and Writings of Frederick Douglass,* vol. 2, edited by Philip Foner

Americans of the day were quite pleased with their achievements. This was often harmless enough. But among the slaveholders this pride had very serious effects. They could not accept even the mildest criticism of "the peculiar institution."

Return to the Preview & Review on page 456.

3. ABOLITIONISM

The Movement to Abolish Slavery

Gradually, a small number of Americans, mostly but not entirely people from the free states, began to argue that slavery was wrong and ought to be **abolished,** or ended. These **abolitionists,** as they were called, were influenced by the same typically American pride and self-confidence that led so many southerners to insist that slavery was the best possible social system. The abolitionists believed in the ideal of freedom. They insisted that America was the land of liberty. They were impatient with any imperfection in their society. It was sinful, they said, to stand by idly while a flaw like slavery existed.

Abolitionists quoted the Declaration of Independence to show that slavery was contrary to American principles. They also put forth religious arguments stressing that all human beings are equal in the eyes of God. It was hard to disagree with these arguments. Nevertheless, most people, even non-slaveholders, considered the abolitionists to be dangerous radicals.

This was so because there seemed no legal way to do away with slavery in the United States. Under the Constitution each state could decide whether or not to allow slavery to exist within its borders. The northern states had abolished it after the Revolution. But nearly all voters in the southern states favored the slave system. There was no chance that the citizens of Virginia or Georgia or Mississippi would ever voluntarily agree to free their slaves.

Slavery could, of course, be abolished by amending the Constitution. But an amendment would require the approval of three fourths of the states. In 1850 half of the 30 states in the Union permitted slavery. No antislavery amendment could possibly be ratified. To campaign for abolition under these circumstances seemed like urging revolution and civil war.

Nevertheless, some important foes of slavery demanded action. One of the prominent early ones was Benjamin Lundy, a saddle maker from New Jersey. Lundy probably became interested in abolition because he was a Quaker. Even during the colonial period many Quakers had spoken out against slavery. In 1821 Lundy began to publish an antislavery newspaper, *The Genius of Universal Emancipation.*

Lundy's paper never had more than 700 subscribers. His influence, however, was quite large. He worked tirelessly for the cause. He urged Congress to abolish slavery in the District of Columbia and to prohibit its spread into the western territories. He bitterly attacked the plan to annex slaveholding Texas. He also demanded that free blacks in the North be treated fairly.

At first Lundy favored granting freedom to the slaves gradually. Perhaps if the children of all slaves born after a certain date were set

Preview & Review

Use these questions to guide your reading. Answer the questions after completing Section 3.
Understanding Issues, Events, & Ideas. Give the significance of the following words in the movement to end slavery: abolish, abolitionists, emancipation, *Appeal to the Colored Citizens of the World,* Underground Railroad.
1. What arguments did the abolitionists make against slavery?
2. How did the following work for abolition: Benjamin Lundy? William Garrison? Angelina and Sarah Grimké? Theodore Weld?
3. How did the following fight slavery: Paul Cuffe? Henry Garnet? Harriet Tubman? Gabriel Prosser? Denmark Vesey? Nat Turner? Frederick Douglass?
4. How did the abolitionists influence opinion in the North?
Thinking Critically. 1. You are a member of the American Anti-Slavery Society. Do you think that William Lloyd Garrison is too radical? Why or why not? **2.** As a volunteer on the Underground Railroad, write a letter describing the escaped slaves, some of the problems you had helping them, and how you solved them.

Benjamin Lundy was an early leader in the movement to abolish slavery.

William Lloyd Garrison, publisher of The Liberator, *proclaimed, "I will be heard." Whom did he blame for the institution of slavery? Do you agree with his argument?*

Angelina Grimké Weld, shown above, and Sarah Grimké appealed to women of the South to reject slavery. Why did they urge its overthrow?

free, the South could accept abolition. When this idea of gradual **emancipation,** or freedom, attracted no southern support, Lundy became more radical. He began to demand immediate emancipation.

Radical and Moderate Voices

In 1829 Benjamin Lundy appointed a young man from Massachusetts, William Lloyd Garrison, as assistant editor of *The Genius of Universal Emancipation*. Garrison turned out to be much more radical than Lundy. Lundy had always hoped to persuade owners to free their slaves. He tried, for example, to show them that slavery was neither efficient nor economical. Garrison simply insisted that it was sinful to own a human being. He denounced not only slaveholders but all Americans who allowed slavery to exist, using religious terms of the Protestant preachers he identified with.

Garrison soon disagreed with Lundy. He left his job as editor and in 1831 began publishing a paper of his own, *The Liberator*. He announced in the first issue:

    ❝ *I will be* as harsh as truth, and as uncompromising as justice. . . . I am in earnest—I will not equivocate—I will not excuse—I will not retreat a single inch—And *I WILL BE HEARD!* **❞**

Garrison's position was so radical that even most northerners who disliked slavery turned against him. He blamed *everyone* who tolerated slavery for the existence of the institution. He urged the northern states to secede from the United States. "No Union with Slaveholders," was one of his slogans. Garrison publicly set fire to a copy of the Constitution. The Constitution, he said, was a "compromise with tyranny" and an "agreement with Hell."

In 1833 Garrison and other abolitionists founded the American Anti-Slavery Society. But Garrison's radical position caused conflict in the organization. The first president of the Society was Arthur Tappan, a well-to-do New York merchant and a devout Presbyterian. He helped to finance the abolitionist movement, but eventually he broke with Garrison. So did Tappan's brother Benjamin, and so did two important southern abolitionists, the sisters Sarah and Angelina Grimké. The Grimké sisters were two of a number of Quakers who opposed slavery.

In 1836 Angelina Grimké published a pamphlet, *Appeal to Christian Women of the South*. The *Appeal* urged southern women to "overthrow this horrible system of oppression and cruelty." She began making speeches attacking slavery before small groups of women in private homes. As her reputation grew, she began to lecture in public to larger groups, as did her sister, Sarah.

In 1838 Angelina Grimké married Theodore Dwight Weld, a clergyman who was a leader of the more moderate opponents of slavery. When Garrison demanded ''immediate emancipation'' of the slaves, he meant exactly that—right now and entirely free. Weld spoke in favor of what he called ''immediate abolition gradually achieved.'' By this he meant that his *goal* was complete freedom for all slaves but that it would take time to change the minds of slaveholders and to persuade northerners to take a stand.

To attract recruits, Weld and his group who were influenced by Charles G. Finney, America's most prominent revivalist, collected and published stories showing how slaves were being mistreated. They organized support for members of Congress who sympathized with their views. They ran candidates of their own in many elections.

Slave Uprisings

It is surely correct to assume that every slave was at least a silent abolitionist. A few were so outraged by slavery that they rose in rebellion against it. The chances of success were slight. Slaveholders feared slave uprisings so much that they reacted to them with terrible brutality. When captured, rebellious slaves were always killed.

One rebel slave was Gabriel Prosser. Every Sunday morning in the spring and summer of 1800 he slipped into Richmond, Virginia. He studied the town, noting the layout and locations of buildings and streets. Quietly, secretly, Prosser planned and gathered followers. Late in August he was ready to strike. Everyone in and around Richmond except known friends of the rebels would die.

Two things stopped Prosser. Two of his followers felt loyalty to their masters. When they learned of the plan to kill everyone around Richmond, they warned their owners. These slaveowners alerted city officials. Still Prosser might have succeeded. More than 1,000 slaves and ex-slaves were ready to strike. But just as they were gathering, a violent storm came up. Heavy rains washed away the roads and bridges into Richmond. Before the group could reorganize, officials seized Prosser. He and 36 others were hanged.

Denmark Vesey of Charleston, South Carolina, was another rebel. Vesey had purchased his freedom after winning some money in a lottery. Yet he was not satisfied with escaping from bondage himself. For years he planned his uprising, gathering a group of slaves and former slaves ready to take up arms. In 1822 he was ready to act, claiming that the Bible had inspired him. At the last moment one of his men lost his nerve and betrayed the plot. Although the rebellion never took place, Vesey and 35 others were hanged.

The bloodiest slave uprising was that organized by Nat Turner, a slave in Southampton County, Virginia. To those who knew him, Turner had seemed the last person who might be expected to resort to violence. He was mild mannered and deeply religious, as indeed many blacks were. Yet in 1831 he and his followers murdered 57 people before being captured. Historians still argue about whether or

"Nat Turner and His Confederates in Conference" was engraved in 1863. Turner leans on a pole, his face drawn with anger. When Turner rebelled, what bloody fate befell Southhampton County?

not Turner was insane. The point is that nearly every slave hated bondage and was eager to see something done to destry the system.

Turner's revolt had important results. In an attempt to quiet the growing antislavery clamor, proslavery people now claimed "Negro slavery, as it exists in the United States, is neither a moral nor a political evil." The revolt also spread fear throughout the white population of the South. Because Turner was a preacher and an educated man, southern states passed stricter laws to control African American preachers and the education of slaves. A member of the Virginia legislature admitted how far they would go to keep slaves from learning.

66 We have, as far as possible, closed every avenue by which light might enter their minds. If you could extinguish [put out] the capacity to see the light, our work would be completed; they would be on the level of the beasts in the fields, and we would be safe.[1] 99

Some slaves learned to read before Turner's revolt. Few did after it. Most states made it illegal to teach a slave to read. You could be put to death if you were caught. People feared that slaves who could read would be more rebellious. Of course slaves were no longer free to read the Bible. But as *De Bow's Review*, a southern magazine, stated:

66 Is there any great moral reason why we should incur [cause] the tremendous risk of having our wives and children slaughtered in consequence of our slaves being taught to read incendiary [those that stir the emotions] publications? Religion is as important to the slave as to the master but is the ability to read essential to salvation? . . . Millions of those now in heaven never owned a Bible. To read is a

[1]From *Eyewitness: The Negro in American History* by William Katz

valuable accomplishment, but it does not save the soul.
. . .[1]"

A few slaves taught themselves to read through heroic efforts or the help of others who could read. On the eve of the Civil War only one or two percent of the slaves were able to read or write. On plantations illiteracy among slaves was almost complete. This illiteracy was one of the worst handicaps of slavery.

Slave Culture

Historians know too little about slave culture. Fortunately, a few slaves wrote or dictated autobiographies. These were full of valuable information. During the 1930s a federally funded writers' project collected an oral history of slavery through interviews with hundreds of ex-slaves. Most were very old when interviewed, and their memories had faded somewhat. But their recollections, along with surviving slave songs, folktales, proverbs, and stories, tell of a rich and complex slave culture.

Slaves managed to shape their own lives within the harsh guidelines of slavery. Most lived in small communities—the quarters— with fellow slaves. There they developed institutions separate from those of white southerners. Their spirituals, slave songs, and tales told of anger and undying hope for freedom and played a central part in the slave culture. Slaves sang not because they were happy or content but because they were told to. And as Frederick Douglass explained in this excerpt, it was the words and the tone of the songs that carried the message of sadness and anger. Slave songs, he said:

". . . were mostly of a plaintive cast [one expressing suffering], and told a tale of grief and sorrow. In the most boisterous outbursts of rapturous sentiment, there was ever a tinge of deep melancholy [sadness]. . . .

I did not, when a slave, understand the deep meaning of those rude, and apparently incoherent songs. I was myself within a circle so that I neither saw nor heard as those without might see and hear. They told a tale which was then altogether beyond my feeble comprehension; they were tones, loud, long, and deep, breathing the prayer and complaint of souls boiling over with the bitterest anguish. Every tone was a testimony against slavery, and a prayer to God for deliverance from chains. The hearing of those wild notes always depressed my spirits and filled my heart with ineffable [unspeakable] sadness. The mere recurrence, even now, afflicts my spirit, and while I am writing these lines, my tears are falling. . . .[2]"

[1]From *De Bow's Review,* 1856
[2]From *My Bondage and My Freedom* by Frederick Douglass

Of course, any direct expression of slaves' feelings might have been suppressed by powerful owners and overseers. But within their communities and amongst themselves in the fields slaves did sing openly of their despair and suffering.

Slaves also developed other aspects of culture that gave them a sense of pride and humanity. Religion among slaves thrived. But it too was often practiced in secret. At night, deep in the woods behind their quarters, slaves would meet to pray. As more and more restrictive laws were passed, this became both more dangerous and more important. It uplifted the tired, beaten spirits of the slaves. It gave them hope.

Other aspects of culture did not develop as fully under the strict codes of slavery. Slave marriages were not recognized by southern law. But most owners encouraged stable marriages on their plantations. Of course, owners had the unquestioned right to break up families. Slaves had to live with this threat. Yet most were able to form lasting marriages and strong families.

Slaves had no legal status. In all southern states they were considered property. They could not own property themselves, marry freely, make contracts, or testify against a white person in court. They could not travel without a pass, or legally possess whiskey or guns. It was against the law for an owner to murder a slave. But severe punishments for disobedience by a slave were legal. Should such a punishment result in death, it was nearly impossible to gain a conviction because slave testimony was inadmissible in court.

Yet by bits and pieces a unique slave culture grew. This amazing achievement has been called by Ralph Ellison, an African American novelist, "one of the great triumphs of the human spirit in modern times."

African American Abolitionists

African Americans in the northern states could speak openly against slavery. Many did so before abolitionism became an important movement. They organized a large number of antislavery societies long before the creation of the American Anti-Slavery Society. The American Society of Free Persons of Color, formed during the National Negro Convention of 1830, was at the forefront of the abolition movement.

These abolitionists varied in their specific ideas. One of the first whom we know much about was Paul Cuffe. Cuffe was born free in Massachusetts Bay in 1759. As a youth he went to sea. Gradually he saved enough to buy a ship. He prospered. Eventually he owned a fleet of six merchant vessels. By 1800 he was probably the richest African American in the United States.

Cuffe favored the return of African Americans to Africa. Most colonizationists wanted to send former slaves to Africa to get rid of them. Cuffe saw colonization as a way for people to free themselves from prejudice and mistreatment. He transported 38 volunteers to West Africa in 1815 at his own expense. He intended to bring a new group each year, but he died before he could carry out his plan.

Henry Highland Garnet was more bitterly antislavery than Paul Cuffe. Garnet was born a slave in 1815 but escaped to the North with his parents when he was a small boy. His father became a shoemaker in New York City. Garnet managed to get a high school education. He went to sea and lost a leg as a result of an accident.

Garnet was a man of fierce determination. He had an eye, a friend said, "that looks through you." During the 1830s and 1840s he preached abolition in these tones:

Abolitionist Henry Highland Garnet is shown in this 1881 engraving.

" Brethren arise, arise! Strike for your lives and liberties. Now is the day and the hour. Let every slave throughout the land do this and the days of slavery are numbered. . . . *Rather die freemen than live to be slaves.*"

He was soon joined by Charles Remond and others. Remond, a well-educated African American from Massachusetts, carried the antislavery crusade throughout the United States and to Great Britain.

Yet Garnet was moderate when compared to David Walker. In Boston in 1829 Walker published an angry *Appeal to the Colored Citizens of the World.* He began his *Appeal*:

" We (the coloured people of the United States) are the most degraded, wretched, and abject [cast down in spirit] set of beings that ever lived since the world began. . . .

The Indians of North and South America—the Greeks— the Irish, subjected under the king of Great Britain—the Jews, that ancient people of the Lord—the inhabitants of the islands of the sea—in fine [in total]; all inhabitants of the earth, (except however the sons of Africa) are called *men,* and of course are, and ought to be free. But we, (coloured people) and our children are brutes [beasts]!! and of course are, and *ought to be* Slaves to the American people and their children forever!! to dig their mines and work their farms; and thus go on enriching them, from one generation to another with our *blood* and our tears!!!![1]"

Walker's essay was a powerful call for bold action. African Americans—free and slave—must strike for freedom—violently, if necessary. If white Americans wanted to prevent racial war, insisted Walker, they had to recognize the rights and humanity of blacks.

Northerners, even some abolitionists, condemned Walker's essay as dangerous. Southerners put a price on Walker's head and tried to halt circulation of his *Appeal.* It is possible that he was later murdered.

[1]From *Appeal to the Colored Citizens of the World* by David Walker

"On to Liberty" by Theodor Kaufmann shows escaping slaves surge forward as they realize that the prize of freedom lies just ahead of them.

Harriet Ross Tubman helped between 200 and 300 escaped slaves make their way to freedom.

Inspired in part by their Christian faith, some African American women joined the attack on slavery. Sojourner Truth was a forceful speaker for abolition and women's rights. Harriet Ross Tubman escaped from Maryland into Pennsylvania when faced with threat of being "sold down the river" after the death of her owner. But she was not satisfied merely to be free or even to make speeches urging the abolition of slavery. She became a specialist at the highly dangerous task of helping slaves escape into the northern states. She made 19 trips into the South and helped between 200 and 300 escaped slaves make their way to freedom.

Tubman was a "conductor" on the **Underground Railroad,** an informal organization that helped escaped slaves to make their way to Canada. Here and there along the route were "stations"—barns, stables, and safe houses—where the escaped slaves could hide. Angry slaveholders offered a reward of $40,000 for Tubman—dead or alive. Robert Purvis, a free African American in Charleston, worked tirelessly for the railroad. His zeal in helping slaves to freedom earned him the title "President of the Underground Railroad."

Frederick Douglass

The most famous African American who became an abolitionist was Frederick Douglass. Douglass had been a slave in Baltimore. In 1836 he ran away but was captured. Two years later he tried again, this time succeeding. He settled in Massachusetts.

One day in 1841 Douglass attended a meeting of the Massachusetts Anti-Slavery Society. Garrison himself was present. Without preparation Douglass stood up and delivered a powerful speech. The members of the society were so impressed that they urged him to become an agent of the society and work full time for abolition.

Abolitionists found that former slaves, like Frederick Douglass, were the best possible advertisements for their cause. These former slaves understood the horrors of slavery as no other person could.

Frederick Douglass proved to a moving and persuasive abolitionist. He was a big, handsome man with what would today be called a magnetic personality. He was an excellent speaker. At first he followed the lead of Garrison, demanding instant abolition. Eventually he decided that the only way to change the system was to work within it. He then began to engage in political activity. He also published his own abolitionist paper, *The North Star*. In it in 1849 he stated his position in clear, direct, and simple language:

Frederick Douglass was the much-admired speaker who, once a slave, now spoke out against the injustices of the peculiar institution with particular conviction. Why do you think people listened so attentively to an abolitionist who was once a slave?

  ❝ The white man's happiness cannot be purchased by the black man's misery. Virtue cannot prevail among the white people, by its destruction among the black people, who form a part of the whole community. It is evident that white and black 'must fall or flourish' together. In the light of this great truth, laws ought to be enacted, and institutions established—all distinctions founded on complexion [skin color] ought to be repealed, repudiated, and forever abolished—and every right, privilege, and immunity, now enjoyed by the white man, ought to be as freely granted to the man of color.[1] ❞

[1] From *The North Star*, November 16, 1849 by Frederick Douglass

These were words he would use time and again in his most famous essay and speech titled *What the Black Man Wants*, and in many other speeches before, during, and after the Civil War.

The Influence of the Abolitionists

In the 1840s and 1850s American abolitionists were a small minority in every part of the country. The followers of William Lloyd Garrison were a small minority of this minority. Nevertheless, the abolitionists had a large influence on public opinion, and Garrison and his followers had a large influence on other abolitionists.

Even people who considered abolitionists dreamers who threatened the peace of the Union were affected by their arguments against slavery. Such people were unwilling to act. But their dislike of slavery grew. Their consciences bothered them. Moderate abolitionists found themselves listening more closely to people like Weld and Stowe. Their own efforts to persuade others to support gradual change had accomplished little.

Many abolitionists became discouraged by their apparent lack of success in ending slavery. But in one important sense they were succeeding better than they knew. They were convincing the people of the North that slavery was a bad institution. They still had to convince them it was possible to free the nation of slavery. 🖳

Return to the Preview & Review on page 465.

CHAPTER 13 REVIEW

1790	ABOLITIONISM	1810	

1793
Whitney invents
cotton gin

1800
Gabriel Prosser
plans revolt

1808
Congress bans
slave importation

1817
American
Colonizat
Society

Chapter Summary
Read the statements below. Choose one, and write a paragraph explaining its importance.
1. Soon after the American Revolution slavery in the United States seemed to be dying out.
2. The increasing importance of cotton to the southern economy revitalized slavery.
3. Many southerners convinced themselves that slavery was good for the slaves.
4. Gradually some Americans began to argue that slavery was wrong and ought to be abolished.
5. Slaves and ex-slaves protested their bondage by revolting or escaping along the Underground Railroad.
6. Although many Americans felt abolitionists were radicals, more and more people grew to dislike "the peculiar institution."

Reviewing Chronological Order
Number your paper 1–5. Then study the time line above and place the following events in the order in which they happened by writing the first next to 1, the second next to 2, and so on.
1. Importation of African slaves banned
2. Whitney's cotton gin
3. Garrison publishes *The Liberator*
4. Prosser plans slave revolt
5. Frederick Douglass joins abolition movement

Understanding Main Ideas
1. Describe the yearly cycle of life on a cotton plantation.
2. How did the lives of the slaves change as cotton production increased?
3. What arguments did some southerners use to defend slavery? What were arguments used by abolitionists to attack slavery?
4. Why did most people consider the abolitionists to be dangerous radicals?
5. Why did William Lloyd Garrison split with many other abolitionists?

Thinking Critically
1. **Determining Cause and Effect**. How did the cotton gin benefit southern farmers? Northern cloth manufacturers? Slaves? How did the cotton gin make life more difficult for slaves?
2. **Analyzing**. Write a script for an argument about slavery between a southern plantation owner and a northern factory owner.
3. **Synthesizing**. You are Frederick Douglass, writing an editorial for your newspaper, *The North Star*. Persuade your readers that in order to achieve the abolition of slavery, they must work within the system, rather than outside it.

Writing About History: Expressive
Write an imaginary interview with Harriet Tubman based on one episode in her life. Use the information in Chapter 13 and in other reference books to prepare your interview.

Practicing the Strategy
Review the strategy on page 457.
Comparing Statistics. Study the graph on page 453, and answer the following questions.
1. What is significant about the date in the title of the graph?
2. What percentage of the white southern population owned no slaves at all?
3. Of the 25 percent who owned slaves, what percentage owned 10 or more? In what kind of occupation do you think these owners were engaged?
4. Why do you think the vast majority of southern whites supported slavery although only a small minority owned slaves?

1
e Genius of Universal Emancipation

2
ey plans slave revolt

1831
First issue of *The Liberator*
★
Nat Turner's revolt

1833
American Anti-Slavery Society

1841
Douglass joins
abolition movement

Using Primary Sources

English-born Frances Anne Kemble was a well-known actress. After a successful stage career, she married an American and moved to Georgia, where her husband and his brother owned several plantations. Read the following excerpt adapted from *Journal of a Residence on a Georgia Plantation in 1838–1839* by Fanny Kemble. As you read, notice how Mrs. Kemble's views differed from those of the plantation owner. Then answer the questions below.

But teaching the slaves is a finable offense. . . . The first offense of the sort is heavily fined, and the second more heavily fined. For the third, one is sent to prison. . . . I certainly intend to teach Aleck to read. I certainly won't tell Mr. Butler [the plantation owner] about it.

I began to see one great advantage in this slavery: you are the absolute ruler on your own plantation. No slave's testimony counts against you, and no white testimony exists but what you choose to admit. Some owners injure their slaves, some brand them, some pull out their teeth, some shoot them a little here and there (all details gathered from ads for runaway slaves in southern papers). They do all this on their plantations, where nobody comes to see.

1. Why was Fanny Kemble afraid to tell the plantation owner that she was teaching Aleck to read?
2. Why do you think plantation owners did not want their slaves to be educated?
3. What evidence from the excerpt suggests that plantation owners could mistreat slaves without fear of punishment by law?

Linking History & Geography

Because of the great distance to Canada, escaped slaves faced many hardships. Below are lists of typical routes. Refer to a map of the United States to help you develop a map showing each route and indicating the number of miles from the first point to the Canadian border. Then describe the hardships an escaped slave might encounter on one of these routes.

1. Charleston, Philadelphia, New York City, Albany, Canada
2. Evansville, Indiana; Indianapolis; Toledo; Detroit; Canada
3. Percival, Iowa; Des Moines; Chicago; Milwaukee; Canada
4. Norfolk, Boston, Montpelier, Canada

Enriching Your Study of History

1. **Individual Project.** Complete *one* of the following projects: make a model or a large-scale drawing of a southern plantation and explain its importance in the economy of the South; *or* make a model or large-scale drawing of a cotton gin and explain how it works and its importance.
2. **Cooperative Project.** In groups, your class will write and present skits showing how the North viewed the South and vice versa. Plot ideas: You return to your plantation from a visit to relatives in a northeastern city, where you attended an abolitionist meeting. Tell your southern friends about the attitudes you encountered. Or, while visiting relatives in the South, you were taken to the cabin of an elderly slave who worked for their family. Describe your impressions to your northern friends.

CHAPTER 14

Reform and Romanticism

F rom the 1830s through the 1850s the effort to get rid of slavery was only one of many reform movements. This was truly an **Age of Reform.** The rapid growth of the country was causing changes of all sorts. These changes were mostly good for the average person. But sometimes they had undesirable side effects. Using machines for mass production reduced the price of goods. But the introduction of machinery often caused skilled workers to lose their jobs. The growth of cities opened up a number of opportunities for thousands of people. But it also led to crowded, unhealthy living conditions. Since Americans were so proud of their society, they found any flaw or weakness in it frustrating and annoying. Because they were so self-confident, they took these imperfections as a challenge. At every hand they could see signs of growth and progress. This made them optimistic about the future. Something *could* be done. Therefore something *must* be done. That was the dominant attitude of the reformers.

State Street in Albany leads to the New York Capitol in 1848. In the center of the street, vendors are selling flowers and fresh fruit from their horse-drawn carts.

Albany Institute of History and Art

Above we see the Jacksonian view of women: to serve men. The women, unless they are very old or very young, serve the meal and stand aside—shy and in the background. Do you think the painter meant to comment on women's role in society?

1. WOMEN AND REFORM

Women in Jacksonian America

One of the strangest things about the movement to free slaves was that many of its most active supporters were themselves not entirely free. When women came forward to speak out against slavery, they were attacked by people who believed that it was "unfeminine" for a woman to speak in public to a mixed audience. Even many male abolitionists took this position. At an international antislavery convention held in London in 1840, the men in charge refused to allow women delegates to participate. Two American delegates, Lucretia Mott and Elizabeth Cady Stanton, had to watch the proceedings from the balcony.

Nowhere were women placed in more lofty positions than in America. Nowhere were they more respected. But they were still treated as second-class citizens. They could not vote, hold public office, or sit on juries. Married women had no control over their own property. In the eyes of the law they were in the same position as children. They were subject to control by their husbands. Single women fared slightly better. At least they could manage their own property.

Women also had few opportunities to get a good education or have an interesting career. They could not be admitted to most high schools. Nearly all people of the time believed that women's brains

Preview & Review

Use these questions to guide your reading. Answer the questions after completing Section 1.
Understanding Issues, Events, & Ideas. Using the following words, describe the women's rights movement: Age of Reform, Women's Rights Convention, Seneca Falls Declaration.
1. What were some of the things women could not do in America in the early 1830s and 1840s?
2. What purpose was given for women's education?
3. In what field were the overwhelming majority of professional women?
4. For what did Susan B. Anthony campaign?
Thinking Critically. 1. Imagine that you are a delegate to the Women's Rights Convention in Seneca Falls, New York. Which right do you consider to be the most important for women to obtain? Why? 2. Write a letter to the editor of a newspaper in 1840, defending a woman's right to speak in public to a mixed audience.

A woman's education was thought a good preparation to "protect women from the dangers with which democratic manners surround them," according to Alexis de Tocqueville.

and nervous systems could not stand the strain of studying difficult subjects such as chemistry and mathematics!

Even most women who tried to improve women's education believed this to be true. Emma Hunt Willard's *Plan for Improving Female Education,* published in 1819, called for teaching young girls religion, housekeeping, literature, and music. The goal was to prepare them for marriage and motherhood, not for a "masculine" career. Willard established the Troy Female Seminary, the first women's high school in America, in 1821. When Catherine and Mary Beecher decided to teach chemistry at their Female Seminary in Connecticut, they assured parents and prospective students that knowledge of chemistry would make their graduates better cooks.

College was still an all-male institution, the final polishing of an educated man, the foundation for public life and the practice of the professions, particularly the ministry. Most people still viewed the role of women as domestic and private. They questioned their need for a college education.

Then in 1833 Charles Finney's Oberlin College in Ohio began to admit women. A few other colleges followed its lead. But real educational opportunities for women came with the founding of women's colleges. The first of these was Mount Holyoke Female Seminary (now Mount Holyoke College), founded by Mary Lyon in 1837.

Mary Lyon was an energetic woman, with red hair and bright blue eyes. She had attended and taught at several coeducational schools and had started the Buckland Female Seminary (a high school) in 1824. After touring several female high schools and visiting with Emma Willard in 1833, Lyon was driven to start a college for women. As she said in 1834, "My heart has so yearned over the adult female youth in the common walks of life, that it has sometimes seemed as if there were a fire shut up in my bones." Mount Holyoke Female Seminary was a rousing success. Soon women's colleges were opening in several states.

Women in the Professions

The ideal woman was expected to be religious, mild mannered, obedient, and totally domestic—nothing more. Practically all careers but marriage and teaching school were considered unfeminine. To be married and "live happily ever after" was supposed to be the goal for every young girl.

Nevertheless, a few women made their careers in male-dominated fields. Elizabeth Blackwell, a teacher, was determined to be a doctor. She read medical books at night. A sympathetic doctor gave her private lessons so that she could qualify for the Geneva Medical College in New York. She graduated first in her class in 1849 and became the first woman licensed to practice medicine in the United States.

Elizabeth Blackwell went on to establish her own hospital, the New York Infirmary for Women and Children, and a medical college for women. Her sister-in-law, Antoinette Brown Blackwell, became the first woman to be ordained a minister. Antoinette Blackwell was also active in many reform movements. Yet she found time to raise six children and to write no fewer than ten books.

Schlesinger Library, Radcliffe College

Elizabeth Blackwell established a medical college for women. Imagine some arguments she had to make to the all-male staff of Geneva Medical College to pursue her goal of practicing medicine.

"I do not wish to see the day come when women of my race in my state shall trail their skirts in the mire of partisan politics. I prefer to look to the American woman as she has always been, occupying her proud estate as the queen of the American home, instead of regarding her as a ward politician."
Congressman Frank Clark, 1915

Points of View

"Men call us angels, and boast of the deference they pay to our weakness! They give us their seats in church, in cars and omnibusses, at lectures and concerts, and in many other ways show us great respect where nothing but form is concerned. . . . But at the same time they are defrauding us of our just rights by crowding us out of every lucrative employment, and subjecting us to virtual slavery."
Amelia Bloomer, 1851

Illustrations from Godey's Lady's Book, *edited by Sara Hale, show the modest dress of the age. If you have a talent to do so, make a fashion sketch of a well-groomed woman of today (or tomorrow).*

Another such professional, Sara Josepha Hale, became the editor of the leading women's magazine of the day, *Godey's Lady's Book.* Hale worked to improve the education of women. She also wrote poetry for children, including "Mary Had a Little Lamb." Much of the writing of these women first appeared in magazines sponsored by religious denominations such as the Methodists' publication, *The Ladies Repository.*

The overwhelming majority of professional women of the period were elementary school teachers. By the 1850s Philadelphia had 699 women and 82 men teaching in its school system. Brooklyn, New York, had 103 women and only 17 men. Yet nearly all the school principals were men, and male teachers were paid higher salaries.

Woman as Guardian of the Home

Teaching fit in neatly with women's role as mother. Childrearing had always been their responsibility. In the 1830s and 1840s it seemed more important than ever. People were beginning to leave the farms for the cities. Instead of the whole family working the land, the father became the "breadwinner," the mother guardian of the home.

Factory work kept fathers away from home from early morning to late evening, six days a week. The mother had almost complete charge of rearing the children. Men no longer shared in most household chores. That was "woman's work."

The Women's Rights Movement

City life and increasing prosperity meant more leisure time for middle- and upper-class women. These women had household servants to help them with their domestic chores. Therefore they could develop new interests and activities. Many became involved in reform. In particular, many became abolitionists.

STRATEGIES FOR SUCCESS

UNDERSTANDING SEQUENCE

Many times history unfolds as a sequence of events. Social progress in the United States from the 1820s through the 1850s provides a good example. Recognizing sequence and relationships among the events will help you understand such periods in the nation's history.

How to Understand Sequence

To understand sequence, follow these guidelines.

1. **Check for dates.** The most obvious clues to a sequence of events are dates.
2. **Look for key words and phrases.** Note terms such as *then, gave rise to, next,* and *finally* that indicate a sequence of events.
3. **Identify relationships among the events.** Determine if one event leads directly to others, and if they in turn lead to still others.
4. **Notice the larger picture.** Remember events in one area might spur events in other areas.

Applying the Strategy

Review Section 1, "Women and Reform." Create a sequential list of the key events mentioned in the section. When completed, your list should resemble the following one.

WOMEN AND REFORM

Plan for Improving Female Education published
Catherine and Mary Beecher open the Female Seminary in Connecticut
Sarah Grimké writes *Letters on the Equality of the Sexes and the Condition of Women*
Women banned from London antislavery conference
Women's Rights Convention in Seneca Falls, New York
Seneca Falls Declaration of Sentiments and Resolutions issued
Sara Josepha Hale becomes editor of *Godey's Lady Book*
Elizabeth Blackwell becomes first woman licensed to practice medicine (1850)
Antoinette Brown Blackwell is first woman to become a fully ordained minister

Note that educational opportunities for women were the first steps in the women's rights movement. Sarah Grimké's book and the exclusion of Lucretia Mott and Elizabeth Cady Stanton from the London antislavery conference led directly to the Seneca Falls Conference. The declaration of women's rights issued at Seneca Falls quickly led to reforms by several states in laws concerning women.

For independent practice, see Practicing the Strategy on page 506.

The Granger Collection

One African American woman and leading abolitionist also spoke out for women.

"The man over there says women need to be helped into carriages and lifted over ditches and over puddles, and have the best place everywhere. Nobody helps me into carriages and over puddles, or gives me the best place—and ain't I a woman? I have ploughed and planted and gathered into barns, and no man could head me—and ain't I a woman?"
Sojourner Truth, 1851

The Granger Collection

Elizabeth Cady Stanton

Women who protested against slavery soon became aware of their own lowly position in society. One argument against slavery was the statement in the Declaration of Independence that all men were created equal. If slaves were entitled to equality, surely "free" women were too. Yet women who tried to speak out against slavery were often prevented from doing so by most male abolitionists.

Both Sarah and Angelina Grimké experienced so much resistance when they made public speeches attacking slavery that they became militant feminists. In *Letters on the Equality of the Sexes and the Condition of Women* (1838), Sarah Grimké wrote that "history teems with women's wrongs" and "is wet with women's tears." In 1838 she wrote:

"It will be scarcely denied, I presume, that, as a general rule, men do not desire the improvement of women. . . . As *they* have determined that Jehovah [God] has placed woman on a lower platform than man, they of course wish to keep her there; and hence the noble faculties of our minds are crushed and our reasoning powers are almost wholly uncultivated [undeveloped]. . . .

Within the last century, it has been gravely asserted [seriously claimed] that, 'chemistry enough to keep the pot boiling, and geography enough to know the location of the different rooms in her house, is learning sufficient for a woman.'[1]"

Women abolitionists began to believe that besides trying to free the slaves, they must try to free themselves from forms of bondage based on sex. Elizabeth Cady Stanton, one of the women who had not been allowed to participate in the London antislavery conference of 1840, wrote:

"I now fully understood the practical difficulties most women had to contend with. . . . The wearied, anxious look of the majority of women impressed me with the strong feeling that some measures should be taken."

In 1848 Stanton, with Lucretia Mott, organized a **Women's Rights Convention** at Seneca Falls, New York. Mott delivered the opening and closing addresses. The delegates to the convention issued a *Declaration of Sentiments* modeled on the Declaration of Independence. What better model could they select? Certainly the purposes of the colonists in writing the Declaration of Independence had been similar to those of the delegates. Both sought greater independence.

Often the delegates chose words that echoed the Declaration of Independence: "When in the course of human events" and "We hold these truths to be self-evident." But they also created a document that stated their views and purposes: "it becomes necessary for one

[1]From *The Liberator,* January 26, 1838

portion of the family of man to assume among the people of the earth a position different from that which they have hereto occupied'' and ''all men *and women* are created equal.''

Just as the first part of the Declaration of Independence had listed grievances of the colonists, the first part of this **Seneca Falls Declaration** listed the grievances of women. The history of mankind, it said, ''is a history of repeated injuries . . . on the part of man toward woman.'' These injuries included denials of the right to vote, the right to equal educational opportunity, and the right to own property. The second part contained resolutions aimed at righting the wrongs listed in the first part. It closed with the demand that women be given ''all the rights and privileges which belong to them as citizens of the United States.''

Similar meetings were soon being held throughout the nation. In the 1850s several national feminist conventions took place. Women were on the move. Their cause won many new supporters. The most important of these was Susan B. Anthony of New York.

In the 1850s Anthony organized campaigns on behalf of equal pay for women teachers and for equal property rights. Her efforts encouraged other feminists to continue the struggle. Soon Massachusetts and Indiana passed more liberal divorce laws. In 1860 New York gave women the right to sue in court and to control their earnings and property. But nowhere were women able to win the right to vote. They made some progress during the Age of Reform, but the vote was not yet theirs. 🗩

A newspaper cartoonist sketched the Women's Rights Convention with the men yawning, stretching, and jeering while the ladies hold up their heads and scowl. How else does the cartoonist poke fun at this serious moment in the story of America? Below is Lucretia Coffin Mott, who organized and led the convention.

Return to the Preview & Review on page 477.

Women and Reform 483

2. REFORMS IN EDUCATION

Preview & Review

Use these questions to guide your reading. Answer the questions after completing Section 2.
Understanding Issues, Events, & Ideas. Describe early education in the United States, using the following words: home school, church school, dame school, adventure school, normal school, *McGuffey's Eclectic Reader,* "the three R's," Lancasterian system.
1. For what reforms in education did Horace Mann work?
2. Why did educators and politicians like the Lancasterian system of education?
3. How did reformers like Mann want to change education?
Thinking Critically. Do you agree with educational reformers of the mid-1800s who said that "democracy could not prosper unless all people could read and write"? Why or why not?

Education in Early America

As you have read, each section of the country developed a distinctive educational system. In each case education was viewed as the responsibility of the family rather than the government. Parents or other relatives taught children at home. In most of these **home schools,** education was restricted to studying the Bible or an almanac to master reading and writing and to learning basic arithmetic. Children whose parents could not read and write received little or no formal eduction.

As the nation grew, rural children and those on the frontier continued to learn at home or in **church schools,** where they were taught by the minister and his wife. Children in towns and cities often attended **dame schools.** Women instructors taught basic reading and writing skills in these schools and charged a nominal fee. The teachers in the dame schools often could barely read and write themselves, so the quality of instruction remained low.

"New England Country School" was painted in about 1878 by Winslow Homer. By then the movement for free public schools had placed schooling in the hands of men and women who were prepared to help children rise in the world.

Addison Gallery of American Art, Phillips Academy, Andover, Massachusetts

Young girls in towns and cities often attended **adventure schools** after completing dame schools. Located in the homes of the instructors, adventure schools stressed music, dancing, drawing, needlework, and handicrafts. In contrast, boys went to private or public grammar schools where they studied Latin and Greek. Boys from wealthier families then enrolled in a college or university where they often trained to become ministers or lawyers.

Free Public Schools

Unlike the women's rights movement, the fight for public education made a great deal of progress during the Age of Reform. Before the 1820s only a handful of communities maintained free schools. By the 1850s villages, towns, and cities all over the nation had established such schools. Education had become a public responsibility. Protestant ministers contributed greatly to this development.

Educational reformers argued that neither democracy nor religion could prosper unless all people could read and write. Schools would train students to be patriotic, hardworking, and moral citizens. In addition, ordinary Americans supported public education because they hoped it would enable their children to rise in the world. The growth of public education for all had far-reaching effects. By 1860, 90 percent of all free adults in America could read and write.

This was largely due to the immense success of the textbooks of Noah Webster, later famous for his American dictionary. His first *Spelling Book* was published in 1783 when Webster was a young schoolteacher in Goshen, New York. Webster emphasized American forms of usage rather than British and wrote a patriotic preface urging Americans to read their own literature. Some 15 million copies of the *Speller* were sold in the next five decades. Webster's *Reader* included speeches of the leaders of the Revolution and was also a best seller.

Another textbook used in many early American schools was Caleb Bingham's *The Columbian Orator*. It was a collection of "original and selected pieces, calculated to improve youth and others in the ornamental and useful art of eloquence," or the art of public speaking. It taught specific speaking skills such as pronunciation, gesturing, and inflection (changes in the loudness and pitch of the voice). It also emphasized the values important to all Americans— freedom, hard work, and respect for human rights. Students read aloud the selections, such as Washington's speech to the French ambassador in 1796.

Noah Webster declared in 1783, "America must be as independent in literature as she is in politics, as famous for arts as for arms." He spent his life molding an American language as part of a growing American culture. How did Webster's work help Americans feel pride in themselves?

66 Born, Sir, in a land of liberty; having early learned its value; having engaged in a perilous [dangerous] conflict to defend it; having, in a word, devoted the best years of my life to secure it [liberty] a permanent establishment in my own country; my anxious recollections, my sympathetic feel-

ings, and my best wishes are irresistibly excited, whensoever, in any country, I see an oppressed nation unfurl [open] the banners of freedom. But above all, the events of the French revolution have produced the deepest solicitude [fondness], as well as the highest admiration. To call your nation brave, were to pronounce but common praise. WONDERFUL PEOPLE! ages to come will read with astonishment the history of your brilliant exploits. . . .['][99]

The first American history textbook was published by John M'Culloch in 1787, when the ink was scarcely dry on the Constitution. Jedidiah Morse soon followed with textbooks on American geography. His geographies described the nation's physical features and told the story of American life. Such textbooks helped students feel great pride in being Americans. They also helped shape Americans' view of what it was to be an American.

In 1836 William McGuffey, a Presbyterian minister, published the first of *McGuffey's Eclectic Readers*. These taught religious lessons as well as reading. The following lessons are from the reader used by eighth graders[2]:

LESSON VII

RULE.—Be careful to pronounce every syllable distinctly and not join the words together.

EXERCISES UNDER THE RULE. To be read over several times by all the students.

We constructed *an arc* and began the problem.

The *surf beat* heavily.

Arm! warriors, arm!

Return to thy dwelling, *all lovely return.* . . .

The Whale Ship.—PROV. LIT. JOURNAL

1. They who go down to the sea in ships pursue a perilous vocation, and well deserve the prayers which are offered for them in the churches. It is a hard life—full of danger, and of strange attraction. The seaman rarely abandons the glorious sea. It requires, however, a pretty firm spirit, both to brave the ordinary dangers of the deep, and to carry on war with its mightiest tenants [whales]. . . .

QUESTIONS.—1. What is the character of the seaman's profession? Particularly of whalemen? 2. What are the most common accidents to which whalers are liable? . . .

ERRORS.—*Ord-na-ry* for or-di-na-ry; *pur-ty* or *per-ty* for pretty; *vict-ry* for vic-to-ry.

SPELL AND DEFINE.—(1) zealously, indisputably, glowingly, . . . (2) proximity, vanquished, leviathan. . . .

[1]From *The Columbian Orator* by Caleb Bingham
[2]From *The Eclectic Fourth Reader* by William H. McGuffey

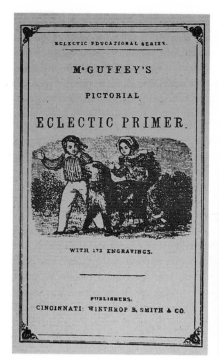

The Granger Collection

Addison Gallery of American Art,
Phillips Academy, Andover, Massachusetts

Winslow Homer was best known for his watercolors. "Homework" offers this portrait of a young pupil reading his lessons while the sun is still strong. Perhaps he is reading a lesson from a McGuffey's Reader *such as the one on the left.*

LESSON LXXVII

RULE.—Be careful to pronounce the little words, like *a, the, and, in,* etc., distinctly, and not to join them to the next word.

No Excellence without Labor.—WIRT.

1. The education, moral and intellectual, of every individual, must be, chiefly, his own work. Rely upon it, that the ancients were right—both in morals and intellect—we give their final shape to our characters, and thus become, emphatically, the architects of our own fortune. . . .

LESSON CVI

RULE.—When similar sounds come at the end of one word, and at the beginning of the next word, they must not be blended into one.

EXERCISE.—He sink*s s*orrowing to the tomb.

Man love*s s*ociety. . . .

Anthony's Oration over Caesar's Dead Body
SHAKESPEARE.

1. Friends, Romans, countrymen! Lend me your ears
I come to bury Caesar, not to praise him.
The evil that men do, lives after them;
The good is oft interred with their bones. . . .

Reforms in Education   487

Generations of textbooks were modeled on McGuffey. Each lesson taught a specific skill, and students answered questions at the end. Each skill built on those already taught. The readers were "eclectic," by which McGuffey meant "selected from the best of various sources." They contained Bible quotations, excerpts, poetry, essays, and articles. Each was chosen partly for the skill it taught and partly for the message it carried. Eventually McGuffey sold some 122 million copies of these books.

Horace Mann

National Portrait Gallery

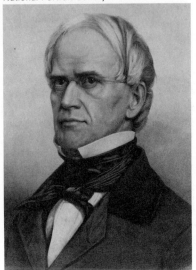

Horace Mann was a great leader in the efforts to improve public education. How did he use the Age of Reform to build on Massachusetts' tradition for education?

The effort to improve public education was particularly strong in Massachusetts. The early Puritans had established elementary and secondary schools in all but the smallest of their towns. Now, in the Age of Reform, the state built on this strong Puritan foundation.

Much of the credit belongs to Horace Mann, a lawyer and state legislator. When Massachusetts established a state board of education in 1837, Mann became its secretary. He worked for laws that required school attendance. He called for special schools to train teachers. He favored higher teacher salaries and better school equipment. Nowhere is his vision better stated than in his 1848 annual report to the Massachusetts Board of Education:

❝ Our means of education are the grand machinery by which the 'raw material' of human nature can be worked up into inventors and discoverers, into skilled artisans and scientific farmers, into scholars and jurists [judges], into the founders of benevolent institutions [those organized for the purpose of doing good], and the great expounders of ethical and theological science [philosophers]. By means of an early education, those embryos of talent may be quickened [made alive], which will solve the difficult problems of political and economical law; . . .[1]❞

Mann alerted Americans to the importance of free public education. His tireless efforts earned him the proud title of "the Father of American public schools."

[1]From *Annual Reports on Education, 1837—49* by Horace Mann

In 1839 Mann founded the first teacher training institute in the United States. Similar schools were soon established throughout the country. These institutes were called **normal schools,** the word coming from *norm,* meaning a "model" or "standard."

Before 1839 teachers had rarely received any direct training. There were no established qualifications a teacher had to meet. One man being interviewed for a job in a mining town was asked only, "Do you retain a clear recollection of the twenty-six letters of the alphabet?" Apparently that was all he was expected to know to "educate" the local children.

Mann was also interested in building new schools. He was exaggerating only a little when he said that "there is more physical suffering endured by our children" in badly constructed schoolhouses "than by prisoners in our jails."

Down through the 1840s wood-frame, one-room "little red schoolhouses" were the rule. In these small buildings 60 or more children of all ages were crowded into one classroom. A single teacher had to deal with first graders and teenagers at the same time. It was difficult to learn with so many distractions. But in the Boston of Horace Mann's day there were few schoolhouses of any kind. Most classes were held in stores and cellars.

By modern standards the best schools of the 1830s and 1840s were very uncomfortable. They had no washrooms. Students sat on narrow, backless benches. Yet, thanks to Horace Mann, by 1848 Massachusetts had built 50 well-equipped and comfortable public schools. Other states soon followed Massachusetts' lead.

The School Curriculum

The main subjects students of the early 1800s learned were known as **"the three R's"**—reading, writing, and 'rithmetic. They were taught quite differently than they are today. Before the 1840s most American schools used a teaching method developed in England by Joseph Lancaster. Lancaster used a monitor system in which teachers instructed older students who, in turn, taught younger pupils their lessons.

The **Lancasterian system** appealed to American educators and politicians because it provided instruction at the lowest possible cost. It did nothing, however, to encourage individual growth or to open the imagination.

In the 1840s and 1850s some educators began to question the Lancasterian system. Reformers like Horace Mann wanted to make education more exciting. Students should be encouraged to give free play to their imaginations. But like all educators, the reformers agreed that the schools' main purpose should be to build character and train children to become good citizens. 📧

Return to the Preview & Review on page 484.

3. RELIGION AND REFORM

Use these questions to guide your reading. Answer the questions after completing Section 3.
Understanding Issues, Events, & Ideas. Use the following words to explain religious reform movements: ideal community, Shakers, Amana community, Oneida community, transcendentalism, Second Great Awakening.
1. How did most Americans view ideal communities?
2. What was life like in a Shaker community?
3. How was God as portrayed by the preachers of the Second Great Awakening different from God as portrayed in the First Great Awakening?
Thinking Critically. In his essay "Self-Reliance" Emerson said, "Nothing is at last sacred but the integrity of your own mind." Find in the dictionary any words that you do not know. Then, explain what you think this sentence means.

Ideal Communities

Relying on education to improve society was likely to be a slow process. Few educational leaders were calling for drastic change. Yet many reformers were dreaming of totally reorganizing society. Some thought it wrong that a few people were much richer than all the others. They hoped to create a world where wealth would be shared equally.

Others thought that family life drew people into a small, closed circle and shut others out. They believed that people should live in community houses and that children should be reared and trained in common, not by their individual parents.

Most Americans considered such schemes foolish and unworkable, if not downright dangerous. Some reformers tended therefore to establish small communities in thinly settled parts of the country. The huge tracts of cheap, undeveloped land still to be found in the United States made it relatively easy to do so. Between 1820 and 1850 at least 58 such **ideal communities** were founded.

Many of these were very short-lived. Some lasted many years. A few evolved into institutions that still survive. The Mormons went west to Utah for much the same reason that the Puritans had come to Massachusetts Bay. Both groups wished to practice their religion without interference from people in their country who considered them dangerous and wrongheaded. The settlement on the Great Salt Lake was the Mormons' ideal community, organized according to their distinct beliefs.

Many other ideal communities were created by religious sects. One of the first to do so was the **Shakers.** This sect was founded by an Englishwoman, "Mother Ann" Lee. Mother Ann believed that she was God. She predicted that the world would soon come to an end. There was no point, therefore, in anyone having children.

Life in Shaker communities, which were called "families," was strictly regulated by a group of elders, half of them men, half women. Members wore simple black clothes. The two sexes lived separately. Everyone was expected to work very hard. All money belonged to the group. Contacts with the outside world were few.

Despite these strict rules the Shakers seemed to enjoy life. Singing, listening to sermons, work itself were all seen as serious religious activities and profoundly satisfying group experiences. New recruits entered the sect. When time passed without the world coming to an end, the Shakers began to adopt orphans in order to renew the membership. By the 1840s there were 20 Shaker communities in America.

The **Amana community,** founded by a German immigrant, Christian Metz, and the **Oneida community,** founded by John Humphrey

Noyes, were two other important communities of this type. Metz founded his settlement in western New York and later moved it to Iowa. The Noyes group began in Vermont and eventually settled in Oneida, New York. Both prospered. They owned much rich farmland and also developed manufacturing.

These colonial Shakers at worship trembled and chanted wordless songs. A church leader claimed that he had seen this form of worship in a vision of Heaven.

People who joined these communities made large personal sacrifices. Obviously most of them were deeply committed to the goals of the group. They were hardworking and skillful. Shaker furniture, simple and graceful, is still highly prized. The handiwork of both Oneida and Amana has evolved into modern manufacturing companies, Oneida making silverware, Amana electrical appliances.

The Transcendental Spirit

Literature and philosophy, rather than religion, were what most interested a group of New Englanders who called themselves the Transcendental Club. Ralph Waldo Emerson, who began his career as a Unitarian minister, was the best known of the group. One of his followers was Henry David Thoreau, the author of *Walden* (1854), which recounts Thoreau's attempt to live simply and in harmony with nature at Walden Pond in Massachusetts. Another follower, Bronson Alcott, became the founder of a cooperative vegetarian community called Fruitlands. When it failed he became largely

Three leaders in the Transcendental movement, from left, Bronson Alcott, Ralph Waldo Emerson, and Henry David Thoreau. What meaning do you give to their phrase, "Hitch your wagon to a star"?

dependent on the success of his daughter, Louisa May Alcott, author of *Little Women*.

Transcendentalism is hard to define. Its central idea was that people could transcend, or rise above, reason by having faith in God's universal spirit and in themselves. "Hitch your wagon to a star," was the advice of one of the transcendentalists.

In Emerson's most famous essay, "Self-Reliance," he made these and many other observations:

> " Trust thyself: every heart vibrates to that iron string.
> Whoso would be a man must be a nonconformist.
> A foolish consistency is the hobgoblin of little minds. . . .
> We are afraid of truth, afraid of fortune, afraid of death, and afraid of each other.
> Nothing is at last sacred but the integrity of your own mind. "

The transcendentalists were idealists, warm and affirmative, who believed in the power of reason and in basic human goodness. They celebrated traits already so much a part of the American character—individualism and self-reliance.

Yet although they were optimists, the transcendentalists did not ignore the problems in American society. They criticized governments, laws, and social institutions. They did not join reform associations, but they did contribute to the spirit of reform. They believed people knew right from wrong, good from bad, and would seek the right and the good if given the chance. Asked Emerson, "What is man born for but to be a Re-former, a Re-maker of what man has made; a renouncer of lies; a restorer of truth and good? . . ."

The Second Great Awakening

The religious views of the first American colonists changed very little with time. The North was still overwhelmingly Protestant. But most

Protestant sects took a more tolerant view of those who disagreed with them than had the Puritans. Early in the 1800s, what is sometimes called a **Second Great Awakening** broke out in various sections of the country. The First Awakening had been a force for toleration. Although preachers like George Whitefield and Jonathan Edwards were hard on sinners, all believers were invited to hear their message.

Many preachers of the revivals that followed the founding of the new nation were even more tolerant, because their message was more optimistic. The Awakening swept through Kentucky and Ohio after 1799 with special force. James McGready preached that sin was wrong but all who repented could be saved. Yet McGready's visions were as frightening as Jonathan Edwards' before him. One description says:

> 66 He could so array Hell before the wicked that they would tremble and quake, imagining a lake of fire and brimstone yawning to overtake them. 99

In the decades that followed frontier people flocked to religious camp meetings, which often lasted for days. Men wept and cried to Heaven. Disciples of McGready, such as Finis Ewing, traveled endlessly through the West bringing their message to isolated farms as well as large camp meetings. They converted sinners by the thousands. Others, like Peter Cartwright, a Methodist, traveled the revival circuit in the West. One biographer wrote of Cartwright:

> 66 His self-reliance, his readiness with tongue and fist, his quick sense of humor, all made him dear to the hearts of the frontier. If . . . intruders attempted to break up his meetings, he was quick to meet force with force and seems to have been uniformly victorious in these physical encounters. 99

The most influential preacher of the movement was Charles Grandison Finney. Finney believed revivals were essential to spreading the word of God. He claimed:

> 66 Almost all the religion in the world has been produced by revivals. God has found it necessary to take advantage of the excitability there is in mankind, to produce powerful excitements among them, before he can lead them to obey. Men are so spiritually sluggish, there are so many things to lead their minds off from religion, and to oppose the purpose of the Gospel, so that it is necessary to raise an excitement among them, till the tide rises so high as to sweep away the opposing obstacles. . . .[1] 99

In his sermons Finney described a democratic Heaven not unlike the United States of America. "God always allows His children as

Charles Grandison Finney stirred his listeners with a vision of a democratic Heaven. How did the Second Great Awakening differ from the first?

---

[1]From *Lectures on Revivals of Religion* by Charles G. Finney

Religion and Reform 493

The Granger Collection

much liberty as they are prepared to enjoy,'' he declared. He preached of the duty of people to take the ''right ground . . . on all subjects of practical morality which come up for decision from time to time.'' Finney inspired Theodore Dwight Weld and other revivalists who preached the gospel while speaking out against slavery, an institution they felt was morally wrong. Another leading revivalist, William Ellery Channing, a Boston Unitarian, did not preach about an angry God but spoke instead about what an exceptionally fine being Christ was.

These ministers preserved the Puritans' concern for high moral standards and social improvements, but played down the passions that had once driven men and women to found new colonies. They advanced the comforting belief that God would provide salvation for all.

Converts flocked to several Protestant sects, most notably the Presbyterian, Baptist, and Methodist, during this period of religious enthusiasm. Others joined one of the new religious groups—such as the Mormons and the Adventists—that arose. Throughout the country church attendance increased. This Second Great Awakening also advanced the cause of moral and social reform, which became a vital function of churches all over America. As Finney said, ''Away with the idea that Christians can remain neutral and keep still, and yet enjoy the approbation [approval] and blessing of God.''

Return to the Preview & Review on page 490.

4. THE ROMANTIC AGE

By the second quarter of the 19th century American writers and painters had become part of the Romantic movement. The Romantic movement had begun in Europe as a revolt against the cold-blooded logic of the Age of Reason and its view of nature governed by fixed scientific laws. Romantics emphasized their feelings and natural instincts over reason and logic. Romantics often viewed nature as a beautiful mysterious teacher. One of the founders of the Romantic movement, the English poet William Wordsworth, wrote:

> ❝ One impulse from a vernal wood
> May teach you more of man,
> Of moral evil and of good,
> Than all the sages can. ❞

The **Romantic Age** began in Europe but seemed particularly American in its praise of ordinary people, individualism, and emotion.

Edgar Allan Poe

Edgar Allan Poe was born in Boston in 1809 and became in his short lifetime a living example of the anguished genius that Romantics often liked to portray. An orphan who had been raised and then rejected by a wealthy Virginian, John Allan, Poe spent much of his life trying to regain Allan's favor. He won appointment to West Point but was discharged for "gross neglect of duty." He drank to excess, took drugs, and once attempted to poison himself. Yet he proved to be a marvelous editor, critic, and poet. In the opinion of many, he invented the detective story. His classics include "The Murders in the Rue Morgue" and "The Purloined Letter." He was one of the first to write what we today call science fiction, and he was a master of the horror tale with such works as "The Pit and the Pendulum," and "The Cask of Amontillado." Poe's poetic description of his childhood reveals much of the romantic in him:

> ❝ From childhood's hour I have not been
> As others were—I have not seen
> As others saw—I could not bring
> My passions from a common spring—
> From the same source I have not taken
> My sorrow—I could not awaken
> My heart to joy at the same tone—
> And all that I loved—*I* loved alone— ❞

Nathaniel Hawthorne and Herman Melville

Nathaniel Hawthorne was born in Salem, Massachusetts, where women were executed as witches in the early days of America. He

Preview & Review

Use these questions to guide your reading. Answer the questions after completing Section 4.
Understanding Issues, Events, & Ideas. In your own words, explain the historical significance of the Romantic Age.
1. How had artists during the Age of Reason viewed nature? How was the view of the Romantics different?
2. How did the experiences of Hawthorne and Melville influence their works?
3. What made Whitman's *Leaves of Grass* startling and original? How did Whitman and Dickinson differ?
4. Who were the writers responsible for "the flowering of New England"?
Thinking Critically. **1.** If you had the opportunity to meet and talk with Poe, Hawthorne, Melville, Whitman, or Dickinson, who would you choose? Why? **2.** Write a biographical sketch of one of the authors discussed in this section.

The Bettman Archive

Edgar Allan Poe shows the tolls of drink and endless hours writing with only a guttering candle for light in this 1848 portrait.

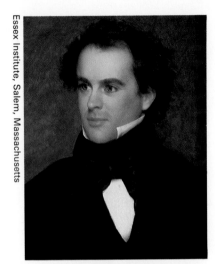

Nathaniel Hawthorne in 1840 was a handsome young author yet to make his reputation. His friend Herman Melville, shown in 1847, would soon begin his masterpiece Moby Dick.

was fascinated by the Puritan past of New England and its continuing influence on the people of his own generation. One of his greatest novels was *The Scarlet Letter* (1850), in which he urged his readers to condemn not sin so much as those who presume to judge the sinner. Another was *The House of the Seven Gables* (1851), a gripping account of the decay of an old New England family. The house in Salem may be visited today. One of his best-known short stories is "My Kinsman, Major Molineux," in which a young man learns to make his way in the world on his own merit.

In 1850, while writing *The House of the Seven Gables,* Hawthorne was introduced by his publisher to another writer in the midst of a novel. This was Herman Melville, who was writing *Moby Dick.* The two became good friends. Melville's life was quite unlike Hawthorne's quiet New England upbringing. As a boy Melville went to sea on a whaler, but jumped ship in the South Seas, where he lived among a tribe of cannibals. Later he became a beachcomber in Tahiti. When he returned to the United States in 1844 he began writing about his adventures. His first book was *Typee* (1846), a description of the South Seas. A sequel, *Omoo* (1847), quickly followed.

Melville's most famous work is *Moby Dick* (1851). Against the background of a whaling voyage—and nobody has described whaling better—he dealt with the problems of good and evil, courage and cowardice, faith, stubbornness, and pride. In the character Captain Ahab—driven to destroy the great white whale, Moby Dick, Melville created one of the greatest figures of American fiction.

Wall Street, not the sea, is the setting of Melville's best-known short story, "Bartleby the Scrivener." In this tale a mild-mannered law clerk finds the courage to tell his employer, "I prefer not to be a little reasonable"—a perfect response for the Romantic Age.

Walt Whitman and Emily Dickinson

The two great romantic poets of the 19th century are Walt Whitman and Emily Dickinson. Whitman, who was born in 1819, was truly a "common man," a supporter of Andrew Jackson, thoroughly at home with tradesmen and laborers. But he was surely not an ordinary man. His collection of poems, *Leaves of Grass* (1850), the last great outpouring of the American romantic movement, was startling and original in form and content with its free verse and plain language. In the poet's words:

  ❝ I celebrate myself, and sing myself,
    And what I assume you shall assume,
    For every atom belonging to me as good belongs to
      you. ❞

His remarkable gift of catching everyday speech and making it poetic is evident in lines like these in which even the Earth is an equal to this celebration of democracy.

> **❝** Earth! you seem to look for something at my hands
> Say, old top-knot, what do you want?
>
> I bequeath myself to the dirt to grow from the grass
> I love,
> If you want me again look for me under your boot-
> soles. **❞**

What a contrast is Emily Dickinson, who was born in Amherst, Massachusetts, in 1830. Shy, reclusive, she would say to Whitman's celebration of self: "I'm Nobody! Who are you?/ Are you—Nobody—too?" Yet these words betray the wondrous gifts of the poet. Only after her death were her poems published, giving us images of America that will be remembered forever. She wrote:

> **❝** This is my letter to the world
> That never wrote to Me—
> The simple news that Nature told
> With tender Majesty.
>
> Her Message is committed
> To hands I cannot see—
> For love of her—Sweet—countrymen—
> Judge tenderly—of me.[1] **❞**

[1]In *The Poems of Emily Dickinson*, edited by Thomas H. Johnson

The Flowering of New England

Besides Emerson, Thoreau, Hawthorne, and Dickinson, many of the great figures of American literature before the Civil War were New Englanders. Henry Wadsworth Longfellow's fame came from poems like "The Village Blacksmith," "Paul Revere's Ride," *The Courtship of Miles Standish*, and *The Song of Hiawatha*. His galloping verses have been recited by generations of schoolchildren: "Listen, my children, and you shall hear/ Of the midnight ride of Paul Revere."

Also prominent in this "flowering of New England," as one critic put it, was John Greenleaf Whittier, a poet as popular in his own day as Longfellow. Whittier was an abolitionist and active in politics. But his poetry is little quoted nowadays. "The Barefoot Boy" was one of his most popular. "Blessings on thee, little man," it begins, "Barefoot boy with cheek of tan."

More weighty was James Russell Lowell, the first editor of the *Atlantic Monthly*. He wrote humorous stories to satirize the Mexican War. Another widely known poet and essayist was Oliver Wendell Holmes, remembered for "The Chambered Nautilus" and "Old Ironsides," a poem about the U.S.S. *Constitution*. 🗐

Walt Whitman in about 1850 scarcely resembles the bearded poet we know from so many later photographs. One senses here that he has not yet found the freedom to "celebrate myself and sing myself." Emily Dickinson kept so to herself that we are fortunate to have her likeness at all.

Return to the Preview & Review on page 495.

Dorothea Lynde Dix, left, and Helen Keller and Anne Sullivan, right.

Preview & Review

Use these questions to guide your reading. Answer the questions after completing Section 5.
Understanding Issues, Events, & Ideas. Using the following words, cite the important attempts to improve society: Perkins Institution, juvenile delinquency, almshouse, house of refuge, Children's Aid Society, temperance, total abstinence, prohibition, National Trades' Union.
1. How did Samuel Howe help blind people? How did Dorothea Dix work to help the insane?
2. Why did reformers want children taken out of almshouses?
3. What was the high point of the temperance campaign?
4. What reforms did Seth Luther seek for factory workers?
Thinking Critically. 1. Charles Brace said, "The best of all Asylums for the outcast child is a farmer's home." Do you agree with Brace? Do you think Brace's statement applies today? **2.** If you were a reformer in the mid-1800s, what aspect of society would you reform? How would you proceed?

5. IMPROVING SOCIETY

Helping the Disadvantaged

Many people were unwilling to live in isolated communities and abandon all the customs and patterns of ordinary life. They were nonetheless sincerely interested in improving society. Some devoted their energies to helping people in need. Samuel Gridley Howe, a Boston doctor, specialized in the education of the blind. In the 1830s he founded a school, the **Perkins Institution.** He developed a method for printing books with raised type so that blind people could learn to "read" with their fingertips. Howe's greatest achievement was teaching Laura Bridgman, a child who was both blind and deaf, to read in this way and to communicate with others through signs called a manual alphabet. Another of his pupils, Anne Sullivan, learned the manual alphabet to communicate with Laura. She later became the teacher of Helen Keller, a remarkable woman who lost her sight and hearing as an infant but became a famous writer and lecturer.

Another Massachusetts reformer, Dorothea Dix, practically revolutionized the treatment of the mentally ill. Dix was a schoolteacher. One day in 1841 she was asked to teach a Sunday school class in a jail in Cambridge, Massachusetts. When she went to the jail, she discovered to her horror that insane and feeble-minded people were being kept there and treated like ordinary criminals. She launched a crusade to improve their treatment. In 1843 she completed her investigation by presenting to the Massachusetts legislature a shocking but true testimony on the conditions she found.

> " I come as the advocate of helpless, forgotten, insane, and idiotic men and women. I proceed, gentlemen, to briefly call your attention to the present state of insane persons confined in this Commonwealth [Massachusetts], in cages, closets, cellars, stalls, pens! Chained, naked, beaten with rods, and lashed into obedience.[1] "

Thereafter, Dix devoted her life to improving the care of prisoners and of the insane. She visited prisons all over the country and wrote reports describing conditions and exposing their faults. Dix insisted that insanity should be treated as a disease and that it could be cured. Through her efforts many states set up asylums for the care of the mentally ill.

Her crusade also lent force to that of prison reformers. These reformers feared social unrest and believed criminals could be rehabilitated to become useful members of society. They successfully called for prisons where first offenders were separated from hardened criminals and for detention schools for juvenile delinquents. But these new prisons stressed solitary confinement and strict discipline, and they probably did little to rehabilitate people who found themselves inside. Over the years the debate on the purpose of prisons would rage. Do they exist solely to separate wrongdoers from society? Or should they be places where criminals are reformed, to be returned to society? The debate continues today. Nonetheless, the prison system that evolved became a model for prison systems throughout the world; Alexis de Tocqueville, for example, came to examine American prisons for the French minister of justice.

Child Care

The social problem of **juvenile delinquency** was also attacked by reformers. As cities grew larger, an increasing number of children and teenagers began to get into trouble with the law. When a boy or girl was caught stealing, for example, the "criminal" was handled the same way that adult thieves were. If convicted, they were thrown into the same jails where older convicts were kept.

Many other children who had not committed crimes wandered homeless about the cities. They were orphans or runaways or youngsters who had been abandoned by their parents. When found, these children were often put into the local poorhouse, called an **almshouse.** Again they were kept along with adults, many of them tramps, drunkards, and similar types.

Reformers realized that this system only increased the chances that young delinquents and wanderers would become dangerous criminals when they grew up. As one put it, the jails turned "little Devils" into "great ones." Instead, the delinquent children should

[1]From Old South Leaflet No. 148 in *Old South Leaflets,* vol. VI

be reformed and the homeless ones protected and taught a trade so that they would be able to earn their livings.

To accomplish these goals, **houses of refuge** were founded as early as the 1820s in New York, Boston, and Philadelphia. Life in these houses was hard, discipline strict. The children rose at dawn, dressed, and were marched off to the washroom. After passing inspection to make sure they were neat and clean, they had an hour or so of lessons. Only then was there a recess for breakfast.

The rest of the day, except for the noon break, was spent working in shops. The boys made such things as cane chair seats, nails, and candles. The girls spent the time sewing. Work ended at about five o'clock. Then, after a light supper, the children marched back to school. The evening classes went on until bedtime.

This system was very harsh by modern standards. Children who violated the rules were often beaten, even put in solitary confinement. But it was a true reform. These houses of refuge represented the first attempt to treat delinquent children differently from adult criminals.

Gradually some of the people who studied juvenile delinquency began to realize that in many cases the children were more victims than criminals. The terrible poverty of the slums made it difficult for them to lead decent, normal lives.

One such person was Charles Loring Brace, one of the first American social workers. Brace founded the **Children's Aid Society** of New York in 1853. The society opened lodging houses where homeless boys and girls could live without actually being confined as they were in a house of refuge. It also established trade schools.

Brace persuaded manufacturers to give some of the children jobs. But his main goal was to be able to relocate homeless children with farm families. He believed that the terrible conditions of slum life in the cities was the main reason why delinquent children were getting into trouble. "The best of all Asylums for the outcast child," he said, is a "farmer's home."

"*Buffalo Newsboy*" *was painted in 1893. At this time boys and girls in trouble with the law were jailed with adults. Homeless children wandered city streets. Have we solved these problems of the Age of the Reform in the 1990s?*

The Attack on "Demon Rum"

Some reformers worked to improve the training of the deaf. Others worked for world peace. Still others tried to get citizens to give up what the reformers considered bad habits, such as drinking or playing games on Sundays. (Many critics considered these people not reformers but busybodies.)

The campaign against alcohol was the most important attempt made to control the personal behavior of citizens. The effort to restrict drinking began as a call for **temperance.** It was a fight against drunkenness, not against drinking in moderation. But it soon became a campaign for **total abstinence**—drinking no alcohol at all—and the **prohibition,** or outlawing, of the manufacture and sale of alcoholic beverages. Those who favored prohibition called drinkers sinners

The Granger Collection

and potential criminals. Again it was Reverend Charles G. Finney who led the effort.

The members of the American Temperance Union, which was founded in 1826, went about the land lecturing and distributing pamphlets. Despite the name they were outright prohibitionists. They urged drinkers to "sign the pledge"—that is, to promise in writing that they would give up alcohol completely. They also formed youth temperance groups to educate young people to the "evils" of alcohol. These clubs, similar to today's Students Against Drunk Driving (S.A.D.D.) groups, even sang a song that carried their message:

> **"** This youthful band
> Do with our hand
> The pledge now sign—
> To drink no wine,
>
> Nor brandy red
> To turn the head,
> nor whiskey hot,
> That makes the sot [drunkard],
>
> Nor fiery rum
> To turn our home
> Into a hell
> Where none can dwell
> Whence peace would fly
>
> Where hope would die
> And love expire
> 'Mid such a fire:—
> So here we pledge perpetual hate
> To all that can intoxicate.[1] **"**

A popular series of engravings made in the 19th century showed a family destroyed by alcohol. In the pleasant family scene on the left we watch as the head of the household persuades his wary wife to join him in a friendly drink. The bottle takes its toll. While the children huddle together their father dozes drunkenly. Meanwhile the mother trades household goods to buy more liquor. Now the table is bare, the cupboard empty, the cat scrawny, and the fireplace cold. Would these engravings be good propaganda for members of the Temperance Society to take "the pledge"? Why?

[1]From *A History of the American People* by Stephen Thernstrom

Improving Society   501

The campaign reached a high point in 1851 when the state of Maine outlawed the manufacture and sale of alcoholic drinks. The person most responsible for the passage of this law, Neal Dow, was a manufacturer who became alarmed because many of the men who worked for him were ruining their lives with drink.

Economic Reform

There were also reformers who wished to change the American economic system. Most people in the nation were better off by far than the average European. But some were not. Many who worked hard had not been able to rise above poverty. Furthermore, as the economy expanded, some people were growing very rich. The gap between wealthy merchants and manufacturers and people of ordinary income seemed to be widening.

Reformers found these trends to be alarming. William Leggett, a New York newspaper editor, asked:

    ❝ Does a man become wiser, stronger, or more virtuous and patriotic because he has a fine house? Does he love his country the better because he has a French cook and a box at the opera?❞

Leggett blamed the growing gap between rich and poor on what he somewhat vaguely called "concentrated money power." He supported Andrew Jackson's attack on the Second Bank of the United States. And he favored reducing tariffs because high tariffs increased the profits of the manufacturers and caused prices to rise.

Leggett's policies were less drastic than those put forth by some other economic reformers. Thomas Skidmore, for example, proposed that rich people not be allowed to leave their wealth to their children. He even proposed that all the personal property of all the people in the country be taken over by the government. It would then be spread among the people in equal shares.

George Henry Evans, publisher of a newspaper called *The Working Man's Advocate*, had a more practical suggestion. Evans's slogan was "Vote Yourself a Farm." He wanted the government to limit the amount of land that any one person could own. He urged Congress to stop the sale of unoccupied land in the West. Publicly owned lands should be divided up into farm plots and given to citizens who were willing to cultivate them. One land reform statement ran:

    ❝ Are you an American citizen? Then you are a joint owner of public lands. Why not take enough of your property to provide yourself a home? Why not vote yourself a farm?❞

William Leggett was one who struggled to close the gap between rich and poor in Jacksonian America. And what of today? Has the gap between rich and poor widened or narrowed, in your opinion?

Efforts to Help Workers

One of William Leggett's favorite proposals was that workers should organize into unions. Although there were some labor organizations during the colonial period, unions had always been considered illegal. They were thought to be conspiracies, plots organized by workers to "control" wages at the expense of employers and the public. Yet by the 1830s many skilled workers were founding unions. In 1834 several trade groups even managed to create a national organization, the **National Trades' Union.** Finally, in 1842, a Massachusetts judge, Lemuel Shaw, ruled in the case of *Commonwealth v. Hunt* that labor unions were not conspiracies unless the members engaged in specific criminal activity. "For men to agree together to exercise their . . . rights," is no crime, Judge Shaw declared. Thereafter, the courts of other states accepted this argument.

Few factory workers organized unions during these years. But the hard conditions and long hours of factory work caused a number of reformers to try to improve the lives of these workers.

Seth Luther, a carpenter and cotton textile worker, was one of the most radical critics of the factory system. Most of the reformers came from farms or from well-to-do city families. They had no actual experience as laborers. Unlike these types, Luther knew what life in the factories was like. He criticized the system vigorously. In particular he denounced the employment of children in factories. Instead of laboring all day over a loom, every child in the nation, he said, should receive a good education at public expense. He called for shorter work hours for all laborers and for better working conditions. He compared the New England textile mills to prisons, the workers to slaves. The employers, he said, "wish to control their men in all things; to enslave their bodies and souls, make them think, act, vote, preach, pray, and worship, as it may suit 'We the Owners.'"

Many less radical reformers supported the movement to reduce the working day from the usual dawn-to-darkness routine to ten

LEADING UNITED STATES INDUSTRIES BY EMPLOYMENT, 1860		
Rank	**Industry**	**Number of Employees**
1	Boots and shoes	123,026
2	Cotton goods	114,955
3	Men's clothing	114,800
4	Lumber	75,595
5	Iron	48,975
6	Machinery	41,223
7	Woolen goods	40,597
8	Carriages, wagons, and carts	37,102
9	Flour milling	27,682
10	Tanning (leather)	22,679

Source: *Eighth Census of the United States, Manufactures, 1860.*

LEARNING FROM TABLES. *This chart shows which American industries had the largest number of workers. Into what business category could you group the top three on the list? Is it surprising that they have the largest number of workers? Explain your reasoning.*

Alexis de Tocqueville is best known for his Democracy in America. *He wrote his observations after an extensive tour of young America in the 1830's.*

hours. Unfortunately, the ten-hour movement made little progress. But in 1840 the federal government set a ten-hour limit on the workday of its own employees.

De Tocqueville's America

As you have read, Alexis de Tocqueville came to America in 1831 to examine its prisons. But he saw much more, and thus became the most famous foreign observer of America as it was swept by the spirit of reform. His book, *Democracy in America*, was full of insights about America. His description, however, is somewhat idealized, rarely mentioning slavery or the other problems facing Americans in the decade before the Civil War.

Perhaps the aspect of America that most amazed de Tocqueville was the high level of involvement of the American people in reform and in politics. He wrote:

“ No sooner do you set foot upon American soil than you are stunned by a kind of tumult; a confused clamour [noise] is heard on every side; and a thousand simultaneous [at the same time] demand immediate satisfaction of their social wants. . . .

Everything is in motion around you; here, the people of one quarter [neighborhood] of the town meet to decide upon building a church; there, the election of a representative is going on; a little farther the delegates of a district are posting [hurrying] to the town in order to consult upon some local improvements; or in another place the labourers of a village quit their plows to deliberate [decide] upon the project of a road or a public school.

Meetings are called for the sole purpose of declaring their disapproval of the line of conduct pursued [followed] by the Government; . . .

The cares of political life take a most prominent place in the occupation of a citizen of the United States, and almost the only pleasure of which an American has any idea is to take part in Government, and to discuss the part he has taken. . . .[1]”

Certainly the Americans described by de Tocqueville were more involved in government and politics than Americans today. As the country has grown into an industrial nation, fewer and fewer people have voted or exercised their civic rights and duties. But then that is one of the virtues of democracy. All are free to choose their levels of participation.

The workings of American democracy fascinated de Tocqueville.

[1]From *Democracy in America* by Alexis de Tocqueville, translated by Henry Reeve

It was far different than the democracy he had observed in France and elsewhere in Europe, where the elite still held most of the power. In America democracy extended to a far greater number of people. The election of Jackson as president had signaled the start of this trend that would continue through the 1800s. De Tocqueville wrote:

66 The Americans have formed a high idea of political rights because they have some political rights. They do not attack those of others, because they do not want their own attacked. Whereas the same person in Europe would be prejudiced against all authority, even the highest, the American obeys the lowest officials without complaint.

Democratic government makes the idea of political rights spread to all citizens, just as the division of property puts the general idea of property rights within reach of all. That, in my view, is one of its greatest advantages.

I'm not saying that it is an easy matter to teach all people to make use of political rights; I only say that when that can happen, the results are important. . . .

In America the people were given political rights at a time when it was difficult for them to misuse them because the citizens were few and their ways of life simple. As they have grown more powerful, the Americans have not greatly increased the powers of democracy. Rather they have extended their democracy by increasing the number of people who have political rights. . . .

Democracy does not confer the most skilful kind of government upon the people, but it produces that which the most skilful governments are frequently unable to awaken, namely, an all-pervading [one that exists throughout] and restless activity, a superabundant force, and an energy which is inseparable from it, and which may, under favourable circumstance, beget [cause] the most amazing results.[1] 99

[1]From *Democracy in America* by Alexis de Tocqueville, translated by Henry Reeve

The End of the Age of Reform

The Age of Reform was a time of high hopes. Today some of the reformers' suggestions seem either undesirable or totally impractical. Others seem quite moderate. At the time the volume and variety of the proposals gave a special excitement to life. But the hectic urge to improve everything at once could not go on forever. What ended it was the conflict between North and South over the future of slavery. 🖰

Return to the Preview & Review on page 498.

CHAPTER 14 REVIEW

1783
Webster
publishes
first *Spelling Book*

1787
First American history book

Chapter Summary
Read the statements below. Choose one, and write a paragraph explaining its importance.
1. From the 1830s through the 1850s the United States experienced an Age of Reform.
2. Reformers fighting for women's rights wanted greater opportunities for women in education and the professions. The Seneca Falls Declaration emphasized the goals of the movement.
3. Textbooks by Noah Webster, John M'Culloch, and William McGuffey helped a distinctly American educational system develop. Horace Mann and others sought to improve education through better teacher training and constructing schools.
4. Some reformers established ideal communities to practice their principles. But most Americans considered such communities foolish.
5. A Second Great Awakening swept the country, revitalizing American religion.
6. The Romantic Age, which began in Europe, seemed particularly American in its celebration of individualism.
7. Reformers also focused their attention on the blind, the insane, juvenile delinquents, orphans, and the poor. Others campaigned against alcohol and for improved working conditions and hours.

Reviewing Chronological Order
Number your paper 1–5. Then study the time line above and place the following events in the order in which they happened by writing the first next to 1, the second next to 2, and so on.
1. Elizabeth Blackwell licensed
2. Seneca Falls Declaration
3. Webster publishes his *Spelling Book*
4. Mann founds first normal school
5. National Trades' Union founded

Understanding Main Ideas
1. How were women treated as second-class citizens in Jacksonian America?
2. What were some of the reforms Horace Mann sought for public education?
3. For what reasons did people try to establish ideal communities between 1820 and 1850?
4. What were some reforms in the treatment of juveniles from 1820 through the 1850s?
5. How did the general public view labor unions?

Thinking Critically
1. **Synthesizing.** Imagine that you are a new teacher in a "little red schoolhouse" in 1840. Write an entry in your diary after your first day of teaching, describing your students, your classroom, and your reactions to them.
2. **Inventing.** Create your own ideal community, basing it on others described in this chapter. Then compose a list of at least seven rules by which members of your community must live.
3. **Editorializing.** Make a list of what you consider necessary to make working conditions "good." Next to each condition on your list, explain why it is important for "good working conditions." Which items on your list could workers in the 1840s hope for? Why?

Writing About History: Persuasive
Write a newspaper advertisement for an ideal community you are founding. Your advertisement should inform readers about life in your community and persuade them to join it. Use the information in Chapter 14 and in reference books to prepare your advertisement.

Practicing the Strategy
Review the strategy on page 481.
Understanding Sequence. Review pages 484–89. Then make a list showing the sequence of developments in American education from colonial times to the 1840s.

THE AGE OF REFORM	1840

20 Second Great Awakening begins	**1826** American Temperance Union	**1830** Mormon religion founded	**1834** National Trades' Union	**1837** *McGuffey's Eclectic Reader*	**1840** Shakers grow to 20 communities	**1848** Seneca Falls Convention	**1853** Brace founds Children's Aid Society
		1831 Howe starts Perkins Institute		**1838** *Letters on the Equality of the Sexes and the Condition of Women*	**1841** Dix begins crusade to help mentally ill	**1849** Elizabeth Blackwell licensed to practice medicine	
				1839 First normal school		**1850** *The Scarlet Letter* ★ *Leaves of Grass*	
						1851 *Moby Dick*	

Using Primary Sources

On July 19, 1848, the delegates at the women's rights convention at Seneca Falls adopted a *Declaration of Sentiments and Resolutions*. As you read the following excerpt, see if you can get a sense of what the delegates were saying. Then answer the questions below.

We hold these truths to be self-evident: that all men and women are created equal; that they are endowed by their Creator with certain unalienable rights. . . . Such has been the patient suffering of women under this government, and such is now the necessity which forces them to demand the equal position to which they are entitled.

The history of mankind is a history of repeated injuries and usurpations on the part of man toward woman, having as its direct object the establishment of an absolute tyranny over her. To prove this, let facts be given to a candid world:

He has never permitted her to exercise her unalienable right to vote.

He has forced her to submit to laws she had no voice in forming.

He has withheld from her rights which are given to the most ignorant and degraded men—both natives and foreigners. . . .

He has made her, if married, in the eye of the law, civilly dead.

He has taken from her all right to property, even the wages she earns. . . .

He has denied her the opportunity of obtaining a thorough education, all colleges being closed to her.

1. Why do you think the women at the convention used words of the Declaration of Independence as the framework of their *Declaration of Sentiments and Resolutions*?

2. Of the rights that the declaration lists as having been denied to women, which do you think has been the most important for women to gain? Why?

3. Do you think that holding a convention and issuing a declaration is an effective way to change the system? If so, why? If not, how would you do it differently?

Linking History & Geography

Organizers of ideal communities soon realized that their communities were best located in somewhat isolated areas. Locate and label the following areas that contained ideal communities on an outline map of the United States: Indiana (New Harmony), Iowa (Amana), western New York (Oneida and Shakers), and Utah (Mormon). What were the advantages of locating these communities in out-of-the-way places? What disadvantages?

Enriching the Study of History

1. **Individual Project**. In the Age of Reform some people realized that they could improve society by helping the disadvantaged. Find out and report on the efforts made by the government or volunteers in your community to help disadvantaged people. If possible, observe some of these efforts and compare the effectiveness of government and private efforts.

2. **Cooperative Project**. In the Lancasterian system of education, older students called monitors, taught younger pupils. Your group will select one student to be a monitor and to teach a topic from this chapter to other group members. Then your group will prepare a report discussing the advantages and disadvantages of this method of education.

Chapter 14 Review 507

UNIT FOUR REVIEW

Summing Up and Predicting

Read the summary of the main ideas in Unit Four below. Choose one statement, then write a paragraph predicting its outcome or consequence in the future.

1. All parts of the country prospered during the Era of Good Feelings. Then regional issues began to threaten the nation's harmony.
2. Jackson's election was a victory for the common man, and a key turning point in American history.
3. Between 1820 and 1850, a feeling of manifest destiny swept the country, and large numbers of people moved westward.
4. The U.S. acquired huge territories, raising serious questions about the spread of slavery.
5. Even as slave labor became an integral part of the southern economy and way of life, a unified abolition movement grew.
6. Reformers sought to improve many aspects of American society.

Connecting Ideas

1. If the presidential election of 1828 could have been televised, do you think that Adams' and Jackson's campaigns would have been different? If so, how? If not, why not?
2. You know that Eli Whitney's cotton gin made life better for some Americans while making it more difficult for others. Name a twentieth-century invention that has had both positive and negative effects on people, and explain your answer.
3. The Seneca Falls Declaration of Sentiments and Resolutions stated, "We hold these truths to be self-evident: that all men and women are created equal." Do you think that women are treated as equals of men in America today? Give evidence to support your point of view.

Practicing Critical Thinking

1. **Making Inferences.** Suppose you were a teenager in the early 1800s. What would your daily life be like if you lived in the Northeast? the South? the West?
2. **Synthesizing.** Imagine that you are a Mormon following Brigham Young to the West. In your travel journal, describe your impressions of your leader.
3. **Evaluating.** You are a slave attempting to persuade your fellow slaves to revolt against your cruel master. What would you say to convince them? Include examples of your mistreatment that justify this action.
4. **Defining Problems.** From the beginnings of your country's history, Americans have believed that educated people make the best citizens in a democracy. If you were unable to read and write, how would your ability to perform your duties as an American citizen be affected?

Exploring History Together

1. Have your group make a map of the United States as it appeared in 1841. Label major states and territories, physical features, and roads, railroads, canals, etc.
2. Imagine that the members of your group are newspaper reporters. Each reporter should write an article about a different American reform movement of the mid-1800s. When the articles are finished, organize them into sections as a newspaper would be.
3. Imagine that your group is the national committee of a major political party. Prepare a "platform" that states how your party stands on the important issues described in this unit. Be sure that your platform addresses each of the major political issues of the 1840s and 1850s.

Reading in Depth

Blassingame, John W. *The Slave Community*. New York: Oxford University Press. Describes the life and culture of American slaves.

Clarke, Mary S. *Bloomers and Ballots*. New York: Viking. Offers a well-documented story of the life of Elizabeth Cady Stanton.

Eggleston, Edward. *The Hoosier School Master*. Evanston, IL.: McDougal-Littell. Studies the life of an Indian teacher in the 1840s.

Johnson, Philip and Carmen Maldonado de Johnson. *A Probe into the Mexican American Experience*. Orlando: Harcourt Brace Jovanovich. Presents in both English and Spanish a brief history of Mexico and southwestern United States.

Petry, Ann. *Harriet Tubman: Conductor on the Underground Railroad*. New York: Archway. Presents an exciting biography of the former slave called the "Moses of her people."

Remini, Robert G. *The Life of Andrew Jackson*. New York: Harper & Row. Provides a dramatic account of the man and his times.

Gettysburg National Military Park/Photography by Henry Groskinsky
Visitors to Gettysburg can view this large circular mural called a cyclorama to see the famous battle waged there.

A DIVIDED AMERICA

UNIT 5

In February 1861 six southern states seceded from the Union and formed the Confederate States of America. Others quickly joined. The crisis laid before the newly elected president of the United States, Abraham Lincoln, was enormous. To preserve the Union, a Civil War must be fought. This unit discusses the political and economic factors that led to secession of the South, as well as the social and psychological reasons that bred distrust and ill will between North and South, particularly over the matter of slavery. The history of the Civil War is then described, including strategies, major battles, and the war's effects on the lives of soldiers, citizens, and slaves. Chapter 17 explains the problems of Reconstruction—the process of bringing the conquered southern states back into the Union. The treatment of the South as a conquered territory and the patterns of racial discrimination and segregation that grew out of Reconstruction make up one of the saddest chapters in the story of America.

Causes of the Civil War

The conflict between the North and South over the future of slavery sputtered and grew into the threat that the southern states would leave the Union if the next president was a Republican. The stage was set by the publication of *Uncle Tom's Cabin*, a novel about slavery that was widely read. Then came the struggle over the Kansas Territory—would it be free or slave?—and the Supreme Court ruling in the Dred Scott case that slaves were a form of property and had "none of the rights and privileges" of citizens of the United States. With the election in 1860 of Abraham Lincoln, the southern states were prepared to secede. Would the secession crisis tear apart the 85-year-old United States of America?

Preview & Review

Use these questions to guide your reading. Answer the questions after completing Section 1.
Understanding Issues, Events, & Ideas. Using the following words, explain how northerners felt about slavery during the 1850s: Fugitive Slave Act, segregation, *Uncle Tom's Cabin*.
1. Why did many northerners support runaway slaves?
2. Why did many northerners object to the Fugitive Slave Law?
3. What point did Stowe try to make in *Uncle Tom's Cabin?* In what way was *Uncle Tom's Cabin* something new in American fiction?
Thinking Critically. You are a northerner living in Massachusetts in 1852 and opposed to the Fugitive Slave Law. Compose the handbill you would pass out at a town meeting to persuade members of your community to protest the law.

1. THE NORTH AND SLAVERY

Slave Catching

Most Americans had expected the Compromise of 1850 to put an end to the slavery controversy. Events quickly proved that it had not done so. The Fugitive Slave Law was very strict. Anyone caught helping a slave escape faced six months in jail and a $1,000 fine. As soon as the new law went into effect southerners began to try to reclaim slaves who had escaped into the free states. Slaves who had escaped to the North found themselves in grave danger of recapture. Persons accused of being runaways could not testify in their own defense. Many blacks in the North who had not run away also felt threatened.

Thousands pulled up stakes and moved to Canada. Among those who left the country were many of the more outspoken African American leaders. "We have lost some of our strong men," Frederick Douglass mourned. He himself did not flee. "The only way to make the Fugitive Slave Law a dead letter," he wrote, "is to make half a dozen or more dead kidnappers." By kidnappers Douglass meant the men who sought to reclaim runaways under the Fugitive Slave Law.

During the next few years about 200 people were captured and

The Brooklyn Museum

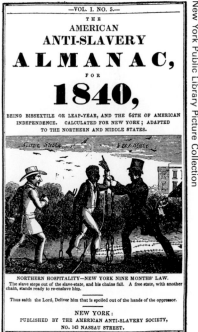

Eastman Johnson painted "A Ride for Liberty—the Fugitive Slave" in about 1862. Johnson was a famous genre *painter—that is, his frequent subject was everyday life. But this is no everyday event for the family riding fearfully north to freedom. What message to fugitives can you find in the* Anti-Slavery Almanac *below?*

sent back into slavery under the new law. This was a small percentage of the number that had escaped. Even these cases, however, had a powerful effect on northern public opinion.

Most northerners were prejudiced against people of African descent, free or slave. Only five states, all in New England, permitted the handful who resided there to vote freely. Some states prohibited them from settling within their borders. Nowhere could they mix with white people. They sat alone on trains or in restaurants, theaters, or hotels. Except in Massachusetts, this **segregation** extended to public schools.

Yet in spite of their prejudices, many northerners were sympathetic to the plight of runaway slaves. Runaways had risked their lives to win freedom. It was hard not to be impressed by them, especially when they had gone on to raise families, learn trades, and become hard-working, law-abiding citizens.

When northerners saw such people seized and dragged off without being given a chance to defend themselves in court, thousands were outraged. In Indiana, for example, a man named Mitchum was arrested and turned over to a southerner who claimed that Mitchum was a slave who had run away 19 years earlier. Whether or not Mitchum had really run away, it seemed cruel and unjust to separate him from his wife and children after so many years.

The North and Slavery 511

A Philadelphia woman, Euphemia Williams, escaped a somewhat different fate. She was arrested, but a judge released her at the last moment. Had he not, her six children, all born in Pennsylvania, would have been enslaved with her. Under southern law whether or not a child was a slave depended on the status of the mother, not the father.

Even northerners who were unmoved by the way the new fugitive slave law affected escaped slaves objected to it. It required citizens of the northern states to help capture runaways when ordered to do so by a law enforcement officer. Thousands considered this a violation of their rights. The abolitionists led the attack on the law.

As you have read, the abolitionist crusade was carried in large part by northern religious leaders. The Quakers had been foremost in the antislavery movement since colonial days. They had been joined by northern ministers and preachers such as Theodore Dwight Weld and Henry Ward Beecher.

In Boston a group headed by the respected clergyman Theodore Parker rescued a runaway couple, William and Ellen Craft. The group so threatened the man who had arrested the Crafts that he fled the city in fear for his life. In Syracuse, New York, a fugitive named Jerry McHenry was freed when a crowd of 2,000 people broke into the jail where he was being held. In Pennsylvania a mob actually killed a slave catcher.

Not many of the runaways who were arrested were freed by force. In most cases they were brought to trial as the law provided. Some were released. Others were sent back into slavery without the public taking much notice. The law was disliked throughout the North, even though little was done to stop it from being enforced. More and more northerners were becoming "uncomfortable" about the existence of slavery in the country.

A Novel About Slavery

Discomfort in the North increased when people began to read *Uncle Tom's Cabin,* a novel about slavery published in 1852. The author, Harriet Beecher Stowe, was not an active abolitionist. In her book she tried to make the point that the slave system was at fault, not the people who owned slaves and profited from their labor. She made the villain of her story, Simon Legree, a northerner.

The plot of *Uncle Tom's Cabin* is as hard to believe as that of a modern soap opera. The main character is the slave Uncle Tom, who accepts slavery with "patient weariness." He speaks to his owners in a soft voice and has "a habitually respectful manner." He is content to remain a slave as long as his master is kind. Indeed, most of the slaves in the book quietly accept slavery and all its injustices.

Tom is first owned by a kindly Kentucky planter named Shelby.

Harriet Beecher Stowe sat for this oil portrait in 1853, one year after publication of Uncle Tom's Cabin.

Next he becomes the property of a noble gentleman from New Orleans named St. Clare. All goes well. Then St. Clare dies. Tom is sold to the Yankee-born Simon Legree, who owns a cotton plantation in Louisiana.

Simon Legree is one of the arch villains of American literature. He enters and exits twirling his moustaches, his lips curled in a sneer. Legree cares only for money. He drives his slaves unmercifully, whipping them repeatedly to make them work harder. He controls them with fierce bulldogs who would "jest as soon chaw one of ye up as eat their dinner," and by Sambo and Quimbo, evil slave overseers whom "Legree had . . . trained in savageness and brutality as systematically as he had his bulldogs." At one point the saintly Tom refuses to whip a slave woman who is too tired to pick as much cotton as Legree wishes. Legree has Tom brutally beaten by Sambo and Quimbo. One lashing follows another. Finally Tom dies of his injuries. As Stowe described the scene:

> 66 Scenes of blood and cruelty are shocking to our ear and heart. What man has the nerve to do, man has not nerve to hear. What brother-man and brother-Christian must suffer, cannot be told us, even in our secret chamber, it so harrows [torments] the soul. And yet, oh my country! these things are done under the shadow of thy laws! Oh Christ! thy church sees them, almost in silence. . . .
>
> 'He's almost gone [dead], Mas'r,' said Sambo, touched in spite of himself by the patience of his victim [Tom].
>
> 'Pay away, till he gives up! Give it to him!—give it to him!' shouted Legree. 'I'll take every drop of blood he has, unless he confesses!'
>
> Tom opened his eyes, and looked upon his master. 'Ye poor miserable critter!' he said, 'there an't no more ye can do! I forgive ye, with all my soul!' and he fainted entirely away.
>
> 'I believe, my soul, he's done for, finally,' said Legree, stepping forward, to look at him. 'Yes, he is! Well, his mouth's shut up, at last,—that's one comfort.'
>
> Yes, Legree; but who shall shut up that voice in thy soul? that soul past repentance [to ask for forgiveness], past prayer, past hope, in whom the fire that never shall be quenched [hell] is already burning.[1] 99

The first and last paragraphs are Stowe's voice. Her words echo the feelings of most abolitionists. She, and they, could not understand how America could allow slavery to continue. Why had the reform movement not boldly tackled the slavery issue? And what of the slaveholders themselves? Why could they not see that slavery was

Point of View

To the author of *Uncle Tom's Cabin* Oliver Wendell Holmes wrote these lines after John Brown had been awarded sainthood by northern abolitionists.

> 66 All through the conflict, up and down
> Marched Uncle Tom and Old John Brown,
>   One ghost, one form ideal,
> And which was false and which was true,
> And which was mightier of the two,
> The wisest sibyl° never knew,
>   For both alike were real. 99
>   Oliver Wendell Holmes

°**sibyl**: a woman prophet

[1]From *Uncle Tom's Cabin* by Harriet Beecher Stowe

Uncle Tom's Cabin was applauded widely in the North, both the novel and a traveling melodrama (a type of play) based on it. Many people saw no spectacle to rival the pursuit of Eliza Harris by bloodhounds on the icebound Ohio River. The poster below praises "the greatest book of the age." Do you think this might be so, or is the publisher simply a good advertiser?

Return to the Preview & Review on page 510.

wrong? *Uncle Tom's Cabin* now thrust those questions in front of all Americans.

Stowe's description of slavery was not very realistic. She had grown up in Connecticut and Ohio. She had seen slaves only once, during a visit to a plantation in Kentucky. Many angry African Americans rejected the patient, submissive Uncle Tom. But while the characters in *Uncle Tom's Cabin* are all either saints or the worst of sinners, the slaves are shown as human beings with deep feelings. This was something new in American fiction.

The book was an immediate popular success. Within a year of publication 300,000 copies were sold. It was made into a play and presented before packed houses in theaters all over the northern states. We cannot know how many of the millions of people who read the book or saw the play became abolitionists as a result. But the historian David Potter was unquestionably correct when he wrote, "The northern attitude toward slavery was never quite the same after *Uncle Tom's Cabin*." 👉

2. THE STRUGGLE FOR KANSAS

Preview & Review

The Kansas-Nebraska Act

The concern of northerners about slavery increased dramatically in 1854. In 1853 Senator Stephen A. Douglas of Illinois had introduced a bill setting up a territorial government for the frontier west of Missouri and Iowa. On the surface it was a routine measure. As settlers pushed the frontier westward, Congress always organized the districts they were entering by setting up governments for them. This had been done repeatedly, beginning with the Northwest Ordinance of 1787.

Douglas' bill, however, ran into trouble. Once California entered the Union, plans for building a railroad to the West Coast sprang up everywhere. Being from Illinois, Douglas favored a route running west from Chicago. No such line could be built until the land beyond Missouri and Iowa had a territorial government.

Southern interests wanted the railroad to run west from New Orleans or some other southern city. All the lands such a route would cross had already been organized. In 1853 the United States had bought from Mexico a tract on the border known as the **Gadsden Purchase.** This land contained a pass through the mountains. A

Engravings such as "The Express Train" were an ever-popular subject for Currier & Ives. What might you have felt as this train passed by?

Use these questions to guide your reading. Answer the questions after completing Section 2. **Understanding Issues, Events, & Ideas.** Use the following words to explain events in Kansas during the 1850s: Gadsden Purchase, Wilmot Proviso, popular sovereignty, Kansas-Nebraska Bill, Ostend Manifesto, free soiler, Beecher's Bibles, Pottawatomie Massacre, guerrilla, "Bleeding Kansas."

1. For what two reasons had Senator Douglas introduced a bill to establish the new territories of Kansas and Nebraska?
2. How did antislavery forces hope to prevent slavery in Kansas? How did proslavery groups influence the Kansas territorial election in 1855?
3. How did northern newspapers report the events in Kansas?

Thinking Critically. You are a free laborer in 1854, planning to move to Kansas. Write a letter to the editor of your local newspaper, explaining why you oppose the Kansas-Nebraska Bill.

Franklin Pierce was elected to the presidency in 1852. He served one unhappy term as president, the Pierces grieving at the loss of their son, who was killed in a train wreck before the inauguration.

railroad could be constructed over this pass and on to the Pacific Ocean. Southerners in Congress did not want to encourage the building of a northern rail line. They refused to vote for the Douglas bill.

Stephen A. Douglas was extremely ambitious. In 1852, when he was only 39, he announced himself a candidate for the Democratic presidential nomination. Other party leaders considered him much too young for that office. They nominated Franklin Pierce of New Hampshire. Pierce went on to defeat the Whig candidate, General Winfield Scott, in the 1852 election.

Douglas did not let this failure discourage him. All his life he had gotten what he wanted. He had made a fortune as a lawyer and real estate investor. He had been a state legislator, a judge, and a member of the House of Representatives before being elected to the Senate. Although he was very short, people spoke of him with awe as the "Little Giant." He seemed to give off energy and determination. He once boasted:

❝ I live with my constituents, drink with them, lodge with them, pray with them, laugh, hunt, dance, and work with them. I eat their corn dodgers and fried bacon and sleep two in a bed with them. ❞

Douglas was a shrewd politician. When he realized that southern congressmen were opposed to his bill, he looked for a way to change their minds. He knew they had held up for two years the passage of a bill creating the Oregon Territory because it contained a clause excluding slavery. He knew they had also defeated the Wilmot Proviso. As you read, in 1846 Congressman David Wilmot of Pennsylvania proposed that slavery be excluded from the lands acquired from Mexico after the Mexican War. The proviso passed the House of Representatives in both 1846 and 1847. But it was defeated in the Senate. Southern senators, led by John C. Calhoun, claimed that the Constitution forbade Congress from passing such a law. It was up to the citizens of each state or territory to decide.

Douglas now came up with a scheme. Why not open the new territory to slavery? To prevent an uproar in the North, however, no new slave territory would be specifically created. Instead, settlers of the area would themselves decide whether or not to permit slavery.

This was the principle of **popular sovereignty** that had already been applied to New Mexico and Utah territories by the Compromise of 1850. As a further compromise the area would be split into two territories—Kansas, west of the slave state of Missouri, and Nebraska, west of the free state of Iowa.

Douglas knew that many northerners would dislike this **Kansas-Nebraska Bill.** But he thought most of them would merely grumble. The possibility of slavery actually being established in the new territories was small. The climate was unsuitable for growing cotton or any other plantation crop. Douglas himself considered slavery a

STRATEGIES FOR SUCCESS

COMPARING MAPS

One of the most important ways to learn history through geography is by comparing maps. You have already been introduced to many of the strategies you need to compare maps. Review the strategies for reviewing map basics, interpreting physical maps, and comparing and contrasting ideas.

How to Compare Maps

To effectively compare maps, follow these guidelines.

1. **Select the maps to be compared carefully.** Make sure the areas covered, the dates of the information, and other important pieces of information provide a reliable picture.
2. **Note similarities and differences.** Examine the patterns and symbols closely.
3. **Apply critical thinking skills.** Make inferences, draw conclusions, and state generalizations about the evidence you find.

Applying the Strategy

The question of extending slavery into the western territories was hotly debated for more than half a century. Three times Congress acted to settle the matter. But it was not resolved by the Missouri Compromise (Compromise of 1820) or the Compromise of 1850. Four short years later Congress once again struggled with the problem before passing the Kansas-Nebraska Act of 1854.

Such a complex matter as the attempts to settle the slavery issue may be better understood by comparing maps of the compromises. Study the maps on this page. Note that they show the changing status of the territories as Congress passed each new compromise. How did the status of California change with the Compromise of 1850? How did the status of Nebraska change with the Kansas-Nebraska Act? What other details can you compare? Based on these maps, what generalizations can you state about the issue of extending slavery?

For independent practice, see Practicing the Strategy on pages 540–41.

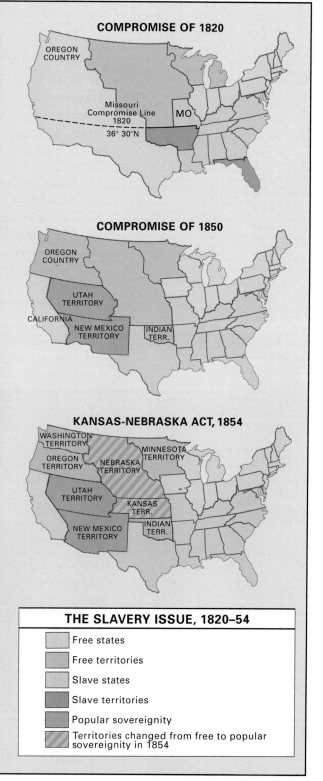

COMPROMISE OF 1820

COMPROMISE OF 1850

KANSAS-NEBRASKA ACT, 1854

THE SLAVERY ISSUE, 1820–54

Free states
Free territories
Slave states
Slave territories
Popular sovereignty
Territories changed from free to popular sovereignty in 1854

terrible institution. But he did not think the development of the West should be held up over the principle of whether or not to permit it. On January 4, 1854, he introduced the bill in the Senate.

The Struggle for Kansas

By 1854 antislavery northerners were outraged. News of the **Ostend Manifesto** (see page 541) had leaked out and was published. Shocked Americans read that President Pierce, pressured by influential southerners, had begun negotiations with Spain to buy Cuba. Northerners saw this as an obvious attempt to add to southern territory. The secrecy surrounding the talks added to their anger.

Now they responded to the Kansas-Nebraska Bill with roars of protest. Although it did not do so specifically, Douglas' bill repealed the ban on slavery in that region which had been imposed by the Missouri Compromise. It was a "criminal betrayal" of the interests of free laborers eager to settle in the new land. It was "an atrocious plot" to make the territory "a dreary region . . . inhabited by masters and slaves."

For months the Kansas-Nebraska Bill was debated in Congress. Finally, with the votes of southerners who approved of the slavery provision, it passed both houses and was promptly signed by President Pierce.

These Missourians are crossing into Kansas by ferry. What side must they have been on in the struggle for control of Kansas?

The Granger Collection

Douglas had hoped that northerners who opposed his bill would quiet down once the issue was settled. Instead they grew more bitter. Antislavery critics were determined to prevent slavery from gaining a foothold in Kansas. Senator William H. Seward of New York said:

" Gentlemen of the Slave States, we will engage in competition for the virgin soil of Kansas, and God give the victory to the side which is . . . right."

Eli Thayer, a member of the Massachusetts legislature, organized the Massachusetts Emigrant Aid Company to help pay the moving expenses of antislavery families willing to settle in Kansas.

And what of these lands so furiously fought for? Broad and flat, they rose gently from east to west to a plateau and the foothills of the Rockies. Tall prairie grass stretched as far as the eye could see. Rainfall was scarce, especially to the west, and trees were few. Shallow rivers flowed east across the rich soils—the Platte and Niobara in the north and the Kansas and Arkansas in the south—to the Missouri and Mississippi rivers.

Hundreds of **free soilers**—those opposed to slavery—might now rush to Kansas and use popular sovereignty to keep slaves out. Alarmed proslavery groups in Missouri therefore hastened across the state line to Kansas. When the first territorial governor took a census of Kansas late in 1854, he found fewer than 3,000 adult males in the territory. But when a territorial legislature was elected in March 1855, more than 6,300 votes were cast! About 5,000 Missourians had crossed over into Kansas to vote. Their ballots were illegal since they were not residents of the territory. Still their votes were counted. As a result a large majority of the men elected to the territorial legislature were proslavery.

The new legislature moved quickly to pass laws authorizing slavery in Kansas territory. It even passed one that provided the death penalty for anyone giving help to runaway slaves. Free Soil Kansans were furious. They refused to recognize the right of this legislature to govern them. Instead they set up their own government at the town of Topeka.

With two governments claiming to rule the same territory, it is not surprising that fighting broke out. Abolitionists in the East began to send guns to the antislavery forces. One such abolitionist was the Reverend Henry Ward Beecher of Brooklyn, New York, a brother of Harriet Beecher Stowe. He was so active and successful in collecting money for guns that people began to speak of the weapons as **Beecher's Bibles**.

Fighting was common in most rough-and-ready frontier communities. In Kansas tension between northern and southern settlers made the situation explosive. Ruffians on both sides armed themselves. In November 1855 a free soil settler was killed by a proslavery man in an argument over a land claim. The dead man's friends then

Reverend Henry Ward Beecher's photograph was taken by Napoleon Sorony in about 1880.

The Struggle for Kansas   519

burned down the killer's cabin. A proslavery sheriff, Samuel Jones, arrested one of these men. *His* friends promptly attacked the sheriff and forced him to release his prisoner. Sheriff Jones, backed by a force of 3,000 Missourians, then set out to track down the rescuers. Luckily the territorial governor put a stop to this activity before more blood could be spilled.

"Bleeding Kansas"

Trouble broke out again in Kansas the following spring. The town of Lawrence had become the headquarters of the antislavery settlers. Bands of armed men marched about the town much the way the Minute Men had paraded about the towns of Massachusetts in 1775. A United States marshal tried to arrest some of the leaders, but they fled before he could do so.

Then, on May 21, Sheriff Jones, again at the head of an army of Missourians, marched into Lawrence. In broad daylight they threw the printing presses of two newspapers into a river. They burned down the Free State Hotel and other buildings. Antislavery Kansans

How would a scene like the one below, titled "Marais des Cygnes Massacre," have fueled the fires raging between North and South over Kansas? The Marais des Cygnes is a river near Topeka. In English its name would be Swamp of the Swans—not quite as musical as Swan Lake.

A CANING IN CONGRESS

While fighting went on in Kansas, angry legislators in Congress traded insults and threats. Words like "liar" were freely tossed about. Prominent among the new personalities engaged in these outbursts was Senator Charles Sumner of Massachusetts. The handsome and well-spoken Sumner was popular in New England as a reformer and abolitionist. His ego was large; his sense of humor poor.

In the debates over Kansas Sumner showed such icy disdain for his foes that he became the most hated man in the Senate. Southern colleagues called him a "filthy reptile" and a "leper."

One day in May 1856 Sumner began a bitter personal attack on Senator Andrew P. Butler of South Carolina, who was not present. Congressman Preston S. Brooks of South Carolina, a nephew of Senator Butler, re-

The Granger Collection

solved to uphold his uncle's honor. Two days after Sumner's speech, Brooks entered the Senate as it adjourned. Sumner remained at his desk writing. Brooks walked up to Sumner and rained blows upon his head with a cane until Sumner fell, bloody and unconscious, to the Senate floor. "I . . . gave him about 30 first-rate stripes," boasted Brooks. "Towards the last he bellowed like a calf. I wore my cane out completely but saved the head which is gold."

Such was Congress on the eve of secession.

---

seethed with rage. Here is how one eyewitness described the attack:

“ The newspaper offices were the first objects of attack. First the office of the *Free State* was destroyed, then that of the *Herald of Freedom*. The presses were broken down to pieces and the type carried away to the river. The papers and books were treated the same way, until the soldiers became tired of carrying them to the river. Then they piled them in the street, and burned, tore, or otherwise destroyed them.

From the printing offices the attackers went to the hotel. By evening, all that remained . . . was a part of one wall. The rest was a shapeless heap of ruins.

The sack of Lawrence occupied the rest of the afternoon. Sheriff Jones, after looking at the flames rising from the hotel and saying that it was "the happiest day of his life," dismissed the troops, and they began their lawless destruction. . . .[1] ”

[1]From *The Englishman in Kansas* by Thomas H. Gladstone

Yale University Art Gallery

These travelers from Missouri have crossed the Kansas border to make trouble for antislavery settlers. How does the artist of "Border Ruffians Invading Kansas" make clear in the men's faces which side he is on?

A few days later a man named John Brown set out to avenge the attack on Lawrence. During his 56 years Brown had moved restlessly from place to place. He tried many businesses but failed time after time. His behavior had often been on the borders of the law, if not outside it. Yet he was sincerely opposed to slavery and devoted to the cause of racial equality. He had come to Kansas in October 1855.

When Brown learned of the attack, he led a party of seven men, four of them his own sons, to a settlement near Pottawatomie Creek, south of Lawrence. In the dead of night they entered the cabins of three unsuspecting families. For no apparent reason they murdered five people. They split open their skulls with heavy, razor-sharp swords. They even cut off the hand of one of their victims.

The **Pottawatomie Massacre** brought Kansas to the verge of civil war. Free soilers and proslavery men squared off to fight as irregular soldiers, or **guerrillas.** Brown was one of many of these. Very few people were killed. But politicians played up the unrest to win support. Soon horror-stricken citizens in the Northeast were reading exaggerated newspaper reports about **"Bleeding Kansas."**

Return to the Preview & Review on page 515.

3. NEW POLITICAL PARTIES

Preview & Review

Use these questions to guide your reading. Answer the questions after completing Section 3.
Understanding Issues, Events, & Ideas. Explain how two new political parties formed in the 1850s, using the following words: nativist, Native American party, Know-Nothings, Republican party.
1. How did the Democratic party suffer from passage of the Kansas-Nebraska Act? Why was the Whig party shattered?
2. In what ways was the political situation unsettled in 1856?
3. What were Buchanan's qualifications for the presidency? Why did the Democrats nominate him?

Thinking Critically. Imagine that you arrived in America from Ireland in 1850. Write a letter to your family in Ireland, explaining why you would *not* join the Native American party or the Republican party.

Political Breakups

The controversy over slavery in the western territories once again became a major political issue. It brought about major shifts in the nation's political parties. The Kansas-Nebraska Act had been a Democratic party measure. Its passage caused that party to lose thousands of supporters in the North. The Whig party, however, was shattered completely. Southern Whigs and their northern allies—known as "Cotton" Whigs—could not remain in the same organization with Northern "Conscience" Whigs. Most of the southerners and "Cotton" Whigs supported the Kansas-Nebraska Act.

The northern Whigs went in two directions. The huge increase of immigration in the 1840s and 1850s hurt the Whig party greatly. For various reasons about 90 percent of the new Irish Catholic citizens became Democrats. German immigrants, many of whom were Catholic, also tended to vote Democratic. Most Whigs, however, belonged to one or another of the Protestant churches. So the Whigs disagreed in both politics and religion wth the new Democrats. As a result many Whigs became **nativists.** They favored strict controls on the admission of foreigners into the country. They joined a new political organization, the **Native American party.** Many former Democrats also joined this new party. Members of the Native American party were often called **Know-Nothings** because when asked about the organization, they replied, "I know nothing."

Perhaps without realizing it, the nativists were trying to make the slavery issue go away by ignoring it. They were also bucking a tide that could not be stemmed without ruining the country. A steady flow of immigrants was essential if the United States was to expand. The very people who joined the Native American party benefited from the work the new immigrants did. By spending their wages, the immigrants stimulated the whole national economy. Fortunately most American-born citizens realized this. The Know-Nothings won some important local elections in the 1850s, but they never replaced either of the two major political parties.

The other new organization that northern Whigs and Democrats joined was the **Republican party.** It sprang up in many northern states immediately after passage of the Kansas-Nebraska Act.

The Republican platform was simple: Keep slavery out of the western territories. Dislike of slavery was not the only reason the party took this stand. Indeed, many Republicans shared the common racial prejudice of most northerners. But they feared that small farmers in the territories could not compete with southerners who could bring their slaves there.

The ranks of voters swelled with newcomers from Ireland, nearly

Milwaukee County Historical Society

all of whom joined the Democratic party. They were poor and unskilled. These Irish interpreted Republican talk about free soil and free men as threatening their jobs. While not in favor of slavery, the Irish found Democratic politics more to their liking.

The Election of 1856

The political situation in 1856 was most unsettled. Neither President Pierce nor Senator Douglas could get the Democratic nomination for the presidency. Their support of the Kansas-Nebraska Act convinced party leaders that these men could not win in the northern states. Instead the Democrats chose James Buchanan of Pennsylvania.

Buchanan seemed well qualified for the presidency. He had been a congressman and also a senator. He was an experienced diplomat, having been minister to both Russia and Great Britain. He had been President Polk's secretary of state. But the chief reason the Democrats picked him was that his service as minister to Britain had kept him out of the country during the bitter fight over the Kansas-Nebraska Act.

The Republicans nominated John C. Frémont, "the Pathfinder." Unlike Buchanan, who was 64, Frémont was a relatively young man in his early forties and something of a national hero. As his nickname indicates, he was an explorer. He had also played an important role in taking California during the Mexican War. A strong, silent type, Frémont had almost no political experience. With voters so divided, that too was a political advantage. Former president Millard Fillmore was also a candidate in 1856. He received the nomination of the Native American party and also was the candidate of the rapidly declining Whig party.

The Republicans did not even attempt to campaign in the South. Fillmore got many northern votes that might otherwise have gone to Frémont, but he did not even come close to winning a single free state. So the contest was between Buchanan and Frémont in the North and between Buchanan and Fillmore in the South. Buchanan's strength in both sections gave him a great advantage among undecided voters and people who put sectional peace ahead of any particular issue.

Buchanan proved to be much more popular than Fillmore in the South. He lost only Maryland. Frémont was the stronger of the two in the North. But Buchanan won narrow victories in Illinois, Indiana, New Jersey, and his home state, Pennsylvania. These gave Buchanan a majority of the electoral vote, 174 to Frémont's 117. Fillmore gained only 8.

Again the danger of the Union breaking up over slavery seemed to have been avoided. Buchanan's conservatism and his long political experience encouraged people to believe that he would proceed cautiously and with good judgment. 🖰

Why did James Buchanan seem well qualified to be president of the United States?

Why was John C. Frémont something of a national hero when he ran for president?

Return to the Preview & Review on page 523.

4. A CONTROVERSIAL COURT

Preview & Review

The Dred Scott Case

Before Buchanan had a chance to demonstrate his abilities, a new crisis erupted. This one was produced by the Supreme Court. For nearly 20 years American courts had struggled with various legal questions surrounding the rights of free blacks and former slaves. In 1841 the nation's attention had been riveted on the Supreme Court as it prepared to issue its decision in the *Amistad* case (page 526). The surprising outcome of that case had heartened abolitionists and given hope to blacks. Abolitionists ignored what was implied in the decision: slaves have no legal rights. Now Americans anxiously awaited the Court's ruling in a case involving a slave named Dred Scott.

We know very little about Dred Scott, the man. He was short and had a dark skin. He could neither read nor write. He must have been a very determined person because he carried on a long struggle for his freedom.

In 1833 Scott had been purchased by John Emerson, an army doctor in St. Louis, Missouri, who used him as a servant. When the army assigned Doctor Emerson to duty at Fort Armstrong in Illinois, he took Scott with him. Then, in 1836, Emerson was transferred to Fort Snelling, a post in the western part of Wisconsin Territory, now Minnesota. Again Scott accompanied him. While there, Scott met and married a slave named Harriet Robinson.

After further moves Emerson was transferred to Florida. He sent the Scotts to St. Louis with his wife. When Emerson died in December 1843, his wife inherited them. Exactly what happened next is not clear. But in 1846, with the help of the family that had originally sold Scott to Emerson, the Scotts sued for their freedom in a Missouri court.

Scott argued that since slavery had been banned in Illinois by state law, he had become free when Emerson brought him to that state. Furthermore, slavery was also illegal in Wisconsin Territory because Wisconsin was in the northern part of the Louisiana Purchase. Slavery had been banned there by Congress in the Missouri Compromise of 1820. In other words, Scott claimed that when he returned to the state of Missouri, he was no longer a slave. Since he had not been reenslaved, he was still free.

This complicated case shuttled from one Missouri court to another for many years. In 1852 the Missouri Supreme Court ruled against Scott. The matter did not end there, however. In 1851 Mrs. Emerson had moved to Massachusetts and remarried. She either sold or gave the Scotts to her brother, John Sanford.

Sanford lived in New York. This offered fresh hope for Scott. Again with the support of friends, he started a new suit for his freedom, this one in the federal courts.

Use these questions to guide your reading. Answer the questions after completing Section 4.
Understanding Issues, Events, & Ideas. Explain the Supreme Court's decision in its controversial 1857 case, using these words: *Dred Scott v. Sandford*, void.
1. What argument did Dred Scott make for his freedom?
2. What did the Supreme Court rule in *Dred Scott v. Sandford?* What argument did Chief Justice Roger Taney make?
3. How was precedent important to the Court's decision?
4. Why was the Court's decision strongly criticized?
Thinking Critically. 1. As a newspaper reporter assigned to cover the Dred Scott case, you have obtained an interview with Scott. Write an article that describes the case from his point of view. **2.** As a justice on the Supreme Court in 1854, you disagree with Taney in *Dred Scott v. Sandford.* List your reasons for disagreeing with his ruling.

Missouri Historical Society

Although little is known about Dred Scott, we do have this portrait made in 1858. It was painted from a photograph of Scott taken earlier.

THE *AMISTAD* MUTINY

One of the most dramatic and widely publicized court cases before *Dred Scott v. Sandford* was the *Amistad* case that began in 1839. In June 1839 a Spanish slaver named the *Amistad* sailed from Havana bound for a plantation in eastern Cuba. The *Amistad* carried four crew members and two Spanish slaveowners with their cargo of fifty-three African slaves. After three days at sea the Africans, led by Joseph Cinqué, revolted. They killed the captain, took control of the *Amistad*, and ordered one of the slaveowners to sail the ship home to Africa. The Spaniard tricked Cinqué and his men for months by sailing a zigzag course up the American coastline. Finally with sails shredded and tattered, the *Amistad* lay becalmed and anchored in Long Island Sound near New London, Connecticut. American naval authorities towed the *Amistad* to New London, where Cinqué and the other Africans were jailed. Here legal proceedings began on behalf of the Spanish owners who demanded that their ship and cargo of slaves be returned to them. Abolitionists immediately took up the Africans' cause, providing them with lawyers and an African interpreter by the name of James Covey.

In September legal proceedings began in the United States Circuit Court in Connecticut and in January moved to the United States District Court. Here Cinqué testified, through Covey, that he had been recently kidnapped in his homeland of Mende in Western Africa. His captors had carried him and others aboard a slaver where they were chained below decks

Cinqué

until the ship reached Havana. There they were sold and put on the *Amistad* where, fearing for their lives, they mutinied and took command of the ship.

Meanwhile, President Van Buren had begun to fear that the *Amistad* case could make slavery a major issue in the 1840 election. He decided that the best way to avoid this possibility was to return the Africans to Cuba for trial by the Spanish. In violation of his presidential power he secretly dispatched a ship to Connecticut with orders to take the Africans into custody and transport them to Cuba. At the last moment Van Buren retracted his order, and by February 1841 the matter had been appealed to the United States Supreme Court under Chief Justice Roger B. Taney. John Quincy Adams defended the Africans. He argued that they were freemen who had been kidnapped and that Van Buren had defied the Constitution's separation of powers by interfering with the judicial system. United

States Attorney General Henry Gilpin headed the prosecution, which argued that the Africans were criminals because they had killed the ship's captain and that they were property as proved in documents carried by their Spanish owners.

On March 9 Justice Joseph Story read the Court's decision: The prosecution had failed to prove the Africans were slaves; therefore, they were free to return home. Freemen had the right to mutiny and to defend themselves if kidnapped; therefore they could not be considered criminals. What were Cinqué's thoughts on hearing the Court's decision? In *Echo of Lions,* novelist Barbara Chase-Riboud has Cinqué speak these prophetic words:

I, too, have become a dangerous man. The war of the Amistad *has become a rallying point for emancipators and the abolitionists and an example to the colored men of America. I am the symbol of insurrection, the amalgamation and lurking violence the slaveholder will not tolerate: that of self-emancipation. I am some marvelous phenomenon, a black man who has defied the courts of America, who has been recognized as having natural as well as legal rights in the highest court of the land. I am a hero. I am a revolutionary.*

What the Court also implied was that had the Africans been slaves, they would have had no rights as human beings. As property, slaves could be legally transported from one state to another. This proved to be the case in 1857 when Taney issued his decision in *Dred Scott v. Sandford.*

The Court and the Constitution

The case of **Dred Scott v. Sandford** began in 1854. Eventually it came to the Supreme Court for final settlement. (The case is incorrectly cited as *Sandford* because of a court clerk's error.) On March 6, 1857, only two days after the start of James Buchanan's term as president, the Court announced its decision.

Chief Justice Roger B. Taney ruled against Scott. "Negroes," he said, were "a subordinate and inferior class of beings." They had "none of the rights and privileges" of citizens of the United States. Scott was not a citizen. Therefore he had no right to bring a suit in a federal court even if he had been free! This amazing statement was enough to keep Scott a slave.

Taney had more to say. Living in Illinois and Wisconsin Territory had not made Scott free. Going to Wisconsin Territory could not have made Scott free because Congress did not have the right to keep slaves out of a federal territory. Taney's argument ran as follows: Slaves were property. Any law which prevented owners from bringing their slaves into a territory would deprive them of property. Since the Fifth Amendment to the Constitution states that "no person shall be . . . deprived of life, liberty, or property without due process of law," the Missouri Compromise was in violation of that amendment. It was unconstitutional and therefore **void**—the law was no longer in force. Of course, Congress had already canceled the Missouri Compromise by passing the Kansas-Nebraska Act.

Taney's argument was particularly annoying to people who were opposed to opening western territories to slavery. The Court was using part of the Bill of Rights to keep people in chains! Furious abolitionists were joined in their outcry by thousands of other people who considered slavery wrong.

Only once before the Dred Scott case had the Supreme Court declared a law passed by Congress to be unconstitutional. That had occurred in 1803, in the case known as *Marbury v. Madison*. Without this precedent to look back to, the justices might not have dared declare that an important law was unconstitutional.

The Dred Scott decision was greeted with a storm of criticism, and with good reason. Whether or not free African Americans were citizens of the United States, many states treated such people as citizens. Everyone agreed that a citizen of one state could sue a citizen of another in the federal courts. Still worse, why was the Supreme Court declaring the Missouri Compromise unconstitutional? That law no longer existed. The Republicans simply had to come out against this part of the decision. It made their reason for existence— keeping slavery out of the territories—illegal.

The justices had acted as they did in hopes of settling the question of slavery in the territories once and for all. Instead they only made the controversy more heated.

Roger B. Taney was the chief justice in both the Amistad *and Dred Scott cases. What shocking reason did he give for his ruling against Scott?*

Return to the Preview & Review on page 525.

5. LINCOLN AND DOUGLAS

Use these questions to guide your reading. Answer the questions after completing Section 5. **Understanding Issues, Events, & Ideas.** Describe the events of the Illinois election of 1858, using the following words: Lecompton Constitution, Lincoln-Douglas Debates, Freeport Doctrine.

1. Why did Senator Douglas speak out against acceptance of the Lecompton Constitution?
2. Why did the Republican party promote Abraham Lincoln's candidacy for the Senate?
3. What position did Senator Douglas take in his debates with Lincoln? What position did Lincoln take?
4. What was Douglas' argument in the Freeport Doctrine? How did it help him in Illinois but hurt him nationally?

Thinking Critically. **1.** Lincoln compared slavery to a cancer and said that abolishing slavery might cause the country to "bleed to death." Do you agree or disagree with Lincoln? Give reasons for your answer. **2.** You have been assigned to cover the Lincoln-Douglas debates for a Chicago newspaper. In your article, explain the issues presented in the debates.

Senator Douglas' Dilemma

Conditions in Kansas Territory grew still worse. Meeting at the town of Lecompton, the proslavery convention in Kansas had drawn up a proposed state constitution authorizing slavery. The delegates represented only a minority of the people of the territory. But since they were Democrats, President Buchanan supported them. He urged Congress to accept this **Lecompton Constitution** and admit Kansas as a state. Of course, antislavery forces in Kansas and throughout the nation objected strongly.

These developments put Senator Stephen A. Douglas in a difficult position. He was a Democrat. (But he was clearly no friend of the president's. Indeed he often used his skills as an orator to express his open contempt for Buchanan.) The president had made the matter a party issue. On the other hand, Douglas sincerely believed in popular sovereignty. And it was obvious that a majority of the people in Kansas were opposed to the Lecompton Constitution and to the opening of the territory to slavery.

To complicate his problem, Douglas had to stand for reelection to the Senate in 1858. If he went against the Democratic party, he would suffer. If he supported the Lecompton Constitution, he might lose his Senate seat, for thousands of Illinois Democrats objected bitterly to that document.

Douglas did not hesitate for long. He announced that he opposed the Lecompton Constitution. When President Buchanan tried to put pressure on him to change his mind, he flatly refused.

When a vote was finally taken on the Lecompton Constitution, the people of Kansas rejected it by a huge majority, 11,300 to 1,788. Southern Democrats and President Buchanan were furious. They blamed Douglas for this defeat.

In Illinois the Democratic party split into factions, one group pro-Buchanan, the other pro-Douglas. Illinois Republicans were of course delighted. It gave them a chance to defeat Douglas and win his seat in the United States Senate.

In those days senators were still chosen by the state legislatures, not by popular vote. Ordinary citizens often had no idea who would be chosen senator when they cast their ballots for their representatives to the state legislature. The 1858 Illinois election did not follow this pattern. Douglas was too important and his quarrel with the president too public. Illinois voters were very much aware that the state representatives they chose would reelect or defeat Douglas. Douglas campaigned hard for his seat. Technically, he and his Republican opponent were speaking in behalf of local candidates for the legislature. But everyone knew that their votes—Democratic or Republican—would decide who Illinois would send to the Senate.

The Lincoln-Douglas Debates

The Republican candidate for the Senate was Abraham Lincoln, a lawyer and former member of the Illinois state legislature. He had served a term in Congress in the 1840s. Lincoln had moved to Illinois in 1830 when he was 21 years old. He had little formal education. As a youth he had attended school only during the few winter weeks when he was not needed to work on his father's farm. But he had read widely on his own. He was a hard worker, and very ambitious.

Lincoln also had a reputation for honesty. Early in his life people began to call him "Honest Abe." He had an excellent sense of humor. Once he saw a woman who was wearing an enormous feathered hat slip and fall in a mud puddle. "Reminds me of a duck," he said to a friend he was with. "What do you mean?" asked the friend. "Feathers on her head and down on her behind," Lincoln replied. These qualities helped him in politics. In 1834 he was elected to the Illinois legislature.

Although Lincoln had prospered as a lawyer, his political career had been only modestly successful. After his term in Congress ended in 1849, he had held no further public office. He had always been a loyal member of the Whig party, but people in Illinois thought of him as a rather ordinary local politician.

All this changed when the Kansas-Nebraska Act revived the question of slavery in the territories. "If slavery is not wrong," Lincoln said, "nothing is wrong." Still, he was not an abolitionist. Slavery was like a cancer, he said, but cutting it out might cause the patient—the United States—to "bleed to death." However, there must be no further extension of slavery in the West. By 1856 Lincoln had joined the new Republican party.

Lincoln expressed his ideas well. He had a remarkable gift for words. What called him to the attention of Republican leaders, however, was his conservatism and good judgment. Although he hated slavery, he did not hate slave owners. He did not blame them for the existence of the institution. He admitted that he did not know how to do away with slavery in states where it already existed.

These views appealed to moderates in the North. To survive as a party, the Republicans had to attack the Dred Scott decision. Their problem was that they did not want to appear to be abolitionists or to favor racial equality. Lincoln seemed the kind of candidate who could manage this difficult task. His good mind and clever tongue were also important because Stephen A. Douglas was a brilliant orator and a master of every detail of the issues of the day.

Lincoln challenged Douglas to debate the issues with him in different sections of Illinois. Douglas agreed. Their meetings attracted large crowds, for each debate was a great local occasion. Because of the importance of the election, newspapers all over the country reported on the debates in detail.

Perhaps Lincoln and Douglas stated their views most clearly in their last debate, at Alton, Illinois, on October 15, 1858. Lincoln said:

> On the point of my wanting to make war between the Free and the Slave States, there has been no issue between us. So, too, when he assumes that I am in favor of introducing a perfect social and political equality between the black and white races. These are false issues. . . . The real issue in this controversy—the one pressing upon every mind—is the sentiment on the part of one class [the Republicans] that looks upon the institution of slavery as a *wrong*, and of another class that does not look upon it as wrong. . . . They [the Republicans] look upon it as being a moral, social, and political wrong; and . . . they insist that it should, as far as may be, *be treated* as a wrong; and one of the methods of treating it as a wrong is to *make provision that it shall not grow larger.* . . .
>
> That is the issue that will continue in this country when these poor tongues of Judge Douglas and myself shall be silent. It is the eternal struggle between these two principles—right and wrong—throughout the world. They are the two principles that have stood face to face from the beginning of time; and will ever continue to struggle. . . .[1]

Lincoln did not want war to settle the slavery issue, and he did not claim complete racial equality. But he did cautiously agree that he, like other Republicans, felt slavery was wrong. And he supported the Republican stand that slavery should not spread to the new territories. Douglas then responded in this meeting that is often called The Great Debate. He said:

> We ought to extend to the negro race . . . all the rights, all the privileges, and all the humanities which they can exercise consistently with the safety of society. Humanity requires that we should give them these privileges; Christianity commands that we should extend those privileges to them. The question then arises. What are those privileges, and what is the nature and the extent of them? My answer is, that that is a question each State must answer for itself. . . . If the people of all the States will act on that great principle, and each State mind its own business, attend to its own affairs, take care of its own negroes, and not meddle in with its neighbors, then there will be peace throughout the North and the South, the East and the West, throughout the whole Union.[2]

The "Little Giant," Stephen A. Douglas, was the Henry Clay of his generation. He was able to put the needs of the nation above self-interest. If you need help to recall Henry Clay, reread pages 438–43.

[1]From Speech at Alton, Illinois, October 15, 1858 by Abraham Lincoln
[2]From Speech at Alton, Illinois, October 15, 1858 by Stephen A. Douglas

Douglas tried to persuade the voters that Lincoln and the Republicans were dangerous radicals. He accused them of being abolitionists and of favoring equality. Lincoln "thinks the Negro is his brother," the Little Giant sneered. As for the western territories, Douglas claimed that all were destined by climate and soil conditions to become free. *Allowing* slave owners to settle in Kansas would not in fact mean that they would do so.

It was obvious that most Illinois voters shared the Little Giant's low opinion of African Americans. Lincoln's own feelings were less extreme but not essentially different. But, Lincoln insisted, all people had the "natural rights" described in the Declaration of Independence: the right to life, liberty, and the pursuit of happiness.

The Freeport Doctrine

On the question of slavery in the territories Lincoln took a firm stand. He put Douglas in a difficult political position by asking him if the people of a territory could exclude slavery *before* the territory became a state. After all, did not the Dred Scott decision mean that slavery could not be banned in any territory?

Lincoln asked Douglas these questions during their debate at Freeport, Illinois. Douglas's answer is now known as the **Freeport Doctrine.** He said:

❝ It matters not what way the Supreme Court may . . . decide. . . . The people have the lawful means to introduce or exclude [slavery] as they please, for the reason that slavery cannot exist . . . unless it is supported by local police regulations. ❞

Obviously, Douglas was correct. If local authorities did not back up the owners, all the slaves could simply walk off and do as they pleased. This being the case, the people of a territory could effectively prevent slaves from being brought into their regions merely by doing nothing.

This argument helped Douglas in Illinois, where many voters were eager to believe that popular sovereignty could work in the territories despite the Dred Scott decision. It hurt him in the slave states, however. Thus it reduced his chances of winning the Democratic presidential nomination in 1860.

On election day in November the voters gave the Democrats a small majority in the state legislature. Douglas was therefore re-elected to the Senate. But Lincoln was helped by the campaign too. The publicity and his effective speeches attracted much national attention. His own account of his feelings is worth recording. "It gave me a hearing," he said. "I believe I have made some marks." But he also said, "I feel like the boy who stumped his toe. I am too big to cry and too badly hurt to laugh." 🖹

Library of Congress

The "Rail Splitter," Abraham Lincoln, is beardless in this early photograph. Reread pages 377–78 to recall Lincoln's early life in Indiana.

Return to the Preview & Review on page 528.

Lincoln and Douglas 531

National Archives

Above, Harpers Ferry lies peacefully in the Shenandoah Valley.

Preview & Review

Use these questions to guide your reading. Answer the questions after completing Section 6.

Understanding Issues, Events, & Ideas. Using the following words, explain the events that led to secession: Harpers Ferry, Homestead Act, border state, Constitutional Unionist party, states' rights, southern regionalism.

1. Why did John Brown and his small army raid Harpers Ferry?
2. How did Brown's raid further divide North and South?
3. How did the four-way race for president help Lincoln get elected?
4. What event prompted the Deep South to secede? What was the southerners' legal argument for their secession?

Thinking Critically. 1. Was John Brown a hero, or was he insane? Cite evidence to support your opinion. **2.** For which candidate would you have voted in 1860? Why?

6. THE THREAT OF SECESSION

The Attack on Harpers Ferry

At this point John Brown again appeared on the national scene. Brown was never punished for his part in the Pottawatomie massacre. He believed that God had commanded him to free the slaves by force. Kansas had seemed the best place to wage this battle. But violence was no longer necessary to keep slavery out of Kansas, and its settlers had little interest in fighting to get rid of it anywhere else.

Brown had to develop a new scheme. He decided to organize a small band of armed followers, march into the South, and seize land in some remote area. What would happen next he never made clear. Apparently he expected slaves from all over the region to run away and join him. With their help he would launch raids throughout the South aimed at rescuing more slaves.

Brown managed to persuade six important Massachusetts abolitionists to give him enough money to organize and supply his attack force. The goal of his tiny 18-man army was a United States government armory in the town of **Harpers Ferry**, Virginia, on the Potomac River northwest of Washington.

On the evening of October 16, 1859, Brown and his commandos crossed the Potomac. They overpowered a watchman and occupied the armory and a government rifle factory. Brown then sent some of his men off to capture two local slaveholders as hostages. One of these was Lewis Washington, a great-grandnephew of George Washington. When workers began to arrive in the morning, Brown also took some of them prisoner. Then he sat back to wait for local slaves to rise up and join his rebellion.

Not one slave did so. But the local authorities reacted promptly. In a matter of hours Brown's force was under siege, pinned down in the armory. A detachment of marines commanded by Lieutenant Colonel Robert E. Lee arrived from Washington. Brown refused to surrender. On October 18 Lee sent the marines forward with fixed bayonets. They quickly overwhelmed the rebels.

Ten of Brown's men were killed, but Brown was taken alive. He was charged with murder, conspiracy, and treason. After a fair but swift trial he was convicted and sentenced to be hanged.

John Brown was almost certainly insane. He was so disorganized that he did not even attempt to let the slaves know that he had come to free them. The affair might have been dismissed as the act of a lunatic if Brown had acted like a disturbed person after his capture, but he did not do so. Indeed, he behaved with remarkable dignity and self-discipline. Shortly after his capture he was interviewed. Clement L. Vallandigham, a congressman from Ohio, and James M. Mason, a senator from Virginia, were among those present. A *New York Herald* reporter wrote notes during the interview and they were later published. Judge for yourself if Brown sounds insane in the following part of the interview:

" *Mr. Vallandigham.* Mr. Brown, who sent you here?

Brown. No man sent me here; it was my own prompting and that of my Maker, or that of the Devil—whichever you please to ascribe it to. I acknowledge no master in human form. . . .

Mason. What was your object in coming?

Brown. We came to free the slaves, and only that. . . .

A Volunteer. How many men, in all, had you?

Brown. I came to Virginia with 18 men only, besides myself. . . .

Mason. How do you justify your acts?

Brown. I think, my friend, you [slaveholders] are guilty of a great wrong against God and humanity,—I say it without wishing to be offensive—and it would be perfectly right for any one to interfere with you so far as to free those you wilfully and wickedly hold in bondage. I do not say this insultingly.

Mason. I understand that.

Brown. I think I did right, and that others will do right who interfere with you at any time and at all times. I hold that the Golden Rule, 'Do unto others as ye would that others should do unto you,' applies to all who would help others gain their liberty.

Lieutenant Stuart. But don't you believe in the Bible?

Brown. Certainly I do. . . .

A Bystander. Do you consider this a religious movement?

Brown. It is, in my opinion, the greatest service man can render to God.

Bystander. Do you consider yourself an instrument in the hands of Providence [God]?

Brown. I do.

Bystander. Upon what principle do you justify your acts?

Brown. Upon the Golden Rule. I pity the poor in bondage that have none to help them: that is why I am here; not to gratify any personal animosity [resentment], revenge, or

Metropolitan Museum of Art

"The Last Moments of John Brown" is the way northerners imagined the leader of the raid on Harpers Ferry being led to his execution. Horace Greeley wrote for his newspaper a description of the woman waiting with her little child: "He stopped a moment, and stooping, kissed the child." But Greeley was not present and in fact only soldiers met Brown. Why would the North have taken such a generous view of John Brown?

vindictive [vengeful] spirit. It is my sympathy with the oppressed and the wronged, that are as good as you and as
precious in the sight of God. . . .

    Bystander. Brown, suppose you had every [slave] in the
United States, what would you do with them?

    Brown. Set them free. . . .[1]"

Even Brown's judge and jailors admired his calm courage. When
he was condemned to death, he said that he had acted in the name
of God:

  "To have interfered as I have done . . . in behalf of His
despised poor, is not wrong, but right. Now, if it is . . .
necessary that I should forfeit my life for the furtherance
of the ends of justice . . . I say, let it be done. I feel no
consciousness of guilt."

Brown became a hero to the abolitionists and to many other
northerners. They considered him a noble freedom fighter. His bloody
murders in Kansas and his reckless assault at Harpers Ferry were
conveniently forgotten. When northerners made Brown a near saint,
southerners in the slave states became even more concerned. They
began to think that northerners intended to destroy slavery, not
merely limit its expansion. Once again, northerners and southerners
looked at each other with suspicion, fear, and even hatred.

The Election of 1860

As the 1860 presidential election drew near, the Democrats became
even more sharply divided. The northern faction supported Senator
Douglas. The southern wing was led by President Buchanan, although he was not a candidate for a second term. The party's
nominating convention was held in April 1860 at Charleston, South
Carolina. Douglas controlled a small majority of the delegates, but
the rules of the convention required a two-thirds majority for nomination. This he could not get. The convention then adjourned.

The delegates gathered again in June in Baltimore. Once more
they failed to agree. This time the party broke formally in two. The
northerners nominated Douglas for president. The southerners selected Buchanan's vice president, John C. Breckinridge of Kentucky.

In the meantime the Republican presidential convention had
taken place in Chicago. To broaden their appeal, party leaders drafted
a program of economic reforms to go along with their demand that
slavery be kept out of the territories. They called for a **Homestead
Act** giving 160 acres (64 hectares), enough land for a family farm, to
anyone who would settle on it. They urged government support for
a railroad to the Pacific and higher tariffs on manufactured goods in

---

The Portent

"Hanging from the
  beam, Slowly swaying
  (such the law),
Gaunt the shadow on
  your green,
    Shenandoah!
The cut is on the crown
  (Lo, John Brown),
And the stabs shall heal
  no more.

Hidden in the cap°
  Is the anguish none
  can draw;
So your future veils its
face,
    Shenandoah!
But the streaming beard
  is shown
The meteor of the war."
    Herman Melville, 1859

° A cap was placed over the head of a man
being hanged.

---

[1] From *The Life and Letters of John Brown* edited by F.B. Sanborn

Reynolda House, Inc.

Thomas Cole's "Home in the Woods" was painted in about 1845. Family farms sprang up everywhere, especially after the Homestead Act of 1862 made land available to anyone who would settle it. After studying this painting closely, what can you say about daily life on the frontier?

order to protect producers from foreign competition. They rejected the idea of nativist support. They promised not to restrict immigration into the country.

Before the convention Senator William H. Seward of New York seemed the person most likely to get the Republican presidential nomination. However, to win the election, the Republicans would have to carry Pennsylvania, Indiana, and Illinois—the northern states that Buchanan had carried in 1856. Seward was thought to be too antislavery to persuade doubtful voters in those states. After much political "horse-trading" the delegates nominated Abraham Lincoln.

Many proslavery radicals had threatened that the southern states would secede from the Union and set up an independent country of their own if a Republican was elected president. This possibility was particularly alarming to many people in the Upper South, the so-called **border states** of Maryland, Delaware, Kentucky, and Missouri. Should civil war break out, it would surely be fought on their soil.

These people formed still a fourth party, the **Constitutional Unionist party,** in 1860. The Constitutional Unionist's platform was simple: They stood for "the Constitution and the Union." In other words, they tried to ignore the controversial issues that were dividing the country. If the party had lived long enough to develop a symbol like the Democratic donkey and the Republican elephant, the symbol should have been an ostrich with its head buried in the sand.

The Constitutional Unionists nominated John Bell, for many years a congressman and senator from Tennessee. Bell was a stiff, rather colorless person. He was chosen because of his long record as a conservative and the fact that although he was a slave owner, he had voted against the Kansas-Nebraska Act.

With four candidates running, no one could hope to get a majority of the popular vote. Lincoln received 1,866,000, nearly all in the northern states. Douglas got 1,383,000, also mostly in the North. Breckinridge received 848,000 and Bell 593,000. But Lincoln won a solid majority of the electoral votes, 180 of the 303 cast.

What had happened was this: In the free states the election was between Lincoln and Douglas. It was a fairly close contest, but Lincoln won in every state. Despite his large popular vote, Douglas got only 12 electoral votes, Missouri's 9 and 3 from New Jersey.

In the slave states Breckinridge and Bell divided the votes. Breckinridge had a majority in all the states of the Deep South. Bell carried the border states of Tennessee, Kentucky, and Virginia.

The Secession Crisis

Although he got much less than half the popular vote, Lincoln had been legally elected president. Even the southerners recognized that this was so. The more radical of them therefore prepared to take their states out of the Union.

LEARNING FROM MAPS. *The outcome of the election of 1860 had long-range consequences. Where was each candidate strongest? How can you explain these regional strengths?*

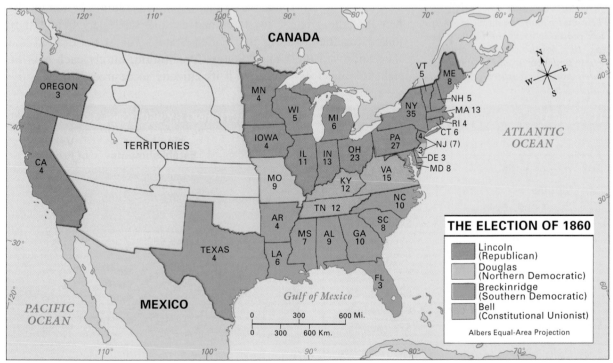

THE ELECTION OF 1860

Lincoln (Republican)
Douglas (Northern Democratic)
Breckinridge (Southern Democratic)
Bell (Constitutional Unionist)

Albers Equal-Area Projection

For several years there had been much talk of the South seceding if a "black Republican" was ever elected president. Lincoln and other northerners had convinced themselves that this talk was merely bluff. Stephen A. Douglas, however, recognized how serious the threat was. As the campaign progressed, he sensed the trend of popular opinion. A month before the election he realized that Lincoln was almost certainly going to win. "Mr. Lincoln is the next president," he told his secretary. "We must try to save the Union. I will go South." During the remaining weeks he campaigned in Tennessee, Georgia, and Alabama. Everywhere he spoke not for himself but for preserving the Union.

His noble effort failed. Within days of the news of Lincoln's election, the legislature of South Carolina summoned a special convention to consider the question of secession. Before the end of the year the delegates to that convention voted to take the state out of the Union. Other southern states followed quickly. Only the states of the Upper South held back, and leaders in these states were seriously considering leaving the Union.

The reasons why the South seceded have puzzled historians for more than a hundred years. Probably no completely satisfactory explanation is possible. But this much can be said: The slave system was at the root of the difficulties between the sections. Southerners felt that the security of their peculiar institution was being threatened. By leaving the United States and setting up a country of their own, they hoped to protect not only slavery but what they considered their whole way of life.

The southern states based their right to leave the Union on the fact that the original 13 states had existed separately before they joined together to form the United States. The states drafted and then approved the United States Constitution. Surely each had the right to cancel its allegiance if its citizens so desired. This was the

LEARNING FROM TABLES. *These tables show the status of American manufacturing in 1860. What was the South's leading product? What problems would leaving the Union cause for southern consumers?*

LEADING U. S. MANUFACTURES, 1860		
Rank	Product	Value
1	Cotton goods	$54,671,082
2	Lumber	$53,569,942
3	Boots and shoes	$49,161,124
4	Flour and meal	$40,083,056
5	Men's clothing	$36,680,803
6	Iron	$35,689,276
7	Machinery	$32,565,843
8	Woolen goods	$25,032,489
9	Carriages, wagons, carts	$23,654,560
10	Leather	$22,785,715

Source: *Eighth Census of the United States, Manufactures, 1860*

MANUFACTURING BY SECTIONS, 1860		
Section	Number of Establishments	Value of of Products
North	73,958	$1,270,937,679
New England	20,671	$468,599,287
Middle Atlantic	53,287	$802,338,392
West	45,562	$455,836,519
Midwest	36,785	$384,606,530
California	8,777	$71,229,989
South	20,631	$155,531,281
Territories	282	$3,556,197

Source: *Eighth Census of the United States, Manufactures, 1860*

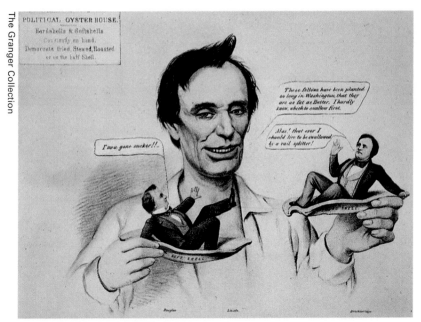

In a rather crude caricature of Abraham Lincoln (but a shadow of the mistreatment he would receive from his critics as president), we see how easily he downed his opponents. "Honest Abe Taking Them on the Half Shell" shows Douglas in Lincoln's right hand, Breckinridge in his left. How does this cartoon capture the outcome of the 1860 election?

doctrine of **states' rights,** first argued by Jefferson in the 1790s. It was given its most complete expression by John C. Calhoun in the 1820s and 1830s when he argued that a state could nullify a federal law it did not consider constitutional.

The ideas of nullification and secession were a challenge to the basic tenets of the Constitution. The Constitution bound all the states together by mutual consent. States agreed to recognize the Constitution as the supreme law of the land. They also recognized federalism–the sharing of power by the national and state governments—and the responsibility of the national government to oversee certain government functions. Now the southern states proposed to cast aside the Constitution in favor of states' rights.

Belief in states' rights was the legal justification of secession, but it was not the reason why the southern states seceded. That was more a matter of **southern regionalism**—loyalty to the region and to the slave system. The national controversy over slavery had weakened the southerners' loyalty to the entire United States. For a person like Lincoln to say, "If slavery is not wrong, nothing is wrong," was a slap in the face to most southerners. No matter that Lincoln and other moderates had no intention of trying to destroy slavery where it already existed, southern defenders of slavery could not accept the idea that the system was "wrong." When Lincoln's point of view triumphed and he became president of the United States, southerners no longer wished to be part of the Union.

Return to the Preview & Review on page 532.

The Threat of Secession   539

CHAPTER 15 REVIEW

THE VERGE OF CIVIL WAR

1850	THE VERGE OF CIVIL WAR	1855

1850
Compromise of 1850 (Fugitive Slave Act)

1852
Uncle Tom's Cabin published

1854
Kansas-Nebraska Bill

Chapter Summary

Read the statements below. Choose one, and write a paragraph explaining its importance.
1. The Fugitive Slave Act and *Uncle Tom's Cabin* increased northerners' discomfort with slavery.
2. The violent and bloody struggle for Kansas between pro- and antislavery groups gave a preview of the Civil War.
3. The controversy over slavery helped end the Whig party and start both the Know-Nothings and the Republican party.
4. The decision in *Dred Scott v. Sandford* continued to focus attention and criticism on slavery.
5. The Lincoln-Douglas debates summarized feelings of both sides of the slavery question and put Lincoln's name before the public.
6. The view of John Brown as a hero after his raid on Harpers Ferry angered southerners.
7. The election of Lincoln rekindled threats of secession based on states' rights and, in fact, several states voted to secede.

Reviewing Chronological Order

Number your paper 1–5. Then study the time line above and place the following events in the order in which they happened by writing the first next to 1, the second next to 2, and so on.
1. Brown's raid on Harpers Ferry
2. *Uncle Tom's Cabin*
3. Lincoln elected president
4. Kansas-Nebraska Bill
5. *Dred Scott v. Sandford*

Understanding Main Ideas

1. How did Douglas hope to persuade southerners to support his Kansas-Nebraska Bill? How did he hope to avoid a northern uproar?
2. How did proslavery and antislavery forces square off in Kansas?
3. What was the Republican platform? In what section of the country was it strongest?
4. What did the Supreme Court decide in the case of *Dred Scott v. Sandford?* Why was the decision strongly criticized?

5. Who were the four candidates for president in 1860, and which was the party of each?
6. How did the Republican party try to broaden its appeal in the election of 1860?

Thinking Critically

1. **Synthesizing**. Imagine that you are a northern abolitionist. Compose a fiery letter criticizing slavery to send to the editor of your local paper.
2. **Creating**. Write the copy for a handbill advertising the play based on *Uncle Tom's Cabin*, to be presented at the Abolition Theatre of Boston, Massachusetts, in 1853. Choose dates and time of performance. Create names of actors for the leading roles.
3. **Evaluating**. In your opinion, what did Lincoln mean when he said every person has a right "to the bread . . . which his own hand earns"? Do you agree or disagree with this statement? Why?
4. **Identifying Issues**. Take the part of a senator from South Carolina after the 1860 election of Abraham Lincoln. In a letter to your closest friend, a senator from New York, explain why your state has chosen to secede from the Union.

Writing About History: Classificatory

Use your historical imagination to write a magazine article about one of the Lincoln-Douglas debates. Describe the setting, and compare the candidates' positions on key issues. Also describe the crowd's reaction to the speakers. Use the information in Chapter 15 and in reference materials to prepare your article.

Practicing the Strategy

Review the strategy on page 517.
Comparing Maps. Study the maps on pages 457 and 551, then answer the following questions.
1. On the map on page 457, what states included cotton-growing areas by 1859?

540   CAUSES OF THE CIVIL WAR

1860

356	1857	1858	1859	1860
umner caned the Senate	*Dred Scott v. Sandford*	Lincoln-Douglas debates ★	Brown's raid on Harpers Ferry	Lincoln elected president ★
★ ottawatomie assacre		Lecompton Constitution rejected ★		South Carolina votes to secede
★ uchanan elected president		Douglas states Freeport Doctrine		

2. How had these areas of cotton growing changed since 1839?
3. On the map on page 551, which states belonged to the Confederacy? Which states were considered "border states," on the side of the Union?
4. Locate the border states on the map on page 457. Why do you think that those states joined the Union side rather than the Confederacy?

Using Primary Sources

Southerners had long wanted to obtain Cuba, arguing that a slave rebellion there might cause American slaves to revolt. In 1854 the United States began negotiations with Spain to buy Cuba. From these talks came the Ostend Manifesto, a secret state department proposal to act if Spain refused. When news of the manifesto leaked out, northerners were outraged, seeing it as a "slaveholder's plot" to add to southern territory. As you read the excerpt from the manifesto, see if you agree with its logic. Then answer the questions below.

Self-preservation is the first law of nature, with states as well as with individuals. . . . After we shall have offered Spain a price for Cuba far beyond its present value, and this shall have been refused, it will then be time to consider the question, does Spain, in possession of Cuba, seriously endanger our internal peace and the existence of our cherished Union?

Should this question be answered in the affirmative, then, by every law, human and divine, we shall be justified in wrestling it from Spain if we possess the power; and this upon the very same principle that would justify an individual in tearing down the burning house of his neighbor if there were no other means of preventing the flames from destroying his own home.

1. What evidence in the excerpt suggests that the states were more concerned with their own in-

terests than with maintaining peace with foreign nations?
2. According to the excerpt, what is the justification for taking Cuba by force? Do you think this logic applies to foreign affairs today? Why or why not?
3. If you were a historian, how might you use the Ostend Manifesto to support the argument that the causes of war develop gradually? Explain your answer.

Linking History & Geography

The Missouri Compromise (1820), the Compromise of 1850, and the Kansas-Nebraska Bill (1854) all revised the geographic limits of slavery. Use the maps on page 517 and the information in Chapters 12 and 15 to answer these questions.
1. Which territories remained free under the Compromise of 1850? Which permitted slavery?
2. What physical features of the West might have limited the spread of slavery naturally?
3. Why do you think southerners continued to fight for the right to bring slavery into the new territories?

Enriching the Study of History

1. **Individual Project**. Prepare a chart to show the political parties that came into being in the 1850s. Include information about the party platforms, candidates, and region of strongest support. Your teacher may wish to display the charts.
2. **Cooperative Project**. Your teacher will divide your class into four teams. Each team will be assigned one of the 1860 presidential candidates: John Bell, John C. Breckinridge, Stephen A. Douglas, or Abraham Lincoln. Each team will prepare and present to the class a short campaign speech to endorse its candidate. Then your class will hold a mock election.

Chapter 15 Review   541

The Civil War

Abraham Lincoln's election sent a signal to southerners to take their states out of the Union. When the Confederacy fired on Fort Sumter, the Civil War began. For four years North and South were locked in battle. Southerners fought the war for the right of self-determination, northerners to keep the Union whole. This chapter relates the major battles and strategies of the war and its burden upon the economies of the North and South. It shows something of the lives of typical Union and Confederate soldiers, as well as of the men and women who came to care for the wounded. The chapter concludes with General Sherman's total war and March to the Sea and the surrender at Appomattox by General Lee to General Grant. And as weary soldiers wended their way home, many wondered "What is lost? What is won?"

Connecticut Historical Society

The American eagle guards its nest of states in this 1861 cartoon. But while the eagle warns against traitors, the southern states in the foreground are hatching rebellion. This war propaganda cartoon leaves no doubt as to the artist's position: "The Union: It Must and Shall be Preserved." Make a poster or draw a picture that shows the breakup of the Union in a different way.

1. THE WAR BEGINS

Between Peace and War

The states of the Deep South left the Union during a time when the United States government was particularly weak. President-elect Lincoln would not take office until March 4, 1861. Furthermore, he showed no interest in dealing with the problem of secession or taking responsibility of any kind before that date. The outgoing president, James Buchanan, seemed paralyzed by the crisis. He announced that secession was illegal. Then he added that it would also be illegal for the federal government to try to prevent a state from seceding!

Matters drifted throughout the winter. Several members of Congress tried to work out compromises that would satisfy the fears of southerners without stirring up northern foes of slavery. None succeeded. More southern states withdrew from the Union. Each seceding state tried to take over federal property within its borders—post offices, army forts, courthouses.

Buchanan did not try to hold on to government property in the states that left the Union. But there were three forts in Charleston, South Carolina, that did not fall into local hands. One of these, **Fort Sumter,** was on an island in Charleston harbor. The others were on the mainland. They were held by about 100 soldiers commanded by Major Robert Anderson.

Gradually, national attention focused on these forts. Would South Carolina use force to seize them? If so, would Buchanan try to defend the forts? Major Anderson was a southerner. But he was also a patriotic soldier who had taken an oath to protect the flag of the United States. Anderson realized that he could not protect all the forts with his tiny force. One night in December 1860 he moved his men to the more easily protected Fort Sumter.

South Carolina troops then occupied the abandoned forts on the mainland. When Buchanan sent an unarmed ship with men and supplies to Fort Sumter, the South Carolinians drove it off with cannon fire from the shore. For the first time shots were fired in anger. Yet no one was injured. Anderson remained in control of Fort Sumter.

The Confederate States of America

On February 4, 1861, 37 delegates representing six southern republics met at Montgomery, Alabama, to create a central government. Southern leaders knew that the seceding states had to design a strong union if they were to stay independent. They had to work fast. They wanted to have the new government in operation before Abraham Lincoln became president of the United States on March 4.

The delegates began work on February 5 and adopted a constitution only three days later. This was possible because the document

Preview & Review

Use these questions to guide your reading. Answer the questions after completing Section 1.
Understanding Issues, Events, & Ideas. Using the following words, explain how the war between the North and South began: Fort Sumter, confederacy, Confederate States of America, Civil War.

1. Why was there no strong presidential reaction in the winter of 1861 to the secession of the Deep South?
2. How did the Confederate constitution reflect the South's belief in states' rights?
3. What was Lincoln's message to the Confederacy in his first inaugural address?
4. What reasoning did President Lincoln give for going to war?

Thinking Critically. 1. Imagine that you are a secretary for President Davis. In your journal, describe Jefferson Davis and explain what you think are his strengths and weaknesses as president of the Confederacy.
2. You are the messenger sent by President Davis to give the order to fire on Fort Sumter on April 12. Write a letter to your cousin in the North, explaining why you think Davis should or should not have issued this order and how you think this action will affect your family.

was almost a copy of the United States Constitution. The differences were small but significant. The new nation was to be a **confederacy** of independent states, not a union. Hence the delegates called it the **Confederate States of America.** The constitution also specifically mentioned slavery and guaranteed the rights of citizens to own slaves. Congress was forbidden to pass any law "denying . . . the right of property in negro slaves."

Despite a stress on the rights of the separate states, the Confederate constitution, like the United States Constitution, was to be the "supreme law of the land." The president was to hold office for six years instead of four. But he could not be reelected. Congress could not spend money unless two thirds of the representatives approved. The constitution could be amended if two thirds of the states approved, not three fourths as under the United States Constitution.

The Confederacy Chooses Jefferson Davis

Jefferson Davis' portrait was made halfway through the war, after he had served two of the six years of his term.

Museum of the Confederacy, Richmond, VA
Photography by Katherine Wetzel

The day after finishing the constitution, the delegates elected Jefferson Davis of Mississippi to be president of the newly formed Confederate States of America. They chose Alexander Stephens of Georgia as vice president.

Davis was in the rose garden at his plantation, Brierfield, overlooking the Mississippi, when a telegram announcing his election was delivered. The president was a tall, slender man with high cheekbones, fair hair, and blue-gray eyes. He was 52 years old, the tenth child of a pioneer family in Todd County, Kentucky. He attended Transylvania University in Lexington, Kentucky, and was graduated from the United States Military Academy in 1828. He resigned his commission in 1835 to become a cotton planter in Mississippi.

Davis had long and varied experience in public life before becoming president of the Confederacy. He was elected to the House of Representatives in 1845. The next year the Mexican War broke out. He gave up his seat in Congress to serve as a colonel in the army. He was wounded in the foot at the Battle of Buena Vista. The wound was quite serious because the bullet drove pieces of his brass spur into his foot. He came back to Mississippi on crutches but recovered fully. In 1847 he was elected to the United States Senate. When Franklin Pierce became president in 1853, he named Davis secretary of war.

Southerners rally for the inauguration of Jefferson Davis, who stands on the balcony of the capitol in Montgomery, Alabama. Judging from the clock, he probably took office at high noon. How was this moment a turning point for the South?

In his inaugural address President Davis insisted that he desired to maintain peaceful relations with the United States. His speech was not very inspiring. Davis was an extremely hard worker, but he did not get on well with people. He often quarreled with members of his cabinet and with other government officials. He could be very stubborn. His feelings were easily hurt by criticism. He wasted far too much of his time handling unimportant details. Once he spent a whole day dictating one 4,000-word letter.

Lincoln Becomes President

In 1861 Jefferson Davis's strengths were much more obvious than his weaknesses. Indeed, when Abraham Lincoln was inaugurated as president of the United States on March 4, many people thought him a far less inspiring leader than the president of the new Confederacy.

Lincoln had chosen a cabinet that reflected a wide variety of attitudes and regions. This was understandable at a time of national crisis. Yet would this backwoods lawyer be able to control such a group? Or would he become a figurehead, a kind of homespun master of ceremonies? He had appointed the best-known Republican in the United States, William H. Seward, as secretary of state. Seward did not resent Lincoln's having defeated him for the Republican presidential nomination. But he did not think Lincoln competent to be president. He was ready, he told his wife, "to save freedom and my country" by making the major government decisions himself.

Lincoln, however, did not intend to be dominated by Seward or anyone else. People like Seward misunderstood him. They took his slow, deliberate, rather uncertain manner to mean confusion and lack of intelligence. Nothing could have been further from the truth.

Lincoln seemed a strange figure, six feet, six inches tall without his stovepipe hat. His voice was thin and high-pitched. He was awkward. At a dance he told his future wife, "I want to dance with you in the worst possible way." "And he certainly did," added Mary Todd Lincoln. She was convinced her husband would one day be president. She had once been courted by Stephen A. Douglas, but after marriage she made Lincoln a fine home and raised his sons in Springfield and Washington.

Lincoln first publicly revealed his depth and determination in his inaugural address. He told the troubled American people:

> Apprehension [fear] seems to exist among the people of the Southern states that by the accession [coming into office] of a Republican administration their property and their peace and their personal security are to be endangered. There has never been any reasonable cause for such apprehension. Indeed, the most ample evidence to the contrary has all the while existed and been open to their inspection. It is found in nearly all the published speeches of him who now addresses you [Lincoln]. I do but quote one of those speeches when I declare that "I have no purpose, directly or indirectly, to interfere with the institution of slavery in the states where it exists. I believe I have no lawful right to do so, and I have no inclination [desire] to do so. . . .
>
> Before entering upon so grave a matter as the destruction of our national fabric, with all its benefits, its memories, and its hopes, would it not be wise to ascertain precisely why we do it? . . .

Mary Todd married Abraham Lincoln in 1842. She was from Kentucky but met Lincoln while visiting relatives in Illinois. How might her Kentucky origins have troubled some people after the Civil War began?

All profess to be content in the Union if all constitutional rights can be maintained. Is it true, then, that any right, plainly written in the Constitution, has been denied? I think not. . . .

One section of our country believes slavery is right, and ought to be extended, while the other believes it is wrong, and ought not to be extended. This is the only substantial [major] dispute. . . .

Physically speaking, we cannot separate. We cannot remove our respective sections from each other, nor build an impassible wall between them. . . . They cannot but remain face to face, and intercourse [dealings], either amicable [friendly] or hostile, must continue between them. . . .

In your hands, my dissatisfied countrymen, and not in mine, is the momentous issue of civil war. The government will not assail [attack] you. You can have no conflict without being yourselves the aggressors. . . .

We are not enemies, but friends. We must not be enemies. Though passion may have strained, it must not break, our bonds of affection. **〞**

Lincoln hoped his words would soothe raw emotions. He assured the South that he would not send troops into the region to prevent secession. He promised again not to interfere with slavery in the states. Nevertheless, secession was illegal, even ''revolutionary,'' he said. ''No state upon its own mere notion can lawfully get out of the Union.'' In any case, secession would not end any of the existing disagreements between the North and South. Conflicts of interest would remain. The only sensible solution was to negotiate as friends. Thus the new president held out every hope that the Union might be preserved.

The Firing on Fort Sumter

The immediate problem Lincoln faced was what to do about Fort Sumter, a problem he inherited from President Buchanan. Major Anderson and his men could not hold out forever without fresh supplies. After considering the question for about a month, Lincoln decided to send food to the besieged garrison but no troop reinforcements or ammunition. He informed the governor of South Carolina of his intention.

The Confederates would not accept even this small ''invasion'' of what they considered their territory. On April 12, acting on orders from President Davis, they began to bombard Fort Sumter. By the next day the fort was in ruins. When his ammunition was almost exhausted, Major Anderson and his weary troops laid down their arms in surrender.

A direct hit on Fort Sumter signals the beginning of the Civil War. Based on the engraving, how would you describe the weapons of this war?

The **Civil War** had begun. Southerners felt that they were fighting for what we would call the right of self-determination. They believed that the people of a state ought to be able to decide what kind of government they wanted for themselves. They had no intention of injuring the states that remained in the Union. What right had the United States to prevent them from going their own way?

Lincoln's answer to this argument was simple: A nation has the right to protect itself against destruction. If one part could separate itself from the rest whenever it disapproved of the result of an election, or the passage of a controversial law, the nation would swiftly break up into many tiny fragments.

Lincoln's reasoning made it possible to go to war for patriotic reasons. Slavery was obviously the major cause of the war. But the war was not fought to abolish slavery. People in the northern states did not suddenly become abolitionists when Confederate cannon began to pound Fort Sumter. They fought ''to save the Union,'' not ''to free the slaves.''

Return to the Preview & Review on page 543.

548   THE CIVIL WAR

Richmond, Virginia, became the capital of the Confederacy, the capitol itself visible at the center.

2. RAISING THE ARMIES

Robert E. Lee

After the attack on Fort Sumter, Lincoln called for 75,000 volunteer soldiers to put down the rebellion. Recruits came forward enthusiastically all over the North. But news that Lincoln intended to use force against the Confederacy caused Virginia, North Carolina, Tennessee, and Arkansas to secede and join the other Confederate states. When Virginia joined the Confederacy, the government shifted its capital from Montgomery, Alabama, to Richmond, Virginia.

In both North and South, recruiting was left to the states. Young men enlisted with high hopes for an exciting adventure that would take them far from farm or factory. A passion for "Zouave" units swept both sides. Prospective soldiers joined these Zouave companies to wear their broad sashes and baggy red breeches.

Since northern and southern soldiers were so much alike, any differences had to come from their generals. Lincoln's first choice for commander of the Union army had been Colonel Robert E. Lee, the officer who captured John Brown. Although Lee was a Virginian, he owned no slaves and was known to have opposed secession. His great hero was George Washington, and he was married to the first president's step-granddaughter.

Lee had been a top student in his class at the United States Military Academy. He always had high grades and graduated second

Preview & Review

Use these questions to guide your reading. Answer the questions after completing Section 2.
Understanding Issues, Events, & Ideas. Describe your experiences as either a Confederate or Union soldier, using the following words: Bull Run, Army of the Potomac, Battle of Seven Pines, Army of Northern Virginia, Seven Days Before Richmond.
1. Why did Lincoln wish Lee to command his army?
2. What advantages did the North have at the beginning of the Civil War? What advantages did the South have?
3. What did the Battle of Bull Run reveal about both sides?
4. In what ways was the Civil War the first modern war?
Thinking Critically. 1. Imagine that you are General Robert E. Lee. In a letter, tell President Lincoln that you cannot lead the Union forces and why. 2. You are a Union soldier under the command of General McClellan. In your diary, record your opinion of McClellan as a man and as a leader.

Raising the Armies   549

Virginia Historical Society

Robert E. Lee sits astride his horse Traveller. Lee was a true national hero because of his strong personal character. Traveller was nearly as celebrated. Visitors after the war pulled the hairs from his tail for souvenirs. Lee's home is today part of the Arlington National Cemetery. From your other reading, is it unusual for a rebel leader to be popular with both friend and foe?

in his class. As a young officer in the Mexican War, he had performed brilliantly. If he had accepted Lincoln's offer, the Civil War might not have lasted as long as it did.

Unfortunately for the United States, Lee put loyalty to his home state of Virginia above the Union. He resigned from the army and joined the Confederates. Lincoln then turned to General Irvin McDowell, who was an efficient officer but without battle experience.

By July 1861 30,000 Union soldiers were training in camps outside Washington. Twenty miles (32 kilometers) to the south other thousands of Confederate soldiers were gathered at Manassas railroad junction, on a small stream called Bull Run. The southern troops at Manassas were commanded by General Pierre Beauregard of Louisiana. Beauregard had also seen action in the Mexican War. In the attack on Mexico City he was twice wounded. It was Beauregard who had commanded the guns that battered Fort Sumter.

North Versus South

In numbers the Confederacy seemed no match for the United States. The North had about 22 million people, the South only 9 million. Nearly 4 million of the southerners were slaves. Since southerners were unwilling to put guns in the hands of slaves, the Confederate army could draw upon only 1,280,000 men between the ages of 15 and 50 to fill its ranks.

In 1860 over 90 percent of the nation's factories were in the northern states. New York, Pennsylvania, and Massachusetts each manufactured more goods than the entire Confederacy. There were only two gunpowder factories in the South, both small. There was not one factory capable of handling orders for uniforms and shoes.

The North also had more than twice as many miles of railroad tracks as the South and twice as many horses, donkeys, and mules. The government had little trouble moving its troops and supplies from the farms and the cities to its armies in the field. Since the United States was already in existence, it had an army, a navy, and ways of raising money. The South had to create these from scratch.

Just to begin operations, Confederate officials were forced to borrow from the state of Alabama and from bankers in New Orleans. The Confederate treasury was originally located in the back room of a bank in Montgomery. The secretary of the treasury and his one assistant had to use their own money to furnish the office.

On the other hand, the Confederacy had certain advantages over the Union. Like the colonists during the Revolutionary War, the southerners were defending their homeland. The invading northern armies had to maintain longer and longer lines of communication as they advanced. The southerners' homes and their whole way of life were at stake. This added to their determination and helped make up for the shortage of men and supplies.

LEARNING FROM MAPS. *This map shows the Union torn apart by the Civil War. Why do you think the border states were so called?*

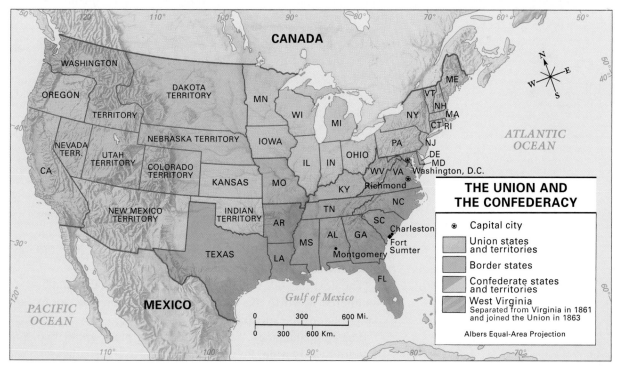

THE UNION AND THE CONFEDERACY

⊛ Capital city

Union states and territories

Border states

Confederate states and territories

West Virginia
Separated from Virginia in 1861 and joined the Union in 1863

Albers Equal-Area Projection

During the Civil War most soldiers still used clumsy, muzzle-loading rifles. Even the most skillful rifleman could get off no more than two shots a minute. This gun had a range of nearly a mile and was deadly accurate up to 250 yards (229 meters). To advance in mass formation against troops armed with such rifles was to invite wholesale slaughter.

Army food ranged from fair to awful. It consisted mostly of salt or pickled beef or pork and bread—cornbread for the Confederate troops and hardtack for the Union. Hardtack was a solid cracker made from wheat. It came in thick, square chunks. The men generally soaked it in their coffee and ate it with a spoon. Coffee was therefore especially important to Union soldiers. They ground the coffee beans by pounding them with a stone or musket butt.

In camp Confederate "Johnny Reb" and Union "Billy Yank" passed the time playing cards, organizing horse races, and taking care of their equipment. Baseball was popular. When bats and balls were not available, the men made do with a board or a section of some farmer's fence rail for a bat. A walnut or stone wrapped with yarn made a usable ball.

Music was a popular pastime in both armies. Soldiers gathered around campfires in the evening to sing songs like "Home, Sweet Home" and "John Brown's Body," the favorite on the Union side. "I don't believe we can have an army without music," said Robert E. Lee. Even northerners found themselves whistling "Dixie," the Confederate anthem.

"Johnny Reb" Meets "Billy Yank"

The Civil War was the bloodiest war Americans have ever waged. Americans fought Americans, yet the diaries and journals of soldiers on both sides described many friendly encounters. Alexander Hunter, a young Confederate soldier, wrote of one such meeting in Virginia. Consider how you would feel fighting the "friendly enemy" he describes here:

    ❝ It was the latter part of August [1863]; orders were given to be prepared to go on [guard] early in the morning; and until a late hour the men were busy cooking rations and cleaning equipment.

    Before the mists had been chased by the rising sun, the company in close column of fours marched down the road. Man and animals were in perfect condition, brimful of mettle [excited] and in buoyant spirits.

    The route lay along the banks of the river; upon the winding course of which, after several hours riding, the regiment reached its destination and relieved the various [guards]. A sergeant and squad of men were left at each post . . . to watch the enemy on the other side of the Rappahannock [River].

    The next day our squad, Sergeant Joe Reid in command, sauntered down to the bank, but seeing no one we lay at length under the spreading trees. . . .

    The Rappahannock, which was at this place about two hundred yards wide, flowing oceanward [to the southeast], its bosom [surface] reflecting the roseate-hued [pink] morn, was as lovely a body of water as the sun ever shone upon. The sound of the gentle ripple of its waves upon the sand was broken by a faint 'halloo' which came from the other side.

'Johnny Reb; I say, J-o-h-n-n-y R-e-b, don't shoot!'

Joe Reid shouted back, 'All right!'

'What command are you?'

The spoken words floated clear and distant across the water, 'The Black Horse cavalry. Who are you?'

'The Second Michigan Cavalry.'

'Come to the bank,' said our spokesman, 'and show yourself; we won't fire.'

'On your honor, Johnny Reb?'

'On our honor, Billy Yank.'

In a second a large squad of blue-coats across the way advanced to the water's brink. The Southerners did the same; then the former put the query [question].

'Have you any tobacco?'

'Plenty of it,' went our reply.

'Any sugar or coffee?' they questioned.

'Not a taste nor a smell.'

'Let's trade,' was shouted with eagerness.

'Very well,' was the reply. '. . . meet us here this evening.'

'All right,' they answered; then added, 'Say, Johnny, want some newspapers?'

'Y-e-s!'

'Then look out, we are going to send you some.'

'How are you going to do it?'

'Wait and see.' . . .

Eagerly he watched. . . . Presently he shouted:

'Here they come!' and then in a tone of intense admiration, 'I'll be doggoned if these Yanks are not the smartest people in the world.'

On the other side were several miniature boats and ships—such as school-boys delight in—with sails set; the gentle breeze impelled [pushed] the little crafts across the river, each freighted with a couple of newspapers. . . .

Drawing lots, Joe Boteler, who found luck against him, started to town, with a muttered curse, to buy tobacco, . . .

Joe returned in the evening with a box of plug tobacco about a foot square; but how to get it across was the question. The miniature boats could not carry it, and we shouted across to the Yanks that we had about twenty pounds of cut plug, and asked them what we must do? They hallooed back to let one of us swim across, and declared it was perfectly safe. . . . I volunteered. Having lived on the banks

A typical young recruit posed for this picture at the beginning of the war.

of the Potomac all my life, I was necessarily a swimmer. . . .

As I approached the shore the news of my coming reached camp, and nearly all the Second Michigan were lined up along the bank.

I felt a little queer [strange], but had perfect faith in their promise [not to shoot] and kept on without missing a stroke. . . . The blue-coats crowded around me and gave me a hearty welcome, . . . and heaped offerings of sugar, coffee, lemons, and even candy . . .

Bidding my friends the enemy good-by, I swam back with the precious cargo, and we had a feast that night.[1] 〞

This aspect of the Civil War is sometimes the hardest to remember: countrymen fought countrymen, brother fought brother. Friends faced each other in battle. And ''brother against brother'' was not just a writer's image. At the Union attack on Hilton Head, South Carolina, Percival Drayton commanded the U.S.S. *Pocahontas*, one of the Union vessels attacking Confederate troops under Brigadier General Thomas F. Drayton, his brother. Both were South Carolinians. Such confrontations were not uncommon, and they made the conflict sadder and more costly to the American people.

The First Modern War

What made the Civil War modern was the change in warfare itself. In earlier times wars had been fought by professional armies—not masses of quickly trained citizen-soldiers. Mercenaries fighting for pay often far outnumbered the patriots in such an army. But that had begun to change during the Revolutionary War. Ordinary Americans swept up by a cause battled the professional British army. The Americans were unwilling to abandon their cause even in the face of heavy losses. This was even more true of both sides in the Civil War.

Battlefield tactics had also changed. In traditional battles armies of nearly equal strength sent long lines of soldiers marching slowly toward each other. But new tactics were developed during the American Revolution and the Napoleonic wars. Virtually all Civil War generals on both sides had been trained in these new strategies at West Point. The basic tactic of modern war was to look for the enemy's weakest point and break through it with superior force. Commanders also now considered geographic, economic, and political aspects of the battle, trying to control the high ground or capture economically or politically important places. Winning generals were often those who were best prepared. They made the best use of the

[1]From *The Blue and the Gray: The Story of the Civil War as Told by Participants*, vol. 1, edited by Henry Steele Commager

SOLDIERING IN THE CIVIL WAR

The typical soldier in the newly formed armies of the North and South had no previous military experience. Most knew how to handle guns, but the rest of soldiering was a mystery to nearly all. To teach recruits how to march, their drill sergeants sometimes tied a piece of hay to each man's left foot and a piece of straw to the right. Then, lining the men up on the drill field, the sergeant would chant, "Hay-foot, straw-foot, hay-foot, straw-foot," until the troops caught on.

Most ordinary soldiers joined the armies with no idea of what actual warfare was like. Some were looking for personal glory. Others joined in hopes of visiting distant places and getting to know Americans from other parts of the country. For North and South, however, love of country was the main motive. The names of volunteer companies reflected this patriotism

Courtesy of the Cooper-Hewitt Museum, Smithsonian Institution/Art Resource NY

and sought to inspire fear in the enemy ranks. Confederate regiments had names like the Southern Avengers, Rejectors of Old Abe, and Barton Yankee Killers. Northern regiments took names like Detroit Invincibles and Union Clinchers.

Most regiments were made up of men from one town or county. Since the soldiers elected their own officers, popularity rather than ability often determined who would be leaders. One Confederate regiment picked a colonel who gave the men two jugs of whiskey.

This system did not make for strict discipline. In one Union regiment drilling on a hot parade ground, a private was heard saying to the company commander, "Tom, let's quit this foolin' around . . . and get a drink."

Winslow Homer caught the youth and innocence of this Union soldier in a watercolor sketch.

geography of the battlefield and concentrated their troops skillfully. For this reason, armies put great effort into collecting information. Planning and reconnaissance—exploring enemy territory—became essential.

The armies were organized and deployed much as an army is today. They were divided into three separate units: cavalry, artillery, and infantry. Each had its particular purpose. The rapidly-moving cavalry gathered information, often riding far behind enemy lines to observe troop movements and the availability and location of supplies and reinforcements. They also studied the lay of the land so that the generals could take the geography of the area into account in designing their strategy and tactics. During a battle, cavalry units might be rushed forward to reinforce weak points, but their basic task was to help in overall planning.

Artillery units manned the big guns. It was hot, noisy, dangerous work. But Civil War leaders knew these guns were crucial in major battles. The artillery pounded away at enemy fortifications, making them vulnerable to attack. Artillery fire also sheltered retreating troops from pursuers. Large numbers of accurate guns could be swiftly moved into position to smother the enemy infantry with heavy fire. The importance of artillery signaled the dawn of modern war.

Cavalry and artillery units were essential parts of a Civil War army. But as always the infantry, or "foot soldiers" as they were called, did most of the fighting. Infantry units consisted of regiments of 1,000 soldiers each. Four regiments composed a brigade.

Even the infantry approached the battle differently from previous wars. Cannon and accurate rifle fire were deadly for troops in the open. So opponents dug trenches and fired at each other from the protection of earthworks. To overwhelm the enemy, the front lines charged toward the trenches into enemy fire, ear-shattering noise, and clouds of dense smoke. At close quarters it was nearly impossible to aim and fire, so soldiers used their bayonets or battered each other with their rifle butts. Often the final stage of the assault was brutal hand-to-hand combat.

War had fundamentally changed. Strategy built on information about enemy positions and the geography of the site determined the outcome of most battles. The tools of war—artillery, shells, and rifles—were more accurate and therefore more deadly. Modern war had become total war. Armies sought to destroy the entire productive capacity of the enemy and the will to fight, not just of its troops but of its civilians too. As the noted Civil War historian Bruce Catton wrote:

> **"** In the Civil War it was all or nothing. . . . Once a little blood had been shed, there was no halfway point at which the two sides could get together and compromise. So the stakes were greatly increased. This too affected the way in which people fought. If you are fighting a total war, the enemy's army is not your own target. What you are really shooting for is the ability to carry on the fight. This means you will hit wherever you can with any weapon that comes into your hand.
>
> Probably it is this more than any other thing that distinguishes modern war: anything goes.[1] **"**

From Bull Run to Richmond

It took time to raise and train an army. The northern people were impatient. "On to Richmond" was the popular cry in Washington. In July 1861, long before the troops were ready, General McDowell ordered them forward. Laughing and joking along the way, the northern soldiers were joined by a parade of carriages filled with congressmen, newspaper reporters, and the curious. The crowd carried picnic lunches and made plans to eat a late supper in Richmond.

[1]From "The First Modern War" by Bruce Catton in *America Goes to War*

On July 21 at **Bull Run** this poorly trained force of 30,000 met the Confederate army, which was not much better prepared. The Confederates, 22,000 strong, had dug into the high ground above Bull Run. McDowell circled west, correctly guessing that the Confederate line was weakest on the left. He was right, and at first the Confederates fell back.

The Yankees almost cracked the southern line. Behind the Rebels lay an open road to Richmond, less than 90 miles (144 kilometers) away. But troops under Thomas J. Jackson stopped the Union advance cold. At the peak of the battle an officer rallied his men with the cry, "There stands Jackson like a stone wall," winning for Jackson the nickname "Stonewall." Then the southerners counterattacked. The Union army was thrown into confusion and panic. Hundreds of soldiers threw down their guns and fled northward toward Washington. If the Confederate soldiers had not been so green, they might have captured the capital before the northern army could regroup. As southern general Joseph E. Johnston commented, "The Confederate Army was more disorganized by victory than that of the United States by defeat."

After this disgraceful defeat President Lincoln put General George B. McClellan in command of the army. McClellan was an excellent organizer. He was also popular with rank-and-file soldiers. He soon whipped the **Army of the Potomac** into excellent shape.

Stonewall Jackson surveys both his men and the lay of the land at the First Battle of Bull Run. How did he win his nickname in this battle?

Raising the Armies   557

STRATEGIES FOR SUCCESS

READING A STATISTICAL CHART

As you learned in the strategy on page 457, statistics are often organized into chart form. An example is below. A chart is especially valuable for use in organizing several sets of numbers. Exact or round numbers may be used in any number of columns to show growth or change. The data shown on a chart is often related, helping you compare the numbers, recognize relationships, and see trends.

How to Read a Statistical Chart

To effectively read a statistical chart, follow these steps.

1. **Identify the type of data.** Read the chart's title. Note headings, subheadings, and labels.
2. **Examine the chart's components.** Study the specific statistics given under each heading. Read across rows and down columns.
3. **Relate numbers and values.** Note quantities. Often a chart will contain a note in parentheses that indicates if the data is to be read in thousands, millions, billions, tons, dollars, or other units. (Be sure to read any footnotes or other special notes at the bottom of the chart as well.)
4. **Use the information.** Ask "what do these statistics tell me?" Draw conclusions and form hypotheses. Compare and contrast the data to note trends and changes.

Applying the Strategy

Study the chart below. Note that it contains information about the Union and the Confederacy on the eve of war. Look at the left column. It lists nine categories of statistics on which you can compare the North and South. Reading across the row for each of these categories gives you both the total number and the percentage of the total for both sides. What was the population of the North? Of the South? As you can see from the chart, the North had more people, nearly three quarters of the total population of the United States.

The North also had more than 10 times the value of manufactured goods and produced more than 10 times the steel as the South. What do these two statistics mean in wartime? The North also had nearly three times the railroad mileage and bank assets as the South, and twice as many farms. Again, what might each of these figures mean on the eve of war? The South did have a small but significant advantage in the value of exports. How might this affect southern war strategy? Review all the statistics, and ask yourself what they meant to each side as the war erupted.

For independent practice, see Practicing the Strategy on page 588.

COMPARING THE NORTH AND THE SOUTH, 1860	North		South	
	Total	%	Total	%
Land Area (square miles)	2,250,000	75.0	750,000	25.0
Population	21,800,000	71.3	8,800,000*	28.7
Farms	1,360,000	67.3	681,000	32.7
Factories	119,500	85.2	20,850	14.8
Value of Manufacturing	$1,730,000,000	91.5	$156,000,000	8.5
Iron Produced (long tons)	2,720,000	94.6	155,000	5.4
Railroad Mileage	21,500	71.0	8,500	28.7
Bank Assets	$345,900,000	72.0	$76,000,000	18.0
Value of Exports	$175,000,000	43.6	$226,000,000	56.4

*Southern population included 3.8 million slaves

Yet McClellan had a number of serious weaknesses as a leader. He was very vain and had too high an opinion of his own abilities. He thought President Lincoln stupid and incompetent. He even had vague visions of taking over control of the government in order to save the Union single-handedly.

These flaws alone would have been bad enough. But McClellan was also overly cautious when it came to fighting. Despite his dashing appearance and bold talk, he never seemed ready to march against the enemy. When he was first appointed, caution was the right policy. The army had to be trained and disciplined. Yet even when this task had been accomplished, McClellan still delayed. Finally, in March 1862, he prepared to attack.

McClellan's plan for capturing Richmond was complicated but sensible. Instead of marching directly south, he moved his army by boat down the Potomac River and through Chesapeake Bay to the mouths of the York and James Rivers, southeast of the Confederate capital. He then advanced up these streams. By the middle of May he had over 110,000 men, a huge force, within 25 miles (40 kilometers) of Richmond.

Instead of striking swiftly at the Confederate capital, McClellan delayed. On May 31 he was moving his army across the Chickahominy River, a branch of the James. While his troops were divided by the river, the Confederate commander, General Joseph E. Johnston, launched a fierce attack. The loss of life in the **Battle of Seven Pines** was heavy on both sides. Yet neither side gained an advantage.

General Johnston was wounded in this battle and had to give up his command. The new leader of the **Army of Northern Virginia** was Robert E. Lee.

The North quickly learned how much it had lost when Lee decided to fight for the Confederates. Although outnumbered, Lee realized how cautious McClellan was. He had reduced his force by ordering General Stonewall Jackson and his men in the Shenandoah Valley north and west of Richmond to attack small Union forces stationed there.

Jackson specialized in the swift movement of troops. Soon his force was closer to Washington than to Richmond. This caused alarm in Washington. President Lincoln ordered large numbers of Union troops to the Shenandoah region. These units were in the wrong place to help McClellan. This was exactly what Lee had hoped for. While the Union soldiers were marching westward, Jackson was hurrying back toward Richmond!

The moment Jackson's brigades had rejoined his own, Lee ordered an all-out attack. What followed is known as the **Seven Days Before Richmond.** The Union army fell back to Harrison's Landing, a base on the James River. Over 15,000 Union soldiers were killed or wounded. The Confederates lost nearly 20,000 men. Neither side could be said to have won the battle. 🔛

As a general, George B. McClellan thought he could save the Union single-handedly. He was sharply critical of President Lincoln. Why is a general who doesn't support his commander-in-chief unlikely to succeed? Give several reasons.

Return to the Preview & Review on page 549.

National Archives

The popular McCormick Reaper helped farmers feed the armies of the North.

3. WAR AND THE ECONOMY

Behind the Northern Lines

By the summer of 1862 northern leaders realized that the Civil War would not be won quickly. It was sure to cost many more thousands of lives and great sums of money. It would affect everyone in the nation—women and men, civilians and soldiers.

The early months of the war brought a business depression and much confusion to many parts of the North and West. The loss of southern trade injured many businesses. Hundreds of millions of dollars owed by southern borrowers could not be collected. Many banks in the North collapsed. About 6,000 companies went bankrupt.

The demands of the army and navy for uniforms, guns, and other supplies soon caused business to pick up again. Union soldiers wore out about 1.5 million uniforms and about 3 million pairs of shoes a year. The clothing and shoe industries boomed. Between 1860 and 1865 the consumption of wool more than tripled.

The Union forces also needed enormous amounts of everything from coal and nails to soap and writing paper. The demand for horses, ambulances, and wagons rose steadily. An army ambulance cost the considerable sum of $170. By October 1862 the army had purchased 3,500 of them.

An army marches on its stomach. But food had to be raised by fewer people because so many young farmers were in uniform. Fortunately, the **mechanical reaper** came into general use at just this time. One reaper could harvest as much wheat as five field hands using scythes and cradles. Cyrus Hall McCormick, the inventor of the reaper, sold about 165,000 of these machines during the war.

The wartime boom caused **inflation.** Prices rose rapidly. The wages of the men and women of the North who produced war supplies and other goods did not keep pace with the rising cost of living. However, work was plentiful. Nearly all people were able to take care of themselves.

Northern Opponents of the War

Many people in the North and West were not willing to fight a war to prevent the southern states from seceding. Some believed that the United States would be better off without the South. Others had no objection to slavery. Still others felt that the southern states had a right to secede.

People who opposed the war came to be popularly known as **Copperheads.** Most of the Copperheads supported the Democratic party. They were sympathetic to the South and argued that it was not worth the cost to force the Confederacy to surrender.

Radical Copperheads organized secret societies with such names as Knights of the Golden Circle and Sons of Liberty. They tried to persuade Union soldiers to desert, and they helped Confederate prisoners to escape. Some Copperheads even smuggled guns and ammunition into the South.

The most important Copperhead leader was Clement L. Vallandigham, a congressman from Ohio. Vallandigham charged that

The Granger Collection

THE COPPERHEAD PARTY.——IN FAVOR OF A VIGOROUS PROSECUTION OF PEACE!

Liberty with her Union shield draws back from the Copperheads in this 1863 cartoon. Copperheads are snakes that strike without warning. These all resemble Clement Vallandigham, the Copperhead leader. What message do you think the cartoonist meant to send?

War and the Economy   561

Lincoln intended to abolish slavery if the United States won the war. He demanded that the government try to negotiate a reunion with the South. In 1863 he was thrown in prison by the military authorities. President Lincoln, however, ordered him released and deported to the Confederacy. Vallandigham went from the South to Canada, and in 1864 he came back to Ohio. Although he resumed his criticisms of the government, Lincoln decided it would be better not to silence him.

Lincoln did not let all critics off so easily. In 1861 he suspended the right of people to *habeas corpus* (from the Latin for "you shall have the body"). This is the legal process for ensuring that an accused person is not imprisoned unlawfully. It is a right guaranteed by the Constitution. But during the war over 13,000 Americans were held in jail without formal charges made against them.

Lincoln insisted that his first duty was to protect the Union. He exercised more power than any earlier president. But Lincoln did not try to be a dictator. The government did not censor newspapers or prevent citizens from voting as they wished in elections. When Union soldiers were sentenced to death for running away during a battle, Lincoln tended to pardon them. He called them "leg cases" rather than cowards, adding, "It would frighten the poor fellows too terribly to kill them." In a more serious mood, while pardoning one deserter, he said, "This boy can do us more good above ground than below ground."

Shortages in the South

Unlike the North the Confederate economy was injured by the war. Paying for the war was the South's most difficult task. It could not raise enough by borrowing or taxing to meet all its bills. As a result the government had to print money that it could not back with gold or silver. It issued over $1 billion in bank notes of questionable value during the war.

The South promised to pay off these notes in gold or silver after the war ended. When the South began to lose the war, people doubted that it would be able to pay its debts. Confederate paper money then fell rapidly in value. By early 1865 50 Confederate paper dollars were worth less than one gold dollar. Prices of goods in the South skyrocketed. In 1864 eggs cost six Confederate dollars a dozen. In the North eggs cost about 25 cents a dozen.

Almost every kind of manufactured product was scarce in the South because the region had been almost entirely agricultural. Shortages of clothing sent people rummaging in their attics in search of spinning wheels and hand looms that their grandparents had used. Soldiers marched in ragged uniforms. Sometimes they had no shoes. For civilians thorns took the place of pins. The blank side of wallpaper served as a substitute for writing paper.

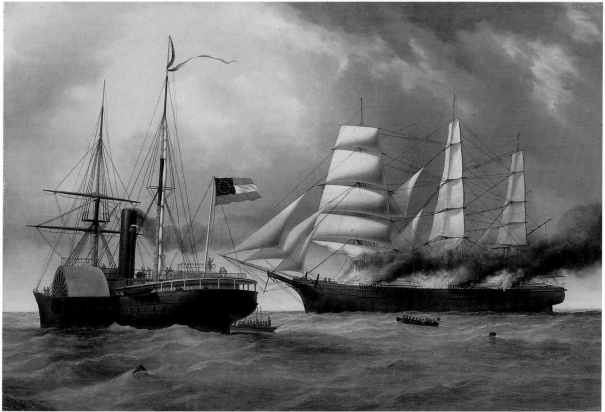

Peabody Museum of Salem

The Blockade

Union leaders eventually developed a war strategy that included several military objectives. First was a blockade of southern ports. The navy remained loyal to the Union. After the fall of Fort Sumter President Lincoln ordered the navy to blockade all southern harbors. This blockade gradually choked off the South's foreign trade. About 6,000 ships had entered and left southern ports in 1860. The next year only 800 managed to slip past northern warships. Thereafter almost none escaped.

Many southern captains tried to break through the blockade. Their ships, like the privateers of earlier wars, were small and fast. These **blockade runners** operated out of Charleston or Savannah or out of Mobile, Alabama, on the Gulf of Mexico.

The British island of Bermuda, only 400 miles (640 kilometers) off the North Carolina coast, was the blockade runners' favorite destination. There they exchanged cotton or other farm products for guns, medicines, blankets, and coffee, as well as for fancy silks and other luxuries. The blockade runners brought in whatever they thought would sell for the best price. Since they were private citizens, the government could not control their activities or order them to import only war supplies.

Winning a victory for the South, the C.S.S. Nashville *is shown burning the ship* Harvey Birch *in this painting by D. McFarlane. Research other naval engagements of the war, including the one between the* Monitor *and the* Merrimack.

Cotton Diplomacy

At the start of the war southern leaders thought that the economies of England and France would collapse without southern cotton. Those nations imported immense amounts of cotton for their textile factories. If their mills were forced to shut down, thousands of workers would lose their jobs. The southerners believed that England and France would enter the war on the side of the Confederacy to prevent this from happening.

Southerners who believed that **cotton diplomacy** would work tried to increase the pressure on England and France by preventing the export of cotton. "We have only to shut off your supply of cotton for a few weeks," one boasted to an English journalist, "and we can create a revolution in Great Britain."

These southerners were wrong. When the war broke out, English warehouses were bulging with cotton. By the time the supply had been used up, the British had discovered that they needed northern wheat more than southern cotton. Most British and French government leaders wanted the Confederacy to win the war. But they were unwilling to enter the war themselves.

Cotton was of little use to the South itself during the war. Planters shifted to growing corn and wheat and to raising pigs and cattle.

The Draft in the South

Another difficulty faced by the Confederacy was raising a large enough army to defend its borders. Thousands of men enlisted. But because the population was small, it became necessary in 1862 to **conscript,** or draft, men to serve as soldiers by law.

This draft was unpopular. It favored the rich, because a man who was conscripted could hire a substitute. Moreover, owners of 20 or more slaves were exempted. The men who had the most to lose if the South were defeated were excused from defending it! Little wonder many southerners complained that the draft law made the conflict "a rich man's war and a poor man's fight."

Religion in Wartime

Often as war intensifies so does religious devotion and enthusiasm. Faced with constant danger and seeing the lives of so many comrades snuffed out, soldiers on both sides sought consolation at religious services. General "Stonewall" Jackson, always a profoundly religious person, encouraged revivals in his Army of Northern Virginia. The United States Christian Commission recruited thousands of northern pastors to serve for short periods as volunteer chaplains. Their reports on the revivals they held in army camps further awakened religious interest in their congregations when they returned home. Church women on both sides collected and sent bandages and bedding to the troops.

Meanwhile, white Protestants representing several northern denominations organized the American Missionary Association. The Association founded congregations of blacks in the "contraband" camps near Hampton, Virginia, and on the Union-controlled Sea Islands along the coast of South Carolina and Georgia.

Slaves in the War

By 1865 the southern government decided to use slaves as soldiers. Slaves had been used by the Confederate army throughout the war as laborers, bakers, blacksmiths, shoemakers, and nurses. Slaves also worked in factories. Half of the 2,400 employees of the Tredegar Iron Works in Richmond, the largest factory in the South, were slaves.

Many persons thought that the slaves would riot or run off by the thousands during the war. Few did. But whenever northern armies invaded a district, some slaves slipped away and crossed the Union lines. Often northern officers put them to work building fortifications. These people became known as **contrabands.**

Slaves also tried to help the Union army whenever possible. The following account tells of two daring and ingenious slaves who spied on the Confederate army:

“ There came into the Union lines a Negro from a farm on the other side of the river, known by the name of Dabney, who was found to possess a remarkably clear knowledge of the topography [lay of the land] of the whole region. . . .

Dabney's wife went across the Rappahannock, and in a few days was installed as laundress at the headquarters of a prominent rebel General. Dabney, her husband, on the north bank, was soon found to be wonderfully well informed as to all the rebel plans. Within an hour of the time that a movement of any kind was projected, or even discussed, among the rebel generals, Hooker [the Union commander] knew all about it. . . .

How he obtained his information remained for some time a puzzlement to the Union officers. At length upon much solicitation [asking], he unfolded his marvellous secret to one of our officers.

Taking him [a Union officer] to a point where a clear view could be obtained at Fredericksburg, he [Dabney] pointed to a little cabin in the suburbs near the river bank, and asked him [the officer] if he saw that clothes-line with clothes hanging to dry. 'Well,' he said, 'that clothes-line tells me in half an hour just what goes on at Lee's headquarters. You see my wife over there . . . moves the clothes on that line so I can understand it in a minute. That there gray shirt is Longstreet [a southern general]; and when she takes it off, it means he's gone down to Richmond. That white shirt means Hill [another southern general]; and when she moves it up to the west end of the line, Hill's corps has moved up stream. That red one is Stonewall. He's down on the right now, and if he moves, she will move the red shirt.' . . .[1]"

From the beginning of the war contrabands tried to join the Union army. But not until Congress passed the militia act in 1862 were "persons of African descent" welcomed in any of the armed forces. That law allowed African Americans in "any military or naval service for which they may be found competent," but most northern leaders placed them in support positions rather than front-line troops. But the law did create a large pool of reinforcements.

The War and Free African Americans

The outbreak of the war filled free African Americans with hope—and with fear. Most of them could not imagine northerners fighting southerners let alone whites fighting whites over slavery. But now it had happened! The war meant an end to the hated Fugitive Slave Law, and if the North won maybe an end to slavery itself. Men and boys rushed to join the Union army. Many later distinguished themselves in battle. Sixteen African Americans won the Medal of Honor for their bravery.

But what if the North lost? Thoughts of a Confederate victory brought fear to free African Americans' hearts, along with many questions. Would they be forced into slavery, even those whose families had never been slaves? They held special prayer meetings in their churches for a Union victory.

And what was the status of free "people of color" *during* the war? There was frightening word that Union soldiers had returned slaves seeking refuge in the Union lines to their owners. President Lincoln's hesitation to make the abolition of slavery an aim of the war added to the confusion.

Immediately after the passage of the militia act free African Americans began organizing military units. Regiments in Union-held Louisiana and South Carolina, and in Kansas were soon at full strength. Colonel Thomas Wentworth Higginson of Massachusetts led the South Carolina regiment. His praise of the African American troops had considerable effect on public opinion. Massachusetts raised two more black regiments, the 54th and 55th. The 54th Massachusetts became the most famous black regiment of the war.

[1]From *The Blue Coats* edited by John Truesdale

Women and the War

Women were not soldiers in the Civil War, but many on both sides took over the management of businesses and farms, while continuing to hold together families. Especially in the South women had great responsibilities. They ran plantations, oversaw slaves, arranged for loans, and collected food and supplies for their families and for the army. They had to do all this in the midst of severe wartime shortages. Many found the experience the most vital incident of their lives. Women in the North were just as captivated by the great turmoil swirling around them.

Some women found jobs in new occupations. More than 400 women—the first to serve in the federal government—were hired as clerks. Women staffed Confederate government offices as well. By the end of the war women had done so well in clerical positions that they were not replaced by men returning from the war. Women on both sides also worked in factories and arsenals. Most of these women were underpaid. Seamstresses received as little as four cents for making a shirt.

Hundreds of women also became nurses. Despite the depressing conditions of wartime work, nursing offered tremendous new opportunities for women. Clara Barton, who was one of the first women attracted to nursing, believed the war had created employment opportunities for women that normally would have taken 50 years. More importantly, women held on to many of the gains after the war.

Urging their oxen onward, fugitive slaves ford the Rappahannock River in this 1862 photograph taken by Timothy O'Sullivan. They are following the retreat of General Pope's army as it makes its way back to Washington after the Second Battle of Bull Run. What probably lies ahead for these so-called contrabands?

Return to the Preview & Review on page 560.

War and the Economy   567

Use these questions to guide your reading. Answer the questions after completing Section 4.
Understanding Issues, Events, & Ideas. Using the following words, explain the important moments of the war in the East: Second Battle of Bull Run; Battle of Antietam; emancipate; Emancipation Proclamation; Battles of Fredericksburg, Chancellorsville, and Gettysburg; Gettysburg Address.
1. What did General Lee believe he must do to end the war?
2. What were the conditions of the Emancipation Proclamation? What was necessary to actually free slaves?
3. What led to the draft riots in 1863?
Thinking Critically. 1. You are a Confederate soldier who survived the Battle of Antietam. Explain the importance of this battle in a letter to your family. 2. Of Fredericksburg, Chancellorsville, or Gettysburg, which battle do you think was the most important to the North? To the South? Give reasons for your answer.

4. THE WAR IN THE EAST

The Second Battle of Bull Run

Northern attention remained focused on a second objective of the war: the capture of Richmond. In the summer of 1862, under orders from Lincoln, McClellan began to withdraw the Union army from its positions near Richmond. The plan was to combine his veterans with a new army being organized south of Washington by General John Pope. As soon as the northerners pulled back, Lee moved northward. He was determined to destroy General Pope's army before McClellan could join with it. He knew that it was not enough simply to defend Richmond. To end the war, he had to deliver such a stinging defeat that the people of the North would lose the will to fight.

In a daring maneuver Lee sent 25,000 men commanded by Stonewall Jackson to hit Pope's army from the rear. Once again Jackson marched swiftly, then struck silently. He cut off the railroad running from Washington to the Union front and set fire to most of Pope's supplies.

In desperation, on August 29 Pope attacked Lee. This **Second Battle of Bull Run** was fought on almost the same ground as the first. The Army of Northern Virginia halted the Union assault and then drove Pope's troops back toward Washington. Dismayed by Pope's failure, Lincoln dismissed him and again gave McClellan command of the Army of the Potomac. Ben Wade, a congressman from Ohio, objected strongly to McClellan's appointment. Lincoln asked him whom he should appoint instead. "Anybody," Wade answered impatiently. "Wade," said Lincoln calmly, "anybody will do for you, but I must have somebody."

Antietam

Lee now marched around the defenses of Washington. On September 4 he crossed the Potomac River to Maryland. McClellan was unsure of Lee's exact position. So he too crossed the river. On September 13 one of McClellan's soldiers found of copy of Lee's battle plans wrapped around some cigars in an abandoned Confederate camp. With this information McClellan was able to track down Lee's army. The armies met in battle on September 17 at Sharpsburg, a town on a branch of the Potomac called Antietam Creek. Lee had fewer than 50,000 men, McClellan about twice that number.

It was a foggy, gray morning when this **Battle of Antietam** began. When the bloody struggle ended at twilight, the Confederates had lost 13,000 men, the Union forces 12,000. One historian wrote:

   ❝ At last the sun went down and the battle ended, smoke heavy in the air, the twilight quivering with the anguished cries of thousands of wounded men. ❞

This is ever the price of war. Here lie Confederate soldiers who have fallen in front of Dunker Church at Antietam in September 1862. Explain from your reading how someone's carelessness led to this loss of life.

For yet another time in this bloody war neither side had won much of an advantage. All next day the exhausted armies faced each other silently. Then, that night, the Confederates retreated back across the Potomac. The North had finally won a battle.

The Emancipation Proclamation

The cost of the war in blood and money was changing the way ordinary people in the North felt about slavery. Anger at southerners more than sympathy for the slaves caused this change. The first result of it came in April 1862 when Congress abolished slavery in the District of Columbia.

Gradually Lincoln came to the conclusion that the United States should try to free all the slaves. He would have preferred to have the states buy the slaves from their owners and then **emancipate** or free them. This idea was known as compensated emancipation.

But Lincoln was a clever politician. He knew that many citizens would oppose paying anything to rebels and slave owners. Others still objected to freeing the slaves for the sake of doing away with an evil institution. Lincoln therefore decided to act under his war powers. He would free slaves not because slavery was wrong but as a means of weakening the rebel government.

Lincoln hesitated until after the Union victory at the Battle of Antietam. Then he issued the **Emancipation Proclamation.**

The Emancipation Proclamation was reprinted in this elaborate poster, the corner of which has been damaged. Tell briefly why true emancipation could not come from a beautiful scroll or even a presidential order while the war was waged. An excerpt appears on page 589.

The War in the East   569

This proclamation stated that after January 1, 1863, "all persons held as slaves within any States . . . in rebellion against the United States shall be . . . forever free."

Notice that the Proclamation did not liberate a single slave that the government could control. It applied only to areas ruled by the Confederates. Slaves in Maryland, Kentucky, Missouri, and even in those parts of the Confederacy that had been captured by Union armies, remained in bondage.

Yet when the armies of the United States advanced into new territory after January 1, 1863, the slaves there were freed. At last the war was being fought for freedom, not only to save the Union. Lincoln also ordered that freed slaves should be encouraged to enlist in the army. In August 1863 Lincoln wrote to Grant that enlisting them "works doubly, weakening the enemy and strengthening us." In December 1863, upon hearing of the bravery of these segregated units, Lincoln said, "It is difficult to say they are not as good soldiers as any." All told, about 180,000 African American soldiers fought for the United States during the Civil War. More than 38,000 lost their

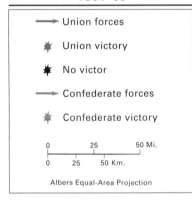

THE WAR IN THE EAST, 1861–63

→ Union forces

✸ Union victory

✷ No victor

→ Confederate forces

✸ Confederate victory

0   25   50 Mi.

0   25   50 Km.

Albers Equal-Area Projection

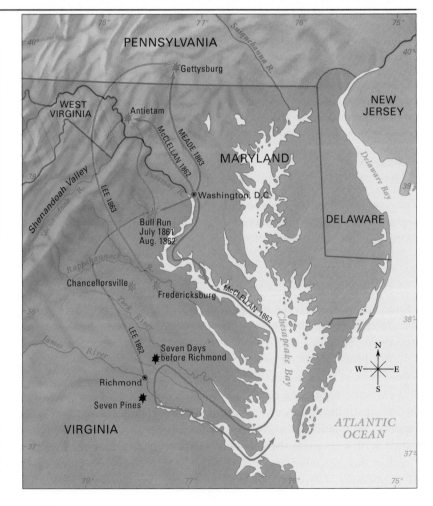

LEARNING FROM MAPS. *Most of the early battles were fought in the East. Why do you think so many battles took place in eastern and northern Virginia?*

The Granger Collection

Notice that the composer of this "Hymn of the Freedman" is identified only as "A Contraband." It was probably a tune used to recruit soldiers. At right is Major Martin R. Delany, who was promoted right on the battlefield for bravery. How many African Americans fought for the Union? How many Hispanic Americans?

lives in the struggle. Several thousand Hispanic Americans fought on both sides. Union admiral David Farragut was the best known.

The Draft Riots

The benefits of the Emancipation Proclamation were slow in coming. Its disadvantages appeared at once. Probably it made southerners more determined than ever to maintain their independence. Many poor northerners resented it because they feared that slaves liberated under the Proclamation would flock into the North to compete with them for jobs. As a result the Democratic party made large gains in the 1862 Congressional elections.

"Rally Round the Flag, Boys!" says this 1864 Michigan recruiting poster. And "Keep Out of the Draft!" which passed the month the poster went to press.

A few months after the Proclamation went into effect, Congress passed a conscription law. Like the Confederate draft, this measure allowed men who were drafted to hire substitutes. They could even avoid military service by paying the government $300.

Poor men could not possibly raise $300, which was as much as a laborer could earn in a year. Many made a connection between the draft law and emancipation. They resented having to risk their lives in order to free slaves who could then compete with them for work.

Draft riots broke out in many parts of the country in the spring and summer of 1863. The worst occurred in New York City, where Irish-born workers ran wild for four days in July. The rioters burned buildings, looted shops, and terrorized innocent local African Americans. Over a hundred African Americans in New York were murdered. These riots should have been a warning. The war might free the slaves, but it was not likely to produce racial harmony, either in the North or South.

Fredericksburg

Meanwhile the Emancipation Proclamation had little effect on the battlefields. When McClellan failed to attack the Confederates as they retreated after the Battle of Antietam, Lincoln again removed him from command of the Army of the Potomac, choosing General Ambrose E. Burnside to succeed him. Unlike McClellan, Burnside was a bold, even reckless officer. He decided to push directly toward

LEARNING FROM CHARTS. *Unlike other wars all the casualties of the Civil War were Americans. Of total Union forces, more than 40 percent were casualties, and nearly 23 percent died. About 33 percent of the Confederate forces were casualties, and almost 24 percent died. Why did such high casualty rates actually favor the North?*

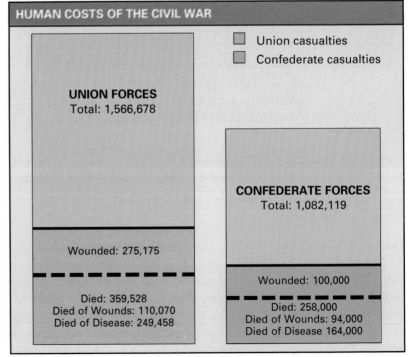

HUMAN COSTS OF THE CIVIL WAR

☐ Union casualties
☐ Confederate casualties

UNION FORCES
Total: 1,566,678

Wounded: 275,175

Died: 359,528
Died of Wounds: 110,070
Died of Disease: 249,458

CONFEDERATE FORCES
Total: 1,082,119

Wounded: 100,000

Died: 258,000
Died of Wounds: 94,000
Died of Disease 164,000

Richmond. In December 1862 he crossed the Rappahannock River over pontoon bridges and occupied the town of Fredericksburg, about 50 miles (80 kilometers) north of Richmond.

The Confederate army was entrenched on a ridge behind Fredericksburg called Marye's Heights. It was an extremely strong position. Looking across the field that lay before the Confederate lines, General E. P. Alexander, Lee's chief of artillery, remarked, "A chicken could not live in that field when we open on it."

Burnside nevertheless attacked. He had 120,000 men to Lee's 75,000. The **Battle of Fredericksburg** was fought on December 13. It began in heavy fog. About eleven o'clock in the morning the fog lifted. The Confederates could see the Union soldiers coming across the frozen plain. They commenced firing.

Burnside sent his blue-coated soldiers charging at Lee's position six separate times. Each time they were driven back by musket and cannon fire, leaving the field littered with their dead. At the end of the day they had suffered 12,000 casualties. Utterly defeated, Burnside crossed back across the Rappahannock. Shortly afterwards, at his own request, Burnside was relieved of command.

Chancellorsville

Lincoln next turned the Army of the Potomac over to General "Fighting Joe" Hooker. General Hooker concentrated his units at Chancellorsville, a village in the densely wooded area of Virginia known

Only the bayonet would do, firing was useless—these the instructions to raw recruits from Pennsylvania in this 1862 assault on Marye's Heights. Why did Confederate troops have such a geographically strong position in this Battle of Fredericksburg?

Binding Up the Wounds of War

Medical treatment in the Civil War was terribly crude by modern standards. Thousands of soldiers died of blood poisoning. Operations were performed without anesthetics. Still worse, about twice as many soldiers died of disease as of wounds.

Typhoid fever took countless lives. No one knew its cause or how to cure it. Army doctors treated pneumonia by bloodletting, a procedure which surely increased the chances that the sick soldier would die.

The best military hospital in the South was run by Sally L. Tompkins in Richmond. President Jefferson Davis made Tompkins a captain. She and Loreta Velásquez were the only women officers of the Confederate army. Like her many counterparts in both North and South, Tompkins saw thousands of amputations performed to halt deadly gangrene.

Bettmann Archive

Clara Barton is shown at the time she ministered to the wounds of war suffered by northern soldiers. Who was her counterpart in the South?

On the Union side heroic work was performed by the nurse Clara Barton. She cared for sick and wounded soldiers at Antietam and Fredericksburg. By wagon caravan she carried supplies from one Union hospital to another, calming the frightened horses when cannon shells exploded in their pathway. In 1864 she was appointed superintendent of nurses for the Union army. Later Barton founded the American Red Cross Society. She served as president of the Red Cross from 1882 to 1904.

as "the Wilderness." While he was preparing to advance, Lee attacked him. This **Battle of Chancellorsville** on May 1–5, 1863, showed Lee at his best. Although he had only 60,000 soldiers to Hooker's 125,000, he divided his army again. Stonewall Jackson's troops slipped quietly around the right side of the Union army. Then Jackson and Lee attacked at the same time. After days of bloody fighting, Hooker retreated. Lee had won another brilliant victory.

The victory was a costly one. General Jackson was wounded by stray bullets from his own lines. Three bullets hit him, one in the right hand and two in the left arm. Nowadays such wounds would not be fatal. But the bone in his arm was badly broken. The arm had to be amputated. Stonewall died from shock and loss of blood.

Historical Picture Service

Stonewall Jackson is shown shortly before his death at Chancellorsville. Study his face. Does Stonewall seem a good nickname for him?

Gettysburg

A month after the battle of Chancellorsville, Lee again invaded the North. He still hoped that a decisive victory on northern soil would cause the United States to give up the struggle.

As gray-clad Confederates marched through Maryland and into Pennsylvania, Union forces raced cross-country to intercept them. General George G. Meade was now in command, the fifth officer to hold this post in less than a year.

On July 1, 1863, one of Meade's units made contact with a Confederate detachment at the town of Gettysburg, in southern Pennsylvania. Lee's soldiers had wandered into the town looking for

shoes. Meade's men were looking for Lee. Lee's army was spread out across the rolling southern Pennsylvania farmland, traveling in three separate columns. Now he quickly concentrated his forces. Meade placed his Union troops outside the town on a ridge shaped like a fishhook. A hill called Cemetery Ridge was the center of their position. Lee's Confederate forces occupied another ridge half a mile away. The center of the Confederate line was on Seminary Ridge.

For two days the battle raged. As the sun set on the second day, Union troops still held a steep knoll called Little Round Top. From there they cut the Rebel ranks to ribbons. That night Lee made the fateful decision to charge the center of Meade's line.

That same night a few miles away, Meade planned for an attack on his center. He moved his strength there. The afternoon of July 3 proved him right. Between one and two o'clock, while Confederate artillery pounded Cemetery Ridge, General George E. Pickett led a charge at the Union position. Howling the eerie "rebel yell," 15,000 infantrymen started to trot across the open ground. For a brief moment some of these Confederates reached the Union trenches on Cemetery Ridge. But Union reserves counterattacked quickly. Pickett's surviving men were driven off. Pickett wrote this account of the battle to his wife:

> 66 Over on Cemetery Ridge the Federals saw a scene never before witnessed on this continent. . . . an army forming in line of battle in full view of the enemy, under their very eyes—charging across a space of nearly a mile [1.6 kilometers] in length over fields of grain and then a smooth expanse—moving with the steadiness of a dress parade, the pride and the glory soon to be crushed by an overwhelming heartbreak.
>
> Well, it is over now. The battle is lost, and many of us are prisoners, many are dead, many wounded, bleeding and dying. Your soldier lives and mourns. If it were not for you, my darling, he would rather, a million times rather, be back there with his dead, asleep for all time in an unknown grave.[1] 99

The battle was over. Lee retreated back into Virginia. Had Meade pursued the Confederates quickly, he might have destroyed them and ended the war. Instead he delayed, and the war dragged on for nearly two more years.

Some months after the **Battle of Gettysburg,** President Lincoln dedicated a cemetery there where thousands of Union soldiers were buried. He delivered a speech so short it left his listeners disappointed. Lincoln's **Gettysburg Address** attracted little attention at

Point of View

A senator from California wrote this impression of Lincoln's delivery of *The Gettysburg Address.*

> 66Mr. Lincoln arose, and laying aside his famous cloak, delivered his celebrated address. It was listened to, I need not say, with the greatest attention, as indeed was everything Mr. Lincoln said on any occasion, but no one at the time regarded it as anything very unusual. . . . There was an impression that his speech was cut short by his emotions. . . . It seemed to me the very least in length, or substance, that might be expected from the President of the United States on such an occasion. . . .99
>
> From *Memoirs of Cornelius Cole,* 1908

[1]From "Pickett's Account" in *Sources in American History*

State Museum of Pennsylvania, Pennsylvania Historical and Museum Commission

"Pickett's Charge at the Battle of Get-tysburg" by Peter F. Rotnermel shows the Union on the left, the Confeder-ates on the right. From your reading, describe the battle using this painting as a point of reference.

the time. It is now recognized as his noblest expression of the purpose of the Civil War and of the ideals of American democracy. Lincoln said:

❝ Four score and seven years ago our fathers brought forth on this continent a new nation, conceived in liberty, and dedicated to the proposition that all men are created equal.

Now we are engaged in a great civil war, testing whether that nation, or any nation so conceived and so dedicated, can long endure. We are met on a great battlefield of that war. We have come to dedicate a portion of that field as a final resting place for those who here gave their lives that that nation might live. It is altogether fitting and proper that we should do this.

But, in a larger sense, we cannot dedicate—we cannot consecrate—we cannot hallow—this ground. The brave men, living and dead, who struggled here, have consecrated it far above our poor power to add or detract. The world will little note nor long remember what we say here, but it can never forget what they did here. It is for us, the living, rather, to be dedicated here to the unfinished work which they who fought here have thus far so nobly advanced. It is rather for us to be here dedicated to the great task re-maining before us—that from these honored dead we take increased devotion to that cause for which they gave the last full measure of devotion; that we here highly resolve that these dead shall not have died in vain; that this nation, under God, shall have a new birth of freedom; and that government of the people, by the people, for the people, shall not perish from the earth. ❞ 🖳

Return to the Preview & Review on page 568.

5. THE WAR IN THE WEST

Cutting the South in Two

In the West the Union objective was to control the Mississippi River. Then it would be impossible for the Confederates to bring men and supplies to the eastern front from Arkansas, Louisiana, and Texas. The South would be cut in two.

The struggle for the river began in 1862. It was long and bitter. Out of it came the great general that Lincoln had been searching for since the beginning of the war. His name was Ulysses S. Grant.

Unlike Robert E. Lee, Grant had done poorly at West Point. He served well enough in the Mexican War. But he found army life boring in peacetime. He began to drink too much. In 1854 he resigned his commission in the army. He tried a number of businesses but succeeded in none. He seemed a totally undistinguished person.

When the Civil War broke out, Grant was working in a leather shop in Galena, Illinois. He joined an Illinois regiment. Since experienced officers were scarce, he was made a brigadier general.

Preview & Review

Use these questions to guide your reading. Answer the questions after completing Section 5.
Understanding Issues, Events, & Ideas. Using the following words, explain the important moments of the war in the West: Fort Henry, Fort Donelson, Battle of Shiloh, Siege of Vicksburg, Port Hudson, Chattanooga.
1. Why was General Grant called "Unconditional Surrender"?
2. What tactics did Grant use to lay siege to Vicksburg?
3. What was General Grant's strategy to end the war?
Thinking Critically. You fought with General Grant at the Battle of Shiloh. In your journal, record the details of the battle, and what happened to Grant afterward.

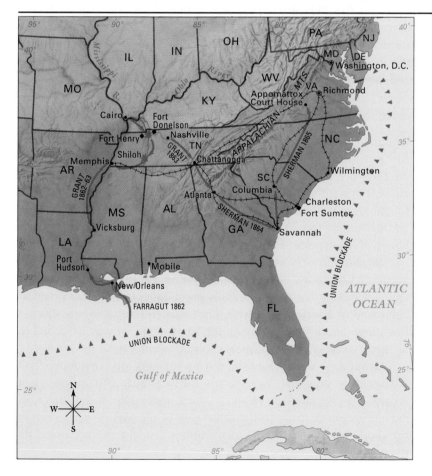

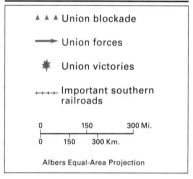

THE BLOCKADE AND THE WAR IN THE WEST, 1862–65

▲ ▲ ▲ Union blockade

→ Union forces

✳ Union victories

++++ Important southern railroads

0   150   300 Mi.
0   150   300 Km.

Albers Equal-Area Projection

LEARNING FROM MAPS. *The war in the West was actually fought in the Mississippi and Tennessee river valleys, where Union forces sought to control the rivers and rail lines. How would Union success there cripple the South?*

The War in the West   577

Grant was a shy, slight man. He did not look like a soldier, much less a general. He was constantly chewing a cigar. He rarely stood up straight. His uniforms were rumpled and ill fitting. Often Grant did not wear his officer's insignia. Yet he was brave and determined, and he turned out to be an excellent military strategist.

In February 1862 Grant successfully attacked **Fort Henry,** a Confederate stronghold on the Tennessee River. He then laid siege to **Fort Donelson,** on the Cumberland River. When the Confederate commander asked Grant what terms he would offer for surrender, Grant replied, "immediate and unconditional surrender." This remark won U. S. Grant the nickname "*U*nconditional *S*urrender" Grant.

Shiloh

Grant next marched his men up the Tennessee River. He intended to destroy railroad lines near Corinth, Mississippi. On April 6, 1862, about 30 miles (48 kilometers) from Corinth, his army was surprised by Confederates under General Albert Sidney Johnston. The resulting **Battle of Shiloh** caught Grant completely off guard. During the first day's fighting, his army was forced back to the river.

Fortunately, 25,000 fresh Union troops arrived during the night. The next day they drove the Confederates back. But Shiloh was an extremely costly victory. In two days about 13,000 Union soldiers were killed or wounded. Grant was so shaken by the surprise attack that he allowed the Confederates to escape. He was relieved of his command. His reputation seemed ruined.

The Siege of Vicksburg

Gradually other Union forces gained control of the Mississippi River. In April 1862 a fleet commanded by Captain David Farragut battered the forts defending New Orleans and Baton Rouge and captured the cities. Farragut's father, Jorge, was one of the many Spaniards who fought against the British in the Revolutionary War. And both David and his father fought for the United States in the War of 1812. In honor of his service, Farragut became the nation's first admiral.

By autumn only a 250-mile stretch (400 kilometers) of the river between Vicksburg, Mississippi, and Port Hudson, Louisiana, was still in Confederate hands. At this point Lincoln put Grant back in command of a powerful army. Grant decided to attack Vicksburg, a town high on cliffs overlooking the Mississippi. It was defended by an army commanded by General John C. Pemberton.

Grant approached Vicksburg from the north in November 1862. His artillery pounded Vicksburg's fortifications. But marshy land around the city made an infantry attack impossible. Grant therefore moved his entire army to the other side of the Mississippi. Then he marched past the Vicksburg fortifications at night and recrossed the river south of the city.

After driving off a Confederate army east of Vicksburg, Grant began the **Siege of Vicksburg,** pinning down Pemberton and his army. The siege began in mid-May. For weeks the Confederates held out. Eventually they ran short of food and ammunition. On July 4, 1863, Pemberton surrendered. Shortly afterwards, the remaining southern stronghold on the river, **Port Hudson,** was also captured. There had been considerable fighting in the states west of the Mississippi River all through the war. After Texas seceded from the Union, men flocked to join the Confederate army enthusiastically. Terry's Texas Rangers, a cavalry unit, and Hood's Texas Brigade fought in many important battles in the eastern theater of the war.

In Texas early in the war local troops recaptured Galveston and Brownsville, which had been seized by Union naval units. Texans also turned back a Union force at Sabine Pass. Then in 1862 they defeated Union troops at Valverde in New Mexico. This enabled the Confederacy to claim control of the New Mexico Territory. However, northern troops counterattacked and defeated the Texans at Glorieta Pass, thus regaining control of the southwestern territories.

After the fall of Vicksburg and Port Hudson, the Confederates continued to control much of Louisiana and Arkansas and nearly all of Texas. Fighting in Texas did not end until May 1865. But it was no longer possible for the Confederates to ship significant amounts of farm products or other supplies across the Mississippi in either direction. The Confederacy had been snipped in two.

David Farragut, to the right leaning from the side of his ship, led Union forces in the 1864 capture of the forts guarding Mobile Bay. The artist, William Heysham Overend, with tongue in cheek, titled this picture "An August Morning with Farragut: the Battle of Mobile Bay." How does the title make clear the artist's admiration for Farragut?

The War in the West   579

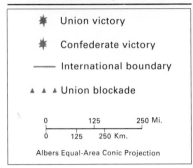

✹ Union victory

✹ Confederate victory

—— International boundary

▲ ▲ ▲ Union blockade

0   125   250 Mi.

0   125 250 Km.

Albers Equal-Area Conic Projection

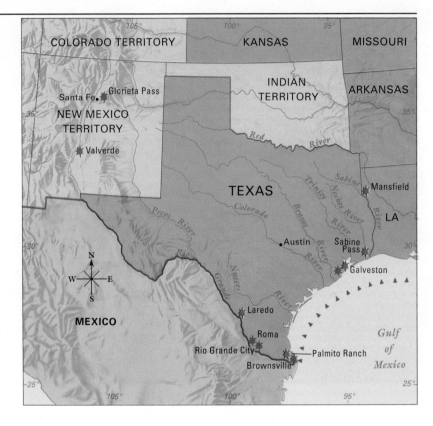

LEARNING FROM MAPS. *Texas forces fought battles in Texas as well as in the New Mexico Territory and several surrounding states. Why do you think Texas military leaders felt it was important to send troops to those distant areas?*

Lincoln Finds His General

Lincoln now put Grant in command of all Union troops west of the Appalachian Mountains. In November 1863 a series of battles was fought around **Chattanooga,** Tennessee, an important railway center and another Union military objective. There Grant defeated a Confederate army under General Braxton Bragg. Bragg retreated into northern Georgia. A few months later, in March 1864, Lincoln called Grant to Washington. He was promoted to lieutenant general and named general-in-chief of all the armies of the United States. Together they planned the war's end.

Grant decided to try to end the war by mounting two great offensives. He himself would lead the Army of the Potomac against Lee, seeking a showdown battle in northern Virginia. A western army commanded by General William Tecumseh Sherman would march from Chattanooga into northern Georgia. Its immediate objective was to capture Atlanta.

Grant had given command of the western army to General Sherman because he was a tough soldier. Sherman had served under Grant at the bloody battle of Shiloh and in the fighting around Chattanooga, and was someone Grant could count on. Sherman's father, an Ohio lawyer and judge, had named his son after the Shawnee leader Tecumseh, whom he admired greatly. 🖅

Return to the Preview & Review on page 577.

6. THE FINAL BATTLES

Grant Versus Lee

In May 1864 Grant crossed the Rappahannock and Rapidan Rivers and marched into the tangled forest of the Wilderness, where Lee had defeated Hooker one year earlier. This time Lee was reluctant to fight. He had only 60,000 men. Grant had more than 100,000.

Grant made Lee fight. For two days Union and Confederate forces hammered away at each other in the **Battle of the Wilderness.** The Army of the Potomac suffered 18,000 casualties, far more than its Confederate enemy.

Scarcely had this battle ended when Grant pressed stubbornly on. He was trying to march around Lee's smaller army and get between it and Richmond. At **Spotsylvania Court House** the two armies clashed again. This time 12,000 Union soldiers fell in a single day.

Again Grant advanced. In another bloody clash, at Cold Harbor, 7,000 Union soldiers died in less than an hour. In one month of fighting Grant had lost 55,000 men, Lee 31,000.

Despite the tremendous human cost, Grant was gaining his objective. Lee was running short of equipment. Union factories were turning out almost unlimited amounts of supplies. The larger population of the North was beginning to tip the scales toward the Union. Lee could not replace all his casualties. But bolstered by a steady stream of volunteers and draftees, the Army of the Potomac was larger after the **Battle of Cold Harbor** than at the start.

In June 1864 Grant crossed the James River in order to strike at **Petersburg,** a town a few miles south of Richmond. Petersburg was an important railroad junction. If Grant could capture it, supplies to Richmond and to Lee's army would be cut off.

Lee's weary veterans managed to stop the Union army outside Petersburg. Grant had to place the city under siege. Both sides dug in. The trenches stretched for miles around the city. For nine months the Confederate defenses held.

Preview & Review

Use these questions to guide your reading. Answer the questions after completing Section 6.
Understanding Issues, Events, & Ideas. Describe the final battles of the Civil War, using the following words: battles of the Wilderness, Spotsylvania Court House, Cold Harbor, Petersburg, Atlanta, Savannah; total war; Appomattox Court House.
1. What was Grant's objective in pressing Lee to battle?
2. How did the capture of Atlanta help Lincoln be reelected?
3. Why did Sherman engage in total war?
4. What were the terms of surrender at Appomattox? Tell whether or not you think these terms were generous.
Thinking Critically. 1. You are a Confederate soldier at Petersburg, which has been under siege for eight months. In your diary, record your impressions of the battle.
2. You are a reporter at Lee's surrender to Grant at Appomattox Court House. Write a headline and front-page news story describing this momentous occasion.

Above, "Summer" shows Robert E. Lee on Traveller with some of his generals at his side in 1863.

The Final Battles 581

Despite his use of total war to bring the South to its knees, Sherman despised war.

> " It is only those who have neither fired a shot nor heard the shrieks and groans of the wounded who cry aloud for more blood, more vengeance, more desolation. War is hell. "
>
> William Tecumseh Sherman, 1865

Sherman's March to the Sea

While Grant was stalled outside Petersburg, General Sherman advanced toward **Atlanta** at the head of a force of 100,000. The Confederate general resisting him, Joseph E. Johnston, had only 60,000 men. He tried to avoid a showdown battle. President Jefferson Davis did not approve of this. He replaced Johnston with General John B. Hood. An aggressive officer, Hood twice attacked Sherman's much larger army. Both attacks failed. On September 2 the Union army marched triumphantly into Atlanta. Hood retreated northward into Tennessee.

News of Sherman's victory reached Washington just before the presidential election of 1864. Lincoln had been renominated by Republicans and pro-war Democrats on a National Union ticket. The vice presidential candidate was Andrew Johnson, a Tennessee Democrat who had remained loyal to the Union. The Democratic candidate was General McClellan. With the war dragging on and on,

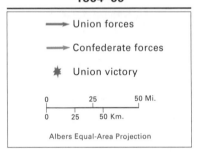

THE FINAL BATTLES, 1864–65

→ Union forces

→ Confederate forces

✳ Union victory

0   25   50 Mi.

0   25   50 Km.

Albers Equal-Area Projection

LEARNING FROM MAPS. The war once again focused on northern Virginia in its closing days. What was the North's primary military objective in that area? Were they ever successful?

Lincoln had expected to lose the election. Now, Sherman's victory helped him and his party immensely. Lincoln was reelected in a landslide, 212 electoral votes to 21.

After capturing Atlanta, Sherman burned the city to the ground. The next day, November 15, his army set out eastward toward the city of **Savannah** on the Atlantic Coast.

As Sherman's army went "marching through Georgia," as the song goes, "from Atlanta to the sea," it left a path of destruction behind it 60 miles wide (96 kilometers). On Sherman's order his troops destroyed or consumed everything in their path.

The Union soldiers slaughtered chickens and cattle. They burned barns and houses. When the men crossed a railroad line, they tore up the rails, piled up and set fire to the ties, and placed the rails on the roaring fire. When the rails were red hot, they bent and twisted them so that they were useless. Sometimes they wound the rails around tree trunks. These were known as "Sherman's neckties."

Sherman was carrying out what is now called **total war.** He sought to destroy the resources of the civilian population as well as the opposing army. He was trying to break the southerners' will to resist. When his harsh policy was questioned, Sherman simply said, "War is cruelty."

On December 21 the Union army entered Savannah. Next Sherman marched north, destroying large sections of South Carolina and North Carolina with the same cold-blooded efficiency.

The entire South was savaged by the war. Two thirds of its railroad mileage was destroyed. The Confederate capital at Richmond met the same fate as the cities in Sherman's path. On April 3, 1865, fires raged through its shattered streets.

Currier & Ives, comfortable with happier subjects, show "The Fall of Richmond" in 1865 as the capital city goes up in flames.

This photograph of William Tecumseh Sherman was taken by Mathew Brady, one of the greatest photographers of the Civil War, in 1865.

The Final Battles   583

Only a month earlier, on March 4, 1865, Lincoln had begun his second term as president. Americans were still fighting Americans. But it was now evident the long and tragic war was drawing to a close. In his second inaugural address Lincoln outlined the policy toward the South he intended to follow. It closed with the words:

> **"** With malice [ill will] toward none, with charity for all, with firmness in the right as God gives us to see the right, let us strive on to finish the work we are in, to bind up the nation's wounds, to care for him who shall have borne the battle and for his widow and his orphan, to do all which may achieve and cherish a just and lasting peace among ourselves and with all nations.**"**

Surrender at Appomattox

In April 1865 Grant finally cut the railroad line to Petersburg. Lee abandoned Petersburg and Richmond and retreated westward. His army was now thinned to 30,000 men. His last hope was to escape into North Carolina and join with the army that Sherman was driving before him. But Grant's pursuing troops sealed off this escape route. On April 8 Lee made the painful decision to surrender.

Lee and Grant met at the home of Wilmer McLean in the village of **Appomattox Court House** on Sunday, April 9. Lee wore his best dress uniform. Grant had on a muddy officer's coat and an ordinary private's shirt, unbuttoned at the neck. Seth M. Flint, a Yankee bugler, described the two men:

> **"** Grant looked like an old and battered campaigner as he rode into the yard. His blue blouse was unbuttoned and underneath could be seen his undershirt. He was unlike Lee.
>
> What a brave pair of thoroughbreds Lee and Traveler were. That horse would have attracted attention anywhere. General Lee's uniform was immaculate and he presented a superb martial [military] figure. But it was the face beneath the gray felt hat that made the deepest impression on me. I have been trying to find a single word that describes it and I have concluded that 'benign' is the adjective I'm after, because it means kindly and gracious. There was something else about him that aroused my deep pity that so great a warrior should be acknowledging defeat. . . .[1] **"**

It was a moving scene. Lee was dignified in defeat, Grant gracious in victory. "I met you once before, General Lee, while we were serving in Mexico," Grant said after they had shaken hands. "I think I should have recognized you anywhere."

[1] From "I Saw Lee Surrender" by Seth M. Flint in *Saturday Evening Post*, vol. 248, no. 5 (April 1940)

Appomattox Court House National Historical Park, Photography by Russ Finley

The two great generals talked briefly about that war of long ago when they had been comrades. Then Grant sat down at a little table and wrote out the terms of surrender. Considering the blood that had been shed and the completeness of the Union victory, the terms were amazingly generous. The Confederates must merely surrender their weapons, promise to be loyal to the Union, and depart in peace. When Lee hinted that his men could benefit greatly if allowed to keep their horses for the spring planting, Grant said, "Let all the men who claim to own a horse or mule take the animals home with them." Both men signed the surrender paper. Flint described what happened next:

> **"** Out came General Lee, his soldierly figure erect, even in defeat. We stiffened and gave him a salute, and the man in gray courteously [politely] returned it. At the moment his soul must have been heavy with sorrow . . . and yet he could return the salute of some Yankee troopers.
>
> After the departure of General Lee, we quickly learned the happy news of the surrender and it spread like wildfire through the army. That night was one of the happiest I have ever known.
>
> When I sounded taps, the sweetest of all bugle calls, the notes had scarcely died away when from the distance—it must have come from General Lee's headquarters—came, silvery clear, the same call. The boys on the other side welcomed peace.
>
> Soldiers don't carry hatred; . . .[1] **"**

[1] From "I Saw Lee Surrender" by Seth M. Flint in *Saturday Evening Post*, vol. 248, no. 5 (April 1940)

The war was over.

At Appomattox Court House, in the quiet of a parlor, the Civil War is ended. How did each great general react to this moving scene?

Return to the Preview & Review on page 581.

The Final Battles 585

LINKING HISTORY & GEOGRAPHY

GEOGRAPHY AND WAR

One of the key influences on war strategy, today as well as yesterday, is geography. In the past, in fact, geography often was more important than strategy—actually determining the outcome of a battle or war. Control of a mountain pass or the high ground gave one side a distinct advantage over another. Can you think of other geographic features that would have a major effect on the progress and outcome of a battle?

Geography and the Civil War

1. How did geography influence the war strategy of the Union?

Lincoln and his military advisers developed a war strategy based on geography. Glance at the map on page 587. What geographic features might influence Union military strategy?

You can see that one key feature of the southern landscape is its long coastline. It stretches from Virginia around Florida to Texas, and is dented with inlets and harbors. Another feature that stands out is the Appalachian Mountains. Note how they effectively divide the Confederacy into east and west. A third prominent physical feature is the Mississippi River, which divides the Confederacy further.

The Union Blockade

2. Why did the Union blockade the southern coastline?

The long southern coastline concerned northern strategists. It concerned them because they knew it would be important to keep the South from getting needed supplies. Remember that most American manufacturing was located in the North. The Confederacy would have to depend on imports carried by ship to replenish their supplies.

What could the Union do? They decided to blockade the entire southern coastline. Union naval ships patrolled the offshore waters, capturing Confederate merchant ships bound for Europe for supplies or returning with them. The blockade, which stretched for 3,500 miles, became increasingly successful. At first, the Union navy could not effectively block the mile upon mile of coastline because Confederate ships were too numerous. As ships were added to the Union navy and lost from the Confederate one, the blockade grew more effective.

The Southern Landscape

3. Why was the Southern landscape a major influence on both war strategy and the war's outcome?

Virtually all the battles of the war were fought on Confederate land. Therefore, the geography of the South was of vital importance to both sides. Why did most of the war unfold in the South?

Remember that although the South fired the first shots of the war, southern strategy was not aggressive. To restore the Union, northern armies had to invade and defeat the Confederacy. The goal of the Confederacy, on the other hand, was to defend itself until the Union tired of fighting. The Confederacy need not invade the North because it sought no Union territory.

Divide and Conquer

4. How did the Union plan to fight the war on Confederate land?

Knowing their armies must invade, Union military advisers devised a plan to divide the South. Remember that the Appalachian Mountains and Mississippi River system already physically divided the South. Control of both would divide Southern armies and block supply routes. It would also require the outmanned Confederate army to fight on two fronts, stretching their limited manpower thin in certain places.

In the West control of the Mississippi and then its major tributaries—the Tennessee and Cumberland rivers—would further divide the South. It would be more and more difficult for reinforcements and supplies to reach Confederate forces. In fact, the Union was so conscious of the importance of geography and of rivers, they named many battles after nearby streams. (The Confederacy named the same battle after the nearest town.) The Battle of Bull Run (the Union name for a battle near a stream in northern Virginia) was also the Battle of Manassas (the Confederate name for the same battle near a small town in the area).

In the East, the North realized that controlling the mountainous spine of the Appalachians would isolate the tidewater South from vast lands of the Confederacy to the west. Union forces could then swiftly surround and capture Richmond and end the war.

A Successful Strategy

5. Did Union strategy work?

Lincoln had the confidence in his plan to stick with it. He knew that it was based on the geography of the land. Each part of the plan capitalized on a different physical aspect. And the war actually unfolded according to the plan Lincoln and his advisors had created.

The blockade eventually crippled the South. Shortages of almost every item became common. Neither southern industry nor southern agriculture could keep up with military or civilian needs. The Union army and navy gained control of the Mississippi and Tennessee river valleys, splitting the Confederacy. From that point on, Union victories divided the Confederacy into smaller and smaller isolated pieces. As the end of the war drew closer, Union troops surrounded Richmond, which was cut off from western reinforcements. Lincoln's confidence in the plan paid off. Strategy built on geography was one of the major keys to northern success in the Civil War.

Applying Your Knowledge

Your class will plan military strategy based on local geography. One group will plan an attack; the other should plan a defense. Consider all the geographic features that might influence a battle taking place in your area. Sketch maps to illustrate the strategies. If possible, visit the site you have selected and note the geographic features in person.

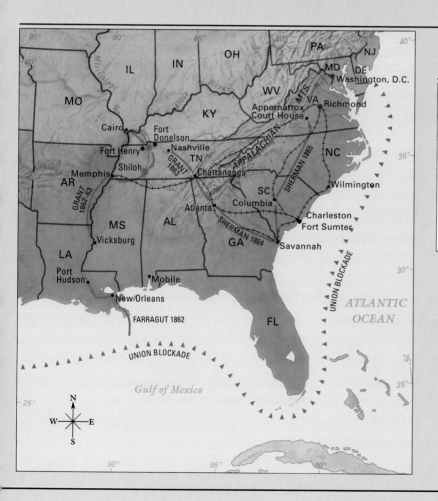

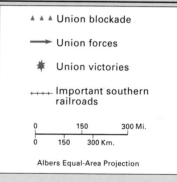

THE BLOCKADE AND
THE WAR IN THE WEST,
1862–65

▲ ▲ ▲ Union blockade

→ Union forces

✷ Union victories

++++ Important southern railroads

| 0 | 150 | 300 Mi. |
| 0 | 150 | 300 Km. |

Albers Equal-Area Projection

CHAPTER 16 REVIEW

1860
Abraham Lincoln elected president

1861
Confederate States of America formed
★
Firing on Fort Sumter
★
Union blockade begins

1862
Union victory
at Antietam
★
Vicksburg Campaign

Chapter Summary

Read the statements below. Choose one, and write a paragraph explaining its importance.
1. In 1861 the states that seceded from the Union formed the Confederate States of America.
2. The Civil War started with the firing on Fort Sumter in Charleston harbor.
3. In numbers the Confederacy was no match for the Union, which had more people, railroads, and manufacturing. The South, however, had a cause and was fighting on its own land.
4. Although both sides were poorly trained for war, the South dominated the early battles.
5. The war had a major impact on the economies of both sides. Northern industrial output and employment boomed even as inflation rose. The South had shortages of many items.
6. The Union army finally won important victories at Antietam and Gettysburg.
7. Draft riots showed that many northerners opposed the Emancipation Proclamation.
8. Union control of the Mississippi River cut the Confederacy in two.
9. Union victories in Virginia forced Lee to surrender in April 1865.

Reviewing Chronological Order

Number your paper 1-5. Then study the time line above and place the following events in the order in which they happened by writing the first next to 1, the second next to 2, and so on.
1. Gettysburg
2. Lee surrenders at Appomattox
3. Confederates fire on Fort Sumter
4. Lincoln appoints Grant
5. Southern leaders form a confederacy

Understanding Main Ideas

1. Describe the life of a typical Civil War soldier.
2. What did the draft riots show about northern attitudes toward African Americans?
3. Why was the Battle of Vicksburg a turning point of the war?
4. How were Grant and Lee similar? How were they different?
5. What were the two parts of General Grant's plan to end the war?

6. Why did General Sherman use total war in his March to the Sea?

Thinking Critically

1. **Analyzing.** Compare and contrast Abraham Lincoln and Jefferson Davis as leaders. From what you have read in this chapter, who do you think was the better leader? Why?
2. **Evaluating.** Choose five Civil War generals and rank them from 1 to 5, according to their military performance. Then explain why you ranked them in this order.
3. **Synthesizing.** Imagine that you are "Billy Yank" or "Johnny Reb" during the Civil War. Write a letter to your parents or to your sweetheart, describing your life as a soldier.
4. **Drawing Conclusions.** Do you think President Lincoln issued the Emancipation Proclamation for ethical reasons, political reasons, or both? Explain.

Writing About History: Expressive

Use your historical imagination to write a letter home as a soldier or nurse in either the Confederate or Union army. Include a description of a general you might have glimpsed in camp, or describe conditions in a hospital for the war wounded. Use the information in Chapter 16 and in other reference books to prepare your letter.

Practicing the Strategy

Review the strategy on page 558.
Reading a Statistical Chart. Study the chart on page 572, then answer the following questions.
1. What is meant by the words "Human Costs" in the title?
2. What kinds of data are being compared in the two columns of this chart?
3. Exactly how many more soldiers did the Union have than the Confederacy?
4. The Union won the war, but who paid the greatest price in casualties? How do you know?

Using Primary Sources

On New Years' Day, 1863 President Lincoln greeted guests at the annual presidential reception

1863
Emancipation Proclamation
★
Draft riots erupt in North
★
Gettysburg

1864
Grant controls Chattanooga
★
Lincoln appoints Grant
★
Sherman burns Atlanta; begins March to the Sea
★
Lincoln reelected

1865
Lee surrenders to Grant

at the White House. Then he slipped away to his private office where, in the presence of a few friends, he prepared to sign the Emancipation Proclamation. Pen in hand, he leaned forward to write his name, and then pausing a moment, said, "I never in my life felt more certain that I was doing right. . . ." With that he wrote his name in bold letters across the bottom of the document. As you read the following excerpt, see if you can feel the turmoil within Lincoln caused by conflicting political and moral values. Then answer the questions that follow it.

Whereas on the twenty-second day of September, A.D. 1862, a proclamation was issued by the President of the United States, containing among other things, the following, to wit:

On the first day of January, A.D. 1863, all persons held as slaves within any state or designated part of a state, the people whereof shall then be in rebellion against the United States, shall be then, thenceforward, and forever free; and the executive government of the United States, including military and naval authority thereof, will recognize and maintain the freedom of such persons and will do no act or acts to repress such persons or any of them, in any efforts they make for their actual freedom. . . .

And by virtue of the power and for the purpose aforesaid, I do order and declare all persons held as slaves within said designated states and parts of states are, and henceforward shall be, free; . . .

And I hereby enjoin the people so declared to be free to abstain from violence, unless in necessary self-defense; and I recommend to them that, in all cases when allowed, they labor faithfully for reasonable wages.

And I further declare and make known that such persons of suitable condition will be received into the armed service of the United States to garrison forts, positions, stations, and other places, and to man vessels of all sorts in said service.

And upon this act, sincerely believed to be an act of justice, warranted by the Constitution upon military necessity, I invoke the considerate judgment of mankind and the gracious favor of Almighty God.

1. Why do you think the Emancipation Proclamation did not specify that slaves in the border states be freed?
2. How do you think the Emancipation Proclamation affected slaves in the Confederate states during the Civil War? Why?
3. If you had been a slave on a southern plantation in 1863, what reasons might you have had to remain on the plantation?

Linking History & Geography
The geography of the South's transportation system helped Union leaders shape their strategy. Use the map on page 577 and the information in the chapter to answer the following questions.
1. What major southern ports were affected by the blockade? Why was control of the Mississippi River an important Union objective?
2. What were three cities connected to Chattanooga by railroad? What seems to be the relationship between railroads and Sherman's march from Atlanta to the sea?
3. About how far apart were the Union and Confederate capitals? How might Union strategy have been different if the Confederate capital had remained in Montgomery, Alabama?

Enriching the Study of History
1. **Individual Project.** Prepare a bulletin board to show the major battles of the Civil War. Give both southern and northern names when there are two. Arrange the battles in the order in which they were fought. Choose appropriate symbols for North and South, northern and southern victories, fighting on land and water, troop movements in the South and West.
2. **Cooperative Project.** Working in two teams, your class will present a newscast following the Battle of Gettysburg. One team will conduct interviews with the commanding generals and surviving soldiers from both armies. The other team will interview spectators who have just heard Lincoln deliver his *Gettysburg Address*. If possible, videotape your program.

Chapter 16 Review   589

Reconstruction

When the Civil War was ended and the slaves were set free, the problem of racial prejudice in the United States was not solved. When the slaves were freed, few thought of returning to Africa. In many cases America had been home for their families for 200 years. Yet African Americans still did not enjoy full citizenship during Reconstruction. Instead, they were now systematically excluded in the clearest form of prejudice, based on race. So-called "Jim Crow laws" and "Black Codes" passed after the Civil War greatly restricted the movement of former slaves. Amendments to the Constitution attempted to do away with race or skin color as a condition of voting, but "separate but equal" facilities, then permitted by the Supreme Court, effectively segregated black people from white. What long night of injustice and terror lay ahead?

Library of Congress

The assassin who tore Abraham Lincoln from a nation finally at peace also took the president from his son Tad. A photographer from Brady Studio made this nice study of father and son.

1. RADICALS AND MODERATES

Lincoln is Assassinated

On the evening of April 9, 1865, President Lincoln received a telegram from General Grant: "GENERAL LEE SURRENDERED THE ARMY OF NORTHERN VIRGINIA THIS MORNING." Next day the whole country had the news. Bells rang out, bands played, flags and banners flew everywhere in the North. A crowd gathered outside the White House. "Tad" Lincoln, the president's 12-year-old son, appeared at the window happily waving a captured Confederate flag. Everyone cheered.

Unfortunately, this happy national mood did not last. On the evening of April 14 Abraham and Mary Todd Lincoln were attending a play at Ford's Theater in Washington. Suddenly a shot rang out. John Wilkes Booth, a little-known actor who sympathized with the South, had slipped into the president's box and fired a bullet into his head. A popular writer described the assassination with these words:

> ❝ Booth kept his eye to the gimlet hole. The head in front of him barely moved. The universe seemed to pause for breath. Then Trenchard [a character on stage] said:' 'Don't know the manners of good society, eh?' Booth did not wait to hear the rest of the line. The derringer was now in his hand. He turned the knob. The door swung inward. Lincoln, facing diagonally away toward the left, was four feet from him. Booth moved along the wall. . . .
>
> The derringer was behind the President's head between the left ear and the spine. Booth squeezed the trigger and there was a sound as though someone had blown up and broken a heavy paper bag. It came in the midst of laughter, so that some people heard it, and some did not. The President did not move. His head inclined toward his chest and he stopped rocking. . . .
>
> A chrysanthemum of blue smoke hung in Box 7. Booth, with no maniacal [crazy] gleam, no frenzy, looked at the people who looked at him and said, 'Sic semper tyrannis! [Thus always to tyrants!] . . . Revenge for the South!'[1] ❞

The next day the president died.

Booth escaped from the theater in the confusion and fled to Virginia. He was hunted down and trapped in a barn. The barn was set on fire, but Booth was killed by a bullet. Whether he was shot by someone else or killed himself is not clear.

The people of the North were shocked and grief-stricken. The Confederacy had surrendered, but the nation was still badly divided.

[1]From *The Day Lincoln Was Shot* by Jim Bishop

Lincoln lay for nine hours in a boarding house near Ford's Theater before he expired from his assassin's bullet. Alexander Hay Ritchie made this etching.

Few people realized the tremendous task of binding the nation's wounds that lay ahead. But now the leader who had guided them through the war was gone. Walt Whitman wrote a memorial to the dead president:

      " O Captain! my Captain! our fearful trip is done,
         The ship has weathered every rack, the prize we sought
            is won,
         The port is near, the bells I hear; the people all
            exulting.
         While follow eyes the steady keel, the vessel grim and
            daring;
           But O heart! heart! heart!
            O the bleeding drops of red,
               Where on the deck my Captain lies,
                  Fallen cold and dead.[1] **"**

The president's death left a terrible void at such a critical time. No one knew it yet, but another great struggle—this one over control of the defeated South—would extend the bitterness of the war for several more years.

President Andrew Johnson

Much now depended on Andrew Johnson, who became president after the **assassination** of President Lincoln. Before the Civil War Johnson had served in both houses of Congress and as governor of Tennessee. The Republicans had picked him to run for vice president in 1864, even though he was a Democrat. He was one of the few

[1] From "O Captain! my Captain!" by Walt Whitman

pro-Union politicians who came from a Confederate state. His home state of Tennessee was not even a member of the Union when he became president!

All through his career Johnson had been a champion of the small farmer. He favored laws to improve public education and provide free farms, or homesteads, for families who would settle on the public lands. He was always critical of great wealth. This helps explain his hatred of the southern planters he called "traitorous aristocrats."

Most Republican politicians expected Johnson to make a fine president. Moderate Republicans believed that "malice toward none" was the best policy and hoped he would extend it to the South. They hoped, as Lincoln had put it in his moving speech at his second inauguration, "to bind up the nation's wounds" quickly.

Johnson pleased the **Moderates** by issuing an **amnesty,** or pardon, to most former Confederates. Those who would take an oath of loyalty to the United States would regain full citizenship. The states of the former Confederacy could hold elections and send representatives and senators to Congress.

On the other hand, Republicans who were determined to protect the rights of the newly freed slaves, called **Radicals,** expected Johnson to act on his well-known dislike of the southern planter class and force the planters to accept the new ways. Congressman Thaddeus Stevens of Pennsylvania was one of the Radical leaders. He demanded that the United States seize the property of the large slaveholders and give it to the ex-slaves. There would be plenty of "rebel land," he said, to give a 40-acre farm (16 hectares) to every adult male ex-slave in the South.

The Aftermath of War

The American Revolution had been a **watershed,** or turning point in history, bringing great political changes. The new nation forged out of that revolution was unique, a government based on the consent of the governed. The Civil War also was a watershed. The secession of the southern states had challenged the very existence of the nation. From the ashes of war a dramatically different society emerged. The Civil War, historian Bruce Catton pointed out, destroyed "the old bases on which society stood. . . . The Civil War was a beginning, rather than an end, simply because it ended forever one of the things on which American society had been built." All Americans had to face the moral and legal questions of slavery. Had the war to end slavery in the United States succeeded? What would now happen to the former slaves?

War's end freed more than 4 million Americans from slavery. But their social and economic positions in the reconstructed nation were still undefined. The war also demolished the life style white southerners had enjoyed before the war. Plantations could no longer rely on slaves for labor, and the war had virtually destroyed the wealth of many planters. The structure of southern society had been disrupted. Was it fair that a few planters had controlled so much of the southern wealth and power? Everyone in the South, rich and poor, now found themselves in a world almost as new as that encountered by the first colonists.

Who in the South gained from the changes? Certainly the slaves gained their freedom. But their world had been torn apart too. They now faced social and economic conditions totally unlike any they had ever known. All were eager to test the limits of their new freedom. Poor whites also gained something. Although they now had to compete with the freed slaves for jobs and status, many hoped to obtain farmlands from the shattered plantations. This gave them hope for a better future.

Northerners' views of southern society changed too. At first many wanted to punish the "rebels." Later, myths about a land of prosperous plantations, fatherly masters, and contented slaves began to emerge. Such a South became the setting for many books and plays published in the years after the war. But the southerners, black and white, knew that these tales were of a South that had never existed.

Finally, the war cost the nation more than 600,000 lives. It caused enormous property losses, especially in the Confederacy. The total war just ended had ravaged farms, railroads, and factories throughout the South. How long would it take to rebuild what the war had destroyed and at what cost?

The Black Codes

The Radicals were also concerned about the way former slaves, called **freedmen**, were being treated in the South. By the end of 1865 all the southern state governments set up under Johnson's amnesty plan had ratified the new **Thirteenth Amendment** to the Constitution, which officially abolished slavery. But white people formed the majority in most parts of the South. They were powerful and well organized. Southern blacks could not protect their new rights without northern help. The new southern governments did not allow black people to vote. Their legislatures swiftly passed regulations called **Black Codes** designed to keep blacks in a condition of semi-slavery.

These codes barred blacks from any kind of work except farming and household service. Some states forced blacks to sign labor contracts with landowners at the beginning of each year. If they left their work, they received no pay. If they refused to sign, they were arrested and charged with being tramps. The "sentence" was to work for one of the landowners for the year.

These Black Codes alarmed most northerners. The results of the new southern elections alarmed them even more. Southern voters,

The Granger Collection

all of them white, chose as leaders many of the same people who had led them during the rebellion. Several Confederate generals were elected to Congress. The Georgia legislature picked Alexander H. Stephens, vice president of the Confederacy, to represent the state in the United States Senate. Stephens had recently been paroled from prison after being charged with treason for his role in the Confederacy.

The newly elected representatives were members of the Democratic party. Admitting them was too much even for Moderate Republicans to accept. Both houses of Congress voted not to admit the new southern representatives. Johnson's plan for **Reconstruction—** bringing southern states back into the Union—was rejected.

Life for many freed slaves did not seem to improve after the Civil War. Such is the plight of these Virginia farmers in about 1900. The butchered hogs had to be lowered into scalding water until their bristles could be scrubbed off. What must have been the joys of freedom? What the sorrows?

Johnson and the Republicans

The Republicans in Congress then began to reconstruct the South according to their own ideas. Before the end of the war Congress had created a **Freedman's Bureau** run by the army to care for refugees. Early in 1866 a new bill was passed increasing the power of the Bureau to protect southern blacks.

President Johnson decided to **veto,** or refuse to approve, this Freedmen's Bureau Bill. He claimed that he approved of the purpose of the bill. He was eager, he said, "to secure for the freedmen . . . their freedom and property and their entire independence." But he argued that it was unconstitutional to apply military law to civilians in peacetime.

Congress therefore attacked the Black Codes by passing a **Civil Rights Act.** This law made blacks citizens of the United States. It

INTERPRETING HISTORY: Reconstruction

Reconstruction is one of the most controversial topics considered by historians. Lincoln hoped Reconstruction would "bind up the nation's wounds" caused by the Civil War. Lincoln based his plan on "malice toward none." But his plan was doomed to failure. As historian Eric Forier said, "What remains certain is that Reconstruction failed, and that for blacks its failure was a disaster whose magnitude cannot be obscured by the genuine accomplishments that did endure."

In the late 19th century white northerners and southerners concentrated on reconciling their differences. The historians of the period, the most influential being William A. Dunning of Columbia University, argued that the Radical Republicans had been cruel and vindictive people, eager for revenge. He also claimed that the freed blacks had proved to be incapable of self-government and that they had been taken advantage of by cynical carpetbaggers. The resulting "Black Republican" governments imposed high taxes on southerners and spent the money either wastefully or for their own direct benefit. Reconstruction became known as "the tragic era."

The first historian to challenge this view was W.E.B. DuBois. He claimed in *Black Reconstruction* (1935) that Reconstruction was an effort by both whites and blacks to create a "true democratic society." It failed because it did not go far enough, explained DuBois: "One fact and one alone explains that attitude of writers toward Reconstruction, they cannot conceive of Negroes as men." DuBois described the achievements of the Reconstruction governments, such as the schools, railroads, and other public institutions that they built. Then in the 1960s, during the intense civil rights movement, historians began to further revise the traditional view. Kenneth Stampp, in *The Era of Reconstruction* (1965), insisted the Radicals were genuine reformers out to defend the rights of blacks and that most black legislators had been good public servants. Moreover, they had never dominated the state governments of the period. Reconstruction failed not because of what it did to southern whites but because it did not implement the reforms necessary to ensure African Americans equal rights.

The most recent authority, Eric Foner, calls Reconstruction "America's Unfinished Revolution." Blacks took advantage of the new educational opportunities eagerly. They used their liberty to move from place to place to escape from backbreaking labor and find new opportunities. They changed the way southern crops, especially cotton, were grown. Their revolution was real, Foner writes, but unfinished in the sense that their full use of their freedom was denied them and even today has not been fully achieved.

---

was necessary to state this specifically because the Dred Scott decision had declared that even free blacks were not American citizens. The bill also forbade the southern states from restricting the rights of freedmen by special laws like the Black Codes.

President Johnson vetoed this bill too. It was a mistake to make blacks citizens, he now insisted. They needed to go through a period of "probation" before receiving this "prize." It was unconstitutional to give blacks "safeguards which go infinitely beyond any that the . . . Government has ever provided for the white race," he said.

As this veto made clear, Johnson's dislike of southern planters did not keep him from being prejudiced against blacks. Great wealth in the hands of a few plantation owners was what he really hated, not slavery. He had once said that he wished every white family in America could have one slave "to take the drudgery" out of life!

In April 1866 both houses of Congress again passed the Civil Rights Act. They obtained the two-thirds majority necessary to **override** the president's veto. This was the first veto of an important law ever to be overridden. Thus the Civil Rights Act became law a year after the war ended. 🖅

Return to the Preview & Review on page 591.

2. THE CIVIL WAR AMENDMENTS

The Reconstruction Acts

Next, Congress passed and sent to the states for ratification what became the **Fourteenth Amendment** to the Constitution. In many ways this measure was even more important than the Thirteenth Amendment. The Republicans in Congress drafted it in order to put the terms of the Civil Rights Act directly into the Constitution.

"All persons born or naturalized in the United States," the amendment said, "are citizens of the United States *and of the State wherein they reside*." This made blacks citizens no matter where in the nation they lived. Then the amendment struck down the Black Codes. "No State shall . . . abridge the privileges and immunities of citizens of the United States; nor shall any State deprive any person of life, liberty, or property, without due process of law."

The Fourteenth Amendment guaranteed equal protection of the laws to all Americans. It did not make racial **segregation,** or separation, illegal. It did not even tell states to allow blacks to vote. It did provide blacks with equal access to the courts, and it forbade laws that applied only to backs but not whites. Nevertheless, most white southerners objected to it strongly. Since the southern states refused to ratify the amendment, it was impossible to get the approval of three fourths of the states, which was necessary to make it part of

Preview & Review

Use these questions to guide your reading. Answer the questions after completing Section 2.

Understanding Issues, Events, & Ideas. Using the following words, explain how the rights of African Americans were affected after the Civil War: Fourteenth Amendment, segregation, Reconstruction Act, impeachment, Tenure of Office Act, Fifteenth Amendment, Civil War Amendments.

1. Why was the Fourteenth Amendment passed?
2. How did Republicans use the Reconstruction Act to force southerners to give blacks the right to vote?
3. Why did the Republican leaders of Congress want to remove President Johnson from office?
4. How would northern blacks have influenced the election of 1868 if they had been allowed to vote?

Thinking Critically. 1. How would you view the Fourteenth Amendment if you were a conservative white southerner? A Radical Republican? An ex-slave in the South? **2.** Which of the Civil War Amendments do you think is the most important? Why?

The Granger Collection

"The First Vote" is the title of this drawing. Discuss whether or not elections such as these counted—or whether the votes were even tallied.

597

Andrew Johnson's course toward the South was watched with special interest by Ulysses S. Grant.

❝But for the assassination of Mr. Lincoln, I believe the great majority of the Northern people, and the soldiers unanimously, would have been in favor of a speedy reconstruction on terms that would be least humiliating to the people who rebelled against their government. . . .❞

From *Personal Memoirs,*
Ulysses S. Grant, 1885

White House Historical Association

Although cartoonists often poked fun at him, there was a kindliness about Lincoln that his photographers captured. Andrew Johnson, shown here in his presidential portrait, lacked this trait. Was it his manner or his policies that riled his critics, according to what you've read?

the Constitution. These amendments became the legal basis of the Civil Rights movement of the 1960s.

President Johnson made his conflict with the Republicans an issue in the Congressional elections of November 1866. He campaigned back and forth across the country, arguing for his own approach. He failed to change many minds. Indeed, most historians believe that Johnson's angry speeches probably lost more votes for his policies than they gained. The Republicans easily maintained their large majorities in both houses of Congress.

After the failure of the southern states to ratify the Fourteenth Amendment, Congress passed the **Reconstruction Act** of March 1867. This stern measure divided what it called "the rebel states" into five military districts. "Sufficient military force" to "protect all persons in their rights" was stationed in each district. To end army rule, each former state would have to draw up a new constitution that guaranteed blacks the right to vote. The state would also have to ratify the Fourteenth Amendment.

In other words, Congress ordered a military occupation of the South. Lincoln's hope that the nation could bind up its wounds in harmony had come to nothing.

White southerners hated military rule, but they hated the idea of racial equality even more. They still refused to ratify the Fourteenth Amendment. A second, and a third, and finally a fourth Reconstruction Act were passed by Congress. Each put more pressure on "the rebel states." At last, in June 1868, southern governments in which blacks participated began to be formed. These governments ratified the amendment. The final state to complete the process was Georgia, in July 1870, more than five years after the end of the Civil War.

President Johnson Is Impeached

Radical Republicans blamed President Johnson for much of the stubborn resistance of white southerners to the Reconstruction Acts. He had urged the states not to accept the Fourteenth Amendment. He had vetoed each of the Reconstruction bills, even though their repassage by large majorities was certain. In February 1868 angry Congressional leaders decided to try to remove the president from office by impeaching him.

The Constitution provides that the House of Representatives, by majority vote, can bring charges against a president. This is called **impeachment.** The charges are judged by the Senate, with the chief justice of the United States presiding over the trial. A two-thirds majority vote is required for conviction and removal from office.

The Radicals brought 11 charges against the president. Most of them were totally without merit. The most serious accusation was that he had violated the **Tenure of Office Act** of 1867 by dismissing Edwin M. Stanton, the secretary of war. This law prohibited the

president from *discharging* appointed officials without the consent of Congress.

Johnson believed that the Tenure of Office Act was unconstitutional. The Constitution states only that Senate approval is necessary for the *appointment* of high officials. In the past no one had challenged the right of a president to remove an appointee without consulting the Senate.

Johnson dismissed Stanton deliberately to bring the issue before the Supreme Court, where it could properly be decided. Impeaching the president was clearly not justified by the facts. Indeed, his term was almost over. But many members of Congress believed that Reconstruction would never be successful unless Johnson were removed from office.

The Senate sits as a court to judge whether or not Andrew Johnson will be convicted in his impeachment trial in 1868. Below is a ticket to the Senate chamber. What is the difference between impeachment and conviction?

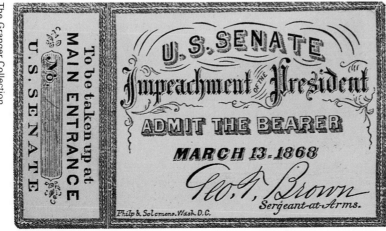

U. S. SENATE

Impeachment of the President

ADMIT THE BEARER

MARCH 13, 1868

Geo. T. Brown
Sergeant-at-Arms.

To be taken up at MAIN ENTRANCE

U. S. SENATE

U. S. SENATE

Philp & Solomons. Wash. D.C.

The Civil War Amendments   **599**

The president was spared conviction by a single vote. On each charge the Senate failed to obtain a two-thirds majority by only one vote.

Andrew Johnson remained in office until March 1869. He was a poor president. All his life he had been a valuable public servant when he was battling for reform, a lone "outsider" stubbornly attacking "the Establishment." When fate made him the head of that Establishment, he proved unable to adjust. He could not work well with other people. He made a dreadful mess of his time in the White House.

Yet Johnson was not an evil man. His Reconstruction policies seem wrong to us today, but he did not deserve to be accused of committing crimes against the nation. His problem was his inability to think of blacks as equal members of society.

The Election of 1868

A majority of the white people of his generation shared Andrew Johnson's low opinion of the character and intelligence of blacks. As we have seen, most northern states did not allow blacks to vote. However, the results of the presidential election of 1868 led to a dramatic change in this situation.

Blacks in the southern states *had* voted in that election. Federal troops stationed there under the Reconstruction Act prevented whites from keeping blacks from the polls. Eager to exercise their civic duty for the first time, many voted, and they naturally cast their ballots overwhelmingly for the Republican party.

The Republican presidential candidate, General Grant, won an easy victory in the electoral college, 214 votes to 80 for the Democratic candidate, Horatio Seymour. But in many northern states the popular vote was extremely close.

Republican politicians also felt that guaranteeing the right to vote for blacks was necessary. Maybe in future elections they could make an important difference. They reasoned that blacks could not have much power in the North. Blacks made up only about one percent of the population in that section. Why not allow them to vote? Certainly blacks would vote solidly Republican. Perhaps the hated Democrats could be kept out of power forever.

Early in 1869 the overwhelmingly Republican Congress drafted still another Constitutional amendment: "The right of citizens of the United States to vote shall not be denied . . . on account of race, color, or previous condition of servitude." Within about a year this **Fifteenth Amendment** was ratified by the states. With the Thirteenth and Fourteenth Amendments, it is one of the **Civil War Amendments** which later formed the basis of the civil rights movement of the 1960s.

Ulysses S. Grant posed for this portrait as president. After leaving the White House, poor and suffering from cancer, Grant wrote his Personal Memoirs, *which became a national best seller. Was Grant as good a president as he was a general?*

Return to the Preview & Review on page 597.

3. FREEDOM AFTER SLAVERY

The Privileges of Freedom

The Civil War Amendments did bring certain freedoms to black Americans. Freedom meant first of all the right to decide what to do with one's own time, from minute to minute and day to day. It meant lifting a terrible weight off the *minds* of nearly 4 million former slaves. It meant freedom to move about.

With freedom from slavery, most blacks had to work less hard. Now they could put down their hoes and stretch their tired muscles for a few minutes without fear of a blow or a harsh word. Parents did not send the youngest children into the fields as their former owners would have done. Old people labored less and rested more. Mothers devoted more time to their homes and children, less to planting, hoeing, and harvesting.

The former slaves also organized religious congregations. Their number and growth surprised whites who had not realized the extent to which Christian beliefs had won the hearts of the slaves. Northern black congregations sent ministers to the South to assist these new organizations.

Another use that blacks made of freedom was to seek education. Very few slaves could read and write. There had been no schools for slave children, and indeed it was against the law in most southern states even to teach a slave to read.

The preacher comes to call, making the children watchful and shy. All here are former slaves. In what ways did freedom change their lives?

Preview & Review

Use these questions to guide your reading. Answer the questions after completing Section 3.

Understanding Issues, Events, & Ideas. What was the significance during Reconstruction of the following words: "Black Republican," Carpetbagger, Scalawag, sharecropping, lien, crop-lien system, world market.

1. What were some of the privileges of freedom for blacks?
2. What were some reasons Carpetbaggers and Scalawags sought public office?
3. Why was it difficult for freedmen to begin farming under the Homestead Act of 1862?
4. What were the unfortunate side effects of the crop-lien system?

Thinking Critically. 1. Imagine that you are a former slave who is now attending school. In your diary, tell why you think education is important for all blacks.
2. Compare and contrast black politicians with white politicians of the Reconstruction period.

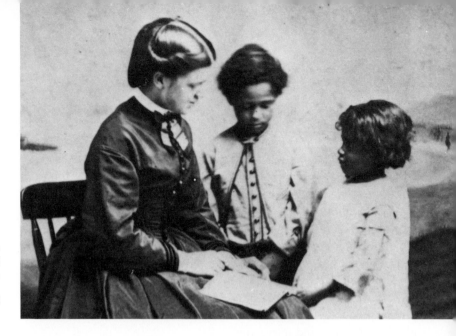

In one of the Freedman's Bureau schools eager pupils gather around their teacher, who no doubt came down from the North as a volunteer. What lie told by prejudiced whites did these schools put to rest?

The Freedmen's Bureau began to oversee schools in the South as soon as the war ended. Many religious and private groups from the North also contributed time, money, and teachers. Nearly every northern denomination founded schools and colleges to educate the most talented among the former slaves. Among the outstanding colleges for blacks started at this time were Howard University, Hampton Institute, and Fisk University.

Blacks responded eagerly to this opportunity for schooling. In South Carolina, for example, a school for blacks was set up in Charleston as soon as the Union army captured the city. By 1867 there were about 20,000 blacks attending school in that state. All over the South elderly ex-slaves could be seen learning their ABC's alongside their grandchildren.

At first most white southerners sneered at the very idea of educating the freedmen. Remember that there had not even been state-supported public schools for whites in the prewar South. But many came to admit that blacks could learn as well as whites. Most blacks who were educated became useful citizens. Thus all but the most prejudiced whites changed their minds. These whites continued, however, to oppose teaching black and white children in the same schools.

Blacks in Government

While the United States army occupied the South, blacks voted and held office in all the states of the former Confederacy. Nothing made white southerners more bitter and resentful than to be "ruled" by the very people they had totally dominated for so long.

"Rule" is not, however, the proper word to describe the role of blacks in southern politics during Reconstruction. Only 22 ever served in Congress and only a handful were elected to high state office during the period. Blacks held many local offices, but they seldom controlled any branch of a local government. The only state legislature that ever had a black majority was South Carolina's between 1868 and 1877.

Most of the members of the **"Black Republican"** governments, as their opponents called them, were whites. Those who came from the northern states were called **Carpetbaggers** because travelers of the period usually carried their belongings in soft-sided bags made of carpeting. The name implied that these "invaders" had no stake in the South but to get rich. Southern white Republicans were referred to scornfully by their Democratic neighbors as **Scalawags**— good-for-nothing rascals.

Carpetbaggers and Scalawags came from all walks of life—military personnel, planters, businessmen, and speculators. Some genuinely wanted to help blacks achieve political influence. Others intended to win power for themselves by controlling black votes. Some were plain thieves. Black politicians in the South also varied widely in ability and devotion to duty. There were fewer Carpetbaggers than Scalawags and blacks in Reconstruction governments. But their undoubted loyalty to the Union and connections in Washington gave them great influence.

During the 1870s white people who objected to blacks holding office emphasized the numerous examples of black corruption and incompetence that came to light. A northern observer, James S. Pike, reported that the 1873 session of the South Carolina legislature was marked by total confusion. "No one is allowed to talk five minutes without interruption," Pike complained. There was "endless chatter" and much "gush and babble." Pike said of one speaker:

66 He did not know what he was going to say when he got up
. . . and he did not know what he had said when he sat
down.99

A black politician in Arkansas collected $9,000 for repairing a bridge that had cost the state only $500 to build in the first place. The black-controlled South Carolina legislature spent $16,000 a year on paper and other supplies. The average spent on these materials before the war was $400. The black South Carolina senators had a kind of private club in the capitol building where fine food and wines and the most expensive cigars were always available. Many black legislators routinely accepted money in exchange for their votes on important issues.

Such things did indeed happen. What white critics failed to mention was that many white politicians were just as corrupt and inefficient. In fact most of the corruption during this time can be traced to whites. One commentator watched the disorderly behavior of members of the United States House of Representatives at about this time. He said that trying to make a speech in the House was like

WHAT YOU GIVE TO ONE CLASS YOU MUST GIVE TO ALL

WHAT YOU DENY TO ONE CLASS YOU SHALL DENY TO ALL

HON. R. B. ELLIOTT'S speech page 7.

Robert B. Elliott of South Carolina addresses his fellow state legislators on civil rights in 1874. What influence do you suppose this well-educated African American had in the state legislature?

trying to speak to a crowd in a passing trolley while standing on the curb of a busy city street.

As for corruption, the main difference between white and black thieves was that the white ones made off with most of the money. After studying the actions of black and white officials during Reconstruction, the historian Joel Williamson concludes that "the most gigantic steals" were engineered by white politicians like "Honest John" Patterson, a Carpetbagger who systematically bribed South Carolina legislators to vote for a bill worth nearly $2 million to a railroad Patterson controlled.

However, the southern state governments also accomplished a great deal of good during these years. They raised taxes in order to improve public education, which had been badly neglected before 1860. They also spent large sums on roads, bridges, railroads, and public buildings damaged during the war. They also expanded public support for medical care and orphans. They began to rebuild the southern economy. And in many cases they established civil rights laws.

STRATEGIES FOR SUCCESS

INTERPRETING A GRAPH OF BUSINESS CYCLES

As you have learned, the United States has a free enterprise economy. This means that businesses are privately owned and operated with little interference by the government. American business is directly affected by the needs and wants of consumers—or the *market.* Prosperity goes in cycles. Events that influence consumers cause the economy to expand or recede. Graphs throughout *The Story of America* illustrate these cycles.

How to Read a Graph of Business Cycles

To read a graph of business cycles, follow these guidelines.

1. **Read the title.** The title identifies the time period illustrated by the graph.
2. **Check the key.** The key explains what the colors and special symbols on the graph mean.
3. **Study the trends.** The graph shows the ups and downs of the business cycle. Periods of expansion rise above the trend line (which may also be called the base line). Periods of recession, or slowdowns, dip below the trend line.
4. **Note the labels.** Historical events that strongly influence economic cycles help explain the reasons for the surge or sag of the economy.

5. **Compare the fluctuations.** The highs and lows differ in intensity and duration (length of time). Compare them to understand the business situation at that time in American history.

Applying the Strategy

Study the graph below. The title, "Business Cycles, 1840–1870" tells you that it illustrates the ups and downs of business from just before the Civil War to immediately after it. Note that the graph shows a period of general expansion, or business growth, from 1840 to 1857. What events helped spur this growth? What happened in 1857 to slow the growth? The Civil War strongly affected American business. Secession caused a recession. Why would this happen? Business recovered to expand during the war as businesses began producing for the war. You can see a brief primary recession immediately after the war as war production ended. Soon however, the economy began to grow again as businesses replaced what was lost in war. What do you think the business cycle from 1870 to 1900 would show?

For independent practice, see Practicing the Strategy on page 619.

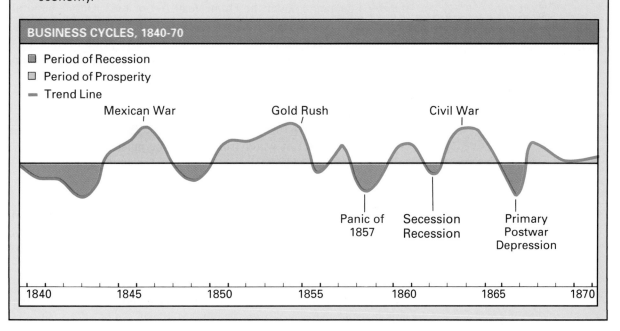

BUSINESS CYCLES, 1840-70

- Period of Recession
- Period of Prosperity
- Trend Line

Mexican War   Gold Rush   Civil War

Panic of 1857   Secession Recession   Primary Postwar Depression

1840   1845   1850   1855   1860   1865   1870

In her diary the mistress of Mulberry Plantation wrote in Sherman's wake.

❝Nothing but tall blackened chimneys to show that any man has ever trod this road before. This is Sherman's track. It is hard not to curse him. I wept incessantly at first. The roses of the garden are already hiding the ruins. My husband said Nature is a wonderful renovator. He tried to say something else and then I shut my eyes and made a vow that if we were a crushed people, crushed by weight, I would never be a slave.❞

Mary Boykin Chesnut, May 2, 1865

The Ravaged Land

Economic ruin and social chaos swept the South. Wherever armies had clashed, houses and barns were shattered or burned, crops ruined, and livestock taken or killed. After the war seed to plant new crops and horses or mules to plow the land were scarce. Even labor was scarce. A quarter of a million southern soldiers had died and many former slaves did not want to work for their former masters.

Many southern industries also were badly damaged, and loans to rebuild or restart them were unavailable. Rubble littered cities that had stood in the path of invading armies.

Southerners set about working their land as best they could. Many whites felt relieved that slavery had ended. But they wondered what lay ahead. Some feared vengeance from former slaves. Others could not adjust to dealing with a free labor force. They had always been members of a group that viewed itself as superior and that thinking continued. In the late spring of 1865, however, both groups knew that unless food crops were planted, there would be nothing to eat in the winter, and unless cash crops were raised, there would be no money to buy seed for next year's crop.

Sharecropping

Nearly all the slaves had been farm workers and nearly all continued to work on the land after they became free. The efforts of Radicals like Thaddeus Stevens to carve up the large plantations and give each black family "forty acres and a mule" never attracted much support among northern whites. In theory, a freedman could get a 160-acre farm (64 hectares) under the Homestead Act of 1862. Only a handful of blacks were able to do so. They lacked the tools, seed money, and the means of getting to the distant frontier. The price of land was only a small part of the cost of starting a farm. As one congressman reported from Georgia in 1866:

❝ The blacks own absolutely nothing but their bodies; their former masters own everything, . . . If a black man draws even a bucket of water from a well, he must first get permission of a white man. . . . If he asks for work to earn his living, he must ask it of a white man.❞

Most of the former slaves therefore continued to cultivate land owned by whites. At first they worked for cash wages. But the South was poor after the war. Most landowners were very short of cash. So a new system called **sharecropping** was worked out.

Sharecropping means sharing the crop. Under this system the landowner provided the laborers with houses, tools, seeds, and other supplies. The sharecroppers provided the skill and muscle needed to

grow the crops. When the harvest was gathered, it was shared, half to two thirds for the landowner, the rest for the sharecropper.

This system allowed black workers to be free of the close daily control they had endured under slavery. Each black family had its own cabin and tilled its own land as a separate unit. Sharecroppers could at least hope that by working hard and saving they might someday have enough money to buy a farm of their own. Then they would be truly free. For this reason most blacks much preferred sharecropping to working for wages.

A long time passed before many sharecroppers owned their farms. Partly this was because most whites tried to keep blacks from obtaining land of their own. The landowners wanted to make sure they had enough workers for their own farms. And they wanted to keep all the blacks dependent upon them.

Some landowners cheated the sharecroppers when the harvest was divided. Local storekeepers also cheated them. Sharecroppers had to buy supplies on credit. They ran up bills at the general store during the growing season. When the crop was sold in the autumn, they used the money to pay off this debt. Frequently the merchant added items to the bill the farmers had never purchased. Blacks who objected were threatened with the loss of credit in the future, or with violence. During Reconstruction, with blacks on local

Winslow Homer painted the cotton pickers whose toils sometimes stained the cotton red with blood. In the engraving below a slave is shown with his sack of cotton. Has freedom made this work easier?

Freedom After Slavery 607

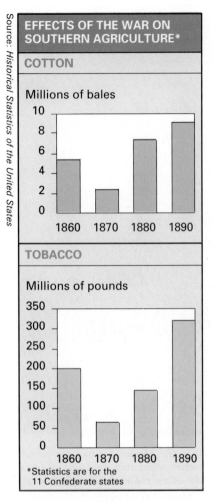

EFFECTS OF THE WAR ON SOUTHERN AGRICULTURE*

COTTON

Millions of bales

TOBACCO

Millions of pounds

*Statistics are for the 11 Confederate states

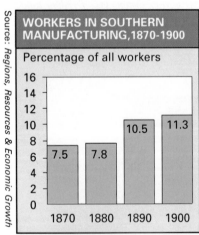

WORKERS IN SOUTHERN MANUFACTURING, 1870-1900

Percentage of all workers

7.5   7.8   10.5   11.3

1870   1880   1890   1900

LEARNING FROM GRAPHS. *What generalization about the southern economy can you draw from these graphs?*

juries, there was some hope for justice. After the end of Reconstruction, with blacks once again barred from juries, the local courts were not likely to give justice to blacks who sued any white person.

Even when dealing with honest landowners and merchants, it was hard to make much more than a bare living as a sharecropper. Prices were high in the stores because the storekeepers also had to borrow to get the goods they sold. They paid high interest rates because money was so scarce in the South. They had to charge high prices to cover that expense. So it was lack of money more than cheating by whites or racial prejudice that kept black sharecroppers from getting farms of their own. White sharecroppers hardly fared better.

The whole system seemed strangely similar to slavery. Blacks were again tied to the land they worked, with little hope of leaving. It gave them, however, the power to control their own day-to-day activities. No longer must they work in gangs, carrying out the orders of a master or overseer. Some sharecroppers, by a combination of good luck and hard work, earned enough to buy land and become truly independent farmers.

The Crop-Lien System

The shortage of money made everyone dependent on bankers and other people with funds to invest. These investors wanted to be sure that the loans they made in the spring were repaid in the fall after the crops had been harvested. They demanded that the landowners pledge the future crop as security for the loan. This meant that they had a claim on the crop, called a **lien,** before it was even planted. If the borrower failed to pay when the loan fell due, the lender could take possession of the crop.

This **crop-lien system** was fair enough on the surface. However, it had an unfortunate side effect. The lenders insisted that the borrowers grow one of the South's major cash crops, such as cotton or tobacco. These were products for which there was a **world market.** They could be converted into cash anywhere and at any time. If the price was low, they could be safely stored until market conditions improved.

The landowners and sharecroppers of the South would have been better off if they could have grown many different things—vegetables and fruits as well as cotton and the other cash crops. By concentrating on one crop, they exhausted the fertility of the soil more rapidly than if they had grown a variety of crops or had alternated crops from year to year. In addition, if they had a larger-than-normal harvest, the price of the cash crop fell steeply because supply was greater than demand.

Everyone was caught up in the system. The bankers put pressure

Brown Brothers

on the landowners and storekeepers. They, in turn, forced the sharecroppers to plant what the bankers wanted. The tendency is to blame the bankers. The charge is that they were greedy and shortsighted. But the bankers really had little choice. It would have been extremely risky, for example, to lend a farmer money to grow tomatoes, for they had to be sold locally when they were ripe or they would rot and become worthless within a few days.

So most southern black people stayed poor. The South itself stayed poor. It took about 20 years for the region to get production back to where it had been when the Civil War broke out. As we shall see, during those years the rest of the country was increasing its output at a rapid rate.

Yet for black southerners the Reconstruction era was a time of genuine progress. Any change from slavery had to be an improvement. They had power over many aspects of their life for the first time. Gradually their standard of living improved. They had more to eat, better clothes, and more comfortable houses. When they supplied these things for themselves by their own labor, they were better off than when they got only what their owners chose to give them. ▭

Sharecroppers stand in front of their cabin, the cotton growing right up to the back porch. What do you suppose the man in the buggy has come for?

Return to the Preview & Review on page 601.

Freedom After Slavery   609

4. TROOPS LEAVE THE SOUTH

Use these questions to guide your reading. Answer the questions after completing Section 4.
Understanding Issues, Events, & Ideas. Describe how white southerners resisted Reconstruction, using the following words: Ku Klux Klan, Amnesty Act of 1872, Compromise of 1877.

1. Why was the outcome of the 1876 presidential election in doubt? How was the president finally selected?
2. Why did another Civil War threaten the nation in 1877?
3. What were the terms of the Compromise of 1877?
Thinking Critically. 1. You are a black living in the South. Write a letter to the editor of your local newspaper, explaining why you have decided not to vote in the presidential election of 1876. **2.** Write a magazine article describing the events that led to the Compromise of 1877.

Resistance to Reconstruction

It is safe to say that the great majority of white southerners strongly resisted the changes forced upon them during Reconstruction, sometimes openly, sometimes in the dead of night. The Black Codes were one attempt to keep blacks in a lowly status. In 1866 the whites also began to form secret organizations to hold blacks down by terror.

The most important of these organizations was the **Ku Klux Klan.** Klan members were determined to keep blacks from voting and thus influencing political events. Klansmen tried to frighten blacks by galloping through the night dressed in white robes, hoods, and masks. They claimed to be the ghosts of Confederate soldiers. They burned crosses on the hillsides, a hint of the terrible tortures that awaited blacks who tried to vote. When blacks refused to be frightened, the Klan often carried out its threats. Hundreds of black southerners were beaten, other hundreds actually murdered by the Klan.

The federal government managed to check the Klan by about 1871. It sent troops to areas where violence had broken out. Many Klan leaders were arrested. Gradually, more white southerners joined in efforts to keep blacks from voting. They joined the Democratic

Blacks attempting to vote are halted by the sharp-featured election judge who keeps his gun at the ready. The man at the door holds a "Republican ticket," but it will not be used in this election. The Republican ticket won in no southern elections. What chance of voting do you think the freedman believed he had?

New York Public Library Picture Collection

party. In 1874 groups in Mississippi began an organized effort, its aim printed prominently in several newspapers, "Carry the election peacefully if we can, forcibly if we must." They formed military companies and marched about in broad daylight. They gave merciless beatings to those blacks they found "uppity" or rebellious. Many blacks fought back against this kind of violence. In some areas small-scale but bloody battles broke out between armed bands of whites and blacks.

The Election of 1876

Since blacks were in the minority in the South and had fewer weapons than whites, they lost most battles when they clashed. Northern whites, meanwhile, began to lose interest in controlling the South by means of the army. They became satisfied that southern whites did not actually intend to reenslave blacks. They began to put the South's problems out of their minds. Gradually the number of troops stationed in the southern states was reduced. Many blacks then chose not to risk voting and exercising their other rights.

In state after state during the 1870s Conservative parties, made up entirely of whites, took over the government from the Republicans. These parties resisted the changes proposed for the South. Many of the members of the parties were former Confederate officials and soldiers. They had been barred from holding office by Section 3 of the Fourteenth Amendment, but the **Amnesty Act of 1872** ended the disability for all but the highest Confederate officials. Former Confederates flocked to the Conservative parties and ran in almost every southern election.

The Republican party was further hurt by the failure of President Grant to live up to expectations as president. The military hero was honest and a true democrat, but he was a poor chief executive. He became the innocent victim of scandals and corruption in his administration. Although he was reelected in 1872 by 800,000 votes more than the Democratic party nominee, Horace Greeley, his party grew weaker. By 1876 the Republicans controlled only three southern states—Louisiana, Florida, and South Carolina. They rejoined their former Confederate partners after the election of 1876. In South Carolina, the last state to be reclaimed politically, the Red Shirts, a band patterned after similar groups in Mississippi, secured the election of a former planter and Confederate general, Wade Hampton.

The presidential election of 1876 pitted Governor Samuel J. Tilden of New York, the Democrat, against Governor Rutherford B. Hayes of Ohio, the Republican. Tilden won in his home state, New York, in neighboring New Jersey and Connecticut, in Indiana, and in all the southern states. This gave him a substantial majority of the electoral vote, 203 to 165. In the popular vote he won by 250,000 votes—4.28 million to 4.03 million.

Switched votes by three southern states kept the story of America from telling of the presidency of Samuel J. Tilden. Tilden won the election but it was Rutherford B. Hayes who became president in 1877. Tilden is above, Hayes below.

Troops Leave the South   611

But when Republican leaders added up the votes on election night, they discovered that switching the electoral votes of the three southern states they still controlled would give the majority to Hayes, 185 to 184! Republican officials in these three states swiftly threw out enough Democratic ballots to change the result. Then they forwarded to Washington "official" results showing Hayes the winner.

Of course the Democrats protested loudly. They filed another set of "official" results that showed Tilden the winner in the three disputed states.

For weeks no one knew who the next president would be. The Constitution did not provide a clear method for solving the problem. According to the Constitution the votes had to be counted. But by whom? Certainly not the Republican-controlled Senate or the Democratic-controlled House of Representatives. Instead, Congress appointed a special commission to settle the issue. It was made up of ten members of Congress—five Democrats and five Republicans, and five members of the Supreme Court. The Supreme Court justices were supposed to be nonpolitical, but three were Republicans, the other two Democrats.

The commission held an investigation and heard evidence from both sides. It soon became clear that both parties had behaved in a completely corrupt manner in the three states in dispute. More Democrats had almost certainly voted than Republicans. But large numbers of blacks who would surely have voted Republican had been kept away from the polls by force and threats.

The Compromise of 1877

When the commissioners finally voted, they split 8 to 7 on each of the disputed states. Every Republican voted for Hayes, every Democrat for Tilden. Obviously they had not paid much attention to the evidence. The Democrats felt cheated. Many were ready to fight to make Tilden president. For a time another Civil War seemed about to break out.

In this crisis the leaders of the two parties worked out what is known as the **Compromise of 1877.** Hayes agreed to recall all the remaining federal troops stationed in the South. He promised to appoint a conservative southerner to his Cabinet. He said also that he supported a proposal sponsored by southerners to build a railroad from Texas to southern California.

In exchange the Democrats promised to guarantee blacks their own rights and not to use their power in the southern states to prevent blacks from voting. After all these details had been settled in a series of informal, behind-the-scenes discussions, the Democrats agreed to go along with the electoral commission's decision. On March 4, 1877, Hayes was inaugurated as president in an orderly, entirely peaceful ceremony. 🖻

Return to the Preview & Review on page 610.

5. THE LONG NIGHT BEGINS

Second-Class Citizens

After the Compromise of 1877 the white citizens of the North turned their backs on the black citizens of the South. Gradually the southern states broke their promise to treat blacks fairly. Step by step they deprived them of the right to vote and reduced them to second-class citizens. Thus began the **Long Night** of racial segregation.

The first step was to pass **poll tax** laws. A poll tax is a charge made for voting. It can be avoided simply by not going to the polls. For poor people, paying a poll tax was a great sacrifice. Many preferred to spend what little money they had in other ways. In most southern states the tax *accumulated* when not paid. That is, a person who skipped one election would have to pay double if he wished to vote at the next year's local election. A person who voted only in presidential elections would pay four times the regular tax.

Another technique for keeping blacks from the polls was to require a **literacy test** for voting. People who could not read could not vote. And those blacks who could read were usually asked to read a difficult, technical legal passage of some kind. Poll taxes and literacy tests did not violate the Fifteenth Amendment because they were not directly based on "race, color, or previous condition of servitude."

These measures prevented many poor white people from voting too. But when they wanted to, the authorities could find ways of allowing whites to vote anyway. One method was to permit people who could not read to vote if they could "understand" and explain a passage that an election official read to them. A white person might be asked to explain a clause in the state constitution that said: "The term of the governor shall be four years." A black person who sought to qualify would then be asked to explain a more complicated passage. And whatever the black said, he would be told his explanation was incorrect and that he had not "understood."

Another technique was the so-called **grandfather clause.** Grandfather clauses provided that literacy tests and poll taxes did not apply to persons who had been able to vote before 1867, or to their children and later descendants. Of course most whites came under this heading, but no blacks did at all. By about 1900 only a handful of black citizens were voting in the southern states. Not until 1915, in *Guinn v. U.S.*, did the Supreme Court rule that grandfather clauses were unconstitutional.

The Court and Segregation

When blacks ceased to have an influence on elections, elected officials stopped paying much attention to their needs and desires. The segregation of blacks and whites in public places became widespread.

Preview & Review

Use these questions to guide your reading. Answer the questions after completing Section 5.
Understanding Issues, Events, & Ideas. Using the following words, discuss the segregation of black Americans: Long Night, poll tax, literacy test, grandfather clause, Civil Rights Act of 1875, Jim Crow law, Civil Rights Cases, *Plessy v. Ferguson,* separate but equal, buffalo soldiers, Tuskegee Institute, Atlanta Compromise, accommodation.
1. Why did southern whites want to keep blacks from voting?
2. What was the result of the Civil Rights Cases decided by the Supreme Court in 1883?
3. What was the importance of the decision in *Plessy v. Ferguson?*
4. What happened to blacks in the 1890s who protested against injustice?
Thinking Critically. 1. You have just read of the Court's ruling on *Plessy v. Ferguson.* Write a letter to your state representative, protesting the ruling. 2. Imagine that you are a black person in the South in 1895. Do you agree or disagree with Booker T. Washington's Atlanta Compromise? Why or why not?

Frederick Douglass had this to say about the plight of blacks in the South after the Civil War.

" No man can be truly free whose liberty is dependent upon the thought, feeling, and actions of others, and who has himself no means in his hands for guarding, protecting, defending, and maintaining that liberty. "
Frederick Douglass, 1882

There had always been a good deal of segregation in the North and South alike. In part it had been based on economics. Poor people could not afford to eat in the same restaurants as rich people, for example, and most blacks were poor. On the other hand, in the decades before the Civil War blacks and whites had often met together informally. This happened perhaps even more in the South than in the North.

After the destruction of the Confederacy, Congress had ruled out segregation in the South. The **Civil Rights Act of 1875** provided specifically that "citizens of every race and color" were entitled to "the full and equal enjoyment" of restaurants, hotels, trains, and all "places of public amusement."

But after 1877 whites began to ignore this law. In part they were more eager now for segregation because blacks were now unquestionably free. Separation had seemed less important to whites when blacks were clearly in lowly positions and under white "command." The typical southern white did not object to sitting next to a black on a streetcar if the black was a nursemaid caring for a white child. The same woman entering the car alone would cause the white to bristle if she tried to occupy the next seat. It became the common practice throughout the South to separate the races in schools, hospitals, orphanages, and other public and private institutions. But this practice was not the law.

That began to change in 1881, when Tennessee passed the first **Jim Crow law.** This law required blacks to ride in separate railroad cars. Florida in 1887 and Texas in 1889 passed similar laws. The name was taken from the black-faced white actors in 19th-century song and dance acts. In time Jim Crow laws extended separation of the races to all places where it had become practice—and beyond.

When blacks began to be turned away from public places like theaters in cities all over the country, some went to court to seek their constitutional rights. In one case, W. H. R. Agee protested against being denied a room in a hotel in Jefferson City, Missouri. In another, Sallie J. Robinson sued because she was forced to ride in a second-class railroad car while traveling from Tennessee to Virginia, even though she had a first-class ticket.

These and other suits, known as the **Civil Rights Cases,** were decided by the Supreme Court in 1883. The majority of the justices ruled that the Civil Rights Act was unconstitutional. It was therefore not illegal for private businesses to practice racial segregation. The guarantees of the Fourteenth Amendment were protections against actions by state governments, not by private persons.

After this, segregation became more and more the rule, especially in the South. Then, in 1896, the Supreme Court heard the case of *Plessy v. Ferguson.* Homer Adolf Plessy, a light-skinned Louisiana black man, was arrested for sitting in a railroad car reserved by Louisiana law for whites. His attorneys argued that the law under

which he was arrested was unconstitutional. Judge John H. Ferguson ruled against Plessy on the grounds that the railroad provided separate but equally good cars for blacks, as required by law. The Supreme Court upheld this reasoning.

The Court's decision permitted other "separate but equal" facilities. Thus segregation was legal, even in public schools, provided the schools for black children were equal to those for whites. The majority ruling stated in part:

> We consider the underlying fallacy [faulty reasoning] of the plaintiff's argument to consist in the assumption that the enforced separation of the two races stamps the colored race with a badge of inferiority. If this be so, it is not by reason of anything found in the act, but solely because the colored race chooses to put that construction upon it. . . . The argument also assumes that social prejudices may be overcome by legislation, and that equal rights cannot be secured to the negro except by an enforced commingling [mixing] of the two races. We cannot accept this proposition. . . . If the civil and political rights of both races be equal one cannot be inferior to the other civilly or politically. If one race is inferior to the other socially, the Constitution of the United States cannot put them upon the same plane.[1]

[1]From *Plessy v. Ferguson*, 163 U.S. 537, 1896.

"Kept In." One sorrowful little girl remains after school, perhaps until she finishes her lessons. Her loneliness is a reminder of the physical barriers of segregation. Where else besides schools was segregation practiced?

Justice John Marshall Harlan came from a family that once kept slaves in Kentucky. But he believed that segregation was in violation of the Constitution. What did he mean by "Our Constitution is color-blind"?

One justice, John Marshall Harlan, born in Kentucky, a slave state, objected to this **separate-but-equal** argument. Harlan's family had owned slaves. But the experiences of Reconstruction had caused him to change his mind about race questions. In his dissent he said:

66 The white race deems itself to be the dominant race in this country. And so it is, in prestige, in achievements, in education, in wealth and power. . . . But in view of the Constitution in the eye of the law, there is in this country no superior, dominant, ruling class of citizens. There is no caste here. Our Constitution is color-blind, and neither knows nor tolerates classes among citizens. In respect of civil rights, all citizens are equal before the law. The humblest is the peer of the most powerful. The law regards man as man, and takes no account of his surroundings or of his color when his civil rights as guaranteed by the supreme law of the land are involved.[1] 99

But in 1896 Harlan's was the minority view both of the Court and among white citizens in all parts of the country.

Efforts to prevent segregation practically ended as a result of these court decisions. Blacks could not stay at hotels used by white travelers. Theaters herded them into separate sections, usually high in the balcony. Blacks had to ride in the rear sections of streetcars. They could not enter "white" parks or swim at "white" public beaches. Even cemeteries were segregated.

The schools, parks, and other facilities open to blacks were almost never as good as those open to whites. The separate-but-equal rule was ignored everywhere. In 1876 South Carolina spent the same amount on the education of each child, black or white. By 1895, when school segregation was complete in South Carolina, the state was spending three times more on each white child.

The Atlanta Compromise

It is easy to imagine how depressed and angry American blacks must have been in the 1890s. Segregation was only the visible surface of the way they were mistreated. In almost any conflict between a black person and a white, the white had every advantage. Blacks were punished more severely when they were convicted of crimes. Many kinds of jobs were entirely closed to blacks. When they did the same work as whites, they received lower pay. If they refused to act humbly and politely to whites, they were insulted or even beaten. If they wanted to adjust to white ideas of how they ought to act, they had to behave like children or clowns.

African Americans even faced discrimination in the armed

[1]From the Dissent of Mr. Justice John Marshall Harlan, *Plessy v. Ferguson,* 163 U.S. 537, 1896.

forces. In 1866, Congress approved several black regiments. Between 1869 and 1890, these regiments, notably the Ninth and Tenth Cavalries, were assigned to fight Indians and protect settlers in the West. Although they too risked their lives, the black soldiers, nicknamed **"buffalo soldiers"** by the Indians, were strictly segregated. Often, if any buffalo soldiers were granted leave to visit a town, local settlers would refuse to serve them in stores, restaurants, or hotels.

Some blacks protested violently against all this injustice. Those who did were dealt with still more violently by the white majority. Lynchings, the killing without trial of supposed criminals by mobs, became ever more frequent.

Faced with these handicaps, many black Americans adopted the strategy proposed by Booker T. Washington, the founder of a trade school for blacks in Alabama, **Tuskegee Institute.** Washington had been born a slave. He obtained an education by working as a janitor at the school he attended. His experiences convinced him that a person of lowly origins could rise in the world by a combination of hard work and a willingness to go along with the wishes and prejudices of powerful people. He had seen firsthand what happened to black people, especially in the South, who openly fought the prejudices of whites.

Washington was expert at obtaining the support of well-to-do whites who wanted to help blacks without actually treating them as equals. His school prospered. He was already well known when, in a speech at Atlanta, Georgia, in 1895, he proposed what became known as the **Atlanta Compromise.**

Blacks should accept the separate-but-equal principle, Washington said. They should learn skilled trades so that they could earn more money and thus improve their lives. And there was nothing shameful about working with one's hands. "There is as much dignity in tilling a field," he said, "as in writing a poem." Furthermore, it would be "the extremest folly" for blacks to demand truly equal treatment from whites. The way to rise in the world was to accept the system and try to get ahead with it.

Washington asked whites only to be fair. Help blacks who went along with segregation, he argued, by making sure that what was separate was really equal.

Most important white southern leaders claimed to be delighted with the Atlanta Compromise. In fact they made very little effort to change the attitude and behavior of average white citizens.

Today Washington seems to have buckled under with the Atlanta Compromise. Yet the failure of Reconstruction had awakened old fears and suspicions about blacks. Once again blacks had to move with caution. Historical imagination helps us see the Atlanta Compromise as a desperate effort to hold on to a few gains. For black people who had to live through those postwar years, going along, **accommodation,** was not cowardice but survival. 🖎

Culver Pictures

Booker T. Washington founded Tuskegee Institute. What reason did he give for starting his famous school?

This classroom scene at Tuskegee Institute was photographed in about 1900. What forms of segregation does this classroom reveal?

Brown Brothers

Return to the Preview & Review on page 613.

The Long Night Begins 617

CHAPTER 17 REVIEW

Reconstruction

1865	THE AFTERMATH OF WAR	1875

1865
Lee surrenders to Grant
★
Lincoln assassinated
★
Reconstruction begins
★
Thirteenth Amendment
1866
Civil Rights Act

1867
Reconstruction Act passed
1868
Johnson impeached and acquitted
★
Fourteenth Amendment
★
Grant elected president

1870
Fifteenth Amendment ratified

1875
Civil Rights Act of 1875
1876
Presidential election disputed

1877
House elects Hayes
★
Compromise of 1877 ends Reconstruction
★
Long Night begins

Chapter Summary
Read the statements below. Choose one, and write a paragraph explaining its importance.
1. Andrew Johnson succeeded to office after the assassination of Lincoln but had trouble working with Congress, which impeached him.
2. Moderate congressmen wanted quick Reconstruction, while Radicals were less forgiving.
3. The Thirteenth Amendment abolished slavery.
4. Congress established the Freedman's Bureau to help newly freed slaves with schools, food, and medical needs.
5. The Fourteenth Amendment guaranteed equal protection of the laws to all Americans. The Fifteenth Amendment made it illegal to deny the right to vote based on race, color, or previous condition of servitude.
6. Organizations such as the Ku Klux Klan were formed to keep blacks in check.
7. The last federal troops were removed from the South under the Compromise of 1877, which made Hayes president.
8. White southerners used many methods to keep blacks as second-class citizens.

Reviewing Chronological Order
Number your paper 1-5. Then study the time line above and place the following events in the order in which they happened by writing the first next to 1, the second next to 2, and so on.
1. Reconstruction Act passed
2. *Plessy v. Ferguson*
3. Grant elected president
4. Atlanta Compromise proposed
5. Lincoln assassinated

Understanding Main Ideas
1. How did the three Civil War Amendments attack the Black Codes?
2. What were the provisions of the Reconstruction Act of 1867? Why did President Johnson veto it? How did Congress react to his veto?
3. How did the election of 1868 show Republicans the importance of the black vote?
4. What were the motives of some Carpetbaggers and Scalawags in the "Black Republican" governments of the South?
5. What situation was resolved by the Compromise of 1877? What were the terms of this agreement?

Thinking Critically
1. **Analyzing.** You are the one senator whose vote is needed to obtain the conviction of President Andrew Johnson on impeachment charges. Why would you vote against removing him from office?
2. **Determining Cause and Effect.** If you were a former slave living in the South in 1870, how would freedom change your life if you were a 58-year-old man? A 22-year-old woman? A 6-year-old boy?
3. **Interpreting.** Study the Thirteenth, Fourteenth, and Fifteenth Amendments in the Reference Section. Then rewrite the amendments in your own words.

Writing About History: Persuasive
You are a newspaper reporter in Washington D.C. Write an editorial on the impeachment trial of Johnson. Your editorial should include both a description of the trial and the reaction of participants. Conclude your editorial by trying to persuade your readers to support or oppose conviction. Use the information in Chapter 1 and in reference books to prepare your report.

The Long Night		
1885		1895

1883
Civil Rights Cases decided

1895
Atlanta Compromise proposed

1896
Plessy v. Ferguson

Practicing the Strategy

Review the strategy on page 605.

Interpreting a Graph of Business Cycles. Study the two charts on page 608, then answer the following questions.

1. What kinds of agriculture are represented in the top chart?
2. What event occurred between 1860 and 1870 that badly damaged the South's agricultural production?
3. How many years passed before southern agricultural production recovered and surpassed the pre-war levels?
4. In the bottom chart there is a sudden jump in the percent of southern workers in manufacturing between 1880 and 1890. What does this suggest about the nature of manufacturing in the South during that time?

Using Primary Sources

For many years after the Civil War Frederick Douglass remained a leading African American spokesman. He continued to encourage blacks to struggle, now against the effects of Reconstruction and the Long Night. In this excerpt from John W. Blasingame's *Frederick Douglass: The Clarion Voice*, Douglass explained why active struggle was necessary. As you read the excerpt, imagine the conditions blacks were struggling against. Then answer the questions that follow it.

> *The whole history of the progress of human liberty shows that all concessions yet made to her august [mighty] claims have been born of earnest struggle. . . . If there is no struggle, there is no progress. Those who profess to favor freedom, and yet deprecate [say bad things about] agitation, are men who want crops without plowing up the ground, they want rain without thunder and lightning. They want the ocean without the awful roar of its many waters.*

1. According to the excerpt, what had caused all progress in human liberty?

2. Do you agree that "If there is no struggle, there is no progress"? Use examples to support your point of view.
3. If you were a government leader during Reconstruction, what plan might you have suggested to help freed slaves begin a new life? Would your plan have been difficult to establish? Why or why not?

Linking History & Geography

Reconstruction meant more than just rebuilding southern governments. It also meant reconstructing land devastated by four years of war. To understand why this aspect of Reconstruction was so important to the South's recovery, answer the following questions.

1. A Virginia farmer in the Shenandoah Valley said soon after the war: "We had no cattle, hogs, sheep, or horses or anything else. The fences were all gone. . . . The barns were all burned; chimneys standing without houses; and houses standing without roofs or doors or windows." What are three things this farmer will have to do to make the farm productive again?
2. Destruction of southern railroads had been a prime Union military objective during the war. How had this isolated the South? What problems would such isolation cause?

Enriching the Study of History

1. **Individual Project**. Imagine you are traveling through the South in 1867. Use your historical imagination to write five diary entries describing Reconstruction.
2. **Cooperative Project**. Members of your group will present a debate of the Atlanta Compromise. Half the group will argue for following Washington's suggestions. The other half will argue against the compromise. After you present your debate, the class will act as a convention and vote on the issue.

Chapter 17 Review   619

UNIT FIVE REVIEW

Summing Up and Predicting
Read the summary of the main ideas in Unit Five below. Choose one statement, then write a paragraph predicting its outcome or future consequence.
1. The failure of the Missouri Compromise and the passage of the Kansas-Nebraska Bill caused even more sectional conflicts over slavery.
2. The election of Abraham Lincoln in 1860 led several southern states to secede. These states formed the Confederate States of America.
3. The firing on Fort Sumter started the Civil War.
4. The Confederacy won most of the early battles, but the Union advantage of sheer numbers and a successful strategy eventually led to victory.
5. Lincoln's plans for a moderate Reconstruction were ended by assassination and Johnson's difficulties with Congress.
6. Although the Civil War Amendments—the Thirteenth, Fourteenth, and Fifteenth—guaranteed civil rights to blacks, white southerners found ways to continue to deny those rights.
7. The Compromise of 1877 ended Reconstruction and several key court decisions led to the start of the Long Night of racial segregation.

Connecting Ideas
1. *Uncle Tom's Cabin* had a strong impact on American attitudes toward slavery and led, in part, to the Civil War. What other book, film, or television program has affected your attitude toward war? How has it affected you?
2. The author says, "When the Civil War was ended and the slaves were set free, the problem of racial prejudice in the United States was not solved." Do you think racial discrimination is still a problem in America? Explain.
3. In 1867 Congress ordered a military occupation of the south. Almost 100 years later, President Eisenhower ordered federal troops to Little Rock, Arkansas, to enforce a Supreme Court ruling on integration. Cite the articles, sections, and paragraphs of the Constitution that give Congress and the president this power.

Practicing Critical Thinking
1. **Evaluating.** Shortly after the news of Lincoln's election, southern states began seceding. If you had been a southerner at that time, would you have been for or against secession? Why?
2. **Synthesizing.** You are Robert E. Lee on April 8, 1865. Your last hope of victory has been dashed. Compose a letter to Jefferson Davis, explaining your decision to surrender.
3. **Analyzing.** In Lincoln's second inaugural address, he called for Americans to act "with malice toward none, with charity for all." How do you think the Reconstruction period would have been different if Lincoln had not been assassinated? Explain.

Exploring History Together
1. Your group will make a diorama or model of a Civil War battlefield. Consult reference books to be sure that your details are accurate. Describe the battle in class, using chess pieces or toy soldiers to show troop movements.
2. Your group will prepare an illustrated chart to show the seesaw struggle for guaranteed rights for blacks during and just after Reconstruction. Include the Black Codes, the Civil Rights Act, the Civil War Amendments, the Long Night, the Civil Rights Act of 1875, the Supreme Court rulings on the Civil Rights Cases and *Plessy v. Ferguson,* and the Atlanta Compromise.
3. Working in groups, your class will research the impeachment trial of Andrew Johnson and act out scenes for and against the president. As Johnson did not appear at his trial, you may wish to set some scenes in the White House. Members of the class acting as the Senate should then decide the case.

Reading in Depth
Beatty, Patricia. *Turn Homeward, Hannalee.* New York: Morrow. Tells the fictional story of a poor southern family during the Civil War, as seen by the sensitive and brave 14-year-old heroine.

Hamilton, Virginia. *Anthony Burns: The Defeat and Triumph of a Fugitive Slave.* New York: Knopf. Tells the story of a runaway slave.

Hansen, Joyce. *Out of This Place.* Houston: Walker. Describes the challenges faced by ex-slaves during the Civil War and Reconstruction.

Kantor, MacKinlay. *Lee and Grant at Appomattox.* New York: Random House. Contains a dramatic account of the surrender.

Miers, Earl and Paul M. Angle. *Abraham Lincoln in Peace and War.* New York: American Heritage. Provides a brief glimpse of Lincoln's life.

Sandburg, Carl. *Abraham Lincoln: The Prairie Years and the War Years.* San Diego: Harcourt Brace Jovanovich. Contains the classic work on the political life of Lincoln (one of six volumes).

Museum of the City of New York

"The Battery, New York" was painted about 1855 by Samuel B. Waugh. This detail shows a shipful of immigrants arriving in New York.

The Development of Modern America

America changed dramatically during the late 1800s and early 1900s. Farmers turned the last frontier of the Great Plains into productive farmland. Inventors and entrepreneurs guided the country into a new era, one in which the United States became the world's greatest industrial nation. Millions of immigrants from around the world came to American shores.

By the early 1900s the United States was a major world power. Reformers struggled to solve problems in society. And a great depression shook the economic and social foundations of the country. But the United States used its resources to defend freedom and win two devastating world wars. It also attempted to stop the worldwide spread of communism.

Throughout the 20th century Americans built on the democratic traditions of the past. African Americans, Hispanics, women, and other groups fought for equal rights. Americans faced the 1990s with confidence that they could handle any challenges the new decade and the future might offer.

621

Use these questions to guide your reading. Answer the questions after completing Section 1.

Understanding Issues, Events, & Ideas. Use the following words to describe the sweeping changes brought about by industrialization and the growth of cities in America in the late 1800s: trust, division of labor, collective bargaining, strike, ethnic neighborhood, political machine, boss, civil service reform, National Grange, Populist party.

1. How did developments in transportation and agriculture spur America's expansion onto the Great Plains?
2. What were the first attempts at government regulation of big business? Why were they necessary?
3. How did financial and economic problems in the late 1800s contribute to the rise of third parties?

Thinking Critically. You are a striking steelworker during the Homestead strike. Use your historical imagination to describe your feelings about the replacement workers, the Pinkertons, and the company's bosses.

1. A CHANGING AMERICA

The Last Frontier

Although manifest destiny had carried settlers from sea to sea before the Civil War, one region was still unsettled. The sprawling Great Plains and the towering Rocky Mountains remained under the control of Indian groups.

The first settlers to approach the plains were accustomed to the wooded lands of the eastern United States and Europe. The virtually treeless plains seemed almost a desert. The government had set aside certain parts of this "Great American Desert" for Indians from the Cherokee, Chickasaw, and other Indian nations evicted from their lands in the 1830s. The rest of the plains belonged to nomadic groups, who constantly roamed across the broad grasslands feeding on the numberless buffalo.

After the Civil War, railroad companies laid their track through the Plains enroute to the Pacific. Miners flocked to the areas in the mountains where gold and silver were discovered.

Thousands of laborers, particularly Irish and Chinese immigrants, laid the tracks, built the bridges, and dug and blasted tunnels through the mountains. Along with the railroad crews came hunters, who in a few short years shot thousands of buffalo, to feed the hungry workers and ship buffalo hides to eastern cities. In 1869 the first railroad, the Union Pacific, connected East and West.

The Plains Indians naturally viewed the people seizing their lands as invaders and resisted them fiercely. But by 1889 Indian resistance had been crushed. With the great buffalo herds all but wiped out and their lands taken by force or by treaty, the Plains Indians had to submit to living on reservations.

The discovery of gold in Colorado and South Dakota, silver in Nevada, and other rich strikes elsewhere caused rushes of prospectors to the West similar to the California Gold Rush of 1849. Mining camps, where life was wild and dangerous, grew up almost overnight and were abandoned just as quickly when the minerals had been extracted.

Working these strikes was different from the placer mining of California. This gold and silver was buried deep in veins of quartz rock. Huge steam-powered drills and other heavy machinery was needed to dig it out. Tunneling operations called for mining engineers. Such operations were expensive. Much money had to be invested. Mining became a big business, often controlled by banks and large corporations.

Ranching on the plains was also a big business. Millons of wild cattle grazed on the grass of Texas. When the value of beef in eastern cities rose in the 1860s, it gave anyone who could get their cattle to market a chance to get rich. Each spring cowhands rounded up herds

of wild cattle and drove them from Texas over government-owned grasslands to railroads in Kansas and Colorado. The cattle, fattened during these "long drives," were then shipped to eastern markets by rail. Many people were soon calling the western plains the "Cattle Kingdom."

But soon the open range was overcrowded. After the extremely cold winter of 1886, much of the open range had to be divided into ranches fenced with barbed wire to confine the cattle so that they could be fed hay in the winter. Barbed wire kept both the animals from roving and enabled farmers to settle much of the plains. New steel plows enabled them to cut through the tough sod.

Many of the events of 19th-century American history were celebrated by Currier & Ives engravings such as the one above. Its title is Across the Continent, *and it was done by Fanny Palmer and James M. Ives in 1868. How many aspects of frontier life can you find in the picture?*

The Rise of Industrial America

After the Civil War, a giant nationwide railroad network was developed. By 1900 it was complete. Railroads stimulated the movement of people and goods, created thousands of jobs, and caused the national economy to grow in numerous other ways. It became possible to ship bulky products cheaply over long distances and thus create a giant national market. Farmers and manufacturers could ship their products to every corner of the country swiftly.

Americans also began to develop new sources of energy after the war. The most important was oil, or petroleum. The first oil well was drilled at Titusville, Pennsylvania in 1859. To light their homes, Americans used kerosene refined from the petroleum as a substitute

An appropriate symbol for America in the 19th century is the ironworks at Pittsburgh. What can you say about the forms of transportation in this engraving? How would environmentalists today appraise this scene?

for whale oil and candles. Soon the demand for kerosene refined from petroleum soared. Later scientists discovered many other uses for petroleum products, the most important being gasoline.

Hand in hand with industrialization went advances in communication. Samuel Morse had already used electricity to invent the telegraph. In 1858 an electric cable was laid across the Atlantic, linking the United States to Europe by telegraph. In 1876 Alexander Graham Bell invented the telephone, and by 1900 more than 1.5 million telephones were in use in the United States. Thomas Alva Edison's "incandescent lamps" made it possible to light entire cities. Electric power became at least as important a source of energy for American industry as oil.

As the American economy grew, business leaders founded large corporations. Some became very rich and powerful and tried to limit competition in order to monopolize production. Several of the largest corporations were controlled by **trusts**—legal agreements designed to regulate production and eliminate competition.

Fearing that these trusts would destroy small companies, form monopolies, and raise prices, the public demanded that the federal government limit the power of trusts. In 1887 Congress established

624   EPILOGUE

the Interstate Commerce Commission, the first government agency charged with regulating industry in order to protect the public. This was the beginning of direct government control of part of the economy, in this case the railroads.

In 1890 Congress passed the Sherman Antitrust Act to protect small companies against large ones. The law stated that companies that "restrained trade" were illegal. A monopoly that used its size to undersell smaller businesses, thus forcing them to close or sell out, was obviously "restraining trade."

Industrialization also affected American workers. Machines simplified what each worker did by breaking down manufacturing into several small steps. But while it was efficient, this **division of labor** made many jobs boring. Each individual worker had only a small part in creating the finished product. More and more industrial jobs involved simply tending machines, and many factories were run with almost military discipline.

Some workers resisted this development by joining unions. The Knights of Labor, formed in 1869, won several important strikes against the railroads, and at the height of its strength in 1886 had 700,000 members. But that year the union was unfairly blamed for a bombing incident in Haymarket Square in Chicago and lost members rapidly.

However, several craft unions organized what became the American Federation of Labor (AFL) at this time. The AFL, led by Samuel Gompers, consisted of skilled workers, such as printers, bricklayers, and cigar makers. It sought to obtain higher wages, shorter work hours, and better working conditions by **collective bargaining** with employers and going on **strike,** or stopping work, when the employers rejected their demands.

The United States was still a rural society; most Americans lived on farms or in villages and towns. But as industry expanded, an urban, or city-dwelling, society developed. The new factories attracted tens of thousands of people from American farms and foreign countries. Agricultural machinery had reduced the need for farm labor and many farmers were attracted by new opportunities in the cities and by the excitement of city life. So were foreigners of all kinds.

America had always been a magnet for the oppressed and the needy. It offered them the promise of freedom and especially the opportunity to improve their standard of living. A young Jewish woman from Russia wrote:

66 So at last I was going to America! Really, really going, at last! The boundaries burst! The arch of heaven soared. A million suns shone out of every star. The winds rushed in from outer space, roaring in my ear, 'America! America!'[1] 99

[1] From *The Promised Land* by Mary Antin

The colossal Statue of Liberty raises the torch of freedom in New York Harbor. It was first known as "Liberty Enlightening the World." Here we see the dedication of the magnificent gift from France. The sculptor, F. A. Bartholdi, wished to pay tribute to the alliance of France with the American colonies during the Revolution. What does the statue symbolize today?

Between 1885 and 1920 more than 20 million immigrants entered the United States. Before 1880 most immigrants had come from western and northern Europe. Thereafter many more came from eastern and southern Europe—Poland, Russia, Italy, and Greece.

The immigrants tended to cluster together in the cities, creating **ethnic neighborhoods.** Many native-born Americans resented them and claimed the newcomers were harder to "Americanize" and physically and mentally inferior. The government restricted immigration from China and Japan, but other attempts to close the door to immigrants failed.

Immigrants found jobs in small shops and dingy sweatshops. They lived in dark, unsanitary apartment buildings called tenements. Social workers, most of them young women college graduates, established settlement houses and other agencies to help educate and care for immigrants and the poor.

National Politics and Culture, 1867–1896

Changes caused by the Civil War and the rapid growth of the economy had important effects on how Americans governed themselves. Voters tended to divide along geographic lines—southerners being Democrats, northerners Republicans—rather than on economic issues. By and large, the political parties failed to solve the important economic problems facing the country.

However, in many northern cities, **political machines,** most of them Democratic, recruited recent immigrants to vote for their candidates. In return political leaders, called **bosses,** supplied jobs, social services, and even small sums of money to the poor, most of whom were recent immigrants. Advances were eventually made, however, in **civil service reform.** Instead of giving government jobs to supporters of the winning political party, applicants had to pass tests. Thereafter employees would be judged on merit and discharged only if they failed to perform their duties properly.

The great changes of the postwar years gave rise to the Age of Realism in American literature and art. Mark Twain, Stephen Crane, Frank Norris, and others wrote of life in the cities and of the problems facing urban, industrialized society. Thomas Eakins, Winslow Homer, James McNeill Whistler, Mary Cassatt, and other artists painted people in everyday settings: a doctor operating on a patient, a fisherman in a storm, a mother caring for a small child.

Because the Democrats and Republicans failed to find solutions for their economic problems, western and southern farmers formed organizations, first the **National Grange** and then the Farmers Alliance. They succeeded in getting some state laws passed regulating the storage of farm products and railroad freight rates. In the 1890s they formed the People's party, or **Populist party,** which demanded reform of the banking system and the free coinage of silver to inflate the money supply in order to raise the prices of farm products.

The most severe depression in the nation's history to that time struck in 1893. Unemployment soared, businesses went bankrupt. Farmers blamed the depression on the government's refusal to put more money into circulation and its failure to regulate business.

The major campaign issue of the election of 1896 was the free coinage of silver, the minting of unlimited supplies of silver into coins. Farmers and debtors favored free coinage, because it would put more money into circulation and cause prices to rise. Business owners and many other people opposed it because it would make the money they already had less valuable. The Democrats nominated William Jennings Bryan, who favored free silver, for president. The Republicans chose William McKinley, who opposed it. He backed money based on gold, which was much rarer and more valuable than silver. The gold standard, he claimed, would guarantee that the country would have "sound money."

The Granger Collection

Free silverites have unhitched their wagon from the Democratic donkey as they roll out of control. This is the view of C. J. Taylor, who made this lithograph in 1896. Bryan has his arms stubbornly folded while Governor Altgeld of Illinois waves a firebrand. Explain why the red banner says "Repudiation."

Return to the Preview & Review on page 622.

Bryan was a wonderful orator and a tireless campaigner. He made speeches all over the country. Mark Hanna, an Ohio businessman, organized McKinley's campaign. He spent enormous amounts of money and used it to publish millions of political pamphlets and employ a small army of speakers.

McKinley won the election, and some historians see the election as symbolizing the modern industrial age. McKinley and the Republicans represented the new power in America—big business and most industrial workers had backed McKinley because he favored high tariffs on foreign manufactured goods, which would protect the wage levels of American workers.

2. AN EXPANDING AMERICA

America in World Affairs, 1865–1912

The Civil War reinforced fears that the European powers would try to take advantage of the United States while engaged in the conflict. In a direct challenge to the Monroe Doctrine, France sent an army into Mexico. But after the war the Mexican people overthrew the French ruler and regained their independence.

Most Americans wanted trade but no political entanglements in European affairs. They knew no European nation was likely to attack them and were happy to isolate themselves from the continent.

Toward the rest of the world, however, Americans were not isolationists. In the spirit of manifest destiny, many believed that all of North and South America—and even the islands of the Pacific—would eventually fall under American influence. The United States was not alone in seeking to control other countries or regions. England, France, and other European nations practiced what was called **imperialism,** a policy of developing colonies or spheres of influence, in Africa and Asia.

The American drive to expand outside the continental United States can be traced back to 1853 when American warships sailed into Tokyo harbor in Japan. Perhaps frightened by the show of naval power, the Japanese agreed to a treaty of friendship with the United States. Next in 1867 the United States purchased Alaska from Russia and occupied the Midway Islands in the Pacific, northwest of Hawaii.

Use these questions to guide your reading. Answer the questions after completing Section 2.
Understanding Issues, Events, & Ideas.

1. Use the following words to describe American expansionism in the late 1800s: imperialism, sphere of influence, dollar diplomacy.

2. Use the following words to discuss the spirit of the progressive: Social Gospel, muckrakers, municipal socialism, conservation.

1. How did policymakers use the Monroe Doctrine to extend American influence in the Western Hemisphere?

2. What role did writers and journalists play in the Progressive Movement?

Thinking Critically. 1. On what basis did some Americans oppose American expansion and imperialism? 2. Progressive muckrakers exposed serious problems in American industry and society, but information—even shocking facts—was not enough to bring about changes. What else, besides informing the public, is needed to effect social change?

The British Library

This detail from a Japanese painted scroll shows one of Commodore Perry's four ships in Edo (Tokyo) Bay. His arrival by steamship in July 1853 was described by the Japanese as "four black dragons" entering their tranquil harbor. Imagine you are aboard one of the small Japanese boats, or sampans, in the foreground. What would be your impression of Perry's steamship?

Colonel Roosevelt and some of his Rough Riders posed for this picture atop San Juan Hill shortly after taking the strategic point.

In 1898 the United States also acquired the Hawaiian Islands.

Americans especially hoped that the countries of Latin America would become markets for America's manufactured goods. In 1889 the nations of North and South America met for the first time in a conference to discuss their common interests. In 1895 the United States also became involved in a boundary dispute between Venezuela and the British colony of Guiana, and forced the British to agree to arbitration. It put both Europe and Latin America on notice that it considered itself the most powerful nation in the hemisphere.

In 1898 the United States became involved in conflict between Spain and Cuba, a Spanish colony. Cuban revolutionaries started a war for independence in 1895. Spain sent its troops to put down the revolt. As tensions mounted in Cuba, President William McKinley sent a battleship, the U.S.S. *Maine,* to Havana harbor to protect Americans in Cuba. While the ship was anchored there, it was rocked by a tremendous explosion. The ship sank, and 260 sailors were killed. Many Americans called for war. When the Spanish refused to agree to free Cuba, Congress declared war on Spain.

The Spanish-American War was a total American triumph. The Philippine Islands, Cuba, and Puerto Rico were easily overwhelmed, and Spanish warships were battered by the American navy. Both Puerto Rico and the Philippines and other Pacific islands became American colonies. While Cuba was given its independence, it too became a kind of dependent, or protectorate, of the United States.

But the peace treaty bitterly divided the American people. Some liked the idea of an American colonial empire. But others thought owning colonies was a violation of democratic principles.

Elsewhere European powers were forcing the weak Chinese government to grant them **spheres of influence,** the right to trade with and develop control of particular areas of that country. American businesses wanted a share of the China market. So in 1899 Secretary of State John Hay issued his Open Door Notes, asking all nations trading with China to agree to allow traders for other countries access to their spheres of influence.

The Spanish-American War and the expansion of trade with Asia made it obvious that a canal across Central America would be valuable to the United States. During the war, it had taken the American battleship *Oregon* 68 days to reach Cuba from the West Coast sailing around South America.

The United States had been considering a canal through Central America since the 1850s. In 1901 the government made an offer to Colombia, which then contained the Isthmus of Panama within its boundaries. In 1903, when Colombia rejected the offer, the people in Panama revolted and created the Republic of Panama. The United States quickly recognized Panama and signed a treaty that granted it the right to build the canal.

On other occasions in the early 1900s, The United States sent troops into Latin American countries to maintain order. This use of troops was called "gunboat" or "big-stick" diplomacy. This use of force to maintain order in the Western Hemisphere was known as the Roosevelt Corollary to the Monroe Doctrine. The United States tried to avoid force through **dollar diplomacy,** investing in the countries of the region and providing financial aid to their governments to prevent revolutions and foreign intervention.

Reformers and the Progressive Movement

The end of the depression of the 1890s and the victory in the Spanish-American War made Americans optimistic. Many people worked to improve society—to make progress. The feeling that reforms were both necessary and desirable was shared by Republicans and Democrats. Progressivism was an *attitude* toward society and politics, not a political organization.

The progressives wanted the government to act on behalf of those who were not sharing in the nation's industrial prosperity. Urban religious leaders practiced what became known as the **Social Gospel,** saying that it was everyone's moral duty to help those who were less fortunate.

Progressives relied on newspapers and magazines to inform the people. Many were pioneer journalists who wrote hard-hitting articles that described social and economic problems and political corruption and demanded reforms. They became known as **muckrakers** because they raked up muck, or dirt, about an issue to make people aware of it.

One muckraker, Lincoln Steffens, reported on "boss-ridden" cities like St. Louis, Minneapolis, and Cincinnati. Ida Tarbell took on big business with a series of critical articles about John D. Rockefeller's Standard Oil monopoly. Upton Sinclair exposed the unsanitary conditions in meat-packing plants in the novel *The Jungle*. Frank Norris' *The Octopus* described the economic stranglehold that the big railroad corporations had on farmers. The horrors of life in the tenements of New York City were made public by Jacob Riis. He wrote:

> 66 Life in the tenements in July and August spells death to an army of little ones whom the doctor's skill is powerless to save. . . . Sleepless mothers walk the streets in the gray of the early dawn, trying to stir a cooling breeze to fan the brow of the sick baby.[1]99

Progressives also tried to make state governments more responsive to the wishes of the people. Governor Robert M. La Follette of Wisconsin was responsible for giving voters more control over how candidates for office were chosen. Other political reforms permitted

[1] From *How the Other Half Lives* by Jacob Riis

Point of View

In a major study of Jewish immigration to America in the late 1800s, the author found this account.

66Not everyone was equally poor. When an immigrant family could occupy a two- or three-room apartment without several boarders, they were considered lucky. Boarders were a natural institution, particularly in the early years when most immigrants came without their families. But even the privilege of being a boarder was not enjoyed by every greenhorn. There were various categories of boarders. A star boarder slept on a folding bed. But I knew a printer who every night unscrewed a door, put it on two chairs; he couldn't pay as much as the one who had the bed.99

From *The World of Our Fathers,* Irving Howe, 1976

Jacob Riis also documented the slums of the cities with his camera. Two of his most famous scenes are "Baxter Street Alley—Rag Picker's Row" (left) and "Street Arabs in Night Quarters, Mulberry Street" (right). Describe in your own words what you think is happening in each photograph.

the voters to propose legislation and to remove unpopular elected officials before their terms ended. Progressives also championed women's right to vote and the Seventeenth Amendment, which provided for the direct election of senators by the people, instead of by the state legislatures.

Progressives favored public ownership of gas and electric companies and streetcar lines—**municipal socialism**—to make city services and utilities cheaper and more efficient. Others urged improved health and housing laws, factory inspection, and limits on child labor and the length of the workday.

Progressives argued that large corporations had too much power over many important industries. They demanded some sort of government control. Some favored breaking up the large combinations by using the Sherman Antitrust Act. Others argued that the big corporations were efficient but should not be allowed to take advantage of consumers. President Theodore Roosevelt did not believe all large companies or trusts were bad. He established a government bureau to investigate their policies. Only if wrong business practices were not corrected should they be broken up.

Roosevelt was responsible for other reforms. At his urging Congress passed the Pure Food and Drug Act providing for federal control of the quality of most foods and drugs and for the supervision of slaughterhouses. Roosevelt also focused the public's attention on **conservation** of natural resources and protection of the environment by placing large areas of forest in national reserves.

The reform policies of Roosevelt's successor, William Howard Taft, were not as successful, and in 1912, Roosevelt decided to oppose him. When "TR" failed to win the Republican nomination, he was nominated by a new Progressive party. Its platform called for a New Nationalism, a government with power to do "whatever . . . the public welfare may require."

The Democrats nominated Governor Woodrow Wilson of New Jersey. Wilson's New Freedom opposed close government regulation of big business and special privileges to interest groups such as labor unions or farmers. Wilson intended to use antitrust laws to break up monopolies and enforce the rules of fair competition.

Wilson won the 1912 election, and both houses of Congress were also controlled by the Democrats. Wilson's industrial and banking reforms were quickly enacted. The Underwood Tariff reduced duties on many products entering the country and established an income tax, made possible by the passage of the Sixteenth Amendment. The Federal Reserve system of banks was created, supervised by the Federal Reserve Board. The Clayton Antitrust Act of 1914 held officers of large corporations personally responsible for antitrust violations and exempted trade unions from antitrust laws. Congress also created the Federal Trade Commission to investigate unfair business practices.

Progressives, however, had a number of prejudices and blind spots. Most were unsympathetic to the new immigrants from eastern Europe. Because most reformers were middle-class and white, they had little understanding of the effects of racial discrimination on black Americans. Most still viewed them as second-class citizens. Southern progressives continued to support rigid segregation.

African American leaders, such as Booker T. Washington and William E. B. Du Bois, disagreed about how to fight for equality in the Progressive Era. Washington favored accepting segregation and working for economic improvements. Du Bois urged blacks to oppose segregation and to be proud of their African origins. Together with other black leaders, he demanded equal economic and educational opportunities for African Americans, protection of the right to vote, and an end to segregation.

National Portrait Gallery

Woodrow Wilson studied law and opened a law office in Atlanta. But he soon returned to college to study history and political science. How did the subjects Wilson studied help prepare him for public office?

Even Uncle Sam seems disturbed by the horde of new arrivals—"Anarchists for Chicago" and "Socialists for New York."

In 1909 white liberals joined with Du Bois in forming the National Association for the Advancement of Colored People (NAACP). This group worked especially to bring an end to lynching, the brutal method of execution being used by southern mobs against blacks.

By 1914 most of President Wilson's goals had been achieved. Then the Great War broke out in Europe and turned the thoughts of Americans toward international problems. 🖅

Return to the Preview & Review on page 629.

America's Pacific Heritage

Since ships first sailed or land caravans carried off its treasure, westerners have been fascinated by the East. Marco Polo was bedazzled even though he came from Venice, a western jewel. The art of the Orient is the oldest in the world, but it was hidden behind the walls of Forbidden Cities. Emigrants from Asia were too poor to own eastern treasures such as we see on these pages, but traders like John Ellerton Lodge filled the holds of the ships the *Kremlin* and *Magnet* with china, silk, ivory, even fireworks that bloomed like chrysanthemums to bring Pacific culture to America.

This dragon comes from a Chinese embroidered chair of the 18th century. Eastern dragons seldom breathed fire and were seen as protectors.

Chinese porcelain has long been prized. The export ware above is an Orange platter in the "Fitzhugh" pattern.

Four children in holiday dress were photographed on the teeming streets of San Francisco's Chinatown before the earthquake of 1906.

The Development of Modern America   635

名里順陳搖馬塔回
恕人共二千四五人

紗 前

海岳 恐太怡

王孫狸桃
包童子武人持々

"Four black dragons spitting fire" is how Japanese artists described Commodore Perry's ships landing at Yokohama.

A gilded bronze Buddha from 10th-century Thailand reminds us that Buddhism has nearly 245 million followers in the East.

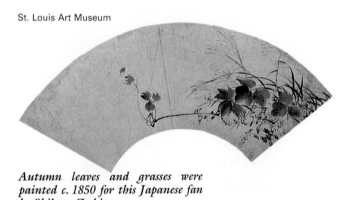

Autumn leaves and grasses were painted c. 1850 for this Japanese fan by Shibata Zeshiu.

A Filipino woman shows her considerable skill at weaving Manila hemp fibers.

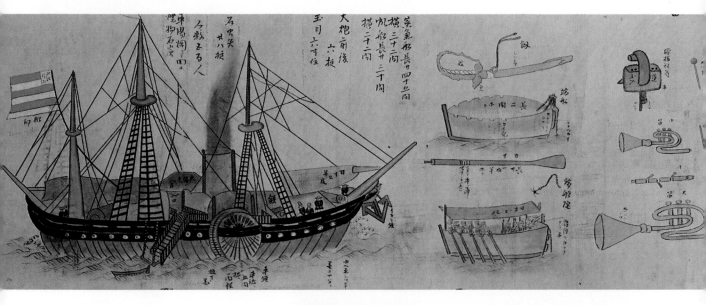

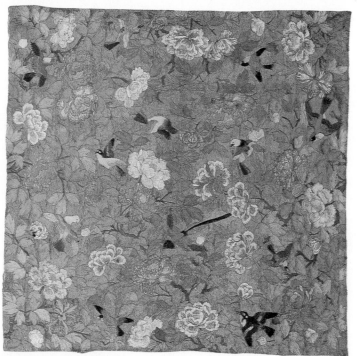

Birds and flowers are the subjects of this 18th-century silk embroidery from Korea.

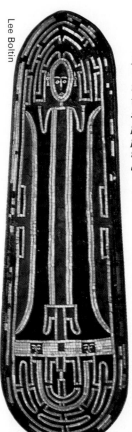

Little known before World War II, the tiny Solomon Islands were home to artisans who created the prized mother-of-pearl inlay for this mid-19th-century ceremonial shield.

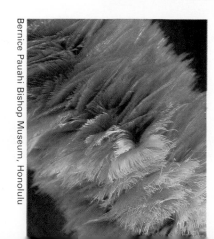

Leis made from the feathers of birds have adorned the nobility of Hawaii even before the rule of Kamehameha III or his successor, Queen Liliuokalani.

637

Isamu Noguchi, one of the greatest sculptors of the 20th century, was born in Los Angeles but taken to Japan when he was two. He called this sleek sculpture piece "California Scenario." It was completed in 1982 and covers 1.6 acres in Costa Mesa, California.

In the shadow of the nation's capitol is the east building of the National Gallery of Art. I. M. Pei, a Chinese American, designed this streamlined structure. Other works by Pei and his partners include the John F. Kennedy Library in Boston and the glass pyramid that is now the entrance to the Louvre museum in Paris.

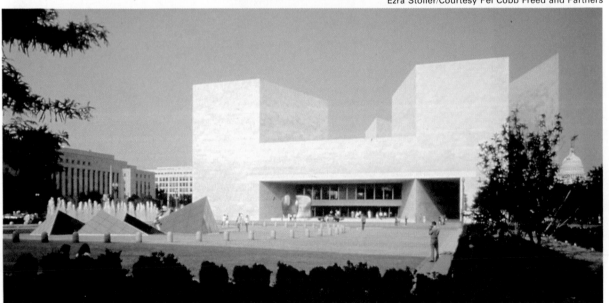

3. A TROUBLED AMERICA

The Great World War

When the Great War broke out between the Central Powers—Germany and Austria (later joined by Turkey and Bulgaria)—and the Allies—Great Britain, France, and Russia—nearly all Americans felt that their country should stay out of it. President Wilson urged treating all the warring nations with "impartiality and fairness and friendliness."

In Europe the war was fought on two fronts. On the Eastern Front Austrian and German armies battled Russians. On the Western Front in Belgium and France, French and British forces fought the Germans.

But the war on the seas was most important for the United States. Trade with both sides was very profitable for American businesses. But the powerful British navy blockaded European ports and kept Germany from obtaining supplies from America. In retaliation the Germany navy used submarines, called U-boats, to attack merchant vessels bound for Allied ports. Although both the blockade and submarine warfare damaged American shipping interests, Americans objected most to German actions. In February 1915 President Wilson warned Germany to stop torpedoing ships without warning. The sinking by German U–boats of the passenger liners the *Lusitania*

A no man's land where shelling has stripped the trees stands behind the trench that separates the French and Germans. Only a few sandbags offer protection from the exploding mortars. The title of this scene in French is "Sur les Champs de Battaille de 1918," or, in English, "On the Field of Battle, 1918."

Use these questions to guide your reading. Answer the questions after completing Section 3.
Understanding Issues, Events, & Ideas. Use the following words to describe the United States after the Great War: Harlem Renaissance, business cycle, welfare state.

1. What events brought the United States into the Great War on the side of the Allies?
2. What economic factors contributed to the Stock Market Crash of 1929?
3. How did Roosevelt's New Deal promote America's recovery from the Great Depression?

Thinking Critically. 1. Prohibition failed, resulting in widespread disregard of the law and in the organization of criminal gangs. Do you think the prohibition of certain drugs today is having a similar effect? Why, or why not? 2. The New Deal brought about drastic changes in an attempt to avert a complete breakdown of the economic system. Using your historical imagination, what do you think American leaders feared would happen without these changes?

Culver Pictures

and the *Sussex* brought Germany and the United States to the brink of war.

After Wilson was reelected in 1916, he urged both sides to settle for "peace without victory." Neither would do so. Then in 1917 Germany renewed its U-boat attacks on merchant ships. On April 2, 1917, Wilson asked Congress to declare war, not to gain territory but to make the world "safe for democracy."

The American economy was then geared up to produce the food and weapons necessary to crush the Central Powers. The antitrust laws were suspended. The railroad system was placed under government management. A War Industries Board oversaw the production and distribution of manufactured goods—and especially materials used for war. Herbert Hoover, United States Food Administrator, organized campaigns to increase production and reduce waste. Both of these efforts were quite successful.

To raise enough men for the army, Congress passed a draft law, the Selective Service Act of 1917. Women, African Americans, and

The "Big Four" of the Great War are, left to right: Vittorio Orlando of Italy, David Lloyd George of Great Britain, Georges Clemenceau of France, and Woodrow Wilson of the United States.

Hispanics took the soldiers' places in the factories, most earning higher wages than ever before.

The Great War was the most devastating the world had ever seen. Yet neither side could gain an advantage until American troops tipped the balance. In March 1918 the Germans launched an all-out attack on Paris. But with Americans at key places, the Allies pushed them back and broke through the German defenses. On November 11, 1918, Germany gave up the war and signed an armistice bringing the war to an end.

President Wilson's peace without victory objective meant that the victors would not be overly harsh toward the Central Powers. His peace proposal, the Fourteen Points, called for guaranteeing freedom of the seas, reducing restrictions on trade, and limiting the manufacture of weapons of war, and guaranteeing all people the right to form countries of their own—national self-determination. Central to Wilson's plan was the creation of a League of Nations that could settle disputes between countries and protect members against attack.

The other Allied leaders accepted many of Wilson's ideas. But they demanded that Germany be blamed for the war and made to pay reparations, that is, the cost of repairing the damage the war had caused.

The Twenties

The Versailles Treaty ended the war and created the League of Nations, but the U.S. Senate refused to ratify the treaty. In the 1920 presidential campaign the Democrats nominated James M. Cox, the Republicans Warren G. Harding. In the election, the first in which women could vote, Harding won by a huge margin. Wilson's hope that the election would show that the people favored the League of Nations was crushed. Soon after the election, the Senate simply passed a resolution declaring that the war was over.

Most Americans were disappointed that the war failed to settle the problems that had caused it. But above all they wanted peace without binding promises to other countries to maintain it. However, economic problems caused by the ending of military production threatened peace at home. Plants that had produced war supplies shut down, leaving thousands of workers unemployed. Soldiers returning to civilian life found it hard to get jobs. Political troubles added to the unrest as people worried that radicals inspired by the Russian Revolution would try to destroy the capitalist system. As a result, the United States experienced a number of paralyzing strikes. Most people blamed them on "foreigners," in part because many of the radicals were recent immigrants. President Wilson's attorney general, A. Mitchell Palmer, ordered raids on the headquarters of suspected communists. This Red Scare caused violations of the civil rights of many people, yet the fear behind it proved to be largely without basis in fact.

A similar mood affected race relations after the war. In the 1920s a new Ku Klux Klan grew in size and influence. The Klan threatened and harassed Jews, Catholics, and African Americans in the North as well as the South. In response, many African Americans were attracted to the ideas of Marcus Garvey, who worked to boost black pride and dignity. But little was done to end discrimination in the United States.

Reformers had long blamed drunkenness for many of America's social problems, and in 1920 the Eighteenth Amendment outlawed the manufacture, transportation, and sale of alcoholic beverages. But in the 1920s prohibition proved impossible to enforce. The 18th Amendment was repealed in 1933 by the Twenty-first Amendment.

The rapid changes of the postwar years aggravated divisions in American society. Some Americans resisted accepting the changes that modern science and technology were causing. Country people were offended by the crime, poverty, and immorality of many city dwellers. But city people scoffed at the simple life of farmers, whom they called "hicks" or "hayseeds."

Yet industrial growth was producing more wealth and leisure time for millions. They looked for new ways to spend this money and time. Interest in music, the arts, sports, and literature increased. While many people sought peace of mind in religion, others rejected rigid, conventional rules of behavior. This new spirit of freedom influenced music, dance, architecture, literature, and painting. Some young women adopted fashions and styles such as "bobbed" hair and short skirts that seemed wild to the older generation.

The best reflection of this mood was a new, distinctly American music known as jazz. African American jazz musicians, who often had little formal training in music, played with a freedom that excited their audiences. Because jazz was popular with whites as well as blacks, it broke down racial barriers, among both musicians and their listeners.

Many African Americans were determined to build pride and a better life for themselves and their children. Segregation had forced them into ghettos, where they shaped their own culture. In New York City's ghetto, Harlem, the **Harlem Renaissance** was born. A cultural revitalization for African Americans, the Harlem Renaissance produced writers such as Langston Hughes, Zora Neale Hurston, and Countee Cullen, along with dozens of musicians, artists, and actors.

New forms of entertainment—movies and radio—also burst upon the national scene during the Roaring Twenties. Attendance at movies soared. Radio held even more fascination for the public. Its low cost and convenience, the excitement of "live" broadcasts of baseball games and political conventions, and the variety of infor-

The New British Museum of American Art, Friends Purchase Fund

"Jazz" by Romare Bearden practically makes its own music with its colors and wonderful composition. Notice how the artist combines all kinds of textures to make one unified image. How is that like jazz itself?

mation it made available combined to give radio its appeal. So too did attendance at spectator sports.

In the 1920s the automobile was a major force in the nation. Henry Ford's assembly-line method of production made the automobile an affordable vehicle for average Americans. His factories turned out millions of low-priced cars. Other manufacturers copied Ford's methods. The automobile boom spread to industries that supplied materials to carmakers: rubber, steel, glass, and paint.

Although society changed dramatically, politics changed very little. Higher tariffs continued to help American manufacturers compete. Tax cuts encouraged new investments. New products for consumers—electric appliances, cameras, wristwatches—increased in number and quality.

Yet the coal and textile industries were depressed. Mines shut down. Unemployment rose. American agriculture also suffered, because European farmers, recovering from the setback caused by the Great War, had recaptured their local markets.

Nevertheless, a "get-rich-quick" attitude flourished. Prices on the stock market soared. But the boom could not last forever. Manufacturers were producing more than consumers could afford to buy. Warehouses became overstocked. Overproduction combined with the collapse of the stock market boom drove the country into the Great Depression.

The Development of Modern America   643

Silver Print, 12½ × 9⅞". Collection, The Museum of Modern Art, New York. Purchase.

The human and physical consequences of the depression meet here. The photograph of the **Migrant Mother** *in California, was taken in one quick ten-minute session by Dorothea Lange in 1936.*

The Great Depression and the New Deal

The stock market crash of 1929 was the beginning of a long period of hard times. Thousands of companies went bankrupt. Hundreds of farmers lost their land. Banks failed, leaving depositors without their savings.

The depression was actually worldwide, an indirect result of the destruction of lives and property caused by World War I. It was triggered in the same way that earlier downturns in the **business cycle** had been. When goods piled up unsold, manufacturers cut production and laid off workers. Unemployed workers had little money, so there was less demand for goods. This caused a further slowdown in production. Prices, wages, and profits all spiraled downward. What made the Great Depression different from other hard times was that it lasted so long. Only in 1939 and 1940, after the outbreak of the Second World War in Europe, did the economy recovery.

Statistics show the depth of the nation's economic woes during this period. From 10 to 15 percent of the workers were without jobs throughout the depression. At the lowest point in 1932 and early 1933 about 25 percent were unemployed. Spending on food, furniture, clothing, and automobiles declined steadily.

Such figures fail to measure the human suffering and despair caused by the Great Depression. It hurt Americans from every walk of life. There was no national unemployment insurance or welfare program at the time.

Although President Herbert Hoover tried to stimulate the economy, he favored voluntary measures that could not be enforced. And few businesses were willing to take risks during the crisis. Hoover preferred to leave responsibility for the publc welfare to state and local governments and private charities. If the federal government provided handouts, he believed, it would undermine individual self-reliance and community spirit.

The Bonus March of the summer of 1932 reflected people's frustration. During the Great War soldiers had been paid only $1 a day, while workers at home prospered. After the war a ''deferred'' bonus, to be paid in 1945, had been authorized by Congress. But during the depression veterans demanded immediate payment. About 15,000 of them marched on Washington to demand this. When Congress refused, Hoover ordered troops to force the protesters to leave their camp near the capital. News of their removal further hurt Hoover's public image.

By late 1932 thousands of people had already lost their homes and apartments. People huddled in ''Hoovervilles,'' shantytowns built on deserted lots. Others—many of them teenagers—''took to the road,'' hitching rides and wandering from place to place looking for work. Blacks, Hispanics, and other minorities were particularly hard hit by the depression.

With President Hoover's popularity at an all-time low, the 1932 Democratic candidate, Franklin D. Roosevelt, was easily elected president. Unlike Hoover, he was determined to take whatever action was necessary to end the depression. In his inaugural address he tried to calm the shaken people, saying:

❝ The only thing we have to fear is fear itself—nameless, unreasoning, unjustified terror which paralyzes needed efforts to convert retreat into advance. . . .[1] **❞**

When Roosevelt—also known as FDR—took office in March 1933, banks all over the country had been forced to close their doors. Roosevelt immediately called a special session of Congress. During the next Hundred Days, Roosevelt, his advisers, and Congressional leaders worked out the New Deal, a plan for national relief, recovery, and reform.

Relief efforts helped the millions of Americans in dire need. Recovery measures sought to revive the economy. Reforms were aimed at keeping the depression from happening again. The Federal Deposit Insurance Corporation (FDIC) insured people's deposits up to $5,000 and helped restore public confidence in the government and the economy. Other measures created jobs, caused farm prices to rise, and spurred business activity directly. The National Industrial Recovery Act permitted industries to set production limits to prevent competition and to fix prices. The law also guaranteed workers the right to join unions and bargain collectively with employers, and it set maximum hour and minimum wage rates.

Another New Deal measure, the Agricultural Adjustment Act, attempted to push farm prices up by cutting down on production. Farmers received "rent" from the federal government if they took some of their land out of cultivation.

In 1934 unemployment was still very high, and industrial production had picked up only slightly. Yet the New Deal was generally considered successful. The government was trying to improve the lives of its people. In the 1934 elections the Democratic party increased its majority in Congress.

FDR's personal popularity soared. He instilled hope through frequent "fireside chats" on the radio in which he explained the problems the nation faced and his plans for dealing with them. Because Roosevelt relied on many expert advisers, known as the Brain Trust, people believed that the best minds in the country were fighting the depression.

But the New Deal did not please everyone. The vast powers claimed by the president and Congress alarmed some Americans. Business leaders objected to the new restrictions on how they conducted their affairs, warning that the New Deal would destroy the free enterprise system. On the other hand, Senator Huey Long of

Well wishers greet President Roosevelt at Warm Springs, Georgia. What words might you have used to describe the new president in his open car?

[1] From *The Public Papers and Addresses, 1933* by Franklin D. Roosevelt

The Development of Modern America   645

Louisiana, Dr. Francis Townshend, Father Charles Coughlin, and other radicals organized protest movements among those who were suffering from the depression.

In 1935 and 1936 the Supreme Court ruled that the National Industrial Recovery Act and the Agricultural Adjustment Act were unconstitutional. In both cases the Court claimed the acts gave the president powers reserved by the Constitution for Congress.

FDR answered his critics by proposing a Second New Deal. The Wagner Labor Relations Act guaranteed unions certain organizing and bargaining rights. The Social Security Act set up a system of old-age insurance and unemployment insurance. A higher income tax on the wealthy and stricter bank regulations were enacted. This approach brought Roosevelt reelection by a landslide victory in 1936.

The New Deal reforms caused a major shift of political loyalties among black voters. Although they had traditionally supported "the party of Lincoln," their interests were repeatedly neglected by Republican politicians. Although many New Deal programs did little to help African Americans, they saw Roosevelt as someone who was trying to treat them fairly. Federal relief projects were particularly important to unemployed blacks. Roosevelt tried hard to prevent racial discrimination in the distribution of government aid. And he appointed a number of African Americans to important government offices.

When the Supreme Court declared many New Deal laws unconstitutional, FDR tried to "reform" the Court by introducing a bill in Congress increasing the number of justices. However, Congress rejected the measure. In 1937 Roosevelt also reduced government expenses drastically in an attempt to balance the budget. The result was a sudden halt to the slim recovery that was under way. This "Roosevelt recession" proved how important government spending had become to the economy.

The New Deal failed to end the depression. Only the increase of foreign purchases of American goods when World War II broke out caused the economy to pick up. But the New Deal revolutionized relations between workers and employers. It spurred the formation of unions and established a precedent for government involvement in settling labor disputes. It also created what we think of today as the **welfare state** and a growing belief that it was the responsibility of the federal government to do whatever was necessary to protect the general welfare. The government became involved in more and more aspects of American life.

The New Deal changed the federal government in significant ways. The power of the presidency grew tremendously because the president and his appointees ran the many new agencies and programs. The importance of government spending on the country's complex modern economy was a major economic lesson of the Great Depression.

Return to the Preview & Review on page 639.

4. A GLOBAL AMERICA

World War II

In the 1920s and 1930s the rise of **totalitarian** governments changed the face of Europe. First in Italy and then in Germany, governments claiming absolute authority over their citizens took over. Dictators Benito Mussolini in Italy and Adolf Hitler in Germany crushed any opposition. Their political system was known as fascism. Japan developed a system of government centered on the worship of an emperor but controlled by military leaders.

In Germany the people were bitter because the Versailles Treaty had humiliated them and crippled their economy. In 1933 the National Socialists, or Nazis, led by Adolf Hitler, took power. The Nazis believed that Germans were the "master race," all others, inferior. They especially disliked and mistreated the Jews. Many Jews fled the country, but the tens of thousands who remained were deprived of their rights and property and thrown into **concentration camps.** Meanwhile, the Japanese army had marched into several provinces of China.

The rise of totalitarianism shocked and angered nearly all Americans. Most sympathized with the victims of aggression. But fear of being drawn into another war was strong.

Although he was worried by the Japanese attack on China, Roosevelt intended to remain neutral. Congress passed a series of neutrality acts to prevent the sale of weapons to warring nations. These laws prevented the United States from helping Ethiopia when Italy invaded that country in 1935. In the case of China Roosevelt was able to get around neutrality restrictions because Japan had not officially declared war.

In 1936 Germany occupied the Rhineland; next it annexed Austria and then Czechoslovakia. Finally, when German troops swept into Poland on September 1, 1939, France and Great Britain declared war.

Congress quickly changed the neutrality laws to favor countries fighting the aggressors. A policy called cash-and-carry made it possible for England and France to purchase American arms if they paid in cash and transported the weapons in non-American ships.

But Hitler's war machine rolled onward, capturing Denmark, Norway, Belgium, the Netherlands, and finally France. Great Britain was in danger of being overwhelmed by a German invasion. To help the British defend themselves, President Roosevelt traded 50 old destroyers, which had been replaced by more modern ships, for leases on British naval and air bases off the coast of the United States. In 1940 FDR was reelected, the first time an American president had been elected to a third term in office. During the campaign he promised not to send Americans "into any foreign wars." Instead

Use these questions to guide your reading. Answer the questions after completing Section 4. **Understanding Issues, Events, & Ideas.**

1. Use the following words to describe the Second World War and the Cold War: totalitarian, concentration camp, Holocaust, genocide, containment, McCarthyism, cold war.

2. Use the following term to discuss the civil rights movement in the late 1950s: nonviolent direct action.

1. America's policy changed from neutrality to aid for the Allies against Nazi Germany. Describe each step of the change.

2. What was the American strategy to ultimately defeat Japan?

3. Explain how the Truman Doctrine, the containment policy, and McCarthyism contributed to the Cold War.

Thinking Critically. In *Brown v. Board of Education,* the Supreme Court ordered public schools to end segregation. You are a soldier assigned to protect the young African American students entering Central High School in Little Rock, Arkansas, in 1957. Use your historical imagination to describe how you feel.

Congress increased aid to Britain by the Lend-Lease Act, which authorized the president to lend or sell war supplies to countries whose defense he considered essential to American security.

To protect American ships transporting supplies to Great Britain against submarine attacks, the United States set up naval bases on Greenland, and later Iceland. By the fall of 1941 an undeclared war was raging in the Atlantic Ocean. American destroyers tracked German submarines and radioed their positions to British planes. In late October an American destroyer, the *Reuben James,* was torpedoed with the loss of more than 100 sailors. Congress authorized the arming of American merchant ships, and the navy was ordered to "shoot on sight" any German submarines encountered.

In September 1940 Japan had made an alliance with Germany and Italy that was known as the Rome-Berlin-Tokyo Axis. By then Japanese troops had conquered much of Southeast Asia. In response, the United States stopped selling scrap iron and oil to Japan, and Roosevelt called for Japanese withdrawal from this region and China. Because Japan depended on the United States for 80 percent of its oil, it would have to either meet his terms or find another source of oil. On December 7, 1941 Japan launched a surprise air attack against the United States naval base at Pearl Harbor, in Hawaii. Japanese leaders felt that if they could destroy America's Pacific Fleet, they

Across the English Channel come boats of every shape and size in the spring of 1940. British, French, and Belgian soldiers had their backs to the channel as the Germans advanced. France was lost, but 340,000 men were saved by the courage and mettle of the British at Dunkirk.

could control the entire Far East.

The attack on Pearl Harbor produced the worst defeat the United States navy has ever experienced. The next day President Roosevelt asked Congress to declare war on Japan. Germany and Italy responded by declaring war on the United States.

As it had in the First World War, the government swiftly took control of the production and distribution of goods. The wartime demand for weapons and supplies brought the Great Depression to an end. Unemployment disappeared. Hundreds of thousands of workers—including many women, African Americans, and Hispanics—found jobs in war industries. A woman riveter recalled:

    ❝ I loved working at Convair [an aircraft factory]. I loved the challenge of getting dirty and getting into the work. . . . Convair was the first time in my life I had the chance to prove that I could do something, and I did.[1]❞

Although the American people were solidly against all the Axis powers, there was no persecution of German and Italian Americans as had occurred during the First World War. Japanese Americans, however, were treated harshly. About 112,000 living in the Far West were rounded up and sent to internment camps in barren parts of the interior. They were forced to sell their homes and property, although they were innocent of any crimes. One young Japanese American man recalled the experience:

    ❝ I remember the pain of being labeled a 'dirty Jap' and a 'dangerous enemy.' For me, a Los Angeles teenager of 17, it was a time when my entire value system was thrown out of kilter.[2]❞

Racial segregation and discrimination against African Americans and Hispanic Americans also continued, even though they were not officially mistreated. Racial unrest, reflected in riots between blacks and whites in northern cities and Hispanics and whites in Los Angeles, occurred frequently.

The countries opposing the Axis in World War II—chiefly, the United States, Great Britain, France, and the Soviet Union, which had been attacked by Germany in June 1941—decided to try to win in Europe before concentrating on the Japanese in Asia. General Dwight D. Eisenhower was supreme commander of the Allied troops in western Europe. His forces first drove the Germans out of North Africa. They then invaded Europe from the south, occupying Sicily quickly and then advancing slowly north through Italy. Meanwhile, an enormous army was being assembled in England for an invasion of France.

[1]From *The Homefront: America During World War II* by Mark Jonathan Harris, et al.
[2]From "Point of View: A Sorry Part of Our History" by Daniel Kuzuhara, in the *Chicago Tribune*, August 26, 1981.

The mushroom cloud of nuclear destruction rose twice over wartime Japan. Such a sight recalls the address to the UN by Pope Paul VI: "Ne jamais plus la guerre": "Never again war."

Months of American and British air attacks on industrial targets and railroads in Germany set the stage for this invasion. On D-Day, June 6, 1944, more than 176,000 men were landed on the beaches of Normandy, in northern France. The fighting was bitter and costly, but in August troops under General George Patton liberated Paris. Early in 1945 the Allies crossed the Rhine River into Germany. In late April advancing American troops met the Soviet forces closing in from the East. On May 8 Germany surrendered.

After their attack on Pearl Harbor, the Japanese conquered the Philippines. Next they targeted Australia, but the American navy battered a Japanese fleet in the Battle of the Coral Sea, off the northeastern Australian coast. Then in the Battle of Midway American carrier-based planes dealt another stinging blow to the Japanese navy, thus gaining control of the central Pacific.

To retake the Philippines and invade Japan, many small islands in the western Pacific had to be taken first. This strategy was called island hopping. Some of the war's bloodiest fighting took place as a result. But by the summer of 1945 American air power was able to batter Japan's cities. Experts calculated that an invasion of Japan would result in millions of American and Japanese casualties. The decision on how then to proceed fell to Harry S Truman, who had become president in April when Roosevelt died suddenly of a stroke.

Since early 1942 scientists had been working on a top-secret project to produce an atomic bomb. In July 1945 Truman was informed that the project had been successful. The United States possessed a bomb powerful enough to destroy an entire city. Truman believed that dropping such a devastating bomb would persuade Japan to surrender. So he ordered the army to use it. In early August two Japanese cities—Hiroshima and Nagasaki—were struck with such terrible destruction that Japan surrendered on August 14, 1945.

World War II demonstrated the horror of total war. The devastation of the atomic bombs and the massive casualty lists shocked people the world over. Equally shocking was the **Holocaust.** The Nazis had carried out a program of **genocide**—an attempt to eliminate an entire racial or ethnic group—against the Jews. During the war, without any military purpose, they killed more than 6 million Jews and also thousands of Slavs, Gypsies, and other innocent people in their death camps.

America in the Cold War

The terrible destruction of the war convinced world leaders that another global war must be avoided. In 1945 delegates from 50 nations drew up a charter for an international organization called the United Nations (UN). Unlike the case with the League of Nations, the United States joined the UN.

Although both the United States and the Soviet Union were

members of the UN, they had great differences. The Soviet Union was a communist society with an economy controlled by the state. Its totalitarian system, ruled by a dictator, was directly opposed to capitalism and democracy. Most Americans admired the way the Soviets had bravely defended their land against the Nazis. Yet suspicions and distrust developed swiftly. In February 1945, Roosevelt, Stalin, and Winston Churchill of Great Britain met at Yalta in southern Russia to discuss the future of Eastern Europe. Stalin insisted that the Soviets have some control over Poland and the other countries of Eastern Europe. The Soviet Union, he noted, had suffered repeatedly from attacks across Polish territory. Roosevelt and Churchill wanted a promise of free elections in Poland, but they conceded the Soviet Union's right to dominate the lands along its borders.

Economists expected the United States to face a serious postwar economic depression. But the depression did not occur. Millions of people had saved money during the war when consumer goods were scarce. Now they spent their savings on homes, automobiles, washing machines, and other goods. Returning soldiers quickly found jobs as companies geared up to meet this demand. The shortages of goods

From this meeting at Yalta on the Crimean Peninsula in the Soviet Union came the compromises of the Cold War. Left to right are Winston Churchill, soon to lose power in England; Franklin Roosevelt, gravely ill after 12 years as president of the United States; and the ruthless Soviet dictator Joseph Stalin. The Big Three worked out the plan that allowed most of Eastern Europe to remain under Soviet control. Why do you think the United States and Great Britain allowed the Soviets to dominate Eastern Europe?

The Development of Modern America 651

after the war caused prices to rise. Workers in turn demanded higher wages. Inflation resulted.

President Truman proposed a reform program known as the Fair Deal. It called for improved old-age and survivors insurance, higher minimum wages, more public housing, and national health insurance. But Congress refused to enact most of his proposals. In 1946 the Republican party won control of both houses of Congress for the first time since the 1920s.

As for foreign policy, Truman sought to keep any more countries from falling under Soviet control. Communist rebels were attempting to overthrow the government in Greece. To block them he proposed offering economic and military aid to "assist free peoples to work out their destinies in their own way." This policy was known as the Truman Doctrine. This became the basis for **containment:** the idea of firm resistance to Soviet expansion anywhere in the world. The result was the **Cold War**—a prolonged standoff fueled by suspicions and threats from both Soviets and the United States.

Most Ameicans supported the idea of helping the people of other countries defend their independence and rebuild their war-torn economies. In 1947 Truman's secretary of state, George Marshall, proposed a broad plan of American aid to the countries of Europe. Under the Marshall Plan, the western European democracies were given $13 billion in aid. This money helped bring about a remarkable recovery in Europe.

After the war the United States, Great Britain, France, and the Soviet Union divided Germany into four zones of occupation. In 1949 the U.S., Great Britain, and France combined their zones to create the Federal Republic of Germany. Angered by this move, the Soviets blocked access to Berlin, which lay entirely within the Soviet zone, but had also been divided into four zones. This threatened to force the Allies to give up their parts of the city. Rather than do so or force a showdown that might lead to war, the Americans organized the Berlin Airlift. For eleven months in 1948-49, food and other necessities for the 2 million residents of West Berlin were flown in on American planes.

The Soviets finally ended the blockade, but during the crisis the United States, Great Britain, France, Italy, and eight other nations organized a mutual defense pact, the North Atlantic Treaty Organization (NATO). The Soviet Union and its "satellites" in eastern Europe formed a similar alliance—the Warsaw Pact.

As the 1948 presidential election approached, the Democratic party was badly divided. Truman won the Democratic nomination, but he faced two challenges in addition to the Republicans. Henry Wallace, who had been Truman's secretary of commerce, ran on the ticket of a new Progressive party. And Governor Strom Thurmond of South Carolina ran on the states' rights, or "Dixiecrat," party ticket. The Dixiecrats left the Democratic party because it had

Through the clouds over Berlin a PC-6 swoops down with its supplies to keep the 2 million residents of West Berlin alive. Why had the Soviets blocked all highways and railroads to Berlin?

adopted a strong civil rights policy—much of it at Truman's urging.

This division of the Democrats caused experts to predict that the Republican presidential candidate, Governor Thomas E. Dewey of New York, would win the election. However, Truman campaigned tirelessly, criss-crossing the nation by train. He criticized the "do-nothing" Republican-controlled Congress for not enacting his Fair Deal. This proved, he insisted, that the Republicans wanted to do away with the reforms of the New Deal. Truman was reelected in one of the great upsets in American political history.

More and more, the Cold War occupied people's attention. Fear of Soviet aggression gripped the nation. The arrests and trials of several Americans accused of giving military secrets to the Soviets led to the fear that traitors infested the government. Then in 1949 communists in China overthrew the nationalist government of General Chiang Kai-shek. A new Red Scare swept the country in 1950 when Senator Joseph McCarthy of Wisconsin claimed that the State Department was full of communists. McCarthy's charges were absurd but widely reported and believed. His use of sensational but unsupported accusations became known as **McCarthyism.**

Soon after the "loss of China" to communism, America faced a similar situation in Korea, a nation freed from Japanese control after World War II. Korea had been divided into two zones, the northern backed by the Soviet Union, the southern by the United States. In June 1950 the North Korean army invaded the South and swiftly pushed the South Korean forces into the southeastern corner of the country.

President Truman immediately applied the containment policy. Acting on behalf of a UN resolution, he ordered American forces into South Korea. The North Koreans were driven back, but when the UN troops, commanded by General Douglas MacArthur, pursued them deep into North Korea, a Chinese army counterattacked. War raged for months.

In 1952 World War II hero Dwight Eisenhower, running as a Republican, was elected president. During the campaign he had announced that if elected he would go to Korea to negotiate a settlement of the war. Soon after his victory he did so. A truce was signed in 1953 reestablishing the original border between the two Koreas.

As president, Eisenhower avoided military involvement in several other crises. He refused to provide American air support for the French in their fight against communist rebels in their colony of Indochina—present-day Laos, Cambodia (Kampuchea), and Vietnam. And in the Middle East, he demanded that France, Great Britain, and Israel cease their attempts to regain control of the Suez Canal from Egypt.

Nonetheless, tensions between the United States and the Soviet Union continued to rise. Soviet scientists launched the world's first earth-circling satellite, the *Sputnik,* in October 1957. This achievement shocked Americans, who had believed that their country led the world in science and technology. Then in 1960 an American high-altitude U-2 spy plane was shot down over the Soviet Union. This further embittered relations between the two countries.

At home the Eisenhower years were prosperous. Eisenhower, though conservative, did not seek to do away with New Deal reforms. Indeed, during his administration, the minimum wage was raised, more public housing was built for low-income families, more workers were covered by the social security and unemployment insurance system, and a cabinet-level department of health, education, and welfare was created.

During Eisenhower's first term the Supreme Court made a momentous decision affecting the struggle for civil rights for African Americans. The Court, headed by Chief Justice Earl Warren, ruled in *Brown v. Board of Education of Topeka* that maintaining ''separate but equal'' public schools was unconstitutional. The Court said:

66 Does segregation of children in public schools solely on the basis of race . . . deprive children of the minority group of equal educational opportunities? We believe it does. . . . We conclude that in the field of public education . . . 'separate but equal' has no place.[1] 99

[1]From *Brown v. Board of Education of Topeka,* Supreme Court of the United States, 347 U.S. 483, 1954.

The decision outlawed separate educational systems for white and black children. Although the Supreme Court realized that getting rid of segregated schools would be difficult, it ordered that the states put the law into effect "with all deliberate speed." Eisenhower thought the *Brown* decision a mistake, but he enforced it when southern whites sought to prevent desegregation by force.

The struggle against all forms of racial discrimination became increasingly vigorous after the *Brown v. Board of Education* decision. So did the white reaction. Isolated acts of violence broke out. The murder in Mississippi of young Emmett Till shocked Americans of all races, especially after an all-white jury found those on trial for his murder not guilty.

In 1956, blacks in Montgomery, Alabama, boycotted the local bus system until it changed its policy of making blacks sit in the backs of buses. During this strike, the young Baptist clergyman Martin Luther King, Jr., gained national recognition as a leader in the drive for equal rights. King preached **nonviolent direct action** as a tactic for bringing about social change. He insisted that love was more powerful than hatred and that appeals to reason were more effective than force. Blacks should avoid violence no matter how badly they were mistreated.

But school integration moved forward very slowly. In 1957 segregation in Little Rock, Arkansas, backed by the governor blocked the enrollment of black children in a Little Rock high school. President Eisenhower sent 1,000 soldiers to make sure the black students were admitted. African Americans also pushed for equal rights by conducting sit-ins at segregated lunch counters, freedom rides on

President Eisenhower ordered U.S. troops to escort the young black students into Central High School in Little Rock, Arkansas. Why had they been denied admission to the school? What effect did photographs such as this one have on the American public in the late 1950s?

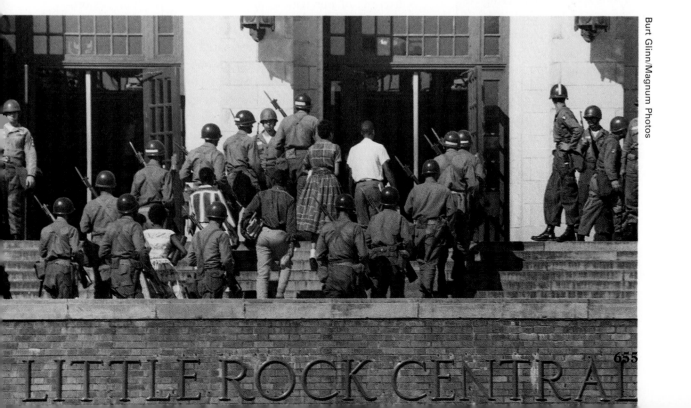

Burt Glinn/Magnum Photos

LITTLE ROCK CENTRAL

"Say I was a drum major for justice," said Martin Luther King, Jr., who knew, as did his followers, that an assassin would someday take his life. Try to listen to his famous speeches on records or tapes.

Point of View

In his famous *Letter from a Birmingham Jail,* Dr. King described the impact of segregation on children.

> 66 You suddenly find your tongue twisted and your speech stammering as you seek to explain to your six-year-old daughter why she can't go to the public amusement park that has just been advertised on television, and see tears welling up in her little eyes when she is told that Funtown is closed to colored children. . . . 99
>
> Martin Luther King, Jr., 1963

buses, and making other protests and marches. Later in 1963 more than 200,000 people, whites and blacks together, gathered in Washington to demonstrate peacefully in favor of civil rights legislation. They heard Reverend King deliver his now-famous "I Have a Dream" speech. King said.

> 66 I have a dream that one day this nation will rise up and live out the true meaning of its creed: 'We hold these truths to be self-evident that all men are created equal.' . . . With this faith we will be able to transform the jangling discords of our nation into a beautiful symphony of brotherhood. . . .[1]99

In 1960 the Republicans nominated Vice President Richard M. Nixon to replace Eisenhower. But in one of the closest presidential elections in American history, Senator John F. Kennedy of Massachusetts won the office. Kennedy called for an idealistic but somewhat vague program, called the New Frontier.

The Cold War, however, continued to dominate the news during the Kennedy administration. The president approved an attempt to overthrow the Soviet-backed government of Fidel Castro in Cuba. It was organized by the American Central Intelligence Agency (CIA). This invasion at a place known as the Bay of Pigs was a total disaster. The prestige of the United States and of Kennedy suffered a heavy blow. Kennedy's hope of promoting goodwill with Latin America by providing economic aid, the Alliance for Progress, achieved only limited results. But one successful program, the Peace Corps, sent volunteers to help people in developing countries.

[1]From "I Have a Dream," copyright © 1963 by Martin Luther King, Jr. Reprinted by permission of Joan Daves.

After the Bay of Pigs disaster, the Soviets constructed a wall across Berlin, sealing off the Soviet zone from the west. The Wall symbolized the iron grip that the Soviets held over all Eastern Europe. Next they confronted the United States in Cuba by building missile bases there. From these bases the Soviets could fire rockets at targets in the United States. Kennedy demanded that Soviet premier Khrushchev remove these weapons from Cuba, and he warned that if missiles were fired, the United States would launch a massive nuclear attack on the Soviet Union. After hesitating briefly, Khrushchev removed the missiles.

Kennedy was unable to get Congress to enact much of his domestic program into law. Measures to reduce taxes and to strengthen civil rights failed, but Congress did fund a program to place Americans on the moon by the end of the 1960s. In 1969 this goal was achieved. But Kennedy was not alive to see it. On November 22, 1963, he was assassinated as he rode in a motorcade through downtown Dallas, Texas.

Return to the Preview & Review on page 647.

NASA

The historical significance of this picture will come with time. In its way it is as rare as Columbus' journal describing the first sighting of the Americas. To report "Man Walks on Moon," The New York Times had to make special headline type large enough for the biggest story of the 20th century. Neil Armstrong took the picture of Edwin Aldrin, his fellow walker on the moon.

657

5. MODERN AMERICA

Use these questions to guide your reading. Answer the questions after completing Section 5.
Understanding Issues, Events, & Ideas. Use the following words to describe events and developments in modern America: standard of living, Sun Belt, domino theory, Vietnamization, affirmative action, acid rain, supply-side economics.
1. What were the main parts of President Johnson's Great Society program?
2. What reasons did American leaders have for committing troops to Vietnam?
3. Describe the problems of urban decay and environmental pollution.
Thinking Critically. Tensions remain between the United States and the other countries of the Western Hemisphere. If you were the president's foreign policy adviser, what steps would you take to reduce the tensions?

The Great Society

The assassination of Kennedy made Lyndon Baines Johnson (LBJ) president. Johnson, who had served for years in Congress, used his knowledge of Congressional politics to push through many of Kennedy's proposals. Energetic and sometimes domineering, he was an expert at persuading reluctant legislators to do what he wanted. Congress passed a new Civil Rights Act and a bill cutting taxes by over $10 billion. The Economic Opportunity Act, passed in 1964, set up the Head Start program to help disadvantaged preschool children, the Job Corps to teach job skills to youths, and VISTA, a domestic version of the Peace Corps.

After defeating Republican Barry Goldwater by a landslide in the 1964 presidential election, LBJ proposed what he called the Great Society program. It included Medicare health insurance for the elderly and housing assistance for the poor.

The economy of the United States that emerged from World War II continued to grow. An excellent transportation network, efficient business organizations, and a large, skilled labor force gave American capitalism an advantage in world markets. Scientific and technological advances increased the nation's economic efficiency. Computers became common in offices, mines, factories, and homes. The use of better chemical fertilizers and insecticides boosted farm production. Advances in medicine, such as the widespread use of penicillin and

Wide World Photos

Lyndon B. Johnson takes the oath from Judge Sarah T. Hughes, Lady Bird and Jacqueline Kennedy at his side.

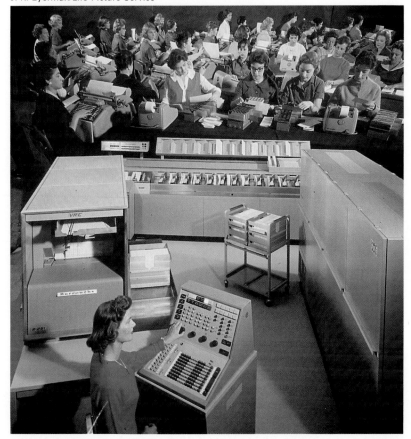

This very interesting double exposure shows one consequence of the computer revolution. A single operator in the foreground does the work of the 31 bank clerks in the background. Why did computers make many people apprehensive?

other antibiotics, provided quick cures for most infectious diseases. Economist John Kenneth Galbraith described America in the 1950s as the Affluent Society. The **standard of living**—the measure of the necessities, comforts, and luxuries available—of the country had never been so high.

American workers underwent significant changes after the war. The need increased for teachers, doctors, lawyers, sales persons, secretaries, clerks, and other office workers. The percentage of women in the work force grew rapidly.

After the war television changed American life in important ways. All but the very poorest families could afford a television. By providing images of news events as they happened, television strongly influenced public opinion.

The population of the United States grew rapidly. Between 1946 and 1960 the rate of population growth tripled. We call this leap in the birth rate a baby boom.

Countless thousands of American families moved from place to place during this time. The South and Southwest, known as the **Sun Belt** because of its warm climate, experienced the most rapid growth. Economic development in the Sun Belt was both a cause and effect of this population shift. Aircraft, electronics, and food processing

The Development of Modern America   659

firms moved to the Sun Belt because living costs were generally lower there. Many retired people also came, especially to Florida.

Americans also tended to move from cities to suburbs. These suburbs required new schools, hospitals, and offices as well as shopping centers containing supermarkets, department stores, and dozens of small shops, always surrounded by acres of parking lots. Suburbanites, mostly members of the middle class and well-paid blue-collar workers, such as carpenters, plumbers, and automobile assembly-line workers, went everywhere by car.

The poor—most of them nonwhite—remained in the cities. Thus a new kind of segregation developed along economic lines. Cities were faced with shrinking income and property taxes because so many well-to-do people moved away. Public housing and inner-city schools were hard hit.

Not everyone shared in the prosperity of the Affluent Society. Working women resented the inequalities of the business world. Most were paid less than men for the same work. A Women's Liberation Movement soon gained momentum. As a result, more and more women were elected to public office. New laws opened more opportunities in business for them.

Ever since passage in 1934 of the Indian Reorganization Act, Indians had been choosing their own leaders and exerting more control over their own affairs. They were no longer under pressure to adopt the ways and values of whites. Indian languages and history were taught in their schools. They relearned ancient arts and crafts. However, the Indian Rights Act of 1968, passed to protect Native Americans against discrimination and mistreatment, actually weakened the tribal governments. Under this law, the older chiefs who dominated many tribal governments gained greater control of tribal affairs. More radical Indians formed the American Indian Movement (AIM) in 1972. AIM organized many protests, including the occupation of Wounded Knee, South Dakota, in 1973.

African American civil rights activists were impatient with the

Among the marchers for Women's Rights are Bella Abzug in her hat and Betty Freidan, right.

pace of reform and demanded more political power and influence. During the "Freedom Summer" of 1964 volunteer workers in the South registered thousands of black voters. Marchers demonstrated against local officials who blocked voter registration. Television coverage of such events impressed viewers with the courage of the demonstrators and the justice of their cause.

But progress was too slow for many blacks. Their frustration erupted in the mid-1960s. Riots broke out in the ghettos. The antiwhite Black Muslims attracted many followers, the best-known being Malcolm X, who called for African Americans to take pride in their race and to reject white society. He said:

> ❝ I am for violence if nonviolence means we continue postponing a solution to the American black man's problem— just to avoid violence. I don't go for nonviolence if it also means a delayed solution. . . .[1]❞

Malcolm X and others spoke of **Black Power.** Extremists formed the Black Panther Party and collected weapons to protect their neighborhoods and to resist police. But as a result of these radical movements, a white backlash occurred.

This young Crow in tribal regalia helps us recall the past.

The Vietnam Era

After the defeat of the French in 1954, nationalists led by the dedicated communist Ho Chi Minh controlled the northern part of Vietnam. South Vietnam had an anticommunist government. The United States supported a government in South Vietnam headed by Ngo Dinh Diem. In South Vietnam a civil war raged between the Viet Cong, South Vietnamese who opposed Diem, and supporters of Diem's government.

American leaders feared that the establishment of a communist government in Vietnam would mean the loss of other Southeast Asian countries, such as Laos and Cambodia, to communism. This **domino theory** held that if one country fell they would all fall. So when President Johnson announced in August 1964 that an American destroyer had been attacked by North Vietnamese gunboats in the Gulf of Tonkin, Congress passed a resolution giving him the authority to "take all necessary measures" to defend American forces there.

By February 1965 President Johnson decided that South Vietnamese government could not defeat the Viet Cong without increased American support. He ordered the air force to bomb targets in North Vietnam and sent two battalions of marines to protect American air bases in South Vietnam. Month after month more American fighting men were sent to Vietnam. But the size of the North Vietnamese army and the Viet Cong in the South grew as well. Little progress toward winning the war was made. With each increase in American

[1] From *Malcolm X Speaks*, edited by George Brietman

The United States became mired in a land war in Asia, just as the French had before them. Critics sharply opposed the war. Much of the antiwar sentiment focused on American soldiers. Later came a time of reconciliation. Many efforts today are directed at helping Vietnam veterans find their place in society. Do you think the government has this responsibility after a war?

involvement, antiwar protestors in the United States grew more vocal. Yet Johnson continued to seek a military victory. America must honor its commitment to South Vietnam, he insisted.

The Vietnam War sharply divided the American people. President Johnson announced that he would not seek reelection in 1968, hoping his withdrawal would heal the split in American society. But before the 1968 election took place, Martin Luther King, Jr., was murdered in Memphis, Tennessee. His death caused protests and riots in 125 cities. Two months later Senator Robert Kennedy of Massachusetts (younger brother of President John F. Kennedy), who was seeking the Democratic presidential nomination, was assassinated. Then, during the Democratic convention in Chicago, police brutally beat and arrested antiwar demonstrators as millions watched on television.

After Kennedy's death Vice President Hubert Humphrey won the Democratic nomination for president easily. However, he lost the election, in part because he supported Johnson's Vietnam policy. Former Vice President Richard Nixon, who had won the Republican nomination, was elected president.

In addition to the dissension caused by Vietnam, President Nixon inherited a number of economic problems that were related to the war. To pay for it, Johnson had greatly increased government spending. But he had avoided raising taxes or cutting domestic programs. Inflation had resulted. In an effort to end this inflation, Nixon ordered a wage-and-price freeze in August 1971.

Like Johnson, Nixon was committed to preventing the communists from conquering South Vietnam. However, he hoped to shift more of the burden of the fighting to the South Vietnamese. This was known as **Vietnamization.** It was clear that the South Vietnamese were ineffective fighters, but by the spring of 1970 about 110,000 Americans had been pulled out of Vietnam. Then, however, in April 1970 Nixon extended the war into Cambodia to attack North Vietnamese supply lines—the so-called Ho Chi Minh Trail.

This escalation of the war set off renewed protests in the United States. College students reacted angrily to the news. At Kent State University in Ohio and Jackson State University in Mississippi students were killed by national guardsmen and police. To quiet the demonstrations, Nixon withdrew the troops in Cambodia and pulled more Americans from Vietnam.

By 1972 fewer than 100,000 American troops remained in Vietnam. Nixon's chief foreign policy adviser, Henry Kissinger, entered into secret negotiations with North Vietnamese leaders. Shortly before the 1972 presidential election Nixon halted air strikes against the North. But after his victory in the election, he resumed the bombing. Finally in January 1973 a peace agreement with the North Vietnamese was signed.

Richard Nixon had also taken steps to resume relations with communist China. He also signed a Strategic Arms Limitation Treaty (SALT) with the Soviet Union, thus reducing tensions between the superpowers.

Yet, after these foreign policy achievements and his landslide reelection, Nixon's power began to crumble. In June 1972, members of his campaign organization were caught burglarizing the Democratic party's headquarters at the Watergate building in Washington, D.C. The president denied that anyone on the White House staff had anything to do with the break-in. But in March 1973 one burglar, James McCord, confessed that important Republican party officials had ordered the break-in. Eventually it came out that high-level White House staff members were indeed involved. A cover-up of the crime planned by Nixon himself had taken place. In July 1974 the House Judiciary Committee passed three articles of impeachment against the president. The Senate seemed likely to impeach Nixon. As a result, on August 9, 1974, Nixon resigned, the only President in American history ever to do so. Vice President Gerald Ford became the new president.

Modern Times

President Ford faced a country in an economic slowdown. Yet prices were on the rise. Ford considered inflation the major problem, but the slump continued. Ford, however, resisted measures aimed at helping the poor and unemployed, such as public housing, health care, and other social programs.

President and Mrs. Nixon are greeted by Mao Tse-tung, the communist leader of China. This was one of two historic visits abroad made by the Nixons. What was the other?

Two marchers in New York's Puerto Rican Day Parade. Baseball is the national pasttime on the island. The girl smiling shyly is holding the Puerto Rican flag. Do you think Puerto Rico might become the 51st state? What arguments are made for and against statehood?

The population of the United States was changing drastically. The Immigration Act of 1965 had opened up the country to many more Latin Americans and Asians. South Koreans, Filipinos, and South Vietnamese flooded into the country seeking economic opportunity and political freedom. As to Hispanic immigration, most came from Mexico, though large numbers from Puerto Rico, Cuba, and Central and South America also arrived.

Dissatisfied with the peaceful protest tactics of Martin Luther King, Jr., African American leaders such as Stokely Carmichael continued the push for Black Power. The white backlash also continued. Some whites picketed against **affirmative action** programs, which compelled employers to give minority workers preference in hiring in order to make up for past imbalances in the work force. Yet despite the backlash, the civil rights movement had changed the nation. Gone forever were the "for whites only" signs and other obvious examples of discrimination.

Economic, political, and social opportunities for women improved dramatically in the 1970s and 1980s. Women entered the work force by the millions during these years. But a proposed Equal Rights Amendment failed to be ratified by the necessary three quarters of the states.

Of the many social problems challenging Americans in the 1970s and 1980s, urban decay and environmental pollution were the most obvious. Neighborhoods and individuals as well as federal, state, and local governments had to deal with them.

A vicious cycle of decay ate away at many of America's central cities. The movement of people to suburbs and the Sun Belt resulted in a decline of public services in the inner cities. Whole neighborhoods wasted away. Schools deteriorated, and the number of dropouts rose. Increasing crime and homelessness worsened the plight of thousands.

Many of America's natural resources also deteriorated. Air and water pollution were on the increase in many regions. Millions of automobiles, buses, and trucks poured exhaust fumes into the air, while power plants and factories released clouds of smoke and cinders. In Los Angeles breathing the almost daily smog became a serious health risk. In the Northeast air pollution caused **acid rain,** which damaged forests and water supplies. Acid rain from America even caused damage in Canada, resulting in strained relations with that country. The pumping of chemical waste products from factories into rivers and lakes threatened water supplies. Chemicals used for killing insects and as fertilizers were also polluting the land and waterways. Accidents to off-shore oil wells and to giant oil tankers spilled millions of gallons of thick, black crude oil into the oceans, fouling miles of beaches and killing seabirds and fish.

The Watergate scandal caused many Americans to lose faith in the government. Governor Jimmy Carter of Georgia won the Democratic nomination for president in 1976 in part claiming that he was an "outsider" unconnected the "Washington establishment." He promised to restore people's confidence in their government. He said:

> ❝ Can our government in Washington, which we love, be decent? . . . I think the answer is yes. We still have a system of government that's the best on earth. The vision that was ours 200 years ago is still there.[1] ❞

In a close election in which barely half the nation's registered voters participated, Carter defeated Ford.

Carter, a deeply religious person, symbolized a reawakening of American morality. He urged Americans to work toward creating a just as well as a prosperous society. He hoped to protect the environment, the workplace, and consumers. Under his administration women, African Americans, and Hispanics received more federal appointments than ever before.

Critics claimed, however, that Carter did not do enough to stimulate the economy and reduce unemployment. Others attacked his environmental and consumer-protection regulations. His civil rights measures came under fire from black and Hispanic leaders for not being strong enough.

In foreign policy, Carter stressed America's commitment to human rights. He refused to aid anticommunist governments that abused the rights of their citizens. When the Soviet Union invaded Afghanistan in 1979, Carter imposed sanctions against the Soviets. He won his greatest praise for his effective role in the peace agreement between Egypt and Israel known as the Camp David Accords. Carter's reputation suffered, however, because of the Iran hostage crisis. In November 1979 an Iranian mob invaded the American embassy in Teheran, Iran, and held 53 Americans in the building prisoner. His inability to gain the release of the American hostages was a blow to America's prestige and thus to his own.

The hostage crisis, plus an inflation rate that reached 13 percent in 1979, reduced Carter's popularity. As a result, the Republican candidate, Ronald Reagan, won a sweeping victory over Carter in the 1980 presidential election. On the day of Reagan's inauguration the American hostages in Iran were finally freed. This gave Reagan a good start as president.

Reagan intended "to curb the size and influence of the Federal establishment." He proposed cutting back government spending on social welfare programs. He also pushed for increased spending on defense. He supported steep tax cuts for the wealthy on the theory that they would invest the money saved on taxes in new business enterprises, which would create jobs and cause the economy to boom. This policy, called **supply-side economics,** greatly increased the national debt. Because of the military buildup, government spending

[1]From *A Government as Good as Its People* by Jimmy Carter

Rachel Carson wrote so movingly of the natural environment that not all her readers realized at first that she was warning America to change its ways before the environment deteriorated and cities decayed. Explain the title Silent Spring.

The triumph of the Carter presidency was bringing together the leaders of two ancient rivals: Egypt represented by Anwar Sadat and Israel represented by Menachem Begin. What agreement did they reach at Camp David before this handshake?

The Development of Modern America

Even his sharpest critics concede that Ronald Reagan, shown here with his wife, Nancy, restored the country's pride in its flag. Once again patriotism was in fashion.

actually went up, but revenues went down because of the tax cuts. Instead of balancing the budget, supply-side economics caused the deficit to reach nearly $200 billion in 1983.

Reagan was a staunch anticommunist. He referred to the Soviet Union as an "evil empire" bent on world domination. His anticommunist foreign policy led him to support the brutal government of El Salvador, which was fighting a war against communist rebels. In Nicaragua he secretly funded armed rebels fighting the pro-communist Sandinistas, the Contras. This policy of backing the Contras eventually led Congress to ban further military aid to these rebels.

Reagan's style and friendly personality made him popular with increasing numbers of Americans. He easily won reelection in 1984 over Democrat Walter Mondale, who had been Carter's vice president. The Reverend Jesse Jackson had made a serious challenge for the Democratic nomination, the first time an African American had done so.

Reagan's second term saw more cuts in social programs, further tax cuts, and still larger deficits. He also favored eliminating government restrictions on many business practices. In some industries this "deregulation" resulted in healthy competition. However, many bank failures and a monumental crisis in the nation's savings and loan industry also resulted from reduced government regulation. American business was challenged by stiffer competition from abroad as well. Inexpensive, high-quality imports from Japan, South Korea, and Taiwan attracted the dollars of American consumers but caused many workers to lose their jobs.

The most unexpected event of the Reagan years was the change in relations with the Soviet Union. The change began soon after Mikhail Gorbachev became premier of the Soviet Union in 1985. He set out to open up Soviet society *(glasnost)* and restructure the economy *(perestroika)*. His focus on internal concerns made him eager to negotiate arms control agreements with the United States. A treaty eliminating medium-range missiles was signed at a summit meeting between Reagan and Gorbachev in 1988.

Much of the glimmer from this achievement was lost when the public discovered that the United States was secretly selling arms to Iran—still viewed as an enemy after the hostage crisis—in hopes of gaining the release of American hostages held by Moslem radicals in Lebanon. More serious still, profits from the arms sale were used to buy arms for the Nicaraguan Contras, even though Congress had prohibited any such military aid. This Iran-Contra Affair led to the discharge and later conviction of several Reagan aides. Reagan claimed not to have known what was going on, which even if true damaged his reputation.

In 1988 Reagan's vice president, George Bush, was elected president, defeating the Democratic candidate, Governor Michael Dukakis of Massachusetts.

America in the World

Relations with its Western Hemisphere neighbors occupies a special place in American policy. The United States and Canada have enjoyed generally good relations, sharing a 5,000-mile border—the world's longest undefended boundary. They are each other's largest trading partner. The countries have disagreed over fishing rights and other matters from time to time. In recent years, they have explored solutions to the acid rain problem, which has damaged Canadian lakes and forests.

Relations between the United States and the nations of Latin America have been more troubled. The United States tended to view these nations as weak, unstable, and in need of American help. To prevent European interference in the hemisphere and to expand trade, the United States often invoked the Monroe Doctrine to justify its own involvement in the region. Between 1898 and 1920 American troops were sent into Central American and Caribbean countries at least 20 times. After World War I American policy gradually changed. Instead of troops, America sent diplomats. President Franklin Roosevelt adopted a "Good Neighbor" policy. He said:

“ The essential qualities of a true Pan Americanism must be
the same as those which constitute a good neighbor, namely,
mutual understanding . . . and a sympathetic appreciation
of the other's point of view.[1] ”

The Platt Amendment, which had given the United States the right to intervene in Cuban internal affairs, was repealed. The United States also took part in international conferences with Latin American countries. A number of mutual defense and trade pacts were negotiated.

World War II brought strengthened cooperation among the

[1]From a speech by Franklin Roosevelt, in *The Evolution of Our Latin American Policy*, edited by James W. Gantenbein

George Bush and Mikhail Gorbachev met in Malta in 1989, just before the communist bloc of eastern countries began to fragment.

nations of the Western Hemisphere. The United States and Canada formed a joint committee to oversee the defense of northern North America. In 1942, the United States joined with most of the countries of Central and South America to coordinate the defense of the rest of the hemisphere.

However, after the war much of Latin America slid into a depression. Desperate for economic help, leaders requested American aid, only to be told that the United States could not afford to help because it was funding the Marshall Plan. This disappointed many Latin Americans, and they began to question their relationships with the United States. Some goodwill was restored by the organization of American States (OAS), which was designed to promote democracy and economic development and to resolve disputes.

In the 1950s the Cold War dominated hemispheric relations. The United States supported several anticommunist governments in Latin America despite human rights abuses by those governments. It also involved itself in the internal affairs of some countries, such as Cuba where the Cuban leader, Fidel Castro, snubbed the United States by instituting communist principles and openly seeking Soviet help. President Johnson sent 20,000 troops to the Dominican Republic in 1965. The United States "cannot, must not, and will not permit the establishment of another communist government in the Western Hemisphere," he insisted. And when revolutionary movements sprang up in Guatemala, Nicaragua, El Salvador, and several other countries President Reagan was convinced that the Soviets and the Cubans were behind them. Claiming that the United States had to forcefully draw the line against communism in Central America, Reagan's administration worked to defeat the rebel Sandinistas who had taken over in Nicaragua. Reagan also sent marines into Grenada to oust a communist dictator and backed the government of El Salvador in its civil war.

The United States also provided economic aid to these countries through programs such as the Alliance for Progress. Important advances were made in education, roads, and health care, and diplomatic relations improved with some Latin American nations.

Drugs, debts, and the environment were the major issues in relations with Latin America in the 1980s. The U.S. government attempted to slow the flow of drugs into the United States in several ways but with little success. Meanwhile, many Latin American countries reached the brink of bankruptcy. Mexico, in particular, faced a financial crisis. The United States provided emergency funding to its neighbor and urged banks to increase their lending to Latin America. Environmental concerns further strained relations with some Latin American countries. People of the Americas and the world joined to stop the destruction of the Amazon rain forest in Brazil.

Dramatic events took place elsewhere as the 1990s began. East and West Germans tore down the Berlin Wall—the hated symbol of

Eric Bouvet/Gamma–Liaison

the Cold War—brick by brick, as they reunited their country. The countries of Eastern Europe—Poland, East Germany, Czechoslovakia, Hungary, Romania, and Bulgaria—threw out their communist governments and held democratic elections. Peaceful mass demonstrations and similar changes swept the republics of the Soviet Union.

In the Middle East Iraq invaded and conquered Kuwait. The United States reacted to this invasion by blocking the flow of goods into and out of Iraq, a move supported by many countries and the United Nations. The United States also sent a large military force to the Middle East.

Everyone hoped that the threat of military action would convince Iraq to withdraw from Kuwait. But Iraqi dictator Saddam Hussein refused to pull his troops out or to negotiate. In January 1991 a United Nations force led by the United States launched an attack on Iraqi military targets. President Bush announced that a war for the liberation of Kuwait had begun. 🖙

The people, not their leaders, decided the Wall separating West and East Germany must come tumbling down. The celebration at the reconciliation of East and West drew millions to the Brandenburg Gate in Berlin.

Return to the Preview & Review on page 658.

The Development of Modern America 669

EPILOGUE REVIEW

1865		1900		1925	

1865
Civil War ends

★
Reconstruction
begins

1869
Knights of
Labor founded

1877
Reconstruction ends

1890
Sherman
Antitrust
Act

1896
Plessy v. Ferguson

1898
Spanish-American War

1909
NAACP formed

1917
U.S. enters
Great War

1928
Ford
introduces
Model A

1929
Great
Depression
begins

1933
New Deal
started

Epilogue Summary
Read the statements below. Choose one, and write a paragraph explaining its importance.
1. Farmers poured onto the Great Plains, taking over the lands of the Plains Indians.
2. American business leaders forged a great industrial nation, but unjust business practices led to demands for government regulation.
3. Workers organized unions to negotiate with powerful employers.
4. Some Americans believed they had a mission to carry American interests worldwide.
5. Progressive reformers successfully attacked some problems, while others remained.
6. The U.S. joined the Great War to make the world safe for democracy.
7. American businesses produced more than the public could buy leading to a severe depression known as the Great Depression.
8. The New Deal was somewhat successful in dealing with the depression but created what we call today the welfare state.
9. The Japanese bombed Pearl Harbor, bringing the U.S. into World War II.
10. A Cold War rivalry between the U.S. and the communist Soviet Union broke out soon after the war. This Cold War last more than 40 years.
11. The United States became one of the world's most affluent countries. But not all groups shared equally in the wealth. This gave rise to the civil rights movement.
12. United States policy in the Western Hemisphere has gradually changed from involvement to cooperation.

Reviewing Chronological Order
Number your paper 1-5. Then study the time line above and place the following events in the order in which they happened by writing the first next to 1, the second next to 2, and so on.

1. America enters World War II
2. Truman Doctrine
3. Sherman Antitrust Act
4. Nixon resigns as president
5. Cuban Missile crisis

Understanding Main Ideas
1. How did big business come to dominate the United States economy by the end of the 1800s? Why did workers organize the union movement?
2. What were some of the problems of urbanization addressed by progressives?
3. What events demonstrate the expansion of America's international influence and power in the years between the Civil and Great wars?
4. What were some of the causes of the Great Depression? What steps did the government take to get the country out of it?
5. What were the roots of the Cold War? In what ways was the Cold War fought?

Thinking Critically
1. **Evaluating.** During the New Deal increased government spending was used to revive the economy, even though this unbalanced the federal budget. What are the disadvantages of such deficit spending? Do you think it is a responsible fiscal policy to stimulate the economy? Why, or why not?
2. **Interpreting.** What was the purpose of Martin Luther King, Jr.'s, strategy of nonviolent resistance? How did he apply it toward his goals? If nonviolent efforts are repeatedly unsuccessful, what results might you expect?
3. **Determining Cause and Effect.** How has the population shift to the suburbs affected America's inner cities? Describe the results of the flight of well-to-do residents and relocation of businesses to the suburbs.

| | 1950 | | | | 1975 | | | 2000 |

1939
Depression ends

1941
U.S. enters World War II

1945
Hiroshima and Nagasaki

★

World War II ends

1947
Truman Doctrine

1949
NATO is formed

1954
Brown v. Board of Education

1962
Cuban Missile Crisis

1963
"I Have a Dream" speech

★

Kennedy assassinated

1965
American involvement in Vietnam escalates

1966
NOW organized

1972
Watergate begins

1973
Wounded Knee

1974
Nixon resigns

1979
Hostages seized in Iran

1980
Reagan elected president

1989
Berlin Wall comes down

1990
U.S. sends troops to Middle East

4. Drawing conclusions. Women are still often paid less than men for the same work. What has caused this inequity? How could this problem be solved?

Writing About History
Spanish conquistadors claimed that their exploits were for "God, gold, and glory." In this way they justified territorial expansion and the control of native peoples for Spain. Compare and contrast Spain's conquest of the New World with America's imperialism. Consider **a.** the motivation for, and means of, conquest; **b.** the means of control over other peoples or nations, and **c.** the justifications for empire.

Using Primary Sources
Some Americans favored American imperialism, as you can see from this speech made to the United States Senate just before a vote on the treaty ending the Spanish-American War. As you read this excerpt, consider the speaker's arguments. Then answer the questions that follow it.

Shall the American people continue their restless march toward the commercial supremacy of the world? Shall free institutions extend their blessed reign until the empire of our principles is established over the hearts of all humanity? . . . Has the Almighty Father given us gifts and marked us with His favor, only to rot in our own selfishness?. . . .

We cannot escape our world duties. We must carry out the purpose of a fate that has driven us to be greater than our small intentions. We cannot retreat from any soil where Providence has placed our flag. It is up to us to save that soil for liberty and civilization. For liberty and civilization and God's purpose fulfilled, the flag must from now on be the symbol of all mankind.

1. According to the speaker why would the other peoples of the world benefit from American expansion?
2. How can you tell that the speaker believes in manifest destiny?

Linking History & Geography
The United States has been involved in several incidents in the Middle East since World War II. To better understand its relative location and the countries of the region, create two maps. On an outline map of the world, label the Mediterranean Sea and the Middle East. Then on an outline map of the Middle East to label all the countries, their capitals, and major bodies of water.

Enriching Your Study of History
1. **Individual Project.** As an oral history project, interview five adults about the Vietnam War. Use a tape recorder if possible. Ask your sources about their experiences, their attitudes about policies, how the war affected their lives, and how they think it affected, and continues to affect, the country. Using your notes or tape recordings, write a script for a documentary of the stories and opinions of your primary sources.
2. **Cooperative Project.** Create a visual time line of the struggle for civil rights. Use copies of photographs from magazines or make original drawings to illustrate events and individuals. Include the dates of key historic moments in the civil rights movement. The graphic time line drawings could become the basis of a school mural.

The Development of Modern America   671

REFERENCE
SECTION

The Reference Section contains a variety of features designed to enhance your understanding of the story of America. *Maps: Portraying the Land* reviews general information about maps and map-reading skills. The atlas includes a world map, maps of Europe, Asia, Africa, and several maps of the United States. A series of graphs and charts present statistical profiles of major American social and economic changes. A Document section contains primary source documents. The glossary lists boldfaced words and their definitions. The index provides page references for the topics discussed in *The Story of America*. An acknowledgments page lists the title and publisher of the primary sources used in *The Story of America*.

MAPS: PORTRAYING THE LAND

We use maps to picture the land. When early people traveled, they noticed differences among places. To describe the new places they had seen, they scratched crude maps on rocks or drew them on leather. Today's maps are the geographer's most important tool. As you read, keep these questions in mind:

1. What features do most maps have in common?
2. Why are maps imperfect pictures of the earth? What are map projections?
3. What are the four most common landforms?
4. On what basis do geographers identify physical regions? Cultural regions?

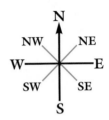

UNDERSTANDING MAPS

Perhaps you have used a map to find your way to a place, such as a friend's house for a party. In order to use any map, you must be able to "read" it, or understand its parts.

Maps

Most of the maps in this textbook have similar parts. These include a **title,** a **legend,** a **directional indicator,** and a **scale.** The title tells you what the map is about. Many map titles also include a date and the area shown. The title of this map is Colonial Products, 1775. The title tells you that the subject is items produced in the colonies in 1775.

The legend, or key, explains the meaning of the symbols used on the map. Areas where tobacco was grown are marked with a tobacco leaf, paper mills with a roll of paper, and other activities with a variety of other symbols. The extent of settlement in 1775 is shaded in brown.

A directional indicator, such as the **compass rose,** helps you find directions on a map. The four cardinal directions—north, south, east, and west—are labeled on the compass rose. North is labeled with an N, south with an S, east with an E, and west with a W. As the compass rose shows, you would travel north to get from Newport to Boston.

You can also determine intermediate directions—northeast, southeast, southwest, and northwest—using the compass rose. Often they are indicated but not labeled. The compass rose at the top of the next column shows the intermediate directions. As you can see on the map, New York City is northeast of Philadelphia.

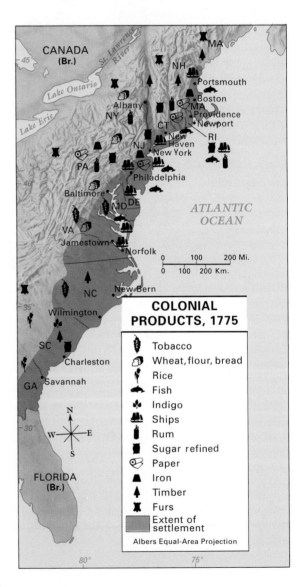

COLONIAL PRODUCTS, 1775

Tobacco
Wheat, flour, bread
Rice
Fish
Indigo
Ships
Rum
Sugar refined
Paper
Iron
Timber
Furs
Extent of settlement

Albers Equal-Area Projection

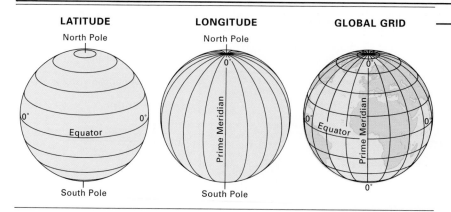

LATITUDE

North Pole

0°   0°

Equator

South Pole

LONGITUDE

North Pole

Prime Meridian

South Pole

GLOBAL GRID

Prime Meridian

Equator

0°   0°

0°

To help you determine distance, maps have a scale. The distances shown on the map are much smaller than the actual distances on the earth's surface. The scale tells you how to relate the two. The line of the scale is divided into equal intervals and labeled in both miles and kilometers. The scale on the map shows that just less than three-quarters of an inch on the map represents 200 miles on the earth's surface. About how far is it from Jamestown to Philadelphia? You should find that it is about 200 miles. The Strategy for Success on page 32 will help you practice using the parts of a map.

Maps in *The Story of America* contain certain special features to enrich your study of them. Around the edges of each map are marks referring to the global grid. This grid, created by the lines of latitude and longitude, helps you locate places on the map. The Strategy for Success on page 46 provides information about latitude and longitude and offers opportunities to practice using them.

Many of the maps in *The Story of America* also have special maps to help you see the location of the area you are studying in relation to other areas of the United States or the world. Such maps are called **locator maps**. The map below has a world locator map to the right of the main map. A box shows the Barbary States in relation to the rest of

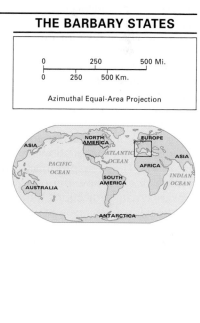

THE BARBARY STATES

0   250   500 Mi.

0   250   500 Km.

Azimuthal Equal-Area Projection

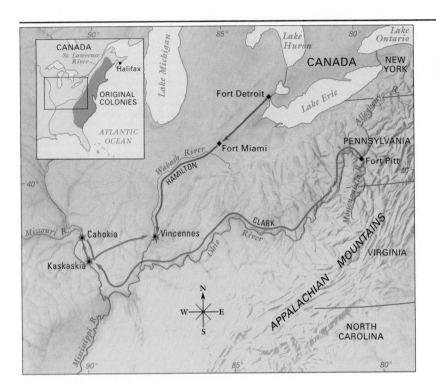

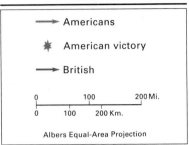

Americans

American victory

British

| 0 | | 100 | | 200 Mi. |
| 0 | | 100 | 200 Km. | |

Albers Equal-Area Projection

the world. As you can see, the Barbary States, on the northern coast of Africa, lay far across the Atlantic Ocean from the United States. In the above map the locator map is in the upper left-hand corner of the main map. It outlines the eastern half of the United States. The map shows the area of study with a box and shades the extent of the original colonies for further reference.

Map Projections

Because maps are flat and the earth is a sphere, maps are imperfect representations of the earth's surface. Globes provide a much more accurate picture of the earth. But they are impractical to carry with you. So **cartographers,** or mapmakers, have devised ways of showing the round earth on flat maps. These **map projections** allow us to get a better idea of how the earth really looks. Mapmakers create projections through complex mathematical formulas, usually using computers to design the maps.

How does a cartographer create a projection? Imagine taking the cover of a softball and using it to make a flat, rectangular picture of the ball. You would have to cut and flatten the cover to fit the rectangle. When you were finished making your picture, parts of the cover would no longer look just as they had when they were on the ball. A cartographer designing a map projection does the

same, deciding what to show most accurately and what to twist and shape, or distort. The interrupted projection at top of the next page gives you an idea of how this process works.

Every map projection, and therefore every map, contains distortions. A projection might distort the shapes of land areas, or their sizes, or distances, or directions. Maps generally are most accurate near the center and more distorted around the edges. Maps of large areas tend to be more distorted than maps of smaller areas. To see how different projections make maps look different, compare the two maps at the bottom of the next page. The map projection on the left is a Robinson projection; the map on the right uses a Peter's projection.

Knowing all this, mapmakers choose the projection that least distorts what they wish to show. One of the earliest projections, the Mercator projection, was used to make maps for sailors. It shows direction accurately—most important for navigation—but it distorts the size of areas away from the equator. The two small maps at the bottoms of pages 682–83 of the Atlas are Mercator projections.

Most of the maps in this textbook are equal-area maps. Equal-area maps show relative sizes quite accurately, although they distort shapes somewhat. The physical map of the United States on

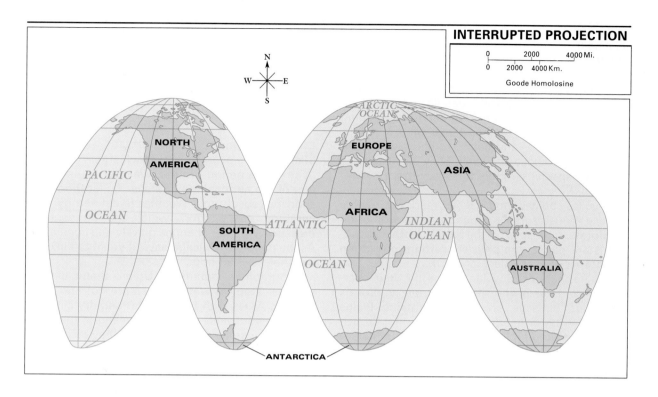

INTERRUPTED PROJECTION

0   2000   4000 Mi.

0   2000 4000 Km.

Goode Homolosine

pages 688–89 of the Atlas is an example of the Albers Equal-Area projection.

You also will note several world maps that use the Robinson projection. The Robinson projection is a compromise, which means it minimizes distortions in size, shape, distance, and direction but does not preserve complete accuracy in any of those properties. It has become widely accepted for world maps. The world map on pages 682–83 of the Atlas is a Robinson projection.

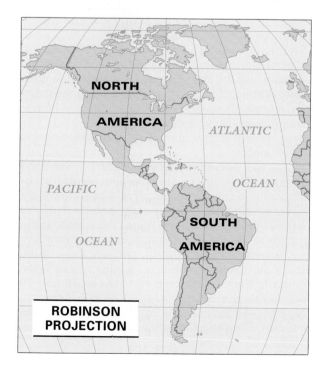

ROBINSON PROJECTION

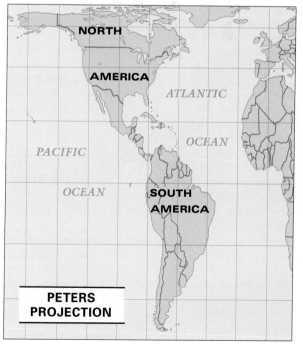

PETERS PROJECTION

Maps: Portraying the Land   677

Types of Maps

Just as there are many map projections, there are many types of maps. Most maps are either political maps or physical maps. Political maps show information such as national and state boundaries and major cities. Physical maps illustrate the natural landscape of an area. They often use shading to illustrate **relief**—the existence of mountains, hills, and valleys—and colors to show **elevation,** or the height above sea level. They also may use colors or special symbols to show other physical features.

Wrinkles, bulges, and gashes mark the earth's surface. These surface variations create different **landforms,** or shapes on the earth's surface. Landforms are part of the **physical setting,** or **natural landscape,** of every place on earth.

Geographers classify landforms by their characteristics. Four of the most common landforms are plains, plateaus, hills, and mountains. **Plains** are nearly flat or gently rolling lands that stretch unbroken to the horizon. The nomadic hunters—those who wandered from place to place—and early explorers who came to America were cheered by the vast plains, knowing they would be easier to cross than mountains. **Plateaus,** too, are relatively flat lands, but unlike plains they rise sharply from the surrounding landscape to 2,000 feet (610 meters) or more on at least one side.

Hills are rounded bulges of land that rise at least 500 feet (152 meters) above the surrounding land to no more than 2,000 feet (610 meters). Various natural forces form hills, but many result from the wearing down, or **erosion,** of mountains. Early settlers found hills obstacles to movement until improvements in wagons and roads in the 1700s made crossing them easier.

The most dramatic landform is the **mountain.** Mountains are often rocky, rugged land that rises sharply from the surrounding land to heights of over 2,000 feet (610 meters). The highest mountain peaks in the United States (not including Alaska and Hawaii) are in the west—the Rocky Mountains, the Sierra Nevada, and the Cascades. Mountain ranges lie near both coasts of the United States. These mountain barriers have influenced American history, from settlement patterns to government policies.

Other maps are called **special-purpose maps** because they illustrate special information. Special-purpose maps include historical maps that show the routes of explorers or boundary changes, population maps that illustrate where the most people live, and economic maps that highlight economic activities.

MAPPING THE UNITED STATES

Maps illustrate a variety of information about the United States. The special-purpose maps that follow show climate regions and cultural regions in the United States.

Climate Regions

Climate is the average of daily weather conditions over a long period of time. **Weather** is the condition of the atmosphere at a specific location for a short period of time. Weather is defined by temperature, precipitation, wind, and atmospheric pressure. Weather changes quickly and constantly. As the people of Chicago say, "If you don't like the weather, wait an hour."

Geographers identify 11 United States climate regions. **Tropical wet** climates are hot and rainy all year. Areas with **tropical wet-and-dry** climates are hot, with most of the rain falling in the summer. These areas are hot because they receive the most direct rays from the sun. In the United States only the Hawaiian Islands have a tropical wet climate. The southern tip of Florida has a tropical wet-and-dry climate. **Humid subtropical** areas found chiefly in the southeastern states have long, hot, and rainy summers. Winters in this region are typically mild but do occassionally have brief cold spells. These areas, too, are relatively warm because the sun's rays are fairly direct.

Continental climates occur in the Northeast and Midwest. These areas have severe winters, but the summers vary from warm to hot.

A **mediterranean** climate occurs on the western edge of North America in California. The winters are mild and dry, the summers hot and dry. A **west coast marine** climate is also found along the western margin of continent north of the Mediterranean region. These areas have cool summers and many days of drizzly rainfall, most of which occurs in the winter.

Little rain falls on areas with **desert** or **semiarid** climates. Such areas occur where landforms or atmospheric conditions cut off rain-bearing winds. Semiarid climates affect nearly one-third of the earth's land. In the United States the largest semiarid areas are the Great Plains and the Intermountain Region, which lie in the rain shadows of the Rocky Mountains and Sierra Nevada respectively. Typically these areas receive between 10 and 20 inches (25 and 50 centimeters) of rain per year. Desert areas, such as the Southwest, receive even less rain, often less than 10 inches (25 centimeters) a year.

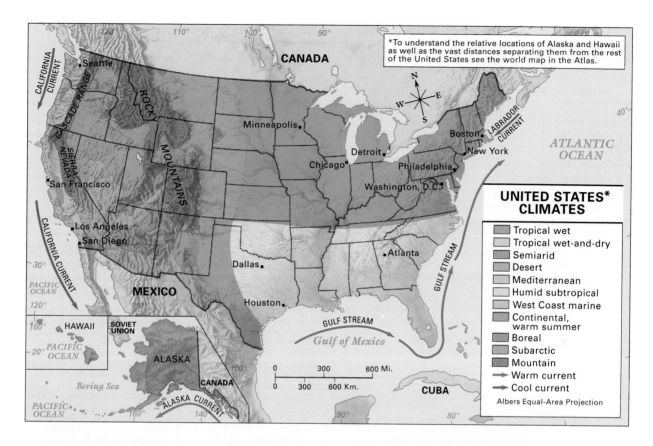

Areas near the North and South poles have high-latitude climates. Because they are far from the equator, the sun's rays strike them at a great angle rather than directly. They are very cold, with no month averaging more than 50° F (10° C). **Boreal** and **subarctic** climates, found in the United States only in Alaska, fit into this climate group. Their long, cold winters and brief summers provide too short a growing season for most crops.

Areas high in the mountains fall into a special climate category—**highland,** or **mountain.** In such areas elevation and landscape cause temperature and precipitation to vary so much that climate generalizations mean little. Each area actually has a climate all its own, called a microclimate.

Cultural Regions

Geographers also use special-purpose maps to illustrate the cultural regions of the United States. The following map identifies seven regions: Northeast, Southeast, Great Lakes, Plains, Southwest, Rocky Mountain, and Pacific Coast. Traditions and history, ethnic makeup, and economic activity link the people within these regions.

The **Northeast** region ranks today as a major manufacturing and commercial area of the nation.

Economic development focuses on such cities as New York, Boston, Philadelphia, Pittsburgh, and Baltimore.

The **Southeast** lies within the Sun Belt, an area characterized by warm weather and rapid growth in population and economic importance. Fertile soil and a mild, moist climate have made the Southeast a key agricultural region from its earliest settlements.

Southeastern farmers grow valuable cash crops such as cotton, tobacco, rice, and peanuts. But the Southeast is changing rapidly. Manufacturing has expanded in the region since the end of the Civil War, making the economy far more diversified. Textile production is the leading industry, and many food processing and chemical companies have recently relocated to the Southeast. Its cities have grown accordingly.

After the Revolutionary War, settlers attracted by the fertile soil of the **Great Lakes** region poured by the thousands across the Appalachians. Farmers from the eastern United States, Scandinavia, Germany, and elsewhere in Europe made the region a center of wheat and corn production. Sites on the Great Lakes and large rivers grew into cities that eventually produced steel, machinery, and other products of America's Industrial Revolution. By the early 1900s Chicago, Cleveland, Detroit, Buffalo, and Cincinnati ranked among the nation's largest cities.

The **Plains** region is America's prime farming region. Crops—especially corn, wheat, and soybeans—wave in fields that stretch as far as the eye can see. Grain elevators stand next to the rail lines that are the arteries of the region. The rich soil, adequate rainfall, and level land of the eastern plains drew farmers from the eastern states and Europe. Many plains communities still reflect the culture of the original settlers, making the plains region a cultural patchwork. People moved onto the dry western plains only after new farming techniques and mechanization made profitable farming there possible.

The states of the **Southwest** are distinguished by a warm, sunny climate and a multicultural population. Most of the Southwest developed slowly. Perhaps more than any other factor, railroads spurred growth in the region. Texas and Oklahoma became the "cattle kingdom," shipping meat by rail to eastern markets. Railroads also

carried settlers to small towns such as Tucson and Phoenix and old Spanish cities such as Santa Fe. Miners came to the Southwest to tap huge ore deposits.

The biggest boom for the area came with the discovery of oil and natural gas in Texas and Oklahoma. Oil refineries and chemical plants soon sprouted throughout the region. Although the oil boom has slowed in recent years, the population and economy of these states continues to grow. Large numbers of people from northern and eastern states have moved to the warm Southwest. This influx has been joined by large numbers of Mexicans who have crossed the border to make a new life in America.

The culture of the Southwest is a mixture of Hispanic, American Indian, and Anglo traditions. Mexican influences are especially strong, as you can see in the local architecture and Spanish place names.

In the **Rocky Mountain** region, development has been difficult. Settlement, farming, and other economic activities take place only in isolated areas. Most of the farming occurs in the eastern part of

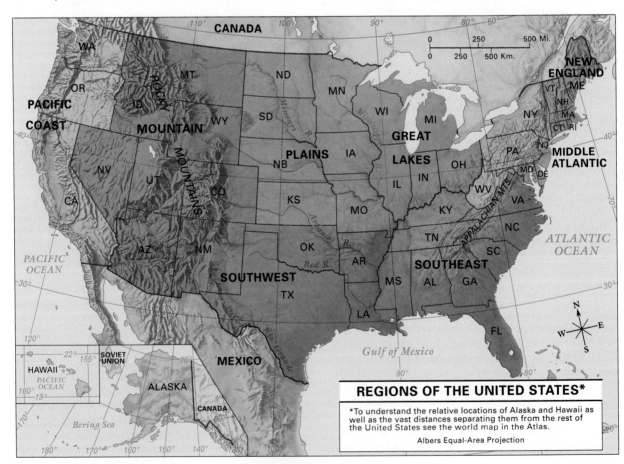

REGIONS OF THE UNITED STATES*

*To understand the relative locations of Alaska and Hawaii as well as the vast distances separating them from the rest of the United States see the world map in the Atlas.

Albers Equal-Area Projection

the region, where the Great Plains reach the foothills of the Rockies, and in valleys and on plateaus among the mountains. Industry is limited in many areas because the rugged terrain restricts access. Forestry and mining are the leading industries.

The **Pacific Coast** is a region of varied physical and cultural settings. The opening of the Oregon Trail in the late 1830s and the discovery of gold in California started a movement of people to the region that has increased steadily. California, Oregon, and Washington have experienced tremendous population and economic growth in the last 50 years, as have Alaska and Hawaii, which became states in 1959.

The Pacific Coast region has a diverse economy. Rich farmlands produce vegetables and fruit, mines yield rich ores, and factories manufacture a wide variety of goods. The population of the region is equally diverse. Asian Americans, Mexican Americans, Pacific Islanders, and Native Americans make up large segments of the population. Their cultural traditions add to the richness of Pacific Coast life.

Map Skills

The ability to read and understand maps can come in handy in everyday life. You may use a street map to find directions or get information from a weather map. Reading maps is, of course, a key part of studying geography, history, and many other subjects. Learning about the global grid, map projections, and types of maps is the first step in learning to read maps. Many of the Strategies for Success in this textbook focus on map skills.

Map Section Review

1. What are the four parts most maps have in common? What is the purpose of each part?
2. Why have cartographers developed map projections to picture the earth?
3. Why do map projections distort features of the earth?
4. What climate regions influence the United States? Where is each region found?
5. Into what cultural regions do geographers often divide the United States?

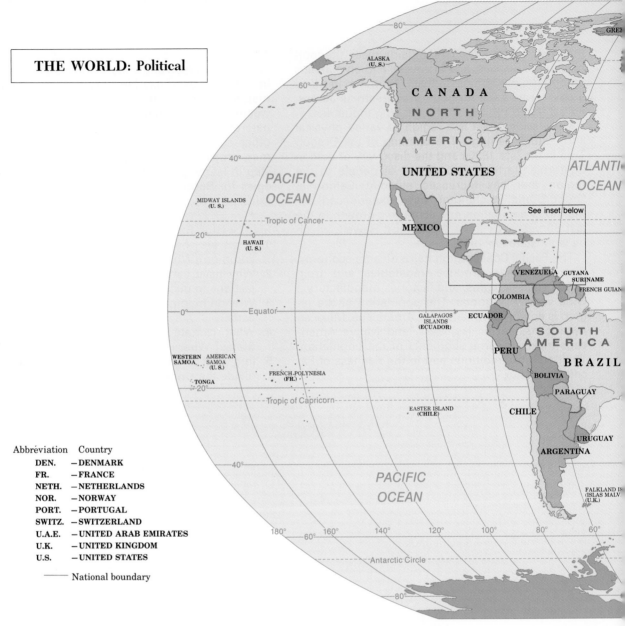

THE WORLD: Political

CANADA
NORTH
AMERICA
UNITED STATES

ALASKA
(U.S.)

GREI

ATLANTI
OCEAN

PACIFIC
OCEAN

MIDWAY ISLANDS
(U.S.)

Tropic of Cancer

MEXICO

HAWAII
(U.S.)

See inset below

VENEZUELA
GUYANA
SURINAME
FRENCH GUIAN

COLOMBIA

GALAPAGOS
ISLANDS
(ECUADOR)

ECUADOR

Equator

SOUTH
AMERICA

PERU

BRAZIL

WESTERN
SAMOA

AMERICAN
SAMOA
(U.S.)

FRENCH POLYNESIA
(FR.)

BOLIVIA

PARAGUAY

TONGA

EASTER ISLAND
(CHILE)

CHILE

Tropic of Capricorn

URUGUAY

ARGENTINA

PACIFIC
OCEAN

FALKLAND IS.
(ISLAS MALV.)
(U.K.)

Antarctic Circle

Abbreviation	Country
DEN.	– DENMARK
FR.	– FRANCE
NETH.	– NETHERLANDS
NOR.	– NORWAY
PORT.	– PORTUGAL
SWITZ.	– SWITZERLAND
U.A.E.	– UNITED ARAB EMIRATES
U.K.	– UNITED KINGDOM
U.S.	– UNITED STATES

———— National boundary

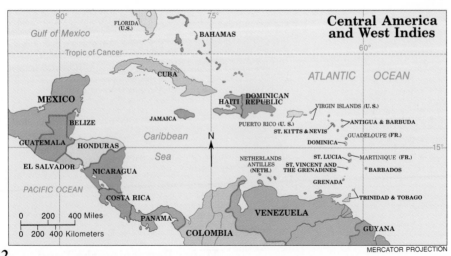

Central America and West Indies

Gulf of Mexico

FLORIDA
(U.S.)

BAHAMAS

Tropic of Cancer

ATLANTIC   OCEAN

CUBA

MEXICO

DOMINICAN
REPUBLIC

HAITI

VIRGIN ISLANDS (U.S.)

JAMAICA

BELIZE

PUERTO RICO (U.S.)

ANTIGUA & BARBUDA

ST. KITTS & NEVIS

GUADELOUPE (FR.)

Caribbean

DOMINICA

GUATEMALA

HONDURAS

N

Sea

EL SALVADOR

NICARAGUA

NETHERLANDS
ANTILLES
(NETH.)

ST. LUCIA

MARTINIQUE (FR.)

ST. VINCENT AND
THE GRENADINES

BARBADOS

PACIFIC OCEAN

GRENADA

COSTA RICA

TRINIDAD & TOBAGO

0   200   400 Miles

PANAMA

VENEZUELA

0   200 400 Kilometers

COLOMBIA

GUYANA

MERCATOR PROJECTION

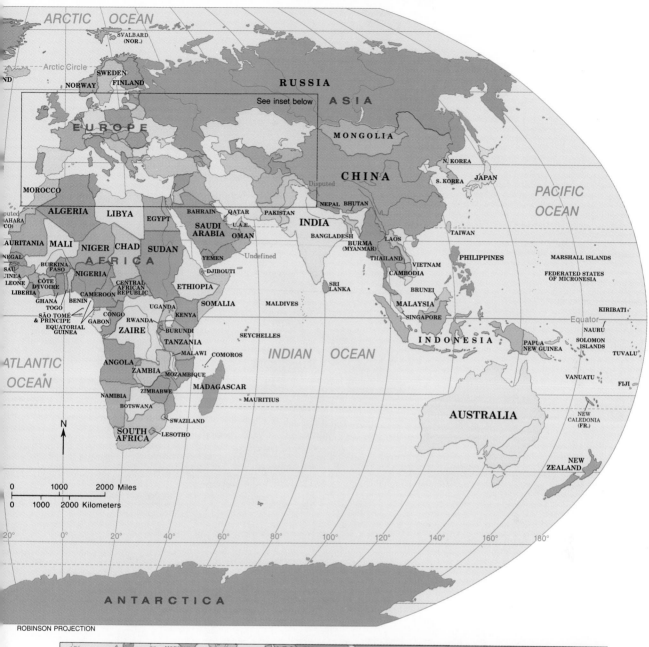

ARCTIC OCEAN

SVALBARD (NOR.)

Arctic Circle

ND

NORWAY   SWEDEN
FINLAND

RUSSIA   A S I A

See inset below

E U R O P E   MONGOLIA

N. KOREA

S. KOREA   JAPAN

MOROCCO   Disputed   CHINA

PACIFIC OCEAN

BAHRAIN   QATAR   PAKISTAN
ALGERIA   LIBYA   EGYPT   NEPAL BHUTAN
                              SAUDI   U.A.E.   INDIA
                              ARABIA   OMAN
AURITANIA   MALI   NIGER   CHAD   SUDAN   BANGLADESH   TAIWAN
                                          YEMEN   Undefined   BURMA   LAOS
NEGAL   A F R I C A   (MYANMAR)
SAU   DJIBOUTI   THAILAND   VIETNAM   MARSHALL ISLANDS
GUINEA   NIGERIA   CAMBODIA   PHILIPPINES   FEDERATED STATES
LEONE   CÔTE   OF MICRONESIA
       D'IVOIRE   CENTRAL   ETHIOPIA   SRI   BRUNEI
LIBERIA   AFRICAN   LANKA
GHANA   CAMEROON   REPUBLIC   MALDIVES   MALAYSIA   KIRIBATI
TOGO BENIN   UGANDA   SINGAPORE
SÃO TOMÉ   CONGO   KENYA   NAURU
& PRÍNCIPE   GABON RWANDA   SEYCHELLES   SOLOMON
EQUATORIAL   ZAIRE   BURUNDI   I N D O N E S I A   ISLANDS
GUINEA   TANZANIA   PAPUA
                                          MALAWI   COMOROS   INDIAN   OCEAN   NEW GUINEA   TUVALU
ATLANTIC   ANGOLA   VANUATU
OCEAN   ZAMBIA   MOZAMBIQUE   FIJI
                  ZIMBABWE   MADAGASCAR   AUSTRALIA
          NAMIBIA   MAURITIUS   NEW
              BOTSWANA   CALEDONIA
                          SWAZILAND   (FR.)
              SOUTH   LESOTHO
N   AFRICA   NEW
                                                                                              ZEALAND

0   1000   2000 Miles
0   1000   2000 Kilometers

20°   0°   20°   40°   60°   80°   100°   120°   140°   160°   180°

A N T A R C T I C A

ROBINSON PROJECTION

15°   0°   NORWAY   SWEDEN   ESTONIA
UNITED   DENMARK   LATVIA   0   250   500 Miles   Europe and
KINGDOM   LITHUANIA   0 250 500 Kilometers   Central Asia
IRELAND   NETH.   RUSSIA
                              BYELARUS   RUSSIA
          BELGIUM   GERMANY   POLAND
ATLANTIC LUXEMBOURG   CZECHOSLOVAKIA   UKRAINE   KAZAKHSTAN
OCEAN   LIECHTENSTEIN
          FRANCE SWITZ. AUSTRIA HUNGARY   MOLDOVA
45°   MONACO ITALY   ROMANIA
                    SAN MARINO YUGOSLAVIA   UZBEKISTAN
          ANDORRA CORSICA   VATICAN CITY BULGARIA   Black Sea   GEORGIA
PORTUGAL   (FR.) SARDINA ALBANIA   ARMENIA   KYRGYZSTAN
          SPAIN   (ITALY) SICILY GREECE   TURKEY   AZERBAIJAN TURKMENISTAN   TAJIKISTAN
                          (ITALY)   CHINA
                          MALTA   CYPRUS SYRIA   AFGHANISTAN
N   LEBANON   IRAN
          MOROCCO   TUNISIA   ISRAEL IRAQ   PAKISTAN
                                    JORDAN   INDIA
          ALGERIA   LIBYA   EGYPT   SAUDI ARABIA KUWAIT   NEPAL
                                                                    Mediterranean Sea
                                                            Caspian Sea

MERCATOR PROJECTION

683

Reykjavík
ICELAND

Arctic Circle

FAROE IS.
(DEN.)

SHETLAND IS.
(U.K.)

•Trondheim

SWEDEN

NORWAY

•Bergen

⊛Oslo

Uppsala•
•Stavanger

Stockholm•

Göteborg•

Glasgow• •Edinburgh

**UNITED
KINGDOM**

DENMARK

North

Belfast•

Copenhagen ⊛

Bornholm
(DEN.)

Sea

Dublin
⊛
IRELAND

Liverpool•

•Manchester

Kalin

Gdans

•Birmingham

•Hamburg

Cardiff•

NETHERLANDS

•Bremen

Berlin ⊛

Bristol•

Thames R.

London•
The Hague⊛ Amsterdam•

Dover•

Rotterdam•

GERMANY

Oder

P O L A

Calais•

BELGIUM Brussels•

•Bonn

River

Le Havre•

LUXEMBOURG

Leipzig•

Elbe

Seine

Paris⊛

Luxembourg•

Frankfurt•

R. Prague⊛ Kra

R.

ATLANTIC

Loire

River

Strasbourg•

Rhine R.

Stuttgart•

R. CZECHOSLOVA

Danube

OCEAN

F R A N C E

Dijon•

•Munich
Vienna⊛

AUSTRIA Budapes

•La Rochelle

Zürich• LIECHTENSTEIN

Bay of
Biscay

Geneva• Bern• SWITZERLAND

HUN

Bordeaux•

Lyon•

A L P S

Garonne

Milan•

Zagreb•

Rhône R.

Turin•

•Venice

•Trieste

R.

Po River

PYRENEES

Genoa•

Nice•

SAN

Bel

Porto•

ANDORRA

Marseille•

MONACO Florence•

APENNINES

MARINO

YUGOSLA

Sarajevo•

PORTUGAL

Ebro River

•Barcelona

Corsica
(FR.)

Adriatic Sea

Lisbon•

Tagus R.

⊛Madrid

Tiber

Rome⊛

S P A I N

Sardinia
(IT.)

R.

I T A L Y

Tir

A L

•Valencia

Seville•

BALEARIC ISLANDS
(SP.)

Tyrrhenian

•Naples

Cádiz•

Sea

Ion

Se

Strait of Gibraltar

M e d i t e r r a n e a n S e a

Palermo•

Sicily

A F R I C A

⊚ **MALTA**

ARCTIC
OCEAN
30°   40°   50°   70°   60°   80°

White Sea

•Arkhangel'sk

U R A L

North Dvina River

M O U N T A I N S

LAND

Lake Ladoga

70°

⊛ Helsinki
of Finland   •St. Petersburg   R U S S I A

⊛ Tallinn
ESTONIA   50°

•Nizhniy Novgorod
(Gor'kiy)

Riga
LATVIA   ⊛ Moscow   Samara
                                   (Kuybyshev)•   *River*

IUANIA
Inius   *Ural*

⊛ Minsk

BYELARUS

w

⊛ Kiev   •Kharkov   Volgograd   *Volga*

Dniester   *River*   ASIA   60°

UKRAINE   Don River   *Caspian*

River

THIAN   MOLDOVA   *R.*
          Kishinev⊛   *Dnieper*   *Sea*   40°
MTS.   •Odessa   of
                              Azov   *Sea*

UMANIA   CAUCASUS   MTS.

Bucharest⊛   •Sevastopol

Danube   River

BALKAN   MTS.   *Black*   *Sea*

⊛ Sofia
BULGARIA   TURKEY
          Istanbul•

N

*Aegean
Sea*

E

⊛ Athens

Crete

EUROPE

⊛   National capital
•   Other city
⊥⊥⊥⊥⊥   Canal
———   National boundary

AZIMUTHAL EQUAL AREA PROJECTION

0   100   200   300 Miles

0   100 200 300   Kilometers

ARCTIC OCEAN

RUSSIA

Lena River

Lena River

Lake Baikal

Ulaanbaatar

MONGOLIA

GOBI (DESERT)

Harbin

Amur River

Sea of Okhotsk

Bering Sea

KAMCHATKA PENINSULA

KURIL ISLANDS (U.S.S.R. & JAPAN)

Vladivostok

Yalu R.

Beijing

Tianjin

Huang He

P'yongyang

N. KOREA

Truce Line

Seoul

S. KOREA

Sea of Japan

Tokyo

JAPAN

Kobe

Osaka

Yokohama

CHINA

Chang

Jiang

Chongqing

Shanghai

Yellow Sea

East China Sea

RYUKYU IS. (JAPAN)

PACIFIC

OCEAN

Xi River

Taipei

TAIWAN

Tropic of Cancer

Guangzhou

Hanoi

MACAO (PORT.)

HONG KONG (U.K.)

LAOS

tiane

oon

Mekong R.

THAILAND

Bangkok

CAMBODIA (KAMPUCHEA)

VIETNAM

Phnom Penh

Ho Chi Minh City

South China Sea

Manila

PHILIPPINES

Philippine Sea

BRUNEI

Bandar Seri Begawan

MALAYSIA

Kuala Lumpur

Singapore

SINGAPORE

Java Sea

Equator

Jakarta

INDONESIA

ASIA

⊛ National capital

• Other city

— National boundary

ROBINSON PROJECTION

687

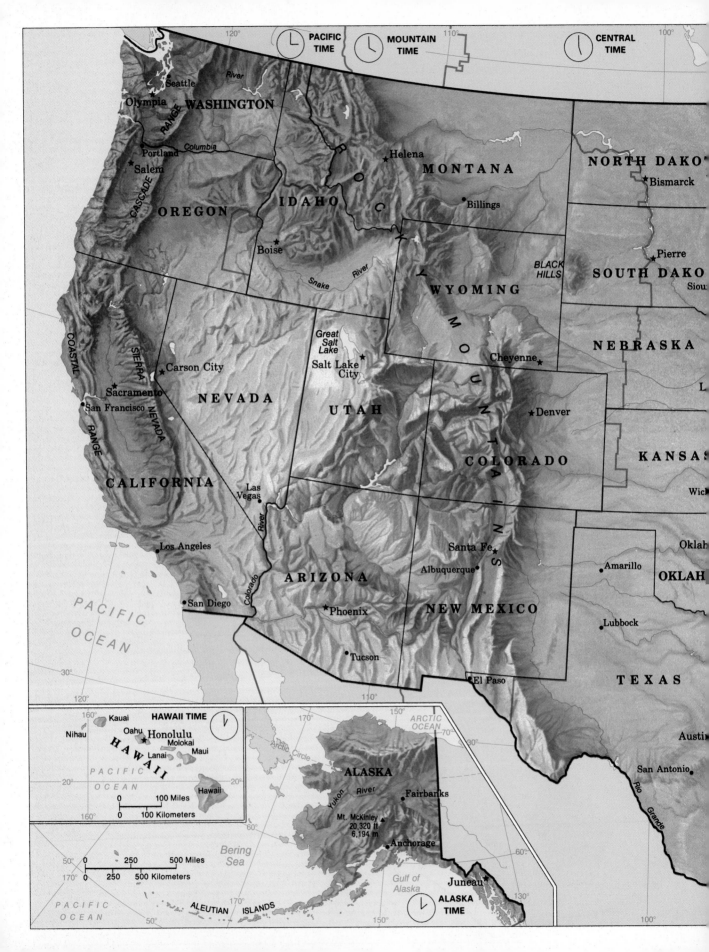

PACIFIC TIME   MOUNTAIN TIME   CENTRAL TIME

120°   110°   100°

RANGE
Seattle
Olympia   WASHINGTON
River
Portland   Columbia
Salem
CASCADE   OREGON   IDAHO   ROC   Helena   MONTANA   NORTH DAKO
Bismarck
Billings
Boise   K   Pierre
Snake   River   SOUTH DAKO
WYOMING   BLACK HILLS   Siou
COASTAL   Great Salt Lake   Y   NEBRASKA
SIERRA   Carson City   Salt Lake City   O   Cheyenne
Sacramento   NEVADA   UTAH   U   Denver   L
San Francisco   RANGE   N   COLORADO   KANSAS
T   Wich
CALIFORNIA   Las Vegas   A   Oklah
River   I   Santa Fe   Amarillo   OKLAH
Los Angeles   N   Albuquerque
ARIZONA   S   Lubbock
Colorado   San Diego   Phoenix   NEW MEXICO
PACIFIC OCEAN   TEXAS
Tucson
30°   El Paso
120°   110°   Austi

HAWAII TIME
160°   Kauai   San Antonio
Nihau   Oahu   Honolulu   170°   ARCTIC OCEAN   Rio
HAWAII   Molokai   150°   70°
Lanai   Maui   Arctic Circle   30°   Grande
PACIFIC   20°   20°   ALASKA
OCEAN   Hawaii   Yukon   River   Fairbanks
0   100 Miles   60°   Mt. McKinley   60°
0   100 Kilometers   20,320 ft 6,194 m
160°   Anchorage
250   500 Miles   Bering Sea   Gulf of Alaska
50°   0   Juneau
170°   0   250   500 Kilometers   ALASKA TIME
PACIFIC OCEAN   ALEUTIAN ISLANDS   150°   130°
50°   170°   100°

EASTERN
TIME

MAINE
★ Augusta

VERMONT
Montpelier •
NEW
HAMPSHIRE
★ Concord
• Boston

Albany ★ **MASSACHUSETTS**
• Rochester
Buffalo •
NEW YORK
★ Providence
Hartford ★ **RHODE ISLAND**
CONNECTICUT

St. Lawrence River
Lake Ontario
Lake Erie

Duluth •
NESOTA
Lake Superior
MICHIGAN
Lake Huron

nneapolis • ★ St. Paul
Mississippi River
WISCONSIN

Milwaukee •
Madison •
Lansing •
Detroit •
River
Lake Michigan

IOWA
• Des Moines
Chicago •
Gary •
INDIANA
OHIO
Columbus •
Cleveland •

Pittsburgh •
PENNSYLVANIA
Harrisburg ★
Philadelphia •
NEW JERSEY
Trenton ★
• New York
Hudson River
GREEN MTS.

ILLINOIS
Springfield ★
Indianapolis ★
Cincinnati •
WEST VIRGINIA
Washington •
Baltimore •
Wilmington •
★ Dover
DELAWARE
Annapolis ★
MARYLAND
70°

ha
Kansas City •
St. Louis •
Frankfort ★
Louisville •
Charleston •
Richmond •
Norfolk •
Chesapeake Bay
40°

Jefferson City ★
Ohio River
KENTUCKY
River
VIRGINIA

MISSOURI

sa
NASHVILLE ★ Nashville
Raleigh •
NORTH CAROLINA
ATLANTIC
OCEAN

ARKANSAS
TENNESSEE
Tennessee River
Memphis •
Mississippi River
Charlotte •
APPALACHIAN MTS.

Little Rock ★
SOUTH
★ Columbia
CAROLINA

Birmingham •
Atlanta •
Charleston •

UNITED STATES: PHYSICAL

⊛ National capital
★ State capital
• Other city
━━ National boundary
─── State boundary

Jackson ★
Montgomery ★
ALABAMA
GEORGIA
Savannah •

Standard time zones are indicated by clocks. (When it is 2 P.M. in western Alaska, it is 6 P.M. along the eastern coast of the United States.)

Albers Equal-Area Projection

MISSISSIPPI
Mobile •
Jacksonville •
★ Tallahassee
30°

Baton Rouge ★
LOUISIANA
Houston •
New Orleans •
FLORIDA
Orlando •

Red River

Gulf of Mexico
Tampa •

N

Miami •

0   250   500 Miles
0   250   500 Kilometers

90°
80°

689

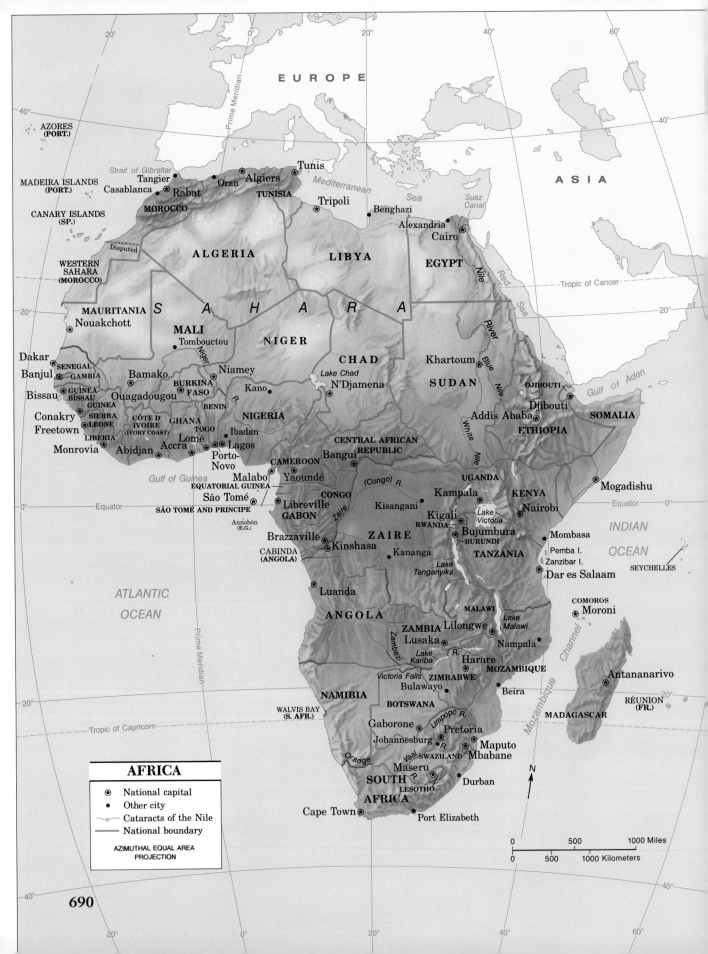

AFRICA

- ⊛ National capital
- • Other city
- ╫ Cataracts of the Nile
- — National boundary

AZIMUTHAL EQUAL AREA
PROJECTION

690

EUROPE

ASIA

Strait of Gibraltar

MADEIRA ISLANDS (PORT.)

AZORES (PORT.)

CANARY ISLANDS (SP.)

Tangier
Casablanca
Rabat
MOROCCO
Oran
Algiers
TUNISIA
Tunis
Tripoli
Benghazi
Mediterranean Sea
Suez Canal
Alexandria
Cairo

WESTERN SAHARA (MOROCCO)
Disputed

ALGERIA
LIBYA
EGYPT
Tropic of Cancer

MAURITANIA
Nouakchott
S A H A R A
MALI
Tombouctou
NIGER
CHAD
Nile
Red Sea
Khartoum
SUDAN
River

Dakar
SENEGAL
Banjul
GAMBIA
Bissau
GUINEA-BISSAU
GUINEA
Conakry
Freetown
SIERRA LEONE
LIBERIA
Monrovia

Bamako
BURKINA FASO
Ouagadougou
Niger R.
Niamey
Kano
N'Djamena
Lake Chad
Blue Nile
DJIBOUTI
Djibouti
Addis Ababa
SOMALIA
ETHIOPIA
Gulf of Aden

CÔTE D'IVOIRE (IVORY COAST)
GHANA
BENIN
TOGO
NIGERIA
Ibadan
Lomé
Accra
Lagos
Abidjan
Porto-Novo

Gulf of Guinea
Malabo
EQUATORIAL GUINEA
São Tomé
SÃO TOMÉ AND PRINCIPE
Annobón (E.G.)

CAMEROON
Yaoundé
CENTRAL AFRICAN REPUBLIC
Bangui
CONGO
Libreville
GABON
Brazzaville
Kinshasa
CABINDA (ANGOLA)
(Congo) R.
Zaire R.
Kisangani
ZAIRE
Kananga
UGANDA
Kampala
RWANDA
Kigali
Bujumbura
BURUNDI
Lake Victoria
KENYA
Nairobi
Mogadishu
White Nile
Equator

TANZANIA
Lake Tanganyika
Dar es Salaam
Mombasa
Pemba I.
Zanzibar I.
INDIAN OCEAN
SEYCHELLES

ATLANTIC OCEAN

Luanda
ANGOLA
ZAMBIA
Lusaka
Zambezi R.
Lake Kariba
Victoria Falls
MALAWI
Lilongwe
Lake Malawi
Nampula
COMOROS
Moroni

Prime Meridian

NAMIBIA
BOTSWANA
WALVIS BAY (S. AFR.)
ZIMBABWE
Bulawayo
Harare
R.
Beira
MOZAMBIQUE
Mozambique Channel
MADAGASCAR
Antananarivo
RÉUNION (FR.)

Tropic of Capricorn

Gaborone
Limpopo R.
Pretoria
Johannesburg
Vaal R.
SWAZILAND
Maputo
Mbabane
Orange R.
Maseru
LESOTHO
Durban
SOUTH AFRICA
Cape Town
Port Elizabeth

N

0   500   1000 Miles
0   500   1000 Kilometers

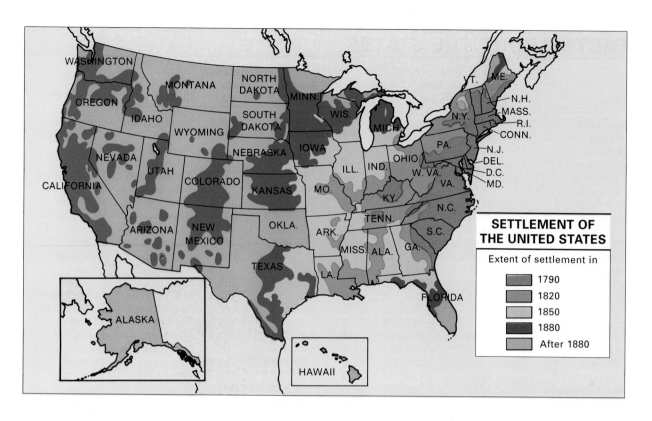

SETTLEMENT OF THE UNITED STATES

Extent of settlement in

- 1790
- 1820
- 1850
- 1880
- After 1880

WASHINGTON
OREGON
IDAHO
MONTANA
NORTH DAKOTA
SOUTH DAKOTA
WYOMING
NEBRASKA
NEVADA
UTAH
COLORADO
CALIFORNIA
ARIZONA
NEW MEXICO
KANSAS
OKLA.
TEXAS
MINN.
WIS.
IOWA
MO.
ARK.
LA.
MICH.
ILL.
IND.
OHIO
KY.
TENN.
MISS.
ALA.
GA.
W. VA.
VA.
N.C.
S.C.
FLORIDA
VT.
ME.
N.H.
MASS.
R.I.
CONN.
N.Y.
PA.
N.J.
DEL.
D.C.
MD.
ALASKA
HAWAII

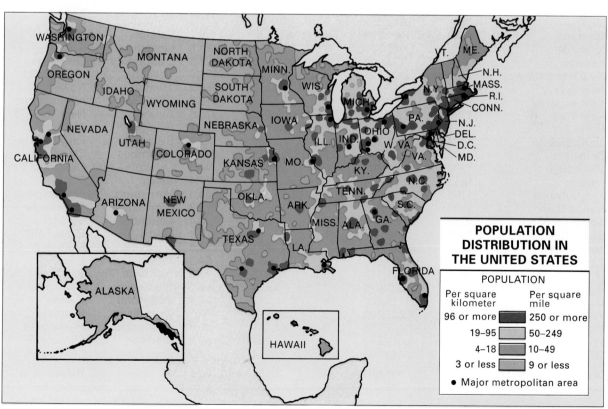

POPULATION DISTRIBUTION IN THE UNITED STATES

POPULATION

Per square kilometer	Per square mile
96 or more	250 or more
19–95	50–249
4–18	10–49
3 or less	9 or less

• Major metropolitan area

WASHINGTON
OREGON
IDAHO
MONTANA
NORTH DAKOTA
SOUTH DAKOTA
WYOMING
NEBRASKA
NEVADA
UTAH
COLORADO
CALIFORNIA
ARIZONA
NEW MEXICO
KANSAS
OKLA.
TEXAS
MINN.
WIS.
IOWA
MO.
ARK.
LA.
MICH.
ILL.
IND.
OHIO
KY.
TENN.
MISS.
ALA.
GA.
W. VA.
VA.
N.C.
S.C.
FLORIDA
VT.
ME.
N.H.
MASS.
R.I.
CONN.
N.Y.
PA.
N.J.
DEL.
D.C.
MD.
ALASKA
HAWAII

FACTS ABOUT THE STATES

State	Year of Statehood	1990 Population	Reps. in Congress	Area (Sq. mi.)	Population Density (Sq. mi.)	Capital	Largest City
Alabama	1819	3,984,000	7	51,609	76.6	Montgomery	Birmingham
Alaska	1959	546,000	1	586,412	0.7	Juneau	Anchorage
Arizona	1912	3,619,000	6	113,909	23.9	Phoenix	Phoenix
Arkansas	1836	2,337,395	4	53,104	43.9	Little Rock	Little Rock
California	1850	29,279,000	52	158,693	151.4	Sacramento	Los Angeles
Colorado	1876	3,272,000	6	104,247	27.9	Denver	Denver
Connecticut	1788	3,226,929	6	5,009	637.8	Hartford	Hartford
Delaware	1787	658,031	1	2,057	307.6	Dover	Wilmington
Florida	1845	12,775,000	23	58,560	180.0	Tallahassee	Jacksonville
Georgia	1788	6,387,000	11	58,876	94.1	Atlanta	Atlanta
Hawaii	1959	1,095,000	2	6,450	150.1	Honolulu	Honolulu
Idaho	1890	1,003,558	2	83,557	11.5	Boise	Boise
Illinois	1818	11,325,000	20	56,400	205.3	Springfield	Chicago
Indiana	1816	5,499,000	10	36,291	152.8	Indianapolis	Indianapolis
Iowa	1846	2,766,658	5	56,290	52.1	Des Moines	Des Moines
Kansas	1861	2,467,000	4	82,264	28.9	Topeka	Wichita
Kentucky	1792	3,665,220	6	40,395	92.3	Frankfort	Louisville
Louisiana	1812	4,180,831	7	48,523	94.5	Baton Rouge	New Orleans
Maine	1820	1,218,053	2	33,215	36.3	Augusta	Portland
Maryland	1788	4,733,000	8	10,577	428.7	Annapolis	Baltimore
Massachusetts	1788	5,928,000	10	8,257	733.3	Boston	Boston
Michigan	1837	9,179,000	16	58,216	162.6	Lansing	Detroit
Minnesota	1858	4,358,864	8	84,068	51.2	St. Paul	Minneapolis
Mississippi	1817	2,534,814	5	47,716	33.4	Jackson	Jackson
Missouri	1821	5,079,385	9	69,686	71.3	Jefferson City	St. Louis
Montana	1889	794,329	1	147,138	5.4	Helena	Billings
Nebraska	1867	1,572,503	3	77,227	20.5	Lincoln	Omaha
Nevada	1864	1,193,000	2	110,540	7.3	Carson City	Las Vegas
New Hampshire	1788	1,103,163	2	9,304	102.4	Concord	Manchester
New Jersey	1787	7,617,418	13	7,836	986.2	Trenton	Newark
New Mexico	1912	1,490,381	3	121,666	10.7	Santa Fe	Albuquerque
New York	1788	17,627,000	31	49,576	370.6	Albany	New York City
North Carolina	1789	6,553,000	12	52,586	120.4	Raleigh	Charlotte
North Dakota	1889	634,223	1	70,665	9.4	Bismarck	Fargo
Ohio	1803	10,778,000	19	41,222	263.3	Columbus	Cleveland
Oklahoma	1907	3,124,000	6	69,919	44.1	Oklahoma City	Oklahoma City
Oregon	1859	2,828,214	5	96,981	27.4	Salem	Portland
Pennsylvania	1787	11,764,000	21	45,333	264.3	Harrisburg	Philadelphia
Rhode Island	1790	988,609	2	1,214	897.8	Providence	Providence
South Carolina	1788	3,407,000	6	31,055	103.4	Columbia	Columbia
South Dakota	1889	693,294	1	77,047	9.1	Pierre	Sioux Falls
Tennessee	1796	4,822,134	9	42,244	111.6	Nashville	Memphis
Texas	1845	16,825,000	30	267,339	54.3	Austin	Houston
Utah	1896	1,711,117	3	84,916	17.8	Salt Lake City	Salt Lake City
Vermont	1791	560,029	1	9,609	55.2	Montpelier	Burlington
Virginia	1788	6,128,000	11	40,817	134.7	Richmond	Norfolk
Washington	1889	4,827,000	9	68,192	62.1	Olympia	Seattle
West Virginia	1863	1,782,958	3	24,181	80.8	Charleston	Huntington
Wisconsin	1848	4,869,640	9	56,154	86.5	Madison	Milwaukee
Wyoming	1890	449,905	1	97,914	4.9	Cheyenne	Cheyenne
District of Columbia		637,651	—	69	10,123.2		Washington

PRESIDENTS OF THE UNITED STATES

No.	Name	Born–Died	Years in Office	Political Party	Home State	Vice President
1	George Washington	1732–1799	1789–97	None	Va.	John Adams
2	John Adams	1735–1826	1797–1801	Federalist	Mass.	Thomas Jefferson
3	Thomas Jefferson	1743–1826	1801–09	Republican*	Va.	Aaron Burr
						George Clinton
4	James Madison	1751–1836	1809–17	Republican	Va.	George Clinton
						Elbridge Gerry
5	James Monroe	1758–1831	1817–25	Republican	Va.	Daniel D. Tompkins
6	John Quincy Adams	1767–1848	1825–29	Republican	Mass.	John C. Calhoun
7	Andrew Jackson	1767–1845	1829–37	Democratic	Tenn.	John C. Calhoun
						Martin Van Buren
8	Martin Van Buren	1782–1862	1837–41	Democratic	N.Y.	Richard M. Johnson
9	William Henry Harrison	1773–1841	1841	Whig	Ohio	John Tyler
10	John Tyler	1790–1862	1841–45	Whig	Va.	
11	James K. Polk	1795–1849	1845–49	Democratic	Tenn.	George M. Dallas
12	Zachary Taylor	1784–1850	1849–50	Whig	La.	Millard Fillmore
13	Millard Fillmore	1800–1874	1850–53	Whig	N.Y.	
14	Franklin Pierce	1804–1869	1853–57	Democratic	N.H.	William R. King
15	James Buchanan	1791–1868	1857–61	Democratic	Pa.	John C. Breckenridge
16	Abraham Lincoln	1809–1865	1861–65	Republican	Ill.	Hannibal Hamlin
						Andrew Johnson
17	Andrew Johnson	1808–1875	1865–69	Republican	Tenn.	
18	Ulysses S. Grant	1822–1885	1869–77	Republican	Ill.	Schuyler Colfax
						Henry Wilson
19	Rutherford B. Hayes	1822–1893	1877–81	Republican	Ohio	William A. Wheeler
20	James A. Garfield	1831–1881	1881	Republican	Ohio	Chester A. Arthur
21	Chester A. Arthur	1830–1886	1881–85	Republican	N.Y.	
22	Grover Cleveland	1837–1908	1885–89	Democratic	N.Y.	Thomas A. Hendricks
23	Benjamin Harrison	1833–1901	1889–93	Republican	Ind.	Levi P. Morton
24	Grover Cleveland		1893–97	Democratic	N.Y.	Adlai E. Stevenson
25	William McKinley	1843–1901	1897–1901	Republican	Ohio	Garrett A. Hobart
						Theodore Roosevelt
26	Theodore Roosevelt	1858–1919	1901–09	Republican	N.Y.	
						Charles W. Fairbanks
27	William Howard Taft	1857–1930	1909–13	Republican	Ohio	James S. Sherman
28	Woodrow Wilson	1856–1924	1913–21	Democratic	N.J.	Thomas R. Marshall
29	Warren G. Harding	1865–1923	1921–23	Republican	Ohio	Calvin Coolidge
30	Calvin Coolidge	1872–1933	1923–29	Republican	Mass.	
						Charles G. Dawes
31	Herbert Hoover	1874–1964	1929–33	Republican	Calif.	Charles Curtis
32	Franklin D. Roosevelt	1882–1945	1933–45	Democratic	N.Y.	John Nance Garner
						Henry Wallace
						Harry S Truman
33	Harry S Truman	1884–1972	1945–53	Democratic	Mo.	
						Alben W. Barkley
34	Dwight D. Eisenhower	1890–1969	1953–61	Republican	Kans.	Richard M. Nixon
35	John F. Kennedy	1917–1963	1961–63	Democratic	Mass.	Lyndon B. Johnson
36	Lyndon B. Johnson	1908–1973	1963–69	Democratic	Texas	
						Hubert H. Humphrey
37	Richard M. Nixon	1913–	1969–74	Republican	Calif.	Spiro T. Agnew
						Gerald R. Ford
38	Gerald R. Ford	1913–	1974–77	Republican	Mich.	Nelson A. Rockefeller
39	Jimmy Carter	1924–	1977–81	Democratic	Ga.	Walter F. Mondale
40	Ronald Reagan	1911–	1981–89	Republican	Calif.	George H. Bush
41	George H. Bush	1924–	1989–	Republican	Texas	R. Danforth Quayle

*The Republican party of the third through sixth presidents is not the party of Abraham Lincoln, which was founded in 1854.

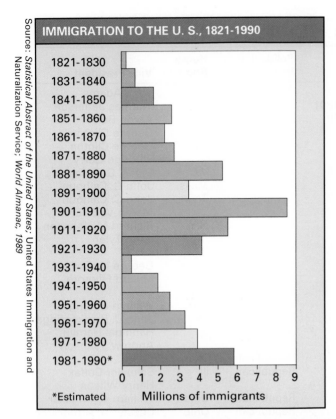

Source: *Statistical Abstract of the United States; United States Immigration and Naturalization Service; World Almanac, 1989*

IMMIGRATION TO THE U. S., 1821-1990

Period	
1821-1830	
1831-1840	
1841-1850	
1851-1860	
1861-1870	
1871-1880	
1881-1890	
1891-1900	
1901-1910	
1911-1920	
1921-1930	
1931-1940	
1941-1950	
1951-1960	
1961-1970	
1971-1980	
1981-1990*	

0 1 2 3 4 5 6 7 8 9

*Estimated   Millions of immigrants

As the graphs on this page indicate, the United States has a rich and varied racial and cultural heritage. This rich heritage is due in large part to immigration. Prior to World War II the majority of immigrants to the United States came from Europe. The Immigration Act of 1965, however, made it easier for non-Europeans to immigrate to the United States. As a result, people from Central and South America, the Caribbean, and Asia now make up the majority of new immigrants.

Source: *Statistical Abstract of the United States*

U. S. IMMIGRATION BY REGION OF ORIGIN, 1890-1939

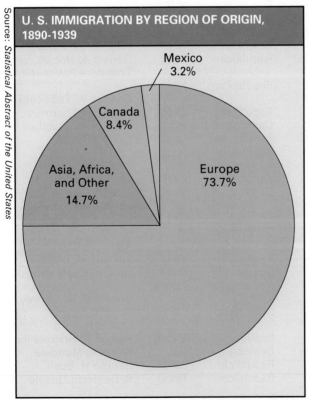

Mexico 3.2%
Canada 8.4%
Asia, Africa, and Other 14.7%
Europe 73.7%

Source: *World Almanac, 1989*

U. S. IMMIGRATION BY REGION OF ORIGIN, 1961-87

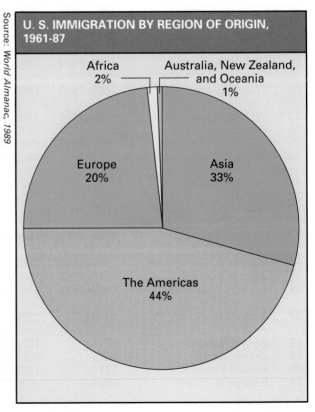

Africa 2%
Australia, New Zealand, and Oceania 1%
Europe 20%
Asia 33%
The Americas 44%

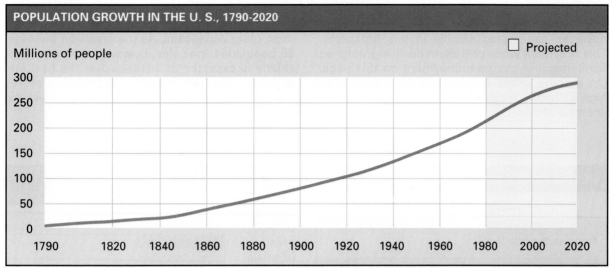

POPULATION GROWTH IN THE U. S., 1790-2020

Millions of people

☐ Projected

Source: Bureau of the Census

Technology also has helped shape American society. The graphs on this page illustrate some of the social consequences of new technologies. Advances in medicine and public sanitation, for instance, have increased the number of years most people live. As a result, the population of the United States has grown. More efficient farming methods have reduced the number of farmers needed to produce food for the American people. This decrease in the demand for farm labor has meant that more workers have been available to fill the jobs created by industrialization. Because these jobs tend to be located in or near cities, the population of the United States has become increasingly urban.

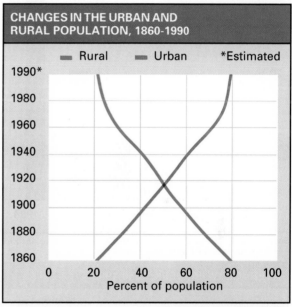

CHANGES IN THE URBAN AND RURAL POPULATION, 1860-1990

■ Rural   ■ Urban   *Estimated

Percent of population

Source: Bureau of the Census

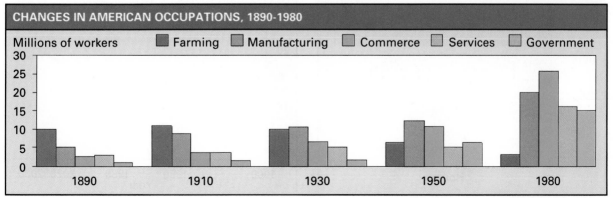

CHANGES IN AMERICAN OCCUPATIONS, 1890-1980

Millions of workers   ■ Farming ■ Manufacturing ■ Commerce ■ Services ■ Government

Source: U.S. Dept. of Agriculture; *Monthly Labor Review*

Over its history the United States has enjoyed strong economic growth. Not everyone in society, however, has shared equally in this prosperity. This is evident when one examines the graphs on family income and unemployment on this page. On average, white Americans have enjoyed the highest family incomes and the lowest rates of unemployment.

Social Security and other government programs have made the retirement years more secure for most older Americans. As the graph on the over-65 population indicates, however, the number of elderly is expected to increase over the next few decades. This increase will place new pressures on the government to develop ways to meet the needs of older Americans.

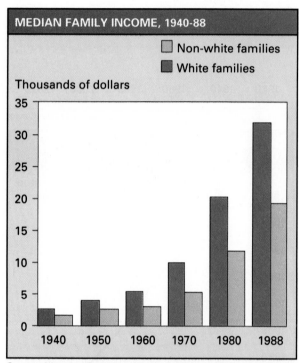

Source: *Historical Statistics of the United States; Statistical Abstract of the United States, 1988;* Bureau of the Census

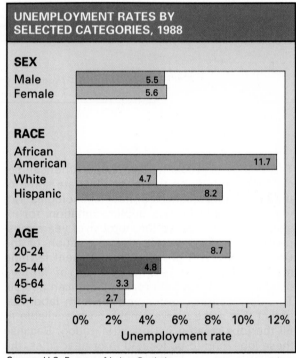

Source: U.S. Bureau of Labor Statistics

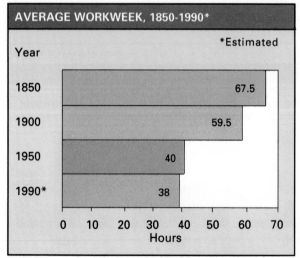

Source: *Statistical Abstract of the United States, 1989*

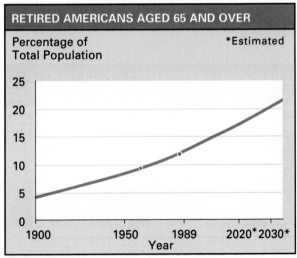

Source: *"Grays on the Go"* in *Time,* Feb. 22, 1988; Bureau of the Census

The federal government must have enough money to finance its programs and activities. The money the government collects for this purpose is called receipts. Most government receipts are in the form of taxes. The money the government spends is referred to as outlays. As can be seen from the graph at the top left, in recent decades the federal government has spent more than it has taken in. This shortfall is called a budget deficit. When the federal government experiences a budget deficit, it must borrow money to finance its spending. This borrowed money is called the national debt. As the graph on the top right shows, paying the interest on the national debt is a major outlay for the federal government.

In recent years, the United States also has experienced a trade deficit. A trade deficit occurs when a nation imports more than it exports. The graph at the bottom of the page shows the relationship between United States import and export values since 1950. The inset traces the rise and fall of United States tariffs.

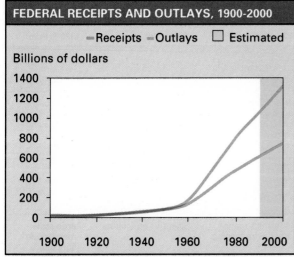

Source: *Statistical Abstract of the United States, 1989*

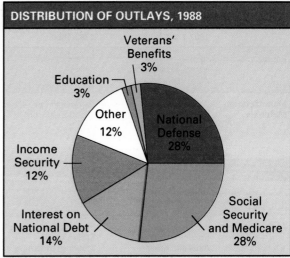

Source: *Statistical Abstract of the United States, 1989*

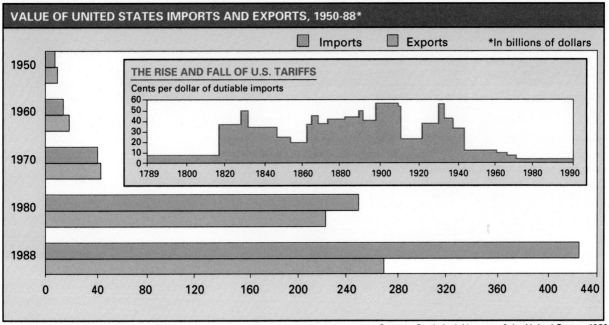

Source: *Statistical Abstract of the United States, 1989*

All societies must face the fact that the resources needed to produce goods and services are limited. Thus each society must decide how best to use its limited resources. A society makes this decision by answering three basic economic questions: (1) What goods and services should be produced? (2) How should these goods and services be produced? (3) For whom should these goods and services be produced?

In the United States these three questions are answered in a free-market environment. By free market, we mean that people are free to produce, sell, and buy whatever they wish and to work for whomever they want. What goods and services are actually produced, however, is determined by the forces of supply and demand. Producers supply those goods and services that are demanded by consumers.

Over time, changes in technology and in the types of goods and services available from other markets around the world have altered the nature of business and industry.

MAJOR ADVANCES IN AMERICAN BUSINESS AND INDUSTRY

	1607-1783	1783-1850	1850-1900	1900-1920	1920-Present
Power	Human muscles Animals muscles Wind and water power	Steam power	Electric power Internal combustion engines		Atomic energy Geothermal energy
Manufacturing Materials	Copper, bronze, iron Wood Clay Plant and animal fibers	Large-scale production of iron	Large-scale production of steel Development of combustion fuels: coal, oil, gas	Large-scale production of light metals and alloys Development of plastics and sythetics	Large-scale production of plastics and synthetics
Factory Methods	Handforges and tools Hand-powered equipment	Machinery powered by water and steam Interchangeable parts	Mass production, with centralized assembly of interchangeable parts	Conveyor-belt assembly line	Automation Computer-operated machinery
Agriculture	Wooden plows Spades and hoes Axes and other hand tools	Iron and steel plows Cotton gin Mowing, threshing, and haying machines	McCormick reaper Barbed-wire fencing	Scientific agriculture	Large-scale mechanized agriculture Corporation farms
Transportation	Horses Animal-drawn vehicles Sailing vessels	Canals Clipper ships Development of railroads and steamships	Large-scale steamship and railroad lines City trolleys, elevated trains	Automobiles, trucks, and buses Development of propeller-driven aircraft	Space exploration Monorail trains Supersonic airplanes
Communication	Hand-operated printing presses Newspapers	Mechanized printing presses Telegraph Mass-circulation books and magazines	Transatlantic cable Telephones Phonographs Typewriters Cameras	Motion pictures Radios	Television Transistors Magnetic tapes Lasers Satellite transmissions
Merchandising and Business Organization	Small shops Peddlers	Individual and family-owned factories and mills General stores	Chain stores Mail-order houses Growth of corporations Trusts	National advertising Holding companies	Shopping centers Conglomerate corporations Multinational corporations

Documents in American History

FROM Magna Carta (1215)

Four hundred years before the English settled in North America, a group of English barons forced their king to sign a document guaranteeing them certain rights. This was the Magna Carta, or Great Charter, signed by King John in 1215. It became a model for all those who demanded democratic government and individual rights for all. The Magna Carta marked a decisive step forward in the development of constitutional government. The guarantees of the Magna Carta—the rights to due process of law; to freedom from unlawful search, seizure, and imprisonment; and to be taxed only with the consent of one's chosen representatives—were restated in the political documents created by Englishmen in the New World.

John, by the grace of God, King of England, Lord of Ireland, Duke of Normandy and Aquitaine, and Earl of Anjou: to his archbishops, bishops, abbots, earls, barons, justiciaries [royal judiciary officers], foresters, sheriffs, governors, officers, and to all bailiffs [sheriff's duputies], and his faithful subjects—Greeting.

Know ye, that we, in the presence of God, . . . have confirmed, for us and our heirs forever;

1. That the English Church shall be free, and shall have her whole rights and her liberties inviolable [safe from sudden change], . . .

We have also granted to all the freemen of our kingdom for us and our heirs forever, all the underwritten liberties, to be enjoyed and held by them and by their heirs, from us and from our heirs. . . .

12. No scutage [tax for military purposes] nor aid [feudal payment] shall be imposed in our kingdom, unless by the common council of our kingdom [representatives]; . . .

14. And also to have the common council of the kingdom, we will cause to be summoned the archbishops, bishops, abbots, earls, and great barons, individually by our letters. . . .

38. No bailiff, for the future, shall put any man to his law upon his own simple affirmation, without credible witnesses produced for that purpose.

39. No freeman shall be seized, imprisoned, dispossessed [deprived of his land], outlawed, or exiled, or in any way destroyed; nor will we proceed against or prosecute him except by the lawful judgment of his peers [equals], or by the law of the land.

40. To none will we sell, to none will we deny, to none will we delay right or justice.

41. All merchants shall have safety and security in coming into England, and going out of England, and in staying in and traveling through England, as well by land as by water to buy and sell, without any unjust exactions [demands], according to ancient and right customs, excepting in the time of war, and if they be of a country at war against us; and if such are found in our land at the beginning of a war, they shall be apprehended [arrested] without injury to their bodies and goods until it be known to us or to our Chief Justiciary how the merchants of our country are treated who are found in the country at war against us; and if ours be in safety there, the others shall be in safety in our land.

42. It shall be lawful to any person, for the future, to go out of our kingdom, and to return, safely and securely by land or by water, saving [preserving] his allegiance to us, unless it be in time of war, for some short space, for the common good of the kingdom. . . .

60. Also all these customs and liberties aforesaid, which we have granted to be held in our kingdom, for so much of it as belongs to us, all our subjects, as well clergy as laity [those not in religious offices], shall observe toward their tenants as far as concern them. . . .

63. Wherefore our will is, and we firmly command that the Church of England be free, and that the men in our kingdom have and hold the aforesaid liberties, rights, and concessions, well and in peace, freely and quietly, fully and entirely, to them and their heirs, of us and our heirs, in all things and places forever, as is aforesaid. It is also sworn, both on our part and on that of the barons, that all the aforesaid shall be observed in good faith and without any evil intention. . . .

Given by our hand in the meadow which is called Runnymede, between Windsor and Staines, this 15th day of June, in the 17th year of our reign.

FROM The Maryland Toleration Act (1649)

The colony of Maryland was founded in 1634. The proprietor of Maryland was Cecilius Calvert, Lord Baltimore. Calvert was a Roman Catholic, but from the beginning he allowed Protestants as well as Catholics to settle in his colony. To insure that the policy of religious toleration continued, in 1648 Calvert authorized the legislature of Maryland to pass a Toleration Act, which guaranteed freedom of worship to all Christians. Jews and others were excluded, but the Maryland Toleration Act was the first law in American history permitting the existence of religious beliefs different from those held by the majority.

Be it . . . enacted that whatsoever person or persons within this province . . . shall deny our Saviour, Jesus Christ, to be the son of God, or shall deny the Holy Trinity (the Father, Son, and Holy Ghost) . . . shall be punished with death and confiscation or forfeiture of all his or her lands. . . .

. . . AND WHEREAS, The enforcing of the conscience in matters of religion has frequently fallen out [turned out] to be of dangerous consequence in those commonwealths where it has been practiced; and for the most quiet and peaceable government of this province, and the better to preserve mutual love and amity amongst the inhabitants thereof. Be it therefore . . . enacted . . . that no person or persons whatsoever within this province . . . professing to believe in Jesus Christ shall . . . henceforth be any ways troubled, molested, or discountenanced [disapproved of] . . . in respect of his or her religion nor in the free exercise thereof within this province . . . nor any way compelled to the belief or exercise of any other religion against his or her consent, so as they be not unfaithful to the Lord Proprietary [proprietor], or molest or conspire against the civil government established or to be established in this province under him or his heirs. And that all and every person and persons that shall . . . wrong, disturb, trouble, or molest any person whatsoever within this province professing to believe in Jesus Christ . . . shall be compelled to pay treble damages to the party so wronged or molested, and for every such offense shall also forfeit twenty shillings sterling in money or the value thereof. . . . Or if the parties so offending . . . shall refuse or be unable to recompense the party so wronged or to satisfy such fine or forfeiture, then such offender shall be severely punished by public whipping and imprisonment during the pleasure of [as his will dictates] the Lord Proprietary, or his Lieutenant or chief governor of this province. . . .

FROM The Rhode Island Colonial Charter (1663)

In 1635 the Massachusetts Bay Colony expelled religious dissenter Roger Williams. Within the year, Williams founded his own settlement on Narragansett Bay and put into practice the principles of religious toleration, democratic government, and fair treatment for Native Americans. In 1644 Williams obtained a charter for his colony of Rhode Island. This charter and the charter of 1663 granted large measures of democracy to the citizens of Rhode Island, and the 1663 charter was the only colonial charter providing for complete religious freedom.

WHEREAS . . . they [the colonists] have freely declared . . . that a most flourishing civil state may stand and best be maintained . . . with a full liberty in religious concernments [affairs] and that true piety rightly grounded upon gospel principles will give the best and greatest security to sovereignty and will lay in the hearts of men the strongest obligations to true loyalty:

Now know ye that we, being willing to . . . secure them in the free exercise and enjoyment of all their civil and religious rights . . . and to preserve unto them that liberty, in the true Christian faith and worship of God, which they have sought . . . to enjoy; . . . do hereby publish, grant, ordain, and declare . . . that no person within the said colony, at any time hereafter, shall be any wise molested, punished, disquieted, or called in question for any differences in opinion in matters of religion . . . but that all and every person and persons may, from time to time, and at all times hereafter, freely and fully have and enjoy his and their own judgments and consciences in matters of religious concernments. . . .

FROM The English Bill of Rights (1689)

By 1688 the English people were tired of King James II's arbitrary use of royal power and his assertion of the "divine right of kings." In a bloodless uprising called the Glorious Revolution, they drove James from the throne. Before granting the throne to William and Mary in 1689, Parliament required them to agree to terms named in a document known as the Bill of Rights. This document clearly established the supremacy of Parliament over the monarch and set forth many of the rights of citizens. The liberties included in the Bill of Rights became part of the Constitution of the United States.

WHEREAS, The late King James II . . . did endeavor to subvert [overthrow] and extirpate [wipe out] the Protestant religion and the laws and liberties of this kingdom . . . and *whereas* the said late King James II having abdicated [given up] the government, and the throne being vacant . . .

. . . the said lords . . . being now assembled in a full and free representative of this nation, . . . do in the first place . . . declare:

1. *That* the pretended power of suspending of laws or the execution of laws by regal authority without consent of Parliament is illegal; . . .

3. *That* the commission [authority] for erecting the late [recent] court of commissioners for ecclesiastical [church-related] causes and all other commissions and courts of like nature are illegal and pernicious [corrupt]; . . .

4. *That* levying money for or to the use of the crown by pretense of prerogative [right] without grant of Parliament . . . is illegal;

5. *That* it is the right of the subjects to petition the king, and all commitments [imprisonments] and prosecutions for such petitioning are illegal.

6. *That* . . . raising or keeping a standing army within the kingdom in time of peace, unless it be with consent of Parliament, is against law. . . .

8. *That* election of members of Parliament ought to be free;

9. *That* the freedom of speech and debates or proceedings in Parliament ought not to be impeached [challenged as to the validity thereof] or questioned in any court or place out of Parliament;

10. *That* excessive bail ought not to be required, nor excessive fines imposed, nor cruel and unusual punishments inflicted.

11. *That* jurors ought to be duly impaneled and returned, and jurors who pass upon men in trials for high treason ought to be freeholders [landholders];

12. *That* all grants and promises of fines and forfeitures of particular persons before conviction are illegal and void;

13. *And that*, for redress of all grievances and for the amending, strengthening, and preserving of the laws, Parliaments ought to be held frequently. . . . Having, therefore, an entire confidence that his said Highness, the Prince of Orange, will perfect the deliverance so far advanced by him and will preserve them from the violation of their rights which they have here asserted and from all other attempts upon their religion, rights, and liberties, the said lords . . . and Commons assembled at Westminster do resolve that William and Mary, Prince and Princess of Orange, be and be declared King and Queen of England, France, and Ireland, and the dominions thereunto belonging. . . .

FROM Thomas Paine's "The Crisis" (1776)

By the time Thomas Paine wrote "The Crisis," the excitement that had followed the American Declaration of Independence had given way to near despair. The British had proved their military superiority time and again. In December 1776 Washington's ragged army was camped in crude shelters on the west bank of the Delaware River. To many the American cause seemed doomed to defeat. It was in these circumstances that Paine's ringing essay was read to the troops. His words were prophetic, for soon American victories at Trenton and Princeton gave supporters of the revolutionary cause new hope.

These are the times that try men's souls. The summer soldier and the sunshine patriot will, in this crisis, shrink from the service of his country; but he that stands it now, deserves the love and thanks of man and woman. Tyranny, like hell, is not easily conquered; yet we have this consolation with us, that the harder the conflict, the more glorious the triumph. What we obtain too cheap, we esteem too lightly; it is dearness [costliness] only that gives everything its value. Heaven knows how to put a proper price upon its goods; and it would be strange indeed if so celestial [divine] an article as FREEDOM should not be highly rated. Britain, with an army to enforce her tyranny, has declared that she has a right (not only to TAX) but "to BIND US in ALL CASES WHATSOEVER," and if being bound in that manner is not slavery, then is there not such a thing as slavery upon earth. Even the expression is impious [lacking in respect]; for so unlimited a power can belong only to God. . . .

I have as little superstition in me as any man living, but my secret opinion has ever been, and still is, that God Almighty will not give up a people to military destruction, or leave them unsupportedly to perish, who have so earnestly and so repeatedly sought to avoid the calamities of war, by every decent method which wisdom could invent. Neither have I so much of the infidel [non-Christian] in me as to suppose that he has relinquished the government of the world, and given us up to the care of devils; and as I do not, I cannot see on what grounds the king of Britain can look up to heaven for help against us: a common murderer, a highwayman, or a housebreaker has as good a pretense as he.

'Tis surprising to see how rapidly a panic will sometimes run through a country. All nations and ages have been subject to them. . . . Yet panics, in some cases, have their uses; they produce as much good as hurt. Their duration is always short; the mind soon grows through them and acquires a firmer habit than before. But their peculiar advantage is that they are the touchstones [tests] of sincerity and hypocrisy and bring things and men to light which might otherwise have lain forever undiscovered. In fact, they have the same effect on secret traitors which an imaginary apparition would have upon a private murderer. They sift out the hidden thoughts of man and hold them up in public to the world. Many a disguised Tory has lately shown his head, that shall penitentially solemnize [regretfully remember] with curses the day on which Howe [General Howe of the British Army] arrived upon the Delaware. . . .

I turn with the warm ardor of a friend to those who have nobly stood, and are yet determined to stand the matter out; I call not upon a few, but upon all: not on *this* state or *that* state, but on *every* state: up and help us; lay your shoulders to the wheel; better have too much force than too little, when so great an object is at stake. Let it be told to the future world, that in the depth of winter, when nothing but hope and virtue could survive, that the city and the country, alarmed at one common danger, came forth to meet and to repulse it. Say not that thousands are gone—[but] turn out your tens of thousands; throw not the burden of the day upon Providence, but *"show your faith by your works,"* that God may bless you. It matters not where you live, or what rank of life you hold, the evil or the blessing will reach you all. The far and the near, the home counties and the back, the rich and the poor, will suffer or rejoice alike. The heart that feels not now is dead; the blood of his children will curse his cowardice who shrinks back at a time when a little might have saved the whole and made them happy. I love the man that can smile in trouble, that can gather strength from distress and grow brave by reflection. It is the business of little minds to shrink; but he whose heart is firm, and whose conscience approves his conduct, will pursue his principles unto death. My own line of reasoning is to myself as straight and clear as a ray of light. Not all the treasures of the world, so far as I believe, could have induced me to support an offensive war, for I think it murder; but if a thief breaks into my house, burns and destroys my property, and kills or threatens to kill me or those that are in it, and to *"bind me in all cases whatsoever"* to his absolute will, am I to suffer it? What signifies it to me whether he who does it is a king or a common man; my countryman or not my countryman; whether it be done by an individual villain, or an army of them? If we reason to the root of things, we shall find no difference; neither can any just cause be assigned [determined] why we should punish in the one case and pardon in the other. Let them call me rebel and welcome. I feel no concern from it. . . .

FROM The Articles of Confederation (1781)

The American colonies cut their ties to Great Britain with the Declaration of Independence, but then they faced the enormous task of forming a central government. To help accomplish this, the Second Continental Congress appointed a committee to draft a constitution. The Articles of Confederation, America's first constitution, was adopted in 1777 but not formally ratified by all the states until 1781. The weaknesses of the government created by the Articles were obvious, but America's first constitution served the nation well. Under it the war of independence was fought and won, and the Land Ordinance of 1785 and the Northwest Ordinance were enacted.

We, the undersigned delegates of the states . . . agree to certain Articles of Confederation and perpetual Union between the States. . . .

Article 1. The style [title] of this confederacy shall be "The United States of America."

Article 2. Each state retains its sovereignty, freedom, and independence, and every power, jurisdiction [authority to act], and right which is not by this confederation expressly delegated to the United States in Congress assembled.

Article 3. The said states hereby severally enter into a firm league of friendship with each other for their common defense, the security of their liberties, and their mutual and general welfare, binding themselves to assist each other against all force offered to [them] or attacks made upon them or [upon] any of them on account of religion, sovereignty, trade, or any other pretense whatever.

Article 4. The better to secure and perpetuate [cause to endure] mutual friendship and intercourse [business connections] among the people of the different states in this union, the free inhabitants of each of these states . . . shall be entitled to all privileges and immunities of free citizens in the several states; . . .

If any person guilty of, or charged with, treason, felony [crime], or other high misdemeanor in any state shall flee from justice, he shall, upon demand of the governor or executive power of the state from which he fled, be delivered up and removed to the state having jurisdiction of his offense.

Full faith and credit shall be given in each of these states to the records, acts, and judicial proceedings of the courts and magistrates of every other state.

Article 5. . . . Delegates shall be annually appointed in such manner as the legislature of each state shall direct to meet in Congress on the first Monday in November in every year. . . .

No state shall be represented in Congress by less than two [members], nor by more than seven members; and no person shall be capable of being a delegate for more than three years in any term of six years; nor shall any person, being a delegate, be capable of holding any office under the United States, for which he, or another for his benefit, receives any salary, fees, or emolument [payment] of any kind. . . .

In determining questions in the United States, in Congress assembled, each state shall have one vote.

Freedom of speech and debate in Congress shall not be impeached or questioned in any court or place out of Congress, and the members of Congress shall be protected in their persons from arrests and imprisonments during the time of their going to and from and attendance on Congress, except for treason, felony, or breach of the peace.

Article 6. No state without the consent of the United States in Congress assembled shall send any embassy to, or receive any embassy from, or enter into any conference, agreement, or alliance or treaty with any king, prince, or state; . . . nor shall the United States in Congress assembled, or any of . . . [the states], grant any title of nobility.

No two or more states shall enter into any treaty, confederation, or alliance whatever between them without the consent of the United States in Congress assembled. . . .

No state shall lay any imposts [taxes on trade] or duties which may interfere with any stipulations [conditions] in treaties entered into by the United States in Congress assembled. . . .

No vessels of war shall be kept up in time of

peace by any state except such number only as shall be deemed necessary by the United States in Congress assembled for the defense of such state or its trade; nor shall any body of forces be kept up by any state in time of peace except such number only as in the judgment of the United States in Congress assembled shall be deemed requisite to garrison [furnish with soldiers] the forts necessary for the defense of such state; but every state shall always keep up a well-regulated and disciplined militia, . . . a due member of field pieces and tents, and a proper quantity of arms, ammunition, and camp equipage [equipment].

No state shall engage in any war without the consent of the United States in Congress assembled, unless such state be actually invaded by enemies, or shall have received certain advice of a resolution being formed by some nation of Indians to invade such state, and the danger is so imminent as not to admit of a delay till the United States in Congress assembled can be consulted. . . .

Article 7. When land forces are raised by any state for the common defense, all officers of or under the rank of colonel shall be appointed by the legislature of each state respectively by whom such forces shall be raised or in such manner as such state shall direct. . . .

Article 8. All charges of war, and all other expenses that shall be incurred for the common defense or general welfare and allowed by the United States in Congress assembled shall be defrayed out of a common treasury, which shall be supplied by the several states, in proportion to the value of all land within each state, granted to or surveyed for any person, as such land and the buildings and improvements thereon shall be estimated according to such mode as the United States in Congress assembled shall from time to time direct and appoint. The taxes for paying that proportion shall be laid and levied by the authority and direction of the legislatures of the several states within the time agreed upon by the United States in Congress assembled.

Article 9. The United States in Congress assembled shall have the sole and exclusive right and power of determining on peace and war, except in the cases mentioned in the sixth article; of sending and receiving ambassadors; [of] entering into treaties and alliances . . .; of granting letters of marque and reprisal [licenses issued by the government to privateers] in times of peace; [of] appointing

courts for the trial of piracies and felonies committed on the high seas. . . .

The United States in Congress assembled shall also be the last resort on appeal in all disputes and differences now subsisting [existing] or that hereafter may arise between two or more states concerning boundary, jurisdiction, or any other cause whatever. . . .

The United States in Congress assembled shall also have the sole and exclusive right and power of regulating the alloy [metal makeup] and value of coin struck by their own authority or by that of the respective states; fixing the standard of weights and measures throughout the United States; regulating the trade and managing all affairs with the Indians, [who are] not members of any of the states, provided that the legislative right of any state within its own limits be not infringed or violated; establishing and regulating post offices from one state to another, throughout all the United States, and exacting such postage on the papers passing through the same as may be requisite to defray the expenses of the said office; appointing all officers of the land forces in the service of the United States, except regimental officers; appointing all the officers of the naval forces and commissioning all officers whatever in the Service of the United States; making rules for the government and regulation of the said land and naval forces and directing their operations. . . .

The United States in Congress assembled shall never engage in a war, nor grant letters of marque and reprisal in time of peace, nor enter into any treaties or alliances, nor coin money, nor regulate the value thereof, nor ascertain the sums and expenses necessary for the defense and welfare of the United States, or [of] any of them, nor emit bills, nor borrow money on the credit of the United States, nor appropriate money, nor agree upon the number of vessels of war to be built or purchased, or the number of land or sea forces to be raised, nor appoint a commander in chief of the army or navy unless nine states assent to the same; nor shall a question on any other point, except for adjourning from day to day, be determined unless by the votes of a majority of the United States in Congress assembled.

Article 10. The Committee of the States, or any nine of them, shall be authorized to execute in the recess of Congress such of the powers of Congress as the United States in Congress assembled, by the consent of nine states, shall from time to time think expedient [necessary] to vest [furnish] them with; provided that no power be delegated to the said Committee for the exercise of which, by the Articles of Confederation, the voice of nine states in the Congress of the United States assembled is requisite. . . .

Article 12. All bills of credit emitted, monies borrowed, and debts contracted by, or under, the authority of Congress, before the assembling of the United States, in pursuance [carrying out] of the present Confederation, shall be deemed and considered as a charge against the United States, for payment and satisfaction whereof the said United States and the public faith are hereby solemnly pledged.

Article 13. Every state shall abide by the determinations [decisions] of the United States in Congress assembled on all questions which by this Confederation are submitted to them. And the Articles of this Confederation shall be inviolably observed by every state, and the union shall be perpetual; nor shall any alteration at any time hereafter be made in any of them; unless such alteration be agreed to in a Congress of the United States and be afterward confirmed by the legislatures of every state.

FROM The Land Ordinance (1785)

The Land Ordinance of 1785 set up a system for the orderly division and sale of western lands. It brought money into the United States treasury and made boundary disputes less serious. It successfully combined the New England idea of carving up the wilderness into large townships with the southern practice of making land available in smaller units to individuals.

Be it ordained [established by law] by the United States in Congress assembled that the territory ceded by individual states to the United States, which has been purchased from the Indian inhabitants, shall be disposed of in the following manner:

A surveyor from each state shall be appointed by Congress or a Committee of the States. . . .

The surveyors, as they are respectively qualified, shall proceed to divide the said territory into townships of six miles square by lines running due north and south and [by] others crossing these at right angles, as near as may be. . . .

The geographer shall designate the townships or fractional parts of townships by numbers progressively from south to north; always beginning each range with No. 1; and the ranges shall be distinguished by their progressive numbers to the westward. The first range, extending from the Ohio to the Lake Erie, being marked No. 1. . . .

The plat [maps] of the townships, respectively, shall be marked by subdivisions into lots of one mile square, or 640 acres . . . and numbered from 1 to 36. . . .

. . . none of the lands within the said territory [shall] be sold under the price of one dollar the acre, to be paid in specie [coin], or loan-office certificates reduced to specie value by the scale of depreciation, or certificates of liquidated debts of the United States, including interest. . . .

There shall be reserved for the United States out of every township . . . four lots. . . . There shall be reserved the lot No. 16 of every township for the maintenance of public schools within the said township. . . .

AND WHEREAS, Congress . . . stipulated grants of land to certain officers and soldiers of the late Continental army . . . for complying with such engagements; be it ordained that the Secretary of War . . . determine who are the objects of the above resolutions and engagements . . . and cause the townships, herein before reserved for the use of the late Continental army, to be drawn for in such manner as he shall deem expedient. . . .

FROM Virginia Statute for Religious Freedom (1786)

Until the beginning of the Revolutionary War, nine of the thirteen colonies still officially supported one particular religion, called an established church. But the practice had been weakened by the "Great Awakening," and by 1787 only Massachusetts, New Hampshire, and Connecticut maintained established religions. In the other states, the support of religious institutions depended on the voluntary contributions of their members.

Thomas Jefferson led the fight for religious freedom and separation of church and state in his native Virginia. This brought him into conflict with the Anglican Church, the established church in Virginia. After a long and bitter debate, Jefferson's statute for religious freedom passed the state legislature. In Jefferson's words, there was now "freedom for the Jew and the Gentile, the Christian and the Mohammedan, the Hindu and infidel of every denomination." When the First Amendment to the Constitution went into effect in 1791, Jefferson's principle of separation of church and state became part of the supreme law of the land.

I. Well aware that Almighty God has created the mind free; *that* all attempts to influence it by temporal [civil] punishments or burdens or by civil incapacitations [lack of fitness for office], tend only to . . . [produce] habits of hypocrisy and meanness and are a departure from the plan of the Holy Author of our religion, who, being Lord both of body and mind, yet chose not to propagate [spread] it by coercions [force] on either, as was in his Almighty power to do; *that* the impious presumption of legislators and rulers, civil as well as ecclesiastical [religious], who, being themselves but fallible and uninspired men, have assumed dominion [rule] over the faith of others, setting up their own opinions and modes of thinking as the only true and infallible [ones], and, such, endeavoring to impose them on others, have established and maintained false religions over the greatest part of the world and through all time; *that* to compel a man to furnish contributions of money for the propagation of opinions which he disbelieves is sinful and tyrannical; *that* even . . . forcing him to support this or that teacher of his own religious persuasion is depriving him of the comfortable liberty of giving his contributions to the particular pastor whose morals he would make his pattern and whose powers he feels most persuasive to righteousness . . . ; *that* our civil rights have no dependence on our religious opinions any more than [on] our opinions in physics or geometry; *that* therefore the proscribing [of] any citizen as unworthy [of] the public confidence by laying upon him an incapacity of being called to offices of trust and emolument unless he profess or renounce this or that religious opinion is depriving him injuriously of those privileges and advantages to which in common with his fellow citizens he has a natural right; . . . *that* to suffer the civil magistrate to intrude his powers into the field of opinion and to restrain the profession or propagation of principles on supposition of their ill tendency is a dangerous fallacy which at once destroys all religious liberty, because he [the magistrate],

being, of course, judge of that tendency, will make his opinions the rule of judgment and approve or condemn the sentiments of others only as they shall square with, or differ from, his own; *that* it is time enough for the rightful purposes of civil government for its officers to interfere when principles break out into overt [open, or public] acts against peace and good order; and, finally, *that* truth is great and will prevail if left to herself, that she is the proper and sufficient antagonist to error and has nothing to fear from the conflict, unless by human interposition disarmed of her natural weapons, free argument and debate, [for] errors [cease] to be dangerous when it is permitted freely to contradict them.

II. *Be it enacted by the General Assembly* that no man shall be compelled to frequent or support any religious worship, place, or ministry whatsoever, nor shall otherwise suffer on account of his religious opinions or belief; but that all men shall be free to profess, and by argument to maintain, their opinion in matters of religion, and that the same shall in no wise diminish, enlarge, or affect their civil capacities.

III. And though we well know that this assembly, elected by the people for the ordinary purposes of legislation only, [has] no power to restrain the acts of succeeding assemblies, constituted with powers equal to her own, and that therefore to declare this act to be irrevocable would be of no effect in law; yet, as we are free to declare, and do declare, that the rights hereby asserted are of the natural rights of mankind, and that if any act shall hereafter be passed to repeal the present or to narrow its operation, such act will be an infringement [violation] of natural rights.

FROM The Northwest Ordinance (1787)

The Northwest Ordinance provided a system of government for the region bounded by the Ohio and Mississippi rivers and the Great Lakes. This territory had been turned over to the central government by the states. By 1787 settlers were flocking to it. These lands might have been governed as colonies and their inhabitants treated as citizens with less than full rights, but Congress rejected that approach. Instead it set up orderly procedures whereby new states were to be created from the old Northwest Territory and admitted to the Union on the same basis as the original thirteen.

It is hereby ordained and declared by the authority aforesaid that the following articles shall be considered as articles of compact between the original states and the people and states in the said territory, and forever remain unalterable, unless by common consent, to wit:

Article 1. No person, demeaning [behaving] himself in a peaceable and orderly manner, shall ever be molested on account of his mode of worship or religious sentiments in the said territory.

Article 2. The inhabitants of the said territory shall always be entitled to the benefits of the writ of habeas corpus and of the trial by jury; of a proportionate representation of the people in the legislature; and of judicial proceedings according to the course of the common law. . . .

Article 3. Religion, morality, and knowledge being necessary to good government and the happiness of mankind, schools and the means of education shall forever be encouraged. The utmost good faith shall always be observed toward the Indians; their lands and property shall never be taken from them without their consent; and in their property, rights, and liberty they shall never be invaded or disturbed unless in just and lawful wars authorized by Congress; but laws founded in justice and humanity shall from time to time be made for preventing wrongs being done to them, and for preserving peace and friendship with them.

Article 4. The said territory and the states which may be formed therein, shall forever remain a part of this Confederacy of the United States of America, subject to the Articles of Confederation, and to such alterations therein as shall be constitutionally made; and to all the acts and ordinances of the United States in Congress assembled, conformable [agreeable] thereto. . . .

Article 5. There shall be formed in the said territory, not less than three nor more than five states; . . . And, whenever any of the said states shall have sixty thousand free inhabitants therein, such state shall be admitted by its delegates into the Congress of the United States on an equal footing with the original states in all respects whatever, and shall be at liberty to form a permanent constitution and state government: *Provided* the constitution and government so to be formed shall be republican [with popularly elected representatives] and in conformity to the principles contained in these articles; and, so far as it can be consistent with the general interest of the Confederacy, such admission shall be allowed at an earlier period, and when there may be a smaller number of free inhabitants in the state than sixty thousand.

Article 6. There shall be neither slavery nor involuntary servitude in the said territory, otherwise than in punishment of crimes whereof the party shall have been duly convicted: *Provided*, always, that any person escaping into the same, from whom labor or service is lawfully claimed in any one of the original states, such fugitive may be lawfully reclaimed and conveyed to the person claiming his or her labor or services as aforesaid. . . .

FROM Federalist #10 (1787)

After months of heated debate, the Constitutional Convention approved a new Constitution and forwarded it to the states for their consideration. The fate of the Constitution was very much in doubt. Those who favored it were known as Federalists. Opponents were called Antifederalists. Arguments for and against filled the newspapers and rang out in social gatherings throughout 1787 and 1788. And in no place did the matter seem more uncertain than in the important state of New York. In New York City a series of 85 letters arguing for the new Constitution appeared in the newspapers. These essays, signed "Publius," were written by Alexander Hamilton, James Madison, and John Jay. The "Federalist Essays," as they came to be called, were influential in convincing New York to ratify the Constitution. In time they were recognized to be what Thomas Jefferson called "the best commentary on the principles of government ever written."

In the following sections from Federalist #10, Madison discusses some of the advantages of the republican form of government created by the new Constitution.

Among the numerous advantages promised by a well-constructed union, none deserves to be more accurately developed than its tendency to break and control the violence of faction [division within the union]. The friend of popular governments never finds himself so much alarmed for their character and fate as when he contemplates their propensity [inclination] to this dangerous vice. . . .

By a faction, I understand a number of citizens, whether amounting to a majority or minority of the whole, who are united and actuated [moved] by some common impulse of passion, or of interest, adverse to the rights of other citizens or to the permanent and aggregate [collective] interests of the community. . . .

The latent [hidden] causes of faction are thus sown in the nature of man; and we see them everywhere brought into different degrees of activity, according to the different circumstances of civil society. A zeal for different opinions concerning religion, concerning government, and many other points, as well of speculation [thought] as of practice; an attachment to different leaders ambitiously contending for pre-eminence and power, or to persons of other descriptions whose fortunes have been interesting to the human passions, have, in turn, divided mankind into parties, inflamed them with mutual animosity [spite], and rendered them much more disposed to vex and oppress each other, than to co-operate for their common good. . . .

It is in vain to say that enlightened statesmen will be able to adjust these clashing interests and render them all subservient to [disposed to serve] the public good. Enlightened statesmen will not always be at the helm; nor, in many cases, can such an adjustment be made at all, without taking into view indirect and remote considerations, which will rarely prevail over the immediate interest which one party may find in disregarding the rights of another or the good of the whole.

The inference to which we are brought is that the causes of faction cannot be removed, and that relief is only to be sought in the means of controlling its effects.

A republic, by which I mean a government in which the scheme of representation takes place . . . promises the cure for which we are seeking.

The influence of factious leaders may kindle a flame within their particular states, but will be unable to spread a general conflagration through the other states. A religious sect may degenerate into a political faction in a part of the confederacy; but the variety of sects dispersed over the entire face of it must secure the national councils against any danger from that source. A rage for paper money, for an abolition of debts, for an equal division of property, or for any other improper and wicked project will be less apt to pervade the whole body of the Union than a particular member of it; in the same proportion as such a malady is more likely to taint a particular county or district than an entire state.

In the extent and proper structure of the Union, therefore, we behold a republican remedy for the diseases most incident [apt to occur] to republican government. And according to the degree of pleasure and pride we feel in being republicans, ought to be our zeal in cherishing the spirit and supporting the character of federalists.

FROM Federalist #15 (1787)

In the section from Federalist essay #15 that follows, Alexander Hamilton effectively summarizes the weaknesses of American government under the Articles of Confederation.

We may indeed, with propriety [correctly], be said to have reached almost the last stage of national humiliation. There is scarcely anything that can wound the pride, or degrade the character, of an independent people, which we do not experience. Are there engagements, to the performance of which we are held by every tie respectable among men? These are the subjects of constant and unblushing violation. Do we owe debts to foreigners, and to our own citizens contracted in a time of imminent peril, for the preservation of our political existence? These remain without any proper or satisfactory provision for their discharge. Have we valuable territories and important posts in the possession of a foreign power, which, by express stipulations, ought long since to have been surrendered? These are still retained, to the prejudice of our interests not less than of our rights. Are we in a condition to resent, or to repel the aggression? We have neither troops, nor treasury, nor government [for the Union]. Are we even in a condition to remonstrate [protest] with dignity? The just imputations on our own faith [true accusations about our actions], in respect to the same treaty, ought first to be removed. Are we entitled, by nature and compact, to a free participation in the navigation of the Mississippi? Spain excludes us from it. Is public credit an indispensable resource in time of public danger? We seem to have abandoned its cause as desperate and irretrievable. Is commerce of importance to national wealth? Ours is at the lowest point of declension [decline]. Is respectability in the eyes of foreign powers a safeguard against foreign encroachments [invasions]? The imbecility of our government even forbids them to treat [negotiate] with us. Our ambassadors abroad are the mere pageants of mimic sovereignty. Is a violent and unnatural decrease in the value of land a symptom of national distress? The price of improved land, in most parts of the country, is much lower than can be accounted for by the quantity of waste land at market, and can only be fully explained by that want of private and public confidence, which are so alarmingly prevalent among all ranks and which have a direct tendency to depreciate property of every kind. Is private credit the friend and patron of industry? That most useful kind which relates to borrowing and lending, is reduced within the narrowest limits, and this still more from an opinion of insecurity than from a scarcity of money. To shorten an enumeration of particulars which can afford neither pleasure nor instruction, it may in general be demanded, what indication is there of national disorder, poverty, and insignificance, that could befall a community so peculiarly blessed with natural advantages as we are, which does not form a part of the dark catalogue of our public misfortunes?

This is the melancholy situation to which we have been brought by those very maxims and counsels, which would now deter us from adopting the proposed Constitution; and which, not content with having conducted us to the brink of a precipice, seem resolved to plunge us into the abyss that awaits us below.

FROM Three Antifederalist Speeches (1788)

Ratification of the new Constitution was widely debated, and in some states ratification was no easy matter. The following speeches were made by opponents of the Constitution at the ratification conventions of Massachusetts and Virginia.

Amos Singletary, Massachusetts—. . . We [fought] with Great Britain, some said, for a threepenny duty on tea; but it was not that—it was because they claimed a right to tax us and bind us

in all cases whatever. And does not this Constitution do the same? Does it not take away all we have, all our property? Does it not lay *all* taxes, duties, imposts and excises? And what more have we to give? They tell us Congress [will be able to] collect all the money they want by impost [tax on imports]. I say there has always been a difficulty about impost. Whenever the [state legislature] was agoing to lay an impost, they would tell us it was more than trade could bear, and that it hurt the fair trader, and encouraged smuggling; and there will always be the same objection—they won't be able to raise money enough by impost, and then they will lay it on the land, and take all we have got. These lawyers, and men of learning, and moneyed men, that talk so finely and gloss over matters so smoothly, to make us, poor illiterate people, swallow down the pill, expect to get into Congress themselves; they expect to be the managers of this Constitution, and get all the power and all the money into their own hands, and then they will swallow up all us little folks, like the great leviathan [sea monster], Mr. President; yes, just as the whale swallowed up Jonah. This is what I am afraid of.

General Thompson, Massachusetts—Sir, the question is, whether congress shall have power . . . ["to provide for the common defense, promote the general welfare"]. . . . I look upon [this section as] big with mischiefs. Congress will have power to keep standing armies. The great Mr. Pitt [a British statesman] says, standing armies are dangerous. . . . We are able to stand our own ground against a foreign power—they cannot starve us out, they cannot bring their ships on the land; we are a nation of healthy and strong men—our land is fertile, and we are increasing in numbers. . . . Let us amend the old confederation. Why not give congress power only to regulate trade?. . . [Where] is the bill of rights which shall check the power of this congress, which shall say, *thus far shall ye come, and no farther*. The safety of the people depends on a bill of rights. . . . There are some parts of this constitution which I cannot digest; and, sir, shall we swallow a large bone for the sake of a little meat? Some say swallow the whole now, and pick out the bone afterwards. But I say, let us pick off the meat, and throw the bone away.

Patrick Henry, Virginia—And here I would make this inquiry of those worthy characters who composed a part of the late federal Convention. I am sure they were fully impressed with the necessity of forming a great consolidated government, instead of a confederation. That this is a consolidated government is demonstrably clear; and the danger of such a government is, to my mind, very striking. I have the highest veneration [regard] for those gentlemen; but, sir, give me leave to demand. What right had they to say, *We, the people?* My political curiosity, exclusive of my anxious solicitude [concern] for the public welfare, leads me to ask, Who authorized them to speak the language of *We, the people*, instead of, *We, the states?* States are the characteristics and the soul of a confederation. . . . The federal Convention ought to have amended the old system [Articles of Confederation]; for this purpose they were solely delegated; the object of their mission extended to no other consideration. You must, therefore, forgive the solicitation of one unworthy member to know what danger could have arisen under the present Confederation, and what are the causes of this proposal to change our government. . . .

This Constitution is said to have beautiful features; but when I come to examine these features, sir, they appear to me horribly frightful. Among other deformities, it has an awful squinting; it squints towards monarchy; and does not this raise indignation in the breast of every true American?

Your President may easily become king. Your Senate is so imperfectly constructed that your dearest rights may be sacrificed by what may be a small minority; and a very small minority may continue forever unchangeably this government, although horridly defective. Where are your checks in this government? Your strongholds will be in the hands of your enemies. It is on a supposition that your American governors shall be honest, that all the good qualities of this government are founded; but its defective and imperfect construction puts it in their power to perpetrate the worst of mischiefs, should they be bad men; and, sir, would not all the world, from the eastern to the western hemisphere, blame our distracted folly in resting our rights upon the contingency of our rulers being good or bad? Show me that age and country where the rights and liberties of the people were placed on the sole chance of their rulers being good men, without a consequent loss of liberty! I say that the loss of the dearest privilege has ever followed, with absolute certainty, every such mad attempt.

If your American chief be a man of ambition and abilities, how easy is it for him to render himself absolute! The army is in his hands, and if he be a man of address [one who is confident and convincing], it will be attached to him, and it will be the subject of long meditation with him to seize the first auspicious [good] moment to accomplish his design; and, sir, will the American spirit solely relieve you when this happens? I would rather infinitely—and I am sure most of this Convention are of the same opinion—have a king, lords, and commons, than a government so replete [filled] with such insupportable evils.

FROM Jefferson's First Inaugural Address (1801)

On March 4, 1801, Thomas Jefferson took the oath of office and became the third president of the United States. Jefferson was a Democratic-Republican, the first non-Federalist to become president. His defeated political opponents wondered what this would mean: How would the government now be different?

Jefferson answered their questions in his First Inaugural Address. He reassured his opponents by stressing his belief that the ideals of democracy and republican government were shared by all. "We are all Republicans; we are all Federalists," Jefferson said. Then he affirmed his belief in the idea of limited government—that that government is best that governs least.

Friends and Fellow Citizens: . . .

All . . . will bear in mind this sacred principle, that though the will of the majority is in all cases to prevail, that will to be rightful must be reasonable; that the minority possess their equal rights, which equal law must protect, and to violate would be oppression. Let us, then, fellow citizens, unite with one heart and one mind. Let us restore to social intercourse [dealings] that harmony and affection without which liberty and even life itself are but dreary things. And let us reflect that, having banished from our land that religious intolerance under which mankind so long bled and suffered, we have yet gained little if we countenance [allow] a political intolerance as despotic, as wicked, and capable of as bitter and bloody persecutions. . . . But every difference of opinion is not a difference of principle. We have called by different names brethren of the same principle. We are all Republicans; we are all Federalists. If there be any among us who would wish to dissolve this Union or to change its republican forms, let them stand undisturbed as monuments of the safety with which error of opinion may be tolerated where reason is left free to combat it. . . .

Let us, then, with courage and confidence pursue our own Federal and Republican principles, our attachment to union and representative government. . . .

About to enter, fellow citizens, on the exercise of duties which comprehend [include] everything dear and valuable to you, it is proper you should understand what I deem the essential principles of our government and consequently those which ought to shape its administration. I will compress them within the narrowest compass they will bear, stating the general principle, but not all its limitations. Equal and exact justice to all men, of whatever state or persuasion religious or political; peace, commerce, and honest friendship with all nations, entangling alliances with none; the support of the state governments in all their rights, as the most competent administrations for our domestic concerns and the surest bulwarks [defenses] against anti-republican tendencies; the preservation of the general government in its whole constitutional vigor, as the sheet anchor [main support] of our peace at home and safety abroad; a jealous care of the right of election by the people—a mild and safe corrective of abuses which are lopped by the sword of revolution where peaceable remedies are unprovided; absolute acquiescence in the decisions of the majority, the vital principle of republics, from which [there] is no appeal but to force, the vital principle and immediate parent of despotism; a well-disciplined militia, our best reliance in peace and for the first moments of war, till regulars may relieve them; the supremacy of the civil over the military authority; economy in the public expense, that labor may be lightly burdened; the honest payment of our debts and sacred preservation of the public faith; encouragement of agriculture, and of commerce as its handmaid; the diffusion of information and arraignment [bringing up] of all abuses at the bar of the public reason; freedom of religion; freedom of the press; and freedom of person under the protection of the habeas corpus, and trial by juries impartially selected. These principles form the bright constellation which has gone before us and guided our steps through an age of revolution and reformation. The wisdom of our sages and blood of our heroes have been devoted to their attainment. They should be the creed of our political faith, the text of civic instruction, the touchstone by which to try the services of those we trust; and should we wander from them in moments of error or of alarm, let us hasten to retrace our steps and to regain the road which alone leads to peace, liberty, and safety.

FROM *Marbury v. Madison* (1803)

In the confusion of President John Adams' last days in office, several commissions for new justices of the peace in the District of Columbia did not get distributed. When President Jefferson found them, he refused to release them to the appointees. This led one of them, William Marbury, to ask the Supreme Court to order Secretary of State James Madison to issue the commissions, which had been properly signed by Adams. Chief Justice John Marshall ruled that the law allowing Marbury to sue in a case like this was not authorized by the Constitution, and was therefore unconstitutional. The decision set an important precedent, that the Supreme Court held the power to rule an act of Congress unconstitutional. This established the principle of "judicial review," whereby courts rule on the legality of government actions.

The government of the United States has been emphatically termed a government of laws, and not of men. . . .

The powers of the legislature are defined and limited; and that those limits may not be mistaken, or forgotten, the Constitution is written. To what purpose are powers limited, and to what purpose is that limitation committed to writing, if these limits may, at any time, be passed by those intended to be restrained? . . . It is a proposition too plain to be contested that the Constitution controls any legislative act repugnant to it; or that the legislature may alter the Constitution by an ordinary act.

. . . a legislative act contrary to the Constitution is not law. . . .

It is emphatically the province [function] and

duty of the judicial department to say what the law is. Those who apply the rule to particular cases must of necessity expound [explain in detail] and interpret that rule. If two laws conflict with each other, the courts must decide on the operation of each.

So if a law be in opposition to the Constitution; if both the law and the Constitution apply to a particular case, so that the court must either decide that case conformably to the law, disregarding the Constitution, or conformably to the Constitution, disregarding the law, the court must determine which of these conflicting rules governs the case. This is of the very essence of judicial duty.

If, then, the courts are to regard the Constitution, and the Constitution is superior to any ordinary act of the legislature, the Constitution, and not such ordinary act, must govern the case to which they both apply.

Those, then, who controvert [deny] the principle that the Constitution is to be considered in court as a paramount law, are reduced to the necessity of maintaining that courts must close their eyes on the Constitution and see only the law.

This doctrine would subvert the very foundation of all written constitutions. It would declare that an act which, according to the principles and theory of our government, is entirely void, is yet, in practice, completely obligatory [binding]. It would declare that if the legislature shall do what is expressly forbidden, such act, notwithstanding the express prohibition, is in reality effectual. It would be giving to the legislature a practical and real omnipotence with the same breath which professes to restrict their powers within narrow limits. It is prescribing [laying down] limits and declaring that those limits may be passed at pleasure.

That it thus reduces to nothing what we have deemed the greatest improvement on political institutions, a written constitution, would of itself be sufficient, in America, where written constructions have been viewed with so much reverence, for rejecting the construction. But the peculiar expressions of the Constitution of the United States furnish additional arguments in favor of its rejection.

The judicial power of the United States is extended to all cases arising under the Constitution.

Could it be the intention of those who gave this power to say that in using it the Constitution should not be looked into? That a case arising under the Constitution should be decided without examining the instrument under which it arises?

This is too extravagant to be maintained. . . .

FROM The Monroe Doctrine (1823)

The Monroe Doctrine was one of the most influential declarations in American history. The principles behind the doctrine were one of the foundations of United States foreign policy for more than a century. Yet it was not a part of the Constitution or even a law passed by Congress. It was part of President James Monroe's annual State of the Union message to Congress.

Monroe was fearful that the European monarchies might try to return the newly independent nations of Latin America to Spain and that Russia would expand its claims from Alaska southward along the Pacific Coast of North America. Acting on the advice of his secretary of state, John Quincy Adams, Monroe boldly stated that the Western Hemisphere was off limits to any future European expansion.

The following passage is an excerpt from Monroe's message.

At the proposal of the Russian Imperial Government, made through the minister of the Emperor [Czar Alexander I] residing here [in Washington, D.C.], a full power and instructions have been transmitted to the minister of the United States at St. Petersburg [the Russian capital city] to arrange by amicable [friendly] negotiations the respective rights and interests of the two nations [the United States and Russia] on the northwest coast of this continent [North America]. . . . The occasion has been judged proper for asserting [stating], as a principle in which the rights and interests of the United States are involved, that the American continents, by the free and independent condition which they have assumed and maintain, are henceforth not to be considered as subjects for future colonization by any European powers. . . .

The citizens of the United States cherish sentiments the most friendly in favor of the liberty and happiness of their fellow men on that side of the Atlantic [Europe]. In the wars of the European powers in matters relating to themselves we have never taken any part, nor does it comport with [fit] our policy to do so. It is only when our rights are invaded or seriously menaced that we resent injuries or make preparation for our defense. With the movements [for independence] in this hemisphere we are of necessity more immediately connected, and by causes which must be obvious to all enlightened and impartial observers. The political system of the allied powers [the Holy Alliance of Russia, Prussia, and Austria] is essentially different in this respect from that of America. This difference proceeds from that which exists in their respective governments; and to the defense of our own, which has been achieved by the loss of so much blood and treasure, and matured by the wisdom of their most enlightened citizens, and under which we have enjoyed unexampled felicity [happiness], this whole nation is devoted. We owe it, therefore, to candor [open honesty] and to the amicable relations existing between the United States and those powers to declare that we should consider any attempt on their part to extend their system [government] to any portion of this hemisphere as dangerous to our peace and safety. With the existing colonies or dependencies of any European power, we have not interfered and shall not interfere. But with the governments who have declared their independence and maintained it, and whose independence we have, on great consideration and on just principles acknowledged, we could not view any interposition [interference] for the purpose of oppressing them, or controlling in any other manner their destiny, by any European power in any other light than as the manifestation of an unfriendly disposition toward the United States. In the war between those new governments and Spain, we declared our neutrality at the time of their recognition, and to this we have adhered, and shall continue to adhere, providing no change shall occur which, in the judgment of the competent authorities of this government, shall make a corresponding change on the part of the United States indispensable to their security.

The late events in Spain and Portugal show that Europe is still unsettled. Of this important fact no stronger proof can be adduced [offered] than that the allied powers [Holy Alliance] should have thought it proper, on any principle satisfactory to themselves, to have interposed by force in the internal concerns of Spain. To what extent such interposition may be carried, on the same principle, is a question in which all independent powers whose governments differ from theirs are interested, even those most remote, and surely none

more so than the United States. Our policy in regard to Europe, which was adopted at an early stage of the wars which have so long agitated that quarter of the globe, nevertheless remain the same, which is, not to interfere in the internal concerns of any of its powers; to consider the government *de facto* [the one actually in power] as the legitimate government for us; to cultivate friendly relations with it, and to preserve those relations by a frank, firm, and manly policy, meeting in all instances the just claims of every power, submitting to injuries from none. But in regard to those continents [North and South America] circumstances are eminently and conspicuously different. It is impossible that the allied powers should extend their political system to any portion of either continent without endangering our peace and happiness; nor can anyone believe that our southern brethren [the people of Latin America and the Caribbean], if left to themselves, would adopt it of their own accord. It is equally impossible, therefore, that we should behold such interposition in any form with indifference. If we look to the comparative strength and resources of Spain and those new governments, and their distance from each other, it must be obvious that she can never subdue [control] them. It is still the true policy of the United States to leave the parties to themselves, in the hope that the other powers will pursue the same course. . . .

Texas Declaration of Rights (1836)

On March 1, 1836, while the Texans were defending the Alamo, a convention met at Washington-on-the-Brazos. The delegates declared the independence of Texas from Mexico and created a government for their new country, the Republic of Texas.

The Texas Constitution was closely modeled on that of the United States. It contained a similar statement of basic rights of individuals that the government could not take away.

All men, when they form a government, have equal rights, and no man or group of men is entitled to special privileges.

All political power comes from the people, and all free governments are founded on their authority. At all times they have the right to change their government in such a manner as they think proper.

No preferences shall be given by the law to any religious group or any mode of worship over another. Every person shall be permitted to worship God according to the dictates of his own conscience.

Every citizen shall be at liberty to speak, write, or publish his opinion on any subject, but is responsible for abusing that privilege.

The people shall be secure in their persons, houses, papers, and possessions from all unreasonable searches and seizures.

A person accused of committing a crime shall have the right of being heard by himself or by a lawyer. In all prosecutions, he shall have the right to a speedy and public trial by an impartial jury.

No citizen shall be deprived of privileges, outlawed, exiled, or in any manner denied the right to vote, except by due course of the law.

No title of nobility or hereditary honors shall ever be granted or conferred in this republic.

No unreasonable bail should be set nor shall the writ of *habeas corpus* be suspended except when the public safety may require it.

Excessive fines shall not be imposed, or cruel or unusual punishment inflicted.

No person shall be imprisoned for debt, even if he cannot pay.

No person's services shall be demanded, nor property taken by the government for public use, unless by his own consent, without just compensation being made according to the law.

Every citizen shall have the right to bear arms in defense of himself and the republic. The army shall at all times be controlled by the government of the people.

FROM The Seneca Falls Declaration and Resolution on Women's Rights (1848)

Inspired by the spirit of reform emerging in the United States in the 1840s, Lucretia Mott and Elizabeth Cady Stanton organized the first American women's rights convention in 1848. At the time, women had few legal rights. They could not vote. They could not practice professions such as medicine, law, and the ministry. And in many states, when women married, control of their property and legal affairs passed to their husbands.

The women assembled at the 1848 Seneca Falls Convention adopted the following document. In words that echoed the Declaration of Independence, it announced their determination to fight for equality with men.

When, in the course of human events, it becomes necessary for one portion of the family of man to assume among the people of the earth a position different from that which they hitherto occupied, but one to which the laws of nature and of nature's God entitle them, a decent respect to the opinions of mankind requires that they should declare the causes that impel [push] them to such a course.

We hold these truths to be self-evident: that all men and women are created equal; that they are endowed by their Creator with certain inalienable rights; that among these rights are life, liberty, and the pursuit of happiness; that to secure these rights governments are instituted deriving their just powers from the consent of the governed. Whenever any form of government becomes destructive of these ends, it is the right of those who suffer from it to refuse allegiance to it, and to insist upon the institution of a new government, laying its foundation on such principles, and organizing its powers in such form, as to them shall seem most likely to effect their safety and happiness. Prudence, indeed, will dictate that governments long established should not be changed for light and transient causes; and accordingly all experience has shown that mankind are more disposed to suffer while evils are sufferable, than to right themselves by abolishing forms to which they are accustomed. But when a long train [list] of abuses and usurpations [seizures of power] pursuing invariably the same object evinces [creates] a design to reduce them under absolute despotism [control by an absolute ruler], it is their duty to throw off such government, and to provide new guards for their future security. Such has been the patient sufferance [suffering] of the women under this government, and such is now the necessity which constrains [causes] them to demand the equal station [status] to which they are entitled.

The history of mankind is a history of repeated injuries and usurpations on the part of man toward woman, having in direct object the establishment of an absolute tyranny over her. To prove this, let facts be submitted to a candid world.

Having deprived her of the first right of a citizen, the elective franchise [right to vote], thereby leaving her without representation in the halls of legislation, he has oppressed her on all sides.

He has made her, if married, in the eye of the law, civilly dead. . . .

Now, in view of this entire disfranchisement [the absence of the right to vote] of one half of the people of this country, their social and religious degradation [reduction to lower status]—in view of the unjust laws above mentioned, and because women feel themselves aggrieved [injured], oppressed [held down], and fraudulently deprived of their most sacred rights, we insist that they have immediate admission to all the rights and privileges which belong to them as citizens of the United States. . . .

RESOLUTIONS

Resolved, That all laws which prevent woman from occupying such a station in society as her conscience shall dictate, or which place her in a position inferior to that of man, are contrary to the great precept [principle] of nature, and, therefore, of no force or authority.

Resolved, That woman is man's equal—was intended to be so by the Creator, and the highest good of the race demands that she should be recognized as such. . . .

Resolved, . . . That it is time she [woman] should move in the enlarged sphere which her great Creator has assigned her.

Resolved, That it is the duty of the women of this country to secure to themselves their sacred right of the elective franchise.

Resolved, That the equality of human rights results necessarily from the fact of the identity [basic sameness] of the race in capabilities and responsibilities.

Resolved, That the speedy success of our cause depends upon the zealous and untiring efforts of both men and women, for the overthrow of the monopoly of the pulpit, and for the securing to women of equal participation with men in various trades, professions, and commerce. . . .

FROM *Dred Scott v. Sandford* (1857)

The Dred Scott decision was one of the most controversial of all Supreme Court rulings. Scott, a slave, had been taken from the slave state of Missouri to the free state of Illinois and then to Wisconsin Territory, where slavery was prohibited by the Missouri Compromise of 1820. Scott's owner later brought him back to Missouri. Scott then brought suit in the courts, claiming that by living in a free territory he had become free. However, Chief Justice Roger B. Taney ruled that Scott was still a slave and that blacks were not citizens of the United States and therefore had no right to sue in court. In addition the Court declared that the Missouri Compromise was unconstitutional.

The judgment aroused a storm of protest throughout the northern states and reopened the bitter national debate over slavery in the western territories.

Chief Justice Taney—. . . The plaintiff . . . was, with his wife and children, held as slaves by the defendant, in the state of Missouri, and he brought this action in the Circuit Court of the United States for that district, to assert [claim] the title of himself and his family to freedom.

The declaration is . . . that he and the defendant are citizens of different states; that is, that he is a citizen of Missouri, and the defendant a citizen of New York.

The defendant pleaded . . . that the plaintiff was not a citizen of the state of Missouri, as alleged [declared] in his declaration, being a Negro of African descent whose ancestors were of pure African blood, and who were brought into this country and sold as slaves. . . .

The question is simply this: Can a Negro, whose ancestors were imported into this country, and sold as slaves, become a member of the political community formed and brought into existence by the Constitution of the United States, and as such become entitled to all the rights and privileges and immunities guaranteed by that instrument to the citizen? One of which rights is the privilege of suing in a court of the United States in the cases specified in the Constitution. . . .

The words "people of the United States" and "citizens" are synonymous terms, and mean the same thing. They both describe the political body who, according to our republican institutions, form the sovereignty, and who hold the power and conduct the government through their representatives. . . . [E]very citizen is one of this people, and a constituent member of this sovereignty. The question before us is, whether the class of persons described in the plea [Africans brought to America as slaves] . . . compose a portion of this people, and are constituent members of this sovereignty. We think they are not, and that they are not included, and were not intended to be included, under the word "citizens" in the Constitution, and can, therefore, claim none of the rights and privileges which that instrument provides for and secures to citizens of the United States. On the contrary, they were at that time considered as a subordinate and inferior class of beings, who had been subjugated by the dominant race, and whether emancipated or not, yet remained subject to their authority. . . .

A Negro of the African race was regarded . . . as an article of property and held and bought and sold as such in every one of the thirteen colonies which united in the Declaration of Independence and afterward formed the Constitution of the United States. . . .

The legislation of the different colonies furnished positive and indisputable proof of this fact. . . .

The language of the Declaration of Independence is equally conclusive: . . .

"We hold these truths to be self-evident: that all men are created equal; that they are endowed by their Creator with certain inalienable rights; that among these are life, liberty, and the pursuit of happiness; that to secure these rights, governments are instituted, deriving their just powers from the consent of the governed."

The general words above quoted would seem to embrace the whole human family, and if they were used in a similar instrument at this day would be so understood. But it is too clear for dispute that the enslaved African race were not intended to be included and formed no part of the people who framed and adopted this declaration. . . .

The right of property in a slave is distinctly and expressly affirmed in the Constitution. The right to traffic in it, like an ordinary article of merchandise and property, was guaranteed to the citizens of the United States, in every state that might desire it, for twenty years. And the government in express terms is pledged to protect it in all future time, if the slave escapes from his owner. . . . And no word can be found in the Constitution which gives Congress a greater power over slave property, or which entitles property of the kind to less protection than property of any other description.

The only power conferred is the power coupled with the duty of guarding and protecting the owner in his rights.

Upon these considerations, it is the opinion of the Court that the Act of Congress which prohibited a citizen from holding and owning property of this kind in the territory of the United States north of the line therein mentioned, is not warranted by the Constitution, and is, therefore, void; and that neither Dred Scott himself, nor any of his family, were made free by being carried into this territory; even if they had been carried there by the owner, with the intention of becoming a permanent resident. . . .

FROM The Mississippi Black Codes (1865)

Soon after the Civil War ended the southern states began to pass laws governing the rights and obligations of the freed slaves. These "black codes," as they came to be called, went much further than simply placing African American citizens in a second-class status. They came close to creating a new slavery. As historian W. E. B. Du Bois observed, in "the original codes . . . there was a plain and indisputable attempt on the part of the Southern states to make Negroes slaves in everything but name."

These examples from the black code enacted in Mississippi show how drastically such laws restricted personal freedom.

Every freedman, free Negro, and mulatto [person of mixed Negro and white ancestry] shall on the second Monday of January, one thousand eight hundred and sixty-six [1866], and annually thereafter, have a lawful home or employment, and shall have written evidence thereof . . . from the Mayor . . . or from a member of the board of police . . . which licenses may be revoked for cause at any time by the authority granting the same. . . .

Every civil officer shall, and every person may, arrest and carry back to his or her legal employer any freedman, free Negro, or mulatto who shall have quit the service of his or her employer without good cause; and said officer and person shall be entitled to receive for arresting and carrying back every deserting employee aforesaid the sum of five dollars, and ten cents per mile from the place of arrest to the place of delivery, and the same shall be paid by the employer and held as a set-off for so much against the wages of said deserting employee. . . .

Any freedman, free Negro, or mulatto, committing riots, routs, affrays [brawls], trespasses, malicious mischief and cruel treatment to animals, seditious speeches, insulting gestures, language or acts, or assaults on any person, disturbance of the peace, exercising the functions of a minister of the gospel without a license from some regularly organized church, vending spirituous or intoxicating liquors, or committing any other misdemeanor, the punishment of which is not specifically provided for by law, shall, upon conviction thereof, in the county court, be fined not less than ten dollars, and not more than one hundred dollars, and may be imprisoned, at the discretion of the court, not exceeding thirty days. . . .

No freedman, free Negro, or mulatto, not in the military service of the United States Government, and not licensed to do so by the board of police of his or her county, shall keep or carry firearms of any kind, or any ammunition, dirk [a long, straight-bladed dagger], or bowie-knife; and on conviction thereof, in the county court, shall be punished by fine, not exceeding ten dollars, and pay the costs of such proceedings, and all such arms or ammunition shall be forfeited to the informer. . . .

All freedmen, free Negroes, and mulattoes in this state over the age of eighteen years, found on the second Monday in January, 1866, or thereafter, with no lawful employment or business, or found unlawfully assembling themselves together, either in the day or night time, and all white persons so assembling with freedmen, free Negroes or mulattoes, or usually associating with freedmen, free Negroes or mulattoes on terms of equality, or living in adultery or fornication with a freedwoman, free Negro or mulatto, shall be deemed vagrants, and on conviction thereof shall be fined in the sum of not exceeding, in the case of a freedman, free Negro or mulatto, fifty dollars, and a white man two hundred dollars and imprisoned, at the discretion of the court, the free Negro not exceeding ten days, and the white not exceeding six months.
. . .

[It] shall be the duty of all sheriffs, justices of the peace, and other civil officers of the several counties in this state to report to the probate courts of their respective counties semiannually, at the January and July terms of said courts, all freedmen, free Negroes and mulattoes, under the age of eighteen, within their respective counties, beats, or districts, who are orphans, or whose parent or parents have not the means, or who refuse to provide for and support said minors, and thereupon it shall be the duty of said probate court to order the clerk of said court to apprentice said minors to some competent and suitable person, or such terms as the court may direct, having a particular care to the interest of said minors: Provided, that the former owner of said minors shall have the preference when, in the opinion of the court, he or she shall be a suitable person for that purpose. . . .

All the penal and criminal laws now in force in this State, defining offenses, and prescribing the mode of punishment for crimes and misdemeanors committed by slaves, free Negroes or mulattoes, be and the same are hereby reenacted, and declared to be in full force and effect, against freedmen, free Negroes, and mulattoes, except so far as the mode and manner of trial and punishment have been changed or altered by law.

Glossary

This glossary contains the words you need to understand as you study American history. After each word there is a brief definition or explanation of the meaning of the word as it is used in *The Story of America*. The page number(s) refer to the page(s) on which the word first appears in the textbook.

Phonetic Respelling and Pronunciation Guide

Many of the key terms in this textbook have been respelled to help you pronounce them. The following Phonetic Respelling and Pronunciation Guide offers the simplest form of usage, and for this Glossary is adapted from *Webster's Ninth New Collegiate Dictionary, Webster's New Geographical Dictionary,* and *Webster's New Biographical Dictionary.* The letter combinations used in the respellings are explained below.

MARK	AS IN	RESPELLING	EXAMPLE
a	alphabet	a	*AL·fuh·bet
ā	Asia	ay	AY·zhuh
ä	cart, top	ah	KAHRT, TAHP
e	let, ten	e	LET, TEN
ē	even, leaf	ee	EE· vuhn, LEEF
i	it, tip, British	i	IT, TIP, BRIT·ish
ī	site, buy, Ohio	y	SYT, BY, oh·HY·oh
	iris	eye	EYE ·ris
k	card	k	KARD
ō	over, rainbow	oh	oh·vuhr, RAYN·boh
ů	book, wood	ooh	BOOHK, WOOHD
ȯ	all, orchid	aw	AWL, AWR·kid
ȯi	foil, coin	oy	FOYL, KOYN
aů	out	ow	OWT
ə	cup, butter	uh	KUHP, BUHT·uhr
ü	rule, food	oo	ROOL, FOOD
yü	few	yoo	FYOO
zh	vision	zh	VIZH·uhn

*A syllable printed in small capital letters receives heavier emphasis than the other syllable(s) in a word.

A

abolished Ended. **465**

abolitionist (ab·uh·LISH·uh·nists) Person who wanted to end slavery in the U.S. **465**

abominable Hateful or offensive. **385**

absolute location Part of geographic theme of location, exactly where on earth a place is. **xxiii**

accommodation Going along with the desires of others. **617**

account Description of facts, conditions, or events. **27**

acid rain Rain containing a high concentration of industrial chemicals that falls as pollution. **664**

adobe (uh·DOH·bee) Building material made of sun-baked brick plastered with mud. **7**

adventure school School for girls that focused on the arts and handicrafts. **485**

advice and consent Senate approval required by the Constitution for major presidential appointments or treaties. **224**

affirmative action Government guidelines compelling employers to give minority workers preference in hiring in order to make up for past imbalances in the work force. **664**

Age of Reform Period in America between about 1830 and 1850 of social concern and improvement. **476**

Alamo (AL·uh·mo) San Antonio fort where 187 Texans died fighting for independence. **410**

Albany Plan of Union First plan for uniting the colonies drafted by Benjamin Franklin in 1754. **100**

Alien and Sedition (si·DISH·uhn) **Acts** Four 1798 laws aimed at foreigners and others in the U.S. who were supposedly undermining the government by helping France. **261**

almshouse Home for poor people. **499**

Amana (uh·MAN·uh) **community** Settlement founded by Christian Metz in early 1800s. **490**

amendment Change or addition to a bill or law such as to the Constitution. **237**

America Name given to lands in the New World—later North, Central, and South America; named after explorer Amerigo Vespucci. **27**

American Colonization Society Group that offered to help former slaves resettle in Africa. **449**

American System Plan developed by Henry Clay in early 1800s for sectional cooperation on legislation. **379**

amnesty (AM·nuhs·tee) Official pardon for crimes committed against the government. **593**

Amnesty Act of 1872 Law that reversed the decision to bar former Confederate officials and soldiers from holding public office. **611**

anguished (AN·gwisht) Distressed or full of sorrow. **495**

annexation (an·ek·SAY·shuhn) Addition of territory to a country. **405**

anthropologist (an·thruh·PAHL·uh·juhst) Scientist who studies the physical, social, and cultural development of people. **9**

antibiotic (ant·ih·by·OHT·ik) Substance such as penicillin which is produced to kill disease-carrying organisms. **659**

Antifederalist Person who supported strong state governments and opposed ratification of the U.S. constitution. **226**

Appalachian Highlands Physical region of the United States that includes the Appalachian mountains and the ridges and valleys associated with them. **xxvi**

Appeal to the Colored Citizens of the World Essay by David Walker urging African Americans to fight for freedom. **471**

appellate (uh·PEL·uht) **court** Lower federal appeals court. **224**

Appomattox (ap·uh·MAT·uhks) **Court House** Virginia town where Lee surrendered to Grant, ending the Civil War. **584**

arch Chief or principal (as in archrival). **513**

archaeologist (ahr·kee·AHL·uh·juhst)
Scientist who studies history and culture by examining the remains of early human cultures. **9**

ardent Very strong. **237**

Army of Northern Virginia Confederate army commanded by Robert E. Lee. **559**

Army of the Potomac Union army near Washington, D.C., during the Civil War. **557**

arsenal Storehouse of weapons. **195**

Articles of Confederation Agreement in 1781 under which the 13 original colonies established a government of states. **185**

artifact (AHRT·i·fakt) Objects made by humans, such as jewelry, tools, or weapons. **9**

assassination (uh·sas·uhn·AY·shuhn) Killing of a government official. **592**

assembly Lawmaking body elected by the people. **110**

astrolabe (AS·truh·layb) Instrument used to measure a ship's latitude or distance from the equator. **19**

Atlanta Major southern city in Georgia that was captured and burned to the ground by General Sherman (1864). **582**

Atlanta Compromise Proposal by Booker T. Washington that both blacks and whites honor the separate-but-equal principle. **617**

atrocious (uh·TROH·shus) Horrifying or disgusting. **518**

attorney general Chief law officer of the nation and legal adviser to the president. **235**

Aztecs (AZ·teks) Powerful Indian nation in Central Mexico at the time of the Spanish invasion in 1519. **29**

B

Bacon's Rebellion Revolt of Virginia colonists led by Nathaniel Bacon in 1676 which resulted in the killing of Indians, the burning of Jamestown, and the removal of the governor. **105**

bank note Paper money supported by gold or silver. **242, 388**

Bank of the United States Central banking system for the nation

Glossary   **719**

created by Congress in 1791 to support American industry. **242**

bankrupt Out of funds or unable to pay debts. **389**

Barbary pirate Seaman from the North African states who in the early 1800s helped seize and rob ships traveling on the Mediterranean Sea. **275**

Battle of Antietam (an-TEET-uhm) Bloody Civil War clash that caused Confederate troops to withdraw from Maryland (1862). **568**

Battle of Buena Vista (bway-nuh-VEE-stuh) American victory by General Taylor in 1847 in Northern Mexico. **420**

Battle of Bunker Hill First major battle of Revolutionary War; actually fought at Breed's Hill. **149**

Battle of Chancellorsville (CHAN-suh-luhrz-vil) Brilliant 1863 Confederate victory in which Stonewall Jackson was killed. **574**

Battle of Cold Harbor Last major victory for Lee and third clash against Union forces led by Grant (1864). **581**

Battle of Cowpens Defeat in 1781 of British in South Carolina. **171**

Battle of Fallen Timbers Decisive fight in 1794 in the Northwest Territory in which Wayne defeated Indians led by Blue Jacket. **248**

Battle of Fredericksburg Victory in 1862 by Confederate forces under Lee that left 12,000 Union soldiers dead. **573**

Battle of Gettysburg Defeat in 1863 of Lee's invasion of the North. **575**

Battle of Horseshoe Bend Defeat of Creek Indians by Andrew Jackson in 1814. **307**

Battle of Long Island Revolutionary War conflict in which British General Howe defeated Washington's forces (1776). **164**

Battle of Monmouth Court House British defeat by George Washington in 1778. **170**

Battle of New Orleans Major fight won by Jackson after the War of 1812 was over (1815). **312**

Battle of Princeton American victory

in Revolutionary War that helped boost American morale. **165**

Battle of Put-in-Bay Perry's defeat of the British navy on Lake Erie in 1813. **305**

Battle of Saratoga Important 1777 American victory in Revolutionary War after which France recognized American independence. **168**

Battle of Seven Pines Civil War clash in which Confederate Commander Johnston was wounded and succeeded by Robert E. Lee. **559**

Battle of Shiloh Costly 1862 Union victory in Mississippi. **578**

Battle of the Thames (TEMZ) Fight in which Harrison won back the Great Lakes region from the British and Tecumseh was killed (1813). **306**

Battle of the Wilderness Clash of Lee's and Grant's forces in the forests southwest of Washington, D.C., resulting in heavy losses on both sides (1864). **581**

Battle of Tippecanoe Fight with the Indians in 1811 that made William Henry Harrison a hero. **299**

Battle of Trenton Revolutionary War victory during which George Washington defeated Hessian mercenaries (1776). **165**

Bear Flag Revolt Defeat of Mexican forces in California by American settlers in 1847. **420**

Beecher's Bibles Name given to guns bought with money raised by abolitionist minister Henry Ward Beecher of New York and sent to antislavery forces in Kansas in the 1850s. **519**

besieged Under attack or surrounded by the enemy. **547**

bias (BY-us) Prejudice. **267**

Bill of Rights Name given to the first ten amendments to the Constitution. **182**

Black Codes Regulations passed by southern governments after Reconstruction to restrict the rights of African Americans. **594**

Black Power Movement in the 1960s by African Americans that supported the use of force and polit-

ical and economic power in the struggle for equal rights. **661**

"Black Republican" Name given to the post-Civil War governments in the South. **603**

Bladensburg Village in Maryland taken by the British in 1814 just before their march on Washington. **308**

"Bleeding Kansas" Name given in eastern newspaper accounts to fighting in Kansas in the 1850s between proslavery and antislavery forces. **522**

blockade runner Small, fast ship used during the Civil War. **563**

bolstered Supported or reinforced. **581**

boom Period of thriving business activity. **392**

border state State such as Maryland, West Virginia, Kentucky, Delaware, and Missouri that held slaves but did not leave the Union during the Civil War. **536**

boreal High-latitude climate found near the North and South poles with brief summers and long, cold winters. **679**

boss Leader of a political machine. **627**

Boston Massacre Incident between British soldiers and Americans in 1770 Boston in which several Americans were killed. **132**

Boston Tea Party Protest in 1773 against British tax on tea during which colonists dumped three shiploads of tea into Boston harbor. **141**

bound Under legal or moral obligation; required. **15**

boycott (BOY-kaht) Refusal to buy certain goods or services as a protest. **128**

breadwinner Primary wage earner in a family. **480**

British Being of Great Britain, which in colonial days was England, Scotland, Wales, or Ireland. **86**

buffalo soldier Nickname given to black soldiers by Indians during the late nineteenth century. **617**

Bull Run Site in Virginia of the first

battle between Union and Confederate armies, a Confederate victory (1861). **557**

business cycle Economic trends that move through periods of prosperity and recession. **644**

busybody Nosy person who interferes in someone else's business. **500**

C

cabinet Officials who head government agencies and are appointed by and advise the president. **235**

The Calhouns of South Carolina Wealthy southern family headed by plantation owner and statesman John C. Calhoun. **374**

canal Waterway dug (especially in the 1800s) for transportation, to link rivers and lakes, and for irrigation. **351**

capitalism Economic system in which individuals own and control the factors of production and government intervention is limited. **242**

carbon-14 dating Process used to determine the age of an ancient object by measuring its radioactive content. **9**

Carpetbagger Northerner who went to the South after the Civil War to profit financially from confused and unsettled conditions. **603**

cartographer Mapmaker. **676**

cash crop Product raised to be sold rather than consumed on the farm. **90**

Cerro Gordo (ser·uh·GAWRD·oh) Mexican town where Americans won an important battle in 1847 in the War with Mexico. **420**

championed Defended or upheld. **462**

charter Official government document granting special rights and privileges to a person or company. **42**

Chattanooga (chat·uh·NOO·guh) Important railway center in Tennessee around which several Civil War battles were fought. **580**

chauvinist (SHOW·vuh·nuhst) Person who has an attitude of superiority toward the opposite sex. **163**

checks and balances. System in which the three branches of government have powers to limit the other branches so that no branch will become too powerful. **224**

Cherokee (CHER·uh·kee) **Nation** Several Indian groups united under Cherokee law. **395**

Children's Aid Society Group founded to help homeless children by relocating them to farm families and lodging houses. **500**

cholera (KOL·er·uh) Deadly intestinal disease. **347**

church school Early American school taught by the minister and his wife. **484**

Circular Letter Plea issued by the Massachusetts legislature to other colonial assemblies that all colonists act together to resist taxation without representation. **130**

circumnavigate (suhr·kuhm·NAV·uh·gayt) To sail completely around the world. **29**

civic Of or relating to citizens and citizenship. **600**

Civil Rights Act of 1866 Law that made African Americans citizens of the United States. **595**

Civil Rights Act of 1875 Law that prohibited segregation of public places. **614**

Civil Rights Cases Lawsuits concerning the constitutional rights of black Americans. **614**

civil service reform Effort to improve government service by adopting an employment system based on skill and merit rather than on politics. **627**

Civil War (1861-1865) Conflict between the northern (Union) and southern (Confederate) states over the issues of slavery and states' rights. **548**

Civil War Amendments Three constitutional amendments (13th, 14th and 15th) guaranteeing civil rights to African Americans. **600**

clan Social or family group. **5**

climate Average of daily weather conditions. **678**

clipper ship Sailing ship of the 19th century built for speed. **432**

Coastal Plain Physical region of the United States that includes the continuous lowland along the Atlantic Ocean. **xxvi**

Coercive (ko·UHR·siv) **Acts** Series of laws passed by the British to punish the colonists for the Boston Tea Party; also called Intolerable Acts. **142**

Cold War Tensions between the U.S. and the Soviet Union after World War II. **652**

collective bargaining Right of a labor union to bargain for all workers employed by a business. **625**

commando Member of a small force of soldiers who specialize in raids in enemy territory. **532**

commenced Began. **133**

commercial revolution Economic expansion in Europe that occurred from 1450 to the 1700s. **18**

commission Committee formed for a specific purpose and with specific powers to act. **101**

Committee of Correspondence Group formed by radicals in colonies to spread the protest of British rule. **143**

common man Ordinary American rather than a representative of the rich and wealthy. **383**

commonwealth Territory in which there is self-government. **58**

compass Instrument used to tell direction. **19**

compass rose Type of directional indicator found on some maps. **674**

compelled Forced or driven. **86**

compensated Given payment to make up for a loss or shortage. **569**

Compromise of 1850 Resolution that temporarily settled disputes between the North and South over slavery issues. **443**

Compromise of 1877 Concessions made by Republicans and Democrats that settled disputed election of 1876 by which Hayes became president. **612**

compulsive Having the power to compel or force. **197**

conceive To think of. **86**

concentration camp Nazi prison where prisoners of war, especially the Jews, were held. **647**

concept Thought or idea. **59**

concession Something given in a compromise. **223**

Concord One of two Massachusetts towns (along with Lexington) where the first battles of the Revolutionary War were fought (1775). **144**

Conestoga (kahn·uh·STOH·guh) **wagon** Sturdy covered wagon used by many of the pioneers who moved westward. **374**

confederacy Alliance of independent states. **544**

Confederate States of America Association of 11 independent southern states formed after their secession from the Union in 1860–61. **544**

confederation Union of groups for a common cause. **9**

conferring Bestowing upon, as in an honor or award. **111**

Congress Legislative, or lawmaking, branch of government made up of the House of Representatives and the Senate. **220**

conquest Something that has been taken over or conquered. **2**

conquistador (kawn·KEES·tuh·dawr) Spanish soldier who helped conquer Mexico and Peru. **31**

Conscience Whigs Northern members of the Whig party who were against slavery (see **Cotton Whigs**). **523**

conscientious Behaving according to what is right or honest. **234**

conscript To draft people by law to serve in the military service. **564**

conservation Planned management of resources to prevent their depletion. **xxiii**

conservative Tending to go by established methods; slow to change. **182**

constitution Written plan of government that includes its laws and principles. **182**

Constitutional Convention Meeting of 12 states (all but Rhode Island) in Philadelphia in 1787 to draft the U.S. Constitution. **197**

Constitutional Unionist Party Political party formed in 1860 that ignored the slavery issue in hopes of preserving the Union. **536**

consumption Using up of, as of goods or services. **560**

containment U.S. policy in the 1950s aimed at limiting the spread of communism. **652**

contempt Disrespect or scorn. **119**

continent One of seven large landmasses on the earth. **xxi**

continental Climate with severe winters and summers that range from warm to hot, such as that found in the northeastern U.S. **678**

continental divide Ridge of the Rocky Mountains that separates rivers flowing generally east from those flowing generally west. **281**

Continental dollars Paper money printed by Congress during the Revolutionary War to pay its debts. **192**

contraband (KAWN·truh·band) Slave who crossed Union lines during the Civil War. **565**

contrary Opposite or not in agreement with. **465**

Convention of 1800 Treaty that prevented war between France and the United States in 1799. **268**

convoy Fleet of ships that is accompanied or escorted by a protective force. **286**

Copperhead Northerner who opposed the Civil War. **561**

Corps of Discovery Group chosen by Lewis and Clark to help them explore the Louisiana Territory. **280**

cotton boll (bol) Seed pod of a cotton plant that grows into a fibrous ball. **450**

cotton diplomacy Belief that England and France would support the Confederacy to insure their supply of cotton. **564**

cotton gin Machine invented by Eli Whitney in 1793 that separated cotton fibers from the seeds. **451**

"Cotton Is King" Southern slogan which meant that cotton, and therefore slavery, was essential to the region. **463**

county court Local government in the southern colonies. **110**

court Official gathering to rule on legality of an action. **182**

cradle Tool used to cut grain. **561**

Creek War Indian attacks in 1813 in Alabama in which more than 400 settlers were killed. **306**

crop-lien (KRAWP·leen) **system** Agreement in which supplies were lent to a farmer by merchants or landowners in exchange for portions of the crops. **608**

crucial (KREW·shuhl) Extremely important. **184**

Crusade One of a series of religious wars between 1100 and 1300 undertaken by the Christians in Europe to regain the Holy Land from the Moslems. **16**

culminated Reached the end or resulted in. **363**

culture Special characteristics of the people who make up a society, such as their language, government, how they make a living, family relationships, and how they educate their children. **4**

Cumberland Road First road built linking East and West from Maryland to Illinois; also called the National Road. **350**

cumbersome Hard to handle because of weight or bulk. **152**

curriculum Courses offered by a school. **450**

D

dame school Urban school in early America taught by women. **484**

dark horse Political candidate who unexpectedly wins a party's nomination. **405**

Declaration of Independence Document adopted by the Second Continental Congress in 1776 that declared American independence from Great Britain and listed the reasons for this action. **157**

Declaratory (di·KLAR·uh·tawr·ee) **Act** Law passed in 1766 by the British parliament that declared the American colonies subject to British law. **128**

deep-seated Firmly established or hard to remove. **85**

Deerfield English settlement in Massachusetts destroyed by the French during Queen Anne's War. **117**

defame To speak badly of or ruin a reputation. **261**

deliberate Slow and careful in acting. **546**

democracy Form of government in which power is vested in the people and exercised by them through a system of free elections. **79**

Democrat Member of the political party begun in the early 1800s that supported strong states' rights and government made up of many classes of people. **382**

Democratic-Republican Member of one of the first two political parties; its members favored policies of Jefferson such as restricting the powers of federal government over the states. **255**

denounced Stated disapproval of or condemned. **503**

department of state Government bureau that advises the president on foreign relations. **234**

depression Period of severe decline in business activity, usually marked by high levels of unemployment. **191**

descendant Offspring. **9**

desert Climate that receives little rain, often less than 10 inches (25 centimeters), such as that in the southwestern U.S. **678**

destined Intended or determined beforehand. **404**

dickering Bargaining to reach an agreement or compromise. **316**

dictator (DIK·tayt·uhr) Ruler with absolute power. **268**

dignified Calm, reserved, or noble. **237**

directional indicator Part of a map that helps you determine directions, such as a compass rose. **674**

dissent Judge's statement of disagreement with the opinion or decision of the majority. **616**

distinct Clearly different or distinguishable. **4**

distortion Twisting or stretching of the true facts. **367**

district court Lower federal trial court in each specified U.S. region. **224**

District of Columbia Federal area designated as the permanent capital of the United States. **255**

diversified (duh·VUHR·suh·fyd) **economy** Economy that depends on both manufacturing and agriculture. **330**

division of labor Separation of the manufacturing steps into specialized tasks to speed and increase production. **625**

doctrine Statement of principles, system of beliefs, or government policy. **97**

doctrine of nullification (nuhl·uh·fuh·KAY·shun) Theory put forth in 1798 that because the Constitution limited power of the federal government over the states, a state had the right to refuse to accept a national law it disagreed with. **268**

dollar diplomacy U.S. policy in the early 1900s of investing money in Latin American countries in hopes that more stable governments would result. **631**

Dominion of New England Territory created by King James II of England in 1686 in an attempt to unify the British colonies. **111**

domino theory Idea that if a country fell to communism, the countries on its borders would also fall; key principle of U.S. foreign policy from the 1950s to the 1970s. **661**

Dorchester Heights Site near Boston of General Washington's first victory against the British in the Revolutionary War. **155**

dormant Not actively growing but protected from the environment (as in the life cycle of plants.) **2**

Dred Scott v. Sandford Supreme Court ruling in 1857 that Scott, a former slave who sued for his freedom, was still a slave despite living in a free state for a time. **527**

drudgery Dull and tiresome work. **596**

dumbfounded Surprised to the point of being speechless. **278**

duty Tariff or tax placed on foreign goods brought into the country. **124**

dynamic Energetic, forceful, or powerful. **97**

E

East India Company British company; given assistance in selling tea in the colonies by the parliament in 1773, leading to the Boston Tea Party. **138**

ecology Study of the interrelationships of organisms and their environments. **xxiii**

economy System of producing, distributing, and consuming goods or services. **35**

egalitarian Marked by the belief in equal social and political rights for all people. **385**

elaborate Complicated or very detailed. **7**

elastic clause "Necessary and proper" clause of the Constitution often used to expand the powers of Congress. **243**

elector Person selected in a state to cast an electoral vote for president. **223**

elevation Height above sea level. **678**

elite (uh·LEET) Small privileged group. **505**

emancipate To free. **569**

emancipation (i·man·suh·PAY·shun) Freedom. **466**

Emancipation Proclamation Decree issued by Abraham Lincoln in 1863 freeing slaves in the South. **569**

Embargo Act Law passed in 1807 prohibiting all exports from the U.S. in response to the impressment of American sailors by the British. **288**

embodied Represented. **199**

empresario Mexican word used to describe businessmen who brought settlers into Texas. **408**

enclosure movement Period when British landowners fenced in their fields and began raising sheep. **44**

endeavor Effort or attempt to accomplish something. **449**

enlightened Informed. **222**

Enlightenment Intellectual movement in the 1700s characterized by a belief in the power of human reason and marked by many scientific discoveries and inventions. **98**

enterprise Project or undertaking. **48**

enumerated (i·NOOH·muh·rayt·d) **articles** Goods produced in the American colonies that could be sold only within the British empire. **114**

environment (in·VY·ruhn·muhnt) Everything in people's surroundings that affect them in any way; nature. **xxi, 6**

"Era of Good Feelings" Period from 1817 to 1821 when the country was prosperous and at peace under President Monroe. **364**

Erie Canal New York waterway completed in 1825 that connected the Hudson River to Lake Erie. **351**

erosion Wearing down. **678**

escapades Wild adventures. **41**

ethical Behaving according to what is considered moral or right. **238**

ethnic neighborhood City community made up of immigrants from the same country. **626**

even-handed Fair or just. **253**

excavate To uncover objects underground by digging. **280**

excerpts Selected or quoted sections of a book or other source. **117**

executive Person or branch of government responsible for enforcing or carrying out the laws. **182**

exempted Released or freed from duty. **564**

exploit (EK·sploit) Heroic and daring act. **303**

extorted Took by force. **142**

extremist Person who holds radical ideas or supports radical measures. **245**

F

faction Group within a group that has its own goals. **535**

fall line Place where the rivers flowing east from the Appalachian Highland drop to the Coastal Plain in waterfalls and rapids. **xxvi**

far-flung Widely spread or distributed. **108**

favorable balance of trade Situation in which a country exports more than it imports, or sells more than it buys. **112**

federalism Sharing of power by the national and state governments. **198**

Federalist Papers Series of newspaper articles written in 1787-88 that explained and defended the U.S. Constitution. **229**

Federalists One of the first two political parties; its members supported a strong central government and a powerful executive branch. **226**

feudal system Structure of society in medieval Europe in which peasants were bound to a lord who, in turn, owed service or payments to a higher ruler. **15**

Fifteenth Amendment Constitutional amendment that guarantees all citizens the right to vote. **600**

figurehead Leader in name only, with little or no power. **222**

First Amendment Constitutional amendment that guarantees freedom of speech, religion, and the press, and the right to assemble peacefully. **266**

First Continental Congress. Meeting of colonial delegates in 1774 at which the colonies demanded repeal of the Intolerable Acts. **143**

Five Nations League of Iroquois groups that inhabited the eastern woodlands of the northern United States. **9**

flank Edge of an army. **171**

fluently With an easy command of the language. **246**

folk tale Story that has been passed down from generation to generation. **9**

foothold Secure position that can be used as a base for further advance. **519**

forge Furnace or shop where iron products are made. **114**

forged Formed or shaped, usually with great effort. **593**

Fort Donelson Confederate fort in Tennessee taken in 1862 by Grant soon after his capture of Fort Henry. **578**

Fort Henry Confederate fort in Tennessee captured by Grant in 1862. **578**

Fort McHenry Fort in Baltimore harbor where Americans stopped a British attack in 1814; this battle was the inspiration for "The Star-Spangled Banner." **310**

Fort Pitt French Fort Duquesne captured and renamed by the British during the French and Indian War. **121**

Fort Sumter Federal fort in Charleston, South Carolina, harbor where an attack by southern forces began the Civil War. **543**

Forty-Niner Nickname given to a prospector who went to California in 1849 in search of gold. **432**

Fourteenth Amendment Constitutional amendment that made African Americans citizens of their states as well as of the U.S., guaranteed their civil rights, and gave them equal protection of the laws. **597**

Fourth of July American Independence Day celebrating the anniversary of the signing of the Declaration of Independence. **157**

framer Author of a document. **254**

free enterprise Economic system that encourages people to develop and market their ideas for profit with little government involvement in the process. **92**

free soiler Person opposed to the spread of slavery. **519**

Free-Soil party Political party founded in 1848 by northern Democrats who were opposed to popular sovereignty. **437**

free state State that did not allow slavery. **436**

Freedman's Bureau Organization run by the army to care for southern blacks after the Civil War. **595**

freedmen Former slaves. **594**

freeman Person who has all the political and civil rights of citizenship in a city, state, or nation. **58**

Freeport Doctrine Stephen Douglas' statement that the people have the ultimate power to decide if slavery should or should not exist in a location. **531**

French Revolution Rebellion beginning in 1789 of the poor French lower classes against the monarchy and upper classes that resulted in the establishment of a Republic. **244**

frigate American warship of the early 1800s. **302**

frontier Edge of a settled region. **79**

Fulton's Folly Name skeptics gave the *Clermont*, Fulton's first steamboat. **354**

Fundamental Orders First written form of government in America; drafted by representatives of the first settlements along the Connecticut River. **58**

fur trade Early American industry involving the sale of hides and furs to Europe. **92**

G

Gadsden Purchase Land along the southern borders of New Mexico and Arizona purchased from Mexico in 1853 to allow construction of the Southern Pacific Railroad. **515**

galleon Heavy sailing ship used as a commercial vessel or a warship in the 15th to 18th centuries. **41**

generalization Broad statement based on loosely associated facts. **6**

genocide Deliberate and planned destruction of a race or cultural group. **650**

geography Study of the the physical and cultural features of the earth. **xxi, 22**

Gettysburg Address Speech containing a classic expression of American democratic ideals delivered by President Lincoln in 1863. **575**

ghost town Abandoned mining town. **435**

glasnost (GLAS·nohst) Spirit of openness and freedom in the Soviet Union begun under Gorbachev. **666**

Glorious Revolution English uprising in 1688 in which the Catholic king James II was replaced by the Protestant monarchs William and Mary. **111**

Gold Rush Surge of 80,000 miners to California to look for gold in 1848. **432**

Goliad Texas town where 350 Texans were killed by Mexican troops in 1836. **410**

government bond Interest-bearing certificate sold by the government to raise revenue. **241**

governor Chief executive of an English colony or American state. **109**

grandfather clause Law which eliminated literacy tests and poll taxes for persons who had voted before 1867 and their descendants. This meant only white men qualified to vote. **613**

grappled Grabbed hold of or struggled with. **273**

Great Awakening Time in the 1700s of widespread religious fervor, a force for toleration in the colonies. **95**

Great Compromise Agreement made at the Constitutional Convention in 1787 to create a House of Representatives elected by the people on the basis of population and a Senate elected by the state legislatures, two members from each state. **220**

Great Lakes Cultural region around the Great Lakes and the upper Ohio and Mississippi rivers. **679**

guano (GWAHN·oh) Manure of seabirds or bats used as fertilizer. **369**

guerrilla (guh·RIL·uh) Fighter who commits sabotage or surprise attacks. **522**

Guilford Court House Site in South Carolina of an American victory in 1781. **171**

H

hail Relentless showering. **312**

hard money Gold or silver coins, or paper money that could be exchanged for gold or silver. **193**

Harlem Renaissance (ren·uh·SAHNS) Period during the 1920s when New York City's Harlem became an intellectual and cultural capital for African Americans. **642**

Harpers Ferry Site of a government arsenal raided in 1859 by John Brown and his commandos. **532**

Hartford Convention Meeting of New England states in 1814 to discuss separation from the Union. **313**

Hawaiian Islands Group of islands in the Pacific Ocean formed by the tops of submerged mountains and annexed by the United States in 1890s. **xxvi**

headright Agreement by colonists to pay their way or that of others to Virginia in exchange for 50 acres of land for each "head" transported from England. **50**

heartened Encouraged. **525**

heavy-handed Harsh. **64**

heralded Proclaimed or announced with enthusiasm. **330**

hereafter Life after death. **19**

highland Climate found in mountains in which elevation and landscape; mountain or microclimate. **679**

hill Rounded bulges of land that rise at least 500 feet (152 meters) above the surrounding land. **678**

Hispaniola (his·puhn·YOH·la) First island settled by Columbus and his crew in 1492; today the site of the Dominican Republic and Haiti. **25**

historical imagination Ability to look at past events objectively by recognizing what people knew and did not know at a particular time. **3**

historical significance Importance of an event to other events. **325**

Holocaust (HO·luh·kawst) Hitler's program to exterminate the Jews. **650**

Holy Land Palestine; important to Christians as the birthplace of Jesus and site of biblical events. **16**

home schools Educational system in which children are taught at home by parents or other relatives. **484**

Homestead Act Law that granted free public land to farmers who agreed to cultivate the land for a given period of time (1862). **535**

House of Burgesses First elected government body was in America, in Virginia in 1619. **50**

house of refuge Place built to house delinquent and homeless children and separate them from adult criminals. **500**

House of Representatives Part of Congress in which the number of delegates each state is entitled to is based on the state's population. **220**

human right Privilege belonging to all human beings. **238**

humid subtropical Climate with long, hot, rainy summers and typically mild winters, such as that found in the southeastern U.S. **678**

I

Ice Age Period when icecaps and glaciers covered large parts of the earth's surface. **2**

ideal community. Settlement established far from other communities in which residents could live as they wished. **490**

ill-advised Unwise or without sound advice. **129**

immigrant Person who comes to another country to live. **343**

immoral Wicked or morally wrong. **440**

immunity Resistance to a disease. **34**

impeachment Formal charge of wrongdoing brought against a government official. **225**

imperialism Practice of establishing and controlling colonies. **629**

impressment Practice used by the British in the early 1800s of forcing sailors of British ancestry to serve in the British navy. **287**

inadmissable Not allowed. **470**

Incas (ING-kuhs) Highly civilized nation of people who lived in the mountains of Peru at the time of the Spanish invasion. **33**

inconclusively Done without settling

anything or reaching a definite result. **294**

indentured servant Laborer who signed a contract agreeing to work for a period of time without wages in return for passage to America. **50**

Independent Treasury System System in the 1840s where debts to government were paid in gold and silver and stored in vaults. **400**

Indies Islands off the east coast of Asia. **18**

indifference Lack of interest. **163**

indigo (IN-dug-goh) Plant that produces a dark blue dye for cloth. **91**

indirect tax Tax on imports that was collected from shippers and paid by consumers in the form of higher prices. **130**

Industrial Revolution Change in production methods in the early 1800s from human to machine power. **335**

industrial technology Tools and machines used to produce goods. **333**

infested Overrun or swarming with. **47**

inflation Rise in price levels resulting from an increase in the amount of money or a decrease in the amount of goods available for sale. **193,**

inflationary (in-FLAY-shuh-ner-ee) **spiral** Continuous rise in prices that occurs when the higher cost of one product or service causes the prices of other goods and services to rise. **392**

inhumanity The quality or state of being cruel or brutal. **458**

insight Clear understanding of the inner or true nature of something. **504**

interchangeable (in-tuhr-CHAYN-juh-buhl) **parts** Production advance involving parts that can be substituted one for the other; an essential for mass production. **334**

Interior Plains United States physical region that includes the vast lowland that stretches from the western slopes of the Appalachians in the east to the foothills of the Rocky Mountains in the west;

the wetter eastern portion is the Central Plains of Central Lowland, and the drier western part is the Great Plains. **xxvi**

Intermountain Region United States physical region that includes the lands between the Rocky Mountains and the Sierra Nevada characterized by dry, rugged plateaus and canyons. **xxvi**

internal improvements Parts of the transportation network such as roads and canals built at public expense. **380**

Intolerable Acts Name colonists gave to the Coercive Acts passed by the British government in 1774 to punish the colonists for the Boston Tea Party. **142**

Islam Religion founded by the prophet Mohammed. **16**

isthmus Narrow strip of land connecting two larger segments of land. **28**

J

Jamestown First successful English colony in America. **47**

Jay's Treaty Treaty in which the British agreed to withdraw troops from western ports and give shipping and trading concessions to the United States. **250**

Jim Crow law Any law that promoted segregation. **614**

joint-stock company Group of investors formed to outfit colonial expeditions in the early 1600s. **44**

jokester Comedian or one who cracks jokes. **194**

justice of the peace Chief official of county courts in the South. **110**

juvenile delinquency Problem of children and teens breaking the law. **499**

K

Kansas-Nebraska Bill Law that allowed the question of slavery in the Nebraska Territory to be decided by popular sovereignty and which created the Kansas and Nebraska territories. **516**

keelboat Shallow, covered riverboat that is towed or poled. **281**

Kentucky and Virginia Resolutions Statements written in 1798 by Jefferson and Madison to question the power of the federal government over the states **267**

King George's War (1744–1748) Third conflict in America between the French and English. **117**

King William's War (1689-97) First in a succession of colonial conflicts between the English and French. **116**

kingpin Leader in a group or undertaking. **76**

King's Mountain Site in South Carolina of Tory defeat in 1780. **171**

Know-Nothings Name given to members of the Native American party during the 1850s. **523**

Ku Klux Klan (koo kluhks KLAN) Secret organization which terrorized African Americans. **610**

L

Lancasterian (lang·kuh·STEER·ee·uhn) **system** Educational system where teachers taught older pupils who then taught younger students. **489**

Land Ordinance of 1785 Law that set up a method for surveying and selling western territories by townships. **189**

Land Ordinance of 1787 Plan for governing the lands in the Northwest Territory as they grew to statehood (also Northwest Ordinance). **189**

landform Shape on the earth's surface. **678**

lathe (LAYTH) Machine that shapes wood by holding and turning it against a cutting tool. **334**

Latin America Countries in Central and South America settled by Spain and Portugal. **322**

Law of Prior Appropriation Principle that rights to water use belong to the person who first uses the water, as long as it is for beneficial purposes such as farming, mining, or manufacturing. **430**

Law of Riparian Rights Principle applied primarily in the East that all property owners whose land borders a river or stream have equal right to the water; they may not increase or decrease its quantity or change its quality. **429**

Lecompton Constitution Proposed Kansas state constitution that would have allowed slavery. **528**

legal rights Privilege given to people by law. **238**

legend Part of a map that explains the meaning of the symbols and colors used on the map. **674**

legislature Elected body given the responsibility of making laws. **110**

Lexington One of two Massachusetts towns (along with Concord) where the first battles of the American Revolution were fought. **144**

Liberia (ly·BIR·ee·ah) Country on West Coast of Africa where some formers slaves settled. **449**

lien (leen) Claim on property as security for a debt. **608**

The Lincolns of Indiana Pioneer family in which President Abraham Lincoln was raised. **377**

Line of Demarcation (dee·mahr·KAY·shahn) Agreement in 1493 that dividing the Atlantic Ocean gave claim to all lands west of the line to Spain and all lands east to Portugal. **25**

literacy test Proof of a person's ability to read and write as a requirement for voting. **613**

livelihood Means of support. **328**

locator map Map that shows the location of the area of the main map in relation to other areas. **675**

The Lodges of Boston Wealthy family who began a political dynasty in the 1800s. **372**

Log Cabin Campaign Whig strategy to win votes for William Henry Harrison based on his reputation as a rugged man of the people. **400**

Long Night Period of racial segregation after the Civil War. **613**

lot One's fate in life. **336**

Louisiana Purchase Acquisition from France made by the United States in 1803 of all the land between the Mississippi River and the Rocky Mountains for $15 million. **278**

Lowell system Method of employing young women to operate power looms in factories in Lowell, Massachusetts, first used in 1813. **339**

Loyalist American during the Revolution who remained loyal to the king of England; also called a Tory. **155**

M

Macon's Bill Number Two (1810) Law that removed restrictions on trade with France and Britain and promised American support to the nation that stopped attacks on American ships. **291**

Maine Free state created by the Missouri Compromise of 1820 to keep a balance of slave and free states in Congress. **437**

mainland Continent or main body of a continent. **543**

mainstay Chief means of support. **8**

malice (MAHL·us) Hatred toward or the desire to hurt others. **593**

manifest destiny Belief popular in the 1840s that the obvious future role of the U.S. was to extend its boundaries to the Pacific Ocean. **412**

manor Land and village ruled over by a feudal lord. **15**

map projection Techinque used by mapmakers to show the spherical earth on a flat map. **676**

Marbury v. Madison Legal case that established the power of the Supreme Court to declare an act of Congress unconstitutional. **273**

market Economic term for the buying and selling of goods and services. **242**

marl Crumbly soil of sand and clay rich in calcium carbonate and used as fertilizer. **369**

Mason-Dixon line Boundary between Maryland and Pennsylvania, traditional line separating North and South. **101**

masonry Stone or brickwork. **65**

mass produce Manufacture, usually using machinery, of goods in large numbers. **333**

Massachusetts Bay Company American colony established by the Puritans in 1630. **58**

matrilineal Descendants or kinship traced down through the mother's side. **5**

Mayflower Compact Document drawn up by the Pilgrims in 1620 that provided a legal basis for self-government. **53**

McCarthyism Use of American suspicion of communists in the 1950s by Senator Joseph McCarthy to gain power by presenting charges of communist infiltration in the state department. **653**

meager Small amount; scanty. **65**

mechanical reaper Machine invented by Cyrus McCormick to harvest wheat. **560**

Mediterranean Climate with hot, dry summers and mild, dry winters, such as that found along the coast of southern California. **678**

mercantilism Economic policy in which a country controls the imports and exports of its colonies. **112**

mercenary (MUHRS·uhn·er·ee) Professional soldier who fights for pay rather than for a cause. **165**

Mexico City Capital of Mexico where Mexican forces surrendered to Americans in 1847. **420**

Middle Passage Slaves' voyage across the Atlantic. **88**

middleman Trader who buys products from one person and sells them at higher prices to a merchant or directly to the consumer. **20**

midwife Woman who assists in childbirth. **336**

militant Aggressive or ready to fight. **482**

mindful Being aware or bearing in mind. **239**

mining camps Village formed by miners working a strike. **434**

Minute Man Revolutionary War civilian-soldier who was trained to fight on short notice. **144**

mission Task for which a person feels called or destined. **33**

Missouri Compromise Act passed in 1820 which allowed Missouri to become a slave state and Maine a free state and attempted to settle the question of slavery's spread by allowing slavery only in territories south of 36° 30′N **437**

moderate Person who avoids extreme political views. **593**

monopoly (muh·NAHP·uh·lee) Exclusive control of a product or service that results in fixed prices and elimination of competition. **139**

Monroe Doctrine Important statement of foreign policy that said the United States would not tolerate European interference in the Western Hemisphere. **323**

Mormon Trail Route to Utah used by Mormon pioneers. **429**

Mormons Religious group begun in the 1820s by Joseph Smith. **427**

Moslems Followers of the Islamic faith. **16**

Mound Builders Prehistoric American Indians who built elaborate ceremonial mounds. **8**

mountain Landform that rises to a height of over 2,000 feet (610 meters); also climate in which elevation and landscape cause temperature and precipitation variations, also highland, or microclimate climate. **679**

movement Geographic theme that describes the continuous movements of people, goods, and ideas. **xxiv**

muckraker (MUHK·rayk·uhr) Reporter who exposed corruption in the early 1900s. **631**

municipal socialism Plan which transferred private ownership of streetcar lines and gas and electric companies to city governments. **632**

mutual (MYOO·choo·ahl). Shared in common. **539**

N

national government Level of government with jurisdiction over all people and all other levels of government. **197**

National Grange (GRAYNJ) Farmers' organization that became politically active during the 1870s. **627**

national judiciary Highest level of courts in a country. **220**

National Road First road built linking East and West from Maryland to Illinois; also called the Cumberland Road. **350**

National Trades' Union Organization formed in 1834 by groups of skilled workers to promote better wages and working conditions. **503**

nationalism Patriotic feelings for one's country. **197**

Native American Party Political organization formed by native-born Americans to oppose immigration and immigrants. **523**

nativist Former Whig who favored strict immigration controls. **343**

natural landscape Vegetation, wildlife, climate and soil of an area; physical setting. **678**

natural resources Riches of nature, such as vegetation, wildlife, minerals, water, and soil. **xxiii**

natural rights Privilege of all people defined by what is instinctively felt to be moral or good. **238**

Nauvoo (naw·VOO) City in Illinois settled by Mormons in the 1800s. **427**

naval stores Product produced from the pine forests of the South, such as pitch used to make ships watertight. **91**

navigation Science of charting the position or course of a ship, aircraft, or similar vehicle. **22**

Navigation Acts British laws between 1651 and 1733 that were a key aspect of mercantilism and that restricted the production of goods by American colonies and forbade trade with countries other than England. **113**

necessary and proper clause Section of the Constitution often used to expand the powers of Congress; also called the "elastic clause." **243**

Negro Fort Florida fort controlled

by runaway slaves that was destroyed by U.S. troops in 1816. **314**

Negro Hill Site of rich gold deposit discovered by two African American prospectors. **435**

neutrality Policy of avoiding permanent ties with other nations. **253**

New England Name given in the early 1600s to the northeasternmost colonies; still used as a label for that section of the United States. **57**

New Jersey Plan Design for Congress presented by William Paterson during 1787 Constitution Convention that favored a one-state, one-vote system. **220**

New Netherland Name given to the colony in the Hudson River area claimed and settled by the Dutch. **64**

New Spain Areas in North and Central America, and the Caribbean claimed and settled by the Spanish. **65**

New Sweden Colony along the Delaware River founded by Swedish settlers. **64**

New World Name given in the early 1500s by explorer Amerigo Vespucci to the lands in Central and South America. **27**

nominal Very small or insignificant, or in name only. **484**

nominating convention Meeting of party members to choose presidential and vice presidential candidates. **384**

Non-Intercourse Act Law passed in 1809 permitting trade with all countries except Britain and France. **291**

nonviolent direct action Method proposed by Martin Luther King for protesting against discrimination without violence. **655**

normal school Teacher training school. **489**

Northeast Cultural region centered on New England and New York that is a major manufacturing and commercial area. **679**

Northwest Ordinance Plan of government for the lands in the Northwest Territory; also Land Ordinance of 1787. **189**

Northwest passage Shipping route from the Atlantic to the East Indies through North America. **44**

Nueces (nooh·AY·suhs) **River** Texas river that Mexican government claimed was the boundary between Mexico and Texas. **418**

Nullification (nuhl·uh·fuh·KAY·shuhn) **Crisis** Episode in 1832 in which South Carolina nullified, or refused to follow, a tariff law causing the national government to threaten force if the law was not followed. **387**

nullify (NUHL·uh·fy) To cancel the legal force of a law. **267**

O

"Old Ironsides" Nickname for the American warship *Constitution* used in the War of 1812. **303**

Olive Branch Petition Plea sent in 1775 to King George III requesting protection of the American colonies from the British Parliament. **151**

one person, one vote Principle of electing legislators from districts with populations of approximately the same size. **104**

Oneida (oh·NYD·uh) **community** Ideal settlement in New York. **490**

open-minded Willing to listen to new ideas. **73**

oppressed Burdened or kept down by a harsh and unjust authority. **407**

ordeal Severe trial or painful experience. **28**

ordinance Public act or law. **387**

ordinance of nullification Legal proposal made by John C. Calhoun that described an orderly way for a state to cancel a federal law it believed unconstitutional. **387**

Oregon Trail Route followed by pioneers to the Northwest. **414**

orrery Mechanical model that illustrates the movement of the sun and planets. **100**

Ostend (ahs·TEND) **Manifesto** Secret proposal that stated that the United States would be justified to take Cuba from Spain by force if Spain refused to sell it; news of the manifesto outraged northerners, who saw it as an attempt by southerners to gain more territory. **518**

outpost Pioneer settlement on the frontier. **306**

outraged Shocked and angered by a serious or terrible offense. **511**

override Constitutional power of Congress to overrule a presidential veto by a two-thirds vote. **225**

overseer Person who supervises other workers. **374**

P

Pacific Coast Physical region of the United States that reaches from the Sierra Nevada and Cascades to the Pacific Ocean; also cultural region that includes Washington, Oregon, California, Alaska, and Hawaii. **xxvi, 681**

Pacific Ocean Largest ocean; west of North and South America; first European sighting by Balboa in 1513 and named by Magellan in 1520. **28**

Panic of 1837 Economic collapse caused by reckless lending and too much paper money in circulation; major cause of westward movement. **392**

Parliament Lawmaking body of England. **109**

Pasha Title of rank or honor n Turkey. **275**

patriot During the American Revolution, a person who favored independence for the American colonies. **144**

patroon Landholder who controlled a huge estate in colonial Dutch New York and New Jersey. **64**

Peace of Ghent Treaty signed in 1814 that ended the War of 1812. **313**

Peace of Paris Agreement in 1783 between Great Britain and the United States that ended the Revolutionary War. **188**

peculiar institution Name some gave to slaveholding. **86**

peppered Repeatedly fired shots at. **145**

perestroika (per·uh·stroy·kuh) Plan to improve and broaden the Soviet economy initiated by Premier Gorbachev. **666**

Perkins Institution School for the blind founded in 1830s by Samuel Gridley Howe. **498**

persistent Continuing steadily despite interference. **2**

"pet bank" State banks chosen in 1833 by President Jackson to receive deposits or funds removed from the Bank of the United States. **391**

Petersburg Town in Virginia where Grant's army kept up a nine-month attack against Lee's army. (1865). **581**

physical setting Natural landscape of an area that includes the landforms, vegetation, climate, and soil. **678**

picaroons (pik·ah·ROONS) French merchant ships that seized cargo from American merchant ships in the 1790s. **257**

piety Devotion to religious duties. **56**

Pilgrims Community of people who moved from Europe to Massachusetts in the 1620s to practice their religion freely; also called Separatists. **53**

Pinckney's Treaty Agreement between Spain and the United States that gave Americans shipping access to the Mississippi and recognized Florida boundary line set by Americans. **251**

pious Having or showing religious devotion. **70**

place Geographic theme relating to the physical features of a location. **xxiv**

plain Nearly flat or gently rolling landform. **678**

Plains Cultural region extending generally from the Mississippi River to the foothills of the Rocky Mountains that is a prime farming region of the U.S. **680**

Plains Indian Member of an Indian group that lived on the grasslands between the Rocky Mountains and the Mississippi River. **8**

plateau Relatively flat land that rises sharply from the surrounding landscape to 2,000 feet (610 meters) or more on at least one side. **678**

Plattsburg New York city where Americans defeated the British during the War of 1812. **306**

Plessy v. Ferguson Supreme Court case that legalized the "separate-but-equal" principle. **614**

plodded Walked slowly and heavily. **351**

Plymouth Site in Massachusetts where the Pilgrims first landed in America in 1620. **55**

political equality Principle that all citizens have the right to vote regardless of wealth. **79**

political machine Big city organization run by bosses who won elections by controlling poor and immigrant voters. **627**

poll tax Fee charged for voting. **613**

polygamy (puh·LIG·uh·mee) Practice of having more than one wife or husband. **427**

Pontiac's (PAHNT·ee·aks) **Rebellion** Indian uprising in 1763 led by Chief Pontiac. **123**

popular sovereignty (SAHV·uh·ruhn·tee) System that allowed settlers in each territory to decide whether or not they would have slavery. **437, 516**

popular vote Vote of the people. **384**

Populist party Third party formed in 1892 that represented the interests of farmers and labor unions; also called People's party. **627**

Port Hudson Mississippi River stronghold in Louisiana captured by Union forces in 1863 to split the Confederacy in two. **579**

Pottawatomie (paht·uh·WAHT·uh·mee) **Massacre** Murder in 1856 of five people by John Brown and followers in revenge for pro-slavery attack on Lawrence, Kansas. **522**

Preamble Introduction to the Constitution that explains its purpose. **197**

precedent Guide for later action. **234**

president Elected head of the executive branch of government. **220**

presidio Spanish fort. **35**

pressing Calling for immediate attention; urgent. **123**

prestige High standing or reputation based on achievement or character. **76**

prevail Triumph or succeed. **98**

privateer (pry·vuh·TIR) American merchant ship which flew the French flag and attacked unarmed British ships in the early 1800s; or member of the crew. **246**

Privy (PRIV·ee) **Council** Advisers to the King of England who set policies governing the American colonies. **109**

Proclamation of 1763 British law closing to colonial settlers the area west of the Appalachians. **123**

profit Gain resulting from sales of goods and services. **242**

profoundly Deeply or intensely. **222**

prohibition Act of forbidding the manufacture, transportation, and sale of alcoholic beverages. **500**

proprietary (pruh·PRY·uh·ter·ee) **colony** Colony granted by the British crown to an individual owner who had all the governing rights. **60**

prospective Likely to be or become. **478**

prospector One who searched for gold or silver. **432**

protective tariff Tax on imports to increase their cost, helping American manufacturers compete. **330**

Protestant Reformation Religious movement in the 16th century aimed at reforming the Catholic church and resulting in the formation of several Protestant religions. **53**

provided Made the condition or established. **185**

proviso Special clause in any document that introduces a condition. **438**

public school Free school funded by taxes and open to all children. **74**

public servant Government official. **183**

Puebla (poo·EB·luh) Site of an important American victory in 1847 in the Mexican War. **420**

pueblo (poo·EB·loh) Indian village of

the Southwestern U.S.; from the Spanish word for town. **7**

Puritans English Protestants who wished to purify the Church of England and who came to America in the early 1600s seeking religious freedom. **58**

putting-out system Method of production in which workers wove cloth on looms in their own homes from thread "put out" by the manufacturer. **336**

Q

Quaker Member of a pacifist religious sect which came to America seeking religious freedom. **67**

quartered Housed or sheltered. **130**

Quebec (kwi·BEK) First permanent French settlement in North America founded in 1608. **62**

Queen Anne's War (1702-1713) French and English conflict after which England gained control of Nova Scotia, Newfoundland and the Hudson Bay. **117**

R

radiated Shone brightly as if sending out rays from a center. **96**

radical Person who favors sudden or extreme changes. **53, 593**

ramrod Marked by rigidity or stiffness. **383**

ranchero (ran·CHER·oh) Mexican landholder who owned a *rancho* **425**

rancho (RAN·cho) Vast estate with cattle grazing lands owned by a Mexican citizen. **425**

rank-and-file Ordinary members rather than the leaders, such as enlisted men or common soldiers as distinguished from the officers. **557**

ratify To approve. **186**

ratifying convention Meeting held in a state for the purpose of approving the Constitution. **226**

Ravaged Violently destroyed. **594**

reactionary Person who opposes political or social change. **255**

reckoning Figuring or calculating. **302**

reclusive Withdrawn from society. **497**

Reconstruction (1867-77) Process after the Civil War of rebuilding and reuniting the nation and its people. **595**

Reconstruction Act Four-part measure passed in 1867 that ordered a military occupation of the South and ordered Southerners to give African Americans constitutional rights. **598**

Red Stick Confederacy Alliance of Creek Indian groups east of the Mississippi allied with Tecumseh to resist white expansion. **298**

refined Polished or well-mannered. **30**

region Geographic theme in which areas of the earth are grouped together by common features. **xxiv**

relationships within places Geographic theme that describes human-environment interactions. **xxiv**

relative location Part of geographic theme of location: where a place is in relation to other places. **xxiii**

relatively Somewhat or to a relative extent. **15**

relief Shading used on maps to show the existence of mountains and valleys. **678**

Removal Act Law passed in 1830 that provided money to help Indian groups move west. **396**

repeal To reject or revoke a law. **268**

Republic of California Name Californians gave to their country after declaring independence from Mexico. **420**

Republic of Texas Country formed after Texans declared independence from Mexico in 1836. **410**

republican Type of government in which power is held by representatives elected by the people. **190**

Republican party Political party formed in 1854 by Northern Whigs and Democrats who opposed slavery. **523**

rescind To cancel. **130**

restrained Quiet or controlled in behavior and manner; held back. **464**

restraint Control that prevents extreme behavior or activity. **224**

revived Brought back to life or renewed. **313**

Revolutionary War Fight for American independence between the American colonies and Great Britain (1775-83); also called the War for American Independence. **147**

Rhode Island system System in Rhode Island mills that used children to operate spinning machines. **337**

rigging Ropes used to work the sails on a ship. **303**

right of deposit Right to load and unload cargo, such as at New Orleans in the early 1800s. **250**

rigorous Challenging, harsh, or severe. **50**

Rio Grande (ree·oh·GRAND·ee) "Great River" that forms the border between Texas and Mexico. **418**

Roanoke (ROH·uh·nohk) Island off the coast of North Carolina where two English settlements failed. **43**

Rocky Mountains Relatively high and rugged mountain chain in the western United States; also a cultural region of the American West that includes the mountains and the valleys and plateaus in between. **xxvi, 680**

Romantic Age Movement in art and literature in the 19th century marked by an interest in nature and an emphasis on natural feelings and emotions, and imagination over logic. **495**

rotation in office Replacing of government jobholders with other members of the political party in power. **385**

rubble Broken pieces of masonry or rock; usually associated with the destruction of houses or buildings. **606**

rural Outside the city. **xxiii**

Rush-Bagot Agreement Agreement between Great Britain and the United States not to allow naval forces on the Great Lakes. **314**

Glossary 731

S

saga Traditional Scandinavian story form that tells about legendary figures and events. **14**

Salt Lake City City in Utah founded by the Mormons in 1847. **428**

San Jacinto (san juh·SINT·oh) Texas town where 1836 defeat of Santa Anna's forces led to Texan independence from Mexico. **410**

San Salvador (san SAL·vuh·dawr) Island where in 1492 Christopher Columbus first landed in the Americas. **24**

satirize Ridicule or make fun of. **497**

Savannah Georgia city captured by Sherman during Civil War (1863). **583**

Scalawag (SKAL·i·wag) Southern white in the Republican party during Reconstruction. **603**

scale Part of a map that tells you how to relate the distance shown on a map with actual distance on the earth. **674**

scavenger (SKAV·en·juhr) Animal or organism that feeds on garbage **347**

Schenectady (skuh·NEK·tuhd·ee) New York town attacked by French and Indians at the start of King William's War in 1689. **116**

sea dog Nickname given to English sea captains in the l6th century. **41**

Sea Island cotton Type of Cotton that grew well only on the Sea Islands along the coasts of Georgia and South Carolina. **450**

seaboard Part of the country by the sea. **342**

seaports Harbor town whose economy depends upon the sea. **80**

secede (si·SEED) To withdraw from, as a state leaving the union. **440**

secession (si·SESH·uhn) Withdrawal from an association or group. **278**

Second Bank of the United States National bank founded in 1816. **388**

Second Battle of Bull Run Confederate victory in Northern Virginia in 1862 that preceded Lee's invasion of Maryland. **568**

Second Continental Congress Meeting of colonial delegates in 1776 at which the Declaration of Independence was written and approved. **150**

Second Great Awakening. Period of religious revival in the 1820s. **494**

sectional conflict Disagreements between the Northeast, South and West over government policies. **371**

secure In this case, to get or obtain. **450**

security Something given as a promise or guarantee of payment. **242**

seethed Boiled with anger. **521**

segregation Separation of people on the basis of racial, religious, or social differences. **511**

self-sufficient Able to take care of oneself. **19**

semiarid Partially dry or getting only light rainfall, typically between 10 and 20 inches (25 and 40 centimeters) per year. **678**

Senate House of Congress to which each state is entitled to elect two senators. **220**

Seneca (SEN·i·kuh) **Falls Declaration** Statement issued by delegates to the 1848 women's rights convention that demanded that women be given the same rights and privileges as men. **483**

separate-but-equal Principle that supported the legality of segregation when races were separated in supposedly equal public schools. **616**

separatist Person who withdrew or separated from the Church of England; also called a Pilgrim. **53**

serf Peasant who under the feudal system was bound to work a master's land. **15**

servitude Slavery. **613**

Seven Days Before Richmond Series of 1862 Civil War battles during which McClellan's Union forces failed to take Richmond, the Confederate capital. **559**

Seven Years' War (1756–1763) European conflict between England and France and their allies; called the French and Indian War in America. **121**

shady Not honest or trustworthy. **257**

Shaker Member of a religious group founded in England in 1747 that established several communities in America. **490**

shaman Religious leader in an American Indian group who used magic or rituals to heal sickness or control events. **393**

sharecropping System in which landowners provided laborers with the supplies needed for farming in exchange for a portion of the crops. **606**

Shays' Rebellion Uprising in 1787 in Massachusetts protesting high state taxes. **195**

shield United States physical region near the upper Great Lakes characterized by thin soils and exposed ancient rock rich in minerals. **xxvi**

ship of the line During the War of 1812 a British ship armed with 70 or more cannons. **302**

shirker One who avoids his or her duties. **165**

shrewd Cunning or clever. **44**

Siege of Vicksburg Union attack led by General Grant in 1863 on a key port in the Mississippi River. **579**

slave Person who is held against his or her will and forced to work for others. **86**

slave state State that permitted slavery. **436**

sniper Sharpshooter who shoots at the enemy from a hidden position. **145**

Social Gospel Idea preached by urban religious progressives that it was a person's moral obligation to help those less fortunate. **631**

society Group of people who live and work together and share similar values and patterns of behavior. **4**

soldier of fortune Professional fighter who is willing to fight for any country or group that will pay him; mercenary. **47**

Sons of Liberty Patriot groups that fought against British authority in the American colonies. **128**

Southeast Cultural region in the Sun Belt that extends south along the Atlantic and Gulf coasts. **679**

southern hospitality Term for the

friendly welcome given strangers by southerners. **75**

southern regionalism Loyalty to the South, its way of life, and its values. **539**

Southwest Cultural region of the U.S. that extends along the U.S.-Mexico border, especially in Texas, New Mexico, and Arizona. **680**

Spanish Armada Large Spanish war fleet defeated by the British in 1588. **42**

spar Pole used to support the sails of a ship. **80**

special interest group Organization that seeks to influence the government to support its own specific cause. **252**

special-purpose map Map that illustrates a special category of information. **678**

specialization (spesh·luh·ZAY·shun) Concentration on the manufacture of a particular product; division of labor in which each person does one specific part of the whole process. **369**

speculator Person who invests money where there is a considerable risk but also the possibility of large profits. **241**

sphere of influence Area controlled in large part by a more powerful country, such as parts of China in the 19th century, which were dominated by European nations. **630**

spinning jenny Mechanical spinning wheel invented by James Hargreaves in 1765. **335**

spoils of office Practice by the party that wins an election of dividing up political rewards. **385**

spoils system Practice by an elected party of rewarding party supporters with appointments to government offices. **385**

Spotsylvania Court House Virginia site of a bloody 1864 Civil War clash between Grant and Lee. **581**

squatter Person who clears and settles a tract of land that he or she does not own. **79**

squeamish Easily shocked or overly sensitive. **221**

stake a claim To declare ownership of an area by marking it with wooden stakes; especially during the Gold Rush. **434**

Stamp Act British law that placed a tax on all printed matter in the colonies. **127**

standard of living The measure of the necessities, comforts, and luxuries available in a society. **659**

starving time Period of severe hunger in Jamestown that lasted from 1609 to 1611. **48**

states' rights Doctrine that holds that the states, not the federal government, have the ultimate power. **268**

status Position or standing. **470**

steam engine Motor patented by James Watt in 1769 and driven by steam. **369**

Stone Age Early period of human cultural development when stone was used to make tools and weapons. **5**

strait Narrow water passage connecting two larger bodies of water. **28**

Strait of Magellan Water passage between the Atlantic and Pacific Oceans at the tip of South America. **28**

straitlaced Morally strict or prudish. **69**

strategy Military plan made to gain an advantage over the enemy. **542**

strike Refusal of employees to work until their demands for better wages or working conditions are met. **625**

stronghold In this case, an area dominated by a particular group such as a political party. **364**

subarctic High-latitude climate found near the North and South poles with brief summers and long, cold winters. **679**

subordinate Under the control of another. **128**

substantial Of a large size or amount. **79**

Sugar Act Law passed in 1764 which taxed the colonists' imports of sugar, wine, and coffee. **124**

Sun Belt Warm weather states in the

South and Southwest where population is increasing. **659**

sunshine patriot Term used by Thomas Paine to describe an American who supported independence only when things were going well. **165**

supply-side economics Policy followed by President Reagan that lowered tax rates in order to increase spending, which would thereby increase tax revenues. **665**

Supreme Court Highest U.S. appeals court, composed of nine justices. **220, 224**

Sutter's Fort Fortified town built by John Sutter on California's American River in 1839. **413**

swashbuckler Swaggering, boasting soldier. **47**

T

tariff Tax on imports; in some countries also placed on exports. **130, 192**

Tariff of Abominations Act of 1828 that placed a high tariff on imports and was bitterly opposed by southern states. **385**

tariff question Disagreement between northeastern and southern states in 1830s over tariffs on imports. **385**

taskmaster A stern boss. **169**

taxation without representation Argument by colonists that they were taxed by the British without being represented in Parliament. **125**

Tea Act English law passed in 1773 that gave the East India Company exclusive rights to sell tea directly to American retailers. **138**

temperance (TEM·puh·ruhns) Movement to restrict the drinking of alcoholic beverages. **500**

tenement (TEN·uh·muhnt) Building in which several families live crowded together, often in unsafe and unsanitary conditions. **348**

tenet Principle or belief outlined in a doctrine or held in common by an organization or group. **539**

Tenure (TEN·yuhr) **of Office Act** Law passed in 1867 that prohibited the president from removing appointed officials without the consent of Congress. **598**

territory Area of land under the jurisdiction of the United States government but not yet a state. **190**

Thanksgiving Day American holiday tradition begun when the Pilgrims gave thanks to God for the help of the Indians and their first harvest in America. **56**

theory Abstract idea or hypothetical set of facts, principles or circumstances. **606**

Thirteenth Amendment Constitutional amendment that abolished slavery. **594**

Three-Fifths Compromise Agreement made by the writers of the Constitution to include three fifths of slaves in counting a state's population. **221**

"Three R's" Basic subjects of early American schools—reading, writing, and 'rithmetic. **489**

ticket List of candidates nominated by a political party. **387**

tidewater Southern coastal areas where rivers were affected by the ocean tides. **91**

title Part of a map that tells you what the map is about. **674**

Toleration Act Maryland law passed in 1649 that granted freedom of religion to all Christians. **61**

Tom Thumb First steam-driven locomotive, built by Peter Cooper in 1830. **355**

Tory Colonist who remained loyal to England during the Revolutionary War. **155**

total abstinence (AB·stuh·nuhns) Drinking no alcohol. **500**

totalitarian (toh·tal·uh·TER·ee·uhn) Type of government in which the state has absolute control over all citizens and no opposition to the government is allowed. **647**

total war Strategy such as that used in the Civil War that calls for the destruction of resources of the enemy's civilian population as well as its army. **583**

tow path Track along the bank of a canal used by men or animals in towing boats. **351**

town common Park-like square in the center of a New England village where the church, meeting house, and school were located. **74**

town meeting Gathering of townspeople to act upon town business; early form of government, especially in New England. **110**

Townshend (TOWN·zuhnd) **Acts** British laws of 1767 that imposed taxes on colonial imports to pay British debts. **130**

township Section of land equalling 36 square miles. **189**

Trail of Tears Name expressing the sadness and hardships of the forced removal of Cherokee Indians from Georgia in 1838. **394**

transcendentalism (trans·en·DENT·uhl·is·uhm) Philosophy promoted by a group of New England idealists that people could rise above reason by having faith in themselves. **492**

Transcontinental Treaty Agreement in 1818 between the U.S. and Spain that extended America's southern boundaries to the Pacific Coast. **316**

Transportation Revolution Advances during the mid-1800s in the speed and ease of transportation; helped join people in the West with those in the East. **357**

tread To walk or step. **234**

treasury Department of the government that manages the nation's finances. **234**

treaty of alliance Agreement among countries of support in case of attack. **168**

Treaty of Dancing Rabbit Creek Treaty of 1830 under which Choctaw Indians agreed to move west of the Mississippi. **397**

Treaty of Greenville Agreement in 1795 in which Indians turned over the southern half of Ohio to American settlers. **250**

Treaty of Guadalupe Hidalgo (gwahd·uhl·OOP·ay·hi·DALL·goh) Agreement that ended the Mexican war

and arranged the sale of vast territories to the United States. **422**

trend General direction or line of development, especially with social change. **502**

triangular trade Name given to the profitable trade between the northern colonies, the West Indies, and England although trade did not always flow in a simple triangular fashion. **93**

tribute In this case, any forced payment of money. **276**

tropical wet Hot and rainy climate, such as that found in Hawaii. **678**

tropical wet-and-dry Climate that is hot and rainy, with most rainfall in the summer, such as that found in the southern tip of Florida. **678**

trust Group of corporations formed by a legal agreement and organized especially for the purpose of reducing competition. **624**

trustee Person who is entrusted with the management of another person's property. **69**

turbulent Causing disturbance. **28**

turnpike Road on which tolls are collected. **349**

Tuskegee (tuhs·KEE·gee) **Institute** School for African Americans in Alabama founded by Booker T. Washington. **617**

Twelfth Amendment Constitutional amendment that clarified the electoral process by separating votes for the president and vice president. **271**

two-party system Political system with two major parties of similar strength; in the U.S. these are now the Democratic and Republican parties. **254**

tyranny (TIR·uh·nee) Oppressive and unjust government. **156**

U

ultimate Final goal or the maximum point possible. **181**

unassuming Not forward or arrogant; modest. **420**

unconstitutional Not in keeping with or supported by the Constitution. **194**

Underground Railroad System by which escaping slaves were secretly helped to reach Canada. **472**

undermine Weaken or hurt by unfair means. **608**

United States of America Country formed by the 13 British colonies which declared independence from Great Britain in 1776. **155**

upland cotton Variety of cotton that withstands cold temperatures, making it hardy enough to grow almost anywhere in the southern states. **451**

uppity Arrogant or acting superior. **611**

urban Of cities and towns. **xxiii**

urban center Area with a population of at least 2,500 persons. **347**

urban frontier Western cities that developed on the edge of settled areas and were used as outposts and depots from which settlers spread. **346**

V

vagrant Tramp or beggar who wanders from place to place. **154**

vain Thinking too highly of oneself; conceited. **270**

Valley Forge General Washington's winter camp in Pennsylvania where in 1777 the Continental army lost thousands of men to harsh weather and desertion. **169**

Veracruz (ver·uh·KROOZ) Mexican seaport captured by Americans in 1847 in War with Mexico. **420**

verge Brink or edge. **522**

veto Presidential power to reject bills passed by Congress. **225, 595**

viceroy Spanish colonial ruler appointed by the king. **65**

Vietnamization Policy of building up the South Vietnamese army so that American troops could be withdrawn. **663**

Viking Scandinavian sailor who

traveled the seas between the 8th and 10th centuries. **14**

Vincennes (vin·SENZ) Site in present-day Indiana of 1778 Revolutionary War battle where Clark's forces defeated the British, securing the Northwest in 1778. **173**

Vinland Name for North America used in ancient Viking sagas. **14**

Virginia Plan Proposal presented at the Constitutional Convention that recommended a government with three separate branches and representation based on population. **220**

virtue Quality of goodness. **400**

void No longer enforced. **527**

volley Firing of many shots at once. **145**

vulcanization Heat and chemical process for hardening rubber. **369**

W

wadding Soft padding material; in colonial days used in packing a bullet in a rifle barrel. **152**

wake Track or path left by a moving ship in the water. **324**

war department Bureau of government in charge of military affairs. **234**

war hawk People from the West and South who favored the War of 1812 against England. **295**

War of 1812 (1812–1814) Conflict between the U.S. and Great Britain over Indian agitation and freedom of the seas. **301**

water-frame Spinning machine invented in 1768 by Richard Arkwright; one of the first inventions of the Industrial Revolution because it used a power source other than human or animal muscle. **335**

watershed Important turning point in history. **593**

weather Condition of the atmosphere at a specific location for a

given time; generally defined by temperature, precipitation, wind, and atmospheric pressure. **678**

welfare state Situation in which the government assumes a large measure of responsibility for the social well-being of the people. **646**

wended Went or proceeded on one's way. **542**

west coast marine Climate with cool summers and many days of drizzly rainfall, most of which falls in the winter. **678**

Whig American who believed in patriotic resistance to King George III; member of a major political party of the 1830s and 1840s. **155**

Willamette Valley Fertile area in Oregon where missionaries began a settlement in the 1830s. **412**

Wilmot Proviso (pruh·VY·zoh) Failed proposal presented in 1846 to prohibit slavery in any land gained from Mexico. **438**

Women's Rights Convention Meeting in Seneca Falls, New York, in 1848 to seek equal rights for women. **482**

world market International demand for goods and services. **608**

X

XYZ Affair Scandal in the 1790s in which the French sought bribes from American diplomats. **257**

Y

Yankee ingenuity (in·juh·NOO·uht·ee) Nickname for American knack for solving difficult problems in clever ways. **92**

Yorktown Battle site in Virginia where in 1871 British general Cornwallis surrendered to George Washington, ending the Revolutionary War. **173**

INDEX

Page numbers in *italics* that have a *p* written before them refer to pictures or photographs; *c,* to charts, graphs, tables, or diagrams; and *m,* to maps.

Virginia Resolutions, 267, 268, 386
Viscaino, Sebastian, 65
Voltaire, François-Arouet Marie, 199
Von Steuben, Friedrich, 169-70, 175
voting Act (1970), 218
voting rights: of African Americans, 214, 511, 600, 602, 610-11, 613; in colonial America, 79-80; Constitutional amendments concerning, 214, 215, 600; democratic reforms and, 384; for 18-year-olds, 218; literacy test and, 613; poll tax and, 613; after Revolutionary War, 183; in Washington, D.C., 217; of women, 215

W

Wade, Ben, 568
wage-and-price freeze, 662
Wagner Labor Relations Act, 646
Walker, David, 471
Wallace, Henry, 652
war department, 234-35
War for American Independence. *See* Revolutionary War
War Hawks, 295, 297, 300, 379, 464
War Industries Board, 640
War of 1812, 300-314, *m301,* 331, 578
Ward, Artemas, 147
Ward, J. Q. A., *p222*
Warren, Earl, 654
Warren, Joseph, 149
Warren, Mercy Otis, 135
wars. *See* names of specific wars
Washington, Booker T., 617, 633
Washington, D.C., 217, 270-71, *p272,* 307-09, *p308. See also* District of Columbia
Washington, Fort, *p189, 248*
Washington, George: as commander-in-chief of army, 151-53, *p151,* 184, 261; at Constitutional Convention, *p196,* 197; death of, 270; in French and English colonial wars, 119, *p120,* 120; as hero to French, 244; inauguration of, 207, *p222,* 231; interest in farming, 100; plans for District of Columbia, 270, *p272;* presidency of, 207, 222, 234-37, *p235, p236,* 242-43, 246-48, 250-53, *p253,* 263, 272, 275, 388; in Revolutionary War,

154-55, *p154* , 164-70, *p169,* 174-75, *p175,* 196; at Second Continental Congress, 151; as slaveholder, 163; view on Indians, 398
Washington, Martha, *p151,* 163, 236-37, *p236*
water rights, 429-31
water-frame, 335
Watergate Affair, 663
Watt, James, 353
Wayne, Anthony, 248, *p248,* 249, 280
weapons: of Civil War, 555-56; production of, 330, 333-34; in Revolutionary War, 152-53, *p 152,* 154; right to own, 211, 237
Weatherford, William. *See* Red Eagle
Webster, Daniel, *p439,* 440, 441-43
Webster, Noah, 485, *p485*
Weeden, John, 194
Weld, Theodore Dwight, 461, 466-67, 512
welfare state, 646
Wellington, Duke of, 308
West: African Americans in, 617; Civil War in, 577-80, *m577, p579, m580;* effect on democracy of, 374-75; in early 19th century, 374-78, *p375, p378;* geography of, 444-45, *m444;* manifest destiny, 412-13; Oregon Trail, 413-14, 416-17; paintings of, *p 62;* relative location of, xxiv; Revolutionary War in, 173, *m173;* water rights in, 429-31; water routes to, *m430;* women in, 377. *See also* frontier; names of specific states
West Indies, 27, *p90,* 93-94, *m94,* 114, 191, 250, 286, 287
westward expansion, 316-17, *p363*
whaling, 449
Wheatley, Phillis, 154
Whig party, 400-01, 404-05, 437, 516, 523, 524
Whigs, in Revolutionary War, 155, 163
Whiskey Rebellion, 252, *p253*
Whistler, James McNeill, 627
White, John, 43, *p43*
white backlash, 661, 664
Whitefield, George, 95-96, *p95,* 98, 493
Whitman, Marcus, 413, 414
Whitman, Narcissa Prentice, 413
Whitman, Walt, 496-97, *p497,* 592

Whitney, Eli, 333-34, 368, 451-52, *p451*
Whittier, John Greenleaf, 497
Wilderness, Battle of, 581, *m582*
Willamette River, 413
Willamette Valley, 412-13, *m444*
Willard, Emma Hunt, 478
William and Mary (king and queen of England), 111-12, *p111*
Williams, Euphemia, 512
Williams, Roger, 59-60, *p59*
Williamson, Joel, 604
Wilmot, David, 438, 516
Wilmot Proviso, 438, 516
Wilson, Woodrow, 633, *p633,* 640-41, *p640*
Winslow, Edward, 71
Winthrop, John, 58, *p58*
Wisconsin, 190, *m190*
Wolcott, Oliver, 334
Wolfe, James, 121, *p122,* 147, 149
women: as abolitionists, 471-72, 477, 480, 482; child-rearing and, 75, 76, 480; during Civil War, 567, 574; in colonial America, 60, 75-76, *p75, p76,* 79, *p80;* education of, 239, 337, 477-79, *p 478,* 485; employment in World War I, 640; employment in World War II, 649; factories and, 336-37, 339-41; in Jacksonian America, 477-79, *p477;* Liberation, 660, *p660;* in Mexico, 408; movement for rights in 1960s, 1970s, and 1980s, 660, *p660,* 664; in professions, 479-80, *p479, p480;* during Revolutionary War, 162-63; voting rights for, 215; in the West, 377; westward journeys of, 414, 416-17; working, 641, 649. *See also* names of specific women
Women's Liberation Movement, 660, *p660*
Women's Rights Convention, 482-83, *p483*
women's rights movement, 337, 480-83, *p482, p483,* 507, 660, *p660*
Worcester v. Georgia, 395
Wordsworth, William, 495
workers: child labor, 337-38, 503; in colonial America, 76-77, 79; in factories, 328, 336-41, 346; 19th-century reform movement and, 503-04, *c503*
world market, 608
Wounded Knee, (S. Dak. 1973), 660

For permission to reprint copyrighted material, grateful acknowledgment is made to the following sources:

Beacon Press: Adapted from *The Broken Spears, The Aztec Account of the Conquest of Mexico,* edited by Miguel Leon-Portilla. Copyright © 1962 by Beacon Press.

Caxton Printers, Ltd.: From excerpt by Wetatonmi from *Hear Me My Chiefs!* by Lucullus V. McWhorter. Copyright 1952 by Lucullus V. McWhorter.

V. Annette Grant: Adapted from "Johnny Reb and Billy Yank" by Alexander Hunter from *The Blue and the Gray: The Story of the Civil War as Told by Participants,* Volume I, edited by Henry Steele Commager. Copyright 1950 by Henry Steele Commager.

Harcourt Brace Jovanovich, Inc.: From *The Constitution: Foundation of Our Freedom* by Warren E. Burger. Essays copyright © 1990 by Warren E. Burger; additional material copyright © 1990 by Harcourt Brace Jovanovich, Inc. From "East Side" from *World of Our Fathers* by Irving Howe. Copyright © 1976 by Irving Howe. "Song for a Youth Temperance Group" from *A History of the American People, Volume One: To 1877* by Stephen Thernstrom. Copyright © 1984 by Harcourt Brace Jovanovich, Inc.

HarperCollins Publishers, Inc.: From *Andrew Jackson and the Course of American Empire, 1767–1821* by Robert V. Remini. Copyright © 1977 by Robert V. Remini.

Alfred A. Knopf, Inc.: From " 'I Am the Sire de Coucy': The Dynasty" from *A Distant Mirror: The Calamitous 14th Century* by Barbara W. Tuchman. Copyright © 1978 by Barbara W. Tuchman.

Macmillan Publishing Company: From *William Penn* by Harry Emerson Wildes. Copyright © 1974 by Harry Emerson Wildes.

Oxford University Press, Inc.: From "Schoolhouses and Scholars" from *The Culture Factory: Boston Public Schools, 1789–1860* by Stanley K. Schultz, pp. 69–92. Copyright © 1973 by Oxford University Press, Inc.

Marian Reiner for Joan Daves: From "Letter From Birmingham Jail" by Martin Luther King, Jr. Copyright © 1963, 1964 by Martin Luther King, Jr.

Saturday Evening Post Company: From "I Saw Lee Surrender" by Seth M. Flint from *The Saturday Evening Post,* July/August 1976, vol. 248, no. 5. Copyright © 1976 by The Saturday Evening Post Company.

Texas Folklore Society: From "Shelling Corn by Moonlight" by Jovita González from *Tone the Bell Easy,* edited by J. Frank Dobie. Copyright 1932 by Texas Folklore Society. Published by Southern Methodist University Press, 1965.

University Press of New England: From "The First Modern War" from *America Goes to War* by Bruce Catton. Copyright © 1958 by William B. Catton

A. P. Watt Limited: From *The Outline of History: Being a Plain History of Life and Mankind* by H. G. Wells. Copyright 1920, 1931, 1940 by H. G. Wells; copyright 1949 by Doubleday & Company, Inc.